T0234550

Lecture Notes in Computer Science 8632

Commenced Publication in 1973
Founding and Former Series Editors:
Gerhard Goos, Juris Hartmanis, and Jan van Leeuwen

Advanced Research in Computing and Software Science
Subline of Lectures Notes in Computer Science

Fernando Silva   Inês Dutra
Vítor Santos Costa (Eds.)

Euro-Par 2014 Parallel Processing

20th International Conference
Porto, Portugal, August 25-29, 2014
Proceedings

 Springer

Volume Editors

Fernando Silva
Inês Dutra
Vítor Santos Costa
Universidade do Porto
CRACS/INESC-TEC and FCUP
Rua do Campo Alegre, 1021
4169-007 Porto, Portugal
E-mail: {fds, ines, vsc}@dcc.fc.up.pt

ISSN 0302-9743   e-ISSN 1611-3349
ISBN 978-3-319-09872-2   e-ISBN 978-3-319-09873-9
DOI 10.1007/978-3-319-09873-9
Springer Cham Heidelberg New York Dordrecht London

Library of Congress Control Number: 2014945461

LNCS Sublibrary: SL 1 – Theoretical Computer Science and General Issues

Typesetting: Camera-ready by author, data conversion by Scientific Publishing Services, Chennai, India

Printed on acid-free paper

Springer is part of Springer Science+Business Media (www.springer.com)

Preface

Euro-Par is an annual series of international conferences dedicated to the promotion and advancement of all aspects of parallel and distributed computing. It covers a wide spectrum of topics from algorithms and theory to software technology and hardware-related issues, with application areas ranging from scientific to mobile and cloud computing. Euro-Par provides a forum for the introduction, presentation, and discussion of the latest scientific and technical advances, extending the frontier of both the state of the art and the state of the practice.

The main audience of Euro-Par are the researchers in academic institutions, government laboratories, and industrial organizations. Euro-Par's objective is to be the primary choice of such professionals for the presentation of new results in their specific areas. As a wide-spectrum conference, Euro-Par fosters the synergy of different topics in parallel and distributed computing. Of special interest are applications that demonstrate the effectiveness of the main Euro-Par topics.

In addition, Euro-Par conferences provide a platform for a number of accompanying technical workshops. Thus, smaller and emerging communities can meet and develop more focused topics or as yet less established topics.

Euro-Par 2014 was the 20th conference in the Euro-Par series, and was organized in Porto, Portugal, by the University of Porto, Faculty of Sciences, Computer Science Department and the Center for Research in Advanced Computing of INESC-TEC. Previous Euro-Par conferences took place in Stockholm, Lyon, Passau, Southampton, Toulouse, Munich, Manchester, Paderborn, Klagenfurt, Pisa, Lisbon, Dresden, Rennes, Las Palmas, Delft, Ischia, Bordeaux, Rhodes, and Aachen. Next year, the conference will be held in Vienna, Austria. More information on the Euro-Par conference series and organization is available on the website at http://www.europar.org.

Euro-Par 2014 covered 15 topics. The paper review process for each topic was managed and supervised by a committee of at least four people: a global chair, a local chair, and two members. Topics with a high number of submissions were managed by larger committees. The final decisions on the acceptance or rejection of the submitted papers were made at a meeting of the conference co-chairs and local chairs of the topics.

The call for papers attracted 267 full-paper submissions, representing 45 countries. A total of 1,070 review reports were collected, giving an average of 4.0 review reports per paper. The Program Committee members hailed from 22 different countries. We selected 68 papers to be presented at the conference and included in the conference proceedings, representing 29 countries from all continents, and resulting in an acceptance rate of 25.5%.

Euro-Par 2014 was very pleased to present three invited speakers of high international reputation, who discussed important developments in very interesting areas of parallel and distributed computing:

1. Pawl Watson (Newcastle University, UK)
2. Henri Bal (Vrije Universiteit, The Netherlands)
3. Ricardo Bianchini (Rutgers University and Microsoft, USA)

As part of Euro-Par 2014, two tutorials and 18 workshops were held prior to the main conference. The two tutorials were:

1. Heterogeneous Memory Models, by Benedict R. Gaster (Qualcomm, Inc.)
2. High-Performance Parallel Graph Analytics, by Keshav Pingali (UT Austin) and Manoj Kumar (IBM)

The 18 workshops were:

1. 12th International Workshop on Algorithms, Models and Tools for Parallel Computing on Heterogeneous Platforms (HeteroPar)
2. 5th Workshop on High Performance Bioinformatics and Biomedicine (HiBB)
3. Second Workshop on Parallel and Distributed Agent-Based Simulations (PAD-ABS)
4. Second Workshop on Runtime and Operating Systems for the Many Core Era (ROME)
5. 7th Workshop on Unconventional High-Performance Computing (UCHPC)
6. 9th Workshop on Virtualization in High-Performance Cloud Computing (VHPC)
7. First Workshop on Applications of Parallel Computation in Industry and Engineering (APCIE)
8. Third Workshop on Big Data Management in Clouds (BigDataCloud)
9. Workshop on Software for Exascale Computing - Project Workshop (SPPEXA)
10. Second Workshop on Dependability and Interoperability in Heterogeneous Clouds (DIHC)
11. Second Workshop on Federative and Interoperable Cloud Infrastructures (FedICI)
12. Third Workshop on On-Chip Memory Hierarchies and Interconnects: Organization, Management and Implementation (OMHI)
13. Second Workshop on Large-Scale Distributed Virtual Environments on Clouds and P2P (LSDVE)
14. 7th Workshop on Resiliency in High-Performance Computing with Clouds, Grids, and Clusters (Resilience)
15. First International Workshop on Reproducibility in Parallel Computing (REP-PAR)
16. First Workshop on Techniques and Applications for Sustainable Ultrascale Computing Systems (TASUS)
17. 7th International Workshop on Multi-/Manycore Computing Systems (MuCoCoS)

18. 7th Workshop on Productivity and Performance – Tools for HPC Application Development (PROPER)

Workshop papers will be published in a separate proceedings volume.

The 20th Euro-Par conference in Porto would not have been possible without the support of many individuals and organizations. We owe special thanks to the authors of all the submitted papers, the members of the topic committees, and the reviewers in all topics for their contributions to the success of the conference. A special word of thanks should go to the global and local chairs, who were always available and did excellent work in managing the reviewing process with a tight deadline. We would also like to express our gratitude to the members of the Organizing Committee. Moreover, we are indebted to the members of the Euro-Par Steering Committee for their trust, guidance, and support. Finally, a number of institutional and industrial sponsors contributed to the organization of the conference. Their names and logos appear on the Euro-Par 2014 website http://europar2014.dcc.fc.up.pt.

It was a pleasure and an honor to organize and host Euro-Par 2014 in Porto. We hope that all participants enjoyed the technical program and the social events organized during the conference, as well as the city of Porto.

August 2014

Fernando Silva
Inês Dutra
Vítor Santos Costa

Organization

Euro-Par Steering Committee

Chair

Christian Lengauer | University of Passau, Germany

Vice-Chair

Luc Bougé | ENS Rennes, France

European Representatives

Marco Danelutto | University of Pisa, Italy
Emmanuel Jeannot | LaBRI-Inria, Bordeaux, France
Christos Kaklamanis | Computer Technology Institute, Greece
Paul Kelly | Imperial College, UK
Thomas Ludwig | University of Hamburg, Germany
Emilio Luque | Autonomous University of Barcelona, Spain
Tomàs Margalef | Autonomous University of Barcelona, Spain
Wolfgang Nagel | Dresden University of Technology, Germany
Rizos Sakellariou | University of Manchester, UK
Henk Sips | Delft University of Technology, The Netherlands
Domenico Talia | University of Calabria, Italy
Felix Wolf | GRS and RWTH Aachen University, Germany

Honorary Members

Ron Perrott | Oxford e-Research Centre, UK
Karl Dieter Reinartz | University of Erlangen-Nuremberg, Germany

Observers

Fernando Silva | University of Porto, Portugal
Jesper Larsson Träff | Vienna University of Technology, Austria

Euro-Par 2013 Organization

Conference Co-chairs

Fernando Silva | University of Porto, Portugal
Inês Dutra | University of Porto, Portugal
Vítor Santos Costa | University of Porto, Portugal

Local Organizing Committee

Joana Dumas	University of Porto, Portugal
Alexandra Ferreira	University of Porto, Portugal
Luís Lopes	University of Porto, Portugal
Pedro Ribeiro	University of Porto, Portugal
Ricardo Rocha	University of Porto, Portugal

Program Committee

Topic 1: Support Tools and Environments

Chair

Thilo Kielmann   Vrije Universiteit Amsterdam, The Netherlands

Local Chair

José C. Cunha   New University of Lisbon, Portugal

Members

Anthony Danalis	University of Tennessee at Knoxville, USA
Bernd Freisleben	University of Marburg, Germany
Tomàs Margalef	Universitat Autonoma de Barcelona, Spain

Topic 2: Performance Prediction and Evaluation

Chair

Alexey Lastovetsky   University College Dublin, Ireland

Local Chair

Francisco F. Rivera   University of Santiago de Compostela, Spain

Members

David E. Singh	University Carlos III of Madrid, Spain
Dimitrios S. Nikolopoulos	Queen's University of Belfast, UK
Leonel Sousa	IST-University of Lisbon, Portugal
Petr Tuma	Charles University, Czech Republic
Wolfgang Nagel	Dresden University of Technology, Germany

Topic 3: Scheduling and Load Balancing

Chair

Helen Karatza   Aristotle University of Thessaloniki, Greece

Local Chair

Jorge Barbosa   University of Porto, Portugal

Members

Alexandru Iosup   Delft University of Technology,
                                   The Netherlands
Andrzej Goscinski   Deakin University, Australia
Cevdet Aykanat   Bilkent University, Ankara, Turkey
Frédéric Suter   IN2P3 Computing Center, CNRS, France
Nick Bessis   The University of Derby, UK
Ramin Yahyapour   Göttingen University, Germany

Topic 4: High-Performance Architectures and Compilers

Chair

Sally A. McKee   Chalmers University of Technology, Sweden

Local Chair

João Paiva Cardoso   University of Porto, Portugal

Members

Changhee Jung   Virginia Tech, USA
Magnus Själander   Florida State University, USA
Rui Hou   Institute of Computing Technology, China
Soner Onder   Michigan Technological University, USA

Topic 5: Parallel and Distributed Data Management

Chair

Josep L. Larriba-Pey   Polytechnic University of Catalonia, Spain

Local Chair

Paolo Romano   IST-University of Lisbon, Portugal

Members

David Dominguez-Sal   Sparsity Technologies, Spain
Kai-Uwe Sattler   Technical University of Ilmenau, Germany
Patrick Martin   Queen's University, Kingston, Canada
Yang-Sae Moon   Kangwon National University, Korea

Topic 6: Grid, Cluster and Cloud Computing

Chair

Uwe Schwiegelshohn   Universität Dortmund, Germany

Local Chair

Hervé Paulino   New University of Lisbon, Portugal

Members

Domenico Talia   University of Calabria, Italy
María S. Pérez-Hernández   Universidad Politécnica de Madrid, Spain
Olivier Beaumont   Inria, France
Rizos Sakellariou   University of Manchester, UK
Satoshi Matsuoka   Tokyo Institute of Technology, Japan
Vijay Saraswat   IBM, USA

Topic 7: Green High-Performance Computing

Chair

Martin Schulz   Lawrence Livermoore National Laboratory,
                                      USA

Local Chair

Luís Lopes   University of Porto, Portugal

Members

Enrique S. Quintana Orti   Universidad Jaime I, Castellon, Spain
Koji Inoue   Kyushu Institute of Technology, Japan

Topic 8: Distributed Systems and Algorithms

Chair

Pascal Felber   Université de Neuchâtel, Switzerland

Local Chair

Luís Veiga   IST-University of Lisbon, Portugal

Members

Corentin Travers   ENSEIRB-MATMECA, France
Fabio Kon   University of São Paulo, Brazil
Paul Grace   University of Southampton, UK
Vincent Gramoli   University of Sydney, Australia

Topic 9: Parallel and Distributed Programming

Chair

Henri Bal   Vrije Universiteit Amsterdam, The Netherlands

Local Chair

João Luís Sobral   University of Minho, Portugal

Members

Ana Varbanescu   University of Amesterdam, The Netherlands
Christian Perez   Inria, ENS-Lyon, France
Fabrice Huet   University of Nice Sophia Antipolis, France
Marco Danelutto   University of Pisa, Italy
Peter Kilpatrick   Queen's University Belfast, UK

Topic 10: Parallel Numerical Algorithms

Chair

Laura Grigori   Inria Paris, France

Local Chair

Rui Ralha   University of Minho, Portugal

Members

Daniel Kressner   EPFL, Switzerland
Rob Bisseling   Utrecht University, The Netherlands

Topic 11: Multicore and Manycore Programming

Chair

Raymond Namyst   University of Bordeaux 1, France

Local Chair

Ricardo Rocha   University of Porto, Portugal

Members

Christoph Kessler   University of Linköpîng, Sweden
Elisabeth Larsson   Uppsala University, Sweden
Frank Mueller   North Carolina State University, USA
Jean-François Méhaut   Grenoble University, France
Jesper Träff   Vienna University of Technology, Austria
Marco Aldinucci   University of Turin, Italy
Mitsuhisa Sato   University of Tsukuba, Japan

Topic 12: Theory and Algorithms for Parallel Computation
Chair
Andrea Pietracaprina   University of Padova, Italy

Local Chair
Pedro Ribeiro   University of Porto, Portugal

Members
Kieran Herley   University College Cork, Ireland
Sergei Vassilvitskii   Google, USA

Topic 13: High-Performance Networks and Communication
Chair
José Flich   Universidad Politécnica de Valencia, Spain

Local Chair
Filipe Araújo   University of Coimbra, Portugal

Members
Cyriel Minkenberg   IBM Research - Zurich, Switzerland
Maurizio Palesi   Kore University, Italy
Tor Skeie   University of Oslo and Simula Research
                                      Laboratory, Norway

Topic 14: High-Performance and Scientific Applications
Chair
Francisco Brasileiro   Universidade Federal de Campina Grande,
                                      Brazil

Local Chair
Pedro Medeiros   New University of Lisbon, Portugal

Members
Adélia Sequeira   IST-University of Lisbon, Portugal
Gilles Fedak   University of Lyon, France
Walfredo Cirne   Google, USA

Topic 15: GPU and Accelerator Computing

Chair

Paul Kelly   Imperial College London, UK

Local Chair

João Lourenço   New University of Lisbon, Portugal

Members

Alexander Heinecke	Technische Universität München, Germany
Anton Lokhmotov	ARM, UK
Christian Plessl	University of Paderborn, Germany
Didem Unat	Lawrence Berkeley Lab, USA
Dora Blanco Heras	University of Santiago de Compostela, Spain
Lee Howes	Qualcomm, USA
Naoya Maruyama	Tokyo Institute of Technology, Japan
Pedro Gonnet	Durham University, UK

Euro-Par 2014 Reviewers

Euro-Par is very grateful to all reviewers for their kind cooperation and effort to achieve an average of four reviews per paper, producing a total of 1,070 reviews.

Abdou Guermouche
Abdullah Gharaibeh
Adélia Sequeira
Afshin Zafari
Agostino Forestiero
Aidan Chalk
Akihiro Nomura
Albert-Jan Yzelman
Alberto Lluch Lafuente
Alberto Sanchez
Alejandro Rico
Aleksandar Ilic
Alex Ramirez
Alexander Fölling
Alexander Heinecke
Alexandra Carpen-Amarie
Alexandre Denis
Alexandru Costan
Alexandru Iosup
Alexey Lastovetsky
Aline Paes

Altino Sampaio
Alvaro Aguilera
Alysson Bessani
Amina Guermouche
Ana Lucia Varbanescu
Ana-Maria Oprescu
Anastassios Nanos
Andra Hugo
Andrea Pietracaprina
Andreas Agne
Andrew Stephen McGough
Andrzej Goscinski
Angelo Furfaro
Angelos Papatriantafyllou
Anita Sobe
Anna Sikora
Anthony Danalis
Anton Lokhmotov
Antonin Steinhauser
Antonio Espinosa
Antonio García-Loureiro

Arash Rezaei
Arlindo Conceição
Armanda Rodrigues
Arnau Prat
Ata Turk
Ayal Zaks
B. Barla Cambazoglu
Barry Rountree
Basilio B. Fraguela
Benjamin Herta
Bernd Freisleben
Bing Tang
Bo Li
Bo Wu
Bogdan Nicolae
Bogdan Prisacari
Bora Ucar
Brice Goglin
Brice Videau
Bruno Ciciani
Bruno Medeiros
Bunjamin Memishi
Carlee Joe-Wong
Carlo Mastroianni
Carmela Comito
Cecília Gomes
Ceriel Jacobs
Cevdet Aykanat
Changhee Jung
Chao Li
Christian Perez
Christian Plessl
Christiane Pousa
Christoph Kessler
Christos Kartsaklis
Claudia Misale
Clemens Grelck
Corentin Travers
Cosmin Dumitru
Cyriel Minkenberg
César De Rose
Daniel Cordeiro
Daniel Franco
Daniel Kressner
Darko Petrovic

David Dominguez-Sal
David E. Singh
David Fiala
Davide Frey
Denis Barthou
Didem Unat
Diego Didona
Diego Rodríguez Martínez
Diego Rughetti
Diego Souza
Dimitar Lukarski
Dimitrios S. Nikolopoulos
Diogo Telmo Neves
Domenico Talia
Dominik Goeddeke
Donald E. Porter
Dong Li
Dora Blanco Heras
Eduardo Cesar
Edwin Yaqub
Elisabeth Brunet
Elisabeth Larsson
Elizeu Santos-Neto
Emilio Francesquini
Emilio Padrón
Emilio Tuosto
Emmanuel Jeannot
Enrique S. Quintana-Orti
Eoghan O'Neill
Eric Aubanel
Erwan Le Merrer
Eugenio Cesario
Fabio Kon
Fabio Luporini
Fabio Tordini
Fabrice Dupros
Fabrice Huet
Fabricio Silva
Fabrizio Marozzo
Farhad Mehdipour
Farhana Zulkernine
Felix Garcia Carballeira
Ferdinando Fioretto
Fernando Birra
Fernando Ramos

Feroz Zahid
Filipe Araújo
Flavien Quesnel
Florian Rathgeber
Flávio Cruz
Francesco Versaci
Francis Russell
Francisco Argüello
Francisco Brasileiro
Francisco D. Igual
Francisco F. Rivera
Francisco Gaspar
Frank Mueller
François Broquedis
François Gindraud
François Trahay
Françoise Baude
Frédéric Suter
Gabriel Marin
Gavin Vaz
Ge Song
George Rokos
George Terzopoulos
George Tzenakis
German Rodriguez
Gheorghe-Teodor Bercea
Gilles Fedak
Giorgis Georgakoudis
Giuliano Mega
Gokcen Kestor
Gorkem Asilioglu
Guangyu Sun
Guilherme Peretti Pezzi
Haipeng Jia
Haiwu He
Hans Vandierendonck
Hartwig Anzt
Heike McCraw
Heinrich Riebler
Heithem Abbes
Helen Karatza
Henri Bal
Henrique Domingos
Hervé Paulino
Hinde Bouziane

Hitoshi Sato
Holger Brunst
Holger Mickler
Hubertus Franke
Håkan Sundell
Idafen Santana-Pérez
Ilia Pietri
Ioannis A. Moschakis
Ismail El Helw
Ivan Tanasic
Ivanilton Polato
Ivor Spence
Jairo Panetta
Jan Westerholm
Javier Celaya
Javier Garcia Blas
Jean-François Méhaut
Jean-Marc Pierson
Jens Doleschal
Jens Domke
Jens Gustedt
Jesper Träff
Jesús Montes
Jiayuan Meng
Jie Shen
Jing Liu
Jizeng Wei
Joan Sorribes
Joana Côrte-Real
John Earnest
John Shalf
Jonathan Rouzaud-Cornabas
Jorge Barbosa
Jose E. Roman
Josep Jorba
Josep L. Larriba-Pey
Joseph Hellerstein
Joseph Schuchart
José C. Cunha
José Carlos Cabaleiro
José Flich
José Germano
José Luis Gonzalez Garcia
José Salavert Torres
José Simão

João A. Silva
João Barreto
João Leitão
João Lourenço
João Luís Sobral
João P. Vilela
João Paiva
João Paiva Cardoso
João Santos
João Silva
Juan Angel Lorenzo del Castillo
Juan C. Pichel
Juan Carlos Moure
Julien Bigot
Julien Forget
Julio Anjos
Julita Corbalan
Jun Wang
Justine Rochas
Jörg Keller
Kadir Akbudak
Kai-Uwe Sattler
Kamer Kaya
Karthikeyan P. Saravanan
Kaveh Razavi
Kees Verstoep
Keiichiro Fukazawa
Kenneth O'Brien
Kento Sato
Kien Le
Kieran Herley
Kiril Dichev
Kirk Cameron
Kiyokuni Kawachiya
Koichi Shirahata
Koji Inoue
Konstantina Mitropoulou
Kuan Lu
Landry Chetsa
Lars Schaefers
Laura Grigori
Laure Gonnord
Lauro Beltrão Costa
Leandro Fontoura-Cupertino
Leandro Marinho

Lee Howes
Leonel Sousa
Lidia Kuan
Lilia Ziane Khodja
Lionel Eyraud-Dubois
Lubomír Bulej
Luigi Nardi
Lukáš Marek
Luís Assunção
Luís Lopes
Luís Veiga
Madhukar Korupolu
Magnus Grandin
Magnus Själander
Maik Srba
Manuel F. Dolz
Marcelo Pasin
Marco Aldinucci
Marco Danelutto
Marco Lackovic
Marcus Carvalho
Marcus Hilbrich
Maria Barreda
Maria Clicia Castro
Maria Couceiro
Martin Děcký
Martin Kreichgauer
Martin Schulz
Martin Tillenius
María S. Pérez-Hernández
Massimo Torquati
Mastoureh Hassannezhad
Mats Brorsson
Matthias Hofmann
Matthieu Dorier
Mauricio Hanzich
Maurizio Drocco
Maurizio Palesi
Merijn Verstraaten
Michael Haidl
Michael Kluge
Michael Wagner
Miguel Areias
Mihai Capota
Mike Rainey

Miquel Àngel Senar
Mircea Moca
Mitsuhisa Sato
Mohammed Tohid
Muhammad Aboelfotoh
Murray Cole
Márcio Castro
Naghmeh Ivaki
Naoya Maruyama
Narayan Desai
Neha Gholkar
Nick Bessis
Nicolai Stawinoga
Nicolas Loriant
Nicolás Guil Mata
Nikola Rajovic
Nishanth Balasubramanian
Nuno Diegues
Nuno Neves
Nuno Oliveira
Nuno Preguiça
Nuno Sebastião
Oleg Lodygensky
Oleksandra Kulankhina
Oliver Schmitt
Olivier Aumage
Olivier Beaumont
Onkar Patil
Ozcan Ozturk
Pablo Quesada Barriuso
Pak Markthub
Paolo Romano
Paolo Trunfio
Pascal Felber
Patrick Carribault
Patrick Martin
Paul Grace
Paul Kelly
Paul Renaud-Goud
Paul Watson
Paulo Ferreira
Paulo Lopes
Paulo Sérgio
Pavol Bauer
Pedro Alonso

Pedro Gonnet
Pedro Medeiros
Pedro Miguens
Pedro Ribeiro
Peter Chronz
Peter Kilpatrick
Peter Libič
Petr Tuma
Philip Church
Pierre Fortin
Pierre Sutra
Pieter Hijma
Porfidio Hernández
Radu Prodan
Rafael Mayo Gual
Rahul Gayatri
Ramin Yahyapour
Ramon Bertran
Ramon Nou
Raphael De Camargo
Raphael Poss
Raquel Lopes
Raul Barbosa
Raymond Namyst
Renan Fischer e Silva
Renato Ferreira
Ricardo Bianchini
Ricardo Dias
Ricardo Rocha
Richard Grunzke
Rio Yokota
Rizos Sakellariou
Rob Bisseling
Robert Dew
Robert Schoene
Roberto Gioiosa
Roberto Palmieri
Roy Bakker
Rui Camacho
Rui Gonçalves
Rui Hou
Rui Ralha
Rui Ramalho
Rui Silva
Rutger Hofman

Saadeldin Moustafa
Sai Narasimhamurthy
Sally A. McKee
Salvatore Venticinque
Samuel Thibault
Sandro Fiore
Sascha Hunold
Satoshi Matsuoka
Scott Beamer
Sebastiano Peluso
Seher Acer
Sergei Gorlatch
Sergei Vassilvitskii
Sergio Bernales
Shadi Ibrahim
Shady Khalifa
Shava Smallen
Shinichi Miura
Shrinivas Anand Panchamukhi
Siamak Azodolmolky
Sima Soltani
Soner Onder
Souley Madougou
Srinath Krishna Ananthakrishnan
Stefan Vijzelaar
Stefania Costache
Stephan Baumann
Stephan Schlagkamp
Stephen Olivier
Stoyan Garbatov
Stylianos Zikos
Subramanian Ramachandran
Sunpyo Hong
Sven van Haastregt
Svetislav Momcilovic
Sérgio Duarte
Sérgio Esteves
Takayuki Aoki
Tamito Kajiyama
Theofrastos Mantadelis

Thilo Kielmann
Thomas Hérault
Thomas Ropars
Tobias Beisel
Tobias Graf
Tobias Hilbrich
Tobias Kenter
Tomàs Margalef
Tomás F. Pena
Toni Cortes
Tor Skeie
Tugrul Dayar
Uwe Schwiegelshohn
Valerio Schiavoni
Vania Marangozova-Martin
Victor Garcia
Victor Goulart
Victor Muntés-Mulero
Vijay Saraswat
Vincent Gramoli
Vincent Weaver
Vitor Duarte
Vladimir Rychkov
Vojtěch Horký
Wagner Meira Jr.
Walfredo Cirne
Wang Yu
Wei Wu
Wesley Bland
Wolfgang Nagel
Xavier Emery
Xiaojun Ruan
Xing Pan
Yang-Sae Moon
Yao Zhang
Yasutaka Wada
Yehia Elshater
Yong Guo
Zafeirios Papazachos
Ziming Zhong

Euro-Par 2014 Invited Talks

Cloud Computing for Healthcare

Paul Watson, Newcastle University, UK

Cloud Computing has the potential to revolutionise healthcare. The expansion of wireless internet, coupled with a massive growth in cheap, mobile sensors offers opportunities to deliver personalised, high-quality healthcare cheaply to people in their own homes. Clouds have an important role to play in realising this potential, as it requires the ability to store and analyse the vast amounts of data that these sensors collect. This presents both problems and opportunities: new scalable, parallel algorithms and platforms are needed to analyse the sensor data, while there are important advantages to be gained by combining the data from a population of users in order to better understand medical conditions and how best to treat them.

The talk will be illustrated with examples from our projects in this area, including the use of sensors to understand older people's activity in order to provide personalised treatment; and also on the analysis of gaming data to help people recover from strokes.

Going Dutch: How to Share a Dedicated Distributed Infrastructure for Computer Science Research

Henri E. Bal, Vrije Universiteit, The Netherlands

The Distributed ASCI Supercomputer (DAS) is a dedicated distributed infrastructure for Dutch Computer Science research. During its 17 year history, DAS witnessed and supported many waves in distributed computing, including wide-area computing (DAS-1), grids and peer-to-peer (DAS-2), e-Science and optical grids (DAS-3), and heterogeneous computing (DAS-4). Unlike many other test beds, the different clusters of DAS are set up by a single organization (the ASCI research school) with one clear vision for each system generation. DAS is designed specifically for Computer Science research, especially for interactive distributed experiments in areas like programming systems, resource management, and networks. With the advent of the fifth generation system, DAS-5, in 2015, DAS has literary become mature and indispensable for Dutch Computer Science.

This presentation first looks back at the impact DAS has had. Despite its relatively modest size and cost, DAS has been used for over 100 PhD theses and for numerous award winning experiments. It enabled large amounts of research funding and it played a key role in huge projects like VL-e and (currently) COMMIT. It also served as a stepping stone for applications like astronomy, multimedia analysis, web-scale reasoning, and climate modelling, each of which won competitions with DAS. Next, the presentation will discuss several ongoing projects in more detail, including programming environments for heterogeneous accelerator-based systems and for big data applications. Here, DAS allows unique and controlled experiments on a variety of hardware. Finally, the presentation tries to draw general conclusions for Computer Science.

Greening Datacenters: Past, Present, and Future

Ricardo Bianchini, Rutgers University and Microsoft, USA

Datacenters host the server infrastructure that powers organizations of many sizes, from universities and enterprises to large Internet services. Collectively, datacenters consume a massive amount of power, representing a financial burden for datacenter operators, an infrastructure burden on power utilities, and an environmental burden on society. However, this problem could be worse if it were not for several advances made over the last decade, especially in the design of large-scale datacenters. In this talk, I will overview the architecture of these datacenters, discuss the main advances made to date, and suggest research directions for the future. Interestingly, some of these directions can benefit directly from the expertise in the parallel computing community.

Euro-Par 2014 Topics Overview

Topic 1: Support Tools and Environments

T. Kielmann, J.C. Cunha, A. Danalis, B. Freisleben, T. Margalef

This topic aims to bring together designers, developers, and users to share their concerns, ideas, and solutions towards more effective tools and environments for parallel and distributed computing. Current challenges are concerned with improved solutions for ease of use, programmability, correctness, reliability, scalability, portability, performance and energy efficiency for current and emerging parallel and distributed computing systems.

This year, a diversity of papers was submitted to this topic, proposing interesting and valuable research contributions. As a result of the reviewing process, 4 papers were accepted for publication. Globally, the accepted papers discuss foundations, design and implementation issues concerning tool development, and present reports of their practical evaluation via concrete applications and benchmarks.

The paper by Aguilar, Furlinger, and Laure, proposes the use of event flow graphs for monitoring MPI applications, as a compromise to balance the lower overhead of profiling tools with the more complete information available from tracers. The paper by Ananthakrishnan and Mueller, presents the ScalaJack tool, by combining customized instrumentation and in-situ data analysis, relying on aspect-orientation techniques for easing code instrumentation, analysis, and code refactoring. The paper by Jiang, Philippen, Knobloch and Mohr, describes extensions to a toolset for instrumenting, measuring and analyzing the performance of parallel programs based on Transactional Memory and Speculative Execution (TM/SE) directives for the IBM BlueGene/Q. The paper by Sofokleous, Loulloudes, Trihinas, Pallis, and Dikaiakos, presents a tool for integrated development of cloud applications, by addressing critical issues of open cloud standard specification, application migration across different cloud providers, and application elasticity.

We would like to thank all the authors who submitted papers to this topic, and the external reviewers, for their contribution to the success of the conference. We also thank the overall coordination and valuable support that was provided by the conference chairs.

Topic 2: Performance Prediction and Evaluation

A. Lastovetsky, F.F. Rivera, D.E. Singh, D.S. Nikolopoulos, L. Sousa, P. Tuma, W. Nagel

In recent years many novel methodologies and tools have been developed for evaluation, design, and model reduction of both existing and emerging parallel and distributed systems. At the same time, the scope of performance evaluation has constantly broadened to include the evaluation of reliability, robustness, energy consumption, and scalability in addition to traditional system functionalities. The aim of this topic, Performance Prediction and Evaluation, is to bring together system designers and researchers involved with the qualitative and quantitative evaluation and modelling of large-scale parallel and distributed applications and systems (e.g., Grids, Cloud computing environments, multi-core and hybrid architectures, and extreme-scale platforms). Authors were invited to submit novel research in all areas of performance prediction and evaluation, and to help bring together current theory and practice.

Heterogeneity, complexity and scale of the new generation of parallel systems, such as hybrid multicore/multi-accelerator nodes, large-scale heterogeneous clusters, Clouds, etc., coupled with the complexity and scale of applications make this topic particularly timely and challenging. This year, twenty three papers were submitted to the topic. Each paper was reviewed by four reviewers and seven papers were selected for presentation. In general, the quality of the submitted papers was high, and many new ideas, methods, and evaluations were presented. The accepted papers cover a wide range of hot topics and altogether give a good view on the challenges currently addressed by the research community.

The paper "DReAM: Per-Task DRAM Energy Metering in Multicore Systems" by Qixiao et al., introduces a new model to capture memory energy-consumption per task in a scenario where multiple tasks, possibly for different applications/users, are running on the multicore platform. They present a novel approach for measuring memory energy consumption on a per-task basis.

In the paper "Characterizing the Performance-Energy Tradeoff of Small ARM Cores in HPC Computation" by Michael A. Laurenzano et. al., an evaluation of energy and performance for HPC codes running on ARM vs. Intel cores is presented. They present an energy estimation model based on the instruction mix and memory operations obtained through static binary analysis. The paper is a measurement report on the performance and power consumption, in which different workloads from different computational kernels compared ARM processors (Cortex A9 and A15) to an Intel Sandy Bridge CPU.

The paper "ParaShares: Finding the Important Basic Blocks in Multithreaded Programs" by Melanie Kambadur and others presents ParaShare, a tool that identifies the basic blocks representing the most time-consuming part of the parallel program. A new metric to score and rank all basic blocks in the program based on their share of parallel execution is introduced. This work also illustrates how the tool can help to identify code whose optimization can bring significant execution time improvement.

The paper "Modeling the Impact of Reduced Memory Bandwidth on HPC Applications" by Ananta Tiwari and others presents a methodology for predicting the performance degradation of the code when the main memory bandwidth is reduced. Machine learning strategies are used to obtain the models. An instrumentation tool developed by the authors is used to obtain data. The accuracy of the method was measured on a number of large scale HPC applications.

Philipp Gschwandtner and others in their paper "Multi-Objective Auto-Tuning with Insieme: Optimization and Trade-O Analysis for Time, Energy and Resource Usage" present a multi-objective autotuner, which tries to optimize three conflicting criteria - execution time, resources, and energy consumption. Detailed analysis and several hints to improve the design of multi-objective autotuners and code optimization are provided.

The paper "Modeling and Simulation of a Dynamic Task-Based Runtime System for Heterogeneous Multi-Core Architectures" by Luka Stanisic et al., presents a simulator of a dynamic runtime system (StarPU) for heterogeneous multi-core architectures on top of a simulation toolkit such as SimGrid. It is used to simulate different linear-algebra applications on hybrid computing systems. This proposal is an example of how to predict the performance of applications on hybrid CPU+GPU systems in a short simulation time.

Finally, the paper "Performance Prediction and Evaluation of Parallel Applications in KVM, Xen, and Vmware" by Choel-Ho Hong and others, presents and evaluates a performance model of parallel applications on three virtualized platforms: VMware, Xen, and KVM. This model predicts the duration of the compute and synchronization phases considering the specific scheduling policies of each hypervisor. Using this, it predicts the application overall execution time. The model is based on the assumption that the parallel application consists of computation and synchronization phases.

We would like to take this opportunity to thank all the authors that submitted their work to this topic and the reviewers for their detailed and constructive reports. We are also grateful to the Euro-Par Organizing Committee for their guidance and help.

Topic 3: Scheduling and Load Balancing

H. Karatza, J. Barbosa, R. Yahyapour, N. Bessis, F. Suter, A. Goscinski, A. Iosup, C. Aykanat

The scheduling and load balancing topic targets in general the optimization of computing resources in several aspect of computation. From the mapping problem of assigning tasks to resources in order to minimize execution time, new approaches concerning energy efficiency become more predominant in today's scheduling research. With the wide range of platforms from high-end infrastructures, with multi-core machines and accelerators, to the highly dynamic cloud infrastructures, new challenges are imposed on resources management.

In "On Interactions Among Scheduling Policies: Finding Efficient Queue Setup Using High-Resolution Simulations", the authors address the issue of effectively designing and implementing a scheduling system in a real production supercomputer center, and they show that choosing the right scheduling algorithm is a key aspect when designing and implementing a scheduling system.

In "ProPS: A Progressively Pessimistic Scheduler for Software Transactional Memory", the authors propose a fine-grain scheduler that monitors concurrency levels between pairs of atomic operations and that dynamically reduces the number of transactions that may start concurrently.

In "A Queueing Theory Approach to Pareto Optimal Bags-of-Tasks Scheduling on Clouds" the authors present a method that minimizes the execution cost while meeting the makespan for data-intensive applications when data is stored outside the cloud so that task's running time is not known a priori.

In "Energy-Aware Multi-Organization Scheduling Problem", the authors model the multi-organization problem as an energy-aware scheduling approach and provide efficient heuristics for a static scenario where all jobs are ready at time zero.

In "Energy Efficient Scheduling of MapReduce Jobs", the authors present a linear programming relaxation technique that guarantees a polynomial time constant-factor approximation to the problem of power-aware map-reduce scheduling in the context of CPU speed scaling. In "SPAGHETtI: Scheduling/Placement Approach for task-Graphs on HETerogeneous architecture", the authors propose a static scheduling algorithm for heterogeneous HPC systems whose complexity is a function of the type of architectures rather than the number of processors.

Finally, we would like to thank all the contributing authors for their work, as well as the reviewers that helped in the selection process.

Topic 4: High Performance Architectures and Compilers

S.A. McKee, J.M.P. Cardoso, C. Jung, M. Själander, R. Hou, S. Onder

The topic High Performance Architectures and Compilers deals with architecture design and compilation for high performance systems. The areas of interest range from microprocessors to large-scale parallel machines (including multi-/many-core, possibly heterogeneous, architectures); from general-purpose to specialized hardware platforms (e.g., graphic coprocessors, low-power embedded systems); and from hardware design to compiler technology. On the compilation side, topics of interest include programmer productivity issues, concurrent and/or sequential language aspects, program analysis, program transformation, automatic discovery and/or management of parallelism at all levels, and the interaction between the compiler and the rest of the system. On the architecture side, the scope spans system architectures, processor micro-architecture, memory hierarchy, and multi-threading, and the impact of emerging trends.

In the 2014 Euro-Par edition of this topic, the selected papers are mainly focused on optimizations to dynamically adapt to computational contexts, techniques to transform GPU specific OpenCL programs to Many Core CPUs, and

OpenMP extensions to specify thread-level speculation and their integration in GCC.

Topic 5. Parallel and distributed Data Management

J.L. Larriba-Pey, P. Romano, D. Dominguez-Sal, K.U. Sattler, P. Martin, Y.S. Moon

Parallel and distributed management of data are fuelled by the need to develop complex services based on the analysis of ever growing volumes of data. In those cases, there are many situations where a complex hierarchy of requirements imply new approaches and techniques to perform locally parallel or geographically distributed operations to explore those data efficiently.

The scientific committee of Topic 5 has selected 5 papers for their high quality and interesting proposals they made. The proposals they make are varied and deal from the management of distributed relational and key-value stores, to reducing the I/O activity by either balancing the load or dinamically compressing the files of the storage system, to mining the top-k most frequent data items. In all, the papers accepted are varied and provide very good insights of the important issues in present management of data.

In particular, paper "Robust and Efficient Large-Large Table Outer Joins on Distributed Infrastructures" proposes a new algorithm to compute the outer join of datasets with large skew in a distributed relational environment. Paper "Ultra-fast Load Balancing of Distributed Key-Value Stores through Network-assisted Lookups" presents a load balancing technique based on hashing for key-value stores that exploits the flexible IP infrastructures of nowadays computers. Paper "Improving Read Performance with Online Access Pattern Analysis and Prefetching" proposes a novel on-line and real-time analyser that allows to reduce the patterns of the read I/O activity, reducing the overhead and storage capacity needs. Paper "Applying selectively parallel I/O compression to parallel storage systems" presents a new dynamic mechanism to decide whether to compress the size of the files in a storage system, reducing their I/O time. Finally, paper "Top-k Item Identification on Dynamic and Distributed Datasets" proposes a gossip protocol to select the top-k most frequent items in a distributed system with single copy of the data.

The chairs of Topic 5 want to thank the members of the committee for their valuable contributions to the review process and the work they did in managing the whole process in a timely fashion and ensuring very high quality.

Topic 6: Grid, Cluster and Cloud Computing

U. Schwiegelshohn, H. Paulino, O. Beaumont, S. Matsuoka, R. Sakellariou, D. Talia, M.S. Pérez-Hernández, and V. Saraswat

Since the operating costs of computing systems are steadily increasing and large computer systems have the potential to increase efficiency in comparison to smaller local installations users are increasingly interested in remotely executing their parallel applications on such systems. In particularly, the use of virtualization has led to a substantial increase of flexibility for these systems. But there are still many open questions that must be addressed by research. For instance, the separation of users and systems due to virtualization produces a new form of market economy requiring business models and service guarantees. Therefore, we need new tools that support monitoring of these guarantees and provide accounting. Also user friendly environments are expected to support users in porting existing applications on these systems and help them to develop applications that efficiently exploit the vast amount of parallelism offered by these systems.

Due to the increasing importance of energy expenses, users and systems administrators are interested in methods to improve system and application management without significantly affecting the quality of service. With respect to this management challenge, it is important to develop methods that allow bridging the above mentioned separation of user and system. Therefore, Topic 6 is devoted to the use and the management of large computer systems. It is the objective of our topic to propose and evaluate new approaches that allow the efficient execution of parallel computing tasks on these systems and therefore to help developers of parallel programs to exploit the vast computing power of these resources without compromising efficiency. In EuroPar 2014, Topic 6 particularly covers workflow management for complex applications, resource management issues, communication in large computer systems, and cooperation between different installations to increase efficiency.

All submitted papers were reviewed by at least 4 reviewers, with 4 papers being selected for inclusion in the program. We are convinced that the contributions of these papers will help us further advance the use of these computer systems for a wide variety of applications.

We would especially like to thank our colleagues, who being experts in the field helped in the reviewing process.

Topic 7: Green High Performance Computing

M. Schulz, L. Lopes, E.S. Quintana Orti, K. Inou

Optimizing power and energy consumption has been identified as one of the most critical issues on our way to exascale. Computations will have to be orders of magnitude more energy efficient than in today's architectures; applications will have to work with fixed total system power caps put in place to not exceed the limited power available; and systems will have to mitigate the impact of power swings during changing workloads. To achieve efficient execution of applications under these constraints, we require new approaches in all aspects of power-aware computing.

Given the importance of the topic, it was introduced for the first time in the program of the conference with the goal of providing a forum to bring together researchers in this developing field. The contributions received focused on subjects such as: the analysis of the energy efficiency of specific CPU/GPU, cache and memory architectures; the impact of power-saving strategies on performance, and; tools to profile energy usage in HPC systems. The two papers selected for publication describe relevant research on energy efficient cache hierarchy configurations for general purpose GPU computing, and on the impact of data movement between nodes in the power consumption of a system, as a function of the way the inter-process communication layer is designed.

Topic 8: Distributed Systems and Algorithms

P. Felber, L. Veiga, P. Grace, V. Gramoli, F. Kon, C. Travers

Parallel computing is increasingly exposed to the development and challenges of distributed systems, such as the lack of load balancing, asynchrony, long latencies, network partitions, failures, malicious and selfish behavior, disconnected operations, well-suited computing models and data structures, heterogeneity. Furthermore, distributed systems are becoming larger, more diverse and more dynamic (changing topology, highly dynamic number of participants).

This topic provides a forum for research and practice, of interest to both academia and industry, about distributed systems, distributed computing, distributed algorithms, and parallel processing on distributed systems.

All submitted papers received at least four reviews, resulting in three papers being accepted for the conference.

The paper *Spanning Tree or Gossip for Aggregation: a Comparative Study* by Lehel Nyers and Mark Jelasity proposes a study assessing the two competing paradigms typically used for distributed aggregation queries: tree-based and gossip-based algorithms. It addresses common stereotypes, e.g. about the fragility of trees and slowness of gossip, and encourages researchers to consider more carefully the best topologies for each particular problem or situation.

The paper *Shades: Expediting Kademlia's Lookup Process* by Gil Einziger and Roy Friedman addresses how to further the Kademlia DHT. It proposes a new caching and augmented routing mechanism, designed to improve lookup performance and better load balance. This is achieved by combining a local cache keeping the most frequently requested items and an additional routing mechanism based on partitioning nodes and items into colors.

Finally, the paper *Analysis and Comparison of Truly Distributed Solvers for Linear Least Squares Problems on Wireless Sensor Networks* by Karl E. Prikopa, Hana Straková and Wilfried N. Gansterer proposes a new such solver, adapted from a matrix factorization method, that requires fewer messages per node to reach high accuracy, with an analytical and experimental comparison of the communication cost of various solvers

We would like to take the opportunity of thanking the authors who submitted a contribution, as well as the Euro-Par Organizing Committee and the external referees who provided highly useful comments. Their efforts have made this conference and this topic possible.

Topic 9: Parallel and Distributed Programming

H. Bal, J.L. Sobral, A. Varbanescu, C. Perez, F. Huet, M. Danelutto, P. Kilpatrick

Developing parallel or distributed applications is a difficult task and it requires adequate programming abstractions and models, efficient design tools, high performance languages and libraries, and experimental validation. This topic provides a forum for presentation of new results and practical experience in this domain. It emphasizes research that facilitates the design and development of high-performance, correct, portable, and scalable parallel programs.

All papers of this topic received 4 reviews that were further discussed among all 7 PC members in a tele-conference meeting. As a result, six strong papers were accepted for the conference, covering important topics such us software and hardware transactional memory, graph analytics, mesh-based simulations, algebraic computations, and random number generation.

Topic 10: Parallel Numerical Algorithms

R.H. Bisseling, L. Grigori, D. Kressner, R.M.S. Ralha

Getting progress in many society-relevant issues relies on the usage of numerical simulations. These numerical simulations very often use sophisticated numerical algorithms and massively parallel computers. Thus the design of robust and scalable parallel algorithms is an important research topic, and this track is composed of four papers that consider several such important numerical algorithms. They include solving linear systems of equations, computing the echelon form of a matrix as used for example in algebraic cryptanalysis, time-domain BEM for the wave equation, or exploiting structure to design efficient computational kernels. Both academic and industrial applications can benefit from the algorithms described in these papers.

The paper *A distributed CPU-GPU sparse direct solver* by Piyush Sao, Richard Vuduc, and Xiaoye Sherry Li, presents a hybrid implementation of the sparse LU factorization which can be used to solve very large sparse linear systems of equations. The hybrid implementation is based on MPI, OpenMP, and Cuda, and it is performed in the context of SuperLU_DIST, a widely used solver implementing the sparse LU factorization for distributed memory computers. SuperLU_DIST is based on static pivoting and right looking sparse LU factorization. In this context, the paper shows that aggregation of data and pipeline execution to overlap computation with communication are important ingredients for obtaining an overall efficient hybrid implementation of the sparse LU factorization.

The paper *Parallel Computation of Echelon Forms* by Jean-Guillaume Dumas, Thierry Gautier, Clement Pernet, and Ziad Sultan, presents parallel algorithms for computing echelon forms over a finite field on shared memory architectures. This problem is relevant in a variety of applications, including algebraic cryptanalysisy. Several algorithms are discussed in this paper, which exploit different partitionings of the matrix, one-dimensional or two-dimensional, block algorithms or recursive algorithms, as well as the usage of fast matrix multiplication Strassen-Winograd algorithm. Several strategies are also developed to balance tiling with delaying modular reductions. Well designed performance experiments compare these different algorithms and outline the role of the different optimizations for obtaining a very efficient parallel implementation.

In the paper *Structured Orthogonal Inversion of Block p-cyclic Matrices on Multicores with GPU Accelerators*, Sergiy Gogolenko, Zhaojun Bai, and Richard Scalettar consider the problem of computing the inverse of block p-cyclic matrices on multicores and GPUs. Such an operation arises in quantum Monte Carlo algorithms. Given that in this case Gaussian elimination with partial pivoting encounters numerical instability, the authors present an algorithm based on a block structured orthogonal factorization, with a judicious distribution of the work between CPUs and GPGPUs using a quantitative performance model. Performance results show that the method is very efficient on hybrid architectures.

In the paper *Time-domain BEM for Wave Equation: Optimization and Hybrid Parallelization*, Berenger Bramas, Olivier Coulaud, and Guillaume Sylvand focus on efficient implementation of an existing time-domain boundary element method to simulate wave propagation. The code developed is part of an industrial computational work-flow at the Airbus Group Innovation and intends to replace an older code. The most intensive computational kernel of the algorithm is, for each time step, the sum of a number of sparse matrix-vector products. Unlike previous works, that consider the parallelization of individual sparse matrix products, the central idea here is to exploit the particular sparsity pattern of the matrices to compute several of such products simultaneously. The experimental results are promising.

Topic 11: Multicore and Manycore Programming

R. Namyst, R. Rocha, C. Kessler, E. Larsson, F. Mueller, J.F. Méhaut, J. Träff, M. Aldinucci, M. Sato

Modern homogeneous and heterogeneous multicore and manycore architectures are now part of the high-end and mainstream computing scene. The complexity of these new architectures created several programming challenges and achieving performance on these systems is a difficult task. This topic seeks to explore productive programming of multicore, many integrated cores, and hybrid systems with accelerators. It focuses on novel research and solutions in the form of programming models, languages, compilers, libraries, runtime systems and analysis tools to increase the programmability of multicore, manycore, and hybrid systems, in the context of general-purpose parallel computing and HPC.

The quality of submissions was very high. Papers have been selected based on the recommendations of at least four reviewers. The six accepted papers address a representative set of issues related to the multicore and manycore programming.

The paper *High-Throughput Maps on Message-Passing Manycore Architectures: Partitioning versus Replication'* by Omid Shahmirzadi, Thomas Ropars and Andre Schiper discusses the challenges in implementing scalable data structures for message-passing manycores.

The paper *A Fast Sparse Block Circulant Matrix Vector Product* by Eloy Romero, Andrés Tomás, Antonio Soriano and Ignacio Blanquer exploits the problem of calculating a sparse matrix vector product where the sparse matrix is block circulant.

The paper *Scheduling data flow program in XKaapi: A new affinity-based algorithm for heterogeneous architectures* by Raphaël Bleuse, Thierry Gautier, João V. F. Lima, Gregory Mounie and Denis Trystram proposes a generic mechanism to automatically optimize the scheduling between CPUs and GPUs on modern multicore GPU-based architectures.

The paper *Delegation Locking Libraries for Improved Performance of Multithreaded Programs* by David Klaftenegger, Konstantinos Sagonas and Kjell Winblad proposes libraries for C and C++ that provide an interface for delegation locks as an alternative to traditional locking.

The paper *A Generic Strategi for Multi-Stage Stencil Applications* by Mauro Bianco and Benjamin Cumming introduces a buffering technique which takes into account intermediate results in the multi-stage procedure to improve memory hierarchy utilization in stencil applications.

The paper *Evaluation of OpenMP Task Scheduling Algorithms for Large NUMA Architectures* by Jerome Clet-Ortega, Patrick Carribault and Marc Perache presents a configurable OpenMP task scheduler for studying and analyzing work-stealing scheduling algorithms for large NUMA architectures.

We are grateful to the authors of all submitted papers for their contribution and interest in this topic and to the program committee members and subreviewers for their dedicated time and knowledge in evaluating and ranking so many submissions.

Topic 12: Theory and Algorithms for Parallel Computation

A. Pietracaprina, P. Ribeiro, K. Herley, S. Vassilvitskii

Parallelism permeates all types of current computing systems, from single CPU machines, to large server farms, supercomputers, clouds, and even Internet-based volunteer computing infrastructures. The effective use of parallelism depends crucially on the availability of faithful, yet tractable, computational models for algorithm design and analysis, and of efficient algorithmic strategies for solving key computational problems on prominent classes of platforms. This topic presents novel contributions that explore foundational issues, models, and algorithms relevant for both traditional and emerging parallel computing scenarios.

All submitted papers were reviewed by the four members of the topic's committee, and two excellent papers were accepted for presentation at the conference. One paper, "Power-Aware Replica Placement in Tree Networks with Multiple Servers per Client" by Guillaume Aupy, Anne Benoit, Matthieu Journault and Yves Robert, studies some variants of the replica placement problem on trees, whose objective is to minimize power consumption. The other paper, "On Constructing DAG-Schedules with Large AREAs" by Scott T. Roche, Arnold L. Rosenberg and Rajmohan Rajaraman, explores the construction of schedules for computational DAGs which maximize the AREA metric, that is, the rate at which the schedules make nodes eligible for execution. In both papers, the authors prove the NP-completeness of the decision versions of the problems under consideration, and provide polynomial-time heuristics, whose efficiency is tested experimentally.

Topic 13: High Performance Networks and Communication

J. Flich, F. Araujo, C. Minkenberg, M. Palesi, T. Skeie

The topic on High-performance networks and communications is devoted to communication issues in scalable compute and storage systems, such as tightly coupled parallel computers, clusters, and networks of workstations, including hierarchical and hybrid designs featuring several levels of possibly different interconnects. All aspects of communication in modern compute and storage systems are of interest, including advances in the design, implementation, and evaluation of interconnection networks, network interfaces, system and storage area networks, on-chip interconnects, communication protocols and interfaces, routing and communication algorithms, and communication aspects of parallel and distributed algorithms.

In this edition, all received papers went through a rigorous selection process with at least four reviews. Two papers were selected for final inclusion in the program. One of the papers deals with programmable networking devices to accelerate the implementation of collective operations, by offloading functionality to the underlying network, while the other one deals with RDMA-based MapReduce, when used over the popular parallel file system "Lustre".

Topic 14: High Performance and Scientific Applications

F. Brasileiro, Pedro Medeiros, A. Sequeira, G. Fedak, W. Cirne

The availability of an abundance of computing resources worldwide has substantially impacted the way that research is nowadays conducted both in the industry and in the academy. The new ways of doing science, rooted on the unprecedented processing, communication and storage infrastructure that became available to researchers encompass activities such as computational modelling and simulation, processing of large amounts of data, often geographically spread, and the visualisation of complex datasets. The constant technological advances that make computers faster and storage more plentiful are not enough to cope with the increased demand generated by more accurate and complex modelling, and an ever increasing quantity of data being generated. There is thus a growing need for a range of high performance applications which can use parallel compute systems effectively, and which have efficient data I/O strategies.

In this track, six papers were selected for presentation at the conference. These papers made valuable contributions for the advance of the state of the art in developing scalable applications for parallel and distributed systems in a variety of domains, including optics, astrophysics, genotyping, and flood forecast, as well as algorithms that can be used in different applications, such as random fields generation, and set intersection. One common characteristic of almost all these works is the use of GPGPU for increasing performance. In the paper "High-Performance Pseudo-analytical Simulation of Multi-object Adaptive Optics over Multi-GPU Systems", Zou et al. developed a novel hybrid pseudo-analytical simulation scheme that allows the accurate and detailed simulation of the tomographic problem. González-Domínguez et al., in "Hybrid CPU/GPU Acceleration of Detection of 2-SNP Epistatic Interactions in GWAS" present EpistSearch, a parallelized tool that uses a novel filter to determine the interactions between all Single Nucleotide Polymorphism pairs of an individual. Lange and Fortin, in "Parallel dual tree transversal on multi-core and many-core architectures for astrophysical N-body simulations" present a parallel dual tree traversal algorithm targeting multi-core CPUs and many-core architectures. The paper "IFM: A Scalable High Resolution Flood Modelling Framework", by Singhal el al. presents a highly scalable, integrated flood forecasting system called IFM, that includes a weather model, a soil model, and an overland water routing model. In the paper "Random Fields Generation on the GPU with the Spectral Turning Bands Method", Hunger et al. introduce a random field generation algorithm based on the turning band method that is optimized for massively parallel hardware such as GPUs. The paper "Fast Set Intersection through Run-Time Bitmap Construction over PForDelta-compressed Indexes" by Klasky and Samatova proposed, implemented and evaluated a fast set intersection approach that couples the storage light-weight PForDelta indexing format with computationally-efficient bitmaps, through a specialized on-the-fly conversion.

Of course the program that we were able to assemble was only possible because of the many high quality contributions that were submitted to the topic. We take this opportunity to thank all the authors for their submissions. We are also indebted to our fellow members of the technical program committee, and the external reviewers, for their judicious assessment of the submissions. Finally, we would also like to acknowledge the invaluable support that has been provided by the conference chairs and the steering committee.

Topic 15: GPU and Accelerator Computing

P. Kelly, J. Lourenço, A. Heinecke, A. Lokhmotov, C. Plessl, D. Unat, D. Blanco Heras, L. Howes, N. Maruyama, P. Gonnet

This topic provides a forum for the presentation of the latest research results and practical experience in GPU and Accelerator Computing. Accelerators of various kinds offer massive performance and power advantages for suitable applications, at every scale from embedded and mobile to supercomputers and datacenters. Examples include graphics processors (GPUs), "manycore" devices, such as Intel's Xeon Phi and other platforms with large numbers of simple cores, as well as more custom devices, customizable FPGA-based systems and streaming dataflow architectures.

The research challenge for this topic is to explore new technologies for realising this potential. We encouraged submissions in all areas related to accelerators: architecture, languages, compilers, libraries, runtime, debugging and profiling tools, algorithms. Papers demonstrating deep engagement with applications and algorithms were particularly welcome, aiming to identify broader insights on the problems of optimization (for performance and power), programmability, performance portability, support for and integration with legacy code.

We thank the many helpful referees, who provided at least four reports on each of the submitted papers. After vigorous, good-natured and pleasurable debate among the program committee members, eight were accepted. So: thank you to the PC members, and to everyone who helped with the refereeing.

The quality of submissions was uniformly high, and without exception, the papers we were unable to accept this time represent sound work which we would encourage the authors to submit next year in more mature form. Thus, thank you also to the authors!

Euro-Par's tight page limit makes it a forum for work which is focussed on interesting new ideas, rather than extensive experimental evaluation of more established material. We believe this makes for a lively programme of presentations, and we are confident there will be plenty of interesting questions and discussion.

Table of Contents

Support Tools Environments

Performance Prediction and Evaluation

Scheduling and Load Balancing

High Performance Architectures and Compilers

Parallel and Distributed Data Management

Grid, Cluster and Cloud Computing

Parallel Numerical Algorithms

Multicore and Manycore Programming

Theory and Algorithms for Parallel Computation

High Performance Networks and Communication

High-Performance and Scientic Applications

GPU and Accelerator Computing

MPI Trace Compression
Using Event Flow Graphs

Xavier Aguilar[1], Karl Fürlinger[2], and Erwin Laure[1]

[1] KTH Royal Institute of Technology,
High Performance Computing and Visualization Department (HPCViz)
and Swedish e-Science Research Center (SeRC),
Lindstedvägen 5, 10044 Stockholm, Sweden
[2] Ludwig-Maximilians-Universität (LMU) Munich,
Computer Science Department, MNM Team,
Oettingenstr. 67, 80538 Munich, Germany

Abstract. Understanding how parallel applications behave is crucial for using high-performance computing (HPC) resources efficiently. However, the task of performance analysis is becoming increasingly difficult due to the growing complexity of scientific codes and the size of machines. Even though many tools have been developed over the past years to help in this task, current approaches either only offer an overview of the application discarding temporal information, or they generate huge trace files that are often difficult to handle.

In this paper we propose the use of *event flow graphs* for monitoring MPI applications, a new and different approach that balances the low overhead of profiling tools with the abundance of information available from tracers. Event flow graphs are captured with very low overhead, require orders of magnitude less storage than standard trace files, and can still recover the full sequence of events in the application. We test this new approach with the NERSC-8/Trinity Benchmark suite and achieve compression ratios up to 119x.

Keywords: MPI event flow graphs, trace compression, trace reconstruction, performance monitoring.

1 Introduction

Current petascale systems provide massive computing power to run scientific simulations in many disciplines ranging, for example, from weather modeling to protein structure analysis. However, their efficient use requires optimized applications with several levels of parallelism, efficient inter-process communication for complex network topologies and optimized memory access through deep memory hierarchies. Therefore, tools to characterize and better understand the performance behavior of applications are an essential part of the HPC landscape.

Performance tools for HPC systems have been widely studied and developed over the last years. These tools can be divided into two families: profilers and

F. Silva et al. (Eds.): Euro-Par 2014, LNCS 8632, pp. 1–12, 2014.

tracers. Profilers generate reports with execution statistics, whereas tracers produce time-stamped event log files. Profilers are less intrusive and more scalable than tracers but profilers do not maintain a record of the structure and sequence of events. In contrast, tracers give the whole picture of what happened during the run time of an application, but are limited in scalability due to the huge amount of data they generate. Current tracing methodologies can produce trace files in the order of gigabytes for only a few minutes of application execution [1]. The size of the trace files also grows drastically as the number of cores used by an application increases. Thus, new scalable methods for performance data collection maintaining sequence and temporal order of the information are needed.

In this paper, we propose a novel approach for application characterization using *event flow graphs* which is designed to combine the advantages of profiling and tracing. This method has the scalability of profiling without discarding the temporal ordering of events performed by the application. We have implemented our solution in the Integrated Performance Monitoring tool (IPM) [2,3], a lightweight and scalable profiling tool for parallel applications. It uses a hash table in memory to store performance data and provides rich metrics about MPI-related events such as MPI timings, communication volume and the communication topology. IPM is open-source and is available freely from http://www.ipm2.org under the LGPL license.

The rest of this paper is structured as follows: In Sect. 2 we define and describe our approach for generating MPI event flow graphs. Section 3 shows some experimental results using the NERSC-8/Trinity Benchmark Suite. In Sect. 4 we review some of the related work in trace compression. The paper ends with future work and conclusions in Sect. 5 and Sect. 6, respectively.

2   MPI Event Flow Graphs

In this work, we use and extend the definitions of Fürlinger et al. [4] for a formal treatment of performance monitoring events. We start with an MPI application with n processes (identified by their ranks $[0..n-1]$), where each process i is characterized by a set of events $E_i \subseteq E$ where E represents all the events that happened during the run time of the application. An event can be any action performed by the application, but in this work we restrict ourselves to MPI operations. In other words, an event is an MPI primitive call.

Each event e has a signature $\delta(e)$ that captures the aspects of the events we are interested in. We can think of the signature as a k-tuple of components $\delta(e) = (\delta^1(e), \delta^2(e), ..., \delta^k(e))$ which represent relevant metrics, such as the type of MPI call, communication partner rank, data transfer size, callsite (source code position), or program region. The mapping from event to signature is not necessarily injective and therefore statistics are recorded for each different signature value. Hence, we can conceptually represent the performance behavior of an MPI process as a table where each row is an event indexed by its signature and each column is a different statistic (number of occurrences, minimal duration, maximal duration, etc.).

In practical terms, the performance behavior is recorded in a hash table in memory which is implemented in IPM with the event signatures $\delta(e)$ being used as the hash keys. The values in this hash table are performance metrics such as the number of occurrences and different timings (minimum, maximum and total duration) of each event. This lets us store performance data in the hash keys as well as in the table entries, thereby reducing the monitoring overhead. Notice that if we include the event timestamp as a component of the signature, we have a model for tracing. If the timestamp is omitted, we lose the temporal dimension of the data and instead have a model for profiling since we cannot know the order in which the events happened during the application's run time. However, as we show in this paper, the temporal ordering of events can nevertheless be fully recovered by keeping track of a (very short) history of the event signatures.

Consider again an MPI application with n processes and a set of events $E_i = \{e_0, e_1, ..., e_m\}$ belonging to process with rank i. Let $\delta(e) : E_i \mapsto S_i$ be the signature function at rank i and $s_i^0 \in S_i$ an initial signature value. Then $\delta'(e)$ with

$$\delta'(e_0) = (s_i^0, \delta(e_0))$$
$$\delta'(e_i) = (\delta(e_{i-1}), \delta(e_i)) \qquad \text{if } i > 0$$

represents the *signature history* for δ. Then, the directed weighted graph $G = (N_i, L_i, w_i, s_i^0)$ with the event signatures forming the set of nodes N_i and the signature history the set of edges L_i

$$N_i = \{\delta(e_i)\} \qquad e_i \in E_i$$
$$L_i = \{\delta'(e_i)\} \qquad e_i \in E_i$$
$$w_i : L_i \mapsto \mathbb{N} \qquad w_i(l) = |\{e_i : \delta'(e_i) = l\}| \qquad l \in L_i$$

is the *event flow graph* for the MPI rank i with s_i^0 as the initial node of the graph. In other words, in the event flow graph the nodes correspond to the MPI calls performed by the application and the edges correspond to the transitions between them. The edge weight (w_i) or edge count is the number of transitions between nodes. Figure 1 depicts a simple MPI application and the corresponding event flow graph for one of its MPI processes, where MPI_Init is the initial node of the graph. Notice that the application has as many graphs as MPI processes.

2.1 Reconstructing Traces from Event Flow Graphs

For the simple example in Fig. 1 we see that the event flow graph completely captures the behavior of an MPI process. It contains all the events performed by the process (nodes of the graph) and the transitions between them (edges between nodes). Therefore, the path $N_i = \{s_i^0, s_i^1 ... s_i^n\}$ from the initial node s_i^0 to the final node s_i^n of the graph corresponds to the event trace for process with rank i. The total number of events (length of the path) in the trace is

$$\sum w_i(l) + 1 \quad \forall l \in L_i$$

```
void main(int argc, char *argv[ ]) {
    MPI_Init(...);
    MPI_Comm_size(...);
    MPI_Comm_rank(..., &myrank);

    for( i = 0; i < 10; i++) {
        if (myrank is even)
            MPI_Send(...);
        else
            MPI_Recv(...);

        MPI_Reduce(...);
    }
    MPI_Finalize( );
}
```

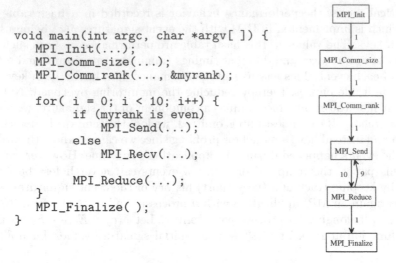

Fig. 1. A simple MPI program and the event flow graph generated for an MPI process with an even rank number

and the number of times that each event e_i appears, also known as node cardinality for the node $\delta(e_i)$, is

$$\sum w_i(in\_edges(\delta(e_i)))$$

In other words, the number of events in the trace is the sum of all edge weights of the graph plus one and each event appears as many times as the total weight of its incoming edges.

In this paper we are only concerned with reconstructing the sequence of events in a trace (time stamps and intervals between events are topics for future work). It is clear that the trace can be easily reconstructed for simple cases such as linear graphs and graphs with a single loop such as the one in Fig. 1. However, there are cases that cannot be reconstructed using flow graphs in this manner. This occurs for applications with conditional branches within a loop, for example, the code snippet in Fig. 2. When reconstructing the trace, we cannot know the order of the calls after the MPI_Barrier across loop iterations.

Thus, we extended our model to cover such cases. Firstly, we added a sequence number to the exit edges of the branch nodes (that is, nodes with more than one exit edge). This new weight is defined as a 2-tuple $< \mathbb{N}, \mathbb{N} >$ where the first element is the sequence number for that edge and the second element is the edge count as defined above. With this extra data, we always know which edge was taken in a branch node when traversing the graph. Figure 3 shows this new extended model.

Secondly, we changed our directed graphs to multidigraphs, that is, directed graphs with more than one edge between the same two nodes. This new graph

```
for( i = 0; i < 10; i++) {
    MPI_Barrier(...);
    if (i < 5)
        MPI_Bcast(...);
    else
        MPI_Gather(...);

    MPI_Reduce(...);
}
```

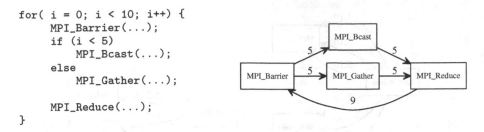

Fig. 2. Example of a conditional branch within a loop and its corresponding event flow graph

model can represent applications in which the conditional branches within a loop vary across loop iterations as depicted in Fig. 3.

```
1: MPI_Comm_rank
2: MPI_Barrier
3: MPI_Send
4: MPI_Barrier
5: MPI_Recv
6: MPI_Barrier
7: MPI_Send
8: MPI_Finalize
```

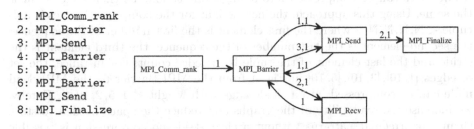

Fig. 3. A sequence of MPI operations and the corresponding multidigraph

2.2 Compressing Edges in Branch Nodes

As shown in the previous section, our new event flow graphs are multidigraphs with sequence numbers in edges that have the same source node. Thereby, we can always reconstruct the event trace associated with an application without any loss of temporal order information by traversing the graph edges in ascending order of their sequence number.

However, creating multiple edges between nodes to record the sequence order can lead to huge graphs. In fact, our experiments showed that this situation is quite common among real applications which sometimes have flow graphs with thousands of edges going out from one node. Nevertheless, those graphs usually exhibit repetitive patterns in terms of the multiple edges between nodes as shown in Fig. 4. In that case, the application calls MPI_Barrier followed by MPI_Recv 10 times, then it calls MPI_Barrier followed by MPI_Send 10 times, afterwards it again calls MPI_Barrier followed by MPI_Recv 10 times, and so on, until MPI_Recv and MPI_Send have each been called 30 times.

As we can see in the figure, the sequence numbers for those edges in the event flow graph follow different arithmetic progressions, that is, the difference between two consecutive numbers in the sequence is constant. In such cases, the

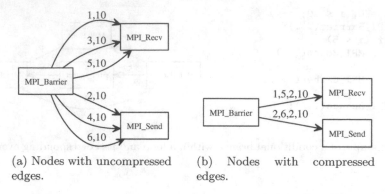

(a) Nodes with uncompressed edges.

(b) Nodes with compressed edges.

Fig. 4. Branch compression of multiple edges between nodes

set of edges can be compressed into a single one as long as their edge count is the same. Using this approach, the new weight for the compressed edges is a 4-tuple $< \mathbb{N}, \mathbb{N}, \mathbb{N}, \mathbb{N} >$ where the first element is the first number of the sequence, the second element is the last number of the sequence, the third element is the stride and the last element of the tuple is the edge count. For instance, the set of edges $[1, 10], [3, 10], [5, 10]$ in Fig. 4 from the MPI_Barrier to the MPI_Send node can be compressed into a single edge with weight $< 1, 5, 2, 10 >$. Hereby, we increase the readability of the graphs and reduce the space needed to store them. For irregular patterns without a clear stride no compression is possible and individual edges need to be stored.

2.3   Implementation in IPM

We have extended IPM to generate MPI event flow graphs as described in the previous section. IPM maintains event statistics such as the total duration, the minimum and maximum time and the number of occurrences for all MPI calls. These statistics are stored in a hash table using the event signatures described in Sect. 2 as the hash key for each event.

To record the transitions between events, we introduced a second hash table that contains pairs of event signatures. This "history" hash table keeps information on transition pairs of event signatures $(\delta(e_{i-1}), \delta(e_i))$. IPM keeps track of the last event signature by storing it in a variable and updating it each time there is a new insertion into the transition hash table. Moreover, IPM also keeps track of branches within loops by checking if there are two pairs in the transition hash table $(< \delta(e_i), \delta(e_j) >, < \delta(e_i), \delta(e_k) >)$ where $\delta(e_j) \neq \delta(e_k)$. If that is so, each element is given a sequence number indicating their arrival order. IPM also joins elements in the transition hash table to compress the number of edges between nodes as described in Sect. 2.2. It keeps track of the old branches for each node. When a branch finishes, IPM checks if the sequence number of the branch follows an arithmetic progression in relation to any of the older branches of that particular node. If that is the case and if both branches have the same edge count, the two branches are compressed into a single branch. Upon program termination, IPM constructs the event flow graph for each MPI process by matching pairs of event edges.

3 Experiments

In order to test our approach for trace reconstruction from MPI event flow graphs, we used the following mini-applications from the NERSC-8/Trinity Benchmarks suite [5]: AMG, an algebraic multigrid solver for linear systems on unstructured grids; GTC, a 3D Particle-in-cell code (PIC) with a non-spectral Poisson solver used for gyrokinetic particle simulation of turbulent transport in burning plasma; MILC, a code for simulating four dimensional SU(3) lattice gauge theory to study quantum chromodynamics (QCD); SNAP, a proxy application that models the performance of a modern discrete ordinates neutral particle transport application, PARTISN [6]; MiniDFT, a plane-wave DFT mini-kernel that computes self-consistent solutions for the Kohn-Sham equations; MiniFE, a mini-application that implements different kernels representative of implicit finite-element applications; MiniGhost, a mini-application that implements a difference stencil across a homogenous three dimensional domain.

The experiments were performed on a Cray XE6 with 2 twelve-core AMD MagnyCours at 2.1 GHz per node. The nodes are interconnected through a Cray Gemini Network, each of them having a total of 32 GB DDR3 memory. The benchmarks were compiled with Intel 12.1.5 and run using the small test case that is provided for each one of them.

3.1 Overhead

Figure 5 shows for each benchmark the percentage of overhead introduced by IPM over their total running time (writing the graph files to disk is also included in the percentage). These experiments were run using strong scaling except for SNAP, MILC and GTC. As depicted in the figure, the overhead introduced to generate the *event flow graphs* is almost negligible, being always below 2%.

3.2 Compression Ratios

Table 1 shows the compression ratio for each benchmark in terms of file size between our flow graph file and a standard trace file for that application generated by IPM, in other words, it shows how many times smaller the event flow graph file is compared to the standard trace file. It is important to be aware that both files contain exactly the same amount of information for each MPI call: call name, bytes sent or received, communication partner and callsite. As our current implementation generates one flow graph per MPI process, the table shows statistics for the minimum, maximum and average compression ratios for all processes within each application. The results in the table demonstrate that the compression depends on the nature of the benchmark. For instance, we have

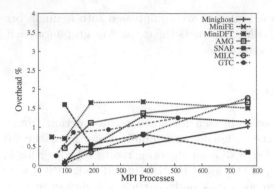

Fig. 5. Percentage of overhead over total running time introduced in the NERSC-8/Trinity benchmarks when generating their event flow graphs

applications such as SNAP with flow graph files 119 times smaller than the standard linear trace whereas in other applications such as AMG the compression ratio is 1.76. In terms of file size, the amount of disk space required to store the traces for a run with 96 cores of SNAP is 1.1 GB whereas the space required for the *event flow graphs* is only 10 MB.

In order to explain this variance in the compression we need to look into some graph metrics. Table 2 gives statistics for the number of nodes, the number of links and the average cardinality of nodes in the graphs. Remember that the node cardinality is the number of instances an event $\delta(e_i)$ happened during the run time of the application as explained in Sect. 2.1. The figures in the tables show that low compression ratios are related to graphs with a large number of nodes with low cardinality such as AMG or MiniDFT. In contrast, graphs consisting of a few nodes with high node cardinality exhibit very good compression ratios.

As explained in Sect. 3, each event is identified uniquely using a signature defined by several metrics. Furthermore, each one of these events is eventually converted into a node in the event flow graph. Therefore, the metrics used as signature elements have an important role in the cardinality of the graph. In our experiments, the event signature was composed of the MPI call name, the MPI rank, the number of bytes associated with the call and the call site. Thus, it is not surprising that applications with huge graphs (such as AMG) have a large number of different call sites and message sizes - this was confirmed by our experiments. The variability in the number of call sites and the sizes of messages leads to a greater number of signatures, and consequently more nodes in the resulting graph.

Finally, we performed another set of experiments with some of the NERSC-8 benchmarks and a five-point stencil code computing a wave 2D equation [7] to measure the increase ratio in file size as we increase the number of simulation time steps. Figure 6 shows that standard trace files increase linearly with the number of simulation steps whereas the event flow graph (EFG) files do not. For most of the benchmarks, the small increment in the graph file size is caused by the addition of new edges to the graphs due to the execution of different call paths as the number of simulation steps increases. (For GTC the number of nodes also increases due to a variation in the size of messages.) However, applications that execute the same loop over time such as the 5-stencil code have constant event flow graph size irrespective of the number of simulation steps. For applications like that, the only difference between graphs from runs with different simulation times is their node cardinality.

Table 1. File compression ratios

Benchmark	Ranks	Min	Max	Avg
AMG	96	1.70	1.85	1.76
GTC	64	37.95	47.65	46.60
MILC	96	38.67	39.44	39.03
SNAP	96	75.37	210.88	119.23
MiniDFT	40	3.14	8.39	4.33
MiniFE	144	15.23	22.25	19.93
Minighost	96	3.84	5.72	4.85

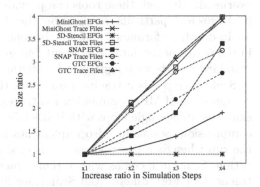

Fig. 6. Increase in file size when increasing simulation steps

Table 2. Number of nodes, edges and cardinality of nodes in the event flow graphs

		Num. of nodes			Num. of edges			Node Cardinality		
Benchmark	Ranks	Min	Max	Avg	Min	Max	Avg	Min	Max	Avg
AMG	96	4973	15115	9,348.94	5052	17287	10,586.47	4.44	4.83	4.59
GTC	64	114	130	114.50	120	151	121.20	96.52	109.53	109.10
MILC	96	6330	6347	6330.18	97426	97443	97426.18	1653.01	1657.31	1657.27
SNAP	96	22	28	24.77	340	1729	1,120.26	7,007.50	17,805.91	14,149.22
MiniDFT	40	512	1087	690.30	873	5851	1,980.38	12.39	63.01	27.29
MiniFE	144	73	280	161.08	75	282	163.08	33.86	50.35	45.10
Minighost	96	89	95	92.33	91	135	111.04	12.13	13.89	13.13

4 Related Work

Performance tools for HPC systems have been studied and developed for years. Extrae and Paraver [8,9], and also ScoreP with Vampir [10,11], are tracing toolsets used to visualize the behavior of MPI applications over time. They provide lossless traces that include all the events that happened while the application was running. However, these traces are huge and their size increases linearly with the number of MPI processes. Therefore, the use of such toolsets is limited by scalability constraints. In contrast, our current work with *event flow graphs* shows that we can capture the events and their temporal order as tracers do while storing it in files that are a few orders of magnitude smaller. However, our approach is still in an early stage and more work is needed to reach the same level of usability and information granularity as that provided by current tracing tools, for example, including continuous data such as timestamps or hardware performance counters in the trace.

Our work is also related to lightweight profiling tools such as mpiP [12] or Gprof [13]. These tools generate profiles of aggregated information with very low overhead. Although these tools can provide a good overview of the performance problems for a particular application, they lack the temporal order of data needed for in-depth performance analysis. In contrast, IPM can provide temporal order in the performance data using *event flow graphs*. Additionally, IPM also provides standard reports with aggregated statistics.

Scalatrace [14] is a tracing framework that provides on-the-fly lossless trace compression of MPI communication traces. It implements intra-node compression describing single loops with RSDs [15] and using techniques such as callpath compression. Scalatrace also implements inter-node compression at the end of the run when each process trace is merged into a single one for the whole application. Scalatrace comes with a replay mechanism for a later analysis of those traces. Our work differs from Scalatrace in the sense that we do not compress series of events, but instead record the behavior of an application using graphs. We believe this approach has better compression ratios and much less overhead as discussed in Sect. 3. Furthermore, our approach also makes it possible to replay traces later for the purposes of performance analysis. Nevertheless, our current implementation still lacks inter-node compression, generating one file per process. This is subject to future work though.

Krishnamoorthy et al. use SEQUITUR to compress traces creating context-free grammars from the sequence of MPI calls [16]. In order to achieve better compression, the trace is not compressed at an event level, but instead every call argument is compressed in a different stream. This loses any program structure in the resulting trace and makes it unreadable. In contrast, our approach keeps the program structure, thus allowing us to easily visualize the traces.

Knüpfer et al. use Complete Call Graphs (CCGs) to compress post-mortem traces according to the call stack [17]. This approach builds a call graph and replaces similar repeated sub-trees with a reference to a single instance. Therefore, CCGs can be very useful for trace analysis tools, reducing their memory footprint and allowing them to deal with bigger traces. However, this method does not eliminate the burden of generating large traces while the application runs.

Flow graphs have been widely used in other areas of computer science such as code generation and analysis. In those contexts, compilers generate flow graphs from their intermediate representation (IR) where nodes are code blocks and edges are branches that a program may take. Our work differs in the sense that the nodes in our graphs are communication events instead of code blocks. In addition, the edges of our event flow graphs are not possible branches but rather transitions that actually happened during the execution.

5 Future Work

Using *event flow graphs* in the analysis of MPI parallel applications opens up many possibilities such as developing new tools to visualize, navigate and interact with graphs. Possible visualization features could be graph coloring depending on different metrics or highlighting differences among graphs to detect load imbalance among processes. The graph approach also allows the use of different algorithms and techniques for automatic graph analysis, for instance, detecting loops in the graph and time spent in those loops. Furthermore, these new performance tools could provide trace reconstruction features for just some sections of the graph or a couple of iterations of a graph cycle.

Our current implementation of the *event flow graphs* in IPM does not keep any time information on call duration in the graph. Thus, trace reconstruction with timestamps is not possible yet. Therefore, we are looking into methods for trace reconstruction that include time information. Furthermore, we want to apply those methods for the reconstruction of any continuous data in the trace, for example, hardware performance counters.

Finally, another aspect we want to explore in the future is inter-node trace compression across ranks. Our current version always generates one flow graph per process. However, it is usual in parallel application that a set of processes has similar or identical behavior. In such cases, the graphs generated by those processes will be similar as well, and thus, they can be compressed into a single graph that could be used to describe that whole set of processes with similar execution.

6 Conclusion

Performance analysis through tracing is the best method to understand the behavior of applications. However, tracing techniques have scalability limitations due to the amount of information that is generated. In this paper we have presented a disruptive approach for performance tracing of MPI parallel applications using *event flow graphs*. This new method combines the scalability and low overhead of profiling methods with the lossless information capabilities of tracing tools. We evaluated our implementation using several mini-applications from the NERSC-8/Trinity Benchmark Suite. The experiments showed promising results, achieving file compression ratios up to 119 with overheads below 2%. Furthermore, the use of applications with longer simulations would allow even better compression ratios because the same paths in the application are executed more times. Although our work is still at an early stage, we believe it has strong potential to be a way towards developing performance analysis tools that are effective at an exascale level.

References

1. Labarta, J., Gimenez, J., Martinez, E., González, P., Servat, H., Llort, G., Aguilar, X.: Scalability of visualization and tracing tools. In: Proc. 11th Parallel Computing Conf. (ParCo 2005), pp. 869–876 (2005)

2. Fuerlinger, K., Wright, N.J., Skinner, D.: Effective performance measurement at petascale using ipm. In: 2010 IEEE 16th International Conference on Parallel and Distributed Systems (ICPADS), pp. 373–380. IEEE (2010)
3. Aguilar, X., Fürlinger, K., Laure, E.: Online performance data introspection with ipm. In: The 15th IEEE International Conference on High Performance Computing and Communications (2013) (to be published)
4. Fürlinger, K., Skinner, D.: Capturing and visualizing event flow graphs of mpi applications. In: Lin, H.-X., Alexander, M., Forsell, M., Knüpfer, A., Prodan, R., Sousa, L., Streit, A. (eds.) Euro-Par 2009 Workshops 2009. LNCS, vol. 6043, pp. 218–227. Springer, Heidelberg (2010)
5. NERSC-8 / Trinity Benchmarks WWW site, http://www.nersc.gov/systems/trinity-nersc-8-rfp/nersc-8-trinity-benchmarks/
6. Alcouffe, R.E., Baker, R.S., Dahl, J.A., Turner, S.A., Ward, R.: Partisn: A time-dependent, parallel neutral particle transport code system. Los Alamos National Laboratory, LA-UR-05-3925 (May 2005)
7. MPICH wiki, http://wiki.mpich.org/mpich/images/1/17/Wave2d.cpp.txt
8. Pillet, V., Labarta, J., Cortes, T., Girona, S.: Paraver: A tool to visualize and analyze parallel code. In: Proceedings of WoTUG-18: Transputer and Occam Developments, vol. 44, pp. 17–31 (1995)
9. Servat, H., Llort, G., Huck, K., Giménez, J., Labarta, J.: Framework for a productive performance optimization. Parallel Computing 39(8), 336–353 (2013)
10. Knüpfer, A., Rössel, C., Mey, D., Biersdorff, S., Diethelm, K., Eschweiler, D., Geimer, M., Gerndt, M., Lorenz, D., Malony, A., et al.: Score-p: A joint performance measurement run-time infrastructure for periscope, scalasca, tau, and vampir. In: Tools for High Performance Computing 2011, pp. 79–91. Springer (2012)
11. Knüpfer, A., Brunst, H., Doleschal, J., Jurenz, M., Lieber, M., Mickler, H., Müller, M.S., Nagel, W.E.: The vampir performance analysis tool-set. In: Tools for High Performance Computing, pp. 139–155. Springer (2008)
12. Vetter, J.S., McCracken, M.O.: Statistical scalability analysis of communication operations in distributed applications. In: ACM SIGPLAN Notices, vol. 36, pp. 123–132. ACM (2001)
13. Graham, S.L., Kessler, P.B., Mckusick, M.K.: Gprof: A call graph execution profiler. ACM Sigplan Notices 17(6), 120–126 (1982)
14. Noeth, M., Ratn, P., Mueller, F., Schulz, M., de Supinski, B.R.: Scalatrace: Scalable compression and replay of communication traces for high-performance computing. Journal of Parallel and Distributed Computing 69(8), 696–710 (2009)
15. Havlak, P., Kennedy, K.: An implementation of interprocedural bounded regular section analysis. IEEE Transactions on Parallel and Distributed Systems 2(3), 350–360 (1991)
16. Krishnamoorthy, S., Agarwal, K.: Scalable communication trace compression. In: Proceedings of the 2010 10th IEEE/ACM International Conference on Cluster, Cloud and Grid Computing, pp. 408–417. IEEE Computer Society (2010)
17. Knupfer, A., Nagel, W.E.: Construction and compression of complete call graphs for post-mortem program trace analysis. In: International Conference on Parallel Processing, ICPP 2005, pp. 165–172. IEEE (2005)

ScalaJack: Customized Scalable Tracing with In-situ Data Analysis*

Srinath Krishna Ananthakrishnan and Frank Mueller

North Carolina State University, USA
mueller@cs.ncsu.edu

Abstract. Root cause diagnosis of large-scale HPC applications often fails because tools, specifically trace-based ones, can no longer record all metrics they measure. We address this problems by combining customized tracing and providing support for in-situ data analysis via Scala-Jack, a framework with customizable instrumentation and pluggable extension capabilities for problem directed instrumentation and in-situ data analysis. We further eliminate cross cutting concerns by code refactoring for aspect orientation and evaluate these capabilities in case studies within and beyond the scope of tracing.

1 Introduction

Experience suggests that HPC codes suffer scalability issues each time the concurrency level increases by an order of magnitude. Analyzing the causes requires knowledge of an application's global and local behavior. Frequently, tracing is used for root cause analysis. Specific application events are identified and traced during execution. Tracing differs from profiling in that it tries to preserve more data, including the chronology of events, while profiling is inherently lossy and focuses on aggregate metrics of loops and nodes. But trace-based tools struggle to isolate problems since instrumentation costs can be prohibitive with exhaustive collection of metrics at events and results in perturbations that can mask the true problem. Traditional approaches employ periodic probing [6] instead of full instrumentation and may employ reduction in data volume through compression. However, this merely postpones the problem of analyzing the data, which requires decompression again. In-situ analysis is an alternative as it reduces data volume inherently and facilities realtime/online root cause analysis. Leveraging user knowledge for instrumentation, problem-specific tracing and analysis capabilities can thus be realized.

Contributions: We have developed ScalaJack to support *active analysis tracing*, i.e., problem-specific extraction and on-the-fly reduction of data through analysis. ScalaJack supports *user-customizable* instrumentation and user callbacks as pluggable extensions for instrumenting interfaces and a means for in-situ data analysis at specific execution points. This supports rapid generation of problem-specific analysis tools. Instrumentation via ScalaJack is *aspect-oriented*

---

* This work was supported in part by NSF grants 1217748, 0958311, and 0937908.

F. Silva et al. (Eds.): Euro-Par 2014, LNCS 8632, pp. 13–25, 2014.

to reduce cross-cutting concerns in source code to improve code readability, reuse, portability and maintainability, which aids in designing large and multi-scalar HPC codes. In experiments, ScalaJack shows scalable trace file sizes with increasing number of tasks and minimal overhead. Aspect-oriented analysis suggests significantly decreased scattering of cross-module code references.

2   Background

ScalaJack is a redesign of ScalaTrace to support customizable instrumentation, user callbacks and aspect-oriented program design. **ScalaTrace** [17] is a state-of-the-art scalable parallel communication tracing library for message-passing MPI programs. MPI events are traced through the PMPI profiling layer. Scala-Trace combines on-the-fly intra-node compression of MPI calls within loops with inter-node compression of events across nodes (in $MPI\_Finalize$). ScalaTrace employs RSDs and PRSDs ([Power] Regular Section Descriptors [14]) structures to represent events in a loop as constant size logs. An RSD is a tuple $< length, event_1...event_n >$ in one loop and a PRSD represents multiple RSDs in nested loops. E.g., two nested for loops with a barrier in the outer and a send in the inner loops correspond to PRSD $< 10, RSD_1, MPI\_Barrier >$ where RSD_1 is $< 10, MPI\_Send >$ for 10 iterations per loop level.

ScalaTrace represents events and parameters through an elastic data representation [24] that morphs scalars, vectors and histograms. Resulting trace files are scalable yet completely lossless, except for delta times between MPI events recorded as lossy histograms. A replay engine allows events to be replayed without original program code, even for non-deterministic histogram data.

Aspect-oriented programming [11] is a software engineering technique to reduce scattering of cross-cutting concerns in source code. An *aspect* is is a piece of code that cannot be factored out into procedural isolation due to cross-cutting *concerns* (e.g., logging, timing, performance monitoring, load balancing) located at *pointcuts* in the code, where *concerns* are the set of all aspects and a *pointcut* separates two regions of disjoint concerns.

Aspect-specific code is moved from the original application's *component* to an aspects specification, i.e., *advice*, which is executed at the original *pointcut* in the code (as a pre- or post-wrapper), often realized via run-time or compile-time support for aspects [12,3].

3   Design and Implementation

ScalaJack reuses compression techniques of ScalaTrace but augments and extends them by introducing an API to define custom events specific to a program and to register callbacks for in-situ analysis of live data. ScalaJack relies on aspects through run-time interpositioning of MPI calls via PMPI and dynamic pre-loading / tagging of event prologues / epilogues.

Figure 1 illustrates how ScalaJack composes generic instrumentation libraries with the application. Custom events are tagged by either augmenting the application with instrumented calls or by enumerating such events in a specification

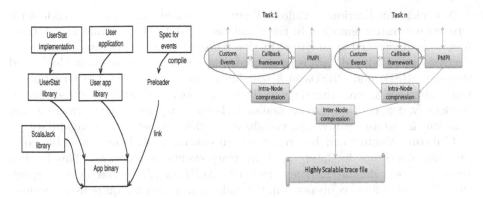

Fig. 1. Instrumentation Composition with ScalaJack

Fig. 2. ScalaJack's High-level Design

file. The user may provide an instrumentation class (UserStat, derived from the Stat class) that implements the methods to start/stop/merge specific trace events, which is compiled separately and linked into the application.

ScalaJack's high-level design is depicted in Figure 2 with novel components (circled) and redesigned existing components (non-circled). Each event is wrapped by ScalaJack with a prologue and epilogue to support tracing *and* invocation of aspect-specific callbacks. Event/user trace data within a task are compressed on-the-fly by exploiting the program's loop constructs while a second phase of compression is performed via inter-node compression over all tasks. This highly compressed single file trace is thus scalable with the number of processes.

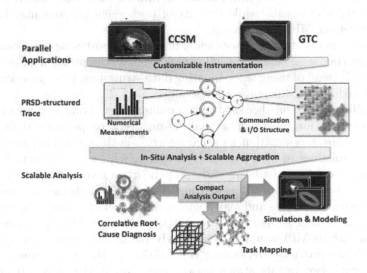

Fig. 3. Typical Application workflow with ScalaJack

A typical application workflow (Figure 3) consists of a parallel code with customized instrumentation to trace and instrument MPI routines or arbitrary functions augmented by in-situ reduction (through analysis) of instrumentation-derived data. Reduced data is co-located with the appropriate event blocks and stored as RSDs and PRSDs in a scalable fashion, preserving the structure of program/trace. Correlating data to the events provides insight into root causes to identify, e.g., performance anomalies. Other tertiary tasks due to cross-cutting concerns integrate readily, e.g., visualization, yielding better code modularity.

Custom Events can bee registered to extend ScalaTrace's scalable compression algorithms for interposing arbitrary events in programs. This level of tracing reduces default instrumentation to $MPI\_Init/Finalize$ events or, optionally, user-defined equivalents in the code, which would require user-provided alternatives for rank/size/barrier (of MPI) for internal ScalaJack functionalities, e.g., inter-node data reduction (not covered in this paper). A custom event API supports (a) event registration and (b) specification of pre-/post-wrappers.

Registration of custom events via the API returns an event code (orthogonal to MPI events) for further ScalaJack calls and internally establishes a control block for optional *flags* for events. Flags may suppress stack signature generation (normally used to identify functions during compression). Signature omission may facilitate joint compression of event sets grouped together by a data-specific criterion or for aggregation.

Custom events invoke user-supplied arbitrary functions when triggered. Registered wrappers for pro- and epilogues resemble functions for custom events and are synonymous to those for MPI events instrumented via the PMPI interpositioning techniques. An auto-generated prelinker provides skeleton code that wraps the original function call. Custom wrappers may coexist with MPI wrappers per event, and both of their data resides in the same, single trace file. Flag-controlled tracing of just Init/Finalize facilitates inter-node compression for MPI-associated user events, while the mix of both event streams may hamper ScalaJack's default MPI compression.

Nested custom events, i.e., trace events inside pre-/post-wrappers, can cause incorrect ordering, e.g., before the epilogue of event 1, the prologue of event 2 is encountered. Instead of using stack-bloating data structures, pre-/post-wrappers are represented as two different events sequences.

User callbacks provide hooks at any communication point and selected call graph nodes, e.g., for in-situ data analysis on event or program data. They also support aspect orientation to separate cross-cutting concerns from main algorithms. Prologues of MPI events cause ScalaJack to create control blocks while epilogues consists of routines that append the events into the trace and engage in intra-node compression of trace data. User callbacks as pre-/post-wrappers serve as *pointcuts* and may augment the trace with user-collected data. User callbacks further support data analysis, optional on-the-fly compression, and, in contrast to MPI wrappers, even early reduction across nodes. A *Stat* (Statistics) class provides overloading capabilities by the user through object orientation with two instantiations for (a) the computation phase before the event and (b) the communication phase of the event. Callbacks are established by overriding Stat's *start/end* methods or by a ScalaJack API call resulting in internal *Stat* instantiation and method overriding. Thus, callbacks before and after each compute/communicate phase are invoked out of the respective pre-/post-wrappers. An optional flag supports suppression of entries into the trace file to let users override Stat's *callback* method, which is invoked just once (without compute/communicate distinction).

User-directed compression: Data from in-situ analysis in callbacks enters the trace as a compressed histogram by default. Users can overload the *ValueSet* class and support their own set of compression routines as callbacks invoked by our reduction framework with data marshaling. This supports *pointcuts* in programs while providing scalability even for customized user data types.

Most aspect-oriented frameworks map aspects to specific events. In contrast, ScalaJack aspects are universal across events but event-specific aspects are realized by light-weight filters. Users can access event objects of *pointcuts* to execute aspects for specific events/conditions, e.g., to access the send count of MPI events. Users can also access event trace queues in their structurally compressed form (PRSDs). This facilitates analysis on the entire trace, e.g., for trace similarity via k-means clustering to group traces based on a distance metric.

4   Evaluation

We assess the scalability of ScalaJack via traces generated by its custom event framework. In addition, the overhead incurred in using ScalaJack over a naïve implementation is studied. We evaluate ScalaJack by refactoring several case studies of typical HPC applications to utilize our aspect-oriented callback framework. Tasks that are tangential to the program are refactored as part of these callbacks. As a result, cross-cutting concerns are removed from the main component of the program, thus improving readability and maintainability.

All experiments were conducted on our ARC cluster with two AMD Opteron 6128 processors with 8 cores each (16 cores) per node and a QDR InfiniBand interconnect. Execution times and trace file sizes were averaged over 10 runs.

Since ScalaJack helps remove cross-cutting concerns in the code, the amount of code related to a concern that is scattered is reduced. To quantify the improvement of using ScalaJack over a naïve implementation with respect to the code footprint, we utilize the degree of scattering (DOS) and degree of focus (DOF) metrics from [8,7]. Concentration ($CONC$) measures how many of the source lines related of a concern s are contained within a component t (e.g., file, class, method intending to a specific task), i.e.,

$$CONC(s,t) = \frac{SLOC_{t,s}}{SLOC_s}$$

where $SLOC_{t,s}$ is the number of source lines of code ($SLOC$) in component t related to concern s, and $SLOC_s$ is the $SLOC$ in all of concern s. It should be noted that $SLOC$ excludes comments, blank lines and annotations for concern assignment. The drawback of $CONC$ is that it does not reflect the amount of scattering of a concern's code and does not allow for different concerns to be compared. This is covered by the degree of scattering (DOS) metric defined by

$$DOS(s) = 1 - \frac{|T|\sum_t^T \left(CONC(s,t) - \frac{1}{|T|}\right)^2}{|T|-1}$$

where T is the set of components for $|T| > 1$ [7]. DOS is a normalized factor between 0 (completely localized) and 1 (completely delocalized). Thus, a reduction in DOS is an indication of less scattering of code across components.

Degree of Focus (DOF) is a dual to the DOS metric and captures how focused a component is. Dedication ($DEDI$) is defined as

$$DEDI(t,s) = \frac{SLOC_{t,s}}{SLOC_t}$$

where $SLOC_{t,s}$ is the number of source lines of code ($SLOC$) in component t related to concern s, and $SLOC_t$ is the $SLOC$ in all of component t. Again, a better metric would be the normalized *degree of focus* (DOF)

$$DOF(s) = \frac{|S|\sum_s^S \left(DEDI(t,s) - \frac{1}{|S|}\right)^2}{|S|-1}$$

where S is the set of concerns for $|S| > 1$. DOF is a normalized factor between 0 (completely unfocused) and 1 (completely focused). Thus, an increase in DOF is desired as it is indicative of reduction in scattering and increase in focus.

Performance analysis: One of the most frequently identified aspects in any program is performance analysis. Developers typically want to identify the performance characteristics of specific regions of their code. In most HPC applications, distinct regions of computation and communication can be identified, and it is often desired to collect performance metrics related to the phases. We evaluate ScalaJack's viability with the IS benchmark of the NAS Parallel Benchmark suite. IS sorts integers through a parallel implementation of bucket sort. As part of the benchmark, each task generates a random number sequence from a seed based on the rank.

We illustrate ScalaJack's capabilities to support performance analysis aspects by choosing PAPI [15] to instrument the L1 data cache misses during the random sequence generation in addition to performing trace analysis on every MPI event in the program. We compare an implementation of the IS benchmark that uses ScalaJack with a naïve implementation with tracing concerns around all MPI functions and performance analysis concerns around the random sequence generation step. We utilize the tracing level of ScalaJack, where all MPI events are traced with custom events and both intra-node and inter-node compression are performed. The naïve version of IS initializes the PAPI library, followed by an instrumentation of the random sequence generation routine of IS with the PAPI API. The return value of this instrumentation routine is then added to the trace. To indicate the changes to perform tracing, a sample MPI routine, MPI_Reduce, is called to add data to the trace. The ScalaJack version differs from the naïve implementation by utilizing PMPI wrappers to trace events (and compress them) while the PAPI API calls are invoked as part of a $StatPAPI$ callback. These callbacks are invoked as part of the prologue and epilogue of the custom event associated with random number generation. This allows for separation of concerns and reusability of the PAPI statistics collection $Stat$ framework.

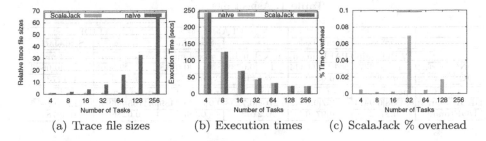

(a) Trace file sizes   (b) Execution times   (c) ScalaJack % overhead

Fig. 4. IS Results

Figure 4(a) compares the trace files generated with ScalaJack and that of the naïve implementation. The trace file sizes shown are relative (normalized) to the ones generated with $n = 4$ tasks for the naïve and the ScalaJack versions, respectively. As can be seen from the graph, traces generated with ScalaJack are highly scalable with an increasing number of processors compared to the traces generated by the naïve implementation. This is owing to the fact that ScalaJack employs intra-node (to compress loops) and inter-node compression to generate a single trace file, while the naïve implementation performs no compression and generates traces for each of the tasks. We compare relative trace file sizes because, on an absolute scale, trace files generated with ScalaJack are larger for lower values of n due to timestamp data of few hundred bytes per event added to the trace. ScalaJack internally times every communication and computation phase of the program and stores them as histograms. This is utilized later by the replay engine and other tools like benchmark generators to create instances of the original program [17,25].

To highlight the overhead incurred in using ScalaJack, we compare the running times of the two implementations of the IS benchmark. As shown in Figure 4(b), ScalaJack introduces very little overhead to the naïve implementation's execution. To put it in a different perspective, Figure 4(c) shows the percentage overhead times of ScalaJack over the naïve implementation. As it can be seen, ScalaJack introduces the highest performance overhead for $n = 32$, i.e., for the best performance of IS under strong scaling, which is when instrumentation overhead (constant across n) contributes the most — but still amounts to just 0.07% overhead for $n = 32$. There is substantial variability in the overhead of ScalaJack over the naïve implementation since each task of the naïve implementation performs I/O to the parallel file system at $MPI\_Finalize$ to write n trace files for n nodes back to disk, each of which may be rather large (in the order of GBs depending on the number loop iterations). This results in I/O contention. In contrast, only $rank$ 0 performs I/O to the file system with ScalaJack after aggregating the traces from all its peers, i.e., a single file of rather moderate size (in the MBs) suffices.

Table 1 (left columns) shows the improvement of using ScalaJack for separation of concerns over the naïve implementation. For IS, the identifiable components are main and PAPI, where the main component implements the benchmark

Table 1. Aspect metrics

	IS				CLAMR				TFIDF			
	naïve		ScalaJack		naïve		ScalaJack		naïve		ScalaJack	
	PAPI	main	PAPI	main	aux	main	aux	main	aux	main	aux	main
CONC(perf,t)	1	0.4777	1	0.0444	1	0.0739	1	0.0118	1	0.3665	1	0.0683
DOS(perf)	0.4992		0.0850		0.1369		0.0234		0.4643		0.1273	
	perf	sort	perf	sort	main	fd	main	fd	main	aux	main	aux
DEDI(main,s)	0.0588	0.9411	0.0057	0.9942	0.2708	0.7293	0.0540	0.9459	0.4155	0.5945	0.1134	0.8666
DOF(main)	0.7782		0.9770		0.2102		0.7955		0.0286		0.5978	

while the PAPI component implements the performance metrics collection routines. The concerns here are identified as perf and sort, where perf is the actual performance metrics collection API invoked at the pointcuts and sort is the rest of the main component that performs the sorting. The goal is to reduce the tangling of code between the two concerns and ScalaJack achieves this. This is reflected by the lower (better) DOS score and a correspondingly higher (better) DOF score for ScalaJack compared to the naïve implementation.

Visualization and Load balancing: We next evaluate the effectiveness of ScalaJack for aspect-oriented application scenarios beyond tracing for performance analysis. We first consider CLAMR [13], an adaptive mesh refinement solver developed at Los Alamos National Laboratory. CLAMR implements a cell-based shallow water code by computing the finite difference on AMR using MPI. CLAMR periodically refines the mesh and also performs load balancing across the nodes to redistribute the meshes. In addition, CLAMR performs OpenGL or MPE-based visualization to display the mesh's current state.

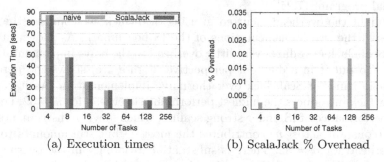

(a) Execution times   (b) ScalaJack % Overhead

Fig. 5. CLAMR Results

Application codes like CLAMR have numerous conflicting concerns that can be effectively addressed using ScalaJack. In the naïve version of CLAMR, tasks like visualization, mesh refinement, load balancing and printing of statistics are not part of the main concern at hand, i.e., computing the finite difference. In CLAMR's ScalaJack version, the various concerns that are tangential to the main concern at hand are refactored into the appropriate prologue/epilogue.CLAMR was evaluated with the custom level of tracing, i.e., only custom events are traced

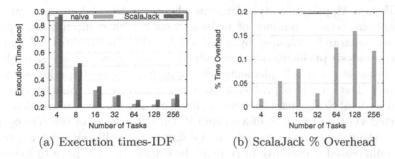

(a) Execution times-IDF   (b) ScalaJack % Overhead

Fig. 6. TF-IDF Results

and no MPI events except for $MPI\_Init/Finalize$. Custom events are config-ured to be created without the stack signature so as to reduce the trace footprint. Since no data is to be written as part of the callbacks, we register user callbacks with the callback mode flag. Since the goal with CLAMR is not tracing but rather refactoring tangential concerns into callbacks, we refrain from comparing trace sizes between naïve and ScalaJack. Instead, to assess the scalability, we compare the execution times of both versions.

Figure 5(a) compares the overhead of ScalaJack through the differences in execution time between the naïve and the ScalaJack versions of CLAMR. Fig-ure 5(b) shows that ScalaJack introduces an overhead of a maximum of 0.03% overhead. This is lower than that of IS because we utilize custom level tracing for CLAMR, which does not trace any MPI events.

Table 1 (middle columns) summarizes the improvements of using ScalaJack to eliminate concerns from CLAMR. With CLAMR, the main component is the code that performs the finite difference, while all cross-cutting concerns are grouped as an auxiliary concern. With ScalaJack, all cross-cutting concerns are performed at the callbacks as part of registered custom events. With CLAMR, the majority of the cross-cutting concern code was that of visualization because the $rank$ 0 task aggregates all mesh values from the other tasks for visualization. Since a major portion of the code is eliminated from the main component, we observe a better (higher) DOF score and thus a better (lower) DOS score.

Data analysis in-situ with trace analysis: As the final case study, we an-alyze ScalaJack's effectiveness with a MapReduce style application that can take advantage of the reduction capabilities of ScalaJack. TF-IDF is a data analysis metric used to assess the importance of a given term with respect to a docu-ment in a dictionary [20]. The two metrics involved are *term frequency* $tf(t, d)$, defined as the frequency of occurrence of a term t in a given document, and *inverse document frequency* $idf(t, D)$ in a set of documents D, defined as the inverse of the frequency of documents that contain a term t within a given dic-tionary of terms. The TF-IDF metric is then defined by

$$tfidf(t, d, D) = tf(t, d) \times idf(t, D)$$

TF-IDF is a MapReduce style problem wherein a set of documents are initially mapped across a number of tasks and each task computes the tf and idf metrics separately followed by a reduction, which aggregates idf metrics. With such analysis problems, efficient reduction strategies that are scalable are required because a naïve implementation might lead to bottlenecks and lower performance. Data analysis problems, such as TF-IDF, can exploit the internal reduction logic of ScalaJack otherwise utilized by inter-node compression. This is supported via the definition of a custom $ValueSet$ instead of the $Histogram$, thus performing data analysis as part of a defined user callback. Such a solution allows for increased reusability of code as developers do not have to explicitly implement communication strategies themselves.

The naïve TF-IDF initially computes the tf and node-local idf and then constructs a communication tree to perform a reduction. The ScalaJack version defines the reduction as a $ValueSet$ of the $StatTFIDF$ object associated with the idf computation event. As part of the event's epilogue, the idf table is added to the $Stat$ object. When inter-node compression is performed at the prologue of $MPI\_Finalize$, the idf tables are compressed as well. With the ScalaJack version, users do not have to be concerned with implementing a communication tree and use ScalaJack's internal reduction tree to perform scalable compression. In our tests, we compare the naïve implementation with the ScalaJack implementation with support for inter-node compression. As with CLAMR, tracing is not the goal here. Hence, we assess the scalability through the overhead of ScalaJack over the naïve implementation.

Figure 6(a) shows the overhead of ScalaJack in comparison to the naïve version. ScalaJack introduces minimal overhead of about 0.16% as reflected in Figure 6(b), thus proving to be light weight. Table 1 (right columns) shows the aspect-related metrics for the TF-IDF case study. With ScalaJack, concerns relating to the communication tree for final idf aggregation are eliminated and are made through an extension of the $ValueSet$ class. This reduces the tangling of code, thus leading to better (higher) DOF and better (lower) DOS scores.

5   Related Work

Our implementation of customizable instrumentation with in-situ data analysis through ScalaJack is closely related to tools that support tracing or profiling of MPI programs. Paraver [19] is a tracing and visualization tool that supports tracing of both shared memory and message passing programs. For MPI programs, Paraver includes a tracing library for intercepting MPI calls and saving them as individual trace files during execution. These trace files are merged offline and then visualized. Paraver and other tracing tools [22,16,9,18] allow users to store user-defined values in a trace but they lack ScalaJack's compression of trace files on-the-fly and the ability to directly affect compression of native trace values (as opposed to user-defined trace values).

VAMPIR [16] is another tracing tool for MPI/OpenMP/CUDA events with support for visualization that stores traces as flat files, which are compressed later through zlib compression. Even though such tools generate trace files with limited scalability, they do not take advantage of the underlying structure of the trace file. Thus, such trace files cannot be efficiently used for replay [24] or code generation [25] supported by ScalaTrace. Recent versions of VAMPIR provide support for marking regions in the trace with specific marker events for identifying potential hotspots in the trace files [4]. These markups can then be used by automated performance analysis tools like Scalasca [9]. With ScalaJack, this can easily be achieved by writing instrumentation data with additional markups directly to the trace file and using plugins for domain-specific compression.

Several tools [22,16,9,18,6,5] support tracing of arbitrary user events through automatic instrumentation via compiler abstractions, dynamic preloading or manual instrumentation of code, both statically and dynamically via binary rewriting. ScalaJack also supports built-in preloading and manual instrumentation but emphasizes separation of cross-cutting concerns via aspect orientation, which simplifies reuse for other programs. In addition, programs not only leverage ScalaJack's compression tree framework to perform reduction of their own data structures efficiently but also improve on intra-node compression and inter-node reduction of default communication tracing data, which is unprecedented.

Arnold et al. [2] identified task behavior equivalence classes using stack signature similarity. They utilized MRNet, a software overlay network that provides efficient multicast and reduction communications [21]. MRNet provides a general framework with generic plugins, each requiring an explicit implementation of compression and reduction. In contrast, ScalaTrace natively supports compression and reduction, i.e., trace-specific plugins directly complement this process or even manipulate internal data structures affecting the trace file format.

Our work is also related to light-weight profiling tools like mpiP [23], gprof [10], and HPCToolkit [1]. While these tools provide simple and high-level information to support a high-level understanding of performance problems, ScalaJack provides facilities to the user for profiling of arbitrary interfaces in their programs in addition to supporting light-weight tracing. Since the instrumentation data is stored along with the trace files, users can correlate events to the data thus helping them to diagnose subtle anomalies dependent on event orders.

6   Conclusion

We have implemented ScalaJack, a framework for customizable instrumentation with in-situ data analysis. ScalaJack provides APIs for users to tag sections of the code that need to be instrumented. This allows users to perform instrumentation at interfaces that are pertinent to the problem at hand instead of having to instrument exhaustively, thereby often compromising scalability. ScalaJack provides direct access to intra-node and inter-node compression algorithms and data structures to preserve the execution structure of a program in a lossless fashion in addition to maintaining scalability.

ScalaJack facilitates in-situ analysis provides by allowing users to perform reduction of data by registering callbacks. In addition to providing native support to compress numeric data into histograms, ScalaJack provides APIs for users to define their own data elements depending on the application. Since the callbacks are synonymous to aspects, users can leverage them to write better code, thus enhancing readability and maintainability. An evaluation of ScalaJack with several case studies has shown that it is very light-weight, posing an overhead of under 0.2% and capable of producing lossless and near-constant trace sizes for event parameters, while resulting in efficient, maintainable source codes with about 75% reduction in the *degree of scattering*. Overall, this demonstrates the fidelity of ScalaJack in facilitating trace generation and analysis for users.

References

1. Adhianto, L., Banerjee, S., Fagan, M., Krentel, M., Marin, G., Mellor-Crummey, J., Tallent, N.: HPCToolkit: Tools for performance analysis of optimized parallel programs. Concurrency & Comp. Practice and Experience 22(6), 685–701 (2010)
2. Arnold, D.C., Ahn, D.H., de Supinski, B.R., Lee, G.L., Miller, B.P., Schulz, M.: Stack trace analysis for large scale debugging. In: International Parallel and Distributed Processing Symposium (2007)
3. Aspect, C.: AspectC: AOP for C. (2004)
4. Brunst, H., Hackenberg, D., Juckeland, G., Rohling, H.: Comprehensive performance tracking with Vampir 7. In: Tools for HPC 2009, pp. 17–29 (2010)
5. Buck, B., Hollingsworth, J.: An API for runtime code patching. International Journal of High Performance Computing Applications 14(4), 317–329 (2000)
6. De Rose, L., Hollingsworth, J., Hoover, T.: The dynamic probe class library – an infrastructure for developing instrumentation for performance tools. In: International Parallel and Distributed Processing Symposium (April 2001)
7. Eaddy, M., Zimmermann, T., Sherwood, K., Garg, V., Murphy, G., Nagappan, N., Aho, A.: Do crosscutting concerns cause defects? IEEE Transactions on Software Engineering 34(4), 497–515 (2008)
8. Eaddy, M., Aho, A., Murphy, G.C.: Identifying, assigning, and quantifying crosscutting concerns. In: Workshop on Assessment of Contemporary Modularization Techniques, pp. 2–2 (2007)
9. Geimer, M., Wolf, F., Wylie, B.J.N., Abraham, E., Becker, D., Mohr, B.: The scalasca performance toolset architecture. In: International Workshop on Scalable Tools for High-End Computing (June 2008)
10. Graham, S.L., Kessler, P.B., Mckusick, M.K.: Gprof: A call graph execution profiler. ACM Sigplan Notices 17(6), 120–126 (1982)
11. Kiczales, G., Hilsdale, E.: Aspect-oriented programming. In: ACM SIGSOFT Software Engineering Notes, vol. 26, p. 313 (2001)
12. Kiczales, G., Hilsdale, E., Hugunin, J., Kersten, M., Palm, J., Griswold, W.G.: An overview of AspectJ. In: Lindskov Knudsen, J. (ed.) ECOOP 2001. LNCS, vol. 2072, pp. 327–354. Springer, Heidelberg (2001)
13. Laboratory, L.A.N.: Cell-based adaptive mesh refinement using MPI and OpenCL GPU code, https://github.com/losalamos/CLAMR
14. Marathe, J., Mueller, F., Mohan, T., de Supinski, B.R., McKee, S.A., Yoo, A.: METRIC: Tracking down inefficiencies in the memory hierarchy via binary rewriting. In: Int'l Symp. on Code Generation and Optimization, pp. 289–300 (March 2003)

15. Mucci, P.J., Browne, S., Deane, C., Ho, G.: PAPI: A portable interface to hardware performance counters. In: HPCMP Users Group Conference (1999)
16. Nagel, W.E., Arnold, A., Weber, M., Hoppe, H.C., Solchenbach, K.: VAMPIR: Visualization and analysis of MPI resources. Supercomputer 12(1), 69–80 (1996)
17. Noeth, M., Ratn, P., Mueller, F., Schulz, M., de Supinski, B.R.: ScalaTrace: Scalable compression and replay of communication traces for high-performance computing. Journal of Parallel Distributed Computing 69(8), 696–710 (2009)
18. of Dresden, T.U.: Score-p: Application instrumentation, https://silc.zih.tu-dresden.de/scorep-current/html
19. Pillet, V., Labarta, J., Cortes, T., Girona, S.: PARAVER: A tool to visualise and analyze parallel code. In: WoTUG-18: Transputer and occam Developments.Transputer and Occam Engineering, vol. 44, pp. 17–31 (April 1995)
20. Rajaraman, A., Ullman, J.: Mining of Massive Datasets. Cambridge Press (2011)
21. Roth, P., Arnold, D., Miller, B.: MRNet: A software-based multicast/reduction network for scalable tools. Supercomputing, 21–36 (2003)
22. Shende, S.S., Malony, A.D.: The tau parallel performance system. Int. J. High Perform. Comput. Appl. 20(2), 287–311 (2006)
23. Vetter, J., Chambreau, C.: mpiP: Lightweight, scalable MPI profiling. CASC/mpip (2005), http://mpip.sourceforge.net/
24. Wu, X., Mueller, F.: Elastic and scalable tracing and accurate replay of nondeterministic events. In: Int'l Conference on Supercomputing, pp. 59–68 (June 2013)
25. Wu, X., Deshpande, V., Mueller, F.: ScalaBenchGen: Auto-generation of communication benchmarks traces. In: International Parallel and Distributed Processing Symposium, pp. 1250–1260 (2012)

Performance Measurement and Analysis of Transactional Memory and Speculative Execution on IBM Blue Gene/Q*

Jie Jiang[1,2], Peter Philippen[1], Michael Knobloch[1], and Bernd Mohr[1]

[1] Forschungszentrum Jülich GmbH,
Institute for Advanced Simulation,
Jülich Supercomputing Centre,
52425 Jülich, Germany
{j.jiang,p.philippen,m.knobloch,b.mohr}@fz-juelich.de
[2] National University of Defense Technology,
School of Computer Science,
Changsha, Hunan Province, 410073, China
jiangjie@nudt.edu.cn

Abstract. The core count of modern processors is steadily increasing, forcing programmers to use more concurrent threads or tasks to effectively use the available hardware. This in turn makes it increasingly challenging to achieve correct and efficient thread synchronization. To support the programmer in this task, IBM introduced hardware transactional memory (TM) and speculative execution (SE) in their Blue Gene/Q system with its 16-core processor, which permits to run 64 simultaneous hardware threads in SMT mode. TM and SE allow for parallelization when race conditions may happen, however upon their detection the respective parts of the execution are rolled back and re-executed serially. This incurs some overhead and therefore usage must be well justified. In this paper, we describe extensions to the community instrumentation and measurement infrastructure Score-P, allowing developers to instrument, measure, and analyze applications. To our knowledge, this is the first integrated performance tool framework allowing to analyze TM/SE programs. We demonstrate its usefulness and effectiveness by describing experiments with benchmarks and a real-world application.

Keywords: Parallel Programming, Performance Analysis, Transactional Memory, Speculative Execution, Blue Gene/Q.

1 Introduction

The number of cores available in modern processors as well as the number of processors inside cache-coherent shared-memory nodes is steadily increasing,

---

* This work is partially supported by the National Basic Research 973 Program of China under Grant No.61312701001, the National High Technology Research and Development Program of China under Grant No.2012AA01A309.

F. Silva et al. (Eds.): Euro-Par 2014, LNCS 8632, pp. 26–37, 2014.

especially in high-end servers and HPC cluster systems. This forces parallel program developers to use more concurrent threads or tasks to effectively use the available hardware, in turn making it increasingly challenging to achieve correct and efficient thread synchronization.

IBM's latest HPC architecture, the Blue Gene/Q, is based on a 16-core PowerPC A2 processor, running up to 64 simultaneous hardware threads in symmetric multi-threading (SMT) mode [1]. To alleviate the implementation of correct and efficient thread synchronization, IBM introduced hardware transactional memory (TM) and speculative execution (SE). The interface to the TM and SE hardware features of the Blue Gene/Q memory subsystem is based on C/C++ pragmas and Fortran directives[1] similar to the ones in the OpenMP specification. The TM programming model is based on an abstraction called a transaction. It is a single-entry and single-exit code block enclosed by a "tm_atomic" directive. It can be used for atomic or critical regions in the code where data access race conditions are expected to be rare and thus the locking overhead in the race-free instances of the region can be avoided. For SE, the corresponding directive has similar semantics as an OpenMP loop work-sharing construct. For example, the "speculative for" directive mimics an "omp parallel for" directive with the additional guarantee to maintain sequential semantics of the code, i.e., the result corresponds to the result of an execution by a single thread. So, TM and SE both allow for parallelization even when race conditions may happen, however upon their detection the respective parts of the execution are rolled back and re-executed serially. However, the benefit of the parallel execution must outweigh the extra management overhead. To help application developers to evaluate the effectiveness of using TM and SE constructs in their codes, the IBM compiler runtime provides a TM/SE monitoring API which allows to collect executions statistics for TM and SE constructs.

In this paper, we describe extensions to the parallel program performance analysis framework Score-P [2], which allows developers to instrument, measure, and analyze MPI, OpenMP, or hybrid MPI/OpenMP parallel applications which also use TM and SE constructs. This integration allows the user to analyze all aspects of parallel performance in one tool environment and to study dependencies and relationships between parallel constructs from the different programming paradigms. For the instrumentation of directive-based parallel programming paradigms, Score-P uses the Open Pragma And Region Instrumenter (OPARI2) tool, which was enhanced to handle IBM TM and SE directives. Measurement results are stored as summary profiles which can be analyzed and viewed by the Cube [3] performance report viewer.

The main contributions of the work described in this paper are:

- A generic extensible tool for automatic instrumentation of directive-based parallel programming paradigms including OpenMP and IBM TM/SE.
- An integrated performance tool framework allowing to analyze MPI, OpenMP, or hybrid MPI/OpenMP parallel programs using TM and SE constructs. To our knowledge, this is the only tool set providing this capability.

---

[1] As in the OpenMP specification, in this paper we will use the term directive for both

The rest of the paper is organized as follows: Section 2 gives a brief overview on related work. Section 3 introduces the performance tool components which were used, adapted, and enhanced, including the IBM TM/SE monitoring API, OPARI, Score-P and Cube. The experiments to evaluate the usefulness and effectiveness of the introduced extensions to our tool infrastructure are described in Section 4. Finally, conclusions and a description of future work close the paper.

2   Related Work

Research on Transactional Memory (TM) has a long history, being first introduced by Herlihy and Moss [4] in 1993 as a theoretical extension to microprocessors. Subsequent research shifted towards Software Transactional Memory (STM) [5], i.e. software ensures the atomicity of the transactions and organizes the rollbacks. Today, STM implementations are available for many programming languages, either as language feature (e.g. Closure) or as a library (e.g. for C/C++, C#, Java).

Several research groups proposed analysis techniques for software transactional memory using different methods. Ansari et al. [6] extended an STM framework to obtain profiling data while Zyulkyarov et al. [7] track data structures that conflict in transactions and determine their influence on the performance of the application. Tracing of transactional memory applications was introduced by Lourencco et al. [8], using a similar approach like the group of Ansari. However, due to the relatively high overhead of STM, this approach is of minor relevance to real-world applications in the field of high-performance computing [9].

IBM presented the first commercially available hardware transactional memory (HTM) system in the Blue Gene/Q (BG/Q) supercomputer [1]. Wang et al. [10] and Schindewolf et al. [11] evaluated the HTM implementation on BG/Q using various benchmarks to determine which applications may benefit from TM. Scientific application developers begin to embrace HTM; performance studies have been performed by Kunaseth et al. [12] for molecular dynamics applications and by Schindewolf et al. [13] for the conjugate gradients method.

On the other hand, the Speculative Execution (SE) functionality of BG/Q has not yet been so well investigated. To the best of our knowledge, no extensive performance study for SE has been performed.

Bihari et al. [14] made a case for adding directives for transactional memory to the OpenMP specification. The importance of a standard way to express TM constructs became visible with the work of Yoo et al. [15], who evaluated the performance of the recently introduced Transactional Synchronization Extensions of Intel's Core architecture processors.

3   Tool Implementation

To gain insight into the behavior and especially into the impact on performance of the new transactional memory and speculative execution features on IBM's

Table 1. Structure used by reporting functions for TM counters

TM record	SE record

```typedef struct TmReport_s {```
``` unsigned long hwThreadId;```
``` unsigned long totalTransactions;```
``` unsigned long totalRollbacks;```
``` unsigned long totalSerializedJMV;```
``` unsigned long totalSerializedMAXRB;```
``` unsigned long totalSerializedOTHER;```
```} TmReport_t;```
	```typedef struct SeReport_s {```
	``` unsigned long totalNONSpecCommitted;```
	``` unsigned long totalSpecCommitted;```
	``` unsigned long totalRollbacks;```
	``` unsigned long totalSerializedJMV;```
	``` unsigned long totalSerializedMAXRB;```
	``` unsigned long totalSerializedOTHER;```
	```} SeReport_t;```

BlueGene/Q architecture, we added support into OPARI2 and to the performance measurement framework Score-P. Source-to-source translation is used to insert probe functions into the application code to instrument the regions of the code that make use of TM and SE. These probe functions are implemented in one of the measurement libraries of Score-P, the so-called TM/SE adapter, and process the data provided by IBM's TM/SE monitoring API to make it usable by the measurement system. The data is recorded and stored in profiles which can be examined with Cube.

This section introduces the IBM TM/SE monitoring API and presents the extensions to OPARI2 that were necessary to perform the instrumentation of the TM/SE directives. Next, the measurement system Score-P and the newly implemented adapter for TM/SE are briefly described. Finally, this section concludes with a detailed description of the newly developed analysis possibilities for transactional memory and speculative execution.

3.1   IBM TM/SE Monitoring API

The SMPRT runtime system on IBM BlueGene/Q provides several intrinsics for application programmers and tool developers to collect accumulative statistic for TM/SE regions.

*tm_get_stats(TmReport_t * stats)* collects the relevant accumulative statistics for all TM regions that a particular hardware thread has executed up to the point of the call, and stores it in a record of type *TmReport_t* as shown in Table 1, left. The main fields of this record include the hardware thread ID, the total number of transactions, the total number of rollbacks, and the total number of serialized executions (instead of successful speculative executions), caused either by JMV[2] conflicts, the maximum number of rollbacks reached, or other reasons. This function can be called both at the beginning and the end of a transaction, the difference reflecting the contribution of the enclosed region. To get thread-specific values, it should be used inside parallel regions (like OpenMP parallel regions).

---

[2] Jail Mode Violations occur in case of irrevocable actions, e.g. I/O.

tm_get_all_stats(TmReport_t * stats) behaves similarly, but it provides the accumulative statistics of all the TM regions that all hardware threads have executed up to the point of the call. This function should be used outside of parallel regions.

se_get_all_stats(SeReport_t * stats) updates the provided record (see Table 1, right) with the sum of the statistics of all the SE regions that all hardware threads have executed up to the call. The statistic counters for speculative execution include the total number of chunks committed by none speculative threads, the total number of chunks committed by speculative threads, the total number of rollbacks for speculative threads, the total numbers of serializations (caused by JMV conflicts, due to reaching the maximum number of rollbacks, and due to other reasons like buffer overflows, hardware races, etc.).

3.2   Instrumenting TM/SE Programs

We use the TM/SE monitoring API described above for collecting runtime accumulative statistics about the execution of TM/SE regions in the application. The necessary instrumentation can be done in various ways; we use source-code based instrumentation to be able to attribute performance data to user-level constructs easily and in a portable way.

The Open Pragma And Region Instrumenter (OPARI2) is a source-to-source instrumentation tool that inserts probe functions and code segments into an application's source code. OPARI2 is developed based on OPARI from the Scalasca performance analysis tool set [16]. The original version was designed to detect and instrument OpenMP directives in C/C++ and Fortran programs. It reads the source file line by line, detects OpenMP directives and runtime functions ignoring strings and comments, and instruments OpenMP constructs by inserting functions as defined by the POMP2 interface [17].

All directives that are to be instrumented are stored in an internal table. While parsing the source code, OPARI2 checks the table whenever a directive is detected. If the directive is to be instrumented, this is done at the beginning and at the end of the source-code region associated with the directive.

Support for TM/SE program instrumentation was integrated into OPARI2 under the precondition of enhancing OPARI2 to have a more modular architecture. The goal was to support different directive-based parallel programming paradigms, starting with OpenMP and IBM's TM/SE, but also keeping OpenACC and Intel MIC LEO (language extensions for offload) in mind. OPARI2 now maintains an internal table of all supported paradigms and directives. Each entry of the table includes the paradigm type, directive name, a flag indicating whether this specific directive should be instrumented, as well as two pointers to functions which perform the necessary instrumentation at the beginning and at the end of the associated source-code region. These directive-specific definitions form the basis of the modularized OPARI2, which makes it straightforward to support new paradigms and directives in the future.

Table 2. Exemplary instrumentation of TM and SE directives for C/C++

Original code	Instrumented code

`#pragma speculative for`
`{`
`...`
`}`
	`PTLS_Speculativefor_enter( int* id,`
	`                const char context_info[] );`
	`#pragma speculative for`
	`{`
	`...`
	`}`
	`PTLS_Speculativefor_exit( int* id );`

`#pragma speculative sections`
`{`
`#pragma speculative section`
` {`
` ...`
 `}`
`...`
`}`
	`PTLS_Speculativesections_enter(`
	`  int* id, const char context_info[] );`
	`#pragma speculative sections`
	`{`
	`#pragma speculative section`
	`  {`
	`    PTLS_Speculativesection_begin(`
	`    int* id, const char context_info[] );`
	`    ...`
	`    PTLS_Speculativesection_end( int* id );`
	`  }`
	`  ...`
	`  PTLS_Speculativesections_exit( int* id );`
	`}`

`#pragma tm_atomic`
`{`
`...`
`}`
	`PTLS_Tm_atomic_enter( int* id,`
	`          const char context_info[] );`
	`#pragma tm_atomic`
	`{`
	`...`
	`}`
	`PTLS_Tm_atomic_exit( int* id ),`

The instrumentation of IBM's transactional memory and speculative execution directives was enabled by defining and adding definitions for all TM/SE directives. That is, new table entries have been created for the tm_atomic, speculative for, speculative do, speculative sections and speculative section directives. The instrumentation is carried out according to the transformation rules as shown in Table 2.

3.3   Measuring TM and SE Programs

To actually measure programs employing the TM/SE techniques the instrumented executable needs to be linked to a measurement library which implements the inserted probe functions. Therefore, we extended the Score-P measurement framework accordingly.

The Score-P Instrumentation and Measurement Infrastructure is a community-driven software framework for recording profiles and traces of parallel program execution [2]. The application under investigation is automatically instrumented, by means of a number of different techniques, and linked to a set of libraries that implement the respective probe functions. Each invocation of a probe function is translated into measurement events such as enter/exit of code regions, or acquire/release of locks. Different metrics like number of visits, time spent in a region, bytes transferred over a network are associated with these events. Furthermore hardware counters providing information about cache misses or floating point operations can be recorded.

There are two main modes of recording and storing data in Score-P: profiling and tracing. In a profile, summarized data is recorded for each callpath executed by the program. Times and number of visits are aggregated; minimum, maximum and average values are stored. The values of performance counters are also recorded. In contrast, in a trace every single instance of an event is recorded. This yields a very detailed view of the program run but comes at the cost of high memory demands during measurement and for storing the trace file itself.

Different methods for performing the instrumentation of an application are available. Many compilers allow for automatic instrumentation of user functions. Here, the compiler inserts probe functions at entries and exits of functions and supplies source-code information. To instrument directive-based parallel programming paradigms, we use OPARI2 as described in Section 3.2. To record MPI-specific events and metrics, PMPI interposition wrappers are used. For analyzing programs that run on GPUs, the CUDA Profiling and Tools Interface (CUPTI) is supported as well.

Each of the aforementioned instrumentation techniques inserts different types of probe functions which provide different types of information to the actual measurement system. To provide the measurement core that records profiles or traces with consistent data, Score-P contains a number of adapters, each taking care of implementing the probe or wrapper functions for a specific kind of instrumentation.

A TM/SE adapter was added in Score-P to enable the measurement of code regions making use of the transactional memory and speculative execution functionality provided by the IBM compilers. These regions, which are instrumented with OPARI2, are first registered with the measurement system. During registration, the type of TM/SE directive is stored together with source code information, consisting of file name and line numbers. Furthermore, the measurement system provides a unique numerical id, which is passed as parameter to the probe function calls surrounding the corresponding TM/SE regions (see Table 2). This allows quick access to the respective region information.

When a region is entered, interface functions provided by the TM/SE runtime are used to obtain data about the number of transactions and rollbacks as well as information about how much of the execution needed to be serialized due to JMV conflicts, too many rollbacks, and other causes, such as buffer overflows, race conditions and concurrent TM/SE regions. These values are passed as custom metrics to the measurement system. The measurement core takes care of keeping count of the number of visits to each region as well as the time spent inside.

4   Experimental Evaluation

In this section, we evaluate our approach with two examples. The first is a quasi-random field update kernel that occurs in similar form in many scientific applications. The second is MP2C, a molecular dynamics application that scales up to the whole JUQUEEN, a 28-rack Blue Gene/Q system at the Jülich Supercomputing Centre.

4.1   Update Kernel

A kernel found in many scientific applications, especially in the area of plasma physics, is an update of charge and power densities of large arrays of particles, in total 6 entries per volume cell. First the values are interpolated and then a reduction on the arrays is performed. Here, multiple threads may concurrently access the same location.

```
!$OMP PARALLEL DO private(xa, i, j1, j2, f1, f2, ci)
do i=1,5000000
  xa = x(i)*oodx
  j1 = aint(xa)
  j2 = j1+1
  f2 = xa-j1
  f1 = 1.0-f2
  ci = charge(i)
  !TM$ TM_ATOMIC SAFE_MODE
  rho(j1,ci) = rho(j1,ci) + re*f1
  rho(j2,ci) = rho(j2,ci) + re*f2
  !TM$ END TM_ATOMIC
end do
!$OMP END PARALLEL DO
```

Listing 1. Update Kernel – TM version

Listing 1 shows an example of such a kernel, although in a very simplified form. In each iteration, it performs a quasi-random update of two entries of an array of about 19 MB, which gives a conflict probability of ~8e-7, so it seems a good candidate for TM.

Figure 1 shows a Cube screenshot of an execution of this kernel on one node of BG/Q with one process and eight threads. Cube's main window consists of three coupled tree-browsers. These show, from left to right, the metric tree, call tree and system tree. A selection of an item in one tree shows the distribution of the value associated with this item in the tree(s) to the right. In this example, the total number of transactions is selected in the metric tree, and we see the expected five million transactions. The call tree in the middle pane shows that they all originate from one TM region. The right pane, the system tree, shows that each thread completed 625,000 transactions.

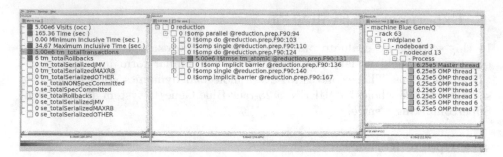

Fig. 1. Cube screenshot of the TM implementation of the update kernel showing five million total transactions distributed homogeneously among the threads

While this seems to be a perfect kernel for TM, with hardly any rollbacks (6 in this example), it has to be noted that the uninstrumented TM implementation is 2 times slower than an implementation with OpenMP atomics and 3 times slower than an implementation with OpenMP reduction. This can also be easily investigated with our toolset. This shows that the tool gives correct information, but a baseline comparison to evaluate TM/SE benefits is still necessary. A detailed performance analysis of this kernel can be found in [18], where tuning opportunities are also shown which are not reflected in our measurements.

4.2 MP2C

MP2C [19] - Massively Parallel Multi-Particle Collision Dynamics - implements a hybrid representation of solvated particles in a fluid. Solutes are simulated atomistically by classical molecular dynamics (MD) which is coupled to the solvent, described by the Multi-Particle-Collision-Dynamics method (MPC). In this work we focus on the MPC part, which can be used as stand-alone implementation for particle-based hydrodynamics. The application is written in Fortran 90 and parallelized with MPI and OpenMP, which are used throughout the code. We investigated the cell collision kernel containing an OpenMP loop counting the particles in a cell and updating a list. In the initial version, this update is guarded with an OpenMP critical directive. We investigated alternative implementations with both TM and SE for this critical section. In the TM case, the OpenMP critical was replaced by an TM atomic, in the SE case the whole loop was executed speculatively.

Figure 2 shows a Cube screenshot of the TM version of the code. We see that 800 million transactions were issued and 560 million rollbacks occurred, i.e. a rollback ratio of 70%. And even worse, more than 3.5 million iterations were serialized because the maximum number of rollbacks was reached. So TM is not a good choice to replace the OpenMP critical in this case.

A much better result was achieved with SE as shown in Figure 3. Here the rollback ratio is only 7% and no serializations occurred. In the system pane this screenshot shows a boxplot of the distribution of rollbacks among the processes,

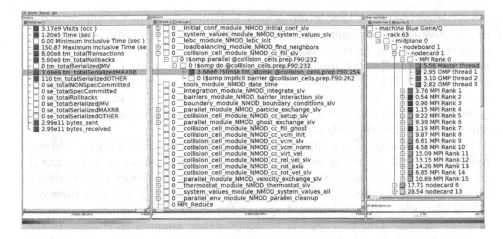

Fig. 2. Cube screenshot of the TM implementation of MP2C. It shows a high variation of serializations due to max. rollbacks among the threads.

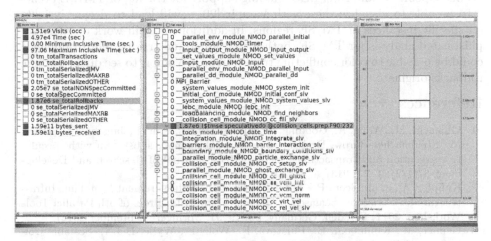

Fig. 3. Cube screenshot of the SE implementation of MP2C, showing the distribution of rollbacks among the processes as a boxplot

with a lower quartile of 3110, an upper quartile of 4410 and a median of 3660, which seems a reasonable distribution.

This example shows that our enhanced tool set easily allows to investigate TM/SE-related performance issues in parallel applications. Furthermore it also allows to compare these results with other implementations like plain OpenMP within the same environment.

5   Conclusion and Future Work

In this paper we presented a unique integrated performance tools framework to measure and analyze applications using IBM TM/SE directives. To this end, we modularized the OPARI2 source-to-source instrumenter to be easily extendable to directive-based programming paradigms other than OpenMP. A respective adapter was added to the measurement infrastructure Score-P. This adapter uses the existing TM/SE monitoring API to query information about the execution of single TM/SE regions. The resulting profile reports can be visualized and analyzed with the Cube performance report viewer. With two examples we proved the applicability of the tool and showed the added value to performance analysis of parallel applications.

One disadvantage of our approach is that TM instrumentation may add significant overhead, especially for regions with small workload, as tm_get_stats() gets called twice per region. We will investigate methods to reduce that overhead, e.g. by minimizing the number of calls to the IBM monitoring API. However, this needs to be carefully balanced against the more limited information available for analysis. Our tool set will be continuously adapted to changes in the existing directive-based programming paradigms, in particular possible TM/SE support in the OpenMP specification. We further plan to integrate other models like OpenACC and Intel LEO. Adding support for tracing of TM/SE events – to be able to visualize these with Vampir [20] – will lead to deeper insights on specific instances of TM/SE regions. In addition, we will work on more sophisticated analysis for TM/SE, both for profiling and tracing. For example, it could be possible to color conflicting transactions in Vampir to see directly where rollbacks originate.

References

1. Ohmacht, M., Wang, A., Gooding, T., Nathanson, B., Nair, I., Janssen, G., Schaal, M., Steinmacher-Burow, B.: IBM Blue Gene/Q memory subsystem with speculative execution and transactional memory. IBM Journal of Research and Development 57(1/2), 1–7 (2013)
2. Knüpfer, A., et al.: Score-P – A Joint Performance Measurement Run-Time Infrastructure for Periscope, Scalasca, TAU, and Vampir. In: Proc. of 5th Parallel Tools Workshop, 2011, Dresden, Germany, pp. 79–91. Springer (September 2012)
3. Geimer, M., Kuhlmann, B., Pulatova, F., Wolf, F., Wylie, B.J.N.: Scalable Collation and Presentation of Call-Path Profile Data with CUBE. In: Proc. of the Conference on Parallel Computing (ParCo), Aachen/Jülich, Germany, pp. 645–652 (September 2007), Minisymposium Scalability and Usability of HPC Programming Tools
4. Herlihy, M., Moss, J.E.B.: Transactional Memory: Architectural Support for Lock-free Data Structures. In: Proc. of the 20th Annual Intl. Symposium on Computer Architecture, ISCA 1993, pp. 289–300. ACM, New York (1993)
5. Shavit, N., Touitou, D.: Software transactional memory. Distributed Computing 10(2), 99–116 (1997)
6. Ansari, M., Jarvis, K., Kotselidis, C., Luján, M., Kirkham, C., Watson, I.: Profiling transactional memory applications. In: 2009 17th Euromicro International Conference on Parallel, Distributed and Network-based Processing, pp. 11–20. IEEE (2009)
7. Zyulkyarov, F., Stipic, S., Harris, T., Unsal, O.S., Cristal, A., Hur, I., Valero, M.: Profiling and Optimizing Transactional Memory Applications. Intl. Journal of Parallel Programming 40(1), 25–56 (2012)

8. Lourenço, J., Dias, R., Luís, J., Rebelo, M., Pessanha, V.: Understanding the behavior of transactional memory applications. In: Proc. 7th Workshop on Parallel and Distributed Systems: Testing, Analysis, and Debugging, p. 3. ACM (2009)
9. Cascaval, C., Blundell, C., Michael, M., Cain, H.W., Wu, P., Chiras, S., Chatterjee, S.: Software Transactional Memory: Why Is It Only a Research Toy? Queue 6(5), 40:46–40:58 (2008)
10. Wang, A., Gaudet, M., Wu, P., Amaral, J.N., Ohmacht, M., Barton, C., Silvera, R., Michael, M.: Evaluation of Blue Gene/Q hardware support for transactional memories. In: Proc. of the 21st International Conference on Parallel Architectures and Compilation Techniques, pp. 127–136. ACM (2012)
11. Schindewolf, M., Biliari, B., Gyllenhaal, J., Schulz, M., Wang, A., Karl, W.: What scientific applications can benefit from hardware transactional memory? In: 2012 International Conference for High Performance Computing, Networking, Storage and Analysis (SC), pp. 1–11. IEEE (2012)
12. Kunaseth, M., Kalia, R.K., Nakano, A., Vashishta, P., Richards, D.F., Glosli, J.N.: Performance Characteristics of Hardware Transactional Memory for Molecular Dynamics Application on BlueGene/Q: Toward Efficient Multithreading Strategies for Large-Scale Scientific Applications. In: Proc. of Intl. Workshop on Parallel and Distributed Scientific and Engineering Computing (2013)
13. Schindewolf, M., Rocker, B., Karl, W., Heuveline, V.: Evaluation of Two Formulations of the Conjugate Gradients Method with Transactional Memory. In: Wolf, F., Mohr, B., an Mey, D. (eds.) Euro-Par 2013. LNCS, vol. 8097, pp. 508–520. Springer, Heidelberg (2013)
14. Bihari, B.L., Wong, M., Wang, A., de Supinski, B.R., Chen, W.: A case for including transactions in openmp ii: Hardware transactional memory. In: Chapman, B.M., Massaioli, F., Müller, M.S., Rorro, M. (eds.) IWOMP 2012. LNCS, vol. 7312, pp. 44–58. Springer, Heidelberg (2012)
15. Yoo, R.M., Hughes, C.J., Lai, K., Rajwar, R.: Performance evaluation of Intel® transactional synchronization extensions for high-performance computing. In: Proc. of SC13: Intl. Conference for High Performance Computing, Networking, Storage and Analysis, p. 19. ACM (2013)
16. http://www.scalasca.org
17. Mohr, B., Malony, A.D., Hoppe, H.C., Schlimbach, F., Haab, G., Hoeflinger, J., Shah, S.: A Performance Monitoring Interface for OpenMP. In: Proc. of Fourth European Workshop on OpenMP (EWOMP), Rome, Italy (September 2002)
18. Maurer, T.: BG/Q Application Tuning – memory hierarchy, transactional memory, speculative execution,
http://www.fz-juelich.de/SharedDocs/Downloads/IAS/JSC/EN/slides/juqueenpt13/juqueenpt13-applicationtuning1.pdf
19. Sutmann, G., Westphal, L., Bolten, M.: Particle based simulations of complex systems with mp2c: hydrodynamics and electrostatics. In: ICNAAM 2010: International Conference of Numerical Analysis and Applied Mathematics 2010, vol. 1281, pp. 1768–1772. AIP Publishing (2010)
20. Brunst, H., Mohr, B.: Performance Analysis of Large-Scale OpenMP and Hybrid MPI/OpenMP Applications with Vampir NG. In: Mueller, M.S., Chapman, B.M., de Supinski, B.R., Malony, A.D., Voss, M. (eds.) IWOMP 2005/2006. LNCS, vol. 4315, pp. 5–14. Springer, Heidelberg (2008)

c-Eclipse: An Open-Source Management Framework for Cloud Applications

Chrystalla Sofokleous, Nicholas Loulloudes, Demetris Trihinas,
George Pallis, and Marios D. Dikaiakos

Department of Computer Science, University of Cyprus, Nicosia, CY1678, Cyprus
{stalosof,loulloudes.n,trihinas,gpallis,mdd}@cs.ucy.ac.cy

Abstract. Cloud application portability and optimal resource allocation are of
great importance in the realm of Cloud infrastructure provisioning. c-Eclipse is
an open-source Cloud Application Management Framework through which users
are able to define the description, deployment and management phases of their
Cloud applications in a clean and intuitive graphical manner. It is built on top of
the well-established Eclipse platform and it adheres to two highly desirable features of Cloud applications: portability and elasticity. In particular, c-Eclipse implements the open, non-proprietary OASIS TOSCA specification for describing
the provision, deployment and re-contextualization of applications across different Cloud infrastructures, thereby ensuring application portability. Furthermore,
c-Eclipse enables Cloud users to specify elasticity policies that describe how the
deployed virtualized resources must be elastically adapted at runtime to match
the needs of a dynamic application-workload. In this paper, we introduce the architecture and implementation of c-Eclipse, and describe its key characteristics
via a use-case scenario that involves a user creating a description of a 3-tier Cloud
application, enriching it with appropriate elasticity policies, submitting it for deployment to two different Cloud providers and, finally, monitoring its execution.

1 Introduction

Application deployment and management in Infrastructure as a Service (IaaS) Clouds
can be a complex and time consuming endeavor, typically requiring manual effort on
the users' behalf and relying on vendor-specific, proprietary tools. Existing IaaS tools
do not provide users with vendor-neutral mechanisms for describing application configuration, deployment, runtime application-scaling preferences, and elasticity policies.
Consequently, the migration of applications between different IaaS providers requires
significant re-configuration and re-deployment effort and time, leading to vendor lock-
in. With the growing number of IaaS-provider service offerings and the increasing
complexity of applications deployed on Clouds, the selection of the most appropriate provider to host an application becomes challenging. While seeking to identify the
deployments that suit best their needs, IaaS clients need to overcome vendor lock-in in
order to test and/or deploy their applications on multiple IaaS providers. Therefore, it
becomes evident that there is a need for *application management tools* that facilitate
the description of applications in a vendor neutral manner, enabling easy application
deployment, management, and migration across different providers, preventing vendor
lock-in.

F. Silva et al. (Eds.): Euro-Par 2014, LNCS 8632, pp. 38–49, 2014.

This article presents **c-Eclipse**, a generic Application Management Framework that:

– is *open-source* and has been implemented on top of the reliable Eclipse platform[1];
– offers graphical tools to *facilitate the description* of an application's structure and its lifecycle management operations;
– *adopts the TOSCA [1] open specification* for blueprinting Cloud applications and consequently packaging them in portable archives that can be processed by any compliant IaaS-provider;
– adopts a language that enables the description of *elasticity policies* for such Cloud applications;
– provides *tools for elasticity policy specification* at different levels of an application's structure.

To this end, c-Eclipse can be promoted by Cloud vendors as an enabling tool for configuring, deploying and managing Cloudified applications on their infrastructure. This is beneficial both for vendors and users; The former can integrate c-Eclipse to their Cloud architectures to attract a wider customer base to use their services via its GUI; the latter are able to describe - the often complex - deployment and management lifecycle of their applications with minimal effort and in a portable way, thus avoiding vendor lock-in.

The rest of the paper is structured as follows: Section 2 presents the related work in Cloud Application Managements platforms. Section 3 gives an overview of the c-Eclipse framework, its architecture, the application description language used and the UI. The c-Eclipse approach for describing elasticity policies for applications is discussed in Section 4. Finally, Section 5 presents a use-case scenario with a 3-tier application described via c-Eclipse and deployed on two separate Cloud infrastructures.

2 Related Work

Many application management frameworks have been developed lately to support Cloud Computing. Some of these frameworks are proprietary, locking their users to specific providers, while others are generic enough allowing management of applications on different infrastructures.

Proprietary: Amazon CloudFormation enables the creation and provisioning of EC2 infrastructure deployments. It uses JSON template files to describe the collection of EC2 resources that compose a deployment. Furthermore, by leveraging Amazon Auto Scaling it enables the specification of policies for automatically scaling the number of EC2 instances in a deployment. Oracle Virtual Assembly Builder (OVAB) [2] simplifies the provisioning of multi-tier applications by capturing the application components into self-contained VM appliances. OVAB can instantiate the appliances on Oracle's Exalogic Elastic Cloud Infrastructure and scale the deployed applications horizontally after a scale command is sent via the command line interface. VMware vCloud Application Director [3] is a provisioning solution that provides the necessary tooling for simplifying the process of designing, customizing and deploying applications on any

---

[1] https://www.eclipse.org/

VMware based Cloud infrastructure. From the well established aforementioned tools, only CloudFormation enables the specification of elasticity policies for automatic scaling, while all of them lock their users to specific IaaS providers.

Generic: Juju [4] is a tool for designing, configuring and deploying applications on a limited number of Cloud platforms. It makes use of shareable and reusable *charms* that encapsulate the configuration, deployment, connectivity and scaling information for an application. Charms are usually Linux oriented, thus limiting the portability of Juju applications. Also, Juju does not allow the specification of elasticity policies. The Agility Platform by ServiceMesh [5] enables the automatic deployment of applications on any Cloud provider, and the dynamic management of their lifecycle by defining auto-scaling rules for adding/removing VMs. Although ServiceMesh allows deployment of applications on different Cloud environments, it comes with a significant financial cost. Wrangler [6] provides a system for automatic deployment and monitoring of distributed applications with complex dependencies on different Cloud infrastructures, through a dedicated XML language. Users can describe a deployment; characteristics of the virtual resources, VM images, authentication credentials; and send it to a coordinating web service.

None of the aforementioned platforms adopts open Cloud standards for describing applications. In an effort to promote Cloud application portability, Winery [7] supports modeling of TOSCA applications via an HTML5-based environment. TOSCA elements are created via the Web-based GUI, which also allows users with prior knowledge of the TOSCA standard to define new types for the TOSCA elements, or configure the existing ones. Furthermore, Winery does not provide a straightforward way of specifying elasticity policies for applications. c-Eclipse on the other hand provides an intuitive GUI that hides all the complex details of the TOSCA standard, enabling thus users to exploit the full potential of the tool. In addition, c-Eclipse enriches the TOSCA specification with *Policy Types* for elasticity, and allows its users to specify the desired elasticity policies for their applications. Finally, Winery relies on BPEL to model applications' management plans, while c-Eclipse makes use of the TOSCA *Lifecycle Interface*. Another platform that uses TOSCA to automate the deployment and scaling of applications over any Cloud technology, is Cloudify [8]. It supports the creation of TOSCA application blueprints via an open-source CLI, however requiring users to master YAML and Python languages. This procedure gets easier when using the full-featured web interface, available only in a payware edition.

3   c-Eclipse Overview

This section presents the c-Eclipse framework focusing on the features that make it attractive to Cloud application developers. Furthermore, it provides a brief overview of the open Cloud application description specification adopted by c-Eclipse. It continues with the description of its architecture together with the necessary requirements when it comes to integration with Cloud vendors. Finally, the c-Eclipse UI is introduced.

3.1   c-Eclipse Features

The c-Eclipse Cloud application management framework incorporates the following characteristics:

- **Ease of Use:** It provides an intuitive and user-friendly GUI that minimizes any complexity regarding the process of Cloud application management, therefore serving as a low-entry barrier to Cloud technologies for new end-users. Not neglecting experienced users, GUI-driven operations can be manually fine-tuned, effectively allowing full workflow control when needed.
- **Elasticity Policies Specification:** It enables the specification of applications' elasticity policies, so that applications can benefit from the dynamic nature of Cloud environments.
- **Monitoring Interface:**It provides interfaces for integration with existing monitoring systems, so that its users can monitor the performance of their deployed applications and their resources thereof.
- **Cloud Vendor Neutral:** Through the adoption of the TOSCA open specification, allows its users to describe applications in a very generic way, so that they can be deployed across different Cloud infrastructures.
- **Platform Independence:** It runs on any OS supported by Eclipse.

3.2 TOSCA Specification for Cloud Applications

TOSCA provides a language to describe the structure of applications, together with their management operations. The structure of an application defines the components an application consists of and the relationships between them. Application components are described in TOSCA by means of *Nodes* (i.e. an application component can be a Tomcat application server in a 3-tier environment). Each Node can have certain semantics that are defined by the properties of the corresponding *Node Type*. Such semantics include the *Requirements* a Node has against its hosting environment, the *Capabilities* it offers and the *Policies* that govern its execution, such as security or elasticity policies. Similarly, TOSCA *Relationships* are used to represent the relations in an application's structure, and have their own semantics defined by their *Relationship Type*. The management aspects of an application are described in TOSCA either by means of lifecycle operations (via the *Lifecycle Interface*) or by more complex *Management Plans*. The *Lifecycle Interface* defines five operations (install, configure, start, stop, uninstall) for describing the management of applications' lifecycle. On the other hand, there is no TOSCA specific way to describe Management Plans. Instead, plans can be specified in any existing process modeling language, such as BPMN, and referenced through TOSCA. Both Lifecycle Operations and Managements Plans require some content to be realized, such as virtual machine images, configuration files etc. These contents are collectively referred to as *Artifacts*.

TOSCA application descriptions can be processed in an imperative or declarative manner. In case of imperative processing [9] the management behaviour of the described application has to be explicitly defined by the user by means of Management Plans. In declarative processing, the management behaviour of the application can be inferred by the semantics of Nodes' and Relationships' Types (i.e. operations specified in the *Lifecycle Interface* of a Type). The latter imposes extra overhead to TOSCA type architects who need to precisely define the semantics of each type, and for the implementers of the TOSCA processing environments who must correctly interpreter the

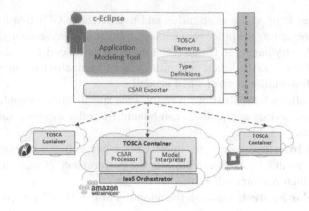

Fig. 1. c-Eclipse Architecture

types' semantics to infer an application's management plans. Consequently, declarative processing makes modeling of Cloud applications easier from the user perspective, since they don't have the extra overhead of defining Management Plans. For this reason, c-Eclipse adheres to the declarative processing approach.

3.3   c-Eclipse Framework Architecture

c-Eclipse is built on top of the Eclipse Platform and follows its OSGi plug-in based software architecture. Its main component is the **Application Modeling Tool**, which facilitates the creation of TOSCA application descriptions. The elements specified in TOSCA and the c-Eclipse specific type definitions for Nodes and Relationships, are stored in the c-Eclipse file system (**TOSCA Elements** and **Type Definitions**), so that they can be accessed by the Modeling Tool. The Application Modeling Tool associates the TOSCA elements and the defined Node and Relationship Types with visual elements that can be used to graphically model an application. The graphical description is translated on the fly into TOSCA, using the semantics of each element in the description. In order to provide such functionalities, c-Eclipse utilizes Graphiti[2], an Eclipse-based graphics framework that enables rapid development of state-of-the-art diagram editors for domain models. Graphiti is based on the Eclipse Modeling Framework (EMF) and offers graphical representations and editing possibilities for EMF objects. To this extend, the Application Modeling Tool transforms TOSCA elements into EMF objects and uses the Graphiti infrastructure to build the graphical editor through which users can schematically describe their applications The TOSCA description along with any artifacts for materializing and managing the described application are packaged into a single archive file (CSAR) by the **CSAR Exporter**. Fig. 1 depicts the high level architecture and the major components of c-Eclipse.

The exported CSAR is passed from c-Eclipse to a TOSCA processing environment operated by a Cloud provider. This environment, referred to as a **TOSCA Container**,

---

[2] https://www.eclipse.org/graphiti/

must be able to process CSAR files and understand the semantics of the contained application description, so that it can deploy and manage the application throughout its lifecycle. Each application modeling tool can define its own types, for various TOSCA elements, with different properties and interfaces. Thus, in order for the TOSCA Container to process a TOSCA description in a declarative manner, which implies deriving based on the type definition of each element the order in which the specified management operations must be executed, the type definitions utilized in a description must also be known to the TOSCA Container. Consequently, a CSAR archive file must contain the following so as to be portable and processable by any TOSCA Container: (1) The XML file specifying the TOSCA-based application description, (2) The definitions of the Node, Relationship and other elements' types that are used in the TOSCA description, and (3) the artifacts that realize an application's management operations and that are referenced in the TOSCA description.

A TOSCA Container might include various components that can be used to process CSARs. Each vendor can decide what components to support and how to provide them within his Cloud architecture. A Container that supports declarative processing of CSARs must implement at least two components: **CSAR Processor** and **Model Interpreter** (Fig. 1). The CSAR Processor receives the CSAR from the **TOSCA Container** and is responsible for the extraction and deployment of the artifacts. Once the artifacts are ready to be used by the TOSCA Container, the Model Interpreter navigates the application's structure and distinguishes the artifacts realizing the management operations of each Node, such as installing/uninstalling instances. Other components that can be implemented by the container, are a **Definition Manager** component in charge of storing the type definitions and making them available to the Model Interpreter and an **Artifact Manager** component for storing the artifacts in appropriate stores.

According to the specification, Cloud providers that wish to become TOSCA-compliant should provide a Container as part of their Cloud architecture. The Container must communicate with an **IaaS Orchestrator** to invoke the necessary IaaS-specific API calls that satisfy the respective TOSCA description. An alternative way of integrating TOSCA modeling tools, such as c-Eclipse, with Cloud providers is to implement a TOSCA Container at the tools' side, with interfaces to multiple Cloud infrastructures. To this extend, Cloud providers should offer the required APIs, so that they can be accessed by the Containers. However, this endeavour entails in-depth knowledge of several complex APIs (sometimes lacking sufficient documentation) and extensive development skills to produce a fully working Container at the tools' side. This was observed and confirmed at first hand, while working towards the evaluation of c-Eclipse in a real scenario (see Section 5), where we implemented simple yet functional TOSCA Containers for two Cloud vendors. Among other, developing a TOSCA Container for a particular IaaS requires to provision for the exchange of authentication tokens, perform validity checks for CSARs, correct deployment/configuration of virtualized instances given defined Node Types, as well as, user requirements and constraints.

Finally, c-Eclipse provides the necessary interfaces so as to be integrated with existing monitoring systems, enabling thus its users to acquire and record the performance of their deployed applications from a single working environment. Currently, it is fully integrated with the JCatascopia [10] monitoring system.

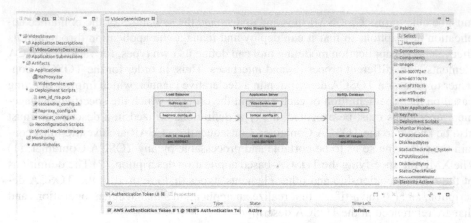

Fig. 2. c-Eclipse UI - (Left) Cloud Project View, (Center) Canvas, (Right) Palette, (Below) Authentication View

3.4 c-Eclipse User Interface

Like any other Eclipse project, c-Eclipse organizes all the files related to an application in a structured hierarchy, as depicted in Fig. 2. A Cloud project, in the Cloud Project View, acts as a placeholder for a single Cloud application and consists of four folders: (i) the *Application Descriptions* folder containing TOSCA descriptions of applications, (ii) the *Application Submissions* folder containing details about application deployments (i.e. Cloud provider, deployment status, total cost etc.), (iii) the *Artifacts* folder with the actual files for the artifacts referenced in the application description, and finally (iv) the *Monitoring* folder including any monitoring data collected by the integrated monitoring system during application's deployments.

Application developers can use the Modeling Tool to describe a Cloud application graphically. The most important part of the tool is the Palette, which includes most of the elements required for creating application descriptions. These are the application components (one component element in the Palette for each distinct Node Type), Relationships (one relationship/connection element in the Palette for each distinct Relationship type), artifacts and monitoring metrics. By simply dragging and dropping pictorial elements from the Palette onto the Canvas of the tool, developers can create a graphical representation of an application. Throughout the application description process, the Modeling tool translates on-the-fly the graphical description into TOSCA and error-proofs the generated TOSCA to assure adherence to the specification, prompting warnings if necessary.

Apart from the default semantics that each Palette element has, additional information can be provided for each element contained in the description, by using the *Properties View* of the tool. For example, the view can be used for uploading custom images for application components, specifying elasticity policies for the whole application and/or for components separately, writing deployment scripts etc. Fig.3 presents a tab in the properties view for specifying elasticity constraints and strategies for a specific application component.

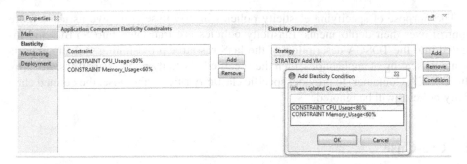

Fig. 3. c-Eclipse Properties View (Elasticity constraints and strategies tab)

Users with expertise in writing XML and with deep knowledge of the TOSCA specification, can manually create or edit an application's TOSCA XML description. Any changes in the XML will be automatically reflected to the corresponding graphical description. This way c-Eclipse attracts broader audience, from entry level to more advanced users.

4   Elasticity Specification in c-Eclipse

Apart from enabling portable automated application deployment and management, c-Eclipse facilitates the specification of applications' elasticity policies so that they can scale at runtime based on user defined policies. Since the TOSCA language does not directly specify how to define elasticity policies for Cloud applications, c-Eclipse exploits the TOSCA *Policy* element to achieve elasticity specification without interfering with applications' portability. TOSCA defines policies as the means by which we can express non-functional behaviour or quality-of-services for an application.

We use two types of elasticity-oriented TOSCA policies in accordance with the SYBL [11] language for elasticity requirements specification: *Elasticity Constraint* and *Elasticity Strategy*. The Elasticity Constraint type is used to express the constraints of an application, related to cost, performance and other application-quality metrics. Here the application user does not specify the exact actions to be enforced when a constraint is violated. Instead, the appropriate actions are determined by the underlying intelligent elastic *Resource Provisioning System* [12]. The Elasticity Strategy type, is used to express specific strategies that should be enforced by the execution environment when specific constraints are violated.

The purpose of defining two distinct TOSCA Policy Types of elasticity is twofold. Cloud users can:

– Specify elasticity constraints and strategies for their applications at different levels of detail, based on their expertise.
– Fully exploit the capabilities of the underlying Resource Provisioning System. In case the underlying system is smart enough to take scaling decisions on its own, the user specifies only the elasticity constraints and relies on the system to decide how to fullfil them.

The purpose of specifying elasticity policies in c-Eclipse is to give its users more control over their deployments. Elasticity policies are translated into SYBL, and injected into the TOSCA description. If the IaaS resource provisioning system supports dynamic scaling of applications, then the specified elasticity policies are translated, (by the TOSCA Container) to provider specific elasticity rules. Otherwise, the defined elasticity policies will be ignored.

5 Use-Case

This section aims at demonstrating the portability and elasticity support capabilities of the c-Eclipse Cloud Application Management Framework. To do so, we present the description, deployment and management phases of an exemplary Cloud application on two environments: (i) Amazon's EC2 infrastructure and (ii) Nephelae[3], our own OpenStack-compliant Cloud research infrastructure.

Before starting the demonstration we needed to implement our TOSCA Containers, as described in Section 3.3, and deploy them on a single virtual instance both on Amazon EC2 and Nephelae. Our simple container for AWS is composed by $\approx$ 450 lines of Code (LOC), implementing 24 needed functions. Similarly, the OpenStack container needed $\approx$ 600 LOC and same number of functions. In order to instrument the application's deployment we also needed a monitoring system to be deployed on both infrastructures. In contrast to EC2[4], Nephelae does not include a native resource and application monitoring solution. Therefore, we instantiate the JCatascopia system for providing the monitoring metrics that will be utilized during the specification of elasticity policies. Finally, we assume each tier instance runs on a Linux-based OS.

Use-Case Scenario: We consider a 3-tier Web application that provides video streaming services to online users. The tiers comprising the application are as follows: (i) a *Load Balancer* which serves as an entry point and distributes incoming user requests across multiple application servers, (ii) the *Application Server* itself, which is materialized through an Apache Tomcat server with the necessary video streaming Web application deployed, and (iii) a *Cassandra*[5] *NoSQL distributed data storage back-end* from where the necessary video content is retrieved.

Application Description Phase: In this first step, the application developer initiates the description process by creating a Cloud project, which will be unique for the above Web application. The necessary folder structure (see Section 3.4) is automatically created, establishing placeholders for individual components required throughout the application management lifecycle. At the same time, the developer is prompted to enter service endpoints and authentication credentials[6] for one or more candidate Cloud provider(s), where the application might eventually be submitted for deployment. The *Authentication Token View* gives an overview of credential details (Fig. 2).

---

[3] http://linc.ucy.ac.cy/Nephelae/
[4] AWS provide the CloudWatch solution for monitoring applications and Cloud resources.
[5] http://cassandra.apache.org/
[6] Credentials are managed in a secure manner using the native Eclipse password manager.

The next step involves creating the application description itself through a guided wizard and subsequently invoking the Modeling Tool, where the respective application structure will be defined. During this phase, the user designs a coarse-grained blueprint of the application structure, avoiding reference to vendor-specific details. This way, the description is portable across different providers. Consequently, at this stage the Palette contains only those generic components that will later-on act as containers for vendor-specific information. Such structural parts include: the application components and the relationships.

For the use-case scenario at hand, the coarse-grained application blueprint is comprised of 3 different application components (Fig. 4). The Load Balancer component is populated with an HA Proxy[7] tarball (orange color box) and a Bash script (white color box) for the respective configuration. Similarly, the Application Server component is populated with the Web application ARchive (WAR) that provides the video streaming functionality and a Bash script for minimal Tomcat configurations. The NoSQL database component is populated with a Bash script for contextualization purposes, such as seed node IP address, listening ports, etc. Additionally, each Component is enriched with a common RSA keypair[8] for shell-access purposes (yellow color box). Finally, the necessary inter-dependencies in the application's structure are specified via the two Relationships shown in Fig. 4. Generic application descriptions are stored in the Application Descriptions folder, and can be used later as customizable templates which can be enriched with vendor-specific information at the deployment phase.

Application Deployment Phase: Once the application developer completes the generic design, it is time to engage in a more fine-grained topology description by providing vendor-specific information. To do so, the user has to invoke the application deployment phase through a context menu action on the description file. This phase is again a wizard driven process requiring the user to select the target Cloud provider where the application deployment will eventually take place. The Palette and Properties Views are now populated with vendor-specific information retrieved by interrogating the IaaS API. In addition to the standard information advertised by the provider such as compute resources availability, volumes and networking configurations, the Palette provides monitoring metrics available by the monitoring systems on EC2 and Nephelae.

To minimize the information displayed and swiftly identify any required component, the Palette includes standard searching and filtering mechanisms. Given that each tier instance of the video streaming service will run on a Linux-based OS, the developer sets the necessary filters to expose available base images that include a 64-bit Ubuntu 12.04 server. For the Application and Database components, the filters are adjusted to search for available Ubuntu-based images that include Apache Tomcat and Cassandra NoSQL, respectively. When suitable images are returned, a simple drag-n-drop operation of their pictorial representations from the Palette to the respective application components (green color box), results to their inclusion within the generated TOSCA description. In the case that matching images are not retrieved, c-Eclipse provides the necessary fields through which the developer can pass specific scripts (or artifact filenames) that will be executed upon contextualization.

---

[7] http://haproxy.1wt.eu/

[8] Only the public key material of the RSA keypair is included within the TOSCA description.

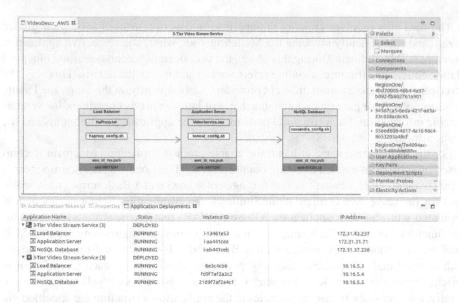

Fig. 4. Application Deployment on Amazon EC2 and Nephelae

What remains to do before inhibiting the actual application deployment process, is for the developer to specify the elasticity-oriented policies. This includes selecting one or more available monitoring metrics from the Palette and assigning them to the components whose resources need to be elastically adapted on runtime. For the video service, it was decided to scale-up only the Application and Database components by adding a new virtualized instance when the CPU utilization threshold exceeded 80% (see Fig. 3). To achieve this, each component was assigned to a CPU probe that reports utilization to the underlying IaaS orchestrator in frequent time intervals.

The customized description, is stored under the Application Submissions folder attributed with the name of the Cloud provider. Upon the completion of the fine-grained description, the application can be submitted to the target Cloud infrastructure for deployment. With a context-menu action, the CSAR Exporter creates the CSAR containing the description with the artifacts, and hands it to the TOSCA Container at the selected IaaS provider.

Application Management Phase: Finally, through, the c-Eclipse *Deployment View*, the application developer can instantly obtain the deployment status without leaving the Eclipse environment. As depicted in the lower part of Fig. 4, a snapshot of the deployments on EC2 and Nephelae is provided, along with provider-specific properties such as component IP addresses, instance IDs, running times etc. A background polling mechanisms refreshes the view and provides the latest information from each IaaS.

6   Conclusion and Future Work

In this paper we present c-Eclipse; an open-source, vendor neutral, Cloud Application Management Framework built on top of Eclipse. c-Eclipse aims at facilitating the deployment and management of Cloud applications, promoting portability of applications across infrastructures, and supporting application elasticity. It adopts an open Cloud standard, and provides a unified environment for describing the structure, deployment and management operations of applications. It then exports the applications' descriptions into portable archives that can be processed by different providers. The functionality of c-Eclipse is presented via a use-case scenario with a 3-tier application being described and deployed on private and public Cloud infrastructures. Though still a prototype, c-Eclipse is currently used in the CELAR Project to deploy elastic Cloud applications. As future work, we will extend c-Eclipse to support existing application configuration management tools, such as Chef (http://getchef.com), to automatically provision and configure applications on new node instances, without requiring the user to write custom deployment scripts. c-Eclipse is available on GitHub at http://github.com/CELAR.

Acknowledgments. This work was partially supported by the European Commission in terms of the CELAR 317790 FP7 project (FP7-ICT-2011-8) and by the European Regional Development Fund and the Republic of Cyprus through the Research Promotion Foundation ("Infrastructure Upgrade /0609/09" project). The authors thank Andreas Papadopoulos, Georgiana Copil and Demetris Antoniades for their fruitful insights.

References

1. OASIS: TOSCA Version 1.0, http://goo.gl/ApNP3C
2. Oracle Virtual Assebly Builder, http://goo.gl/Eetq0V
3. VMware vCloud Application Director, http://goo.gl/j7LyU7
4. Ubuntu Juju, https://juju.ubuntu.com/
5. ServiceMesh Agility Platform, http://www.servicemesh.com
6. Juve, G., Deelman, E.: Automating Application Deployment in Infrastructure Clouds. In: Proceedings of the 2011 IEEE 3rd International Conference on Cloud Computing Technology and Science, pp. 658–665. IEEE Computer Society (2011)
7. Kopp, O., Binz, T., Breitenbücher, U., Leymann, F.: Winery: A Modeling Tool for TOSCA-Based Cloud Applications. In: Basu, S., Pautasso, C., Zhang, L., Fu, X. (eds.) ICSOC 2013. LNCS, vol. 8274, pp. 700–704. Springer, Heidelberg (2013)
8. GigaSpaces Cloudify, http://goo.gl/rYGceK
9. Binz, T., Breitenbücher, U., Haupt, F., Kopp, O., Leymann, F., Nowak, A., Wagner, S.: Open-TOSCA - A Runtime for TOSCA-Based Cloud Applications. In: Basu, S., Pautasso, C., Zhang, L., Fu, X. (eds.) ICSOC 2013. LNCS, vol. 8274, pp. 692–695. Springer, Heidelberg (2013)
10. Trihinas, D., Pallis, G., Dikaiakos, M.D.: JCatascopia: Monitoring Elastically Adaptive Applications in the Cloud. In: 14th IEEE/ACM International Symposium on Cluster, Cloud and Grid Computing (2014)
11. Copil, G., Moldovan, D., Truong, H.L., Dustdar, S.: SYBL: An Extensible Language for Controlling Elasticity in Cloud Applications. In: 13th IEEE/ACM International Symposium on Cluster, Cloud and Grid Computing, pp. 112–119 (2013)
12. CELAR EU FP7 Project, http://celarcloud.eu/

Modeling and Simulation of a Dynamic Task-Based Runtime System for Heterogeneous Multi-core Architectures

Luka Stanisic[1], Samuel Thibault[2], Arnaud Legrand[1],
Brice Videau[1], and Jean-François Méhaut[1]

[1] CNRS, Inria, University of Grenoble, France
firstname.lastname@imag.fr
[2] University of Bordeaux, Inria, France
samuel.thibault@labri.fr

Abstract. Multi-core architectures comprising several GPUs have become mainstream in the field of High-Performance Computing. However, obtaining the maximum performance of such heterogeneous machines is challenging as it requires to carefully offload computations and manage data movements between the different processing units. The most promising and successful approaches so far rely on task-based runtimes that abstract the machine and rely on opportunistic scheduling algorithms. As a consequence, the problem gets shifted to choosing the task granularity, task graph structure, and optimizing the scheduling strategies. Trying different combinations of these different alternatives is also itself a challenge. Indeed, getting accurate measurements requires reserving the target system for the whole duration of experiments. Furthermore, observations are limited to the few available systems at hand and may be difficult to generalize. In this article, we show how we crafted a coarse-grain hybrid simulation/emulation of StarPU, a dynamic runtime for hybrid architectures, over SimGrid, a versatile simulator for distributed systems. This approach allows to obtain performance predictions accurate within a few percents on classical dense linear algebra kernels in a matter of seconds, which allows both runtime and application designers to quickly decide which optimization to enable or whether it is worth investing in higher-end GPUs or not.

1 Introduction

High-Performance Computing architectures now widely include both multi-core CPUs and GPUs. Exploiting the tremendous computation power offered by such systems is however a real challenge. Programming them efficiently is a first concern, but managing the combination of computation execution and data transfers can also become extremely complex, particularly when dealing with multiple GPUs. In the past few years, it has become very common to deal with that through the use of an additional software layer, a runtime system, based on the task programming paradigm [3,4,7]. Applications are expressed as a task graph

F. Silva et al. (Eds.): Euro-Par 2014, LNCS 8632, pp. 50–62, 2014.

with data dependencies, i.e., a Directed Acyclic Graph (DAG), and provide both CPU and GPU implementations for the tasks. The runtime can then schedule the tasks over all available computation units, and automatically initiate the entailed data transfers. Scheduling heuristics such as HEFT or work stealing are used to automatically optimize that execution [3]. Application programmers are thus relieved from scheduling concerns and technical details.

As a result, the concern becomes choosing the right task granularity, task graph structure, and scheduling strategies optimizations. Task granularity is of a particular concern on hybrid platforms, since a tradeoff must be found between large tasks which are efficient on GPUs but expose little task parallelism, and a lot of small tasks for CPUs but are less efficient on GPUs. The task graph structure itself can have an influence on execution time, by requiring more or less communication compared to computation, which can be an issue depending on the available bandwidth on the target system. Last but not least, optimizing scheduling strategies has been a concern for decades, and the introduction of hybrid architectures only makes it even more challenging.

Getting accurate measurement results for all combinations is not trivial and it requires reserving the target system for a long period, which can become prohibitive. Moreover, experimenting over a wide range of different platforms is also necessary to make sure that the resulting strategy choices are generic, and not only suited to the few target systems which were available to developers. Finally, since execution time on real machine exhibit variability, dynamic schedulers tend to make varying scheduling decisions, and the obtained performance is thus far from deterministic. This makes performance comparisons more questionable and debugging of non-deterministic deadlocks inside such runtimes even harder.

Simulation is a technique that has proven extremely useful to study complex systems and which would be a very powerful way to address these issues. Performance models can be collected for a wide range of target architectures, and then used for simulating different executions, running on a single commodity platform. Since the execution can be made deterministic, experiments become *completely reproducible*, also making debugging a lot easier. Additionally, it is possible to try to extrapolate target architectures, for instance by trying to increase the available PCI bandwidth, the number of GPU devices, etc. and thus even estimate performance which would be obtained on hypothetical platforms. Cycle-accurate simulation of GPUs has hence received a lot of attention recently. However, the current solutions are extremely costly and not precise enough for helping runtime and application designers (see Section 2). Instead, we claim that a top-down modeling approach should be used.

In this article, we show how we crafted a coarse-grain hybrid simulation/emulation of StarPU [3] (see Section 3), a dynamic runtime system for heterogeneous multi-core architectures, on top of SimGrid, a simulation toolkit specifically designed for distributed system simulation. Although our work is based on the StarPU runtime system, it could be applied to other runtimes. Our contribution are the following:

- we present in details models that are essential for good performances and quantify their impact on overall prediction (Sections 5, 6, and 7);
- we validate our models by systematically comparing traces acquired in simulation with those from native executions in a wide variety of settings;
- we show that our approach allows to obtain predictions accurate within a few percents for both Cholesky and LU factorizations on four different generations of GPUs, within a few seconds on a commodity laptop, and we illustrate how it allows to conduct preliminary exploratory studies easily (Section 8).

2   Related Work

In most other scientific fields, simulation is used to evaluate complex phenomena and to address all the difficulties raised by the conduction of real experiments such as cost, reproducibility, and extrapolation capability. As a result, many detailed micro-architecture level simulators of GPUs have been developed in the last years. For example GPGPU-Sim [5], one of the most commonly used cycle-accurate GPU simulator, runs directly NVIDIA's parallel thread execution (PTX) virtual instruction set and simulates every detail of the GPU. It is thus very useful for obtaining insights into architectural design problems for GPUs. However, no comparison to an actual GPU is provided in [5] and although the trends predicted by GPGPU-Sim are certainly interesting, it is not clear that it can be used to perform accurate performance prediction of a real hardware. A few other GPU-specific simulators have therefore been developed (e.g., Barra [9] for the NVIDIA G80 or Multi2Sim [11] for the AMD Evergreen GPU). Such specialization allow Multi2sim to report predictions within 5 to 30% of native execution for several OpenCL benchmarks. While this prediction is quite impressive, it comes at the price of a very long simulation time as every detail of the GPU is simulated. The average slowdown of simulations versus native execution is reported to be $44,000\times$ while the one of GPGPU-Sim on a similar scenario is about $90,000\times$[11].

In the context of tuning HPC runtimes, expectations in term of simulation accuracy are extremely high. It is thus difficult to rely on a simulator that may provide the right trends but with a 50% over/under estimation. Choosing the right level of granularity or the correct scheduling heuristic can not be done without precise and quantitative predictions. Such errors come from an inadequate level of details and can be avoided. Therefore, we propose to use a top-down modeling approach such as promoted by the SimGrid project [8], which provides a *versatile* simulation toolkit to study the behavior of large-scale distributed systems like grids, clouds, or peer-to-peer systems. SimGrid builds on fluid network models that have been proven as a reasonable alternative to both simple analytic models and expensive, difficult-to-instantiate packet-level simulations [12] and have recently been extended to simulate accurately MPI applications on Ethernet networks [6]. In a fluid model, communications, represented by *flows*, are simulated as single entities rather than as sets of individual packets and the bandwidth allocated to flows is constrained by the network resource capacity. While such models ignore all transient phases between two steady-state operation points, they are very flexible and allow to easily account for network topology and heterogeneity as well as many non-trivial phenomena (e.g., RTT-unfairness of TCP or cross-traffic interferences) [12] at a very low simulation cost. In the next sections, we explain how StarPU has been ported on top of SimGrid and how multi-GPU architectures have been modeled within SimGrid.

3 Porting StarPU over SimGrid

StarPU relies on a task-based abstraction with a clear semantic, which eases the modeling. A StarPU execution consists in scheduling a graph of tasks with data dependencies (i.e., a Directed Acyclic Graph) on the different computing resources, while taking care about data localization. Hence, from the modeling perspective, there are three main components to take into account: StarPU scheduling, computation on the different computing resources, and communication between the computing resources.

Since StarPU scheduling is generally dynamic and opportunistic, the decisions taken when simulating should be as close as possible to the ones taken in a native execution. The most natural approach is thus to execute the StarPU code related to scheduling decisions and to replace actual task execution with SimGrid calls. Yet, to make sure that simulation is carried out in a reproducible and controlled way, SimGrid exports a specific thread API (similar to the POSIX one) that allows the SimGrid kernel to control the scheduling of all application threads. In simulation, such threads run in mutual exclusion and are scheduled upon completion of simulated data transfers and simulated computations. Therefore, any direct regular call to the POSIX threads had to be abstracted as well. Likewise, in simulation mode, any memory allocation on CPUs or GPUs has to be faked as no actual data processing is done and no actual GPU is necessarily available on simulation machines. Last, since schedulers may use runtime statistics to take scheduling decisions, time had to be abstracted as well to make sure that simulation time (instead of current time) is used in a consistent way. When running on top of SimGrid, StarPU applications and runtime are thus *emulated* since the actual code is executed, but any operation related to thread synchronization, actual computations of CPU-intensive kernels, or data transfer is in fact *simulated*. More precisely, the control part of StarPU is executed to dynamically inject computation and communication tasks in the simulator.

For simplicity reasons, each CPU and GPU is represented as a SimGrid host with specific characteristics and it comprises one or several threads which manage synchronization and signaling to StarPU, whenever transfer or computation kernels end. The characteristics of the GPUs and of the communication interconnect are measured beforehand on the target machine and expressed in term of processing power, bandwidth, and latency. As a result, such approach is very different from the classical ones described in Section 2 where architecture is modeled in detail and coarse-grain performances are derived from fine-grain simulation of GPU internals.

Table 1. Machines used for the experiments

Name	Processor	Number of Cores	Frequency	Memory	GPUs
hannibal	Intel Xeon X5550	2×4	2.67GHz	2×24GB	$3 \times$QuadroFX5800
attila	Intel Xeon X5650	2×6	2.67GHz	2×24GB	$3 \times$TeslaC2050
conan	Intel Xeon E5-2650	2×8	2.0GHz	2×32GB	$3 \times$TeslaM2075
frogkepler	Intel Xeon E5-2670	2×8	2.6GHz	32GB	$2 \times$K20

In such a modeling, the overhead of the runtime (e.g., the time needed to take scheduling decisions, to manage synchronizations or to manage internal queues) is not accounted for in the simulation and only the parts related to the application execution are simulated. As we will see in the rest of the article, such a naive emulation coupled with a simple modeling of computation and communications may be enough for some applications on some platforms but can lead to gross inaccuracies in others. Showing merely a few examples where simulation and native execution match would hence not be a validation. Instead, we tried to (in)validate our model by conducting as much experiments as possible in a large variety of settings until we find a situation where our simulation fails producing a good prediction. These critical experiments were generally very instructive as they allowed us to understand how to improve our modeling.

In the rest of the article, we present the different sources of errors we identified and the kind of prediction that can be done once they are fixed.

4 Experimental Setting

We conducted series of experiments to (in)validate our modeling approach. All conclusions were drawn from analyzing and comparing GFlop/s rate, makespans and traces of StarPU on one hand (called *Native* in the following), and StarPU on top of Simgrid (called *SimGrid* in the following) on the other.

Before running applications, StarPU needs to obtain a calibration of the platform, which consists in measuring bandwidths and latencies for communication between each processing unit, together with evaluating timings of computation kernels [2]. Such information is used to guide StarPU schedulers' decisions when delegating tasks to available workers. StarPU has thus been extended to generate at the same time a (XML) SimGrid description of the platform, which can later be used for simulation purposes. It is important to understand that only the calibration, which is meant to be run once and for all on the target system before conducting any performance investigation, is used in the *SimGrid* simulation and that it is not linked to the application being studied. The only condition is that the application can use only computation kernels that have been measured, of course. Such a clear separation allowed all the simulations presented in this paper to be performed on personal commodity laptops. This separation also allows to simulate machines we don't have access to, knowing merely their characteristics (i.e., computation kernel runtimes and memory bandwidth).

To study the validity of our models, we used the systems described in Table 1. These NVIDIA GPUs have distinct characteristics and belong to different

Table 2. Typical duration of runtime operations

Operation	Transfer queue management	GPU memory allocation (cudaMalloc)	GPU memory deallocation (cudaFree)	Pinned RAM allocation (cudaHostAlloc)
Time	$10\mu s$	$175\mu s$	$125\mu s$	$650\mu s$/MB

generations, which intends to demonstrate the validity of our approach on a range of diverse machines. Regarding applications, we decided to focus on two common dense linear algebra kernels: *cholesky* and *LU* factorization. Regarding task granularity, we fixed a relatively large block size (960 × 960) as it is representative of what is typically used to achieve good performances. In our experiments, CPUs were only controlling the execution and scheduling of the tasks while GPUs had the roles of workers, meaning that whole computation was done entirely on multiple GPUs. We focused on this kind of scenario as GPUs have stable performance and provide a significant fraction of computational power in dense linear algebra. We also investigated situations involving both CPUs and GPUs a the same time. Although the initial results were excellent, we could not include them in this article due to lack of room and decided to instead present in detail the specifics of GPU modeling.

This whole work was done in the spirit of open science and reproducible research. Both StarPU and Simgrid software are free software available online. All experiment results presented in this paper are publicly available on *figshare* [13]. Supplementary data, which is not presented in this paper due to space limitation, are also available at the same location along with all the scripts, raw data files and traces which allow to regenerate this document.

Finally, assessing the impact of our various modeling attempts is quite difficult. Some of them are specifically linked to the modeling of the StarPU runtime, while others are more linked to the modeling of communications or to the computation variability. Obtaining a good predictive power is the combination of a series of improvements. Hence, comparing different runtime modeling options with a native execution while having a poor modeling of communications and computations would not be very meaningful. So instead, we evaluate our different runtime modeling options while using the best options for communication and computation modeling. Likewise, when we evaluate various communication modeling options, we always use the best modeling option of runtime and computations, which allows us to evaluate how much accuracy we may lose by overlooking this particular aspect.

5   Modeling Runtime System

Since StarPU is dynamic, inaccurate emulation of the control part would produce different scheduling decisions and would damage prediction of the overall execution time. We show how, in some cases and if not treated correctly, this can produce misleading results, and present how these issues were eliminated.

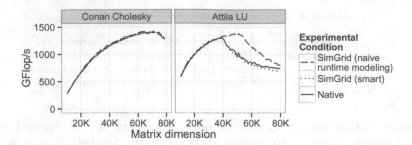

Fig. 1. Illustrating the influence of modeling runtime. Careless modeling of runtime may be perfectly harmless in some cases, it turns out to be misleading in others.

As we already mentioned, process synchronizations, memory allocations of CPU or GPU, submission of data transfer requests are all faked in simulation mode, whereas such operations in native execution do take time and have an impact on the overall performance. Several delays were included in the simulation to account for their overhead (Table 2 depicts typical duration of such operations). Another (probably the most) influential parameter for accurate modeling of runtime proved to be the size of GPU memory. Such hardware limits force the scheduler to swap data back and forth between the CPUs and GPUs. These data movements saturate the PCI bus, producing a tremendous impact on overall performance. It is thus critical to keep track of the amount of memory allocated by StarPU during the simulation to make sure the scheduler will behave in the same way for both real native executions and simulations.

Figure 1 illustrates the importance of taking into account the runtime parameters described above. Each curve depicts GFlop/s rate of experiments representing 90 different matrix dimensions (matrix dimension 80,000 corresponds to ≈25GB). Solid line *Native* shows the execution of StarPU on the native machine, while the other two are the results of the simulation: *naive* for execution without any runtime adjustments and *smart* with all of them included. The left plot depicts a situation where all these optimizations have very little influence as both *naive* and *smart* lines are almost overlapping with the *native* line. On the other hand, for some other machines and applications (plot on the right), having a precise modeling of runtime is critical as otherwise, simulation may highly overestimate the performance for the larger matrix size. Nonetheless, we remind that the excellent predictions achieved in these examples are also the result of the careful modeling of communications and computations, which we will present in the next Sections.

6   Modeling Communication in Hybrid Systems

Due to the relatively low bandwidth of the PCI bus, applications running on hybrid platforms often spend a significant fraction of the total time transferring data back and forth between the main RAM and the GPUs. Modeling communication between computing resources is thus of primary importance. As a

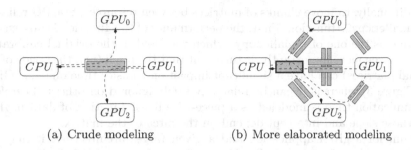

(a) Crude modeling   (b) More elaborated modeling

Fig. 2. Communication and topology modeling alternatives. In the crude modeling, a single link is used and communications do not interfere with each others. The more elaborated modeling allows to account for both the heterogeneity of communications and the global bandwidth limitation imposed by the PCI bus.

first approximation (see Figure 2(a)), the transfer time between resources could be modeled as a single link with a latency and a transfer rate corresponding to typical characteristics of the PCI bus. However, such modeling does not account for many architectural aspects. First, the bandwidth between CPU and GPU is asymmetrical. Second, communication characteristics are not uniform among all pairs of CPUs and GPUs, as it depends on the chipset architecture. We decided to account for it by using a dedicated uplink and a downlink with different characteristics for each pair of resources (see Figure 2(b)). Furthermore, any communication between two resources has to go through a common shared link (in bold), which represent the maximum capacity of the PCI bus. Modeling contention in such a way is however insufficient as depending on resources involved in a communication, data transfers may be serialized or not. For example, although most CUDA transfers are serialized whenever they involve the same resource, on some systems it is possible to transfer both from GPU_0 to GPU_1 and from GPU_1 to GPU_0 at the same time.

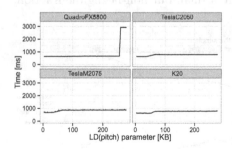

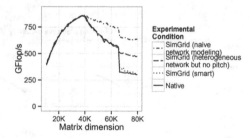

Fig. 3. Transfer time of 3,600 KB using cudaMemcpy2D depending on the pitch of the matrix

Fig. 4. Performance of the LU application on hannibal (QuadroFX5800 GPUs) using different modeling assumptions

Additionally, to move chunks of matrices between resources, StarPU relies on the `cudaMemcpy2D` function. First, the performance of this function is not exactly the same as the one of `cudaMemcpy`, which was used in the original calibration process. Even more importantly, it turns out that the pitch (i.e., the stride of the original matrices) can have a significant impact on transfer time on some GPUs (see Figure 3) whereas it can be relatively safely ignored on others. Therefore, communication time is modeled as a piece-wise linear function of data payload and whose slope and intercept depend on the pitch of the matrix.

Again, for a given application and a given target architecture, it may not be necessary to take care of all such details to obtain a good prediction. For example, as illustrated on Figure 4, a naive network modeling such as the one on Figure 2(a) proved excellent predictions when matrix dimension is smaller than 40,000. Beyond such size, a more precise modeling of the network (as in Figure 2(b)) is necessary. Beyond 66,240, the behavior of `cudaMemcpy2D` changes drastically and has to be correctly modeled to obtain a good prediction of the performances.

7   Modeling Computation

When running simulation, the actual result of the application is of no interest. Hence the execution of each kernel is replaced by a virtual delay accounting for its duration. In our initial approach, we used the mean duration of each computation kernel, which was benchmarked by StarPU during the calibration phase. Although this was producing satisfactory results, using a fixed value leads to a deterministic schedule in simulation. This may bias the simulation and does not allow to verify the ability of the scheduling algorithms to handle the variability of the resources.

Therefore, we modified StarPU to capture the timing of every computation during a *Native* execution. Such collection of data can then be used to analyze the computation time distribution which can be approximated using irregular histograms [10], as regular ones (with uniform bin-width) revealed very inefficient at representing details of distributions where a small but non-negligible fraction

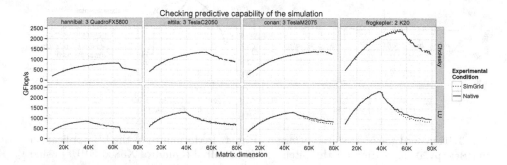

Fig. 5. Checking predictive capability of our simulator in a wide range of settings

of values are an order of magnitude larger than the vast majority of measurements. Such approximation can then be used in the simulation by generating pseudo-random variables from the histograms.

Although this technique allows to obtain different simulated schedules by changing the seed of the simulation, no significant gain in term of accuracy could be observed for the applications and machines we used so far. The makespan is always very similar in both cases (mean duration vs. random duration following an approximation of the original distribution). Nonetheless, we strongly believe that in some more complex use cases, e.g., sparse linear algebra algorithms, using fine models like histograms may provide more precise predictions.

8   Prediction Accuracy in a Wide Range of Settings

As we explained in the previous section, a careless modeling of any aspect of runtime, communications or computations, can lead to gross inaccuracies for particular combinations of machines and applications. We show in this section that we managed to cover the most important issues, which enables us to obtain excellent prediction of performances. Figure 5 depicts the performance as a function of the size of the matrix for the two applications LU and Cholesky and for the four different hybrid systems we described in Table 1. For most combinations, the prediction obtained with SimGrid is very accurate. The only two scenarios where the error is larger than a few percents is for the LU kernel on conan and frogkepler when our prediction slightly overestimates the (bad) performances for large matrices. The trend is however perfectly predicted as well as the size beyond which performance drops.

A closer look at traces (see Figure 6) allows to see that this approach does not only provide a good estimation of the total runtime but also offers an accurate simulation of the scheduling details. Since even with the same parameters, native traces differ from an execution to another, a point-to-point comparison with a

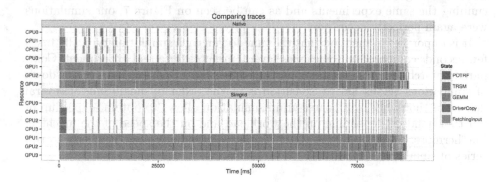

Fig. 6. Comparing execution traces (native execution on top vs. simulated execution at the bottom) of the Cholesky application with a $72,000 \times 72,000$ matrix on the Conan machine. Traces are not perfectly identical since the execution is not deterministic but the behavior of the simulation is representative of the real execution.

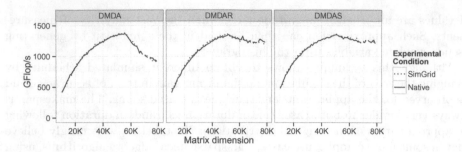

Fig. 7. Cholesky on Attila: studying the impact of different schedulers

simulation trace would not make sense. However, we can check that both traces are indeed extremely close, which allows to study and understand the potential weaknesses of a scheduler.

For example, the reason for the performance drop observed on Figure 5 and which is more and more critical with newer GPUs can be explained by the need to move data back and forth between the GPUs and the main memory whenever matrix size exceeds the memory size of the GPUs. The scheduler we used in Figure 5 is the *DMDA* (Deque Model Data Aware) scheduler. Although it schedules tasks where their termination time (including data transfer time) will be minimal, it does not take care of the number of available data buffers on each GPU. Such greedy strategy may be harmful as GPU may be overloaded with work and forced to evict some data, as it cannot handle the whole matrix. Two other strategies *DMDAR* and *DMDAS* were designed to tend to execute tasks whose data is already on the GPU, before tasks whose data is not yet available. Therefore, we decided to check whether these two other schedulers could stabilize performances at the peak or not. To this end, we first ran the corresponding simulations and obtained a positive answer (Figure 7). Later, when the target system became accessible again, we confirmed these results by running the same experiments and as can be seen on Figure 7, our simulations were again perfectly accurate.

It is important to mention that the time to run each simulation typically takes few seconds compared to sometimes several minutes for a real experiment. Compared to architecture-level simulators (see Section 2) whose average slowdown of simulations versus native execution is of the order of magnitude of several dozens of thousands, our coarse-grain simulation allows to obtain a speedup of ten to a hundred depending on the workload and on the speed of the machine. Furthermore, since the target system is not required anymore, it is easy to run series of simulations in parallel.

9   Conclusion and Future Work

In this article, we have explained how to model and simulate using SimGrid a task-based runtime system on a hybrid multi-core architecture comprising several GPUs. Unlike fine-grain GPU simulators that have been proposed in the past and which focus on architectural details of GPUs, our coarse-grain approach allows to accurately predict the actual running time and to perform extremely quickly extensive simulation campaigns to study various alternatives. We demonstrated the precision of our simulations using the critical method, i.e., by testing our models and by conducting as much experiments as possible in a large variety of settings (two standard dense linear algebra applications, four different generations of GPUs, several scheduling algorithms) until we found a situation where our simulation failed at producing a good prediction, in which case we fixed our modeling. Such a tool is extremely interesting for both StarPU developers and users as it allows (i) to easily and accurately evaluate the impact of various parameters or scheduling alternatives (ii) to tune and debug applications on a commodity laptop (instead of requiring a dedicated access to a high-end machine) *in a reproducible way* (iii) to obtain reliable comparison of performance estimations that may allow to detect problems with some real experiments(perturbation, configuration issue, etc.).

Now that we have proven the efficiency of this approach on dense linear algebra kernels, we intend to continue with this work in three directions. First, we plan to explore using both CPUs and GPUs as computation units. While initial investigation on classical hybrid multi-core computers showed perfect results, we expect that dealing with large NUMA machines comprising hundreds of cores will be much harder. Second, StarPU was recently extended to exploit clusters of hybrid machines by relying on MPI [1]. Since SimGrid's ability to accurately simulate MPI applications has already been demonstrated [6], combining both works should allow to obtain good performances predictions of complex applications on large-scale high-end HPC infrastructures. Third, many numerical applications have been recently ported on top of StarPU, including dense (MAGMA and PLASMA) and sparse linear algebra (QR-MUMPS), and FMM methods. Such applications are less regular and are thus likely to be more challenging to model. However, a reliable performance evaluation methodology would bring considerable insights to the developers.

Acknowledgments. This work is partially supported by the SONGS ANR project (11-ANR-INFRA-13). We warmly thank Paul Renaud-Goud for his help with the initial investigation of validity and Emmanuel Agullo for motivating this study and providing insights on its usefulness.

References

1. Augonnet, C., Aumage, O., Furmento, N., Namyst, R., Thibault, S.: StarPU-MPI: Task Programming over Clusters of Machines Enhanced with Accelerators. In: Träff, J.L., Benkner, S., Dongarra, J.J. (eds.) EuroMPI 2012. LNCS, vol. 7490, pp. 298–299. Springer, Heidelberg (2012)
2. Augonnet, C., Thibault, S., Namyst, R.: Automatic Calibration of Performance Models on Heterogeneous Multicore Architectures. In: Lin, H.-X., Alexander, M., Forsell, M., Knüpfer, A., Prodan, R., Sousa, L., Streit, A. (eds.) Euro-Par 2009 Workshops. LNCS, vol. 6043, pp. 56–65. Springer, Heidelberg (2010)

3. Augonnet, C., Thibault, S., Namyst, R., Wacrenier, P.A.: StarPU: A Unified Platform for Task Scheduling on Heterogeneous Multicore Architectures. Concurrency and Computation: Practice and Experience 23, 187–198 (2011)
4. Ayguadé, E., Badia, R.M., Igual, F.D., Labarta, J., Mayo, R., Quintana-Ortí, E.S.: An Extension of the StarSs Programming Model for Platforms with Multiple GPUs. In: Sips, H., Epema, D., Lin, H.-X. (eds.) Euro-Par 2009. LNCS, vol. 5704, pp. 851–862. Springer, Heidelberg (2009)
5. Bakhoda, A., Yuan, G.L., Fung, W.W.L., Wong, H., Aamodt, T.M.: Analyzing CUDA workloads using a detailed GPU simulator. In: ISPASS, pp. 163–174 (2009)
6. Bedaride, P., Degomme, A., Genaud, S., Legrand, A., Markomanolis, G., Quinson, M., Stillwell, L.M., Suter, F., Videau, B.: Toward better simulation of mpi applications on ethernet/tcp networks. In: 4th International Workshop on Performance Modeling, Benchmarking and Simulation of HPC Systems (PMBS) (November 2013)
7. Bosilca, G., Bouteiller, A., Danalis, A., Herault, T., Lemarinier, P., Dongarra, J.: DAGuE: A Generic Distributed DAG Engine for High Performance Computing. In: IEEE International Symposium on Parallel and Distributed Processing, pp. 1151–1158. IEEE Computer Society (2011)
8. Casanova, H., Legrand, A., Quinson, M.: SimGrid: A Generic Framework for Large-Scale Distributed Experiments. In: Proceedings of the 10th IEEE International Conference on Computer Modeling and Simulation (UKSim) (April 2008)
9. Collange, S., Daumas, M., Defour, D., Parello, D.: Barra: A Parallel Functional Simulator for GPGPU. In: IEEE/ACM International Symposium on Modeling, Analysis and Simulation of Computer and Telecommunication, pp. 351–360 (2010)
10. Denby, L., Mallows, C.: Variations on the histogram. Journal of Computational and Graphical Statistics 18(1), 21–31 (2009)
11. Ubal, R., Jang, B., Mistry, P., Schaa, D., Kaeli, D.: Multi2Sim: A Simulation Framework for CPU-GPU Computing. In: Proceedings of the 21st International Conference on Parallel Architectures and Compilation Techniques, PACT 2012, pp. 335–344. ACM, New York (2012)
12. Velho, P., Schnorr, L., Casanova, H., Legrand, A.: On the validity of flow-level TCP network models for grid and cloud simulations. ACM Transactions on Modeling and Computer Simulation 23(3) (October 2013)
13. Companion of the StarPU+SimGrid article. Hosted on Figshare (2014), http://dx.doi.org/10.6084/m9.figshare.928095, online version of this article with access to the experimental data and scripts (in the org source)

Modeling the Impact of Reduced Memory Bandwidth on HPC Applications[*]

Ananta Tiwari[1], Anthony Gamst[2], Michael A. Laurenzano[3], Martin Schulz[4], and Laura Carrington[1]

[1] Performance Modeling and Characterization Lab,
San Diego Supercomputer Center, USA
{tiwari,lcarring}@sdsc.edu
[2] Computational and Applied Statistics Lab, San Diego Supercomputer Center, USA
acgamst@math.ucsd.edu
[3] Department of Computer Science and Engineering, University of Michigan, USA
mlaurenz@eecs.umich.edu
[4] Lawrence Livermore National Laboratory (LLNL), USA
schulzm@llnl.gov

Abstract. To deliver the energy efficiency and raw compute throughput necessary to realize exascale systems, projected designs call for massive numbers of (simple) cores per processor. An unfortunate consequence of such designs is that the memory bandwidth per core will be significantly reduced, which can significantly degrade the performance of many memory-intensive HPC workloads. To identify the code regions that are most impacted and to guide them in developing mitigating solutions, system designers and application developers alike would benefit immensely from a systematic framework that allowed them to identify the types of computations that are sensitive to reduced memory bandwidth and to precisely identify those regions in their code that exhibit sensitivity. This paper introduces a framework for identifying the properties in computations that are associated with memory bandwidth sensitivity, extracting those same properties from HPC applications, and for associating bandwidth sensitivity to specific structures in the application source code. We apply our framework to a number of large scale HPC applications, observing that the bandwidth sensitivity model shows an absolute mean error that averages less than 5%.

1 Introduction

The trend towards multi-core systems has accelerated over the last decade and has had a profound impact on HPC systems. Multi-core designs allow for greater energy efficiency by increasing the compute performance of the processors through replicating simple and more energy conserving cores on a processor chip, potentially at lower voltages, without requiring complex and power hungry single core enhancements. With energy and power often being cited as the most critical issues on the road to practical exascale systems, it is foreseeable that this trend

---

[*] The rights of this work are transferred to the extent transferable according to Title 17 §105 U.S.C.

F. Silva et al. (Eds.): Euro-Par 2014, LNCS 8632, pp. 63–74, 2014.

will continue. Some studies already project hundreds to thousands of cores per processor [7]. While multi-core systems certainly offer advantages in terms of energy efficiency, they also pose new challenges. As the number of cores per processor is scaled up, the memory bandwidth feeding the cores, in particular the off-chip bandwidth which is limited by pin constraints and slowly rising memory speeds, will result in performance challenges that can seriously undermine the performance achievable by multi-core processors.

Different HPC computations will suffer different degrees of performance degradation when faced with reduced per core memory bandwidth, i.e., performance degradation is not a simple linear function of bandwidth vs. performance, but rather a complex function that also involves the characteristics of the workload (e.g., arithmetic intensity, memory access patterns and work distribution among cores). We therefore need a systematic methodology to understand and predict how sensitive a given computation or algorithm is to reduced per core memory bandwidth. This paper presents a modeling framework that allows such a characterization and can be used to predict how different computations within an application, computational phase or even basic block will behave under a given reduced memory bandwidth. Our methodology uses fine-grained application and hardware characterization to build predictive models through machine learning based models. In particular, we make the following contributions:

- We introduce predictive models for memory bandwidth sensitivity that are effective across a range of code granularities. We detail the machine learning algorithm used to construct the models and how to train them using empirical measurements that capture both data flow and computational properties of applications.
- We evaluate our models using a diverse set of real scientific workloads. We show that the framework accurately pinpoints regions within these codes where reduced bandwidth of current and future generation multi-core systems could pose significant performance challenges.
- We apply our framework to HYPRE [14], a library for solving large sparse linear systems of equations, and show how it can accurately predict bandwidth sensitivity scores for different solver implementations and thereby help select implementations that are less sensitive to reduced memory bandwidth.

2   Predicting Performance Sensitivity

The amount of available memory bandwidth can have a crucial performance impact on the different computational phases of a large scale application. Understanding the level of this impact, where in the execution it is occurring, and algorithmic choices that might minimize this impact are critical for application developers as the core count on current and future multi-core systems grows. Performance prediction via fine grain models of an application can address these questions. Developing such detailed performance models requires a test system for model validation (Section 2.1), a modeling technique amenable to the complex and diverse space of HPC computations (Section 2.2), and techniques to capture the details or characterization of computations (Section 2.3).

2.1   Model Validation System

To validate that the models accurately predict an application's sensitivity to reduced per core memory bandwidth, we need a test system where we can change the per core memory bandwidth. To design such a system, we first focus on the parameters involved in determining theoretical memory bandwidth (TBW), which can be calculated as follows:

$$\text{TBW} = mem\_freq \times L \times W \times I \qquad (1)$$

TBW is the product of memory bus frequency (mem_freq), the number of lines of data transferred per clock cycle (L), the bus width (W) and the number of memory channels (I). The test system that we use in our study consists of DDR-N (Double Data Rate) DRAM modules on a motherboard that supports dual channel memory; therefore, L and I parameters are fixed at 2. Bus width W is 64 bits for our test-bed. Thus, to approximate systems with lesser memory bandwidth, we rely on changing the mem_freq parameter, the frequency of the memory bus.

While it is not possible, on current systems, to change the memory bus frequency from the OS-level, modern systems allow choosing between different bus frequencies at boot time (through the BIOS setup). Our test system consists of a single node from the Gordon Supercomputer [25]. The dual-socket node contains two 8-core 2.6 GHz Intel Xeon E5-2670 (SandyBridge) processors and 64 GB of DDR3 memory. The default frequency rating of the DDR3 modules is 1333 MHz. The BIOS setup allows two additional frequencies – 1067 MHz and 800 MHz.

To demonstrate that lowering the memory bus frequency in the BIOS results in a test bed with reduced per core memory bandwidth, we present a study that utilizes the memory read bandwidth test in `lmbench` [24] for the three available memory bus speeds on our system. The results in Figure 1 show four plateaus indicating the L1 cache, L2 cache, L3 cache, and main memory bandwidths for the test-bed at the three memory bus frequencies.

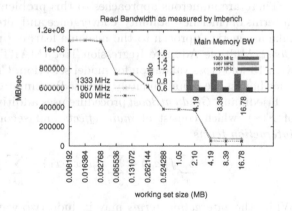

Fig. 1. `lmbench` results for different bus frequencies

As expected, the L1, L2, and L3 cache plateaus do not show any change across different memory bus frequencies. The fourth plateau, for working set sizes above 4.19 MB, indicates the main memory bandwidth and shows changes. These changes are replotted in the histogram sub-graph within Figure 1. In this subfigure the bandwidths for 1067 MHz and 800 MHz are normalized to the bandwidths at 1333 MHz. Memory read bandwidth is reduced by roughly 17.5% when we decrease the memory bus frequency by 20% from 1333 MHz to 1067

MHz. This reduction is roughly 37.7% when going from 1333 MHz to 800 MHz (or by 40%). These results demonstrate that changing the memory bus frequency allows us to approximate the behavior we are looking to study – reduced per core memory bandwidth and its effect on the performance of compute phases within HPC applications.

2.2   Model Methodology

To model the performance sensitivity we utilize machine learning techniques produce estimates $\widehat{F}(\mathbf{x})$ of that function $F(\mathbf{x})$ which is the optimal predictor of the *output variable* y from the *input variables* $\mathbf{x} = \{x_1, ..., x_n\}$ in the class of functions $\mathcal{F}$, in the sense that

$$F(\mathbf{x}) = \arg\min_{f \in \mathcal{F}} EL\left(f(\mathbf{x}), y\right)$$

where L is a non-negative loss function, for example, $L(s,t) = (s-t)^2/2$, and $Eh(x,y) = \int h(\mathbf{x}, y)dP(\mathbf{x}, y)$ is the expectation operator corresponding to the joint distribution P of $\mathbf{x}$ and y. The function F is an approximation to the optimal predictor G of y, which may involve input variables other than $\mathbf{x}$ and may be in a different class of functions from $\mathcal{F}$; that is, G may have a different functional form or be more or less smooth than functions in $\mathcal{F}$. Any particular technique and specific, finite set of *training data* $\{(\mathbf{x}_i, y_i)\}_{i=1}^{n}$, will produce a specific estimate $\widehat{F}(\mathbf{x})$ of $F(\mathbf{x})$. Different data sets and different techniques will generally produce different estimates.

There are numerous approaches to this problem, each with various tradeoffs in terms of efficiency, stability, convergence and interpretability. In this work, we take a generic approach to the machine learning problem, using the *Gradient-Boost*, Multiple Additive Regression Tree (MART) approach of Friedman [15], with 10-fold cross validation for model selection. Cross-validation is used to produce honest (i.e. approximately unbiased) estimates of the error of fitted models.

Friedman's *GradientBoost* procedure uses additive (ANOVA-type) expansions of $F(\mathbf{x})$, which consist of *main effects* and second-, third-, and higher-order *interaction terms*

$$F(\mathbf{x}) = \sum_{j} f_j(x_j) + \sum_{j,k} f_{jk}(x_j, x_k) + \sum_{j,k,l} f_{jkl}(x_j, x_k, x_l) + \dots. \qquad (2)$$

While the *interaction terms* may include two-way, three-way, or even higher-order interactions, care must be taken when fitting the model to (finite) training sets to avoid over-fitting, which has a negative effect on the ability of the predictor to generalize; that is, to produce reasonable predictions from input variables not already in the training set. The *GradientBoost* procedure uses two *regularization* techniques to limit the risk of over-fitting. The first is to limit the number of terms M included in the additive expansion (2), and the second (essentially) multiplies the predicted values associated with each of the fitted terms by a *learning rate* parameter, which slows the optimization process through *incremental shrinkage*, reduces the risk of converging to (sub-optimal) local minima, and (essentially) determines the effective number of (unique) trees K in the final predictor. There is an inverse relationship between these two control parameters, such that solutions with a larger number of additive components are more likely to converge successfully when a smaller learning rate is used, and vice versa [15]. Naturally, there is still a risk of over-fitting and approximately optimal values of K and M must be selected from the range of candidate values. We use 10-fold cross validation for this purpose. In k-fold cross validation (in our case, $k{=}10$), the training dataset is randomly partitioned into k subsets of approximately equal size. k different models are then constructed, each using $(k-1)$ of the k partitions as training input so that 1 of the k sets can be set aside for model validation. Each of the k models are then validated against the validation set and the model that yields the minimum error is selected.

MART was selected in part because the regression trees, upon which the technique is based, are computationally efficient, relatively robust to missing data and monotone transformations of the input variables, and allow us to make very minimal smoothness assumptions (see [8,9]). We describe the training set, error estimates and the predictive accuracy of our fitted models on real application hotspots in Section 3.

2.3 Computational Characterization

In order to develop models that capture a computation's sensitivity to per core bandwidth we need to first capture low-level details of how an application interacts with and exercises the underlying hardware subcomponents or application characterizations. We develop these detailed characterizations by gathering what we will refer to as an application signature. These signatures are collected by a set of static and dynamic binary analysis tools and include per basic-block, per loop and per function information. This information consists of the operations required by the application in the form of instruction mix and counts, data locality properties, metrics that capture the application's interaction with the memory subsystem such as cache hit rates, load and store operations, etc.

At the center of the characterization and analysis tool-suite is our x86 binary instrumentation toolkit, PEBIL [21]. PEBIL works directly on the binary and there is no re-compilation or re-linking required – steps we wish to avoid because they can interfere with the original behavior of the application. The fact that PEBIL works on the binary directly also makes the use of the tools easy to use on large-scale applications.

Static Analysis: The static analysis tool written on top of PEBIL produces information about the approximate structure of the program and the operations that occur within those structures (e.g., functions and loops). The tool also records type and size of classes of operations (e.g., memory and floating operations) that are within those control structures. The static analysis tool records the average size of memory operands in each block and measures the number of instructions between register or memory definitions and their usage (i.e., data dependencies).

Dynamic Analysis: To gather detailed information about data movement within an application, the memory characterization tool written on top of PEBIL instruments every memory access in the application and pipes the address stream to be processed on-the-fly by a series of different tools (e.g. reuse distance calculation, working set size analysis and a cache simulator for system of interest). The cache simulator tool, for example, produces the cache hit rates for a set of target systems of interest for each of the application's loops. Another dynamic analysis tool keeps visit count information for the application's control units (e.g., basic block visit counts). Visit count information when combined with the static instruction mix information gives detailed information on the instruction make-up of the application.

The characterization data is managed using an SQL relational database. All the static and dynamic data for an application is collected into the database, which can be queried for computational characterization information that form the application signature. The signature includes an entry for each of the control structure units of a given application (such as basic blocks) and consists of information about instruction mix, cache behavior, data dependencies, etc.

3   Results

We utilized the test system and the modeling methodology to investigate the performance sensitivity of HPC applications to the reduced per core memory bandwidth. The test system (described in Section 2.1) was used to both train and validate the models (see Section 3.1). We then evaluated our models on a set of real applications and the results are presented in Sections 3.2 and 3.3.

3.1   Model Training

To create a model that captures how the performance of various types of computations are affected by reduced per core memory bandwidth, we use a set of benchmarks along with source code transformation frameworks to generate a diverse set of small computations to train the model. The benchmarks come from pcubed benchmarking framework [22], which can be configured to yield computations with specific computational, memory, and data flow properties. We supplement these pcubed loops with kernels derived from different computational domains – dense linear algebra (e.g. matrix-matrix multiplication and matrix-vector multiplication), stencil computations, etc. In addition, for some of the kernels, we generate variants using two source-to-source compiler transformation tools – Orio [26] and CHiLL [11]. Some of the optimizations that we used to generate these variants include loop unrolling, cache/register tiling and scalar replacement. Each of these variants is configured to run with multiple working set sizes. Together with pcubed, kernels and kernel variants, we had a total of 2900 computations that formed our training set. All of the training computations were timed using the three memory bus frequency settings on the test system. We take six measurements for each; we discard the min and max measurements and average the remaining four. Also, for each test we generate a characterization signature using the tools described in Section 2.3.

Predictive models are constructed using the machine learning problem presented in Equation 3. The predictors listed in right hand side of the equation show the entries that make up a loop signature. mem_freq is the memory bus frequency and d1m, d2m, d3m are the number of memory accesses per instruction that hit on L1, L2 and L3 caches respectively. dmm is the number of accesses per instruction that miss on L3. loads, stores, int_ops and branch_ops are the number of load, store, integer and branch operations per instruction. fprat is the the ratio of the number of floating point operations to the number of memory operations. fops_ins is the number of floating point operations per instruction. int_dud and fp_dud are integer and floating point def-use distances respectively. The outcome (degradation) is log-transformed to stabilize the residual variance.

$$\log(\texttt{degradation}) = F(\texttt{mem\_freq}, \texttt{d1m}, \texttt{d2m}, \texttt{d3m}, \texttt{dmm}, \texttt{loads}, \texttt{stores}, \texttt{int\_ops}$$
$$\texttt{branch\_ops}, \texttt{fprat}, \texttt{fops\_ins}, \texttt{int\_dud}, \texttt{fp\_dud}) \tag{3}$$

We use 10-fold cross validation for model selection, optimizing both the number of trees and the interaction depth empirically via a parameter sweep. The model reported here is based on $\widehat{K} = 800$ trees, each with an interaction depth of at most $\widehat{M} = 5$, where both $\widehat{K}$ and $\widehat{M}$ were selected by cross validation, as described in Section 2.2. Squared error loss is used to fit the multiple additive regression tree model. The model selected via the 10-fold cross-validation is then used to make predictions for all the points in the training set. The predictions are highly accurate with just 2% absolute mean error.

3.2   Model Evaluation on Real Applications

We evaluated the predictive capability of the model on real applications at a fine grain level by looking at the individual computational phases or loops of the applications. Our evaluation application suite consisted of the following applications: 1) four benchmarks (CG, MG, LU and FT) from the NAS parallel benchmarks [4], 2) miniFE and miniGhost from the Mantevo benchmarks [1], 3) AMG2006 [29], which is parallel algebraic multigrid solver for linear systems arising from problems on unstructured grids, and 4) SMG2000 [10], which is a parallel semicoarsening multigrid solver for the linear systems arising discretizations of the diffusion equation. miniFE is a finite-element mini-application that implements kernels representative of unstructured, implicit finite-element applications. miniGhost is a Finite Difference mini-application which implements a difference stencil across a homogenous 3D domain.

We started by generating the characterization signatures for the applications using our analysis tool-suite. We identified a total of 42 computational phases or hotspots in these applications. Using a loop timer tool built on top of PEBIL, we instrumented the binaries to collect timing information for each of these loops to verify the models. We then executed the applications using the three bus frequency configurations.

To evaluate the models, we fed the characterization signatures for the application's hotspots to our model to predict the performance degradation when

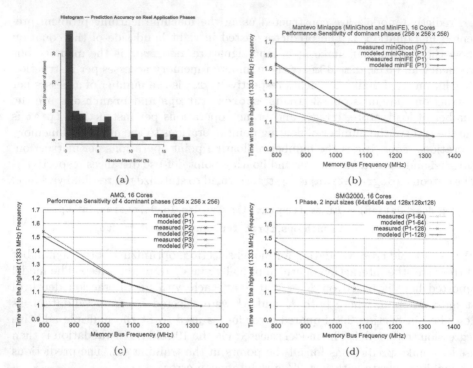

Fig. 2. (a) Overall prediction accuracy for application phases. (b), (c) and (d) demonstrate the accuracy of models on different application behaviors.

running at the two lower frequencies. Overall prediction results (histogram) are shown in Figure 2(a). Note that the error calculation reported here are 'out of sample', i.e., the characterization signatures for the application hotspots are not seen during the model training process and thereby demonstrates the predictive accuracy of our models. Overall the models predict the outcome well – average absolute mean error is 4%. For more than 91% of the application hotspots, the prediction error is less than 10%. Some of the outlying hotspots with higher error rates have at least one characteristics in common – the per visit time on these loops is very small. So, it is possible that the method we use to measure time does not accurately capture the time spent on these loops.

After validating the models, we used the models to investigate the behavior of the different computational phases within the applications. Figure 2(b) shows that different applications of the same benchmark suite (e.g. mantevo) can exhibit different reduced memory bandwidth sensitivity and that our model accurately predicts those sensitivities. In particular, miniFE's key hotspot consists of an sparse matrix product, with the matrix stored in compressed sparse row format. Indirect addressing and random memory access patterns thus make this hotspot highly sensitive to the memory bandwidth.

We also looked at the diversity of computational phases within a single application. Figure 2(c) shows the results for the three most dominant loops in

AMG2006. These three phases have different sensitivity to reduced bandwidth and our models accurately capture this behavior. The figure also shows that applications are comprised of phases that exhibit different sensitivities and that only fine-grained models can capture the complex behavior in these applications.

Finally, the working set size can also impact how individual phases react to reductions in memory bandwidth. In Figure 2(d) we investigate a single phase of the SMG2000 application to analyze how its sensitivity changes as the problem size is changed. The figure illustrates how the model is able to accurately capture the change in the phase's sensitivity as the application's input size is changed.

3.3 Algorithm Selection

We applied our framework to HYPRE [14], a library for solving large sparse linear systems of equations. With this set of experiments, we want to demonstrate how our models can accurately predict bandwidth sensitivity scores for different solver implementations and thereby help developers select and/or design algorithmic implementations that are less sensitive to reduced memory bandwidth for future multi-core systems.

We focused on the linear algebraic System (IJ) interface, which provides access to general sparse matrix solvers. We selected three best-performing solvers – Algebraic Multigrid (AMG), Parasails and hybrid-AMG. Solver choice can be made at run-time and to isolate just the phases related to different algorithms, we first profiled the three runs using different algorithms to eliminate the common phases or loops (only those that have the same computational properties). We then timed these phases at the highest frequency and used our model to predict how reduced per core memory bandwidth affects the unique phases in each of the solver instantiations. Results for the analyzed phases are presented in Table 1. The predictions that our model makes are, at worst, off by 3.6%. Parasails is the best solver for our test system and beats the second best choice (hybrid-AMG) by 1.28x. It is, however, also the most sensitive to the reduced bandwidth – slowing down by 1.37x when run at 800MHz bus frequency. hybrid-AMG, on the other hand, is the least sensitive. The speedup advantage Parasails has on hybrid-AMG diminishes to 1.09x at 800MHz. If we were to make a reasonable assumption that on future many-core systems the per core memory bandwidth will be below the range that we could simulate using our test system, then hybrid-AMG solver will deliver better performance for those systems.

Table 1. Exploring the choices of solver algorithms – all times in seconds and the (slowdown) is wrt to time @1333MHz

Algo	Measured Time@1333	Measured Time@1067 (slowdown)	Predicted Time@1067 (slowdown)	% Error @1067	Measured Time@800 (slowdown)	Predicted Time@800 (slowdown)	% Error @800
AMG	2.96	3.14 (1.06)	3.18 (1.07)	1.08	3.46 (1.17)	3.59 (1.21)	3.76
Parasails	2.06	2.29 (1.11)	2.30 (1.11)	0.40	2.84 (1.37)	2.87 (1.39)	1.06
hybrid-AMG	2.85	2.99 (1.05)	3.04 (1.07)	1.65	3.28 (1.15)	3.40 (1.19)	3.58

4   Related Work

Many researchers have investigated the idea of utilizing different power states of memory modules for greater energy efficiency [13, 23, 27]. These efforts exploit memory stalls to drive their optimization for energy usage. Our work is distinct in that we take a model-based approach to predict performance degradation at different bus frequencies; these models should enable fine-grain optimizations. Deng et al. [12] use DVFS techniques to limit main memory energy consumption on single- and multi-core systems. They utilize modeling to determine optimal DVFS settings for the applications. Our work is distinct from theirs in that they use a simulator rather than a real system. Thus, they are restricted to small executions (e.g. <100M instructions), whereas our work models large applications for the full execution and validates the models on a real system.

Performance models for HPC applications have been utilized to improve system designs, inform procurements, and guide application tuning [3, 17, 19]. Kerbyson et al. [20] utilize application-specific knowledge to construct performance models. These models are highly accurate, however, the mostly manual modeling exercise has to be largely repeated when the structure of the code or the algorithmic implementation changes. Vetter et al. [2] combine analytical and empirical modeling approaches to incrementally construct realistic and accurate performance models. Code modification must be made in the form of adding annotations or "modeling assertions" around key application constructs. Others [5, 16, 28] have also used application-specific approaches to generate performance and power models, however, they are difficult to automate and generalize because they require guidance from domain experts. Our models do not assume any domain- or application-specific knowledge and strictly base their predictions on what they learn about the computational properties of the application.

There has also been work done on using model-based methodology to predict the scalability of HPC applications. Barnes et al. [6] use regression-based approaches on training data consisting of execution observations with different input sets on a small subset of the processors and use the models to predict performance on a larger number of processors. Others [18] have used machine learning to model input parameter sensitivity of HPC applications. These modeling techniques are application-specific and the training points for regression and machine learning are drawn from the application's input parameter space.

5   Conclusion

This paper presented a model-based framework that can be used to identify computational phases within large-scale applications that are sensitive to reduced per-core memory bandwidth – a phenomenon which we anticipate will be further exacerbated as systems scale up the number of cores on a processor. Our framework assumes no domain-specific knowledge about the application and strictly makes predictions about the memory bandwidth sensitivity of the application's phases based on characterization information that we can collect using our binary analysis tools. We evaluated the framework using various scientific workloads and showed that the framework accurately predicts ($<5\%$ absolute mean error in prediction) how sensitive the diverse phases and algorithms within these workloads are to the reduced per core memory bandwidth.

Acknowledgements. This work was supported in part by the DOE Office of Science, Advanced Scientific Computing Research, under award number 62855 "Beyond the Standard Model – Towards an Integrated Modeling Methodology for the Performance and Power"; PNNL lead institution; Program Manager Sonia Sachs. The authors acknowledge partial support from LLNL under subcontract B600667. This work was also supported in part by the DoD and used elements at the Extreme Scale Systems Center, located at ORNL and funded by the DoD. Partial support also came from the DOE Office of Science through the SciDAC award titled SUPER (Institute for Sustained Performance, Energy and Resilience). Part of this work was performed under the auspices of the U.S. Department of Energy by Lawrence Livermore National Laboratory under Contract DE-AC52-07NA27344 (LLNL-CONF-655084).

References

1. Mantevo Project, http://mantevo.org/
2. Alam, S., Vetter, J.: A framework to develop symbolic performance models of parallel applications. In: 20th International Parallel and Distributed Processing Symposium, IPDPS 2006, p. 8 (April 2006)
3. Bailey, D.H., Snavely, A.: Performance modeling. Understanding the past and predicting the future. In: Cunha, J.C., Medeiros, P.D. (eds.) Euro-Par 2005. LNCS, vol. 3648, pp. 185–195. Springer, Heidelberg (2005)
4. Bailey, D.H., Barszcz, E., Barton, J.T., Browning, D.S., Carter, R.L., Dagum, L., Fatoohi, R.A., Frederickson, P.O., Lasinski, T.A., Schreiber, R.S., Simon, H.D., Venkatakrishnan, V., Weeratunga, S.K.: The nas parallel benchmarks summary and preliminary results. In: Proceedings of the 1991 ACM/IEEE Conference on Supercomputing, Supercomputing 1991. ACM, New York (1991)
5. Barker, K., Davis, K., Kerbyson, D.: Performance modeling in action: Performance prediction of a cray xt4 system during upgrade. In: IEEE International Symposium on Parallel Distributed Processing, IPDPS (2009)
6. Barnes, B.J., Rountree, B., Lowenthal, D.K., Reeves, J., de Supinski, B., Schulz, M.: A regression-based approach to scalability prediction. In: Proceedings of the 22nd Annual International Conference on Supercomputing, ICS 2008 (2008)
7. Bergman, K., Borkar, S., Campbell, D., Carlson, W., Dally, W., Denneau, M., Franzon, P., Harrod, W., Hiller, J., Karp, S., Keckler, S., Klein, D., Lucas, R., Richards, M., Scarpelli, A., Scott, S., Snavely, A., Sterling, T., Williams, R.S., Yelick, K.: Exascale computing study: Technology challenges in achieving exascale systems (2008), http://www.cse.nd.edu/Reports/2008TR-2008-13.pdf
8. Breiman, L.: Random forests. Machine Learning 45(1), 5–32 (2001)
9. Breiman, L., Friedman, J., Stone, C.J., Olshen, R.A.: Classification and Regression Trees. Chapman & Hall, CRC (1984)
10. Brown, P.N., Falgout, R.D., Jones, J.E.: Semicoarsening Multigrid on Distributed Memory Machines. SIAM J. Sci. Comput. 21(5), 1823–1834 (2000)
11. Chen, C., Chame, J., Hall, M.W.: CHiLL: A framework for composing high-level loop transformations. TR 08-897, Univ. of Southern California (June 2008)

12. Deng, Q., Meisner, D., Bhattacharjee, A., Wenisch, T.F., Bianchini, R.: Coscale: Coordinating cpu and memory system dvfs in server systems. In: 45th Annual IEEE/ACM International Symposium on Microarchitecture, MICRO (2012)
13. Diniz, B., Guedes, D., Meira Jr., W., Bianchini, R.: Limiting the power consumption of main memory. In: ACM SIGARCH Computer Architecture News, vol. 35, pp. 290–301. ACM (2007)
14. Falgout, R.D., Meier Yang, U.: hypre: A library of high performance preconditioners. In: Sloot, P.M.A., Tan, C.J.K., Dongarra, J. J., Hoekstra, A.G. (eds.) ICCS 200. Part III. LNCS, vol. 2331, pp. 632–641. Springer, Heidelberg (2002)
15. Friedman, J.: Greedy function approximation: A gradient boosting machine. Annals of Statistics 29(5), 1189–1232 (2001)
16. Hoefler, T.: Bridging performance analysis tools and analytic performance modeling for HPC. In: Guarracino, M.R., et al. (eds.) Euro-Par-Workshop 2010. LNCS, vol. 6586, pp. 483–491. Springer, Heidelberg (2011)
17. Hoisie, A., Kerbyson, D.J., Mendes, C.L., Reed, D.A., Snavely, A.: Special section: Large-scale system performance modeling and analysis. Future Generation Comp. Syst. 22(3), 291–292 (2006)
18. Ipek, E., de Supinski, B.R., Schulz, M., McKee, S.A.: An approach to performance prediction for parallel applications. In: Cunha, J.C., Medeiros, P.D. (eds.) Euro-Par 2005. LNCS, vol. 3648, pp. 196–205. Springer, Heidelberg (2005)
19. Kerbyson, D., Vishnu, A., Barker, K., Hoisie, A.: Codesign challenges for exascale systems: Performance, power, and reliability. Computer 44(11), 37–43 (2011)
20. Kerbyson, D.J., Jones, P.W.: A performance model of the parallel ocean program. Int. J. High Perform. Comput. Appl. 19(3), 261–276 (2005)
21. Laurenzano, M., Tikir, M., Carrington, L., Snavely, A.: Pebil: Efficient static binary instrumentation for linux. In: 2010 IEEE International Symposium on Performance Analysis of Systems Software (ISPASS), pp. 175–183 (March 2010)
22. Laurenzano, M.A., Meswani, M., Carrington, L., Snavely, A., Tikir, M.M., Poole, S.: Reducing energy usage with memory and computation-aware dynamic frequency scaling. In: Jeannot, E., Namyst, R., Roman, J. (eds.) Euro-Par 2011, Part I. LNCS, vol. 6852, pp. 79–90. Springer, Heidelberg (2011)
23. Lebeck, A.R., Fan, X., Zeng, H., Ellis, C.: Power aware page allocation. ACM SIGPLAN Notices 35(11), 105–116 (2000)
24. McVoy, L., Staelin, C.: lmbench: Portable tools for performance analysis. In: Proceedings of the 1996 Annual Conference on USENIX Annual Technical Conference, ATEC 1996, Berkeley, CA, USA, pp. 23–23. USENIX Association (1996)
25. Norman, M., Snavely, A.: Accelerating data-intensive science with Gordon and Dash. In: 2010 TeraGrid Conference (2010)
26. Norris, B., Hartono, A., Gropp, W.: Annotations for productivity and performance portability. In: Petascale Computing: Algorithms and Applications, Computational Science, pp. 443–462. Chapman & Hall / CRC Press (2007)
27. Pandey, V., Jiang, W., Zhou, Y., Bianchini, R.: Dma-aware memory energy management. In: HPCA, vol. 6, pp. 133–144 (2006)
28. Tiwari, A., Laurenzano, M., Carrington, L., Snavely, A.: Modeling power and energy usage of hpc kernels. In: Proceedings of the Eighth Workshop on High-Performance, Power-Aware Computing, HPPAC 2012 (2012)
29. Yang, U.: Parallel algebraic multigrid methods in high performance preconditioners. In: Garbow, B.S., Dongarra, J., Boyle, J.M., Moler, C.B. (eds.) Numerical Solution of Partial Differential Equations on Parallel Computers. LNCS, vol. 51, pp. 209–236. Springer, Heidelberg (1977)

ParaShares: Finding the Important Basic Blocks in Multithreaded Programs

Melanie Kambadur, Kui Tang, and Martha A. Kim

Columbia University, New York, NY
{melanie,martha}@cs.columbia.edu, kt2384@columbia.edu

Abstract. Understanding and optimizing multithreaded execution is a significant challenge. Numerous research and industrial tools debug parallel performance by combing through program source or thread traces for pathologies including communication overheads, data dependencies, and load imbalances. This work takes a new approach: it ignores any underlying pathologies, and focuses instead on pinpointing the exact locations in source code that consume the largest share of execution. Our new metric, *ParaShares*, scores and ranks all basic blocks in a program based on their share of parallel execution. For the eight benchmarks examined in this paper, ParaShare rankings point to just a few important blocks per application. The paper demonstrates two uses of this information, exploring how the important blocks vary across thread counts and input sizes, and making modest source code changes (fewer than 10 lines of code) that result in 14-92% savings in parallel program runtime.

1 Introduction

With massive scale data to analyze, explosive growth in server and mobile core counts, and multithreading making its way into mainstream language specifications such as C++ [22], parallel software is officially ubiquitous. All parallel applications share the same fundamental goal of making the best use of resources: time, power, money, or some combination of these. To honor this goal, programs must be performant, bug-free, scalable, and not overly difficult to write or debug. Parallel program optimization poses particular challenges, as developers must uncover and address a nearly unbounded catalog of potential inefficiencies arising at any level of the stack, from relatively high level algorithmic and design choices, to program inputs, to source language implementation, to thread library selection, to operating system configurations, and the target hardware platform. Correcting performance inefficiencies requires programmers to have knowledge of, and potentially, take action at, multiple levels of the stack.

Many research and industrial tools have been introduced over the years to help programmers correct parallel performance inefficiencies. Generally these tools employ one of two broad strategies. The first is to look for specific kinds of errors, sometimes within targeted program regions such as a program's critical path. For example, tools may identify load imbalances [4], long waits [16,8], lock contention [23,6], I/O blocking [18], or unnecessary I/O [5]. One issue with this

F. Silva et al. (Eds.): Euro-Par 2014, LNCS 8632, pp. 75–86, 2014.

approach is that each type of inefficiency may need its own tool or search procedure. The second general strategy is to troll for multiple or broader types of problems by tracking hardware and system events. Some tools track thread traces and program runtimes to predict which threads will scale poorly in future runs [9,12]. Other tools take a hardware perspective, monitoring instruction counts, CPU utilization, thread preemption rates, and cache latencies [14,7,26,15,21,1]. Unfortunately, linking hardware events back to software can pose a number of challenges. For example, event data may need to be aggregated across parallel threads. Additionally, it is often difficult to connect certain events precisely to software, meaning that areas of code identified as problematic may be large.

This paper utilizes a third strategy for performance debugging. *ParaShares* identify very tiny regions of code that take up the majority of multithreaded execution, agnostic to the type or cause of underlying performance pathologies. Their only goal is to precisely point programmers to the lines in their program that would benefit most from optimizations. A ParaShare is a rankable score that measures each basic block's share of a total parallel program's execution. The rankings are similar to hot block analyses that report the most frequently executed basic blocks and their CPU use. However, ParaShares factor in the degree of program parallelism at each block execution, providing a more accurate reflection of a block's contribution to wall-clock execution time. The weighting scheme downgrades the importance of blocks that execute during highly parallel program phases. As a result, it ranks blocks that mostly run during serial phases relatively higher in importance as they tend to consume a greater fraction of runtime.

Per block parallelism weights are enabled by parallel block vector (PBV) profiling [17], a recent technique which was introduced for the purpose of improving micro-architectural design. In the next section, we explain this new application of PBVs in more detail, comparing ParaShares to existing analyses and motivating the use of such a precise and fine-grained performance debugging tool (Sect. 2). We then present a step by step procedure for collecting and analyzing ParaShares (Sect. 3). Finally, using ParaShares for eight benchmark applications, we examine how the key optimization points move as input size and parallelism vary (Sect. 4.1), and make small, ParaShare-targeted source code changes that, although only a few lines apiece, speed the benchmarks 14–92%(Sect. 4.2).

2   ParaShares

ParaShares are a new way to rank the basic blocks in a parallel program according to their relative multithreaded runtime contributions. This section defines ParaShares, describes how they differ from traditional hot block analyses, gives readers a first look at experimentally collected ParaShares, and makes a case for analyses that focus on fine-grained regions of code.

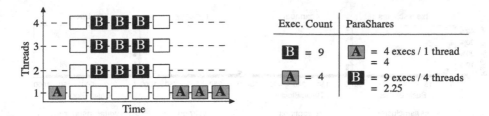

Fig. 1. ParaShares rank basic blocks to identify those with the greatest *impact on parallel execution*, weighting blocks by the runtime parallelism exhibited by the application each time the block was executed

2.1 The Basic Concept

Basic blocks are small program fragments, constrained to be a linear sequence of instructions with a single entry point and a single exit point. As the program executes, some blocks will be executed very frequently, while others may execute rarely or not at all. The frequently executed blocks are called "hot" and are important optimization targets as they constitute a large share of an application's dynamic work. Hot block analysis has traditionally been used for a variety of purposes, including JIT translation [24], garbage collection optimizations [13], simulation points analysis [19], code cache management [20], and parallel performance debugging, for example, in Intel's VTune Amplifier [15].

ParaShares makes a subtle but important twist on traditional hot block analyses, weighting each basic block by the degree of parallelism exhibited by the program when the block was executed. Figure 1 illustrates the significance of this change. On the left is a program trace that highlights the execution patterns of two blocks of interest, A (gray) and B (black). For simplicity, we assume that both blocks have the same number of instructions and equal execution times, though in actual ParaShare computations this unlikely assumption is amended (Sect. 3.1). Simple counting reveals that B executes 9 times whereas A executes only 4, giving B a higher rank of importance. However, A may consume more of the program's execution time because its executions occur during serial phases of the program. To account for this nuance, ParaShares divides the executions by the degree of parallelism at execution time, in this example dividing B's 9 executions by the 4 threads that ran while B executed, and dividing A's 4 blocks by 1 for the single running thread. As a rule, parallelism is counted at the start of a basic block's execution to resolve any overlaps in block executions between threads. The resulting scores capture parallel execution shares more effectively, and in this case rank A and B in the opposite order of importance versus traditional execution counts.

2.2 A First Look at Real Applications

Figure 2 gives a first look at ParaShare block rankings for real applications, eight programs from the Parsec Version 3.0 [3] and Splash-2 [25] benchmark

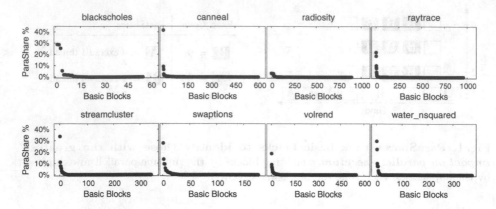

Fig. 2. ParaShare rankings identify important blocks to target for multi-threaded performance optimizations. These graphs show the ParaShare percentages (ordered from greatest to least share) of all the basic blocks in eight benchmark applications.

suites, namely `blackscholes`, `canneal`, `radiosity`, `raytrace`, `streamcluster`, `swaptions`, `volrend`, and `water_nsquared`. The Splash2x variant of Splash that is packaged with Parsec was used for its provision of multiple input sets. All of the applications are written in C and C++ and parallelized using pthreads with a variety of design patterns, including a mix of data and task parallelism. Each program was run alone using 24 threads and native input set sizes on a Dell PowerEdge R420 server. The server is dual socket with Intel Sandybridge E5-243 chips, each with six cores and two-way hyper-threading for a total of 24 effective cores. The system has 24GB of DRAM and runs Ubuntu 12.04.2 with the 3.9.11 version of the Linux kernel. The graphs show that just a few basic blocks (on the x-axis) per program dominate the ParaShare rankings (on the y-axis). The small number of important blocks is no surprise. However, ParaShare's ability to highlight blocks that are important in terms of wall-clock time instead of processor execution times combined across threads makes it possible to massively improve program performance with just minor code changes, as demonstrated later in Sect. 4.2.

2.3   Benefits of Fine Granularity

The well known 90-10 rule of thumb says that 90% of program execution time resides in just 10% of code. For our benchmarks, the rule holds: functions that consume roughly 90% of the execution represent 2.3-17.3% of the lines in the overall programs, or an average of 7.7%. Table 1 shows the exact line counts per benchmark, as well as line counts for the functions consuming 90% of the execution based on ParaShare computations.

The table also shows the number of lines of code contained in the basic blocks that are responsible for 90% of the ParaShare execution. Using block-granularity

Table 1. A case for fine-grained identification of performance inefficiencies. To examine the functions that take up 90% of the parallel execution, a programmer must examine an average of 338.5 lines per program. To examine the basic blocks that consumed the same amount, they would need to look at an average of 50 lines per program.

Benchmark Application	Total Lines	90% Exec By Func Lines	90% Exec By Block Lines	50% Exec By Block Lines
blackscholes	564	68	34	21
canneal	1362	204	70	6
radiosity	11836	276	42	4
raytrace	10963	431	51	8
streamcluster	2539	439	12	5
swaptions	1550	359	28	10
volrend	4227	585	133	89
water_nsquared	2079	338	29	18

hotspots rather than function hotspots saves programmers from looking at an average of 289 lines per benchmark. In fact, basic block hotspots save enough that we could coin a new 90-2 rule of thumb, because 90% of the parallel execution is taken up by just 2.4% of the program source lines according to our precise ParaShares analysis. The top 50% of program execution could be covered by searching an even more targeted set of code; programmers would need to look at only 20 source lines per application, or 1% of the overall program. The block versus function savings is particularly important in unfamiliar applications with lengthy functions and lots of loops — a feature common to some of the scientific benchmarks used in this study. For example, volrend has one function with three sets of doubly nested loops, and we found more than a few instances where a single function contained four or more loops.

3 Collecting and Analyzing ParaShares

This section describes the framework for translating source code to ParaShare rankings, examines the robustness of ParaShare rankings across trials, and experimentally demonstrates that ParaShare weighting can significantly change top blocks' relative importance versus traditional profiling.

3.1 The Collection Framework

From a user's perspective, ParaShares are straightforward to collect. They require recompilation, a single program run with the usual inputs and usual outputs, and the execution of a post-processing script. Under the covers, ParaShares are more complex, as depicted in the framework in Figure 3. The first two steps come from previous work, while the remaining steps are new to this work.

Step 1. Compile the source program with Harmony. ParaShares use parallel block vectors, or PBVs [17], to count how many times each basic block

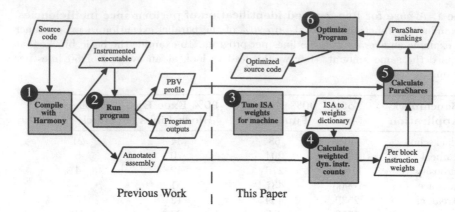

Fig. 3. The Collection Framework. To collect ParaShares, programmers re-compile their program with a specialized compiler, then execute it once with normal inputs. Profiling files produced at compile and execution time are analyzed in post-processing to give the programmer a list of ParaShares and corresponding source code locations.

executes at each thread count exhibited over the course of a program's execution. PBVs are collected via compiler instrumentation, requiring source programs to be compiled with Harmony [11], an extended version of LLVM. Compilation with Harmony produces two outputs: an annotated assembly code file and an instrumented executable file.

Step 2. Execute the program once to collect a PBV. After compilation with Harmony, a single program run with normal inputs produces a PBV profile as well as the usual program outputs.

Step 3. (Optional) Tune machine specific parameters. Optionally, ParaShares can incorporate machine specific instruction weights to account for differences in opcode processing or memory access times. If used, these weights should be stored in a dictionary mapping instruction types to latency factors. Opcode dependent latency factors are often already available online; for example, latency factors for our machine are available in [10]. These latency factors suggest multiplying conditional operations by two, add instructions by one, and divide instructions by 30, as well as multiplicative factors for other types of instructions. Due to the overwhelming significance of total instruction count, our applications' ParaShare rankings showed minimal sensitivity to these latency factors. However, latency factors could have more of an effect for other applications and architectures.

Step 4. Calculate per block static instruction counts. Next, the total (possibly weighted) instruction count per basic block is calculated. The instruction contents of each block are available in the annotated assembly file produced earlier by Harmony. With weighting, a sum of the weights of each instruction in the block produces a total block weight ($Weight_b$). As an unweighted alternative, a simple count of the instructions per block suffices.

Step 5. Calculate ParaShare rankings. The ParaShare for each block b is computed using the block's static instruction weight and dynamic thread weight. Specifically, the sum of each block's executions at thread count t ($Execs_{b,t}$) are divided by t. This formula is loosely related to the runtime calculation used in Quartz [2], but we apply it here at a smaller granularity and for a different purpose. The ParaShare of block b is the product of this dynamic thread weight and the static block weight, where max is the maximum number of threads that ever executes concurrently in the program:

$$\mathrm{ParaShare}_b = \sum_{t=1}^{max} \frac{\mathrm{Execs}_{b,t}}{t} \times \mathrm{Weight}_b$$

As necessary for further analysis, the absolute ParaShare for each basic block can be normalized to the program's total ParaShare (the sum of ParaShares across blocks).

Step 6. Use the ParaShare rankings for performance optimizations or other analyses. Finally, ParaShares can be mapped back to the source code via compiler debug information in the assembly code.

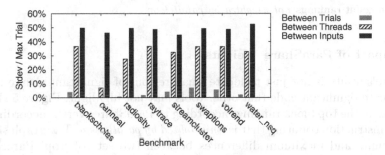

Fig. 4. Robustness of the metrics. Runtimes and basic block execution counts can change across program trials, but the differences are small relative to the differences in ParaShares collected across varying thread counts or input set sizes.

3.2 ParaShare Robustness

A program's parallel behavior may be inconsistent across runs, changing block execution counts or overall program runtime. Despite these variations, a single profiling run can produce representative ParaShares, particularly if the purpose of collection is to examine and optimize the hottest blocks with the highest ParaShares. Figure 4 plots the standard deviations of a program's total ParaShares as a fraction of the maximum program total ParaShare across ten trials. Across runs with the same thread count and input, this division was never more than 7% and averaged only 3.2%. The variation is small when compared with variations between trials given different maximum thread counts (31% on average) or different input sizes (48%). In addition to the magnitude of the overall program ParaShare staying consistent between trials, the ranking of individual basic blocks varies minimally, and changes only in lower ranked blocks with ParaShares of 2% or less. This is not the case across thread counts and input sizes as explored in Sect. 4.1.

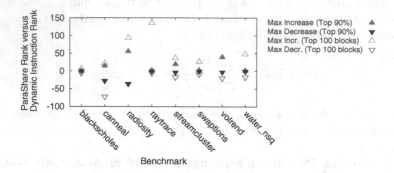

Fig. 5. ParaShares versus unweighted rankings for the blocks representing 90% of ParaShare execution and for the larger set of the top 100 blocks per application. ParaShares often significantly impact the relative importance of a block versus dynamic instruction count rankings *not weighted by parallelism*.

3.3   Impact of ParaShare Weights

ParaShare's utility is not just to locate small regions of significant source code, but to locate significant code that other tools may not highlight. Figure 5 shows differences in the top block rankings according to ParaShares versus according to dynamic instruction counting that is *unweighted by parallelism*. The graph shows the minimum and maximum differences between two sets of 'top' ParaShare blocks: first, those blocks representing 90% of the execution of 24-thread count runs (as previously depicted in Fig. 2, this block count varies by application), and second, the top 100 ParaShare blocks per program. From the first set of differences, we see significant changes in four of the eight applications. One block in `radiosity` is ranked 55 spots higher by ParaShares than by dynamic instruction counts, and another is ranked 36 spots lower by ParaShares. In the second, larger set of 100 block differences, rankings change significantly amongst almost all of the applications. Individual blocks (in `raytrace`) jump as many as 135 spots in the ParaShare rankings, and fall as many as 72 spots (in `canneal`).

4   ParaShares in Real Applications

This section uses ParaShares to explore real applications in more detail, examining how important blocks differ across inputs and thread counts and using ParaShares for targeted micro-optimizations.

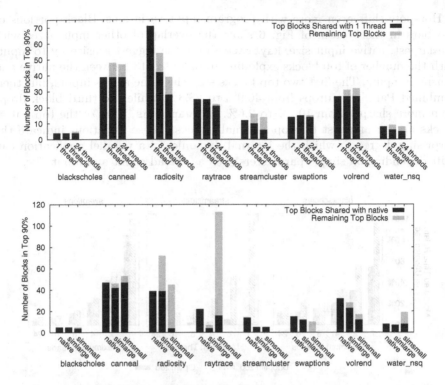

Fig. 6. Top ParaShare blocks vary across thread counts and input sizes.
These differences suggest that optimizations may need to be targeted to the level of
expected parallelism and to input size for maximum effect.

4.1   How Top Blocks Differ

A small handful of basic blocks dominates the ParaShare ranks and overall execution. These top blocks can vary significantly across thread counts and input
sizes, suggesting that as environmental circumstances change, optimizations may
need to be re-applied or re-targeted for maximum effect. The top of Fig. 6 plots
the number of blocks that make up the top 90% of each application when run
with 1, 8, and 24 threads. The number of hot blocks can change significantly. For
example, when run with 1 thread, 71 blocks comprise the top 90% of radiosity,
but this number shrinks to 39 when the application runs with 24 threads. The
black part of each bar indicates how many of the top 90% were also in the top
90% of a serial run. Thus, the 39 key blocks in 24-threaded radiosity include
11 blocks that were not important to single-threaded radiosity. While it is
not evident in the plot, the ranking of blocks within the top 90% changes as
well: the block with the highest ParaShare in single-threaded radiosity falls
to 26th place in 24-threaded radiosity. The highest ranking block in single-
threaded streamcluster remains atop the list in 24-threaded streamcluster,
but the second place block falls off of the list entirely, dropping from 19% of the
ParaShare to 0.3%, and the third ranked block falls to the ninth spot.

Hotspots shift even more with program input variations. Black portions of the bars in the bottom of Fig. 6 show the overlap of other input sizes with the largest, native input size. Raytrace shows the biggest sensitivity to input, with the number of top blocks exploding from 22 to 113 between the native and simsmall inputs. The first two top blocks stay the same across inputs, but their combined ParaShare drops from 40.9% to 28.3%, while the third block drops even more sharply from 10.2% to 2.6%. In swaptions, none of the top native blocks appear amongst the top simsmall blocks. These variations indicate the surprising degree to which the internal dynamics of a parallel application can shift depending on simple parameters such as thread count and input size.

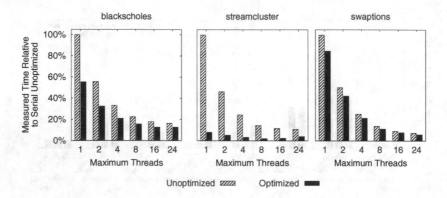

Fig. 7. ParaShares pinpoint inefficiencies that lead to significant opportunities for optimization. With the extremely targeted profiling provided by ParaShares, we were able to improve benchmark performance by up to 92% through source code changes less than 10 lines long.

4.2   Performance Tuning

Using ParaShares to target particularly important lines of source code, we made extremely simple and short source code changes to reduce application runtimes 14-92%. Figure 7 shows the effect of optimizations to blackscholes, streamcluster, and swaptions. Both optimized and unoptimized versions were compiled with LLVM's -O3 optimization set. Our manual optimizations improve computation time, but do not make any algorithmic or parallelization changes. As a result, the savings shrink as thread counts increase, but they remain significant (up to 82%) even at large thread counts.

In blackscholes, the top two blocks consume nearly 60% of the overall runtime given 24 threads and native input sizes. These blocks are found in the kernel function which calculates financial option values. By collapsing the original 20 temporary variables in the function to 3, we alleviated register pressure resulting in a 44.6% performance improvement at one thread and 22% at 24 threads. For streamcluster, the top blocks are found in the dist() function, which computes the squared Euclidean distance between two Points, each of which is a struct with pointers to arrays of `float` coordinates. Inspecting the line of code in question (the body of a nested for loop), we guessed that the compiler missed an opportunity for common subexpression elimination, then modified the code to force it to do so. This change halved the loop body's original four array lookups and two subtractions and reduced register pressure, saving 92% of the serial runtime, and 64% of the 24 thread runtime. Finally, the top blocks in `swaptions` correspond to a few nested loops within the `HJM_SimPath_Forward_Blocking.cpp` file. We experimentally unrolled these loops one to four times to find the optimum unrolling level for each. In addition to the inability of the compiler to dynamically test a variety of unrolling levels, these opportunities may have been missed because the loops involve nested accesses to custom data structures. In total, our loop optimizations resulted in a 15% savings for a single threaded swaptions execution, and a 19.7% savings for a 24-thread execution.

Given the simplicity of our optimizations, the performance savings are disproportionately large. Across a datacenter or many nodes in a distributed system, the savings could be even more important, and potentially financially significant as well. Best of all, we were able to make the optimizations quickly, because ParaShares allowed us to focus our efforts on just a few lines of code rather than thousands.

5   Conclusions

ParaShares provides a new lens through which to analyze multithreaded application performance. In contrast to most parallel performance optimization techniques, ParaShares do not target a specific type of inefficiency or level of the system stack. Instead, ParaShares track parallelism from the code's point of view, weighting each basic block execution by the whole program's parallelism at the time of the execution. This fine-grained scoring makes it simple to localize important lines of code, even in large or unknown programs. Once important code is localized, more extensive analysis and optimizations can be precisely targeted, leading to small code changes with big performance effects.

References

1. Adhianto, L., Banerjee, S., Fagan, M., Krentel, M., Marin, G., Mellor-Crummey, J., Tallent, N.R.: HPCToolkit: Tools for performance analysis of optimized parallel programs. Concurrency and Computation 22(6) (April 2010)
2. Anderson, T.E., Lazowska, E.D.: Quartz: A tool for tuning parallel program performance. SIGMETRICS 18, 115–125 (1990)
3. Bienia, C.: Benchmarking Modern Multiprocessors. PhD thesis. Princeton University (2011)
4. Bohme, D., Wolf, F., de Supinski, B.R., Schulz, M., Geimer, M.: Scalable critical-path based performance analysis. In: IPDPS (2012)
5. Chabbi, M., Mellor-Crummey, J.: Deadspy: A tool to pinpoint program inefficiencies. In: CGO (2012)

6. Chen, G., Stenstrom, P.: Critical lock analysis: Diagnosing critical section bottlenecks in multithreaded applications. In: SC (2012)
7. Chen, K.-Y., Chang, J., Hou, T.-W.: Multithreading in Java: Performance and scalability on multicore systems. Transactions on Computers 60(11) (November 2011)
8. Du Bois, K., Eyerman, S., Sartor, J.B., Eeckhout, L.: Criticality stacks: Identifying critical threads in parallel programs using synchronization behavior. In: ISCA (2013)
9. Du Bois, K., Sartor, J.B., Eyerman, S., Eeckhout, L.: Bottle graphs: Visualizing scalability bottlenecks in multi-threaded applications. In: OOPSLA (2013)
10. Granlund, T.: Instruction latencies and throughput for AMD and Intel x86 processors (February 2012), http://gmplib.org/~tege/x86-timing.pdf
11. Harmony Parallel Block Vector Collection Tool, http://arcade.cs.columbia.edu/harmony
12. He, Y., Leiserson, C.E., Leiserson, W.M.: The Cilkview scalability analyzer. In: SPAA, pp. 145–156 (2010)
13. Huang, X., Blackburn, S.M., McKinley, K.S., Moss, J.E.B., Wang, Z., Cheng, P.: The garbage collection advantage: Improving program locality. In: OOPSLA (October 2004)
14. Huang, Y., Cui, Z., Chen, L., Zhang, W., Bao, Y., Chen, M.: HaLock: Hardware-assisted lock contention detection in multithreaded applications. In: PACT (2012)
15. Intel® Corporation. Intel® Parallel Amplifier (2011), http://software.intel.com/en-us/articles/intel-parallel-amplifier/
16. Joao, J.A., Suleman, M.A., Mutlu, O., Patt, Y.N.: Bottleneck identification and scheduling in multithreaded applications. In: ASPLOS (2012)
17. Kambadur, M., Tang, K., Kim, M.A.: Harmony: Collection and analysis of parallel block vectors. In: ISCA (June 2012)
18. Miller, B.P., Callaghan, M.D., Cargille, J.M., Hollingsworth, J.K., Bruce, R., Karen, I., Karavanic, L., Kunchithapadam, K., Newhall, T.: The Paradyn parallel performance measurement tools. IEEE Computer (1995)
19. Perelman, E., Hamerly, G., Van Biesbrouck, M., Sherwood, T., Calder, B.: Using simpoint for accurate and efficient simulation. In: SIGMETRICS, vol. 31. ACM (2003)
20. Shi, H., Wang, Y., Guan, H., Liang, A.: An intermediate language level optimization framework for dynamic binary translation. SIGPLAN Notices 42(5) (May 2007)
21. STMicroelectronics, Inc. PGProf: Parallel profiling for scientists and engineers (2011), http://www.pgroup.com/products/pgprof.htm
22. Stroustrup, B.: C++11 the new ISO C++ standard (2013), http://www.stroustrup.com/C++11FAQ.html
23. Tallent, N.R., Mellor-Crummey, J.M., Porterfield, A.: Analyzing lock contention in multithreaded applications. In: PPoPP (2010)
24. Topham, N., Jones, D.: High speed CPU simulation using JIT binary translation. In: MOBS, vol. 7 (2007)
25. Woo, S., Ohara, M., Torrie, E., Singh, J., Gupta, A.: The SPLASH-2 programs: Characterization and methodological considerations. In: ISCA (1995)
26. Yoo, W., Larson, K., Baugh, L., Kim, S., Campbell, R.H.: ADP: Automated diagnosis of performance pathologies using hardware events. In: SIGMETRICS (2012)

Multi-Objective Auto-Tuning with Insieme: Optimization and Trade-Off Analysis for Time, Energy and Resource Usage

Philipp Gschwandtner, Juan J. Durillo, and Thomas Fahringer

University of Innsbruck, Institute of Computer Science, Austria
{philipp,juan,tf}@dps.uibk.ac.at

Abstract. The increasing complexity of modern multi- and many-core hardware design makes performance tuning of parallel applications a difficult task. In the past, auto-tuners have been successfully applied to minimize execution time. However, besides execution time, additional optimization goals have recently arisen, such as energy consumption or computing costs. Therefore, more sophisticated methods capable of exploiting and identifying the trade-offs among these goals are required. In this work we present and discuss results of applying a multi-objective search-based auto-tuner to optimize for three conflicting criteria: execution time, energy consumption, and resource usage. We examine a method, called RS-GDE3, to tune HPC codes using the Insieme parallelizing and optimizing compiler. Our results demonstrate that RS-GDE3 offers solutions of superior quality than those provided by a hierarchical and a random search at a fraction of the required time (5%) or energy (8%). A comparison to a state-of-the-art multi-objective optimizer (NSGA II) shows that RS-GDE3 computes solutions of higher quality. Finally, based on the trade-off solutions found by RS-GDE3, we provide a detailed analysis and several hints on how to improve the design of multi-objective auto tuners and code optimization.

1 Introduction

The performance of a software application crucially depends on the quality of its source code. The increasing complexity and multi/many-core nature of hardware design have transformed code generation, whether done manually or by a compiler, into a complex, time-consuming, and error-prone task which additionally suffers from a lack of performance portability. To mitigate these issues, a new research field, known as *auto-tuning*, has gained increasing attention. *Auto-tuners* are an effective approach to generate high-quality portable code. They are able to produce highly efficient code versions of libraries or applications by generating many code variants which are evaluated on the target platform, often delivering high performance code configurations which are unusual or not intuitive.

Whilst earlier auto-tuning approaches were mainly targeted at execution time [1], other optimization criteria such as energy consumption or computing costs are gaining interest nowadays. In this new scenario, a code *configuration* that

F. Silva et al. (Eds.): Euro-Par 2014, LNCS 8632, pp. 87–98, 2014.

is found to be optimal for low execution time might not be optimal for another criterion. Therefore, there is no single solution to this problem that can be considered optimal, but a set, namely the Pareto set, of solutions (i.e. code configurations) representing the optimal trade-off among the different optimization criteria. Solutions within this set are said to be non-dominated: any solution within it is not better than the others for all the considered criteria.

This multi-criteria scenario requires a further development of auto-tuners, which must be able to capture these trade-offs and offer the user either the whole Pareto set or a solution within it. Although there is a growing amount of related work considering the optimization of several criteria [2, 3, 4, 5, 6], most of them consider two criteria simultaneously at most, and many fail in capturing the trade-off among the objectives.

In this paper we investigate the auto-tuning of parallel codes using the Insieme compiler to optimize three different criteria: execution time, resource usage and energy consumption. For tuning the codes, we consider as optimization knobs: dynamic concurrency throttling (DCT, later on referred to as used cores), loop tiling, and frequency and voltage scaling (DVFS). We examine the obtained results in detail to analyze and illustrate the complex interactions between optimized software and hardware. To the best of our knowledge, this is the first work exploring an auto-tuner to optimize parallel programs for more than two objectives and analyzing trade-offs among these objectives. Our main findings of this work demonstrate that: (1) RS-GDE3 can be successfully applied to a three-objective optimization problem without any modifications or restrictions and (2) the trade-off between execution time and energy consumption, dependent on efficient parallelization, can be explained by investigating resource usage. Furthermore, we compare RS-GDE3 with a state-of-the-art multi-objective optimizer (NSGA-II) that has been adjusted to deal with three objectives. The results show that RS-GDE3 derives solutions with better quality than an NSGA-II-based solution.

The paper is structured as follows: Section 2 describes the auto-tuning infrastructure used for this work. The experiment design, the objectives of interest, the target codes and hardware platform are outlined in Section 3. Section 4 presents our results and their detailed analysis. Finally relevant related work is listed in Section 5 and Section 6 concludes.

2   Insieme Compiler

2.1   Auto-Tuning Infrastructure

Our work is based on the Insieme compiler, a multi-objective auto-tuning optimizing compiler and runtime system for parallel codes [7].

Figure 1 illustrates the overall architecture of Insieme. An input code is loaded by the compiler (1), analyzed and prepared (2) to be tuned prior to execution. During this process, a set of tunable *parameters* are identified, encompassing loop tile sizes, number of cores involved in the computation as well as the frequency setting of the CPUs. Afterwards, the optimizer conducts auto-tuning (hence we use the terms *auto-tuner* and *optimizer* interchangeably) by iteratively selecting sets of *configurations* for each code to be evaluated (executed) on the target

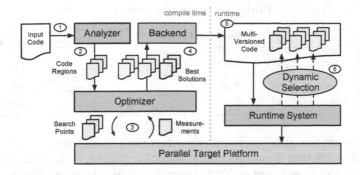

Fig. 1. Overview of the Insieme compiler, adapted from [7]

system (3). At the end, the optimizer derives a Pareto set consisting of the best configurations found. These are passed to the backend (4) and compiled into multi-versioned code (5). The runtime system can then dynamically select the preferred code version to be executed (6).

2.2 Optimizers

The main search engine of Insieme, described in previous work of the authors [7], is called RS-GDE3 and aims at computing the Pareto set of code configurations. RS-GDE3 combines an approximation technique from the class of Differential Evolution (DE) and a search space reduction mechanism based on Rough Set theory. The goal of this latter technique is to reduce the search to a small area where RS-GDE3 assumes the location of the optimal configurations. This method was successfully applied to an optimization problem with two conflicting objectives in [7], whereas we apply it for the first time to three objectives in this work. However, RS-GDE3 is a true multi-objective optimizer that can handle an arbitrary number of objectives within the scope of Pareto optimality.

In addition to RS-GDE3, the Insieme compiler includes two other search engines, which are used in this paper to compare with, based on a hierarchical and a random search. The hierarchical search evaluates points on an equidistant grid defined over each tunable parameter. Random search generates a set of code configurations by randomly setting the values of each tunable parameter.

3 Experiment Design

3.1 Objectives

In this work we try to optimize parallel programs for three objectives and investigate the trade-offs between them: **execution time**, **resource usage**, and **energy consumption**.

Execution time is inherently an objective of interest, as providing results within the shortest possible time is desirable for most programs.

We furthermore include *resource usage*, denoted by $r(x) = x \cdot t_p(x)$ with x being the number of cores involved in executing the program and $t_p(x)$ denoting

Table 1. Code Characteristics

Code	Problem Size	Compu- tation	Memory	Tile Sizes	No. of Cores	CPU Freq. (Ghz)	Total No. of Configurations
mm	1200^2	$\mathcal{O}(N^3)$	$\mathcal{O}(N^2)$	$(1{-}600)^3$			$1.11 \cdot 10^{11}$
dsyrk	1200^2	$\mathcal{O}(N^3)$	$\mathcal{O}(N^2)$	$(1{-}600)^3$		1.2–2.7	$1.11 \cdot 10^{11}$
jacobi-2d	10000^2	$\mathcal{O}(N^2)$	$\mathcal{O}(N^2)$	$(1{-}5000)^2$	1–32	+ Turbo	$1.28 \cdot 10^{10}$
3d-stencil	600^3	$\mathcal{O}(N^3)$	$\mathcal{O}(N^3)$	$(1{-}300)^2$		Boost	$4.61 \cdot 10^7$
n-body	500000	$\mathcal{O}(N^2)$	$\mathcal{O}(N)$	$1{-}1000,$ $1{-}500000$			$2.56 \cdot 10^{11}$

the parallel execution time, as an objective to reflect computing costs. Most economic cost models that focus on computational resources, such as the ones used by cloud providers, are based on CPU hours [8]. Similarly, many academic computing centers base their accounting on CPU hours even if users are not charged. Hence, we believe that resource usage (reflecting computing costs – economic or otherwise) is an important optimization goal for parallel applications.

As a third objective of interest we consider *energy consumption*. Reducing it is of interest to both HPC center operators and users (as future cost models might include energy consumption due to its increasing workload dependence). To optimize also for energy, we require information about the energy consumption of parallel programs. The CPU is the largest contributor of the overall energy consumption of a non-accelerated HPC node that can also be influenced the most by the workload executed. Hence, we focus our energy optimization efforts on this component and rely on the Intel RAPL interface. It offers estimations with a resolution of 15.3 microjoules at a rate of 1 KHz for the entire CPU package. Recent related work showed RAPL to be accurate enough for purposes such as ours [9]. It should be noted that we use RAPL due to its wide availability, however the Insieme compiler can use any energy measurement/modeling system that meets the necessary accuracy and resolution requirements.

Let E_i be the energy consumption of a code executed on any number of cores of CPU socket $i \in P$ where P denotes the set of all sockets that have cores participating in the execution of a parallel program. Then $E_{total} = \sum_{i \in P} E_i$ denotes the overall energy consumption of the code. For brevity, we refer to execution time only as time and to energy consumption as energy throughout the rest of the paper.

3.2   Benchmarks and Target Platform

Our benchmarks consist of a matrix multiplication kernel (*mm*, using an ijk loop order), a BLAS-3 linear algebra kernel (*dsyrk*, computing $B = A * A^T + B$), two stencil codes (*jacobi-2d* and a generic 3x3x3 *3d-stencil*) and an implementation of an *n-body* simulation. Except for the *mm* and *dsyrk* codes, all of them exhibit distinct computation and memory complexities as listed in Table 1 and hence considerably different memory reuse and access patterns. Furthermore, although identically categorized in terms of complexity, the memory access patterns of *mm* and *dsyrk* are very different since the (on-the-fly) transposition of A eliminates the unaligned matrix access conducted within the *mm* code. Table 1 also lists the tunable parameters and their ranges for each code.

Table 2. Parameter Settings of the Optimizer

Algorithm	Parameters
RS-GDE3	$|C| = 30$, $CR = 0.5$, $F = 0.5$
Hierarchical Search	21 values per tiling parameter (2D tiling problems) 8 values per tiling parameter (3D tiling problems) 6 different numbers of cores 6 different frequencies

The target platform is a quad-socket shared-memory system equipped with Intel Xeon E5-4650 Sandy Bridge EP processors, each offering 8 cores clocked at 1.2–2.7 GHz (up to 3.3 GHz with Turbo Boost). Each core features private L1 and L2 caches of 64 and 256 KB each in addition to the CPU-wide shared L3 cache of 20 MB. The system provides 128 GB of main memory, uses a Linux operating system with a 3.5.0 kernel and our backend compiler is GCC 4.6.3. Hyper-Threading was not used in any of our experiments.

3.3   Configuration of the Optimizers

We have run the three optimizers available within the Insieme framework: RS-GDE3, hierarchical search, and random search. The parameters for RS-GDE3 and hierarchical search are described in the following and summarized in Table 2. In the case of RS-GDE3, we need to set the size of set C of code configurations (processed by RS-GDE3), the parameters CR and F required by the DE method, and the termination condition of the algorithm. These values have been determined during a preceding tuning phase , have an impact on the optimization results and may differ for different architectures. As termination condition, RS-GDE3 stops when it does not generate a better code configuration for m consecutive iterations (to be set by the user, 5 in our case).

For the hierarchical search only the sampling grid needs to be defined. It depends on the number of tunable parameters and defines the total number of configurations to be evaluated. We have configured the hierarchical search with a grid such that at least 15000 different configurations are examined. For generating the grid we only need to specify how many equidistant values we consider for every tunable parameter (note that for the number of cores, we only select powers of 2).

Finally, for the random search, we need to specify the number of configurations to be examined (also 15000 for this work) and the probability distribution to be used (uniform probability distribution).

3.4   Comparison Criteria

To systematically compare different search-based optimization strategies we use two different metrics: (1) the *efficiency* of each strategy, and (2) the *quality* of the configuration set obtained.

Efficiency. N denotes the total number of configurations evaluated and reflects the effort of the auto-tuner. Furthermore, time-to-solution and energy-to-solution respectively refer to the amount of time and energy spent by a search method to arrive at a final configuration set S.

Table 3. Performance Comparison of the Different Evaluated Algorithms

Code	Hierarchical Search				Random				RS-GDE3			
	N	$|S|$	$|S|'$	$V(S)$	$\overline{N}$	$\overline{|S|}$	$\overline{|S|}'$	$\overline{V(S)}$	$\overline{N}$	$\overline{|S|}$	$\overline{|S|}'$	$\overline{V(S)}$
mm	18432	18	2%	0.00	15000	4.4	0%	0.33	956.2	23.4	98%	0.48
dsyrk	18432	21	5%	0.00	15000	2.2	11%	0.17	1149.6	24.8	98%	0.31
jacobi-2d	15876	31	78%	0.69	15000	17.2	5%	0.55	1243.6	29.8	75%	0.76
3d-stencil	15876	30	22%	0.75	15000	24.8	60%	0.61	981.4	28.2	77%	0.76
n-body	15876	26	0%	0.50	15000	30	17%	0.70	1801.4	29.6	87%	0.77

Quality. Assessing the quality of a configuration which optimizes only one objective can be achieved by simply analyzing its value in that objective. However, comparing configurations of a multi-objective optimization problem is more complex since it requires comparing sets –the computed trade-offs– instead of single values. The *hypervolume* $V(S)$ of a set of non-dominated configurations S is a metric proposed in [10] that solves this problem. It consists of the normalized volume –an area in case of a dual-objective problem– containing configurations that are worse than those contained in S. In other words, for any configuration enclosed by that volume there is a configuration in S with better values for all the considered objectives. Obviously, the larger the hypervolume the better the quality of the configurations in S. The largest hypervolume value $(V(S) = 1)$ belongs to the utopia point (unattainable optimal configuration), i.e. the point consisting of the optimum value for each criterion.

We also propose another metric to evaluate the quality of S: the freedom in selection. The metric aims to quantify how many different high quality configurations a technique exposes to the user. Simply using $|S|$ to measure this does not completely address the problem: e.g. a configuration set obtained by strategy A could contain a lot of points dominated by the single point computed with strategy B. For this reason, we also employ $|S|'$, denoting the relative amount of configurations which are not dominated by the configurations computed by any other of the auto-tuners used. Hence, the higher the percentage, the higher the quality of the configurations contained within S.

Since random search and RS-GDE3 are stochastic algorithms, results of a single run are not sufficient for a meaningful comparison. In our evaluation we use the arithmetic means $\overline{N}$, $\overline{|S|}$, $\overline{|S|}'$ and $\overline{V(S)}$, derived over five runs, as directly comparable substitutes.

4   Experimental Results

4.1   RS-GDE3 Evaluation

Table 3 gives an overview of the performance of RS-GDE3 compared to hierarchical and random search with respect to the three considered metrics. It shows that RS-GDE3 needs only 5–12% of the number of evaluations compared to the hierarchical and random search strategies to provide configurations that dominate between 77% and 100% of the configurations offered by the other two. In addition, the configuration sets offered by RS-GDE3 span larger hypervolumes than the configuration sets provided by hierarchical and random search.

Beyond the already low number of evaluations compared to hierarchical and random search, RS-GDE3 requires even less time and energy for finding the final configuration set since it quickly converges on good solutions during the search. Hence, only 0.7–7.2% of the time and 1.2–8% of the energy are required by RS-GDE3 compared to hierarchical and random search. It should be noted that the optimization problem cannot be simplified by sequentially optimizing parameters (e.g. finding an optimal tile size first and then tuning the number of cores), as the optimal choices for these settings are inter-dependent [7].

4.2 Energy-Time Trade-Off as a Function of Resource Usage

Related work has already shown the existence of a trade-off between time and power consumption [5]. It is easily explained by different levels of CPU usage: faster configurations commonly use a higher number of cores, naturally demanding a higher power budget. Trade-offs between time and energy have been less studied in literature and are more difficult to obtain/explain since energy also depends on time. Thus, any optimization providing a trade-off between time and energy must in-/decrease power consumption disproportionally high compared to the de-/increase in time. Our experiments show that the trade-off between time and energy varies with the resource usage and can expose different behaviors. In the rest of this section, we analyze these results and describe which parameters/situations are responsible for such trade-offs.

For the sake of clarity, we summarize our results using a graphical representation as the one presented by Figure 2a. It shows the time, energy, and resource usage behavior of the set of code configurations computed by RS-GDE3 for different benchmark codes (in this case *mm*). These configurations (described in Table 4) are first ranked according to the number of sockets used; configurations using the same number of sockets are further sorted by increasing resource usage.

In all our evaluated problems (see Figure 2) we can observe two different parts: a part where time and energy are highly positively correlated, and a second one indicating a trade-off between the two. In all the cases, the first part always corresponds to configurations using a single CPU socket. As a consequence, we structure our discussion in two blocks: the *single-socket* and the *multi-socket* case. It should be noted that RS-GDE3 computed configurations that use up to four sockets for all problems except for *jacobi-2d*. This is explained by an average scaling behavior of the *jacobi-2d* code, which reaches its minimal execution time by using 10 cores instead of the maximum of 32. The remaining four codes scale well on our target hardware.

The Single-Socket Case. The results show that the configurations using only one socket can be further divided into a subset where reducing time also reduces the energy, and a subset where reducing time increases the energy. Without loss of generality we focus our discussion on the example of matrix multiplication (Figure 2a). When taking resource usage into consideration, we observe that time and energy are highly correlated when resource usage is low; however, this only holds until the resource usage reaches a critical point (configuration no. 5

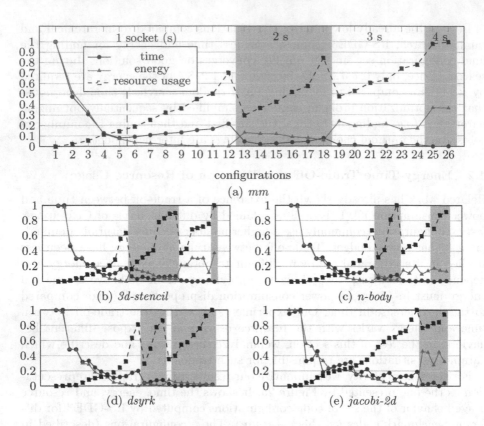

(a) *mm*

(b) *3d-stencil*

(c) *n-body*

(d) *dsyrk*

(e) *jacobi-2d*

Fig. 2. RS-GDE3 computed trade-offs among time, energy and resource usage

in Figure 2a), when both, energy and time, become conflicting objectives (i.e. energy can be further reduced from that point onwards while time increases).

A detailed analysis of the computed configurations (listed in Table 4) reveals that they use almost identical tile sizes. These values correspond to an optimal (local or global) tile size configuration found by the auto-tuner. Thus, once this optimal tile size configuration has been found, there are only two tunable parameters influencing the behavior of a code: the number of cores and the clock frequency.

Due to our sorting, the left-most configuration in Figure 2a is the one with the lowest resource usage (only one core in use, at the highest frequency). From this point, increasing the number of used cores reduces the time, and at the same time also the energy. The reason for this behavior can be explained with the power consumption breakdown of the CPU: using a single core requires most off-core entities of a socket to be active, such as the last level cache or the memory controller. Generally, increasing the number of used cores does not require providing additional power to activate those entities. Hence, doubling the number of used cores for example does not usually require double the power. Thus, as both time and power per used core decrease, the overall energy is also reduced. In fact, our experiments show that configurations no. 1–5 in Figure 2a, where time and

Table 4. Details of all *mm* configurations depicted in Figure 2a

Conf. No.	1	2	3	4	5	6	7	8	9	10	11	12	13
Tile Size A	37	30	24	31	30	30	30	30	30	30	30	30	21
Tile Size B	248	248	248	248	236	248	248	248	248	248	248	248	248
Tile Size C	6	6	6	6	6	6	6	6	6	6	6	6	6
No. of Cores	1	2	3	6	8	8	8	8	8	8	8	8	12
CPU Freq. (GHz)	2.7	2.7	2.7	2.7	2.7	2.7	2.5	2.3	2.2	2.0	1.9	1.6	2.7

Conf. No.	14	15	16	17	18	19	20	21	22	23	24	25	26
Tile Size A	18	30	18	30	32	31	25	21	30	15	24	21	24
Tile Size B	248	248	248	248	248	248	248	248	248	248	248	248	248
Tile Size C	6	6	6	6	6	6	6	6	6	6	6	5	6
No. of Cores	16	16	16	16	16	19	20	23	23	24	24	32	32
CPU Freq. (GHz)	2.7	2.6	2.3	2.2	1.7	2.7	2.6	2.7	2.3	2.7	2.3	2.7	2.7

energy do not conflict, only differ in the number of used cores. Note that this holds only for scalable codes such as the ones used in our experiments. If a code does not scale sufficiently, parallelization may lead to a disproportionally low decrease in time compared to the increase in power, and the overall energy will increase as well. Since we target HPC codes, we assume scalability for the rest of the analysis. Our first observation can then be stated as follows: *1. Assuming scalable codes, parallelism is a way of reducing both time and energy when using a single socket computing system if the other parameters are kept invariable.*

The second way of modifying the behavior with regard to the left-most configuration is via frequency tuning. Lowering the frequency – despite possibly decreasing the energy – increases time. The results of RS-GDE3 show that frequency tuning leads to dominated configurations if it is applied before fully exploiting parallelism. The reason explaining this is very simple. For every other configuration, the optimizer finds a configuration with increased parallelism reducing the time and obtaining a higher energy reduction than by using lower frequencies. Our second observation can be stated then as: *2. In a single-socket scenario, parallelism allows for higher rates of energy reduction than frequency tuning and, in addition, reduces time.*

Once the maximum number of cores has been reached, the auto-tuner exploits frequency tuning. These configurations correspond to the second part of the graph, where energy and time are conflicting objectives. As follows from our previous discussion, decreasing the time is no longer possible since parallelism has been already exploited and all cores are working at their maximum frequencies. Decreasing the frequency will naturally increase the execution time but energy reductions can be achieved, caused by the cube root rule [11]: the power consumption of a CPU scales cubically as long as its voltage changes with the frequency in a correlated fashion; however, the performance of a code usually scales at most linearly with the CPU clock frequency. Hence, a trade-off between time and energy is formed and continues up to the energy-optimal frequency setting. This energy-optimal setting is workload-dependent and was found to be around 1.5 GHz on our target platform by our auto-tuner, as lower frequencies show an increase in energy (because the CPU voltage cannot be scaled down accordingly by the hardware). Thus, as lower frequencies would worsen all three objectives, such configurations are rejected by the optimizer. Our third observation in this case is: *3. When parallelism has been already exploited, energy can still be further reduced by the sake of slightly increasing time, via applying frequency tuning.*

The Multi-socket Case. Again, without loss of generality we focus on the results depicted by Figure 2a. According to the results illustrated in that graph, moving to a configuration using an increased number of sockets has been successfully exploited by the auto-tuner. In such situations, RS-GDE3 has always found a configuration which reduces the time compared to configurations using a lower number of cores (see for example the first configurations using two, three, or four sockets in Figure 2a). However, this jump to a higher number of sockets always comes with an increase in energy. Thus, our observation (1) in the previous section does not hold in the case of using multiple sockets due to the required energy to operate additional sockets. This fact allows us to state our fourth observation: *4. Multiple sockets can be exploited to decrease the execution time of an application but not to further reduce its energy.*

Our experiments also reveal that, when using more than one socket, the number of cores leading to optimal trade-off configurations does not gradually increase as in the single socket case, but almost instantly reaches the maximum number. This results in our fifth observation: *5. Optimal trade-off configurations using more than one socket span over the maximum number of available cores.*

We also observe that the energy can be reduced by the sake of increasing the time. This situation corresponds to observation (3), where the auto-tuner reduced the frequency for energy savings. Therefore, that observation also applies to the case of configurations involving several sockets at a full utilization level.

In addition to the results presented so far, we investigated whether Turbo Boost might have any effect on our observations. Our experiments showed that, while Turbo Boost allows RS-GDE3 to generate additional solutions (with lower execution time and higher energy compared to not using Turbo Boost, therefore extending the solution set in one direction), all our observations are valid whether Turbo Boost is enabled or disabled.

4.3   Comparison of RS-GDE3 with NSGA-II

We have shown the potential of our RS-GDE3 method for three-objective auto-tuning compared to a hierarchical and a random search. The aim of this section is to empirically evaluate RS-GDE3 when compared to other multi-objective optimizers that have been adjusted to deal with three objectives. Nevertheless, it should be noted that without such modification, none of them can be used for auto-tuning with three conflicting objectives. To that end, we chose NSGA-II [12], the most popular algorithm for multi-objective optimization. For a fair comparison, we configured NSGA-II to evaluate the same number of configurations as RS-GDE3. Table 5 lists the results of this comparison for each of our benchmark codes. It shows that the Pareto sets obtained by RS-GDE3 span larger hypervolumes than the ones achieved by NSGA-II, hence providing better solutions. Furthermore, RS-GDE3 offers at least the same number of solutions as NSGA-II. Thus, overall, RS-GDE3 outperforms NSGA-II.

Table 5. Performance Comparison of RS-GDE3 with NSGA-II

Code	RS-GDE3 $|S|$	$V(S)$	NSGA-II $|S|$	$V(S)$
mm	17	0.65	17	0.64
dsyrk	20	0.93	8	0.78
jacobi-2d	30	0.83	30	0.74
3d-stencil	25	0.93	20	0.87
n-body	30	0.88	30	0.82

5 Related Work

There is a wide range of related work in the field of auto-tuning. One possible approach is machine learning (ML), however it has never been used in a truly multi-objective fashion. Search-based methods as used in Active Harmony [1] pose an alternative to ML. They have been successfully applied for computing the whole set of Pareto efficient solutions for up to two criteria, (e.g. execution time and efficiency [7] or execution time and compilation time [4]).

The recent concern for power and energy consumption is reflected in the growing amount work applying auto-tuning to optimize them. Whether they consider power or energy, in addition to execution time, most of them fail to capture the full trade-off and only compute a single solution. Some works use models for power/energy and execution time and apply dynamic programming for optimization [2], while others obtain real power measurements [3]. Similar efforts include exploiting slack time for example in OpenMP [6]. However, hardly any of these approaches compute the full Pareto set of solutions. Reducing this trade-off to a predefined number of solutions may limit the freedom of selecting a solution and render detailed trade-off analyses impossible. To the best of our knowledge, [13, 14] are two of the few works investigating that trade-off.

To the best of our knowledge, this is the first application of an auto-tuner to optimize three objectives. We also provide a detailed analysis of the identified trade-offs. While present in several related works, they do not directly deal with optimization or auto-tuning. They rather analyze trade-offs for changing hardware or software configurations. Predominantly using manually preselected solutions, instead of automatically obtained ones, many investigate DVFS or DCT [15], while some evaluate application model changes [16].

6 Conclusion

In this work, we have shown the application of a multi-objective auto-tuner which optimizes for three conflicting criteria: execution time, resource usage and energy consumption. We compared RS-GDE3 with a hierarchical and a random search and showed that it requires at least 93% less time and 92% less energy to obtain solutions of equal or higher quality in a benchmark composed of five representative codes. A comparison to a modified state-of-the-art optimizer, NSGA-II, shows that RS-GDE3 offers solutions of higher quality. We identified the complex relationships between the three objectives and the effect of our tunable parameters on them. Our results have been outlined with clear observations to be used to guide the development of auto-tuners and code optimization.

Acknowledgements. This research has been partially funded by the Austrian Research Promotion Agency under contract 834307 (AutoCore) and by the FWF Austrian Science Fund under contracts I01079 (GEMSCLAIM) and W 1227-N16 (DK-plus CIM).

References

[1] Tapus, C., Chung, I., Hollingsworth, J.: Active harmony: Towards automated performance tuning. In: IEEE 2002 Conference on Supercomputing (2002)

[2] Li, D., de Supinski, B.R., Schulz, M., et al.: Strategies for energy-efficient resource management of hybrid programming models. IEEE Transactions on Parallel and Distributed Systems 24(1), 144–157 (2013)

[3] Tiwari, A., Laurenzano, M.A., Carrington, L., Snavely, A.: Auto-tuning for energy usage in scientific applications. In: Alexander, M., et al. (eds.) Euro-Par 2011 Workshops. Part II. LNCS, vol. 7156, pp. 178–187. Springer, Heidelberg (2012)

[4] Hoste, K., Eeckhout, L.: Cole: Compiler optimization level exploration. In: Proc. of the 6th Intl. Symposium on Code Generation and Optimization. ACM (2008)

[5] Rahman, S., Guo, J., Bhat, A., et al.: Studying the impact of application-level optimizations on the power consumption of multi-core architectures. In: Proc. of the 9th Conference on Computing Frontiers. ACM (2012)

[6] Dong, Y., Chen, J., Yang, X.: et al.: Energy-oriented openmp parallel loop scheduling. In: International Symposium on Parallel and Distributed Processing with Applications, ISPA 2008. IEEE (2008)

[7] Jordan, H., Thoman, P., Durillo, J., et al.: A multi-objective auto-tuning framework for parallel codes. In: IEEE 2012 Conference on Supercomputing (2012)

[8] Fox, A., Griffith, R.: Joseph, et al.: Above the clouds: A berkeley view of cloud computing. Dept. Electrical Eng. and Comput. Sciences, University of California, Berkeley, Rep. UCB/EECS 28 (2009)

[9] Hähnel, M., Döbel, B., Völp, M., et al.: Measuring energy consumption for short code paths using RAPL. SIGMETRICS Perform. Eval. Rev. 40(3) (January 2012)

[10] Zitzler, E., Thiele, L.: Multiobjective evolutionary algorithms: A comparative case study and the strength pareto approach. IEEE Transactions on Evolutionary Computation 3(4) (1999)

[11] Flynn, M., Hung, P., Rudd, K.: Deep submicron microprocessor design issues. IEEE Micro, 19(4) (1999)

[12] Deb, K., Pratap, A., Agarwal, S., Meyarivan, T.: A fast and elitist multiobjective genetic algorithm: Nsga-ii. IEEE Transactions on Evolutionary Computation 6(2), 182–197 (2002)

[13] Freeh, V., Lowenthal, D.: Using multiple energy gears in mpi programs on a power-scalable cluster. In: Proc. of the 10th ACM SIGPLAN PPoPP. ACM (2005)

[14] Balaprakash, P., Tiwari, A., Wild, S.: Multi-objective optimization of hpc kernels for performance, power, and energy. In: 4th International Workshop on Performance Modeling, Benchmarking, and Simulation of HPC Systems, PMBS 2012 (2013)

[15] Freeh, V., Lowenthal, D., Pan, F., et al.: Analyzing the energy-time trade-off in high-performance computing applications. IEEE Transactions on Parallel and Distributed Systems, 18(6) (2007)

[16] Lively: C., Wu, X., Taylor, V., et al.: Energy and performance characteristics of different parallel implementations of scientific applications on multicore systems. International Journal of High Performance Computing Applications 25(3) (2011)

Performance Prediction and Evaluation of Parallel Applications in KVM, Xen, and VMware

Cheol-Ho Hong[1], Beom-Joon Kim[2], Young-Pil Kim[1],
Hyunchan Park[1], and Chuck Yoo[1]

[1] Korea University, Seoul, South Korea
[2] LG Electronics, Seoul, South Korea

Abstract. Cloud computing platforms are considerably attractive for
parallel applications that perform large-scale, computationally intensive
tasks. These platforms can provide elastic computing resources to the
parallel software owing to system virtualization technology. Almost every cloud service provider operates on a pay-per-use basis, and therefore,
it is important to estimate the performance of parallel applications before
deploying them. However, a comprehensive study that can predict the
performance of parallel applications remains unexplored and is still a research topic. In this paper, we provide a theoretical performance model
that can predict the performance of parallel applications in different
virtual machine scheduling policies and evaluate the model in representative hypervisors including KVM, Xen, and VMware. Through this
analysis and evaluation, we show that our performance prediction model
is accurate and reliable.

1 Introduction

Cloud computing is an attractive approach to enable research scientists to utilize
nearly limitless computation resources in a reliable and flexible manner. By using cloud services, research scientists can deploy parallel applications to perform
large-scale, computationally intensive tasks reliably without worrying about the
configuration or the arrangement of the hardware platforms for the deployment
[17]. Moreover, owing to the elastic characteristic of cloud computing, they can
flexibly adjust the capacity of the computing resources according to the requirements of each parallel application. As a result, the use of cloud computing for
parallel applications is currently increasing at a fast rate [3].

Virtualization is the main technology of cloud computing. Whether cloud
vendors provide IaaS (Infrastructure as a Service), PaaS (Platform as a Service),
or SaaS (Service as a Service) for their customers, every stack of those services
has a virtualization layer on top of the lower physical layers. Virtualization
offers elastic and flexible virtual computing environments that are essential for
cloud computing by providing each user the illusion of possessing an OS on
a real hardware platform. In virtualization software, a hypervisor virtualizes all

F. Silva et al. (Eds.): Euro-Par 2014, LNCS 8632, pp. 99–110, 2014.

hardware resources such as the CPU, memory, and I/O devices of a real physical machine, providing each of the virtualized resources to a virtual machine (VM). Recent popular hypervisor titles for cloud computing include KVM [8], Xen [2], and VMware ESXi [6].

Because almost every cloud service provider operates on a pay-per-use basis, the question of whether a hypervisor can run parallel applications with acceptable performance at lower cost has become an important issue. In virtualization, the main factor that decides the performance of parallel applications is the CPU scheduler of each hypervisor [16][11]. The scheduler multiplexes all virtual CPUs (VCPUs) in a system according to its particular policy. Because of this additional scheduling layer, it is difficult to estimate the performance of parallel applications in virtualization before deploying them, even though performance in the native environment is already known.

In this paper, we provide a comprehensive performance model that can predict the performance of parallel applications in different scheduling policies and evaluate the model in the representative hypervisors. The main contributions of this paper related to previous studies are as follows:

- We provide theoretical performance modeling and prediction for parallel applications in virtualization. Previous research studies [17][12][13] only address virtualization overheads based on experiments. To the best of our knowledge, no other research studies have suggested practical performance models yet.
- We present the evaluation results of the performance model on the representative hypervisors. Throughout the evaluation, we show that our performance prediction model is accurate and reliable to such an extent as to predict the performance of parallel applications in virtualization before directly deploying them.

The remainder of this paper is structured as follows: In Section 2, we explain the background of VM scheduling policies. In Section 3, we provide the performance prediction model. Section 4 shows the performance evaluation results. Section 5 explains related work. Finally, we present our conclusions in Section 6.

2   Background

2.1   Scheduling Policy

One of the main tasks of a VM scheduler is to choose which virtual CPU should be assigned to a physical core. A VM scheduler schedules all VCPUs in a system according to its policy that has purposes such as improving responsiveness, throughput, and utilization.

KVM. The Completely Fair Scheduler (CFS) [8] was introduced as the Linux CPU scheduler from the Linux kernel 2.6.23. The goal of the CFS is to give each VCPU a fair amount of CPU time by maintaining a balance between them. For this purpose, the CFS scheduler tracks the virtual runtime that is the amount of CPU time given to each VCPU at a certain point. In scheduling VCPUs, the CFS selects VCPUs with smaller virtual runtimes-that means some VCPUs have not received sufficient CPU time compared to other VCPUs-thus maintaining the balance. In addition to this basic policy, it considers I/O-intensive VCPUs by giving them a comparable share of CPU time when they request the CPU.

Xen. In recent versions of Xen, the credit scheduler [2], which is a proportional fair-share CPU scheduler, is used by default. The credit scheduler schedules domains fairly based on the credit amount that is determined by the weight each domain receives. Credit refers to CPU time or CPU bandwidth for which each domain can run. Three VCPU priorities are defined in the current Xen implementation: UNDER (value of -1), OVER (-2), and BOOST (0). The priority of the VCPU is determined by the remaining credit amount of the VCPU when the global account thread is running. If the credit amount of the VCPU is positive, the priority of the VCPU is UNDER. Conversely, if the credit amount is negative, the priority of the VCPU becomes OVER. BOOST priority is introduced to improve I/O performance of domains in terms of both bandwidth and latency.

VMware. The relaxed coscheduler [15] in VMware is based on the proportional-share-based algorithm in which each VM has resource specifications such as shares, reservation, and limit. The scheduler maintains the consumed CPU resource of each VM, and makes scheduling decisions based on the recorded data. If a VM consumes less CPU than allowed, the VM is temporarily assigned a higher priority than other VMs, and it is chosen to run next. When a VM is selected to run, the ESXi scheduler uses a co-scheduling policy, also known as gang scheduling, which executes all VCPUs of a single VM at the same time. This scheduling policy is beneficial to parallel applications because threads that frequently attempt to synchronize with each other can decrease their waiting time by running the VCPUs concurrently.

3   Performance Prediction

In this section, we theoretically show how the execution time of a parallel program is determined in the virtualization environments. For simplicity, we make some assumptions needed to build our VM scheduling model and policy. First, we assume that the number of threads in a parallel application does not exceed the number of VCPUs in the VM. This assumption is rational because CPU-intensive applications commonly run using a number of threads equal to or less than the number of cores [10]. Second, each thread is fixed to a VCPU to avoid the cost of thread migration in a guest OS. Third, each parallel thread is assumed to be blocked rather than spin when the thread has to wait for other threads during synchronization. In virtualization, this wait policy is generally configured in order to prevent superfluous CPU spinning.

3.1   VM Scheduling Model and Policy

To predict the performance of parallel programs in virtualization, we formalize the VM scheduling model and policy. $P = \{P_1, P_2, ..., P_{|P|}\}$ represents physical CPUs, where $|P|$ is the number of physical CPUs in the system. $V = \{V_1, V_2, ..., V_{|V|}\}$ indicates VMs running on the physical CPUs, where $|V|$ is the number of VMs in the system. The weight of VM V_i is represented by $\omega(V_i)$, which is a relative proportion of CPU consumption. Therefore, we have $\sum_{i=1}^{|V|} \omega(V_i) = 1$. $C(V_i) = \{v_{i1}, v_{i2}, ..., v_{i|C(V_i)|}\}$ indicates VCPUs running on VM V_i, and the number of VCPUs is $|C(V_i)|$.

We need to define the fair amount of received CPU by VCPU v_{ij} from time 0 to t, which we call $F(t, i, j)$. $F(t, i, j)$ is determined by the number of processors, the weight proportion of the VM, and the number of VCPUs in the VM. Reflecting these factors, we define $F(t, i, j)$ as

$$F(t, i, j) = \frac{|P| \times \omega(V_i)}{|C(V_i)|} \times t \tag{1}$$

Then, we define the amount of CPU time that a VCPU actually uses in the scheduling interval $[t_1, t_2)$ as $R(t_1, i, j)$. Then, we can derive the next scheduling time t_2 as follows. To guarantee fairness in sharing CPU time, the hypervisor scheduler should meet the following condition: $F(t_2, i, j) = F(t_1, i, j) + R(t_1, i, j)$. Therefore, using Equation (1), we have $\frac{|P| \times \omega(V_i)}{|C(V_i)|} \times t_2 = \frac{|P| \times \omega(V_i)}{|C(V_i)|} \times t_1 + R(t_1, i, j)$. Then, we obtain the following equation.

$$t_2 = t_1 + \frac{R(t_1, i, j) \times |C(V_i)|}{|P| \times \omega(V_i)} \tag{2}$$

3.2   Execution Time of a Single Phase

A parallel application distributes the total work into several parallel threads. Each thread then consists of multiple phases, each of which has one computation part and one subsequent synchronization part. Through the latter part, all computations in the same phase must be finished before the next phase begins. To obtain the execution time of a single phase in virtualization, we define the execution time of the computation part of VCPU v_{ij} during the mth phase as $compT(m, v_{ij})$ and the synchronization part as $syncT(m, v_{ij})$. Then, the execution time of the mth phase, $execP(m)$, is as follows: $execP(m) = compT(m, v_{ij}) + syncT(m, v_{ij})$.

compT. The value of the computation part itself may be longer than a time slot of the hypervisor. We define the length of the computation part of VCPU v_{ij} during the mth phase as $C(m, v_{ij})$. Then, we have $C(m, v_{ij}) = M_m \times S + Frac(m, v_{ij})$, where $M_m \geq 0$, S is the length of a time slot, and $Frac(m, v_{ij})$ is the remainder of the time. This computation part is executed using $(M_m + 1)$ time slots. Let us assume that this computation part starts at t_1 and the remaining part starts at t_p. According to Equation (2), the second time slot of this computation part has to start at the following point: $t_2 = t_1 + \frac{S \times |C(V_i)|}{|P| \times \omega(V_i)}$. Similarly, $t_3 = t_2 + \frac{S \times |C(V_i)|}{|P| \times \omega(V_i)} = t_1 + (2 \times \frac{S \times |C(V_i)|}{|P| \times \omega(V_i)})$. The (M_m+1)th time slot starts at t_p. Then, it should have the following value: $t_p = t_1 + (M_m \times \frac{S \times |C(V_i)|}{|P| \times \omega(V_i)})$. Then, the execution time of the computation part of the mth phase, $compT(m, v_{ij})$, is as follows: $compT(m, v_{ij}) = t_p + Frac(m, v_{ij}) - t_1$. Then, we obtain the following equation:

$$compT(m, v_{ij}) = (M_m \times \frac{S \times |C(V_i)|}{|P| \times \omega(V_i)}) + Frac(m, v_{ij}) \tag{3}$$

syncT. The synchronization part follows the computation part, and the main purpose of this part is to wait for other threads to finish their computation parts while being blocked. Let us assume that the former computation part starts at t_1, and the next computation part starts at t_2. To guarantee fairness in sharing CPU time, the hypervisor should then execute the next part at the following point according to Equation (2): $t_2 = t_1 + \frac{Frac(m, v_{ij}) \times |C(V_i)|}{|P| \times \omega(V_i)}$, where $Frac(m, v_{ij})$ is the remainder of $C(m, v_{ij})$ (see subsection $compT$). Then, the execution time of the synchronization part of the mth phase, $sync\_preT(m, v_{ij})$, is as follows: $sync\_preT(m, v_{ij}) = t_2 - t_1 - Frac(m, v_{ij})$. Then, we obtain the following equation: $sync\_preT(m, v_{ij}) = \frac{Frac(m, v_{ij}) \times |C(V_i)|}{|P| \times \omega(V_i)} - Frac(m, v_{ij})$.

This value is derived on the assumption that the hypervisor ideally maintains fairness between VMs. However, in our previous research [7], we showed that this value can be significantly larger in real hypervisors. The credit scheduler and the CFS adopt an asynchronous scheduling policy; therefore, they are not synchronization-aware. The problem, then, is that those VCPUs required to participate in each synchronization phase are not guaranteed to be scheduled within the t_2 value. Consequently, the execution time of the synchronization part is increased, and this situation degrades the performance of parallel applications. Conversely, when a coscheduling policy is selected, it makes all VCPUs in a VM run on physical CPUs simultaneously. Therefore, this scheduling method can make a synchronization environment similar to that of a non-virtualized OS, therefore mitigating the increase in synchronization time.

To reflect the characteristic of each scheduling policy, we introduce a proportional constant, H. The H value can be obtained by conducting experiments in each virtualization environment. We repeatedly run our micro benchmark programs with a medium computation size (the details are provided in Section 4.1) and measure the average synchronization time. Then, we compare the measured value of each program with the calculated $sync\_preT(m, v_{ij})$ value to produce the H value. We could check that the different programs produce similar H values in the same hypervisor. We determined that the values are 1.7 in KVM, 1.15 in Xen, and 0.7 in VMware. We multiply H by the intermediate value of the synchronization part. Then, we obtain the following equation:

$$syncT(m, v_{ij}) = H \times Frac(m, v_{ij}) \times (\frac{|C(V_i)|}{|P| \times \omega(V_i)} - 1) \tag{4}$$

execP. Because we have $execP(m) = compT(m, v_{ij}) + syncT(m, v_{ij})$, we obtain the following equation by adding Equations (3) and (4).

$$execP(m) = M_m \times \frac{S \times |C(V_i)|}{|P| \times \omega(V_i)} + Frac(m, v_{ij}) \times (1 + H \times (\frac{|C(V_i)|}{|P| \times \omega(V_i)} - 1)) \quad (5)$$

3.3 Execution Time of a Parallel Program

Because a parallel application consists of multiple phases, the completion time of a parallel application is the sum of the execution times of each phase in the software. When the parallel application has $|J|$ phases, the total completion time, *completionT*, is obtained using Equation (5) as follows.

$$
\begin{aligned}
completionT &= \sum_{m=1}^{|J|} execP(m) \\
&= \sum_{m=1}^{|J|} \{M_m \times \frac{S \times |C(V_i)|}{|P| \times \omega(V_i)} + Frac(m, v_{ij}) \times (1 + H \times (\frac{|C(V_i)|}{|P| \times \omega(V_i)} - 1))\}
\end{aligned}
\quad (6)
$$

$|C(V_i)|$, $|P|$, $\omega(V_i)$, S, and H are predetermined in the virtualization environment. The value of M_m and $Frac(m, v_{ij})$ can be obtained from $C(m, v_{ij})$, which is the length of the computation part of VCPU v_{ij} during the mth phase, because $C(m, v_{ij}) = M_m \times S + Frac(m, v_{ij})$. The $C(m, v_{ij})$ value can be obtained in the non-virtualized environment manually by calculating the total number of instruction cycles or automatically by using profiling tools that utilize Profiler for OpenMP (POMP) and Opari [9]. Therefore, we can predict the performance of parallel applications in virtualization without directly deploying them.

4   Performance Evaluation

4.1   Experimental Setup and Method

For all experiments in this paper, we used an Intel Xeon E5-2620 hexa-core platform that has six cores running at 2.0 GHz with 15 MB of L3 cache and 16 GB of main memory. To realize exact one-to-one mapping between physical cores and VCPUs, the hyper-threading technology is turned off. The system is hosted by KVM 1.4.2, Xen 4.1.3, and VMware ESXi 5.0 on separate hard disk drives. We use all guest OSs as Linux with the kernel version 2.6.32. In the experiments, with regard to Xen, we did not use domain0, which is an administrator VM and is responsible for processing I/O requests, leaving it mainly in the idle state. We let the number of VCPUs of all VMs equal to the number of physical CPUs (six) in order to make each group of VCPUs exploit the underlying physical CPUs efficiently and thoroughly.

In all Linux VMs, we use GCC 4.7.1, which supports the version 3.1 of the OpenMP specification, and we set the waiting policy of OpenMP as *PASSIVE* that blocks VCPUs when the synchronization condition is not met in order to prevent superfluous CPU spinning at the user-level. To prevent kernel-level lock-holder preemption (LHP) [14], we applied a Linux patch for paravirtualization VMs [4] in Xen, and activated Intel Pause Loop Exiting (PLE), which is a hardware-based feature, in KVM and VMware.

To evaluate the execution time prediction of a single phase as provided in Equation (5), we develop a new micro benchmark program that is intended to measure the overhead of a single phase that is composed of one computation part and one subsequent synchronization part. The program can receive the computation size of a thread as an input parameter so that we can make parallel programs of any size. We create 4 individual child benchmark programs with computation sizes of a single phase as approximately 3,500 (small), 15,000 (medium), 35,000 (large), and 150,000 (very large) kilo-cycles per thread (in the latest x86 architecture).

To evaluate the execution time prediction of a parallel program, provided in Equation (6), we use NAS Parallel Benchmarks (NPB) [1] that are programs used to evaluate the performance of parallel supercomputers. In this research, we use NPB version 3.2.1 for the OpenMP programming model and set the problem size to A. The benchmark programs consist of *CG, EP, FT, IS, MG, BT, LU, LU-HP,* and *SP*.

4.2   Prediction for a Single Phase

In this section, we show whether the performance prediction model provided in Section 3.2 is accurate and reliable. For the experiment, a target VM executing each child benchmark program was individually run on each hypervisor. The target VM had 6 VCPUs with 6 threads per our benchmark program that was based on the assumption explained in Section 3. To adjust the target VM weight, we deployed multiple CPU-bound VMs running our single-threaded CPU-intensive program that simulates background workloads. Because we configured the number of VCPUs in all VMs as 6, we can set the weight of the target VM to 100%, 50%, 33%, 25%, 20%, and 17% by launching each background VM one by one. For example, to set the weight of the target VM to 20%, we deploy the target VM and 4 background VMs. For accuracy, we run our micro benchmark program repeatedly more than 20,000 times in each hypervisor and then calculate the average execution time of the computation and synchronization part separately during the run of a single VCPU.

To predict the performance of each program, we run each benchmark program in the native Linux environment, and produce values of $C(m, v_{ij})$ which is the length of the computation part of VCPU v_{ij}. Then, the M_m and $Frac(m, v_{ij})$ values can be obtained as shown in Table 1, given that the time slice of KVM

Table 1. Parameters required to predict the performance of a single phase. The unit of time is ms.

Hypervisor	Benchmark	$C(m,v_{ij})$	M_m	S	$Frac(m,v_{ij})$	H	$|C(V_i)|$	$|P|$
KVM	3,500K	1.67	0	6	1.70	1.7	6	6
	15,000K	8.36	1	6	2.40	1.7	6	6
	35,000K	16.72	2	6	4.70	1.7	6	6
	150,000K	83.59	13	6	5.60	1.7	6	6
Xen	3,500K	1.67	0	30	1.70	1.15	6	6
	15,000K	8.36	0	30	8.40	1.15	6	6
	35,000K	16.72	0	30	16.70	1.15	6	6
	150,000K	83.59	2	30	23.60	1.15	6	6
VMware	3,500K	1.67	0	30	1.70	0.7	6	6
	15,000K	8.36	0	30	8.40	0.7	6	6
	35,000K	16.72	0	30	16.70	0.7	6	6
	150,000K	83.59	2	30	23.60	0.7	6	6

is 6 ms, that of Xen is 30 ms, and that of VMware is 30 ms. Other values such as H, $|C(V_i)|$, and $|P|$ are also provided in the table. The H value is obtained by the experiments as explained in Section 3.2. Then we use Equation (5) to predict the time of each program.

The execution times of a single phase for KVM, Xen, and VMware, for which the weight was changed from 100% to 17%, are shown in Figure 1. We also provide the measured synchronization ($SyncT$) and computation ($CompT$) time which comprise the execution time, in order to help the analysis of the execution overhead. The ratio of the difference between the measured and predicted time to the measured time, defined as $\frac{predicted\_time - measured\_time}{measured\_time}$, follows each graph. As the graphs show, our prediction model can estimate the execution time of a single phase quite accurately in Xen and VMware, and approximately in KVM. In most cases, the value of the ratio is within 19% in KVM (19% in average), 15% (9% in average) in Xen, and 6% (4% in average) in VMware.

The KVM result shows that the scheduler imposes an additional overhead when the weight is 50% in all benchmark programs. It seems that the CFS cannot properly deal with the situation in which the workloads are apparently asymmetric. The result also shows that our prediction model is not accurate for the small program (3,500 K). This is because the actual synchronization time was shorter than the prediction, and we are investigating the exact reason for this. In Xen, our prediction model underestimates the execution time of the small program because the actual synchronization time was longer than expected. This situation seems to be related to the minimum preemption time of Xen (2 ms). The small program must be repeatedly blocked and unblocked during a relatively short time. However, Xen prevents VCPUs from preemption during the first 2 ms in order to prohibit starvation. When the small program cannot preempt the current VCPU, this seems to cause extra synchronization overhead. The VMware result shows that the scheduler can solidly process parallel applications without fluctuation as it adopts the coscheduling policy for synchronization.

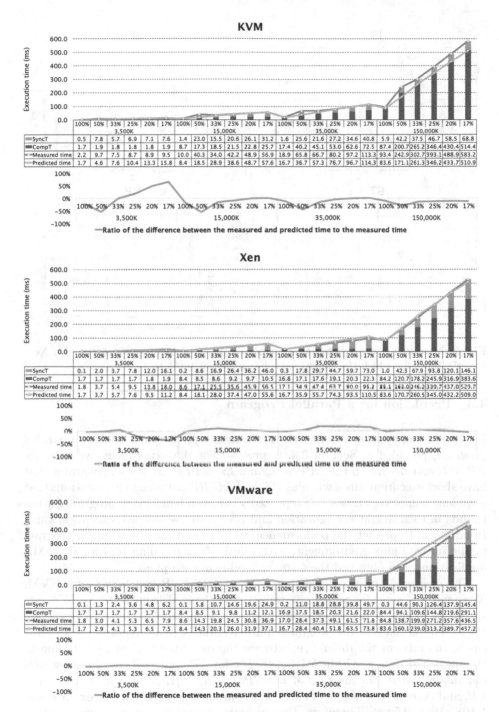

Fig. 1. Execution time of a single phase for KVM, Xen, and VMware, for which the weight was changed from 100% to 17%, and the ratio of the difference between the measured and predicted time to the measured time

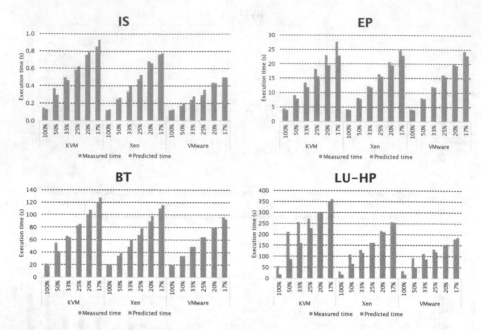

Fig. 2. Measured and predicted time values of the NPB benchmarks for KVM, Xen, and VMware, for which the weight was changed from 100% to 17%

4.3 Prediction for a Parallel Program

In this section, we show whether the performance prediction model for a parallel program, provided in Section 3.3, is precise. For the experiment, we used *IS*, *EP*, *BT*, and *LU-HP* in the NPB program. *IS* and *EP* are kernel programs that have short execution times whereas *BT* and *LU-HP* are pseudo applications that have long completion times. We repeatedly ran each benchmark program for ten rounds in each weight configuration and produced the average execution time. In addition, to predict the performance, we deployed each benchmark program in the native Linux environment, with ompP [5], a profiling tool for OpenMP applications, and obtained the $C(m, v_{ij})$ value of each phase.

The measured and predicted time values of the NPB benchmarks for KVM, Xen, and VMware, for which the weight was changed from 100% to 17%, are shown in Figure 2. For *IS*, *EP*, and *BT*, our prediction model could estimate the execution times of the programs quite accurately in all hypervisors. In most cases, the ratio of the difference between the measured and predicted time to the measured time is within 5% for *IS*, 8% for *EP*, and 13% for *BT*. However, our model suffered in the case of *LU-HP*. *LU-HP* is the hyperplane version of *LU*, and is composed of lots of small size computation parts (in our experiment, $1,108,416 \times 0.5$ms). Therefore, the program seemed to cause severe synchronization overheads across all hypervisors as explained in Section 4.2. When we changed the H value for the small size computation part to 6 in KVM, 4 in

Xen, and 2.9 in VMware, we could predict the execution times more correctly as depicted in Figure 2.

5 Related Work

There are several studies to resolve the synchronization problem of virtualization. Relaxed coscheduling [15] of VMware ESXi is a representative coscheduling algorithm for synchronization. Instead of forcing all VCPUs of a VM to be simultaneously scheduled, the scheduler enables the VCPUs to be scheduled within the *skew* value. As another coscheduling approach, Weng et al. [16] proposed hybrid scheduling in the Xen hypervisor. For only concurrent VMs, the scheduler determines to coschedule VCPUs; other VCPUs are scheduled asynchronously. The researchers also provided simple modeling for the performance of parallel applications. However, because the proposed model assumes that the size of the computation part is equal to a single time slice, it is inadequate for the real hypervisors.

There are several studies to explain the virtualization overhead of Xen. Xu et al. [17] revealed that the performance of Xen VMs could reach the performance in the native environment only when few synchronization operations are used, and the number of VCPUs in the VM does not exceed the number of physical CPUs. Tao et al. [12][13] quantified the performance deficit of OpenMP applications in Xen VMs . They showed that the inefficiency of the kernel blocking operation decreases the performance of some parallel applications in the virtual environment. However, these studies only show preliminary results, and therefore, they are insufficient to predict the performance of parallel applications in virtualization.

6 Conclusion

In this paper, we proposed a performance model that can predict the performance of parallel applications in various scheduling policies. First, we provided theoretical performance modeling and prediction for parallel applications in virtualization, Second, we showed the evaluation results of the performance model on the representative hypervisors. We hope that our research will contribute toward further studies on parallel computing performed in a virtual environment.

Acknowledgements. This work was supported by the National Research Foundation of Korea(NRF) grant funded by the Korea government(MEST) (No.2010-0029180) with KREONET.

References

1. Bailey, D., Barszcz, E., Barton, J., Browning, D., Carter, R., Dagum, L., Fatoohi, R., Frederickson, P., Lasinski, T., Schreiber, R., et al.: The nas parallel benchmarks summary and preliminary results. In: Proceedings of the 1991 ACM/IEEE Conference on Supercomputing 1991, pp. 158–165. IEEE (1991)

2. Barham, P., Dragovic, B., Fraser, K., Hand, S., Harris, T., Ho, A., Neugebauer, R., Pratt, I., Warfield, A.: Xen and the art of virtualization. In: ACM SIGOPS Operating Systems Review, vol. 37, pp. 164–177. ACM (2003)
3. Buyya, R., Yeo, C., Venugopal, S., Broberg, J., Brandic, I.: Cloud computing and emerging it platforms: Vision, hype, and reality for delivering computing as the 5th utility. Future Generation Computer Cystems 25(6), 599–616 (2009)
4. Friebel, T., Biemueller, S.: How to deal with lock holder preemption. Presentation at Xen Summit North America (2008)
5. Fürlinger, K., Gerndt, M.: ompp: A profiling tool for openmp. In: Mueller, M.S., Chapman, B.M., de Supinski, B.R., Malony, A.D., Voss, M. (eds.) IWOMP 2005/2006. LNCS, vol. 4315, pp. 15–23. Springer, Heidelberg (2008)
6. Haletky, E.: Vmware esx and esxi in the enterprise (2011)
7. Hong, C., Yoo, C.: Synchronization-aware virtual machine scheduling for parallel applications in xen. IEICE Transactions on Information and Systems 96(12), 2720–2723 (2013)
8. Kivity, A., Kamay, Y., Laor, D., Lublin, U., Liguori, A.: kvm: The linux virtual machine monitor. In: Proceedings of the Linux Symposium, vol. 1, pp. 225–230 (2007)
9. Mohr, B., Malony, A.D., Shende, S., Wolf, F.: Towards a performance tool interface for OpenMP: An approach based on directive rewriting. Forschungszentrum, Zentralinst. für Angewandte Mathematik (2001)
10. Nishitani, Y., Negishi, K., Ohta, H., Nunohiro, E.: Implementation and evaluation of openmp for hitachi sr8000. In: Valero, M., Joe, K., Kitsuregawa, M., Tanaka, H. (eds.) ISHPC 2000. LNCS, vol. 1940, pp. 391–402. Springer, Heidelberg (2000)
11. Sukwong, O., Kim, H.: Is co-scheduling too expensive for smp vms? In. In: Proceedings of the Sixth Conference on Computer Systems, pp. 257–272. ACM (2011)
12. Tao, J., Fürlinger, K., Marten, H.: Performance evaluation of openmp applications on virtualized multicore machines. In: Chapman, B.M., Gropp, W.D., Kumaran, K., Müller, M.S. (eds.) IWOMP 2011. LNCS, vol. 6665, pp. 138–150. Springer, Heidelberg (2011)
13. Tao, J., Fürlinger, K., Wang, L., Marten, H.: A performance study of virtual machines on multicore architectures. In: PDP, pp. 89–96 (2012)
14. Uhlig, V., LeVasseur, J., Skoglund, E., Dannowski, U.: Towards scalable multiprocessor virtual machines. In: Proceedings of the 3rd Virtual Machine Research and Technology Symposium, pp. 43–56 (2004)
15. VMWare. The cpu scheduler in vmware vsphere 5.1., https://www.vmware.com/files/pdf/techpaper/VMware-vSphere-CPU-Sched-Perf.pdf
16. Weng, C., Wang, Z., Li, M., Lu, X.: The hybrid scheduling framework for virtual machine systems. In: Proceedings of the 2009 ACM SIGPLAN/SIGOPS International Conference on Virtual Execution Environments, pp. 111–120. ACM (2009)
17. Xu, C., Bai, Y., Luo, C.: Performance evaluation of parallel programming in virtual machine environment. In: Sixth IFIP International Conference on Network and Parallel Computing, NPC 2009, pp. 140–147. IEEE (2009)

DReAM: Per-Task DRAM Energy Metering
in Multicore Systems

Qixiao Liu[1,2], Miquel Moreto[1,2], Jaume Abella[1],
Francisco J. Cazorla[1,2,3], and Mateo Valero[1,2]

[1] Barcelona Supercomputing Center, Barcelona, Spain
[2] Universitat Politecnica de Catalunya, Barcelona, Spain
[3] Spanish National Research Council (IIIA-CSIC), Barcelona, Spain

Abstract. Interaction across applications in DRAM memory impacts
its energy consumption. This paper makes the case for accurate per-
task DRAM energy metering in multicores, which opens new paths to
energy/performance optimizations, such as per-task energy-aware task
scheduling and energy-aware billing in datacenters. In particular, the
contributions of this paper are (i) an ideal per-task energy metering
model for DRAM memories; (ii) DReAM, an accurate, yet low cost, implementation of the ideal model (less than 5% accuracy error when 16 tasks
share memory); and (iii) a comparison with standard methods (even distribution and access-count based) proving that DReAM is more accurate
than these other methods.

1 Introduction

Energy demand and cost of computing systems have grown during the last years,
and the trend is expected to hold in the coming future [1]. Conversely, computing
hardware-related costs (e.g., servers) have remained roughly constant or even decreased in datacenters, desktops and laptops. This leads to scenarios where energy
costs are as significant as hardware-related costs. For instance, energy already accounts for 20% of the total cost of ownership in a large-scale computing facility [2].
This cost virtually doubles if we also include the cost of the cooling infrastructure
needed to dissipate the temperature induced by such a high energy consumption.
Similarly, laptops and desktops may use in the order of 50-200 Watts depending on
the computing power and peripherals attached. Assuming a cost of 0.11€/kWh and
3 years of non-stop operation (so 26,280 hours), a computer dissipating 120 Watts
sustainedly would reach an energy cost of 350€. This cost is in the same order of magnitude as the computer itself and it is expected to grow since energy cost is expected
to grow [1]. Therefore, managing energy consumption is of paramount importance.

As processor design moves towards multi-threaded and many-core processors,
in which an increasing number of different applications run simultaneously in
the same processor, providing per-task energy metering becomes critical. Metering the energy consumed by each task accurately would provide the following benefits. First, the amount of hardware resources allocated to a given task
(e.g., cores, memory space) impact both its execution time and energy consumption. If per-task energy can be accurately estimated, one may optimize, not only

F. Silva et al. (Eds.): Euro-Par 2014, LNCS 8632, pp. 111–123, 2014.

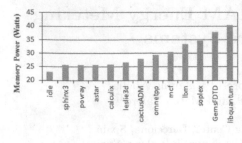

Fig. 1. Average memory power of a set of SPEC CPU 2006 benchmarks running alone on an Intel Sandy Bridge server, with 8 cores and a 64GB DDR3 memory running at 1.6GHz. Memory power is obtained using the Running Average Power Limit (RAPL) interfaces [6] and total system power with a *FitPC* external multimeter. We correlate total power data with the data collected from the hardware energy counters using time stamps. Representative benchmarks were selected based on previous characterization studies [7].

each task's performance, but its energy consumption or a combined energy-delay metric.Second, per-task energy metering can be used by the operating system (OS) to schedule tasks better so that energy consumption is minimized while still completing tasks when needed. And third, traditionally, datacenters charge users based on the resources they are allocated. The increasing fraction of energy-related costs in datacenters and the need for more accurate billing pushes for new billing approaches based on the actual energy consumption of each task rather than on the nominal resources allocated or on simply distributing energy evenly among running applications [3].

In that respect, despite memory power keeps increasing, reaching 30-50W in high-performance computers [4], there is a lack of understanding of per-task energy consumption in memory. To elaborate on the need of accurate per-task memory energy metering, we measured the power dissipation of different SPEC CPU 2006 benchmarks on an Intel Sandy Bridge server, see Figure 1. In this experiment memory represents between 25% and 34% of the total system power and it is comparable to the entire processor socket power. Further, different tasks incur different power consumption: e.g., 25.7W (`482.sphinx3`) versus 40.4W (`462.libquantum`). However, while per-task energy metering solutions exist for processors [5], to the best of our knowledge, no mechanism exists to accurately measure the per-task memory energy consumption in multicore systems.

We propose, for the first time, an ideal method and an efficient implementation of such method to fairly measure the energy consumed in DRAM memories when concurrently running several tasks. Our approach relies on tracking both the activity incurred by running tasks and the memory state they induce.

Overall, the contributions of this work are as follows:

- An ideal per-task energy metering model for DRAM memories, as needed for performance/energy optimization, task scheduling and billing in multicore systems. This is the reference model against which per-task energy metering mechanisms in DRAM memories can be compared to.
- DReAM, an accurate, yet low cost, implementation of the ideal model. DReAM is within 5% average error with respect to the ideal model at the expense of less than 0.1% power and area overhead in the processor.
- A comparison of DReAM with other energy metering approaches proving that DReAM is far more accurate than those other approaches.

2   Background and Related Work

In recent years, there has been an increasing interest for energy metering in different environments from datacenters [3] to smartphones [8,9]. Previous proposals, however, focus on providing accurate energy metering for single-core architectures or multicore architectures in which a single (multi-threaded) application is executed. These scenarios are relatively easy to handle since, when an application is scheduled on the CPU, it is accounted the whole energy consumption of the system (e.g., using a simple meter). Other proposals [4,10] make use of performance-monitoring counters (PMCs) or system events, such as OS system calls, to breakdown the energy consumption of the system across its components (e.g., memory, processor, etc.). In many cases, the results of the power model are compared against approaches using circuit-based mechanisms such as current sense resistors. Some Intel servers model DRAM power per channel, but they are unaware of per-task interactions in each channel as well as DRAM bank state interactions across requests [11].

Recently, Shen et al. [12] proposed a request-level OS mechanism to attribute power consumption to each server request based on PMCs [13]. Similarly, Kestor et al. [14] derive the energy of moving data along the memory hierarchy by designing a set of micro-benchmarks. However, both approaches cannot take into account the impact of inter-task interferences unless appropriate solutions provide accurate per-task energy metering in multicores. Our work in [5] provides Per-Task Energy Metering (PTEM) for on-chip resources (cores, caches, etc.). Our proposal in this paper, DReAM, provides such support for DRAM memories.

DRAM memory energy consumption can be split into dynamic, refresh and background. Dynamic energy corresponds to the energy spent to perform those *useful* activities triggered by the programs running. For instance, the energy spent to retrieve data from memory on a read operation or the termination power due to terminating signals of other ranks on the same channel. Refresh energy corresponds to the energy consumed to refresh periodically all memory contents. Background energy includes the energy consumed due to *useless* activity not triggered by the program(s) being run as well as the energy wasted due to imperfections of the technology used to implement the circuit.

3   Metering Per-Task Energy Consumption

In this section we present an idealized model for per-task energy metering without considering hardware cost. The result of this model is later used as the reference for DReAM model to meter per-task energy with a low-cost implementation. We assume a multicore architecture where an on-chip memory controller serves as the bridge to the off-chip memory. Next we describe the memory model considered in this paper, how energy is consumed in the different memory blocks, and our models to split energy among different tasks.

3.1   Memory Model

We focus on DDRx SDRAM as it is one of the most common memory technologies. A DDRx SDRAM memory system is composed by a memory controller and

Table 1. Memory commands, timing, power states and background power breakdown for a read operation in close-page mode

Category	Sub	C1	C2	C3	C4	C5	C6
Command	T_0	—		ACT	READ	PRE	—
	T_1			—			
Timing	T_0	—	t_{XP}	t_{RCD}	t_{RTP}	t_{RP}	—
State	$Bank_0$	PD	S	A		S	PD
	$Bank_1$				S		
	$Bank_2$						
	$Bank_3$						
Power	Rank	P_{PD}	P_S	P_A		P_S	P_{PD}
	T_0	$\frac{P_{PD}}{2}$	$P_S - \frac{P_{PD}}{2}$	$P_A - \frac{P_{PD}}{2}$		$P_S - \frac{P_{PD}}{2}$	$\frac{P_{PD}}{2}$
	T_1			$\frac{P_{PD}}{2}$			

one or more DRAM devices. The memory controller controls the off-chip memory system acting as the interface between the processor and DRAM devices.

A memory *rank* consists of multiple devices, which in turn consist of multiple banks that can be accessed independently. Each bank comprises rows and columns of DRAM cells (organized in arrays) and a row-buffer to cache the most recently accessed rows in the bank. Rows are loaded into the row-buffer using a row activate command (ACT). Such command opens the row, by moving the data from the DRAM cells to the row-buffer sense amplifiers. Once a bank is open, any read/write operation (R/W) can be issued. Finally, a precharge command (PRE) closes the row-buffer, storing the data back into the row. The memory controller can use two different policies to manage the row-buffer: close-page that precharges the rows immediately after every access, and open-page that leaves the rows in the row-buffer open for potential future accesses to the same rows.

Different models can be adopted to access memory. Those models determine which ranks, devices, banks and arrays are accessed on each operation. We adopt the same model as *DRAMsim2*, which in turn models Micron DDR2/3 memories [15]. In this model, all devices in a rank are accessed upon every access. In each device, only one bank is accessed, in which all arrays are accessed. Each array provides the specified row to the sense amplifier on every access, where a number of contiguous columns are accessed over successive cycles to serve an incoming access. In our model, we use a single rank, 8 devices per rank, 8 banks per device and 8 arrays per bank configuration. In one cycle, one bank per device is accessed, thus providing 64 bits in total for the rank. A burst of 8 cycles provides 64 bytes on every access to memory, therefore matching the cache line size for the last level cache (LLC) in the processor.

Under this configuration, all devices are always in the same power state, which is equivalent to consider the power state at rank level. In each device, banks can be in different states. Note, however, that our approach can be easily adapted to other models. This is not detailed in this paper due to lack of space.

3.2   Memory Energy Consumption

The energy model for the main memory is based on the current profiles provided by Micron [16] and it splits energy consumption into dynamic, refresh and background energy. This is analogous to the methodology used in [17], where the same data from Micron is used as input. Micron energy model determines the background electric current level, and so the background power dissipation of each rank. Devices can be in three different states: Power Down (PD), Standby (S), and Active (A). In each state, power dissipation is P_{PD}, P_S and P_A respectively. PD state is the one with the lowest power dissipation.

Table 1 shows the effect on memory of a read command. We observe that the device is in PD state when the memory controller is not processing any request. Note that in our configuration all devices in the rank are in the same state and therefore, rank and device states match. When the memory controller receives a memory access request from task 0 (T_0), it sends a clock enable (CKE) signal to transition the rank from PD to S state. The device stays in S state as long as all banks are powered up and idle. This includes the time the device is waiting for the memory controller to send those commands corresponding to the requests in the memory controller's queues. During the S state, background power is higher than in PD state ($P_S > P_{PD}$). S state lasts t_{XP}, as depicted in Table 1. Eventually, some banks are activated so that the device as well as some banks transition to A state. The device and the accessed banks (Bank0 in the example) are in A state during part of the activation period (t_{RCD}) and while the read/write command is served (t_{RTP} in the example for a read command). While in A state, the device incurs the highest power dissipation, P_A, with $P_A > P_S$. Once the only command being processed is the PRE command, the device and accessed banks transition to S state. When no command is executed and no memory access request exists in the memory controller buffer, the memory controller sends the clock disable signal returning the device to PD state.

As stated before, modern memory controllers may implement either open-page or close-page policies. The close-page policy is the focus in this paper, although we have observed similar trends for open-page policy.

3.3 Per-Task Energy Metering for Close-Page Policy

Our idealized model relies on the fact that background power dissipation of a device depends solely on its current state, which can be induced by different, concurrent accesses. Therefore, our model attributes background energy to each task based on the state it imposes on memory. Memory occupancy is discarded as input for the model since background energy does not depend on it.

1) During PD only background power is consumed, which cannot be attributed to any task since during PD no task has any memory activity. Hence, we divide background power evenly across all tasks running in the processor. 2) Whenever a device transitions from PD to S state, the extra background power incurred due to S state, i.e. $P_S - P_{PD}$ is distributed uniformly across all tasks with inflight commands that force the memory devices to stay in S state. 3) When a device is in A state (active), the extra power incurred (i.e. $P_A - P_S$) is distributed evenly across all tasks enforcing A state. For instance, Table 1 shows the case where one task, T_0, issues a *read* command (first row) and the other task T_1 issues no command. Assuming that those are the only tasks using the

Table 2. Memory commands, timing, power states and background power breakdown for several operations in close-page mode.

Command	T_0	—		ACT	READ	PRE	—	
	T_1		—	ACT	READ	PRE		—
Timing	T_0	—	t_{XP}	t_{RCD}	t_{RTP}	t_{RP}	—	
	T_1		—	t_{RRD}	t_{RCD}	t_{RTP}	t_{RP}	...
State	$Bank_0$	PD	S		A	S		S	PD
	$Bank_1$			S		A			
	$Bank_2$					S			
	$Bank_3$								
	Rank	P_{PD}	P_S		P_A		P_S	P_{PD}	
Power	T_0	$\frac{P_{PD}}{2}$	$P_S - \frac{P_{PD}}{2}$	$P_A - \frac{P_S}{2}$	P_A	$\frac{P_S}{2}$	$\frac{P_{PD}}{2}$		
	T_1	$\frac{P_{PD}}{2}$	$\frac{P_S}{2}$	$\frac{P_A}{2}$	$P_A - \frac{P_S}{2}$	$\frac{P_S}{2}$	$P_S - \frac{P_{PD}}{2}$	$\frac{P_{PD}}{2}$	

memory system, during the whole period T_1 is responsible only for half of the P_{PD} power (last row). T_0 is responsible for half of the P_{PD} and all P_S and P_A extra power (penultimate row).

When multiple commands are processed in parallel, we follow the same principle of attributing power to those tasks that impose the memory to be on a given state. In the example in Table 2, we show a particular case where both T_0 and T_1 issue commands in parallel. First, the device is in PD state. Eventually, T_0 makes the device transition to S, so T_0 is responsible for the extra background power. Then, devices transition to A state and T_1 starts its activate command. Both tasks are equally responsible for P_{PD} and P_S power, but only T_0 is responsible for P_A power. Later, T_1 also enforces memory to be in A state so that the total power must be uniformly distributed across both tasks. Finally, as commands finish, tasks T_0 and T_1 stop enforcing high-power states and power dissipation is attributed only to those tasks imposing each particular state.

3.4   Ideal Per-Task Energy Metering Model

We generalize the memory energy consumed by each task as follows.

1) The background (bg) energy attributed to a task can be generalized as follows for both open- and close-page policies:

$$E_{bg,\ total}^{mem}(Tk_i) = P_{PD} \times ExecTime(Tk_i)/\#Tk + \sum_{j=0}^{ExecTime(Tk_i)} \left((P_S - P_{PD}) \times \frac{\delta_{i,j}^S}{\#Tk_{S,j}} \right)$$

$$+ \sum_{j=0}^{ExecTime(Tk_i)} \left((P_A - P_S) \times \frac{\delta_{i,j}^A}{\#Tk_{A,j}} \right) \qquad (1)$$

In the first addend each running task is metered an even part of P_{PD}, where $ExecTime(Tk_i)$ stands for the execution time of task i in cycles and $\#Tk$ for the number of tasks running in the processor – not necessarily the maximum number of tasks allowed in the processor–. The second and third addends meter $P_S - P_{PD}$ and $P_A - P_S$ for tasks enforcing those states. $\#Tk_{S,j}$ and $\#Tk_{A,j}$ correspond to the number of tasks imposing S and A states respectively in cycle j; and $\delta_{i,j}^S$ and $\delta_{i,j}^A$ indicate if the task i makes memory be in S and A state respectively, in cycle j. In other words, $\delta_{i,j}^A$ is 1 if task i is executing a *read, write* or *activate* (last t_{RCD} cycles) command in cycle j, and 0 otherwise; and $\delta^S_{i,j}$ is 1 if task i is executing a *precharge* or activate (first t_{XP} cycles) command or if it has pending commands in the memory controller while all banks are idle in cycle j, and 0 otherwise. Note that, as stated before, memory occupancy is not considered for metering energy to tasks since the memory regions not used by the task under consideration cannot be turned off when idle. Hence, background power remains the same regardless of the memory space used.

2) Dynamic energy for a task depends on the number of operations it performs, as shown in the following equations:

$$
\begin{aligned}
E^{mem}_{dyn,\ total}(Tk_i) = {}& E^{mem}_{read} \times \#RD(Tk_i) + E^{mem}_{write} \times \#WR(Tk_i) \\
& + E^{mem}_{ACT} \times \#ACT(Tk_i) + E^{mem}_{PRE} \times \#PRE(Tk_i)
\end{aligned}
\tag{2}
$$

where E^{mem}_{read}, E^{mem}_{write}, E^{mem}_{ACT} and E^{mem}_{PRE} stand for the energy of each command, and $\#RD(Tk_i)$, $\#WR(Tk_i)$, $\#ACT(Tk_i)$ and $\#PRE(Tk_i)$ stand for the number of memory internal commands executed by task i.

3) *Refresh* operations may have some side effects such as delaying some commands issued by running tasks. However, this fact does not alter the energy model. Also, refresh commands consume some energy to access the corresponding rows. Since refresh operations are distributed evenly over time at a fixed rate and they are not originated by any particular task, their energy is split evenly across all running tasks. Thus, refresh energy per task is as follows:

$$
E^{mem}_{refr,\ total}(Tk_i) = E^{mem}_{refr} \times \#Ref \times ExecTime(Tk_i)/\#Tk
\tag{3}
$$

E^{mem}_{refr} corresponds to the dynamic energy of a refresh command. $\#Ref$ corresponds to the average number of refresh operations performed per cycle.

4   DReAM, A Practical Approach to Per-Task Energy Metering

Implementing the exact computation of the *idealized* energy model is expensive — if at all feasible — due to the large number of events to be tracked, the frequency at which they must be tracked, and the lack of information that the processor has about the memory state. On the other end, metering memory energy evenly among running tasks or proportionally to the number of accesses that they perform requires minor changes to current architectures. However, these approaches exhibit low estimation accuracy as shown later in Section 5.2. Therefore, we propose DReAM, our per-task energy metering approach that trades off energy metering accuracy and implementation complexity.

In DReAM memory model, dynamic and refresh energy can be easily tracked as in the idealized model. This requires the memory vendor to provide the dynamic energy per access type, namely E^{mem}_{read}, E^{mem}_{write}, E^{mem}_{ACT} and E^{mem}_{PRE} for tracking dynamic energy and E^{mem}_{refr} for tracking refresh energy, as well as the average number of refresh operations per cycle ($\#Ref$). These parameters are already provided by chip vendors like Micron for DDR2/3 memories [16], so our model imposes no change to current DDR2/3 memories. In the memory controller,

Table 3. DReAM hardware requirements

Block	Memory Vendor	Extra Logic
Memory	E_{read}^{mem}, E_{write}^{mem}, E_{ACT}^{mem}, E_{PRE}^{mem}, E_{PD}^{mem}, E_{refr}^{mem}, $\#Ref$	$\#RD$, $\#WR$, $\#ACT$, $\#PRE$, $\#RD(Tk_i)$, $\#WR(Tk_i)$, $\#ACT(Tk_i)$, $\#PRE(Tk_i)$, $IntMem$ cycle counter

we only require per-task activity counters, namely $\#RD(Tk_i)$, $\#WR(Tk_i)$, $\#ACT(Tk_i)$ and $\#PRE(Tk_i)$. Total background energy, $E_{bg,total}^{mem}$ can be obtained by metering memory energy consumption [10] and subtracting dynamic and refresh energy. The PD background power is constant and hence easy to track. Meanwhile, the remaining background energy, E_{rem}^{mem}, is due to active and standby periods (i.e. $E_{bg,total}^{mem} = E_{PD}^{mem} + E_{rem}^{mem}$).

Our model distributes E_{PD}^{mem} uniformly across all tasks, while E_{rem}^{mem} is distributed based on access frequencies per task. To that end, we divide the execution into intervals of $IntMem$ processor cycles and track the number of memory accesses sent to the memory controller (in a per-task basis) in the current interval. Thus, background energy is obtained as follows:

$$E_{bg,\,total}^{mem}(Tk_i) = \frac{P_{PD}^{mem} \times ExecTime(Tk_i)}{\#Tk} + \sum_{j=0}^{\frac{ExecTime(Tk_i)}{IntMem}} \#accesses_j^{Tk_i} \times \frac{E_{rem}^{mem}(j)}{\#TOTaccesses_j}$$

(4)

where P_{PD}^{mem} is the PD background power, $\#accesses_j^{Tk_i}$ tracks the number of memory accesses of task i during interval j, and $\#TOTaccesses_j$ tracks the total number of memory accesses in interval j. $E_{rem}^{mem}(j)$ is the non-power-down background energy in interval j, obtained by subtracting all other sources of energy consumption from the total energy measured in the interval. Sensitivity to the sampling interval ($IntMem$) is studied in the evaluation section.

Putting All Together

The DReAM approach requires little hardware overhead. DReAM mostly requires setting up some counters similar to the PMCs currently available in most high-performance processors. DReAM support does not interfere the execution of programs since it is not in any critical path. Table 3 summarizes those parameters required from the memory vendor and the extra logic (i.e. counters) that must be set up. Counters with the "(Tk_i)" suffix must be replicated for each task.

Regarding the interface with the software, the OS is responsible for keeping track of the energy consumed by every task running in the system. DReAM exports a special register, called Memory Energy Metering Register (MEMR), that acts as the interface between DReAM and the OS. The OS can access that register to collect the energy estimates made by DReAM. This typically will happen when a context switch takes place. At that moment, the OS reads the MEMR using the hardware-thread index (or CPU index) for the task that is being scheduled out (T_{out}). Then, the OS aggregates the energy consumption value read in the *task struct* for T_{out}. Right after the new task (T_{in}) is scheduled in, the memory state

Table 4. System Configuration

Main memory	
Frequency and size	1000MHz, 8GB
Technology and supply voltage	65nm, 1.2V
Row-buffer management policy	close-page
Address mapping scheme	Shared Bank
Chip details	
Core count	1, 4, 16 cores, single-threaded
Fetch, decode, issue, commit bandwidth	2 instructions/cycle
Instruction & Data L1	32KB, 4-way, 32B/line (2 cycles hit)
Instruction & Data TLB	256 entries fully-associative (1 cycle hit)
LLC Size	256KB/core, 16-way, 64B/line (3 cycles hit + 12 cycles L1 miss penalty and bus round trip) 256KB (1 core), 1MB (4 cores), 4MB (16 cores)

may remain at a particular state due to an access triggered by the task that has been scheduled out. Although, DReAM attributes background energy consumption to T_{in}, this occurs during few cycles (in the order of tens or hundreds of cycles). Under a processor frequency of 2GHz, 500 cycles are equivalent to $0.25\mu s$, while context switches occur at much higher granularity, every 10-100ms.

As in [5], the time the OS spends working on behalf of a given task is attributed to the calling task. The remaining energy consumed by the OS can be evenly attributed to all running tasks. In any case, DReAM provides the hardware support needed to attribute OS energy to tasks as required.

5   Evaluation

5.1   Experimental Setup

We use *DRAMsim2* [15] to model off-chip main memory, a cycle-accurate memory system simulator for DDR2/3 memories including a memory controller and DRAM memory. The processor is modeled with *MPsim* [18]. *DRAMsim2* has been connected to *MPsim* so that LLC misses are propagated to the memory controller, which manages those memory requests. A power model based on Micron memories has been implemented in *DRAMsim2*.

We consider three Chip Multi-Processor (CMP) configurations with 1, 4 and 16 single-threaded cores. The second level cache (L2) is partitioned with 256KB 16-way per core. Therefore, L2 size is 256KB, 1MB and 4MB for 1, 4 and 16 cores respectively. These configurations have been chosen to discount the effect of on-chip inter-task interferences due to shared resources (e.g., shared L2 cache), thus allowing to consider memory effects only. Details about the configuration can be found in Table 4. Other parameters are analogous to those in [5].

For the DRAM memory we model a 8GB memory since it is enough to support the workloads used in this paper. DRAM memory is single-rank with 8 devices per rank, 8 banks per device and 8 arrays per bank. DRAM memory row-buffer management policy is close-page across all the evaluation section.

Benchmarks. We use traces collected from the whole SPEC CPU 2006 benchmark suite using the reference input set. Each trace contains 100 million instructions, selected using the SimPoint methodology [19]. Running all N-task combinations is infeasible as the number of combinations is too high. Hence, we classify benchmarks into two groups depending on their memory access frequency. Benchmarks in the high-frequency group (denoted H) are those presenting a memory access frequency higher than 5 accesses per 1,000 cycles when running in isolation, that is: *mcf, milc, lbm, libquantum, soplex, gcc, bwaves, leslie3d, astar, bzip2, zeusmp, sphinx3* and *omnetpp*. The rest of the benchmarks access with low frequency (denoted L). From these two groups, we generate 3 workload types denoted L, H and X depending on whether all benchmarks belong to group L, H or a combination of both.

We generate 8 workloads per group and processor setup randomly, except for the 1-core setup where all benchmarks run in isolation. In the case of X, half of the benchmarks belong to L and the other half to H.

Metrics. In order to evaluate the accuracy of DReAM, we use as the reference the ideal model. In each experiment, we measure the *off estimation* or *prediction error* of each model with respect to the idealized model, which is computed as follows, where N is the number of tasks in a workload.

$$WldPredError = \frac{\sum_{i=0}^{N} |Energy_{ideal_i} - Energy_{model_i}|}{Energy_{measured}} \tag{5}$$

We then take the average *WldPredError* across all benchmarks in each workload analyzed in each processor setup.

5.2 DReAM Energy Estimation

In this section we show the accuracy of DReAM with respect to the ideal model presented in Section 3. We also include the ES model that uniformly splits energy across all running tasks regardless of their activity and memory behavior, together with a simple Proportionally To memory Accesses model (PTA) that splits energy across tasks proportionally to their memory accesses.

DReAM Sampling Interval (IntMem). The memory energy consumption prediction of DReAM varies with different sample period (interval) lengths. When choosing the interval length, we seek for a reasonable tradeoff between accuracy and hardware cost, by regulating the interval period from 128 to half million processor cycles. As expected, higher sampling frequency increases accuracy. However, discrepancy between short and long sampling periods is not huge (from 4.6% to 7.4% average *WldPredError*). Some meaningful average *WldPredError* increase is observed when moving from a 512-cycles sampling interval to a 1024-cycles interval. Further increasing the interval size until reaching half million cycles has little impact on accuracy since deviation from the ideal model quickly flattens. Thus, we have chosen two different interval sizes with different accuracy/cost tradeoff: 512 and 50K cycles sampling intervals.

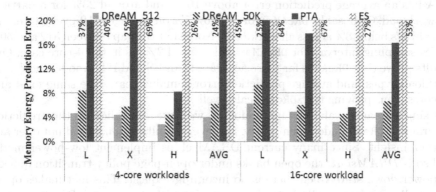

Fig. 2. Per-task DRAM energy prediction error for 4-core workloads

DRAM Energy Consumption Prediction. Next we evaluate the off estimation for 4-core and 16-core processor setups with respect to the ideal model.
The left half of Figure 2 shows the result for the 24 workloads (8 of each type)
under the 4-core setup. We observe that, in general, the ES model is highly inaccurate averaging over 45% prediction error across all workloads, and ranging
from 26% to 69% for all workload types. Prediction is more accurate for L and
H workloads than for X ones. This is expected since benchmarks in L and H
workloads are more homogeneous, so their individual power consumption is also
more homogeneous than in X workloads. PTA model improves the estimation
accuracy, with an average prediction error around 24%. PTA accuracy is high
for H workloads since the large number of accesses of H benchmarks makes
energy cost more proportional to the number of accesses (dynamic energy becomes dominant). However, benchmarks in L group seldom access memory, so
their memory energy is mainly background energy, which PTA fails to predict
accurately.

Our `DReAM` model improves prediction accuracy significantly over both ES and
PTA. When the sample period granularity is 512 cycles, the prediction error is
always below 10%, and 3.9% on average. If the sampling period increases to 50K
cycles, the prediction error may reach 14.0% at most for one particular workload,
and 6.1% on average. The right half of Figure 2 shows results under the 16-core
setup. First, we observe that ES and `DReAM` accuracy remains similar to that of
the 4-core setup. In contrast, PTA accuracy slightly improves. The average prediction error across all workloads for the ES model rises to 53%. The error increment
mainly comes from L workloads. A similar effect occurs for `DReAM`, thus making L
workloads to exhibit the lowest prediction accuracy. Trends for PTA are similar
to those for the 4-core setup, thus exhibiting higher accuracy for H workloads, although accuracy for the 16-core setup is higher. This is due to the fact that, with
4 cores, a large deviation for one benchmark has significant impact in average results, but such average impact becomes lower across 16 tasks. However, maximum
error for individual benchmarks in each workload still remains high. Nevertheless,

PTA has an average prediction error above 10%, and around 23% for a particular workload. Opposably, DReAM error is below 5% on average (512-cycles interval) and always below 8% across all workloads. Note that the gap between 512 and 50K cycles sampling intervals for DReAM is still around 2%, as in the 4-core case. Our results prove that DReAM is far more accurate than ES and PTA models across all workload types, and average prediction error remains nearly the same for 4 and 16 cores, thus proving that DReAM scales well.

Using the same evaluation methodology, we have also validated the prediction accuracy of DReAM under open-policy. However, results obtained did not offer any further insight. Since many current DRAM chips implement low-power mode, and so is *DRAMsim2*, the open banks under open-page policy transition quickly to power down state when there is no incoming request. This fact makes open-page policy perform similarly to close-page in multicore systems. Results are not shown due to space constraints.

DReAM Energy Overhead. DReAM requires some hardware support in the form of counters to track memory activity. Those counters are placed in the memory controller, which in general is on-chip, so the memory devices remain unchanged.

As shown in Table 3, DReAM needs few counters (5 shared counters and 4 extra counters per thread). 32-bit counters suffice to track the corresponding events. Further, few of those counters are accessed on each memory access and at the end of a sampling interval. We have considered the energy consumption for two different sampling intervals: 512 and 50K cycles. Area and power overheads have been derived with power models analogous to those of Wattch [20]. Wattch-like power models are built on top of CACTI 6.5 simulation tool [21]. Results for 4-core and 16-core configurations show that the total energy and area overhead for DReAM is largely below 0.1% of the memory system.

Furthermore, relative overheads do not change noticeably if the core count is increased, which proves that DReAM scales well. Energy overheads for 512 cycles sampling intervals are higher than for 50K intervals, but still under 0.1% for the whole chip.

6   Conclusions

Different programs show highly different energy profiles in different components. However, per-task memory energy metering has not been considered so far. In this paper, we propose, for the first time, an ideal model to measure per-task DRAM memory energy and devise DReAM, an efficient and accurate implementation of such ideal model. We show how DReAM achieves a prediction error between 3.9% and 4.7% w.r.t. the ideal model with negligible overhead for 4 and 16 core setups respectively. The error is largely below the error introduced by approaches such as even distribution and proportional-to-accesses distribution.

Acknowledgements. This work has been partially supported by the Spanish Ministry of Science and Innovation under grant TIN2012-34557, the HiPEAC

Network of Excellence, by the European Research Council under the European Union's 7th FP, ERC Grant Agreement n. 321253, and by a joint study agreement between IBM and BSC (number W1361154). Qixiao Liu has also been funded by the Chinese Scholarship Council under grant 2010608015.

References

1. Barroso, L.: The Price of Performance. Queue 3(7) (2005)
2. Hamilton, J.: Internet-Scale Service Infrastructure Efficiency. In: ISCA (2009)
3. Jimenez, V., Gioiosa, R., Cazorla, F., Valero, M., Kursun, E., Isci, C., Buyuktosunoglu, A., Bose, P.: Energy-aware accounting and billing in large-scale computing facilities. IEEE Micro 31(3), 60–71 (2011)
4. Bircher, W.L., John, L.K.: Complete system power estimation: A trickle-down approach based on performance events. In: ISPASS (April 2007)
5. Liu, Q., Moreto, M., Jimenez, V., Abella, J., Cazorla, F.J., Valero, M.: Hardware support for accurate per-task energy metering in multicore systems. ACM Trans. Archit. Code Optim. 10(4) (December 2013)
6. Intel Corp.: Intel 64 and ia-32 architectures software developer's manual (2012)
7. Phansalkar, A., Joshi, A., John, L.K.: Analysis of redundancy and application balance in the SPEC CPU2006 benchmark suite. In: ISCA, pp. 412–423 (2007)
8. Pathak, A., Hu, C., Zhang, M., Bahl, P., Wang, W.M.: Fine-grained power modeling for smartphones using system call tracing. In: EuroSys. (2011)
9. Chung, Y.F., Lin, C.Y., King, C.T.: ANEPROF: Energy profiling for android java virtual machine and applications. In: ICPADS (2011)
10. David, H., Gorbatov, E., Hanebutte, U.R., Khanna, R., Le, C.: RAPL: Memory power estimation and capping. In: ISLPED (2010)
11. Intel Corp.: Intel xeon processor E5-2600 product family uncore performance monitoring guide (March 2012)
12. Shen, K., Shriraman, A., Dwarkadas, S., Zhang, X., Chen, Z.: Power containers: an os facility for fine-grained power and energy management on multicore servers. In: ASPLOS (2013)
13. Bellosa, F.: The benefits of event-driven energy accounting in power-sensitive systems. In: ACM SIGOPS European Workshop, pp. 37–42 (2000)
14. Kestor, G., Gioiosa, R., Kerbyson, D., Hoisie, A.: Quantifying the energy cost of data movement in scientific applications. In: IISWC, pp. 56–65 (September 2013)
15. Rosenfeld, P., Cooper-Balis, E., Jacob, B.: DRAMSim2: A cycle accurate memory system simulator. IEEE Comput. Archit. Lett. (2011)
16. Micron: Calculating memory system power for DDR3. Micron Technical Notes (2007)
17. Deng, Q., Meisner, D., Ramos, L., Wenisch, T., Bianchini, R.: Memscale: Active low-power modes for main memory. In: ASPLOS (2011)
18. Acosta, C., Cazorla, F., Ramirez, A., Valero, M.: The MPsim simulation tool. Technical Report UPC-DAC-RR-CAP-2009-15, UPC (2009)
19. Sherwood, T., Perelman, E., Calder, B.: Basic block distribution analysis to find periodic behavior and simulation points in applications. In: PACT (2001)
20. Brooks, D.M., Tiwari, V., Martonosi, M.: Wattch: A framework for architectural-level power analysis and optimizations. In: ISCA (2000)
21. Muralimanohar, N., Balasubramonian, R., Jouppi, N.: CACTI 6.0: A tool to understand large caches. HP Tech Report HPL-2009-85 (2009)

Characterizing the Performance-Energy Tradeoff of Small ARM Cores in HPC Computation

Michael A. Laurenzano[1,2], Ananta Tiwari[1,3], Adam Jundt[1], Joshua Peraza[1], William A. Ward, Jr.[4], Roy Campbell[4], and Laura Carrington[1,3]

[1] EP Analytics
[2] Dept. of Computer Science and Engineering, University of Michigan, USA
[3] Performance Modeling and Characterization Lab.,
San Diego Supercomputer Center, USA
[4] High Performance Computing Modernization Program, U.S. Dept. of Defense, USA
{michaell,ananta.tiwari,adam.jundt,joshua.peraza,
laura.carrington}@epanalytics.com,
{william.ward,roy.campbell}@hpc.mil

Abstract. Deploying large numbers of small, low-power cores has been gaining traction recently as a system design strategy in high performance computing (HPC). The ARM platform that dominates the embedded and mobile computing segments is now being considered as an alternative to high-end x86 processors that largely dominate HPC because peak performance per watt may be substantially improved using off-the-shelf commodity processors.

In this work we methodically characterize the performance and energy of HPC computations drawn from a number of problem domains on current ARM and x86 processors. Unsurprisingly, we find that the performance, energy and energy-delay product of applications running on these platforms varies significantly across problem types and inputs. Using static program analysis we further show that this variation can be explained largely in terms of the capabilities of two processor subsystems: single instruction multiple data (SIMD)/floating point and the cache/memory hierarchy; and that static analysis of this kind is sufficient to predict which platform is best for a particular application/input pair. In the context of these findings, we evaluate how some of the key architectural changes being made for upcoming 64-bit ARM platforms may impact HPC application performance.

1 Introduction

As large-scale high performance computing (HPC) systems have grown in size and the scope of problems being solved, reducing their power consumption has become a first-class problem. Indeed, many argue that power consumption is one of the primary constraints on the size of upcoming HPC systems [4][5][20][27][30]. We see this impacting industry, academia, and government, where substantial effort and resources are being marshaled to improve energy efficiency in HPC centers. On the other hand, the problems being solved on HPC systems, ranging

F. Silva et al. (Eds.): Euro-Par 2014, LNCS 8632, pp. 124–137, 2014.

from basic research to solving day-to-day problems in defense and industry, have HPC users demanding more and more performance out of their systems.

In response to these forces, HPC system architects have sought out designs that deliver higher performance with lower power budgets. One of the design alternatives that has gathered much attention along these lines is to use a large number of small, low-power cores in place of a smaller number of large, power-hungry cores. In particular, ARM processors, the dominant platform in the embedded and mobile computing domains, are being considered. The argument for using a large number of ARM cores is twofold. First, low-power cores are often more energy efficient than high-end cores [17]. Second, having come from domains which have always been power constrained, ARM designs in particular have been engineered to be frugal with power; careful attention having been given to include only those features that are worth the extra power they consume [7]. However, the question remains: *are those features well-suited to HPC applications?*

Current 32-bit ARM platforms such as ARMv7 have limitations that preclude their immediate use in modern HPC systems: only 4GB of memory are supported per process [15], and the ISA and hardware support for vector math is limited [8]. Ameliorating these limitations is one of the purposes of ARMv8, a 64-bit version of the ARM architecture, which is set to be released in early to mid 2014. Among other improvements, ARMv8 includes the ability to natively address significantly more than 4GB of memory, along with support for IEEE754 double-precision (DP) math and vectorized DP operations [14]. Still, it remains unclear whether these improvements will impact the ability of ARMv8 to deliver satisfactory performance to broad classes of HPC applications, and to what extent they will improve upon existing ARMv7 processors.

In this work, we characterize the performance and energy of ARM and x86 platforms by drawing compute kernels and applications from a number of HPC problem domains. These benchmarks are methodically characterized in terms of their performance and power on several ARMv7 (32-bit) and x86 processors. We examine performance, energy and energy-delay product (EDP), finding that these metrics vary by least an order-of-magnitude on a given implementation, and that they depend on the specific features of the application being run. We employ static program analysis on the benchmark kernels to characterize their behavior in terms of memory and floating point operations. From these characteristics, we develop simple regression models for performance, energy, and EDP disparities across applications, finding that these are largely explainable as functions of the memory and floating point characteristics of the compiled application. Building upon this insight, we present a model for estimating how performance is likely to change with improvements in the CPU and memory of upcoming 64-bit ARMv8 systems, finding that both have significant impacts on the performance of a broad class of applications.

The rest of this paper is structured as follows. Section 2 discusses work in the literature related to this paper. Section 3 explains the experimental methodology used in this work to assess the performance and power characteristics of HPC applications. Section 4 presents a methodical evaluation of two ARM platforms on a number of compute kernels and application benchmarks, followed by a discussion of the factors underlying the performance and energy characteristics of the applications and how these characteristics are likely to be impacted by the introduction of 64-bit ARM platforms. Finally, Section 5 concludes.

2   Related Work

This section describes the related literature in two areas that intersect with our work: using ARM cores in HPC and HPC Performance Modeling.

2.1   ARM in High Performance Computing

Rajovic et al. [26] evaluate the performance and energy efficiency of the Tegra 2, Tegra 3, and Quadro 1000M on a set of HPC microkernels. The Tegra 2 and 3 contain two and four core ARM Cortex-A9 processors respectively, and the Quadro 1000M is a discrete mobile GPU. Padoin et al. [24] compare the scalability and energy efficiency of a PandaBoard, Snowball, and Tegra 2 when running High Performance Linpack. Ou et al. [23] compare energy and cost efficiency of a PandaBoard containing an ARM Cortex-A9 with an Intel Core2 Q9400 on three applications: web server throughput, an in-memory database, and video transcoding. They find that the PandaBoard achieved the greatest energy efficiency gains in less computationally intensive applications (the in-memory database in their study). Fürlinger et al. build a cluster of second-generation Apple TV devices which utilize an ARM Cortex-A8 [13]. They evaluate CPU and memory performance compared to a BeagleBoard and system performance per watt running High Performance Linpack compared to systems on the Green500 list.

Blem et al. [7] focus on the specific microarchitectural implementations of ARM and x86 processors, comparing an ARM Cortex-A8, ARM Cortex-A9, Intel Sandybridge, and an Intel Atom. By showing that the Atom could achieve similar energy consumption to the Cortex-A9 when controlling for microarchitectural features, they conclude that ISA is not major determinant of energy efficiency, instead finding that ARM and x86 implementations are simply different engineering design points.

Our work complements this existing body of literature. Our contribution is to document the performance and energy impact ARM cores have on a wide range of HPC computational benchmarks, as well as to show that the variability in performance and energy can largely be attributed to FP/SIMD computation and interactions with the memory subsystem.

2.2   HPC Application Performance Modeling

Kerbyson et al. propose some of the seminal ideas in predictive application performance and scalability modeling, showing that it is possible to accurately model the performance for a single application and that the model depends on specifics of the implementation of that application [18][19]. Several other works show how to use an application-independent approach to modeling performance, using a variety of application characteristics collected as traces of the running application, then mixing those with the results of measurement microkernels that are deployed on the system to predict performance for the application/system pair [10][28]. Snavely et al. [29] show that while a cycle accurate simulator could be very accurate, it was infeasible for a full-scale HPC application. Instead, they show that it is possible to tractably predict performance using a few important features.

Carrington et al. [9] show that simple combinations of metrics are infeasible to use for precisely predicting HPC application performance. In this work we show that even simple, static features of HPC applications can be employed to provide useful insights into the direction and magnitude of their performance and energy characteristics, even while precise performance prediction with those features may not be feasible.

3   Analysis and Measurement Methodology

The aim of this work is to characterize an extensive set of HPC application benchmarks in terms of their performance, energy and energy-delay product (EDP) on a several ARM processor configurations. This section discusses the methodological considerations made to develop these characterizations. We begin by discussing the performance measurement methodology, followed by a discussion of a methodology for attributing the wall-level power draw to the workload running on a system. Last, we describe a set of program analysis tools and methodologies that are deployed in the evaluation to develop energy models.

3.1   Performance Measurement

This work evaluates a number of HPC application kernels and benchmarks for performance and power. Our approach to measuring performance on application kernels is to manually insert timing instrumentation around the key computational loops, avoiding measurement of initialization and finalization code such as parsing arguments, reading files, allocating/freeing memory and output validation. The performance of these activities is important, yet in benchmark kernels they tend to be greatly over represented as a fraction of runtime relative to their runtime in full application codes. Many HPC benchmarking packages such as the NAS Parallel Benchmarks [6], pcubed [21] and polybench [25] adopt a similar rationale, providing (sometimes multiple) timers around important phases of computational work.

3.2   Attributing Power to a Workload

The goal of our power measurement methodology is to isolate the power draw consumed only by the CPUs running the application. To isolate the power draw in this fashion we measure system-wide power draw during long-running computational kernels at several core counts, with the purpose of deriving the power contribution only of the cores actively involved in the computation. We begin with the formulation of system-wide power shown in Equation 1.

$$W^i_{system} = i * W_{active} + (N - i) * W_{idle} + W_{other} \tag{1}$$

The elements of Equation 1 are i, the number of active cores, W^i_{system}, the measured power using i active cores and N, the total number of available cores on the system. The goal of producing an equation in this form is to derive W_{active}, the power draw of a single active core, W_{idle}, the power draw of a single idle core and W_{other}, the power draw of all other system components. Because there are three unknowns (W_{active}, W_{idle} and W_{other}), measurements at three core counts ($i = c_1, c_2, c_3$) is sufficient to produce system of equations, shown in Equation 2, to which we can apply any of a number of numerical techniques to approximate the unknowns. In this work we use Gaussian elimination.

$$\begin{bmatrix} W^{c_1}_{system} \\ W^{c_2}_{system} \\ W^{c_3}_{system} \end{bmatrix} = W_{active} \begin{bmatrix} c_1 \\ c_2 \\ c_3 \end{bmatrix} + W_{idle} \begin{bmatrix} N - c_1 \\ N - c_2 \\ N - c_3 \end{bmatrix} + W_{other} \begin{bmatrix} 1 \\ 1 \\ 1 \end{bmatrix} \tag{2}$$

This framing of the problem makes several assumptions. First, it assumes that W_{active}, W_{idle} and W_{other} do not depend on the number of cores that are active. For this assumption to hold, the workload must be carefully selected so that each additional running instance of the kernel produces a similar additional power draw increase. This means ensuring that running instances do not compete with one another for processor resources like cache and interconnect, which would introduce execution stalls and reduce circuit-level switching activity. Second, this formulation resolves W_{active}, W_{idle} and W_{other} only for a particular benchmark. Empirically, however, we found that W_{idle} and W_{other} for a particular system are stable across a range of computational kernels, indicating that these values are relatively independent of the workload running on the system. Therefore, we utilize this methodology for only a few kernels on each system to estimate W_{idle} and W_{other} for the system, allowing us to isolate the power per active core for **any workload** by plugging the full system power measurement for that workload W^i_{system}, along with W_{idle} and W_{other}, into Equation 1.

3.3   Program Static Analysis Tools

In this work we employ two binary analysis tools to analyze application codes. In particular, we use the EPAX toolkit [12] to analyze the static properties of ARM binaries and the PEBIL toolkit [22] on x86 binaries. Static binary analysis is the act of examining a compiled binary program to extract information about the properties of the code and data that reside within that program. EPAX and PEBIL accomplish this by reading the executable from disk, parsing and disassembling its contents, then writing out a file containing a number of details about the machine-level instructions in the program as well the relationship between those instructions such as their membership in high-level structures such as basic blocks, loops, and functions. In this work, we use EPAX on ARM binaries and PEBIL on x86 binaries to extract a number of features we expect to be salient to HPC applications, including counts of floating point and vector (SIMD) operations, along with the counts and properties of memory operations. When possible to gather at compile-time, we augment the information gathered by EPAX and PEBIL with information about the sizes of key data structures within the important computational loops. As we show in Section 4.3, this array of static properties is enough to make informative predictions about the direction and magnitude of the relative amount of energy consumed when running the application on ARM and x86 systems.

Table 1. Platform configurations

	Intel Sandy Bridge	ARM Cortex-A9	ARM Cortex-A15
Name	Dell Poweredge T620	Dell Copper	nCore BrownDwarf Y-class
Platform	x86_64 64-bit	ARMv7 32-bit	ARMv7 32-bit
Processor	8-core 2.6GHz Xeon E5-2670	4-core 1.6GHz Marvell MV78460	4-core 1.4GHz TI 66AK2E05
D-Cache	Shared 20MB L3, Priv. 256KB L2, Priv. 32KB L1	Shared 2MB L2, Priv. 32KB L1	Shared 4MB L2, Priv. 32KB L1
Memory	32GB 1333MHz DDR3	4GB 1333MHz DDR3	2GB 1600MHz DDR3
FP/SIMD	SSE, AVX	VFPv3-D32, no SIMD	VFPv4, NEON
Notes	*Turbo and HT disabled*	-	*c66x DSP cores disabled*

Table 2. Benchmarks and applications

Type	Programs		Summary
Compute Kernels	PolyBench[25]	adi, atax, bicg, cholesky, doitgen, dynprog, fdtd 2d, fdtd ampl, gemver, gesummv, grammschmidt, jacobi 2d, mvt, seidel, symm, trisolv, trmm	linear algebra, data mining, stencils
	Other	covcol, dct, dsyr2k, dsyrk, matmulinit, mm, stencil-3d, strmm, strsm, swim, tce	
Application Benchmarks	Mantevo[16]	miniMD, CoMD, miniGhost	molecular dynamics, finite element, finite difference, quantum chromodynamics, plasma physics
	CORAL[1]	AMGmk, MILCmk	
	Trinity[11]	miniFE, GTC	

4 Evaluation

4.1 Experimental Setup

We utilize three distinct platforms throughout this evaluation, summarized in Table 1. These test platforms consist of a high-end Intel Sandy Bridge E5-2670, a popular configuration among the largest modern supercomputers [2]. We also use two energy-efficient ARM server platforms: a Cortex-A9 based Dell Copper server and a Cortex-A15 based nCore BrownDwarf Y-class supercomputer. For power measurement, we use a Yokogawa WT310 digital power meter [3] to measure AC power draw of the entire system at the wall. Power measurements for each benchmark run are then isolated using the approach described in Section 3.2.

On our test platforms we deploy 28 compute kernels and 7 application benchmarks, summarized in Table 2. Many of the compute kernels are drawn directly from the Polyhedral Benchmark Suite [25], while others are augmented versions thereof or hand-written compute kernels of our devising. For each compute kernel we generate a total of eight configurations, consisting of the cross product of double- and single-precision (DP and SP) versions of the benchmarks and data set sizes that are large enough that they fit into each of the four levels of the memory hierarchy on all systems (L1 , L2 and L3 Cache[1] as well as main memory). This yields a total of 224 compute kernels. The sizes of the four data sets were chosen carefully so that both the DP and SP versions fit into the same level of the memory hierarchy on all systems (SP data types generally consume half the memory of their DP counterpart). For our particular test platforms, we use 10-15KB of SP data for L1, 80-100KB of SP data for L2, 700-900KB of SP data for L3 and 50-70MB of SP data for main memory. The seven application benchmarks are also described in Table 2, which are drawn from the Mantevo [16], CORAL [1] and NERSC-8 Trinity [11] benchmark suites and represent applications from among a number of unique computational domains. For most applications we use both DP and SP versions. The exception to this is miniMD, for which we were unable to compile the DP version on either of the ARM platforms. Benchmarks and applications are compiled with gcc, using optimization level -O3 and vectorization support flags: -funsafe-math-optimizations -mavx on the Sandy Bridge and -funsafe-math-optimizations -mfpu=neon[2] on both ARM systems. We pin threads to cores to ensure that no thread migration occurs during any experimental runs. All performance, power, energy and EDP numbers presented are the average of three runs.

4.2 Performance and Energy Characterization

We begin the evaluation by presenting performance and energy characterizations of the compute kernels and benchmark applications on all systems. Figure 1 shows distributions of the performance 1(a)-1(b), energy 1(c)-1(d) and EDP 1(e)-1(f) for the compute kernels, grouped according to floating point precision (SP/DP) and which memory level the kernel exercises (L1/L2/L3/MM) and normalized to the Intel Sandy Bridge system, where values greater than

---

[1] Neither the Cortex-A9 nor the Cortex-A15 have L3 cache, and thus they have two sizes that fit into main memory.

[2] Without -funsafe-math-optimizations, SIMD NEON instructions will fail to materialize on the ARM systems because those instructions do not adhere to the IEEE754 standard.

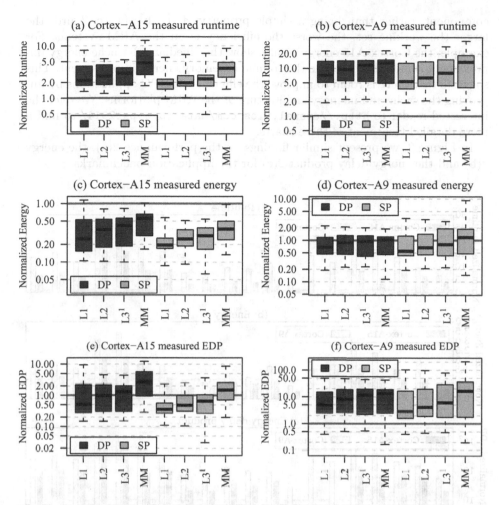

Fig. 1. Distributions of the runtime (a)-(b), energy (c)-(d) and energy-delay product (e)-(f) for single-core compute kernels on ARM Cortex-A15 and Cortex-A9, relative to Intel Sandy Bridge. Distributions are shown as box plots, which highlight the the maximum (upper tail), 75th percentile (box upper-bound), median (line within box), 25th percentile (box lower-bound) and minimum (lower tail). Interested readers can find more detailed charts at http://epanalytics.com/data/euro-par2014/.

one for runtime indicate ARM performance suffers relative to the Sandy Bridge system, and values less than one for energy and EDP identify benchmarks that are more energy efficient when executed on the ARM systems. Three interesting trends can be observed. First, in almost all cases the SP versions of the kernels show better characteristics on the ARM systems over their DP counterparts, an issue that should be resolved on future 64-bit ARM systems. Second, there is substantial variation in runtime even within a particular grouping of kernels, suggesting that performance, energy and EDP have a substantial software component, rather than being a simple property of the hardware. Third, the larger the working set, the worse the efficiency is on the ARM systems. For example, the Cortex-A15 energy results show that median L1-Cache energy improvement is more than double that of main memory energy improvement. This suggests that there is room to improve the efficiency of HPC applications by improving the cache and memory architecture of the ARM platforms. We refer the interested reader to http://epanalytics.com/data/euro-par2014/ to find a more detailed treatment of these charts.

In Figure 2, we present similar findings on the performance 2(a), the energy 2(b) and the energy-delay product 2(c) for the application benchmarks.

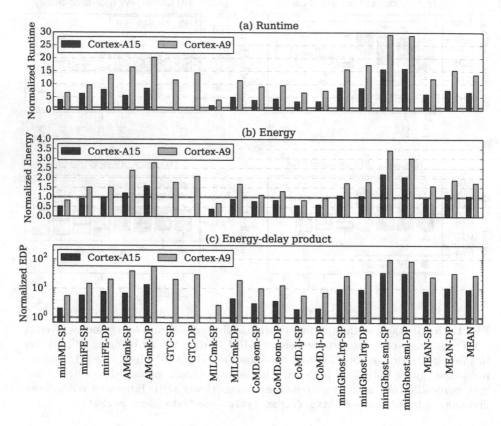

Fig. 2. Runtime (a), energy (b) and energy-delay product (c) for quad-core application benchmarks on an ARM Cortex-A15 and Cortex-A9, relative to an Intel Sandy Bridge. Note that (c) is plotted on a log scale.

4.3   Attributing Energy Characteristics to Static Program Features

In Section 3.3, we described two static binary analysis tools, PEBIL for x86 and EPAX for ARM, which were employed to collect information about the the

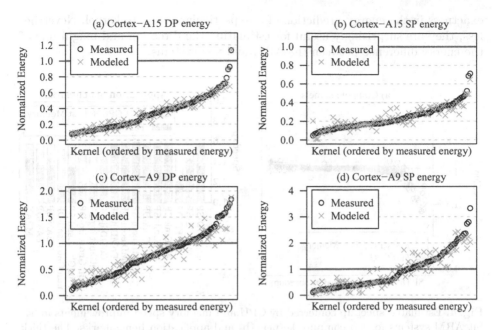

Fig. 3. Measured and modeled energy for Cortex-A15 (a)-(b) and Cortex-A9 (c)-(d). A statistical measure of the variation in kernel energy that is explained by the models (adjusted R-squared) is (a) 90%, (b) 64%, (c) 80% and (d) 76%.

memory/cache and floating point/SIMD operations that reside within the key loops of the compute kernels. Specifically, we collect the counts of instructions, memory operations, floating point operations, the number of bytes moved per memory operation, and the size of the key data structure(s) in the loop. We then use multivariate linear regression to build models of the energy consumption (normalized to Sandy Bridge) of the compute kernels as a function only of these terms and some of their simple variants (e.g., floating point ops per instruction), along with 10-fold cross validation on the models. Figure 3 shows the measured and modeled energy consumption for the Cortex-A15 3(a)-3(b) and the Cortex-A9 3(c)-3(d), again normalized to the Intel Sandy Bridge.

Two interesting features are apparent from Figure 3. First, we observe that the models capture a significant fraction of the variation in energy across the compute kernels. Visually, this can be seen where the shape of the modeled energy points follows the shape of the measured energy points. A statistical measure of this property is given by the *adjusted R-squared* of the model [31]. Adjusted R-squared is the percentage of variation captured by the model, where a perfect model would capture 100%. The models shown in Figures 3(a), 3(b), 3(c) and 3(d) have adjusted R-squared measures of 90%, 64%, 80% and 76% respectively. Qualitatively, the models account for the majority of the energy variation across benchmarks. Second, the models are able to correctly predict which system uses the least energy to run a particular compute kernel in 210 of the 224 kernels. We take care to note that these models are imprecise, lacking exactness in the energy prediction of any particular compute kernel. Nevertheless, they are surprisingly useful for estimating the direction and magnitude of the energy difference between the ARM and x86 systems.

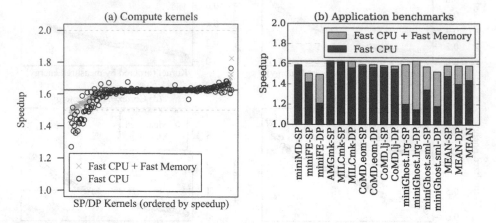

Fig. 4. Estimated speedup conferred by CPU and memory speed improvements in 64-bit ARM systems for (a) compute kernels (b) and application benchmarks. The thick red line shows the theoretical speedup that would be achieved if scaling by the CPU clock rate increase $(2.6/1.6 = 1.625)$.

4.4   Implications for 64-Bit ARM

Implementations of 64-bit ARM platforms are expected to arrive in early to mid 2014. It is widely anticipated that 64-bit ARM will improve upon the current 32-bit implementations by offering higher clock rates, improvements in the memory architecture, and more complete vector math support, for example by supporting 2-wide DP SIMD operations and fully adhering to the IEEE754 standard. We estimate the impact of these factors on performance by examining the relationship those factors have to performance on the Sandy Bridge system. In particular, we dial down the memory and processor clock frequencies on the Sandy Bridge system to 800MHz and 1.6GHz respectively to measure the speedup between the low and high clock rate runs, which represents how much benefit is conferred to the application by running on hardware which has faster compute and memory resources. Similarly, we estimate the impact of faster CPU only by dialing down only the memory. The estimated speedups produced by this approach are presented in Figure 4, showing in 4(a) that increasing a slow clock rate by a factor of 1.625 confers a speedup of at least 1.625x for a majority (81%) of compute kernels. This suggests that clock rate increases in 64-bit ARM systems are likely to show substantial improvements for the performance of many HPC applications. In 4(b), we present the application benchmarks speedups when speeding up only the CPU clock rate (blue/dark), and both the CPU and memory clock rates (orange/light). From these results and the results in 4(a), we can infer that increases in the speed of the cores, as opposed to the memory, account for the largest share of the speedups in the applications. We conclude from these insights that improvements in the clock rates of 64-bit ARM implementations are likely to have a substantial benefit to HPC applications, while memory speed plays a significant but quantitatively less important role.

5   Conclusion

Using a large number of small, low-power cores has been gaining ground as a design strategy to improve the energy efficiency of upcoming HPC systems. As ARM is the dominant platform in the mobile and embedded computing segments, many believe that ARM is a viable competitor to the high-end x86 systems that make up a substantial fraction of large-scale HPC systems today. In this work, we methodically documented the performance and energy characteristics of a number of HPC computations on several current ARM platforms. We found that performance and energy efficiency of the ARM systems varies by up to an order-of-magnitude and depends on the computational and memory characteristics of the application. Moreover, we showed that this variability can be described as a function of two important processor subsystems: the floating point/SIMD unit and the cache/memory hierarchy. Finally, we investigated the performance implications that 64-bit ARM systems will have, finding that HPC applications stand to benefit substantially from changes in the CPU and memory subsystems.

Acknowledgments. This work was supported in part by the U.S. Department of Defense HPCMP PETTT program (Contract No: GS04T09DBC0017 though DRC) and by the U.S. Air Force Office of Scientific Research under AFOSR Award No. FA9550-12-1-0476. We also wish to thank Mr. Tim Carroll and Dr. Mark Fernandez of Dell for providing early access to the Cortex-A9 based Dell Copper ARM server.

References

1. CORAL Benchmark Codes (2013), https://asc.llnl.gov/CORAL-benchmarks/
2. The Top 500 list (November 2013), http://www.top500.org
3. Yokogawa: WT300 Series Digital Power Meters, http://tmi.yokogawa.com/ us/products/digital-power-analyzers/digital-power-analyzers/wt300- series-digital-power-meters/
4. Asanovic, K., Bodik, R., Catanzaro, B.C., Gebis, J.J., Husbands, P., Keutzer, K., Patterson, D.A., Plishker, W.L., Shalf, J., Williams, S.W., et al.: The landscape of parallel computing research: A view from berkeley. Technical report, Technical Report UCB/EECS-2006-183, EECS Department, University of California, Berkeley (2006)
5. Attig, N., Gibbon, P., Lippert, T.: Trends in supercomputing: The european path to exascale. Computer Physics Communications 182(9), 2041–2046 (2011)

6. Bailey, D.H., Barszcz, E., Barton, J.T., Browning, D.S., Carter, R.L., Dagum, L., Fatoohi, R.A., Frederickson, P.O., Lasinski, T.A., Schreiber, R.S., et al.: The nas parallel benchmarks summary and preliminary results. In: Proceedings of the 1991 ACM/IEEE Conference on Supercomputing, 1991, pp. 158–165. IEEE (1991)

7. Blem, E.R., Menon, J., Sankaralingam, K.: Power struggles: Revisiting the risc vs. cisc debate on contemporary arm and x86 architectures. In: HPCA, pp. 1–12 (2013)

8. Buttari, A., Dongarra, J., Langou, J., Langou, J., Luszczek, P., Kurzak, J.: Mixed precision iterative refinement techniques for the solution of dense linear systems. International Journal of High Performance Computing Applications 21(4), 457–466 (2007)

9. Carrington, L., Laurenzano, M., Snavely, A., Campbell, R.L., Davis, L.P.: How well can simple metrics represent the performance of hpc applications? In: Proceedings of the 2005 ACM/IEEE Conference on Supercomputing, SC 2005, p. 48. IEEE Computer Society, Washington, DC (2005)

10. Carrington, L., Snavely, A., Gao, X., Wolter, N.: A performance prediction framework for scientific applications. In: Sloot, P.M.A., Abramson, D., Bogdanov, A.V., Gorbachev, Y.E., Dongarra, J. J., Zomaya, A.Y. (eds.) ICCS 2003, Part III. LNCS, vol. 2659, pp. 926–935. Springer, Heidelberg (2003)

11. Cordery, M., Austin, B., Wassermann, H., Daley, C., Wright, N., Hammond, S., Doerfler, D.: Analysis of cray xc30 performance using trinity-nersc-8 benchmarks and comparison with cray xe6 and ibm bg/q (2013)

12. Analytics, E.P.: EPAX Toolkit: Binary Analysis for ARM (2014), http://epaxtoolkit.com/

13. Fürlinger, K., Klausecker, C., Kranzlmüller, D.: Towards energy efficient parallel computing on consumer electronic devices. In: Kranzlmüller, D., Toja, A.M. (eds.) ICT-GLOW 2011. LNCS, vol. 6868, pp. 1–9. Springer, Heidelberg (2011)

14. Goodacre, J.: Technology preview: The armv8 architecture. White Paper (November 2011)

15. Goodacre, J., Cambridge, A.: The evolution of the arm architecture towards big data and the data-centre. In: Proceedings of the 8th Workshop on Virtualization in High-Performance Cloud Computing, p. 4. ACM (2013)

16. Heroux, M.A., Doerfler, D.W., Crozier, P.S., Willenbring, J.M., Edwards, H.C., Williams, A., Rajan, M., Keiter, E.R., Thornquist, H.K., Numrich, R.W.: Improving performance via mini-applications. Sandia National Laboratories, Tech. Rep. (2009)

17. Hölzle, U.: Brawny cores still beat wimpy cores, most of the time. IEEE Micro 30(4) (2010)

18. Kerbyson, D.J., Alme, H.J., Hoisie, A., Petrini, F., Wasserman, H.J., Gittings, M.: Predictive performance and scalability modeling of a large-scale application. In: Proceedings of the 2001 ACM/IEEE Conference on Supercomputing (CDROM), Supercomputing 2001, pp. 37–37. ACM, New York (2001)

19. Kerbyson, D.J., Jones, P.W.: A performance model of the parallel ocean program. Int. J. High Perform. Comput. Appl. 19(3), 261–276 (2005)

20. Kogge, P., Bergman, K., Borkar, S., Campbell, D., Carson, W., Dally, W., Denneau, M., Franzon, P., Harrod, W., Hill, K., et al.: Exascale computing study: Technology challenges in achieving exascale systems (2008)

21. Laurenzano, M.A., Meswani, M., Carrington, L., Snavely, A., Tikir, M.M., Poole, S.: Reducing energy usage with memory and computation-aware dynamic frequency scaling. In: Jeannot, E., Namyst, R., Roman, J. (eds.) Euro-Par 2011, Part I. LNCS, vol. 6852, pp. 79–90. Springer, Heidelberg (2011)

22. Laurenzano, M.A., Tikir, M.M., Carrington, L., Snavely, A.: Pebil: Efficient static binary instrumentation for linux. In: 2010 IEEE International Symposium on Performance Analysis of Systems & Software, ISPASS 2010, pp. 175–183. IEEE (2010)

23. Ou, Z., Pang, B., Deng, Y., Nurminen, J.K., Yla-Jaaski, A., Hui, P.: Energy- and cost-efficiency analysis of arm-based clusters. In: Symposium on Cluster, Cloud and Grid Computing, CCGRID (2012)

24. Padoin, E.L., de Oliveira, D.A., Velho, P., Navaux, P.O., Videau, B., Degomme, A., Mehaut, J.-F.: Scalability and energy efficiency of hpc cluster with arm mpsoc

25. Pouchet, L.-N.: PolyBench: The Polyhedral Benchmark suite (2012), http://www.cse.ohio-state.edu/~pouchet/software/polybench/

26. Rajovic, N., Rico, A., Vipond, J., Gelado, I., Puzovik, N., Ramirez, A.: Experiences with mobile processors for energy efficient hpc. In: Design, Automation and Test in Europe Conference and Exhibition, DATE (2013)

27. Shalf, J., Dosanjh, S., Morrison, J.: Exascale computing technology challenges. In: Palma, J.M.L.M., Daydé, M., Marques, O., Lopes, J.C. (eds.) VECPAR 2010. LNCS, vol. 6449, pp. 1–25. Springer, Heidelberg (2011)

28. Sharkawi, S., DeSota, D., Panda, R., Stevens, S., Taylor, V., Wu, X.: Swapp: A framework for performance projections of hpc applications using benchmarks. In: Proceedings of the 2012 IEEE 26th International Parallel and Distributed Processing Symposium Workshops & PhD Forum, IPDPSW 2012, pp. 1722–1731. IEEE Computer Society, Washington, DC (2012)

29. Snavely, A., Carrington, L., Wolter, N., Labarta, J., Badia, R., Purkayastha, A.: A framework for performance modeling and prediction. In: Proceedings of the 2002 ACM/IEEE Conference on Supercomputing, Supercomputing 2002, pp. 1–17. IEEE Computer Society Press, Los Alamitos (2002)

30. Snir, M., Gropp, W., Kogge, P.: Exascale research: Preparing for the post–moore era (2011)

31. Vogt, W.P., Johnson, R.B.: Dictionary of statistics & methodology: A nontechnical guide for the social sciences. Sage (2011)

On Interactions among Scheduling Policies: Finding Efficient Queue Setup Using High-Resolution Simulations

Dalibor Klusáček[1,2] and Šimon Tóth[1,2]

[1] CESNET a.l.e., Zikova 4, Prague, Czech Republic
[2] Faculty of Informatics, Masaryk University
Botanická 68a, Brno, Czech Republic
{xklusac,toth}@fi.muni.cz

Abstract. Many studies in the past two decades focused on the problem of efficient job scheduling in HPC and Grid-like systems. While many new scheduling algorithms have been proposed for systems with specific requirements, mainstream resource management systems and schedulers are still only using a limited set of scheduling policies. Production systems need to balance various policies that are set in place to satisfy both the resource providers and users (or virtual organizations) in the system. While many works address these separate policies, e.g., fairshare for fair resource allocation, only few works try to address the interactions between these separate solutions. In this paper we describe how to approach these interactions when developing site-specific policies. Notably, we describe how (priority) queues interact with scheduling algorithms, fairshare and with anti-starvation mechanisms. Moreover, we present a case study describing how an advanced simulation tool was used to find new configuration for an actual resource manager deployed in the Czech National Grid, significantly increasing its performance.

Keywords: Scheduling, Queues, Fairshare, Simulation.

1 Introduction

For many years, researchers have been searching for a perfect job scheduling algorithm that would improve the performance of HPC and Grid-like systems. Still, there are few algorithms that are being used in practice [18] as can be seen in many production schedulers applied in nowadays general resource management systems. For example, the core of the system is generally based on the trivial first come first served (FCFS) approach and backfilling is typically the most advanced option available [2,1,17,18]. Since backfilling has been proposed in 1995 [13], it is obvious that there is some misunderstanding between the research community and system administrators concerning "what is really important".

In this paper we show that the problem of operating a production scheduler is far more complex than just choosing a proper scheduling algorithm. Using our experience from Czech National Grid Infrastructure *MetaCentrum* [14] we

F. Silva et al. (Eds.): Euro-Par 2014, LNCS 8632, pp. 138–149, 2014.

explain several additional challenges that appear when searching for a functional solution. These problems are related to the fact that real systems must meet far more complicated requirements than those that are typically considered in classical research papers. For example, real life systems have to focus on maintaining fairness among users of the system [9,19], rather than just trying to optimize simple criteria like the average slowdown or makespan. In practice, it quickly turns out that those widely used "theoretical" models and optimization goals are mostly impractical in real life [5,18].

The contribution of this paper is based on our ability to provide detailed insight into a real, complex job scheduling system. In detail, we explain several important features that current resource managers offer to the system administrator in order to establish robust, efficient and fair computing infrastructure (Section 2). In Sections 3 and 4, we provide a real life example from MetaCentrum, describing how the actual resource manager has been reconfigured in order to increase the overall performance and fairness. Furthermore, Section 5 demonstrates how advanced simulation and evaluation tools can be used to evaluate new possible setups of complex scheduling systems prior actual deployment. We conclude the paper in Section 6.

2   Main Components of a Resource Management System

Resource managements systems are rather conservative in their choices of scheduling policies and mostly rely on well established and robust approaches [18]. The desired overall behavior is then achieved through the interactions of a chosen set of policies and additional mechanisms. This section describes these commonly employed components of resource management systems and their impacts.

2.1   Ordering Policy

Ordering policies determine the order of jobs in which they are then processed by a scheduling policy. Resource management systems usually provide a set of static ordering policies (ordering between two jobs does not change once established) as well as dynamic policies. Jobs can be either kept in the order of their arrival (static ordering), or can be ordered dynamically according to their length (Shortest Job First, Longest Job First), according to their resource requirements (Largest CPU/Memory Requirements First,...) or their (user configured) priority. Combinations of ordering policies are also possible [1,7].

Fairshare is a dynamic priority ordering policy designed to provide user-to-user fairness. Job ordering is usually based on users previous resource consumption [7,12]. Typically, the more resources a user consumes the lower her priority becomes. Fairshare self-balances itself around an equilibrium where all users have consumed the same amount of resources. Practical implementations of fairshare also *reflect aging* [7] by periodically decreasing all recorded consumption using so called decay factor [1]. This is suitable for systems with faster job turnaround times that put higher emphasis on more recent resource consumption.

2.2   Scheduling Policy

Commonly used scheduling policies range from trivial FCFS, aggressive back-filling (no reservations), to EASY [13] or Conservative backfilling [7], each with it's own shortcomings. *FCFS* guarantees the execution of jobs in the order of arrival by considering the first job only (provided by the ordering policy). FCFS will wait until the first job can be executed and only then continues processing the rest of the jobs. *EASY backfilling* [13] builds on top of FCFS but instead of strictly following the job order as mandated by the ordering policy it only guarantees the earliest possible start for the first job. Other jobs are allowed to start, as long as they do not interfere with the first job's reservation. *Conservative backfilling* extends EASY by providing reservation for every job that cannot start immediately. Remaining jobs are allowed to start as long as they do not interfere with any previously established reservation. The notions of "first job" and the order of jobs are mandated by the ordering policy as was described in Section 2.1.

Job starvation is an undesirable process where a particular job (or a user) is subject to excessive wait time due to the presently configured policies. The notion of excessive is of course subject to interpretation. For example, fairshare ordering priority will deliberately cause starvation of users with recent high resource consumption, which is however considered desirable. FCFS and Conservative backfilling algorithms provide anti-starvation mechanisms, guaranteeing that jobs are not undesirably delayed. More aggressive forms of backfilling like EASY or aggressive backfilling need to be combined with other mechanisms in order to prevent starvation, as they can delay the execution of certain jobs without any bounds [15].

2.3   Queue Configuration

Previously presented policies provided by resource management systems are relatively simple. At the same time, a single policy cannot cover the usually complex requirements used in production systems. To deal with more complex requirements, resource management systems provide the notion of queues which can be configured separately. Then, it is the interaction between queue-specific policies and the global system policies that dictates the overall behavior of the system.

Queues can handle different policies, that are mostly represented by a set of various limits [1,2,17]. These limits then apply on jobs that are executed from that queue. The limits usually cover per-user, per-group and per-queue limitations concerning the maximum number of running jobs and/or amount of particular resource type (e.g., CPU cores). Queues can also be configured to have access to only a subset of available resources, e.g., limiting a queue to a particular cluster of machines. Such policy establishes pools of resources, where several queues can compete for a limited set of resources, thus preventing a (potentially dangerous) saturation of the entire system.

While such configuration can increase resource fragmentation [7], it is necessary when dealing with different classes of users accessing the system. We need to be very careful when saturating the system with jobs from a single user, or even when saturating the system with a single class of jobs. For example, saturating the system with long running jobs (i.e., jobs with expected runtime of several weeks) will naturally lead to great deterioration in performance characteristics of the system (e.g., huge wait times for shorter jobs).

Such situations are approached in different manners. For example, in Zeus cluster in PL-Grid, all long jobs as well as jobs that require whole node(s) are planned ahead using reservations which enables the forward detection of potential problems [4]. In Ohio Supercomputer Center several combined approaches are used together. For example, long serial jobs are only allowed if a user is able to reasonably explain why he or she needs to run such a long experiment [16]. Moreover, parallel jobs have in general smaller maximal runtime limit compared to sequential jobs. Also, per-user and per-group limits are used together with fairshare accounting [16].

Surprisingly, we are not aware of any work that would describe how to determine suitable combinations of global policies and queue configurations. Clearly, a more in-depth analysis must be performed to better understand these issues. We provide such a case study in the following text.

3   Configuration of MetaCentrum Resource Manager

So far, we have provided an overview of several techniques that are available in current resource management systems. In the remaining text we demonstrate how these techniques interact together. We also describe how existing setup can be significantly improved by proper reconfiguration, using a real-life based example from MetaCentrum (Sections 4 and 5).

Before we start, we would like to stress out that there is no widely accepted and universal definition describing "the one and only suitable setup of the system". In fact, different people and/or organizations may have different notion of "what is efficient" when it comes to job scheduling. In this paper, we use examples coming from the Czech NGI MetaCentrum. The approaches and solutions presented in the following sections are presented in the context of this system. Still, we believe that they are applicable to a wide range of systems.

3.1   Historical Setup

Historically, MetaCentrum used three major queues (long, normal, short) that had different maximum walltime limits per job (30 days, 24 hours, 2 hours), different priorities (70, 50, 60) and different limits on maximum running concurrent jobs of one user (70, 300, 250). Together with the user limits, long and short queues were also limited to a subset of machines. Using the combination of priorities, user limits and limited resource pools the system originally provided balanced performance for each of the three job classes (under 2 hours, 2-24 hours, up to 30 days). There was also a low priority (20) queue called backfill that only accepted single node jobs (max limit per user is 1000) that run up to 24 hours. Beside these, there were several other queues for special purposes, e.g., administrator's testing queue. Still, majority of jobs used those 4 main queues. A scheme of the historical setup is shown in Fig. 1.

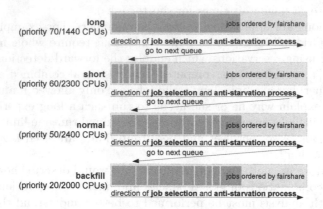

Fig. 1. Historical queues setup as applied in MetaCentrum

Jobs were dynamically ordered within queues using priorities based on fair-share [7]. A backfill-like algorithm was used to scan the queues, starting with the highest priority queue. It immediately started every job that could execute. Those jobs that could not start immediately received reservations using an *anti-starvation* mechanism (see Section 2). A reservation blocked every node that was potentially suitable to execute a job, that is any node that is capable of providing the requested amounts of resources and properties. This approach has been applied as classical reservations computed according to estimated completion times of jobs were very imprecise. This was caused by the fact that users of the system often did not provide detailed runtime estimates, instead simply choosing one of the job classes available (under 2 hours, 2-24 hours, up to 30 days). By reserving all suitable nodes the scheduler was able to guarantee the earliest possible start time, at the cost of decreasing opportunities for backfilling.

3.2 Problems with Historic Setup

The major problem with the historic setup was that *it only used one queue for jobs longer than 1 day.* Therefore, this queue had to be used by every job that was expected to last longer than 24 hours. At the same time, it was also used by very long jobs that are "dangerous" as we have explained in Section 2.3. Therefore, the queue had quite strict limits concerning number of available CPUs (1440), while short, backfill and normal had significantly larger pools of CPUs (2300, 2000 and 2400, respectively). While such a restriction was necessary, it was obvious that it limits efficient usage of resources.

For example, our historic workload logs indicated that majority of utilized CPU time was based on jobs from long queue. An example of job arrivals and

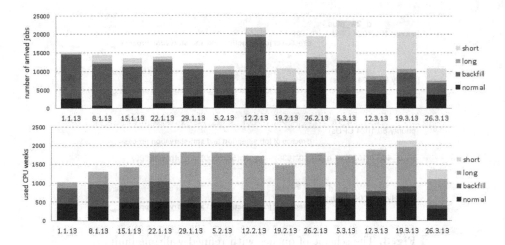

Fig. 2. Job arrivals (top) and used CPU time (bottom) per week and queue

CPU time distribution with respect to queues is shown in Fig. 2. Clearly, long queue, having the least CPUs was at the same time responsible for the most of the overall utilization (see Fig. 2 (bottom)).

4 Proposed Modifications of the Scheduling Scheme

After performing detailed analysis of historic workloads, MetaCentrum management decided that a new setup of the whole scheduling system must be developed. We now present main features of the two new setups that were proposed and evaluated (Section 5), in order to remove aforementioned inefficiencies.

4.1 Conservative Extension

The first considered modification was rather conservative. The main goal was to increase the pool of available CPUs for longer jobs. In the first step, long queue has been refined into 5 queues. The one with the longest maximum job walltime limit is called q_2w_plus (up to 30 days) and has the maximum priority. Next, there are q_2w, q_1w, q_4d, q_2d with decreasing priorities and walltime limits (2 weeks, 1 week, 4 days and 2 days, respectively). Normal and short queues are now called q_1d and q_2h while q_4h is a new queue with walltime limit being 4 hours. The scheme of the system with newly refined queues is shown in Fig. 3.

Once the long queue has been replaced with several new queues it is now possible (and safe) to increase the number of CPUs for selected newly created queues as is shown in Fig. 3. Importantly, we have significantly increased the number of CPUs for jobs lasting at most 2 weeks, while very long jobs (q_2w_plus) obtain at most 1024 CPUs[1]. No other modifications were considered in this scheme.

---

[1] Different queues may share some CPUs, i.e., in general, CPUs available for a given queue are not exclusively reserved for such a queue.

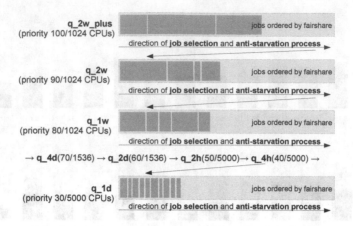

Fig. 3. The scheme of queues with refined walltime limits

4.2   Complex Extension

While the conservative modification described in the previous section was rather simple and straightforward, we also tried to develop a more complex modification that would also address overall fairness and efficiency of the anti-starvation mechanism.

Concerning fairshare, we have replaced the original single-resource aware mechanism that only reflected CPU consumption with a new multi-resource aware solution that also reflects RAM consumption. As discussed in the literature, single-resource based fairshare is highly unfair for heterogeneous systems and workloads [6,8,12]. Beside the fairshare metric itself, we have also started to consider the *effect of newly added queues on fairness*. For example, if a job has low priority (due to the fairshare) but ends up in a high priority queue (due to its walltime) it will often start much earlier than a high priority job residing in a low priority queue, which is highly unfair. Therefore, we have proposed more complex modification of the scheduling scheme, which extends the previous conservative, multi-queue setup. In this case, the queues are only used to (1) *setup CPU limits* and (2) *provide information on job's maximum walltime* (if not specified directly by a user). All (major) queues have the same priority, i.e., the ordering in which a job is being selected for execution is now only based on a given user's fairshare. Therefore, those queues are now only "virtual" and the actual scheduling process is performed over *one single queue* that contains all jobs from those "virtual" queues, as depicted in Fig. 4.

In the second step, we have proposed a modification of the anti-starvation mechanism. So far, all suitable nodes were reserved for starving job (see Section 3.1), which often led to resource wasting. Since the queues are now more fine-grained with respect to maximum job runtime, we can compute estimated job completion times far more precisely and only reserve those CPUs that are expected to be the soonest available. The calculation of reservations uses runtime

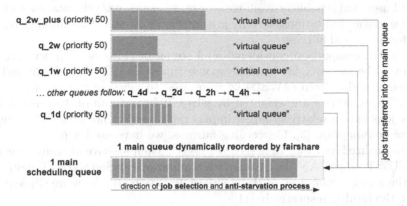

Fig. 4. "Virtual queues" with only 1 main scheduling queue managed by fairshare

estimates (or refined queue walltime limits) of currently running jobs. Reservations are updated in every scheduling cycle with respect to dynamic changes like early completing jobs or changes in fairshare-based priorities.

5   Experimental Evaluation

The two possible modifications of the scheduling scheme described in Section 4 were experimentally evaluated through detailed simulations. It must be said that according to MetaCentrum management, the conservative extension was the prime candidate to become the new production setup in MetaCentrum. The intuition within the management was that *it is a simple and safe evolution of the historical setup.* On the other hand, we believed that the complex extension was more suitable for our purposes, as it introduces new and important features including *multi-resource fairshare and optimized anti-starvation mechanism.* Therefore, it was necessary to perform detailed simulations, analyzing pros and cons of these two candidates.

5.1   Simulation Environment

The simulations were performed using our GridSim-based job scheduling simulator *Alea* [10]. Alea provides advanced capabilities that allow for very detailed and complex simulations. These capabilities include support of several scheduling algorithms, complex job specifications (based on standard qsub syntax used in real systems), multi-resource aware fairshare policies, multi-queue setups including related limits, etc. Alea is regularly used in MetaCentrum to test new setups prior their deployment in the production service.

5.2   Simulation Results

The simulations used a historic workload from MetaCentrum, covering 5 months of execution in 2013. This workload contains 376,722 jobs coming from 302 different users and is publicly available at: www.fi.muni.cz/~xklusac/workload. Due to the space limitations, we only present the most important findings related to performance and fairness.

The initial comparison considered all 3 scenarios (historic, conservative and complex). The avg. weighted wait/response time (AWWT/AWRT) [3] and the avg. weighted slowdown (AWSD) [3] were used to measure the general performance. These metrics are weighted by jobs CPU consumption to prevent that smaller jobs have a relatively larger impact on a metric than jobs with a higher resource consumption [3]. Concerning fairness, we have used a per-user metric called normalized user wait time (NUWT) [11][2]. Then we have measured the avg. of all NUWT values (ANUWT) and their standard deviation (NUWT-dev). The lower the average value and/or the standard deviation are, the more efficient and fair are the results, respectively [11].

The results for these metrics are shown in Table 1 with the best results being highlighted by bold font. Clearly, the complex extension is highly improving, delivering (nearly) best results in all criteria. In fact, the slightly worse NUWT-dev is acceptable as the ANUWT has decreased significantly compared to the historic scenario. Surprisingly, the conservative approach has worse results than both considered setups, which was not anticipated. In fact, all criteria have shown large deterioration compared to historic and complex scenarios. Importantly, the large standard deviation of normalized user wait times (NUWT-dev) suggested that the deteriorating results are likely related to insufficient fairness.

Table 1. General results concerning performance and fairness

	AWWT	AWRT	AWSD	ANUWT	NUWT-dev
historic	33795	629448	2.32	0.11	**0.50**
conservative	56207	647769	4.37	1.07	13.52
complex	**18346**	**609909**	**1.66**	**0.08**	0.56

The initial experiment was a surprise, indicating that *conservative extension is not a good solution* due to a significant deterioration in both performance and fairness related metrics. To better understand the situation, we have measured how the two new setups influence the wait times of users in the system. For this purpose, we have measured the percentage of users/jobs having their wait time (WT) improved or deteriorated compared to the original (historic) setup. Also, we have measured the average improvement/deterioration of wait times for these jobs. The overall results are presented in Table 2. For most criteria, the complex setup behaves similar to the conservative. A closer inspection reveals that the actual problem is the huge difference in the avg. wait time for delayed jobs. Complex increases the avg. job wait time by 2.1 hours while conservative

---

[2] In NUWT, the total user wait time is normalized by the amount of user-consumed CPU time. It uses the same idea as classical *max-min* fairshare [6], i.e., users with high CPU consumption may wait longer than (so far) less active users.

Table 2. Detailed results showing impact on users wait times

	users with impr. WT(%)	jobs with impr. WT(%)	avg. WT impr. (hours)	users with deter. WT(%)	jobs with deter. WT(%)	avg. WT deter. (hours)
conserv.	26.5	**13.9**	6.7	19.2	**2.7**	55.7
complex	**31.1**	13.4	**7.2**	**13.9**	3.2	**2.1**

increases it by 55.7 hours on average! Such a huge increase corresponds with the overall unsatisfactory results seen in Table 1.

Still, further analysis was required to exactly identify the source of the problem. So far, the data indicated that this a fairness-related problem caused by huge wait times of particular jobs. Therefore, we have decided to construct heatmaps showing the avg. wait time of jobs (shown by color intensity) with respect to time (x-axis) and queues (y-axis) for both considered extensions. Fig. 5 shows the results for conservative (top) and complex (bottom) approaches. Using this "high resolution" tool, we can better understand why the conservative approach performs much worse compared to the complex extension.

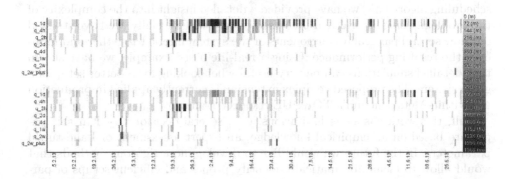

Fig. 5. Heatmap of avg. wait time (in minutes) wrt. queues and time for conservative (top) and complex (bottom) extensions

As was mentioned in Section 4, the conservative approach uses fixed ordering of queues which is potentially dangerous as low priority queues may be "blocked out" by higher priority queues, which is unfair with respect to global fairshare. This "blocking effect" is a result of the applied (historic) "greedy" anti-starvation mechanism. Fig. 5 (top) shows such situations on several occasions where the low priority q_1d and q_4h queues exhibit significant delays compared to higher priority queues. As can be seen, this situation does not appear for complex approach (see Fig. 5 bottom) as (1) all queues are only virtual and all jobs are strictly ordered using fairshare and (2) an optimized anti-starvation mechanism is used.

To sum up, the experiments surprisingly demonstrated that a simple conservative extension of known setup is not a good solution. They revealed previously unexpected results such that it is not sufficient to simply increase the pool of available CPUs for longer jobs, without also improving fairness-related features and the anti-starvation mechanism. For example, it turned out that as soon as longer jobs can use more CPUs it means that also the (original) *anti-starvation mechanism can occupy more CPUs* which blocks all other waiting jobs. Moreover, it was shown that a multi-queue based solution with fixed queue ordering is dangerous as it *ignores global fairshare*. From this point of view, the complex extension increases fairness as now a user with high fairshare-based penalty cannot cheat by sending his or hers jobs into a higher priority queue, such as q_2w, or so. Similarly, shorter jobs having high priorities are not unfairly overtaken by longer jobs (from high priority queues). Also, thanks to the new multi-resource aware fairshare mechanism [12] we are now able to properly establish fairness priorities subject to (highly) heterogeneous resources and jobs.

6   Conclusion and Future Work

We have shown that an efficient job scheduling is a very complex problem when realistic scenarios are considered. Unlike many prior works that only consider scheduling algorithms, we have provided a detailed insight into the complexity of the problem, using several real-life based examples. Especially, we have stressed out how several particular components of the system interact together and influence the resulting performance. Using a real-life based example, we have shown that detailed simulations can be very useful when looking for a better setup of a given system. The proposed complex extension is currently applied in production use within MetaCentrum's TORQUE resource manager.

Still, this work has some limitations, e.g., several decisions used in this paper are based on an empirical knowledge, an expert assessment or hand-tuned parameters. In the future we would like to develop more rigorous methods that would allow to (semi)automatically identify proper and efficient setups of particular policies. For starters, it would be very helpful to have some method for an efficient dynamic adaptation of various queue limits.

Acknowledgments. We highly appreciate the support of the Grant Agency of the Czech Republic under the grant No. P202/12/0306 and the support provided by the programme LM2010005 funded by the Ministry of Education, Youth, and Sports of the Czech Republic is highly appreciated. The access to the MetaCentrum computing facilities and workloads is kindly acknowledged.

References

1. Adaptive Computing Enterprises, Inc. Maui Scheduler Administrator's Guide, version 3.2 (January 2014), http://docs.adaptivecomputing.com

2. Adaptive Computing Enterprises, Inc. Moab workload manager administrator's guide, version 7.2.6 (January 2014), http://docs.adaptivecomputing.com
3. Ernemann, C., Hamscher, V., Yahyapour, R.: Benefits of global Grid computing for job scheduling. In: GRID 2004: Proceedings of the 5th IEEE/ACM International Workshop on Grid Computing, pp. 374–379. IEEE (2004)
4. Flis, L., Lason, P., Magrys, M., Ozieblo, A., Twardy, M.: Effective utilization of mixed computing resources on zeus cluster. In: Cracow Grid Workshop, pp. 105–106. ACC Cyfronet AGH (2012)
5. Frachtenberg, E., Feitelson, D.G.: Pitfalls in parallel job scheduling evaluation. In: Feitelson, D., Frachtenberg, E., Rudolph, L., Schwiegelshohn, U. (eds.) JSSPP 2005. LNCS, vol. 3834, pp. 257–282. Springer, Heidelberg (2005)
6. Ghodsi, A., Zaharia, M., Hindman, B., Konwinski, A., Shenker, S., Stoica, I.: Dominant resource fairness: Fair allocation of multiple resource types. In: 8th USENIX Symposium on Networked Systems Design and Implementation (2011)
7. Jackson, D., Snell, Q., Clement, M.: Core algorithms of the Maui scheduler. In: Feitelson, D.G., Rudolph, L. (eds.) JSSPP 2001. LNCS, vol. 2221, pp. 87–102. Springer, Heidelberg (2001)
8. Joe-Wong, C., Sen, S., Lan, T., Chiang, M.: Multi-resource allocation: Fairness-efficiency tradeoffs in a unifying framework. In: 31st Annual International Conference on Computer Communications (IEEE INFOCOM), pp. 1206–1214 (2012)
9. Kleban, S.D., Clearwater, S.H.: Fair share on high performance computing systems: What does fair really mean? In. In: Third IEEE International Symposium on Cluster Computing and the Grid, pp. 146–153. IEEE Computer Society (2003)
10. Klusáček, D., Rudová, H.: Alea 2 – job scheduling simulator. In: 3rd International ICST Conference on Simulation Tools and Technique, ICST (2010)
11. Klusáček, D., Rudová, H.: Performance and fairness for users in parallel job scheduling. In: Cirne, W., Desai, N., Frachtenberg, E., Schwiegelshohn, U. (eds.) JSSPP 2012. LNCS, vol. 7698, pp. 235–252. Springer, Heidelberg (2013)
12. Klusáček, D., Rudová, H.: Multi-resource aware fairsharing for heterogeneous systems. In: Job Scheduling Strategies for Parallel Processing (2014)
13. Lifka, D.A.: The ANL/IBM SP Scheduling System. In: Feitelson, D.G., Rudolph, L. (eds.) IPPS-WS 1995 and JSSPP 1995. LNCS, vol. 949, pp. 295–303. Springer, Heidelberg (1995)
14. MetaCentrum (January 2014), http://www.metacentrum.cz/
15. Mu'alem, A.W., Feitelson, D.G.: Utilization, predictability, workloads, and user runtime estimates in scheduling the IBM SP2 with backfilling. IEEE Transactions on Parallel and Distributed Systems 12(6), 529–543 (2001)
16. Ohio Supercomputer Center. Batch Processing at OSC (February 2014), https://www.osc.edu/supercomputing/batch-processing-at-osc
17. PBS Works, PBS Professional 12.1, Administrator's Guide (January 2014), http://www.pbsworks.com
18. Schwiegelshohn, U.: How to design a job scheduling algorithm. In: Job Scheduling Strategies for Parallel Processing (2014)
19. Wierman, A., Harchol-Balter, M.: Classifying scheduling policies with respect to unfairness in an M/GI/1. In: 2003 ACM SIGMETRICS International Conference on Measurement and Modeling of Computer Systems, pp. 238–249. ACM (2003)

ProPS: A Progressively Pessimistic Scheduler for Software Transactional Memory*

Hugo Rito and João Cachopo

INESC-ID, Instituto Superior Técnico, Universidade de Lisboa, Portugal
{hugo.rito,joao.cachopo}@ist.utl.pt

Abstract. Software Transactional Memory (STM) is one promising abstraction to simplify the task of writing highly parallel applications. Nonetheless, in workloads lacking enough parallelism, STM's optimistic approach to concurrency control can adversely degrade performance as transactions abort and restart often.

In this paper, we describe a new scheduling-based solution to improve STM's performance in high-contention scenarios. Our Progressively Pessimistic Scheduler (ProPS) uses a fine-grained scheduling mechanism that controls the amount of concurrency in the system gradually as transactions abort and commit with success.

Experimental results with the STMBench7 benchmark and the STAMP benchmark suite showed that current coarse-grained, conservative transaction schedulers are not suitable for workloads with long transactions, whereas ProPS is up to 40% faster than all other scheduling alternatives.

Keywords: Performance, Software Transactional Memory, Transaction Conflict, Transaction Scheduling.

1 Introduction

Software Transactional Memory (STM) [11] turned into one of the most promising abstractions to bridge the gap between mainstream programmers and parallel programming. Unfortunately, the performance of STM-based applications may vary greatly, depending on the application's workload: Even though STMs exhibit very good performance for read-dominated workloads, the same cannot be said about highly contended workloads in which frequent transaction reexecutions place a significant stress on the system, hindering its performance [1,3,7].

Transactions reexecute whenever they conflict, which happens when the STM runtime speculatively executes two or more concurrent transactions that cannot both commit due to conflicting memory accesses.

A transaction scheduler [12,2,4] is an STM component that uses runtime information to predict conflicts and, thus, prevent transactions that are likely to

---

* This work was supported by national funds through FCT – Fundação para a Ciência e a Tecnologia, under project PEst-OE/EEI/LA0021/2013.

F. Silva et al. (Eds.): Euro-Par 2014, LNCS 8632, pp. 150–161, 2014.

conflict from running concurrently. The assumption is that in workloads lacking inherent parallelism, executing a large number of transactions concurrently can degrade performance as transactions restart often. So, to limit the amount of restarts and the amount of wasted work, a transaction scheduler serializes conflicting transactions either at transaction begin or at transaction restart.

Unfortunately, most scheduling policies are too conservative as they over-serialize transactions—that is, two non-conflicting transactions are scheduled to execute one after the other when they could safely overlap.

In the next section, we discuss how STMs may benefit from transaction scheduling in high-contention workloads and we explain why coarse-grained and conservative scheduling policies, as those used by existing transaction schedulers, are unable to extract the latent parallelism of STM-based applications.

In this paper, we tackle the problem of efficient transaction scheduling and we make the following contributions:

- A new fine-grained progressively pessimistic scheduling policy (ProPS) for STM that collects information regarding the maximum concurrency level between pairs of atomic operations and, then, uses that information to gradually reduce concurrency as contention increases (Section 3).
- An overview of ProPS's implementation in the FlashbackSTM [10]. This fully decentralized implementation of our novel fine-grained scheduling policy has zero runtime overhead for read-only transactions (Section 4).
- A thorough evaluation of ProPS with both the STMBench7 benchmark [6] and the STAMP benchmark suite [8]. Results show that ProPS is up to 40% faster than ATS [12], CAR [2], and Shrink [4] (Section 5).

2 Why We Need Better Transaction Scheduling

The key observation behind transaction scheduling is that conflicts are dynamic, meaning that the order in which transactions execute influences the number of conflicts that occur. Moreover, in many STM-based programs, transactions execute independently of each other in a nondeterministic order. Hence, by changing the order in which transactions execute, a transaction scheduler may reduce the amount of wasted work in high-contention workloads and increase throughput.

In practice, transaction schedulers use serialization to order transactions with expected conflicts one after another, trading off concurrency between threads for less wasted work. To exemplify, consider the execution scenario 1 depicted at the top half of Figure 1. In this scenario, thread T_1 makes two calls to atomic operation $OP1$ while thread T_2 tries to execute atomic operation $OP2$ once.

Without a transaction scheduler, the concurrent execution of $OP1$ and $OP2$ has an adverse effect on performance because both atomic operations conflict and, thus, only Tx_1 (first) and Tx_3 (later) commit with success without conflicting. Transaction Tx_2, on the other hand, aborts and reexecutes twice before committing with success, which happens only when executing solo in the system.

With a transaction scheduler, after detecting the conflict between Tx_1 and Tx_2 (and to prevent Tx_2 from restarting again) the scheduler may force new

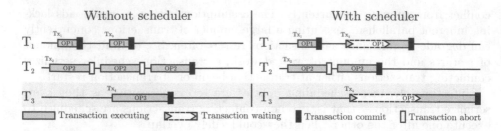

Fig. 1. Execution of operations $OP1$, $OP2$, and $OP3$ without a transaction scheduler and with a naive transaction scheduler by two concurrent threads (scenario 1) and three concurrent threads (scenario 2). Only $OP1/OP2$ conflict when executed concurrently.

transactions to serialize after Tx_2—that is, the scheduler delays Tx_3's start to after the successful commit of transaction Tx_2. With this decision, the scheduler reduces to half the number of transaction restarts, therefore reducing the execution time.

Ideally, the transaction scheduler is accurate enough to execute concurrently only transactions that will not conflict. Though possible in some particular cases, in general this is very hard to accomplish due to the dynamic nature of transactions and, thus, schedulers serialize transactions based on previous observations. Current scheduling solutions, however, are still too coarse-grained, too conservative, and, for those reasons, may serialize non-conflicting transactions.

Coarse-grained scheduling solutions [12] monitor the number of aborts to detect periods of high-contention, in which case they serialize all transactions. Such schedulers assume that, when contention is high, a transaction that aborts and restarts immediately has high probability to conflict again, leading to another transaction abort. Thus, to prevent conflict-prone transactions from conflicting again, the scheduler serializes all transactions that abort.

Despite their low overhead, these *all-or-nothing* approaches to scheduling have limited applicability because transactions are serialized not due to the transaction's expected behavior but because of the behavior of the system as a whole. To exemplify, consider scenario 2 of Figure 1 that extends scenario 1 with a third thread (T_3) executing a single atomic operation $OP3$.

With the transaction scheduler, the reexecution of transaction Tx_2 forces all subsequent transactions (Tx_3 and Tx_4, in this case) to serialize. Yet, as the execution without the scheduler shows, this coarse-grained scheduling policy is over-serializing transactions. Only Tx_2 and Tx_3 need to execute one after the other because only the pair $OP1/OP2$ conflict when executed concurrently. The pairs $OP1/OP3$ and $OP2/OP3$ do not conflict and may execute concurrently with performance benefits as we observe in the scenario without scheduling.

Our naive scheduling policy is an over-simplification of Yoo and Lee [12]'s Adaptive Transaction Scheduler (ATS). In ATS, each thread maintains a contention intensity (CI) value, which is decreased after each successful commit and increased after each abort, and threads serialize in a central queue whenever their CI value is above a predetermined threshold. ATS's scheduling policy is very simple and has nearly no overhead, but is too coarse-grained and unnecessarily reduces concurrency in high contention scenarios, as described before.

Conservative scheduling solutions [2], on the other hand, serialize transactions based on the fact that the atomic operations they execute conflicted with each other, at least once, in the past. By using per-transaction information, the scheduler attempts to predict more accurately how a particular transaction configuration will behave when executed again concurrently. Going back to the previous example, a conservative scheduler may learn that operations $OP1$ and $OP2$ conflict, in which case it will serialize all their future executions.

CAR-STM [2] is a conservative scheduling policy that maintains a per-core transaction queue and, when a transaction restarts, the dispatcher serializes the restarting transaction in the per-core queue containing the transactions with maximum probability of conflicting with it. Even though less conservative than ATS, with a large number of concurrent threads or under high contention, CAR-STM's per-core queues may constitute a performance bottleneck.

The problem with both scheduling policies is that they ignore the fact that transactions are dynamic—that is, a transaction's behavior may change as the state of the application also changes. This means that, for instance, operations $OP1$ and $OP2$ in our example may be able to execute concurrently in the future, if they access disjoint memory locations.

Recognizing this runtime property of transactions, the Shrink [4] scheduler uses the memory locations recently accessed by a thread to predict the read-set of future transactions executed by that thread. At transaction start, Shrink verifies whether any of the memory locations in the transaction's predicted read-set is being written by other concurrently executing transactions and, if that is the case, the starting transaction serializes by acquiring a global shared lock. However, it is unclear how the read-set of a transaction may help predict the read-set of a different transaction executing a distinct atomic operation, even considering the fact that both transactions are executed in succession by the same thread. Also, Shrink intercepts all read accesses to memory, adding a non-negligible overhead to the most common STM operation: the transactional read.

In summary, transaction schedulers' pessimistic approach to concurrency may reduce the number of conflicts between transactions but at the cost of reducing too much the parallelism in the application. The decision to serialize transactions that would execute without conflicting greatly hinders the throughput of the system and constitutes a fundamental obstacle to the effectiveness of scheduling. The challenge, then, is to develop a fine-grained, more optimistic transaction scheduler that is able to increase parallelism between transactions.

3   A Progressively Pessimistic Scheduling Policy

Although system-wide information may help describe the runtime behavior of the system as a whole, the transaction scheduler acts upon individual transactions and, for that reason, the scheduler needs fresh transaction-specific information to perform fine-grained scheduling decisions that minimize the number of transactions that are unnecessarily serialized.

To allow such fine-grained scheduling our new Progressively Pessimistic Scheduler (ProPS) maintains a *concurrency level* matrix (CL) between pairs of atomic operations—that is, for each atomic operation of type i and each atomic operation of type j, the value of CL_{ij} describes how many transactions executing atomic operations of type i may execute concurrently with one transaction executing atomic operation of type j.

In the beginning, all CL_{ij} values are equal to MAX_THREADS, which corresponds to the maximum number of concurrent threads in the systems (typically the number of processors in the machine), and ProPS uses CL values to adapt the amount of concurrency in the system: At transaction begin of atomic operation i, the scheduler calculates the minimum CL_{ij} value between the starting transaction and all other in-flight transactions. Atomic operations with a minimum CL value of MAX_THREADS proceed normally. Yet, as an operation's minimum CL value decreases, ProPS reduces the number of transactions executing that operation.

When a transaction of type i aborts due to a conflict with another transaction of type j, ProPS reduces the concurrency level between atomic operations of type j and i using equation 1 below, where k is a value in $[0, 1]$.

$$CL_{ji} = CL_{ji} \times k \tag{1}$$

By limiting the number of transactions of type j that may start concurrently with transactions of type i only, our new scheduling policy reduces the STM's level of optimism in a fine-grained way. Future transactions for different atomic operations are unaffected by this reduction and, thus, may proceed normally at transaction begin if their minimum CL value is equal to MAX_THREADS.

When a transaction of type i finally commits with success, for each operation of type j ProPS updates operation's i CL_{ij} values using equation 2 below, where α is a value in $[0, 1]$, and $numRestarts \geq 0$ corresponds to the number of times that the committing transaction restarted before this successful commit.

$$CL_{ij} = min(\text{MAX\_THREADS}, CL_{ij} + \text{MAX\_THREADS} \times \alpha \div (1 + numRestarts)) \tag{2}$$

Note that, by design, ProPS exponentially reduces concurrency as transactions conflict but increases concurrency only linearly at transaction commit. This design decision allows the scheduler to react very fast to periods of high contention, while, at the same time, to steadily revise its predictions as transactions start committing with success. Furthermore, at transaction commit, our scheduling policy uses the number of times the transaction aborted before committing with success to control how fast the scheduler restores concurrency, benefiting transactions that seldom conflict.

4   The ProPS Implementation

We implemented ProPS in the FlashbackSTM [10], a word-base, multi-version STM implemented as a pure Java library that extends the lock-free version of the JVSTM [5] with the concept of memo-transactions [9]. In the FlashbackSTM,

```
1   static double[][] CL; static TxInfo[] txs; TxInfo myInfo
2
3   upon tx.begin:
4     myInfo.id = tx.id; myInfo.numRestarts = 0
5     do
6       cl = MAX_THREADS; enemies = 1; worstEnemy = nil
7       for each inFlightTx in txs do
8         if (CL[tx.id][inFlightTx.id] < cl)
9           cl = CL[tx.id][inFlightTx.id]; enemies = 1; worstEnemy = inFlightTx
10        else if (inFlightTx == worstEnemy)
11          ++enemies
12      while (cl ÷ enemies < 1)
13      limitConcurrency(cl ÷ enemies)
14
15  upon tx.abort caused by enemyTx:
16    myInfo.numRestarts++
17    CL[enemyTx.id][myInfo.id] = CL[enemyTx.id][myInfo.id] * k
18
19  upon tx.commit:
20    txs[myInfo.pos] = nil
21    for each opId in atomicOperations do
22      CL[myInfo.id][opId] = min(MAX_THREADS,
23        CL[myInfo.id][opId] + MAX_THREADS × α ÷ (1 + myInfo.numRestarts))
```

Listing 1.1. The ProPS implementation. The scheduler is fully decentralized as each thread decides whether to wait or to begin immediately by itself.

reads are very fast, always consistent, and read-only transactions never conflict with other transactions. Read-write transactions, on the other hand, may conflict but only with other already committed read-write transactions.

To control the execution and the order in which read-write transactions commit, we changed the FlashbackSTM in two ways. First, we changed read-write transactions so that they report to the scheduler at transaction begin time, commit time, and abort time. Second, we changed the bytecode manipulator so that it assigns a unique identifier (ID) to each atomic operation.

Note that our modifications to the FlashbackSTM have zero runtime overhead for read-only transactions: Given that read-only transactions never conflict in the FlashbackSTM, they do not need to be scheduled and, thus, never report to the transaction scheduler as read-write transactions do. In Listing 1.1 we show the pseudocode of ProPS, which works in a fully decentralized way because each thread decides whether to wait or to begin immediately by itself.

ProPS stores per-thread information in a TxInfo object and system-wide information in a global CL matrix and in a global txs array. The thread-local TxInfo instance gathers information about the transaction currently in execution by the thread, such as the ID of the atomic operation, and the number of transaction restarts. On the other hand, the global CL matrix stores the concurrency level between pairs of atomic operations, as described in the previous section, whereas the global txs array contains all in-flight transaction currently in the system.

At begin time, the scheduler updates the thread's TxInfo instance with information regarding the new transaction (line 4) and uses the CL matrix to calculate the transaction's minimum cl value, depending on the operation's ID and the current system configuration (lines 5–12).

The limitConcurrency function (line 13) may delay the execution of a transaction because it forces the starting transaction to acquire a position in the txs array with a compare-and-swap (CAS) operation. When a transaction successfully acquires a given position in the txs array, it may begin its execution (otherwise, it will have to keep trying until it succeeds); when the transaction finishes, it releases its position in the txs array, as shown in line 20.

The size of the array corresponds to the maximum number of read-write transactions that the scheduler will allow to execute concurrently—in our current implementation, the size of the array corresponds to the number of cores in the machine—and the scheduler uses the minimum cl value of each starting transaction to control the number of positions in the array that may be used. With a cl value equal to MAX_THREADS, the scheduler behaves similarly to an optimistic scheduler. Lower cl values make ProPS progressively more pessimistic.

At transaction abort, the scheduler increments the number of restarts (line 16) and reduces the concurrency level (line 17). At commit time, a committing transaction increments its concurrency level with all atomic operations (lines 21–23).

It is worth mentioning that we made our implementation as lightweight as possible. For instance, accesses to the CL matrix are not explicitly synchronized and, thus, threads may read stale data. We argue, however, that adding random imprecisions to the scheduler is preferable than to pay the high cost of synchronization because, in this particular context, suboptimal scheduling decisions do not change the semantics of the programs, only their performance.

5   Experimental Results

To evaluate our approach, we used the STMBench7 benchmark [6] and the STAMP benchmark suite [8]. We ran these benchmarks using the Flashback-STM either with no scheduler (shown as *Default*) or with one of the following schedulers: ProPS, ATS [12], CAR [2], and Shrink [4].

We configured ProPS with a k-value of 0.5, an α-value of 0.05. We tested with several values for these parameters and used the values that produced the best results. Due to space constraints, we do not show in this paper a sensitivity analysis for these parameters, but the results do not vary too much within a reasonable range for these values.

Neither one of the pessimistic schedulers used in our tests had an implementation for the FlashbackSTM, so we provided our own optimized implementation of each scheduling policy. To collect fair and comparable results, all four schedulers share the same FlashbackSTM code base and the same scheduling interface.

We ran our tests on a machine with four AMD Opteron 6168 processors, each with 12 cores, for a total number of 48 cores. All processors shared a Supermicro H8QG6 motherboard with 128Gb of RAM. The machine was running CentOS

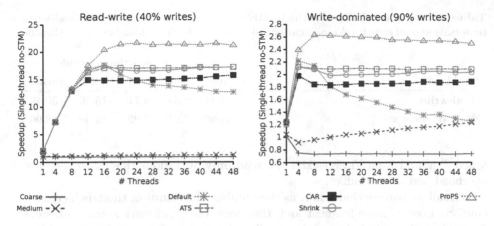

Fig. 2. Speedup of the STMBench7 benchmark with all long read-write traversals and all structural modifications disabled, for each of the two workloads

release 6.4 and Java SE version 1.7.0_21. We made 20 runs of each benchmark with 1 up to 48 threads in increments of 4 threads per test, and we removed the top 5 best and worst results, presenting only the average of the ten remaining values. The speedup results use as baseline the execution time of the benchmark running single-threaded without any STM instrumentation.

5.1   STMBench7 Benchmark: Short Transactions

The STMBench7 benchmark was designed to test STMs under high-contention scenarios, making it appropriate to understand how non-negligible concurrency among transactions that often results in reexecutions affects performance.

We measured the time it took for the benchmark to complete a fixed number of operations with all long read-write traversals and all structural modifications disabled in a read-write workload (40% writes out of 130000 total operations) and in a write-dominated workload (90% writes out of 60000 total operations).

In Figure 2, we present speedup results for the STMBench7 benchmark using both the FlashbackSTM with the various schedulers and two lock-based approaches: coarse-grained locks and medium-grained locks.

Although STM's indirect memory accesses add overhead, on both workloads with one thread the STM version of the benchmark is faster than the non-instrumented version of the benchmark. This happens because some operations execute repeated method calls. These methods, when executed inside Flashback-STM's memo-transactions, populate a per-transaction memo-cache with information about their runtime behavior. The STM then uses this information to identify repeated work that may be skipped, thus improving performance.

Comparing the results obtained with the various schedulers, we see that, regardless of the workload, ProPS outperforms all other approaches. The results for the read-write workload with the STM are specially good when compared to locks, because this workload benefits both from our less pessimistic approach to

Table 1. Percentage of aborts of the STMBench7 benchmark with all long read-write traversals and all structural modifications disabled, for both workloads with 48 threads

		Transaction scheduler			
Workload	Default	ATS	CAR	ProPS	Shrink
Read-write	59.41	9.34	8.71	15.96	30.49
Write-dominated	65.06	7.93	6.92	16.50	28.96

scheduling and from FlashbackSTM's read-only operations that have very low overhead and never conflict.

Overall we can conclude that, as the number of concurrent threads increases, conflicts become more frequent and, therefore, the benchmark starts to benefit from scheduling. The influence that conflicts have on performance is more evident on the write-dominated workload where the FlashbackSTM without scheduling achieves its peak speedup with 4 threads and then performance abruptly plunges to the point that, with 48 threads, the benchmark executes as fast as with 1 thread. With scheduling, on the other hand, the benchmark is able to maintain the performance stable as the number of threads increases.

Despite the drastic reduction in the abort rate (Table 1), none of the pessimistic schedulers' peak performance surpasses the peak performance of the Default scheduler. As the results with ATS and CAR clearly show, even on write-dominated, conflict-prone workloads a lower abort rate may not translate into better performance if the scheduler is too pessimistic and serializes transactions that could otherwise execute concurrently without conflicts.

Instead of serializing all transactions when contention is high as traditional pessimistic schedulers do, ProPS's progressively pessimistic scheduling policy gradually reduces concurrency when transactions start conflicting. Thus, even though the abort rate goes up to 16.50%, ProPS outperforms all other alternatives, showing that there is latent parallelism in the benchmark that is not explored by the pessimistic schedulers.

5.2 STMBench7 Benchmark: Mixed Transactional Workload

The previous results were obtained with two workloads that execute short transactions predominantly. Now, we explore how the various schedulers behave for a workload with very long transactions: For that, we use again the STMBench7 benchmark, but now with all long read-write traversals enabled.

For these tests, we changed the number of operations executed on each workload to 4000 operations on the read-write workload and to 2000 operations on the write-dominated workload. This change was necessary to maintain an average execution time of roughly 30 seconds with 48 threads. We present the speedup results in Figure 3.

As we can see, all pessimistic schedulers perform worse than the FlashbackSTM with no scheduler, a result somewhat surprising because the use of a scheduler

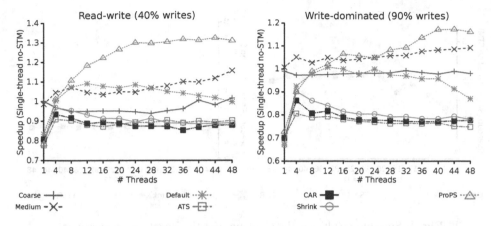

Fig. 3. Speedup results relative to a sequential execution of the STMBench7 benchmark with all structural modifications disabled, for each of the two workloads

should reduce the amount of wasted computation due to conflicting transactions, and STMBench7 is known for having a highly conflicting workload. Yet, despite its high abort rate, the Default approach extracts more parallelism from the benchmark with its optimistic approach, and, thus, it has better performance.

These results show that the performance issues caused by over-serialization are specially bad in applications that execute large numbers of threads in a mixed transactional workload where the size of transactions may vary greatly.

Furthermore, our results strongly indicate that the assumption behind most pessimistic scheduling policies—that in high contention workloads transactions that conflicted at least once in the past will always conflict with each other again in the future—is usually wrong and, for that reason, schedulers need to take into consideration the dynamic nature of transactions when deciding.

ProPS's more optimistic approach to concurrency, coupled with fine-grained information about the conflict probability between atomic operations, is able to make better scheduling decisions, extract more parallelism from the benchmark, and improve performance up to 35% in these two highly contented workloads.

Finally, despite the additional overhead imposed by the STM, the Flashback-STM with ProPS outperforms locks and scales better on both workloads. Even on the worst case scenario where 90% of transactions are read-write and may read up to 1 million memory locations, ProPS is able to extract the benchmark's latent parallelism and scale up to 40 threads. In this very demanding workload, medium-grained locks are only 10% faster with 48 threads than with 1 thread, whereas ProPS with 48 threads executes 70% faster than with 1 thread and surpasses the performance of medium-grained locks for 16 or more threads.

5.3   STAMP Benchmark Suite

STAMP has eight different applications but we limited our study to Genome and Vacation as these applications represent two important execution scenarios:

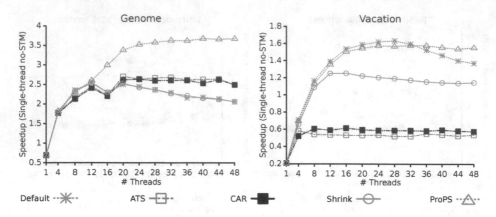

Fig. 4. Speedup results for the Genome and the Vacation applications

Genome executes millions of short transactions (98% of read-write transactions read less than 3 memory locations), whereas Vacation predominantly executes long transactions that perform up to 7226 transactional reads. Each application executed with the following parameters: For Genome, "-g 32768 -s 64 -n 66777216", and for Vacation, "-n 1800 -q 90 -u 90 -r 16384 -t 300000".

Figure 4 shows the speedup results for the various schedulers. Once again, ProPS consistently outperforms all other transaction schedulers.

Genome's results highlight the usefulness of our scheduler in an application that executes millions of micro transactions. ProPS is always as good or better than all other schedulers, improving performance up to 40%. Yet, ProPS does not scale past 24 threads and we believe that the cost of creating and terminating a high number of short lived transactions justifies this performance plateau.

The Vacation benchmark reinforces the idea that current pessimistic schedulers are not suitable for workloads with long transactions: Again, all pessimistic schedulers perform significantly worse than Default. Most transactions in this benchmark are long and, therefore, the decision to serialize any transaction that would be able to execute without conflicting greatly hinders the performance of the system. ATS, CAR, and Shrink use coarse-grained, conservative heuristics that fail to predict the behavior of each individual transaction and end up serializing almost all threads. ProPS, on the other hand, is the first transaction scheduler to perform well on these types of workloads.

6   Conclusions

In this paper we proposed ProPS, a new transaction scheduler for STM systems that gradually adapts the amount of concurrency in the application as transactions abort and commit. When compared to other scheduling policies, our new scheduling policy is fine-grained, because ProPS calculates CL_{ij} values for each pair of atomic operations i and j, and is *progressively pessimistic*, because rather than serializing all transactions when contention is high, ProPS gradually reduces concurrency as CL values decreases.

Experimental evaluation with the STMBench7 benchmark and the STAMP benchmark suite demonstrated the usefulness of our novel scheduling policy as ProPS was able to outperform and scale better than all other scheduling alternatives in a variety of workloads and applications. Unlike conservative solutions, our less pessimistic approach to scheduling performs well in workloads with long transactions and with a lot of latent parallelism.

References

1. Cascaval, C., Blundell, C., Michael, M., Cain, H., Wu, P., Chiras, S., Chatterjee, S.: Software transactional memory: Why is it only a research toy? Queue 6, 46–58 (2008)
2. Dolev, S., Hendler, D., Suissa, A.: CAR-STM: Scheduling-based collision avoidance and resolution for software transactional memory. In: Proceedings of the 27th ACM Symposium on Principles of Distributed Computing, PODC 2008, pp. 125–134 (2008)
3. Dragojević, A., Felber, P., Gramoli, V., Guerraoui, R.: Why STM can be more than a research toy. Commun. ACM 54, 70–77 (2011)
4. Dragojević, A., Guerraoui, R., Singh, A., Singh, V.: Preventing versus curing: Avoiding conflicts in transactional memories. In: Proceedings of the 28th ACM Symposium on Principles of Distributed Computing, PODC 2009, pp. 7–16 (2009)
5. Fernandes, S., Cachopo, J.: Lock-free and scalable multi-version software transactional memory. In: Proceedings of the 16th ACM Symposium on Principles and Practice of Parallel Programming, PPoPP 2011, pp. 179–188. ACM (2011)
6. Guerraoui, R., Kapalka, M., Vitek, J.: STMBench7: A benchmark for software transactional memory. SIGOPS Oper. Syst. Rev. 41, 315–324 (2007)
7. McKenney, P., Michael, M., Triplett, J., Walpole, J.: Why the grass not be greener on the other side: A comparison of locking vs. transactional memory. SIGOPS Oper. Syst. Rev. 44, 93–101 (2010)
8. Minh, C., Chung, J., Kozyrakis, C., Olukotun, K.: STAMP: Stanford transactional applications for multi-processing. In: IEEE International Symposium on Workload Characterization, IISWC 2008, pp. 35–46. IEEE (2008)
9. Rito, H., Cachopo, J.: Memoization of methods using software transactional memory to track internal state dependencies. In: Proceedings of the 8th International Conference on the Principles and Practice of Programming in Java, PPPJ 2010(2010)
10. Rito, H., Cachopo, J.: FlashbackSTM: Improving STM performance by remembering the past. In: Kasahara, H., Kimura, K. (eds.) LCPC 2012. LNCS, vol. 7760, pp. 266–267. Springer, Heidelberg (2013)
11. Shavit, N., Touitou, D.: Software transactional memory. In: Proceedings of the 14th Annual ACM Symposium on Principles of Distributed Computing, PODC 1995, pp. 204–213. ACM (1995)
12. Yoo, R., Lee, H.: Adaptive transaction scheduling for transactional memory systems. In: Proceedings of the 20th Annual Symposium on Parallelism in Algorithms and Architectures, SPAA 2008, pp. 169–178. ACM (2008)

A Queueing Theory Approach to Pareto Optimal Bags-of-Tasks Scheduling on Clouds

Cosmin Dumitru[1], Ana-Maria Oprescu[1], Miroslav Živković[1],
Rob van der Mei[2], Paola Grosso[1], and Cees de Laat[1]

[1] System and Network Engineering Group,
University of Amsterdam (UvA),
Amsterdam, The Netherlands
C.Dumitru@uva.nl
[2] Department of Stochastics,
Centre for Mathematics and Informatics (CWI),
Amsterdam, The Netherlands
R.D.van.der.Mei@cwi.nl

Abstract. Cloud hosting services offer computing resources which can scale along with the needs of users. When access to data is limited by the network capacity this scalability also becomes limited. To investigate the impact of this limitation we focus on bags–of–tasks where task data is stored outside the cloud and has to be transferred across the network before task execution can commence. The existing bags–of–tasks estimation tools are not able to provide accurate estimates in such a case. We introduce a queuing–network inspired model which successfully models the limited network resources. Based on the Mean–Value Analysis of this model we derive an efficient procedure that results in an estimate of the makespan and the executions costs for a given configuration of cloud virtual machines. We compare the calculated Pareto set with measurements performed in a number of experiments for real–world bags–of–tasks and validate the proposed model and the accuracy of the estimated configurations.

1 Introduction

Bag–of–tasks (BoT) applications are common in science and engineering and are composed of multiple independent tasks, which can be executed without any ordering requirements. Therefore, the execution of a typical BoT application can be parallelized. As the number of tasks within a particular BoT application may be large, the application may also be computationally (i.e. resource) demanding. The execution parallelism and resource demanding properties of BoT applications make them suitable for deployment and execution within the cloud environment. Since the cloud environment has large (theoretically unlimited) resources, the widely–adopted pay–as–you–use model implies the assignment of budgets and/or execution deadlines. Characteristics of tasks, such as the running time, are not given a priori, and therefore need to be estimated [12]. Taking into

F. Silva et al. (Eds.): Euro-Par 2014, LNCS 8632, pp. 162–173, 2014.

account the lack of prior knowledge of the tasks' running times, this presents
the challenges for the resource management system with the conflicting goals of
minimizing the execution cost while meeting the total execution time deadlines.
In general, there are two types of BoT applications, namely *compute–intensive*
and *data–intensive* applications. We focus in this paper on *data–intensive* BoT
applications where each task requires the *large–sized* data to be available at the
location where data processing takes place *before* actual processing. In a typical
scenario involving such BoT applications, the Master (owned by the cloud user)
has a BoT, and each task is to be executed by one of the K Virtual Machines
(VMs), VM_1, VM_2, ..., VM_K. As the VMs are instantiated in the cloud and
become ready, they connect to the Master. When a VM connects (1) , the Master
randomly selects a task from a BoT, and assigns (2) it to the VM. In order to accomplish the assigned task, the VM has to retrieve the data of a–priori unknown
large size via Internet from a remote server (3), and during the retrieval process,
this VM may compete for the network and remote server resources with other
VMs. Naturally, the more VMs that compete for network and remote server resources, the longer the retrieval time, and consequently, the larger the makespan.
Similarly, the larger the data to be retrieved, the longer the retrieval time and
the makespan. However, predicting by how much these factors will impact the
makespan remains a considerable challenge.

In this paper we analyze the significance of the data transfer performance
uncertainty to the makespan. This uncertainty further affects the accuracy of
the schedules presented to the user as (nearly) optimal. This is a consequence of
the approach in which state–of–the–art schedulers cannot identify the network
contention induced by a large number of VMs participating in an execution, or
large data transfers (or both). This leads to incomplete executions, or dramatically violated makespan constraints. We derive a queueing–theory based model
that allows efficient investigation of the impact of data transfer to the makespan.
Based on the model and performed analysis, we derive the procedure that allows
efficient numerical derivation of the makespan, which further allows to calculate
the Pareto optimal solutions for execution costs and makespan.

- We derive and discuss a queueing–theory based model of the cloud system
  used for the BoT applications. This model takes into account the data transfer, and requires only the average size of the data set within the BoT. The
  average size of the data may be estimated using well–known procedure for
  estimating bags stochastic properties [12].
- We analyze the model using Mean–Value Analysis (MVA) [8] and develop
  the simplified, yet efficient procedure that allows us to determine the data
  retrieval time, and to estimate the makespan.
- We validate the proposed model against the traces of two different types of
  real–world BoT applications executions on real–world clouds. In addition,
  we use the MVA method to derive Pareto optimal configurations.

The paper is organized as follows: in Section 2 we describe the related work.
In Section 3 we describe the system model which accounts for the large data

transfers. Further we analyse the proposed model using an MVA approach. Section 4 discusses the results of the model validation, and illustrates the Pareto front of the makespan in case of data–intensive BoT applications using the large data sets. We present our conclusions in Section 5.

2   Related Work

This work is closely related to a number of topics: resource selection and scheduling in clouds,performance prediction, and data-aware scheduling. In this section we provide a short overview of related work.

Efficient resource scheduling with regard to minimizing makespan or other objectives has been explored within the context of cluster, grid and cloud technologies. A common approach assumes full capacity information of available resources and by employing various heuristics optimal schedules are obtained. The majority of approaches just ignore the data access/transfer requirements and expect that the network behaves as an infinite resource.

In [14] the authors consider network resources in the cloud resource selection phase, but they are performance constant, regardless of the workload. The assumption made here is that input data is replicated across the available resources. A genetic algorithm is used to obtain the Pareto frontier of combination of resources that would lead to optimal schedules for a given workload.

The Budget Aware Task Scheduler (BaTS) [12] uses a stochastic approach to determine the workload's properties and uses the collected information to generate an approximated Pareto set of schedules suitable for the workload, along with a predicted makespan [16]. While this system is efficient in predicting the behavior of compute-intensive workloads, the potential impact of the limited network resources on the makespan is ignored. The scheduler presented in [10] is able to predict the execution time of more complex workloads, like DAG workflows and it is data-aware, but it expects full information on tasks runtime including the data transfer time. Moreover, this data transfer time does not change over time with the addition of new, possibly different resources (scaling up).

When network resources are involved and data access becomes a bottleneck, two popular approaches are taken. One optimizes based on data locality, that is, jobs are scheduled on resources that are close to the data sources [7], [6]. An orthogonal approach replicates data [11], such that the same data is stored at multiple locations and compute jobs which require the same data can be spread across the best available resources, thus lowering the chances of contention. Systems like Gfarm [15] and Hadoop [17] ensure that data is replicated system-wide in order to avoid data access bottlenecks. The replication strategy and the number of replicas influences the performance of the system.

However, both approaches require either compute resources located conveniently close to the data or extra steps (and costs) to replicate the data before the application starts. None of the approaches described above take into account the changing data transfer time when predicting performance. Besides, to the best of our knowledge, the queue–network models and Mean Value Analysis were not used for the makespan calculation of data–intensive bags–of–tasks.

3   System Model

In this section we introduce our model of the data–intensive BoT system previously described. First we describe the details of the observed system; then we explain the queueing–theory based model of the system, and we end this section by describing Mean Value Analysis of the given model.

One of the major assumptions for BoT systems is that all tasks from given BoT are independent from one another, i.e. the tasks could be executed without any ordering requirements. The assignment of a single task T_i from a total of N BoT tasks to virtual machines is random, and we neglect the communication overhead (for this assignment) between a particular virtual machine and the master. There are in total K virtual machines, and once the task T_i is assigned to VM_k, $k = 1, 2, \ldots, K$, the virtual machine downloads the data from the data storage. We note the random variable representing the download time of task T_i as T_d, and the expected value of task download time is noted by $T_D = \mathbb{E}[T_d]$.

Once the data corresponding to T_i has been downloaded by VM_k, this virtual machine immediately starts execution of the assigned task. When processing of task T_i is completed, VM_k requests new task assignment from the master. We neglect the time that VM needs to store (i.e. upload) task's output data to a remote destination. As each VM in the system either downloads data or processes the task, the number of tasks (jobs) allowed in the system is constant and equals K. We note the compute rate of VM_k by μ_k, and therefore the average time $\mathbb{E}[S_k]$ a task has been served by VM_k is given as $\mathbb{E}[S_k] = \dfrac{1}{\mu_k}$, $k = 1, 2, \ldots, K$.

Due to the fact that we neglect the upload data process as well as the communication between master and VMs, our system can be modeled as the closed queueing network. The VMs represent a queueing system where every new task arrival experiences immediate service and does not wait – this system is modeled as the one with infinite number of servers, of which at most K are used.

As single data storage is used for the data download, the download happens over shared network resources. Therefore it could be modeled as single–server Processor Sharing (PS) queue, in which the server download rate is μ_S. The PS queue that models download process in our case could be either the Discriminatory Processor Sharing (DPS) or Egalitarian Processor Sharing (EPS) queue. This is due to the fact that download rate experienced by a VM_k is limited by the maximum download rate, μ_k^D, and these download rates may be different for different VMs. When the number of download sessions is small, i.e. when the sum of all the service demands at the server is below μ_S, we have DPS. Otherwise, when the number of download sessions is large, the download process is modeled as EPS. In the EPS model, each of the download tasks present in the system obtain a fair share of the capacity. In such a case the download rate experienced by VM_k is $\frac{\mu_S}{\#dtasks}$. The data download rate for task T_i experienced by VM_k is given as the following:

$$\mu_k^D \text{ if } \sum_{l=1}^{\#dtasks} \mu_l^D \leq \mu_S \text{ and } \frac{\mu_S}{\#dtasks} \text{ if } \sum_{l=1}^{\#dtasks} \mu_l^D > \mu_S \quad (1)$$

The model we presented can be considered as a closed BCMP queuing network [4], i.e. there are multiple classes of the tasks as their processing rates depend on the class of the task. This is due to the fact that a task is already mapped to a VM of a certain type before it reaches the server. Next to it, the download rates may differ, as given by equation 1. In order to calculate the makespan, we need the expected time, $\mathbb{E}[T]$ a task spends in the system. As the data requests are generated only when the task assigned to VM_k is completed, the expected time $\mathbb{E}[T_k]$ that tasks assigned to VM_k spend in the system, equals to the sum of the expected download time $\mathbb{E}[T_k^D]$, and the expected service time i.e.:

$$\mathbb{E}[T_k] = \mathbb{E}[T_k^D] + \mathbb{E}[S_k] = \mathbb{E}[T_k^D] + \frac{1}{\mu_k} \quad k = 1, \dots, K. \tag{2}$$

The average download times $\mathbb{E}[T_k^D]$ are dependent on the number of download tasks, and using equation 1 we have

$$\mathbb{E}[T_k^D] = \begin{cases} \frac{1}{\mu_k^D} & \text{if } \sum_{l=1}^{\#dtasks} \mu_l^D \leq \mu_S \\ \frac{\mathbb{E}[\#dtasks]}{\mu_S} & \text{if } \sum_{l=1}^{\#dtasks} \mu_l^D > \mu_S \end{cases} \tag{3}$$

In order to evaluate the expected number of download tasks $\mathbb{E}[\#dtasks]$ from equation 3 we would need the equilibrium state probabilities of our system. While methods to obtain a product form for the equilibrium state probabilities exist [5], they require computing all the states of the network and their complexity increases with the number of nodes in the network. The computing of states may take time, which impact the time required for the makespan calculation. Besides, in order to calculate $\mathbb{E}[T_k^D]$ we need information about each task size. In order to solve these two issues we derived an aggregated model, based on Mean Value Analysis.

3.1   A Mean Value Analysis Approach

The first step in our approach is to transform the given model into the model in which all virtual machines would have the same compute rate ($\bar{\mu}_k = \bar{\mu}$) as well as download rate ($\bar{\mu}_k^D = \bar{\mu}^D$). The second step is to analyse such model for tasks of average size. This is the essence of the Mean Value Analysis (MVA) approach.

We model the VMs as the queueing system with the infinite number of servers, of which at most K are used. The aggregated compute rate (μ_{agg}) of this system remains the same,

$$\mu_{agg} = \sum_{k=1}^{K} w_k \mu_k \quad \text{where} \quad w_k = \frac{\mu_k}{\sum_{k=1}^{K} \mu_k} \tag{4}$$

where w_k represents the probability that some arbitrary task will be executed on machine k in the non–aggregated system. The service rate of VM_k is

$$\bar{\mu} = \frac{\mu_{agg}}{K}. \tag{5}$$

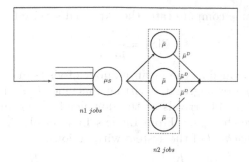

Fig. 1. The aggregated model of the considered system

The similar reasoning holds for the aggregated download rate μ_{agg}^D, i.e.

$$\mu_{agg}^D = \sum_{k=1}^{K} w_k \mu_k^D \quad \text{where} \quad w_k = \frac{\mu_k^D}{\sum_{k=1}^{K} \mu_k^D}. \tag{6}$$

The maximum download rate of VM_k in this system is therefore

$$\bar{\mu}^D = \frac{\mu_{agg}^D}{K}. \tag{7}$$

As in the original model, the actual data download rate is dependent on the number of tasks that simultaneously access the data storage. The data download rate is now equal for all virtual machines VM_k, and let $\mu_S(j)$ be the service rate of the data storage server when the number of download tasks $\#dtasks = j$. Using equation 7 we obtain the following expression for $\mu_S(j)$

$$\mu_S(j) = \begin{cases} \bar{\mu}^D & \text{if } \frac{j}{K} \cdot \mu_{agg}^D \leq \mu_S \\ \frac{\mu_S}{j} & \text{if } \frac{j}{K} \cdot \mu_{agg}^D > \mu_S \end{cases} \tag{8}$$

Due to the aggregation process we can now calculate the stationary probabilities of the system states. The system state is described as (n_1, n_2) where n_1 represents the number of the tasks that are downloaded while n_2 represents the number of the tasks that are processed by (n_2) VMs. It holds that $n_1 + n_2 = K$, and $n_1, n_2 \geq 0$. Let $\pi_1(j|K)$ be the conditional probability that the number of download tasks is j under condition that the total number of tasks in the network is K. We define $\pi_2(j|K)$ accordingly. The mean service time experienced by an arriving job at the data storage node (the average download time) is derived using MVA for the single chain product form closed networks [8]. The MVA analysis is based on two important results from the queuing theory: *the arrival theorem* [13,8] and *Little's Law* [9].

From the arrival theorem we obtain the expected download rate when there are K tasks in the network as the following

$$\mathbb{E}[T^D(K)] = \sum_{j=1}^{K} \pi_1(j-1|K-1)\frac{j}{\mu_S(j)} \tag{9}$$

As VMs have the same compute rate, the expected service time is constant, i.e.

$$\mathbb{E}[S] = \frac{1}{\mu_{agg}}. \tag{10}$$

The *visit rate* is defined as the mean number of visits made by a task at the download server (v_D) or aggregated virtual machines (v_S). In our case, $v_D = v_S = \frac{1}{2}$ as the number of arrivals at the download server and the aggregated virtual machines are the same. From Little's Law we obtain the total system arrival rate, i.e. *throughput* of the system with K jobs:

$$\lambda(K) = \frac{K}{v_D\mathbb{E}[T^D(K)] + v_S\mathbb{E}[S]} = \frac{K}{\frac{1}{2}\mathbb{E}[T^D(K)] + \frac{1}{2}\mathbb{E}[S]}. \tag{11}$$

The queue length distribution at the download server is derived from

$$\pi_1(j|K) = \frac{v_1 \cdot \lambda(K)}{\mu_S(j)}\pi_1(j-1|K-1), j = 1, \dots K. \tag{12}$$

The probability of an empty queue is derived from

$$\pi_1(0|K) = 1 - \sum_{j=1}^{K} \pi_1(j|K). \tag{13}$$

Using recurrence formulae 9–13 we can derive $\mathbb{E}[T^D(K)]$. For a total of N tasks within the BoT, the total makespan obtained using the MVA is

$$M = \frac{N}{\frac{K}{\mathbb{E}[T^D(K)]+\mathbb{E}[S]}}. \tag{14}$$

The computation complexity of the MVA-based estimation algorithm is $O(K^2)$ where K is the number of VMs. As in practice K is relatively small, the MVA approach is well–suited to estimate the Pareto frontier of optimal configurations for a given workload.

4   Evaluation and Discussion

We evaluate the accuracy of our MVA-based prediction procedure for data-intensive bags–of–tasks using an experimental setup consisting of two real-world applications and multiple cloud instance types. We also investigate the efficiency of our MVA-based procedure when employed towards constructing Pareto fronts.

All experiments were performed using the Amazon EC2 [1] cloud region Ireland. The characteristics of the Amazon EC2 instance types used in our experiments are presented in Table 1. The compute performance of each instance consists of the number of virtual CPUs (vcpus) and their allocated shares, ECU (EC2 Compute Unit), the equivalent of a 2007 AMD Opteron CPU. We chose to focus on these three types because they exhibit different computation-to-network-to-price ratios and therefore allow us to analyze the behavior of the MVA-based procedure in different real-world scenarios. The storage server hosting the input data was located in the Netherlands. For instance reservation and task execution we used the Budget- and Time-constrained Scheduler[12].

Table 1. Amazon EC2 Instance Details

Type	CPUs (ECU)	Memory(GB)	Network	Cost($/h)
m1.s	1(1)	1.7	Low	0.047
m1.m	1(2)	3.75	Moderate	0.095
m1.l	2(4)	7.5	Moderate	0.190

Applications. We considered two image processing applications, each display-ing a different compute-to-data ratio: *OpenJpeg* a JPEG2000 software encoder [3] and a *ImageMagick* suite component, which compresses images to the JPEG for-mat [2] and applies a sharpening filter. The input data used for our experiments consisted in a subset of 7500 TIFF image frames in 4K resolution of the open source movie *Sintel*. The average file size was 24.3 MB. For both applications, we estimated the expected performance of each EC2 instance type (see Table 1) us-ing BaTS' sampling module. During the sampling procedure, we also performed network bandwidth measurements to assess the storage server's capacity. We remark that, according to our sampling results, for the same input data, the *OpenJpeg* application has a higher average execution time since the compression algorithm used is more computationally-intensive.

Experiments. To evaluate the accuracy of our MVA-based prediction proce-dure, we compare it against the data-oblivious prediction mechanism of BaTS, referred to as 'simple', and against real executions ("exec") of several scenarios having the same input data (bag), but different cloud instance configurations:

1-1-1 consists in one instance of each type: m1.s, m1.m, m1.l
5-5-5 consists in five instances of each type: m1.s, m1.m, m1.l
10-10-10 consists in ten instances of each type: m1.s, m1.m, m1.l

Since real executions are subject to external noise (such as network traffic or cloud instance performance variability), we repeat the execution of each scenario three times and derive corresponding error bars to obtain the 'exec' makespans.

All results for both types of applications are collected in Figure 2. For each configuration, we present the MVA-based makespan estimate, the 'simple' makespan estimate and the 'exec' makespan (with error bars). Each configu-ration is labeled using the types and respective number of instances, in the following format: `type:no_instances[+type:no_instances[...]]`. All execu-tions were performed three times and the makespans averaged. The variance of each execution was relatively low(0.10-0.20), especially for the 'larger' con-figurations. In the case of 'small' (3 machines) configurations the variance is slightly higher(0.20-0.25). We assume that this is due to both varying network conditions and to the slight variability in performance of the instances. The cloud provider is not able to provide a perfectly identical instance in terms of performance due to the shared environment. Also small configurations are more sensitive to varying Internet conditions.

We selected these three configurations as they offer a good insight with regard to the behavior of the MVA prediction method in the presence of varying numbers and types of instances. The '1-1-1' configuration has a low number of instances and thus can be used to benchmark the behavior of both the MVA and simple prediction methods. The '5-5-5' configuration starts to encounter contention at the storage server, especially in the case of the *ImageMagick* application, which as previously mentioned, exhibits a lower compute-to-data ratio. We already see here that the 'simple' estimation is no longer accurate enough. The '10-10-10' configuration manages to saturate the storage server in the case of both applications. The MVA method is able to include the fact that the data storage server has become the bottleneck. In all cases the MVA value is close to the measured execution time. This shows that the simplification we have made in our model, where all the different types of instances are aggregated and then homogenized does not considerably affect the accuracy of the MVA method.

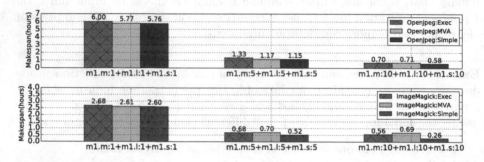

Fig. 2. Measured (exec), MVA Predicted and simple predicted makespans for three configurations

We can now use this result to apply the MVA method to a real scenario in which the user is faced with the task of selecting from a list of configurations, which exhibit different performance and cost. We obtained the Pareto fronts (PFs) of each application, using both the MVA-based and 'simple' estimates, as shown in Figure 3. Each point in the graph represents an unique configuration with its corresponding cost and makespan. The PFs were obtained by exhaustively computing the makespan and budget estimates of all possible configurations, considering a maximum of 10 instances per type, and then selecting the non-dominated set of configuration, i.e. for a configuration from the Pareto Set is . As the maximum number of instances and instance types increases, this approach becomes extremely slow (the total number of configurations grows exponentially). However, here we focus on the efficiency of employing our MVA-based method when constructing PFs and further usage of approximations algorithms is beyond the scope of this paper. In the case of the PF of the *ImageMagick* application we observe a 'tipping point', i.e. a point in the objective space where the speedup obtained by selecting a more expensive configurations starts decreasing considerably. This is less visible in the case of the *OpenJpeg* application, as the saturation point is not fully achieved not even in the case of the most expensive configuration. This is related, as previously mentioned, to the different compute-to-data ratio of the application.

The 'simple' PF offers a set of configurations which, as empirically shown in the first set of experiments does not represent the 'true' Pareto Front, due to the naive method's inaccuracy in the presence of network bottlenecks. By selecting a configuration from this set, the user could potentially make inefficient use of his budget.

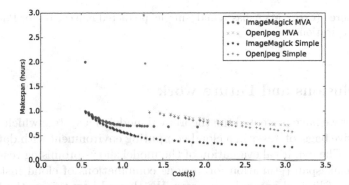

Fig. 3. Pareto fronts for two application types: OpenJpeg and ImageMagick

To empirically evaluate the accuracy of each MVA-based Pareto front, we selected for real execution four configurations: the global cheapest, the cheapest from the group of very fast schedules, i.e. the ones at the right of the 'tipping point', and two other configurations such that they equally divide the price interval between the first two selected configurations. Figure 4 shows the execution makespan (exec), the 'simple' makespan estimate and the MVA-based makespan estimate for each configurations and for each application considered. Each configuration was executed three times and Figure 4 presents the average over the three executions together with the error. Again, we remark that the variance is small, similar to that observed for the first presented experiments.

For all the configurations, the execution times, and both the MVA and simple estimates are close to each other. This is due to the special properties held by the schedules located on the Pareto front. These configurations make best use of the available resources and inherently avoid contention; when contention is reached, the configuration is less efficient with respect to cost and makespan and therefore would not be present in the non-dominated set of configurations (Pareto front).

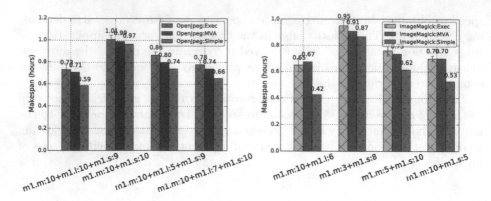

Fig. 4. Measured (exec), MVA-based and 'simple' predicted makespans for Pareto front selected configurations

5   Conclusions and Future work

In this paper we have presented the theoretical model of a system which executes data–intensive bags–of–tasks in a cloud computing environment with data access bottlenecks. The empirical evaluation of the model shows promising results with respect to makespan estimation for various combinations of cloud instances in the presence of limited network resources. We showed how this method (MVA) can be successfully applied to an existing scheduler to obtain Pareto fronts for data–intensive bags–of–tasks workloads. The MVA procedure requires information about the mean behavior of the system's components and thus no other statistical properties can be derived, besides means. While this can be seen as a limitation of the prediction ability of our model, it makes it on the other hand very robust and computationally efficient. As future work we plan to model the system as a more complex queueing network, which would allow us to obtain more properties of the system, such as service time distributions.

Funding has been provided by the Dutch national research program COMMIT.

References

1. Amazon ec2 - amazon elastic compute cloud, https://aws.amazon.com/ec2/ (accessed: January 27, 2014)
2. Imagemagick: Convert, edit, or compose bitmap images, http://www.imagemagick.org/ (accessed: Januray 27, 2014)
3. Openjpeg - jpeg2000 codec, http://www.openjpeg.org/ (accessed: January 27, 2014)
4. Baskett, F., Chandy, K.M., Muntz, R.R., Palacios, F.G.: Open, closed, and mixed networks of queues with different classes of customers. J. ACM 22(2), 248–260 (1975)

5. Bolch, G., Greiner, S., de Meer, H., Trivedi, K.S.: Queueing Networks and Markov Chains: Modeling and Performance Evaluation with Computer Science Applications. Wiley-Interscience, New York (1998)
6. Cirne, W., Paranhos, D., Costa, L., Santos-Neto, E., Brasileiro, F., Sauve, J., Silva, F.A.B., Barros, C., Silveira, C.: Running bag-of-tasks applications on computational grids: The mygrid approach. In: Proceedings of the 2003 International Conference on Parallel Processing, 2003, pp. 407–416 (2003)
7. Frey, J., Tannenbaum, T., Livny, M., Foster, I., Tuecke, S.: Condor-g: A computation management agent for multi-institutional grids. Cluster Computing 5(3), 237–246 (2002)
8. Lavenberg, S.S.: Computer Performance Modeling Handbook. Academic Press, Inc., Orlando (1983)
9. Little, J.D.C.: A proof for the queuing formula: $L = \lambda w$. Operations Research 9(3), 383–387 (1961)
10. Mao, M., Humphrey, M.: Auto-scaling to minimize cost and meet application deadlines in cloud workflows. In: Proceedings of 2011 International Conference for High Performance Computing, Networking, Storage and Analysis, SC 2011, p. 49:1–49:12. ACM, New York (2011)
11. McClatchey, R., Anjum, A., Stockinger, H., Ali, A., Willers, I., Thomas, M.: Data intensive and network aware (diana) grid scheduling. Journal of Grid Computing 5(1), 43–64 (2007)
12. Oprescu, A.-M., Kielmann, T., Leahu, H.: Budget estimation and control for bag-of-tasks scheduling in clouds. Parallel Processing Letters 21(02), 219–243 (2011)
13. Reiser, M., Lavenberg, S.S.: Mean-value analysis of closed multichain queuing networks. J. ACM 27(2), 313–322 (1980)
14. Taheri, J., Zomaya, A.Y., Siegel, H.J., Tari, Z.: Pareto frontier for job execution and data transfer time in hybrid clouds. Future Generation Computer Systems (2013)
15. Takefusa, A., Tatebe, O., Matsuoka, S., Morita, Y.: Performance analysis of scheduling and replication algorithms on grid datafarm architecture for high-energy physics applications. In: HPDC, vol. 3, p. 34 (2003)
16. Vintila, A., Oprescu, A.-M., Kielmann, T.: Fast (re-)configuration of mixed on-demand and spot instance pools for high-throughput computing. In: Proceedings of the First ACM Workshop on Optimization Techniques for Resources Management in Clouds, ORMaCloud 2013, pp. 25–32. ACM, New York (2013)
17. White, T.: Hadoop: The Definitive Guide, 1st edn. O'Reilly Media, Inc. (2009)

SPAGHETtI: Scheduling/Placement Approach for Task-Graphs on HETerogeneous archItecture

Denis Barthou[1,2] and Emmanuel Jeannot[2]

[1] Bordeaux Institute of Technology, France
[2] Inria, LaBRI, France

Abstract. We propose a new algorithm, called SPAGHETtI, for static scheduling tasks on an unbounded heterogeneous resources where resources belongs to different architecture (e.g. CPU or GPU). We show that this algorithm is optimal in complexity $O(|E||A|^2 + |V||A|)$, where $|E|$ is the number of edges, $|V|$ the number of vertices of the scheduled DAG and $|A|$ the number of architectures – usually a small value – and that it is able to compute the optimal makespan. Moreover, the number of resources to be used for executing the schedule is given by a linear time algorithm. When the resources are bounded we provide a method to reduce the number of necessary resources up to the bound providing a set of compromises between the makespan and the size of the infrastructure.

1 Introduction

Directed acyclic graphs (DAGs) have been used to model [7,8,15], execute [2,5,12] and predict [14] the performance of parallel applications. There exists many scheduling algorithms for mapping tasks of a DAG onto the resources of parallel machines [13,17,20]. A lot of work have been proposed to schedule task graphs on heterogeneous resources when execution and communication time depend on the machine that executes a task [3,16,17]. However, recent advances in High-Performance Computing (HPC) have led to two important considerations:

- HPC systems feature a relatively low heterogeneity. Contrary to proposed solutions of the literature where each individual machine can perform differently, one often face a fix number of architectures (e.g. CPU, GPU, MIC, etc.) where performance is homogeneous.
- HPC systems and their applications are of very large-scale. Top end HPC systems can have as many as hundreds of thousands of processors. The tiled version of the dense Cholesky factorization for instance has more than 10 million tasks (matrix of order 204800 and tiles size of 512). Therefore, the complexity to schedule the DAGs is crucial in this setting.

In this paper, we propose a new static scheduling algorithm designed for this kind of systems. Instead of considering each individual processor independently it considers the architectures of the target machine. Within each architecture the communication and execution time is considered homogeneous. Thanks to

F. Silva et al. (Eds.): Euro-Par 2014, LNCS 8632, pp. 174–185, 2014.

that feature, for an unbounded number of resources, it is able to schedule the input graph optimally in terms of makespan, with an optimal complexity of $O(|E||A|^2 + |V||A|)$ where $|E|$ is the number of edges, $|V|$ of vertices of the DAG and $|A|$ the number of architectures and potentially resorting to task duplication.

The remaining of the paper is organized as follows. In Section 2, we discuss the related work. The models are described in Section 3. The algorithm is detailed in Section 4. How to go from an unbounded number of resources to a bounded number is discussed in Section 5. Experimental results are provided in Section 6.

2 Related Work

Static scheduling task graphs on homogeneous resources is NP-hard even for two machines (reduction from 2-partition [9]). However, for unbounded resources and no communication cost it is clearly in P as it requires to use new resources (resource augmentation) to have a schedule of the length of the critical path. In the case of communication cost, optimal scheduling can be found for some special input graph only (without [19] or with [1] duplication).

There exists a lot of static scheduling heuristics for heterogeneous scheduling (see [6] for some examples. If duplication is not allowed, HEFT [17] provides a good schedule in a reasonable complexity $O(|V|^2 p)$, with p the number of processing units. In [6], it has been experimentally shown that HEFT is one of the best heuristics (in terms of makespan) for random graphs among 20 different heuristics. In case duplication is allowed, TANH [3] is a heuristic of interest for our study as it provides a low complexity $(O(|V|(p\log p) + |V|^2))$ and is optimal under some hypothesis. The authors show that TANH provides an optimal schedule (in terms of makespan) if a "*A fork node i that is not a join node is assumed to have the same execution time on all processors.*" Such hypothesis does not hold in many cases. For instance in the Cholesky task graph, the POTRF task is a fork task that is not a join task and its runtime is very different if you execute it on a CPU or on a GPU.

In conclusion static scheduling heuristics have a complexity that depends on the number of processors and are not able in the general case, due to NP-completeness, to provide an optimal schedule.

3 Models and Definitions

We consider an application modeled by a directed acyclic task graph (DAG) $G = (V, E)$ where V is the set of tasks to be executed and E represents precedence constraints between tasks. The execution model of the DAG is close to the macro-dataflow model where a task can be executed only after all its predecessors have terminated and when communications from its predecessors and this task have been performed. However, it differs in the way costs are modeled.

We want to model a large platform where we have different architectures. Think for instance of a node with a set of multicore processors (a NUMA machine with several hundreds of cores) with some accelerators (e.g. GPU cards having each several hundreds of CUDA cores or Xeons Phi each featuring 60 cores with 4 threads each). In this case, we assume that the communication cost between two architectures is the same whatever the actual instances that are sending and receiving the data. Moreover, the communication costs are considered constant when data move within one architecture (whether this task is executed on the same instance as its predecessor or not). This later assumption is different from the standard DAG scheduling model where a distinction is made if the communication is occuring within the same instance (has no cost) or between different instances (has a non zero cost). This is justified as follows. First, in our model, this constant cost can be zero in order to neglect intra-architecture communications compared to inter-architecture communications. Second, we want to produce a schedule where high-level decisions are taken such has: "*On which architecture should I schedule this task ?*" We think the impact of locality on a multi-architecture machine is more important than locality inside one given homogeneous architecture. Third, the assumption of constant communication time within an architecture makes all the difference theoretically speaking: it is this assumption that allows us to find an optimal solution. Finally, the experiment section will show that it leads to predictable execution time and is therefore reasonable in real settings.

Formally, let ω be the communication time function, defined for each edge of the graph, and τ is the execution time function, defined for each vertex. We consider a set of different architectures, A. The communication time for a given edge depends on the architecture executing the vertices of this edge. Hence, the function ω is defined over $E \times A^2 \to \mathbb{R}$: For each edge, we have a communication matrix of order $|A| * |A|$ that provides the communication times of this edge depending on the source and destination architecture. Similarly the execution time function is defined as $V \times A \to \mathbb{R}$: for each task we have a vector of execution time of order $|A|$ (see an example in Fig. 1).

Definition 1 (Start time). *For a task graph G and an architecture set A, the start time is a function:*

$$\theta : V \times A \to \mathbb{N}$$
$$i, j \to t$$

that associates to task i and architecture j a time t for i to start on j. We denote the starting time of task i on architecture j: $\theta_i[j]$.

The start time is a total function, defined for all vertices and architectures. It does not imply that tasks are systematically duplicated on all architectures, but only represents possible starting times according to architectures. The earliest completion time is defined as the minimal time to start a task, added to the time to execute the task, considering all possible architectures: $C_i^{earliest} = \min_{j \in A} \theta_i[j] + \tau_i[j]$ The makespan is then simply deducted: $C_{\max} = \max_{i \in V} C_i^{earliest}$. The makespan usually involves the latest completion time, when tasks are duplicated. The earliest completion time is equal to the latest completion time for non-duplicated tasks. This is not a limitation, since it is always possible to define an additional sink task, having as predecessors the tasks initially with no successors. Besides, our mapping algorithm will ensure that the tasks with an earliest completion time equal to the makespan are not duplicated.

The mapping function defines more precisely the resource executing task i:

Definition 2 (Mapping). *A mapping of a task graph G is a function*

$$\mu : V \times A \to \mathbb{N} \cup \{\bot\}$$
$$i, j \to r$$

that associates to each task i and architecture j the resource number r that executes i. When i is not executed on architecture j, r corresponds to the special value $\bot$. When the same task is mapped to different architectures, there is duplication. We denote the resource executing task i on architecture j: $\mu_i[j]$.

Definition 3 (Constraints). *Given a graph G, a set of architectures A and a vector of resources $r = (r_k)_{k \in A}$, the functions μ and θ define resp. a valid mapping and schedule if and only if the following constraints are checked:*

1. *Resource constraint. One task is executed at a time on the same resource.*

$$\forall i, j \in V, k \in A, i \neq j, \mu_i[k] = \mu_j[k] \neq \bot \Rightarrow (\theta_i[k] + \tau_i[k] \leq \theta_j[k])$$
$$\vee (\theta_j[k] + \tau_j[k] \leq \theta_i[k]) \quad (1)$$

2. *Architecture constraint. Resources are bounded by r:*

$$\forall i \in V, k \in A, \mu_i[k] \leq r_k \quad (2)$$

3. *Dependence constraints. The start time follows the precedence constraint and communication costs:*

$$\forall (i, j) \in E, \forall k, \exists h, \theta_j[k] \geq \theta_i[h] + \tau_i[h] + \omega_{ij}[h, k] \quad (3)$$

4   The SPAGHETtI Algorithm

We consider here the computation of the minimum makespan when there is no resource constraint (1) and no architecture constraint (2). Within this formulation, it is possible to define a schedule and a mapping function giving for each task the architecture(s) where it executes.

4.1   Minimizing Makespan

Consider first the case where there is only one architecture available, i.e. $|A| = 1$. Then ω and τ are only functions of tasks. The optimal makespan can be evaluated by computing the earliest start time of each task. According to the dependence constraint (3), this start time fulfills the following property:

$$\theta_j^{earliest} = \max_{(i,j) \in E} (\theta_i^{earliest} + \tau_i + \omega_{ij})$$

We can arbitrarily define the earliest start time for tasks with no predecessor in G as 0. This formulation then corresponds to a longest path problem on the DAG G (critical path). This can be solved in $\mathcal{O}(|V|+|E|)$ time with a topological sort and then the evaluation in topological order of the function $\theta^{earliest}$.

Now, consider the case where $|A| \geq 1$. The dependence constraint defines the value of the earliest start time as:

$$\theta_j^{earliest}[k] = \max_{(i,j)\in E} \min_{h\in A}(\theta_i^{earliest}[h] + \tau_i[h] + \omega_{ij}[h,k]).$$

Using $(\min, +)$ notation algebra, where the addition corresponds to a min and multiplication to $+$, the min term can be rewritten into: $\sum_{h\in A}(\theta_i^{earliest}[h] * \tau_i[h] * \omega_{ij}[h,k]$. This corresponds to a matrix vector product with θ_i and τ_i vectors indexed by A and $\omega_{i,j}$ a square matrix of rank $|A|$. The vector definition of $\theta_j^{earliest}$ is therefore:

$$\theta_j^{earliest} = \max_{(i,j)\in E} \theta_i^{earliest} * \text{diag}(\tau_i) * \omega_{i,j} \tag{4}$$

with max the component-wise maximum and $\text{diag}(\tau_i)$ the diagonal matrix obtained from the vector. This recursive definition of $\theta_j^{earliest}$ is similar to the case where $|A| = 1$, and leads to the definition of the SPAGHETtI algorithm.

Algorithm 1. Compute the earliest starting time for each vertex in G

Input: $G = (V, E)$ // The input DAG
Input: τ // Function defining the duration time vector
Input: ω // Function defining the communication time vector
1 **forall the** $i \in G$ **do** // Assign a time vector, for all architectures
2    $\theta_i \leftarrow 0$
3 $C_{\max} \leftarrow 0$
4 $S \leftarrow \text{Topological\_sort}(G)$
5 **forall the** $i \in S$ **do** // Visit G in topological order, starting with *source*
6   **for** *every vertex j predecessor of i in G* **do**
7      $\theta_i = \max(\theta_i, \theta_j * \text{diag}(\tau_j) * \omega_{j,i})$// Element-wise maximum on vectors
8    $C_{\max} \leftarrow \max(C_{\max}, \max_{k\in A} \theta_i[k] + \tau_i[k])$

Figure 1 shows an example of the schedule and makespan computed by SPAGHETtI on a graph, for two architectures, CPU and GPU. CPU values are put in the first row/column of vectors and matrices, GPU in the second. For instance, CPU→CPU communication between a and e takes 1, CPU→GPU takes 3. The earliest starting time for task a is 0 for both architectures. The starting time for task b, when started on CPU, is at least the time to complete a on CPU and then communicate with b, or complete a on GPU and communicate accross architectures. This leads to a starting time of 2. This is the same case for GPU, and for task c. Task e on CPU cannot complete before either task a has completed on CPU and CPU→CPU communication has finished (duration 1), or task a has completed on GPU and GPU→CPU communication has finished (duration 4): the earliest starting time for e on CPU is therefore 2. We let the reader continue the reasoning and check the values of the table on the right.

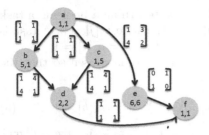

Task	$\theta_{CPU}^{earliest}$	$\theta_{GPU}^{earliest}$	Mapping
a	0	0	CPU
b	2	2	GPU
c	2	2	CPU
d	7	7	CPU
e	2	3	CPU
f	8	9	CPU

Fig. 1. On the left, the task graph with the values of τ for each task and ω for each edge. On the right, the earliest starting time for each task, given when the task starts on CPU and on GPU. Then the last column corresponds to the architecture where the task is mapped in order to reach the optimal makespan (9 in this example).

Theorem 1. *Algorithm 1 computes the optimal makespan of G with the optimal complexity $\mathcal{O}(|A|^2 * |E| + |A| * |V|)$.*

Proof. First, let us show that the SPAGHETtI algorithm computes indeed the optimal makespan. Assume that Algorithm 1 does not compute the optimal makespan. There exists a scheduling function θ' verifying the dependence constraint (3) such that for all architectures k, $\theta'_{sink}[k] \leq \theta_{sink}[k]$ and for at least one architecture, this inequality is strict. Such relation is denoted $\theta'_{sink} < \theta_{sink}$. Consider a task i_0, minimal according to the topological order, such that $\theta'_i < \theta_i$. θ_{i_0} is defined as:

$$\theta_{i_0} = \max_{(j,i_0) \in E} (\theta_j * \text{diag}(\tau_j) * \omega_{j,i_0}).$$

As $\theta_j = \theta'_j$ for all the predecessors j of i_0 and there exists a $k \in A$ such that $\theta'_{i_0}[k] < \theta_{i_0}[k]$, we have:

$$\theta'_{i_0}[k] < \max_{(j,i_0) \in E} \min_{h \in A} (\theta'_j[h] * \tau_j[h] * \omega_{j,i_0}[h,k]).$$

Thus there exists a predecessor j of i_0 such that for all architecture $h \in A$:

$$\theta'_{i_0}[k] < \theta'_j[h] * \tau_j[h] * \omega_{j,i_0}[h,k].$$

This is in contradiction with the dependence constraint (3), and contradicts the definition of θ'. Hence Algorithm 1 computes the optimal makespan.

Now line 7 corresponds to $O(|A|^2 * |E|)$ operations, the $|A|^2$ term coming from the matrix vector product $\theta_j * \text{diag}(\tau_j) * \omega_{j,i}$. Line 8 takes $O(|A| * |V|)$ operations due to the max operation. The total complexity corresponds to the size of the inputs. Since the makespan may depend on all of them, this shows the complexity is optimal. □

4.2 Mapping Tasks to Architectures

Finding a mapping function corresponds to finding one or several architectures for each task, compatible with earliest starting time constraints. As there is no resource constraints, μ is here an indicator function returning a boolean: a task i is mapped on an architecture $j \in A$ if $\mu_i[j] = 1$ otherwise $\mu_i[j] = 0$. A task is duplicated on two different architectures $j, k, j \neq k$ if $\mu_i[j] = \mu_i[k] = 1$.

For all tasks with no successor in G, the architecture is chosen so that the earliest completion time can be attained:

$$\forall h \in A, h = \min\{k \in A \mid \theta_i[k] + \tau_i[k] = C_i^{earliest}\} \Rightarrow \mu_i[h] = 1. \qquad (5)$$

Note that these tasks are not duplicated, since h is uniquely defined. The makespan corresponds to the earliest completion time of one of these tasks, hence the mapping here is chosen so that the optimal makespan is reached.

For all the other tasks, the dependence constraint guides the choice of architecture that can execute them: Consider a task $i \in G$ and an edge $(i, j) \in E$. Assume j is mapped on architecture $k \in A$, then the schedule computed by the SPAGHETtI algorithm ensures there exists an architecture $h \in A$ such that $\theta_i[h] \leq \theta_j[k] - \tau_i[h] - \omega_{ij}[h, k]$. This defines a value for μ_i:

$$\forall (i, j) \in E, \forall k, l \in A,$$
$$\mu_j[k] = 1 \wedge l = \min\{h \in A \mid \theta_i[h] \leq \theta_j[k] - \tau_i[h] - \omega_{ij}[h, k]\} \Rightarrow \mu_i[l] = 1. \quad (6)$$

An alternative definition of μ can prevent useless task duplication, whenever possible. Instead of Equation (6), the following equation can be used:

$$H_i = \{h \mid \forall (i, j) \in E, \forall k \in A, \mu_j[k] = 1 \Rightarrow \theta_i[h] \leq \theta_j[k] - \tau_i[h] - \omega_{ij}[h, k]\},$$
$$H_i \neq \emptyset \Rightarrow \mu_i[\min H_i] = 1. \, (7)$$

When this equation does not define a value for μ_i, Equation (6) has to be used and duplication is necessary. Equations (5), (6) and (7) define recursively the function μ: Starting from tasks with no successor, μ is defined for all tasks in a reverse topological order. The definition of μ shows that this computation requires $\mathcal{O}(|A|^2|E|)$ operations when applying definitions (6) or (7) and $\mathcal{O}(|A||V|)$ operations when applying definition (5). This is the optimal complexity since, as for the schedule, it corresponds to the size of the inputs G, τ and ω. Therefore, this procedure, combined with the SPAGHETtI algorithms provides a solution that is optimal in terms of makespan and complexity.

Figure 1 shows the result of the mapping computation on the task graph. As the task f as a lower completion time $8 + 1 = 9$ when executed on CPU, this is the mapping of this task. Task e and d are indifferently mapped to CPU or GPU (here CPU, ordered first). For task b, there is only one possible mapping to ensure that d is scheduled at time 7: b has to be scheduled on GPU.

4.3   Determining the Number of Resources for Each Architecture

The required amount of resources for each architecture is not given by the previous algorithms. To determine this number of resources we use a greedy algorithm that allocates task to architecture instances, extending the previous architecture mapping computed in the previous section and computing the actual instance $\mu_i[k]$ of task i when mapped on architecture k. For each architecture we consider the tasks by increasing start time and we allocate them to the first resource of the architecture that can respect the start scheduling constraints. If no resource is available we proceed with resource augmentation and create a new instance of this architecture. Therefore, the number of resources used is the minimal number of resources that respect the schedule (i.e. the task start time). Moreover, this allocation is optimal in terms of platform dimensioning only if there is no sufficient slack in the schedule to delay tasks in order to save resources.

5   Exploring Tradeoffs for Heterogeneous Machines

Here, we deal with the case where the number of resources is higher than the available ones. There exists several ways of reducing the number of resources used by a schedule. In homogeneous setting an effective way was explored by the Pyrros project [19] where, after DSC [20] clusters were merged using the *work profiling method* of [10]. Another technique, presented in the context of register allocation, consists in adding some dependence edges in the graph in order to reduce the number of simultaneously live variables [18].

In heterogeneous environments, merging architectures has no meaning. We propose here a method similar to the one proposed for register allocation, where instructions are replaced by tasks and resources are processing units instead of registers. We reduce the inherent parallelism of the task graph by iteratively adding edges and then re-computing the schedule, the mapping and the number of resources until we reach the target number of resources. The procedure is depicted in Algorithm 2.

Algorithm 2. Adding n edges to the DAG G to reduce its parallelism

---

   Input: $G = (V, E)$ // The input DAG
   Input: n // Number of edges to add
1   $S \leftarrow$ Topological_sort(G)
2   $I \leftarrow$ Interference_graph(G);
3   **forall the** n *edges to be added* **do** // We will add n edges
4      $i \leftarrow$ Highest_degree_node(I)
5      $j \leftarrow$ Highest_degree_node(neighbor(i))
6   **if** $i \prec_S j$ **then** // If i is before j in the topological order
7 | Add (i, j) in G // Communication cost is set to 0
8   **else**
9 | Add (j, i) in G // Communication cost is set to 0
10   Remove (i, j) in I // and decrease degree of i and j

To add edges to the graph in order to reduce its parallelism, we first sort nodes in topological order. Then, we build the *interference graph I* of the DAG. In the interference graph, vertices are the same as in the original DAG. There is an edge between two vertices if there is no path between them in the DAG (they could be scheduled in parallel). In this interference graph we choose the node i of highest degree and a neighbor of i of highest degree. Then, this edge is added to the DAG G and the interference graph is updated. We iterate until

n edges have been added. Therefore we add a batch of n edges before applying again the SPAGHETtI algorithm. The rational behind adding several edges at the same time is to amortize the interference graph construction. The rational behind choosing the highest degree nodes in the interference graph is that a node with high degree has a lot of freedom in terms of parallelism and we are therefore more likely to impact the whole graph parallelism by reducing the parallelism of this kind of nodes. We avoid adding cycles in the original DAG: the added edge is directed so that it respects the topological order (line 6).

Moreover, each time we add a set of n edges, we compute the makespan of the new SPAGHETtI's schedule. This outputs a new compromise between the execution time and the number of resources. Hence, with this procedure we explore a full set of compromises (time vs. resources) until we reach the required bound. This is helpful for decision makers to correctly dimension their platform. In the following experiments, n was chosen between 10 and 100.

6   Experimental Results

We have implemented all the algorithms and procedures of the previous section. They take an input DAG, the communication and computation cost of each task on each architecture and the target number of resources for each architecture. In the following experiments intra-architecture communications are always zero.

We have also designed a simple runtime system that executes the static schedule on the given environments. In our experiments we have used nodes featuring 2 6-cores intel Xeons (X5650) at 2.67GHz with 36 Gb of RAM and 3 NVIDIA Tesla M2070 GPU at 1.15 GHz with 6 Gb of memory.

We have coded the dense tiled Cholesky factorization [11]. It features 4 kernels (POTRF, TRSM, SYRK and GEMM) that are executed using the Intel MKL library 12.1.9 for the CPUs and the CUBLAS version 4.2 for the GPUs. The Cholesky DAG can be seen here [4].

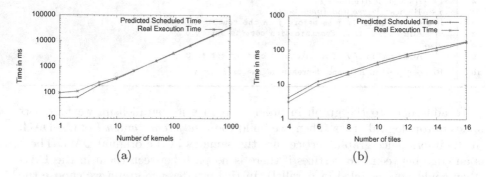

Fig. 2. Model validation experiments on (a) a chain of SYRK kernels alternatively on CPU and GPU, (b) on a tiled Cholesky factorization with 4096x4096 tile size

Model Validation. To validate our model we have executed a real schedule, measured the execution time of each kernel and compared the predicted schedule time with the measured values.

In Fig. 2(a), we execute a chain of SYRK kernels that are scheduled alternatively between a GPU and CPU. We see that as the chain size increases, the performance between the predicted time and the actual execution time becomes closer. This validates our execution and inter-architecture communication model.

In Fig. 2(b), we execute the Cholesky factorization[1] using tile size of 4096 and the decomposition of the matrix varies between 4 and 16 tiles (hence, the order of the matrix varies between 16384 and 65536). Here, we see that the predicted execution time is just a little higher than the real execution time. This validates the kernel execution time and communication time within a GPU as all the tasks, in this case, are scheduled on the GPUs.

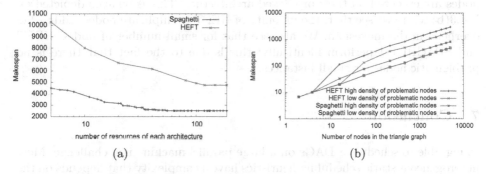

Fig. 3. HEFT and SPAGHETtI comparison (a) for bounded number of resources for the Cholesky Graph, (b) for unbounded number of resources in case of duplication

Comparison with HEFT. Being a list scheduling algorithm, HEFT is not able to make a short-term sacrifice to achieve a gain in the long term. This is exemplified with Fig. 3(a). In this Figure, we schedule a Cholesky DAG of 1540 nodes on two different architectures. Communicating within an architecture is free but communicating between architecture is very costly. In this case, the first task to be scheduled is faster on architecture 1 than on architecture 2 and the other tasks are faster on architecture 2. HEFT will execute the first task on architecture 1 and stay on this architecture until the end of the execution. On the other hand, the execution cost of the tasks on architecture 2 can amortize the communication time: SPAGHETtI pays the cost of executing the first task on architecture 2 and continues to execute all the tasks on this architecture. The optimal makespan is 2505 for 191 resources of architecture 2. We output all the compromises found by our method between 191 and 5 resources. For 191 resources, SPAGHETtI's makespan is 1.9 faster than the HEFT one. But if we reduce the number of resources to 5 for both architectures, SPAGHETtI still

---

[1] The factorization was checked correct by post-processing the result.

outperforms HEFT by a factor of 2.2. We explain the increase of performance ratio as follows. For a large number of resources SPAGHETtI does not need to use duplication but when the number of resources decreases, SPAGHETtI finds that duplication reduces the makespan even more. Indeed, it starts using this feature when the number of available resources is lower than 105.

In order to assess the importance of duplication, we have tested the case of a *triangle DAG*, where from time to time, two nodes (called *problematic nodes*) sharing the same predecessors, have an opposite behavior in terms of execution time (one is more efficient on one architecture while the other is more efficient on the other architecture) and in terms of communication time (going from the architecture they favor to the other architecture is very costly). The other tasks are homogeneous (they have the same execution time on every architectures). In this case, it is better to duplicate nodes that are predecessors of these problematic nodes in order to avoid to pay the communication cost while these nodes are executed on their privileged architecture. This is what is depicted on Fig 3(b) where we see that, the inability of HEFT to duplicate nodes, adds a big overhead in the makespan. We also see that for small number of nodes, HEFT and SPAGHETtI perform identically: this is due to the fact that there is no problematic nodes for small instances.

7   Conclusion

Being able to schedule a DAGs on a large parallel machine is a challenge. Most heterogeneous static scheduling heuristics have a complexity that depends on the number of resources. In this paper we propose to classify the resources by architecture in order to reduce the complexity of the scheduling process and to cope with modern HPC environments where the heterogeneity is relatively low. We also use a model where the communication time depends only on the source and destination architecture and not on the instances of these architecture. Thanks to this hypothesis, we are able to provide an optimal mapping strategy with a very low complexity. We then show that we can find the minimal number of resources required to respect the schedule start time and we are able to propose a set of compromises (makespan vs. platform size) in order to help decision makers to dimension their environment depending on the time-to-solution constraint they impose. Results show that the proposed model is verified in some real settings and that we are able to amortize the execution of some task on suboptimal resources or to duplicate tasks when necessary.

Future works are directed towards a better optimization of the part where we switch from unbounded to bounded resources. We plan to do this by exploiting the slack of the schedule and map tasks on suboptimal resources as long as the schedule length is not increased.

Acknowledgement. We would like to thank Valentin Fréchaud for his help in the implementation and test of the SPAGHETtI method.

References

1. Ahmad, I., Kwok, Y.K.: On exploiting task duplication in parallel program scheduling. IEEE Transactions on Parallel and Distributed Systems 9(9), 872–892 (1998)
2. Augonnet, C., Thibault, S., Namyst, R., Wacrenier, P.A.: Starpu: A unified platform for task scheduling on heterogeneous multicore architectures. Concurrency and Computation: Practice and Experience 23(2), 187–198 (2011)
3. Bajaj, R., Agrawal, D.P.: Improving scheduling of tasks in a heterogeneous environment. IEEE Transactions on Parallel and Distributed Systems 15(2), 107–118 (2004)
4. Bosilca, G., Bouteiller, A., Danalis, A., Herault, T., Lemarinier, P., Dongarra, J.: Dague: A generic distributed dag engine for high performance computing, innovative computing laboratory technical report. Tech. rep., ICL-UT-10-01 (2010)
5. Bosilca, G., Bouteiller, A., Danalis, A., Herault, T., Lemarinier, P., Dongarra, J.: Dague: A generic distributed dag engine for high performance computing. Parallel Computing 38(1), 37–51 (2012)
6. Canon, L.-C., Jeannot, E., Sakellariou, R., Zheng, W.: Comparative evaluation of the robustness of dag scheduling heuristics. In: Grid Computing, pp. 73–84. Springer (2008)
7. Chong, F.T., Sharma, S.D., Brewer, E.A., Saltz, J.: Multiprocessor runtime support for fine-grained, irregular dags. Parallel Processing Letters 5(04), 671–683 (1995)
8. El-Rewini, H., Lewis, T., Ali, H.: Task Scheduling in Parallel and Distributed Systems. Prentice Hall (1994)
9. Garey, M., Johnson, D.: A Guide to the Theory of NP-Completeness. W.H. Freeman and company, New York (1979)
10. George, A., Heath, M.T., Liu, J.: Parallel cholesky factorization on a shared memory multiprocessor. Linear Algebra and its applications 77, 165–187 (1986)
11. Gustavson, F.G., Karlsson, L., Kågström, B.: Distributed sbp cholesky factorization algorithms with near-optimal scheduling. ACM Transactions on Mathematical Software (TOMS) 36(2), 11 (2009)
12. Jeannot, E.: Automatic multithreaded parallel program generation for message passing multiprocessors using parameterized task graphs. In: International Conference on Parallel Computing (2001)
13. Leung, J.Y.T. (ed.): Handbook of Scheduling. Chapman & Hall/CCR (2004)
14. Mak, V.W., Lundstrom, S.F.: Predicting performance of parallel computations. IEEE Transactions on Parallel and Distributed Systems 1(3), 257–270 (1990)
15. Sinnen, O.: Task scheduling for parallel systems, vol. 60. Wiley. com (2007)
16. Tang, X., Li, K., Liao, G., Li, R.: List scheduling with duplication for heterogeneous computing systems. J. of Parallel and Distributed Computing 70(4), 323–329 (2010)
17. Topcuoglu, H., Hariri, S., Wu, M.Y.: Performance-effective and low-complexity task scheduling for heterogeneous computing. IEEE Transactions on Parallel and Distributed Systems 13(3), 260–274 (2002)
18. Touati, S.-A.-A., Eisenbeis, C.: Early control of register pressure for software pipelined loops. In: Hedin, G. (ed.) CC 2003. LNCS, vol. 2622, pp. 17–32. Springer, Heidelberg (2003)
19. Yang, T., Gerasoulis, A.: Pyrros: Static Task Scheduling and Code Generation for Message Passing Multiprocessor. In: Supercomputing 1992, pp. 428–437. ACM, Washington D.C (1992)
20. Yang, T., Gerasoulis, A.: DSC Scheduling Parallel Tasks on an Unbounded Number of Processors. IEEE Trans. on Parallel and Distributed Systems 5(9) (1994)

Energy-Aware Multi-Organization Scheduling Problem*

Johanne Cohen[1], Daniel Cordeiro[2], and Pedro Luis F. Raphael[2]

[1] Laboratoire de Recherche en Informatique (LRI, UMR 8623),
Université Paris-Sud, Bât 650 Ada Lovelace, 91405 Orsay, France
Johanne.Cohen@lri.fr
[2] Department of Computer Science,
University of São Paulo, Rua do Matão, 1010; 05508-090 São Paulo/SP, Brazil
{danielc,plfr}@ime.usp.br

Abstract. Scheduling algorithms for shared platforms such as grids and clouds granted users of different organizations access to powerful resources and may improve machine utilization; however, this can also increase operational costs of less-loaded organizations.

We consider energy as a resource, where the objective is to optimize the total energy consumption without increasing the energy spent by a *selfish organization*. We model the problem as a energy-aware variant of the Multi-Organization Scheduling Problem that we call MOSP-ENERGY.

We show that the clairvoyant problem with variable speed processors and jobs with release dates and deadlines is NP-hard and also that being selfish can cause solutions at most $m^{\alpha-1}$ far from the optimal, where m is the number of machines and $\alpha > 1$ is a constant. Finally, we present efficient heuristics for scenarios with all jobs ready from the beginning.

1 Introduction

Cooperative computational platforms such as grid computing or community clouds are typically organized as a federated system where users and computational resources, belonging to different organizations — *i.e.*, different administrative domains — share resources and exchange jobs with each other, in order to simultaneously maximize the profits of the collectivity and their own interests. Those platforms create novel research and business possibilities that, in turn, require ever more computational power. Examples of such organizations are research laboratories, universities or company departments.

Current distributed systems and their underlying algorithms allow an efficient redistribution of the jobs over the available resources, improving the overall utilization of the platform. Specialized algorithms for cooperative computing are capable of incite the creation of these platforms by guaranteeing that no organization will worsen its own results (in terms of performance) by sharing its resources with the others, even when the other behave in a selfish way.

---

* This work was partially funded by the São Paulo Research Foundation (FAPESP #2012/03778-0).

F. Silva et al. (Eds.): Euro-Par 2014, LNCS 8632, pp. 186–197, 2014.

The participation on such communities can have a side-effect that is often neglected by its users: the unpredictable increase of the operational costs for the organization. Less loaded organizations could save energy by putting its machines on stand-by, turning them off, or even decreasing the speed of the processors for non-priority jobs. The co-existence of these jobs with jobs migrated from other organizations can make this practice unfeasible.

It is crucial to optimize the allocation of the jobs for the whole platform in order to achieve good system performances. Moreover, it is important to do that in such a way that no organization will be harmed by sharing its own resources. The goal of this work is to study this problem considering energy costs also as a kind of resource that should be exchanged between the participants.

1.1 Related Work

The evolution of the processors technology has been driven by the demand of increased performance and reduced sizes. These demands resulted on chips with high power density and temperatures. On large scale server farms, energy-efficiency became an important issue because of the energy costs. Furthermore, part of this energy is converted into heat, which degrades processor's performance and reliability. Technologies as Intel's "Turbo Boost" or AMD's "Power-Now" were developed to offer speed-scaling capabilities, that allow the system to set the speed of the processors in order to control energy consumption.

The *Dynamic Speed Scaling* scheduling model was first studied by Yao, Demers and Shenker [9]. They considered a problem where n jobs with release dates r_i, deadlines d_i and processing volumes w_i, must be scheduled in a variable-speed processor with the objective of minimizing the energy consumption on that processor. The energy consumption is given by the integral over time of the power function $P(s(t)) = s(t)^\alpha$, where $s(t)$ is the speed in which the processor is running on time t and $\alpha > 1$ is a constant real number that depends on the technical characteristics of the processor — usually $\alpha \in [2,3]$. There are two assumptions to simplify the model: the processor spectrum of speeds is continuous and can be any real number between $0 \le s \le +\infty$.

They have proposed an optimal greedy algorithm for the problem, known as the *YDS algorithm*. It iteractively finds the *maximum density interval*, that is, the time interval $[t, t']$ such that the sum of the processing volumes of the jobs completely inside that interval, divided by the length of the interval, is maximum. By the convexity of the power function, this value gives the optimal speed on that interval (in the sense that no other feasible schedule can use less power on that interval.) The jobs in the interval are then scheduled using the Earliest Deadline First policy at this speed, jobs partially in the interval have their release dates and deadlines adjusted.

Albers et al. [1,2] studied the problem with m variable-speed processors with and without preemption and job migration. When migration is not allowed, the problem is NP-Complete; otherwise there is a polynomial algorithm to find the optimal solution. They also proved that, if the jobs have *agreeable deadlines* (*i.e.*, given two jobs, if $r_1 \le r_2$ then $d_1 \le d_2$), the problem can be optimally solved in polynomial-time by distributing the jobs in a round-robin fashion, prioritizing jobs with smaller release dates.

Scheduling on cooperative platforms were first studied by Pascual et al. [5,8]. They proposed the Multi-Organization Scheduling Problem (MOSP). In their model, independent organizations, sharing resources on a grid-like fashion, have a local performance objective for their jobs besides the global makespan. Their main contribution is the analysis of a centralized 3-approximation algorithm for the makespan that always incite these organizations to cooperate.

The concept of selfishness on individualists organizations has been broaden by Cohen et al. [4]. Studying workloads of bag-of-tasks jobs, they have analyzed situations where selfish organizations could change the schedule of the jobs assigned to its own machines and proposed algorithms that avoid schedules where the devised global schedule could be changed by re-inserting local jobs earlier. When all organizations behave selfishly, any approximation algorithm has a ratio greater than or equal to $(2 - N/2)$ regarding the optimal makespan with local constraints and presented several 2-approximation algorithms for the global makespan that always respect the selfishness restriction. They have also analyzed the decentralization of the decision making using Algorithmic Game Theory [3].

1.2   Contributions and Outline of this Paper

Scheduling algorithms for modern cooperative platforms composed of resources shared between independent participants granted its user access to powerful resources and improved the utilization of machines that were, most of the time, idle. With the increasing need for more computational power, the energy consumption on these machine also became an issue.

We modeled the problem as a Multi-Organization Scheduling Problem (MOSP) with respect to the system total energy consumption. We have multiple organizations, each one with a processor that can operate at variable speed (as in classic Dynamic Speed Scaling problems), and its own set of jobs. The goal is to find a global schedule, migrating jobs from one organization to another, that minimizes the total energy consumption.

Each organization has what is called a *selfish restriction*, that being a energy restriction that makes unfeasible any schedule that increase the energy consumption of that organization compared to what would be if the same organization was alone (even if the global energy consumption decrease with that schedule.)

An interesting aspect of this problem is that the energy consumption is given by a convex function on the speed of the processor, making its analysis significantly different from the original MOSP problem.

On Section 2 we formally define the problem. Section 3 shows that the general problem is NP-hard and that the ratio between the energetic consumption of solutions that respect the selfish constraint to the cost of solutions that does not respect may be unbounded for some instances of the problem. Heuristics for the problem with several organizations executing jobs that must meet a deadline are presented in Section 4, and their energy savings are experimentally analyzed in Section 5. Finally, some conclusion remarks are presented in Section 6.

2   Problem Description and Notations

The general problem studied in this paper is how to perform energy-aware scheduling on cooperative platforms formed by a federation of organizations. Different independent organizations, interconnected in a grid-like fashion, share resources and exchange jobs, expecting an improvement on their performance and costs. We are interested in studying how to redistribute the load between the organizations, decreasing the total energy-cost of the entire platform.

We call this problem the Energy-Aware Multi-Organization Scheduling Problem (MOSP-ENERGY), after the Multi-Organization Scheduling Problem (MOSP), that first studied scheduling on grid computing platforms. Formally, we define our cooperative platform as a federation of N organizations. Each organization $O^{(k)}$, $1 \leq k \leq N$, shares a machine that supports continuous *dynamic speed scaling* (*i.e.*, processors can operate at any arbitrary speed s that can be changed by the scheduler over time) and intend to execute $n^{(k)}$ jobs. A job $J_i^{(k)}$, $1 \leq i \leq n^{(k)}$, is defined by its release date $r_i^{(k)}$, its deadline $d_i^{(k)}$ and its processing volume $w_i^{(k)}$. The job with the biggest deadline of $O^{(k)}$ is defined as $d_{\max}^{(k)} = \max_i d_i^{(k)}$. Job preemption is allowed.

At a given time, if the chose speed is s, the power required to operate the processor is given by $P(s) = s^\alpha$, where α is a constant real number that depends on the type and model of the processor, usually with a value between 2 and 3. The energy consumption on one machine is given by the integral of $P(s)$ over time. The total energy consumption of the system is the sum of the power consumption of the machines of all organizations.

In order to encourage the creation of these cooperative platforms, we impose a hard constraint on the feasibility of the schedules: no organization can have its costs increased by cooperating. We call this the *selfish restriction* of the organizations. In other words, if an organization $O^{(k)}$ can execute its jobs consuming a total energy of $E_{\text{local}}^{(k)}$ only using its own machines, then a feasible schedule S must ensure that $E_S^{(k)} \leq E_{\text{local}}^{(k)}$ (otherwise the organization could just leave the platform). The optimization problem to be solved can be stated as:

$$\text{minimize } E_S \text{ subject to } E_S^{(k)} \leq E_{\text{local}}^{(k)}, \forall k$$

3   Complexity Analysis

3.1   The Cost of Having Selfish Organizations

Respecting MOSP-ENERGY selfish restriction restrains the set of feasible schedules. This limitation have an impact on the quality of the optimal solutions. For the general (*i.e.*, without the selfish restriction) energy minimization problem for multiple machines, it is known that:

Lemma 1 (Albers et al. [2]). *For any set of jobs, the energy of an optimal schedule on m processors is at least $1/m^{\alpha-1}$ times that of an optimal schedule on one processor.*

The worst case for MOSP-ENERGY is when all but one organizations are idle. The overloaded organization may not be able to migrate its jobs to the others in order to respect the selfish restriction. The optimal solution without the selfish restriction would be able to redistribute the load among all the m machines. So, the following corollary holds:

Corollary 1. *The ratio between the best solution that respects* MOSP-ENERGY *selfishness restriction to the best solution that does not respect it is* $m^{\alpha-1}$.

3.2   Computational Complexity

This section studies how hard is to find an optimal solution for the MOSP-ENERGY problem. We study, without loss of generality, the simpler case with 1 machine per organization. Lets consider the decision version of the MOSP-ENERGY defined as follows:

Instance: a set of N organizations (for $1 \leq k \leq N$, organization $O^{(k)}$ has $n^{(k)}$ jobs and 1 processor with variable speed) and an integer K.

Question: does there exist a schedule S such that the selfish restriction $E_S^{(k)} \leq E_{\text{local}}^{(k)}$ is respected for all $O^{(k)}$ and such that its total energy consumption E_S is less than or equal to K?

We will show that:

Theorem 1. *The* MOSP-ENERGY *problem is NP-Complete.*

Proof. It is straightforward to see that MOSP-ENERGY $\in NP$. Our proof is based on a reduction from the well-known PARTITION problem [6]:

Instance: a finite set of positive integers $A = \{a_1, \ldots, a_n\}$.

Question: is there two disjoint subsets A_1 and A_2 of A such that $\sum_{a_i \in A_1} a_i = \sum_{a_j \in A_2} a_j$?

Given an instance of PARTITION, we construct an instance of MOSP-ENERGY with $N = 2$ organizations as follows. Let t and t' be two integers representing two different deadlines where $t < t'$. Let D be an integer representing a processing volume; we will discuss their values later.

Organization $O^{(1)}$ has only one job, $J_1^{(1)}$, with $r_1^{(1)} = 0$, $d_1^{(1)} = t$ and $w_1^{(1)} = D$. Organization $O^{(2)}$ has $n+1$ jobs: $J_1^{(2)}, \ldots, J_{n+1}^{(2)}$. The first job of $O^{(2)}$ is identical to the one from $O^{(1)}$: $r_1^{(2)} = 0$, $d_1^{(2)} = t$, $w_1^{(2)} = D$. The remaining n jobs have $r_i^{(2)} = 0$, $d_i^{(2)} = t'$ and $w_i^{(2)} = a_i$.

Let $\beta = \sum_{a_i \in A} a_i$. We define an integer K as:

$$K = \frac{2D^\alpha}{t^{\alpha-1}} + \frac{\left(\frac{\beta}{2}\right)^\alpha}{(t'-t)^{\alpha-1}} + \frac{\left(\frac{\beta}{2}\right)^\alpha}{(t'-t)^{\alpha-1}}$$

And choose the values of D, t and t', such that: $\frac{D}{t} > \frac{D+\beta}{t'}$. Choosing $D \geq 5\beta$ and $t' \geq 3t+1$ satisfy these conditions.

Now we can easily build an instance for MOSP-ENERGY from the set A in polynomial time, as depicted in Fig. 1(a). In this instance, the optimal local energy consumption of $O^{(1)}$ (computed by the YDS algorithm) is given by $E_{local}^{(1)} = \frac{D^\alpha}{t^{\alpha-1}}$.

Now, we will compute the cost of the local energy consumption of organization $O^{(2)}$. This cost can also be computed using the YDS algorithm. Recall from Section 1.1 that the optimal speed to execute a job is calculated using the concept of interval of maximum density, $i.e.$, the time interval such that the sum of the processing volumes of the jobs that start and finish in it, divided by the length of the interval, is maximum. This density is the speed on which the jobs inside this interval will be executed in the optimal schedule, hence, the total energy spent by a job is determined by its speed in an optimal schedule.

D, t and t' was chosen in such a way that $\frac{D}{t} > \frac{D+\beta}{t'}$. Thus, the interval of maximum density for both organizations will always be the interval on which the jobs of processing volume D and deadline t are. This means that in the optimal local schedule for $O^{(2)}$, job $J_1^{(2)}$ must be executed alone from time 0 until time t. From time t until time t', all the remaining jobs are executed. The energy spent by $O^{(2)}$ is then given by $E_{local}^{(2)} = \frac{D^\alpha}{t^{\alpha-1}} + \frac{\beta^\alpha}{(t'-t)^{\alpha-1}}$.

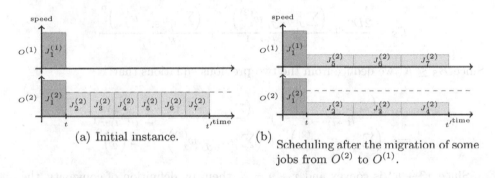

(a) Initial instance.   (b) Scheduling after the migration of some jobs from $O^{(2)}$ to $O^{(1)}$.

Fig. 1. Reduction of the MOSP-ENERGY problem from PARTITION

Now we must show that this transformation is a reduction. First, suppose that the set A can be split into two disjoint subsets A_1 and A_2 such that $\sum_{a_i \in A_1} a_i = \sum_{a_j \in A_2} a_j$. In order to respect the selfish restriction and avoid an increase on the local cost of organization $O^{(1)}$, neither the first job from $O^{(1)}$ nor $O^{(2)}$ can migrate. The only way to decrease the total energy cost is to migrate some of the other jobs. We will split the last n jobs of $O^{(2)}$ into 2 subsets, $\mathcal{J}_1$ and $\mathcal{J}_2$ such that if $a_i \in A_1$ than the job $J_{i+1}^{(2)}$, with $w_{i+1}^{(2)} = a_i$, belongs to set $\mathcal{J}_1$. Otherwise, it belongs to $\mathcal{J}_2$.

We can migrate the jobs of one of the subsets, say $\mathcal{J}_1$, to organization $O^{(1)}$. As consequence of our assumptions on D, t and t', the migrations does not change $E_{local}^{(1)}$. After all migrations, the cost of organization $O^{(2)}$ will be given by:

$$E_{\mathcal{S}}^{(2)} = \frac{D^\alpha}{t^{\alpha-1}} + \frac{\left(\sum_{J_i^{(2)} \in \mathcal{J}_1} w_i^{(2)}\right)^\alpha}{(t'-t)^{\alpha-1}} + \frac{\left(\sum_{J_j^{(2)} \in \mathcal{J}_2} w_j^{(2)}\right)^\alpha}{(t'-t)^{\alpha-1}}$$

Since $\sum_{J_i^{(2)} \in \mathcal{J}_1} w_i^{(2)} = \sum_{J_j^{(2)} \in \mathcal{J}_2} w_j^{(2)} = \frac{\beta}{2}$, the global energy consumption on this schedule is equal to:

$$E_{\mathcal{S}} = E_{\mathcal{S}}^{(1)} + E_{\mathcal{S}}^{(2)} = \frac{2D^\alpha}{t^{\alpha-1}} + \frac{2\left(\frac{\beta}{2}\right)^\alpha}{(t'-t)^{\alpha-1}} = K$$

Thus, the local constraints are respected and the total energy spent is K.

Suppose now that there is a valid schedule for this instance such that its total cost is less than or equal to K. It implies that some jobs from organization $O^{(2)}$ must have migrated. We can split the jobs from $O^{(2)}$ into two subsets $\mathcal{J}_1$ and $\mathcal{J}_2$ such that $J_i^{(2)} \in \mathcal{J}_1$ if job $J_i^{(2)}$ was migrated to $O^{(1)}$, otherwise $J_i^{(2)} \in \mathcal{J}_2$. Now, we split the set A in two subsets A_1 and A_2 in such a way that $a_i \in A_i$ if and only if $J_{i+1}^{(2)} \in \mathcal{J}_1$; otherwise, it belongs to $\mathcal{J}_2$. The global energy consumption of this schedule is given by:

$$E_{\mathcal{S}} = \frac{2D^\alpha}{t^{\alpha-1}} + \frac{\left(\sum_{J_i^{(2)} \in \mathcal{J}_1} w_i^{(2)}\right)^\alpha}{(t'-t)^{\alpha-1}} + \frac{\left(\sum_{J_j^{(2)} \in \mathcal{J}_2} w_j^{(2)}\right)^\alpha}{(t'-t)^{\alpha-1}}$$

Since $E_{\mathcal{S}} \leq K$, we deduce from the two previous equations that:

$$\frac{\left(\sum_{J_i^{(2)} \in \mathcal{J}_1} w_i^{(2)}\right)^\alpha}{(t'-t)^{\alpha-1}} + \frac{\left(\sum_{J_j \in \mathcal{J}_2} w_j^{(2)}\right)^\alpha}{(t'-t)^{\alpha-1}} \leq \frac{2\left(\frac{\beta}{2}\right)^\alpha}{(t'-t)^{\alpha-1}}$$

$$\implies \left(\sum_{J_i^{(2)} \in \mathcal{J}_1} w_i^{(2)}\right)^\alpha + \left(\sum_{J_j^{(2)} \in \mathcal{J}_2} w_j^{(2)}\right)^\alpha \leq 2\left(\frac{\beta}{2}\right)^\alpha$$

Since $x^\alpha + y^\alpha$ is convex and $x + y = \beta$, then, by definition of convexity, the function $x^\alpha + y^\alpha$ is minimum when $x = y$ and $x^\alpha + y^\alpha \geq 2(\frac{\beta}{2})^\alpha$. In our case, this means that:

$$2\left(\frac{\beta}{2}\right)^\alpha \leq \left(\sum_{J_i^{(2)} \in \mathcal{J}_1} w_i^{(2)}\right)^\alpha + \left(\sum_{J_j^{(2)} \in \mathcal{J}_2} w_j^{(2)}\right)^\alpha \leq 2\left(\frac{\beta}{2}\right)^\alpha \tag{1}$$

Now, we split set A into two subsets A_1 and A_2 such that $a_i \in A_1$ if $J_i^{(2)} \in \mathcal{J}_1$; otherwise $a_i \in A_2$. From Eq. 1, $\sum_{a_i \in A_1} a_i = \sum_{J_i^{(2)} \in \mathcal{J}_1} w_i^{(2)} = \frac{\beta}{2}$.

In other words, it means that $\sum_{a_i \in A_1} a_i = \sum_{a_i \in A_2} a_i$. This proves that set A can be split into two disjoint subsets A_1 and A_2 such that $\sum_{a_i \in A_1} a_i = \sum_{a_j \in A_2} a_j$ if and only if there is a valid schedule to this instance such that its total cost is less than K. This concludes our proof.

4   Heuristics

We developed heuristics for the MOSP-ENERGY problem for instances of bag-of-tasks jobs that are available at the beginning of the batch ($r_i = 0$). Without loss of generality, we assume that all $w_i = 1$ and only deadlines are free to vary.

The main idea of these heuristics is to migrate jobs from a more costly organization to a less costly one, always respecting the selfish restrictions. This is achieved by adjusting the release date of the migrated jobs to values higher then the higher deadline of the host organization. If one migrates a job to an interval that overlaps with any job from the hosting organization, the processor may have to increase its speed to be able to respect all the deadlines, resulting in an increase of the energy cost to execute the jobs of hosting organization. This may happen if value of the maximum density interval is changed. Avoiding these migrations ensures that the energy to run the host's jobs will remain unchanged. Fig. 2(a) illustrates the idea, showing the result of a possible migration.

We start considering how to redistribute energy as a resource among $N = 2$ organizations and then present a generic heuristic for N organizations.

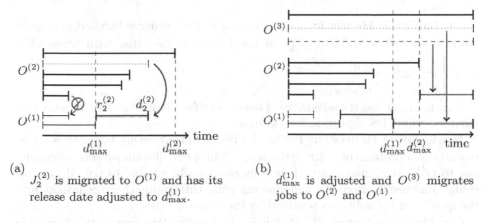

(a) $J_2^{(2)}$ is migrated to $O^{(1)}$ and has its release date adjusted to $d_{\max}^{(1)}$.

(b) $d_{\max}^{(1)}$ is adjusted and $O^{(3)}$ migrates jobs to $O^{(2)}$ and $O^{(1)}$.

Fig. 2. Schema of the heuristics migrations

4.1   Heuristics for $N = 2$ Organizations

Consider an instance of the MOSP-ENERGY problem with only $N = 2$ organizations. Assume, without loss of generality, that $d_{\max}^{(1)} \leq d_{\max}^{(2)}$.

Our heuristics — based on the YDS algorithm (see Section 1.1) — iteratively find the maximum density interval of the more costly organization on each iteration. After performing the migrations, we use the original YDS algorithm on each organization to compute the minimum processor speed to execute each job.

At each iteration, the heuristics compute the maximum density interval $[r_\Delta^{(2)}, d_\Delta^{(2)}]$ of the organization with the biggest $d_{\max}$ (in our case, $O^{(2)}$) and the list of jobs $J_{\Delta_i}^{(2)} \in \mathcal{J}_\Delta^{(2)}$ that lies inside it. We have three cases to consider:

(i) if $d_{\Delta_i}^{(2)} \leq d_{max}^{(1)}$ the heuristic cannot migrate $J_{\Delta_i}^{(2)}$ without increasing the energy spent by the other organization's local jobs;

(ii) if $r_{\Delta_i}^{(2)} \geq d_{max}^{(1)}$ the heuristic can migrate the job "as is" (without changing its release date and deadline). For $N = 2$, this case is equivalent to the problem for m machines and can be optimally solved on polynomial-time [2];

(iii) if $r_{\Delta_i}^{(2)} < d_{max}^{(1)}$ and $d_{\Delta_i}^{(2)} > d_{max}^{(1)}$ the job can be migrated, but its release date must be adjusted, has shown in Fig. 2.

Our heuristics differ on how to handle the third case, which we call the *border jobs*, since they intersects the border defined by $d_{max}^{(1)}$. We will describe how each heuristic tackles the border problem in the following sections.

Greedy Heuristic. The first heuristic deals with the border jobs in a greedy way. At each iteration, we compute the maximum density interval of $O^{(2)}$. If the jobs on $\mathcal{J}_{\Delta}^{(2)}$ does not intersects the border, we solve the problem as explained before. If the jobs are in the border, we choose the job with biggest deadline. If the migration of this job (adjusting its release date to $d_{max}^{(1)}$) decreases the total energy cost of the platform, the job is migrated. Otherwise, the job remains in its original state on $O^{(2)}$. We repeat this process until there are no more jobs to consider on $O^{(2)}$.

Probabilistic Heuristic. In this heuristic, the border is handled in a probabilistic way. A job $J_i^{(2)} \in \mathcal{J}_{\Delta}^{(2)}$ in the border is migrated with probability

$$p_i = \begin{cases} \frac{d_i^{(2)} - d_{max}^{(1)}}{d_{\Delta}^{(2)} - d_{max}^{(1)}} & \text{if } d_i^{(2)} > d_{max}^{(1)} \\ 0 & \text{otherwise.} \end{cases}$$

This heuristic has the advantage of being very fast in practice, whereas Greedy must run the YDS algorithm several times.

Brute-Force Heuristic. The border problem that we are trying to solve is, essentially, a problem of splitting the set $\mathcal{J}_{\Delta}^{(2)}$ into two disjoint subsets, migrating one to $O^{(1)}$. For small inputs, it is computationally feasible to try all possible splits. The results from the experiments with this approach gives insight into the quality of the solutions provided by the other heuristics.

Consider the subset of $\mathcal{J}_{\Delta}^{(2)}$ that is in the border. We enumerate all possible partitions of $\mathcal{J}_{\Delta}^{(2)}$ in two disjoint subsets (one set will be migrated and the other will remain on $O^{(2)}$) and test which one minimizes the total energy cost. This heuristic is, of course, exponential in the number of jobs in $\mathcal{J}_{\Delta}^{(2)}$.

4.2   Heuristic for N Organizations

Using the ideas presented on Section 4.1, we have designed a simple polynomial-time heuristic for the case when we have more than two organizations. The heuristic is based on the Iterative Load Balancing Algorithm (ILBA [5]).

The basic principle of our heuristic is to redistribute the energy expenditure of the organizations starting with the two organizations that have the smallest deadlines and iteratively add the jobs from the most costly organizations. One-by-one, each organization has its energy decreased.

The heuristic enumerates the organizations by non-decreasing values of their $d_{\max}$, *i.e.*, $d_{\max}^{(1)} \le d_{\max}^{(2)} \le \cdots \le d_{\max}^{(N)}$ and considers, one-by-one, each organization $O^{(k)}$ for $k = \{2, \ldots, N\}$. The choice of which jobs from $O^{(k)}$ should be migrated is done based on the concept of the maximum density interval (MDI). The algorithm computes the MDI of its jobs and migrates the border job with biggest deadline to the organization among $O^{(1)}, \ldots, O^{(k-1)}$ that decreases the most the total energy.

When there is no more job worth migration on the density interval, the value of $d_{\max}$ of all organizations $O^{(1)}, \ldots, O^{(k-1)}$ is updated — see Fig. 2(b) — and the algorithm checks if there is a new MDI on $O^{(k)}$ with jobs worth migration. If yes, it repeats the migration process. If not, the algorithm will try to redistribute the jobs of the next organization ($O^{(k+1)}$).

This process is repeated until all organizations had been considered. Note that by updating the $d_{\max}$ value after considering each MDI, we never increase the energy spent to execute the jobs already scheduled. Consequently, MOSP-ENERGY selfish restrictions are always respected.

5 Experimental Evaluation

We designed a series of experiments to evaluate the heuristics presented on the previous section. The experiments were evaluated using randomly generated workloads akin to typical environment found on academic cooperative platforms [5]. We evaluated the algorithms with instances containing a random number of machines, organizations and jobs with different deadlines. Two different scenarios were considered.

In the first, the number of initial jobs in each organization follows a Zipf distribution with exponent equal to 1.4267 and the jobs' deadlines are uniformly distributed. In the second, the $C_{\max}$ of these organizations follows the same Zipf distribution, and $d_i^{(k)} = C_{\max}^{(k)}$, $\forall i, k$ and the jobs are uniformly distributed among the organizations. The intuition about the scenarios is that the first configuration best models the distribution of jobs among organizations in shared platforms [7], where the second models the selfish restriction of the original MOSP problem, with the deadlines representing the initial makespan of the organizations.

Table 1. Results for $N = 2$ organizations. For different numbers of jobs per organization, we show how each heuristic performs if compared to no cooperation at all.

# Jobs/Org	% Greedy	% Probabilistic	% Brute-Force
5	0.69	1.85	2.45
10	0.94	2.12	3.09
15	2.29	1.61	3.21
20	1.79	1.27	4.97
50	0.78	0.67	7.44
100	0.32	0.30	3.08

Table 2. Results for $N = 10$ and 20 organizations, showing how the iterative algorithm performs if compared to no cooperation at all

N	# Jobs/Org	Energy Saved (%)	N	# Jobs/Org	Energy Saved (%)
10	5	11.87	20	5	15.64
10	10	6.81	20	10	9.81
10	15	5.47	20	15	6.11
10	20	4.64	20	20	5.04
10	30	2.86	20	30	3.24

Table 3. Performance results for $N = 2$ organizations on the second scenario

# Jobs/Org	% Greedy	% Probabilistic	% Brute-Force
5	4.22	5.86	6.72
10	4.12	3.19	5.94
15	2.08	2.96	6.81

Tables 1 and 2 summarizes the results obtained by our heuristics for the first scenario. Our preliminary tests showed that the maximum d_{max} does not affect significantly the results for the first scenario. So, due to the lack of space, all results for this scenario are presented for $d_{max} = 50$. Varying the number of jobs per organization, we show how much each heuristic can save on the total energy usage if compared to the total energy usage that could have been obtained without migrations (applying the YDS algorithm for each organization individually.) Each result is presented as the average of 200 experiments.

The results shows that for $N = 2$ organizations, the energy saving is limited by the selfish restriction of the organizations. The Greedy heuristic is able to save more energy than Probabilistic when the ratio between the number of jobs to the number of organizations is higher. The results obtained with Brute-Force are presented for the sake of comparison. For $N = 10$ and $N = 20$, our iterative algorithm was able to obtain savings up to 11.87% and 15.64%, respectively. Further investigation is needed for instances with higher number of jobs per organizations. In this case, the organizations have a higher probability of have similar d_{max}. This fact hampers the ability of improving the solutions because of MOSP-ENERGY selfish restriction.

Tables 3 and 4 summarizes the results obtained by our heuristics for the second scenario. The results show a significant energy reduction — up to 27.45% — if the notion of deadline is related only to the initial makespan.

Table 4. Performance results for $N = 10$ and 20 organizations on the second scenario

N	# Jobs/Org	Energy Saved (%)	N	# Jobs/Org	Energy Saved (%)
10	5	17.99	20	5	20.08
10	10	19.10	20	10	25.50
10	15	19.13	20	15	27.45

6 Concluding Remarks

In this work, we have studied the problem of scheduling on cooperative platforms considering energy as a communal resource. The objective of the Energy-Aware Multi-Organization Scheduling Problem (MOSP-ENERGY) is to minimize the total energy consumption of the entire platform, while assuring that the energy cost to execute jobs from a particular organization will not increase.

Balancing energy consumption is significantly different from the load balancing problem because of the convexity of the cost function. We have proved that the MOSP-ENERGY problem is NP-hard and that the ratio between the best solution respecting the organizations' selfish restriction to the solution that minimized the total energy is equal to $m^{\alpha-1}$.

We have designed heuristics to show how one can redistribute the energy between organizations respecting the selfish restriction. Our experimentals shows that we can save as much as 27% energy of the total spent by the platform.

This study was a first step on a better understanding of the role of energy costs on cooperative platforms. Further research will investigate approximation algorithms for the problem and fairness issues on the distribution of the energy costs between the organizations even if the jobs from different organizations belong to the same maximum density interval.

References

1. Albers, S., Antoniadis, A., Greiner, G.: On multi-processor speed scaling with migration. In: ACM Symposium on Parallelism in Algorithms and Architectures, pp. 279–288 (2011)
2. Albers, S., Müller, F., Schmelzer, S.: Speed scaling on parallel processors. In: ACM Symposium on Parallel Algorithms and Architectures, pp. 289–298 (2007)
3. Cohen, J., Cordeiro, D., Trystram, D., Wagner, F.: Coordination mechanisms for selfish multi-organization scheduling. In: IEEE International Conference on High Performance Computing, pp. 1 9 (December 2011)
4. Cohen, J., Cordeiro, D., Trystram, D., Wagner, F.: Analysis of multi-organization scheduling algorithms. In: D'Ambra, P., Guarracino, M., Talia, D. (eds.) Euro-Par 2010, Part II. LNCS, vol. 6272, pp. 367–379. Springer, Heidelberg (2010)
5. Dutot, P.F., Pascual, F., Rzadca, K., Trystram, D.: Approximation algorithms for the multiorganization scheduling problem. IEEE Transactions on Parallel and Distributed Systems 22(11), 1888–1895 (2011)
6. Garey, M.R., Johnson, D.S.: Computers and Intractability: A Guide to the Theory of NP-Completeness. W. H. Freeman (January 1979)
7. Iosup, A., Dumitrescu, C., Epema, D., Li, H., Wolters, L.: How are real grids used? The analysis of four grid traces and its implications. In: 7th IEEE/ACM International Conference on Grid Computing, pp. 262–269 (September 2006)
8. Pascual, F., Rzadca, K., Trystram, D.: Cooperation in multi-organization scheduling. In: Kermarrec, A.-M., Bougé, L., Priol, T. (eds.) Euro-Par 2007. LNCS, vol. 4641, pp. 224–233. Springer, Heidelberg (2007)
9. Yao, F., Demers, A., Shenker, S.: A scheduling model for reduced CPU energy. In: Symposium on Foundations of Computer Science, pp. 374–382. IEEE (1995)

Energy Efficient Scheduling of MapReduce Jobs*

Evripidis Bampis[1], Vincent Chau[2], Dimitrios Letsios[1], Giorgio Lucarelli[1],
Ioannis Milis[3], and Georgios Zois[1,3]

[1] Sorbonne Universités, UPMC Univ Paris 06, UMR 7606, LIP6, F-75005, France
{Evripidis.Bampis,Dimitrios.Letsios,Giorgio.Lucarelli,
Georgios.Zois}@lip6.fr
[2] IBISC, Université d'Évry, France
vincent.chau@ibisc.univ-evry.fr
[3] Dept. of Informatics, AUEB, Athens, Greece
milis@aueb.gr

Abstract. MapReduce has emerged as a prominent programming model
for data-intensive computation. In this work, we study power-aware
MapReduce scheduling in the speed scaling setting first introduced by
Yao et al. [FOCS 1995]. We focus on the minimization of the total
weighted completion time of a set of MapReduce jobs under a given budget of energy. Using a linear programming relaxation of our problem, we
derive a polynomial time constant-factor approximation algorithm. We
also propose a convex programming formulation that we combine with
standard list scheduling policies, and we evaluate their performance using
simulations.

1 Introduction

MapReduce has been established as a standard programming model for parallel computing in data centers or computational grids and it is currently used
for several applications including search indexing, web analytics or data mining.
However, data centers consume an enormous amount of energy and hence, energy
efficiency has emerged as an important issue in the data-processing framework.
Several empirical works have been carried-out in order to study different mechanisms for the reduction of the energy consumption in the MapReduce setting
and especially for the Hadoop framework [6–8]. The main mechanisms for energy saving are the *power-down* mechanism, where in periods of low-utilization
some servers are switched-off and the *speed-scaling* mechanism (or DVFS for
Dynamic Voltage Frequency Scaling) where the servers' speeds may be adjusted
dynamically [18]. Until lately, most work in the MapReduce framework were focused on the power-down mechanism, but recently, Wirtz and Ge [17] showed

* This work was partially supported by the European Union (European Social Fund
- ESF) and Greek national funds, through the Operational Program "Education
and Lifelong Learning", under the programs THALES-ALGONOW (E. Bampis, G.
Lucarelli, I. Milis) and HERACLEITUS II (G. Zois), and the project "Mathemati-
cal Programming and Non-linear Combinatorial Optimization" under the program
PGMO (E. Bampis, V. Chau, G. Lucarelli).

that for some computation intensive MapReduce applications the use of intelligent speed-scaling may lead to significant energy savings. In this paper, we study power-aware MapReduce scheduling in the speed scaling setting from a theoretical point of view.

In a typical MapReduce framework, the execution of a MapReduce job creates a number of Map and Reduce tasks. Each Map task processes a portion of the input data and outputs a number of key-value pairs. All key-value pairs having the same key are then given to a Reduce task which processes the values associated with a key to generate the final result. This means that each Reduce task cannot start before the completion of the last Map task of the same job. In other words, there is a complete bipartite graph implying the precedences between Map and Reduce tasks of a job. However, the Map tasks of a job can be executed in parallel and the same holds for its Reduce tasks.

In what follows we consider a set of MapReduce jobs that have to be executed on a set of speed-scalable processors, i.e., on processors that can adjust dynamically their speed [18]. Each job consists of a set of Map tasks and a set of Reduce tasks, with every task having a positive work volume. Each job is also associated with a positive weight representing its importance/priority, and a release date (or arrival time). Like in [4, 5], we consider that the Map and the Reduce tasks of each job are *preassigned* to the processors and in this way we take into account data locality, i.e. the fact that each Map task has to be executed on the server where its data are located. Given that the preemption of tasks, i.e. the possibility of interrupting a task and resuming it later, may cause important overheads we do not allow it. This is also the case often in practice: Hadoop does not offer the possibility of preemption [12]. The scheduler has to decide the time interval and the speed over time at which a task is executed, taking into account the energy consumption. High processor's speeds are in favor of performance at the price of high energy consumption. Our goal is to schedule all the tasks to the processors, so as to minimize the total weighted completion time of jobs respecting a given budget of energy.

Related Work. Chang et al. [4] consider a set of MapReduce jobs with their Map and Reduce tasks preassigned to processors and their goal is to minimize the total weighted completion time of jobs. They proposed approximation algorithms of ratios 3 and 2 for arbitrary and common release dates, respectively. However, they do not consider neither distinction nor dependencies between Map and Reduce tasks of a job. Moreover, their model falls into a well-studied problem known as *concurrent open-shop* (or *order scheduling*) for which the same approximation results are known (see [10] and the references therein). Extending on the above-mentioned model, Chen et al. [5], proposed a more realistic one which takes into account the dependencies among Map and Reduce tasks and derived an 8-approximation algorithm for the same objective. Moreover, they managed to model also the transfer of the output of Map tasks to Reduce tasks and to derive a 58-approximation algorithm for this generalization. In a third model proposed by Moseley et al. [12], the dependencies between Map and Reduce tasks of a job are also taken into account while the assignment of tasks to processors is not given in advance. The authors studied the preemptive variant for both the case of identical and unrelated processors. They proposed constant approximation ratios of 12 and 6, respectively. For the unrelated processors case, they focused on the special case where each job has a single Map and a single Reduce task. For the latter case on a single map and a single reduce processor they also proposed a QPTAS which becomes a PTAS for a fixed number of processing times of tasks.

In the energy-aware setting, Angel et al. [2] proposed approximation algorithms for the problem of minimizing the total weighted completion time on unrelated parallel processors, under a model where the processing time and the energy consumption of the jobs are speed dependent. Moreover, Megow et al. [11] recently proposed a PTAS for the problem of minimizing the total weighted completion time on a single speed-scalable processor.

Our Results and Organization of the Paper. We adopt the MapReduce model of [4] where the tasks are preassigned to processors but extended with dependencies between Map and Reduce tasks as in Chen et al. [5, 12] in the speed scaling setting [18]. In Section 2, we present formally our problem and we introduce our notation. In Section 3, we present a constant-factor approximation algorithm. Using discretization of the possible speed values we give an interval indexed LP relaxation of our problem and we transform an optimal solution to this LP to a feasible solution for our problem by list scheduling in the order of tasks' α-points (see e.g. [9, 13]). This leads to a $O(1)$-energy $O(1)$-approximation algorithm, that is an algorithm that may use energy augmentation. More specifically, we call a schedule c-energy ρ-approximate if its objective function is at most ρ times far from the objective function of an optimal schedule and it exceeds the given energy budget by a factor of at most c (see e.g. [14]). Our algorithm describes a tradeoff between the approximation ratio and the energy augmentation as a function of α. By appropriately choosing α, our result becomes a constant-factor approximation for our problem. In Section 4, we are interested in natural list scheduling policies such as FIRST COME FIRST SERVED (FCFS) and HIGHEST DENSITY FIRST (HDF). However, in our context we need to determine the speeds of every task in order to respect the energy budget. For that, we propose a convex programming relaxation of our problem, for a prespecified order of jobs, which can be solved in polynomial time by the Ellipsoid algorithm. Then we combine the solution of this relaxation with FCFS and HDF and we compare experimentally their effectiveness.

2   Problem Statement and Notation

In the sequel we consider a set $\mathcal{J} = \{1, 2, \ldots, n\}$ of n MapReduce jobs to be executed on a set $\mathcal{P} = \{1, 2, \ldots, m\}$ of m speed-scalable processors. Each job is associated with a positive weight w_j and a release date r_j and consists of a set of Map tasks and a set of Reduce tasks that are preassigned to the m processors. We denote by $\mathcal{T}$ the set of all tasks of all jobs, and by $\mathcal{M}$ and $\mathcal{R}$ the sets of all Map and Reduce tasks, respectively. Each task $T_{i,j} \in \mathcal{T}$ is associated with a non-negative work volume $v_{i,j}$.

We consider each job having at least one Map and one Reduce task and that each job has at most one task, either Map or Reduce, assigned to each processor. Map or Reduce tasks can run simultaneously on different processors, while the following precedence constraints hold for each job: every Reduce task can start its execution after the completion of all Map tasks of the same job.

For a given schedule we denote by C_j and $C_{i,j}$ the completion times of each job $j \in \mathcal{J}$ and each task $T_{i,j} \in \mathcal{T}$, respectively. Note that, due to the precedence constraints of Map and Reduce tasks, $C_j = \max_{T_{i,j} \in \mathcal{R}} \{C_{i,j}\}$. By $C_{max} = \max_{j \in \mathcal{J}} \{C_j\}$ we denote the makespan of the schedule, i.e., the completion time of the job which finishes last. Let also, $w_{\min} = \min_{j \in \mathcal{J}} \{w_j\}$, $v_{\min} = \min_{T_{i,j} \in \mathcal{T}} \{v_{i,j} : v_{i,j} > 0\}$, $w_{\max} = \max_{j \in \mathcal{J}} \{w_j\}$, $r_{\max} = \max_{j \in \mathcal{J}} \{r_j\}$ and $v_{\max} = \max_{T_{i,j} \in \mathcal{T}} \{v_{i,j}\}$.

In this paper, we combine this abstract model for MapReduce scheduling with the speed scaling mechanism for energy saving [18] (see also [1] for a recent review). In this setting, the power required by a processor running at time t with speed $s(t)$ is equal to $P(s(t)) = s(t)^\beta$, for a constant $\beta > 1$ (typically, $\beta \in [2,3]$) and its energy consumption is power integrated over time, i.e., $E = \int P(s(t))dt$.

Due to the convexity of the speed-to-power function, a key property of our problem is that each task runs at a constant speed during its whole execution. So, if a task $T_{i,j}$ is executed at a speed $s_{i,j}$, the time needed for its execution (processing time) is equal to $p_{i,j} = \frac{v_{i,j}}{s_{i,j}}$ and its energy consumption is $E_{i,j} = \frac{v_{i,j}}{s_{i,j}} s_{i,j}^\beta = v_{i,j} s_{i,j}^{\beta-1}$.

Moreover, we are given an energy budget E and the goal is to schedule non-preemptively all the tasks to the m processors, so as to minimize the total weighted completion time of the schedule, i.e., $\sum_{j \in \mathcal{J}} w_j C_j$, without exceeding the energy budget E. We refer to this problem as MAPREDUCE problem.

All omitted proofs can be found in the full version of this work, available at http://arxiv.org/abs/1402.2810.

3   A Linear Programming Approach

In this section we present an $O(1)$-energy $O(1)$-approximation algorithm for the MAPREDUCE problem. Our algorithm is based on a linear programming relaxation of the problem and it transforms the solution obtained by the linear program to a feasible schedule for the MAPREDUCE problem using the technique of α-points. Note that, by allowing energy augmentation we are able to describe a tradeoff between energy and performance. Moreover, we can derive a constant-factor approximation ratio (without energy augmentation) for the MAPREDUCE problem by appropriately choosing some parameters.

3.1   Linear Programming Relaxation

To give a linear programming formulation of our problem, we first discretize the possible speed values. In order to do this, we need to compute an upper and a lower bound on the speed of each task. An upper bound of $\left(\frac{E}{v_{\min}}\right)^{\frac{1}{\beta-1}}$ is easily obtained since the energy consumption of any task can not exceed the energy budget. A lower bound on the speed values is $\frac{v_{\min}}{\mathcal{C}}$, where $\mathcal{C}$ is an upper bound to the makespan of any optimal schedule; $\mathcal{C}$ can be computed by considering all jobs executed after the maximum release date. Then, by loosing a factor of $(1+\epsilon)$ with respect to an optimal solution, we can prove the following.

Lemma 1. *There is a feasible $(1+\epsilon)$-approximate schedule for the* MAPREDUCE *problem in which each task $T_{i,j} \in \mathcal{T}$ runs at a speed $s \in \mathcal{V}$, where $\mathcal{V}$ is the set of all possible discrete speed values and $\epsilon \in (0,1)$.*

Next, we discretize the time horizon $(0, \mathcal{C}]$ of an optimal schedule by partitioning it into the intervals $(0, \lambda], (\lambda, \lambda(1+\delta)], (\lambda(1+\delta), \lambda(1+\delta)^2], \ldots, (\lambda(1+\delta)^{u-1}, \lambda(1+\delta)^u]$, where $\delta > 0$ is a small constant, $\lambda > 0$ is a constant that we will define later, and u is the smallest integer such that $\lambda(1+\delta)^{u-1} \geq \mathcal{C}$. Let $\tau_0 = 0$ and $\tau_t = \lambda(1+\delta)^{t-1}$, for $1 \leq t \leq u+1$. Moreover, let $I_t = (\tau_t, \tau_{t+1}]$, for $0 \leq t \leq u$, and $|I_t|$ be the length of the interval I_t, i.e., $|I_0| = \lambda$ and $|I_t| = \lambda\delta(1+\delta)^{t-1}$, $1 \leq t \leq u$. Note that, the number of intervals is polynomial to the size of the instance and to $1/\delta$, as $u = \lceil \log_{1+\delta} \frac{\mathcal{C}}{\lambda} \rceil + 1$.

Let $p_{i,j,s} = \frac{v_{i,j}}{s}$ be the potential processing time for each task $T_{i,j} \in \mathcal{T}$ if it is executed entirely with speed $s \in \mathcal{V}$. For each $T_{i,j} \in \mathcal{T}$, $t \in \{0, 1, \ldots, u\}$ and $s \in \mathcal{V}$, we introduce a variable $y_{i,j,s,t}$ that corresponds to the portion of the interval I_t during which the task $T_{i,j}$ is executed with speed s. In other words, $y_{i,j,s,t}|I_t|$ is the time that task $T_{i,j}$ is executed within the interval I_t at speed s, or equivalently, $\frac{y_{i,j,s,t}|I_t|}{p_{i,j,s}}$ is the fraction of the task $T_{i,j}$ that is executed within I_t at speed s. Note that the number of $y_{i,j,s,t}$ variables is polynomial to the size of the instance, to $1/\epsilon$ and to $1/\delta$. Furthermore, for each task $T_{i,j} \in \mathcal{T}$, we introduce a variable $C_{i,j}$, which corresponds to the completion time of $T_{i,j}$. Finally, let C_j, $j \in \mathcal{J}$, be the variable that corresponds to the completion time of job j. (LP) in the next page, is a linear programming relaxation of the problem where each task $T_{i,j} \in \mathcal{T}$ runs at a single speed $s \in \mathcal{V}$.

Our objective is to minimize the sum of weighted completion times of all jobs. For each task $T_{i,j} \in \mathcal{T}$, the corresponding constraint (1) ensures that $T_{i,j}$ is entirely executed. Constraints (2) enforce that the total amount of processing time that is executed within an interval I_t cannot exceed its length. In [16], the authors proposed a lower bound for the completion time of a job. This lower bound can be adapted to our problem and for the completion time of a task $T_{i,j} \in \mathcal{T}$ leads to a corresponding constraint (3). Constraints (4) ensure that the completion time of each job is the maximum over the completion times of all its tasks. Constraint (5) ensures that the given energy budget is not exceeded. Note that the value s^β for each $s \in \mathcal{V}$ is a fixed number. Constraints (6) imply the precedence constraints between the Map and the Reduce tasks of the same job, as they enforce that the fraction of a Map task that is executed up to each time point should be at least the fraction of a Reduce task of the same job executed up to the same time point; hence, each Map task completes before all Reduce

(LP) : minimize $\sum_{j \in \mathcal{J}} w_j C_j$

subject to :

$$\sum_{s \in \mathcal{V}} \sum_{t=0}^{u} \frac{y_{i,j,s,t}|I_t|}{p_{i,j,s}} = 1, \qquad\qquad \forall T_{i,j} \in \mathcal{T} \tag{1}$$

$$\sum_{j:T_{i,j} \in \mathcal{T}} \sum_{s \in \mathcal{V}} y_{i,j,s,t} \leq 1, \qquad\qquad \forall i \in \mathcal{P}, 0 \leq t \leq u \tag{2}$$

$$C_{i,j} \geq \frac{1}{2} \sum_{s \in \mathcal{V}} y_{i,j,s,0}|I_0| \left(\frac{1}{p_{i,j,s}} + 1 \right) +$$

$$\sum_{t=1}^{u} \sum_{s \in \mathcal{V}} \left(\frac{y_{i,j,s,t}|I_t|}{p_{i,j,s}} \tau_t + \frac{1}{2} y_{i,j,s,t}|I_t| \right), \quad \forall T_{i,j} \in \mathcal{T} \tag{3}$$

$$C_j \geq C_{i,j}, \qquad\qquad \forall T_{i,j} \in \mathcal{T} \tag{4}$$

$$\sum_{T_{i,j} \in \mathcal{T}} \sum_{s \in \mathcal{V}} \sum_{t=0}^{u} y_{i,j,s,t}|I_t|s^{\beta} \leq E \tag{5}$$

$$\sum_{t=0}^{\ell} \sum_{s \in \mathcal{V}} \frac{y_{i,j,s,t}|I_t|}{p_{i,j,s}} \geq \sum_{t=0}^{\ell} \sum_{s \in \mathcal{V}} \frac{y_{i',j,s,t}|I_t|}{p_{i',j,s}},$$

$$\forall T_{i,j} \in \mathcal{M}, T_{i',j} \in \mathcal{R}, 0 \leq \ell \leq u \tag{6}$$

$$y_{i,j,s,t} = 0, \qquad \forall T_{i,j} \in \mathcal{T}, s \in \mathcal{V}, t : \tau_t < r_j \tag{7}$$

$$y_{i,j,s,t}, C_{i,j}, C_j \geq 0, \qquad \forall T_{i,j} \in \mathcal{T}, s \in \mathcal{V}, 0 \leq t \leq u \tag{8}$$

tasks of the same job. Constraints (7) do not allow tasks of a job to be executed before their release date.

In what follows, we denote an optimal solution to (LP) by $(\bar{y}_{i,j,s,t}, \bar{C}_{i,j}, \bar{C}_j)$.

3.2   The Algorithm

In this section we use (LP) to derive a feasible schedule for the MAPREDUCE problem. Our algorithm is based on the idea of list scheduling in order of α-points [9, 13]. In general, an α-point of a job is the first point in time where an α-fraction of the job has been completed, where $\alpha \in (0,1)$ is a constant that depends on the analysis. In this paper, we will define the α-point $t_{i,j}^{\alpha}$ of a task $T_{i,j} \in \mathcal{T}$ as the minimum ℓ, $0 \leq \ell \leq u$, such that at least an α-fraction of $v_{i,j}$ is accomplished up to the interval I_{ℓ} to (LP), i.e.,

$$t_{i,j}^{\alpha} = \min \left\{ \ell : \sum_{t=0}^{\ell} \sum_{s \in \mathcal{S}} \frac{\bar{y}_{i,j,s,t}|I_t|}{p_{i,j,s}} \geq \alpha \right\}.$$

Thus, once our algorithm has computed an optimal solution $(\bar{y}_{i,j,s,t}, \bar{C}_{i,j}, \bar{C}_j)$ to (LP), it calculates the corresponding α-point, $t_{i,j}^{\alpha}$, for each task $T_{i,j} \in \mathcal{T}$. Then we create a feasible schedule as follows: For each processor $i \in \mathcal{P}$, we consider a priority list σ_i of its tasks such that the tasks with smaller α-point have higher priority. A crucial point in our analysis is that we consider that a task $T_{i,j} \in \mathcal{T}$ becomes *available* for the algorithm after the time $\tau_{t_{i,j}^\alpha+1} > r_j$. Moreover, if $T_{i,j} \in \mathcal{R}$ then we need also all tasks $T_{i',j} \in \mathcal{M}$ to be completed in order $T_{i,j}$ to be considered as available. For each task $T_{i,j} \in \mathcal{T}$, we use a constant speed $s_{i,j} = \frac{v_{i,j}}{p_{i,j}}$, where

$$p_{i,j} = \gamma \sum_{t=0}^{t_{i,j}^\alpha} \sum_{s \in \mathcal{V}} \bar{y}_{i,j,s,t}|I_t|$$

is the processing time of $T_{i,j}$ used by our algorithm, and $\gamma > 0$ is a constant that we define later and describes the tradeoff between the energy consumption and the weighted completion time of jobs. In fact, speed $s_{i,j}$ is determined by the needs of the analysis and it serves as a tool in order to upper bound the energy augmentation used for the execution of $T_{i,j}$ and also the completion time of $T_{i,j}$ in a schedule produced by the algorithm. At each time point where a processor $i \in \mathcal{P}$ is available, our algorithm selects the highest priority available task in σ_i which has not been yet executed. Note that our algorithm always create a feasible solution as we do not insist on selecting the highest priority task if this is not available. ALGORITHM $\mathcal{MR}(\alpha, \gamma)$ gives a formal description of our method.

ALGORITHM $\mathcal{MR}(\alpha, \gamma)$

1: Compute an optimal solution $(\bar{y}_{i,j,s,t}, \bar{C}_{i,j}, \bar{C}_j)$ to (LP).
2: **for** each task $T_{i,j} \in \mathcal{T}$ **do**
3:    Compute the α-point $t_{i,j}^\alpha$, the processing time $p_{i,j}$ and the speed $s_{i,j}$.
4: **for** each processor $i \in \mathcal{P}$ **do**
5:    Compute the priority list σ_i.
6: **for** each time where a processor $i \in \mathcal{P}$ becomes available **do**
7:    Select the first available task, let $T_{i,j}$, in σ_i which has not been yet executed.
8:    Schedule $T_{i,j}$, non-preemptively, with processing time $p_{i,j}$.
     Let $C_{i,j}$ be the completion time of task $T_{i,j}$.
9: **for** each job $j \in \mathcal{J}$ **do**
10:    Compute its completion time $C_j = \max_{i \in \mathcal{P}} C_{i,j}$.

Note that the processing time of a task $T_{i,j} \in \mathcal{T}$ to an optimal solution to (LP) is $\bar{p}_{i,j} = \sum_{t=0}^{u} \sum_{s \in \mathcal{V}} \bar{y}_{i,j,s,t}|I_t|$. Hence, the energy consumption $\bar{E}_{i,j} = \sum_{t=0}^{u} \sum_{s \in \mathcal{V}} \bar{y}_{i,j,s,t}|I_t|s^\beta$ for the execution of $T_{i,j}$ to an optimal solution to (LP) may be smaller or bigger than the energy consumption $E_{i,j}$ for the execution of $T_{i,j}$ by the algorithm. The next lemma gives a relation between these two quantities.

Lemma 2. *Let $\bar{E}_{i,j}$ and $E_{i,j}$ be the energy consumption of the task $T_{i,j} \in \mathcal{T}$ in an optimal solution to (LP) and in the solution of* ALGORITHM $\mathcal{MR}(\alpha, \gamma)$, *respectively. It holds that $E_{i,j} \leq \frac{1}{\gamma^{\beta-1}\alpha^\beta} \bar{E}_{i,j}$.*

We also need to lower bound the completion time $\bar{C}_{i,j}$ of the task $T_{i,j} \in \mathcal{T}$ given by the (LP). This is done by the following lemma.

Lemma 3. *If* $\lambda < \alpha \frac{v_{\min}}{s_{\max}}$, *then for each task* $T_{i,j} \in \mathcal{T}$ *it holds that* $\bar{C}_{i,j} \geq$ $(1 - \alpha) \cdot \tau_{t_{i,j}^{\alpha}}$.

Using Lemmas 2 and 3 as well as Lemma 1 we can prove the following theorem.

Theorem 1. ALGORITHM $\mathcal{MR}(\alpha, \gamma)$ *is a* $\frac{1}{\gamma^{\beta-1}\alpha^{\beta}}$*-energy* $\frac{\gamma^2+3\gamma+1}{1-\alpha}(1+\varepsilon)$*-approximation algorithm for the* MAPREDUCE *problem, where* $\gamma > 0$ *and* $\alpha, \varepsilon \in (0,1)$.

By choosing $\gamma = \frac{1}{\alpha^{\beta}-\sqrt[\beta]{\alpha}}$, no energy augmentation is used and ALGORITHM $\mathcal{MR}(\alpha, \gamma)$ becomes a constant-factor approximation for the MAPREDUCE problem, and the following theorem holds.

Theorem 2. *There is a* $\frac{\alpha^{\beta}-\sqrt[\beta]{\alpha})^2+3\alpha^{\beta}-\sqrt[\beta]{\alpha}+1}{(\alpha^{\beta}-\sqrt[\beta]{\alpha})^2(1-\alpha)}(1+\varepsilon)$*-approximation algorithm for the* MAPREDUCE *problem, where* $\alpha, \varepsilon \in (0,1)$.

In Fig.1 we depict the tradeoff between energy augmentation and approximation ratio for some practical values of β.

For special instances of our problem where there are no precedence constraints between Map and Reduce tasks or even all jobs have a common release date (as in [4]) our results are improved as follows.

Corollary 1. *There is a* $\frac{\alpha^{\beta}-\sqrt[\beta]{\alpha}+1}{\alpha^{\beta}-\sqrt[\beta]{\alpha}(1-\alpha)}(1 + \varepsilon)$*-approximation algorithm for the* MAPREDUCE *problem without precedence constraints between Map and Reduce tasks, and a* $\frac{1}{\alpha^{\beta}-\sqrt[\beta]{\alpha}(1-\alpha)}(1 + \varepsilon)$*-approximation algorithm for the* MAPREDUCE *problem without precedence constraints between Map and Reduce tasks and jobs with common release dates, where* $\alpha, c \subset (0,1)$.

Our ratios are optimized by selecting the appropriate value of α for each β. Table 1 gives the achieved ratios for practical values of β.

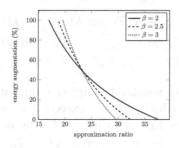

Fig. 1. Tradeoff between energy augmentation and approximation ratio when $\beta = \{2, 2.5, 3\}$

Table 1. Approximation ratios for the MAPREDUCE problem for different values of β

β	general	no precedence	no precedence & no release dates
2	37.52	9.44	6.75
2.2	34.89	8.84	6.29
2.4	33.01	8.41	5.97
2.6	31.59	8.09	5.72
2.8	30.50	7.84	5.53
3	29.62	7.64	5.38

4   A Convex Programming Approach

We are interested in natural list scheduling policies such as FIRST COME FIRST
SERVED (FCFS) and HIGHEST DENSITY FIRST (HDF). However, in our context
we need to determine the speeds of every task in order to respect the energy
budget. For that, we propose a convex programming relaxation of our problem
when an order of the jobs is prespecified.

4.1   The Convex Program

Let $\sigma = \langle 1, 2, \ldots, n \rangle$ be a given order of the jobs. Consider now the restricted
version of the MAPREDUCE problem where, for each processor $i \in \mathcal{P}$, the tasks
are forced to be executed according to this order. We shall refer to this problem as
the MAPREDUCE(σ) problem. Note that, the order is the same for all processors.
We write $j \prec j'$ if job $j \in \mathcal{J}$ precedes job $j' \in \mathcal{J}$ in σ. We propose a convex
program that considers the order σ as input and returns a solution that is a
lower bound to the optimal solution for the MAPREDUCE(σ) problem.

In order to formulate our problem as a convex program, for each task $T_{i,j} \in \mathcal{T}$,
let $p_{i,j}$ be a variable that corresponds to its processing time and $C_{i,j}$ a variable
that determines its completion time. Let also C_j, $j \in \mathcal{J}$, be the variable that
corresponds to the completion time of job j. Then, (CP) is a convex programming
relaxation of the MAPREDUCE(σ) problem.

$$(\textbf{CP}) : \text{minimize} \sum_{j \in \mathcal{J}} w_j C_j$$

subject to :

$$\sum_{T_{i,j} \in \mathcal{T}} \frac{v_{i,j}^{\beta}}{p_{i,j}^{\beta-1}} \leq E \tag{9}$$

$$r_{j'} + \sum_{k=j'}^{j} p_{i,k} \leq C_{i,j}, \qquad \forall T_{i,j}, T_{i,j'} \in \mathcal{T}, j' \prec j \tag{10}$$

$$C_{i',j} + p_{i,j} \leq C_{i,j}, \qquad \forall T_{i,j} \in \mathcal{R}, T_{i',j} \in \mathcal{M} \tag{11}$$

$$C_{i,j} \leq C_j, \qquad \forall T_{i,j} \in \mathcal{T} \tag{12}$$

$$s_{i,j}, C_{i,j}, C_j \geq 0, \qquad \forall T_{i,j} \in \mathcal{T}, j \in \mathcal{J}$$

The objective function of (CP) is to minimize the weighted completion time of
all jobs. Constraint (9) guarantees that the energy budget is not exceeded; note
that we have substituted the energy consumption $E_{i,j}$ of each task $T_{i,j}$ by its
equivalent $E_{i,j} = p_{i,j} s_{i,j}^{\beta} = p_{i,j}(\frac{v_{i,j}}{p_{i,j}})^{\beta}$, where $s_{i,j} = \frac{v_{i,j}}{p_{i,j}}$ is the speed of task $T_{i,j}$.
Constraints (10) and (11) give lower bounds on the completion time of each task
$T_{i,j} \in \mathcal{T}$, based on the release dates and the precedence constraints, respectively.
Note that, if we do not consider precedences between the tasks, then (CP) will
return the optimal value of the objective function, instead of a lower bound on

it, as constraints (10) describe in a complete way the completion times of the tasks. However, this is not true for constraints (11) which are responsible for the precedence constraints. Finally, constraints (12) ensure that the completion time of each job is the maximum over the completion times among all of its tasks.

As the optimal solution to (CP) does not necessarily describe a feasible schedule, we need to apply an algorithm that uses the processing times found by (CP) and the order σ so as to create a feasible schedule for the MAPREDUCE(σ) problem, and hence for the MAPREDUCE problem. It suffices to apply, the lines 6-8 of ALGORITHM $\mathcal{MR}(\alpha, \gamma)$, by considering the same order for all processors.

4.2   Experimental Evaluation of Scheduling Policies

We propose different orders of jobs and discuss how far is an optimal solution for the MAPREDUCE(σ) problem using these orders with respect to an optimal solution for the MAPREDUCE problem. Consider the following standard orders.

FIRST COME FIRST SERVED (FCFS): for each pair of jobs $j, j' \in \mathcal{J}$, if $r_j < r_{j'}$ then $j \prec j'$ in σ.

HIGHEST DENSITY FIRST (HDF): for each pair of jobs $j, j' \in \mathcal{J}$, if $\frac{w_j}{\sum_{T_{i,j} \in j} v_{i,j}} > \frac{w_{j'}}{\sum_{T_{i,j'} \in j'} v_{i,j'}}$ then $j \prec j'$ in σ.

The following proposition gives negative results concerning the approximation ratio that we can achieve if we use the FCFS or the HDF order.

Proposition 1. *There are instances for which the optimal solutions to the* MAP-REDUCE(FCFS) *and the* MAPREDUCE(HDF) *problems are within a factor of* $\Omega(n)$ *from the optimal solution to the* MAPREDUCE *problem.*

In what follows we compare the FCFS and HDF policies with respect to the quality of the solution they produce. Our simulations have been performed on a machine with a CPU Intel Xeon X5650 with 8 cores, running at 2.67GHz. The operating system of the machine is a Linux Debian 6.0. We used Matlab with cvx toolbox. The solver used for the convex program is SeDuMi.

The instance of the problem consists of a matrix $m \times n$ that corresponds to the work of the tasks, two vectors of size n that correspond to the weights and the release dates of jobs, a precedence graph for the tasks of the same job, the energy budget and the value of β. Similarly with [5], the instance consists of $m = 50$ processors and up to $n = 25$ jobs. Each job has 20 Map and 10 Reduce tasks, which are preassigned at random to a different processor. The work of each Map task is selected uniformly at random from $[1, 10]$, while the work of each Reduce task $v_{i,j} \in \mathcal{R}$ is set equal to a random number in $[1, 10]$ plus $\frac{3 \sum_{T_{i',j} \in \mathcal{M}} v_{i',j}}{|\{T_{i',j} \in \mathcal{M}\}|}$, taking into account the fact that Reduce tasks have more work to execute than Map tasks. The weight of each job is selected uniformly at random from $[1, 10]$ and the release date of a job, is given as a Bernoulli random variable with probability $1/2$ for every interval $(t, t+1]$. The energy budget that is used equals $E = 1000$, while β is set $\beta = 2$. We have also set the desired accuracy of the returned solution of the convex program to be equal to 10^{-7}. For each number of jobs, we have repeated the experiments with 10 different matrices. The results we present below, concern the average of these 10 instances. The benchmark and the code used in our experiments are freely available at http://www.ibisc.univ-evry.fr/~vchau/research/mapreduce/.

As mentioned before, the (CP) does not lead to a feasible solution for our problem. In order to get such a solution we apply the following algorithm. At each time t where a processor becomes available we select to schedule the task $T_{i,j}$ of higher priority such that: (i) $T_{i,j}$ is already released at t, (ii) if $T_{i,j}$ is a Reduce task, then all Map tasks of the same job must have been already completed at t, and (iii) $T_{i,j}$ has not been yet executed.

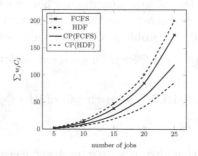

Fig. 2. Comparing solutions for FCFS and HDF (scaled down by a factor of 10^3)

As shown in Fig. 2 the heuristic based on FCFS outperforms the heuristic based on HDF. In fact, the first heuristic gives up to $16 - 21\%$ better solutions than the second one for different values of n. Surprisingly, the situation is completely inverse if we consider the corresponding solutions of the convex programs. More precisely, the convex programming relaxation using HDF leads to $26\% - 43\%$ smaller values of the objective function compared to the convex programming relaxation using FCFS. Moreover, we can observe that the ratio between the final solution of each heuristic with respect to the lower bound for the MapReduce(σ) problem given by the convex program is equal to 1.46 for FCFS and 2.43 for HDF; the variance is less than 0.1 in both cases.

5   Conclusions

We presented a constant-factor approximation algorithm based on a linear programming formulation of the problem of scheduling a set of MapReduce jobs in order to minimize their total weighted completion time under a given budget of energy. Moreover, in the direction of exploring the efficiency of standard scheduling policies, we presented counterexamples for them, as well as, we experimentally evaluated their performance, using a convex programming relaxation of the problem when a prespecified order of jobs is given. It has to be noticed that our results can be extended also to the case where multiple Map or Reduce tasks of a job are executed on the same processor. An interesting direction for future work concerns the online case of the problem. However, it can be proved that there is no an $O(1)$-competitive deterministic algorithm (see Theorem 13 in [3]). A possible way to overcome this is to consider resource (energy) augmentation, or to study the closely-related objective of a linear combination of the sum of weighted completion times of the jobs and of the total consumed energy.

References

1. Albers, S.: Algorithms for dynamic speed scaling. In: STACS, pp. 1–11 (2011)
2. Angel, E., Bampis, E., Kacem, F.: Energy aware scheduling for unrelated parallel machines. In: Green Computing Conference, pp. 533–540 (2012)
3. Bansal, N., Pruhs, K., Stein, C.: Speed scaling for weighted flow time. SIAM J. on Computing 39(4), 1294–1308 (2009)
4. Chang, H., Kodialam, M.S., Kompella, R.R., Lakshman, T.V., Lee, M., Mukherjee, S.: Scheduling in mapreduce-like systems for fast completion time. In: INFOCOM, pp. 3074–3082 (2011)
5. Chen, F., Kodialam, M.S., Lakshman, T.V.: Joint scheduling of processing and shuffle phases in mapreduce systems. In: INFOCOM, pp. 1143–1151 (2012)
6. Feller, E., Ramakrishnan, L., Morin, C.: On the performance and energy efficiency of Hadoop deployment models. In: BigData Conference, pp. 131–136 (2013)
7. Feng, B., Lu, J., Zhou, Y., Yang, N.: Energy efficiency for MapReduce workloads: An in-depth study. In: ADC, pp. 61–70 (2012)
8. Goiri, I., Le, K., Nguyen, T.D., Guitart, J., Torres, J., Bianchini, R.: GreenHadoop: leveraging green energy in data-processing frameworks. In: EuroSys, pp. 57–70 (2012)
9. Hall, L.A., Shmoys, D.B., Wein, J.: Scheduling to minimize average completion time: Off-line and on-line algorithms. In: ACM-SIAM SODA, pp. 142–151 (1996)
10. Mastrolilli, M., Queyranne, M., Schulz, A.S., Svensson, O., Uhan, N.A.: Minimizing the sum of weighted completion times in a concurrent open shop. Oper. Res. Letters 38(5), 390–395 (2010)
11. Megow, N., Verschae, J.: Dual techniques for scheduling on a machine with varying speed. In: Fomin, F.V., Freivalds, R., Kwiatkowska, M., Peleg, D. (eds.) ICALP 2013, Part I. LNCS, vol. 7965, pp. 745–756. Springer, Heidelberg (2013)
12. Moseley, B., Dasgupta, A., Kumar, R., Sarlós, T.: On scheduling in map-reduce and flow-shops. In: ACM-SPAA, pp. 289–298 (2011)
13. Phillips, C.A., Stein, C., Wein, J.: Minimizing average completion time in the presence of release dates. Math. Programming 82(1-2), 199–223 (1998)
14. Pruhs, K., van Stee, R., Uthaisombut, P.: Speed scaling of tasks with precedence constraints. Theory Comput. Syst. 43, 67–80 (2008)
15. Roemer, T.A.: A note on the complexity of the concurrent open shop problem. Journal of Scheduling 9, 389–396 (2006)
16. Schulz, A.S., Skutella, M.: Scheduling unrelated machines by randomized rounding. SIAM J. Discr. Mathematics 15(4), 450–469 (2002)
17. Wirtz, T., Ge, R.: Improving MapReduce energy efficiency for computation intensive workloads. In: IGCC, pp. 1–8 (2011)
18. Yao, F.F., Demers, A.J., Shenker, S.: A scheduling model for reduced cpu energy. In: IEEE- FOCS, pp. 374–382 (1995)

Automated Transformation of GPU-Specific OpenCL Kernels Targeting Performance Portability on Multi-Core/Many-Core CPUs*

Dafei Huang[1,2], Mei Wen[1,2], Changqing Xun[1,2], Dong Chen[1,2], Xing Cai[3],
Yuran Qiao[1,2], Nan Wu[2,3], and Chunyuan Zhang[1,2]

[1] Department of Computer, National University of Defense Technology
[2] State Key Laboratory of High Performance Computing,
Changsha, China
[3] Simula Research Laboratory, Oslo, Norway
hdafei@acm.org

Abstract. When adapting GPU-specific OpenCL kernels to run on multi-core/many-core CPUs, coarsening the thread granularity is necessary and thus extensively used. However, locality concerns exposed in GPU-specific OpenCL code are usually inherited without analysis, which may give side-effects on the CPU performance. When executing GPU-specific kernels on CPUs, local-memory arrays no longer match well with the hardware and the associated synchronizations are costly. To solve this dilemma, we actively analyze the memory access patterns by using array-access descriptors derived from GPU-specific kernels, which can thus be adapted for CPUs by removing all the unwanted local-memory arrays together with the obsolete barrier statements. Experiments show that the automated transformation can satisfactorily improve OpenCL kernel performances on Sandy Bridge CPU and Intel's Many-Integrated-Core coprocessor.

Keywords: OpenCL, Performance portability, Multi-core/many-core CPU, Code transformation and optimization.

1 Introduction

Heterogeneous computing systems, which incorporate two or more types of compute devices, are nowadays widely available from supercomputers to smart phones. A typical combination has been CPU plus GPU accelerator, while Intel's many-integrated-core (MIC) coprocessor is an increasingly popular choice of accelerator, such as in the currently No.1 supercomputer of the world: Tianhe-2. Programming, however, can be a challenge for using the heterogeneous devices for computations. The common strategy is to program separately for each type of the compute devices. Such a device-specific approach requires extensive

---

* Supported by the National Nature Science Foundation of China under No. 61033008, 61272145, and 61103080; 863 Program under No. 2012AA012706.

F. Silva et al. (Eds.): Euro-Par 2014, LNCS 8632, pp. 210–221, 2014.

programming effort, thereby difficult with respect to code maintenance and portability. An ideal scenario is thus to have the same source code base for multiple architectures, while maintaining a good level of performance portability.

OpenCL was designed with cross-platform code portability in mind. The advantage of adopting OpenCL programming is thus that a unified source code can work on different hardware architectures. On the other hand, however, performance portability does not come for free with OpenCL. The majority of existing OpenCL programs are GPU-specific, written with a bias or consensus toward getting good performance through making use of a massive number of threads, the round-robin instruction scheduling pattern, and the GPU-specific memory hierarchy [4][14]. These GPU-specific implementations, when executed directly on CPUs with heavy-weight cores, typically cannot achieve good performance [10].

Code transformation can provide a GPU-specific OpenCL program with performance portability to multi-core/many-core CPUs. A common technique of transformation is to enforce a coarser thread granularity, using the so-called *work-item coalescing* or *serialization* [12,13]. Moreover, work-items within a work-group are a primary source of vector- and instruction-level parallelism, both of which are typically exploited by a single CPU thread. However, the prior work concerning OpenCL code transformation has largely neglected to incorporate CPU-specific performance properties, such as spatial and temporal data locality [6], or directly inherit data locality features from a GPU-specific OpenCL kernel, often resulting in poor performance on CPUs [12,13]. What's more, when handling local memory and barriers, the existing code transformations have mainly concentrated on functionality and semantics but not performance, and without relevant analysis.

We will propose in this paper a new approach to transforming GPU-specific OpenCL kernels into a high-performance form that suits multi-core/many-core CPUs. It is based on a precise analysis of memory accesses, with help of a linear array-access descriptor. The resulting code transformation can thus remove all the unnecessary arrays that are allocated in OpenCL's local memory. In addition, all the unnecessary thread synchronizations are properly removed, instead of blindly using the known technique of *loop fission*. Thereafter, a post optimizer performs CPU-specific loop-level optimizations. The automatically transformed OpenCL kernels can be effectively executed on the multi-core/many-core architecture by using POSIX threads.

2   Related Work

There are many publications that address the challenge of adapting OpenCL code for the multi-core/many-core architecture targeting performance portability using code transformation, which directly translates GPU-specific OpenCL code into another code fit for CPUs.

Previous research activities that implement OpenCL for CPU platforms vary widely in the chosen approach to coalescing work-items and capturing

SIMD parallelism. The Twin Peaks method [6] utilizes `setjmp` and `longjmp` to merge fine-grain work-items into a single OS-thread, and performs vectorization within a work-item, but does not explore inter work-item parallelism. Region serialization methods [12,13] coalesce work-items by constructing thread loops and performing loop fission to reproduce the similar functionality of inter work-item synchronizations. They rely on an auto-vectorization technology within loop iterations to exploit parallelism. Intel's implementation of OpenCL for x86, being the least explicitly disclosed or studied, directly targets SIMD instructions and efficiently exploits vector-parallelism within a work-group [7]. None of the above implementations, however, handles data locality well enough, since they just depend on if the locality exposed on the GPU-specific code is suitable for the targeting CPU, so they may result in a strided access pattern by executing one or more work-items as long as possible, instead of interleaving the accesses of the work-items that can share the elements on one cache line. Stratton et al. rely on CEAN expression to do a more advanced handling of spatial locality [14]. Seo et al. adopt another approach from a different viewpoint [11], by automatically adapting the work-group size for better performance on multi-core CPU architecture.

No existing work can properly handle the issue of unnecessary use of local memory and synchronization. The state of the art usually uses arrays in OpenCL's global memory (main memory as to CPU) to simulate the ones in local memory, while ignoring the existence of caches on CPU. As for barriers, the Twin Peaks method directly uses jump instructions to simulate the function, which results in excessive overhead and breaks the locality in kernel code. Other approaches fully depend on the technique of loop fission, which also results in overhead of loop control instructions and variable extensions.

3   A Linear Descriptor of Array Access

An accurate identification of local and global memory access patterns is the key to a high-quality transformation from GPU-specific kernels to the CPU-matching counterparts. However, previously proposed descriptors of array access patterns have been designed for the scenario of nested loops, or not accurate enough to extract dependencies between work-items in the context of parallel SPMD OpenCL kernels [3][5].

We propose a precise linear descriptor of array accesses, based on the observation that most array accesses in a GPU-specific kernel can be expressed linearly. For example, the only exception to linear array accesses that can be found in Nvidia Computing SDK and the SHOC benchmark suite consists of indirect array accesses.

For each array that is accessed in any loop within a GPU-specific OpenCL kernel, our new array-access descriptor expresses the array index as a linear subscript function of only initial variables, that is: the work-item/work-group IDs, the loop induction variable, and the input arguments to the OpenCL kernel. In addition, a set of linear constraints, i.e., equalities and inequalities, are derived

```
     __kernel void matrixMul( __global float* C, __global float* A, __global float* B,
                              __local float* As, __local float* Bs, int uiWA, int uiWB )
     {
1        int aBegin = uiWA * BLOCK_SIZE * Gid.y;
2        int aEnd   = aBegin + uiWA - 1;
3        int aStep  = BLOCK_SIZE;
4        int bBegin = BLOCK_SIZE * Gid.x;
5        int bStep  = BLOCK_SIZE * uiWB;

6        float Csub = 0.0f;
7        for (int a = aBegin, b = bBegin; a <= aEnd; a += aStep, b += bStep)
8        { AS[Lid.x + Lid.y * BLOCK_SIZE] = A[a + uiWA * Lid.y + Lid.x];
9          BS[Lid.x + Lid.y * BLOCK_SIZE] = B[b + uiWB * Lid.y + Lid.x];
10         barrier(CLK_LOCAL_MEM_FENCE);
11         for (int k = 0; k < BLOCK_SIZE; ++k)
12            Csub += AS[k + Lid.y*BLOCK_SIZE] * BS[Lid.x + k*BLOCK_SIZE];
13         barrier(CLK_LOCAL_MEM_FENCE);  }
14       C[(Gid.y*GROUP_SIZE_Y+Lid.y)*GLOBAL_SIZE_X + (Gid.x*GROUP_SIZE_X+Lid.x)] = Csub;
     }
```

Fig. 1. The original GPU-specific kernel of matrix multiplication

from the conditions of branches and loops to accurately pinpoint the range of the array index. As an illustrating example, Figure 1 shows the OpenCL kernel implementation of matrix multiplication, $C = A \times B$, available from Nvidia GPU Computing SDK. (It should be noted that some of the variables are renamed for clarity, and `Lid` denotes the local work-item ID, whereas `Gid` denotes the global work-group ID.) Within the outer loop of the kernel function there are six different array accesses: write access to `AS` and read access to `A` on line 8, write access to `BS` and read access to `B` on line 9, read access to both `AS` and `BS` on line 12. Descriptors of the array accesses to `AS` and `A` (line 8,12) are listed in Figure 2, where f denotes the linear subscript function, *Constraint* denotes the set of linear constraints, and $Iter_x (x = a, b, k)$ represent the normalized loop induction variables. For read access `A[a+uiWA*Lid.y+Lid.x]`, the linear function is f_A^{read}, derived by replacing a with its corresponding linear expression without any intermediate variable. The $Constraints_A^{read}$ limits the ranges of the variables in f_A^{read}, by combining loop conditions and intrinsic constraints on work-group and work-item IDs.

$$
\begin{cases}
f_A^{read} = (uiWA \times BLOCK\_SIZE \times Gid.y + BLOCK\_SIZE \times Iter_a) + uiWA \times Lid.y + Lid.x \\
Constraint_A^{read} = \{Iter_a \geq 0 ;\ Iter_a < uiWA/BLOCK\_SIZE;\ Gid.y \geq 0;\ Gid.y < GLOBAL\_SIZE; \\
\qquad\qquad Lid.x \geq 0;\ Lid.x < BLOCK\_SIZE;\ Lid.y \geq 0;\ Lid.y < BLOCK\_SIZE\}
\end{cases}
$$

$$
\begin{cases}
f_{AS}^{write} = Lid.x + Lid.y \times BLOCK\_SIZE \\
Constraint_{AS}^{write} = \{Lid.x \geq 0;\ Lid.x < BLOCK\_SIZE;\ Lid.y \geq 0;\ Lid.y < BLOCK\_SIZE\}
\end{cases}
$$

$$
\begin{cases}
f_{AS}^{read} = Iter_k + Lid.y \times BLOCK\_SIZE \\
Constraint_{AS}^{read} = \{Iter_k \geq 0;\ Iter_k < BLOCK\_SIZE;\ Lid.y \geq 0;\ Lid.y < BLOCK\_SIZE\}
\end{cases}
$$

Fig. 2. Array access descriptors of accesses to `AS` and `A` in matrix multiplication

The derivation of a linear array-access descriptor, such as shown in Figure 2, is fully automated by taking advantage of the *Static Single Assignment* in LLVM infrastructure.

4   Transforming GPU-Specific OpenCL Kernels

4.1   Analysis-Based Coalescing

Work-item coalescing (or *serialization*) aims to merge the work-items of an entire work-group into a single CPU thread. The standard technique of coalescing is to construct a nested *thread loop*, where the loop levels correspond to the dimension of a work-group, the loop induction variables match the local work-item IDs, and the loop body is the original GPU-specific kernel code. A complicating factor, however, arises with thread synchronization. The state of the art is to adopt *loop fission* wherever synchronization appears. An example can be found in Figure 3.

```
Kernel_Name(Kernel_Args...)   Kernel_Name(Kernel_Args...)
{                             {
    Kernel_Body_1...              for(Lid.z=0; Lid.z<GROUP_SIZE_Z; Lid.z++)
    barrier();                      for(Lid.y=0; Lid.y<GROUP_SIZE_Y; Lid.y++)
    Kernel_Body_2...                  for(Lid.x=0; Lid.x<GROUP_SIZE_X; Lid.x++)
}                                       { Kernel_Body_1... }
                                  for(Lid.z=0; Lid.z<GROUP_SIZE_Z; Lid.z++)
                                    for(Lid.y=0; Lid.y<GROUP_SIZE_Y; Lid.y++)
                                      for(Lid.x=0; Lid.x<GROUP_SIZE_X; Lid.x++)
                                        { Kernel_Body_2... }
                              }
  (a) Original kernel with barrier    (b) Coaleced kernel using thread loop and loop fission
```

Fig. 3. Work-item coalescing by constructing thread loops

Considering the negative effects of blindly adopting loop fission, our remedy is to adopt an accurate dependence analysis, based on the linear descriptor of array accesses from Section 3, so that unnecessary thread synchronizations are eliminated, thereby avoiding loop fission.

Another performance-critical factor, in connection with work-item coalescing, is the use of OpenCL's local memory. Local memory array emulated by a segment of the slow main memory attached to a CPU may result in performance penalty, due to unnecessary data copies and additional thread synchronizations. This performance dilemma has received insufficient attention in the state of the art of work-item coalescing. Our novel contribution is therefore to eliminate all the unnecessary local-memory arrays during coalescing. This again will be based on the precise analysis of memory access patterns.

Eliminating Unnecessary Local-Memory Arrays

The functionality of local memory usage in GPU-specific kernels can be classified into three types:

1) Buffering: To improve temporal and spatial data locality within the kernel code, newly accessed data that are to be reused are buffered in OpenCL's local memory, so that long-latency global memory accesses are replaced by faster local memory accesses.
2) Reorganization: Data are loaded from OpenCL's global memory and stored in local memory using a different pattern, which allows coalesced memory accesses and effectively avoids bank conflicts. A representative example is

the transposed matrix multiplication $(C = A \times A^T)$ kernel [8], where tiles of matrix A are loaded in rows but stored into columns of a local-memory array.

3) Enabling communication and reducing computation: Intermediate results of a work-item are stored in OpenCL's local memory before another work-item uses them. This type of usage not only reduces duplicated computations among different work-items, but also enables inter work-item communication.

On the multi-core/many-core architecture, functionality No. 3 also has to use OpenCL's local memory, thus work-item coalescing should not change this usage of local memory. For functionality No. 2, although data copy overhead arises due to the data reorganization, subsequent more efficient accesses to the reorganized data may still draw overall performance benefits. Regarding functionality No. 1, however, the usage of OpenCL's local memory becomes obsolete because the same effect can be achieved by the cache hierarchy on CPUs. Therefore, such a usage of local memory should be eliminated during coalescing. This requires an automated code analysis that can distinguish between the three usage types, together with automated replacement of local-memory array accesses with the corresponding global-memory array accesses.

Loads from local-memory arrays can be translated to direct global memory loads, provided the following two conditions are both satisfied:

(1) For a pair of local array write and read, by examining their array access descriptors, if some of the variables in the write descriptor are substituted with the variables of the read descriptor, the two descriptors become identical including the subscript functions and constraints.

(2) In this local array read-write pair, the write data is from a global memory read, which can be checked by using a definition-use chain.

After replacing the local array read with its corresponding global array read. The local array write will become dead code, and can be removed by compiler afterwards. An example is the following local array read-write pair from Figure 2:

$$\left\{ \begin{array}{l} f_{AS}^{write} = Lid.x + Lid.y \times BLOCK\_SIZE \\ Constraint_{AS}^{write} = \{Lid.x \geq 0;\ Lid.x < BLOCK\_SIZE; \\ \qquad\qquad Lid.y \geq 0;\ Lid.y < BLOCK\_SIZE\} \end{array} \right. \qquad (4.1)$$

$$\left\{ \begin{array}{l} f_{AS}^{read} = Iter_k + Lid.y \times BLOCK\_SIZE \\ Constraint_{AS}^{read} = \{Iter_k \geq 0;\ Iter_k < BLOCK\_SIZE; \\ \qquad\qquad Lid.y \geq 0;\ Lid.y < BLOCK\_SIZE\} \end{array} \right. \qquad (4.2)$$

If we substitute $Lid.x$ in (4.1) with $Iter_k$ from (4.2), the two descriptors become identical, which satisfies condition (1). Moreover, the write data of (4.1) is read from global array A according to line 8 in Figure 1, which satisfies condition (2):

$$\begin{array}{l} f_A^{read} = (uiWA \times BLOCK\_SIZE \times Gid.y + BLOCK\_SIZE \\ \qquad \times Iter_a) + uiWA \times Lid.y + Lid.x \end{array} \qquad (4.3)$$

So a transformation from local memory load to direct global memory load is legal, by performing the substitution of $Lid.x$ with $Iter_k$ in (4.3), and using it to replace (4.2):

$$f_{AS}^{read} = Iter_k + Lid.y \times BLOCK\_SIZE \quad \Rightarrow$$
$$f_A^{read} = (uiWA \times BLOCK\_SIZE \times Gid.y + BLOCK\_SIZE \quad (4.4)$$
$$\times Iter_a) + uiWA \times Lid.y + Iter_k$$

However, for local arrays with the data reorganization functionality, it is legal but not performance-beneficial. So an intuitive or heuristic condition is induced here to guarantee that a local array does not have the functionality of data reorganization:

(3) Looking at the linear subscript functions of a local array write and its respective global memory read, the variable $Lid.x$ has the same coefficient in the two functions (or that $Lid.x$ does not exist).

For example, in formulas (4.1) and (4.3), $Lid.x$ has coefficient 1 in both f_{AS}^{write} and f_A^{read}, and array accesses by (4.1) and (4.2) are the only accesses to local array AS. By using the condition above, we can conclude that local array AS does not have the functionality of data reorganization. By removing all the local arrays that only have the functionality of data buffering, and replacing them with direct accesses to global arrays, we can thus ensure good performance after work-item coalescing. Lines 8,9,12 in Figure 5 (line numbers remain the same as in Figure 1) shows the codes after eliminating the unnecessary local arrays AS and BS.

Dependence Analysis and Synchronization Elimination

Synchronization elimination happens after the unnecessary local arrays, the main source of synchronizations, are removed. However, we cannot simply delete all the barriers, since these may serve other local arrays that are not removed, or the synchronizations may use global memory. To check whether a barrier can be safely eliminated, dependence analysis is needed. Here, dependence analysis is very different from the typical scenario, because it is the dependence between different work-items that we care about.

When performing dependence analysis for a certain barrier, we first divide the kernel into basic blocks (barriers are also boundaries of the basic blocks). Then we examine every pair of array accesses (one of the accesses must be a write operation and both touch the same local or global array) that are located separately in two basic blocks before and after the barrier. The process is shown in Figure 4, where rectangles with dashed edge show the partitioning of basic blocks with different control structures, and arrows show the basic blocks within which array access pairs must be examined. The left part emphasizes that the examinations are for different work-items. For each examination, we combine the two descriptors of the access pair to form a linear *Diophantine Inequation System*. If there is a solution to the inequation system where not all the three pairs of local IDs are required to be equal, actual dependence exists and the barrier cannot be removed.

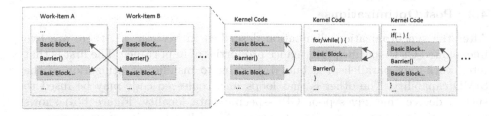

Fig. 4. An illustration of dependence analysis

$$\begin{cases} \begin{cases} f_1 = \overrightarrow{Coe_1} \cdot \overrightarrow{Var_1}^{\mathrm{T}} + Const & \overrightarrow{Var_1} = (..., Lid.z, Lid.y, Lid.x) \\ Constraint_1 \end{cases} \\ \begin{cases} f_2 = \overrightarrow{Coe_2} \cdot \overrightarrow{Var_2}^{\mathrm{T}} + Const & \overrightarrow{Var_2} = (..., Lid.z', Lid.y', Lid.x') \\ Constraint_2 \end{cases} \\ \Rightarrow \begin{cases} f_1 = f_2 \\ Constraint_1 \\ Constraint_2 \end{cases} \end{cases} \qquad (4.5)$$

Equation (4.5) shows the construction of an inequation system. The upper part shows two descriptors to be examined (Coe denotes the vector of coefficients, Var denotes the vector of variables, and $Const$ denotes a constant), and the lower part is the resultant system, generated by forcing the subscript functions to be equal while the both constraints are satisfied. Note that each local ID is no longer treated as the same variable in f_1 and f_2, so we use different names. A barrier must be reserved if the inequation system has a solution without the restriction $\{Lid.x = Lid.x'; Lid.y = Lid.y'; Lid.z = Lid.z'\}$.

By using the above dependence analysis, we can eliminate all the removable barriers in a GPU-specific kernel, and then enclose the kernel body by a thread loop. For non-removable barriers, loop fissions are inserted. Figure 5 shows the matrix multiplication kernel after coalescing, where both the barriers in the original kernel are eliminated.

```
     for (int Lid.y=0 ; Lid.y<BLOCK_SIZE; Lid.y++)
       for (int Lid.x=0 ; Lid.x<BLOCK_SIZE; Lid.x++) {
…      ...
6        float Csub = 0.0f;
7        for (int Itera=0, Iterb=0; Itera<=uiWA/BLOCK_SIZE; Itera++, Iterb++)
8,9      { //Dead Code
10         //Removed barrier(CLK_LOCAL_MEM_FENCE);
11         for(int Iterk=0; Iterk<BLOCK_SIZE; ++Iterk)
12           Csub += A[(uiWA*BLOCK_SIZE*Gid.y+BLOCK_SIZE*Itera)+uiWA*Lid.y+Iterk]
                   * B[(BLOCK_SIZE*Gid.x+BLOCK_SIZE*uiWB*Iterb)+uiWB*Iterk+Lid.x];
13         //Removed barrier(CLK_LOCAL_MEM_FENCE); }
14       C[(Gid.y*GROUP_SIZE_Y+Lid.y)*GLOBAL_SIZE_X+(Gid.x*GROUP_SIZE_X+Lid.x)] = Csub;
     }
```

Fig. 5. Code snippet of the matrix multiplication kernel after work-item coalescing

4.2   Post Optimizations

After the synchronization elimination described in Section 4.1, there are two unexploited CPU-specific performance properties of importance. The first is that inter work-item parallelism is buried, leading to insufficient utilization of the SIMD capability. The other is that loops in a coalesced code may be fused to such a degree that gives poor CPU-specific data locality. Figure 6(a) shows the unoptimized access sequences to arrays A and B, where iterative accesses to array A go through the whole long row, and accesses to B go through the whole column, resulting in successive cache misses. Furthermore, no SIMD parallelism is exploited.

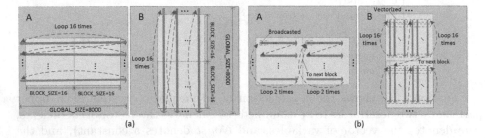

Fig. 6. Different access sequences to arrays A and B

We adopt two post optimizations of the coalesced code. They are combinations of traditional loop-level optimizations, but of vital effects on final performance.

Vectorization: The best loop level for performing vectorization should be that with induction variable Lid.x. This is because the coalesced memory accesses of a GPU-specific kernel often result in sequential and short-stride memory accesses across that loop level. So loop-interchange is firstly performed before ordinary vectorization so that Lid.x-loop becomes the innermost. The resultant effect as shown in Figure 6(b) is that, each scalar element of A is expanded into a vector, and each set of eight adjacent accesses to B is vectorized to produce a new vector. Then computational operations are fully vectorized so that the works of eight work-items are accomplished simultaneously.

Data locality re-exploitation: Our process of data locality re-exploitation has two steps, blocking of long non-thread-loops and loop interchange. As the result shown in Figure 6(b), the iterative array accesses are restricted in small blocks, so that the CPU cache can play a very good role.

The code snippet as the final output of the kernel transformation targeting the Sandy Bridge architecture can be found in Figure 7.

5   Performance Evaluation

We have implemented a fully automated tool chain that performs kernel transformation based on the Clang compiler front end and the LLVM compiler

```
for(int Itera=0, Iterb=0; Itera<=uiWA/BLOCK_SIZE; Itera++, Iterb++)
  for(int vLid.x=0; vLid.x<BLOCK_SIZE/8; vLid.x++)
    for(int Lid.y=0; Lid.y<BLOCK_SIZE; Lid.y++)
      for(int Iterk=0; Iterk<BLOCK_SIZE; ++Iterk)
        Csub[Lid.y][vLid.x]= vec_float8_add( Csub[Lid.y][vLid.x],
              vec_float8_mult(
              vec_float8_broadcast(A[(uiWA*BLOCK_SIZE*
                Gid.y+BLOCK_SIZE*Itera)+uiWA*Lid.y+Iterk]),    //broadcast
              vec_float8_load(B+BLOCK_SIZE*Gid.x+BLOCK_SIZE*uiWB*Iterb+
                uiWB*Iterk+vLid.x*8)                           //load
                          )               );                  //mult, add
```

Fig. 7. Final code snippet of the transformed matrix multiplication kernel

infrastructure [2]. The tool chain transforms a GPU-specific OpenCL kernel into a function, whose input arguments include the original ones from the GPU-specific kernel plus a set of work-group IDs. The vector operations are enabled by using Intel intrinsics. Each call to this function is equivalent with executing a corresponding work-group.

To run an entire OpenCL program that has both host and kernel code, the kernel transformation tool chain is integrated into an open source OpenCL implementation called FreeOCL [1], where POSIX threads are used to execute work-groups concurrently.

Experiments are carried out on two hardware platforms: (1) two Intel Xeon E5-2650 eight-core CPUs that have 16 physical cores together, as a typical multi-core CPU, (2) an Intel Xeon Phi 5110p coprocessor with 60 physical cores, as an emerging many-core CPU. The new OpenCL implementation, including our automated kernel transformation tool chain (denoted by OurOCL), is compared against the OpenCL implementation from Intel SDK for OpenCL Applications 2013, which is the official OpenCL runtime provided by Intel (denoted by IntelOCL).

Six kernels are used as the benchmarks. They cover a wide range of computational intensities and intrinsic memory localities. The first five kernels are optimized for running on GPUs so that they are well GPU-specific, where Stencil2D comes from SHOC and the remaining four kernels are from Nvidia GPU Computing SDK. The sixth kernel, NaiveMatrixMul, is the baseline matrix multiplication from [9], which is not so GPU-specific, and can show the potentiality of our method when few optimization features can be inherited.

IntelOCL is usually the most powerful commercial OpenCL runtime on Intel platforms, so we compare running the kernels via OurOCL, where kernels will be auto-transformed before execution, against running the same kernels via IntelOCL. When running the benchmarks, only the kernel execution times are recorded. Table 1 shows all the speedups of kernel executions relative to the CPU+IntelOCL configuration. The table indicates that OurOCL can improve the performance of GPU-specific kernels on multi-core CPUs by an average factor of 3.24x, not including the NaiveMatrixMul kernel. The average performance improvement of MIC+OurOCL over MIC+IntelOCL is 2.06x (3.53x/1.71x).

Table 1. Performance comparison with Intel OpenCL implementation and OpenMP

Kernel name	Scale	CPU + IntelOCL	CPU + OurOCL	CPU + OMP	MIC + IntelOCL	MIC + OurOCL	MIC + OMP
oclMatrixMul	8000 × 8000	1	3.02	0.37	1.94	3.95	3.74
oclFDTD3d	320×320×320 Radius=16 Timestep=5	1	6.02	2.20	2.22	5.88	4.13
Stencil2D	4096 × 4096 1000 iters	1	2.53	1.16	1.83	2.42	1.95
oclDCT8x8	10240 × 10240	1	3.42	2.27	1.43	4.17	4.52
oclNbody	327680	1	1.20	0.74	1.13	1.24	1.38
*NaiveMatrixMul	8000 × 8000	1	33.48	4.10	4.55	43.76	41.43
Average (except NaiveMatrixMul)		1	3.24	1.35	1.71	3.53	3.14

IntelOCL is very good at utilizing the inter-work-group and inter-work-item parallelism by using the multiple cores and SIMD units. But its synchronization overhead is experimentally found to be somewhere between that of the region-based methods and the Twin Peaks method [14]. So the performance boost of OurOCL should be mainly attributed to the elimination of barriers and local-memory arrays, and partly the locality re-exploitation. The oclNbody kernel gets the minimum performance improvements on both platforms, because it is the most compute-intensive. The overheads induced by barriers and redundant memory copies only account for a small part of the kernel execution time. As for the two stencil computation kernels: oclFDTD3d and Stencil2D, improvements on MIC are much lower than those on CPU. This is because only a small portion of the execution time is used for computation as the two kernels are highly memory-intensive, so MIC can hardly show its superior parallel capability. The intensity of memory accesses also results in the slightly lower performances on MIC than those on CPU. On the other hand, the NaiveMatrixMul kernel obtains huge performance boosts because of both overhead removal and data locality improvement.

Performances of corresponding OpenMP implementations are also presented. The OpenMP implementations are based on the serial host implementations that can be found in every adopted benchmark, by properly adding OpenMP directives. (Execution of the OpenMP implementations on MIC uses the native mode.) We note that multi-core/many-core specific optimizations were already performed in some of the host implementations such as oclDCT8x8, and the *icc* can also automatically carry out various optimizations. Generally, improved OpenCL performances on both CPU and MIC are comparable with or even better than the OpenMP implementations. This shows that our automated code transformation can indeed greatly enhance performance portability.

6   Conclusion

To improve the performance portability of OpenCL programs from GPUs to CPUs, code transformation is widely accepted. This paper presents a novel transformation methodology for GPU-specific OpenCL kernels targeting performance portability on multi-core/many-core CPUs, aiming at solving the potential problems induced by using local-memory arrays on CPUs, including redundant data copies and the accompanying costly synchronizations. A new array-access descriptor that can accurately uncover the array access patterns of OpenCL work-items lays the foundation of our work.

Experiments are done on Sandy Bridge CPU and Knights Corner MIC, which show that, for GPU-specific kernels, our new OpenCL implementation outperforms the powerful Intel OpenCL runtime on both platforms.

References

1. FreeOCL: multi-platform implementation of OpenCL 1.2 targeting CPUs, https://code.google.com/p/freeocl/
2. The LLVM compiler infrastructure, http://llvm.org/
3. Balasundaram, V., Kennedy, K.: A technique for summarizing data access and its use in parallelism enhancing transformations. In: SIGPLAN 1989 Conference on Programming Language Design and Implementation, Portland, USA, pp. 41–53 (1989)
4. Baskaran, M.M., Bondhugula, U., Krishnamoorthy, S., Ramanujam, J., Rountev, A., Sadayappan, P.: A compiler framework for optimization of affine loop nests for GPGPUs. In: 22nd International Conference on Supercomputing, Island of Kos, Greece, pp. 225–234 (June 2008)
5. Bastoul, C.: Code generation in the polyhedral model is easier than you think. In: 13th International Conference on Parallel Architectures and Compilation Techniques, Antibes Juan-les-Pins, France, pp. 7–16 (September 2004)
6. Gummaraju, J., Morichetti, L., Houston, M., Sander, B., Gaster, B.R., Zheng, B.: Twin peaks: A software platform for heterogeneous computing on general-purpose and graphics processors. In: 19th International Conference on Parallel Architectures and Compilation Techniques, Vienna, Austria, pp. 205–216 (September 2010)
7. Intel Corporation: Intel SDK for OpenCL Applications XE 2013 Optimization Guide (2013)
8. Nvidia: OpenCL Best Practices Guide (February 2011)
9. Nvidia: OpenCL Programming Guide for the CUDA Architecture (February 2011)
10. Pennycook, S., Hammond, S., Wright, S., Herdman, J., Miller, I., Jarvis, S.A.: An investigation of the performance portability of OpenCL. Journal of Parallel and Distributed Computing 73(11), 1439–1450 (2013)
11. Seo, S., Lee, J., Jo, G., Lee, J.: Automatic OpenCL work-group size selection for multicore CPUs. In: 22nd International Conference on Parallel Architectures and Compilation Techniques, Edinburgh, UK (September 2013)
12. Stratton, J.A., Grover, V., Marathe, J., Aarts, B., Murphy, M., Hu, Z., Hwu, W.M.W.: Efficient compilation of fine-grained SPMD threaded programs for multicore CPUs. In: 8th Annual IEEE/ACM International Symposium on Code Generation and Optimization, Toronto, Canada, pp. 111–119 (April 2010)
13. Stratton, J.A., Stone, S.S., Hwu, W. M.W.: MCUDA: An effective implementation of CUDA kernels for multi-core CPUs. In: Amaral, J.N. (ed.) LCPC 2008. LNCS, vol. 5335, pp. 16–30. Springer, Heidelberg (2008)
14. Stratton, J.A., Kim, H.S., Jablin, T.B., Hwu, W.M.W.: Performance portability in accelerated parallel kernels. Tech. Rep. IMPACT-13-01, University of Illinois at Urbana-Champaign (May 2013)

Switchable Scheduling for Runtime Adaptation of Optimization

Lénaïc Bagnères[1] and Cédric Bastoul[2]

[1] University of Paris-Sud and Inria, Orsay, France
lenaic.bagneres@inria.fr
[2] University of Strasbourg and Inria, Strasbourg, France
cedric.bastoul@unistra.fr

Abstract. Parallel applications used to be executed alone until their termination on partitions of supercomputers: a very static environment for very static applications. The recent shift to multicore architectures for desktop and embedded systems as well as the emergence of cloud computing is raising the problem of the impact of the execution context on performance. The number of criteria to take into account for that purpose is significant: architecture, system, workload, dynamic parameters, etc. Finding the best optimization for every context at compile time is clearly out of reach. Dynamic optimization is the natural solution, but it is often costly in execution time and may offset the optimization it is enabling. In this paper, we present a static-dynamic compiler optimization technique that generates loop-based programs with dynamic auto-tuning capabilities with very low overhead. Our strategy introduces switchable scheduling, a family of program transformations that allows to switch between optimized versions while always processing useful computation. We present both the technique to generate self-adaptive programs based on switchable scheduling and experimental evidence of their ability to sustain high-performance in a dynamic environment.

1 Introduction

Static compilers are facing the challenge of generating efficient codes for increasingly dynamic execution environments. Two decades ago, optimizing compilation was referred as building "supercompilers for supercomputers" [20]. Compiler techniques had to optimize aggressively for complex parallel machines but in a very static context: usually one program with few dynamic parameters, one well defined architecture/system and one user. Iterative compilation and auto-tuning approaches have been developed on top of static compilation as efficient solutions to find the best optimization parameters and to adapt to various (but fixed) architectures and problem sizes [2,19,12]. The large adoption of multicore systems and the emergence of cloud computing brings new dynamic factors that are not captured by iterative compilation or auto-tuning, such as the existence of competing workloads or the possible migration of the process to another architecture. This situation raises the need for more dynamic optimization schemes.

F. Silva et al. (Eds.): Euro-Par 2014, LNCS 8632, pp. 222–233, 2014.

Just in time compilation is a convenient solution to address dynamic execution environments. However, it requires very low algorithmic complexity of the underlying techniques to avoid to offset the optimization it is enabling. Current state-of-the-art static automatic optimization and parallelization techniques rely on an algebraic representation of programs that allows precise analyses as well as very aggressive program transformations to optimize codes, known as the *polyhedral model* [7,3,11]. Unfortunately, most polyhedral-based techniques show exponential complexity [17]. Hence, they are challenging to include in a dynamic compilation framework, except when a runtime analysis allows to use this model while it was not possible at static compile time [9]. Our proposal is a mixed static-dynamic technique, which benefits from the power of polyhedral frameworks at static compile time, while being able to change the optimization decision at runtime during the computation itself.

The potential benefit of such a technique is significant because the dynamic nature of the execution environment comes from several factors that directly impact performance. First of all, a compiled program may be run on different architectures with different features such as various cache memories or number of cores, which have dramatic impact on the best optimization choice. A decision at the early stage of the execution is not enough: virtual machines and cloud computing technology allow the architecture to change during execution. Next, the application may depend on dynamic parameters such as problem size (e.g., array size). Hence the best optimization is likely to be different depending on those parameters that will be known only at runtime. Finally, the operating system and the system workload are also paramount because processes may affect each other, e.g., through cache pollution or by stressing the system scheduler.

Our approach is to design at compile-time programs that can adapt at runtime to the execution context. The originality of our solution is to rely on *switchable scheduling*, a selected set of program restructuring which allows to swap between program versions at some meeting points without any rollback. A first step selects pertinent switchable versions according to their performance behavior on some execution contexts. The second step builds a self-adaptive program including selected versions. Then at runtime the program keeps choosing the best version thanks to a low overhead sampling and profiling of the versions, ensuring during the process that every computation contributes to the final result. We performed an experimental study on dozens of execution contexts and demonstrate superior adaptability of our generated codes with respect to state-of-the-art static optimization technique.

2   Background

The application domain of our technique is loop-based kernels with affine control and memory accesses, i.e., such that loop bounds, conditions and array subscripts are affine forms of outer loop counters and constant parameters. This class of computational kernels is known as SCoPs for Static Control Parts. SCoPs can be modeled using an algebraic representation called the *polyhedral model*. Because

of the restriction on the input program form, each dynamic *instance* of a given
SCoP statement can be modeled as an integer point in a union of polyhedra
called the *iteration domain* of that statement. For example, let us consider the
input code in Figure 1(a). Figure 1(b) shows the iteration domain of the statement S(i,j). Each loop enclosing the statement in the code corresponds to a
dimension of the domain. Several compilers have the ability to raise SCoPs to a
polyhedral form such as *GNU GCC*[1] and *LLVM*[2].

Once a SCoP is raised to the polyhedral model, an optimizer can compute a
scheduling by means of *scheduling relations* that express logical execution dates
for all statement instances, e.g., to achieve data locality or to expose parallelism while satisfying data dependences. In the following, we will only consider
scheduling that does not alter the original program semantics. Figures 1(c1) and
1(c2) show two different possible scheduling relations. They map original *input*
dimensions, which express original statement instances, to target *output* dimensions, which express their new order. Scheduling relations are expressive enough
to encode a complex composition of program transformations (including, e.g.,
loop interchange, fusion, fission, skewing, tiling etc.) [8]. Those in Figures 1(c1)
and 1(c2) correspond respectively to the identity transformation and to the re-
versal of the inner loop. Many efficient scheduling algorithms have been designed,
notably the Pluto algorithm for automatic optimization and parallelization [3]
and the Letsee technique based on iterative optimization [11].

Finally a code generator for scanning polyhedra such as CLooG [1] can produce a syntactic program that implements the new scheduling from the iteration
domains and the scheduling relations. Figures 1(d1) and 1(d2) present the programs generated back from the corresponding polyhedral representations after
the code generation step. The complete Figure 1 summarizes the usual workflow
of a polyhedral framework with two different scheduling relations that result in
two *versions* of the input program. Most previous works aim at finding only *one*
good version. Our work improves this scheme with dynamic capablities, to be
able to chose the right version for the right execution context.

3   Switchable Scheduling

In a polyhedral compilation framework, a program version is generated from the
input program information and a scheduling. The scheduling is in turn expressed
as a list of scheduling relations, one for each statement. In this work, we focus
on particular sets of scheduling called *switchable scheduling*. Two scheduling
are switchable if and only if there exist meeting points in the corresponding
generated versions such that it is possible to continue the execution from any
of these versions at those meeting points without affecting the program result.
Translated to the polyhedral model terminology, it means that there must exist
a couple of logical dates called *switching dates*, one for each scheduling, such that
the sets of instances that have been scheduled prior to these dates in each version

---

[1] http://gcc.gnu.org/wiki/Graphite
[2] http://polly.llvm.org

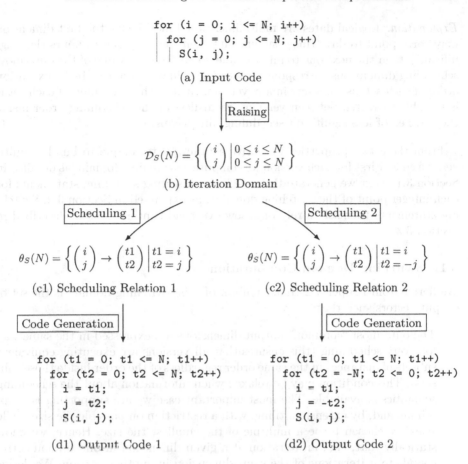

Fig. 1. Polyhedral Transformation Workflow For Two Example Versions

is the same, regardless of their respective order. To simplify their computation, and without loss of generality, we require that switching dates correspond to existing instance schedules. The set of switching dates for a scheduling θ to a scheduling θ' is called its *switching domain to θ'*.

Property 1. To a given switching date in a scheduling there may exist only a unique corresponding switching date in another scheduling.

Explanation. Each instance of the original program has a unique image in the target program. Hence, given a set of already executed instances before a meeting point in a version, the corresponding meeting point in another version, if it exists, is the unique instance that will be executed directly after that set.   □

Property 2. If the outermost dimensions of two scheduling are mapping input dimensions in the same order, then the first instance scheduled at any value of these outermost dimension belongs to the switching domain of the corresponding scheduling to the other scheduling.

Explanation. Logical dates are multidimensional like clocks: the first dimension may correspond to days (most significant) then the next one to hours (less significant), then the next one to minutes and so on. To each value of the outermost scheduling dimensions corresponds a set of scheduled instances. If the execution order of such sets is the same in any version, then at the beginning of each set it is possible to switch between versions, regardless of the scheduling order inside the set, i.e., of less significant scheduling dimensions.   □

From these two properties we derive a practical technique to build a multiversion code. First for each version we compute a switching domain, as detailed in Section 3.1. Next we generate the code itself, inserting switching statements for each integer point of the switching domains, as explained in Section 3.2. Switching statements themselves rely on a low overhead runtime system described in Section 3.3.

3.1   Switching Domain Computation

We derive from Property 2 that a (subset of) the switching domain is the set of output vectors such that:

1. The outermost "common" output dimensions are expressed in the same way for every scheduling (this ensures that all versions are executing equivalent subsets of instances in the same order regardless of the order inside those subsets). This condition may be relaxed when information about the scheduling semantics is available. The most important case we are supporting is stripmining and, by extension, tiling, with a restriction on possible tile sizes. Tile sizes are chosen to be a multiple of the smallest tile size. Hence, we know statically that, e.g., an iteration at a given dimension in one version corresponds to n iterations of the same dimension in another version. We derive from this a simple affine constraint on the existence of meeting points.
2. The remaining output dimensions are set to the lexicographic minimum of the possible values (to ensure the logical date of the switching statement is at most the same as the first instance scheduled inside the subset). Moreover, we add another output dimension set to 0 to ensure the switching statement is executed before the first instance of the subset.

Switching domains are easy to compute from the scheduling using the PIP tool [6] to compute the lexicographic minimum of the innermost output dimensions. Figures 2(d1) and 2(d2) show the switching domains corresponding to the scheduling in Figures 1(c1) and 1(c2): the first dimension has the same expression in both scheduling and has the same range, the second one is set to the minimum value for each version, and a new one has been added and set to 0.

The code generation step detailed in Section 3.2 uses switching domains to insert "switching statements" in the final code: to each integer point in this domain will correspond an execution of the switching statement. It is not desirable to execute the switching statement at each meeting point because of the overhead it may introduce. Switching domains can be easily restricted to fit the need.

A first solution is to intersect it with a convenient lattice. In this way, switching statements will be executed at constant intervals along scheduling dimensions. A second solution with the same effect is to apply a special strip-mine onto some scheduling dimensions. In this case, selected scheduling dimensions are decoupled into three dimensions in the switching domains and the scheduling relations. The outer dimension iterates over strips, the middle one is set to 0 for the switching domain and to 1 for all the scheduling relations, and the inner one is set to 0 for the switching domain and iterates over integer points inside strips for the scheduling relations. This does not affect the order of the instances, but it inserts a switching date before each strip. While the first solution is simpler, the second one allows to consider switching along parallel dimensions: the dimension over strips has to be sequential, but the one over points inside strips may be parallel.

3.2 Multi-Version Code Generation

Generating a code that includes multiple versions of the original program with the ability of switching between them is a three step process. First we extend the original scheduling with one innermost output dimension set to 1. It ensures that the switching statement will be executed before any existing instance if they are scheduled at the same logical date, since that output dimension has been set to 0 for the switching domain[3]. Figures 2(e1) and 2(e2) show the extended schedulings of Figures 1(c1) and 1(c2). Next, we generate the code from the original domains and scheduling as in a classical polyhedral framework, with the CLooG tool [1]. The only difference is that we generate a code for each version and that we add the corresponding switching domain to each code generation problem. Each integer point of the switching domain corresponds to an execution of the switching statement. Finally some glue code is added to support switching: additional variables are created to communicate current common output coordinates while switching and labels/gotos are inserted to jump to the end of the code once one version terminates.

The switching statement itself is made of two parts. First, the *switching source* includes calling the runtime to decide about switching or not, communicating of current common output coordinates and actual switching (through goto statements). Second, the *switching sink* includes a label to be used as the target of a switch, receiving the common output coordinates and setting back the remaining output coordinates to the lexicographic minimum. Figure 2(f) shows the final code (spanning two columns) for our running example started in Figure 1. The switching source corresponds to the `if` part of the switching statement while the sink corresponds to the `else` part.

3.3 Runtime

The runtime switching decision system is as simple as possible to minimize the overhead. It is based only on the execution time and has two modes called

---

[3] If the last output dimension is not a common dimension, another solution without scheduling extension is to subtract 1 to its expression in the switching domain.

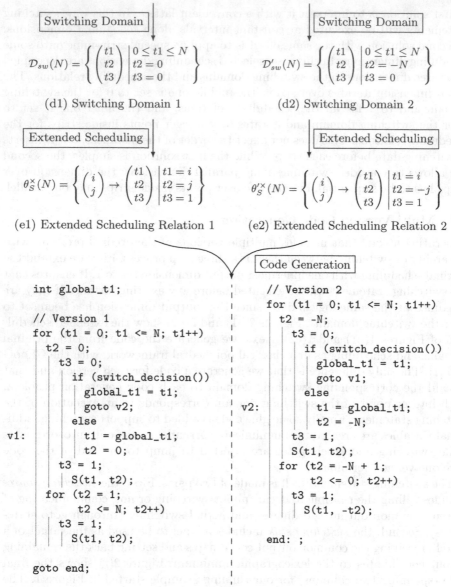

$$\mathcal{D}_{sw}(N) = \left\{ \begin{pmatrix} t1 \\ t2 \\ t3 \end{pmatrix} \middle| \begin{array}{l} 0 \leq t1 \leq N \\ t2 = 0 \\ t3 = 0 \end{array} \right\}$$

(d1) Switching Domain 1

$$\mathcal{D}'_{sw}(N) = \left\{ \begin{pmatrix} t1 \\ t2 \\ t3 \end{pmatrix} \middle| \begin{array}{l} 0 \leq t1 \leq N \\ t2 = -N \\ t3 = 0 \end{array} \right\}$$

(d2) Switching Domain 2

$$\theta_S^{\times}(N) = \left\{ \begin{pmatrix} i \\ j \end{pmatrix} \to \begin{pmatrix} t1 \\ t2 \\ t3 \end{pmatrix} \middle| \begin{array}{l} t1 = i \\ t2 = j \\ t3 = 1 \end{array} \right\}$$

(e1) Extended Scheduling Relation 1

$$\theta_S'^{\times}(N) = \left\{ \begin{pmatrix} i \\ j \end{pmatrix} \to \begin{pmatrix} t1 \\ t2 \\ t3 \end{pmatrix} \middle| \begin{array}{l} t1 = i \\ t2 = -j \\ t3 = 1 \end{array} \right\}$$

(e2) Extended Scheduling Relation 2

Code Generation

```
        int global_t1;                      // Version 2
                                            for (t1 = 0; t1 <= N; t1++)
        // Version 1                          t2 = -N;
        for (t1 = 0; t1 <= N; t1++)           t3 = 0;
          t2 = 0;                             if (switch_decision())
            t3 = 0;                             global_t1 = t1;
            if (switch_decision())              goto v1;
              global_t1 = t1;                 else
              goto v2;                 v2:      t1 = global_t1;
            else                                t2 = -N;
v1:           t1 = global_t1;                 t3 = 1;
              t2 = 0;                         S(t1, t2);
          t3 = 1;                           for (t2 = -N + 1;
          S(t1, t2);                             t2 <= 0; t2++)
          for (t2 = 1;                        t3 = 1;
              t2 <= N; t2++)                  S(t1, -t2);
            t3 = 1;                         end: ;
            S(t1, t2);

        goto end;
```

(f) Final Code Including Two Versions That May Switch To Each Other

Fig. 2. (Our Alternative End of Fig. 1) Generation of a Multi-Version Code

watching and *sampling*. In watching mode, the runtime simply checks that the performance is stable by measuring the time spent between two calls. Since switching statements are inserted at constant strides along output dimensions and SCoP execution time is typically not affected by data values, this measure is precise enough for our purpose. If it is the first call to the runtime or if the watching mode detected a performance variation, due to, e.g., changes on the execution context or on the workload executed between two calls to the runtime, the sampling mode is enabled. This mode switches quickly between versions to detect the best performing one. Then a switch is performed to that version while the runtime is set back to the watching mode. A very important property of this strategy is that every computation contributes to the final result: no rollback is necessary if a bad optimization decision has been made.

4   Selecting Pertinent Versions

A key aspect of our optimization strategy is the selection and the ordering of the switchable versions to be part of the multi-version code. For this purpose we rely on a dedicated version generation phase and on an extensive empirical study of the version behavior.

To generate versions, we rely on the polyhedral compiler PoCC[4] which uses both the Pluto algorithm [3] and the Letsee iterative optimization engine [11] to compute efficient scheduling. Generating switchable versions is done by enforcing additional constraints discussed in Section 3.1: from a base version, other versions are generated by calling Letsee or Pluto with different strategies and/or tile sizes, such that they share common output dimensions. Different scheduling may often end up to the same executable code (a shifting on an output dimension may be removed by a loop normalization by the compiler). Such versions are discarded.

Once a set of versions has been generated for a given input code, they are evaluated separately by running them on pre-defined contexts. Contexts include various architectures, data sizes and system workloads. One context is a combination of these factors. Only the versions that are the best in at least one context are considered to be selected. Our results show that they are still too many. Some of them are performing the same way in several contexts; those duplicates are detected and discarded (in our study, we accept a performance loss of 10%). Finally to select a pre-defined maximum number of versions (in our study, 8), we associate an "efficiency" coefficient to each version on each context (depending on how far it is from the best version) and we model and solve the choice as a linear optimization problem to maximize the overall efficiency.

The order in which the selected versions are used during sampling by the runtime described in Section 3.3 is critical: small loops are likely to be entirely executed before the sampling is done. For this reason, best performing versions in most contexts including small problem sizes are used for sampling first.

5   Experimental Results

We evaluate the switchable scheduling approach on a selection of realistic execution contexts. Experimental results demonstrate the ability of this technique to generate programs that can adapt themselves to their environment. Overall,

---

[4] http://pocc.sf.net

its geomean speedup over a fixed optimization of a state-of-the-art automatic optimization and parallelization is **1.49** for our test cases.

Our experimental setup is three-dimensional. First, target architectures includes one ARM and several flavours of Intel x86 architectures: Olimex A20 ARM Cortex-A7 dual-core, Intel Core2 Quad CPU Q9550 2.83GHz, Intel Core2 Quad CPU Q6600 2.40GHz and Intel Core2 Quad CPU Q8200 2.33GHz. This selection notably spans different number of cores and cache sizes. Next, problem size ranges are small and medium as they are defined in the target benchmarks. Lastly, 5 workloads have been investigated: the target process may be running alone, with low (one process) or high (one process per core) computation intensive workload and with low or high memory access intensive workload.

We consider 12 benchmarks, typical compute-intensive kernels extracted from the PolyBench suite[5]. Our selection focuses on kernels including one main loop since it is the main target of our technique. We report below for all benchmarks a short description. Column #versions gives the number of different versions that have been generated using PoCC (duplicates have been removed); #best reports the number of best versions reported in the 40 contexts; and #nodup removes from the previous column the versions that behave in the same way as another one if we accept up to a 10% performance loss. It illustrates that the best version is indeed dependant on the execution context, but also that a limited number of versions is enough most of the time, hence with a reasonable impact on the generated code size.

benchmark	description	#versions	#best	#nodup
2mm	Linear algebra (BLAS3)	40	9	2
adi	Stencil (2D)	67	9	4
choleski	Cholesky Decomposition	16	12	4
durbin	Toeplitz system solver	23	17	4
fdtd-apml	Stencil (3D)	50	10	2
gemm	Matrix-multiply and addition	37	18	4
gramschmidt	Gram-Schmidt decomposition	59	12	2
jacobi-1d	Stencil (1D)	24	11	3
jacobi-2d	Stencil (2D)	19	7	4
lu	Matrix decomposition	19	8	2
mvt	Matrix Vector Product and Transpose	16	8	2
seidel-2d	Stencil (2D)	17	7	4

Figure 3 reports normalized mean performance for all execution contexts for each benchmark, worst corresponds to the worse (context-wise) version, baseline is the mean of all versions, roughly corresponding to the average performance a random strategy is likely to provide, best corresponds to the best (context-wise) solution, pluto is the default static Pluto (version 0.10) solution and switchable is the switchable scheduling solution. Overall, the difference between baseline and best with geomean **4.98** is the maximum speedup of the solution, it corresponds to an iterative compilation strategy, a high potential already demonstrated by previous work [12]. switchable corresponds to our solution with an overall geomean speedup of **4.36** against a random strategy, including a sensible yet acceptable overhead of the switching strategy, and of **1.49** over the default Pluto solution. size growth shows the compiled switchable scheduling kernel size growth

---
[5] http://polybench.sf.net

with respect to Pluto's solution, a limited increase. Sampling on bad versions may degrade performance significantly (e.g., gemm case). Also in jacobi-1d case, our strategy has lower performance than Pluto. This corresponds to situations where Pluto's solution is good enough while the overhead of switchable scheduling overcomes its benefits. We may complement our technique with a dynamic test as Pradelle et al. suggested [13] to prevent using switchable scheduling in such situation.

benchmark	worst	baseline	best	pluto	switchable	size growth
2mm	0.38	1	3.56	1.48	3.14	1.13
adi	0.13	1	4.46	2.98	4.08	1.07
choleski	0.74	1	1.89	1.35	1.52	1.02
durbin	0.25	1	2.14	1.74	1.90	1.04
fdtd-apml	0.08	1	2.77	2.19	2.61	1.07
gemm	0.31	1	8.42	1.39	5.70	1.04
gramschmidt	0.10	1	18.27	17.34	17.36	0.99
jacobi-1d	0.17	1	19.15	16.30	15.71	1.10
jacobi-2d	0.25	1	8.24	4.08	7.87	1.38
lu	0.24	1	4.42	3.02	4.82	1.04
mvt	0.55	1	2.28	1.54	2.12	1.06
seidel-2d	0.26	1	5.37	2.21	4.97	1.11

Fig. 3. Potential and Operational Performance Results (mean of all contexts, the baseline is the mean performance of all versions in all contexts)

6 Related Work

The root of our work belongs to compiler optimization in the polyhedral model [7] and loop versioning [4]. The Pluto algorithm is a state-of-the-art compiler technique relying on the polyhedral model to build complex loop transformations with excellent parallelism-locality trade-offs using a target independent cost model [3]. It has been coupled with iterative frameworks to optimize for specific targets [12]. Those techniques create unspecialized or overspecialized optimization which may not be adequate for various execution contexts.

Static compiler techniques have been used to help runtime systems to optimize dynamically. The ADAPT framework provides runtime generation and specialization of code sections [18]. Because of the runtime overhead it fits well to programs with large execution time while we are using static techniques as much as possible to minimize runtime costs. Qilin provides adaptive mapping for parallel programs [10]. Unlike our method, it is not addressing the dynamic workload dimension of the execution context. Emani et al. proposed an adaptive mapping technique which primarily targets dynamic workload variations [5]. It impacts the OpenMP runtime behaviour whereas we target code restructuring.

Aggressive dynamic optimization techniques include thread-level speculation [14,15]. They generate an optimistically optimized version and in case of mistake, they rollback to a conservative version. In comparison, we target a different program class that can be analyzed precisely at compile time, and in case of a bad choice, no rolling back is necessary since every computation is useful by construction. Dynamic optimization involving polyhedral compilation is emerging. EvolveTile is a framework to perform a dynamic tile size selection [16]. Our approach also supports such optimization but with more restrictions on tile sizes and shapes because of the switchable scheduling class constraints. However, our technique supports a wider range of optimizations. Pradelle et al. target the same program class as our technique and involve versioning as well [13]. Their approach is to use profiling to build predictive tests according to dynamic factors to choose the best version of a kernel before executing it. Our approach is acting at a finer grain as we focus on switching from kernel versions during computation. VMAD is an infrastructure for dynamic profiling with the unique ability to discover static behavior, which is not visible at static compilation time [9]. VMAD supports dynamic version selection. Some forms of switchable scheduling are possible within this framework and are under investigation.

7   Conclusion

This paper addresses the problem of taking advantage of the best optimization while computing in an ever more dynamic environment, focusing on static control loop nests. Our proposal differs from just-in-time compilation approaches which have to rely on low-overhead techniques as well as static compilation approaches that generate a code which can be either too generic or too specialized. Instead, we propose a mixed static-dynamic scheme which builds on state-of-the-art static polyhedral compilation techniques with empirical study to select pertinent optimizations and a low-overhead runtime mechanism to switch to the best optimization during computation, depending on the current execution context. Our technique introduces a special class of optimization called switchable scheduling and a code generation method to build a program that takes advantage of multiple such optimizations. Experimental evidence demonstrate both the potential of this approach and its effectiveness at generating codes that perform well on various environments.

Ongoing work includes a code generation technique to allow versions to lie inside their own functions, to benefit from per-version low-level compiler optimization options. More aggressive versioning and switchable-scheduling generation under time constraint are also under investigation.

References

1. Bastoul, C.: Code generation in the polyhedral model is easier than you think. In: PACT 2013 IEEE International Conference on Parallel Architecture and Compilation Techniques, Juan-les-Pins, France, pp. 7–16 (September 2004)
2. Bodin, F., Kisuki, T., Knijnenburg, P.M.W., O'Boyle, M.F.P., Rohou, E.: Iterative compilation in a non-linear optimisation space. In: W. on Profile and Feedback Directed Compilation, Paris (October 1998)

3. Bondhugula, U., Hartono, A., Ramanujam, J., Sadayappan, P.: A practical automatic polyhedral parallelizer and locality optimizer. In: PLDI 2008 ACM Conf. on Programming language Design and Implementation, Tucson, USA (June 2008)
4. Byler, M., Davies, J.R.B., Huson, C., Leasure, B., Wolfe, M.: Multiple version loops. In: International Conference on Parallel Processing (August 1987)
5. Emani, M., Wang, Z., O'Boyle, M.: Smart, adaptive mapping of parallelism in the presence of external workload. In: 2013 IEEE/ACM International Symposium on Code Generation and Optimization (CGO), pp. 1–10 (2013)
6. Feautrier, P.: Parametric integer programming. RAIRO Recherche Opérationnelle 22(3), 243–268 (1988)
7. Feautrier, P.: Some efficient solutions to the affine scheduling problem, part II: multidimensional time. Int. J. of Parallel Programming 21(6), 389–420 (1992)
8. Girbal, S., Vasilache, N., Bastoul, C., Cohen, A., Parello, D., Sigler, M., Temam, O.: Semi-automatic composition of loop transformations for deep parallelism and memory hierarchies. Int. J. of Parallel Programming 34(3), 261–317 (2006)
9. Jimborean, A., Mastrangelo, L., Loechner, V., Clauss, P.: VMAD: An Advanced Dynamic Program Analysis & Instrumentation Framework. In: O'Boyle, M. (ed.) CC 2012. LNCS, vol. 7210, pp. 220–239. Springer, Heidelberg (2012)
10. Luk, C.-K., Hong, S., Kim, H.: Qilin: Exploiting parallelism on heterogeneous multiprocessors with adaptive mapping. In: MICRO-42. 42nd Annual IEEE/ACM International Symposium on Microarchitecture, pp. 45–55 (December 2009)
11. Pouchet, L.-N., Bastoul, C., Cohen, A., Cavazos, J.: Iterative optimization in the polyhedral model: Part II, multidimensional time. In: ACM SIGPLAN Conference on Programming Language Design and Implementation (PLDI 2008), Tucson, Arizona, pp. 90–100. ACM Press (June 2008)
12. Pouchet, L.-N., Bondhugula, U., Bastoul, C., Cohen, A., Ramanujam, J., Sadayappan, P.: Combined iterative and model-driven optimization in an automatic parallelization framework. In: SC 2010, New Orleans, USA (November 2010)
13. Pradelle, B., Clauss, P., Loechner, V.: Adaptive Runtime Selection of Parallel Schedules in the Polytope Model. In: 19th High Performance Computing Symposium - HPC 2011. United States, Boston (2011)
14. Rauchwerger, L., Padua, D.: The LRPD test: speculative run-time parallelization of loops with privatization and reduction parallelization. In: Proceedings of the ACM SIGPLAN 1995 Conference on Programming Language Design and Implementation, PLDI 1995, pp. 218–232. ACM, New York (1995)
15. Steffan, J.G., Colohan, C., Zhai, A., Mowry, T.C.: The stampede approach to thread-level speculation. ACM Trans. Comput. Syst. 23(3), 253–300 (2005)
16. Tavarageri, S., Pouchet, L.-N., Ramanujam, J., Rountev, A., Sadayappan, P.: Dynamic selection of tile sizes. In: 18th IEEE Int. Conf. on High Performance Computing (HiPC 2011), Bangalore, India (December 2011)
17. Upadrasta, R., Cohen, A.: Sub-polyhedral scheduling using (unit-)two-variable-per-inequality polyhedra. In: ACM Symposium on Principles of Programming Languages, POPL 2013, Rome, Italy, pp. 483–496 (2013)
18. Voss, M., Eigenmann, R.: ADAPT: Automated de-coupled adaptive program transformation. In: Int. Conf. on Parallel Processing, pp. 163–170 (2000)
19. Whaley, C., Petitet, A., Dongarra, J.J.: Automated empirical optimization of software and the ATLAS project. Parallel Computing 27(1–2), 3–35 (2000)
20. Wolfe, M.: High performance compilers for parallel computing. Addison-Wesley Publishing Company (1995)

A New GCC Plugin-Based Compiler Pass
to Add Support for Thread-Level Speculation
into OpenMP

Sergio Aldea, Alvaro Estebanez,
Diego R. Llanos, and Arturo Gonzalez-Escribano

Dpto. Informática, Universidad de Valladolid
Campus Miguel Delibes, 47011 Valladolid, Spain
{sergio,alvaro,diego,arturo}@infor.uva.es

Abstract. In this paper we propose a compile-time system that adds support for Thread-Level Speculation (TLS) into OpenMP. Our solution augments the original user code with calls to a TLS library that handles the speculative parallel execution of a given loop, with the help of a new OpenMP `speculative` clause for variable usage classification. To support it, we have developed a plugin-based compiler pass for GCC that augments the code of the loop. With this approach, we only need one additional code line to speculatively parallelize the code, compared with the tens or hundreds of changes needed (depending on the number of accesses to speculative variables) to manually apply the required transformations. Moreover, the plugin leads to a faster performance than the manual parallelization.

Keywords: Thread-Level Speculation, TLS, OpenMP, Source code generation, GCC plugin.

1 Introduction

The availability of multicore architectures allows users not only to run several applications at the same time, but also to run parallel code. However, the manual development of parallel versions of existent, sequential applications is an extremely difficult task because it needs (a) an in-depth knowledge of the problem to be solved, (b) understanding of the underlying architecture, and (c) knowledge of the parallel programming model to be used. Many parallel languages and parallel extensions to sequential languages have been proposed to exploit the capabilities of modern multicore system. The most successful proposal in the domain of shared memory system is OpenMP [1], a directive-based parallel extension to sequential languages as Fortran, C, or C++, that allows the parallelization of user-defined code regions. OpenMP does not ensure the correct execution of the code according to sequential semantics, making the programmer responsible for such tasks. Possible dependence violations that may occur between iterations during execution need to be addressed by the programmers.

F. Silva et al. (Eds.): Euro-Par 2014, LNCS 8632, pp. 234–245, 2014.

On the other hand, automatic parallelization offered by compilers only extracts parallelism from loops when the compiler can assure that there is no risk of a dependence violation at runtime. Only a small fraction of loops falls into this category, leaving many potentially parallel loops unexploited. Thread-Level Speculation (TLS) techniques allow the extraction parallelism from fragments of code that can not be analyzed at compile time, namely, the compiler can not ensure that the loop can be safely run in parallel. TLS can deal with those situations in which dependence violations may occur, leading the parallel loop to correctly finalize its execution. The main problem of these techniques is that the code needs to be manually augmented in order to handle the speculative execution and monitor the possible dependences. Programmers have to modify those accesses to variables that may lead to a dependence violation, also known as *speculative* variables.

In our prior work [2], we proposed the idea of extending OpenMP to allow the user to mark variables as speculative, and a compile-time system that enables the automatic transformation of the code to support its execution by a TLS runtime library. The transformations proposed are transparent to programmers, who do not need to know anything about the TLS parallel model. These key aspects of our proposal solve the problems stated above. Programmers only have to classify variables depending on their accesses, letting our solution perform all the changes needed in the source code. To do so, we have proposed a new OpenMP clause (`speculative`) to handle those variables whose use may lead to any dependence violation.

In this paper we present the development of a GCC plugin-based compiler pass to give support to the new clause `speculative` into GCC OpenMP implementation. This pass transforms the loop with the corresponding `omp parallel for` directive, inserting the runtime TLS calls needed to (a) distribute blocks of iterations among processors, (b) perform speculative loads and stores of `speculative` variables (pointed out using the new clause), and (c) perform partial commits of the correct results calculated so far. The TLS runtime library used [3] is based on the same design principles as the speculative parallelization library developed by Cintra and Llanos [4,5].

Our experimental comparison between manual and automatic transformation of the user code shows that the runtime performance of the code generated by our compilation system is even faster than the performance returned by a manually-transformed code. Besides, the number of lines that should be changed by the programmer to speculatively parallelize a loop is reduced to only one, instead of the significant amount of lines needed in a manual intervention, which depends on the number of accesses to speculative variables inside the loop.

2   Thread-Level Speculation in a Nutshell

Speculative parallelization (SP), also called Thread-Level Speculation (TLS) or Optimistic Parallelization [6] assumes that sequential code can be optimistically executed in parallel, and relies on a runtime monitor to ensure that no dependence violations are produced. A dependence violation appears when a given

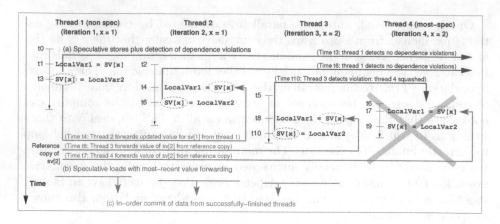

Fig. 1. Example of speculative execution of a loop and summary of operations carried out by a runtime TLS library

thread generates a datum that has already been consumed by a successor in the original sequential order. In this case, the results calculated so far by the successor (called the offending thread) are not valid and should be discarded. Early proposals [7,8] stop the parallel execution and restart the loop serially. Other proposals stop the offending thread and all its successors, re-executing them in parallel [4,9,10,11].

Figure 1 shows an example of thread-level speculation. The figure represents four threads executing four consecutive iterations, and the sequence of events when the loop is executed in parallel. The value of x was not known at compile time, so the compiler was not able to ensure that accesses to the SV structure do not lead to dependence violations when executing them in parallel. Note that, at runtime, the actual indexes of SV[x] are known.

Speculative parallelization works as follows. Each thread maintains a version copy of the entire SV vector, called the *speculative data structure*. At compile time, all reads to SV are replaced by a function that performs a *speculative load*. This function obtains the most up-to-date value of the element being accessed. This operation is called *forwarding*. If a predecessor (that is, a thread executing an earlier iteration) has already defined or used that element then the value is forwarded (as Thread 2 does in Fig. 1). If not, then the function obtains the value from the main copy of the vector (as Thread 3 does in the figure).

Regarding modifications to the shared structure, all write operations should be replaced at compile time by a *speculative store* function. This function writes the datum in the version copy of the current processor, and ensures that no thread executing a subsequent iteration has already consumed an outdated value for this structure element, a situation called "dependence violation". If such a violation is detected, the offending thread and its successors are stopped and restarted.

If no dependence violation arises for a given thread, it should *commit* all the data stored in its version copy to the main copy of the speculative structure. Note that commits should be done in order, to ensure that the most up-to-date

```
#pragma omp parallel for default(none)  private(i, Q, aux)  speculative(a)
  for (i = 0; i < MAX; i++) {
    Q = i % (MAX) + 1;
    aux = a[Q-1];

    Q = (4 * aux) % (MAX) + 1;
    a[Q-1] = aux;
  }
```

Fig. 2. Example of FOR loop annotated with the speculative clause

values are stored. After performing the commit operation, a thread can receive a new iteration or block of iterations to continue the parallel work.

Finally, the original loop to be speculatively parallelized should be augmented with a scheduling method that assigns to each free thread the following chunk of iterations to be executed. If a thread has successfully finished a chunk, it will receive a brand new chunk not executed yet. Otherwise, the scheduling method may assign to that thread the same chunk whose execution had failed, in order to improve locality and cache reutilization.

In short, at compile time TLS requires that the original code be augmented to perform speculative loads, speculative stores, and in-order commits. In addition, it also requires that the loop structure be rearranged in order to follow the re-execution of squashed operations. Without computational support, this is a task that programmers have to carry out manually. Our plugin solves this limitation, automatically performing all these changes required by the TLS runtime library that gives support. Programmers just need to use the new OpenMP clause we have proposed to point out which variables may lead to a dependence violation.

3   New OpenMP Clause: speculative

The new OpenMP clause we defined [2] is called speculative, and it needs to be used as part of a parallel for directive. The new clause is used as follows, where list contains variables that may lead to any dependence violation:

```
#pragma omp parallel for speculative (list)
  for-loop
```

With this extension, programmers are able to write OpenMP programs as usual, but annotating those variables that could lead to a dependence violation as speculative. With this method, programmers do not have to take care of handling these violations, being the speculative engine the responsible of such task. Once a programmer annotates each variable to its type, the plugin augments the code to add support for the TLS runtime library.

Figure 2 shows an example of the use of the proposed clause. Variable i is private, since it is the variable that controls the iterations of the FOR loop. Variables Q and aux are private, because they are always written before being read in the context of an iteration. Finally, variable a is speculative, because

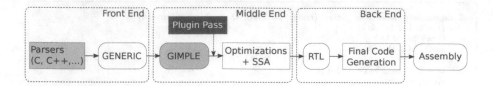

Fig. 3. GCC Compiler Architecture [12,13] simplified. The main OpenMP related components, highlighted in grey, are the C, C++ and Fortran parsers, and the GIMPLE IR level. The black box represents the location of our plugin pass.

accesses to this variable can lead to dependence violations. Eventually, a particular iteration will read from a a non-updated value and therefore the execution will be incorrect. As we have seen in Sect. 2, a speculative scheme would allow this loop to finish correctly.

4   Parsing the New speculative Clause

Although the plugin mechanism enables us to perform all the changes needed by the TLS runtime library, plugins do not allow the extension of the parsed language. Therefore, adding a new OpenMP clause recognized by GCC requires not only the creation of a plugin, but also modifying the GCC code itself. In order to parse the new clause speculative, we have extended the GNU OpenMP (GOMP), an OpenMP implementation for GCC. The main parts of the GCC architecture related within OpenMP are highlighted in grey in Fig. 3. GOMP has four main components [14]: parser, intermediate representation, code generation, and the runtime library called libGOMP. In relation to GOMP, we have focused on modifying its parsing phase and the intermediate representation (IR). The generation of new code to support TLS is located in the plugin developed, and mainly this new code consists of calls to the TLS library functions needed for the speculative execution.

The parser identifies OpenMP directives and clauses, and emits the corresponding GENERIC representation. We have modified the C parser and the IR to add support for the new clause speculative. First, we have created the GENERIC representation of the new clause like other standard clauses. Then, the compiler has been prepared to recognize and parse the clause as part of the parallel loop construct. When the new clause has been parsed and the IR is generated, our plugin detects the clause and starts all the transformations needed on the code.

5   Plugin-Based Compiler Pass Description

Once the new clause proposed is recognized by GCC, programmers can set the speculative variables, and the plugin developed can augment the original code.

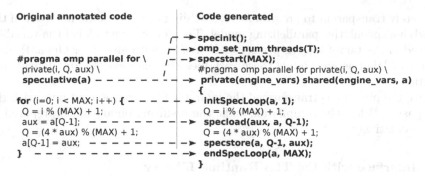

Fig. 4. Code of Fig. 2 annotated and the resulting, transformed pseudo-code. initSpecLoop() and endSpecLoop() are macros that expand to more code, hidden here for legibility reasons.

The use of plugins provides several advantages, such as faster building of prototypes, easier modifications and contributions, and the use of GCC as a research compiler. Using plugins programmers can load external shared modules, which are inserted as new passes into the compiler. We will take advantage of this feature to develop our plugin and add support to TLS into OpenMP. We have chosen to modify GCC because it is a mainstream mature compiler, and we expect that extending GCC functionalities will have a higher impact. Moreover, as long as GCC supports more than 30 architectures, this increases the compatibility of our proposal.

The new pass is added once the compiler has transformed the code into GIMPLE, and just before GCC does the first pass related to OpenMP (omplower). Therefore, our pass is added before pass_lower_omp in passes.c. In this point, we have the code in a GIMPLE representation, and the FOR-loop marked with the omp parallel for directive preserves all the clauses written by the programmer. Therefore, we have the information about which variables are shared, private, and speculative, the latter thanks to the new clause proposed. After this pass, GCC processes speculative variables as shared, while their handling as speculative will be carried out at runtime by the TLS library.

Figure 4 shows a brief example of the transformations made by the plugin. The parser detects the new speculative clause, and the new compiler pass automatically performs all the transformations needed to speculatively parallelize the loop. If the plugin does not find the speculative clause on the pragma, the semantic of the loop remains identical to any other standard OpenMP loop. With the list of variables and data structures that should be speculatively updated, the plugin replaces each read of one of these variables or data element with a specload() function call. Similarly, all write operations to speculative variables are replaced with a specstore() function call. Loads or stores involving other variables do not require additional changes in the code, since all flavors of *private* and *shared* variables keep their respective semantics in the context of a speculative execution. The plugin also adds all the structures and functions needed to run the TLS system that parallelize the code. This process is completely transparent to programmers, shielding them from the intricacy of the underlying speculative parallelizing model. They only have to label the variables involved in the target loop as *private* or *shared*, as with any other OpenMP program, and label as *speculative* those variables that can lead to any dependence violation.

Once the plugin has transformed the loop, GCC operation continues with the next passes. When the compilation ends, the resulting binary file is prepared to run speculatively.

5.1   Interface with the TLS Runtime Library

The plugin-based compiler has to augment the code with the functions and structures needed for the speculative execution, and defined by the TLS runtime library. The library used [3] is largely based in Cintra's and Llanos' work (see [4,5] for details). The plugin has to replace accesses over speculative variables with `specstore()` or `specload()` functions. This task requires the plugin to detect code lines where a write and/or read is applied, to extract the type of the speculative variable or the particular field of an speculative structure, and to perform the changes needed, including the addition of new variables to handle the temporal values required. The plugin is also able to detect reductions applied on speculative variables, replacing them by the appropriate function calls to the TLS runtime library that handle them.

The TLS runtime library also requires other functions and structures, some of them sketched in Fig. 4, that the plugin has to correctly insert into the code. Regarding the original loop, the plugin replaces the parallelized loop with a new loop that drives the speculative execution. This new loop iterates over the threads, and has the same body as the original, although it is augmented with extra code that ensures the correct distribution of iterations over the threads, and commits the data stored in the speculative variables. The definition of the new loop and the code inserted before the body of the original loop is gathered in the macro `initSpecLoop()` (Fig. 4) for simplicity. The code lines which are required to be inserted after the body of the original are gathered in the macro `endSpecLoop()`.

Besides modifying the target loop and its body, the plugin also adds three functions before the loop. The first one, `specinit()`, initializes the TLS runtime library, and it has to be called once in a program. Therefore, the plugin detects the `main` function of a program, and adds the call to `specinit()` as the first statement. The other two functions required are `specstart()` and `omp_set_num_threads()`, which are always placed before each parallelized loop. `specstart()` initializes the execution of the following parallel loop, while `omp_-set_num_threads()` set the number of threads for its parallel execution.

5.2   Handling Complex Statements

The plugin is able to handle all definitions and uses of scalar variables, not only simple assignments. This includes dealing with complex statements, that are required to maintain the same order in which the multiple speculative loads and stores are executed. The plugin first resolves the loads, creating new temporal variables that take part of the expression that assign a value to the speculative variable. After replacing the loads for the corresponding `specload()`, the plugin handles the store into the speculative variable by placing a `specstore()`. An example of this situation is a writing into a speculative array with a speculative variable as index.

Programmers may write other constructs that the plugin can deal with, such as assignments from one pointer to another, accesses involving directions or the data pointed by the pointer, assignments between entire data structures or only fields of those structures, and speculative variables involved in casting operations.

5.3   Using the Plugin to Compile the User Code

From the point of view of programmers, to speculatively parallelize a source code with our system they only have to add an OpenMP parallel loop directive and set a few parameters to the compiler. First, programmers should add the OpenMP directive in the target loop, and classify its variables according to their usage in `private` and its variants, `shared`, `speculative`.

Second, to compile the program, programmers should indicate the size of the block of iterations that will be issued for speculative execution, as well as the number of threads they want to launch. We have developed a wrapper script that launches the compilation of the plugin plus the speculative engine, and it is run as follows:

```
$ atlas -threads T -block B -c example.c
```

Just by using the speculative clause, a programmer can speculatively parallelize a code, while the rest of transformations needed are transparently performed by the plug-in and the compiler.

6   Validation

In order to check the correctness of our plugin and the code that it generates, we have developed a battery of regression tests. These regression tests include more than 50 loops with one or more speculative variables, scalar variables, pointers, elements from multidimensional arrays, or elements from data structures. They also cover situations with speculative variables that have different types, and loops executing a number of iterations that are variable and defined in runtime. These regression tests are developed with the aim of covering possible situations that we can find in a source code, allowing us to check the correction of the plugin before addressing real applications. One of these tests is shown in Fig. 5, where we check the correct operation of the plugin with speculative accesses over variables with different sizes, and speculative accesses to data structures, including assignments between entire structures.

We have also tested the plugin with real-word applications that are not parallelizable at compile time due to several data dependencies, requiring runtime

```
1:  int i, j, array[MAX], array2[MAX];
2:  struct card{ int field; };
3:  struct card p1 = {3}, p2 = {99999}, p3 = {11111};
4:  char aux_char = 'a';
5:  double aux_double = 3.435;
        ...
6:  #pragma omp parallel for default (none) private(i,j) shared(array1, p2) \
7:     speculative(p1, p3, aux_char, aux_double, array2)
8:  for ( i = 0 ; i < NITER ; i++ ) {
9:    for ( j = 0 ; j < NITER ; j++ ) {
10:      if (i <= 1000) p1.field = array[i % 4] + j;
11:      else array2[i % 4] = p1.field;

12:      if (i > 2000) aux_char = i %20 + 48 + aux_char % 48;
13:      else aux_char = i % 20 + array[i % 4] % 10 + 48;

14:      if (i > 1500) aux_double = array[i % 4] / (i+1) + aux_double;
15:      else array2[i % 4] = (int) (aux_double / i*j) + (array2[(i+j) % 4] + i*j) % 1234545;

16:      if (i*j > 10000) p1 = p2; else p3 = p1;
17:    }
18: }
```

Fig. 5. Example of the kind of situations that the plugin can deal with

speculative parallelization. These applications are the 2-dimensional Convex Hull problem (2D-Hull) [15], the Delaunay Triangulation using the Jump-and-Walk strategy [16], the 2-dimensional Minimun Enclosing Circle (2D-MEC) problem [17], and a C implementation of TREE [18]. The plugin is able to speculatively parallelize the target loops in these benchmarks correctly.

7   Relative Performance and Programmability

Automatic parallelization moves the workload from the programmer to the compiler. This is a great deal if the performance achieved by the automatic approach is as good as the obtained by the manual one. In Table 1 we summarizes the relative performance of both automatic and manual approaches. Note that the numbers are not the speedups obtained, but their relative comparison. The experimental results show that the automatic transformation leads to a faster code than the one obtained by manually replacing accesses to speculative variables with function calls. The reason is that the manual transformation of the source code may prevent the application of certain compiler optimizations. In contrast, our automatic transformation system works with the GIMPLE intermediate representation, after the first phases of the compiler have been triggered. The performance achieved by the applications parallelized using the `speculative` clause is 24% faster than the performance scored by the manual parallelization on geometric average. The maximum speedup achieved in each application is shown in Table 1. Data have been obtained running each experiment three times, and then obtaining the average. Experiments were carried out on a 64-processor server.

Regarding programmability, using the proposed clause dramatically reduces the number of lines required in comparison with the former, manual way of

Table 1. Number of lines required in both automatic and manual approaches, their relative performance, and the maximum speedup achieved for each application, where 'p' indicates the number of processors. 2D-Hull and MEC are executed with a 10M-points dataset, Delaunay with a 1M-points dataset, and TREE with a dataset of 4096 nodes.

Application	# of lines Auto	# of lines Man.	Relat. perfor. by # of proc. 8	16	32	48	64	Maximum Speedup
2D-Hull	1	139	1.301	1.288	1.404	1.287	1.205	**12.97** (56p)
Delaunay	1	191	1.261	1.255	1.212	1.106	1.122	**3.11** (32p)
2D-MEC	1	50	1.335	1.369	1.416	1.285	1.410	**2.63** (24p)
TREE	1	42	1.125	1.106	1.077	1.198	1.218	**6.47** (40p)
Geom. Mean	1	86	1.253	1.251	1.269	1.217	1.234	**5.12**

parallelizing a code using the TLS library. Parallelizing a code with the proposed `speculative` clause only requires one line of code –the modified OpenMP pragma–, while parallelizing the same code manually requires tens to thousands new lines, depending on the number of accesses to speculative variables.

Such reduction in the number of required lines is not the only advantage. Parallelizing the code with the plugin only requires classifying the variables within the loop according to their usage, whereas the manual alternative is not only a hard, error-prone task, but also a deep knowledge of the TLS library.

8   Related Work

As far as we know, there are not proposals to extend OpenMP to support software-based TLS. Instead, in the literature there are some approaches that extend OpenMP to support Transactional Memory (TM) [19], and hardware speculation, such as the pragma implemented in the IBM C/C++ compiler for Blue Gene/Q [20]. Early works propose the use of pragma directives, OpenMP-based [21] or not [22], to enable speculative parallelism at a hardware level. However, these proposals do not define any particular new OpenMP directive.

More recently, proposals are focused on TM. Proposals such as [23,24,25] extend OpenMP to support TM, providing new directives and clauses in order to mark and wrap critical sections A similar proposal is Soc-TM [26], but focused on TM programming for embedded systems.

Although some of these proposals implement the code generation required, as far as we know, there are not any specific work that proposes or implements OpenMP extensions to support Thread-Level Speculation. This empty hole is what we aim to fill with this paper, proposing a new OpenMP clause, and a plugin-based compiler pass that supports the TLS runtime library [3] based on the technique that Cintra and Llanos' speculative engine [4,5] implements.

Other research groups have also experimented with the GCC (since version 4.5) plugin mechanism. Among them, some plugins are designed to make the development of GCC plugins easier than with the standard procedure, such as

GCC Melt [27], MilePost GCC [28], or a GCC Python plugin [29]. We decided to develop our transformation system as a GCC plugin in order to avoid dependencies to third-party, not-so-mature systems.

9   Conclusions

We present a compile-time system that automatically adds the code needed to handle the speculatively parallel execution of a loop, and uses a new OpenMP clause (speculative) to find those variables that may lead to a dependence violation. We have used the plugin mechanism provided by GCC to support the new OpenMP clause. Using this clause, programmers can point out the speculative variables, and they do not need to know anything about the speculative parallelization model. In order to parallelize a code, programmers are only required to add one line (the OpenMP pragma plus the speculative clause), instead of the significant amount of lines required by the manual parallelization, which depends on the number of accesses to speculative variables. Moreover, the performance of the generated codes is even faster that the manually parallelized codes.

We expect that implementing this new clause in a mainstream compiler, together with the automation of the whole process of the speculative parallelization, will help Thread-Level Speculation to be mature enough for its inclusion in mainstream compilers.

Acknowledgments. This research is partly supported by the Castilla-Leon Regional Government (VA172A12-2, PIRTU); Ministerio de Industria, Spain (CENIT OCEANLIDER); MICINN (Spain) and the European Union FEDER (MOGECOPP project TIN2011-25639, CAPAP-H3 network TIN2010-12011-E, CAPAP-H4 network TIN2011-15734-E).

References

1. Chandra, R., Menon, R., et al.: Parallel Programming in OpenMP, 1st edn. Morgan Kaufmann (October 2000)
2. Aldea, S., Llanos, D.R., González-Escribano, A.: Support for thread-level speculation into OpenMP. In: Chapman, B.M., Massaioli, F., Müller, M.S., Rorro, M. (eds.) IWOMP 2012. LNCS, vol. 7312, pp. 275–278. Springer, Heidelberg (2012)
3. Estebanez, A., Llanos, D.R., Gonzalez-Escribano, A.: New Data Structures to Handle Speculative Parallelization at Runtime. In: Proceedings of HLPP 2014 (2014)
4. Cintra, M., Llanos, D.R.: Toward efficient and robust software speculative parallelization on multiprocessors. In: Proceedings of PPoPP 2003 , pp. 13–24 (June 2003)
5. Cintra, M., Llanos, D.R.: Design space exploration of a software speculative parallelization scheme. IEEE Trans. Parallel Distrib. Syst. 16(6), 562–576 (2005)
6. Kulkarni, M., Pingali, K., et al.: Optimistic parallelism requires abstractions. In: Proceedings of PLDI 2007, pp. 211–222 (2007)
7. Gupta, M., Nim, R.: Techniques for speculative run-time parallelization of loops. In: Proc. of the 1998 ACM/IEEE Conference on Supercomputing, pp. 1–12 (1998)

8. Rauchwerger, L., Padua, D.: The LRPD test: Speculative run-time parallelization of loops with privatization and reduction parallelization. In: Proceedings of PLDI 1995, pp. 218–232 (1995)
9. Dang, F.H., Yu, H., Rauchwerger, L.: The R-LRPD test: Speculative parallelization of partially parallel loops. In: Proceedings of 16th IPDPS, pp. 20–29 (2002)
10. Xekalakis, P., Ioannou, N., Cintra, M.: Combining thread level speculation helper threads and runahead execution. In: Proceedings of ICS 2009, pp. 410–420 (2009)
11. Gao, L., Li, L., et al.: SEED: A statically greedy and dynamically adaptive approach for speculative loop execution. IEEE Trans. Comput. 62(5), 1004–1016 (2013)
12. GNU Project: GCC internals (2013), http://gcc.gnu.org/onlinedocs/gccint/
13. Novillo, D.: GCC an architectural overview, current status, and future directions. In: Proceedings of the Linux Symposium, Tokyo, Japan, pp. 185–200 (September 2006)
14. Novillo, D.: OpenMP and automatic parallelization in GCC. In: Proceedings of the 2006 GCC Developers' Summit, Ottawa, Canada (2006)
15. Clarkson, K.L., Mehlhorn, K., Seidel, R.: Four results on randomized incremental constructions. Comput. Geom. Theory Appl. 3(4), 185–212 (1993)
16. Devroye, L., Mücke, E.P., Zhu, B.: A note on point location in Delaunay triangulations of random points. Algorithmica 22, 477–482 (1998)
17. Welzl, E.: Smallest enclosing disks (balls and ellipsoids). In: Maurer, H. (ed.) New Results and New Trends in Computer Science. LNCS, vol. 555, pp. 359–370. Springer, Heidelberg (1991)
18. Barnes, J.E.: TREE. Institute for Astronomy. University of Hawaii (1997), ftp://hubble.ifa.hawaii.edu/pub/barnes/treecode/
19. Larus, J., Kozyrakis, C.: Transactional memory. Commun. ACM 51(7), 80–88 (2008)
20. IBM: Thread-level speculative execution for C/C++. IBM XL C/C++ for Blue Gene, Tech. report (2012)
21. Packirisamy, V., Barathvajasankar, H.: OpenMP in multicore architectures. University of Minnesota, Tech. Rep (2005)
22. Martínez, J.F., Torrellas, J.: Speculative synchronization: Applying thread-level speculation to explicitly parallel applications. In: Proceedings of ASPLOS 2002, pp. 18–29 (2002)
23. Baek, W., Minh, C.C., et al.: The OpenTM transactional application programming interface. In: Proceedings of 16th ISCA, pp. 376–387. IEEE Computer Society (2007)
24. Milovanović, M., Ferrer, R., Unsal, O.S., Cristal, A., Martorell, X., Ayguadé, E., Labarta, J., Valero, M.: Transactional memory and OpenMP. In: Chapman, B., Zheng, W., Gao, G.R., Sato, M., Ayguadé, E., Wang, D. (eds.) IWOMP 2007. LNCS, vol. 4935, pp. 37–53. Springer, Heidelberg (2008)
25. Wong, M., Bihari, B.L., de Supinski, B.R., Wu, P., Michael, M., Liu, Y., Chen, W.: A case for including transactions in OpenMP. In: Sato, M., Hanawa, T., Müller, M.S., Chapman, B.M., de Supinski, B.R. (eds.) IWOMP 2010. LNCS, vol. 6132, pp. 149–160. Springer, Heidelberg (2010)
26. Ferri, C., Marongiu, A., et al.: SoC-TM: Integrated HW/SW support for transactional memory programming on embedded MPSoCs. In: Proceedings of CODES+ISSS 2011, pp. 39–48. ACM Press (2011)
27. Starynkevitch, B.: MELT: A translated domain specific language embedded in the GCC compiler. In: Proceedings of IFIP DSL 2011, pp. 118–142 (2011)
28. Fursin, G., Kashnikov, Y., et al.: Milepost GCC: machine learning enabled self-tuning compiler. Int'l. Journal of Parallel Programming 39(3), 296–327 (2011)
29. Malcolm, D.: GCC python plugin v0.12.(2013), https://fedorahosted.org/gcc-python-plugin/ (last visit: May 2014)

Improving Read Performance with Online Access Pattern Analysis and Prefetching

Houjun Tang[1,2], Xiaocheng Zou[1,2], John Jenkins[1,3], David A. Boyuka II[1,2],
Stephen Ranshous[1,2], Dries Kimpe[3], Scott Klasky[2],
and Nagiza F. Samatova[1,2,*]

[1] North Carolina State University, Raleigh, NC 27695, USA
[2] Oak Ridge National Laboratory, Oak Ridge, TN 37830, USA
[3] Argonne National Laboratory, Argonne, IL 60439, USA
samatova@csc.ncsu.edu

Abstract. Among the major challenges of transitioning to exascale in HPC is the ubiquitous I/O bottleneck. For analysis and visualization applications in particular, this bottleneck is exacerbated by the write-once-read-many property of most scientific datasets combined with typically complex access patterns. One promising way to alleviate this problem is to recognize the application's access patterns and utilize them to prefetch data, thereby overlapping computation and I/O. However, current research methods for analyzing access patterns are either offline-only and/or lack the support for complex access patterns, such as high-dimensional strided or composition-based unstructured access patterns. Therefore, we propose an online analyzer capable of detecting both simple and complex access patterns with low computational and memory overhead and high accuracy. By combining our pattern detection with prefetching, we consistently observe run-time reductions, up to 26%, across 18 configurations of PIO-Bench and 4 configurations of a micro-benchmark with both structured and unstructured access patterns.

1 Introduction

Scientists who work with simulations such as S3D combustion [1] and GTS core plasma fusion [2] spend a significant amount of time analyzing the massive amount of data generated. With the increasing gap between CPU and I/O, the performance of scientific analysis and visualization applications are often I/O-bound [3], thus read performance becomes a key area for optimization. An essential component of this process is to better understand the application's I/O behavior or its access patterns.

An access pattern is a sequence of accesses that exhibits a certain regularity. Many common access patterns occur as a result of iterative computations [4]. For example, if a matrix is stored in row-major format, reading consecutive rows of the matrix results in a contiguous pattern, whereas reading one column induces a simple-strided pattern with the file pointer incremented by the same amount (row size) between each request. Scientific applications exhibit these

---

* Corresponding author.

F. Silva et al. (Eds.): Euro-Par 2014, LNCS 8632, pp. 246–257, 2014.
© Springer International Publishing Switzerland 2014

patterns and others, including higher dimensional strided access patterns and composition-based or correlation-based unstructured access patterns.

Recognizing access patterns in an application is a key to potentially reducing future file read time. Scientific applications often read and analyze data alternately, thus by overlapping the two phases with prefetching can significantly reduce the overall execution time of the application. Accurate prefetching can be achieved with access pattern analysis.

In order to achieve high prefetching accuracy, it is necessary to acquire comprehensive knowledge of the application's access patterns. Various methods have been proposed [5–8], however, these tools are all offline-based and not capable of detecting complex access patterns (such as composition-based unstructured access patterns). Offline-based tools assume access history of one or more previous runs beforehand, which is unrealistic to obtain for scientific applications nowadays that run for hours or even days. In addition, offline based algorithms cannot be directly applied to online analysis as 1) they assume the presence of full access history, which may not fit in the memory; and 2) they detect a pattern after its full occurrence, which provides no useful information for the current optimization strategy.

We propose a method for online analysis that requires no prior information of the application. To the best of our knowledge, our method is the first one capable of performing online analysis of various complex access patterns. The contributions of this work are as follows:

Online, Low-Overhead Pattern Analysis with High Accuracy. We adopt a "pattern growth" approach and efficient pattern detection algorithms to enable online analysis with overhead less than 5% in all test cases. The overall run-time reduction is up to 26% via pattern-aware prefetching with accuracy up to 99%;

Support for Various Access Patterns. We develop an analyzer capable of detecting structured access patterns as well as composition-based and correlation-based unstructured access patterns;

Low Memory Footprint. To retain low memory footprint during run-time, we merge I/O traces with their corresponding access patterns in a compact format and keep a limited number of recent trace records in memory.

2 Background

Many I/O access patterns classification approach have been proposed [5, 9, 10]. Compared with them, we additionally support unstructured access pattern. Although the access pattern classification is similar, the algorithms to detect the patterns are different for offline and online analysis, as explained in Section 3.1.

2.1 Structured Access Pattern

Structured access patterns include contiguous, simple-strided, and kd-strided patterns. Fig. 1 illustrates the former two kinds. A contiguous pattern occurs when consecutive read requests are accessing a contiguous region of data in a file. It can be further divided into uniform and variable size patterns. For strided patterns, a stride is the difference between starting offsets of consecutive requests, and is fixed within each dimension. Simple-strided pattern is a special case of kd-strided when $k = 1$. A kd-strided pattern can be viewed as a series of $k - 1$d-strided segments with its k dimensional stride. For example, a 2d-strided pattern with the following offsets: $\{1, 3, 5, 11, 13, 15, 21, 23, 25\}$, is composed of three simple-strided segments $\{1,3,5\}$, $\{11,13,15\}$, and $\{21,23,25\}$, with the second dimensional stride of 10. Kd-strided pattern is often found when accessing a sub-volume or sub-plane of multi-dimensional data.

2.2 Unstructured Access Pattern

Unstructured access patterns are accesses that exhibit patterns with less regularity compared to structured ones. The number of accesses is linear to the number of parameters representing them, while exponential for structured ones. There are two particular instances that we found useful for scientific applications, which are referred as composition-based and correlation-based unstructured access patterns. The composition-based patterns capture the repeating intervals between structured patterns or individual accesses, which is further explained in Section 3.3. Previous research in [7] exploited block correlations in storage systems. We include this kind of pattern and referred it as correlation-based unstructured access patterns. For example, from an offset sequence of $\{10, 20, 30, 40, 50, 10, 70, 20, 30, 80, 10, 40, 20, 30\}$, the correlation-based pattern is $\{10|\,20, 30\}$ and $\{20|\,30\}$, meaning that the data starting from offset $20, 30$ is frequently accessed after 10, while 30 is often accessed after 20. The threshold value of frequent accesses is 3, which is the number of times an offset occurs to be considered in a pattern. The request size is omitted for simplicity.

3   Method

Our online analyzer performs access pattern analysis of applications during their run-time and utilize the pattern information to guide prefetching for better performance. Fig. 2 illustrates the overview of our framework.

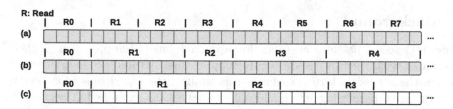

Fig. 1. Each block represents 1 byte of data stored in row-major format, with shaded blocks being accessed. (a) Contiguous with uniform size: 8 requests ($R0$ to $R7$) each access 4 bytes. (b) Contiguous with variable size: 5 requests with sizes of $4, 8, 4, 8, 8$ bytes. (c) Simple-strided: 4 requests each access 4 bytes of data with 8 bytes between the starting offsets of consecutive requests.

3.1   Online Access Pattern Analysis

We adopt a rule-based model for access pattern detection in our online analyzer, which is the key component the framework. We maintained a "pattern library" that contains a collection of rules. These rules provide a concise description of the access sequences that are recognized as access patterns. The input is a sequence of accesses and the output is the detected access patterns and corresponding prefetching instructions.

Each time a read request is traced, the analyzer first performs a lookup in the pattern history to decide whether to activate a previously detected pattern and start prefetching or use it for analysis. The pattern analysis procedure includes the following steps: 1) create a new pattern if current records in the trace buffer match any detection rules in the pattern library; 2) "grow" the current pattern if the following accesses belong to it and inform the prefetcher to prefetch data that are predicted to be accessed next; 3) commit the access pattern to the pattern history when the new access do not fit in; 4) attempt to coalesce the current pattern with previous structured ones to form a higher level pattern; 5) look back in the pattern history and check if there is any pattern that matches the current one. More details of this procedure are explained in later examples of structured and unstructured pattern analysis.

Unlike offline analysis with a complete access history, online analysis must be incremental to detect a pattern during its occurrence. Thus we adopt the above "pattern growth" approach: as new accesses arrive, they are compared to the current active pattern before being inserted to the trace buffer. The pattern library consists of detection and coalesce rules for detecting structured and unstructured access patterns. The difference between them are the objects they operate on: detection rule operates on offset of accesses while coalesce rule operates on patterns. The analysis is performed periodically instead of upon every new request to reduce computation overhead. Three threshold values (T_{struct}, T_{corr}, and T_{comp}) are used to trigger the analysis of structured, correlation-based unstructured, and composition-based unstructured access patterns.

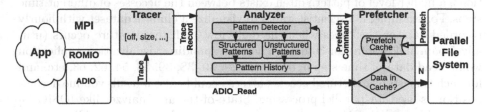

Fig. 2. An overview of our framework: each time a read request is made, the tracer extracts the read request's information while it is being passed to the prefetcher. The requested data are copied to user buffer if found in the prefetch cache or a normal file read is issued to the parallel file system, the components added are in shaded shapes.

3.2   Structured Access Pattern Analysis

Different detection rules are used for contiguous and simple-strided access patterns. A contiguous pattern is determined by having at least 3 consecutive accesses with no gap in between. A simple-strided pattern comes with same offset differences (stride) between at least 3 consecutive accesses with identical request size. Kd-strided pattern is composed of $(k-1)$d-strided segments and is detected by the coalesce rule, which checks the stride and the number of accesses of two strided patterns with the same dimension. Note that each dimension of a kd-strided pattern must have at least three $(k-1)$d-strided segments.

Take a 2d-strided pattern with the following offsets {1, 3, 5, 11, 13, 15, 21, 23, 25, 31, 33, 35} as an example. The second dimensional stride can not be determined until 31 is accessed that signals the end of the third simple-strided segment. With three simple-strided segments detected and committed, they are coalesced to a 2d-strided one(step 1 to 4 of the pattern analysis procedure). An earlier detection is possible if a previous 2d-strided pattern with the same stride and number of accesses of first dimension exists in the pattern history: we temporarily mark the current simple-strided pattern of {1, 3, 5} as the 2d-strided one and start prefetching (step 5). Once a mismatch happens, it is restored to the previously detected pattern and continue the analysis procedure. Only the most recent pattern that qualifies is used in case multiple candidates exist, as same pattern tends to occur close in time. The time complexity for detection rule is $O(n \times T_{struct})$, and for the coalesce rule is $O(N_{spattern})$, where n is the number of total accesses, and $N_{spattern}$ is the number of detected structured access patterns. Though the time complexity depends on the whole trace and could be quite large, the frequency of the analysis is expected to be high and as a result for each analysis procedure the workload is relatively small.

3.3   Unstructured Access Pattern Analysis

Previous analyzers usually deal with access patterns build from individual accesses. However, when accessing time-series data generated by scientific simulations, a higher level of pattern often exists between the accesses of different time steps. For example, if a scientist wants to visualize a climate dataset with hourly recorded data at the times when the daily low/high temperature occurs (usually 5-6am and 2-3pm) for 30 days. The corresponding visualization application would read data of time step 5, 6, 14, 15, 29, 30, 38, 39, 53, 54, 62, 63, etc. and for each time step, structured access patterns could exist if a sub-volume decomposition is used for parallel processing. State-of-the-art analyzer like IOSIG [5] is only able to detect the structures ones within each time step, while not recognizing the higher level of composition-based unstructured pattern with time step intervals repeating 29 times of {1, 8, 1, 14}.

The detection rule for composition-based pattern detection is to find offset delta (the difference between any two consecutive offsets) sequences that repeat at least twice. Two separate delta sequences are created from the offset of accesses and the starting offset of structured access patterns. To efficiently detect such patterns, we build suffix trees incrementally that has linear time and space complexity. The corresponding pattern can be easily obtained from its suffix tree after each time of analysis.

For correlation-based access patterns, steps 2 and 4 are skipped because a correlation-based pattern stays the same once generated. In step 5, patterns are merged into one if a previous pattern with the same "entry" is found. Only accesses with request size larger than R_{size} are considered because the cost of analyzing those accesses outweighs the cost brought on by prefetching. In addition, we only focus on frequent accesses (occurs more than T_{freq} times) with their next N_{next} accesses. And the time complexity is $O(n \times N_{next})$ The frequent access is referred as the "entry" of a pattern. A candidate set of accesses that have the potential of becoming frequent, which have a frequency between $T_{freq} - \epsilon$ and T_{freq}, is maintained for incremental analysis. The analyzer then forms the pattern of each frequent access as the entry and a list of its following frequent accesses. Each time the entry is accessed, this pattern is activated and the following accesses are prefetched as much as possible.

3.4   Trace Storage with Low Memory Footprint

Our framework requires limited additional memory usage during application's run-time. The tracer extracts useful information from read requests and passes them to the analyzer to determine whether to store them in the trace buffer. Trace records are compressed to a pattern representation if possible. The memory used for structured access patterns are significantly reduced due to its regularity. A 2d-strided pattern with 1024 accesses needs approximately 102KB in memory while only 134B with a pattern representation. The unstructured access patterns require more storage than structured but still use much less memory than keeping all its accesses. In addition, since online analysis focuses on current access patterns, only recent trace records are kept in the trace buffer. The tracer is implemented in the ADIO layer of MPI-IO, on which MPI optimizations like data sieving can be captured and utilized, as well as allowing the usage of other PMPI-based methods, such as Darshan [11].

3.5   Informed Prefetching

The prefetcher prefetches data informed by the analyzer and checks if data in the prefetch cache can be used for current request. Depending on the accecc pattern, the size of prefetched data varied, and we only consider relatively large data size ($> 1KB$) as smaller request sizes do not benefit from prefetching. It is also implemented in ADIO layer and prefetches data per MPI process using a prefetching thread. To avoid extra overhead caused by communication between processes, both the analysis and prefetching are per-process based. We adopted a conservative prefetching strategy to minimize the cost of mis-prefetching: the prefetcher starts to prefetch data when a stable access pattern is detected and stops immediately when the previously prefetched data is not used, which indicates the detected access pattern is terminated.

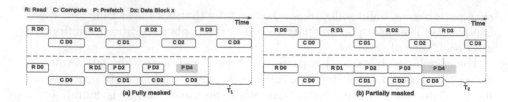

Fig. 3. Prefetching is fully and partially masked by computation

4 Experimental Results

4.1 Experimental Setup

Our experiments were conducted on Argonne LCRC Fusion cluster. Each node is equipped with Intel Xeon 8-core (dual quad-core) 2.53 GHz processor, 36 GB memory, and 250GB local disk. The attached local disk to each node enables us to set up our own PVFS2 servers and create an isolated environment. We used 8 server nodes running PVFS2 2.8.2 file system with default strip size of 64KB. These nodes are connected with InfiniBand QDR and Gigabit Ethernet. Additionally, we implemented our framework based on MPICH 3.0.4.

4.2 Structured Access Pattern Performance

We used the PIO-Bench [12], a widely used synthetic parallel file system bench-mark suite, and conducted experiments with contiguous, simple-strided, and 2d-strided access patterns to evaluate the performance with structured access pattern detection.

As mentioned in Section 1, the benefit of prefetching comes from overlapping I/O and computation. Fig. 3 illustrates four periodic read (R D0 to R D3) that are fully and partially masked by the computations via informed prefetching and the total time of T_1 and T_2 is reduced. To mimic real application's behavior, we insert computation time between each file read operation of PIO-Bench. To determine the computation time, we collected the time of running GNU Scientific Library functions such as find minimum number, first 100 smallest numbers, mean, standard deviation, and sorting. The ratio of computation time to read time for different size of data are shown in Table 1. We found the ratio of 0.5, 1.0, and 2.0 could represent different scenarios of real computation time and thus are used in our experiments. The results of simple-strided is similar to those of 2d-strided and due to space limitation, we only show the results using ratio of 0.5 and 1.0 that represent I/O intensive and compute intensive scenarios, contiguous and 2d-strided access pattern, and read request of 128KB and 1MB.

From the results shown in Fig. 4 we can see a reduction in the application's total running time in all cases with the percentage of up to 26% and an average of 17% for contiguous access pattern and 16% for 2d-strided. The performance gain of the informed prefetching with access pattern analysis are more pronounced

Table 1. Ratio of computation time to read time for a given size of data

Size	min	min100	mean	sd	sort
128KB	0.027	0.061	0.183	0.353	1.388
1MB	0.028	0.031	0.221	0.428	1.899
16MB	0.034	0.027	0.244	0.473	2.586

Table 2. Prefetching accuracy of three structured access patterns

Pattern Type	Size	Read #	Accuracy
Contiguous / Simple-strided	128KB	1024	99.9%
	1MB	512	99.8%
	16MB	32	96.5%
2d-strided	128KB	1024	99.8%
	1MB	512	99.6%
	16MB	32	92.0%

when the computation to read time ratio is 1.0 because read time is fully masked by computation. For ratio with 2.0, the time reduction percentage is between that of 1.0 and 0.5, which is expected because the potential of run-time reduction is less when computation takes most of the time.

4.3   Unstructured Access Pattern Performance

The random strided pattern of PIO-Bench is a composition-based unstructured access pattern, however, this pattern is too simple compared to real scientific applications. Thus we developed a micro-benchmark with both structured and unstructured access patterns. We found the results for correlation-based patterns are similar to those in [7] and thus it is not included in our micro-benchmark. The micro-benchmark simulates the file read behavior of an application mentioned in Section 3.3, which performs 3D visualization of climate datasets with hourly data at time steps when daily low/high temperature occurs. A sub-volume decomposition is used to perform parallel I/O for each time step. We experimented with two types of decompositions: row-wise and column-wise, as shown in Fig. 5. For each time step, the 3D data is broke into "slices" and each process reads one slice. The resulting access pattern contains both structured (simple/2d-strided within each time step) and composition-based unstructured pattern (repeating kd-strided with time step interval rotates from $\{1, 8, 1, 14\}$). Similar to the previous experiments, we set the computation time to the average time of each file read. In addition to using plain row-major file layout, we also tested with files stored with block layout. Scientific applications like ScaLAPACK benefits from this kind of layout as they use blocks as the unit for communication and computation. The normal row-major file layout can also be viewed as the block layout with block size of 8B (the size of double).

The total data size of each time step read by all processes is 1GB and we vary the decomposition type, file layout type, and the number of processes. All processes are synchronized before the first read and the maximum elapsed time is reported. Fig. 6 compares the performance results by row and column decomposition with different file layout types. The row decomposition of different block sizes have similar results, and column decomposition with row-major layout takes much longer time since it has most dis-contiguous accesses, and are omitted due to space limitation. For all cases, we observe the time reduction ranges from 13% to 26% with prefetching, which proves the effectiveness of the analyzer.

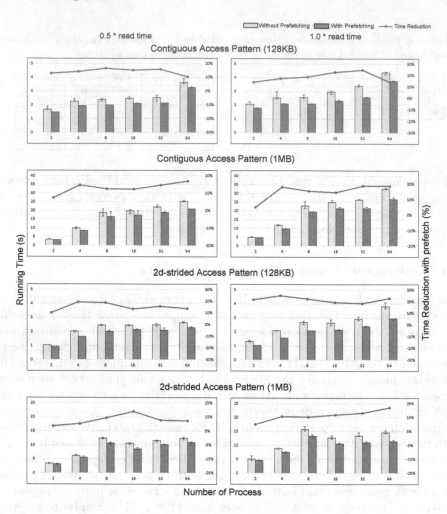

Fig. 4. Performance of contiguous and 2d-strided access patterns

4.4   Overhead of Trace Collection and Access Pattern Analysis

The overhead of our trace collector and analyzer is defined as the time difference between the two runs with our framework and with original MPICH. To test the overhead of trace collection and analysis, we run with the previous configurations by setting the computation time to, the median of 10 different runs is used. Due to space constraint, we only show results of two different cases in Fig. 7. Similar overhead is observed in other cases and all are less than 5%.

4.5   Accuracy of Access Pattern Detection

To evaluate the effectiveness of our pattern detection algorithm, we use prefetching accuracy as a metric. It is calculated by dividing the amount of subsequently

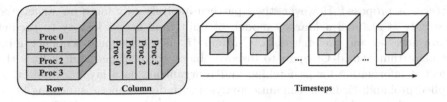

Fig. 5. Two types of domain decomposition used in our evaluation

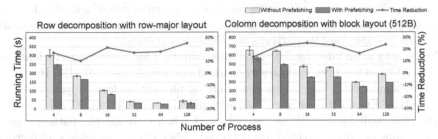

Fig. 6. Performance of row/column domain decomposition with different block size

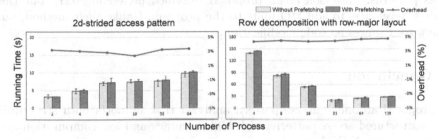

Fig. 7. Overhead of trace collector and analyzer with 2d-strided and unstructured access pattern

used and prefetched data by the total used data. The high accuracy means the prediction of analyzer is accurate. Table 2 shows the prefetching accuracy of three structured access patterns. The high percentage is expected as these patterns are highly structured and remain stable for a period of time.

5 Related Work

Various methods have been proposed to utilize access patterns for I/O optimization. Gong et. al [13] proposed a parallel run-time layout optimization framework to speed up queries on large complex scientific datasets. In database community, utilizing access patterns to guide prefetching proves to be effective [14]. Unlike their methods that deal with file layout organization and database objects, respectively, our work only involves MPI-IO and is on byte level.

Most of the existing pattern analyzers [5–8] perform analysis in the offline-based fashion. In [5], a notation called I/O signature that represents access patterns is proposed. However, their pattern analysis only focus on structured ones. Oly et al. used a Markov model [6] built from access history to predict future accesses and prefetch data. C-Miner [7] uses a frequent sequence mining algorithm named CloSpan to discover block correlations, and utilizes the detected information for prefetching and reorganizing data layout. Choi et. al applied probabilistic latent semantic analysis with deterministic annealing [8] to discover file or variable access patterns. These methods require prior knowledge of the application and can not be directly applied to online analysis. We enabled our trace collection and analysis to be online, which is more desirable for scientific applications nowadays. Our analyzer can also be used in offline manner that generates same access patterns as offline-based ones.

Prefetching is an effective latency-hiding solution for improving efficiency of parallel I/O and has been extensively studied and widely used [15–18]. However, the traditional prefetching strategies such as file-system level approaches are conservative. Even with advanced parallel file systems such as PVFS [19] and Lustre [20], high bandwidth is not achieved when only simple patterns such as contiguous or simple strided are detected. They cannot provide satisfactory performance for the modern scientific simulations with a large number of complex access patterns. Patterson et al. proposed informed prefetching [21], but this requires developers to add I/O hints to the program. Unlike their method, our framework requires no code modification.

6 Conclusion

We proposed an online access pattern analyzer that supports both structured and unstructured access patterns with high accuracy and low computation and memory overhead. With the pattern-aware prefetching, our method results in up to 26% run-time reductions on top of less than 5% overhead with both kind of access patterns in 22 benchmark evaluations.

Acknowledgements. We would like to thank the Leadership Computing Facilities at Argonne National Laboratory and Oak Ridge National Laboratory for the use of resources. Oak Ridge National Laboratory is managed by UT-Battelle for the LLC U.S. D.O.E. under Contract DE-AC05-00OR22725. This work was supported in part by the U.S. Department of Energy, Office of Science, Advanced Scientific Computing Research and the U.S. National Science Foundation (Expeditions in Computing and EAGER programs).

References

1. Chen, J.H., Choudhary, A., De Supinski, B., DeVries, M., Hawkes, E., Klasky, S., Liao, W., Ma, K., Mellor-Crummey, J., Podhorszki, N., et al.: Terascale direct numerical simulations of turbulent combustion using S3D. Computational Science & Discovery 2(1), 15001 (2009)

2. Wang, W., Lin, Z., Tang, W., Lee, W., Ethier, S., Lewandowski, J., Rewoldt, G., Hahm, T., Manickam, J.: Gyro-kinetic simulation of global turbulent transport properties in tokamak experiments. Physics of Plasmas 13, 092505 (2006)

3. Zhu, Y., Jiang, H., Qin, X., Feng, D., Swanson, D.R.: Improved read performance in a cost-effective, fault-tolerant parallel virtual file system (ceft-pvfs). In: CCGrid 2003, pp. 730–735. IEEE (2003)

4. Di Biagio, A., Speziale, E., Agosta, G.: Exploiting thread-data affinity in openmp with data access patterns. In: Jeannot, E., Namyst, R., Roman, J. (eds.) Euro-Par 2011, Part I. LNCS, vol. 6852, pp. 230–241. Springer, Heidelberg (2011)

5. Byna, S., Chen, Y., Sun, X.H., Thakur, R., Gropp, W.: Parallel I/O prefetching using MPI file caching and I/O signatures. In: SC 2008, pp. 1–12. IEEE (2008)

6. Oly, J., Reed, D.A.: Markov model prediction of I/O requests for scientific applications. In: ICS 2002, pp. 147–155. ACM (2002)

7. Li, Z., Chen, Z., Srinivasan, S.M., Zhou, Y.: C-Miner: Mining Block Correlations in Storage Systems. In: FAST, pp. 173–186 (2004)

8. Choi, J.Y., Abbasi, H., Pugmire, D., Podhorszki, N., Klasky, S., Capdevila, C., Parashar, M., Wolf, M., Qiu, J., Fox, G.: Mining hidden mixture context with adios-p to improve predictive pre-fetcher accuracy. In: 2012 IEEE 8th International Conference on E-Science (e-Science), pp. 1–8. IEEE (2012)

9. Crandall, P.E., Aydt, R.A., Chien, A.A., Reed, D.A.: Input/output characteristics of scalable parallel applications. In: Proceedings of the IEEE/ACM SC 1995 Conference on Supercomputing, pp. 59–59. IEEE (1995)

10. Madhyastha, T.M., Reed, D.A.: Learning to classify parallel input/output access patterns. TPDS 13(8), 802–813 (2002)

11. Carns, P., Latham, R., Ross, R., Iskra, K., Lang, S., Riley, K.: 24/7 characterization of petascale I/O workloads. In: Cluster 2010, pp. 1–10 (2010)

12. Shorter, F.: Design and analysis of a performance evaluation standard for parallel file systems. PhD thesis, Clemson University (2003)

13. Gong, Z., Boyuka, D., Zou, X., Liu, Q., Podhorszki, N., Klasky, S., Ma, X., Samatova, N.F.: Parlo: Parallel run-time layout optimization for scientific data explorations with heterogeneous access patterns. In: CCGrid 2013, pp. 343–351 (2013)

14. Han, W.S., Moon, Y.S., Whang, K.Y.: Prefetchguide: Capturing navigational access patterns for prefetching in client/server object-oriented/object-relational dbmss. Information Sciences 152, 47–61 (2003)

15. Baer, J.L., Chen, T.F.: An effective on-chip preloading scheme to reduce data access penalty. In: Proceedings of the 1991 ACM/IEEE Conference on Supercomputing 1991, pp. 176–186. IEEE (1991)

16. Dahlgren, F., Dubois, M., Stenstrom, P.: Fixed and adaptive sequential prefetching in shared memory multiprocessors. In: ICPP 1993, vol. 1, pp. 56–63. IEEE (1993)

17. Dahlgren, F., Dubois, M., Stenstrom, P.: Sequential hardware prefetching in shared-memory multiprocessors. TPDS 6(7), 733–746 (1995)

18. Ding, X., Jiang, S., Chen, F., Davis, K., Zhang, X.: Diskseen: Exploiting disk layout and access history to enhance I/O prefetch. In: USENIX Annual Technical Conference, vol. 7, pp. 261–274 (2007)

19. Carns, P.H., Ligon III, W.B., Ross, R.B., Thakur, R.: Pvfs: A parallel file system for linux clusters. In: Proceedings of the 4th Annual Linux Showcase and Conference, pp. 391–430 (2000)

20. Braam, P.J., Zahir, R.: Lustre: A scalable, high performance file system. Cluster File Systems, Inc. (2002)

21. Patterson, R.H., Gibson, G.A., Ginting, E., Stodolsky, D., Zelenka, J.: Informed prefetching and caching, vol. 29. ACM (1995)

Robust and Efficient Large-Large Table Outer Joins on Distributed Infrastructures

Long Cheng[1,2,3], Spyros Kotoulas[2], Tomas E. Ward[1], and Georgios Theodoropoulos[4]

[1] National University of Ireland Maynooth, Ireland
[2] IBM Research, Ireland
[3] Technische Universität Dresden, Germany
[4] Durham University, UK
long.cheng@tu-dresden.de, spyros.kotoulas@ie.ibm.com
tomas.ward@eeng.nuim.ie, theogeorgios@gmail.com

Abstract. Outer joins are ubiquitous in many workloads but are sensitive to load-balancing problems. Current approaches mitigate such problems caused by data skew by using (partial) replication. However, contemporary replication-based approaches (1) introduce overhead, since they usually result in redundant data movement, (2) are sensitive to parameter tuning and value of data skew and (3) typically require that one side is small. In this paper, we propose a novel parallel algorithm, Redistribution and Efficient Query with Counters (REQC), aimed at robustness in terms of size of join sides, variation in skew and parameter tuning. Experimental results demonstrate that our algorithm is faster, more robust and less demanding in terms of network bandwidth, compared to the state-of-the-art.

1 Introduction

Outer joins are popular in complex queries and frequently used in OLAP [1, 2] and large-scale data analysis, to name but a few applications. Unlike inner joins, the operation does not discard tuples from either relation that do not match with tuples in the other [3]. For example, for a left outer join (⋈) between two inputs R and S on their attributes a and b, the following query returns not only the matched tuples in the form of <x,a,y>, but also <x,a,*null*>, when values do not match.

```
select R.x R.a S.y
from R left outer join S  on R.a = S.b     (Query 1)
```

Currently, as for inner joins, implementations for distributed outer joins utilise one of two distributed patterns [4]: *redistribution-based* and *duplication-based outer joins*. To study the core performance characteristics of these approaches, we focus on analyzing the parallelism within a single outer join operation between two relations R and S on an n-node system (assuming both R and S are in the form of <key, value> pairs and $|R| < |S|$ in the following).

For redistribution-based approaches, parallel outer joins contain three phases: *partition*, *redistribution* and *local outer joins*. In the first phase, the relations R_i and S_i, initially arbitrarily partitioned across each computation node i, are partitioned into distinct sets R_{ik} and S_{ik} ($k \in [1,n]$) respectively, according to the hash values of their join key attributes. Each of these sets is distributed to a corresponding remote node k in the second phase. After that, the sequential outer joins of local fragments commence. This scheme can achieve near linear speed-up under ideal balancing conditions

F. Silva et al. (Eds.): Euro-Par 2014, LNCS 8632, pp. 258–269, 2014.

for distributed systems [5]. However, when the processed data has significant *attribute value skew*, the join performance will dramatically decrease due to the emergence of computational hot spots [6].

Duplication-based distributed outer joins differ significantly from inner joins. There are two distinct stages involved: (1) An inner join between R and S, composed by a *duplication* and *local inner join* phase in which the former phase duplicates (broadcasts) R_i at each node to all other nodes, and the latter is the same as that for sequential inner joins, formulating the intermediate results T_i at each node i; (2) An outer join between R and T, which is similar to the redistribution-based method described above. The *duplication* in this method can efficiently reduce hot spots resulting from *attribute value skew*. Nevertheless, this operation is costly and only suitable for small-large table outer joins. Additionally, such a scheme will still encounter performance bottlenecks when there exists *join product skew* [7], because in such scenarios the redistributed T could be very large (e.g. Cartesian product) or suffer from skew itself.

As data skew occurs naturally in various applications [8], and join performance is challenged by large scale data in the era of Big Data, it is important for practical data systems to perform efficiently in such contexts. In this work, we propose a new outer join algorithm, redistribution and efficient query with counters (REQC), for robustly and efficiently processing large-large table outer joins on distributed architectures. We summarize the contributions of this paper as following:

- We apply the join geography of semijoins to parallel outer joins on distributed systems. We find that this semijoin-like scheme is better suited for skew handling in massive distributed joins.
- We further develop the semijoin-based scheme into the REQC algorithm, in order to increase performance and robustness.
- Experimental results on 192 cores and 1 billion tuples indicate that our method is both efficient and robust. Moreover, we compare our approaches with five different baselines taken from the literature which we implement on the same platform. Our findings indicate that our method is faster, more robust and requires less network communication, across a range of skew and parameter values.

The rest of this paper is organized as follows: In Section 2, we report on related work. We present our REQC algorithm in Section 3 and its detailed implementation in Section 4. We evaluate our approach in Section 5 while we conclude the paper and suggest directions for future work in Section 6.

2 Related Work

2.1 Related Work on Joins

Data skew is a significant problem for multiple communities, such as databases [9], data management [10], data engineering [11] and web data [8]. Joins with extreme skew can be found in the semantic web field (e.g. in [8], the most frequent item in a real-world dataset appeared in 55% of entries).

Research in parallel joins on shared-memory systems [9] and GPUs [12] has already achieved significant performance speedups through improvements in architecture at the hardware-level of modern processors. Nevertheless, as applications grow in scale, their associated scalability is limited by either the number of threads available or the system memory and I/O.

Various techniques have been proposed for distributed inner joins to handle skew [7, 13–15]. Often, the assumption is that inner join techniques can be simply applied to outer joins, as identified in [4]. However, applying such techniques for outer joins directly may lead to poor performance [16].

Current research on outer joins focuses on join reordering, elimination and view matching [3, 17, 18]. State-of-the-art methods designed specific for outer join implementation achieve significant performance improvements [4], however, they are based on the duplication-based method and cannot be applied to large-large table outer joins.

Distributed semijoins have been extensively studied, primarily in two domains: (1) joins in P2P systems, for reducing network communication based on the high selectivity of a join [13], such as descrbied in [19]; (2) pre-joins in distributed systems which seek to avoid sending tuples which will not participate in a join, such as the method described in [7], for a common implementation, and [20], for application to the MapReduce framework. In contrast, we apply a semijoin pattern with **full parallelism** to outer joins on a distributed architecture **directly**, and propose our efficient and robust REQC algorithm on this basis.

2.2 Details on the State-of-the-Art

PRPD. Xu et al. [15] propose a hybrid distributed geography called PRPD (*partial redistribution & partial duplication*) for inner joins, by combining the two conventional patterns described. For a single skew relation S (assume R is uniformly distributed), the high skew tuples S_{loc} of S are retained locally and other tuples S_{redis} are redistributed based on hashing. For R, the tuples R_{dup} with keys contained in S_{loc} are broadcast to all the nodes, and the rest R_{redis} are redistributed as normal. The final joins are composed by $R_{redis} \bowtie S_{redis}$ and $R_{dup} \bowtie S_{loc}$ at each node.

As the high skew tuples of S are not redistributed at all and, instead, just a small number of tuples from R are broadcast, the *attribute value skew* can be highly reduced. This hybrid scheme has shown to be very efficient in processing inner joins, and could be applied to outer joins directly. Nevertheless, we have to redistribute the results of $R_{dup} \bowtie S_{loc}$ in an outer join, which could be very costly: since S_{loc} is highly skewed, the cardinality of the intermediate results can be very large. This condition will be demonstrated in our evaluation in Section 5.

DER. Xu et al. [4] also propose another algorithm called DER (*duplication and efficient redistribution*), aimed at optimizing outer joins. This method comprises two stages: (1) R_i at each node i is duplicated to all the nodes to start inner joins. At this stage, not only are the matched results T kept but also the ids of all *non-matched* rows in the table R; (2) Only the recorded ids are redistributed according to their hash values and, then, the final join results are assembled on that basis.

In fact, this optimization provides for an efficient way to extract non-matched results of an outer join. Notice that the *join* in the first stage of the conventional duplication-based scheme is an *inner join* instead of an *outer join*. The reason for this is that the duplication could bring either redundant or erroneous non-matched outputs. To alleviate this problem, redistributing the intermediate results is adopted. In comparison, DER uses a clever way around this: non-matched tuples of R are redistributed and these tuples are indicated by a row-id from the table R. As such, the redistributed part is small and network communication and computational workload are greatly reduced. The experimental results show that the DER algorithm can achieve significant speedups over competing methods.

As DER must broadcast R, it is designed to work best for small-large table outer joins. When associated with the PRPD algorithm, the broadcasted part R_{dup} is typically small. As identified by [16], we can integrate DER into PRPD to fix the cardinality problem as described for $R_{dup} \bowtie S_{loc}$ previously. The experiments in [16] have shown that this hybrid method (referred to PRPD+DER) is efficient on handling skew in large-large outer joins. Regardless, we will demonstrate that our proposed REQC algorithm can outperform this optimized technique.

QC. Recently, Cheng et al. [21] introduced a novel parallel join approach called *query-based distributed joins*, for handling data skew of inner joins on distributed architectures. An approach on that basis named *query with counters* (QC) [16] specified for *outer-joins* proved to be faster than the state-of-the-art in the presence of highly-skewed data. Regardless, the method performs bad when processing low-skew data. In comparison, the proposed REQC approach further refines that basic algorithm and we will show that this new method is more robust and also capable of higher performance than [16] in our evaluation in Section 5.

3 Our Approach

3.1 Semijoin for Outer Joins

The approach of semijoin-based distributed joins is shown in Figure 1(a), where the two communication patterns (*redistribution* and *retrieve*) makes it different from the conventional join approaches and the commonly-used semijoins. Under such a scheme, the implementation of the outer join in *Query 1* is organized as the following four steps:

1. Tuples in R_i at each node i are redistributed to remote nodes based on the hash values of their attributes a. This process is shown as ① in the figure.
2. The *unique* keys[1] $\pi_b(S_i)$ of S_i at each node i are sent to the corresponding node as well, according to their hash values. This process is shown as ② in the figure.
3. All received tuples $\bigcup_{i=1}^{n} R_{ik}$ at each node k probe all received keys $\bigcup_{i=1}^{n} \pi_b(S_{ik})$, organizing the matched results T_k and output the non-matched results. After that, each key fragment $\pi_b(S_{ik})$ probe T_k and send back the matched tuples to node i. The process of sending these back is shown as ③ in the figure.
4. The returned tuples join with tuples of S_i at each node to produce matched results.

The final outer join results are composed from the output of the non-matched part in Step 3 and the matched part in Step 4. As we only distribute the *unique* keys of S, this scheme can be very efficient for handling data skew in distributed outer joins. More exactly, (1) even when S is high skewed, each node will receive only one key (or maximum of n keys if these tuples appear on the n nodes); and (2) each transferred key is treated the same in the following look-up operations. We will exam the performance of this approach in our later evaluations.

3.2 REQC Algorithm

To distinguish the matched and the non-matched tuples and then send the former back to the requester, we implement $\{[\bigcup_{i=1}^{n} R_{ik} \ltimes \bigcup_{i=1}^{n} \pi_b(S_{ik})] \ltimes \pi_b(S_{ik})\}$ at each node

---

[1] Here, we use the operator π_b for presenting the duplicate-removing *projection* on the join attribute b of the relation S.

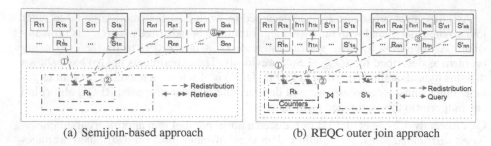

(a) Semijoin-based approach   (b) REQC outer join approach

Fig. 1. The semijoin-based outer join approach and our proposed REQC method. The dashed square refers to the remote computation nodes and objects.

k as described in the third step of the above method. This process is complex and could be time costly, since there is significant computation involved. In the meantime, when S has low skew, the two-sided communication of large numbers of transferred keys and returned tuples can become costly, decreasing the join performance. To remedy these problems, we propose our REQC algorithm, shown in Figure 1(b), based on three optimizations:

1. Tuples in each S_i are first divided into two parts before the joins: (a) the non- or low-skewed part S_i', is hash-redistributed to all the nodes, and (b) the high-skewed part h_i, using the semijoin-based scheme.
2. Each received tuple fragment S_{ik}' and key fragment $\pi_b(h_{ik})$ probes the received tuples $\bigcup_{i=1}^n R_{ik}$ at each node k. To identify the non-matched results, a *counter* is added to each tuple and it increases by one when this tuple is probed. Then, the non-matched tuples will be the ones with the counter value still at zero after all probings.
3. Only the retrieved *values* are sent back during the probing process of the key fragments, and the *value* is set to *null* when a key's probes have failed. The transferred keys are kept locally and the returned values follow the same sequence as these keys. Then, the <key, value> pair can be easily rebuilt based on their sequence (e.g. the index in an array), to compute the final join with h_i at each node i.

With these optimizations, we can efficiently improve the performance of the semijoin-based approach as follows: (1) even when S shows low skew, all tuples will be redistributed, avoiding the two-sided communications issue and consequently improving the robustness; (2) a simple probe operation is applied to the retrieval of the matched results for $\pi_b(h_{ik})$, which is much simpler than the previously mentioned join operations; (3) only values rather than entire tuples are returned, therefore the inter-machine communication is reduced. Though we also return the non-matched values as *nulls*, bringing additional communication, the number of $\pi_b(h_i)$ is always very small, making this effect negligible.

We refer to our algorithm as *redistribution and efficient query with counters* because (1) the process of transferring keys to remote nodes and retrieving the corresponding values looks like a *query*; (2) *counters* are used to distinguish non-matched results; and (3) only tuples corresponding to keys with high skew are processed by *querying*. We refer to the algorithm with only the latter two optimizations as QC (*query with counters*) [16]. As shown in our later evaluation, QC is always faster than the semijoin-based approach, implying that the introduction of *counters* is itself beneficial for such operations.

Moreover, compared with the state-of-art techniques PRPD+DER [4,15] described in Section 2, our approach does not involve any redundancy in join (or lookup) operations, because our method is totally duplication-free and all nodes only receive the tuples that they will eventually use. This should make the approach more efficient, and we will conduct a detailed performance comparison in Section 5. Additionally, the join framework of our approach is more straightforward and can be applied to other kinds of joins directly (e.g. the returned *null* can be applied directly for right outer-joins and the *counters* for anti-joins etc).

4   Implementation

In this section, we present a detailed implementation of the proposed REQC approach. We compare our algorithm with the state-of-art techniques PRPD+DER [4, 15]. Since [4, 15] do not provide any code-level information, and in the interests of making a fair comparison, we have implemented all these methods with the parallel language X10 [22].

4.1   Pre-partitioning of Skew Tuples

We have to measure the local skew so as to partition the relation S at each node for our algorithm as well as the PRPD+DER method. Efficient skew measurement is beyond the scope of this work. As we are more interested in a high performance in-memory implementation we add two pre-processing steps before each test: (1) for each test parameterized by t, each node pre-reads the keys appearing more than t times into an ArrayList and considers these the required skew keys; and (2) Tuples in S_i at each node i are divided into S_i' and h_i based on an assessment of the skewed keys, and each of them is kept in an ArrayList as well. These pre-processing steps make our later performance comparison more fair and meaningful because: (1) the total join performance is very sensitive to the chosen skew keys and operations like sampling cannot guarantee the same set of keys are selected, (2) the extra time cost for skew extraction is removed, so that the focus is on the analysis of runtime performance only, and (3) in a real system, there are opportunities to perform these operations as part of other processing activities.

4.2   Parallel Join Processing

We describe our implementation at each node as the following four steps. As the local join process is well studied and techniques such as the sort-merge and hash joins are commonly used, we have selected the hash-join for our implementations.

R Distribution: As shown in Figure 2 lines 1-8, tuples of R at each computation node are partitioned into n chunks, and each tuple is assigned according to the hash value of its key by a hash function $h(key) = key \ mod \ n$. After that, all collected tuples in the chunk $R\_c(i)$ is transferred to the remote node i. Note that the term *here* means the id of current node.

Push Query Keys: Similar to the previous step, tuples of S' are also hash-redistributed to remote nodes. For the high skewed part h, tuples are kept in *hashmap* and only the

R Distribution:
1: Initialize R_c:array[array[tuple]](n)
2: **for** $tuple \in list\_of\_R$ **do**
3:     $des \leftarrow$ hash$(tuple.key)$
4:     $R\_c(des).add(tuple)$
5: **end for**
6: **for** $i \leftarrow 0..(n-1)$ **do**
7:     Push $R\_c(i)$ to $r\_R\_c(i)(here)$ at node i
8: **end for**

Push Query Keys:
9: Initialize S'_c:array[array[tuple]](n)
        h_c:array[hashmap[tuple]](n)
10: **for** $tuple \in list\_of\_S'$ **do**
11:     $des \leftarrow$ hash$(tuple.key)$
12:     $S'\_c(des).add(tuple)$
13: **end for**
14: **for** $tuple \in list\_of\_h$ **do**
15:     $des \leftarrow$ hash$(tuple.key)$;
16:     $h\_c(des).put(tuple)$
17: **end for**
18: **for** $i \leftarrow 0..(n-1)$ **do**
19:     Extract unique keys of $h\_c(i)$ to $local\_key$(i)
20:     Push $local\_key(i)$ to $r\_key\_c(i)(here)$,
            $S'\_c(i)$ to $r\_S'\_c(i)(here)$ at node i
21: **end for**

Return Queried Values:
22: Initialize T:hashmap, r_value_c:array[value]
23: **for** $i \leftarrow 0..(n-1)$ **do**
24:     **for** $tuple \in r\_R\_c(here)(i)$ **do**
25:         Put $<tuple.key, (tuple.value, 0)>$ into T
26:     **end for**
27: **end for**
28: **for** $i \leftarrow 0..(n-1)$ **do** // probing received keys

29:     **for** $key \in r\_key\_c(here)(i)$ **do**
30:         **if** $key \in T$ **then**
31:             $r\_value\_c.add(T.get(key).value)$
32:             $T.get(key).counter{+}{+}$
33:         **else**
34:             $r\_value\_c(i).add(null)$
35:         **end if**
36:     **end for**
37: **end for**
38: **for** $i \leftarrow 0..(n-1)$ **do**
39:     Push $r\_value\_c(i)$ to $value\_c(i)(here)$ at node i
40: **end for**

Result Lookup:
41: **for** $i \leftarrow 0..(n-1)$ **do** // joins of high skew part h
42:     **for** $value \in value\_c(here.id)(i)$ **do**
43:         **if** $value \neq null$ **then**
44:             Lookup corresponding key over $h\_c(i)$
45:             Output matched results
46:         **end if**
47:     **end for**
48: **end for**
49: **for** $i \leftarrow 0..(n-1)$ **do** // joins of low skew part S'
50:     **for** $key \in r\_S'\_c(here)(i)$ **do**
51:         **if** $key \in T$ **then**
52:             Output the matched result
53:             $T.get(key).counter{+}{+}$
54:         **end if**
55:     **end for**
56: **end for**
57: **for** $key \in T$ **do**
58:     **if** $T.get(key).counter == 0$ **then**
59:         Output non-matched results
60:     **end if**
61: **end for**

Fig. 2. Implementation of proposed REQC algorithm at each node

unique keys are pushed to remote nodes. Lines 9-21 of Figure 2 present the details of this process. There, each HashMap in h_c supports the data structure of $1 \rightarrow n$ mapping, so as to efficiently hold skewed tuples. In addition both the h_c and $local\_key\_c$ are kept in memory for computing the final joins, as mentioned in Section 3.2. We synchronize the operation here to guarantee the completion of the data transfer at each node before the next phase commences.

Return Queried Values: This phase starts after the grouped query keys have been transferred to the appropriate remote nodes. The implementation at each node is similar to a sequential hash join. For each received tuple of R, as shown in lines 22-27 of Figure 2, a $<key,(value, 0)>$ pair is placed in the local hash table T, where the 0 means the initialized $counter = 0$ of this tuple. After that, as shown in lines 28-40, the received keys start to access T sequentially to obtain their values. In this process, if the mapping of a key already exists, its value is retrieved, otherwise, the value will be considered as *null*. In both cases, the value of the query key is placed into an array r_value_c so that it can be sent back to the requester(s). All these processes take place in parallel at each node, and we also synchronize the operations here.

Result Lookup: The join results of the high skewed tuples at each node can be looked-up after all the values of the query keys have been pushed back. Since the query keys and their respective values are held in order inside arrays, we can easily look up the keys in the corresponding hash tables to organize the join results. In the meantime, the received tuples of S' probe the hash table T to retrieve the matched results for the low skewed tuples. After that step, we can easily scan the *counter* of each tuple in T to organize the non-matched results. This process is described in lines 41-61 of Figure 2. The entire join process terminates when all individual nodes terminate.

5   Evaluation

Platform. Our evaluation platform is the *High-Performance Systems Research Cluster* located at IBM Research Ireland. Each computation unit of this cluster is an iDataPlex node with two 6-core Intel Xeon X5679 processors running at 2.93 GHz, resulting in a total of 12 cores per physical node. Each node has 128GB of RAM and a single 1TB SATA hard-drive and nodes are connected by Gigabit Ethernet. The operating system is Linux kernel version 2.6.32-220 and the software stack consists of X10 version 2.3 compiling to C++ and gcc version 4.4.6.

Datasets. Our evaluation is implemented on two relations R and S, which are both two-column tables. We fix the cardinality of R to 64 million tuples and S to 1 billion tuples and set both their key and payload to 8-byte integers. We assume that R and S meet the foreign key relationship, namely every tuple in S is guaranteed to find exactly one join partner in R [11], and we only add skew to S, following the Zipf distribution. The skew tuples are evenly distributed on each computing node and the skew factor is set to 0 for uniform, 1 for the low skew (top ten popular keys appear 14% of the time) and 1.25 for high skew dataset (top ten popular keys appear 52% of the time). Joins with such characteristics and workloads are common in data warehouses and column-oriented architectures as well as being prevalent in recent studies [9–11].

Setup. In all experiments, we only count the number of matches, we do not actually output join results. Moreover, for PRPD, PRPD+DER and our REQC algorithm, in which skewed tuples need to be pre-extracted, we implemented a test series with different parameters t (recall that tuples where the key appears more than t times is considered as skewed) for each dataset, as shown in Figure 4. When presenting results, we always choose the t with the best runtime achieved.

5.1   Runtime

Performance. We examined the runtime performance of the six algorithms as described previously: the conventional redistribution-based algorithm (referred to *Hash*), PRPD [15], PRPD+DER [4, 15], semijoin-based outer joins (referred to as *Semijoin*), QC [16] and the proposed REQC approaches. We implement our tests using 16 nodes (192 hardware cores) of the cluster and present the results in Figure 3. It can be seen that: (1) when S is uniform, the first three methods and REQC perform nearly the same, much faster than *Semijoin* and QC; (2) with low skew, PRPD+DER and REQC outperforms the other four algorithms; and (3) with high skew, the latter four algorithms perform much better than *Hash* and PRPD.

We can also observe that the time cost of *Hash* and PRPD increases sharply with the increase in data skew. In contrast, for the other four algorithms, it decreases. Moreover, PRPD always performs the worst, meaning that the approach for inner joins cannot

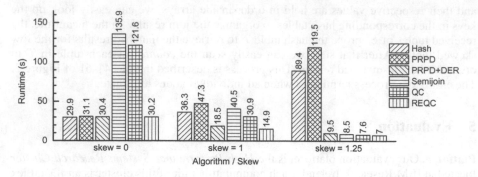

Fig. 3. Runtime comparison of the six algorithms under varying skew (192 cores)

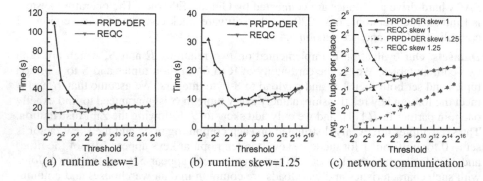

(a) runtime skew=1   (b) runtime skew=1.25   (c) network communication

Fig. 4. Runtime and network communication of PRPD+DER and REQC with increasing threshold t over different skews (192 cores)

be applied to outer joins directly. In the meantime, QC is always faster than *Semijoin*, demonstrating that the latter two optimizations described in Section 3.2 do improve join performance by themselves. Furthermore, runtime performance of PRPD+DER and REQC changes much more gradually than the other four algorithms with increasing skew, demonstrating their robustness under varying skew. Finally, it is also worth highlighting that our proposed REQC approach is always faster than the state-of-the-art PRPD+DER algorithm, about 24%-36% depending on skew value.

REQC vs PRPD+DER. We conduct a more detailed comparison of our REQC and PRPD+DER, based on a series of tests with different parameters t, corresponding to what the system considers a popular key. The results are presented in Figure 4(a) and 4(b). It can be seen that REQC always outperforms PRPD+DER for any given t. In addition, the runtime difference for different t values are only minor for our REQC algorithm while those in PRPD+DER change more rapidly, demonstrating that our approach is more robust with respect to input parameters. In fact, tuning t would require additional, more complex or costly operations, meaning that the performance difference between the two approaches would be even greater for applications which include these steps.

Table 1. Number of tuples (max/avg) received at each core using 192 cores (millions)

Max. / Avg.	Hash	PRPD	PRPD+DER	Semijoin	QC	REQC
skew=0	5.9 / 5.9	5.9 / 5.9	5.9 / 5.9	8.7 / 8.7	5.9 / 5.9	5.9 / 5.9
skew=1	62.4 / 5.9	62.4 / 5.9	3.5 / 3.5	3.0 / 3.0	2.1 / 2.1	2.3 / 2.3
skew=1.25	239.8 / 5.9	239.8 / 6.0	1.3 / 1.3	0.7 / 0.7	0.6 / 0.6	0.8 / 0.8

5.2 Network Communication and Load Balancing

Network Communication. We count a single key or payload as 1/2 of a tuple, and record *the average number of received tuples at each core* for each algorithm as shown in Table 1. We can see that *Semijoin* results in the highest number of tuples while the other five algorithms receive the same number of tuples when the dataset is uniform. This is expected, since (1) tuples in the first three algorithms and REQC are just simply redistributed; (2) the number of transferred keys and the payload of QC is equal to the number of tuples; and (3) *Semijoin* not only moves all the keys, but also all the retrieved tuples. With an increase in skew, the average received tuples in the *Hash* and PRPD methods generally does not change. The reason is that all tuples are still redistributed in *Hash* and PRPD needs to redistribute the large number of intermediate results. In contrast, the other four show a significant decrease, as they do not move high skew tuples. In addition, our REQC algorithm transfers less data than PRPD+DER.

We also track the detailed number of received tuples for different threshold t values for REQC and PRPD+DER and present the results in Figure 4(c). It can be seen that in PRPD+DER that number first decreases and then increases, showing a trade-off between the number of duplicated and redistributed tuples. For REQC, the number of received tuples is always increasing, however, it is less than PRPD for any given t. In our tests, the best performance achieved in REQC is always better than PRPD+DER. For example, $t = 4$ for REQC and $t = 64$ for PRPD+DER in the condition $skew = 1$. That is why REQC transfers less data than PRPD+DER in Table 1, notably 34%-38% less, under skew.

Load Balancing. We analyze the load balancing properties of each algorithm based on *the maximum number of received tuples at each core*. We can see that the first two algorithms encounter serious load-balancing problems when the data exhibits skew. In contrast, the latter four algorithms achieve perfect load balancing under varying skew.

5.3 Scalability

We finally test the scalability of our REQC algorithm. We implement our test on a distributed architecture with 2 nodes (24 cores), 8 nodes, 12 nodes and 16 nodes (192 cores) on all three datasets. The detailed time-cost is shown in Figure 5, where each step there is consistent with the implementation explained in Section 4.2.

We can see that our algorithm generally scales well with the number of cores under varying skew. More specifically when data is uniformly distributed, the second and fourth step scale well and dominate the runtime. In addition, the time cost of the third step is nearly 0, the reason is that there are no *query* keys for remote nodes. With low skew, all four steps decrease with increase in the number of cores, and the second step becomes the most expensive part of the execution. Moreover, for high skew, the second

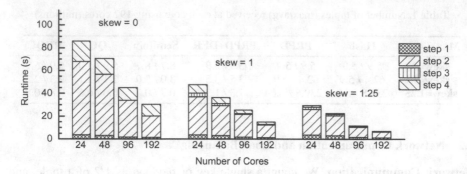

Fig. 5. The detailed time cost of the REQC algorithm with increasing the number of cores

step is always the dominating factor in performance. All of this demonstrates that the *query* processing of the third step in our algorithm is very lightweight, and the process in the second step (namely tuple hash-partitioning, local hash table building for high skew tuples and data transfers) has a high impact on the join performance.

6   Conclusions

In this paper, we have introduced a new algorithm, *redistribution and efficient query with counters*, for robustly and efficiently computing large-large table outer joins on distributed architectures. We have presented a detailed implementation of our approach and the experimental results demonstrate that our implementation is robust, efficient and scalable. Furthermore, compared to state-of-the-art techniques [4, 15], our algorithm always performs better with less network communication under skew conditions.

Data duplication is widely used in data engineering to reduce data movement and load imbalance. As our algorithm is duplication-free, we anticipate that our proposed method will not only be a supplement to existing schemes on parallel joins to minimize runtime but also for other domains. We intend to apply our approach in the semantic web domain, where workloads present very high skew [8].

Acknowledgments. This work is supported by the Irish Research Council and IBM Research Ireland.

References

1. Galindo-Legaria, C., Rosenthal, A.: Outerjoin simplification and reordering for query optimization. ACM Transactions on Database Systems (TODS) 22(1), 43–74 (1997)
2. Rao, J., Pirahesh, H., Zuzarte, C.: Canonical abstraction for outerjoin optimization. In: Proceedings of the 2004 ACM SIGMOD International Conference on Management of Data, SIGMOD 2004, pp. 671–682. ACM (2004)
3. Bhargava, G., Goel, P., Iyer, B.: Hypergraph based reorderings of outer join queries with complex predicates. ACM SIGMOD Record 24(2), 304–315 (1995)
4. Xu, Y., Kostamaa, P.: A new algorithm for small-large table outer joins in parallel DBMS. In: Proceedings of the 26th IEEE International Conference on Data Engineering, ICDE 2010, pp. 1018–1024 (2010)

5. De Witt, D., Gray, J.: Parallel database systems: The future of high performance database systems. Commun. ACM 35(6), 85–98 (1992)
6. DeWitt, D.J., Naughton, J.F., Schneider, D.A., Seshadri, S.: Practical skew handling in parallel joins. In: Proceedings of the 18th International Conference on Very Large Data Bases, VLDB 1992, pp. 27–40 (1992)
7. AI Hajj Hassan, M., Bamha, M.: An efficient parallel algorithm for evaluating join queries on heterogeneous distributed systems. In: Proceedings of The 16th annual IEEE International Conference on High Performance Computing, HiPC 2009, pp. 350–358 (2009)
8. Kotoulas, S., Oren, E., van Harmelen, F.: Mind the data skew: distributed inferencing by speeddating in elastic regions. In: Proceedings of the 19th International Conference on World Wide Web, WWW 2010, pp. 531–540. ACM (2010)
9. Kim, C., Kaldewey, T., Lee, V.W., Sedlar, E., Nguyen, A.D., Satish, N., Chhugani, J., Di Blas, A., Dubey, P.: Sort vs. hash revisited: Fast join implementation on modern multi-core CPUs. Proc. VLDB Endow. 2(2), 1378–1389 (2009)
10. Blanas, S., Li, Y., Patel, J.M.: Design and evaluation of main memory hash join algorithms for multi-core CPUs. In: Proceedings of the 2011 ACM SIGMOD International Conference on Management of Data, SIGMOD 2011, pp. 37–48. ACM (2011)
11. Balkesen, C., Teubner, J., Özsu, G.A., Main-memory, M.T.: Hash joins on multi-core CPUs: Tuning to the underlying hardware. In: Proceedings of the 29th International Conference on Data Engineering, ICDE 2013, pp. 362–373 (2013)
12. He, B., Yang, K., Fang, R., Lu, M., Govindaraju, N., Luo, Q., Sander, P.: Relational joins on graphics processors. In: Proceedings of the 2008 ACM SIGMOD International Conference on Management of Data, SIGMOD 2008, pp. 511–524. ACM (2008)
13. Kossmann, D.: The state of the art in distributed query processing. ACM Comput. Surv. 32(4), 422–469 (2000)
14. Zhang, X., Kurc, T., Pan, T., Catalyurek, U., Narayanan, S., Wyckoff, P., Saltz, J.: Strategies for using additional resources in parallel hash-based join algorithms. In: Proceedings of the 13th IEEE International Symposium on High Performance Distributed Computing, HPDC 2004, pp. 4–13 (2004)
15. Xu, Y., Kostamaa, P., Zhou, X., Chen, L.: Handling data skew in parallel joins in shared-nothing systems. In: Proceedings of the 2008 ACM SIGMOD International Conference on Management of Data, SIGMOD 2008, pp. 1043–1052. ACM (2008)
16. Cheng, L., Kotoulas, S., Ward, T., Theodoropoulos, G.: Efficient handling skew in outer joins on distributed systems. In: Proceedings of the 14th IEEE/ACM International Symposium on Cluster, Cloud and Grid Computing, CCGrid 2014, pp. 295–304 (2014)
17. Hill, G., Ross, A.: Reducing outer joins. The VLDB Journal 18(3), 599–610 (2009)
18. Larson, P.Å., Zhou, J.: View matching for outer-join views. The VLDB Journal 16(1), 29–53 (2007)
19. Koloniari, G., Pitoura, E.: Peer-to-peer management of XML data: Issues and research challenges. ACM Sigmod Record 34(2), 6–17 (2005)
20. Blanas, S., Patel, J.M., Ercegovac, V., Rao, J., Shekita, E.J., Tian, Y.: A comparison of join algorithms for log processing in MapReduce. In: Proceedings of the 2010 ACM SIGMOD International Conference on Management of Data, pp. 975–986. ACM (2010)
21. Cheng, L., Kotoulas, S., Ward, T., Theodoropoulos, G.: QbDJ: A novel framework for handling skew in parallel join processing on distributed memory. In: Proceedings of the 15th IEEE International Conference on High Performance Computing and Communications, HPCC 2013, pp. 1519–1527 (2013)
22. Charles, P., Grothoff, C., Saraswat, V., Donawa, C., Kielstra, A., Ebcioglu, K., von Praun, C., Sarkar, V.: X10: An object-oriented approach to non-uniform cluster computing. In: Proceedings of the 20th Annual ACM SIGPLAN Conference on Object-Oriented Programming, Systems, Languages, and Applications, OOPSLA 2005, pp. 519–538. ACM (2005)

Top-k Item Identification
on Dynamic and Distributed Datasets

Alessio Guerrieri, Alberto Montresor, and Yannis Velegrakis

University of Trento, via Sommarive 5, Trento, Italy

Abstract. The problem of identifying the most frequent items across multiple datasets has received considerable attention over the last few years. When storage is a scarce resource, the topic is already a challenge; yet, its complexity may be further exacerbated not only by the many independent data sources, but also by the dynamism of the data, i.e., the fact that new items may appear and old ones disappear at any time. In this work, we provide a novel approach to the problem by using an existing gossip-based algorithm for identifying the k most frequent items over a distributed collection of datasets, in ways that deal with the dynamic nature of the data. The algorithm has been thoroughly analyzed through trace-based simulations and compared to state-of-the-art decentralized solutions, showing better precision at reduced communication overhead.

1 Introduction

One of the classical problems in computer science is the development of efficient algorithms to compute statistical functions over a dataset. Among these, identifying the most frequent items has attracted considerable attention over the last years. In particular, two challenging scenarios have been considered: very large but static datasets [12] and continuous streams of data [15].

Recent advances in information and communication technology have dramatically changed the computational landscape in which these problems are applied: useful information is now often found across many physically distributed and independent sources. For retrieving the most frequent items, one needs to collect and integrate information from multiple, dynamic datasets, posing challenges on the computation of a global function over the data located at distant nodes.

Computing the most frequent items over a collection of dynamically changing and independent data sets is part of the problem of *continuous distributed monitoring* [9]. This problem finds application in many different scenarios, such as computing the popularity of topics in social services like Twitter and Facebook, discovering global security attacks in communication networks, or identifying popular web pages for ranking search results.

The straightforward solution to this problem is to send all the information to a central node, which can in turn compute the statistics. As this approach is impractical for very large and dynamic datasets, a number of variations to this idea have been proposed aiming to reduce both the traffic and the load on

F. Silva et al. (Eds.): Euro-Par 2014, LNCS 8632, pp. 270–281, 2014.

the central node. One approach is to perform periodic polling or more sophisticated random sampling [20] instead of continuous monitoring. Since the interest is only on the k most popular elements, one can send information only when the local set of top-k items changes, or when there is a number of changes above a threshold [11]. An intermediate solution tries to predict the interesting items and communicate them to the central node, using either knowledge of the data distribution [5], entropy statistics [3] or sketches as a form of a compact data representation [10]. This centralized approach can be applied when this information must be gathered in a single location to use it as a reference when needed.

However, using a central node may not be preferable in all applications. Individual sources may not be willing to send all their information to a central node and allow it to acquire a global view of the entire system that goes well beyond the original goal – identifying the most frequent items. If the number of sources is really large, the central node may become a serious bottleneck, not only in terms of communication but also in terms of computation. Finally, in a highly distributed environment, individual sources may need to have always available the information that the central node has computed and use it for their own purposes.

We advocate here a completely decentralized approach for computing the top-k most frequent items in a large collection of independent dynamically changing datasets, based on the idea of gossip-based protocols for information propagation [13]. Intuitively, each source has an estimate of what are the most frequent items globally. Initially, the only information a source has is the set of local frequencies. Periodically, each source performs a random gossip exchange with another source, sending and receiving their current estimates. Both sources then update their estimates using the old local estimate and the estimate received from the other source. This process is repeated until the estimates converge to the actual top-k items.

This idea has been recently applied to the identification of top-k items [19] in a collection of static datasets. The algorithm in [19] is shown to be very efficient, converging to the correct top-k items in a logarithmic time with respect to the size of the network. In this work we push this technique even further, by considering dynamic datasets where new items may be added – while existing items may be removed – at any time.

The contributions of this work are the following: (i) we formally define the problem of computing the top-k most frequent items in a distributed, dynamic environment (Section 2); (ii) we extend the algorithm presented in [19] by considering the case in which the collection of data is not fixed but varies over time (Section 3); (iii) we prove that our novel algorithm converges with very high probability despite the modifications to the original one (Section 4); (iv) we experimentally test our solution on trace-driven datasets, showing that, even without a central node, our approach manages to achieve a very good precision at the expense of a communication overhead which is shared among all sources (Section 5). We conclude the paper by analyzing related work (Section 6) and summarizing our results (Section 7).

2   Problem Statement

We consider a finite collection $\mathcal{P}$ of networked nodes. Each node can communicate – if it chooses to do so – with any other node in $\mathcal{P}$, provided they know its identifier; process identifiers may be obtained either through a static list, or through a peer sampling service [14]. We consider a universe $\mathcal{I}$ of items, a time domain $\mathcal{T}$ and a function $F : \mathcal{P} \times \mathcal{I} \times \mathcal{T} \to \mathbb{N}$, referred to as the *local frequency* of an item $i \in \mathcal{I}$ in a node $p \in \mathcal{P}$ at a time $t \in \mathcal{T}$, and denoted as $F_p^t(i)$ for brevity. Intuitively, the function represents the number of times an item has been observed in a node until a specific moment.

We define the *global frequency* of an item i at a time t, denoted as $F^t(i)$, to be the cumulative frequency in all the nodes, i.e.,

$$F^t(i) = \sum_{p \in \mathcal{P}} F_p^t(i)$$

We are interested in finding the k most frequent items across the whole node network. Let i_k^t denote the k-th item in the sequence of all the items in the node network sorted in decreasing order of global frequency at the time t. The set we are interested in is the set $MF^t \subseteq \mathcal{I}$ of the items with global frequency more than or equal to $F^t(i_k^t)$, i.e.,

$$MF^t = \{i \mid i \in \mathcal{I} \wedge F^t(i) \geq F^t(i_k^t)\}$$

Note that the cardinality of MF^t may be larger than k since there may be several items with the same global frequency as i_k^t.

We consider two different cases of the problem. In the first we assume that the frequency of the items can only increase in time. This finds application in scenarios where one is interested in the number of times the items have appeared in the nodes since the beginning of the operation of the system. We refer to this case as the *streaming scenario*. In the second case, we are interested in counting the appearances of items within a recent time window. This applies in scenarios where one needs to ignore appearances of items that have occurred long time ago and take into consideration only the recent appearances. This means that the function F for an item may increase or decrease in time. We refer to this case as the *sliding window scenario*.

3   Gossip-Based top-k Discovery

Since we assume no centralized authority or node with global knowledge, we would like every node of the network to be able to provide an answer to the top-k problem. Each node will estimate the *average global frequency*, i.e. the global frequency of an item divided by the network size; given that the network size is constant, this estimate can be used instead of global frequency to compute the top-k set.

We adopt a solution that is based on a gossip-based aggregation protocol [13], where the local knowledge of a node is expanded with knowledge collected from

---

Algorithm 1: Gossip algorithm executed by node p

Data: Nodes $\mathcal{P}$, int k, int *sleep*, int s, int Δ_{round}

MAP $est_p \leftarrow \emptyset$

SET $old \leftarrow \emptyset$

int $rounds \leftarrow 0$

function *main*()

    repeat *every* Δ_{round} *time units*

        $rounds \leftarrow rounds + 1$

        if *extractTop*(est_p, k) $\neq old$ **then**

            $rounds \leftarrow 0$

            $old \leftarrow$ extractTop(est_p, k)

        if $rounds \leq sleep$ **then**

            NODE $q \leftarrow$ random($\mathcal{P}$)

            send $\langle$REQUEST, extractTop(est_p, s)$\rangle$ **to** q

upon receive $\langle$REQUEST, MAP $est_q\rangle$ **from** q **do**

    MAP $\Delta \leftarrow \emptyset$

    foreach $i \in est_q$ **do**

        $\Delta[i] \leftarrow \frac{1}{2}(est_p[i] - est_q[i])$

        $est_p[i] \leftarrow est_p[i] - \Delta[i]$

    send $\langle$REPLY, $\Delta\rangle$ **to** q

upon receive $\langle$REPLY, MAP $\Delta\rangle$ **do**

    foreach $i \in \Delta$ **do**

        $est_p[i] \leftarrow est_p[i] + \Delta[i]$

function *modifyLocalFrequency*(ITEM i, **int** $\delta_{F_p(i)}$)

    $est_p[i] \leftarrow est_p[i] + \delta_{F_p(i)}$

function *updateWindow*(**list** *activeItems*)

    $cutoff \leftarrow$ currentTime $-$ windowSize

    while *activeItems*.*head*().*timestamp* $< cutoff$ **do**

        modifyLocalFrequency(*activeItems*.head().id, -1)

        activeItems.removeHead()

---

other nodes in the network. The nodes try to estimate the average global frequency of each item by updating any local estimate they may have to reflect also the estimates of the other nodes. If this is repeated continuously in a gossip fashion, then the information about the frequency of the most frequent items is epidemically propagated to all the nodes in the system. Previous work [19] has shown that not only this approach makes the frequencies of the various items in the individual nodes to converge to the true *average global frequencies* of the respective items, but also that they do so at an exponential rate [13].

The results of previous works [13,19] are based on the assumption that the local frequencies are not changing, i.e., that the input remain static while the gossip algorithm is applied. We are interested in the case in which the local frequencies of the items are continuously changing, making the global frequencies continuously increase (in the case of the streaming scenario) or continuously fluctuate (in the case of the sliding window scenario). Our gossip-based algorithm is an extension of the one for the static case [19]. It propagates the changes that occur in a distributed fashion all over the network, using the parallel participation of the nodes to obtain a very good approximation of the average global frequencies.

The algorithm is shown in Algorithm 1. Each node p maintains a map structure $est_p : \mathcal{I} \to \mathbb{R}$ that represents p's estimate for the average global frequency of each item i, i.e., an estimate for the value $F^t(i)/|\mathcal{P}|$. Since $|\mathcal{P}|$ is constant, the top-k items in the map structure should coincide with the top-k among the estimated global frequencies. The node does not need to keep the local frequencies of the items in a different structure from the estimates. Whenever there is a change in the local frequency of an item, it is enough to record it in est_p by changing the estimate for the respective item accordingly. This is implemented by calling the function modifyLocalFrequency and providing to it the item and the change in its local frequency. Furthermore, we consider a function extractTop that given a map structure M and a number s, returns a new map structure with only the entries of M with a frequency in the top s values.

Each node p works in periodic *rounds*, during which it may initiate a gossip exchange with a random node q. A gossip exchange consists of a REQUEST message sent from p to q, followed by a REPLY message sent by q to p. In the request message, the node p includes the $s \geq k$ items from est_p with the s highest frequencies, alongside their estimated frequencies. Sending more than k items in the request results in faster convergence; this is a trade-off, however, as higher values of s result in larger communication costs.

When the request is received by node q, q updates its own estimates by subtracting $\Delta[i] = \frac{1}{2}(est_q[i] - est_p[i])$ from the estimate $est_q[i]$ of every item i that the received message contained. It then responds to the request by sending a reply message to p containing a map with the value $\Delta[i]$ of every item i whose estimate frequency was modified. Upon receipt of the response from q, for every item i for which the value $\Delta[i]$ is contained in the response message, the value est_p is updated to the value $est_p + \Delta[i]$. As a result, when the gossip exchange between the two nodes is completed, both nodes will have their estimates for the top-k items of p, updated to the average of the values that these two nodes had before the gossip.

$$est_q[i] \leftarrow est_q[i] - \Delta[i] = \frac{1}{2}(est_q[i] + est_p[i])$$

$$est_p[i] \leftarrow est_p[i] + \Delta[i] = \frac{1}{2}(est_q[i] + est_p[i])$$

In other words, a gossip exchange between any two nodes p and q substitutes the old values $est_p[i]$ and $est_q[i]$ with their average $\frac{1}{2}(est_q[i] + est_p[i])$.

Since it is possible that the global top-k items remain unchanged for potentially long periods, our algorithm communicates only when nodes observe variations in their current top-k lists, thus using fewer messages and bandwidth. We allow our nodes to be in one of two different states: *active* or *dormant*. Active nodes periodically initiate gossip exchanges with other nodes. Dormants only participate in exchanges initiated by other nodes. An active node becomes dormant when the last *sleep* number of exchanges have not changed its set of top-k items. A dormant node becomes active again whenever a variation in the set of top-k items occurs, either because of information received from other nodes, or because of variations in the local frequencies. The above approach ensures that the number of exchanges is reduced whenever there are no important changes, but can automatically and rapidly increase when needed.

For the case of a sliding window scenario each node keeps in a list the sequence of items it has received. When the topmost item in the list is out of the window, it is removed from the queue and its frequency in the local frequency table is decreased by 1. The sum of the local frequencies for that item is thus kept equal to the number of its active instances in the network. If this approach requires too much memory, we can divide the window into smaller time chunks and keep, for each of these chunks, the frequencies of all items the node has received in that time chunk. The window will not move continuously, but in chunk-steps: each time a chunk has become obsolete all its contents will be thrown away. In our experiments we assume that each node has enough memory to store the sequence of items it has received during the window and will update the local frequency table every time an item has become obsolete.

4 Protocol Convergence Analysis

Previous work [19] has computed a probabilistic upper bound on the number of rounds in the static case, showing that the convergence time grows logarithmically with the network size. If we assume that the local frequencies of the items do not change, then our problem is reduced to the case of [19].

In our case, the presence of the *sleep* parameter plays an important role. When the top-k of a node has not changed for *sleep* consecutive rounds, it will become dormant and will stop initiating exchanges until either it meets a node with a different top-k set, or its local top-k changes because of the arrival of new local data. The introduction of the *sleep* parameter creates the possibility, however low, that part of the network might converge to a wrong answer.

To study the probability of such a situation, we devised the following scenario. Let C be the set of nodes containing a wrong top-k; furthermore, consider the case where all top-k sets maintained by nodes in C are

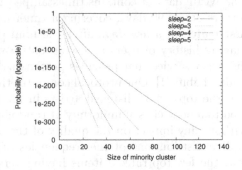

Fig. 1. Probability of convergence to a wrong answer, with different values of *sleep* ($n = 1000$).

equal. Let $n = |\mathcal{P}|$ and $c = |\mathcal{C}|$. If, for *sleep* rounds of the protocol, nodes only contact nodes of their kind (nodes in nodes in $\mathcal{C}$ only contact those in $\mathcal{C}$, and those in $\mathcal{P} - \mathcal{C}$ only contact those in $\mathcal{P} - \mathcal{C}$), the entire network might become dormant before a common answer is reached. The probability of this event to occur in a complete graph is the following:

$$\left(\frac{c-1}{n-1}\right)^{c \cdot sleep} \cdot \left(\frac{n-c-1}{n-1}\right)^{(n-c) \cdot sleep}$$

As shown in Figure 1, the probability of the network becoming dormant while a group of nodes still contain a wrong answer get exponentially small with the size of the disagreeing group. Since nodes are also prone to exit from their dormant state whenever the arrival of new data changes the composition of the local top-k, we can conclude that the network will converge to the correct top-k with very high probability.

5   Results

We performed extensive simulations of our algorithm using PeerSim [18], a peer-to-peer simulator written in Java. If not stated otherwise, each experiment is repeated 20 times.

Our objective is to design a protocol that identifies the items in MF^t as accurately as possible. Unfortunately, it is impossible to guarantee that the output of our protocol corresponds exactly to MF^t at each time t, because of the delay occurring between the arrival of an item and the discovery of this fact by all nodes in the network. We will therefore measure the quality of a proposed protocol by checking for each node in the network, at each time t, the number of items that appear both in its output and in MF^t. We then compute the average across the entire network and, when needed, average across all time instants to get the average precision of the network across the entire experiment.

Evaluation Framework. We tested the algorithm on two different scenarios. The WCUP dataset contains timestamped URL requests to the 1998 World Cup servers across 90 days, covering a timeframe starting from a month before the first match to a few days after the final [4]. The LAST.FM dataset records the playing history of users across an entire year on the Last.fm website, a music discovery service that provides personalized recommendations based on the listening habits [1]. Our protocol computes the top-k most accessed pages in WCUP and the top-k most listened artists in LAST.FM. Each single data item is delivered to a node chosen uniformly at random. Different policies have been studied, without any impact on the quality of the solution.

The distributions of the frequencies of our chosen datasets follow a power law, the few top ranked items having very large frequency while all the many lower ranked items have very small frequency. This property guarantees a certain degree of separation between the top-k items and all the lesser frequent items.

Table 1 contains all the default parameters for the experiments listed in the current section. In our experiments, the d nodes that form the neighbor set of each node are chosen uniformly at random, property that could be achieved by using a peer sampling protocol. The amount of data items s sent per round is set to $2k$. Such value has been experimentally validated in a previous paper [19] as a good compromise between convergence speed and bandwidth. Larger values for s do not induce a very large improvement in convergence speed (and thus precision), but have a much steeper cost in terms of message size.

Table 1. Default values of our parameters, where not explicitly stated otherwise

N	number of nodes in the network	100
d	degree of nodes in the network	20
k	number of most frequent items	40
s	amount of data items per round per node	2k
Δ_{round}	length of each round	1 hour
$sleep$	sleeping factor	5
W	size of the sliding window	1 day

Streaming Results. We first analyze how does our algorithm behave in the streaming model, when it has to compute the top-k over all the items that have arrived since the start of the experiment. To measure precision, in each instant t we compare the top-k of each node in that instant against the global top-k computed using all data delivered from instant 0 to instant t.

In Figure 2 we show the precision of our algorithm against the size of the network, using a round length of one hour. The larger the system, the more time is needed for information to reach all nodes; consequently, a slightly lower precision is obtained. Still, since an increase from 100 to 1000 nodes causes a decrease in just 0.5% in precision, the algorithm remains highly scalable.

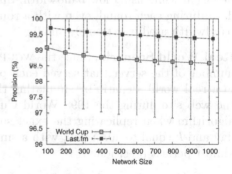

Fig. 2. Algorithm precision using variable network size

The *sleep* parameter is very influential in decreasing both the amount of messages and the workload of each node. Figure 3a shows that a small value for *sleep* can decrease the amount of messages sent by a huge margin across the entire experiment. Figure 3b instead shows that the highest the value for *sleep*, the slower the nodes will become dormant. If *sleep* is too low, the nodes will quickly become dormant and the algorithm will be slower to react to changes to the global top-k. By choosing the value for this parameter it is possible to achieve the desired trade-off between precision and bandwidth.

Sliding Window Results This second group of experiments illustrate the performance and behavior of our approach in a sliding window scenario, when each

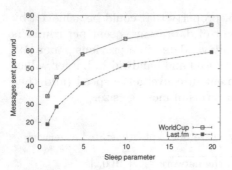
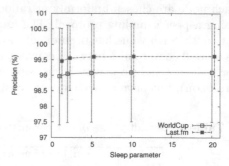

(a) Average number of messages sent on average by a single node per round against *sleep*

(b) Average precision across the entire experiment against *sleep*

Fig. 3. Analysis of the *sleep* parameter in the two datasets

occurrence of a data item is deleted after W rounds have passed. We assume that each node has enough memory to store all the local items that are still within the time window and updates the local frequency table whenever one local item expires.

Figure 4 shows how the algorithm behaves with a sliding window 1-day long. By decreasing the round length of the protocol we can achieve almost perfect precision while using low bandwidth. Since each node will send around 1KB of data during each round, even with a round length of one minute the amount of bandwidth used is extremely small.

Real World Scenario. Since the WCUP dataset also contains the identification number of the server that served each page request, we can test our algorithm in a real world scenario by simulating the network of 20 servers that managed the web site during the 1998 World Cup. Figure 5 shows the precision of our algorithm when replicating the exact same setting, with a window length of 1 day and k equal to 40. Again, with a small round length the algorithm achieves almost perfect precision.

Comparison. To our knowledge, there are no other decentralized top-k algorithm that work on sliding windows. We therefore compare our approach with another decentralized top-k algorithm in the basic, streaming scenario.

In Figure 6 we compare our approach with the gossip-based decentralized sampling approach in [16]. Since both approaches use gossip, it is possible to directly compare their performance by using the same round length and measuring the amount of bandwidth used. Figure 6 shows that our approach obtains better results using only a very small fraction of the bandwidth. When compared on the LAST.FM dataset, the larger difference is caused by the larger dataset.

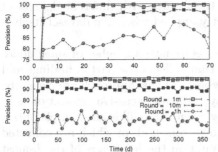

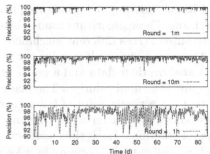

Fig. 4. Precision across time, using different window sizes (WCUP on top, LAST.FM on the bottom)

Fig. 5. Precision in the realistic WCUP scenario with $k = 40$, using different round lengths

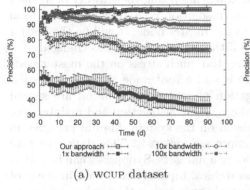

(a) WCUP dataset

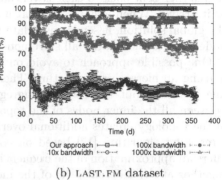

(b) LAST.FM dataset

Fig. 6. Comparison of our algorithm with the gossiping sampling approach

6 Related Work

Finding the most frequent items is a classic problem with applications in many different fields. According to the specific application and the properties of the dataset, wildly different requirements need to be satisfied. In the most basic case, where the dataset is stored in a single machine and the amount of memory available is enough to store the frequencies of each item, the problem becomes quite trivial. If the amount of memory is not large enough, the problem moves into the streaming scenario. Theoretical work [2] proved that it is possible to estimate items frequency to a constant factor in logarithmic space. The most common approach is to define compressed data structures to store the approximated frequency of the interesting items, the items that may be part of the top-k set. Among the many synopsis in the literature [12], the "COUNT SKETCH" data structure [7] allows a single pass algorithm that is able to compute an arbitrarily close approximation of the top-k in logarithmic space. Other algorithms [8] can also work in a sliding window scenario, by keeping track of both frequent items and items that might become frequent in the future, with different degrees of precision. These algorithm cannot be directly applied when the dataset itself is distributed across different machines.

A common approach to solve our problem is to have a number of *slave* nodes that analyze their data and a *master* node that collects the partial findings and computes the final solution. The main drawbacks of this approach are clear: the system has a single point of failure and may cause an excessive amount of computation on the master node. Cao and Wang's algorithm [6] is an example of this type of solutions. Each slave computes its own top-k, all of which are collected by the master node to compute a lower bound on the frequency of the k-most frequent item. This information is given to the slaves, that recompute their solution to include only those items that have local frequencies above the threshold. Babcock and Olston's approach [5] instead computes a starting approximation of the top-k set in each slave node and in the master node. The temporary solution is then sent back to each slave, that starts analyzing the entirety of its data as it arrives. When a slave sees that its own solution is "different enough" from the global solution, it sends an update to the master node. It will be the master node's job to then notify all slave nodes if the global solution has changed.

One possible approach to avoid putting too much stress on the master node is using an hierarchical structure. There is still a root node that computes the final solution, but the costs of aggregation of temporary solution are spread between all the inner nodes of the topology. The construction and maintenance of the topology creates additional overhead on the system. Manjhi presents an interesting algorithm [17] based on compressed synopsis. This data structure offers an approximation of the frequencies of a datasets. Synopsises can be joined together at the different level of the hierarchical topology to obtain in the root node an estimate of the top-k set. This simple approach is then enhanced by the idea of a precision gradient. The level of compression of the synopsis is not kept constant in the system, but is adapted at each different level of the topology to minimize the communication costs.

A completely decentralized algorithm is inherently more robust and should guarantee better subdivision of work between the nodes. Lahiri and Tirthapura [16] presented a gossip algorithm based on uniform random sampling. The intuition behind this algorithm is that the top-k of a dataset should be similar to a large enough random sampling of the dataset. The algorithm thus computes a random sampling of all the data in the distributed system via repeated aggregation. Since the entire sample must be sent around, the amount of data sent is much bigger than in our algorithm.

7   Conclusions

In this work we have extended an existing approach to find the k most frequent items across a distributed collection of datasets, without relying on a central node that collects global knowledge about the data. The method we discussed is based on a gossip protocol that allows local information in a node to be epidemically propagated to other sources. The algorithm presented has special features to deal with continuously changing data. Trace driven experiments illustrate that despite the dynamic changes in the global frequencies, the system is able to react quickly and provide a good approximation from any node of the network.

References

1. Last.fm, http://www.lastfm.com
2. Alon, N., Matias, Y., Szegedy, M.: The space complexity of approximating the frequency moments. In: Proc. of STOC 1996, pp. 20–29. ACM (1996)
3. Arackaparambil, C., Brody, J., Chakrabarti, A.: Functional monitoring without monotonicity. In: Albers, S., Marchetti-Spaccamela, A., Matias, Y., Nikoletseas, S., Thomas, W. (eds.) ICALP 2009, Part I. LNCS, vol. 5555, pp. 95–106. Springer, Heidelberg (2009)
4. Arlitt, M., Jin, T.: 1998 World Cup web site access logs (August 1998), http://www.acm.org/sigcomm/ITA/
5. Babcock, B., Olston, C.: Distributed top-k monitoring. In: Proc. of SIGMOD 2003, pp. 28–39 (2003)
6. Cao, P., Wang, Z.: Efficient top-k query calculation in distributed networks. In: Proc. of PODC 2004, pp. 206–215. ACM (2004)
7. Charikar, M., Chen, K., Farach-Colton, M.: Finding frequent items in data streams. Theoretical Computer Science 312(1), 3–15 (2004)
8. Chi, Y., Wang, H., Yu, P., Muntz, R.: Moment: Maintaining closed frequent itemsets over a stream sliding window. In: Proc. of ICDM 2004. IEEE (2004)
9. Cormode, G.: Continuous distributed monitoring: A short survey. In: Proc. of AlMoDEP 2011, pp. 1–10. ACM (2011)
10. Cormode, G., Garofalakis, M.N.: Sketching probabilistic data streams. In: Proc. of SIGMOD 2007, pp. 281–292 (2007)
11. Cormode, G., Muthukrishnan, S., Yi, K.: Algorithms for distributed functional monitoring. ACM Transactions on Algorithms 7(2), 21 (2011)
12. Gibbons, P.B., Matias, Y.: Synopsis data structures for massive data sets. In: External Memory Algorithms, pp. 39–70. American Mathematical Society (1999)
13. Jelasity, M., Montresor, A., Babaoglu, O.: Gossip-based aggregation in large dynamic networks. ACM TOCS 23(3), 219–252 (2005)
14. Jelasity, M., Voulgaris, S., Guerraoui, R., Kermarrec, A.-M., van Steen, M.: Gossip-based peer sampling. ACM TOCS 25(3) (August 2007)
15. Karp, R., Shenker, S., Papadimitriou, C.: A simple algorithm for finding frequent elements in streams and bags. ACM Trans. Database Syst. 28(1), 51–55 (2003)
16. Lahiri, B., Tirthapura, S.: Identifying frequent items in a network using gossip. J. Parallel Distrib. Computing 70(12), 1241–1253 (2010)
17. Manjhi, A., Shkapenyuk, V., Dhamdhere, K., Olston, C.: Finding (recently) frequent items in distributed data streams. In: Proc. of ICDE 2005. IEEE (2005)
18. Montresor, A., Jelasity, M.: PeerSim: A scalable P2P simulator. In: Proc. of P2P 2009, pp. 99–100 (September 2009)
19. Sacha, J., Montresor, A.: Identifying frequent items in distributed data sets. Computing 95(4), 289–307 (2013)
20. Tirthapura, S., Woodruff, D.P.: Optimal random sampling from distributed streams revisited. In: Peleg, D. (ed.) DISC 2011. LNCS, vol. 6950, pp. 283–297. Springer, Heidelberg (2011)

Applying Selectively Parallel I/O Compression to Parallel Storage Systems

Rosa Filgueira[1], Malcolm Atkinson[1], Yusuke Tanimura[2], and Isao Kojima[2]

[1] University of Edinburgh, School of Informatics, Edinburgh EH8 9AB, U.K.
{rosa.filgueira,mpa}@ed.ac.uk
[2] Information Technology Research Institute, AIST, Tsukuba, Japan
{yusuke.tanimura,isao.kojima}@aist.go.jp

Abstract. This paper presents a new I/O technique called *Selectively Parallel I/O Compression* (SPIOC) for providing high-speed storage and access to data in QoS enabled parallel storage systems. SPIOC reduces the time of I/O operations by applying transparent compression between the computing and the storage systems. SPIOC can predict whether to compress or not at runtime, allowing parallel or sequential compression techniques, guaranteeing QoS and allowing partial and full reading by decompressing the minimum part of the file. SPIOC maximises the measured efficiency of data movement by applying run-time customising compression before storing data in the Papio storage system.

Keywords: Parallel File System, Data Intensive Computing, Compression algorithms, Adaptive systems.

1 Introduction

Large scale Data-Intensive Computing plays an important role in many scientific activities and commercial applications, whether it involves data mining of commercial transactions, experimental data analysis and visualization, or intensive simulation such as climate modelling. The challenge [1] is to develop a new framework to support Data-Intensive Computing that provides persistent storage for large datasets as well as balanced computing so the data can be analyzed. Parallel file systems (PFSs) such as Lustre [2], General Parallel File System (GPFS) [3], and Papio [4] are a type of distributed file system that distributes file data across multiple servers and provides for concurrent access by multiple tasks of a parallel application. For transferring completely a large dataset to or from PFS, the data are striped via several I/O streams. This type of file system, is commonly used in Data-Intensive Computing for obtaining high-performance I/O. While PFS, can scale in capacity and access bandwidth to support a large number of clients and petabytes of data, they cannot mask the imbalance between I/O throughput and compute power, the expensive storage network, and the limitation of hard disk drive (HDD) throughput. Therefore, the rate at which data can be delivered from disk to compute engine is a limiting factor, causing the data transfer channel to become a serious bottleneck.

Our aim is to reduce this bottleneck by decreasing the overall I/O time needed for transferring completely datasets between the computer and storage system (and vice versa). To reach our objective, in this paper we present three new compression strategies: *Sequential Compression*, *Parallel Compression* and *Selectively Parallel I/O Compression* (SPIOC), which are located on the client's side. Each strategy is an improvement over the previous one, and they apply run-time lossless compression (sequential or

F. Silva et al. (Eds.): Euro-Par 2014, LNCS 8632, pp. 282–293, 2014.

parallel). SPIOC also decides whether to compress or not, and which technique should be use (sequential or parallel) depending on the features of the client's machine.

We have chosen Papio as the storage system, because it was designed for large scale cluster computing. Papio provides QoS guarantees by employing an advanced reservation approach. While Papio executes each I/O operation with the I/O throughput requested by users, our techniques reduce the number of strips needed for completing the data transfer. Therefore, the combination of Papio and SPIOC allows us to reduce the time needed for writing and reading files while satisfying the reservation requests from users.

The remainder of this paper is: Section 2 introduces related work. Section 3 describes our system for selecting the compression algorithm. Section 4 explains the compression strategies. Section 5 presents an extensive evaluation. We conclude with a summary and a discussion of potential future work.

2   Related Work

2.1   The Papio Parallel File System

Papio is a storage system that supports parallel I/O and the performance reservation functionality [4]. Papio has a client API library, which allows users to reserve I/O performance with desired throughput (e.g. MB/sec), access type (read or write), and access time (from start to end). Papio allocates storage resources according to these reservations. When the requested throughput is higher than that provided by a single Storage Server (SS), multiple SSs are used, increasing the I/O parallelization. An I/O stream is the channel which the data flow between the client's application and one SS. Therefore, the total number of I/O streams (called *stripe_count*) is set to the number of SSs assigned to the reservation. Furthermore, Papio's API allows users to cut up a file into parts for performing the I/O operations (read_PAPIO and write_PAPIO). Each part is called a *chunk*. In each I/O operation, the *chunk* is striped over all of the I/O streams. The minimum unit of transfer via an I/O stream in Papio is called a stripe of *stripe_size* bytes. So, according to the level of I/O parallelization, more stripes can be transferred in parallel because more I/O streams are used. The total amount of data (*stream_width*) written or read each time by the I/O streams is *stripe_size* * *stripe_count*.

Figures 1(a), 1(b) show examples of application programs which write a 130MB file to Papio by using different *chunk* sizes. In both examples, the user's I/O throughput reservation is 300MB/sec. As the requested I/O throughput is higher than a single SS (100MB/sec), three SSs are assigned to the execution of the applications. In Figure 1(a), the entire file is written as one *chunk*, which requires one *write_PAPIO* operation, and in Figure 1(b), the file is written in several *chunks* of 10MB, which requires 13 *write_PAPIO* operations. Finally, each *write_PAPIO* operation stripes the *chunk* (*stripe_size* is 1MB in the examples), written in parallel via 3 parallel I/O streams. If the requested I/O throughput was 100MB/sec, only 1 SS would be assigned, and the stripes would be written sequentially. For both examples, *stream_width* is 3MB, and the number of stripes is 130.

Similar performance is obtained if users use a single or several *chunks*. Timing measurements by using those methods with the environment explained in Section 6 are at[1]. However, we have to be aware that if *chunk_size* is smaller than *stream_width*, Papio will wait for the next *chunk* to fill the streams, causing a performance degradation called *stream delay*.

---

[1] Supplementary details:
http://effort.is.ed.ac.uk/Compression/WritingMethods.pdf

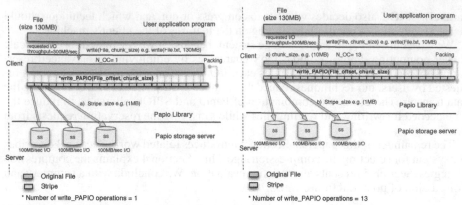

(a) Writing a file by using a single *chunk* to Pa- (b) Writing a file by using a several *chunks* to
pio   Papio

Fig. 1. Methods for writting files to Papio

2.2 Applying Compression to File Systems

The following are examples of how compression can be applied to files before storing
them in the file system, with parallel or sequential strategies, and using different lossless
compression algorithms.

APCFS [5] is a file system which supports fast autonomous compression at high
compression rates by applying multiple compression techniques. It is designed as a virtual layer inserted over an existing file system, compressing and decompressing data
by intercepting kernel calls. FuseCompress [6] provides a mountable Linux filesystem
which transparently compresses its content. FuseCompress supports several compression algorithms. However, when users want to read partial data by specifying an offset,
FuseCompress will decompress data from the beginning of the file to the specified offset.

ZBD [7] is a chunk-layer driver that transparently compresses and decompresses
data as they flow between the file-system and storage devices. ZBD maintains high
performance by leveraging modern multicore CPUs through explicit work scheduling.
In [8], two real-time methods are presented to identify the data that will yield significant
space savings when compressed. The first method estimates the compressibility of the
data. The second method examines data being written to the storage system in an online
manner and determines its compressibility.

All those approaches perform transparent compression to files before storing them,
and some of them have adaptive methods for deciding wether to compress or not. Our
work covers those two aspects, in addition it reduces the I/O time needed for transferring
the data guaranteeing the I/O throughput requested by users. We also apply adaptive
parallel techniques to reduce as much as possible the compression time. Furthermore,
our techniques allow us to perform partial reads decompressing the minimum part of
the file. Finally, the file system where we apply our compression techniques is a parallel
storage system, while others apply their techniques to serial file systems.

3 Selecting the Compression Algorithm

Depending on the datatype and redundancy levels, some algorithms can achieve a higher
compression ratio than others, or may need more time to perform the compression and

decompression operations. So, an adaptive method that selects the most suitable compression algorithm depending on a users priorities (speed vs compression ratio) and data features is desirable.

In [9], we implemented a strategy called *Runtime Adaptive Strategy* (RAS) for applying compression to the communications among MPI processes, and it has been productively by [10]. The decisions taken by RAS relies on two modules: The *Network Behaviour module*, which estimates the speedup achieved by sending a message with and without compression, and the *Compression Behaviour Module* which has a library called *Compression Library* with several compression algorithms and it produces a *heuristics file*, which stores the compression algorithm to use depending on the message datatype and its redundancy level.

The *Compression Behaviour Module* allows us to select a compression algorithm based on two criteria: high compression ratio; high compression and decompression speed. Our goal is to improve the I/O performance by reducing as much as possible the transfer time. Overhead introduced by the compression should be as small as possible. Therefore, we have tuned the *Compression Behaviour Module* to give us the best algorithm for each datatype (primitive or derived) based in the second criterion.

The compression strategies presented in this paper are completely different from our previous work. However, we have decided to use the *Compression Behaviour Module* to select the compression algorithm for each file datatype. As well as modifying this module to work with files instead of MPI messages, in this work we have added two new lossless data compression algorithms to our *Compression Library*: LZ4 [11] and *Snappy* [12]. So, the new version of the *Compression Behaviour module* has access to the following algorithms: *RLE, Huffman, LZO, Snappy* and *LZ4*.

In the current work we have performed an exhaustive empirical study with synthetic and real files to improve the *heuristics file,* by using the environment described in Table 2. We have developed a synthetic file generator to test integers, floats and double numbers and character string datatypes. The files generated have sized 100KB, 500KB, 900KB, 1MB, 2MB. We have added redundancy to the data as described in [13]: 0%, 25%, 50%, 75% and 100%. On the other hand, real files from different sources, and with different sizes and datatypes have been selected :

- The UCI Machine Learning repository[2]: *3D_spatial _network* (float), *pop_failure* (float), *regression_tom* (integer and float), *regression_twitter* (integer and float), and *ad* (integer and float)
- The Canterbury corpus[3]: *E.coli* (text), *Bible.txt* (text), *World192.txt* (text), *plrabn12.txt* (text), *pi.txt* (text) and *kennedy.xls* (excell)
- The Text Compression Benchmark[4]: *enwiki8* (text), *enwiki9* (text)
- The BISP3D application [14]: *Mesh3* (integer), *Mesh4* (integer).

The studies show that the shortest compression and decompression times are achieved by *LZ4, Snappy, LZO, RLE, Huffman* in ascending order as shown in Table 1.The results for the synthetic files can be founded at[5]. Notice that the highest compression ratios are not always achieved by the faster algorithms. But as the aim this work is to provide high-speed storage and access to Papio, fast algorithms are preferred over high-compression algorithms. *LZ4* is the fastest algorithm, independent of the datatype, size,

---

[2] http://archive.ics.uci.edu/ml/

[3] http://corpus.canterbury.ac.nz/

[4] http://mattmahoney.net/dc/text.html

[5] Supplementary information:
http://effort.is.ed.ac.uk/Compression/SyntheticResults.htm

Table 1. Compression ratio, and compression and decompression times for real files

File	Size(MB)	Compression ratio					Time compr. + decompr(sec)				
		RLE	HUFF	LZO	Snappy	LZ4	RLE	HUFF	LZO	Snappy	LZ4
3D_spatial	20	1.00	2.14	1.67	1.61	1.65	10.4	54.00	8.45	6.33	5.36
pop_failure	0.25	1.17	2.3	1.63	1.65	1.52	12.89	74.69	15.07	11.74	10.00
regression_tom	15	1.24	3.51	4.95	4.79	4.70	10.61	35.33	3.70	2.80	2.46
regression_twitter	217	1.20	2.99	4.08	4.27	3.81	7.06	36.04	4.18	3.24	3.26
ad	9.8	1	5.2	33.05	16.6	38.65	9.6	24.04	0.98	0.83	0.60
E.coli	4.5	1.01	4	2.03	2.14	1.60	14.72	46.01	9.91	5.97	4.69
Bible.txt	3.9	1.00	1.82	2.02	2.03	1.93	20.01	92.49	7.92	5.33	4.82
World192.txt	2.4	1.02	1.58	1.98	1.99	2.00	10.81	123.02	7.76	5.34	5.05
plrabn12.txt	0.47	1.00	1.74	1.55	1.51	1.49	10.09	125.13	16.43	12.05	10.79
pi.txt	0.97	1.00	2.35	1.22	1.20	1.26	11.53	85.07	14.00	14.02	11.89
kennedy.xls	1	1.00	2.22	2.84	2.42	2.74	11.02	62.21	6.29	5.51	4.88
enwki8	35	1.00	1.56	1.79	1.76	1.97	6.44	75.07	8.25	6.33	6.10
enwiki9	954	1.00	1.54	1.99	1.97	1.75	6.08	76.25	7.55	5.61	5.16
Mesh3	14	1.00	2.40	7.81	7.61	6.50	8.18	49.01	4.98	3.74	3.29
Mesh4	26	1.00	2.26	2.48	2.55	2.05	8.18	42.81	5.42	5.64	3.59

or redundancy level, so we have updated the *heuristics file* used by the *Compression Behaviour Module* by selecting this algorithm for all datatypes and redundancy levels. However, in future works this selection can be different if the selection criteria change, or if a new algorithm is introduced which satisfies our requirements, for some or all datatypes and redundancy levels.

4 Adding Compression to Papio

4.1 Sequential Compression Strategy

The first of three strategies proposed in this work is *Sequential Compression*, which aims to reduce the total time needed for writing a file into Papio Storage Server, guaranteeing the I/O speed specified by the user. To reach this aim, this strategy divides the file into several *chunks* and compresses them before writing to the storage system because if a user selects a part of file to read, only the *chunks* which belong to the selection will be decompressed. Otherwise, the whole file must be decompressed.

This strategy applies an algorithm which returns the compression parameters: the number of *chunks* to be compressed (*N_CC*), the size of the *chunks* to compress (*compression_chunk_size*), the compression ratio (*compression_ratio*), and the compression algorithm to use (*algo*) according to the *heuristics file*.

Firstly, the algorithm checks the compression *heuristic file* to determine the compression algorithm to use. Then, a compressibility study is performed to get the compression ratio. Today there is not established method for estimating compression ratio rather than just compressing. In [15], we find an analytically proof which affirms that accurately estimate the compression cannot be performed unless reading practically all the data. But this, will take too long. So, this algorithm selects three slices located randomly from the middle until the end of the file and it studies their compressibility. The size of each slice is 5% of the *chunk_size*. Later, the algorithm calculates the compression ratio getting an average of the compressed size of those slices. Finally, in order to avoid writing to Papio in very small *chunks*[6], the algorithm ensures that each *compressed chunk* is approximately the same size as the *chunk_size* specified by the user. So, knowing

---

[6] We want to prevent that the *compressed chunks* are not smaller than *stream_width* to avoid the *stream delay* problem.

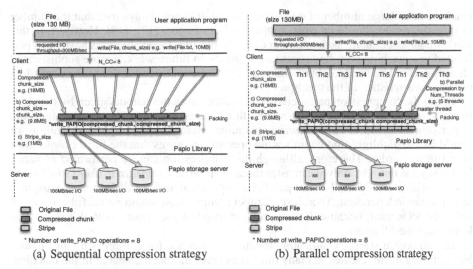

(a) Sequential compression strategy   (b) Parallel compression strategy

Fig. 2. Adding compression to Papio write operation

the compression ratio, this algorithm computes the new *chunk* size to compress (compression_chunk_size = $\lceil chunk\_size \times compression\_ratio \rceil$) and the number of *chunks* to compress (N_CC= $\lceil file\_size / compression\_chunk\_size \rceil$). Pseudo code of the algorithm at[7]. The outcome of this algorithm, is that the number of stripes is reduced.

Figure 2(a) illustrates the *Sequential Compression Strategy*. The number of *chunks* (*N_OC*) has been reduced from 13 uncompressed *chunks* to 8 *compressed chunks*. Note that the *chunk_size* is 10MB in 1(b) and the *compression_chunk_size* is 18MB in 2(a). However, the *compressed chunks* size is *chunk_size*. In the example, the number of stripes has been reduced from 130 to 80. However, we need extra memory for allocating the *compressed chunks*. The write API of Papio has been modified to implement this algorithm and to write the compressed *chunks* calling the compression API of the *Compression Library*. So, the compression is completely transparent to the user. Finally, this strategy stores in Papio a mapping file with information needed for decompressing the file. To achieve an improvement in the I/O write operations with this strategy equation (1) must hold:

$$\frac{Time\_write * N\_OC}{(Time\_write * N\_CC) + (Time\_comp * N\_CC)} > 1 \qquad (1)$$

Where *Time_write* is the time needed for writing a *chunk* of data in Papio, and *Time_comp* is the time for compressing a *chunk* of data.

4.2 Parallel Compression Strategy

This strategy divides the file in *chunks* to compress in the same way as the previous one. The main difference, is that *Parallel Compression Strategy* reduces as much as possible the compression time, compressing several *chunks* in parallel. To benefit from multithreaded compression we should use $<= nc$ threads, where *nc* is the number of cores available to the application [16]. Any number of threads higher than the number of cores could cause performance degradation. There are studies that show, that when a

---

[7] Supplementary details:
http://effort.is.ed.ac.uk/Compression/SequentialCompression.pdf

machine has a large number of cores ($>= 24$ nc), it is not always true that the number of threads created should be equal to the number of cores [17], [18]. However, in this work we have set the nc as the number of cores, because the evaluations have been performed in a machine with few cores (see Table 2). In future work, a more sophisticated algorithm could be used to obtain the suitable number of threads at run time depending on the characteristics of the machine.

To get the compression parameters, this strategy uses the outputs given by the algorithm described in Section 4.1. However, this strategy also applies another algorithm to perform the compression and write operations. Before explaining the algorithm, we would like to highlight that Papio's write operation requires that the file's *chunks* must be written in order. Therefore, although the compression can be performed in parallel by several threads, only the master thread can write *compressed chunks* following a sequential order. Note that the parallel compression and parallel streams (striping) in Papio are independent. Therefore, parallel compression would be useful even when only one SS is used, because the compression speed of each *chunk* with this strategy is lower than the SS speed.

The algorithm starts by allocating the memory needed for compressing the *chunks*. Next, the algorithm creates as many threads as cores has been detected in the machine. In case that the number of *chunks* to be compressed (N_CC) is smaller than the number of cores, the algorithm creates N_CC threads. Later, to each thread a *chunk* (which size *compression_chunk_size*) is assigned to compress. Compressions are performed in parallel, and each thread writes the compressed data in its allocated buffer. For compressing, each thread calls the compression API of the *Compression Library*.

In the mean time the master thread waits until the first thread has finished the compression of its *chunk*, and then writes the *compressed chunk* to Papio. The information of the *compressed chunk* is added to the mapping file. Blocks are compressed in groups of the number of threads. So, as soon as the first *compressed chunk* of each group is written to Papio, a new group of *chunks* are assigned to threads to be compressed. In that way, the master thread only waits for the fist *compressed chunk*, and ideally, the remaining *chunks* are going to be compressed by the time the master writes the compressed ones. For pseudo code of the algorithm see at[8].

The Figure 2(b) shows an example by applying *Parallel Compression Strategy*. The number of *chunks* to compress is 8 (N_CC), as in the previous example. However, the first 5 *chunks* are compressed in parallel. In this example, we not only have reduced the number of stripes from 130 to 80, but also the compression time. To achieve an improvement in the I/O write operations with this strategy equation (2) has to be hold:

$$\frac{Time\_write * N\_OC}{(Time\_write * N\_CC) + (Time\_comp) + (Time\_total\_wait)} > 1 \qquad (2a)$$

$$Time\_total\_wait = Time\_wait * (N\_CC/Num\_Threads) \qquad (2b)$$

Note that the *Time_wait* could be most of the time zero or near zero. This happens when the time spent by the threads to compress in parallel a group of *chunks* (*Time_comp*) is less than the time spent by the master to write those *compressed chunks* (*Time_write* ∗ *Num_Threads*). Otherwise, *Time_wait* would be the difference between these two times.

4.3 Selectively Parallel IO Compression Strategy

While storage system compression can save disk space, compressing data can adversely affect, increasing sometimes the I/O time when the compression is applied. So, if writing a compressed file decreases the write performance, it probably will also decrease

---

[8] Supplementary information:
http://effort.is.ed.ac.uk/Compression/ParallelCompression.pdf

read performance. Therefore, we have designed *Selectively Parallel I/O Compression Strategy* (SPIOC) whose decision algorithm only turns compression on when the estimated time of compressing and writing the file is lower than writing the file without compression. Also, in case the machine is single core, the file will be compressed and written sequentially. Otherwise, multiple threads can be created for compressing and writing the file in parallel.

SPIOC decision algorithm uses the algorithm explained in Section 4.1 for obtaining the compression parameters. Firstly, the algorithm checks the compression ratio. If the compression ratio is not higher than a predefined threshold (*threshold_1*, set up as 1.20), the compression will be turned off, and the file will be written without compression. Otherwise, the next step is to estimate the time for writing the file with and without compression, applying the equation (1) in case of single core, an the equation (2) in case of multi core. Because Papio guarantees the I/O throughput specified by the user, we already know the time needed for writing a *chunk* in Papio (*time_write*). On the other hand we have modified the algorithm explained in Section 4.1 to measure the time for compressing the slices of file used for checking the compression ratio and to estimate which is the time needed to compress a *chunk* of data (*Time_comp*). Only when the estimated reduction by the decision algorithm is higher than a predefined threshold (*threshold_2*, set up as 1.20), the compression is activated, and *Sequential_Compresion* or *Parallel_Compression* strategy is applied depending on the machine's features (single or multi core). Otherwise, the file is written without compression

The values of the thresholds have been set after preliminary studies using the environment explained in Section 6. Those values could be different depending on the characteristics of the machine where the applications are executed. Ideally, they should be adjusted at run time by the decision algorithm. However, this feature is beyond the scope of this work. As the previous algorithms, this one also has been implemented by modifying the write API of Papio. Because SPIOC is an improvement over the two previous strategies, it has been chosen as the strategy to use in Papio. Furthermore, with this strategy the compression is not always applied, so the information stored in the mapping file has been modified by adding a new line, to indicate wether the file is stored compressed.

5   Adding Decompression to Papio

In order to make readings of compressed and non-compressed files stored in Papio transparent by applying SPIOC, a decompression algorithm has been designed and implemented for the read operations, as shown[9]. This algorithm performs full and partial read operations by decompressing the minimum part of the file. This means that if a user wants to read some portion of a file, the algorithm calculates which *compressed chunks* it has to read and decompresses only those ones. Unlike write operations, Papio allows read operations to be performed without following a specific order. Therefore, in this case, multiple threads can read and decompress the *chunks* in parallel.

The algorithm starts by reading the mapping file associated with the file that is going to be read from Papio. The mapping file states whether the file has been compressed or not, and information about each *compressed chunk* written to Papio. Only the *compressed chunks* that need to be read from Papio are obtained by mapping the parameters provided by the user.

---

[9] Supplementary information:
http://effort.is.ed.ac.uk/Compression/ReadCompression.pdf

Table 2. Machine specifications

Nodes	Description
32 Compute nodes	Intel Xeon E5540 (2.53GHz, 4 cores) CPU x 2, 48GB memory, Broadcom NetXtreme-II (10 GbE)
8 Storage servers	Intel Xeon E3-1230 (3.2GHz, 4 cores) CPU, 8GB memory, Intel X520-DA2 (10 GbE)
1 Management server	AMD Opteron 6128 CPU (2GHz, 8 cores), 8GB memory, Intel X520-DA2 (10 GbE)

In case of compression, the next step is to read the selected *compressed chunks* from Papio and decompress them in parallel by several threads. For decompressing, each thread calls our decompression API of the *Compression Library*. The master thread waits until all threads finish their operations, and if it is needed, more threads are created in the following iterations. However, if the file is stored without compression, the file is read as in the original version of Papio.

6   Evaluation

We have evaluated our three compression strategies by using a High-Performance Cluster described in Table 2. Several files have been used to evaluate our proposal. However, we only show results for the seven largest files (Table 3) with the most different characteristics, to demonstrate how our strategies adapt to different scenarios. The file sizes displayed in the Table 3 correspond to originals (uncompressed). Using any of our compression strategies these are reduced to $\frac{size*compression\_ratio}{100}$.

Figure 3(a) shows a comparative in terms of speed up between *Sequential Compression* and *Parallel Compression* strategies. As previously described, in Papio a higher level of I/O parallelization is used whenever a higher I/O throughput is requested, because more stripes are written at the same time. By presenting the speedup values depending on I/O throughput, we show how our techniques perform at different levels of I/O paralelization. We have used the first five files described in table 3, and three different I/O throughputs: 100MB/sec, 200MB/sec and 300MB/sec. The *Parallel Compression Strategy* set up the threading level to 8 automatically. We define speed up as

Table 3. Details of files used for our evaluation

File	Size	Category	Type	Comp. Ratio
lgd_element.rdf [19]	17GB	geographic	text	11.96
all_geonames.rdf [20]	6.3GB	geographic	text	12.76
enwik9.txt [21]	950MB	linguistics	text	1.75
strain_cat.txt [22]	433MB	earth science	float	1.3
biggan_learn.bvecs [23]	13GB	computer vision	multidata	1.05
tiny_metadata.bin [24]	38GB	computer vision	binary	8.13
dna_15.cel [25]	1.9GB	biology	numeric	1.52

Table 4. Estimated and real speed up values for sequential and parallel compression

File/Strategy	100 MB I/O Speed Up		200 MB I/O Speed Up		300 MB I/O Speed Up	
strain_cat	estimated	real	estimated	real	estimated	real
Sequential	0.78	0.84	0.49	0.43	0.33	0.38
Parallel	1.28	1.34	1.21	1.24	1.20	1.21
all_geonames	estimated	real	estimated	real	estimated	real
Sequential	8.14	8.72	4.36	4.5	3.04	2.9
Parallel	12.58	13.45	12.25	12.35	11.97	11.68

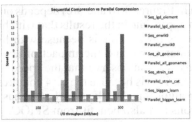
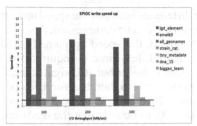
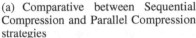

(a) Comparative between Sequential Compression and Parallel Compression strategies

(b) Speed up by applying SPIOC in the write operations.

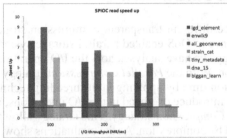

(c) Speed up by applying decompression in the read operations

Fig. 3. Evaluations results

$\frac{Original\_time\_IO\_operation}{Strategy\_time\_IO\_operation}$. As the results show, in most cases both strategies reduce the time needed for writing the different files by using different I/O throughput. The speed ups obtained by *Parallel Compression Strategy* are higher than *Sequential Compression Strategy*, because the compression overhead has been almost hidden. However, we can observe that there are some cases where using those strategies write performance is decreased. For example, writing the file *biggan_learn.bvecs* with any of those strategies. Because the compression ratio of that file is very low, the overhead introduced by applying compression is higher than the benefit from writing *compressed chunks* to Papio.

Table 4 shows how SPIOC detects when the compression is going to improve the I/O performance, and when not, estimating the speed up in each case. We have used *strain_cat.txt* and *all_geonames.rdf* files, with different I/O throughput, and we have applied sequential (by using 1 thread) and parallel (by using 8 threads) compression techniques and measured the real speed up for each case. The estimated speed up by SPIOC has been recorded. The results demonstrate that the estimated values by SPIOC are very close to the real ones, with an error between 3%- 7%.

The performance of SPIOC has been evaluated, see Figures 3(b) and 3(c), with all the files described in the table 3. SPIOC set up automatically the threading level to 8. Experiments demonstrate how SPIOC reduces I/O time for reading/writing Papio in most cases, and only in few cases, the I/O performance has not been improved, but it has not been degraded. Note that for *biggan_learn.bvecs* file the compression has been deactivated. The reason is that SPIOC has detected that the compression ratio of this file is smaller than the *threshold_1*. If we used a single core machine for evaluating SPIOC, it would also deactivate the compression for *strain_cat.txt* file because the estimated speed ups for sequential compression (shown in table 4) are smaller than *threshold_2* for any of the I/O throughputs.

The difference between the speed ups shown in Figures 3(b) and 3(c) depends on how much each file can be compressed. Also, we can appreciate in the results that with higher I/O throughput, the speed up gained by SPIOC is lower. This is because with higher I/O throughput, less time is required for I/O operations, and the impact of applying compression is lower but still significant. Finally, we can observe that the speed up for write operations is higher than for read operations. This is because the LZ4 compression algorithm is 20% faster than the decompression algorithm. So, the *threshold_2* has been set up to 1.20, to be sure that the reads operations can also benefit from SPIOC.

7   Conclusions and Future Work

We have presented three different transparent compression strategies in order to improve the I/O performance in QoS enabled parallel storage systems. With the *Sequential Compression* strategy, we have analysed how the I/O operations could be improved by applying compression. With the *Parallel Compression* strategy we have studied how to reduce the compression time by applying multithreading techniques. Since in some cases compression may introduce overhead in the I/O operations, we have designed the *Selectively Parallel I/O Compression* strategy. This strategy allows us to predict the I/O time reduction achieved by compression. As the evaluations show, SPIOC is able to improve the I/O operations, adapting the compression techniques at run time, and turning it on, only when is beneficial.

In future work, we would like to improve SPIOC by detecting the optimal value for the thresholds and threading level at run time depending on the characteristics of the computer nodes and files. And to provide users the option to choose the compression algorithm criteria that suit their requirements. Other improvements could apply different compression algorithms to the file's *chunks* depending on their datatypes, and apply our strategies to collective I/O operations provided by the Papio. Finally, SPIOC could be applied to other file systems which have similar QoS features to Papio's. For other systems where available throughput is not aware, *Sequential Compression* and *Parallel Compression* strategies are still applicable.

Acknowledgment. The research has been supported by the NERC UK Grant (NE/H02297X/1). We would like to thank the AIST institute for providing the infrastructures to evaluate the work.

References

1. Gu, Y., Grossman, R.L.: Toward efficient and simplified distributed data intensive computing. IEEE Trans. Parallel Distrib. Syst., 974–984 (2011)
2. CFS Inc., Lustre: A scalable, high-performance file system, cluster File Systems Inc. white paper, version 1.0 (2002)
3. Schmuck, F., Haskin, R.: GPFS: A shared-disk file system for large computing clusters. In: Proc. of the First Conference on File and Storage Technologies (FAST), pp. 231–244 (January 2002)
4. Tanimura, Y., Hidetaka, K., Kudoh, T., Kojima, I., Tanaka, Y.: A distributed storage system allowing application users to reserve i/o performance in advance for achieving sla. In: GRID, pp. 193–200 (2010)
5. Kella, K.K., Khanum, A.: Apcfs: Autonomous and parallel compressed file system. International Journal of Parallel Programming 39(4), 522–532 (2011)

6. Fusecompress, a linux file-system that transparently compresses its contents (2011), http://code.google.com/p/fusecompress/
7. Klonatos, Y., Makatos, T., Marazakis, M., Flouris, M.D., Bilas, A.: Transparent online storage compression at the block-level. TOS 8(2), 5 (2012)
8. Harnik, D., Kat, R., Sotnikov, D., Traeger, A., Margalit, O.: To zip or not to zip: Effective resource usage for real-time compression. Presented as Part of the 11th USENIX Conference on File and Storage Technologies. USENIX, Berkeley (2013), https://www.usenix.org/conference/fast13/zip-or-not-zip-effective-resource-usage-real-time-compression
9. Filgueira, R., Singh, D.E., Carretero, J., Calderón, A., García, F.: Adaptive-compi: Enhancing mpi-based applications' performance and scalability by using adaptive compression. IJHPCA 25(1), 93–114 (2011)
10. Filgueira, R., Atkinson, M., Nuñez, A., Fernández, J.: An adaptive, scalable, and portable technique for speeding up mpi-based applications. In: Kaklamanis, C., Papatheodorou, T., Spirakis, P.G. (eds.) Euro-Par 2012. LNCS, vol. 7484, pp. 729–740. Springer, Heidelberg (2012)
11. Real time data compress (2012), http://fastcompression.blogspot.co.uk/p/lz4.html
12. Russell, J., Cohn, R.: Snappy. Book on Demand (2012), http://books.google.co.uk/books?id=PXajMQEACAAJ
13. Filgueira, R., Singh, D.E., Calderón, A., Carretero, J.: Compi: Enhancing mpi based applications performance and scalability using run-time compression. In: Ropo, M., Westerholm, J., Dongarra, J. (eds.) EuroPVM/MPI 2009. LNCS, vol. 5759, pp. 207–218. Springer, Heidelberg (2009)
14. Loureiro, A., González, J., Pena, T.F.: A parallel 3D semiconductor device simulator for gradual heterojunction bipolar transistors. Int. Journal of Numerical Modelling: Electronic Networks, Devices and Fields 16, 53–66 (2003)
15. Raskhodnikova, S., Ron, D., Rubinfeld, R., Smith, A.: Sublinear algorithms for approximating string compressibility. Algorithmica 65(3), 685–709 (2013), http://dblp.uni-trier.de/db/journals/algorithmica/algorithmica65.htmlRaskhodnikovaRRS13
16. Fan, D., Zhang, H., Wang, D., Ye, X., Song, F., Li, G., Sun, N.: Godson-t: An efficient many-core processor exploring thread-level parallelism. IEEE Micro 99(1), 5555
17. Pusukuri, K.K., Gupta, R., Bhuyan, L.N.: Thread reinforcer: Dynamically determining number of threads via os level monitoring. In: Proceedings of the 2011 IEEE International Symposium on Workload Characterization. IISWC 2011, pp. 116–125. IEEE Computer Society, Washington, DC (2011)
18. Pusukuri, K.K., Gupta, R., Bhuyan, L.N.: Adapt: A framework for coscheduling multithreaded programs. ACM Trans. Archit. Code Optim. 9(4), 45:1–45:24 (2013)
19. Linked geo data (July 18, 2009), http://downloads.linkedgeodata.org/releases/2009-07-01/
20. Geo names (September 2009), http://www.geonames.org/ontology/documentation.html
21. Mahoney, M.: Large text compression benchmark (August 2013), http://mattmahoney.net/dc/text.html
22. Bell, A.F., Greenhough, J., Heap, M.J., Main, I.G.: Challenges for forecasting based on accelerating rates of earthquakes at volcanoes and laboratory analogues. Geophysical Journal International 185(2), 718–723 (2011)
23. Jégou, H., Douze, M., Schmid, C.: Product quantization for nearest neighbor search. IEEE Transactions on Pattern Analysis & Machine Intelligence 33(1), 117–128 (2011) (to appear)
24. Torralba, A., Fergus, R., Freeman, W.T.: 80 million tiny images: A large data set for nonparametric object and scene recognition. IEEE Transactions on Pattern Analysis and Machine Intelligence 30(11), 1958–1970 (2008)
25. Greshock, J., Bachman, K.E., Degenhardt, Y.Y., Jing, J., Wen, Y.H., Eastman, S., McNeil, E., Moy, C., Wegrzyn, R., Auger, K., Hardwicke, M.A.: Molecular target class is predictive of in vitro response profile. Cancer Res. 70(9), 3677–3686 (2010)

Ultra-Fast Load Balancing of Distributed Key-Value Stores through Network-Assisted Lookups

Davide De Cesaris[1,2], Kostas Katrinis[1], Spyros Kotoulas[1], and Antonio Corradi[2]

[1] IBM Research, Dublin, Ireland
[2] DEIS, University of Bologna, Bologna, Italy

Abstract. Many systems rely on distributed caches with thousands of nodes to improve response times and off-load underlying systems. Large-scale caching presents challenges in terms of resource utilization, load balancing, robustness and flexibility of deployment. In this paper, we propose a novel distributed caching method based on dynamic IP address assignment. Keys are mapped to a large IP address space statically and each node is dynamically assigned multiple IP addresses. As a result, we have a system with minimal need for central coordination, while eliminating the single point of failure in competitive solutions. We evaluate our system in our datacenter and show that our approach localizes the effect of load-balancing to only loaded cache servers, while leaving cache clients unaffected and also providing for finely-granular rebalancing.

1 Introduction

Massive distributed caches play an important role in large-scale computing infrastructures. For example, Facebook has reported [1,2] that they store tens of TB in a modified implementation of memcached, distributed over hundreds of nodes in a cluster. A set of challenges emerge, when managing caches of this size:

- *Robustness* The system should be robust against node failure and should not have a single point of failure. On the other hand, distributed protocols should have low overhead and be able to respond to failures quickly.
- *Load-balancing* In most caches, key lookups would follow a very irregular pattern, presenting significant skew, as also described in [1]. Typically, HTTP requests and other lookups would follow a power law [3]. Key popularity may shift with time or rapidly change, due to unexpected events.
- *Scalability* Any distributed protocol should be able to scale to large numbers of nodes and have minimal performance impact.
- *Flexibility* It is common and highly desirable to tap into unused resources in a data center. We would like caching techniques that are flexible in terms of demand of computational resources.

This paper introduces Network-Assisted Lookups (NAL), a method to do rapid load-balancing of key-value stores by exploiting the existing IP infrastructure. The key points in our approach are:

F. Silva et al. (Eds.): Euro-Par 2014, LNCS 8632, pp. 294–305, 2014.
© Springer International Publishing Switzerland 2014

- *IP protocol as a distributed location registry.* Our system relies on a static mapping of keys to a large space, the static mapping of this space to IP addresses and the dynamic allocation of IP addresses to machines as a way to load balance the system.
- *Exploit existing resources.* The resources in the system need not be homogeneous or have similar throughput.
- *Scalability.* The proposed method scales linearly and is limited only by the number of available (private) IP addresses in the datacenter, which is not a problem in the foreseeable future.
- *Robustness.* Our method relies on IP address re-allocation on the network. As such, there is no central point of failure in the system.

We prototyped NAL in our lab datacenter and evaluated it using key access patterns that are characteristic for skewed data access in a range of trending and established workloads. Our results manifest that NAL manages to be as efficient as competitive approaches (consistent hashing), while achieving to reduce convergence time after load-balancing and also localizing the effect of block rebalancing to clients "causing" the imbalance.

This paper is structured as follows. Section 2 presents related approaches and delves deeper into the most competitive one, namely consistent hashing, showing its scalability limit via experimental evaluation we conducted. Section 3 presents the architecture of NAL and discusses the workings of the various components, while Section 4 elaborates in our load-balancing algorithm for distributed caching in NAL. We present evaluation results we obtained using our NAL prototype implementation in Section 5 and conclude in Section 6.

2 Related Art and Motivation

Distributed data-management/processing frameworks typically spread data blocks/records across two or more store locations (e.g. servers). For instance, distributed caching systems such as Memcached [4] and Redis [5] cache recently accessed key-value pairs (e.g. database records) across distributed cache server processes. The latter are typically started at servers, where spare compute, memory and network resources have been harvested. Further examples are parallel/distributed databases and distributed batch data-processing frameworks employing distributed filesystems (e.g. HDFS [6] in Hadoop). A precondition for these distributed stores is the existence of a lookup service entity that maps an identifier to the actual location of the data that needs to be retrieved. Typically, a data record/block is identified by a key. Then, by means of the mapping entity, the key is mapped to the identity (e.g. destination IP socket) of the physical/virtual host (server), where the corresponding data record/block resides. Unless otherwise qualified, we employ in the remainder of this paper the term "key" to refer to data identifiers and the term "block" (or "data block") to refer to the payload value (e.g. binary object or database record) that is the data unit uniquely identified by exactly one key and retrieved to a processing node as the result of a key lookup and data fetch action.

An additional functional requirement for a data lookup service is the ability to dynamically update the location of data blocks. The latter may change at runtime as the result of a load/store balancing action or to maintain a desired replication factor to counter data node failures. At the occurrence of any amendment of a block's location (referred to as "block migration" hereafter), the key-to-location mapping entity needs to be updated accordingly to ensure non-intermittent access to distributed data blocks. Distributed stores relying on a centralized lookup service address this requirement by sending location updates to a nameserver. At large-scale, the centralized name service becomes quickly the bottleneck and typically replication (e.g. clustering) is employed to guarantee reasonable lookup latency. However, replication has scalability limitations due to cost and complexity proportionality between the data volume stored and the lookup service capacity required. Distributed hash-tables (DHTs) such as Chord [7]) constitute a scalable and resilient solution; still, they are harder to implement and may degrade performance due to operating at the application/session layer. In addition, having block location "encoded" among data nodes - as is the case with DHTs - can pose security concerns (e.g. in a public cloud environment multiple tenants share the same physical memory resources) and/or contradict the service model. A typical example of the latter case is when the service model mandates the service provider as the sole provider of a persistent and highly-available distributed filesystem service to multiple datacenter tenants. Offering a distributed file service using a DHT and with high availability guarantees may be hard to achieve within such a model, given that e.g. tenants may choose to reboot servers, where part of the block location information is stored.

Following the above discussion on limitations of alternative solutions, we narrow our attention to distributed caching as the best solution for being extended to provide for dynamic data re-balancing. Although various hashing techniques are possible, we focus here on *consistent hashing* [8], a technique that is known to significantly reduce the miss rate during cache server addition/removal. Figure 1a depicts the standard continuum-based implementation of consistent hashing, assuming in this example four data (cache) servers and an integer continuum set S ($S = \{0, 1, 2.., N\}, N = 2^{32} - 1$). Also, each data server is assigned a unique integer in the continuum (e.g. Data-Server-1 $\leftarrow N/4$). Server selection for a given key k occurs as follows: the key is first hashed to an integer value x in the integer set S. The server selected for retrieving the block identified by k is then the server that is assigned to the smallest integer in $\{x, x + 1, .., N\}$. For instance, on the left-hand side of Figure 1a, the block corresponding to $k1$ (resp. $k2$) will be fetched from data server-1 (resp. data server-3).

In commodity distributed caching deployments (e.g. memcached [4]), consistent hashing is static, i.e. servers are statically assigned to the continuum, albeit not necessarily following a uniform key load per server (e.g. to cater for heterogeneity of available memory at each server). Here, we exercise the scalability of extending consistent hashing with load-balancing capabilities, specifically via dynamic re-hashing. The approach has been proposed before in different contexts (e.g. processor memory hierarchy [9]), albeit with scalability requirements not to the level required in this use-case. Figure 1a exemplifies dynamic load-balancing via re-hashing in our toy four-server setup. Initially (left-hand side sub-figure), each server is assigned (for brevity) an equal number of keys along the continuum. Due to data skewness, a fraction of keys served by *Data-server-3* becomes hot (relative to average key popularity), leading to sub-optimal cache performance. To remedy this, the continuum is rebuilt, shifting part of the hot key range to *Data-Server-2* (right-hand side in Figure 1a) and thus providing for a balanced

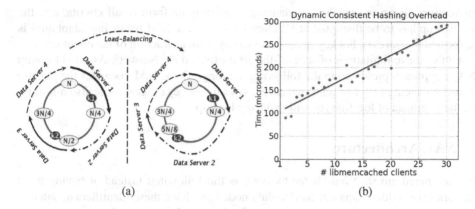

Fig. 1. Consistent Hashing: (a) Load-balancing through dynamic continuum rebuilding on four cache servers and (b) evaluation of time overhead due to load-balancing

caching load, adaptive to recent key access patterns. This approach assumes the existence of a centralized key access pattern monitoring and adaptation entity that is though off the lookup and retrieval path.

To evaluate the performance of dynamic consistent hashing to provide for dynamic load-balancing at scale, we created a prototype setup in memcached, using the provided consistent hashing implementation in libmemcached (*libketama* [10]). The latter provides for the ability to dynamically re assign keys to memcached servers through a weighting mechanism. We also implemented a baseline centralized controller with the sole functionality of notifying memcached clients to rebuild their continua (dynamic re-hashing), together with communicating the set of weights that each client should use as input during each re-hashing cycle to assign memcached server in its continuum. The latter occurs via a simple application-level UDP protocol between the controller and the memcached client.

Using this setup, we measured the time overhead of completing a load-balancing action, specifically by measuring the time that each memcached client takes to finish rebuilding its continuum data structure and reporting the maximum value over the entire set of clients. For each client set size, we repeat the experiment for 5000 times and report the average time overhead over all 5000 repetitions. Figure 1b depicts the results of this experiment with a memcached client set size (actual servers) ranging from 1 to 30. By applying linear regression to the measurements, we obtain the following expression for estimating the time overhead T_{dch} of dynamic consistent hashing (in microseconds) as a function of the number of cache clients x:

$$T_{dch}(x) = 100 + 6.6 \cdot x \tag{1}$$

In extrapolation for a conservative size of a web application comprising 1000 clients, the last equation yields a load-balancing overhead of approximately 7ms just for rebuilding the hashing data structures (i.e. not accounting for the cache misses that will inevitably occur during any cache re-balancing action, regardless of the approach). Obviously, this is a significant penalty, when sub-10ms queries is the desired operating range of target applications. Even worse, the re-balancing penalty is uniform to **all clients**, e.g. the key lookup has to be disrupted at all clients, even if the load-balancing adaptation is performed to address a hot key range accessed by a small fraction of the client set.

All the above limitations of state-of-the art motivated the Network-Assisted Lookup (NAL) approach presented in the following. Among others, NAL localizes the penalty of load-balancing only to clients that access keys in hot key ranges, while also minimizing the overhead of location resolution during lookup.

3 NAL Architecture

The key paradigm shift introduced by NAL is the following: instead of having fixed network service identifiers attached to data nodes and have these identifiers updated at the lookup service, whenever the location of a data block is changed due to migration, NAL employs a static key-to-location mapping created once and for all at key hash generation time and provides for accurate lookup of arbitrarily migrated data blocks by updating the network identity of the actual location of a block.

Figure 2 materializes the above abstract statement, depicting the architectural amendments to a distributed application (e.g. web application) employing memcached with Network-Assisted Lookups. The embodiment assumes deployment on an IT infrastructure employing an Ethernet 802.3/IPv4 network stack; due to this setup being "standard" in commodity datacenters, we assume it in the rest of this work, whereby a generalization of the approach to alternative network technologies is beyond the scope of this paper. One of the many application servers comprising the distributed application is shown at the top of Figure 2, where a memcached client is running. Although the memcached client part is typically embedded into the application logic, we depict it for the sake of presentation as a standalone service termed "lookup service". Unlike the "standard" memcached practice of having each key hashed to the single network identifier (hostname or IP address) of a cache server process that potentially holds the data block identified by the respective key, the NAL architecture takes a **static** hashing

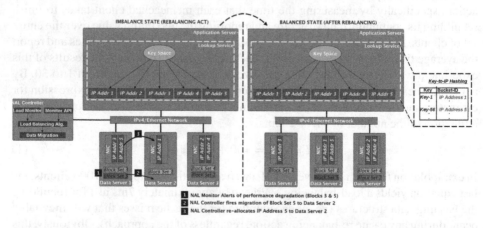

Fig. 2. Network-assisted Lookup Architecture and Data Migration Example

approach of keys to IP addresses, the latter not being bound to a specific cache server process.

The NAL Controller facilitates dynamic binding of IP addresses (that buckets are mapped to) to memcached cache servers, whereby each IP address (and thus hash bucket) corresponds to a set of data blocks ("Block Set"). Leveraging on the feature provided by modern operating systems to have Network Interface Cards (NICs) identified by a plurality of IP addresses, the controller is capable of assigning multiple IP addresses to the NIC of a memcached server and thus mapping multiple buckets to the server. Dynamic address binding is in fact the last step taken by the controller at the event of a block set migration event. Additional functionality implemented at the controller is the continuous monitoring of cache servers' load - either embedded as part of the controller implementation or by interfacing existing memcached monitoring tools via a dedicated API - and the execution of a load-balancing algorithm (cf. section 4) at the detection of caching performance degradation as the result of one or more server overload.

Figure 2 depicts also an example showcasing how the NAL approach achieves dynamic load-balancing without breaking the linear scalability of the distributed caching service. At the event of the NAL controller deducing a cache server overload incident (e.g. Data Server 1 being overloaded in the example of Figure 2), the controller takes a re-balancing action by picking a block set and migrating it from the overloaded (Data Server 1) to a less utilized cache server (Data Server 2). For this, the controller maintains a data structure that maps a bucket identifier to the list of keys that hash to the specified bucket. The re-balancing action completes by also migrating the IP address that the migrated block set statically maps to: in the example of Figure 2, this occurs by de-allocating IP Address 5 from Data Server 1 and allocating it via a newly created aliased interface to Data Server 2. Deriving from this example, it follows that re-balancing in NAL involves interaction **only between a constant number of servers, leaving application/frontend servers untouched** and providing for seamless key lookup while driving the system to a more balanced state and thus yielding better end-user performance.

Load-Balancing Granularity Analysis at Scale. Based on the above specification, it is straightforward that the bucket size used by a NAL deployment drives the granularity of load-balancing, since a bucket of keys (i.e. a block set) is the minimum unit of migration. Let C_{size} be the total cache size (in bytes) available in the system (i.e. the sum of memory allocated to each cache process in the system) and $addr$ be the number of IP addresses dedicated within the datacenter to NAL use. Then, assuming uniform block set size, the *block set size* BS_{size} (in bytes) is lower bounded by

$$BS_{size} \geq \frac{C_{size}}{addr} \tag{2}$$

Due to NAL statically binding an IP address to a bucket and thus to a block set, it follows that the maximum number of block sets that a cache server can hold equals the maximum number of IP addresses $addr_{node}$ that the cache server's network interface can be identified by. Assuming a uniform distribution of total cache size to cache servers, let r be the average cache size ratio of the total cache size C_{size} that is allocated to a cache server. Then, the *block set size* BS_{size} (in bytes) is also lower bounded by

Table 1. NAL dimensioning examples

Cache Size (Total)	Cache Size (Server)	Minimum Bucket Size
64 GBytes	0.5 GBytes	0.125 MBytes
64 GBytes	6.4 GBytes	1.6 MBytes
256 GBytes	0.5 GBytes	0.125 MBytes
256 GBytes	25.6 GBytes	6.4 MBytes
1 TBytes	1.024 GBytes	0.256 MBytes
1 TBytes	10.24 GBytes	2.56 MBytes
1 TBytes	102.4 GBytes	25.6 MBytes
32 TBytes	**32.768 GBytes**	**8.192 MBytes**
32 TBytes	327.68 GBytes	81.92 MBytes
32 TBytes	2 TBytes	512.0 MBytes
132 TBytes	131.072 GBytes	32.768 MBytes
132 TBytes	2 TBytes	512.0 MBytes
512 TBytes	524.288 GBytes	131.072 MBytes
512 TBytes	2 TBytes	512.0 MBytes

$$BS_{size} \geq \frac{C_{size} \cdot r}{addr_{node}} \qquad (3)$$

and by combining Equations 2 and 3 we get the feasible set of block set sizes

$$max(\frac{C_{size}}{addr}, \frac{C_{size} \cdot r}{addr_{node}}) \qquad (4)$$

Equation 4 governs the finest granularity of load-balancing and is obviously dependent on system dimensioning. To develop a practical feeling of this bound, we first seek to specify the maximum number of IP addresses we could assign to a network interface ($addr_{node}$ in Eq. 4). Experimentation on a modern albeit "commodity" server running Redhat Enterprise Linux 6.3 revealed that we could assign up to 8192 addresses to a network interface and seamlessly communicate with the server under test on the various IP addresses assigned to it. In the rest, we assume a maximum bound of $addr_{node} = 4096$ IP addresses per cache server. We further set the total number of IP addresses available to NAL to $addr = 16M$, thus allocating an entire /8 IPv4 subnet to NAL. Given the abundance of private IP addresses in a datacenter, the latter choice is not expensive. Using the above setup, we plug target total cache size values to Equation 4, covering a range of systems, from small-scale campus hosting to the largest social networking websites (Facebook reported [2] 800 servers offering at least 28 Tbytes of in-memory cache in 2008). We also assume a broad range of average cache memory size allocated to each per cache server, with the ratio r alternating among following values: 0.1%, 1%, 5% and 10%. Table 1 lists the minimum bucket sizes supported by the various setups generated by the process previously described. Evidently, the minimum bucket size supported is always by multiple orders of magnitude smaller compared to the per server average cache memory size. Taking the 2008 Facebook memcached setup [2] as an example (shown in bold font in Table 1), each cache server has 35 Gbytes of memory allocated to each memcached server (assuming uniform distribution of total cache size to servers). In this example, an approximately 8 Mbytes bucket size is possible, yielding the possibility to do load-balancing at more than 1/1000th of cache size on a per server basis.

It follows from the above that **NAL provides for very fine-grained dynamic load-balancing, even when dimensioned for the most aggressive distributed caching setups that can be thought of today**. Obviously, there is a trade-off between the selected bucket size and the number of buckets in terms of bucket management overhead. It must be noted that the numbers shown in Table 1 are only indicative of the minimum bucket size, while it is still possible to dimension the system with a much larger bucket size to strike a good balance between load-balancing granularity and management overhead.

4 Load Balancing Algorithm

This section presents the load-balancing algorithm we implemented within our proof of concept prototype for the sake of evaluating the NAL approach. It must be though noted that due to the modularity of the NAL Controller (cf. Figure 2), our algorithm can be replaced by any alternative algorithm that interfaces with the rest of the controller modules.

It is straightforward that a well balanced distributed caching system should strive to minimize data access latency and thus global rate of cache evictions, obviously bounded by the caching system dimensions and constrained on the actual key access pattern. Around this intuition, our algorithm shown in Listing 1.1 works as follows:

- At the beginning of each load-balancing iteration, the algorithm reads via the Controller monitor API the eviction rates of all cache servers and computes the average eviction rate across the system.
- In case no outlier is identified, specifically no cache server with eviction rate diverging more than a predefined threshold from the average eviction rate, then no load-balacing action is taken,
- or else the algorithm enters the core of its load-balancing logic towards deciding the list of block sets (sets of key-value stores) that are to be migrated from the most overloaded to the least loaded server.
- The choice of the destination server depends on the state of the caches: if there are nodes without evictions, the algorithm chooses the server with the lower number of requests per second, otherwise it picks the server with the lowest number of evictions per second. The last critical decision taken by the load-balancing algorithms deals with the how many and which block sets to migrate.
- In terms of which block sets to migrate, the algorithm picks the block sets with the lowest number of requests per second, thus keeping the hot blocks at the overloaded data server. The intuition here is that, despite keeping all hot blocks in the overloaded server, the migration of blocks from the latter will free up cache memory and thus decrease the eviction rate due to more hot blocks being able to be kept in cache. An additional advantage of this approach is the continuity of service from cache for a higher number of clients, for the hot block sets are highly demanded. Would it be the hot block sets that were migrated, this would lead to an eviction storm that would impact a larger number of client requests (hot requests).

– The number of block sets to migrate is driven by the parameter N. This allows for adopting a coarse-grained approach when the system becomes very imbalanced, while employing a more fine-grained adaptation (by dynamically setting the parameter N) when the skew between eviction rates is reduced and the system is more stable.

Listing 1.1. Pseudo-code of Load-balancing Algorithm with NAL

```
Set M // overload threshold (eviction rate)
Set N // normalization factor for deciding popularity of blocks to be migrated
LOOP
{
  FOR all the nodes in cache server list
  {
    READ #evictions/sec into array E
  }
  AvgEvcts=Average(E)
  FOR each item e in E
  {
    Max_Evcts = Max(Abs(e-AvgEvcts),Max_Evcts)
  }
  IF Max_Evcts < M // system is balanced
  {
    WAIT T_check seconds
  }
  ELSE // start load-balancing/block migration
  {
    S = node with max #evictions/sec
    Max_reqs = #requests/sec of S
    L = list of x nodes with least evictions
    IF L is not empty
    {
      D = node with min #evictions/sec
    }
    ELSE
    {
      D = node of L with min #requests/sec
    }
    Min_reqs = #requests/sec of D
    Reqs_to_move = (Max_reqs - Min_reqs) / N
    B = list of less accessed Block Sets of S with sum of #requests/sec greater
        than or equal to Reqs_to_move
    MOVE B from S to D
    WAIT T_check seconds
  }
}
```

Our algorithm scales with the number of cache servers and is highly responsive within the dimensions of the most aggressive setups (O(100) servers). As part of our ongoing work, we are currently formalizing its efficacy against equivalent standard algorithms (e.g. bin packing), while also experimenting with hierarchical monitoring so as to relieve the strain on the controller from having to poll all cache servers for cache performance statistics.

5   Evaluation

We deployed our proof of concept prototype implementation of NAL in our lab datacenter using 30 servers in total. All servers comprise two Intel Xeon X5670 6C processors,

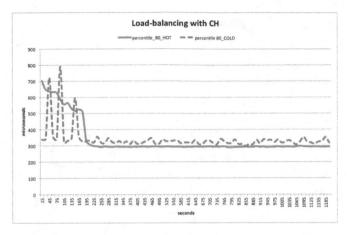

Fig. 3. Evolution of 80th-percentile of key-value pair retrieval latency when load-balacing with dynamic consistent hashing

128GB DDR3 RAM and an 1TB SATA disk, while interconnecting via a full-bisection 10GigE network. Eight (8) of the servers are used as cache servers (memcached), one (1) server is running the persistent data store (MySQL database with 10M entries of average size 100K each) and the rest of the servers are running client access code, i.e. code that fetches key-value pairs randomly from the hierarchical data store.

Each client initially attempts to fetch a key-value pair from the cache (using libmemcached) and only in the case of a cache miss, it then fetches the requested key-value pair from the database server. To drive the system to an imbalanced state for the purpose of evaluating the efficacy and performance of NAL, a fraction of the client set requests keys following a Zipf distribution, while the rest of the clients request keys uniformly. This is a known key access pattern evident in various applications, e.g. web applications requesting a popular web page or object, batch document/chunk processing frameworks etc., and is exactly the root cause of imbalance in distributed data stores. We initially run the system with uniform key access across all clients until the system stabilizes to a constant average eviction rate (steady state) and then a fraction of the clients enter the Zipf access pattern mode. Figures 3 and 4 depict the 80th percentile of key-value retrieval latency across all clients in the system for dynamic consistent hashing and NAL respectively [1], whereby we have dissected the client set to a hot (clients using Zipf access pattern) and a cold (clients following uniform access pattern) set. By inspecting the two charts, one can easily observe the anticipated superiority of NAL over dynamic consistent hashing: a) while consistent hashing causes a latency fluctuation to the cold set of clients due to dynamic continuum rebuilding regardless of the type of client, **NAL leaves cold clients unaffected, while halving the latency of hot clients** and b) NAL manages to achieve a balanced state by almost 2x faster than consistent hashing, due to the localized nature of the balancing act, as opposed to consistent hashing convergence time, which is proportional to the number of clients.

---

[1] We start reporting results at the time Zipf distribution mode comes into effect,i.e. steady state latency is not shown

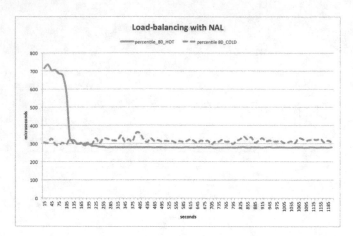

Fig. 4. Evolution of 80th-percentile of key-value pair retrieval latency when load-balacing with NAL

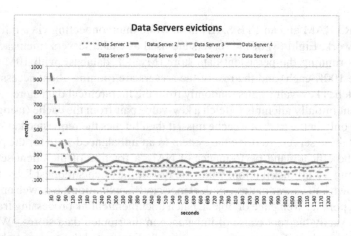

Fig. 5. Time series of eviction rates across cache servers when load-balancing with NAL

To showcase the granular adaptation brought by our load-balancing algorithm, we also depict in Figure 5 the time series of eviction rates across the eight cache servers when using NAL. We observe that the algorithm reduces initially the eviction rate of the most overloaded server (Data Server 2), then proceeding with the newly most overloaded server (Data Server 3) and finally maintaining a fairly balanced system by fine-tuning among all servers. We note here that throughout our evaluation, CPU load due to the NAL Controller has never exceed 1%, memory footprint was only 4.25MB and control network throughput in-and-out of the controller was always less than 4 Kbytes/s.

6   Conclusions

This paper presented a novel scheme that facilitates scalable, fast and fine-granular load-balancing in distributed key-value data management systems. Leveraging on the ability of modern servers and operating systems to alias network interfaces, we disconnect key lookup from actual key-value pair location and thus cancel the need for dynamically updating the location of a key, whenever the key-value pair location changes. We have presented a comprehensive architecture that in turn we prototyped in our lab datacenter, showing through experimentation that our approach achieves equal efficacy to state-of-the-art, while being 2x faster for the setup size tested. In larger setups, we expect the convergence gain of our approach to be proportional to cache system size, when compared to competitive approaches.

References

1. Nishtala, R., Fugal, H., Grimm, S., Kwiatkowski, M., Lee, H., Li, H.C., McElroy, R., Paleczny, M., Peek, D., Saab, P., et al.: Scaling memcache at facebook. In: Proceedings of the 10th USENIX Conference on Networked Systems Design and Implementation, pp. 385–398. USENIX Association (2013)
2. Facebook Note: Scaling memcached in facebook (2012), https://www.facebook.com/note.php?note_id=39391378919
3. Adamic, L.A., Huberman, B.A.: Zipfs law and the internet. Glottometrics 3, 143–150 (2002)
4. Fitzpatrick, B.: Distributed caching with memcached. Linux J. 2004, 5 (2004)
5. Redis: Redis website (2014), http://redis.io/
6. Shvachko, K., Kuang, H., Radia, S., Chansler, R.: The hadoop distributed file system. In: Proceedings of the 2010 IEEE 26th Symposium on Mass Storage Systems and Technologies, MSST 2010, pp. 1–10. IEEE Computer Society, Washington, DC (2010)
7. Stoica, I., Morris, R., Karger, D., Kaashoek, M.F., Balakrishnan, H.: Chord: A scalable peer-to-peer lookup service for internet applications. SIGCOMM Comput. Commun. Rev. 31, 149–160 (2001)
8. Karger, D., Sherman, A., Berkheimer, A., Bogstad, B., Dhanidina, R., Iwamoto, K., Kim, B., Matkins, L., Yerushalmi, Y.: Web caching with consistent hashing. Computer Networks 31, 1203–1213 (1999)
9. Chang, K., Loh, G.H., Thottethodi, M., Eckert, Y., Connor, M.O., Subramanian, L., Mutlu, O.: Enabling efficient dynamic resizing of large dram caches via a hardware consistent hashing mechanism. Technical Report 2013-001, Electrical and Computer Engineering Department,Carnegie Mellon University (2013)
10. Libmemcached: Libmemcached website (2014), http://libmemcached.org

Virtual Machine Consolidation in Cloud Data Centers Using ACO Metaheuristic

Md Hasanul Ferdaus[1], Manzur Murshed[2],
Rodrigo N. Calheiros[3], and Rajkumar Buyya[3]

[1] Faculty of Information Technology, Monash University,
Churchill Vic 3842, Australia
[2] School of Information Technology, Faculty of Science,
Federation University Australia, Churchill Vic 3842, Australia
[3] Department of Computing and Information Systems,
The University of Melbourne, Australia

Abstract. In this paper, we propose the AVVMC VM consolidation scheme that focuses on balanced resource utilization of servers across different computing resources (CPU, memory, and network I/O) with the goal of minimizing power consumption and resource wastage. Since the VM consolidation problem is strictly NP-hard and computationally infeasible for large data centers, we propose adaptation and integration of the Ant Colony Optimization (ACO) metaheuristic with balanced usage of computing resources based on vector algebra. Our simulation results show that AVVMC outperforms existing methods and achieves improvement in both energy consumption and resource wastage reduction.

1   Introduction

Cloud computing, a very recent paradigm shift in IT industry, is growing rapidly with the goal of providing virtually infinite amount of computing, storage, and communication resources where customers are provisioned these resources according to their demands as a pay-per-use business model [1]. To meet the rapid growth of customer demands for computing power, cloud providers such as Amazon and Google are deploying large number of planet-scale power-hungry data centers across the world, even comprising more than 1 million servers [2]. Reports show that energy is one of the critical TCO (Total Cost of Ownership) variables in managing a data center, and servers and data equipment account for 55% of energy used by data centers [3]. Large data centers also have enormous effects on the environment: higher energy consumption consequently drive in more carbon emission. Furthermore, inefficient use is one of the key factors for the extremely high energy consumption: in traditional data centers, on average servers operate only at 10-15% of their full capacity most of the time, leading to expenses on over-provisioning of resources [4]. Since cloud promises virtually unlimited resources through elastic provisioning and absolute reliability and availability, over-provisioning of resources in cloud data centers is a common phenomenon.

F. Silva et al. (Eds.): Euro-Par 2014, LNCS 8632, pp. 306–317, 2014.

Virtualization technologies allow data centers to address such resource and energy inefficiency by placing multiple Virtual Machines (VM) in a single physical server through live VM migration techniques. Reduction of energy consumption is achieved by switching idle physical servers to lower power states (e.g., suspended) while still preserving application performance requirements.

In this paper, we propose AVVMC, a VM consolidation algorithm that focuses on balanced resource utilization of servers for different resource types. We present adaptation techniques of the popular *Ant Colony Optimization* (ACO) [5] metaheuristic with vector algebra-based multi-dimensional server resource utilization capturing method [6]. Through simulation-based evaluation, we show that AVVMC outperforms four other existing VM consolidation methods in different performance metrics.

2 Related Works

VM consolidation techniques have been very attractive to reduce energy costs and increase resource utilization in virtualized data centers. Consequently, a good amount of research works have been done in this area and depending on the modeling techniques used, different problem solving techniques are proposed. Most of the works that apply greedy heuristics primarily model VM consolidation as variants of the bin packing problem and propose extensions of simple greedy algorithms such as First Fit Decreasing (FFD) [7], Best Fit [6], Best Fit Decreasing [8], and so on [9, 10]. However, as VM consolidation is a NP-hard problem, greedy approaches are not guaranteed to generate near optimal solutions. Moreover, most of the approaches use mean estimators that fail to capture the multi-dimensional aspect of server resource utilization [6].

Using constraint programming (CP) model, Van et al. [11] proposed VM provisioning and placement techniques to achieve high VM packing efficiency in cloud data centers. Entropy [12] is a server consolidation manager proposed for clusters with the goal of minimizing the number of active servers and VM migration overhead. However, by the use of CP the proposed frameworks effectively restrict the domain of the total number of servers and VMs in data center, and thus limit the search space.

Recently, ACO metaheuristics have successfully been used to address 1-dimensional bin packing problem and VM consolidation. Levine et al. [13] first proposed an ACO-based solution for bin packing problem combined with a local search algorithm. Later, Brugger et al. [14] used a later version of the ACO metaheuristic that demonstrated superior performance over genetic algorithm for large problem instances. Feller et al. [15] used another version of ACO to address VM consolidation and has shown better results than FFD. However, the evaluation is shown by varying only the number of cores demanded by VMs while keeping other resource demands unchanged and as a result the evaluation is simplified to one-dimensional resource. Another recent work [16] proposed a multi-objective ACO algorithm to reduce resource wastage and power consumption in cloud data centers. This work considers two types of resources (i.e.

CPU and memory) and demonstrates performance improvement over genetic and other ACO-based algorithms.

3   Virtual Machine Consolidation

Most of the popular cloud providers offer different categories of VMs with specification for each type of resource. These VM instances differ in their individual resource capacity: some instances are larger than others, whereas some instances have relatively higher capacity of one type of resource compared to other resources. Moreover, cloud VM instances host various types of applications and active VMs exhibit dynamic resource demands in run-time that can be captured and used to perform workload prediction and estimation [17]. Because of the above properties of VM instances and dynamic workloads, complementary resource demands across difference resource dimensions are common in cloud data centers [6]. Furthermore, as clouds offer an on-demand pay-as-you-go business model, customers can demand for creation and termination of any number of VMs according to their requirements. As a result, VMs are created and terminated in the cloud data centers dynamically, which causes resource fragmentation in the servers, and thus leads to degradation in server resource utilization. VM consolidation is a tool to address the above issues in virtualized data centers that tries to pack the active VMs in the minimum number of physical servers considering multi-dimensional resource demands with the goal of energy saving and maximization of server resource utilization.

3.1   Modeling VM Consolidation as Multi-dimensional Vector Packing Problem

Multi-dimensional Vector Packing Problem (mDVPP) is a NP-hard combinatorial optimization problem where a number of items have to be packed into the minimum number of bins provided that bins capacities are not violated [18]. We model the physical machines (PMs) as bins and the VMs as items to pack into the bins. Let P denotes the set of n PMs and V denotes the set of m VMs in the data center. The set of d types of resources available in the PMs is represented by R. Each PM P_i ($P_i \in P$) has a d-dimensional *Resource Capacity Vector* (RCV) $C_i = \langle C_i^1, \ldots, C_i^k, \ldots, C_i^d \rangle$, where C_i^k denotes the total capacity of resource R_k of PM P_i. Similarly, each VM V_j ($V_j \in V$) is represented by its d-dimensional *Resource Demand Vector* (RDV) $D_j = \langle D_j^1, \ldots, D_j^k, \ldots, D_j^d \rangle$, where D_j^k denotes the demand of resource R_k of VM V_j. The *Resource Utilization Vector* (RUV) $U_i = \langle U_i^1, \ldots, U_i^k, \ldots, U_i^d \rangle$ of PM P_i is computed as the sum of the RDVs of the hosted VMs:

$$U_i^k = \sum D_j^k \text{ for } \forall x_{i,j} = 1 \tag{1}$$

where x is the *Placement Matrix* that models the VM-to-PM placements and is defined as follows:

$$x_{i,j} = \begin{cases} 1 & \text{if } V_j \text{ is placed in } P_i \\ 0 & \text{otherwise} \end{cases} \tag{2}$$

We also introduce the *PM Allocation Vector* y, where each element y_i equals 1 if PM P_i is hosting at least 1 VM, or 0 otherwise:

$$y_i = \begin{cases} 1 & \text{if } \sum_{j=1}^{m} x_{i,j} \geq 1 \\ 0 & \text{otherwise} \end{cases} \tag{3}$$

The goal of the AVVMC VM consolidation algorithm is to place the VMs in the available PMs in such a way that: 1) resource utilization of active PMs is maximized across all dimensions and 2) power consumption of active PMs is minimized. Since available models for server power consumption primarily focus on CPU utilization [19], any placement decision that results in lesser number of active PMs compared to others have higher resource utilization across all dimensions and lesser energy consumption. So, we formulate the objective function f as a single minimization function on y:

$$min f(y) = \sum_{i=0}^{n} y_i \tag{4}$$

Finally, the PM resource capacity constraint (i.e. for each resource type, demands D^k of hosted VMs not to exceed host PM's resource capacity C^k) is expressed as follows:

$$\sum_{j=1}^{m} D_j^k x_{i,j} \leq C_i^k, \forall i \in \{1, \ldots, n\}, \forall k \in \{1, \ldots, d\} \tag{5}$$

And the following ensures that each VM is assigned to at most one PM:

$$\sum_{i=1}^{n} x_{i,j} \leq 1, \forall j \in \{1, \ldots, m\} \tag{6}$$

3.2   Modeling Multi-dimensional Resource Utilization Based on Vector Algebra

When placing VMs in a PM, capturing the measure of overall resource utilization for multiple resource types is one of the most important factors for any server consolidation algorithm: saturation of only one resource type can lead to no further improvement in utilization while leaving other types of resource underutilized. In order to capture both balanced and overall resource utilization, we augment and integrate the vector algebra-based complementary resource utilization capturing technique [6] in our ACO-based solution. Our model considers CPU, memory, and network I/O as relevant server resources in the context of VM consolidation. We consider storage resource is provided on-demand through SAN/NAS-based storage backbone (e.g., Amazon EBS). PM's normalized resource capacity is expressed as a unit cube (*Resource Cube*), with the three dimensions representing three types of resources. RCV and RUV represent the total capacity and current resource utilization of PM, respectively. To capture the degree of imbalance in current resource utilization of a PM, the *Resource Imbalance Vector* (RIV) is used which is computed as vector difference between RUV's projection on RCV and RUV itself. Given $RUV = C\hat{i} + M\hat{j} + I\hat{k}$ of a PM after placing a VM (C, M, and I are current utilization of CPU, memory, and network I/O), $RIV = (C - H)\hat{i} + (M - H)\hat{j} + (I - H)\hat{k}$, where $H = (C + M + I)/3$. When selecting VMs for placement in a PM, the VM that shortens the magnitude of RIV most is the VM that mostly balances the resource utilization of the PM across different dimensions. The magnitude of RIV is given by the following:

$$magRIV = \sqrt{(C - H)^2 + (M - H)^2 + (I - H)^2} \tag{7}$$

We use *magRIV* to define the heuristic information for the proposed AVVMC algorithm along with the overall resource utilization of PM (Eq. 13).

3.3   Modeling Resource Utilization and Wastage

The overall resource utilization of PM p is modeled as the summation of the normalized resource utilization U_p^r of each individual resource $r \in R$ (Eq. 1): $Utilization_p = \sum_{r \in R} U_p^r$, where $R = \{CPU, MEM, IO\}$. Similarly, resource wastage is modeled as the summation of the remaining resources (normalized) of each individual resource:

$$Wastage_p = \sum_{r \in R}(1 - U_p^r) \tag{8}$$

3.4   Modeling Power Consumption

Power consumption of servers is dominated by their CPU and can be expressed as a linear expression of CPU utilization [19]. So, we model the energy drawn by a PM p as a linear function of its CPU utilization $U_p^{CPU} \in [0, 1]$:

$$E(p) = \begin{cases} E_{idle} + (E_{full} - E_{idle}) \times U_p^{CPU} & \text{if } U_p^{CPU} > 0 \\ 0 & \text{otherwise} \end{cases} \tag{9}$$

where E_{full} and E_{idle} are the average energy drawn when a PM is fully utilized (i.e. 100% CPU busy) and idle, respectively. Due to the non-proportional power usage (i.e. high idle power) of physical servers, we consider turning off or suspending idle servers after the VM placement. Therefore, the estimate of the total energy consumed by a VM placement decision x is computed as follows:

$$E(x) = \sum_{p=1}^{n} E(p) \tag{10}$$

4   Proposed Solution

4.1   Adaptation of ACO Metaheuristic for VM Consolidation

ACO metaheuristics are computational methods that take inspiration from the foraging behavior of some ant species [5]. In ACO, a number of artificial ants build solutions to the considered optimization problem by choosing feasible solution components and exchanging information on the quality of these solutions via pheromone. In the proposed AVVMC algorithm, we adapt *Ant Colony System* (ACS) [20], a later version of ACO and consider each VM-to-PM assignment as a solution component. Pheromone levels are associated to all VM-to-PM assignments representing the desirability of assigning a VM to a PM (Eq. 11 and Eq. 18) and heuristic values are computed dynamically for each VM-to-PM assignment representing the favorability of assigning a VM to a PM in terms of both overall and balanced resource utilization of the PM (Eq. 13).

4.2   AVVMC Algorithm

The AVVMC algorithm pseudocode is shown in Algorithm 1. Pheromone levels are implemented using a $n \times m$ matrix τ. Each ant starts with an empty solution, a set of PMs, and a randomly shuffled set of VMs [line 6-12]. Inside the while loop, an ant is chosen at random and is allowed to choose a VM to assign next to its current PM among all the feasible VMs (Eq. 16) using a probabilistic decision rule (Eq. 15) [line 11-22]. If the current PM is fully utilized or there are no feasible VMs left to assign to the PM, a new empty PM is taken to fill in [line 14-16].

When all the ants have finished building their solutions, all the solutions in the current cycle are compared to the so far found *global-best-solution* (GBS) against their achieved objective function values f (Eq. 4). The solution with minimum value of f is chosen as the current GBS [line 23-28]. The pheromone reinforcement amount is computed based on (Eq. 19) and the pheromone levels of each VM-PM pair is updated to simulate the pheromone evaporation and deposition according to (Eq. 18) [line 29-34]. The algorithm reinforces the pheromone values only on the VM-PM pairs that belong to the GBS. Afterwards, the whole process of searching new solutions repeats. The algorithm terminates when no further improvement in the solution quality is observed for the last $nCycleTerm$ cycles [line 35]. Different parts of the algorithm are formally defined below.

Definition of Pheromone and Initial Pheromone Amount. At the beginning of any ACO algorithm, ants start with a fixed amount of initial pheromone for each VM-PM solution component. Following the approach used in the original ACS algorithm [20], we use the measure of quality of the solution produced by a reference baseline algorithm (FFD heuristic based on L_1 norm mean estimator) to compute the initial amount of pheromone:

$$\tau_0 := PE_{FFDL1Norm} \tag{11}$$

Algorithm 1. The AVVMC Algorithm.

1: Input: Set of PMs P and their RCV C_i, set of VMs V and their RDV D_j, set of ants $antSet$.
   Set of parameters $\{nAnts, nCycleTerm, \beta, \omega, \delta, q_0\}$
2: Output: Global-best-solution GBS
3: Initialize parameters, set pheromone value for each VM-PM pair $(\tau_{v,p})$ to τ_0, $GBS :=$
   $\emptyset, nCycle := 0$
4: **repeat**
5:   **for all** $ant \in antSet$ **do**
6:     $ant.solution := \emptyset; ant.pmList := P$
7:     $ant.p := 1; ant.vmList := V$
8:     Shuffle $ant.vmList$
9:   **end for**
10:   $antList := antSet; nCycle := nCycle + 1$
11:   **while** $antList \neq \emptyset$ **do**
12:     pick an ant at random from $antList$
13:     **if** $ant.vmList \neq \emptyset$ **then**
14:       **if** $FV_{ant}(ant.p) = \emptyset$ **then**
15:         $ant.p := ant.p + 1$
16:       **end if**
17:       Choose a VM v from $FV_{ant}(ant.p)$ accord. to Eq. 15
18:       $ant.solution.x_{p,v} := 1; ant.vmList.remove(v)$
19:     **else**
20:       $ant.solution.f := p; antList.remove(ant)$
21:     **end if**
22:   **end while**
23:   **for all** $ant \in antSet$ **do**
24:     **if** $ant.solution.f < GBS.f$ **then**
25:       $GBS := ant.solution$
26:       $nCycle := 0$
27:     **end if**
28:   **end for**
29:   Compute $\Delta\tau$
30:   **for all** $p \in P$ **do**
31:     **for all** $v \in V$ **do**
32:       $\tau_{v,p} := (1 - \delta) \times \tau_{v,p} + \delta \times \Delta\tau_{v,p}$
33:     **end for**
34:   **end for**
35: **until** $nCycle = nCycleTerm$

where $PE_{FFDL1Norm}$ is the *Packing Efficiency* of the solution produced by the FFD heuristic. The PE of any solution sol produced by an algorithm is given by:

$$PE_{sol} = \frac{nVM}{nActivePM} \tag{12}$$

Definition of Heuristic Information. During the solution building process, the heuristic value $\eta_{v,p}$ represents a measure of benefit of selecting a solution component $v - p$. As the goal of AVVMC is to reduce the number of active PMs by packing VMs in a balanced way, we define the heuristic value favoring both balanced resource utilization in all dimensions and higher overall resource utilization:

$$\eta_{v,p} = \omega \times |log_{10}magRIV_p(v)| + (1 - \omega) \times Utilization_p(v) \tag{13}$$

where $magRIV_p(v)$ is the magnitude of RIV of PM p after assigning VM v to it (Eq. 7). Logarithm of $magRIV_p(v)$ is taken to give higher heuristic values to the v-p pairs that result in smaller magnitudes of RIV. $Utilization_p(v)$ is the overall resource utilization of PM p if VM v is assigned to it:

$$Utilization_p(v) = \sum_{r \in R} (U_p^r + D_v^r) \qquad (14)$$

And ω is a parameter that trades off the relative importance of balanced versus overall resource utilization as per our definition.

It can be shown that $magRIV$ is in the interval $[0.0, 0.82]$. Since logarithm of zero is undefined, we used the range $[0.001, 0.82]$ in the evaluation and thus $|log_{10} magRIV|$ results in the range $[0.086, 3.0]$ which is compatible to $Utilization_p$ in terms of metric that results in the interval $[0.0, 3.0]$.

Pseudo-random Proportional Rule. When constructing a solution, an ant k selects a VM s to be assigned to PM p with the following *pseudo-random proportional rule* [20]:

$$s = \begin{cases} argmax_{v \in FV_k(p)} \{\tau_{v,p} \times [\eta_{v,p}]^\beta\} & \text{if } q \le q_0 \\ S & \text{otherwise} \end{cases} \qquad (15)$$

where q is a random number uniformly distributed in $[0, 1]$, q_0 is a parameter in interval $[0, 1]$, $\tau_{v,p}$ is the current pheromone value associated with the v-p VM-PM pair (Eq. 18), and β is a non-negative parameter that determines the relative importance of pheromone amount versus heuristic value in the decision rule. $FV_k(p)$ defines the list of feasible VMs for ant k to assign to PM p:

$$FV_k(p) = \left\{ v \mid \sum_{p=1}^{n} x_{p,v} = 0 \bigwedge U_p^r + D_v^r \le C_p^r \text{ for } \forall_r \in R \right\} \qquad (16)$$

When $q \le q_0$, then the v-p pair resulting highest $\tau_{v,p} \times [\eta_{v,p}]^\beta$ value is chosen as the solution component (exploitation), otherwise a VM v is chosen with probability $P_k(v, p)$ using the following random-proportional rule (exploration):

$$P_k(v, p) = \begin{cases} \dfrac{\tau_{v,p} \times [\eta_{v,p}]^\beta}{\sum_{u \in FV_k(p)} \tau_{v,p} \times [\eta_{v,p}]^\beta} & \text{if } v \in FV_k(p) \\ 0 & \text{otherwise} \end{cases} \qquad (17)$$

Global Pheromone Update. In order to favor the solution components of the GBS for subsequent iterations and to simulate pheromone evaporation, the global update rule is applied on the pheromone values of each $v-p$ pair according to the following equation:

$$\tau_{v,p} := (1 - \delta) \times \tau_{v,p} + \delta \times \Delta\tau_{v,p} \qquad (18)$$

where δ is the global pheromone decay parameter $(0 < \delta < 1)$ and $\Delta\tau_{v,p}$ is the pheromone reinforcement applied to each $v-p$ pairs and is computed as follows:

$$\Delta\tau_{v,p} = \begin{cases} PE_{GBS} & \text{if } v - p \in GBS \\ 0 & \text{otherwise} \end{cases} \qquad (19)$$

5   Performance Evaluation

Because of the lack of access to large scale testbeds or real cloud infrastructures and ease of reproducibility, we resorted to simulation-based evaluation to compare the performance of the proposed AVVMC to the following existing works in literature: 1) an adapted version of Max-Min Ant System (MMAS) metaheuristic for VM consolidation (MMVMC) [15], 2) a greedy algorithm (VectorGreedy) [6] for solving consolidation that uses vector algebra for mean estimation of multi-dimensional resources, 3) a modified version of the FFD algorithm (FFD-Volume) [7] that uses volume-based mean estimator, and 4) another modified FFD algorithm (FFD-L1Norm) based on L_1 norm mean estimator.

The simulated data center consists of a cluster of homogeneous PMs and VM resource demand for each resource type is expressed in percentage of total resource capacity of PM. We used reference-based VM resource demands: $Ref = z\%$ means each randomly generated VM resource demand D^r falls in the interval $[0, 2z]$ for $r \in \{CPU, MEM, IO\}$. Considering the fact that clouds deploy high-end servers and try to host as many VMs as possible in each active server to increase resource utilization, we conducted our simulation for the scenarios where expected average PE would be more than 4, otherwise there would not be much scope for consolidation and benefit of using specialized algorithms. Therefore, we used reference values of $Ref = 10\%, 15\%, 20\%$, and 25% with their corresponding expected average PE of 10, 6.7, 5, and 4. The simulation is conducted through 10 independent simulation runs and each run was repeated for 100 times and finally, the results are generated after taking their average.

The optimal values of the parameters used in AVVMC are measured through rigorous parameter sensitivity analysis in the preliminary phases of the experiment and are set as follows: $nAnts = 5, nCycleTerm = 5, \beta = 2, \delta = 0.5, q_0 = 0.8$, and $\omega = 0.5$. Parameters for the other algorithms are taken as reported in the respective papers.

Table 1 summarizes performance of various algorithms for 1000 VMs in terms of 1) the number of active PMs, 2) achieved VM packing efficiency, and 3) power consumption according to the overall power consumption model (Eq. 10). For the purpose of simulation, we set E_{idle} and E_{full} to 162 watts and 215 watts, respectively as used by Gao et al. [16]. Table 1 shows that for all the four reference values, AVVMC outperforms other algorithms in all the above performance metrics. It also shows that AVVMC achieves PE near the expected average values. One interesting observation from column 6 of Table 1 is that AVVMC achieves comparatively better performance over MMVMC and VectorGreedy for larger reference values (i.e. larger VM sizes), whereas it achieves comparatively better performance over FFD-based algorithms for smaller reference values (i.e. smaller VM sizes). The reason is that metaheuristic-based solutions have higher flexibility to refine the solutions for smaller reference values (i.e. when higher number of VMs can be packed in a single PM) compared to larger reference values. On the other hand, FFD-based greedy solutions achieve higher overall resource utilization and need lesser number of active PMs for larger reference values (i.e. when VMs are larger).

Table 1. Simulation results across various performance metrics

Ref	Algorithm	# Active PM	Achieved PE	Power Con. (Watt)	% Imp. (Power)
10%	AVVMC	100	10.00	21280.03	
	MMVMC	103	9.71	21759.55	2.20
	VectorGreedy	108	9.26	22582.51	5.77
	FFDL1Norm	117	8.55	23927.11	11.06
	FFDVolume	118	8.47	24165.25	11.94
15%	AVVMC	156	6.41	33114.59	
	MMVMC	163	6.13	34331.21	3.54
	VectorGreedy	167	5.99	34990.55	5.36
	FFDL1Norm	178	5.62	36824.39	10.07
	FFDVolume	177	5.65	36594.35	9.51
20%	AVVMC	215	4.65	45244.68	
	MMVMC	226	4.42	46945.68	3.62
	VectorGreedy	240	4.17	49225.02	8.09
	FFDL1Norm	242	4.13	49628.40	8.83
	FFDVolume	242	4.13	49677.00	8.92
25%	AVVMC	267	3.75	56325.08	
	MMVMC	286	3.50	59438.72	5.24
	VectorGreedy	310	3.23	63289.46	11.00
	FFDL1Norm	296	3.38	61008.50	7.68
	FFDVolume	296	3.38	61099.22	7.81

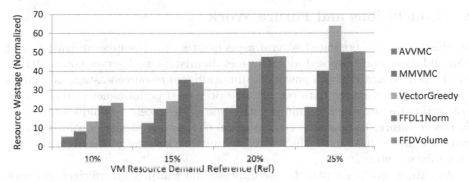

Fig. 1. Bar chart representation of total resource (normalized) wastage of AVVMC and other algorithms

Fig. 1 shows a bar chart representation of the total resource (normalized in percentage) wastage of active PMs that host 1000 VMs according to (Eq. 8) for the VM placement solutions produced by the different consolidation algorithms. The figure shows that AVVMC significantly reduces the resource wastage compared to other algorithms. This is because AVVMC tries to improve the overall resource utilization with preference to consolidate VMs with complementary resource demands in each server and thus reduces resource wastage across different resource dimensions.

In order to assess AVVMC for time complexity, simulation is conducted for larger number of VMs and the solution computation time is plotted (Fig. 2). The algorithm is written in Java language and ran on a Dell Workstation having Intel Core i5-2400 3.10 GHz CPU (4 cores), and 4 GB of RAM. It is observed that computation time increases non-linearly with the number of VMs with small gradient and for 2000 VMs, AVVMC takes around 25 seconds on average.

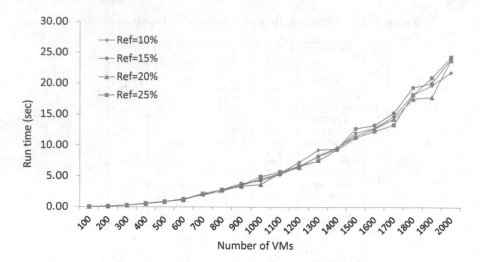

Fig. 2. Solution computation time of AVVMC for large problem instances

6   Conclusions and Future Work

In this paper, we presented several aspects of server resource utilization and consolidation, and proposed an ACO metaheuristic-based server consolidation mechanism to address both power consumption and resource wastage minimization in large virtualized data centers. We presented performance evaluation by comparing the proposed technique with some of the recent techniques proposed in the literature. We also showed evaluation of time complexity of solution computation and argued about the feasibility and effectiveness of the algorithm for cloud data centers.

As future work, we plan to incorporate mechanisms for efficient network resource utilization in cloud infrastructures during VM placement and consolidation decisions. We also expect to consider current VM assignments and reconfiguration (including VM live migrations) overheads during VM placement decision making phase. In this way, an overall VM placement framework will be designed and implemented that will be aware of both energy consumption and compute-network resource utilization.

References

1. Buyya, R., Yeo, C.S., Venugopal, S., Broberg, J., Brandic, I.: Cloud computing and emerging IT platforms: Vision, hype, and reality for delivering computing as the 5th utility. Future Generation Computer Systems 25(6), 599–616 (2009)
2. Miller, R.: Ballmer: Microsoft has 1 million servers (July 2013),
   http://www.datacenterknowledge.com/archives/2013/07/15/
   ballmer-microsoft-has-1-million-servers/
3. Perspectives, I.: Using a Total Cost of Ownership (TCO) model for your data center (October 2013), http://www.datacenterknowledge.com/archives/2013/10/
   01/using-a-total-cost-of-ownership-tco-model-for-your-data-center/

4. Barroso, L., Holzle, U.: The case for energy-proportional computing. Computer 40(12), 33–37 (2007)
5. Dorigo, M., Birattari, M., Stutzle, T.: Ant colony optimization. Computational Intelligence Magazine. IEEE 1(4), 28–39 (2006)
6. Mishra, M., Sahoo, A.: On theory of VM placement: Anomalies in existing methodologies and their mitigation using a novel vector based approach. In: 2010 IEEE International Conference on Cloud Computing (CLOUD), pp. 275–282. IEEE (2011)
7. Wood, T., Shenoy, P., Venkataramani, A., Yousif, M.: Sandpiper: Black-box and gray-box resource management for virtual machines. Computer Networks 53(17), 2923–2938 (2009)
8. Beloglazov, A., Buyya, R.: Adaptive threshold-based approach for energy-efficient consolidation of virtual machines in cloud data centers. In: Proceedings of the 8th International Workshop on Middleware for Grids, Clouds and e-Science. ACM (2010)
9. Li, X., Qian, Z., Chi, R., Zhang, B., Lu, S.: Balancing resource utilization for continuous virtual machine requests in clouds. In: 2012 Sixth International Conference on Innovative Mobile and Internet Services in Ubiquitous Computing (IMIS), pp. 266–273. IEEE (2012)
10. Li, X., Qian, Z., Lu, S., Wu, J.: Energy efficient virtual machine placement algorithm with balanced and improved resource utilization in a data center. Mathematical and Computer Modelling 58(5), 1222–1235 (2013)
11. Van, H.N., Tran, F., Menaud, J.M.: Performance and power management for cloud infrastructures. In: 2010 IEEE 3rd International Conference on Cloud Computing (CLOUD), pp. 329–336 (July 2010)
12. Hermenier, F., Lorca, X., Menaud, J.M., Muller, G., Lawall, J.: Entropy: a consolidation manager for clusters. In: Proceedings of the 2009 ACM SIGPLAN/SIGOPS international conference on Virtual execution environments, VEE 2009, pp. 41–50. ACM, New York (2009)
13. Levine, J., Ducatelle, F.: Ant colony optimization and local search for bin packing and cutting stock problems. Journal of the Operational Research Society 55(7), 705–716 (2004)
14. Brugger, B., Doerner, K.F., Hartl, R.F., Reimann, M.: Antpacking-an ant colony optimization approach for the one-dimensional bin packing problem. In: Gottlieb, J., Raidl, G.R. (eds.) EvoCOP 2004. LNCS, vol. 3004, pp. 41–50. Springer, Heidelberg (2004)
15. Feller, E., Rilling, L., Morin, C.: Energy-aware ant colony based workload placement in clouds. In: Proceedings of the 2011 IEEE/ACM 12th International Conference on Grid Computing, pp. 26–33. IEEE Computer Society (2011)
16. Gao, Y., Guan, H., Qi, Z., Hou, Y., Liu, L.: A multi-objective ant colony system algorithm for virtual machine placement in cloud computing. Journal of Computer and System Sciences (2013)
17. Wood, T., Cherkasova, L., Ozonat, K., Shenoy, P.: Predicting application resource requirements in virtual environments. HP Laboratories, Technical Report HPL-2008-122 (2008)
18. Caprara, A., Toth, P.: Lower bounds and algorithms for the 2-dimensional vector packing problem. Discrete Applied Mathematics 111(3), 231–262 (2001)
19. Fan, X., Weber, W.D., Barroso, L.A.: Power provisioning for a warehouse-sized computer. ACM SIGARCH Computer Architecture News 35(2), 13–23 (2007)
20. Dorigo, M., Gambardella, L.: Ant colony system: A cooperative learning approach to the traveling salesman problem. IEEE Transactions on Evolutionary Computation 1(1), 53–66 (1997)

Workflow Scheduling on Federated Clouds

Juan J. Durillo and Radu Prodan

University of Innsbruck, Innsbruck, Austria
`juan,radu@dps.uibk.ac.at`

Abstract. Federated Clouds, or the orchestration of multiple Cloud services for fulfilling applications' requirements, is receiving increasing attention. Despite their many advantages, federated Clouds also present some downsides since different services may reside in different geographically located areas. This paper focuses on evaluating the advantages and disadvantages, from the point of view of performance and financial costs, of using a federation of Clouds for executing scientific workflows. It evaluates a wide range of different workflow types with different requirements in terms of computation and communication (produced and consumed data), and discusses which kind of workflow applications can benefit from a Cloud federation and how.

1 Introduction

Workflows emerged as a popular paradigm used by scientists and engineers to model scientific and industrial applications. Workflow applications are usually executed on parallel and distributed systems to minimize their completion time or makespan. A challenging task here is to determine the "optimal" mapping or schedule of the workflow tasks onto the available resources that produces the shortest makespan, a well-known NP-complete problem.

Nowadays, Cloud computing is becoming attractive for companies and institutions to access to parallel and distributed resources. Despite the promise of theoretically infinite number of resources, data centers acting as Cloud providers have limited capacity to be shared among many clients. In overloaded situations, a provider infrastructure may not be large enough to accommodate all customers' requests, which negatively impacts its popularity. To mitigate this problem, several providers limit the maximum number of instances that can be simultaneously used by a single user, for example to 20 by *Amazon EC2*. In response to this, *federated Clouds* [12] aim to coordinate (federate) the Cloud infrastructure of several institutions, offering access to their services and, therefore, significantly increasing the resources available to an application. A Cloud federation can be viewed as a marketplace where providers sell and buy on-demand computational capacity and offer it transparently to their customers. In this case, if a single provider does not have enough resources for accommodating a customer request, it can buy the missing capacity from the marketplace.

Federated Clouds bring new opportunities when using commercial Clouds, as different providers may offer resources with different performance and pricing

F. Silva et al. (Eds.): Euro-Par 2014, LNCS 8632, pp. 318–329, 2014.

models. In such situations, a customer may be interested in scheduling low-priority tasks on the slow resources offered by a cheap provider, and high-priority critical tasks on the expensive fast resources offered by a high-performance provider. Scheduling a workflow application becomes therefore a *multi-objective optimisation* problem with at least two in-conflict criteria, *makespan* and *financial cost*, to which a single solution does not exist. In fact, the solution to this kind of problems consists of a set of tradeoff solutions between the conflicting criteria, known as *Pareto front*. Moreover, federated Clouds pose additional drawbacks limiting the range of applications that can benefit from them. For example, resources belonging to different providers may be located in different areas connected via best-effort Internet, which is particularly problematic in the context of data-intensive applications. In addition, companies may impose restrictions over sensitive data that must stay within the frontiers of a single institution, limiting optimisation opportunities. In this situations, it is not clear whether federated Clouds are an appealing alternative for workflow applications.

In this paper we investigate the potential of a federation of Clouds for multi-criteria workflow scheduling. We tackle the problem from the point of view of a broker coordinating the services of two federated Clouds with different performance and price models: *Amazon EC2* and *GoGrid* [1]. We analyse how that federation can be used to schedule workflow applications with different shapes (degree of parallelism), different number of activities, and different requirements in terms of computation and communication. The contributions of this paper are threefold: (1) we describe the multi-objective workflow scheduling problem on federated Clouds using the Multi-Objective Heterogeneous Earliest Finish Time (MOHEFT) algorithm; (2) we analyse whether federated Clouds improve the execution of workflow application; and (3) we analyse of the tradeoff between the workflow execution and its financial cost on federated Clouds.

The rest of the manuscript is organized as follows. Next section contains related work. In Section 3 we describe our architecture and research problem, followed by the Cloud-aware MOHEFT scheduling algorithm in Section 4. Sections 5 and 6 describe the experimental setup and the obtained results. Finally, Section 7 contains the conclusions and the future work.

2 Related Work

Previous attempts to multi-objective workflow scheduling consisted in transforming the problem into a mono-objective optimization one using user preferences [3,9,11], imposing constraints over the optimisation criteria [16,8], or optimising single objectives individually [4]. More recently, several approaches computing the whole set of tradeoff solutions emerged grouped in two main lines: (1) genetic algorithms-based techniques for optimizing makespan and cost [23], makespan and energy consumption [13], or makespan, cost and reliability [18]; and (2) list-based heuristics for optimizing makespan and cost or makespan [5,6]

---

[1] http://www.gogrid.com/products/cloud-hosting

and energy consumption [7]. Only few of these works targeted workflow scheduling on Clouds and none of them considers Cloud federations.

While most related research deals with the placement of Virtual Machines (VM) onto Physical Machines (PM) [14,15,20,21], scheduling of tasks onto VMs has been scarcely studied on the context of a Cloud federation. In this sense, [10] analyses and proposes several heuristics for task scheduling onto resources belonging to the same provider but geographically located in different areas. Though not purely a federation of Clouds, the authors address a similar problem to the one arising in a federated system. The authors in [17] present a semantic architecture to build schedulers for federated Cloud with emphasis on the system architecture with no special focus to the optimality of the scheduler. None of these approaches consider a purely multi-objective formulation of the problem.

3   Model

We describe in this section the architecture, workflow, and resource model underneath our approach, together with the makespan and financial cost objectives.

3.1   Architecture

Fig. 1 depicts our system architecture whose main component is the broker coordinating resources belonging to different Cloud providers. This broker receives a workflow application as input and is in charge of computing several schedule solutions trading off makespan and financial cost. Once these tradeoff solutions are computed, it selects a schedule out of them, usually user-guided and biased by external conditions. Solution selection mechanisms are out of the scope of this paper, which focuses on computing an optimal and representative set of tradeoff solutions. Once a solution has been selected, the broker is in charge of resource provisioning and deploying the workflow activities for execution. In order to compute the tradeoff schedules, the broker needs to know the workflow, the available resource types, and how to compute the makespan and financial cost entailed by different schedules.

3.2   Workflow Model

We model a *workflow* as a directed acyclic graph: $W = (A, D)$ consisting of n activities $A = \bigcup_{i=1}^{n} \{A_i\}$, interconnected through control flow and data flow dependencies; $D = \{(A_i, A_j, Data_{ij}) \mid (A_i, A_j) \in A \times A\}$, where $Data_{ij}$ represents the size of the data which needs to be transferred from activity A_i to activity A_j. We use $pred(A_i) = \{A_k \mid (A_k, A_i, Data_{ki}) \in D\}$ to denote the *predecessor* set of activity A_i, (i.e. activities to be completed before starting A_i). We assume that the computational workload of every activity A_i is known and is given by the number of machine instructions to be executed.

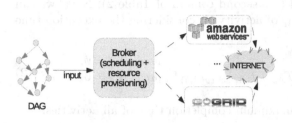

Instance	Speed [GFLOPS]	Price [$/h]	GFLOPS/ $
Amazon EC2 Instances			
m1.small	2.0	0.1	19.6
m1.large	7.1	0.4	17.9
m1.xlarge	11.4	0.8	14.2
c1.medium	3.9	0.2	19.6
c1.xlarge	50.0	0.8	62.5
GoGrid Instances			
GG.large	8.8	0.16	46.4
GG.xlarge	28.1	0.76	37.0

Fig. 1. System architecture

Fig. 2. EC2 and GoGrid performance and prices

3.3   Resource Model

The broker assumes that our hardware platform consists of a set of m *heterogeneous resources* $R = \cup_{j=1}^{m} R_j$, which can be of any type as our case studies in this paper Amazon EC2 and GoGrid. In particular, we consider in this paper the five Amazon EC2 resources and the two GoGrid instances analysed in [2] and summarized in Table 2. For a given resource R_j of a certain type, we know its average performance measured in GFLOPs and its price per hour of computation. The final price of a schedule is based the resources' usage and the data stored and transferred. This price depends on four components: (1) price per hours of resource usage PE_{R_i}, (2) price per MB of data storage PS_{R_i}, (3) price per MB of data received PI_{R_i}, and (4) price per MB of data sent PO_{R_i}. The prices of these components depend on the Cloud provider. As mentioned before, Cloud providers may impose some constraints too. While in theory a user can access an infinite pool of resources, most providers restrict this number to a maximum of N instances that can be simultaneously acquired. These N resources can be of any type and do not have to be kept invariant during execution. We use $sched(A_i)$ to denote the resource on which the task A_i is *scheduled* for execution.

3.4   Makespan

To compute the makespan, it is necessary to define the *execution time* $t_{(A_i,R_j)}$ of an activity A_i on a resource $R_j = sched(A_i)$ as the sum of the time required for transferring the biggest input data from any $A_p \in pred(A_p)$ and the time required to execute A_i on R_j:

$$t_{(A_i,R_j)} = \max_{A_p \in pred(A_i)} \left\{ \frac{Data_{pi}}{b_{pj}} \right\} + \frac{workload(A_i)}{s_j}, \tag{1}$$

where $Data_{pi}$ is the size of the data to be transferred between A_p and A_i, b_{pj} is the bandwidth between the resource where task A_p was executed and the resource R_j (corresponding to the bandwidth of the local network in case both resources belong to the same provider, or to the Internet connection in case they belong to different providers), $workload(A_i)$ represents the length of the task A_i in machine instructions, and s_j the speed of the resource R_j in number of machine instructions per second (see second column of Table 2). Next, we can compute the *completion time* T_{A_i} of activity A_i considering the execution time of itself and its predecessors:

$$T_{A_i} = \begin{cases} t_{(A_i, sched(A_i))}, & pred\,(A_i) = \emptyset; \\ \max\limits_{A_p \in pred(A_i)} \left\{ T_{A_p} + t_{(A_i, sched(A_i))} \right\}, & pred\,(A_i) \neq \emptyset. \end{cases} \quad (2)$$

We define the *makespan* as the maximum completion time of all activities:

$$T_W = \max_{i \in [1,n]} \left\{ T_{(A_i, sched(A_i))} \right\}. \quad (3)$$

3.5   Financial Cost

The *financial cost* for executing an activity depends on two terms: the computation cost $C^{(comp)}$ and the cost of data transfer and storage $C^{(data)}$. We assume that all providers charge the customers using an hourly based model (i.e. per hour of computation). We define $C^{(data)}_{(A_i, R_j)}$ as the cost of the data transfers $In(A_i)$ and $Out\,(A_i)$ and storage $Data\,(A_i)$ resulting from executing activity A_i on resource R_j:

$$C^{(data)}_{(A_i, R_j)} = Data\,(A_i) \cdot t_{(A_i, R_j)} \cdot PS_{R_i} + In(A_i) \cdot PI_{R_i} + Out\,(A_i) \cdot PO_{R_i}, \quad (4)$$

In defining the cost $C^{(comp)}_{R_j}$ of using a resource R_j, we assume that for each task A_i executed on R_j we record two timestamps: $t^{(start)}_{A_i}$ when the activity starts and $t^{(end)}_{A_i}$ when the activity finishes its execution. We consider without loss of generality that the times for transferring the input $In\,(A_i)$ and the output data $Out\,(A_i)$ are included in the interval between $t^{(start)}_{A_i}$ and $t^{(end)}_{A_i}$.

Let us consider now the set of all p activities scheduled on resource R_j denoted as $\{J_1, \ldots, J_p\}$, where $p < n$ and $sched\,(J_i) = R_j, i \in [1,p]$, sorted based on their start timestamp: $t^{(start)}_{J_1} < \ldots < t^{(start)}_{J_p}$. Based on this ordering, we cluster these activities in $q \leq p$ different *groups* $G^{(j)}_k$, $1 \leq k \leq q$. All activities in one group are executed consecutively without releasing the resource. After the activity with the largest start timestamp in the group completes, the resource is released.

We construct the first group $G^{(j)}_1 = \{J_1, \ldots, J_r\}, r \leq p$ following three rules:

1. The first activity J_1 belongs to the first group: $J_1 \in G^{(j)}_1$;
2. Every activity $J_i \in G^{(j)}_1, 2 \leq i \leq r$, starts before the current leased hour expires and before the machine is released:

$$t^{(start)}_{J_i} < t^{(start)}_{J_1} + \left\lceil \frac{t^{(end)}_{J_{i-1}} - t^{(start)}_{J_1}}{3600} \right\rceil \cdot 3600. \quad (5)$$

We convert the total time of using a resource to hours by dividing it by 3600 and using the ceiling operator. This equation guarantees a contiguous resource allocation of activities within one hour slot;

3. The next activity not part of the first group $J_{r+1} \notin G_1^{(j)}, r + 1 \leq p$, starts after the last hour of computation elapses and the resource is released:

$$t_{J_1}^{(start)} + \left\lceil \frac{t_{J_r}^{(end)} - t_{J_1}^{(start)}}{3600} \right\rceil \cdot 3600 < t_{J_{r+1}}^{(start)}. \tag{6}$$

Successive groups are built until the last activity J_p has been assigned to one group. The second group $G_2^{(j)}$ is constructed in the same way starting from J_{r+1} instead of J_1, and similarly for the rest of the groups. Once all groups have been created, we define the cost $C_{R_j}^{(comp)}$ of using the resource R_j as the number of hours required for executing all groups multiplied by the cost per hour:

$$C_{R_j}^{(comp)} = PE_{R_j} \cdot \sum_{k=1}^{q} \left\lceil \frac{\sum_{A_i \in G_{R_j}^{(k)}} t_{(A_i, R_j)}}{3600} \right\rceil. \tag{7}$$

The cost of executing the workflow $W = (A, D)$ is the sum of the cost of all m the used resources and the cost for transferring and storing the data:

$$C_W = \sum_{j=1}^{m} C_{R_j}^{(comp)} + \sum_{(A_i, A_j, Data_{ij}) \in D} C_{(A_i, R_j)}^{(data)}. \tag{8}$$

4   Cloud-Aware MOHEFT Algorithm

We employ a method for computing the tradeoff solutions as an extension of the MOHEFT [6] algorithm customised for dealing with the characteristics of federated Cloud environments. MOHEFT is an instance of a class of multi-objective greedy algorithms as defined in [5], based on extending the HEFT [19] algorithm to consider multiple simultaneous criteria. MOHEFT, summarized in Algorithm 1, requires the instance types offered by all Cloud providers, the maximum number of resources that can be simultaneously rented from each provider N, and the desired number of tradeoff solutions K.

Firstly, MOHEFT ranks the tasks in the workflow using the B-rank metric and creates a set S of K empty schedules (lines 2 and 3). Afterwards, it iterates over the list of tasks and extends every solution in S by mapping the next task onto different possible instances. For every task, the algorithm builds a list of possible resources where the task can be executed, either by reusing an instance already assigned to a previous task, or by acquiring a new instance (lines 10 and 14, respectively). This list is used for building new schedules that also consider the current task. The newly produced schedules are stored in a temporary set S', initially empty. After each iteration, S' replaces S before the next task in the list is considered. Obviously, this strategy results in an exhaustive search if we do not include any restrictions. To avoid this, MOHEFT saves only the best K tradeoff solutions from the temporary set S' to the set S, selected based on the objective functions and the diversity of the set, i.e., how different these

---

Algorithm 1. Cloud-aware MOHEFT algorithm.

Require: $W = (A, D), A = \bigcup_{i=1}^{n} A_i$ ▷ Workflow application
Require: $N = (N_1, ..., N_c)$ ▷ Maximum instances allowed in each of the c Cloud providers
Require: $I = \bigcup_{i=1}^{m} I_i$ ▷ Different instance types offered by all c Cloud providers
Require: K ▷ Desired number of trade off solutions
Ensure: $S = \bigcup_{i=1}^{K} sched_W, sched_W = \{(A_i, sched(A_i)) | \forall A_i \in A\}$ ▷ Set of K tradeoff schedules
1: **function** MOHEFT(W, N, I, K)
2:     $Rank \leftarrow$ B-RANK(A)   ▷ Order tasks according to the B-rank
3:     **for** $k \leftarrow 1, K$ **do**   ▷ Create K empty workflow schedules
4:        $S_k \leftarrow \emptyset$
5:     **end for**
6:     **for** $i \leftarrow 1, n$ **do**   ▷ Iterate over the ordered tasks in the $Rank$ list
7:        $S' \leftarrow \emptyset$
8:        **for** $k \leftarrow 1, K$ **do**   ▷ Iterate over all tradeoff schedules
9:           $R \leftarrow \emptyset$ ▷ Build a set of possible instances for executing next task
10:           **for** $r \leftarrow 1, |S_k|$ **do**   ▷ Reuse instance where tasks in S_k are executing
11:              $(A', R') = S_{kr}$
12:              $R \leftarrow R \cup R'$
13:           **end for**
14:           **for** $r \leftarrow 1, m$ **do**   ▷ Consider a new instance of each type
15:              $R \leftarrow R \cup I_r$
16:           **end for**
17:           **for** $j \leftarrow 1, |R|$ **do**   ▷ Iterate over all resources
18:              $s \leftarrow S_k \cup (Rank_i, R_j)$ ▷ Extend all intermediate schedules
19:              **if** VIOLATIONCONSTRAINTS(s, N) **then**   ▷ Check if too many VMs from a provider
20:                 $T_s \leftarrow \infty$ ▷ Mark schedule as non-valid
21:                 $C_s \leftarrow \infty$
22:              **end if**
23:              $S' \leftarrow S' \cup \{s\}$ ▷ Add new mapping to intermediate schedules
24:           **end for**
25:        **end for**
26:        $S' \leftarrow$ SORTCROWDDIST(S', K)   ▷ Sort according to the crowding distance
27:        $S \leftarrow$ FIRST(S', K)   ▷ Choose K schedules with the highest crowding distance
28:     **end for**
29: **return** S
30: **end function**

---

solutions are (see [6]). To deal with the restriction on the maximum number of instances that can be simultaneously rented from a provider, MOHEFT discards any schedule that violates this constraint (line 19) by setting its financial costs and makespan to infinite. This way, the partial solution will be always worse (dominated) than any other schedule and will be discarded in line 26.

5 Experimental Setup

We describe in this section the workflow and resource setups used in evaluating our approach.

5.1 Workflow Applications

We consider in our evaluation two types of workflow applications: synthetically-generated and real-world.

We generated the synthetic workflows as described in [22] considering two kinds of shapes: *Type-1* workflows with many independent activities sharing one successor and one predecessor, and *Type-2* workflows where most tasks have different successors and predecessors. *Type-1* workflows represent applications which can clearly benefit from a high number of resources since many activities can be executed in parallel. In *Type-2* workflows, the number of parallel activities is lower than in the former case, hindering but not preventing the benefit of parallel execution. In both cases, we consider workflow instances with a number of activities between 100 and 1000. We generated the length of each activity using a Gaussian distribution with the execution time of around 10 seconds on an average single core instance. For both types, we considered three classes with different data requirements: *Low* where each activity produces/consumes around 10MB of data, *Medium* producing/consuming around 100MB, and *High* producing/consuming around 1GB.

The Persitence of Vision Raytracer (POV-Ray) [1] application is a free tool for creating three dimensional graphics used by scientists in biochemistry, medicine or architecture visualisation. It consists of rendering a set of images/frames, merging them, and storing the result in a file. The number of frames to merge determines the number of activities in the workflow. The volume of data consumed by this application also depends on the number of frames which have to be transferred to the merger activity after being rendered. We consider here three instances of this application rendering 512, 1024, and 4096 frames.

5.2   Resources

We carried out the experiments in a federated infrastructure with two IaaS Cloud providers: Amazon EC2 and GoGrid. We use for modelling the workflows' makespan the average performance in millions of floating point operations per second (GFLOPs) of five different instance types of Amazon EC2 and three instances of GoGrid, as reported the Iosup et al. in [2] after extensive benchmark experimentation (see Table 2). We assume that the resources of the same provider are connected using a local 1000mbps network and the different providers are connected using a 150mbps wide area network. We consider that a user can simultaneously rent 20 instances from both Amazon EC2 and GoGrid, which can be of any of the types summarized in Table 2. Although these limits can be usually extended upon request, we intend in this paper evaluate how MOHEFT can deal with the default configurations.

6   Experimental Results

In this section, we analyse the schedules computed by MOHEFT for each type of workflow when using a federation of EC2 and GoGrid Cloud and a maximum of $K = 10$ tradeoff solutions. These tradeoff solutions will be graphically depicted in Figures 3, 4, and 5, showing for each solution (numbered $0 - 9$ on the horizontal axis) the makespan and cost normalized in the interval $[0, 1]$. This normalisation is done using the maximum and minimum values within the Pareto front for both the makespan and financial cost. Therefore, a value of makespan $= 0$ after the normalisation indicates the solution with the shortest makespan

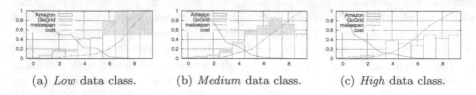

(a) *Low* data class.   (b) *Medium* data class.   (c) *High* data class.

Fig. 3. Normalized *Type-1* workflow tradeoff schedules

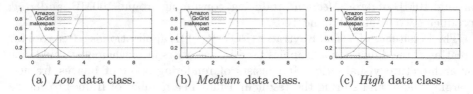

(a) *Low* data class.   (b) *Medium* data class.   (c) *High* data class.

Fig. 4. Normalized *Type-2* workflow tradeoff schedules

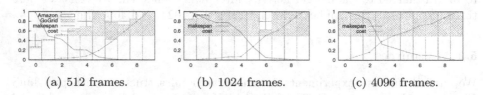

(a) 512 frames.   (b) 1024 frames.   (c) 4096 frames.

Fig. 5. Normalized POV-Ray workflow tradeoff schedules

in the Pareto front, and a value of makespan = 1 indicates the solution with the largest makespan within the Pareto front. The same is applicable to the cost. These graphs also show the percentage of instances simultaneously used from the maximum allowed by each provider. This information is showed in form of bar charts, where the height of each bar indicates the percentage normalised in the [0,0.5] interval. We use a total of 40 resources (20 from each provider) as explained before, therefore, a bar with a height of 0.5 indicates that 20 provider machines have been used. We use two different bar textures to differentiate between the two considered providers. In all the experiments of this section, graphs depict the information for workflows consisting of 1000 activities; experiments with a different number of activities have shown the same behavior but have been omitted here due to space limitations.

6.1   Type-1 Workflows

Fig. 3 summarizes the results obtained for workflows *Type-1*. We focus first our analysis on the advantages of using the Cloud federation and comment afterwards on the makespan and cost of the computed solutions. The three graphs show that the benefits of using a federation of Clouds decreases with the volume of the data managed by the application. When the data volume is low, the workflow makespan can be further decreased by considering the joined use of services from the federation. We observe this behavior in Fig. 3a, where the three tradeoff schedules with smallest makespan (labelled 7, 8, 9) uses all available machines provided by the federation (the percentage of machines used from both providers is 0.5). As long as the data volume increases, aggregating resources from different providers does not reduce the makespan, despite the fact that the number of independent activities in the workflow is high. In particular, when the data volume is medium, the percentage of machines used from the federation decreased and never receased the maximum of 40. Finally, when the data volume is high, the federated Cloud does not bring any advantage and the computed schedules only use machines of one or the other provider. Regarding the makespan and financial cost, we observe in all cases that a schedule with an overhead of less than 10% with respect to the shortest computed makespan dramatically increases the costs. For example, the difference between the makespan of the schedules labelled 6 and 9 is smaller than 5%, while the difference in financial costs are up to 80% (see Fig. 3a). A deeper analysis of the results also reveals that cheap solutions rarely consider federated resources and rather use resources from a single provider. A possible explanation for this behavior is the hourly based price model offered by the providers, cheap solutions trying to increase resource utilisation instead of launching simultaneous instances.

6.2 Type-2 Workflows

Fig. 4 depicts the results obtained for *Type-2* workflows. In all the evaluated scenarios, MOHEFT produced less than $K = 10$ tradeoff schedules which indicates that the tradeoff between makespan and financial cost is lower for this kind of workflows than for those of *Type-1*. Regarding to the used resources, only few instances are required to execute this kind of workflows as a consequence of the lower number of activities which can be executed in parallel. Therefore, the use of a Cloud federation does not bring any benefit in this situation. The analysis of the makespan versus cost reports in this case the same behavior as before: reducing the makespan overhead to less than 10% over the shortest one implies a strong economical investment, while schedules with more than 10% overhead imply a small price fraction.

6.3 POV-Ray

As explained before, each activity of the POV-Ray workflow renders a frame and transfers it to a final activity which merges all the frames and stores them into a file. Each frame is of around 1MB in size; therefore, the POV-Ray application can be considered as a *Type-1* workflow and expects to achieve benefits from using a federation of Clouds. As summarized in Fig. 5, it is obvious that the federation helps in reducing the makespan of this application. The three evaluated cases show that the higher the number of activities, the higher the benefit from the federation. This result is a consequence of the high degree of parallelism showed by this workflow application and the low volume of data required.

7 Conclusions and Future Work

In this paper we tackled the problem of multi-objective workflow scheduling from the perspective of a Cloud federation and presented a Cloud-aware of the multi-objective HEFT algorithm, called MOHEFT. We analyse the potential of MOHEFT to schedule workflow applications with different properties: workflow shape, size, and amount of data to be transferred among workflow activities. Experimental results using Amazon EC2 and GoGrid as independent providers illustrated that federated Clouds can help in shortening the makespan for workflow applications which do not require transferring large amounts of data among activities. In situations when data transfers dominate the computation time, the workflow does not benefit from a federation of Clouds and performs better in a single provider configuration. In future work we will extend the analysis for other real-world applications and a wider set of Cloud providers. We will also analyse extensions to MOHEFT to better deal with federated Clouds and workflows dealing with big data problems.

References

1. http://www.povray.org/
2. Alexandru, I., Ostermann, S., Yigitbasi, M., Prodan, R., Fahringer, T., Epema, D.: Performance analysis of cloud computing services for many-tasks scientific computing. In: IEEE Transactions onf Parallel and Distributed Systems (2010)
3. Assayad, I., Girault, A., Kalla, H.: A bi-criteria scheduling heuristics for distributed embedded systems under reliability and real-time constraints. In: International Conference on Dependable Systems and Networks, DSN 2004, Firenze, Italy. IEEE (June 2003)
4. Bessai, K., Youcef, S., Oulamara, A., Godart, C., Nurcan, S.: Bi-criteria workflow tasks allocation and scheduling in cloud computing environments. In: Proceedings of the 2012 IEEE Fifth International Conference on Cloud Computing, CLOUD 2012. IEEE Computer Society, Washington, DC (2012)
5. Canon, L.-C., Emmanuel, E.: Mo-greedy: An extended beam-search approach for solving a multi-criteria scheduling problem on heterogeneous machines. In: International Heterogeneity in Computing (2011)
6. Durillo, J., Fard, H., Prodan, R.: Moheft: A multi-objective list-based method for workflow scheduling. In: 4th IEEE International Conference on Cloud Computing Technology and Science (December 2012)
7. Durillo, J.J., Nae, V., Prodan, R.: Multi-objective workflow scheduling: An analysis of the energy efficiency and makespan tradeoff. In: CCGRID (2013)
8. Fard, H., Prodan, R., Barrionuevo, J., Fahringer, T.: A multi-objective approach for workflow scheduling in heterogeneous environments. In: 2012 12th IEEE/ACM International Symposium on Cluster, Cloud and Grid Computing (CCGrid) (May 2012)

9. Garg, S.K., Buyya, R., Siegel, H.J.: Scheduling parallel applications on utility grids: Time and cost trade-off management. In: Proceedings of the Thirty-Second Australasian Conference on Computer Science, ACSC 2009, Australian Computer Society, Inc., Darlinghurst (2009)
10. Garg, S.K., Yeo, C.S., Anandasivam, A., Buyya, R.: Environment-conscious scheduling of hpc applications on distributed cloud-oriented data centers. J. Parallel Distrib. Comput. 71(6) (June 2011)
11. Hakem, M., Butelle, F.: Reliability and scheduling on systems subject to failures. In: Proceedings of the 2007 International Conference on Parallel Processing ICPP 2007. IEEE Computer Society, Washington, DC (2007)
12. Kurze, T., Klems, M., Bermbach, D., Lenk, A., Tai, S., Kunze, M.: Cloud Federation. In: Proceedings of the 2nd International Conference on Cloud Computing, GRIDs, and Virtualization, CLOUD COMPUTING 2011. IARIA (September 2011)
13. Mezmaz, M., Melab, N., Kessaci, Y., Lee, Y., Albi, E.-G.T., Zomaya, A.Y., Tuyttens, D.: A parallel bi-objective hybrid metaheuristic for energy-aware s cheduling for cloud computing systems. Journal of Parallel and Distributed Computing (71) (2011)
14. Rao, L., Liu, X., Liu, W.: Minimizing electricity cost: Optimization of distributed internet data centers in a multi-electricity-market environment. In: In Proc. of INFOCOM (2010)
15. Ren, S., He, Y., Xu, F.: Provably-efficient job scheduling for energy and fairness in geographically distributed data centers. In: Proceedings of the 2012 IEEE 32nd International Conference on Distributed Computing Systems, ICDCS 2012. IEEE Computer Society, Washington, DC (2012)
16. Sakellariou, R., Zhao, H., Tsiakkouri, E., Dikaiakos, M.D.: Scheduling workflows with budget constraints. In: Gorlatch, S., Danelutto, M. (eds.) Integrated Research in Grid Computing. CoreGrid series. Springer (2007)
17. Santana-Perez, I., Perez-Hern'ndez, M.S.: A semantic scheduler architecture for federated hybrid clouds. In: 2012 IEEE Fifth International Conference on Cloud Computing (2012)
18. Talukder, A.K.M.K.A., Kirley, M., Buyya, R.: Multiobjective differential evolution for scheduling workflow applications on global grids. Evolution 21(13) (2009)
19. Topcuoglu, H., Hariri, S., Wu, M.-Y.: Performance-effective and low-complexity task scheduling for heterogeneous computing. IEEE Transactions on Parallel and Distributed Systems 13(3) (March 2002)
20. Urgaonkar, R., Kozat, U.C., Igarashi, K., Neely, M.J.: Dynamic resource allocation and power management in virtualized data centers. In: NOMS. IEEE (2010)
21. Yao, Y., Huang, L., Sharma, A., Golubchik, L., Neely, M.: Power cost reduction in distributed data centers: A two time scale approach for delay tolerant workloads. IEEE Transactions on Parallel and Distributed Systems 99 (2013) (PrePrints)
22. Yu, J., Buyya, R., Ramamohanarao, K.: Workflow scheduling algorithms for grid computing. In: Xhafa, F., Abraham, A. (eds.) Meta. for Sched. in Distri. Comp. Envi. SCI. vol. 146, pp. 173–214. Springer, Heidelberg (2008)
23. Yu, J., Kirley, M., Buyya, R.: Multi-objective planning for workflow execution on grids. In: Proceedings of the 8th IEEE/ACM International Conference on Grid Computing, GRID 2007. IEEE Computer Society Press, Washington, DC (2007)

Locality-Aware Cooperation for VM Scheduling in Distributed Clouds

Jonathan Pastor[1], Marin Bertier[2], Frédéric Desprez[4], Adrien Lebre[1], Flavien Quesnel[1], and Cédric Tedeschi[3]

[1] ASCOLA Research Group, Mines Nantes / Inria / LINA, Nantes, France
[2] ASAP Research Group, INSA / Inria / IRISA, Rennes, France
[3] Myriads Research Group, Université de Rennes 1 / Inria / IRISA, Rennes, France
[4] Avalon Research Group, LIP ENS Lyon UMR 5668, Lyon, France
firstname.lastname@inria.fr

Abstract. The promotion of distributed Cloud Computing infrastructures as the next platform to deliver the Utility Computing paradigm, leads to new virtual machines (VMs) scheduling algorithms leveraging peer-to-peer approaches. Although these proposals considerably improve the scalability, leading to the management of hundreds of thousands of VMs over thousands of physical machines (PMs), they do not consider the network overhead introduced by multi-site infrastructures. This overhead can have a dramatic impact on the performance if there is no mechanism favoring intra-site *v.s.* inter-site manipulations.

This paper introduces a new building block designed on top of a network with Vivaldi coordinates maximizing the locality criterion (*i.e.,* efficient collaborations between PMs). We combined such a mechanism with DVMS, a large-scale virtual machine scheduler and showed its benefit by discussing several experiments performed on four distinct sites of the Grid'5000 testbed. With our proposal and without changing the scheduling decision algorithm, the number of inter-site operations has been reduced by 72%. This result provides a glimpse of the promising future of using locality properties to improve the performance of massive distributed Cloud platforms.

Keywords: Cloud Computing, locality, peer-to-peer, overlay network, Vivaldi, DVMS, virtual machine scheduling.

1 Introduction

Introduced few years ago [6], the new trend to deliver Cloud Computing resources, in particular Infrastructure as a Service (IaaS) solutions, consists in leveraging several infrastructures distributed world-wide. If such distributed Cloud Computing platforms deliver undeniable advantages to address important challenges such as reliability, latency or even in somehow jurisdiction concerns, most mechanisms that were previously used to operate centralized IaaS platforms must be revisited to offer the same level of transparency for the end-users.

Keeping such an objective in mind, the use of the P2P paradigm has to be strongly investigated. This is particularly true for scheduling algorithms in

F. Silva et al. (Eds.): Euro-Par 2014, LNCS 8632, pp. 330–341, 2014.

charge of assigning virtual machines (VMs) on top of physical machines (PMs) according to their effective needs (and reciprocally usages), to preserve a good quality of service (QoS). Indeed and although major improvements have been done, centralized approaches [8] are neither scalable nor robust enough. Hierarchical solutions [4] that can be seen as good candidates face important limitations: First, finding an efficient partitioning of resources is a tedious task as matching a hierarchical overlay network on top of a distributed infrastructure is often not natural. Secondly, in addition to requiring complex failover mechanisms to face crashed leader/super peer and network disconnections, hierarchical structures have not been designed to react swiftly to physical topology changes such as node apparitions/removals and network performance degradations. P2P algorithms allow to address both concerns, *i.e.*, scalability as well as resiliency of infrastructures. Although promising approaches have been proposed to address the scheduling problem of VMs in a P2P fashion [13,3], they are still facing limitations coming from the overlay network they rely on. The approach proposed in [13] maps a ring overlay network on a distributed infrastructure which prevents making any distinction between close nodes and distant ones. Similarly, the approach described in [3], while adopting an orthogonal, gossip-based approach, still suffers from building a randomized overlay network, thus breaking the physical topology.

Considering that both the network latency and the bandwidth between peers have a strong impact on the reactivity criterion of the scheduling problem, *locality* properties of peers should be considered to favor efficient VM operations. In other words, to reduce as much as possible the time to switch from one schedule (*i.e.*, a mapping between VMs and PMs running in the infrastructure) to another one, it is crucial to make cooperation first between peers in the closest neighborhoods before contacting peers belonging to other sites. Moreover, it is noteworthy that this notion of locality is dynamic, and varies over time according to the network bandwidth/latency and disconnections.

The contribution of this paper is a new building block that enables to tackle the *locality* concern in distributed VM scheduling algorithms such as the two aforementioned ones. We estimate the locality through a cost function of the latency/bandwidth tuple between peers in the network, thus enabling each peer to select its closest neighbors. We rely on Vivaldi [2], a simple decentralized protocol allowing to map a network topology onto a logical space while preserving locality. On top of Vivaldi, a shortest path construction, similar to the well-known Dijkstra algorithm, is performed each time there is a need for cooperation between two nodes taking part in the schedule. We illustrate the advantage of this new building block by changing the overlay network in the DVMS proposal [13]. We selected DVMS as we have a good expertise of it and because it is, as far as we know, the only one that guarantees to find a solution if one exists [12].

The remainder of this article is structured as follows. In Section 2, we discuss some background regarding the DVMS proposal and the P2P technics to handle the locality aspects. Section 3 gives an overview of our proposal by introducing the short path algorithm on top of Vivaldi and the way we integrate it into

DVMS. In Section 4, we validate the proposal by analyzing its benefits with respect to the previous version of DVMS by discussing experiments conducted on Grid'5000. Related works are discussed in Section 5. Finally, we discuss perspectives and conclude this article in Section 6.

2   Background

2.1   DVMS

DVMS [12,13] (Distributed Virtual Machine Scheduler) is a framework that schedules VMs cooperatively and dynamically in large-scale distributed systems. It is deployed as a set of agents that are organized following a ring topology and that cooperate with one another to guarantee that VM demands are satisfied during their executions. Concretely, when a node [1] cannot guarantee the QoS for its hosted VMs or when it is under-utilized, it starts an iterative scheduling procedure (ISP) by querying its first neighbor to find a better placement; it thus becomes the initiator of the ISP. If the neighbor cannot satisfy the request, it is forwarded to the following free node until the ISP succeeds. When a viable mapping has been found, the leader (*i.e.*, the last peer that has taken part to the ISP) reconfigures the system by performing adequate VM migrations. Such an approach allows each ISP to send requests only to a minimal number of nodes and even though an ISP can reserve all nodes if the corresponding problem is particularly hard to solve (thus guaranteeing that a solution will always be found if it exits), experiments have shown that in most cases ISPs involve only few nodes. Moreover, the DVMS proposal allows several ISPs to occur independently at the same moment throughout the infrastructure; in other words, scheduling is performed on partitions of the system that are created dynamically, which significantly improves the reactivity of the system. To prevent conflicts that could occur if several ISPs performed concurrent operations on the same PMs or VMs, it should be emphasized that PMs are reserved for exclusive use by a single ISP.

An example involving three partitions is shown in Figure 1; in particular, we can see the growth of partition 1 between two steps. Explaining in detail the notion of "first out" is beyond the scope of this article but readers can consider that the "first out" relation enables to handle communications efficiently, as each node involved in a partition can forward a request directly to the first node on the outside of its partition [13].

We formally proved the correctness of DVMS using temporal logic, and we validated the first version of the prototype at large scale (by means of simulations involving up to 80k VMs and 8k nodes and with experiments on the Grid'5000 testbed involving up to 4.7k VMs and 470 nodes [12]).

As discussed earlier, one limitation of this approach is related to its ring topology that prevents it from taking into account the actual network topology.

---

[1] In the following, *node* and *PM* will refer to the same entity (*i.e.*, a physical server of the infrastructure).

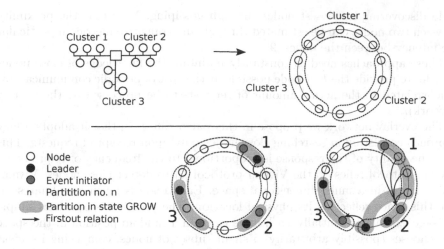

Fig. 1. Solving three problems simultaneously and independently with DVMS. The ring has been matched on top of three distinct clusters.

In other words, if the ISP strategy enables to limit the size of one partition to a minimal number of nodes, these nodes are selected without considering the network conditions at the time the ISP starts. This can lead to inefficient situations where VM migrations occur between two nodes that are far from each other, which lasts longer than a migration between two close nodes. Obviously the ring can be built to limit the distance between peers globally (*i.e.*, peers of the same region/area would be grouped together as illustrated in Figure 1). However, in such a case, at least two nodes of each group are directly connected to two far nodes. Note that an approach such as the one proposed in [5], which consists in deploying one ring per site and relying on a *super-ring* to interconnect few representatives of each local ring, would not solve many problems. Besides problems inherent to hierarchical and structured overlay networks, this solution would not provide a good answer to locality: When going out of the local ring, it would still not be possible to find the next closest ring.

2.2 Overlay Networks and Locality

As illustrated in the previous paragraph, one of the primary downsides of overlay networks lies in that they break the physical topology by connecting nodes that have no physical proximity. Besides hierarchical attempts in building locality-aware overlay networks [5,17,18], we can first mention the locality improvement mechanisms of the Pastry structured overlay network [15]. In order to reduce the latency of the routing process, each node is given the opportunity to choose the closest nodes to fill its routing table. Learning the existence of new nodes relies on a periodic exchange of parts of routing tables.

Similar mechanisms have been adopted within unstructured overlay networks to make their logical connections reflect the physical proximity of nodes, each node discovering its closest nodes through gossiping. Note that the proximity between two nodes can be estimated through any transitive metric, in particular the latency between the nodes [9].

These approaches need to constantly maintain the knowledge of close nodes in order to provide the *best* node possible at the cost of periodic communications (uncorrelated to the actual amount of requests to be processed by the overlay network).

The overlay network we propose in this paper differs in that it adopts a lazy approach consisting in searching close nodes only upon receipt of requests. This way, the quality of the response is proportional to the frequency of requests.

Our protocol relies on the Vivaldi protocol [2] to detect close nodes. Vivaldi places nodes in a multi-dimensional space. Each node is given coordinates inside this space reflecting its physical location. The protocol is based on simple message exchanges. Initially, each node is given a random position in the space and chooses (possibly arbitrarily) a small subset of nodes, composing its *view*. Then, each node starts estimating the round trip time between itself and another node chosen randomly in its view, and adapts its distance with this node in the space accordingly, coming closer to it or moving away from it. The nodes can repeat this step independently (each with another node from its view), to improve the accuracy of the positioning. A globally accurate positioning of nodes can be obtained very quickly (in a small number of such steps) if nodes have a few long-distance nodes in their view and if the network is not excessively dynamic. These long distance links can be easily maintained.

Recall that Vivaldi does not allow to directly know the nodes that are close in the network, but to be able to recognize them through their coordinates. Our overlay relies on the examination of Vivaldi coordinates of nodes discovered during the processing of requests sent to it.

3 Contributions

The aim of this paper is to revisit a distributed scheduling algorithm, the DVMS proposal, in order to take account of locality criteria. To this aim, we focus first on the overlay network, and second, we propose an abstraction that allows combining DVMS with a locality-aware overlay network without being intrusive in its source code.

3.1 Locality-Aware Overlay Network

We here present our lazy locality-aware overlay network that underlies the VM scheduling platform we developed. It is made of two layers.

The lower layer is mainly an implementation of the Vivaldi protocol (which core mechanisms were described earlier) making nodes (that are initially interconnected arbitrarily) aware of their position in the infrastructure.

Based on these coordinates, the upper layer is responsible for building a locality-aware overlay dynamically. This layer takes its roots in the classic Dijkstra's shortest path algorithm to collect a set of close nodes starting from a given position.

Searching for Close Nodes. Once the Vivaldi map is achieved, and each node knows its coordinates, we are able to estimate how *close* two given nodes are by calculating their distance in the map. However, recall that the view of each node does not *a priori* contain its closest nodes [2]. Therefore, we need additional mechanisms to locate a set of nodes that are close to a given initial node. Vivaldi gives a *location* to each node, not a neighborhood.

We use a modified, distributed version of the classic Dijkstra's shortest path algorithm that leverages the Vivaldi map to build such a neighborhood. More specifically, its goal is to build a **spiral**[3] interconnecting the nodes in the plane that are the closest ones from a given initial node.

Let us consider that our initial (or root) point is the node n_R. The first step is to find a node to build a two-node spiral starting with n_R. This is done by selecting the node from n_R's network view, say n_i, which exhibits the smallest distance with n_R. n_i becomes the second node in the spiral. From this point on, n_R remembers n_i as its successor and n_i remembers n_R as its predecessor. n_R also sends its network view to n_i, which, on receipt, creates its **spiral view** that contains the N nodes closest to n_R taken from both n_R and n_i network views. It will allow n_i to find the next node to build the spiral. Assuming this closest node from n_R in n_i's spiral view is n_j, n_j will be added in the spiral by becoming the successor of n_i. n_j receives n_i's spiral view and creates and fills its own spiral view with nodes closest to n_R contained in both n_i's spiral view and n_j's network view. This algorithm is repeated until the amount of nodes requested by the application have been interconnected in the spiral.

Note that there is a risk to be blocked at some point, having a spiral view containing only nodes that are already in the spiral, hindering from extending it further. However, this problem can be easily addressed by introducing few long-distance nodes when the spiral view is created/updated.

Learning. Applying the protocol described above, the quality of the spiral is questionable in the sense that the nodes that are actually close to the root node n_R may not be included. To improve the *quality* of the spiral, *i.e.*, to reduce the average distance from each of its nodes to the initial node, we rely on a learning mechanism coming with no extra communication cost: When a node is contacted to become the next node in one spiral, and when it receives the associated spiral view, it can also keep in its network view the nodes that are closer to itself, thus potentially increasing the quality of a future spiral construction. Such an improvement through learning is illustrated in Figure 2. Note that learning may also be used to constantly improve already built spirals. While providing obvious advantages, allowing it comes at the cost of changing links in the spirals dynamically, which may not match all applications' constraints.

---

[2] In the following, we call this view the **network view**, to distinguish it from the **spiral view** to be introduced later.

[3] Our use of the term *spiral* is actually a misuse of language, since the graph drawn in the plane might contain crossing edges.

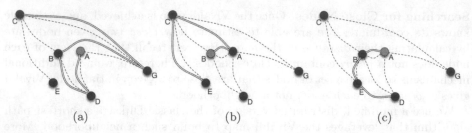

Fig. 2. Learning mechanism: (a) The initial view of each node is materialized by the dashed lines. Given these views, the spiral obtained from node A is represented by the double thick lines. In particular, this spiral allowed A and B to discover each other. (b) If B starts building a spiral, it will start by contacting A. This spiral construction allows also E and B to discover each other. (c) If A is requested to start another spiral, it will exhibit an increased locality awareness.

3.2   PeerActor: A Building Block to Abstract Overlay Networks

As a P2P scheduling algorithm, the DVMS proposal can be divided in two major components: (i) The ring overlay network and (ii) the protocol in charge of detecting and resolving scheduling issues. As our goal consists in taking into account locality criteria without changing the DVMS protocol, we designed a building block, *i.e., the Peer actor*, which enables us to revisit DVMS by abstracting the overlay network it relies on. At a coarse-grain level, the Peer actor can be seen as a generic layer for high level distributed services, providing network abstractions and robust communications between agents deployed on each node. By leveraging the Peer actor API, developers can focus on the service itself without dealing with node apparitions/removals and network disconnections.

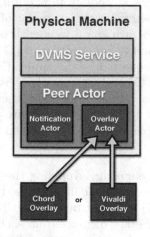

Fig. 3. DVMS on top of the Peer actor

From the software point of view, the Peer actor relies on modern software frameworks (Scala and Akka) following the actor model rules. In such a model, each instance will collaborate by exclusively exchanging messages, and priority will be given to collaboration between close instances when using the locality-based overlay (LBO).

As illustrated in Figure 3, the Peer actor contains two sub actors: The *Notification actor* and the *Overlay network actor*. The Notification actor enables services to subscribe to events that will be triggered by other services, as for detecting overloading of nodes or for handling crash of neighbours. The Overlay network actor is in charge of sending/receiving messages through the network. In order to compare both approaches, ring-based *v.s.* locality-aware, we developed two different Overlay network actors: The first one provides a Chord-like overlay [16], while the second one delivers the locality-aware overlay described in Section 3.1.

4   Experiments

The main objective of the experiments we conducted was to estimate the impact of locality on the performance of a distributed scheduling algorithm. A significant portion of the reconfiguration time is spent in live migration of virtual machines, which depends of network parameters such as latency and bandwidth. One way to improve the performance of distributed scheduling algorithms is to promote collaborations between close resources, which can be reached by maximizing the ratio *nb intrasite migrations/nb migrations*.

4.1   Experimental Protocol

To compare our experiments, we implemented a dedicated injector that makes load changes of VMs during a predefined time. VMs are launched on PMs in a round-robin manner, *i.e.*, each PM hosts roughly the same number of VMs at the beginning. The experiment consists in repeatedly changing target CPU loads of VMs. Every t seconds, the injector that is deployed on a dedicated node selects one VM and changes its CPU load according to a Gaussian distribution. t is a random variable that follows an exponential distribution with rate parameter λ. The Gaussian distribution is defined by a mean (μ) as well as a standard deviation (σ) that are given at the beginning of the experiment. The parameters are $\lambda = Nb\_VMs/300$ and $\mu = 70$, $\sigma = 30$. Concretely, the load of each VM starts from 0% and varies on average every 5 minutes in steps of 10 (with a significant part between 40% and 100% of CPU usage). The duration of each experiment was set to 3600 seconds.

Figure 4 depicts our testbed. For each experiment, we booked 40 compute servers spread over 4 geographical sites (10 PMs per site) and 1 service server from the Grid'5000 testbed. The compute servers were used to run VMs and DVMS while the service node runs the aforementioned injector. Each compute node was equipped with 8 cores and hosted a number of VMs proportional to its number of CPU cores ($nbVM = 1.3 \times nb\ cores$), leading to a global number of 416 VMs. Although such a number is rather small regarding the latest experiments that have

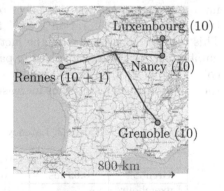

Fig. 4. Testbed

been performed on DVMS [12], our goal is not to validate once again the scalability criteria but to focus on the locality aspect of such an algorithm.

4.2   Results

Maximization of Intra-Site Migrations. Table 1 compares the ratio between intra-site migrations and the total number of migrations, using Chord or our LBO network. The results show that the impact of locality is significant: Using LBO leads to an average number of 86.3% of intra-site migrations while using a Chord-based DVMS decreases this ratio to 49.6%.

Table 1. Comparison of intra-site migrations ratio (DVMS/Chord vs. DVMS/LBO)

	Chord	LBO
Average	0.496	0.863
Minimum	0.378	0.798
Maximum	0.629	0.935

Dynamic Clustering. During our investigation of the results brought about LBO, we noticed that many of the inter-site migrations were performed between Luxembourg and Nancy sites. In Table 2, it is noticeable that Luxembourg and Nancy have a latency that is significantly below usual inter-site latencies (Nancy and Luxembourg are separated by only 100 kilometers), while Rennes and Grenoble have almost the same latency with all their respective remote sites. Indeed, servers located in Luxembourg and Nancy are more likely to collaborate with each other, while those located on Rennes and Grenoble will find collaborators regardless of their location. This explains why many of the inter-site migrations were performed between Luxembourg and Nancy. This means that LBO enabled DVMS to learn which site is more interesting to perform VM migration. Promoting low latency inter-site collaboration made many inter-site migrations acceptable compared to those executed by the Chord version.

Reactivity. Table 3 depicts metrics that allow for an objective comparison of the efficiency of both overlay networks. In addition to reducing the number of inter-site migrations, the side effect of using the LBO is to reduce the solving time: The partition duration is 46% lower than that encountered with Chord. This result is consistent with the fact that with our locality-aware overlay, the number of sites that are involved in partitions becomes very close to one. Indeed collaborating with closer nodes allows exchanging information between nodes of the partition much faster, thus increasing once again the reactivity of the system.

Table 2. Latency measured between sites

	Grenoble	Luxembourg	Nancy	Rennes
Grenoble	0.09 ms	16.55 ms	14.24 ms	15.92 ms
Luxembourg		0.17 ms	2.70 ms	13.82 ms
Nancy			0.27 ms	11.42 ms
Rennes				0.23 ms

Table 3. Comparison of partitions metrics using DVMS/Chord and DVMS/LBO

	Chord	LBO
Average number of sites involved	1.645	1.082
Average duration to detect a valid configuration (msec)	154.63	98.50

5 Related Work

Many virtual infrastructure managers have been proposed to deal with specific concerns. In this section, we will focus on some of their limitations, especially regarding locality, scalability, and fault-tolerance.

The most common managers are the centralized ones, like Entropy [7,8], since they are easy to deploy. They are generally designed to work on a cluster. In this context, they do not take account of the network topology, and they cannot manage VMs efficiently in a multi-site/multi-cluster deployment. Moreover, they are prone to fault-tolerance, scalability, and reactivity issues; to avoid these limitations, one possibility is to rely on more decentralized approaches, like hierarchical or distributed ones.

Hierarchical managers, like Snooze [4], may be more suited to handle locality. For instance, it is possible to setup (i) one manager per cluster, and (ii) one (fault-tolerant) super manager that monitors cluster managers and chooses on which cluster a new VM should start. The main problem with this approach is that, in the absence of cooperation between cluster managers, VMs cannot be migrated from one cluster to another, which is especially annoying if one cluster is overloaded. Moreover, the super manager is not necessarily aware of the network topology and therefore may not be able to interact efficiently with cluster managers if the latter are distributed among several sites. Furthermore, the super manager limits the scalability of this approach; to deal with this issue, researchers have designed distributed approaches.

Many distributed approaches have been proposed to manage VMs [1,3,10,11,14,19]. Some of them are limited in terms of scalability since they (i) require a global view of the infrastructure to take a decision [14,19] and/or (ii) rely on a centralized service node that is not fault-tolerant [11,19]. Some approaches lead to a huge number of migrations [1,11] without necessarily optimizing the chosen scheduling criterion [1]. Moreover, none of these approaches have been designed to take account of the network topology and therefore manage VMs efficiently in a multi-site deployment.

To summarize, a locality-aware distributed approach is required to (i) avoid issues related to scalability and single points of failures, and to (ii) manage VMs efficiently in heterogeneous network environments like those found in multi-site/multi-cluster deployments. Our work in this paper targets such a challenge.

6 Conclusion

Cloud Computing has entered our everyday life at a very high speed and huge scale. From classic High Performance Computing simulations to the management of huge amounts of data coming from mobile devices and sensors, its impact can no longer be minimized. While promoted for a long time, delivering Cloud Computing capabilities by leveraging only few large-scale data centers does not enable to cope with the demand of Cloud resources anymore, and a new model consisting in leveraging several micro/nano data centers distributed WANwide is more and more investigated. The main challenge is thus to revisit most of the mechanisms that are common to current IaaS management systems to leverage more decentralized algorithms. Among the different contributions that have been proposed, a large number have focused on the scheduling issue of the VMs to achieve the scalability required but at the expense of the locality criteria. However, manipulating VMs WANwide degrades significantly the performance as well as the quality of the service of the whole system.

Hence, the first step toward such a highly distributed Cloud infrastructure is to take into account this notion of locality between Cloud Computing resources. In this paper, we showed how such locality criteria can be considered by delivering a new building block using P2P algorithms and a Vivaldi overlay network connected to the DVMS proposal, an efficient and flexible VM scheduler. Our first experiments over Grid'5000 showed that, connecting 4 different sites and scheduling VMs over them, we could gain up to 72% of inter-site operations. It is worth noting that one experimental observation we had during this work was that the proposed overlay network was actually able to reflect the underlying topology, and in particular to build a hierarchical overlay dynamically if the underlying topology is hierarchical.

Our future work will consist in refining the decision model used in scheduling mechanisms to enable them to consider the cost difference between intra-site and inter-site migrations, thus promoting intra-site migrations in multi-site partitions. More generally, the association between locality-based overlay networks and Peer Actors will become a building block for revisiting every single service composing IaaS systems. It will enable to deliver a new generation of Utility Computing as depicted by the Discovery Initiative[4].

Acknowledgments. Experiments presented in this paper were carried out using the Grid'5000 experimental testbed, being developed under the INRIA ALADDIN development action with support from CNRS, RENATER, and several Universities as well as other funding bodies (see https://www.grid5000.fr).

References

1. Barbagallo, D., Di Nitto, E., Dubois, D.J., Mirandola, R.: A Bio-inspired Algorithm for Energy Optimization in a Self-Organizing Data Center. In: Weyns, D., Malek, S., de Lemos, R., Andersson, J. (eds.) SOAR 2009. LNCS, vol. 6090, pp. 127–151. Springer, Heidelberg (2010)
2. Dabek, F., Cox, R., Kaashoek, M.F., Morris, R.: Vivaldi: A Decentralized Network Coordinate System. In: 2004 Conf. on Applications, Technologies, Architectures, and Protocols for Computer Comm. SIGCOMM 2004, pp. 15–26 (2004)

---

[4] http://beyondtheclouds.github.io/

3. Feller, E., Morin, C., Esnault, A.: A Case for Fully Decentralized Dynamic VM Consolidation in Clouds. In: CloudCom 2012: 4th IEEE International Conference on Cloud Computing Technology and Science (December 2012)
4. Feller, E., Rilling, L., Morin, C.: Snooze: A Scalable and Autonomic Virtual Machine Management Framework for Private Clouds. In: CCGRID 2012: 12th Int. Symp. on Cluster, Cloud and Grid Comp, pp. 482–489 (May 2012)
5. Garcés-Erice, L., Biersack, E.W., Ross, K.W., Felber, P., Urvoy-Keller, G.: Hierarchical Peer-To-Peer Systems. Parallel Processing Letters 13(4), 643–657 (2003)
6. Greenberg, A., Hamilton, J., Maltz, D.A., Patel, P.: The Cost of a Cloud: Research Problems in Data Center Networks. SIGCOMM Comput. Commun. Rev. 39(1), 68–73 (2008)
7. Hermenier, F., Demassey, S., Lorca, X.: Bin Repacking Scheduling in Virtualized Datacenters. In: Lee, J. (ed.) CP 2011. LNCS, vol. 6876, pp. 27–41. Springer, Heidelberg (2011)
8. Hermenier, F., Lawall, J., Muller, G.: BtrPlace: A Flexible Consolidation Manager for Highly Available Applications. IEEE Transactions on Dependable and Secure Computing 99 (2013) (PrePrints)
9. Jelasity, M., Babaoglu, O.: T-Man: Gossip-based Overlay Topology Management. In: Brueckner, S.A., Di Marzo Serugendo, G., Hales, D., Zambonelli, F. (eds.) ESOA 2005. LNCS (LNAI), vol. 3910, pp. 1–15. Springer, Heidelberg (2006)
10. Marzolla, M., Babaoglu, O., Panzieri, F.: Server consolidation in Clouds through gossiping. In: WoWMoM 2011: Proceedings of the 12th IEEE International Symposium on a World of Wireless, Mobile and Multimedia Networks, pp. 1–6. IEEE Computer Society, Washington, DC (2011)
11. Mastroianni, C., Meo, M., Papuzzo, G.: Self-economy in cloud data centers: Statistical assignment and migration of virtual machines. In: Jeannot, E., Namyst, R., Roman, J. (eds.) Euro-Par 2011, Part I. LNCS, vol. 6852, pp. 407–418. Springer, Heidelberg (2011)
12. Quesnel, F., Lebre, A., Pastor, J., Sudholt, M., Balouek, D.: Advanced Validation of the DVMS Approach to Fully Distributed VM Scheduling. In: ISPA 2013: 12th IEEE International Conference on Trust, Security and Privacy in Computing and Communications, pp. 1249–1256 (July 2013)
13. Quesnel, F., Lèbre, A., Sudholt, M.: Cooperative and Reactive Scheduling in Large-Scale Virtualized Platforms with DVMS. Concurrency and Computation: Practice and Experience 25(12), 1643–1655 (2013)
14. Rouzaud-Cornabas, J.: A Distributed and Collaborative Dynamic Load Balancer for Virtual Machine. In: Guarracino, M.R., et al. (eds.) Euro-Par-Workshop 2010. LNCS, vol. 6586, pp. 641–648. Springer, Heidelberg (2011)
15. Rowstron, A., Druschel, P.: Pastry: Scalable, Decentralized Object Location, and Routing for Large-Scale Peer-to-Peer Systems. In: Guerraoui, R. (ed.) Middleware 2001. LNCS, vol. 2218, p. 329. Springer, Heidelberg (2001)
16. Stoica, I., Morris, R., Karger, D., Kaashoek, M.F., Balakrishnan, H.: Chord: A Scalable Peer-to-Peer Lookup Service for Internet Applications. In: ACM SIGCOMM Computer Communication Review, vol. 31, pp. 149–160. ACM (2001)
17. Xu, Z., Mahalingam, M., Karlsson, M.: Turning Heterogeneity into an Advantage in Overlay Routing. In: INFOCOM (2003)
18. Xu, Z., Zhang, Z.: Building Low-Maintenance Expressways for P2P Systems. Tech. Rep. HPL-2002-41, Hewlett-Packard Labs (2002)
19. Yazir, Y.O., Matthews, C., Farahbod, R.: Neville, S., Guitouni, A., Ganti, S., Coady, Y.: Dynamic Resource Allocation in Computing Clouds Using Distributed Multiple Criteria Decision Analysis. In: Cloud 2010: IEEE 3rd Int. Conf. on Cloud Computing, Los Alamitos, CA, USA, pp. 91–98 (July 2010)

Can Inter-VM Shmem Benefit MPI Applications on SR-IOV Based Virtualized Infiniband Clusters?*

Jie Zhang, Xiaoyi Lu, Jithin Jose, Rong Shi, and Dhabaleswar K. (DK) Panda

Department of Computer Science and Engineering,
The Ohio State University
{zhanjie,luxi,jose,shir,panda}@cse.ohio-state.edu

Abstract. Single Root I/O Virtualization (SR-IOV) technology has been introduced for high-performance interconnects such as InfiniBand. Recent studies mainly focus on performance characteristics of high-performance communication middleware (e.g. MPI) and applications on SR-IOV enabled HPC clusters. However, current SR-IOV based MPI applications do not take advantage of the locality-aware communication on intra-host inter-VM environment. Although Inter-VM Shared Memory (IVShmem) has been proven to support efficient locality-aware communication, the performance benefits of IVShmem for MPI libraries on virtualized environments are yet to be explored. In this paper, we present a comprehensive performance evaluation for IVShmem backed MPI using micro-benchmarks and HPC applications. The performance evaluations show that, through IVShmem, the performance of MPI point-to-point and collective operations can be improved up to 193% and 91%, respectively. The application performance can be improved up to 96%, compared to SR-IOV. The results further show that IVShmem just brings minor overhead compared to native environment.

Keywords: IVShmem, SR-IOV, Virtualization, MPI, InfiniBand.

1 Introduction

Distributed computing infrastructures are becoming increasingly virtualized, owing to the ease of system management and administration. They provide desirable features to meet demanding requirements of computing resources in modern computing systems, including server consolidation, performance isolation and ease of management, along with guaranteeing security, and live migration [21]. Virtual Machine (VM) technologies have already been widely adopted in industry computing environments, especially data-centers. For instance, data-center providers, Amazon's Elastic Compute Cloud (EC2) [1], rely on virtualization to consolidate computational resources for applications from different customers, with required Quality of Service guarantees on the same underlying hardware. Even though virtualization has gained significant momentum in the enterprise computing domain, its adoption in the High Performance Computing (HPC) domain remains lower. One of the biggest hurdles in realizing this objective comes from lower performance of virtualized I/O devices, offered by virtualized computing environments [13]. The performance of virtualized I/O devices is likely to be

---

* This research is supported in part by National Science Foundation grants #OCI-1148371, #CCF-1213084 and #CNS-1347189.

F. Silva et al. (Eds.): Euro-Par 2014, LNCS 8632, pp. 342–353, 2014.

the key driver in the adoption of virtualized cloud computing systems in HPC domains. High performance MPI libraries such as MVAPICH2 [19], OpenMPI [20], can provide sub-microsecond latencies. However, realizing such performance in virtualized environment is still a challenge.

The recently introduced Single Root I/O Virtualization (SR-IOV) [23] offers an attractive alternative for virtualizing I/O devices, when compared to existing software-based virtualization techniques. According to the SR-IOV specification, a PCIe device can present itself as multiple virtual devices and each virtual device can be dedicated to a single VM. Our earlier study [13] indicates that SR-IOV can attain near to native performance for inter-node point to point communication, at the MPI level. However, one of the main drawbacks of SR-IOV is that it does not support VM locality aware communication. Thus, inter-VM communications within the node also have to go through SR-IOV channel, leading to performance overheads. On the other hand, VM communication schemes such as Inter-VM shared memory (IVShmem) [16], offer shared memory backed communication for VMs within a single host. Consequently, we carry out a primitive-level experiment using Perftest-1.2.3 [2], as shown in Figure 1. The experiment compares the primitive level latencies between SR-IOV based IB communication and shared memory communication, and underscore the performance overheads. For 64 bytes message size, the latencies observed are 0.96 and 0.20 μs, for SR-IOV(IB-Send) and IVShmem, respectively. These performance overheads motivate this study, to explore whether IVShmem scheme can benefit MPI communication within a node on SR-IOV enabled InfiniBand clusters.

In this paper, we study the performance characteristics of IVShmem and explore its applicability in VM locality aware communication for MPI libraries on SR-IOV enabled InfiniBand clusters. We propose a high performance prototype design of MPI library, for intra-host inter-VM communication using IVShmem. Then we conduct a comprehensive performance evaluation using micro-benchmarks and HPC applications. The evaluation results indicate that IVShmem scheme has big potential to

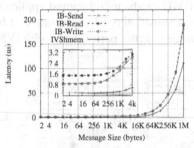

Fig. 1. Primitive-Level Latency Comparison between SR-IOV enabled IB and IVShmem

benefit intra-host inter-VM communication on SR-IOV enabled InfiniBand clusters. This paper mainly focuses on evaluating the performance improvement potential of IVShmem backed MPI communication, on SR-IOV based InfiniBand clusters. We make the following key contributions as part of this paper:

1. Identify the performance overheads associated with SR-IOV for intra-host inter-VM communication
2. Detailed performance evaluations of IVShmem, and exploring its performance improvement potential for VM locality aware communication
3. Performance analysis and scalability evaluations of IVShmem backed MPI library using micro-benchmarks and HPC applications

4. Performance comparisons between IVShmem backed and native mode MPI libraries, using HPC applications

The evaluation results indicate that IVShmem can improve point to point and collective operations by up to 193% and 91%, respectively. The application execution time can be decreased by up to 96%, compared to SR-IOV. The results further show that IVShmem just brings small overheads, compared with native environment.

The rest of the paper is organized as follows. Section 2 provides an overview of IVShmem, SR-IOV, and InfiniBand. Section 3 describes our prototype design and evaluation methodology. Section 4 presents the performance analysis results using micro-benchmarks and applications, scalability results, and comparison with native mode. We discuss the related work in Section 5, and conclude in Section 6.

2   Background

Inter-VM Shared Memory (IVShmem) (e.g. Nahanni) [16] provides zero-copy access to data on shared memory of co-resident VMs on KVM platform. IVShmem is designed and implemented mainly in system calls layer and its interfaces are visible to user space applications as well. As shown in Figure 2(a), IVShmem contains three components: the guest kernel driver, the modified QEMU supporting PCI device, and the POSIX shared memory region on the host OS. The shared memory region is allocated by host POSIX operations and mapped to QEMU process address space. The mapped memory in QEMU can be used by guest applications by being remapped to user space in guest VMs. Evaluation results illustrate that both micro-benchmarks and HPC applications can achieve better performance with IVShmem support.

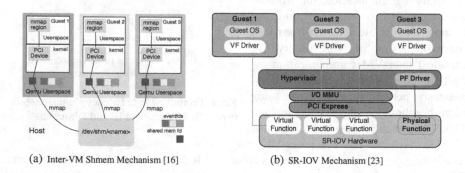

(a) Inter-VM Shmem Mechanism [16]   (b) SR-IOV Mechanism [23]

Fig. 2. Overview of Inter-VM Shmem and SR-IOV Communication Mechanisms

Single Root I/O Virtualization (SR-IOV) is a PCI Express (PCIe) standard which specifies the native I/O virtualization capabilities in PCIe adapters. As shown in Figure 2(b), SR-IOV allows a single physical device, or a Physical Function (PF), to present itself as multiple virtual devices, or Virtual Functions (VFs). Each virtual device can be dedicated to a single VM through the PCI pass-through, which allows each VM to directly access the corresponding VF. Hence, SR-IOV is a hardware-based approach to implement I/O virtualization. Furthermore, VFs are designed based on the existing non-virtualized PFs. Therefore, the drivers of the current adapters can also be used to drive the VFs in a portable manner.

InfiniBand [12] is an industry standard switched fabric designed for interconnecting nodes in HPC clusters. The TOP500 rankings released in November 2013 indicate that more than 41% of the computing systems use InfiniBand as their primary high performance interconnect.

3 Prototype Design and Evaluation Methodology

In this section, we first propose the prototype design for IVShmem based MPI communication and then discuss various dimensions for evaluating the performance impact of IVShmem for intra-host inter-VM communication on SR-IOV based InfiniBand clusters. The results of evaluation for each dimension are described in Section 4.

3.1 Prototype Design

As introduced in Section 2, SR-IOV and IVShmem are two different mechanisms that can be used for intra-host inter-VM communication. To better illustrate, the two inter-VM communication schemes are presented in Figure 3(a). For SR-IOV scheme, which is shown in the solid line, each VM is configured with a dedicated Virtual Function, so that an MPI process in Guest-1 can communicate with another MPI process in Guest-2 without concerning whether Guest-2 is co-located with Guest-1 in a same physical node or not. This does not deliver the best approach to high performance communication. In order to take advantage of shared memory between VMs co-located in a given host, guest VMs need to detect which VMs are co-located with themselves, so that they can map the same memory region into their own memory spaces. Based on what we discussed in Section 2, IVShmem provides a mechanism to expose a host memory region to all co-resident VMs as virtual PCI devices. And finally, this memory region can be mapped to user spaces of guest systems. We implement a prototype MPI library by utilizing IVShmem. Therefore, the communication between co-resident VMs can happen along the IVShmem channel as shown in the dashed line in Figure 3(a), instead of the SR-IOV channel, as shown in the solid line.

3.2 Evaluation Dimensions

We follow a five-pronged approach to evaluate the performance improvement potential of IVShmem for intra-host inter-VM communication on SR-IOV based InfiniBand clusters, as shown in Figure 3(b).

Point to Point Communication: Point to point communication is a basic communication scheme in MPI communication. On virtualized environments with SR-IOV support, our earlier studies [13] showed related performance evaluations. In this paper, we mainly evaluate the performance improvement potential of IVShmem for point to point communication including both two-sided and one-sided operations.

Collective Communication: Collective communication is an important and frequently used communication scheme of MPI. However, current SR-IOV solution does

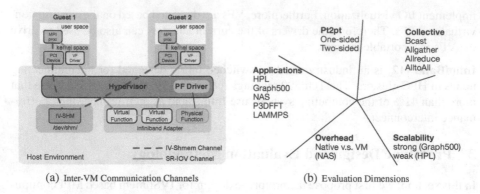

(a) Inter-VM Communication Channels   (b) Evaluation Dimensions

Fig. 3. Inter-VM Communication Channels and Evaluation Dimensions

not take advantage of the locality aware collective communication on intra-host inter-VM environment, which leads to performance overhead. Therefore, we evaluate the performance improvement potential of IVShmem for four widely used collective operations across VMs on a single node in this paper.

Application Execution Time: MPI has established itself as the de-facto standard of programming model for HPC applications. Clearly, the performance of MPI libraries will significantly impact the execution time of these HPC applications. Thus, we choose five representative HPC applications (as shown in Table 1) to evaluate the performance benefits of IVShmem.

Table 1. Representative HPC Applications for Evaluation

Name	Description
P3DFFT	Parallel Three-Dimensional Fast Fourier Transforms, dubbed P3DFFT [5], is a library for large-scale computer simulations in a wide range of sciences, such as physics, climatology and chemistry.
HPL	High Performance Linpack (HPL) is the parallel implementation of Linpack [7] and the performance measure for ranking the computer systems of the Top 500 supercomputer list.
LAMMPS	LAMMPS stands for Large-scale Atomic/Molecular Massively Parallel Simulator [22]. It is a classical molecular dynamics simulator from Sandia National Laboratory.
Graph500	Graph500 [24] is one of the representative benchmarks of Data intensive supercomputer applications. It exhibits highly irregular communication pattern.
NAS	NAS [3] contains a set of benchmarks which are derived from the computing kernels, which is common on Computational Fluid Dynamics (CFD) applications. These represent the class of regular iterative HPC applications.

Virtual Machine Scalability: As the emergence of virtualization technology, we can achieve easier system management and performance isolation. However, the performance characteristics might vary significantly as the number of VMs increase. This paper evaluates the performance impact of IVShmem scheme by adjusting the number of VMs within a physical node in SR-IOV enabled InfiniBand clusters.

Performance Overhead: Earlier studies indicate that high performance VM environments are able to achieve low cost of CPU and memory virtualization [25]. I/O virtualization, however, leads to longer I/O latency, since I/O devices are usually shared by multiple VMs within a host. In this paper, we evaluate the performance overheads of SR-IOV and IVShmem compared to native environment.

4   Performance Evaluation

In this section, we describe our experimental testbed and discuss our evaluation of two-sided and one-sided point to point, collective operations, and HPC applications. Since this paper focuses on performance evaluation of IVShmem scheme on InfiniBand clusters with SR-IOV support, we use one node with multiple cores for evaluation.

4.1   Experiment Setup

Our testbed is an InfiniBand cluster, where each node has dual 8-core 2.6 GHz Intel Xeon E5-2670 (Sandy Bridge) processors with 20MB L3 shared cache, 32 GB main memory and equipped with Mellanox ConnectX-3 FDR (56 Gbps) HCAs with PCI Express Gen3 interfaces. We use RedHat Enterprise Linux Server release 6.4 (Santiago) with kernel 2.6.32-279.19.1.el6.x86_64 as the host OS.

We use the Mellanox OpenFabrics Enterprise Distribution MLNX_OFED_LINUX 2.1-1.0.0 to provide the InfiniBand interface with SR-IOV support and KVM as the Virtual Machine Monitor (VMM). Each VM is pinned to a single core and has 1.5 GB main memory. The OS used in each VM is RedHat Enterprise Linux Server release 6.4 (Santiago) with kernel 2.6.32-131.0.15.el6.x86_64.

All applications and libraries used in this study are compiled with gcc 4.4.6 compiler. All MPI communication performance experiments use MVAPICH2 2.0rc1 and OSU Micro-Benchmarks. Experimental results are averaged by 5 runs to ensure fair comparison. Our tests are conducted with different numbers of VMs on one node, 8 for power of two case, and 15 for full-subscribed case (while reserving one core for host OS).

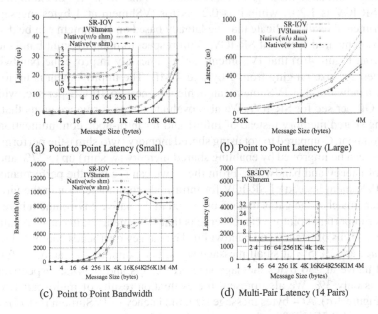

(a) Point to Point Latency (Small)

(b) Point to Point Latency (Large)

(c) Point to Point Bandwidth

(d) Multi-Pair Latency (14 Pairs)

Fig. 4. Two-sided Point to Point Performance

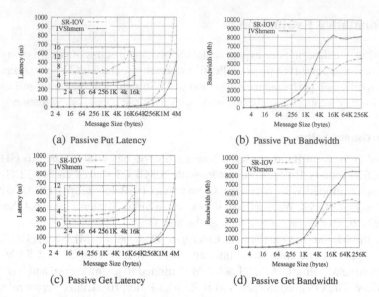

(a) Passive Put Latency

(b) Passive Put Bandwidth

(c) Passive Get Latency

(d) Passive Get Bandwidth

Fig. 5. One-sided Point-to-Point Performance

4.2 Point to Point Communication Performance

In this section, we evaluate the MPI level point to point performance for intra-node inter-VM communication in terms of latency and bandwidth. Figure 4(a) and Figure 4(b) show the two-sided point to point latencies of small and large message sizes, respectively. We can observe that, IVShmem based MPI library achieves lower latency for both small and large message sizes, compared to the SR-IOV. For example, the latency of SR-IOV is $1.2\mu s$, while it is $0.22\mu s$ for IVShmem at 4 bytes message size. The experimental results indicate that the latency based on IVShmem can be decreased up to 82%, compared to that of SR-IOV. With respect to point to point bandwidth, we can see from Figure 4(c) that IVShmem can significantly improve the bandwidth for various message size ranging from 1 byte to 4 MB. The improvement is up to 158%. The peak bandwidth that IVShmem can achieve is near to 10 GB per sec, while it is around 6 GB per sec for SR-IOV. We also evaluate the performance gains that comes from using shared memory instead of InfiniBand for intra-node communication in native environment. Compared to not using shared memory (w/o shm), the performance of native MPI can be improved by enabling shared memory (w shm) up to 77% and 191% in terms of latency and bandwidth. From these, we can see that the performance gains of using IVShmem instead of SR-IOV for intra-node communication in the virtualized environment matches the gains that we observed in the native environment here.

Another important point we can observe is that IVShmem attains near to native performance in terms of latency and bandwidth. The latency overheads compared to native performance are 3%-5% at small message sizes. For example, the latencies for IVShmem and native at 256 bytes message size are $0.35\mu s$ and $0.34\mu s$, respectively. The overhead is only 3%. We also present the evaluation results of multi-pair latency (7 pairs) in Figure 4(d). At 4 bytes message size, the latency of IVShmem is $0.77\mu s$, while it is $2.72\mu s$ for SR-IOV. When the message size varies from 1 byte to 4 MB, IVShmem can decrease the latency by up to 86%, compared to SR-IOV. Thus, IVShmem can significantly improve the point to point communication performance for MPI library compared to SR-IOV, and can also achieve near to native performance.

The recent MPI standard [18] has introduced one-sided communication model. In this model, one process's memory can be updated directly by another process. Unlike MPI two-sided communication model in which both sender and receiver are involved for data transfer, one-sided communication allows one process to specify all necessary parameters, and synchronization is done explicitly to ensure the completion of communication. As it can be seen from Figure 5(a) and Figure 5(b), IVShmem based MPI one-sided passive Put operation achieves lower latency and higher bandwidth, compared to SR-IOV. The latency is decreased up to 85% at 1 KB message size, while bandwidth can be improved up to 193% at 16 bytes message size. Similarly, the evaluation results shown in Figure 5(c) and 5(d) indicate that IVShmem also benefits one-sided passive Get operation in terms of latency and bandwidth. Similar performance improvements are observed for passive Get operation. The results indicate that IVShmem scheme can significantly improve performance of one-sided and two-sided point-to-point communications operations.

4.3 Collective Communication Performance

We select four widely used collective communication operations in our evaluations: Broadcast, Allgather, Allreduce and Alltoall. Figure 11(a) to Figure 11(d) show that, compared to SR-IOV, IVShmem significantly cuts down the latencies of the above four collective operations across 15 VMs. For example, at 4 bytes message size, the latency of broadcast operation for IVShmem is $0.5\mu s$, while it is $4.15\mu s$ for SR-IOV. From 1 byte to 1 MB message size, the latencies can be decreased up to 91%, 87%, 85% and 88% through IVShmem for the above four collective operations, respectively. Based on our experimental evaluations, IVShmem can remarkably improve MPI collective communication performance within one node.

4.4 Application Performance

As discussed in Section 3, many of the HPC applications rely on MPI performance. In this section, therefore, we evaluate the performance benefit of IVShmem using real HPC applications. According to above evaluations on four collective communication operations, we use several HPC applications, each one as a representative mainly corresponding to one or two particular collective operations. From Figure 6(a) to Figure 6(d), we depict the evaluation results of different test programs in P3DFFT library, which are test_inverse.c, test_rand.c, test_sine.c and test_spec.c. The inverse evaluation results using 15 VMs are shown in Figure 6(a). As we can see, the execution times can be decreased by 96%, 79%, 40% through IVShmem for input size 128, 256, 512, respectively. The execution times of rand also can be reduced by 96%, 76%, 37%. Similar results can be observed for sine and spec. This is because the majority of the total execution time is spent in MPI_Alltoall operation. However, as the problem size increases, the proportion of communication drops down, and thus the performance improvement decreases. The evaluation results indicate that IVShmem can effectively reduce the execution time of the above four P3DFFT test programs. And it also verifies the evaluation results of collective communication in Section 4.3.

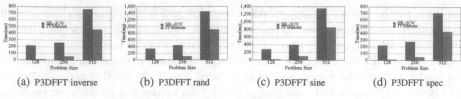

(a) P3DFFT inverse   (b) P3DFFT rand   (c) P3DFFT sine   (d) P3DFFT spec

Fig. 6. P3DFFT Performance on 15 VMs

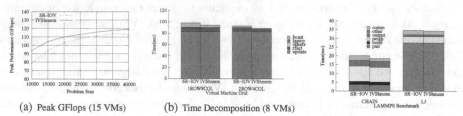

(a) Peak GFlops (15 VMs)   (b) Time Decomposition (8 VMs)

Fig. 7. HPL Performance

Fig. 8. LAMMPS Performance

The HPL evaluation results are presented in Figure 7. Here, we first measure the peak performance achieved by launching tests on 15 VMs as shown in Figure 7(a). Both SR-IOV and IVShmem achieve peak performance when the problem size is larger than 40,000. In our evaluations, IVShmem outperforms SR-IOV by around 4%-18% in GFLOPS, for various experiments. To better analyze the communication cost, we decomposed the time of HPL benchmark by using 8 VMs with various VM grid configuration. From Figure 7(b), we observe that the main communication benefit in HPL is coming from Broadcast. Through IVShmem, the broadcast latency can be decreased by 66% and 50% for 2x4 and 1x8 grids, respectively.

We also profile the time decomposition of Chain and LJ benchmark in LAMMPS. Figure 8 shows that IVShmem can decrease the communication time by 36% and 13% for Chain and LJ, respectively. And the total execution time can be decreased by up to 8% for Chain.

4.5 Virtual Machine Scalability

In this section, we evaluate the virtual machine scalability to explore the performance impact on increasing the number of virtual machines in a single host. Such evaluation helps to determine the optimal number of virtual machines to be deployed within a single host. We measure the weak scalability of HPL with fixed memory usage of each VM and increasing number of VMs. Figure 9(a) shows that IVShmem brings 2%-7% benefits compared to SR-IOV. We also use Graph500 benchmarks to evaluate the strong scalability of IVShmem and SR-IOV. As shown in Figure 9(b), IVShmem exhibits better scalability and decreases the execution time up to 35%, compared to SR-IOV.

4.6 Performance Overhead

For performance overhead evaluation, we used NAS to run seven different computing kernels of class B: IS, MG, CG, LU, FT, BT and SP. The first 5 kernels ran across 8 VMs, while BT and SP ran across 9 VMs, based on the requirement of these two application kernels. It can be noted from Figure 10, IVShmem reduces the execution

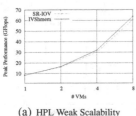
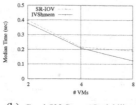
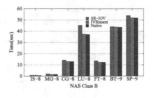

(a) HPL Weak Scalability   (b) Graph500 Strong Scalability

Fig. 9. Virtual Machine Scalability

Fig. 10. Performance Overhead Comparison

times for NAS Parallel Benchmarks - IS (21%), MG (19%), LU (17%), compared to SR-IOV. We also ran them on native environment, and we observe that IVShmem only introduces around 5% overhead compared to native performance. Our evaluation results indicate that IVShmem introduces a small overhead.

5 Related Work

I/O virtualization can be broadly classified into two categories – software based and hardware based. Earlier studies such as [17] and [4] have shown network performance evaluation of software-based approaches in Xen. Studies [14,6,11] have demonstrated that SR-IOV is significantly better than software-based solutions for 10GigE networks. In [14], the authors have provided a detailed performance evaluation on the environment of SR-IOV capable 10GigE in KVM. They have studied several important factors that affect network performance in both virtualized and native systems. Further, studies [9,15,10] with Xen have demonstrated the ability to achieve near-native performance in VM-based environment for HPC.

Our previous study of the performance characteristics of using SR-IOV with InfiniBand [13] has shown that while SR-IOV enables low-latency communication, MPI libraries need to be designed carefully and offer advanced features for improving intra-node, inter-VM communication. Previously, we proposed designs for improving intra-node inter-VM communication by using an Inter-VM Communication Library (IVC) and re-designed the MVAPICH2 library to leverage the features offered by the IVC [8]. However, this solution was based on the Xen platform and did not show the studies with SR-IOV enabled InfiniBand clusters. In addition, an implementation of IVShmem [16] provided the detailed introduction of Nahanni, a IVShmem implementation. Based on the implementation, the authors developed the MPI-Nahanni user-level library, which is ported to the Nemesis channel in MPICH2 library. Their design used memory-mapped shared memory provided by Nahanni in order to accelerate inter-VM communication on the same host.

Different from the previous work, this paper presents a comprehensive performance improvement potential study of IVShmem for intra-host inter-VM communication based on MVAPICH2 library on SR-IOV enabled InfiniBand clusters. Performance evaluation shows promising results of IVShmem based MPI communication using point to point, collective micro-benchmarks and several representative HPC applications. This paper is the first paper to carry out performance studies with IVShmem on SR-IOV enabled InfiniBand clusters.

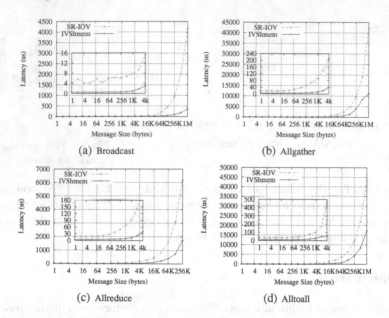

Fig. 11. Collective Communication Performance on 15 VMs

6   Conclusion and Future Work

In this paper, we have studied the performance improvement potential of IVShmem for intra-host inter-VM MPI communication. We have briefly introduced the prototype design of a high performance MPI library for intra-host inter-VM communication using IVShmem. And then we have conducted detailed performance evaluations using MPI micro-benchmarks and representative HPC applications. Our performance evaluations using micro-benchmarks show that IVShmem based MPI library improves point to point (two-sided and one-sided) and collective performance by up to 193% and 91%, respectively. Application evaluation results indicate that based on IVShmem, the execution times of NAS, P3DFFT, LAMMPS benchmarks were decreased by up to 21%, 96%, 8%, respectively, compared to SR-IOV. And the peak performance of HPL is improved by 18% using IVShmem. The evaluations using Graph500 and NAS also demonstrate that IVShmem based MPI library shows good scalability and introduces minor overhead, compared to native performance.

In the future, we plan to continue our research along this direction, and provide a high performance MPI library design to dynamically switch between IVShmem and SR-IOV for efficiently supporting locality aware MPI communication across nodes on SR-IOV enabled InfiniBand clusters.

References

1. Amazon EC2, http://aws.amazon.com/ec2/
2. CPMD Consortium, http://www.openfabrics.org/downloads/perftest/
3. NAS Parallel Benchmarks,
   http://www.nas.nasa.gov/Resources/Software/npb.html

4. Apparao, P., Makineni, S., Newell, D.: Characterization of Network Processing Overheads in Xen. In: Proceedings of the 2nd International Workshop on Virtualization Technology in Distributed Computing, VTDC 2006. IEEE Computer Society, Washington, DC (2006)
5. Pekurovsky, D.: P3DFFT: A Framework for Parallel Computations of Fourier Transforms in Three Dimensions. SIAM Journal on Scientific Computing 34(4), C192–C209 (2012)
6. Dong, Y., Yang, X., Li, J., Liao, G., Tian, K., Guan, H.: High Performance Network Virtualization with SR-IOV. Journal of Parallel and Distributed Computing (2012)
7. Dongarra, J.J., Duff, L.S., Sorensen, D.C., Vorst, H.A.V.: Numerical Linear Algebra for High Performance Computers. Society for Industrial and Applied Mathematics (1998)
8. Huang, W., Koop, M.J., Gao, Q., Panda, D.K.: Virtual Machine aware Communication Libraries for High Performance Computing. In: Proceedings of the 2007 ACM/IEEE Conference on Supercomputing, SC 2007, pp. 9:1–9:12. ACM, New York (2007)
9. Huang, W., Liu, J., Abali, B., Panda, D.K.: A Case for High Performance Computing with Virtual Machines. In: Proceedings of the 20th Annual International Conference on Supercomputing, ICS 2006, New York, NY, USA (2006)
10. Huang, W., Liu, J., Koop, M., Abali, B., Panda, D.: Nomad: Migrating OS-bypass Networks in Virtual Machines. In: Proceedings of the 3rd International Conference on Virtual Execution Environments, VEE 2007, New York, NY, USA (2007)
11. Huang, Z., Ma, R., Li, J., Chang, Z., Guan, H.: Adaptive and Scalable Optimizations for High Performance SR-IOV. In: Proceedings of 2012 IEEE International Conference on Cluster Computing (CLUSTER), pp. 459–467. IEEE (2012)
12. Infiniband Trade Association, http://www.infinibandta.org
13. Jose, J., Li, M., Lu, X., Kandalla, K., Arnold, M., Panda, D.: SR-IOV Support for Virtualization on InfiniBand Clusters: Early Experience. In: Proceedings of 13th IEEE/ACM International Symposium on Cluster, Cloud and Grid Computing (CCGrid), pp. 385–392 (May 2013)
14. Liu, J.: Evaluating Standard-Based Self-Virtualizing Devices: A Performance Study on 10 GbE NICs with SR-IOV Support. In: Proceedings of IEEE International Symposium on Parallel & Distributed Processing (IPDPS), pp. 1–12. IEEE (2010)
15. Liu, J., Huang, W., Abali, B., Panda, D.K.: High Performance VMM-bypass I/O in Virtual Machines. In: Proceedings of the Annual Conference on USENIX 2006 Annual Technical Conference, ATC 2006, Berkeley, CA, USA (2006)
16. Macdonell, A.C.: Shared-Memory Optimizations for Virtual Machines. PhD Thesis. University of Alberta, Edmonton, Alberta, Fall (2011)
17. Menon, A., Santos, J.R., Turner, Y., Janakiraman, G.J., Zwaenepoel, W.: Diagnosing Performance Overheads in the Xen Virtual Machine Environment. In: Proceedings of the 1st ACM/USENIX International Conference on Virtual Execution Environments, VEE 2005, pp. 13–23. ACM, New York (2005)
18. MPI Forum: MPI: A Message Passing Interface. In: Proceedings of Supercomputing (1993)
19. MVAPICH2: High Performance MPI over InfiniBand and iWARP,
    http://mvapich.cse.ohio-state.edu/
20. OpenMPI: Open Source High Performance Computing, http://www.open-mpi.org/
21. Rosenblum, M., Garfinkel, T.: Virtual Machine Monitors: Current Technology and Future Trends. Computer 38(5), 39–47 (2005)
22. Plimpton, S.: Fast Parallel Algorithms for Short-Range Molecular Dynamics. J. Comp. Phys. 117, 1–19 (1995)
23. Single Root I/O Virtualization,
    http://www.pcisig.com/specifications/iov/single_root
24. The Graph500, http://www.graph500.org
25. Huang, W., Liu, J.X., Abali, B., Panda, D.K.: A Case for High Performance Computing with Virtual Machines. In: The Proceedings of 20th Annual International Conference on Supercomputing (ICS), Queensland, Australia, June 28-30 (2006)

Power-Aware L$_1$ and L$_2$ Caches for GPGPUs

Ehsan Atoofian and Ali Manzak

Electrical Engineering Department,
Lakehead University,
Thunder Bay, Canada
{atoofian,amanzak}@lakeheadu.ca

Abstract. General Purpose Graphics Processing Units (GPGPUs) employ several levels of memory to execute hundreds of threads concurrently. L$_1$ and L$_2$ caches are critical to performance of GPGPUs but they are extremely power hungry due to the large number of cores they need to serve. This paper focuses on power consumption of L$_1$ data caches and L$_2$ cache in GPGPUs and proposes two optimization techniques: the first optimization technique places idle cache blocks into drowsy state to reduce leakage power. Our evaluations show that cache blocks are idle for long intervals and putting them into drowsy mode immediately after each access reduces leakage power dramatically with negligible impact on performance. The second optimization technique reduces dynamic power of caches. In GPGPU applications, many warps have inactive threads due to branch divergence. Existing GPGPU architectures access cache blocks for both active and inactive threads, wasting power of caches. We use active mask of GPGPUs and access only the portion of cache blocks that are required by active threads. By dynamically disabling unnecessary sections of cache blocks, we are able to reduce dynamic power of caches significantly.

Keywords: GPGPU, CUDA, Memory hierarchy, Cache, Power.

1 Introduction

Early Graphics Processing Units (GPUs) exploited software-managed local memories (or scratch-pad) instead of caches. GPU workloads include large amount of streaming data which are difficult to cache. However, recent general purpose GPU applications demonstrate high level of data locality which makes them suitable for caches. In response, GPU vendors have included caches in their designs. For instance, NVIDIA introduced up to 48KB L$_1$ cache per core in Fermi [9] and AMD's Fusion GPU [13] offers 16KB L$_1$ cache per core. Both vendors' recent GPUs have global coherent L$_2$ caches. NVIDIA increased size of L$_2$ cache from 768KB in Fermi architecture [9] to 1536KB in GK110 [11]. It is expected that the size of caches grows in future.

Large caches consume significant static and dynamic power. This problem exacerbate in future: voltage reduction has slowed down in recent years, limiting dynamic power reduction through voltage scaling. Lowering the threshold voltage results in significant increase in static power. Therefore, it is necessary to optimize caches to reduce power consumption.

F. Silva et al. (Eds.): Euro-Par 2014, LNCS 8632, pp. 354–365, 2014.
© Springer International Publishing Switzerland 2014

Several architectural and circuit level techniques have been proposed to deal with the power of caches in processors [6, 14]. However, GPGPUs provide unique opportunities to reduce power of caches due to their architecture. For example, once a cache block is accessed by a thread, it takes several hundreds of clock cycles until the same block is accessed again. This is mainly due to the round-robin scheduling policy [5] used in GPGPUs. So, once a thread is executed, it should wait until GPGPU schedules other threads before it is executed again. The long inter-access delay can be used to reduce leakage power by placing cache blocks into drowsy mode [8] immediately after each access. The other opportunity for optimization of caches in GPGPUs is related to underutilization of cache blocks. Due to branch divergence, some applications are not able to fully utilize warp slots each cycle. Hence, dynamically disabling access to inactive cache blocks can reduce dynamic power.

In summary, this paper makes the following contributions:

1) The inter-access delay of L_1 and L_2 cache blocks is in the range of several hundreds of clock cycles. We exploit this property and propose a method that dynamically changes the state of cache blocks between ON and drowsy.

2) The number of active threads within a warp varies across the cycles. We exploit GPU active-mask feature to detect inactive portions of cache blocks before an instruction is scheduled for execution. We disable bit-lines, word-lines, and sense amplifiers of inactive SRAM cells to reduce dynamic power in L_1 and L_2 caches.

The remainder of the paper is structured as follows. Section 2 describes our baseline GPGPU model. Section 3 explains the motivation behind this work. Section 4 details our optimization techniques. Section 5 discusses our measurement methodology and reports the results. Section 6 describes related work and Section 7 concludes the paper.

2   Background

In this section, we provide a brief description of GPGPU architecture. For consistency, we use NVIDIA and CUDA terminology in this paper. However, our techniques are general and can be applied to a broader range of GPGPUs from other vendors.

A GPGPU consists of many Streaming Multiprocessors (SMs) and each SM typically has 8 to 32 Processing Elements (PEs). For instance, NVIDIA's Fermi series has 16 SM and each SM has 32 PEs. Figure 1 shows architecture of a GPGPU. Each SM is associated with a private L_1 data cache and read-only constant and texture caches along with a low latency shared memory. The memory is organized as several DRAM banks and each bank is associated with a slice of shared L_2 cache. SMs and L_2 cache are connected through an interconnection network. In this work, we use a 2D mesh topology for interconnection network since it is simple to implement and is throughput-effective [4].

A CUDA program is composed of one or more kernel functions that are launched and executed on the GPGPU (Figure 2). Each kernel divides its work into identically sized groups, called Cooperative Thread Arrays (CTAs). Every CTA is assigned to an SM for execution. To improve utilization of resources in an SM, more than one CTA can be assigned to the SM. The maximum number of CTAs per SM is limited by SM resources such as number of threads, size of shared memory and register file, etc. [10]. For example if a CTA requires 8KB of shared memory and the baseline SM has 32KB available, then only 4 CTAs can be launched simultaneously on the same SM. From a programmer's point of view, all threads within a CTA execute each instruction in the kernel concurrently. However, on the real hardware, because of resource constrains, software threads are actually executed in groups of threads called warps. A warp has 32 threads on current NVIDIA GPUs. The SM executes one warp at a time. If a warp is stalled due to a long latency instruction, then the SM selects another warp for execution.

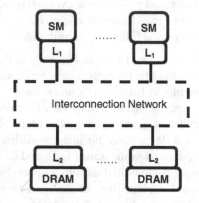

Fig. 1. GPGPU architecture

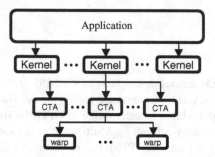

Fig. 2. GPGPU application hierarchy

A GPGPU kernel commonly accesses global memory space which is shared by all threads. When threads access data in the global memory, their accesses go through a two-level cache hierarchy. The L_1 caches are private to SMs but the L_2 cache is shared by all SMs. The L_1 caches are not coherent. They follow write-evict, write-no-allocate policy [10]. On the other side, the L_2 cache is coherent and uses write-back with write-allocate policy [10]. The cache blocks in GPGPUs are wide. For instance, in Fermi family, the cache blocks in L_1 and L_2 caches are 128 bytes. So, if all load or store instructions of a warp map to the same cache line, then all threads of the warp can be completed in a single transaction.

In this work, we employ a two-level scheduler [17]. The scheduler partitions warps into two groups: an active group holding warps eligible for execution and an inactive group of pending warps. Warps that are waiting for long latency events such as loads from DRAM are placed in the pending set. Once a warp is ready for execution, it is removed from the pending list and is inserted into the active list. This approach avoids stall cycles in a one level round-robin based scheduler [5] since warps progress with different speeds and the probability that all warps stall due to a long latency memory operation reduces significantly.

3   Motivation

In this section, we explain motivation behind our work and characterize several workloads used in this study to show power saving opportunities in GPGPUs. We use applications from NVIDIA SDK [18], Rodinia Benchmark suite [20], and Parboil Benchmark suite [21] (for detail of experimental framework, please refer to Section 5). The second column in Table 1 shows abbreviations for the benchmarks.

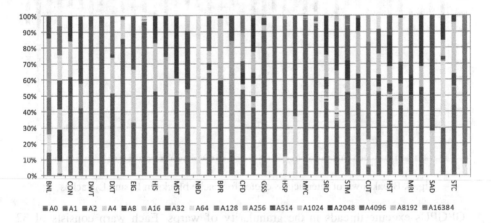

Fig. 3. Breakdown of accesses to cache blocks in L_1 and L_2 caches

Figure 3 shows breakdown of accesses to the cache blocks in L_1 and L_2 caches. For each benchmark, the first bar corresponds to the L_1 cache and the second bar corresponds to the L_2 cache. Each bar in the graph is divided into 16 sections. The top most component of a bar labeled A16384 shows number of blocks that are accessed 16384 times or more. Similarly, the bottom most component labeled A0 shows the number of blocks that are not accessed by any SMs. In L_1 caches, 50% of cache blocks are accessed 16 times or less. In L_2 cache, 50% of cache blocks are accessed 8 times or less. Since most of memory requests are serviced by L_1 caches, cache blocks in L_2 are idle more often. In DWT, GSS, and MYC, more than 88% of the cache blocks are never used for execution of the programs. These cache blocks can be put into drowsy mode to reduce power consumption.

Next, we focus on cache blocks that are accessed by PEs. Figure 4 shows break-down of inter-access cycles for cache blocks in L_1 and L_2 caches. For each bench-mark, the first bar corresponds to the L_1 caches and the second bar corresponds to the L_2 cache. We measure the number of cycles elapsed between two consecutive access-es to the same cache blocks. For L_1 caches, more than 50% of cache blocks have in-ter-access cycle of 128 or more. For L_2 cache, more than 50% of cache blocks have inter-access cycle of 64 or more. On average, the inter-access cycle for L_1 and L_2 caches are 2442- and 2840-cycle, respectively. In the two-level scheduler, after a warp is scheduled for execution, it should wait until all the other warps in the active list are scheduled. The only time that a warp is scheduled for execution in two con-secutive cycles is when there is no other warp in the active list. Hence, quite often, there is a gap between two executions of a warp. This inter-access delay provides opportunity to put the cache blocks into drowsy mode immediately after they have been accessed.

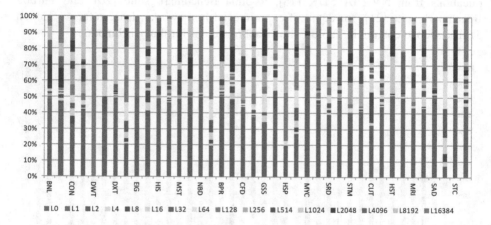

Fig. 4. Breakdown of inter-access cycles for cache blocks in L_1 and L_2 caches

GPGPUs execute threads in the granularity of warps. Each warp consists of 32 threads executing instructions in a lock-step manner. A fully utilized warp has 32 active threads executing one instruction at a time. In Graphics applications, quite often warps utilize all 32 slots. However, this may not be true for general purpose applications. General purpose applications exhibit more complex control flow behav-ior due to frequent branch instructions. Conditional branch instructions can cause threads within a warp take different paths, or diverge. Since GPGPUs allow a warp to have only one active PC at any given time, GPGPUs execute taken and not-taken paths in two phases. In the first phase, threads in the taken path execute and all threads in the not-taken path are idle. In the second phase, threads in the not-taken path execute and the rest are idle. Existing GPGPU implementations access cache blocks for all 32 threads within a warp although many warps may have fewer than 32 threads. The last two columns in Table 1 show the percentage of active threads within the warps that access L_1 and L_2 cache blocks, respectively. It is important to note that L$_2$ cache is accessed when a miss occurs in any of the L$_1$ caches including data, texture, and shared L$_1$ caches. This is the main reason that block utilization in L$_2$ cache is lower than block utilization in L$_1$ data caches. While in some benchmarks, i.e. CUT, all warps have 32 active threads throughout the entire execution, some others, i.e. MYC, have very low cache block utilizations. Unnecessary accesses to the cache blocks in benchmarks with low warp utilization waste power. By avoiding these unnecessary accesses, we can reduce dynamic power in caches.

Table 1. GPGPU Benchmarks and Warp Utilization

Benchmark	Abbr.	L$_1$ block Utilization	L$_2$ block Utilization
binomialOptions	BNL	99%	98%
convolutionSeparable	CON	100%	81%
dwtHaar1D	DWT	100%	95%
dxtc	DXT	100%	1%
eigenvalues	EIG	100%	33%
histogram	HIS	100%	94%
MersenneTwister	MST	100%	73%
nbody	NBD	100%	14%
backprop	BPR	91%	81%
cfd	CFD	100%	93%
gaussian	GSS	65%	37%
hotspot	HSP	100%	96%
myocyte	MYC	4%	2%
srad_v1	SRD	99%	99%
streamcluster	STM	98%	99%
cutcp	CUT	100%	100%
histo	HST	100%	98%
mri-gridding	MRI	100%	99%
sad	SAD	93%	93%
sgemm	STC	100%	100%

4   Reducing Power of L$_1$ and L$_2$ Caches

In this section, we present static and dynamic power reduction techniques based on opportunities discussed in Section 3.

4.1   Static Power Reduction Using Drowsy Cells

Inter-access cycles in Figure 4 show that cache blocks are not accessed for long intervals and it is possible to save power of cache blocks when they are idle. Several techniques have been proposed to reduce leakage power of cache cells by turning off cache blocks when they are not needed [1, 22]. The drawback of these techniques is that data in cache blocks are lost when they are turned off and the extra power needed to access interconnection network and L_2 cache (if L_1 miss occurs) or main memory (if L_2 miss occurs) to reload data may negate any power saving and may degrade performance. To avoid these pitfalls, we put cache blocks into drowsy mode [8].

A drowsy cell exploits dynamic voltage scaling to reduce leakage power. Each cache block can switch between high and low (drowsy) supply voltages. When a cache block is idle its voltage is set to low supply voltage. Due to short-channel effects in deep-submicron processes, leakage current reduces significantly in idle cache blocks. The combined effect of reduced leakage current and voltage results in a dramatic saving in static power. Whenever an SM sends a request to a cache, the cache controller checks the condition of the voltage of the cache line. If the accessed line is in normal mode, no extra delay is incurred, because the power mode of the line can be checked concurrently with the read and comparison of the tag. However, if the line is in drowsy mode, we need to prevent the discharge of the bit-line of the cache line because it may read out the wrong data. We need to wait an extra cycle to switch the supply voltage back to normal mode before reading out the data.

One implication of drowsy cell is that execution time of programs may increase since drowsy cells require extra time to wake-up. We use a two-level scheduler [17] to select a warp for execution. Each cycle, the scheduler selects a ready warp from the active list and sends it for execution. To hide wake-up latency of drowsy cells, the scheduler should send the source operands of a load/store instruction to the memory unit before the associated instruction is issued. To handle this, the scheduler can issue a warp and concurrently look into active warps to find the warp that is going to be issued in the next cycle. Thus, one can eliminate the overhead of drowsy cells with 1-cyle wake-up delay. Similarly, the scheduler can look into active list and send information of the warp to the memory unit n cycles ahead and may wake-up drowsy cells to hide n cycles of wake-up delay. So, the two-level scheduler is able to hide the latency of drowsy cells. However, we also evaluate a scheduler which is not able to check the warps ahead of time. In Section 5, we explore the performance impact of drowsy cells with different wake-up latencies assuming that it is not feasible to hide the latency of drowsy cells.

4.2   Reducing Dynamic Power Using Active Mask

In the previous section, we used drowsy cells to reduce leakage power when a cache block is idle. However, when the cache block is accessed all bytes within the block are placed in ON state. For example, in Fermi family, each cache block is 128-byte. So, when SM executes a load/store instruction, the whole 128-byte is woken up. Accessing such a large number of SRAM cells incurs significant dynamic power because of activating word-lines, bit-lines, and sense amplifiers.

As shown in Table 1, the percentage of active threads varies across the benchmarks. Because of branch divergence, some warps cannot fill the whole 32 slots. However, in existing implementations of GPGPUs, a warp with partial utilization still activates the whole cache block. This means that we have to pre-charge word-line (WL), bit-line (BL), bit-line-bar (BLB), and sense amplifiers for the whole cache block although a subset of the cache block is used for warp execution. One way to reduce dynamic power of the cache blocks is to access only portions of cache blocks that are accessed by active threads. GPUs use an active mask which indicates active threads within a warp. The mask is a vector of 32 bits and each bit corresponds to a thread. When a branch instruction diverges, the bits corresponding to active threads are set and the rest are cleared. Hence, we can use active mask to disable portions of cache blocks associated with inactive threads.

We use the Divided Word Line (DWL) [23] technique to implement active mask aware access to caches. Figure 5 illustrates the structure of DWL. In DWL, the WL is segmented into several Small WLs (SWLs). Each SWL enables or disables accessing to the portion of cache block attached to it. For our work, each SWL covers 4-byte of the cache block. The output of a row decoder is connected to SWLs. GPU architecture is suited for easy integration of DWL into caches. A warp's active mask has all information required to determine which SWL should be active or inactive. Each SWL is activated by an AND gate which has two inputs, the horizontal line coming from the row decoder and the vertical line coming from the active mask. DWL reduces dynamic power since whenever a cache block is accessed those bytes within the cache block that correspond to the inactive threads are disabled.

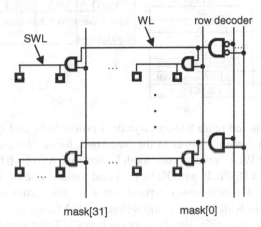

Fig. 5. Structure of DWL

5   Methodology and Results

We used GPGPU-Sim (version 3.1.1) [3] to evaluate our power aware optimization techniques. GPGPU-Sim is a publicly available, detailed cycle-based simulator for GPGPUs. We configure the simulator to closely match NVIDIA's Fermi GTX480 as recommended in the GPGPU-Sim manual (Table 2). We use a collection of benchmarks from CUDA SDK [18], Rodinia Benchmark suite [20], and Parboil Benchmark suite [21] (Table 1). We ran the benchmarks until completion or for 1 billion instructions, whichever comes first.

5.1   Experimental Results

In this section, we report power saving in L_1 and L_2 caches. Figure 6 shows static, dynamic, and total power saving in L_1 and L_2 caches. For each benchmark, the first bar represents static power in caches with drowsy mode relative to the static power of the baseline scheme. Bars less than one show power reduction. In order to quantify the leakage current in caches, we modeled a cache based on 6T SRAM cells in HSPICE. We used the technology files from Predictive Technology Models (PTM) [12] with feature size of 32-nm and nominal voltage of 0.9V. We found that the state of SRAM cells can be maintained if V_{dd} is reduced up to 0.2V. While an ideal drowsy cell can work at 0.2v, in practice it is necessary to add safety margin to take into account noise and also mismatch between transistors. Table 3 shows static power for nominal voltage and reduced voltages in a row of L1 and L2 caches. Even when V_{dd} is reduced to 0.4v, the static power is less than 8% of static power when cache cells operate at full V_{dd}. For the rest of this section, we assume drowsy cells operate at 0.4v.

Table 2. GPGPU-Sim Configuration

Number of SMs	16
Warps/Shader	48
Threads per warp	32
PEs/SM	32
Registers per core	32768
L_1 (size/assoc/line)	16KB/4-way/128B
L_2 (size/assoc/line)	768KB/16-way/128B
Memory controller	FR-FCFS

Table 3. Static power in a row of L_1/L_2

$V_{dd}(v)$	0.2	0.3	0.4	0.9
Static Power L_1/L_2(mw)	0.04/0.26	0.056/0.36	0.08/0.53	1.08/6.7

The second column in Figure 6 shows dynamic power in L_1 and L_2 caches with active mask relative to dynamic power of the baseline scheme. We extracted resistance and capacitance of SWLs based on the model used in CACTI v6.0 [15]. Similar to static power, we used HSPICE with PTM [12] and feature size of 32-nm to estimate dynamic power. The dynamic power depends on warp utilization of the benchmarks (Table 1). Benchmarks with low warp utilization, i.e. MYC, show significant dynamic power saving. On the other side, benchmarks such as CUT that usually have 32 active threads do not benefit from this technique. Benchmarks with moderate warp utilization, i.e. GSS, have limited dynamic power saving. On average, the dynamic power reduces by 7% and 24% in L_1 and L_2 caches, respectively.

The third column in Figure 6 shows the relative total power saving. The combined system first changes the state of a requested cache block from drowsy to active. Then, based on active mask, it decides which portion of the cache block should be activated. Benchmarks with low warp utilization, i.e. MYC, have the highest power saving because they take advantage of both the leakage and the dynamic power saving techniques. On average, the total power is reduced by 90% and 96% in L_1 and L_2 caches, respectively.

As we discussed in Section 4.1, a two level scheduler can activate a cache block ahead of time and avoid any penalty due to wake-up delay. However, if it is not feasible to hide wake-up latency (for example if GPGPU uses a scheduler other than the two level scheduler), we assume that this delays execution of the warps. To quantify the effect of wake-up latency, we ran the benchmarks with one and two extra cycles overhead. Note that these latencies are in addition to the latency of the baseline cache. Figure 7 shows performance of a GPGPU with drowsy cache relative to the baseline scheme. Bars less than one show slow-down. A GPGPU has many warps and if a warp is stalled due to cache delay, the GPGPU can issue and execute another warp. Hence, the performance changes slightly with wake-up delay. On average, the performance of the benchmarks changes by less than 0.3% when wake-up delay is one and two cycles. In some benchmarks, i.e. STM, execution time reduces when wake-up delay increase. We analyzed these benchmarks and found that the sequence of executed warps changes with wake-up delay. In the new sequence, cache miss rate reduces and this improves performance of these benchmarks slightly.

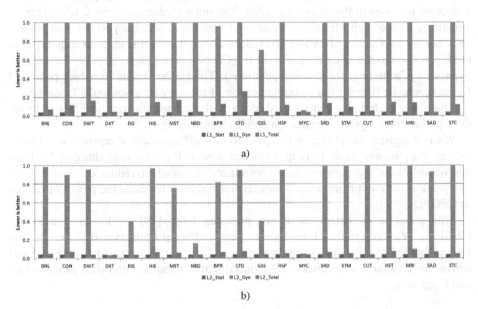

Fig. 6. Static, dynamic, and total power saving in a) L$_1$ and b) L$_2$ caches

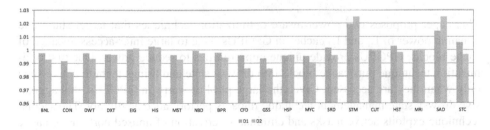

Fig. 7. Performance impact of drowsy cache with one and two cycles wake-up delay

6   Related Work

Gebhart et al. [2] proposed a unified local memory which can dynamically change the capacity of register, shared memory, and cache on a per application basis. Existing implementations of GPGPUs use a one-size-fit-all policy and hard-partition local storage of an SM in design time. However, GPGPU applications have diverse local storage requirements and a single memory unit is often most critical to performance of a given application. Gebhart et al. [2] proposed a unified memory architecture that aggregates different memory units and allows a flexible allocation based on applications' requirements. The tuning that this flexibility enables improves both performance and energy of GPGPUs.

Sankaranarayanan et al. [7] proposed adding tinyCache to reduce power of L_1 data cache. A tinyCache is a small filter inserted between a PE and an L_1 data cache and intercepts accesses to the shared L_1 cache. The main challenge of tinyCache is cache coherency. Since each PE has a private tinyCache, it is necessary to maintain coherency across tinyCaches of an SM. To reduce coherence overhead, Sankaranarayanan et al. proposed to either evict content of tinyCache into L_1 cache (e.g. for barriers) or bypass tinyCache (e.g. for atomic operations). TinyCache is able to reduce power of L_1 data cache by filtering out a sizable portion of memory accesses to the L_1 cache.

The above techniques can be used along with our optimization techniques to reduce power consumption of caches in GPGPUs further.

Warped register file [16] uses compiler to turn off unallocated registers and places the rest into drowsy mode to reduce leakage power. It also avoids charging bit-lines and word-lines of registers associated with inactive threads to reduce dynamic power. Our work is different from warped register file since we focus on the power of caches in GPGPUs.

This paper is an extension of our previous work [19] on L_1 data caches in GPGPUs. We have studies inter-access cycle and warp utilization in L_2 cache and found that the behavior of L_2 cache is similar to L_1 cache. We applied drowsy cell and active mask to the cache blocks and reduced static, dynamic, and total power of L_1 and L_2 caches.

7   Conclusion

This paper proposes two power-aware optimization techniques that target static and dynamic power of L_1 and L_2 caches in GPGPUs. Due to large inter-access distance of cache blocks, GPGPUs provide unique opportunities to reduce power. Our first optimization technique puts cache blocks into drowsy state and brings them to active state only when they are accessed. Given the large pool of warps in GPGPUs, this aggressive drowsy state management technique impacts performance negligibly. The second technique exploits active masks and eliminates activation of unused portions of cache blocks. These two optimization techniques combined are able to reduce power of L_1 and L_2 caches by 90% and 96%, respectively.

Acknowledgment. This work was supported by the National Sciences and Engineering Research Council of Canada.

References

1. Kaxiras, S., Hu, Z., Martonosi, M.: Cache decay: Exploiting generational behavior to reduce cache leakage power. In: Proceedings of ISCA, pp. 240–251 (2001)
2. Gebhart, M., et al.: Unifying primary cache, scratch, and register file memories in a throughput processor. In: Proceedings of MICRO-45, pp. 96–106 (2012)
3. Bakhoda, A., Yuan, G., Fung, W., Wong, H., Aamodt, T.: Analyzing CUDA workloads using a detailed GPU simulator. In: Proceedings of ISPASS (April 2009)
4. Bakhoda, A., Kim, J., Aamodt, T.: Throughput-effective On-chip Networks for Manycore Accelerators. In: MICRO (2010)
5. Fung, W., Sham, I., Yuan, G., Aamodt, T.: DynamicWarp Formation and Scheduling for Efficient GPU Control Flow. In: MICRO (2007)
6. Boettcher, M., et al.: MALEC: A Multiple Access Low Energy Cache. In: Design, Automation & Test in Europe Conference & Exhibition (DATE), pp. 368–373 (2013)
7. Sankaranarayanan, A., Ardestani, E.K., Briz, J.L., Renau, J.: An Energy Efficient GPGPU Memory Hierarchy with Tiny Incoherent Caches. In: ISLPED, pp. 9–14 (2013)
8. Flautner, K., et al.: Drowsy caches: Simple techniques for reducing leakage power. In: Proceedings of ISCA, pp. 148–157 (2002)
9. NVIDIA Corp. NVIDIA's Next Generation CUDA Compute Architecture: Fermi (2009)
10. NVIDIA. CUDA Programming Guide Version 5.0 (2013)
11. NVIDIA Corp. NVIDIA's Next Generation CUDA Compute Architecture: Kepler GK110 (2012)
12. Arizona state university predictive technology model, http://ptm.asu.edu
13. Demers, E.: Evolution of AMD graphics, AMD Fusion Developer Summit (2011)
14. Agrawal, A., Jain, P., Ansari, A., Torrellas, J.: Refrint: Intelligent refresh to minimize power in on-chip multiprocessor cache hierarchies. In: Proceedings of HPCA (2013)
15. Muralimanoharet, N., et al.: Optimizing NUCA Organizations and Wiring Alternatives for Large Caches with CACTI 6.0. In: Proceedings of MICRO (2007)
16. Abdel-Majeed, M., Annavaram, M.: Warped Register File: A Power Efficient Register File for GPGPUs. In: Proceedings of HPCA (2013)
17. Gebhart, M., et al.: Energy-efficient mechanisms for managing thread context in throughput processors. In: Proceedings of the ISCA, pp. 235–246 (2011)
18. NVIDIA. CUDA C/C++ SDK code samples (2013)
19. Atoofian, E.: Reducing Static and Dynamic Power of L1 Data Caches in GPGPUs. In: Proceedings of HPPAC, Phoenix AZ (2014)
20. Che, S., Boyer, M., Meng, J., Tarjan, D., Sheaffer, J., Lee, S.-H., Skadron, K.: Rodinia: A Benchmark Suite for Heterogeneous Computing. In: IISWC (2009)
21. Stratton, J.A., et al.: Parboil: A Revised Benchmark Suite for Scientific and Commercial Throughput Computing (2012)
22. Zhou, H., et al.: Adaptive mode-control: A static-power-efficient cache design. In: Proceedings of International Conference on Parallel Architectures and Compilation Techniques (2001)
23. Yoshimoto, M., et al.: A divided word-line structure in the static ram and its application to a 64k full cmos ram. IEEE Journal of Solid-State Circuits 18(5), 479–485 (1983)

Power Consumption Due to Data Movement in Distributed Programming Models

Siddhartha Jana[1], Oscar Hernandez[2], Stephen Poole[2], and Barbara Chapman[1]

[1] Computer Science Department,
University of Houston,
Houston, Texas
{sidjana,chapman}@cs.uh.edu
[2] Computer Science and Mathematics Division,
Oak Ridge National Laboratory,
Oak Ridge, Tennessee
{oscar,spoole}@ornl.gov

Abstract. The amount of energy consumed due to data movement poses a serious challenge when implementing and using distributed programming models. Message-passing models like MPI provide the user with explicit interfaces to initiate data-transfers among distributed processes. In this work, we establish the notion that from a programmer's standpoint, design decisions like the size of the data-payload to be transferred and the number of explicit MPI calls to service such transfers have a direct impact on the power signatures of communication kernels. Upon closer look, we additionally observe that the choice of the transport layer (along with the associated interconnect) and the design of the data transfer protocol, both, contribute to these signatures. This paper presents a fine-grained study on the impact of the power and energy consumption due to data movement in distributed programming models. We hope that results discussed in this work would motivate application and system programmers to include energy consumption as one of the important design factors while targeting HPC systems.

1 Introduction and Related Work

One of the primary challenges on the pathway to Exascale Computing is the 20MW power consumption envelope established by the U.S. Department of Energy's Exascale Initiative Steering Committee [11]. The direct outcome of this has been a rising concern about the energy and power consumption of large-scale applications that rely on various communication libraries for efficient data movement in distributed systems. As part of this work, we establish the notion that the factors responsible for the performance of such libraries, also govern the power-profiles of such applications. Fig. 1 lists many such factors throughout the hardware and software stack.

This work is an extension of our previous experience of studying the impact of one-sided communication in PGAS models (OpenSHMEM) [7]. We had

F. Silva et al. (Eds.): Euro-Par 2014, LNCS 8632, pp. 366–378, 2014.

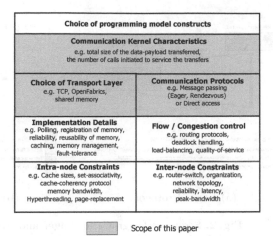

Choice of programming model constructs	
Communication Kernel Characteristics e.g. total size of the data-payload transferred, the number of calls initiated to service the transfers	
Choice of Transport Layer e.g. TCP, OpenFabrics, shared memory	**Communication Protocols** e.g. Message passing (Eager, Rendezvous) or Direct access
Implementation Details e.g. Polling, registration of memory, reliability, reusability of memory, caching, memory management, fault-tolerance	**Flow / Congestion control** e.g. routing protocols, deadlock handling, load-balancing, quality-of-service
Intra-node Constraints e.g. Cache sizes, set-associativity, cache-coherency protocol memory bandwidth, Hyperthreading, page-replacement	**Inter-node Constraints** e.g. router-switch, organization, network topology, reliability, latency, peak-bandwidth

Scope of this paper

Fig. 1. Factors impacting the energy and power consumption across the hardware and software stack

learned that managing small-sized data transfers on RDMA-capable networks are more energy efficent that handling large bulk transfers. In this paper, we present empirical evidence highlighting the contribution of design factors within the software stack to the power consumption by the underlying system. Our takeaway from this study is that the protocols used to implement such interfaces, play a significant role in impacting its power-cost. In addition, since the design of communication libraries are tuned to specific interconnect solutions, the choice of the transport layer adopted for servicing data transfers plays an equally significant role.

In Section 2, we discuss the impact of the above factors on the behavior of two-sided communication interfaces within MPI, the de facto standard for distributed memory model. This is an extension of past work on analyzing the impact of data-transfer characteristics on one-sided communication interfaces [7]. We discuss the characteristics of our testbed and our experimental methodology in Section 3. This is followed by a description of our observations of the impact on power consumption by CPU cores and the DRAM while relying on Ethernet (via traditional TCP) and Infiniband (via OFED or OpenFabrics Enterprise Distribution [1]) fabrics (Section 4). All of these are discussed with respect to the implementation of two basic message-passing schemes - the Eager and Rendezvous protocols. Finally in Section 4, we summarize our findings by discussing the total power efficiency achievable for each of the above configurations. We hope this work motivates the practice of taking power-metrics into consideration while designing middleware solutions for Exascale-era machines.

2   Factors Affecting Power and Energy Profile of Remote Data Transfers

Two-sided data-transfer in distributed-memory models like MPI, sockets, etc. require the active participation of both the sender and the receiver of the data.

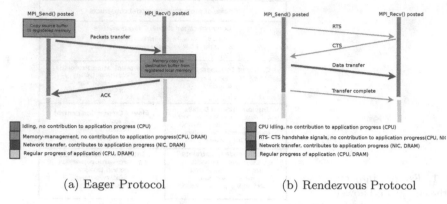

(a) Eager Protocol   (b) Rendezvous Protocol

Fig. 2. Sequence Diagrams for Eager and Rendezvous protocols

The impact on the achievable latency and bandwidth of such transfers depend on the design of the transport layer (and the associated interconnect) and the data transfer protocol. As part of this work, we learned that the impact of these factors on the energy metrics is very important.

2.1   Choice of Transport Layer and the Associated Interconnect

If the target platform relies on an OS-based TCP protocol for servicing data transfers, CPU cores undergo multiple switches between user and supervisor operating modes. In addition, relying on Ethernet-based fabric has the potential of degrading the achievable efficiency both in performance and energy consumption (as discussed later). To avoid this, a communication library may exploit kernel-bypass mechanisms and RDMA-based capabilities of the OFED stack on top of modern interconnects like InfiniBand, etc.

2.2   Design of Data-Transfer Protocols

Data transfers within message-passing libraries are based on two well-established paradigms - the eager and rendezvous protocols. The primary phases involved in these protocols are depicted in the line diagrams in Fig. 2.

Rendezvous protocols incorporate RTS-CTS[1] handshaking to ensure that the sender waits for an explicit request from the receiver before servicing the actual transfer. Such an exchange ensures that the receiver's buffer is ready for being overwritten with the incoming payload. This method has proven to be beneficial for large bulk transfers since the overhead of the handshaking operation gets eclipsed by the gain in the throughput of the end-to-end data movement [2]. For small message sizes, however the additional round trip proves expensive.

Eager protocols help mitigate the above overhead by reducing the time and energy spent by the sender waiting for the receiver to post the destination buffer

---

[1] Request-To-Send / Clear-To-Send two-sided handshake signal.

address. The sender may choose to start transfering its data to a pre-allocated buffer without waiting for the receiver to send a CTS signal. This is easily facilitated by an underlying interconnect solution that supports RDMA-based transfers. Once the receiver calls MPI_Recv(), it can copy-out the data from this pre-allocated buffer. Not surprisingly, the impact of latency of such techniques is bounded by the costs of memory registration and the additional in-memory copies both at the sender's and the receiver's end.

2.3 Power versus Latency

Energy efficient communication depends on a number of factors listed in Fig. 1. Through this text, we hope to establish the difference between optimizing for energy versus power. It must be noted that one doesn't always have to sacrifice the lowest possible latency to achieve energy-efficiency[2]. Consider the plots shown in Fig. 3.

The plots (a) and (b) depict the average power consumed by CPU cores (Y-axis) and the corresponding latency (X-axis) incurred while transferring a 32KB payload across the network (MPI Send-Recv over InfiniBand). If this payload is divided into 64 fragments, the energy consumption by the CPU cores is about 6 mJ and the transfer takes about 370 μs to complete. The average power consumption during this transfer is about 16.21 Watts (Fig. 3a). If instead, we chose to split this payload into only 2 fragments (16KB each), the energy consumption drops to 0.33 mJ (by 94.5%) and latency to 20 μs (by 94.6%). However, this comes at the cost of a rise in power consumption to 16.565W, i.e. an increment by 1.8% (Fig. 3b). Thus, despite the higher power consumption, choosing the latter option enables the CPU cores to service the transfer using lesser energy.

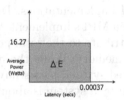

(a) Using 64 fragments to transfer data. Energy=6mJ

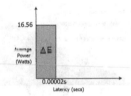

(b) Using 2 fragments to transfer data. Energy=0.33mJ

Fig. 3. Power Versus Latency. Use of a 32KB data payload transferred using MPI_Send() over InfiniBand

3 Experimental Setup

Our study was aimed at performing a fine-grained analysis of the impact on different components of a distributed system, namely, the cores, the socket, the motherboard, the memory unit, and the entire compute-node as a whole.

---

[2] It is very important to remember that optimizing for energy consumption is not always equivalent to optimizing for power.

Table 1. Test-Platform characteristics

RAPL monitored Node		PowerPack monitored SystemG Node	
Processor	Intel Xeon CPU E5-2670	Processor	Intel Xeon CPU E5462
Microarchitecture	Intel's Sandy Bridge	Microarchitecture	Intel's Sandy Bridge
Operating Frequency	2.6 GHz	Operating Frequency	2.8 GHz
Maximum Thermal Design Power (TDP)	115 Watts	Maximum Thermal Design Power (TDP)	80 Watts
Hyperthreading support	Disabled	Hyperthreading support	Disabled
Infiniband card	Mellanox MT26428, fw-ver:2.7.0	Infiniband card	Mellanox MT26428, fw-ver:2.5.9
Linux kernel version	2.6.32 x86_64	Linux kernel version	2.6.32 x86_64
Compiler	gcc version 4.4.6	Compiler	gcc version 4.4.4
Compiler flags used	-O3	Compiler flags used	-O3
Energy Sampling rate	1ms	Power Sampling rate	10ms

The experiments were performed for two different implementations of MPI - Open MPI [4] and MVAPICH2 [9]. We observed similar behavior between the two MPI implementations. Due to space constraints, we discuss the impact of only Open MPI's implementation of data transfers on two major components [5] that contribute to the total power consumption of a system, viz. the CPU cores and the memory. While the network card forms an important component of a distributed system, past study indicates that its impact on the total power consumption by a system is about 1% [3]. We therefore omit any further discussion on the impact of NIC from the rest of the text.

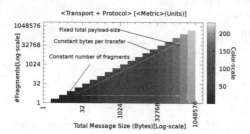

Fig. 4. Layout of the plots in this paper

Note on Interpreting the Graphical Plots. We briefly discuss the method of interpreting the plots presented in the following sections. Each plot illustrates empirical results in terms of an energy metric. It corresponds to a specific transport layer and a communication protocol.

The coordinate axes (log-scale) correspond to two controllable factors that define a communication phase in an application - the total size of data transferred during that phase (X-axis) and the number of explicit MPI-calls (Y-axis) used to transfer that payload. Throughout this text, we refer to the latter as the count of *fragments*[3]. The shade of a point in this coordinate space indicates the value of monitored metric that is represented by the color-scale to the right of each plot.

Microbenchmark Used for Evaluating the Impact of Data Transfers. The pseudo-code and the sequence diagram of the synthetic microbenchmark

---

[3] It must be noted that each fragment may further be divided into smaller chunks by the underlying layers based on the middleware design, NIC hardware contraints, etc.

Table 2. Synthetic microbenchmark used for evaluating energy and power consumption by varying the total size of data payload and the number of fragments

Sequence Diagram	Code snippet

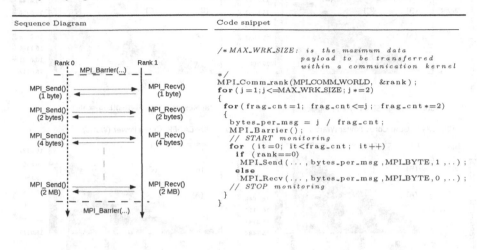

```
/* MAX_WRK_SIZE: is the maximum data
                payload to be transferred
                within a communication kernel
*/
MPI_Comm_rank(MPI_COMM_WORLD, &rank);
for( j=1; j<=MAX_WRK_SIZE; j*=2)
{
  for( frag_cnt=1; frag_cnt<=j; frag_cnt*=2)
  {
    bytes_per_msg = j / frag_cnt;
    MPI_Barrier();
    // START monitoring
    for (it=0; it<frag_cnt; it++)
      if (rank==0)
        MPI_Send(..., bytes_per_msg, MPI_BYTE, 1, ..);
      else
        MPI_Recv(..., bytes_per_msg, MPI_BYTE, 0, ..);
    // STOP monitoring
  }
}
```

used to study the impact of the explicit data transfers are presented in Table 2. It must be noted that the type of transfers being evaluated use traditional MPI blocking two-sided point-to-point interfaces.

Test Platform for Monitoring Energy and Power Consumption. We incorporated two different power-monitoring schemes:

- *Intel's Running Average Power Limiting (RAPL):* The energy consumption by the CPU cores were monitored using the RAPL interface [6] which are exposed as model specific registers on SandyBridge platforms. These were read using VampirTrace [8] via PAPI [10]
- *PowerPack on SystemG:* The power consumption by the memory unit, was measured using the PowerPack 4.0 framework on the SystemG cluster at Virginia Tech. The power consumption is measured directly using the four VDC pins that supply power to the module [5].

4 Empirical Observation and Analysis

In this section, we present our observations of the impact on the energy and power consumption by the CPU cores and memory due to the factors discussed in the previous section.

4.1 Using TCP over Ethernet

Using Rendezvous Protocol. Consider the power consumption by the CPU cores servicing the sender process (Fig. 5a(I)). While handling small data payloads ($< 1KB$) the CPU cores suffer a high power cost (region A). The reason

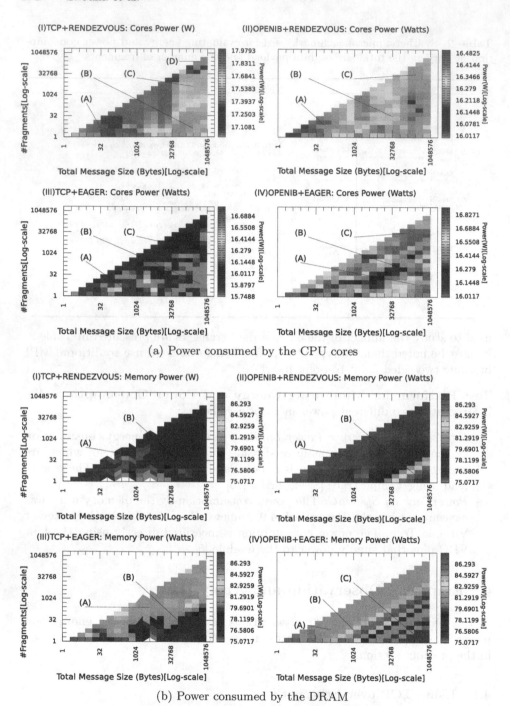

(a) Power consumed by the CPU cores

(b) Power consumed by the DRAM

Fig. 5. Power consumed by the CPU cores and the DRAM while servicing remote data transfers by the sender process

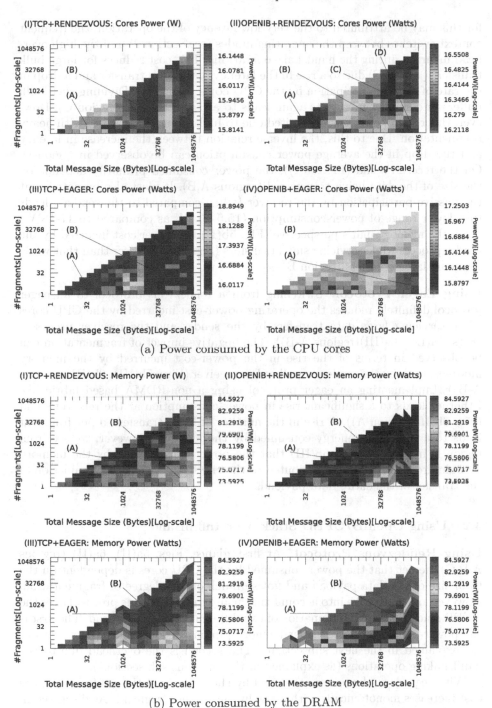

(a) Power consumed by the CPU cores

(b) Power consumed by the DRAM

Fig. 6. Power consumed by the CPU cores and the DRAM while servicing remote data transfers by the receiver process

for this may be attributed to the very low latency of the operation, the frequent context switches between the operating modes (see Section 2) and the high overhead incurred during the handshake operations. This cost reduces for large bulk transfers ($> 32KB$) due to a rise in the latency of the data transfer and a drop in the rate of active participation by the CPU cores (region B). Dividing such bulk buffers into smaller fragments again leads to a rise in the cost (region-C). However, this rise in power-cost in limited due to high latency that arises with heavy fragmentation. Due to this, the inverse relation between the increase in latency and the drop in the average power consumption can be observed in region-D. On the receiver's end (Fig. 6a(I)), the power consumed primarily depends on the size of the data being transferred (regions A,B). It must also be noted that the passive participation by the receiver (when compared to the sender), leads to a lower range of power-consumption (15.5-16.2W as compared to 17-18W). From the memory unit's perspective (Fig. 5b(I)) the power cost incurred by the sender process while servicing small transfers (region A) is lesser than that while servicing large transfers (region B).

Using Eager Protocol. Switching from a rendezvous protocol to an eager protocol definitely reduces the operating power-cost incurred by the CPU cores while servicing large data transfers by the sender and the receiver processes (Figs. 5a(III), 6a(III)(regions A-B)). The negative impact of fragmentation can be observed in terms of the rise in the power-cost incurred by the memory modules, both by the sender as well as the receiver (Figs. 5b(III), 6b(III)(regions A-B)). Implementing an eager protocol using a non-RDMA based fabric like Ethernet leads to a significant rise in power-consumption at the receiver's end (Fig. 6b(III)(region A)). A rise in the number of bytes transferred per fragment leads to a rise in the energy consumed by the memory. However, we see from region B in Figs. 5b(III), 6b(III) that the power consumption by the memory module drops. This can be attributed to the rise in the latency in completion of the transfer of the entire data payload.

4.2   Using OpenIB/OFED Stack over InfiniBand

Using Rendezvous Protocol. At first glance, Figs. 5a(II), 6a(II) (regions A,B,C), depict that the power consumed by the CPU cores is dependent on the total size of the data payload and not so much on the degree of fragmentation. However, one must take into account that using the rendezvous protocol over the OFED stack leads to a combination of two different types of overhead. The first is the power-penalty of using either memory-pinning or local memcpy operations (as explained in the next subsection). The second is the overhead due to the handshaking operations (as explained in the previous sub-sections).

With regards to the power consumed by the memory at the sender's side, the cost increases monotonically with a rise in the size per fragment. As discussed in the following bullet point below, using the OFED stack is accompanied with the power-penalty of either memory-pinning or local memcpy operations. This cost varies with the number of bytes transferred with each fragment (Fig.5b(III)).

Using Eager Protocol. Parallel diagonally-colored bands in Figs. 5a(IV), 5b(IV), 6a(IV), 6b(IV) show that the power consumed by the cores and the memory unit, both depend on the number of bytes transferred within each fragment. As discussed before, either the memory space containing these fragments are dynamically pinned-down (registered) with the NIC or its contents are copied over to some pre-registered buffer. The performance penalty of dynamic registration of small buffers is expensive. Thus, a runtime implementation would typically perform a local copy of the contents into a pre-registered buffer. Our experience shows that the power cost of this memory copy increases with rise in the fragment size (i.e. bytes/fragment). This can be observed in region-C. As the size of each fragment increases, an implementation would typically start dynamically registering user buffers with the NIC. Either way, this keeps the CPU cores active. It is during this inflection point that we observe a slight drop in the cores power consumption. Further increase in the size of fragment again leads to a rise in this cost (region A).

Complementary to the CPU power consumption, the power-cost incurred by the memory rises with the size per fragment (region A). It too hits a cool spot (region B) and then rises up monotonically with a rise in the achievable bandwidth on the NIC.

4.3   Summary: Achievable Energy-Efficiency during Data Transfers

To study the net impact of the choice of the communication protocols and the transport layer, we evaluated the power efficiency using a metric tuned towards

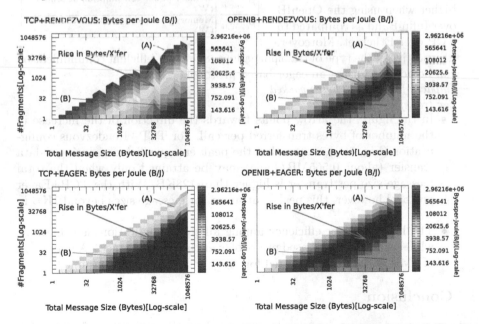

Fig. 7. A summary of the total bytes transferred per Joule of energy consumed by the sender and the receiver while participating in remote data transfers

communication-intensive kernels. The energy-efficiency of a compute-intensive application kernel is given by the total number of machine/floating-point operations per second per watt of power consumed (MOPS/Watt or FLOPS/Watt). To evaluate the cost of data transfer operations, we use a similar metric - the net bandwidth achievable per watt of power consumed by the participating processes; in other words - the number of bytes that can be transferred across the network for each joule of energy consumed by the sender and receiver. For a point-to-point communication model like MPI, this may be represented by the equation below:

$$\frac{Bw}{P_{net}} = \frac{Bw}{(P_{s,cpu}+P_{s,mem}+P_{r,cpu}+P_{r,mem})} = \frac{B_{payload}}{\Delta E_s + \Delta E_r} \quad \left(\frac{Bytes}{Joule}\right)$$

(1)

The symbols used in this equation are listed in Table 3. The net impact on this metric is discussed in Fig: 7. The primary observations are:

Table 3. Symbols in Eqn.1

Symbols	Metric
Bw	Achievable bandwidth (bytes/sec)
P_{net}	Net average power consumed (W)
$B_{payload}$	Total number of bytes transmitted
ΔE_s	Energy consumption by sender (J)
ΔE_r	Energy consumption by receiver (J)
$P_{s,cpu}$	Cores power consumption at sender (W)
$P_{r,cpu}$	Cores power consumption at receiver (W)
$P_{s,mem}$	Memory power consumption at sender (W)
$P_{r,mem}$	Memory power consumption at receiver (W)

- The net bandwidth achievable using an interconnect directly impacts the maximum value of energy-efficiency. Thus the peak bytes transmitted per joule is an order of a magnitude higher when using the OpenIB over InfiniBand as compared to TCP over Ethernet. Moreover, irrespective of the type of transport adopted, energy-efficient communication can be achieved using an eager-based protocol.
- *Impact of number of bytes packed per transfer:*
  - In the figure, the arrow points towards the direction of the increase in the number of bytes transferred per call. For TCP+Rendezvous configuration (Fig. 7(I)), we see that the peak energy efficiency during a data transfer (about 0.565MB/Joule) may be attained only when the total message size per transfer is higher than 128KB. With the TCP+Eager protocol however, this peak is attained for message sizes beyond 1KB in size.
  - The highest power efficiency among all the configurations is achievable while using an eager-based protocol over the OpenIB stack - A maximum of 3MB of data is transferred for every joule of energy consumed.

5   Conclusion

Data movement across large-scale systems has the potential of impacting not only the performance of distributed programming models, but also the power-signatures. In this paper, we established the notion that the choice of the transport layer and the design of communication protocols play a significant role in terms of the energy and power consumption. The empirical results discussed in this paper highlighted the behavior of this impact on the CPU cores and the memory. It was observed that the power consumption by CPU cores and the memory bandwidth is not only impacted by the latency of the remote transfers, but also the memory bandwidth between the CPU cores and the memory.

While using traditional TCP over Ethernet, energy savings can be obtained by choosing an eager-based protocol over a rendevous-based one. While using an eager protocol, an efficiency of upto 600bytes/joule may be obtained. Despite these savings, it must be noted that mapping an eager protocol over a non-RDMA based fabric leads to high power consumption by the memory. While using an RDMA-capable network like InfiniBand, the use of eager-based protocol lends itself naturally to the semantics of the transport layer (OpenFabrics OFED, in our case).

Irrespective of the type of transport and protocol, higher efficiency (bytes transferred per joule) can be achieved by aggregating user buffers into contiguous larger fragments before servicing the transfer. In addition, the net bandwidth achievable during a transfer impacts this efficiency. We hope that results of energy-efficiency as well as a detailed study of the impact on the various sub-components of the system would motivate the design of "power-aware" middleware for use with HPC applications.

As the next step, we plan to extend this study to evaluate the impact on large-scale multi-node systems. It is equally essential to study the contribution of communication kernels to the energy profiles of large scale real world HPC applications.

Acknowledgments. This work is supported by the U.S. Dept. of Defense via the Extreme Scale Systems Center and used resources at the Oak Ridge Leadership Computing Facility, which is supported by the Office of Science (U.S. Dept. of Energy) under Contract No. DE-AC05-00OR22725. Thanks are due to the support teams of VampirTrace from the Zentrum für Informationsdienste und Hochleistungsrechnen (ZIH, Technische Universität Dresden, Germany), Power-Pack from the Scalable Performance Lab (Virginia Tech, U.S.A.) and PAPI from the Innovative Research Lab (University of Tennessee at Knoxville, U.S.A.).

References

1. OpenFabrics Alliance: The Case for Open Source - RDMA (August 2011), https://www.openfabrics.org/index.php/ofa-documents/presentations/doc_download/228-the-case-for-open-source-rdma-.html
2. Barrett, B.: OpenMPI Data Transfer (December 2012), http://www.open-mpi.org/video/internals/Sandia_BrianBarrett-1up.pdf, detailed overview of the Open MPI data transfer system
3. Feng, X., Ge, R., Cameron, K.: Power and Energy Profiling of Scientific Applications on Distributed Systems. In: Proceedings of the 19th IEEE International Parallel and Distributed Processing Symposium 2005, pp. 34–34 (April 2005)

4. Gabriel, E., Fagg, G.E., Bosilca, G., Angskun, T., Dongarra, J.J., Squyres, J.M., Sahay, V., Kambadur, P., Barrett, B., Lumsdaine, A., Castain, R.H., Daniel, D.J., Graham, R.L., Woodall, T.S.: OpenMPI: Goals, Concept, and Design of a Next Generation MPI Implementation. In: Proceedings, 11th European PVM/MPI Users' Group Meeting, Budapest, Hungary, pp. 97–104 (September 2004)

5. Ge, R., Feng, X., Song, S., Chang, H.C., Li, D., Cameron, K.W.: Powerpack: Energy Profiling and Analysis of High-Performance Systems and Applications. IEEE Transactions on Parallel and Distributed Systems 21(5), 658–671 (2010)

6. Intel Corporation: Intel(R) 64 and IA-32 Architectures Software Developer's Manual Vol. 3B: System Programming Guide, Part-2 (February 2014), http://www.intel.com/content/www/us/en/architecture-and-technology/64-ia-32-architectures-software-developer-vol-3b-part-2-manual.html

7. Jana, S., Hernandez, O., Poole, S., Hsu, C.-H., Chapman, B.M.: Analyzing the Energy and Power Consumption of Remote Memory Accesses in the Openshmem Model. In: Poole, S., Hernandez, O., Shamis, P. (eds.) OpenSHMEM 2014. LNCS, vol. 8356, pp. 59–73. Springer, Heidelberg (2014), http://dx.doi.org/10.1007/978-3-319-05215-1_5

8. Knüpfer, A., Brunst, H., Doleschal, J., Jurenz, M., Lieber, M., Mickler, H., Mller, M., Nagel, W.: The Vampir Performance Analysis Tool-Set. In: Resch, M., Keller, R., Himmler, V., Krammer, B., Schulz, A. (eds.) Tools for High Performance Computing, pp. 139–155. Springer, Heidelberg (2008), http://dx.doi.org/10.1007/978-3-540-68564-7_9

9. Liu, J., Wu, J., Panda, D.: High Performance RDMA-Based MPI Implementation Over Infiniband. International Journal of Parallel Programming 32(3), 167–198 (2004), http://dx.doi.org/10.1023/B%3AIJPP.0000029272.69895.c1

10. Mucci, P.J., Browne, S., Deane, C., Ho, G.: PAPI: A Portable Interface to Hardware Performance Counters. In: Proceedings of the Department of Defense HPCMP Users Group Conference, pp. 7–10 (1999)

11. Shalf, J., Dosanjh, S., Morrison, J.: Exascale Computing Technology Challenges. In: Palma, J.M.L.M., Daydé, M., Marques, O., Lopes, J.C. (eds.) VECPAR 2010. LNCS, vol. 6449, pp. 1–25. Springer, Heidelberg (2011)

Spanning Tree or Gossip for Aggregation: A Comparative Study

Lehel Nyers[1] and Márk Jelasity[2],*

[1] University of Szeged, Hungary, and Subotica Tech, Subotica, Serbia
[2] MTA-SZTE Research Group on Artificial Intelligence, and University of Szeged, Hungary

Abstract. Distributed aggregation queries like average and sum can be implemented in several different paradigms including gossip and hierarchical approaches. In the literature, these two paradigms are routinely associated with stereotypes such as "trees are fragile and complicated" and "gossip is slow and expensive". However, a closer look reveals that these statements are not backed up by thorough studies. A fair and informative comparison is clearly needed. However, it is a very hard task, because the performance of protocols from the two paradigms depends on different subtleties of the environment and the implementation of the protocols. We tackle this problem by carefully designing the comparison study. We use state-of-the-art algorithms and propose the problem of monitoring the network size in the presence of churn as the ideal problem for comparing very different paradigms for global aggregation. Our experiments help us identify the most important factors that differentiate between gossip and spanning tree aggregation: the time needed to compute a truly global output, the properties of the underlying topology, and the sensitivity to dynamism. We demonstrate the effect of these factors in different practically interesting topologies and scenarios. Our results help us to choose the right protocol in the knowledge of the topology and dynamism patterns.

1 Introduction

Fully distributed aggregation is an important problem where we wish to execute queries such as sum, average, minimum, or maximum over unreliable networks (sensor networks, physical networks of routers, overlay networks, etc.), in which no central servers are directly accessible.

At least two paradigms are known for solving this problem. On the one hand, *gossip* algorithms were proposed to achieve large degrees of robustness. Gossip protocols do not rely on fixed topologies: nodes exchange information with random neighbors to implement a diffusion-like computation pattern, and as a result the system converges to a state where all the nodes know the query result. From the vast literature, here we focus on the adaptive approaches only. In [1], the authors propose the restarting technique to convert any one-shot algorithm into an adaptive one. Apart from restarting, other approaches have been proposed that focus on error correction through some form of bookkeeping at the nodes [2–5].

* M. Jelasity was supported by the Bolyai Scholarship of the Hungarian Academy of Sciences. This work was supported by the European Union and the European Social Fund through project FuturICT.hu (grant no .: TAMOP-4.2.2.C-11/1/KONV-2012-0013).

F. Silva et al. (Eds.): Euro-Par 2014, LNCS 8632, pp. 379–390, 2014.

The other paradigm is *hierarchical aggregation*, a popular method in sensor networks [6]. It was also proposed for general process groups [7]. Tree-based aggregation remained unpopular in some areas, for example, peer-to-peer networks due to the widely held assumptions about its lack of robustness. There are a few notable exceptions: the Astrolabe framework [8], which is in fact only a virtual tree with completely unstructured gossip communication patterns behind it; the GAP protocol and its variants [5,9–11] that actually build a spanning tree over a distributed network; and PRISM [12], a hierarchical approach that is built on top of a distributed hashtable, with a focus on detecting and signaling imprecise output.

Unfortunately, the literature is strongly influenced by stereotypes about both approaches like "spanning tree protocols are fragile" and "gossip protocols are slow and expensive". It is tacitly assumed that these statements have been conclusively settled. However, when surveying the literature, this does not turn out to be the case. In fact, we are not aware of any studies with a focus on a principled comparison among very different paradigms for aggregation. For example, Merrer et al [13] compare algorithms for size estimation, but they do not include spanning tree methods that are in the focus of our interest. Chitnis et al consider a very basic tree protocol that has no capabilities for reconfiguration, and briefly compare it with gossip [14]. The environment they consider is sensor networks. Due to the limited scope and suboptimal representatives of gossip and tree protocols, this work does not settle the problems we raised. Wuhib et al [5] propose an adaptive gossip protocol and compare it to GAP. Interestingly, GAP outperformed the gossip protocol in all scenarios examined (which were inspired by aggregation tasks in wired networks of routers). While this is a very nice result, it is far from complete due to the particular selection of the communication topology and the aggregation problem.

Our main contribution is that we propose a careful experimental design to shed light on the strengths and the weaknesses of both approaches. We experiment with competitive, state-of-the-art representatives of spanning tree and gossip protocols, and model different network environments. We identify the key aspects that determine the performance of the protocols in order to help application developers select the best solution in a given practical setting.

2   System Model

We assume that the system consists of N nodes that form a network with the help of reliable channels such as a TCP connections or physical links. Nodes communicate by exchanging messages over these channels only. Messages can be delayed. In addition, nodes can join and leave at any time. We assume the existence of a failure detector that sends a message to the node when a neighbor node fails. Leaving nodes and crashed nodes are treated identically. Leaving nodes can join again, and while offline, they retain their state. When they join again, they reconnect to their previous neighbors.

3   The Protocols in Our Comparison

The common problem these algorithms solve is the monitoring of aggregate values. That is, at any point in time t we have a network of $N(t)$ nodes all of which have a value. Let the set of values at time t be $A(t) = \{a_1(t), \ldots, a_{N(t)}(t)\}$. The task is to continuously calculate (monitor) a global function $f(A(t))$. A given algorithm for solving this problem typically supports a well-defined set of aggregate functions f.

Due to lack of space we cannot present a complete description of all the protocols we examine in our experimental study. Instead, we describe the key ideas behind them, along with comments about our own implementation, where applicable. Our full implementation can also be downloaded.[1]

3.1 GAP (General Aggregation Protocol)

GAP is an adaptation of the classical self-stabilizing BFS construction algorithm of Dolev et al [15] that is based on message passing instead of shared tables. We implemented the version of GAP described in [9].

In GAP, there is a special node that acts as the root of the spanning tree. The root is fixed and guaranteed to remain available. The tree grows from the root as all the nodes discover their shortest path towards the root, starting with the neighbors of the root, and so on. GAP implicitly assumes a relatively stable underlying network. Each node in the network maintains a table that contains an entry for each neighbor and the node itself. Each table entry contains the level in the tree, and classifies the neighbor as parent, child, or peer. The parent of each node is always the neighbor with the minimal level (say, ℓ), and the node's own level is always $\ell + 1$. A table entry also contains the aggregate value in the subtree rooted in the neighbor. These values are used to calculate the node's own aggregate.

A node gets several types of messages related to changes in the topology (failed or new neighbors) or changes in the aggregate value (locally or in a subtree of a child node). When receiving a message, the node updates its own tables if necessary in such a way that the invariants of the tree structure and aggregate calculation are restored. Our implementation uses the "cache-like" policy [9] for maintaining the table, which means that table entries change only due to explicit messages and never due to predictions.

GAP can be implemented in a reactive or a proactive manner. In the former case, all changes are immediately reported to the neighbors. In the latter case, changes accumulate during a time period and are reported at once in a round-based fashion. We implemented the proactive round-based version, as it has better load balancing and generates fewer messages on average in dynamic environments.

The original publication of GAP did not mention that it is also important that the connections with neighbors need to preserve the order of the messages, otherwise inconsistent states can occur. This can be achieved with an appropriate transport layer, or at the application level as well.

3.2 Adaptive Gossip Protocols

We used the push-sum algorithm as a starting point [16]. In this algorithm (as in all gossip variants) the basic idea is that the nodes engage in a diffusive computation, during which nodes periodically send to each neighbor a proportion of the "mass" they store and also receive mass from neighbors. This way the nodes can collectively compute the average of all the values. Other aggregates, such as the network size can also be computed: if a single node has a value of 1, and all the other nodes have a value of 0 then the average is $1/N$, which can be used to recover the network size N.

---

[1] http://peersim.sourceforge.net/

The push-sum algorithm is by default a one-shot algorithm, unsuitable for monitoring. There are two approaches to achieve adaptivity. The first is the restart-based approach and the second is what we call the "bookkeeping" approach. We included in our set of algorithms a representative of both classes. In both cases, in each round a node with k neighbors sends one kth of its mass to each of the neighbors.

Restarted push-sum. The key idea is that the algorithm is run in *epochs* of some fixed length, after which the gossip protocol is restarted automatically in a distributed way [1]. In effect, the restart mechanism takes a snapshot of the system at the beginning of the epoch that involves the nodes that were live at that time, and then the aggregate of this snapshot is computed during the epoch. After the completion of the epoch, the computed aggregate value is used as the output of the algorithm, hence the output is delayed by roughly two epoch lengths at most. Depending on the topology of the network, epochs can be rather short (as few as 20 rounds) due to the quick convergence of gossip.

LiMoSense, a bookkeeping approach. Instead of restarting, a gossip protocol might attempt to repair the state of the nodes as a reaction to failure. This can be achieved if some variant of bookkeeping for the underlying gossip algorithm (e.g. push-sum) is implemented that makes it possible to "undo" those computations that had to do with a failed node, or that makes it possible to repair message drop failure by comparing books with neighbors. The main design goal of such protocols is the classical requirement of self-stabilization, that is, to be able to eventually converge after failures and dynamism stop. A state-of-the-art representative of such protocols is LiMoSense [2]. We use this protocol in our comparison study.

3.3   Common Properties

When comparing different paradigms, we should focus on application areas and systems where the paradigms in question all are feasible and have a similar cost. In other words, there are systems that are *obviously* suitable only for one or the other algorithm. Here, we do not focus on these obvious cases.

First, the system is assumed to have a *special stable node* that is guaranteed to remain available in the network. GAP crucially relies on such a node to act as the root of the tree for tree building and maintenance. Such a node is not critical for gossip but—given that due to GAP we need to assume a stable root—gossip protocols can and will take advantage of it too. For example, when calculating the network size, the node that has the initial value of 1 can be the root (see Section 4.1). Note that GAP does not rely on the root for reading out the value: it can be modified to propagate the global aggregate to all the nodes.

Second, all the protocols are *round based* with a period (round length) of Δ. They generate a very *similar amount of traffic* in each round: each node sends one message to each neighbor in each round. In the case of GAP this can be substantially reduced, but only when the network becomes static and there is no failure either. This is because no messages need to be sent if there is no change in the aggregated value or in the underlying topology. In our implementation, GAP broadcasts in each round even if there is seemingly no change. The reason is that—since we work with systems that constantly change—this results in a negligible amount of extra traffic, and it solves a subtle issue of the original algorithm related to churn.

4 Experimental Setup and Methodology

We used the PeerSim [17] simulator with the event-based engine in all our experiments.

4.1 Network Size as the Aggregation Problem of Choice

Calculating the average of distributed values is often the baseline problem used to evaluate generic distributed aggregation algorithms. This, however, is rather problematic because the performance then depends crucially on the distribution of the values. If the distribution is concentrated around the average, then one cannot differentiate between the ability of an algorithm to provide real global results and between the local sampling effect, that is, when the average of local samples is similar to the global average by pure chance. This is true in the case of both gossip and spanning tree algorithms.

It is vital that here we wish to compare the *global* behavior of the algorithms, that is, how they behave in scenarios where they need to consider the entire data set. The performance of such global tasks can be considered a *worst case*, which can only improve when local neighborhoods already offer a good approximation of a given query. Of course it is of interest how certain algorithms react to specific distributions, and one could even develop algorithms that explicitly exploit specific known distributions, if such prior knowledge is available. However, without prior knowledge getting a quick result due to local sampling is just a matter of chance, so when comparing very different generic paradigms, we consider a robust worst case analysis more informative and preferable.

Our choice is the network size estimation problem. For this problem, the spanning tree approach counts each node according to the tree hierarchy: all nodes have a value of 1, and the tree calculates the sum. The gossip protocols here will calculate the average in a network of N nodes were the initial value is 0 at all nodes except the root, where it is 1, which gives $1/N$ as a result [1]. In both cases, the point is that the problem is clearly global, where a useful answer is available only after the algorithm has globally converged.

4.2 Network Topologies

Our protocols need undirected topologies, so where the original topology definition is directed, it has to be understood with the directionality of the edges dropped. All networks are of size $N = 1000$ unless otherwise stated.

NewsCast. A dynamic topology defined in [18]. In a nutshell, without describing NEWS-CAST in detail, each node will have a new set of random neighbors in each cycle using the same cycle period as the aggregation protocol. The number of neighbors is $k = 30$. The motivation is that gossip protocols are often implemented over such dynamic topologies so that nodes can communicate with random samples from the network in each cycle, as assumed in theoretical discussions of gossip protocols.

Random k-out. A static topology in which every node connects to a set of k random neighbors. After dropping directionality, the average degree is $2k$. The motivation is that randomly sampled, but static, topologies have been proposed recently as the optimal choice in commercial P2P platforms over the Internet [19].

Binary Tree. An undirected balanced binary tree is formed. In our experiments the root node of the aggregation protocols is placed at different levels of the tree from 0 (the root of the binary tree) to $\lceil \log_2 N \rceil$, the leaf level of the tree. We include this artificial topology to be able to illustrate a major difference between gossip and spanning tree approaches.

Barabasi-Albert (BA). To test heavy tailed degree distributions, we include the BA network that is constructed incrementally. New nodes connect to old nodes already in the network according to the preferential attachment rule, that is, with a probability proportional to the degree of the old node [20]. New nodes get $k = 2$ edges when they are added to the topology. In our experiments the root node of the aggregation protocols is placed at nodes with different degrees in this topology.

4.3   Failure and Churn Scenarios

We used the same model of message delay in all experiments: each message is delayed by a uniform random time drawn from the interval $[0, 0.2\Delta]$. Our preliminary experiments revealed very little sensitivity to message delay in all the protocols, so we do not focus on this aspect. We consider no message drop failures. This is because in most scenarios that are reasonable for a spanning tree the underlying topologies in question are static, so it is feasible to apply a reliable transport layer such as TCP.

The protocols require a failure detector. We assume a timeout-based detector with a timeout of 5Δ in all experiments. Our preliminary experiments suggested very little sensitivity to this parameter as well, so we keep it fixed throughout the study.

Node churn was modeled based on statistics from a BitTorrent trace [21] as well as known empirical findings [22]. We draw the online session length for each node independently from a log-normal probability distribution with two different parameter settings. The first setting that we call *fast churn* is $\mu = 3$ and $\sigma^2 = 1$, which results in a mean of ~ 33. The unit of the resulting online session lengths is the communication period Δ. This—considering that Δ can be expected to be in the range of seconds—is a rather short session length so it represents a very dynamic scenario. The second set of parameters that we call *slow churn* is $\mu = 6$ and $\sigma^2 = 2$, which results in a mean of ~ 1096.

Offline session lengths are determined implicitly by fixing the number of nodes that are online at the same time. The ratio of online nodes was set to a range of values from $\alpha = 1$ to $\alpha = 0.2$. As stated previously, nodes that re-join the network retain the state they had when leaving the network.

4.4   Evaluation Methodology and Metrics

We are interested in static behavior. As mentioned above, we assume a constant churn pattern with a static expected network size αN, where α is the ratio of online nodes in the scenario in question. In this setting, we expect a good monitoring algorithm to consistently signal $\hat{N}(t) = \alpha N$ as the approximated network size in cycle t.

To measure how close a given algorithm is to this optimal behavior, we run each scenario 10 times for 10,000 cycles, and collect statistics of the absolute error $|\alpha N - \hat{N}(t)|/(\alpha N)$ over the last 9,000 cycles in each run. We ignore the first 1,000 cycles in order to allow the system to reach an equilibrium state. We plot the average and the standard deviation (with error bars).

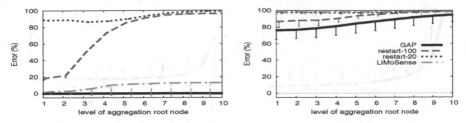

Fig. 1. Binary tree, no churn (left) and fast churn, 80% of the nodes online (right). The horizontal axis shows the level of the aggregation root node in the physical topology (0: root, 10: leaves).

5 Results

First, we demonstrate some weaknesses of the gossip approaches and GAP that are not so evident at first sight. This will shed light on which scenarios to avoid for these paradigms. Subsequently, we look at the two realistic topologies: static random k-out and the BA topology, and take a closer look at some interesting subtleties that are important in these cases, and that define which approaches are preferable.

5.1 The Achilles Heel of Gossip

Let us start with the Achilles heel of gossip protocols. In principle, gossip protocols for aggregation have been shown to work on any connected topology, that is, they are guaranteed to converge. However, if the communication topology is not a fully connected graph, but instead a *static* graph with relatively small average degree, then the convergence speed is well-known to depend on the mixing time of a certain random walk on this topology [23]. On the other hand, the convergence time of GAP depends on the diameter (that is, the maximal minimal path length) that bounds the maximal number of steps information needs to take to reach the root.

It is often the case that graphs with a low diameter also have a rapid mixing time, but trees are exceptions. For example, the rooted balanced binary tree has a diameter of $O(\log N)$ whereas it has a mixing time of $O(N)$ (see, for example, [24], Example 7.7).

For this reason, at least in the failure-free scenario, we expect gossip protocols to suffer, and this is indeed the case as Figure 1 (left) shows. GAP achieves full precision very quickly, whereas even LiMoSense does not reach convergence within 10,000 rounds when the node that is assigned the role of the root node is closer to the leaves in the physical topology, let alone restart that is inherently limited in the number of rounds until convergence. (We remind the reader not to confuse the root node of the aggregation with the root of the physical topology.) However, when we introduce churn, all algorithms suffer since the underlying topology is very fragile. Still, GAP performs best (see Figure 1 (right)).

The results also reveal another important point, namely it does matter a lot where the root node is placed within the underlying physical topology. It is much harder to break out of a region closer to the leaves for the diffusion process as it is from the root (recall that for gossip the aggregation root is initialized with a value of 1, while the remaining nodes have a value of 0).

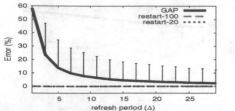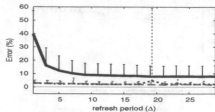

Fig. 2. NewsCast with $k = 30$, no churn (left) and fast churn, 80% of the nodes online (right). The horizontal axis shows the neighborhood refresh period of NewsCast in rounds (Δ).

5.2   The Achilles Heel of Spanning Trees and Bookkeeping Gossip Protocols

In many cases, gossip protocols assume a random set of neighbors in each round [1] that is given by a dynamic protocol for peer sampling [18]. This radically dynamic neighbor set is ideal for vanilla gossip, however, if bookkeeping is involved, it becomes a serious problem, since the tables will grow indefinitely until they reach the size of the whole network. This is not scalable, since all entries have an associated failure detector as well, which need to maintain a communication link with each node. For this reason, the members of the old neighbor set should be treated as failed nodes, to get scalability. This, however, completely destroys the ability of the protocol to converge if the aggregation task is global, like network size estimation. All in all, with dynamic peer sampling bookkeeping gossip cannot be applied at all with any hope of success.

For GAP, the changing neighbor set raises similar issues: growing tables (and eventually a spanning tree with a star topology) or the option of treating old neighbors as failed. In our implementation, we opt for the second approach, as the option of growing tables is clearly not scalable.

Figure 2 shows simulation results with the NewsCast dynamic topology. Clearly, for fast refreshing periods the only feasible protocol is restarted gossip. Yet in the case of slower refreshing (when the topology becomes relatively stable on the short run) GAP is competitive. LiMoSense is the least favorable option in this scenario.

5.3   The k-Out Topology

We examined the k-out topology for different values of k. Without churn, all the protocols can achieve an error that is practically 0% for $k \geq 2$, except restart-20 that achieves 25% error for $k = 2$. Clearly, an epoch length of 20 is not sufficient for such a low value of k. Note that the lower the value of k is the greater the mixing time becomes.

Figure 3 contains our experiments involving churn. Our first observation is that GAP and restart are rather insensitive to the speed of churn, whereas LiMoSense is very sensitive. In the slow churn scenario its results are dramatically better. This is because fast churn is highly disruptive for this algorithm due to the constant attempts to repair the state of the system when a neighbor leaves.

At the same time, in slow churn all the algorithms become rather unstable when the offline session lengths are long (that is, when α is small). This is because—although the network is relatively stable—in such scenarios the aggregation root can become disconnected and can remain so for a relatively long time, which temporarily causes extremely large errors.

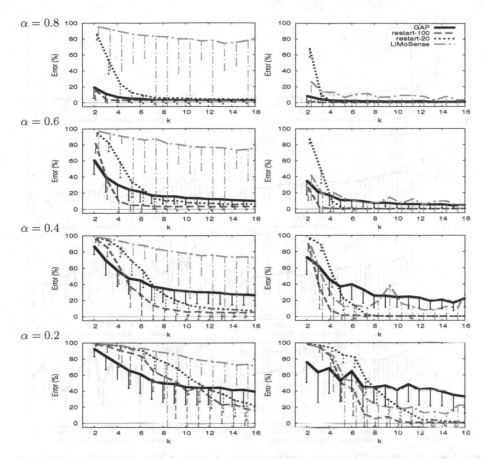

Fig. 3. Results with k-out topology, fast churn (left column) and slow churn (right column). The horizontal axis shows values of k. The proportion of online nodes is given by α.

As for GAP, we can observe an interesting case that is consistent with our findings over the binary tree topology: when k is very small, GAP has a slight advantage due to not depending on the mixing time of the topology. Note that for a very small k the random k-out topology behaves locally like a tree as there is a rather small probability for finding short circles, which slows gossip protocols down.

For large values of k gossip protocols can take advantage of the very good mixing properties and can beat GAP, esp. with an epoch length of 100. GAP also profits from an increasing k (and therefore a decreasing diameter, and more options to repair the tree) but not as much as gossip protocols.

5.4 The Barabasi-Albert Topology

We generated one BA topology with $k = 2$ as previously described. In this fixed topology we placed the aggregation root at nodes with different degrees. Our results involving churn are shown in Figure 4.

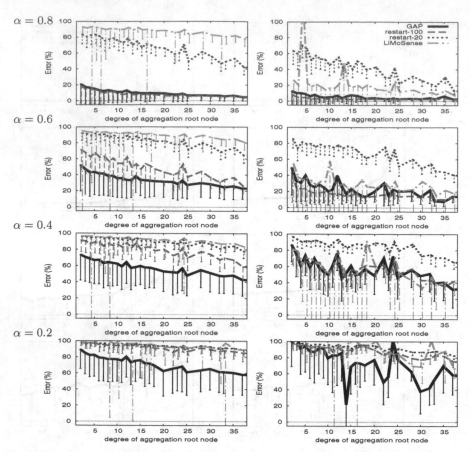

Fig. 4. Results with the BA topology, fast churn (left column) and slow churn (right column). The horizontal axis shows the degree of the node where the aggregation root is placed. The proportion of online nodes is given by α.

We can observe a strong dependence of the precision of the aggregation result on the position of the aggregation root in the underlying BA topology. Central nodes with a large degree achieve a significantly better approximation. This is also true for the gossip protocols, which here also rely on a fixed "root" node (see Section 3.3).

As in the k-out topology, without churn (not shown), all the protocols can achieve an error that is practically 0%, except restart-20 that achieves an error of 35% to 5% depending on the centrality of the root. Restart-20 performs poorly throughout the experiments, clearly indicating that an epoch length of 20 is not sufficient. At the same time, restart-100 is among the best options in most scenarios.

Clearly, in these scenarios GAP provides the most stable performance. As with the k-out topology, gossip protocols continue to be sensitive to the speed of churn: with LiMoSense it is more so, but the restart variants also show sensitivity, with restart-100 being the most robust.

As in the k-out topology, in slow churn we observe a very large variance for small α and for a low degree aggregation root. The reason is the same: the aggregation root can get disconnected.

Table 1. Summary of conclusions

	sensitivity to changing		delay due to	
	membership	topology	convergence	epoch length
spanning tree	moderate	high	diameter	none
bookkeeping gossip	high	high	mixing time	none
restarted gossip	moderate	none	mixing time	epoch length

6 Discussion and Conclusions

In this paper, we compared three different paradigms for global distributed aggregation: approaches based on a spanning tree, restarted gossip, and bookkeeping gossip. We argued that network size estimation is an appropriate problem for the purposes of this comparison. We stressed the role of different topologies, and shed light on the weak and strong points of the approaches.

Table 1 summarizes some of the conclusions we arrived at in the evaluation section. In our experiments the effective network size was constant, so the effect of the delay due to the epoch length remained hidden. However, the epoch length must be chosen such that it lies in the range of the mixing time so as to allow for proper convergence. This means that restarted gossip will double the delay of bookkeeping gossip in the worst case, while it is not sensitive to a dynamic topology (due to not relying on failure detectors and neighborhood tables) and it is less sensitive to churn for the same reason.

As for the spanning tree, the convergence time of gossip (that depends on the mixing time) is typically at least an order of magnitude larger than the diameter in most topologies, even in the random k-out topology (which has a low mixing time), let alone more practical topologies. Our experiments clearly support this insight. This means that a spanning tree is much faster than the other methods, and its advantages mainly result from this property, along with the ability to self-repair equally quickly, when the topology is not too dynamic.

Overall, when selecting the right protocol, one needs to consider the structure of the topology and the patterns of dynamism in the membership (churn) and the topology itself. If the topology is relatively stable, a spanning tree approach is preferable even in high churn, while for dynamic topologies a restarted gossip protocol with the right epoch length is more suitable. We could identify no scenarios where bookkeeping gossip is clearly preferable, when truly global aggregation is needed. If local sampling approximates the global aggregate well, we face a very different problem that requires a different approach for analysis. Nevertheless, results on global problems always represent a lower bound on performance. The ultimate solution is most likely a combination of gossip and tree approaches in an adaptive way, based on the automated detection of topology and dynamism properties; an interesting venue for future research.

References

1. Jelasity, M., Montresor, A., Babaoglu, O.: Gossip-based aggregation in large dynamic networks. ACM Transactions on Computer Systems 23(3), 219–252 (2005)
2. Eyal, I., Keidar, I., Rom, R.: Limosense – live monitoring in dynamic sensor networks. In: Erlebach, T., Nikoletseas, S., Orponen, P. (eds.) ALGOSENSORS 2011. LNCS, vol. 7111, pp. 72–85. Springer, Heidelberg (2012)

3. Jesus, P., Baquero, C., Almeida, P.S.: Fault-tolerant aggregation by flow updating. In: Senivongse, T., Oliveira, R. (eds.) DAIS 2009. LNCS, vol. 5523, pp. 73–86. Springer, Heidelberg (2009)

4. Mehyar, M., Spanos, D., Pongsajapan, J., Low, S.H., Murray, R.M.: Asynchronous distributed averaging on communication networks. IEEE/ACM Trans. Netw. 15(3), 512–520 (2007)

5. Wuhib, F., Dam, M., Stadler, R., Clemm, A.: Robust monitoring of network-wide aggregates through gossiping. In: Proc. 10th IFIP/IEEE Intl. Symp. on Integrated Management (IM 2007), pp. 21–25 (May 2007)

6. Madden, S., Franklin, M.J., Hellerstein, J.M., Hong, W.: TAG: A tiny aggregation service for ad-hoc sensor networks. In: Proc. 5th Symp. on Operating Systems Design and Implementation (OSDI 2002), pp. 131–146 (2002)

7. Gupta, I., van Renesse, R., Birman, K.P.: Scalable fault-tolerant aggregation in large process groups. In: Proc. Intl. Conf. on Dependable Systems and Networks (DSN 2001). IEEE Computer Society Press (2001)

8. Birman, K.P., van Renesse, R., Vogels, W.: Scalable data fusion using astrolabe. In: Proc. Fifth Intl. Conf. on Information Fusion (FUSION 2002), vol. 2, pp. 1434–1441 (2002)

9. Dam, M., Stadler, R.: A generic protocol for network state aggregation. In: Proc. Radiovetenskap och Kommunikation, RVK 2005 (2005)

10. Prieto, A.G., Stadler, R.: A-gap: An adaptive protocol for continuous network monitoring with accuracy objectives. IEEE Trans. on Netw. and Serv. Manag. 4(1), 2–12 (2007)

11. Krishnamurthy, S., Ardelius, J., Aurell, E., Dam, M., Stadler, R., Wuhib, F.Z.: Brief announcement: the accuracy of tree-based counting in dynamic networks. In: ACM Symp. on Principles of Distr. Comp. (PODC), pp. 291–292. ACM (2010)

12. Jain, N., Mahajan, P., Kit, D., Yalagandula, P., Dahlin, M., Zhang, Y.: Network imprecision: A new consistency metric for scalable monitoring. In: Proc. 8th USENIX Conf. on Operating Systems Design and Implementation (OSDI 2008), pp. 87–102. USENIX Association (2008)

13. Le Merrer, E., Kermarrec, A.M., Massoulie, L.: Peer to peer size estimation in large and dynamic networks: A comparative study. In: Proc. 15th IEEE Intl. Symp. on High Performance Distr. Comp. (HPDC 2006), pp. 7–17 (2006)

14. Chitnis, L., Dobra, A., Ranka, S.: Aggregation methods for large-scale sensor networks. ACM Trans. Sen. Netw. 4(2), 9:1–9:36 (2008)

15. Dolev, S., Israeli, A., Moran, S.: Self-stabilization of dynamic systems assuming only read/write atomicity. Distributed Computing 7(1), 3–16 (1993)

16. Kempe, D., Dobra, A., Gehrke, J.: Gossip-based computation of aggregate information. In: Proc. 44th Annual IEEE Symp. on Foundations of Computer Science (FOCS 2003), pp. 482–491. IEEE Computer Society (2003)

17. Montresor, A., Jelasity, M.: Peersim: A scalable P2P simulator. In: Proc. 9th IEEE Intl. Conf. on P2P Comp. (P2P 2009), pp. 99–100. IEEE (September 2009), extended abstract

18. Jelasity, M., Voulgaris, S., Guerraoui, R., Kermarrec, A.M., van Steen, M.: Gossip-based peer sampling. ACM Transactions on Computer Systems 25(3), 8 (2007)

19. Roverso, R., Dowling, J., Jelasity, M.: Through the wormhole: Low cost, fresh peer sampling for the internet. In: Proc. 13th IEEE Intl. Conf. on P2P Comp. (P2P 2013). IEEE (2013)

20. Albert, R., Barabási, A.L.: Statistical mechanics of complex networks. Reviews of Modern Physics 74(1), 47–97 (2002)

21. Roozenburg, J.: Secure decentralized swarm discovery in Tribler. Master's thesis, Parallel and Distributed Systems Group, Delft University of Technology (2006)

22. Stutzbach, D., Rejaie, R.: Understanding churn in peer-to-peer networks. In: Proc. 6th ACM SIGCOMM Conf. on Internet Measurement (IMC 2006), pp. 189–202. ACM (2006)

23. Boyd, S., Ghosh, A., Prabhakar, B., Shah, D.: Randomized gossip algorithms. IEEE Transactions on Information Theory 52(6), 2508–2530 (2006)

24. Levin, D.A., Peres, Y., Wilmer, E.L.: Markov Chains and Mixing Times. AMS (2008)

Shades: Expediting Kademlia's Lookup Process*

Gil Einziger, Roy Friedman, and Yoav Kantor

Computer Science Department, Technion, Haifa 32000, Israel
{gilga,roy,ykantor}@cs.technion.ac.il

Abstract. Kademlia is considered to be one of the most effective key based routing protocols. It is nowadays implemented in many file sharing peer-to-peer networks such as BitTorrent, KAD, and Gnutella.

This paper introduces *Shades*, a combined routing/caching scheme that significantly shortens the average lookup process in Kademlia and improves its load handling. The paper also includes an extensive performance study demonstrating the benefits of Shades and compares it to other suggested alternatives using both synthetic workloads and traces from YouTube and Wikipedia.

1 Introduction

Distributed Hash Tables (DHT) are at the heart of most peer-to-peer (P2P) systems. Consequently, a plethora of papers and ideas on how to implement DHTs has been published, e.g., [4,19]. DHTs tend to differ from each other in the routing scheme they employ, as well as the space and message overhead they incur for maintaining their overlay. During the last few years, Kademlia has become one of the most widely used DHTs in practice [20,22]. This is largely due to its proven robustness to churn, enabled by its unique partially parallel lookup mechanism and large routing tables. Further, Kademlia's applications extend beyond P2P. For example, a variant of Kademlia was suggested for high performance computing in grids and clusters [25].

Like many other DHTs, Kademlia's routing phase may involve contacting a logarithmic number of nodes, which may be too slow for time sensitive applications [18,21]. For example, one of the lessons of the CoralCDN project [10], a successful DHT based content delivery network, is that DHT lookup latency was a performance bottleneck for their system.

Since typical workloads of Internet based applications are often highly skewed, caching lookup results along the search path has the potential of reducing the average lookup time experienced by users. However, due to Kademlia's unique routing and dynamic bucket manipulation schemes, caching is less effective in Kademlia than in more rigid DHTs like Chord [9].

To tackle this problem, we introduce a novel caching and augmented routing mechanism for Kademlia called Shades (the entire code of Shades is available as open source at [2]). That is, each node maintains a small local cache that is

---

* This work is partially supported by the Technion HPI Research School.

F. Silva et al. (Eds.): Euro-Par 2014, LNCS 8632, pp. 391–402, 2014.

managed using an effective cache filtering mechanism called *TinyLFU*. TinyLFU maintains a compressed approximate statistics of all items encountered and uses this as an admission filter that only admits popular items into the cache and is able to do so in a very time and space efficient manner, as reported in [8]. Further, Shades augments Kademlia's routing decisions using a secondary hashing technique that we call *colors*. As described later in this paper, colors are used to help caches specialize in items of their own color, thereby increasing the skewing in the observed access distribution of the requests they encounter, resulting in much higher hit rates. In particular, a limited number of lookup requests are issued to nodes whose id hashes to the same color as the key of the item being searched rather than according to the usual Kademlia lookup process. In addition, the hints from TinyLFU's statistics are used to limit the number of such deviations from the normal lookup process and only apply them when there is statistical evidence that they are likely to help. Finally, we employ an *overload protection* mechanism to prevent Kademlia nodes from becoming overwhelmed with requests[1].

We have experimented with Shades and compared it to plain Kademlia and other previous caching suggestions for Kademlia, namely *KadCache* – the caching suggestion of the Kademlia authors [20], the local cache suggested in [12] – a.k.a. *Local* and *Kaleidoscope* [9]. These experiments were conducted using both synthetic workloads mimicking ones that are often found in real applications, as well as real traces from YouTube and Wikipedia. In these results, we have found that Shades significantly reduces the number of nodes participating in the lookup process compared to plain Kademlia, KadCache, Local and Kaleidoscope. At the same time, it also achieves competitive message and bandwidth overheads relative to the other suggested caching schemes.

The rest of this paper is organized as follows: We start by describing Shades (and Kademlia) in Section 2. Section 3 survey an additional related work. Performance evaluation is presented in Section 4. Finally, we conclude with a discussion in Section 5.

2 Shades

As indicated before, Shades includes three components: a highly effective small cache, an augmented routing that is based on secondary hashing (colors) whose goal is to direct lookup traffic to caches that are likely to have the data, and an overload protection mechanism. The caching mechanism is described below in Section 2.1, the routing scheme is presented in Section 2.2, and the overload protection is explained in Section 2.3.

2.1 Caching Mechanism

With Shades, each node in the system maintains a small local cache in addition to its Kademlia storage. When a node receives a lookup request, it can either

---

[1] This latter optimization does not improve the lookup hop-count, but rather the overall latency by avoiding routing to nodes that are overloaded.

return the k-closest nodes, return a cached result or return the stored value. The difference between Kademlia storage and the cache is that the former has to store all items that the node is assigned to according to the Kademlia DHT algorithm. On the other hand, the goal of the cache is to boost the performance of the system by storing selective items. In particular, in order to keep the cache size small and since real world workloads tend to exhibit access locality, intuitively the cache should include the most frequently requested items.

For the cache management, we have chosen to employ the cache architecture of TinyLFU [8]. In TinyLFU, there is a separation between cache eviction policies and admission policies. TinyLFU maintains an approximated statistics over all recently encountered items such that a new item will replace the cache victim only if it is more frequent than the cache victim as illustrated in Figure 1(a). Since the statistics are kept over a large collection of past requests and can potentially be very big, TinyLFU only maintains an approximation of this statistics. To keep the statistics fresh, TinyLFU perform a periodic *Reset* operation, this operation halves all counters. As reported in [8], the memory overhead associated with TinyLFU is comparable to a memory pointer per cache line. Since TinyLFU can work with any eviction policy, we complement TinyLFU, with a *Lazy LFU* eviction policy. This policy attempts to find the least frequently used item in the cache, however does so lazily, performing a single search step per cache lookup, resulting in $O(1)$ query complexity, and hit rate similar to a true LFU cache.

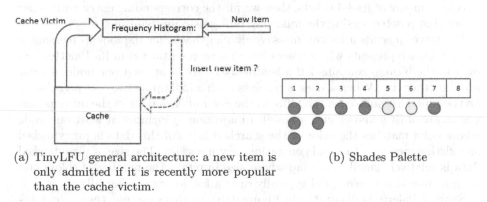

(a) TinyLFU general architecture: a new item is only admitted if it is recently more popular than the cache victim.

(b) Shades Palette

Fig. 1. An illustration of TinyLFU and Shades Palette

2.2 Routing

As mentioned before, Shades augments the standard Kademlia routing scheme by utilizing a secondary key called *color* in order to partition cache content between nodes and create a distributed large cache out of many small individual caches. Unlike the Kademlia key that comes from a large domain to prevent collisions, the color domain is small and collisions are desirable.

During the parallel iterative lookup process, Shades may issue cache lookup requests to nodes that have the same color as the requested key even if these nodes do not advance in Kademlia's XOR distance metric [20].[2] For this reason, we call such deviations a *side step*. Hence, while intuitively a side step improves the chances of hitting a cache due to the use of colors, in the case of a cache miss, it prolongs the lookup process since it does not advance toward the key in the XOR metric. In order to avoid paying this price for cache misses, Shades only takes side steps if the item is relatively likely to be cached already. To that end, Shades relies on TinyLFU to keep track of the likelihood that the item would indeed be in the cache, as detailed later in this section.

Finally, once the lookup is done, the search result is only stored in caches that are interested in caching it. Since TinyLFU only admits items to the cache if they are more frequent then the cached items, Shades ensures that the cached result is shared with a node that is likely to admit it. In the rest of this section, we first describe an auxiliary data structure used by the routing mechanism of Shades and then provide the details of the protocol.

Palette. Since going over all the k-buckets in order to find a matching color candidate can be time consuming, each node p maintains a mapping between colors and the nodes matching these colors that p is award of. This mapping, implemented as a hash table, is called the *Palette* of node p. For each color i, when node p has at least one node of color i in any of its k-buckets, then the ith entry of p's Palette points to these nodes. However, if p does not have any node of color i in any of its k-buckets, then we fill the corresponding entry with other nodes that p detects using the following pull gossip mechanism.

Whenever p sends a lookup message, it piggybacks on the lookup message a bitmap that represents which colors have no representatives in its Palette. I.e., bit i in the bitmap contains 1 if p is already aware of at least one node of color i and 0 otherwise. When a node q receives such a lookup message, it piggybacks on the reply one node corresponding to the color of each 0 bit in the bitmap that q is aware of (if q knows such a node). In addition, q includes at least one node whose color matches the color of the searched key. All this data is piggybacked on existing messages to avoid generating new messages. The size of piggybacked data is relatively small: a bitmap whose size in bits is the number of colors and at most one id per color (and typically only a few ids or none at all).

Shades' Palette is illustrated in Figure 1(b). In this example, there are 8 different colors. The dark tokens represent the nodes that appear in the k-buckets whereas the bright tokens are nodes discovered through the bitmap gossip mechanism. In this example, color 8 does not have any representative. Therefore the bitmap [11111110] will be added to any outgoing Kademlia message. If any of the nodes that receive such a message knows of a node that matches color 8, it will include this node in its response.

Shades Routing Protocol. The routing protocol for key lookup, performed by node p, goes as follows. Denote c the searched key's color. While node p is not

---

[2] The distance metric used by Kademlia to decide on hashed ids proximity is XOR.

aware of c-colored nodes, p performs traditional Kademlia lookups. When node p is aware of c-colored nodes, either from its data structures or through replies received from other nodes, it performs multiple cache lookups denoted as *side steps*. These cache lookups are performed simultaneously to Kademlia's routing protocol. We call these cache lookups side steps since they are not necessarily advancing the search according to the Kademlia XOR metric.

Let q be the c-colored node that is closest to the searched key. The first side step is performed by sending a request to node q, which does not have to be in the k-candidates list. q checks whether the requested key is in its cache. If so, it sends back the (key, value) item from the cache. Otherwise, q returns a response that contains the following additional information:

– Is the item needed? I.e., will this specific cache admit this item if encountered based on the mechanism described in Section 2.1.
– Is the item popular? I.e., is this item likely to be admitted to other caches.

When p receives the response from q, it acts according to the response: In case of a cache hit, the lookup is finished. Otherwise, if the item is not popular, then no more side steps are performed and the lookup is continued as in Kademlia. If the item is popular, then another side step can be taken. Note that by this point, p received more c-colored nodes from responding nodes. If p discovered more than one c-colored node, it favors contacting the closest one according to the XOR metric.

At the end of the lookup, if the lookup is successful, p sends the (key,value) item to the c-colored node that is closest to the searched key and has noted in its response that the value is needed. This node stores the result in the cache for future requests.

Shades, as Kademlia, has up to α outstanding queries at any given time. When not performing a side step, all the outstanding queries advance according to the key XOR distance metric as in Kademlia. While performing a side step, $\alpha - 1$ of the outstanding queries advance according to the key distance metric in addition to the one outstanding side step.

Note that in order to perform a side step, p needs to know a node with the same color as the searched key. Recall that the Palette significantly increases the probability that p knows such a node. This enables our protocol to usually perform the first side step right in the start of a lookup, which is important since the benefit of hitting a cache early is far greater than hitting it later.

2.3   Congestion Control

When we started experimenting with Kademlia in general and Shades in particular, we encountered a severe congestion problem when running test cases with many nodes (this can be seen in the result in Section 4.5 below). For this reason, we implemented a simple congestion control mechanism .

In that mechanism every message is attached an additional bit that is set if the sender's incoming message queue was more then 75% full when the message was sent. Once a node receives a message with a set congestion bit, it marks the sending node as a candidate for replacement. That is the receiver encounter a possibility to replace the congested, it will do so without sending a ping message. The result of this mechanism is that congested nodes reduce their representation in routing tables and therefore receive less incoming traffic.

3   Related Work

Several works have investigated how to use caching to reduce the lookup cost in DHTs. For example, in [12] it is suggested to add to Kademlia a local cache named *Fast Table*. This table stores the results of previous lookups the node has performed. When a node receives a lookup request, it first checks its Fast Table to see if it contains cached results for it. This approach was shown in [9,12] to yield a reduction in average lookup length. As mentioned in the introduction, we refer to this scheme as Local in this paper.

Another important caching suggestion appears in the original Kademlia paper [20]. In this suggestion, every time a node performs a lookup operation, it sends a store value request to the last node it contacted that did not have the value. This suggestion, called KadCache in this paper, was evaluated in [9] for its message cost and (lack) of load balance capabilities. In this paper, we extend that evaluation of KadCache to cover its latency aspects. As we show in the performance section of this paper, Shades reduces considerably the number of contacted nodes compared to both Local and KadCache, and usually also improves the communication overhead.

The work most related to Shades is Kaleidoscope [9]. Kaleidoscope also uses colors to augment the combined routing and caching process of Kademlia to obtain better caching, but focuses on communication overhead reduction. In Kaleidoscope, messages are first forwarded to a node of a matching color along the lookup path, and only then an iterative lookup starts. Since Kaleidoscope never deviates from the lookup path, it cannot efficiently use as many colors as Shades, and therefore achieves lower cache hit rates than Shades. Further, the more colors Kaleidoscope uses, the longer it take to reach each cache.

Unlike Kaleidoscope, Shades may deviate from the lookup path of Kademlia if there is probabilistic evidence that doing so is likely to find a cached result nearby. Shades bases its decisions on a compressed approximated statistics in order to both manage its cached content, and also decide on the maximal number of cache lookups that may deviate from the Kademlia lookup path. So while both Kaleidoscope and Shades rely on the notion of colors as a secondary hashing mechanism, each takes this concept in a completely different direction.

The main differences between Kaleidoscope and Shades are summarized in Table 1. As can be seen, Shades uses more colors than Kaleidoscope and therefore forms a more effective distributed cache. Further, Shades benefits more from each cache hit as it performs the first cache lookup earlier than Kaleidoscope. Shades also uses a more advanced cache policy that is also used to decide how many times we deviate from the lookup path, and what node is most suitable to store the cached value at the end of the lookup. Finally, the last line of the table titled "share policy" indicates that shades stores the results of successful lookups in caches of matching colors that were encountered along the lookup process only if these caches are likely to benefit from them. In contrast, Kaleidoscope always pushes the results of lookups to such caches. This helps Shades save messages. Evidently, in our performance evaluation section, we show that Shades contacts substantially fewer nodes than Kaleidoscope, obtains significantly better load sharing, and generates similar overall traffic as Kaleidoscope.

Table 1. Comparison between Kaleidoscope and Shades

	Kaleidoscope	Shades
# Colors	17	150
On path lookups	Unlimited	Unlimited
Deviates from path	No	Yes
Time of first cache lookup	During lookup	First step
Cache policy	LRU	TinyLFU+LazyLFU
Share policy	Always	Only if needed

Other methods to reduce Kademlia's lookup latency includes careful parameter configuration [22], techniques to fill k-buckets with nodes of geographical proximity [16], a new metric based on geographical distance [11] and a recursive lookup scheme [15]. We believe that many of these suggestions can be deployed alongside with Shades as they either reduce the latency of individual messages, or optimize the configuration parameters of the protocol. In contrast, Shades slightly changes the algorithm and satisfies lookups using information from fewer nodes.

Other DHT's like OneHop [13], Kelips [14] and Tulip [3] achieve O(1) lookups at the cost of background traffic overheads. In contrast, Shades does not generate any background traffic. Systems that include O(1) lookups include, e.g., Dynamo [7] and ZHT [17]. Both systems target high performance data centers. Given that a variant of Kademlia was also suggested for this context [25], Shades can be adopted to that domain as well.

4   Performance Measurements

4.1   Methodology and Setup

In this section, we evaluate the performance of Shades. We also compare Shades to Kaleidoscope [9], Local [12], and the caching scheme suggested by the original Kademlia paper [20] (a.k.a. KadCache). For the evaluation, we used a Java implementation of Shades, Kaleidoscope, KadCache, and Local. We have experimented with several different sizes of networks by running multiple Java VMs (one VM per 80 nodes) on two servers and emulating the users lookup requests that are picked from a given, pre calculated workload. We used both synthetic and real life workloads. The real workloads are distributions that were taken from a real YouTube data set [6] and a real Wikipedia data set [23].

In the synthetic distributions, each node in the system periodically picks an item out of 1,000,000 possible keys according to the specific distribution and issues a lookup request for that key. In the YouTube distributions, we used a data set that contains statistics of over 161k newly created videos. These videos were monitored weekly during 21 weeks starting from 16th April, 2008. We used the number of views per week in order to directly generate a distribution that reflects the popularity of each video during that week. As for the Wikipedia trace, it contains an ordered list of requests that were accepted by Wikipedia servers during a period of two months. It is very extensive and contains 10% of the traffic for Wikipedia at that time period. Unfortunately, this trace does not contain client information. Therefore, we simply picked a continuous flow of 5 million requests, cut it into small chunks and randomly but equally assigned them nodes. Each request is then assigned to a key and is searched for during the experiment.

In all experiments, caches are given a warm-up period in which each node in the system issues 500 lookup requests. After the warm-up period, each node in the system issues 500 additional lookup requests. Statistics of message send/receive, incoming/outgoing bandwidth and the latency are monitored locally by each node and are collected via HTTP at the end of the experiment. Our experiments where performed on the real system code with the following parameters: bucket size $k = 7$; network sizes: 500, 2,500 and 5,000 nodes; request distributions: Zipf 0.7, Zipf 0.9. Zipf distributions with similar values were found, e.g., in Web caching and file sharing applications [5]. Notice that in the case of 5,000 nodes, the experiment includes a total of 5,000,000 requests, half during the warmup period and the other half during the measurement interval.

4.2 Metrics and Definitions

Since the wall-clock latency depends on a large number of factors and is therefore very noisy, we have decided to focus on measuring the number of *contributing nodes* for each lookup, i.e., the number of nodes whose replies were utilized while performing the lookup, instead of wall-clock latency. We note that this number may be different from the number of contacted nodes, e.g., if three parallel lookups are sent and the first reply returns the value, then the number of contributing nodes is 2 (the initiator and the node that returned the cached result), even though 3 nodes were contacted. Since Kademlia works with concurrent iterative lookup, this is not exactly the latency in hops. Yet, since our experiments were conducted with $\alpha = 3$, dividing the number of contributing nodes by α (3) gives a relatively good estimation to the number of hops used in the lookup process. We have also studied the cache hit rates as well as the amount of traffic generated both in terms of message count and overall bandwidth.

4.3 Number of Colors

Varying the number of colors has a complex effect. On the one hand, increasing the number of colors enhances the observed frequency of correctly colored items

Table 2. Effect of the number of colors on the performance of Shades

Performance And The Number of Colors				
	Wikipedia		YouTube	
	Shades(50)	Shades(150)	Shades(50)	Shades(150)
Local	0.28	0.26	0.21	0.2
First side step	0.47	0.5	0.59	0.64
Second side step	0.5	0.53	0.65	0.69

more aggressively, thereby increasing their weight in the cache. On the other hand, since the cache size is limited, it comes at the expense of general items, hurting the performance of the local cache.

Hence, the number of colors is a tradeoff parameter. Picking the correct number mainly depends on what the system goals are. In order to explain this tradeoff, we measured the hit rates of the local cache, the first side step and the second side step for different color configurations. This check neglects searches that end due to other reasons within their first few steps.

The results in Table 2 present the different hit rates achieved using 50 and 150 colors. As expected, 50 Colors achieves higher local cache hit rates, but lower chromatic cache hit rates. We feel that Shades offers a more attractive tradeoff with 150 colors than with 50 colors.

This configuration achieves over 50% hit rate within the first two side steps with both Wikipedia and YouTube workloads. In the latter, it reaches 65% hit rate for the first side step and over 70% hit rate after the second side step.

Hence, as long as the increase in hit rate after the first side step is significant, we suggest increasing the number of colors in order to achieve lower latency. The rest of our measurements focus on the 150 colors configuration of Shades.

4.4   Comparison to Other Caching Mechanisms

In this section, we compare Shades to previously suggested caching schemes as well as to a plain Kademlia. We use concurrency of $\alpha = 3$ and measure how many nodes contributed to the lookup resolution.

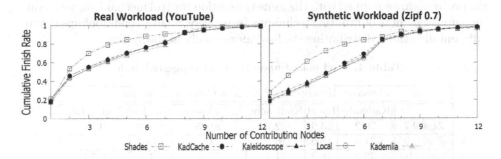

Fig. 2. Number of contributing nodes required to perform a lookup

To get a better feel for the latency improvement of Shades, we exhibit the average and median lookup latency measured by the number of contributing nodes. The median represents how many nodes are required on average to resolve half of the lookups.

Table 3 presents the median latency values for all the protocols evaluated. Shades reduces the median latency by as much as 22% − 34% compared to the best alternative for every workload.

Unlike median, average latency can be manipulated in many ways and is sensitive to edge values. For example, lookups that are resolved at the local cache significantly reduce the average latency without impacting the median latency. Also the minority of very long lookups increase the average latency without increasing the median latency. Our results are presented in Table 3.As can be seen, Shades improves also the average latency by ≈ 18 − 23% in comparison to the best alternative of each workload.

Table 3. Average and median latency during the measurements

Average And Median Latency (Contributing Nodes)											
	Kademlia		Local		KadCache		Kaleidoscope		Shades		Shades/Best	
Metric	A	M	A	M	A	M	A	M	A	M	A	M
Zipf 0.7	5.34	5.47	5.29	5.29	5.16	5.18	5.12	5.1	4.08	3.27	0.79	0.64
Zipf 0.9	4.01	3.76	3.92	3.42	4.01	3.76	4.20	3.15	3.03	2.18	0.77	0.69
YouTube	3.72	2.69	3.41	2.66	3.40	2.44	3.40	2.64	2.74	1.9	0.81	0.78
Wikipedia	4.32	3.48	4.06	3.44	4.14	3.23	4.15	3.2	3.31	2.21	0.82	0.69

We expect Shades' latency advantage to become more dominant with larger networks. Since the lookup paths of Kademlia grow longer with the network size, the impact of finishing a large portion of the searches within the first two hops becomes greater in large networks.

4.5   Load Distribution

Table 4 compares the average number of messages handled by the most congested 50 nodes in the network (1% busiest nodes). As can be observed, for each workload Shades improves the load placed on these nodes by 22%-43%. Since all routing protocols are equipped with the same congestion control mechanism, we credit the improvement to our routing technique. Intuitively, Shades sends lookups in two different directions, distributing the load more evenly in the system.

Table 4. Load placed upon the most congested nodes

Messages Handled By 1% Most Congested Nodes						
	Kademlia	Local	KadCache	Kaleidoscope	Shades	Shades/Best
Zipf 0.7	26.2	23.9	22.7	20.05	11.45	0.57
Zipf 0.9	21.4	18.6	16.7	17	13.00	0.78
YouTube	22.4	18.2	21.1	17.9	13.3	0.74
Wikipedia	26.6	17.6	19.9	17	13.3	0.78

5   Discussion

We have presented Shades, a combined caching/routing scheme that augments Kademlia, yielding a significant improvement in latency. Through simulations that are based on artificial Zipf-like distributed workloads as well as real traces from YouTube and Wikipedia, we have found that Shades reduces the median number of nodes contributing to each lookup by 22-36% compared to the best of breed among the other schemes in the workloads tested and a 30-40% reduction compared to plain Kademlia. Shades obtains a load reduction on the busiest nodes (hot-spots) of 22-43% with respect to the best scheme and 40-56% compared to plain Kademlia. With reported latencies of 5.8-7.6 seconds for tuned Kademlia based systems such as [18,21], our improvements can have a significant impact on the user experience of these systems.

Shades also generated fewer messages than Kadcache and Local, and a similar bandwidth consumption as the best of breed among them. In some workloads Kaleidoscope offers slightly lower message and bandwidth costs than Shades, but the differences are small.

Another interesting aspect of Shades is that its latency with a small cache of 100 items is better than any of the other caching schemes we have compared against even when they are equipped with an unbounded cache. Shades is an open source project [2], implemented as an extension to OpenKad [1].

When using caching, there is always the question of keeping the cache content consistent. There are many applications in which data is immutable, in which case the problem does not exist. In particular, in such systems explicit versioning is often used instead of updates (e.g., http://www.saphana.com/). In other cases, using periodic revalidation against the main copy or deleting items from the cache after a TTL is enough to ensure timely eventual consistency [24].

References

1. OpenKad, http://code.google.com/p/openkad/
2. Shades source code, https://code.google.com/p/shades/
3. Abraham, I., Badola, A., Bickson, D., Malkhi, D., Maloo, S., Ron, S.: Practical locality-awareness for large scale information sharing. In: van Renesse, R., Castro, M. (eds.) IPTPS 2005. LNCS, vol. 3640, pp. 173–181. Springer, Heidelberg (2005)
4. Androutsellis-Theotokis, S., Spinellis, D.: A Survey of P2P Content Distribution Technologies. ACM Computing Survey 36, 335–371 (2004)
5. Breslau, L., Cao, P., Fan, L., Phillips, G., Shenker, S.: Web caching and zipf-like distributions: Evidence and implications. In: INFOCOM, pp. 126–134 (1999)
6. Cheng, X., Dale, C., Liu, J.: Statistics and social network of youtube videos. In: 16th Int. Workshop on Quality of Service, IWQoS 2008, pp. 229–238 (June 2008)
7. DeCandia, G., Hastorun, D., Jampani, M., Kakulapati, G., Lakshman, A., Pilchin, A., Sivasubramanian, S., Vosshall, P., Vogels, W.: Dynamo: Amazon's highly available key-value store. SIGOPS Oper. Syst. Rev. 41(6), 205–220 (2007)
8. Einziger, G., Friedman, R.: Tinylfu: A highly efficient cache admission policy. In: 22nd Euromicro Int. Conf. on Parallel, Distributed and Network-Based Processing (PDP), pp. 146–153 (February 2014)

9. Einziger, G., Friedman, R., Kibbar, E.: Kaleidoscope: Adding colors to kademlia. In: Proc. of the 13th IEEE Int. Conf. on P2P Computing (September 2013)
10. Freedman, M.J., Freudenthal, E., Mazières, D.: Democratizing content publication with coral. In: Symposium on Networked Systems Design and Implementation, NSDI 2004, pp. 18–18. USENIX Association, Berkeley (2004)
11. Groß, C., Stingl, D., Richerzhagen, B., Hemel, A., Steinmetz, R., Hausheer, D.: Geodemlia: A robust p2p overlay supporting location-based search. In: Proc. of the 12th IEEE Int. Conf. on P2P Computing. IEEE (September 2012)
12. Guangmin, L.: An Improved Kademlia Routing Algorithm for P2P Network. In: Int. Conf. on New Trends in Information and Service Science, pp. 63–66 (2009)
13. Gupta, A., Liskov, B., Rodrigues, R.: One hop lookups for peer-to-peer overlays. In: Proc. of the 9th Conf. on Hot Topics in Operating Systems, HOTOS 2003. USENIX Association, Berkeley (2003)
14. Gupta, I., Birman, K., Linga, P., Demers, A., van Renesse, R.: Kelips: Building an efficient and stable p2p dht through increased memory and background overhead. In: Kaashoek, M.F., Stoica, I. (eds.) IPTPS 2003. LNCS, vol. 2735, pp. 160–169. Springer, Heidelberg (2003)
15. Heep, B.: R/kademlia: Recursive and topology-aware overlay routing. In: 2010 Australasian Telecommunication Networks and Applications Conf (ATNAC), 31 October- November 3, pp. 102–107 (2010)
16. Kaune, S., Lauinger, T., Kovacevic, A., Pussep, K.: Embracing the peer next door: Proximity in kademlia. In: Eighth Int. Conf. on P2P Computing, P2P 2008, pp. 343–350 (September 2008)
17. Li, T., Zhou, X., Brandstatter, K., Zhao, D., Wang, K., Rajendran, A., Zhang, Z., Raicu, I.: Zht: A light-weight reliable persistent dynamic scalable zero-hop dht. In: Parallel & Distributed Processing Symposium, IPDPS (2013)
18. Liu, B., Wei, T., Zhang, J., Li, J., Zou, W., Zhou, M.: Revisiting why kad lookup fails. In: Proc. of the 12th Int. Conf. on P2P Computing, pp. 37–42. IEEE (2012)
19. Lua, E., Crowcroft, J., Pias, M., Sharma, R., Lim, S.: A Survey and Comparison of P2P Overlay Network Schemes. IEEE Communications Surveys Tutorials 7(2), 72–93 (2005)
20. Maymounkov, P., Mazières, D.: Kademlia: A P2P Information System Based on the XOR Metric. In: Proc. of the 1st Int. Workshop on P2P Systems (IPTPS), pp. 53–65 (2002)
21. Steiner, M., Carra, D., Biersack, E.W.: Faster content access in kad. In: Proc. of the 8th Int. Conf. on P2P Computing, pp. 195–204. IEEE Computer Society, Washington, DC (2008)
22. Stutzbach, D., Rejaie, R.: Improving lookup performance over a widely-deployed dht. In: INFOCOM 2006. 25th IEEE Int. Conf. on Computer Communications. Proc., pp. 1–12 (2006)
23. Urdaneta, G., Pierre, G., van Steen, M.: Wikipedia workload analysis for decentralized hosting. Elsevier Computer Networks 53(11), 1830–1845 (2009)
24. Vogels, W.: Eventually consistent. Communications of the ACM 52(1), 40–44 (2009)
25. Wozniak, J.M., Jacobs, B., Latham, R., Lang, S., Son, S.W., Ross, R.B.: C-mpi: A dht implementation for grid and hpc environments. In: Preprint ANL/MCS-P1746-0410, 04/2010 (2010)

Analysis and Comparison of Truly Distributed Solvers for Linear Least Squares Problems on Wireless Sensor Networks

Karl E. Prikopa, Hana Straková, and Wilfried N. Gansterer

University of Vienna, Vienna, Austria
Faculty of Computer Science

Abstract. The solution of linear least squares problems across large loosely connected distributed networks (such as wireless sensor networks) requires distributed algorithms which ideally need very little or no co-ordination between the nodes. We first provide an extensive overview of distributed least squares solvers appearing in the literature and classify them according to their communication patterns. We are particularly interested in *truly distributed* algorithms which do not require a fusion centre, cluster heads or any multi-hop communication. Beyond existing methods, we propose the novel least squares solver PSDLS, which utilises a recently developed distributed QR factorisation algorithm. All communication between nodes is exclusively performed within the push-sum algorithm for distributed aggregation.

We analytically compare the communication cost of PSDLS and the existing truly distributed algorithms. In all these algorithms, the communication cost of reaching a predefined accuracy depends on many factors, including network topology, problem size, and settings of algorithm-specific parameters. We illustrate with simulation experiments that our novel PSDLS solver requires significantly fewer messages per node than the previously existing methods to reach a predefined solution accuracy.

1 Introduction

We consider the problem of solving the linear least squares problem

$$\min_{x} \|b - Ax\|_2 \tag{1}$$

for $x \in \mathbb{R}^m$ in a truly distributed way, where $A \in \mathbb{R}^{n \times m}$ with $n \geq m$ and $b \in \mathbb{R}^n$. We are interested in solving such problems over a loosely connected, decentralised network, e.g. a wireless sensor network (WSN), where each node holds part of the input data. In particular, we assume that A is distributed row-wise over the N nodes of the network and that the element $b(i)$ resides on the same node as the ith row of A. For $n > N$, each node contains a block of consecutive rows of A.

Many applications in WSNs require the distributed solution of a linear least squares problem, e.g., the reconstruction of physical fields [1], target tracking [2],

F. Silva et al. (Eds.): Euro-Par 2014, LNCS 8632, pp. 403–414, 2014.

the solution of the seismic tomography inversion problem [3] when monitoring volcanic activity or localisation [4]. WSNs typically consist of a large number of inexpensive sensor nodes which act autonomously but cooperate with each other to achieve a common goal. Working in a fully decentralised manner allows for decisions to be made on any node. In combination with actuators, the nodes can take autonomous actions in the physical world. Asynchronous communication is an important challenge to be considered in the design of a truly distributed algorithm. The sensor nodes are normally constrained in terms of their resources, primarily their energy supply and computation capabilities. One of the sources of high power consumption is communication. The energy required by the nodes to communicate with other nodes is directly proportional to the communication range. This implies that communicating with the immediate neighbourhood of a node is significantly cheaper than communicating with very distant nodes. Preserving energy also increases the lifespan of the nodes and in turn of the entire network.

As we will summarise in the following section, many distributed least squares solvers can be found in the literature, but most of them do not operate in a truly distributed manner without the need for centralised fusion centres, cluster heads or multi-hop communication. Multi-hop communication requires routing tables, and setting those up requires additional communication. The overhead is particularly large if the routing tables have to be updated frequently.

Dynamic changes and distributed fault tolerance are also important factors in the design of a distributed algorithm for WSNs. Although such difficult scenarios are beyond the scope of this paper, they can be implicitly considered by the use of gossip algorithms for aggregation. The push-sum algorithm [5] used by the PSDLS algorithm proposed in this paper can be directly replaced by fault-tolerant alternatives which are able to recover from silent message loss and temporary or permanent link failures [6,7].

Synopsis. In Section 2, we provide an extensive review of the existing literature about distributed least squares solvers and classify them based on their communication patterns. In Section 3, we introduce the new push-sum-based distributed least squares solver PSDLS. Section 4 provides an analytical comparison of the communication cost of PSDLS and the truly distributed algorithms appearing in the literature up until now. Simulation results are presented in Section 5, and our conclusions are summarised in Section 6.

2   Existing Distributed Least Squares Solver

In this section, we summarise the efforts presented in the literature for solving the linear least squares problem (1) in a distributed setting. We categorise existing algorithms into three groups: (*i*) *Centralised approaches* using a fusion centre or approaches which require *global communication*, (*ii*) *clustered approaches* where the communication of each node is limited to a subset of the network (cluster) with a cluster head, and (*iii*) *truly distributed approaches* where the communication of each node is limited to its immediate neighbourhood *without* using any multi-hop communication.

2.1 Centralised Approaches or Global Communication

A strategy that has been studied extensively is the use of a central unit (*fusion centre*) which performs the computation for the entire network. The fusion centre approach first collects the data from all nodes in the network (global communication), then solves problem (1) at the fusion centre and finally distributes the result to all nodes (global communication). The positioning of the fusion centre is crucial for communication cost and scalability (cf. [3]). There are several drawbacks to this approach: Potential congestion effects (particularly around the fusion centre [8]) can lead to delays and in the worst case to data loss. Multi-hop communication and setting up routing tables incur additional overhead. Last, but not least, the fusion centre becomes a single point of failure. Research on fusion centre approaches often focusses on the efficient accumulation of the data at the fusion centre (see, e.g., [9]). Other efforts perform only parts of the computation at the fusion centre and offload other parts onto the individual nodes (see, e.g., [4]). However, these approaches still require global (multi-hop) communication of each node with the fusion centre.

Reichenbach et al. [4] consider the problem that each node needs to determine its location and analyse three methods for solving the least squares problem arising in this context: normal equations, QR factorisation and singular value decomposition. For all three methods, they split the computation into two parts in order to distribute them between a high performance base station and wireless sensor nodes. The base station computes the computationally intensive tasks and then sends the result to the nodes, which only have to perform low complexity computations to determine their location. This approach significantly reduces the amount of computation performed on the sensor nodes, saving more than 47% of floating-point operations for normal equations and more than 99% for the QR factorisation and the SVD. The disadvantage is the communication cost incurred by the nodes having to send their measurements to the fusion centre either over long distances or with multi-hop communication and non-static routing.

One example for exploiting a specific routing structure is presented by Borgne et al. [9], where the measured data is aggregated at each node towards the fusion centre along a routing tree. The authors extend the basic set of available aggregation functions (minimum, maximum, sum, count and average) to a regression operator which uses the sensor node measurements as input, reducing the amount of data based on the regression model. The advantage of this approach is the reduction of the communication range of the nodes to a localised neighbourhood. However, the final result is only available at the fusion centre, which in the event of a failure leads to the breakdown of the entire computation.

The distributed multisplitting method [10], based on the parallel multiplitting method by Reanut [11], applies the well-known fixed-point iteration methods Jacobi, Gauss-Seidel and successive over-relaxation to the normal equations.

The matrix A is distributed column-wise over the nodes and weighting matrices are used to recombine the solutions of the local problems, which are independent problems resulting from the linear multisplitting of A. Note that in this method, the solution x is not replicated, but distributed across the nodes. In each iteration a vector of size n has to be broadcast to all other nodes (global communication).

The distributed modified conjugate gradient least squares (D-MCGLS) algorithm [10] exploits the fact that the conjugate gradient method can be applied to the symmetric and positive definite normal equations. It is also based on a parallel method, MCGLS by Yang and Brent [12], which is targeted at distributed memory architectures. Yang and Brent have improved the parallel performance of the standard CGLS method by reducing the global synchronisation points for the inner products. D-MCGLS requires A to be distributed row-wise. If A is not symmetric, for each local row of A, the node also needs to have the corresponding column locally. Each node has to use the same initialisation for x. In each iteration, a vector of length m and a scalar value have to be broadcast to all other nodes in the network (global communication).

2.2   Clustered Approaches

A first step towards a more decentralised setting than the fusion centre approaches summarised in Section 2.1 is based on clustering. The network is divided into clusters. In each cluster, one node acts as the cluster head, which often is more powerful than the other nodes in the cluster. The division is based on a certain criterion, e. g., on the geographical location of the nodes or on the predefined communication radius of the cluster head. The cluster heads act as intermediate fusion centres for the clusters. The nodes of a cluster only communicate with their cluster head and with nodes within the same cluster. Compared to the fusion centre approaches, a multi-tier model is used where only the cluster heads communicate with the fusion centre, reducing the communication cost and also the risk of congestion.

Behnke et al. [13] address issues arising with the clustered version of the distributed least squares algorithm presented in [4]. They report that the algorithm does not scale well with an increasing number of nodes and on large networks does not work at all due to the assumption that each node can communicate with all cluster heads which distribute the precomputed parts of the solution. They develop the scalable distributed least squares (sDLS) algorithm to overcome these drawbacks by limiting the communication of each node to its cluster head. To achieve this, each node is provided with individual precomputed data, in turn reducing the size of the data transferred to each node and also the computations to be performed by each node. Communication and computation costs are therefore independent of the network size and enable scalability of the algorithm also in large networks.

Shakibian and Charkari [14] propose a clustered, multi-swarm version of the particle swarm optimisation algorithm (MMS-PSO) for solving a least squares problem as a minimisation problem. Each cluster head manages the member nodes acting as a sub-swarm of the process. They also use a fusion centre to get the final global result from all cluster heads through weighted averaging. The authors claim that their method decreases the latency through clustering and converges faster than a fusion centre approach.

Summarising, clustering reduces but does not eliminate the risk of a single point of failure affecting the entire network. The cluster heads usually have to be more powerful than the other nodes to be able to handle the higher volume of messages received. If a cluster head fails, the complete area covered by the cluster and its data are lost until a new cluster head takes over.

2.3   Truly Distributed Approaches

The most decentralised approach is to limit the communication of the nodes to their immediate neighbourhood (defined by the communication range). Each communication partner has to be reachable in a single hop as multi-hop communication would incur additional overhead through routing and thus increase the energy consumption of the resource restricted nodes.

Zhou et al. [15] propose a distributed least squares solver which they claim is robust against reported node failures. The algorithm is designed for $m = 1$ and higher dimensions are not considered in [15]. The distributed iterative algorithm exchanges the values of A and b with the neighbours and updates them using a Metropolis weight based on the degree of the node's neighbours, which are determined before the iterative algorithm initialises. In the event of a node failure, convergence is still guaranteed, but the result will no longer be correct. Therefore, the authors extend their algorithm, trying to reduce the magnitude of the occurring error. A disadvantage is that node failures have to be detectable. Once detected, the weights used in the computation have to be updated throughout the network, which poses a global updating problem requiring communication across the entire network. In the event of a node failure, the magnitude of the error depends on the network topology. Although the algorithm presented in [15] is truly distributed, we do not consider it in our analysis and in our simulations because it is restricted to the special case $m = 1$.

Sayed et al. [2,16,17] propose a diffusion-based least mean square estimator (diffLMS) using steepest-descent iterations for solving the normal equations. Diffusion strategies are seen as an alternative to consensus strategies for distributed optimisation problems, both limiting the communication to the neighbourhood. A and b are both distributed row-wise. In each iteration, diffLMS consists of two main steps, an adaption step and a combination step, and delivers an estimate of the solution x in each node. The authors provide two variants of their algorithm, adapt-then-combine (ATC) and combine-then-adapt (CTA), which differ in the order of these computation steps (for details, see Section 4).

Another fully distributed approach is the distributed least mean squares method (D-LMS) by Schizas, Mateos and Giannakis [18,19,20]. D-LMS is based on Lagrange multipliers and uses the least squares residual and the difference between the estimates of x from the neighbourhood in a correction step to compute the least squares solution iteratively. The data distribution of A and b is again row-wise. At each step an estimate for the solution x is available in each node. D-LMS communicates twice in each iteration, once to broadcast the current estimate to all neighbours and a second time to send individual correction vectors to each neighbour (single-hop unicast – for details, see Section 4).

3   A Push-Sum-Based Least Squares Solver

In this section, we introduce the Push-Sum Distributed Least Squares Solver (PSDLS), shown in Algorithm 1, for problem (1). The matrix A and the vector b are distributed row-wise across the participating nodes. The parts of A and b available locally at node u will therefore be denoted by A^u and b^u, respectively. The solution x is approximated at each node. The local instance of a vector v which occurs at every node u will be referred to as v_u, and $v_u(i)$ refers to the ith element of v_u. In particular, x_u refers to the approximation of the entire solution vector x at node u. The algorithm does not require any knowledge about the global topology of the network and it does not assume any specific connections between the nodes. Each node only needs to know its neighbours. In such a setup, the push-sum algorithm [5] provides a truly distributed way for summing or averaging values across the nodes of the network. If each node knows the total number of nodes N in the network, then the sum of the values over all nodes can be computed using distributed averaging. Note that N can also be estimated in a truly distributed way [21]. Alternatively, the push-sum algorithm can be used to compute the sums directly without the need to know N at every node. However, based on our experience, this variant leads to slightly slower convergence.

Algorithm 1. Push-Sum Distributed Least Squares Solver (PSDLS)

Input: $A \in \mathbb{R}^{n \times m}$ with $n > m$, $b \in \mathbb{R}^n$, both distributed row-wise over N nodes
Output: $x_u \in \mathbb{R}^m$ on every node
1: **in each** node u **do**
2:    $[Q^u, R_u] \leftarrow \text{vdmGS}(A^u)$
3:    $z_u \leftarrow \text{dmmv}(Q^{u\top}, b^u)$
4:    $x_u \leftarrow \text{solve } R_u x_u = z_u$ ▷ local

PSDLS is a direct least squares solver first computing a distributed QR factorisation of A (line 1.2[1]) and subsequently solving *locally* a linear system with the triangular matrix R_u at every node (line 1.4). For the distributed QR factorisation we use the gossip-based distributed modified Gram-Schmidt orthogonalisation method *vdmGS* introduced in [22,23]. vdmGS returns the orthonormal matrix $Q \in \mathbb{R}^{n \times m}$ distributed row-wise (denoted by Q^u) and the complete upper-triangular matrix $R \in \mathbb{R}^{m \times m}$ in every node (denoted by R_u). Consequently, $Q^\top$ is distributed column-wise across the nodes. To compute the right-hand side of the linear system (line 1.3), the distributed matrix-vector multiplication *dmmv* described in [23] is used, which accepts the matrix argument

---

[1] Line x.y refers to line y in Algorithm x.

distributed column-wise and the vector argument distributed row-wise. The solution of the linear system (back substitution) can be computed locally and does not need any further communication with the other nodes because every node has its local estimate of R. At the end of the algorithm, each node u has its own local approximation x_u of the solution of the least squares problem (1).

4   Communication Cost of Distributed LS Solvers

We compare the communication cost of the novel PSDLS method, both variants of diffLMS described in [16] and D-LMS described in [20] in terms of number of messages and amount of data sent per node.

diffLMS. There are different versions of the diffLMS algorithm aside from the order of execution in ATC and CTA mentioned previously. diffLMS can also exchange the observations b^u and matrix rows A^u with the neighbouring nodes to improve the estimate of the solution. This requires an additional step for exchanging the information which increases the communication cost. For better comparison with [16], we will limit the analysis to the versions without the additional information exchange.

In the ATC version of the diffLMS method, shown in Algorithm 2, each node u first computes an intermediate value $\psi_u \in \mathbb{R}^m$, which adds a step-size μ of the least squares residual to the current estimation of x_u, where A^u and b^u correspond to the rows of A and b available locally on node u. The intermediate value ψ_u is subsequently broadcast to the local neighbourhood D_u. Each node then updates its estimate of x_u with a weighted sum of all received ψ_i ($i \in D_u$), and its own ψ_u, the weights being denoted as $\omega_u(i)$. A proof of convergence and several possible weighting matrices are given in [16].

The CTA variant of diffLMS performs exactly the same operations but in a different order. The intermediate values ψ_u are first broadcast to the neighbourhood, then each node computes its estimate of x_u and in the last step the new intermediate value ψ_u. According to [2, p.31], "... *the difference between the*

Algorithm 2. Diffusion Least Mean Square (diffLMS) - ATC and CTA

Input: $A \in \mathbb{R}^{n \times m}$ with $n > m, b \in \mathbb{R}^n$, both distributed row-wise over N nodes
For all nodes u: x_u and ψ_u initialised with zero
Output: $x_u \in \mathbb{R}^m$ on every node

Adapt-then-Combine (ATC)	**Combine-then-Adapt (CTA)**
1: **in each node** u **do**	1: **in each node** u **do**
2: **while** not converged **do**	2: **while** not converged **do**
3: $\psi_u \leftarrow x_u + \mu A^{u^\top}(b^u - A^u x_u)$	3: Broadcast ψ_u to D_u
4: Broadcast ψ_u to D_u	4: $\psi_u \leftarrow \omega_u(u)x_u + \Sigma_{i \in D_u}\omega_u(i)x_i$
5: $x_u \leftarrow \omega_u(u)\psi_u + \Sigma_{i \in D_u}\omega_u(i)\psi_i$	5: $x_u \leftarrow \psi_u + \mu A^{u^\top}(b^u - A^u \psi_u)$
6: **end while**	6: **end while**

Algorithm 3. Distributed Least-Mean Squares Solver (D-LMS)

Input: $A \in \mathbb{R}^{n \times m}$ with $n > m, b \in \mathbb{R}^n$, both distributed row-wise over N nodes
  For all u and $\forall i \in D_u$: x_u and v_u^i initialised with zero
Output: $x_u \in \mathbb{R}^m$ on every node
1: **in each** node u **do**
2:     **while** not converged **do**
3:         Broadcast x_u to D_u
4:         **for each** node $i \in D_u$ **do**
5:             $v_u^i = v_u^i + \frac{c}{2}(x_u - x_i)$
6:         Send v_u^i to each corresponding node $i \in D_u$
7:         $x_u = x_u + \mu[2A^{u\top}(b^u - A^u x_u) - \Sigma_{i \in N_u}(v_u^i - v_i^u) - c\Sigma_{i \in N_u}(x_u - x_i)]$
8:     **end while**

---

implementations lies in which variable we choose to correspond to the updated weight estimate.". In ATC, x_u is the result of the combination step (line 2.5 of ATC), in CTA it is the result of the adaption step (line 2.5 of CTA). However, mathematically and numerically this does not result in the same solution.

D-LMS. The D-LMS method is shown in Algorithm 3. A node u first broadcasts its current estimate x_u to its neighbourhood D_u (line 3.3). Then an individual correction vector v_u^i is computed for each neighbour $i \in D_u$ using the received estimation x_i and its own estimation x_u (line 3.5). These values are then sent to each corresponding node i. In the last step of each iteration (line 3.7), the new estimate x_u is computed using a least squares residual from A^u and b^u, the locally available parts of A and b, and the correction terms v_u^i and v_i^u received from the neighbourhood. This term is added to the current x_u and weighted with a step-size parameter μ resulting in an estimate x_u of the solution x in each node. Proof of convergence is given in [18].

Comparison of Communication Cost

The cost of a broadcast to all neighbours ("local broadcast") depends on the topology and on the type of connection. Therefore, we introduce the broadcasting parameter $B(d)$ for denoting the number of messages required for broadcasting to d neighbours. In a wireless setting, a single message is required to perform a broadcast to all neighbours, thus $B(d) = 1$. However, in a setting with point-to-point communication (e. g., wired connections), d messages are required for sending a message to d neighbours, thus $B(d) = d$. For a global broadcast beyond the neighbourhood in any network other than a fully connected one, additional messages are needed for multi-hop message relaying over intermediate nodes.

The communication patterns and costs for ATC and CTA are identical. In each iteration, each node u broadcasts a vector of size m to its neighbourhood D_u. In k_1 iterations, node u sends $k_1 B(|D_u|)$ messages. D-LMS requires communication in two of its steps. In line 3.3, a local broadcast is required to distribute the vector x_u of size m to the neighbours. Line 3.6 sends $|D_u|$ individual messages of size

Table 1. Comparison of the communication cost for diffLMS, D-LMS and PSDLS

Algorithm	Number of messages sent per node	Total amount of data sent per node
diffLMS	$k_1 B(|D_u|)$	$k_1 B(|D_u|) m$
D-LMS	$k_2 (B(|D_u|) + |D_u|)$	$k_2 (B(|D_u|) + |D_u|) m$
PSDLS	$2mR$	$\frac{1}{2} (m^2 + 7m) R$

m to distribute the correction term. This results in $k_2(B(|D_u|) + |D_u|)$ messages and $k_2(B(|D_u|) + |D_u|)m$ data values sent per node.

Although PSDLS is not an iterative method, we have to consider the number of rounds R required by each push-sum algorithm. Note that in practice R may vary slightly for different push-sum calls due to the randomisation. In the distributed QR decomposition, for the first $m - 1$ columns of the matrix A two push-sum calls have to be executed, the first one summing scalars and the second one summing vectors. In column l of A the length of these vectors is $m - l$. For column m only one scalar push-sum call has to be executed. The matrix-vector product $Q^\top b$ requires one more push-sum call on vectors of length m. Consequently, the number of messages sent per node is $2mR$. In each push-sum call, the values *and* a weight have to be transmitted [5].

Table 1 summarises the analytical results of this section. We conclude that independently of the number of iterations k_1 and k_2, D-LMS sends $|D_u|$ more messages and more data per iteration than diffLMS. For comparing the communication cost, information about the number of iterations k_1 and k_2 required by diffLMS and D-LMS, respectively, and the number of push-sum rounds R required by PSDLS is necessary. As our simulation results in Section 5 illustrate, these quantities differ significantly across the three methods.

5   Experiments

The simulation results presented in this section demonstrate the different convergence speeds in terms of average number of messages sent per node and therefore provide some qualitative insight into typical values of k_1, k_2 and R for the algorithms compared in this paper. Our simulations are based on Matlab implementations of the algorithms. The implementation of the push-sum algorithm is round-based and synchronised. The neighbours are selected at random from a uniform distribution. For all methods, A and b are distributed row-wise over all N nodes. Without loss of generality, we consider the special case $n = N$, i.e., each node holds one row of A and one element of b. Like in [16], the relative degree weight matrix was used for both diffLMS and D-LMS.

In order to evaluate the accuracy of the approximate solution x_u computed by the algorithms, we evaluated the relative error

$$\max_{u=1,..,N} \|x_u - x^*\|_\infty / \|x^*\|_\infty, \tag{2}$$

where x^* is the solution computed sequentially in Matlab.

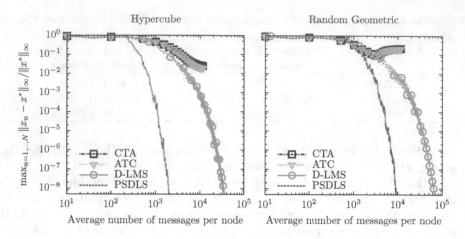

Fig. 1. Comparison for $N = n = 64, m = 8$ on different topologies: hypercube (left) and random geometric (right). The step-sizes are $\mu_{\text{ATC}} = \mu_{\text{CTA}} = 0.01$ and $\mu_{\text{D-LMS}} = 0.2$.

diffLMS and D-LMS are both iterative methods, whereas the PSDLS is a direct method with an iterative building block (the push-sum algorithm) in each step. For a fair comparison of the methods, the instances of the push-sum algorithm in PSDLS were not terminated based on reaching a predefined accuracy, but based on a predefined maximum number of rounds.

The behaviour of diffLMS and D-LMS strongly depends on the choice of the step-size parameter μ. Based on our experience, in particular the convergence speed of diffLMS is very sensitive to the choice of μ, and for bad choices of μ the methods even diverge. The best choice for μ in terms of convergence speed seems to vary greatly with m, the topology and the average node degree. Unfortunately, the literature does not give any guidance on how to choose μ. Thus, we performed extensive simulations across a wide range of values for μ and chose the values at which the respective algorithm eventually achieves the highest accuracy.

Figure 1 shows the convergence behaviour of the different algorithms for $N = 64$ nodes arranged in a hypercube and as a random geometric graph on the unit square with a communication radius 0.2. The horizontal axis shows the average number of messages sent per node and the relative error (2) achieved for this number of messages sent per node is plotted on the vertical axis. The experiments show that the diffLMS methods do not reach the targeted accuracy of 10^{-8} and after 12000 messages only achieve an accuracy of 10^{-2} on a hypercube. On a random geometric graph diffLMS diverges at around 3100 messages and does not even reach 10^{-1}. On a hypercube network, the D-LMS algorithm achieves an accuracy of 10^{-8}, but requires around 32600 messages to be sent per node. The PSDLS method converges significantly faster than the other algorithms requiring only about 1950 messages per node to reach an accuracy of 10^{-8}, which is a factor of 16 less than D-LMS. The amount of data sent per node is also significantly lower for PSDLS, sending only 5400 values compared to 261000 values sent by

D-LMS. Similar behaviour can be observed for the random geometric graph. PSDLS converges more than 7 times faster than D-LMS and sends only 0.05% of the data sent by D-LMS.

6 Conclusion

We surveyed existing distributed least squares solvers and classified them based on their communication pattern. We introduced a novel truly distributed least squares solver PSDLS based on the push-sum algorithm, which limits the communication to the immediate neighbourhood of each node and does not require a fusion centre or clustering.

We analysed and compared the communication cost of all existing truly distributed methods in terms of the number of messages and the amount of data sent per node. Numerical simulations showed that the number of messages per node required for a solution accuracy of 10^{-8} is more than a factor of seven lower for the novel PSDLS algorithm than for the other truly distributed methods.

Future work will consider fault tolerance in distributed least squares solvers.

Acknowledgement. This work was partly supported by the Austrian Science Fund (FWF): S 10608-N13 (NFN SISE).

References

1. Reise, G., Matz, G., Gröchenig, K.: Distributed field reconstruction in wireless sensor networks based on hybrid shift-invariant spaces. IEEE Transactions on Signal Processing 60(10), 5426–5439 (2012)
2. Sayed, A.H.: Diffusion adaptation over networks. In: Academic Press Library in Signal Processing, vol. 3, pp. 323–454. Academic Press, Elsevier (2014)
3. Shi, L., Song, W.Z., Xu, M., Xiao, Q., Kamath, G., Lees, J., Xing, G.: Imaging seismic tomography in sensor network. In: IEEE International Conference on Distributed Computing in Sensor Systems (DCOSS), pp. 304–306 (2013)
4. Reichenbach, F., Born, A., Timmermann, D., Bill, R.: A distributed linear least squares method for precise localization with low complexity in wireless sensor networks. In: Gibbons, P.B., Abdelzaher, T., Aspnes, J., Rao, R. (eds.) DCOSS 2006. LNCS, vol. 4026, pp. 514–528. Springer, Heidelberg (2006)
5. Kempe, D., Dobra, A., Gehrke, J.: Gossip-based computation of aggregate information. In: Proceedings of the 44th Annual IEEE Symposium on Foundations of Computer Science, pp. 482–491 (2003)
6. Gansterer, W.N., Niederbrucker, G., Straková, H., Schulze Grotthoff, S.: Scalable and fault tolerant orthogonalization based on randomized distributed data aggregation. Journal of Computational Science 4(6), 480–488 (2013)
7. Niederbrucker, G., Straková, H., Gansterer, W.N.: Improving fault tolerance and accuracy of a distributed reduction algorithm. In: SC Companion: High Performance Computing, Networking, Storage and Analysis, pp. 643–651 (2012)
8. Khan, M.I., Gansterer, W.N., Haring, G.: Static vs. mobile sink: The influence of basic parameters on energy efficiency in wireless sensor networks. Computer Communications 36(9), 965–978 (2013)

9. Le Borgne, Y.A., Nowe, A., Abughalieh, N., Steenhaut, K.: Distributed regression for high-level feature extraction in wireless sensor networks. In: 2010 Seventh International Conference on Networked Sensing Systems (INSS), pp. 249–252 (2010)

10. Shi, L., Song, W.Z., Kamath, G., Xing, G., Liu, X.: Distributed least-squares iterative methods in networks: A survey. Submitted to Computing Journal (2013)

11. Renaut, R.A.: A parallel multisplitting solution of the least squares problem. Numerical Linear Algebra with Applications 5(1), 11–31 (1998)

12. Yang, L., Brent, R.: Parallel MCGLS and ICGLS methods for least squares problems on distributed memory architectures. The Journal of Supercomputing 29(2), 145–156 (2004)

13. Behnke, R., Salzmann, J., Lieckfeldt, D., Timmermann, D.: SDLS - Distributed least squares localization for large wireless sensor networks. In: International Conference on Ultra Modern Telecommunications & Workshops, pp. 1–6 (2009)

14. Shakibian, H., Charkari, N.: MMS-PSO for distributed regression over sensor networks. In: IEEE Conference on Multisensor Fusion and Integration for Intelligent Systems (MFI), pp. 68–73 (2010)

15. Zhou, Q., Kar, S., Huie, L., Poor, H.V.: Robust distributed least-squares estimation in sensor networks with node failures. In: IEEE Global Telecommunications Conference, pp.1–6 (2011)

16. Cattivelli, F., Sayed, A.: Diffusion LMS strategies for distributed estimation. IEEE Transactions on Signal Processing 58(3), 1035–1048 (2010)

17. Tu, S.Y., Sayed, A.: Diffusion strategies outperform consensus strategies for distributed estimation over adaptive networks. IEEE Transactions on Signal Processing 60(12), 6217–6234 (2012)

18. Schizas, I.: Consensus in ad hoc WSNs with noisy links - Part II: Distributed estimation and smoothing of random signals. IEEE Transactions on Signal Processing 56(4), 1650–1666 (2008)

19. Mateos, G., Schizas, I.D., Giannakis, G.B.: Performance analysis of the consensus-based distributed LMS algorithm. EURASIP Journal on Advances in Signal Processing 2009(1), 68:6–68:6 (2009)

20. Schizas, I.D., Mateos, G., Giannakis, G.B.: Distributed LMS for consensus-based in-network adaptive processing. IEEE Transactions on Signal Processing 57(6), 2365–2382 (2009)

21. Sluciak, O., Rupp, M.: Network size estimation using distributed orthogonalization. IEEE Signal Processing Letters 20(4), 347–350 (2013)

22. Straková, H., Gansterer, W.N., Zemen, T.: Distributed QR factorization based on randomized algorithms. In: Wyrzykowski, R., Dongarra, J., Karczewski, K., Waśniewski, J. (eds.) PPAM 2011, Part I. LNCS, vol. 7203, pp. 235–244. Springer, Heidelberg (2012)

23. Straková, H., Gansterer, W.N.: A distributed eigensolver for loosely coupled networks. In: 21st Euromicro International Conference on Parallel, Distributed and Network-Based Processing (PDP), pp. 51–57 (2013)

High-Performance Computer Algebra:
A Hecke Algebra Case Study

Patrick Maier[1], Daria Livesey[2], Hans-Wolfgang Loidl[3], and Phil Trinder[1]

[1] School of Computing Science, University of Glasgow, Glasgow, UK
[2] School of Natural and Computing Sciences, University of Aberdeen, Aberdeen, UK
[3] School of Mathematical and Computer Sciences, Heriot-Watt University, Edinburgh, UK

Abstract. We describe the first ever parallelisation of an algebraic computation at modern HPC scale. Our case study poses challenges typical of the domain: it is a multi-phase application with dynamic task creation and irregular parallelism over complex control and data structures.

Our starting point is a sequential algorithm for finding invariant bilinear forms in the representation theory of Hecke algebras, implemented in the GAP computational group theory system. After optimising the sequential code we develop a parallel algorithm that exploits the new skeleton-based SGP2 framework to parallelise the three most computationally-intensive phases. To this end we develop a new domain-specific skeleton, `parBufferTryReduce`. We report good parallel performance both on a commodity cluster and on a national HPC, delivering speedups up to 548 over the optimised sequential implementation on 1024 cores.

1 Introduction

Computational algebra is an important area of symbolic computation with many complex and expensive computations that would benefit from parallel execution. The area is served by a variety of systems, many specialising in some mathematical domain, for example GAP [7], a computational algebra system (CAS) specifically designed for group theory and combinatorics.

Some discrete mathematical problems are embarrassingly parallel, and this has been exploited for years even at Internet scale, e.g. the "Great Internet Mersenne Prime Search". Other problems have more complex coordination patterns and both parallel algorithms and parallel CAS implementations have been developed, e.g. ParGAP [5]. Many parallel algebraic computations exhibit high degrees of irregularity, at multiple levels, with numbers and sizes of tasks varying enormously (up to 5 orders of magnitude) [16]. They tend to use complex user-defined data structures, exhibit highly dynamic memory usage and complex control flow, often exploiting recursion. They make little, if any, use of floating-point operations.

This combination of characteristics means that symbolic computations are not well suited to conventional HPC paradigms with their emphasis on iteration over floating point arrays, and has motivated the development of scalable domain-specific scheduling and management frameworks like SymGrid-Par [16] and SymGridPar2 (SGP2) [20].

This paper outlines the first ever modern HPC-scale parallelisation of a problem in computational group theory, namely finding the invariant bilinear forms of Hecke algebra representations. These bilinear forms, and Hecke algebras more generally, are an

F. Silva et al. (Eds.): Euro-Par 2014, LNCS 8632, pp. 415–426, 2014.

important tool in the study of symmetries that arise in many branches of mathematics, e. g. in topology and knot theory, with applications in theoretical physics and chemistry.

Our starting point is a sequential algorithm for computing bilinear forms, implemented in GAP. Prior to parallelising, we optimise the sequential algorithm, reducing sequential runtime by a factor of 350 (Section 2).[1] The paper makes the following research contributions.

(1) The development of a parallel algorithm for finding above bilinear forms. The parallelisation exploits the new SGP2 framework designed for scalable GAP computations. Core elements of SGP2 are a set of algorithmic skeletons, implemented in the parallel Haskell DSL HdpH [21], and a GAP binding for Haskell. We parallelise the three most time-consuming phases of the algorithm: (a) solving homomorphic images of linear systems over finite fields, (b) solving interpolation problems over rationals, and (c) bilinear invariance check (over polynomial matrices). All algebraic computations are performed by sequential GAP instances and coordinated by HdpH (Section 4).

(2) Some SGP2 skeletons are generic, e. g. the `parMap` parallel map of a function over a list. Other skeletons are specific to the algebraic domain. Specifically to compute with homomorphic images, a technique that is typical for a large class of algebraic algorithms, we have developed a new algebraic skeleton `parBufferTryReduce` that repeatedly checks whether the homomorphic results accumulated thus far are sufficient to reconstruct the final result (Section 3).

(3) Many mathematicians have access to commodity clusters rather than HPCs, so SGP2 is designed for both. We report good speedup and efficiency for a range of bilinear form problems, both on a Beowulf cluster and on medium-scale configurations of the HECToR UK supercomputer [12]. For example, one problem instance achieves a speedup of 548, coordinating 992 GAP instances on 1024 cores (Section 5).

2   Algorithm for Finding Invariant Bilinear Forms

Background.   Using the terminology of [8], let $R = \mathbb{Z}[x, x^{-1}]$ be the ring of Laurent polynomials in an indeterminate x. For the purpose of this paper, it suffices to know that a *Hecke algebra*[2] $\mathcal{H}$ is an R-algebra with a basis $\{T_w \mid w \in W\}$ over R, where W is a finite Coxeter group with set of generators S. In this paper, we only consider Hecke algebras of type E_m ($m = 6, 7, 8$), that is, W is the exceptional Coxeter group E_m, and the cardinality of the set of generators S is m.

An n-dimensional *representation* ρ of a Hecke algebra $\mathcal{H}$ is an R-algebra homomorphism from $\mathcal{H}$ to $M_n(R)$, the R-algebra of $n \times n$ matrices over R. Note that ρ is *generated* by the matrices $\rho(T_s)$, $s \in S$. $\mathcal{H}$ is known to have a finite number of so-called *cell* representations ρ. Moreover, Howlett and Yin [13] have brought each of these cell representations ρ into a form where all m matrices $\rho(T_s)$ are sparse.

Graham and Lehrer [11] and Geck [8] show that for any given ρ there exists a nontrivial symmetric matrix $Q \in M_n(R)$, unique up to scalar multiplication, such that

---

[1] Such dramatic optimisations are not unusual in computer algebra as the typical high-level presentation of computational mathematics often omits opportunities for sequential optimisation.

[2] More precisely, $\mathcal{H}$ is a one-parameter generic Iwahori-Hecke algebra.

$$Q \cdot \rho(T_s) = \rho(T_s)^\mathsf{T} \cdot Q \tag{1}$$

for all generators $\rho(T_s)$. We call Q the *matrix of an invariant bilinear form*.

Depending on the representation ρ, finding the invariant bilinear form Q may require substantial computation. For each algebra type, the table below lists the number of cell representations ρ, the range of dimensions of ρ and the range of spreads of degree bounds of Laurent polynomials in Q. These numbers (and hence the difficulty of the problem) vary by several orders of magnitude.

Hecke algebra type	E_6	E_7	E_8
number of cell representations ρ	25	60	112
dimension of ρ	6–90	7–512	8–7168
spread of degree bounds of polynomials in Q	29–54	45–95	65–185

Sequential Algorithm for Computing Q. In principle, Q can be computed by viewing Equation (1) as a system of linear equations and solving for the entries of Q. However, solving linear systems over $\mathbb{Z}[x, x^{-1}]$ is too expensive to obtain solutions for high dimensional representations.

Instead, we solve the problem by interpolation. We view each entry of Q as a Laurent polynomial with $u - l + 1$ unknown coefficients, where $u - l + 1$ is the spread between lower degree bound l and upper degree bound u. Solving Equation (1) at $u - l + 1$ data points will provide enough information to compute the unknown coefficients by solving linear systems over the rationals instead of $\mathbb{Z}[x, x^{-1}]$. To avoid computing with very large rational numbers (due to polynomials of high degree), we solve homomorphic images of Equation (1) modulo small primes and use the Chinese Remainder Theorem to recover the rational values.

The algorithm takes as input m generators $\rho(T_s)$ of dimension n, lower and upper degree bounds l and u, and a finite set of small primes P. From the degree bounds, we construct a set V_{lu} of $u - l + 1$ small integers (excluding zero) to be used as data points for interpolation. The primes in P must be chosen large enough not to divide any of the integers in V_{lu}. The algorithm runs in three phases:

1. For all $p \in P$ and $v \in V_{lu}$, GENERATE a modular interpolated solution Q_{vp} of (1) by instantiating the unknown x with v and solving the resulting system modulo p.
2. For all $v \in V_{lu}$, REDUCE the modular matrices Q_{vp} by rational Chinese remaindering and obtain a rational interpolated solution Q_v of (1). Construct each Laurent polynomial q_{ij} in Q by gathering the (i, j)-entries of all Q_v and solving a rational linear system for the coefficients q_{ij}. Since Q is symmetric, there are $(n + 1)n/2$ such systems, each of dimension $u - l + 1$.
3. For all generators $\rho(T_s)$, CHECK that the resulting Q satisfies (1) over $\mathbb{Z}[x, x^{-1}]$.

After some (offline) pre-processing, the theory of Hecke algebras admits a particularly efficient way to GENERATE Q_{vp}. Instead of solving a linear system, the rows of Q_{vp} are computed by a *spinning basis algorithm* [9,17], multiplying, or *spinning*, the basis vector e of a pre-determined one-dimensional sub-space with n pre-determined products of the generators $\rho(T_s)$.

We observe that Q often has many identical entries. Therefore, the gather step of the REDUCE phase filters duplicates to avoid repeatedly solving the same linear systems. Typically, avoiding duplicates reduces the workload of REDUCE by a factor of 5 to 10.

Sequential Optimisations. Profiling the GAP code on Hecke algebras of type E_6 lead to a number of improvements. The three most important ones are:

1. Avoiding unnecessary copying during the GENERATE phase by reducing the size of lambda abstractions encoding the generators.
2. Reducing the memory footprint by storing generators in a sparse matrix format.
3. Spinning the basis more efficiently by exploiting associativity.

For type E_6 these optimisations reduced sequential runtime of the algorithm (cumulative over all representations) by a factor of about 350, and the memory footprint by an order of magnitude from several GB to hundreds of MB.

3   The SymGridPar2 Framework

SGP2 System Architecture. GAP [7] is the leading free system for computational discrete algebra. It is designed to be natural to use for mathematicians; to be powerful and flexible for experts and to be freely extensible so that it can encompass new mathematics. GAP supports very efficient linear algebra over small finite fields, multiple representations of groups, subgroups, cosets and different types of group elements, and backtrack search algorithms for permutation groups.

This case study used the most recent stable GAP distribution, GAP 4.6, which does not support parallelism. Hence the sequential GAP 4.6 instances are coordinated over the network by a distributed middleware, the SymGridPar2 (SGP2) framework [20]. The middleware occupies one core per multicore node and controls (via a RPC-like protocol) independent GAP 4.6 instances running on the remaining cores (Figure 1).

SGP2 itself is implemented in HdpH [21], a domain-specific language (DSL) for distributed-memory task parallelism, embedded in Haskell. SGP2 consists of two parts: (1) a GAP binding, enabling calls from HdpH to GAP, including automatic marshaling, and (2) a number of general-purpose and domain-specific parallel skeletons.

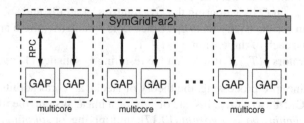

Fig. 1. SGP2 system architecture

```
-- HdpH types
type Par a                              -- parallel computation, returns result of type 'a'
type Closure a                          -- serialisable value/computation of type 'a'
type Task a = Closure (Par (Closure a)) -- serialisable parallel computation
                                        -- returning serialisable result of type 'a'

-- sample general-purpose skeletons
parMap    :: Closure (a → b) → [Closure a] → Par [Closure b]
parReduce :: Closure (a → a → a) → [Closure a] → Par (Closure a)

-- novel domain-specific skeleton; repeatedly reduces the results of a lazy list of input tasks
-- until the reducer computes a result
parBufferTryReduce :: ([Closure a] → Par (Maybe (Closure b))) -- reducer
                      → Int                                    -- reducer batch size
                      → Int                                    -- number tasks eval'd in parallel
                      → [Task a]                               -- lazy list of input tasks
                      → Par (Maybe (Closure b))                -- result
```

Fig. 2. HdpH types and some SymGridPar2 skeleton signatures

SGP2 Programming Model. HdpH is a monadic DSL, embedding a high-level co-ordination language into Haskell. Figure 2 introduces two central types of the HdpH DSL: Par, the monad type constructor for parallel computations, and Closure, the type constructor for serialisable values including unevaluated computations, or thunks. A Task is defined as a serialisable monadic computation returning a serialisable result. Thanks to serialisability, tasks and their results can be distributed over the network, and HdpH exploits this to provide automatic load management by work stealing.

At the lowest level, HdpH exposes fork/join style primitives for parallel program-ming. Using the primitives the HdpH library defines a number of general-purpose poly-morphic skeletons (Figure 2), e. g. parallel maps (applying a function closure to a list of closures, in parallel) and reductions. The skeletons evaluate their input lists strictly as they coordinate monadic computations, and hence are unsuitable for computing with potentially infinite lazy lists.

Our case study requires solving an unknown number of subproblems in parallel until there are enough intermediate results to construct the solution. More specifically, the algorithm of Section 2 requires the use of an unknown number of primes in the GEN-ERATE phase. A typical Haskell program would parametrise the GENERATE phase with an infinite lazy list of primes, and rely on demand from the REDUCE phase to decide how many primes are actually needed. As the monadic context of HdpH precludes lazy lists, we capture this domain-specific pattern[3] in a new skeleton that combines a task farm with a reducer.

The new parBufferTryReduce skeleton takes as input (in reverse order) a lazy list of tasks, the number of tasks to evaluate in parallel, the reducer batch size and the re-ducer function. A call to parBufferTryReduce f b n tasks continually forks from the head of list tasks, aiming to keep n tasks under evaluation, accumulating a list accu of intermediate results (not necessarily in the order of tasks). The reducer f is executed every time the length of accu is a multiple of the batch size b. The skeleton

---

[3] This pattern is common in algebraic computations that generate modular subproblems, e. g. linear system solving based on modular arithmetic and Chinese remaindering.

returns a result as soon as the reducer finds one; it returns `Nothing` only if the reducer fails to produce a result even after all `tasks` are evaluated.

The HdpH DSL greatly simplifies developing domain-specific skeletons, particularly skeletons with complex parallel coordination such as `parBufferTryReduce`. A case in point is the implementation of the latter spanning less than 90 lines of code.

4   Parallel Algorithm for Finding Invariant Bilinear Forms

Each of the three phases of the sequential algorithm (Section 2) contains significant amounts of parallelism. Deciding what and how to parallelise is guided by the ratio between computation and communication costs on the distributed target architectures.

Parallel Phases. Figure 3 shows the parallel structure of the algorithm to compute Q, with lower and upper degree bounds l and u, for an n-dimensional cell representation given by m generators $\rho(T_s)$; P is the set of primes used in the GENERATE phase.

The GENERATE *phase* forks $|P|(u-l+1)$ parallel tasks, each taking as input a pair of integers $(p, v) \in P \times V_{lu}$, where V_{lu} is defined as in Section 2. Each task runs the spinning basis algorithm to compute an $n \times n$ matrix Q_{vp} of integers modulo p. Thus the input size of GENERATE tasks is small and constant but the output size is quadratic in the dimension.

The REDUCE *phase* first constructs $k \le (n + 1)n/2$ interpolation problems by Chinese remaindering and filtering duplicates, then forks k parallel tasks solving the interpolation problems. Each task takes as input a vector of $u - l + 1$ rational values, solves a linear system of $u - l + 1$ equations over the rationals, and returns a vector of $u - l + 1$ polynomial coefficients. Thus input and output size of REDUCE tasks depend (linearly) on the degree spread (and on the size of the rational numbers, which depends on the choice of P.)

The CHECK *phase* forks m parallel tasks, each checking the validity of Equation (1) w. r. t. one generator $\rho(T_s)$. To this end, each task requires as input the whole matrix Q, i. e. $(n + 1)n/2$ polynomials with up to $u - l + 1$ rational coefficients. Thus the input size of CHECK tasks is quadratic in the dimension and linear in the degree spread (and depends on the size of the rational coefficients), whereas the output is a single bit.

Overall Coordination. Figure 3 depicts a parallel structure where REDUCE synchronises on the completion of GENERATE, which depends on the set of primes P. Instead,

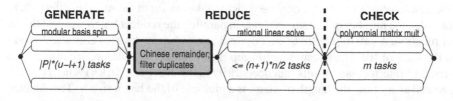

Fig. 3. Structure of parallel algorithm for computing invariant bilinear forms Q

the `parBufferTryReduce` skeleton (Section 3) decouples GENERATE from RE-
DUCE: The list `tasks` is a (possibly lazy and infinite) list of GENERATE tasks, the
reducer `f` runs the REDUCE phase followed by the CHECK phase, and the batch size `b`
determines the frequency of (attempted) reductions.

Note that most tasks in Figure 3 run on GAP workers and have a small memory footprint. However, the big task constructing the interpolation problems at the beginning of
the REDUCE phase is executed on a dedicated GAP instance, the *GAP master*, because
it must gather all Q_{vp} matrices and mangle them simultaneously, which may require
substantial amounts of memory.

5   Evaluation of Parallel Performance

We evaluate the parallel algorithm (Section 4) on all cell representations (reps) for
Hecke algebra of type E_7 and on the smaller reps of type E_8. The reps for type E_6 don't
warrant parallel execution as their sequential runtimes are less than 150s. We evaluate
on three different architectures:

- up to 16 nodes of a commodity cluster (Beowulf, 8 cores/node, 2.0GHz Intel Xeon
  CPUs, 12GB RAM/node, Gigabit Ethernet),
- up to 32 nodes of a Cray XE6 (HECToR [12], 32 cores/node, 2.3GHz AMD Inter-
  lagos CPUs, 32GB RAM/node, Cray Gemini interconnect), and
- a large memory NUMA server (Cantor, 48 cores, 2.8GHz AMD Opteron CPUs,
  512GB RAM).

Figure 4 displays our results, organised into 2 columns: to the left data about the E_7 reps
3 to 60, to the right about the E_8 reps 3 to 16; reps 1 and 2 for E_7 resp. E_8 are trivial and
easy to solve sequentially.

Problem size. The top row of Figure 4 plots the representations' dimensions and degree
spreads (right y-axis) as well as the numbers of GENERATE and REDUCE tasks (left y-
axis); recall that the number of CHECK tasks is constant at 7 and 8, respectively.

We observe that the number of GENERATE tasks tracks the degree spreads curve,
whereas the number of REDUCE tasks oscillates by an order of magnitude or more
though its trend is rising with the dimension.

To obtain reproducible results, the set of primes was chosen somewhat bigger than
minimal, and the batch size parameter of the `parBufferTryReduce` skeleton was
set so high that the reducer runs only once, after the GENERATE phase is completed.

Runtime. The second row of Figure 4 plots parallel runtimes, on 16 Beowulf nodes
(using $15 * 7 + 1 = 106$ GAP workers) in the case of E_7, and on Cantor (using 40
GAP workers) in the case of E_8. The graph for E_8 also plots the total work, i.e. the
cumulative runtime of all tasks, and the time spent in the sequential part of the REDUCE
phase. The graph for E_7 only plots the parallel work, i.e. the cumulative runtime of all
parallel tasks.[4] The reported times reflect single experiments as a statistically significant
number of repetitions would be prohibitively expensive.

---

[4] We failed to record the runtime of the sequential REDUCE step for E_7, thus can't provide total
  work; parallel work is an under-approximation.

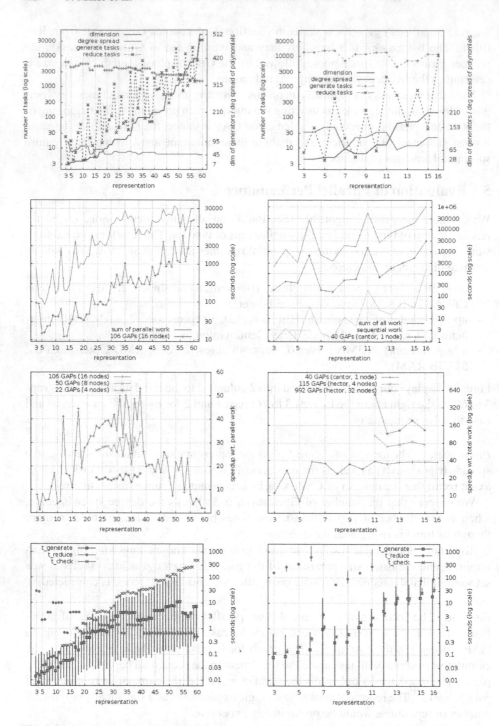

Fig. 4. Performance of parallel algorithm for finding invariant bilinear forms Q, E_7 to the left, E_8 to the right. Top to bottom: problem size, runtime, speedup, size of GAP tasks.

We observe that the amount of (total, parallel, sequential) work and the parallel runtime oscillate noisily due to the dramatic oscillation in the number of REDUCE tasks. The trend of work and runtime appears to grow with the dimension; the degree spread appears to have no influence.

Speedup. The third row of Figure 4 plots speedups on 16 Beowulf nodes (E_7, using 106 GAP workers) and on Cantor (E_8, using 40 GAP workers).

Since sequential runtimes are not available, we compute speedups w. r. t. parallel work (for E_7) or total work (for E_8). This method systematically underestimates the true speedup (particularly for E_7) as it fails to account for some of the costs of sequential execution, e. g. more time spent on sequential garbage collection.

We observe that most E_7 reps up to 22 are too small to produce significant speedups on 16 Beowulf nodes. Reps 39 and above, and particularly reps above 55, suffer from Amdahl's law due to significant time spent in the sequential part of REDUCE. Similarly, the E_8 reps up to 5 are too small for good speedups on Cantor. However, we cannot observe the effect of Amdahl's law for E_8; there is so much parallel work that speedups for reps 11 to 16 are close to the maximum of $40\times$ despite rep 16 spending more than 1000 seconds in the sequential phase.

For the E_7 reps 23 to 38, we also investigate strong scaling from 4 to 8 to 16 Beowulf nodes. We observe that speedup oscillations increase with scale, i. e. some representations scale, others don't; best speedup ($53\times$) is achieved for rep 38, corresponding to a best case efficiency of 50%. The picture is similar for the E_8 reps 11 to 15 when investigating strong scaling from 4 to 32 nodes on HECToR; rep 11 achieves the top speedup of $548\times$, top efficiency of 55%, but the other reps do not scale so well. Note that for multi-phase symbolic computations with irregular and dynamic parallelism an efficiency of 40% is good, as previously reported on smaller architectures [15,16,26].

Task size. The bottom row of Figure 4 shows the average, minimum and maximum runtimes of GENERATE, REDUCE and CHECK tasks; the time recorded is GAP compute time, excluding communication and marshaling overheads.[5]

We observe that CHECK tasks are generally expensive but regular, and REDUCE tasks are largely regular, with only some reps showing moderate irregularity (E_7 rep 48 is an outlier). However, GENERATE tasks are wildly irregular, varying by at least two orders of magnitude. The average cost of GENERATE and CHECK tasks appears to grow with the dimension, whereas the cost of REDUCE tasks appears to depend strongly on the degree spread.

Limitations. Two issues preclude solving the remaining E_8 reps with the current algorithm. First, the sequential time spent in the REDUCE phase, which grows quadratically with the dimension, obliterates speedups beyond dimension 200 (for E_7). The parallel algorithm needs to be redesigned to scale to dimensions between 1000 and 2000 (which are typical of E_8), let alone the maximum of 7168.

---

[5] Overheads for calling GAP, including marshaling and data transfer, vary with task input and output size. For E_7 GENERATE tasks on Beowulf, for instance, overheads generally stay two orders of magnitude below average task size, ranging from about 10^{-4} to about 0.1 seconds.

The second issue is the memory consumption, growing quadratically in the dimension, of the GAP master at the start of the REDUCE phase. The 12GB RAM of a Beowulf node prove insufficient already from E_8 rep 12, dimension 168.

6   Related Work

Computational Algebra Skeletons. This paper gives further evidence to the success of a parallel pattern, or skeleton, approach [2] in the domain of computational mathematics. We combine specialist domain knowledge, in the area of computational group theory, with language and systems knowledge, specifically for high-level orchestration of parallelism on large-scale clusters. This continues our work on domain-specific parallel patterns for symbolic computation, and some recent examples are as follows. We have designed a parallel Orbit, that achieves a speedup of up to 36 on a 64-core machine [14]; a critical-pair-completion pattern, with the Gröbner Bases computation as one instance that achieves a speedup of 6.9 on an 8-core machine; and the multiple-homomorphic images pattern, that achieves speedups of up to 11.9 on a 16-node cluster [18].

Parallel Computational Algebra. Several computer algebra systems offer dedicated support for parallelism (see [10, Sec 2.18] and [25]). Distributed Maple [26] provides a portable Java-based communication layer to permit interaction of Maple instances over a network. It uses future-based language constructs for synchronisation and communication, and has been used to parallelise several computational geometry algorithms. The Sugarbush [1] system is another distributed-memory extension of Maple, which uses Linda as coordination language. A distributed-memory parallel extension to GAP is the GAPMPI [3] package, which provides access to MPI functionality from within GAP. In contrast to this model of explicit message passing, our approach provides higher level abstractions, such as the parBufferTryReduce skeleton.

The TOP-C system provides task-oriented parallelism on top of a distributed shared-memory system [4], implementing several symbolic applications, including parallel computations over Hecke algebras [6] on networks of SPARC workstations.

Several efforts of parallelising computational algebra have targeted previous generations of HPC architectures. Sibert et al [27] describe the implementation of basic arithmetic over finite fields on a Connection Machine. Roch et al [24] discuss the implementation and performance of a parallel Gröbner basis algorithm on the Floating Point System hypercube Tesseract 20 with 16 nodes. Another parallel Gröbner basis algorithm is implemented on a Cray Y-MP by Neun and Melenek [23] and later on a Connection Machine by Loustaunau and Wang [19]. We are not aware of any other work within the last 20 years that targets HPC for computational algebra.

More recently main-stream computer algebra systems have developed interfaces for large-scale distribution, aiming to exploit Grid infrastructures [22]. The community effort of defining a protocol for symbolic data exchange on such infrastructures allows interchange between different computer algebra systems [16]. In contrast to these Grid-based infrastructures, our technology targets massively parallel supercomputers.

Invariant Bilinear Forms for Hecke Algebra Representations. The invariant bilinear forms Q carry data that enables us to find so-called *Jantzen filtrations* [17], which simplify the general understanding of transformations of Hecke algebra representations.

Such bilinear forms Q for Hecke algebras of type E_7 and E_8 have previously been computed by Geck and Müller in an ad-hoc way; their paper [9] describes the mathematical basis for their approach but does not consider parallelism or evaluate performance. This paper and [17] are part of an ongoing project, started by Geck, to build a systematic GAP database of bilinear forms Q for Hecke algebras of type E_6, E_7 and E_8.

7 Conclusion

We have described what we believe is the first ever parallelisation of an algebraic computation on a modern HPC. The computation of invariant bilinear forms for Hecke algebra representations is multi-phase and exhibits irregular parallelism over the complex control and data structures typical of computer algebra. The parallelisation exploits the new skeleton-based SGP2 framework and required the development of a new domain-specific skeleton, `parBufferTryReduce`. The performance on a medium-scale HPC configuration and a commodity cluster is good, if noisy, reflecting the complexity of the problems solved. For example, for medium-size Hecke algebra representations (23 to 38) of type E_7 we obtain speedups of between 25 and 53 on 16 Beowulf nodes (128 cores, 106 GAP workers). For small E_8 representations (11 to 15) we obtain speedups of between 116 and 548 on 32 HECToR nodes (1024 cores, 992 GAP workers).

In related and ongoing work we report good performance results for small algebraic kernels on far larger HPC configurations, e. g. weak scaling of the `sumEuler` kernel (summing up Euler's φ function over large intervals) on up to 32K HECToR cores [20]. Core failures are predicted to rise along with the number of cores. To insure large and expensive symbolic computations against core failures, we have implemented and are evaluating automatic recovery of idempotent computations in SGP2 [28].

Acknowledgements. This research was supported by the grants HPC-GAP (EPSRC EP/G05553X), AJITPar (EPSRC EP/L000687/1), RELEASE (EU FP7-ICT 287510).

References

1. Char, B.W.: Progress report on a system for general-purpose parallel symbolic algebraic computation. In: ISSAC 1990, Tokyo, Japan, pp. 96–103. ACM Press (1990)
2. Cole, M.I.: Algorithmic Skeletons: Structured Management of Parallel Computation. MIT Press (1989)
3. Cooperman, G.: GAP/MPI: Writing parallel programs in GAP easily. Tech. rep., Northeastern University, Boston, USA (1998)
4. Cooperman, G.: TOP-C: Task-oriented parallel C for distributed and shared memory. In: Cooperman, G., Jessen, E., Michler, G.O. (eds.) Workshop on Wide Area Networks and High Performance Computing. LNCIS, vol. 249, pp. 109–117. Springer, London (1999)

5. Cooperman, G.: Parallel GAP: Mature interactive parallel computing. In: Groups and Computation III, Columbus, OH, USA, pp. 123–138. De Gruyter (2001)
6. Cooperman, G., Tselman, M.: New sequential and parallel algorithms for generating high dimension Hecke algebras using the condensation technique. In: ISSAC 1996, Zürich, Switzerland, pp. 155–160. ACM Press (1996)
7. GAP Group: GAP – groups, algorithms, and programming (2007), http://www.gap-system.org
8. Geck, M.: Hecke algebras of finite type are cellular. Invent. Math. 169, 501–517 (2007)
9. Geck, M., Müller, J.: James' conjecture for Hecke algebras of exceptional type, I. J. Algebra 321(11), 3274–3298 (2009)
10. Grabmeier, J., Kaltofen, E., Weispfenning, V.: Computer Algebra Handbook. Springer (2003)
11. Graham, J.J., Lehrer, G.I.: Cellular algebras. Invent. Math. 123, 1–34 (1996)
12. HECToR: UK National Supercomputing Service, www.hector.ac.uk
13. Howlett, R.B.: W-graphs for the irreducible representations of the Hecke algebras of type E_7 and E_8, private communication with J. Michel (December 2003)
14. Janjic, V., et al.: Space exploration using parallel orbits. In: Advances in Parallel Computing, ParCo 2013, Munich, Germany, vol. 25, pp. 225–232. IOS Press (2014)
15. Konovalov, A., Linton, S.: Parallel computations in modular group algebras. In: PASCO 2010, Grenoble, France, pp. 141–149. ACM Press (2010)
16. Linton, S., et al.: Easy composition of symbolic computation software using SCSCP. J. Symb. Comput. 49, 19–95 (2013)
17. Livesey, D.: High Performance Computations with Hecke Algebras: Bilinear Forms and Jantzen Filtrations. Ph.D. thesis, University of Aberdeen (2014)
18. Loidl, H.W., et al.: Comparing parallel functional languages: Programming and performance. Higher-order and Symbolic Computation 16(3), 203–251 (2003)
19. Loustaunau, P., Wang, P.Y.: Towards efficient parallelizations of a computer algebra algorithm. In: Frontiers of Massively Parallel Computation, McLean, VA, USA, pp. 67–74. IEEE (1992)
20. Maier, P., Stewart, R., Trinder, P.W.: Reliable scalable symbolic computation: The design of SymGridPar2. Computer Languages, Systems & Structures 40(1), 19–35 (2014)
21. Maier, P., Trinder, P.: Implementing a high-level distributed-memory parallel Haskell in Haskell. In: Gill, A., Hage, J. (eds.) IFL 2011. LNCS, vol. 7257, pp. 35–50. Springer, Heidelberg (2012)
22. Maple Grid Computing Toolbox, http://www.maplesoft.com/products/toolboxes/GridComputing
23. Neun, W., Melenk, H.: Very large Gröbner basis calculations. In: Zippel, R.E. (ed.) CAP 1990. LNCS, vol. 584, pp. 89–99. Springer, Heidelberg (1992)
24. Roch, J.L., Sénéchaud, P., Françoise Siebert-Roch, F., Villard, G.: Computer algebra on MIMD machine. In: Gianni, P. (ed.) ISSAC 1988. LNCS, vol. 358, pp. 423–439. Springer, Heidelberg (1989)
25. Roch, J.L., Villard, G.: Parallel computer algebra. Tech. rep., IMAG, France, tutorial at ISSAC 1997 (1997)
26. Schreiner, W., Mittermaier, C., Bosa, K.: Distributed Maple: parallel computer algebra in networked environments. J. Symb. Comput. 35(3), 305–347 (2003)
27. Sibert, E.E., Mattson, H.F., Jackson, P.: Finite field arithmetic using the Connection Machine. In: Zippel, R.E. (ed.) CAP 1990. LNCS, vol. 584, pp. 51–61. Springer, Heidelberg (1992)
28. Stewart, R.: Reliable Massively Parallel Symbolic Computing: Fault Tolerance for a Distributed Haskell. Ph.D. thesis, Heriot-Watt University (2013)

Generic Deterministic Random Number Generation in Dynamic-Multithreaded Platforms

Stefano Mor[1,2,3,4,*], Jean-Louis Roch[1,3,4], and Nicolas Maillard[2]

[1] Univ. Grenoble Alpes, LIG, F-38000 Grenoble, France
[2] Instituto de Informática, Univ. Federal do Rio Grande do Sul, Porto Alegre, Brazil
[3] CNRS, LIG, F-38000 Grenoble, France
[4] Inria
{Stefano.Mor,Jean-Louis.Roch}@imag.fr, nicolas@inf.ufrgs.br

Abstract. On dynamic multithreaded platforms with on-line scheduling such as work-stealing, randomized computations raise the issue of reproducibility. Compliant with *de facto* standard sequential Deterministic Random Number Generators (DRNGs) noted R, we propose a parallel DRNG implementation for finite computations that provides deterministic parallel execution. It uses the stateless sub-stream approach, enabling the use of efficient DRNG such as Mersenne Twister or Linear Congruential. We demonstrate that if R provides fast jump ahead in the random sequence, the re-seeding overhead is small, polylog in expectation, independently from the parallel computation's depth. Experiments benchmark the performance of randomized algorithms employing our solution against the stateful DRNG DotMix, tailored to the Cilk Plus dynamic multithreading runtime. The overhead of our implementation `ParDRNG< R>` compares favorably to the linear overhead of DotMix re-seedings.

Keywords: Random Numbers, Dynamic-Multithreading, Generic, DotMix, Cilk.

1 Introduction

Deterministic Random Number Generators (DRNGs), stateful abstractions that generate a random number stream from a given initial seed, provide reproducibility to random experiments and are useful in the debug of randomized algorithms.

Dynamic multithreading, defined by Leiserson *et al.* [1] as a synonym of task parallelism, is a processor-oblivious parallel programming model where keywords enable parallelism on the serial code without reference to the number of available processors. A scheduler, such as non-blocking randomized work stealing, manages the execution. These platforms guarantee deterministic results, despite the intrinsic non-determinism introduced by the scheduler, except if the result relies on stateful components. Such is the case of DRNGs. State-of-the-art DRNGs for dynamic multithreaded environments overcomes this by fixing a tailored generation algorithm, trading-off abstraction of implementation properties (*e.g.*, randomness, cryptography, regularity, *etc.*) for performance.

Contribution. As an alternative to fixed implementations for parallel DRNGs, we propose a generic parallel API called `ParDRNG<R>` that ensures deterministic parallel executions on dynamic multithreading platforms. `ParDRNG<R>`

---

* Scholarship holder CNPq - Brazil, Eiffel Laureate - French Ministry of Foreign Affairs.

F. Silva et al. (Eds.): Euro-Par 2014, LNCS 8632, pp. 427–438, 2014.
© Springer International Publishing Switzerland 2014

uses as underlying engine a sequential DRNG R and inherits its qualities without compromising parallel efficiency. Its main insight is the use of R's capability of "jumping-ahead" in the generated stream to ensure determinism; the application partitions the random sequence on-the-fly among the parallel tasks, and each task re-seeds its DRNG through a jump-ahead to generate only random numbers belonging to its subsequence. To ensure efficiency, these re-seeds occur only when triggered by a steal operation performed by the work stealing scheduler. We prove this method to introduce an overhead upper-bounded by the parallel work (*work-efficiency*) even when efficient jump-ahead is absent, and that the theoretical re-seeding overhead is polylog (*work-optimality*) whenever R provides at least polylog jump operations on the random sequence.

Related Works. Coddington [2] enumerates a useful array of techniques to parallelize conventional DRNGs, like "leapfrog" (cyclic partition among processors) and "sequence splitting" (block partition among processors) but these are not processor-oblivious. On the other hand, counter-based DRNGs [3] have excellent statistical properties and can be used in deterministic parallel executions. However, considering performance, each random generation from the counter requires an operation equivalent to re-seeding, and thus a linear overhead. The polylog overhead of ParDRNG<R> compares favourably. Moreover, R can itself use counter-based generators (*e.g.*, AES). The "re-seed through jump" strategy is also discussed by Haramoto *et al.* [4], which argued in favor of parallel programs to build a fast jump-ahead algorithm over Mersenne Twister, what resulted in the implementation of SIMD-oriented Fast Mersenne Twister (SFMT). This is also the case of L'Ecuyer's RNGStreams library (on the top of its MRG32k3a generator [5]). Both approaches deliver a jump with high constant cost, compensated by the large range skipped — which, contrary to ParDRNG<R>, is defined at compile time. Languages like Haskell also follow this sub-stream approach, offering their own splittable generators to the programmer. All these implementations offer a static set of properties, since the generation algorithm is fixed.

Comparison. ParDRNG<R> is compared performance-wise with the stateful, counter-based DRNG DotMix [1], written in C++ for the Cilk Plus dynamic multithreading platform. DotMix supports infinite simulations, but requires any execution to match the same directed acyclic task graph (DAG). ParDRNG<R> supports non-deterministic DAGs, but only finite computations. The polylog overhead of ParDRNG<R> compares favorably with the linear overhead of DotMix re-seedings. Also contrary to DotMix, the programmer may choose different underlying engines providing different sets of properties. *E.g.*, our approach can be made secure by using underlying cryptographic generators.

Outline. Definitions for DRNGs, with general interface and required complexity are at Sec. 2. The main reasoning over work-efficient and work-optimal generic algorithms and its applicability to random number generators are on Sec. 3. Experiments and performance comparison with DotMix are reported on Sec. 4. Concluding remarks are on Sec. 5.

All the relevant data structures and algorithms are written in C++11 with template facilities, aiming reproducibility and pragmatic analysis, although knowledge on the language is not mandatory.

2   Sequential DRNGs and Generic Interface

A DRNG acts as a deterministic stream that provides new random numbers based on its current *state*. The initial state is given by a *seed* value. Random streams have a finite orbit, called its *period*, which corresponds to a sequence of numbers that will eventually be repeated over successive generations.

Two DRNG classes are distinguished to generate the stream $\langle r_n \rangle$ from a function r with finite output set and good statistical properties [3]. *Conventional* DRNGs iterate $r_n = r(r_{n-1})$ (*e.g.*, Mersenne Twister [6], Linear Congruential, Tausworth [7], BBS [8]); while *counter-based* DRNGs independently compute $r_n = r(n)$ (*e.g.*, Philox [3], DotMix). Thus, counter-based are parallel, but conventional DRNGs appear serial: implementations benefit from the previous value r_{n-1} to efficiently generate r_n with less overhead than counter-based ones. In addition, some conventional DRNGs provide efficient jump-ahead over multiple output values in less time than it takes to repeatedly invoke r [3].

A generic interface for DRNGs is now defined in order to set a common notation and complexity requirements for our parallel algorithms. It is assumed that the DRNGs work around integer types, for compatibility.

Function NEXT . Input: a reference to a DRNG. Return: the next random number produced by the DRNG– sets its internal state. Complexity is $\Theta(1)$.

Function SEED. Input: a reference to a DRNG and optionally an unsigned integer serving as the seed for the generator. Return: generator's seed after the call. Each call with the second parameter re-seeds the generator and resets the internal state. Complexity is $\Theta(1)$.

Function CLONE . Input: two DRNG references, source and destination. Return: nothing. Copies the state from source to destination. Complexity is $\Theta(1)$.

Function JUMP. Input: a reference to a DRNG and a natural number n. Return: nothing. Performs a *jump-ahead* operation, advancing the generator's state as if NEXT was called n times. Different constraints on the DRNGs usually allow faster implementations. Thus, the cost of jump is modelled as three variations of a function $\delta : \mathbb{N} \to \mathbb{N}$.

- *Linear* : $\delta(n) = O(n)$. Direct implementation. It requires no extra memory in order to operate, what may be prohibitive for other versions. Trade-offs between memory and space are considered by Haramoto *et al.* [4].
- *Log* : $\delta(n) = O(\log_2 n)$. Could be implemented, *e.g.*, by exponentiation over current state, like the BBS generator [8].
- *Const* : $\delta(n) = O(1)$. Could be implemented, *e.g.*, by extending the Log version through pre-computation of the required powers in its finite period.

Function GENERATE . The kernel of this paper. Input: a (seeded) DRNG of type R and non-negative memory range of size n. Output: a sequence of n numbers generated by the DRNG filling the range. Its reference sequential implementation is

```
template <OutputIterator I, DRNG R>
void GENERATE (I first, I last, R& r) {
    while (first != last) *(first ++) = ValueType<I> (NEXT (r)) ;
}
```

The generic parameter R denotes an arbitrary sequential DRNG. For this reason the interface is named `ParDRNG<R>`. Parallel implementations of **Generate** are detailed that do not presuppose thread-safeness for the functions provided by R.

3   Parallel DRNGs and Analysis

Dynamic-multithreading is examined through task-based computations. A *task* is an indivisible set of machine instructions. Two tasks can be executed in parallel unless related by a sequential dependency. Tasks are executed by *workers* (threads in this paper). A worker is *inactive* when it is idle and *active* otherwise. A *top* is a totally ordered integer time stamp regarding the execution of a parallel program. Current top is denoted s, previous top $s-$ and next top $s+$. The top before the execution is 0 and first top is 1. When a synchronization between worker i and j occurs at s, it is noted by $s(i,j)$. The platform provides a *scheduler*, an algorithm that decides which worker executes which task at each top.

As recurrent notation, a parallel algorithm operates over P workers and input size n and has work $T(n) = W(n) + V(n)$, where $W(n)$ is the sequential work and $V(n)$ is the parallelism overhead. The total work with an unbounded number of processors is the parallel algorithm's depth.

The discussion is contextualized over Cilk Plus' dynamic multithreading platform [9], the most recent incarnation of Cilk [10]. It provides a fork-join abstraction where user threads are spawned as parallel procedures (keyword `cilk_spawn`) and joined in a blocking way (keyword `cilk_sync`). This implies a processor-oblivious model of computation.

Cilk Plus assigns continuations (ready tasks) to workers through a randomized work stealing scheduler [10]. It is implemented as a collection of worker threads with a double-ended queue (deque) with two extremes, a front and a back. Parallel continuations produced by the worker are placed in its deque's front. Idle workers with an empty deque keep randomly selecting victim workers until choosing one with a non-empty deque. In this case, it steals the continuation at the deque's back. Idle workers with a non-empty deque remove and execute continuations from its deque's front. The runtime stops when all workers are idle. The main invariants are the fact that a stolen task is executed without entering the deque (prevents deadlocks) and the spawned task is immediately executed, while the spawner goes to the deque's front (depth-first execution). This model is considered in the implementations that follow.

3.1   Work-Efficiency

A parallel algorithm is defined to be work-efficient *iff* $T(n) = W(n) + V(n) = O(W(n))$, *i.e.*, its overhead is not asymptotically larger than the work parallelized. Consider a naive implementation of parallel generate:

```
1    template <ForwardIterator I, DRNG R>
2    void PARALLEL_GENERATE (I first, I last, R& r0) {
3        DistanceType<I> n = distance (first, last) ;
4        if (n < parallel_grain ()) return GENERATE (first, last, r0) ;
5        halve (n) ;
6        R r1 = r0 ; // CLONE
7        JUMP (r1, n) ;
8        I middle = successor_n (first, n) ;
9        cilk_spawn PARALLEL_GENERATE (first, middle, r0) ;
10       cilk_spawn PARALLEL_GENERATE (middle, last, r1) ;
11   }
```

Let n' be the parallel threshold returned by `parallel_grain()`. Also, let $\alpha = \Theta(1)$ be the work performed by NEXT and $\beta = \Theta(1)$ be the same for the assignment of DRNGs (function CLONE, Sec. 2). Thus, regarding DRNG operations, naive parallel generate has total work $T(n) = \alpha n'$ when $n < n'$. Otherwise, $T(n) = \beta + \delta(\lfloor n/2 \rfloor) + T(\lceil n/2 \rceil) + T(\lfloor n/2 \rfloor)$. In closed form (only for powers of two, which maintain asymptotic behavior by the Akra-Bazzi Method): $T(n) = \alpha n + \beta(n-1) + \sum_{i=0}^{\log_2(n)-n'-1} 2^i \delta \left(n/2^{i+1}\right)$. Subtracting from both sides $W(n) = \alpha n + \beta$, delivers the overhead: $V(n) = \beta(n-2) + \sum_{i=0}^{\log_2(n)-n'-1} 2^i \delta \left(n/2^{i+1}\right)$ (1) determined by δ. Both Const and Log versions of δ are work-efficient because of its overhead $O(n)$ when applied in Equation (1); while Linear version has overhead $O(n \log_2 n)$, and thus is not.

It is possible to reduce the number of jump-ahead operations when the spawned routines run sequentially. Jumps are only performed to guarantee that determinism is preserved when the recursive calls operate in parallel. Since parallelism only unfolds in the presence of steals, execution can jump exclusively when a continuation is stolen; otherwise the original DRNG is used. This tactic effectively moves the determinism overhead to computation's depth, in a fashion inspired by the *work-first* principle of Cilk's scheduler [10].

Some meta-programming is applied over the work stealing scheduler, still at application level: an extra parameter is appended to the recursive function call with the id of the worker that invoked the method originally. Current worker's id (obtained by calling `__cilkrts_get_worker_number()` through wrapper (generic) function `me ()`) is compared to caller to determine whether actual parallel execution is in course. The code is written using tail recursion optimization, replacing the final recursive call by a loop. Also, in order to use the same DRNG in absence of steals, the DRNGs are passed by reference and cloned only whenever needed. This implies an occasional cancellation of the tail recursion optimization, but only when a successful steal takes place:

```
1   template <ForwardIterator I, DRNG R, Natural N>
2   void PARALLEL_GENERATE (I first, I last, R& r0, N worker = me ()) {
3       DistanceType<I> n = distance (first, last) ;
4       while (n > parallel_grain ()) {
5           halve (n) ;
6           I middle = successor_n (first, n) ;
7           R r1 = r0 ; // CLONE
8           cilk_spawn PARALLEL_GENERATE (first, middle, r0, worker) ;
9           if (worker != me ()) { // steal
10              JUMP (r1, n) ;
11              return PARALLEL_GENERATE (middle, last, r1, me ()) ;
12          }
13          first = middle ;
14      }
15      return generate (first, last, r0) ;
16  }
```

3.2 Analysis

As demonstrated by Blumofe *et al.* [11], the expected number of total steal attempts for a parallel execution with depth T_∞ and scheduled by randomized work stealing is $O(PT_\infty)$. Nevertheless, the performance of our method is bounded by the number of successful steals, *i.e.*, the steal attempts over non-empty deques. Next we employ a counting technique that estimates the size of an specific subset of the performed steal attempts (*e.g.*, successful ones) and does not depend on execution's depth. This generalizes the bound to non-deterministic DAGs.

First, let each worker $1 \leq i \leq P$ to have associated a *local counter* φ_i, and their union to be the *global counter*:

Definition 1 (Local Counter). *Let S be the poset of all events during a parallel execution (identified by the respective tops). A local counter is any function $\varphi_i : S \to \mathbb{R}^+$ where: (1) If i is inactive at $s \in S$, then $\varphi_i(s) = 0$. (2) If i is active at $s \in S$, then $\varphi_i(s) > \varphi_i(s-)$.*

Definition 2 (Global Counter). *Let Σ be a (possibly non maximal) subset of S containing only synchronization operations. A global counter is any function $\varphi : S \to \mathbb{N}^P$ with $s \mapsto (\varphi_1(s), \cdots, \varphi_P(s))$ where: (1) Function φ_i is a local counter for worker i. (2) If $s(i,j) \in \Sigma$, then $\min(\varphi_i(s+), \varphi_j(s+)) \geq \min(\varphi_i(s-), \varphi_j(s-)) + 1$*

Henceforward all successful steals are considered to be the interesting synchronizations, *i.e.*, the ones in Σ. The local counter $\varphi_i(s)$ is the size of worker i's deque at s. The global counter is the total number of successful steals. Limit M is defined as the maximum size of any deque during computation.

An upper-bound for all local counters also bounds the global counter:

Lemma 1. *During a randomized work stealing execution over P workers, let Σ be subset of steal operations, φ be a global counter over Σ. Also let u be a random variable whose value is the number of occurrences of the steals in Σ and $\mathbb{E}(u)$ be its expected value. If there is a constant M such that $\varphi_i(s) \leq M$ for all $1 \leq i \leq P$ active at s, then $\mathbb{E}(u) \leq M(P-1)H_{(P-1)}$, where $H_{(P-1)} = \sum_{k=1}^{P-1} 1/k$ is the harmonic number, and $\pi^2(P-1)^2/6$ is the expected variance.*

Proof (Sketch). First, any synchronization operation is named "local step". Let $\phi_{\min}(\varphi, s)$ be a function that returns the value of the minimal non-zero local counter at top s. A local counter is increasing while i is active. A round of consecutive local step where each processor has been victim of at least a steal request in Σ is named a "global step". Yet a global step is a coupon collector's problem, thus the expected number of consecutive successful steals in Σ is $(P-1)H_{(P-1)}$, with variance $\pi^2(P-1)^2/6$. By Def. 2 the number of such steps is less than M which states $\mathbb{E}(u) \leq M(P-1)H_{(P-1)}$.

Fig. 1 shows a snapshot at top s of a global counter from Def. 2 (bounded by M) and function $\phi_{\min}$ used in the proof sketch of Lemma 1.

The cost of a jump-ahead operation was modelled to be a function of current sub-range's size. Thanks to Lemma 1, the next corollary bounds in expectation the overhead introduced by each successful steal of a given range size:

Corollary 1. *Let u_m be a random variable whose value is the number of occurrences of the steals of size m in Σ. Then, $\mathbb{E}(u_m) \leq (P-1)H_{(P-1)}$.*

Proof (Sketch). Once a steal of size m is suffered, it cannot be suffered again until processor becomes idle (size is strictly decreasing). Thus, for any size m, the maximum M is 1. The remaining follows directly from Lemma 1.

JUMP's overhead is bounded by summing the costs of different u_m. Since half of the range is put at deque's front at each spawn, there are $\log_2 n$ different steal sizes to appear, minus size n. Therefore, the expected overhead is: $V(n) = (n-1)\beta + H_{(P-1)}(P-1)\sum_{i=0}^{\log_2(n)-1} \delta(2^i)$. For a fixed P the expected overhead is $O(n)$ when using the Linear version of δ. Thus, in expectation, work-efficiency is always assured.

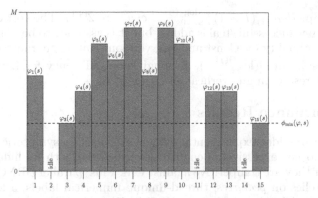

Fig. 1. Example of a Global Counter at top s. Here, $P = 15$ and each active worker i has an value $\varphi_i(s)$. In this example, $\phi_{\min}(\varphi, s) = \varphi_3(s) = \varphi_{15}(s)$. Workers 2, 11, an 14 are inactive (idle); they are not accounted in the calculus of $\phi_{\min}(s)$, and have $\varphi(s) = 0$.

The proof considers a loose bound of one idle worker per top. Nevertheless, the local steps are generally performed in parallel, mitigating the $P-1$ factor. Also, as $P \to \infty$, the harmonic number $H_{(P-1)}$ approximates $\log(P-1) + \gamma + 1/2(P-1) + o(1)$, where $\gamma \approx 0.58$ is the Euler-Mascheroni constant. Indeed, asymptotically for large value of P, Theorem 3 in Tchiboukdjian *et al.* [12] states that the expected total number of steals is asymptotically less than $3.65 \cdot M \cdot (P-1)$.

3.3 Work-Optimality

A parallel algorithm is defined to be work-optimal *iff* $V(n) = O(\log_2^{O(1)} n)$.

Our technique can be refined in order to obtain work-optimal parallel generation. The problem may be reduced to eliminate the fixed overhead introduced by CLONE. In order to track the quantity of random numbers generated until a given execution point, a counter is used, which is passed (by copy) as parameter to recursive calls. This eliminates unnecessary DRNGs copies, in exchange for paying the price of longer jumps. Nevertheless, the jumps are mitigated by parallelism and "cheap" when the DRNG provides polylog time jump-ahead. The algorithm also relies on the polymorphic behavior of function *seed* described at Sec. 2 and a seed constructor:

```
1   template <ForwardIterator I, DRNG R, Natural N0, Natural N1>
2   void PARALLEL_GENERATE (I first, I last, R& r0, N0 worker = me (), N1 hist = 0) {
3       DistanceType<I> n = distance (first, last) ;
4       while (n > parallel_grain ()) {
5           halve (n) ;
6           I middle = successor_n (first, n) ;
7           cilk_spawn PARALLEL_GENERATE (first, middle, r0, worker, hist) ;
8           hist += n ;
9           if (worker != me ()) { // steal
10              R r1 (SEED (r0)) ; // seed constructor
11              JUMP (r1, hist) ;
12              return PARALLEL_GENERATE (middle, last, r1, me (), hist) ;
13          }
14          first = middle ;
15      }
16      return generate_seq (first, last, r0) ;
17  }
```

Now we are able to cut off the $\beta(n-2)$ term from on Equation (1). Even the more expensive JUMP calls are yet upper-bounded by the most expensive possible jump: $H_{(P-1)}(P-1)\sum_{i=0}^{\log_2(n)-1} \delta(n - n/2^{i+1})$. The cost of call to seed constructor per successful steal is added, but it is assumed to be a small constant. Now work-optimality for Const and Log versions can be guaranteed, because its overhead results in $O(\log_2^{O(1)} n)$, although work-efficiency for Linear version is lost, since it results in an overhead of $O(n \log_2 n)$.

4   Performance Results

This section provides experimental evidence that the asymptotic limits shown previously do not excessively penalize the execution with its hidden constants and whether they are competitive against Cilk Plus' parallel DRNG, DotMix [1].

DotMix relies on *pedigrees*, thread-unique numerical labels, a feature its authors persuaded Intel to include in its Cilk Plus implementation. A given reference to a global DotMix generator compresses the pedigree and then "RC6-mixes" (hashes) the result with a small collision probability. To maintain pedigrees on the runtime overcharges it with less than 1% overhead. DotMix show statistical quality rivaling (with high variance) the one of Mersenne Twister upon the Dieharder random number test suite.

All experiments were performed using computer "Turing" from the Group of Parallel and Distributed Computing of the Universidade Federal do Rio Grande do Sul (Brazil): Linux 3.2.0-40-generic #64-Ubuntu SMP x86_64. CPUs Intel Xeon X7550 2GHz ×32 (2 thread per core), Caches d32K + i32K/256K/18432K. Mem. Total: 132,018,988 kB. Intel's ICPC 2013 compiler with O2 optimizations is used because it is currently the only compiler that supports Cilk Plus' pedigrees. Other relevant software are Cilkpub 1.03 (for DotMix) and Boost C++ Libraries 1.55. Sources are available in http://www.inf.ufrgs.br/~sdkmor/Europar2014/.

Three sequential DRNGs from Boost C++ serve as the underlying engine of the generic scheme: Mersenne Twister 19937 (MT19937) [6], Linear Congruential (Rand48), both over 64-bit integers, and Tausworth Generator (Taus88) [7], over 32-bit integers. The only Boost generator that implements a jump operation in log time is Rand48, the others executing in linear time. A Blum Blum Shub (BBS) [8] crypto-secure generator over 512-bit integers with logarithmic time jump was also implemented. In all tests, work-optimal algorithms are used with Rand48 and BBS and the work-efficient versions with the others.

There are four test algorithms: Generate, Introsort, Maximal Independent Set (by Luby's Method), and Fibonacci, designed to evaluate performance in an increasing level of adversity against our methods. The algorithms run for a number of workers $1 \leq P \leq 32$ as well as a sequential version. In order to provide statistical confidence the pointed plots are the means of 50 executions for each P and sequential version, lying within a 95.45% confidence interval. The standard deviation is at worst case under 8% of the mean, a reasonable range for randomized algorithms. T_s (resp. T_P) denotes the sequential time (resp. parallel time on P processors) with DRNG R (resp. ParDRNG<R>). Yet T_1 is the time of ParDRNG<R> scheduled on one processor.

The comparison criteria is total execution time. Since the algorithms do not have a common sequential implementation (because of different implementations of the generator components), speedup and efficiency measurements are not

Table 1. Average time (in milliseconds, rounded up) of parallel algorithms' execution. Shown sequential time T_s and parallel times T_1 and T_2.

DRNG	Generate			Intro Sort			MIS			Fibonacci		
	T_s	T_1	T_2	T_s	T_1	T_2	T_s	T_1	T_2	T_s	T_1	T_2
Rand48	559	529	268	5649	5730	2994	39	67	43	17	194	97
Taus88	703	660	1033	6132	6412	3661	38	67	45	30	193	146
MT19937	877	901	611	6451	6577	3680	38	66	43	30	327	199
DotMix	4201	1713	863	6227	9798	5217	51	67	42	129	389	195
BBS	25954	25602	13006	6316	6424	3503	149	182	102	701	910	455

meaningful when compared against each other, since a slow sequential implementation may wrongly boost the results. This way, we take out the unfairness of comparing relative speedups, but are use it to show anomalies in sequential executions.

In fact, some DotMix benchmarks running in sequential showed unusual measurements for T_s and T_1, but are as expected for T_2 and above. Thus, for clearness of comparison, these execution times are displayed separately; measurements on T_s, T_1, and T_2 are in Tab. 1 and measurements for T_P with $P > 2$, are in Fig. 2. The unusual behavior of DotMix is contextualized within each benchmark. Highlights on the implementations and reviews over the results follow.

Generate. Implementation of `PARALLEL_GENERATE`. Generates 10^8 64-bit random numbers in parallel. The sequential version for all DRNGs is a for loop calling method `NEXT`. The parallel version of DotMix is a call to its own `fill_buffer` function, implemented with the same tail-recursion optimization of our codes, with parallel a threshold of 2,048. Target implementation has the same grain size for comparison fairness. Boost generators and BBS have a minor difference between T_s and T_1, with BBS being much slower because of its extensive use of integer modulus. DotMix, has a T_1 that is $2.45\times$ faster than its T_s. Since DotMix is projected with a parallel-first principle, `fill_buffer` is optimized regarding pedigree initialization (scope bounding), which is mandatory in order to generate deterministic results, introducing large sequential overhead, what does not affect `ParDRNG<R>`. A speedup comparison between T_1 and T_2 shows Rand48 (work-optimal), BBS, and DotMix with ≈ 1.97 of speedup while work-efficient MT19937 has ≈ 1.47 of speedup. Taus88, work-efficient and 32 bits, has speed-down of ≈ 0.63. DotMix scales until $P = 11$ processors, being better than MT19937 for $P > 4$ processors (it scales up to 6 processors). DotMix is never better than Rand48. Taus88 does not profit at all from `ParDRNG<R>`, probably due to 32 to 64-bit casting. Even BBS is faster for 26 or more processors. Overall we are competitive with DotMix for fast underlying generators.

Randomized Introsort. STL's sort, it is a quicksort algorithm that is switched to heapsort whenever its tree depth goes beyond $2 \log_2 n$. We use a modified partition procedure to always divide the interval by half for comparison fairness between DRNGs. The pivots are generated in an "online" fashion, as they are needed. To determine how many terms are to be jumped, it is supposed that each recursive call will advance the generator as much as the size of the subsequence it takes as input. This implies an "over-estimation overhead", because for under threshold instances the algorithm is switched to a non-randomized sort and yet, the DRNGs need to be advanced accordingly to the subsequence. DotMix, because of its use of pedigrees, is not implemented with this overhead. We

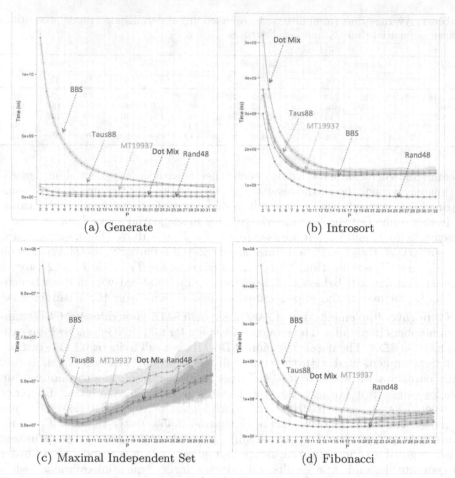

(a) Generate

(b) Introsort

(c) Maximal Independent Set

(d) Fibonacci

Fig. 2. Average time (in nanoseconds) of parallel algorithms' execution. Shown parallel times from T_2 to T_{32}. The respective colored areas around the points are the confidence interval of 95.45%.

sort 10^8 integers. All generators have $T_s \approx T_1$, except DotMix, that has large overhead $T_1 \approx 1.58T_s$ without optimized `fill_buffer`. Indeed, until $P = 13$ DotMix has the worst performance, even when comparing to BBS, whose slow performance seems to be mitigated by the work-optimal implementation, placing it at the same level and sometimes better than its work-efficient rivals. For $P > 13$ DotMix is at most statistically equal to the work-efficient implementations. Rand48, being fast and work-optimal, is the incontestable winner. Taus88 has a significant gain, since no type casting is necessary.

Maximal Independent Set. Implementation of Luby's method, it is divided in three steps, repeated until the input is marked as empty: (1) select nodes with probability $1/2^i$, where i is the node's degree; (2) unselect lowest degree node of two neighbor selected nodes; (3) move the remaining selected nodes to the MIS and removes its neighbors from input. Steps (1) and (2) are performed in parallel for each node, but step (2) only executes after (1). We use random numbers for the probabilistic selection in step (1), but the parallel generate function is initialized by a step (0) to generate random numbers in an "off-line" fashion at each round – to the highest level of over-estimation. To provide comparison fairness, the same numbers are selected despite a given generators output. The input is a grid graph with 10^6 nodes. The implementation was written to have irregular scalability: at each step a worker may have assigned a node already marked as unselected, performing no useful work. For small P this behavior eliminates node removal operations, but the parallel performance degradetes fast for larger values. For the fixed values we generate and for the selected input graph, performance loss begins between 6 and 8 workers. When considering both this highly irregular scalability and the maximun level of over-estimation the non-secure DRNGs have the same statistical performance — with larger confidence interval due to the other non-DRNG operations the algorithm performs – while BBS penalizes execution because of its integer modulus operations not being mitigated by online generation.

Fibonacci. A randomized recursive calculus of 30th Fibonacci term that uses three random numbers (before, after and between the recursive calls) and adds them to the recursive sum. As in Introsort, the random numbers are also generated "online", as needed. We use it to illustrate the weakness of our design (it is also a weak point for DotMix because of its depth [1]); the distance of jump is not calculated in constant time, because although we are able to calculate how much previous calls will advance the main generator, this calculus involves computing how many nodes the tree will spawn. This is as much computational work compared to the computation being performed. We used the fast doubling Fibonacci algorithm to mitigate this cost. This decrease of arithmetical work prevents the randomized algorithm to be work-optimal. For this algorithm, DotMix is statistically paired with the work-efficient implementations, although slightly faster for $P > 5$. Taus88 is nearly always better than MT193937, which reinforces its previous improvements for online algorithms. Rand48 is the best until $P - 25$, when it becomes statistically equal to DotMix. For the same range BBS is the worst, being statistically equal to MT19937 afterwards.

5   Concluding Remarks

Despite the fact that we rely on Cilk Plus to implement our designs, our scheme is not dependent on it. Its coding is simple to be written in another dynamic multi-threaded environment and the theoretical analisys does not rely on a fixed execution's depth. This implies correctness even on the presence of a non-deterministic DAG, such as those on adaptive algorithms [13].

We have significant performance gains as described in Sec. 4. We are competitive with DotMix for off-line generation algorithms and generally faster with online generation and fast underlying generators. With our generic scheme we are able to choose the desired point between quality and speed of several DRNGs. In addition, it is possible to be drastically more performatic than DotMix or other parallel DRNGs with fixed implementations by selecting underlying DRNGs whose generated sequence is especially effective for a particular application.

An hybrid solution of our approach and DotMix is compelling. However, because DotMix does not have an equivalent to jump-ahead operation, the linear version becomes mandatory. In our tests, this approach was more than $10\times$

slower than SFMT, a 128bit generator. As shown at Tab. 1, DotMix is faster when using its own internal generate function. However, maybe there is some optimization inside DotMix to allow it. We plan to verify it as future work. Also, we plan to extend the jump on steals technique to numerical algorithms.

In `ParDRNG<R>` the number of required random numbers must be known *a priori* to the computation. This is a strong limitation to our method. There is, however, a range of algorithms that are suited to it besides direct parallel generation, such as randomized sorts, randomized graph generation, randomized genetic algorithms (crossing over), *etc.* Additionally, one may overcome this limitation by guessing large non-overlapping ranges between the different workers, thus enabling algorithms to not know exactly how many numbers they will need in runtime, given an upper-bound. Combining over-estimation and polylog jumps mitigates largely the overheads. This is similar to what is done, for instance, by SFMT [4] and RNGStreams [14].

References

1. Leiserson, C.E., Schardl, T.B., Sukha, J.: Deterministic parallel random-number generation for dynamic-multithreading platforms. In: Proc. of PPoPP 2012, pp. 193–204. ACM, New York (2012)
2. Coddington, P.: Random number generators for parallel computers. The NHSE Review 2 (1997)
3. Salmon, J.K., Moraes, M.A., Dror, R.O., Shaw, D.E.: Parallel random numbers: As easy as 1, 2, 3. In: Proc. of SC 2011, pp. 16:1–16:12. ACM, New York (2011)
4. Haramoto, H., Matsumoto, M., L'Ecuyer, P.: A fast jump ahead algorithm for linear recurrences in a polynomial space. In: Golomb, S.W., Parker, M.G., Pott, A., Winterhof, A. (eds.) SETA 2008. LNCS, vol. 5203, pp. 290–298. Springer, Heidelberg (2008)
5. Fischer, G.W., Carmon, Z., Ariely, D., Zauberman, G., L'Ecuyer, P.: Good parameters and implementations for combined multiple recursive random number generators. Oper. Res. 47(1), 159–164 (1999)
6. Matsumoto, M., Nishimura, T.: Mersenne twister: A 623-dimensionally equidistributed uniform pseudo-random number generator. ACM Trans. Model. Comput. Simul. 8(1), 3–30 (1998)
7. L'Ecuyer, P.: Maximally equidistributed combined tausworthe generators. Mathematics of Computation 65(213), 203–213 (1996)
8. Blum, L., Blum, M., Shub, M.: A simple unpredictable pseudo random number generator. SIAM J. Comput. 15(2), 364–383 (1986)
9. Intel Corporation: Intel cilk plus language specification (2013)
10. Frigo, M., Leiserson, C.E., Randall, K.H.: The implementation of the cilk-5 multi-threaded language. In: Proc. of PLDI 1998, pp. 212–223. ACM, New York (1998)
11. Blumofe, R.D., Leiserson, C.E.: Scheduling multithreaded computations by work stealing. J. ACM 46(5), 720–748 (1999)
12. Tchiboukdjian, M., Gast, N., Trystram, D., Roch, J.-L., Bernard, J.: A tighter analysis of work stealing. In: Cheong, O., Chwa, K.-Y., Park, K. (eds.) ISAAC 2010, Part II. LNCS, vol. 6507, pp. 291–302. Springer, Heidelberg (2010)
13. Traoré, D., Roch, J.-L., Maillard, N., Gautier, T., Bernard, J.: Deque-free work-optimal parallel stl algorithms. In: Luque, E., Margalef, T., Benítez, D. (eds.) Euro-Par 2008. LNCS, vol. 5168, pp. 887–897. Springer, Heidelberg (2008)
14. L'Ecuyer, P., Simard, R.J., Chen, E.J., Kelton, W.D.: An object-oriented random-number package with many long streams and substreams. Operations Research 50(6), 1073–1075 (2002)

Implementation and Performance Analysis
of SkelGIS for Network Mesh-Based Simulations

Hélène Coullon[1,2] and Sébastien Limet[1]

[1] Univ. Orléans, INSA Centre Val de Loire, LIFO EA 4022, F-45067 Orléans Cedex 2
{helene.coullon,sebastien.limet}@univ-orleans.fr
[2] Géo-Hyd Antea Group, 101 rue Jacques Charles, 45160 Olivet, France

Abstract. The implicit parallelism is an active domain of computer-science to hide intricate details of parallelization from the end-user. Some solutions are specific to a precise domain while others are more generic, however, the purpose is always to find the adapted level of abstraction to ease the high performance and parallel programming. We present SkelGIS, a *header-only* implicit parallelism C++ library to solve mesh-based scientific simulations. In this paper is detailed the implementation of SkelGIS for the specific case of *network simulations*, where the space domain can be represented as a *directed acyclic graph* (DAG). This implementation is based on a modified, optimized and parallelized version of the *Compressed Sparse Row* format, which is completely described in this paper. Finally, experiments on different kinds of clusters and different sizes of DAGs are evaluated.

1 Introduction

Taking advantage of the full potential of emerging parallel high performance systems becomes increasingly difficult. In novel processor architectures such as GPUs and many-cores processors, the memory hierarchy becomes complex, and CPU clusters are growing toward a capability of millions and billions of cores. Even if those extremes are not common nowadays, it becomes difficult and time consuming to write efficient parallel codes, especially for non-computer scientists. This is why *implicit parallelism* is one of the most active domain of computer research. It consists in providing programming tools to improve the level of productivity and performance of parallel codes, while hiding the intricate details of new architectures and low level parallel libraries.

Most scientific simulations are based on partial differential equations (PDEs). Some of those equations can be solved analytically, some of them cannot. This technique is difficult and most resolutions are proceeded for specific boundary or initial conditions. Thus, most PDEs are commonly solved using numerical methods such as finite difference, finite volume or finite element methods. Those methods produce mesh-based simulations where the time domain is discretized by a set of iterations and the space domain is discretized by a set of points (finite difference) or a set of cells to form a mesh (finite volume and finite element). One or more numerical schemes are obtained from numerical methods. A scheme

F. Silva et al. (Eds.): Euro-Par 2014, LNCS 8632, pp. 439–450, 2014.

represents a computation to apply at each time iteration on the mesh and is of the form:

$$\{U_{t-1}(x), U_{t-1}(y); y \in N(x)\} \longmapsto U_t(x), \tag{1}$$

where x represents an element of the mesh, $U_t(x)$ is the set of quantities to compute for element x at the time iteration t, $N(x)$ is the neighborhood of x required to compute $U_t(x)$. In other words, quantities of the element x at a time iteration t is a function of quantities for this element and its neighborhood at time iteration $t-1$. In computer science, this kind of computation is called a *stencil* and is intensively studied.

Some simulations have the particularity to identify two kinds of places in the space domain, for which the behavior is different and where different numerical schemes are applied to simulate the real phenomena. For example, in a blood flow simulation in the human arterial network, the behavior is different in an artery and at a conjunction node where arteries join. In this case, the domain is first discretized as a *network*, before each kind of element is again discretized to a mesh. A network is represented as a graph and contains two kinds of elements: nodes and edges. For the same blood flow example, the arteries are represented by the edges of the graph and the conjunction nodes by the nodes of the graph. A node could have more or less incoming and outgoing edges (arteries), thus a network is an irregular structure. Networks are used a lot in different kind of simulations as, for example, arterial or vein simulations, road or rail traffic simulations, water-flow or pollutant transfer simulations etc. Thus, it is very important to offer implicit parallelism solutions to write parallel network-simulations. However, existing implicit parallelism solutions, to solve mesh-based PDEs, do not propose an easy way to write network-simulations. SkelGIS is a header-only C++ library to write parallel mesh-based simulations on distributed memory architectures, using MPI. The parallelization of codes is totally hidden from the user through four concepts: *distributed data structures* (DDS), *data mappings*, *appliers* and *interfaces*. Those concepts have already been implemented for Cartesian two-dimensional regular mesh [5,6]. In this paper is presented the implementation of the implicit parallelism library SkelGIS, for the specific case of network simulations, and more precisely for networks which can be represented by directed acyclic graphs (DAGs). The implementation of SkelGIS for network simulations, and its efficiency, are based on an adaptation, a re-indexation and a parallelization of the *compressed sparse row* (CSR) format, which is described in this paper. Moreover, performances of the solution have been evaluated until 8000 cores on a blood flow simulation.

The rest of this paper is organized as follows. Section 2 explains the CSR format for sparse matrices and graphs. Then, Section 3 describes the adaptation of the CSR format for networks. Section 4 details the implementation of the whole SkelGIS solution for network simulations. Performance of SkelGIS is evaluated in Section 5 and related work are discussed in Section 6. Finally, Section 7 concludes this work.

2   The Compressed Sparse Row Format

The work presented in this paper is based on an adaptation of the Compressed Sparse Row (CSR) format [3] for network simulations. Two different views of the CSR format are presented in this section, first the sparse matrix view and then the graph view.

The 3-array variation of the CSR format handles the storage of sparse matrices with three arrays. The first array, named *values*, contains the non-zero values of the matrix, stored line by line. The second array is named *columns*. The element i of the array *columns* contains the column index of the associated i^{th} element of *values*. Finally, the third array is named *rowIndex*. The element i of the array *rowIndex* contains the index, in the array *values*, of the first non-zero element of the ith row of the matrix. A dummy entry, equal to zero, is added at the beginning of the *rowIndex* array. This way, the row i contains $rowIndex[i+1] - rowIndex[i]$ non-zero elements. To access a non-zero element with its row and column indexes (i, j) it is needed to find j between elements $columns[rowIndex[i]]$ and $columns[rowIndex[i+1] - 1]$. The index where j is found in *columns* is the index of the searched non-zero value in *values*. CSR, as other formats, only stores non-zero values of a sparse matrix. Thus, the CSR has a light memory footprint. However, it suffers from a lack of efficiency to access a non-zero value with its row and column index (i, j). Nevertheless, CSR is very efficient to represent connectivity in a graph as shown below.

CSR can be used to store undirected graphs. An *undirected graph* is denoted by $G = (V, E)$ where V is a finite set of *vertices* or *nodes* and $E \subseteq V \times V$ is the set of *edges*. The matrix $Sp(G)$ associated to a graph G represents the adjacency matrix of the graph G (e.g. Figure 1(a)). In the case of undirected graphs, $Sp(G)$ is symmetric. In a graph $G = (V, E)$, v_i and $v_j \in V$ are said *neighbor vertices* if $(v_i, v_j) \in E$. In other words, two vertices are neighbor vertices if a non-zero value is placed at (v_i, v_j) and (v_j, v_i) in $Sp(G)$. $\forall v \in V, N(v)$ denotes the set of neighbors of the vertex v. The degree of a vertex $v \in V$, denoted by $deg(v)$, is the number of incident edges to v, i.e. $deg(v) = |N(v)|$. In the row v of the matrix $Sp(G)$, $N(v)$ represents column indexes where a non-zero value is present. In an undirected graph $G = (V, E)$ where $V = \{v_0, ..., v_{n-1}\}$, the *cumulative degree* of a vertex $v_i \in V$ is denoted $cdeg(v_i)$ and defined by $cdeg(v_i) = \sum_{j=0}^{i} deg(v_j) = \sum_{j=0}^{i} |N(v_j)|$. In the matrix $Sp(G)$, $cdeg(v_i)$ represents the number of non-zero elements in the row v_i added to the number of non-zero elements in previous rows. Thus, it is possible to represent G with two arrays. The first one of size $n+1 = |V|+1$, called *cdeg*, is defined by $cdeg[i+1] = cdeg(v_i), \forall i \in [0, n[$, where $cdeg[0] = cdeg(v_{-1}) \stackrel{def}{=} 0$. The second array, denoted N (for neighborhood), is of size $cdeg[n] = cdeg(v_{n-1})$ and $\forall v_i \in V, N(v_i) = \{v_{N[j]} | j \in [cdeg[i], cdeg[i+1][\}$. This two-arrays representation corresponds to the CSR format where arrays *cdeg* and N of G are respectively equal to the arrays *rowIndex* and *columns* of $Sp(G)$. Figure 1(a) illustrates a simple undirected graph. The node 0 of this graph has two neighbors, 1 and 2, as a result, the second cumulative degree value is 2. Node 1 has three neighbors therefore $cdeg[2] = 2 + 3 = 5$. Iterating this process on each node of the graph leads to $cdeg = [0, 2, 5, 6, 7, 11, 12, 13, 14]$ for this graph. Neighbors of node 0 are 1 and 2 and those of node 1 are 0, 3 and 4 etc. Finally, $N = [1, 2, 0, 3, 4, 0, 1, 1, 5, 6, 7, 4, 4, 4]$. It can be noticed that the neighborhood of node 4, for example, can be easily accessed since $cdeg[4] = 7$ and $cdeg[5] - 1 = 10$ give the first and the last index of N where are stored indexes of the neighbors of node 4, as a result nodes 1, 5, 6 and 7 are the neighbors of node 4.

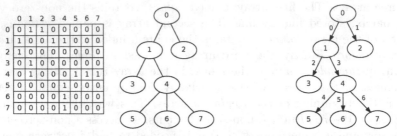

(a) An undirected graph G and its associated sparse adjacency matrix Sp(G).

(b) The equivalent directed graph G'.

Fig. 1. Examples of graphs

Unlike in the sparse matrix case, where elements are accessed by $(row, column)$ indexes, in the graph case elements are accessed by row index only and then the neighborhood of the node can be accessed in $O(1)$. Supposing that the data associated to each nodes are stored in a table X such that $|X| = |V|$, then accessing neighbor values of a node v_i simply consist in accessing X from index $N[cdeg[i]]$ to $N[cdeg[i+1] - 1]$.

3   A Distributed Data Structure for DAGs

This paper deals with the implementation of SkelGIS for the specific case of networks which can be represented with directed acyclic graphs (DAGs). This section shows how CSR can be used to implement DAGs, how it can be optimized to fit scientific simulation needs, and how it can be efficiently parallelized. A distributed version of the CSR format has already been proposed by Edmonds et Al [8]. However this distributed version is not specifically improved and optimized for scientific mesh-based simulations.

A *directed graph* $G = (V, E)$ is a graph where each edge $e = (v_1, v_2) \in E$ is directed from v_1 to v_2 and where v_1 and v_2 are respectively called the *source* and *destination* nodes of e. A *directed acyclic graph* (DAG) is a directed graph $G = (V, E)$ such that for all node $v \in V$, there is no path, following successive directed edges, from v to itself. In scientific simulations on DAGs, a node could need incoming edges and nodes, and outgoing edges and nodes, to be computed. An edge, on the other hand, needs its source and destination nodes to be computed. First, in a DAG $G = (V, E)$, for a node $v \in V$ and an edge $e \in E$, $S(e)$ denotes the source node of e and $D(e)$ denotes the destination node of e. Two arrays represent this information, S and D of size m where $S[i] = S(e_i)$ and $D[i] = D(e_i)$ for all $e_i \in E$. $N_V^+(v)$ denotes the set of output nodes of v such that $N_V^+(v) = \{v'|(v, v') \in E\}$. $N_E^+(v)$ denotes the set of output edges of v, thus $N_E^+(v) = \{e \in E|S(e) = v\}$. Symmetrically $N_V^-(v)$ and $N_E^-(v)$ denotes the sets of input nodes and edges of a vertex v. Finally, a *root* node v of a DAG G verifies $|N_E^-(v)| = 0$, and a *leaf* node verifies $|N_E^+(v)| = 0$. Cumulative degrees are the same for edges and nodes because the number of incoming edges and nodes are the same, and the number of outgoing edges and nodes are equal too. Then, $\forall v_j \in V$, $|N_E^+(v_j)| = |N_V^+(v_j)|$ and $|N_E^-(v_j)| = |N_V^-(v_j)|$. In a DAG $G = (V, E)$, where $V = \{v_0, ..., v_{n-1}\}$), for a vertex $v_i \in V$: $cdeg^+(v_i) = \sum_{j=0}^{i} |N_E^+(v_j)|$ denotes the output cumulative degrees of a node v_i and $cdeg^-(v_i) = \sum_{j=0}^{i} |N_E^-(v_j)|$ denotes the input cumulative degrees of a node v_i. $cdeg^+$ and $cdeg^-$ denote arrays of size $n + 1$ such that $cdeg^+[i + 1] = cdeg^+(v_i)$ and $cdeg^-[i + 1] = cdeg^-(v_i)$, where $cdeg^+[0] = cdeg^-[0] = 0$. Finally, as in Section 2, it is possible to define arrays N_V^+, N_E^+, N_V^-, and N_E^- of size $cdeg^+[n]$ and $cdeg^-[n]$.

Figure 1(b) represents a directed graph which has the same structure as the graph of Figure 1(a). Node 0 has no input neighbor but has two output neighbors, as a result the second value of $cdeg^+$ is 2 and the second value of $cdeg^-$ is 0 etc. Associated neighbor nodes are stored in N_V^+ and N_V^-, the corresponding edges are stored in N_E^+ and N_E^-. The whole representation of this DAG is given by the following eight arrays : $cdeg^+ = [0, 2, 4, 4, 4, 7, 7, 7, 7]$, $cdeg^- = [0, 0, 1, 2, 3, 4, 5, 6, 7]$, $N_E^+ = [0, 1, 2, 3, 4, 5, 6]$, $N_E^- = [0, 1, 2, 3, 4, 5, 6]$, $N_V^+ = [1, 2, 3, 4, 5, 6, 7]$, $N_V^- = [0, 0, 1, 1, 4, 4, 4]$, $S = [0, 0, 1, 1, 4, 4, 4]$ and $D = [1, 2, 3, 4, 5, 6, 7]$.

Some modifications of the DAG data structure are needed to parallelize it on distributed memory architectures. Indeed, in this case, the DAG has to be partitioned into sub-graphs (of equivalent sizes) which are distributed among processors. Here is not discussed the way the graph is partitioned but only how to optimize local representation of each sub-graph to keep benefits of the data structure. Each processor receives a part of the graph where indexes are global, which means that the initial local indexing may be non-continuous. Therefore a re-indexing is needed to represent the local sub-graph. Figure 2(a) illustrates the extraction of the sub-graph managed by the processor 1 from a DAG $G = (V, G)$. This sub-graph $G_1 = (V_1, E_1)$ has eight nodes, $|V_1| = 8$, and seven edges, $|E_1| = 7$. Connections with the rest of the DAG G are drawn with dashed lines. These dashed elements are denoted as *halo* elements and represent needed information from other processors to compute the stencil.

The re-indexation of local edges is very simple, it goes from up to bottom and from left to right at each level (Figure 2(b)). The re-indexation of local nodes, on the other hand, sorts nodes in several classes to optimize the use of cache lines and to minimize the number of conditions in the SkelGIS code. First, roots and leaves are distinguished from other nodes. Actually, in most simulations, roots and leaves are computed differently to manage the physical border of the domain. Grouping those nodes together in memory allows a better use of cache lines.

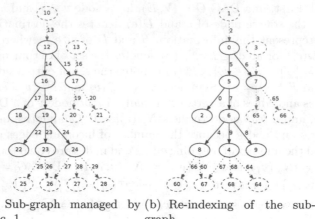

(a) Sub-graph managed by proc. 1

(b) Re-indexing of the sub-graph.

Fig. 2. Sub-graph managed by proc. 1 (blue) and its connections with those of proc. 0 (red) and 2 (green).

Moreover, it makes possible to move through those elements avoiding conditions in the code (to test if a node is a root or a leaf). Secondly, remaining local nodes are partitioned into two sets: those needing communications to get halo elements and the others. This makes possible an efficient overlap of computations with communications [9], using non-blocking routines of MPI. As for roots and leaves, those two classes improve cache use and avoid conditions in the code. Thus, performances of final programs will be improved by the re-indexation.

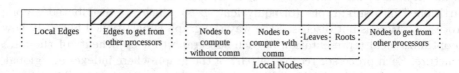

Fig. 3. Re-indexation for edges and nodes

Figure 3 illustrates the different classes used for re-indexation and an example is shown Figure 2. The eight arrays of the local data structure of the processor 1 are: $cdeg^+ = [0, 2, 5, 7, 7, 7, 7, 7, 7]$, $cdeg^- = [0, 1, 2, 2, 3, 4, 5, 6, 7]$, $N_E^+ = [2, 3, 4, 5, 6, 0, 1]$, $N_E^- = [0, 3, 1, 5, 6, 4, 2]$, $N_V^+ = [7, 1, 6, 4, 5, 0, 3]$, $N_V^- = [2, 0, 2, 1, 1, 1, 0]$, $S = [2, 2, 0, 0, 1, 1, 1]$ and $D = [0, 3, 7, 1, 6, 4, 5]$. This data structure must be completed with information on connections with halo elements of the rest of the DAG. To manage these incoming and outgoing information, the halo elements are added to the local DAG structure with indexes starting from the greater local index of local nodes and edges. This way, the cache line optimization obtained by the re-indexation is kept. To insert external nodes in the local data structure, cumulative degrees arrays $cdeg^+$ and $cdeg^-$ and associated tables N_E^+, N_E^-, N_V^+, N_V^- must be updated. In Figure 2(b), one can note that local nodes 2 and 3 receive one input edge and node from processor 0. Thus, $cdeg^-$ is modified at indexes 3 and 4, adding one to each. As $cdeg^-$ represents cumulative degrees, nodes 3 to $|V_1|$ and 4 to $|V_1|$ have to be updated. Modifications on N_V^- consist in adding new indexes to store halo elements to receive from other processors. Thus, indexes 8 and 9 are inserted at the right place. The parallel data structure for processor 1 is then $cdeg^+ = [0, 2, 5, 7, 9, 11, 16, 16, 16]$, $cdeg^- = [0, 1, 2, 3, 5, 6, 7, 8, 9]$, $N_E^+ = [0, 2, 3, 4, 5, 6, 0, 1, 9, 10, 11, 12, 13, 14, 15]$, $N_E^- = [0, 3, 7, 1, 8, 5, 6, 4, 2]$, $N_V^+ = [7, 1, 6, 4, 5, 0, 3, 10, 11, 12, 13, 13, 14, 15]$ and $N_V^- = [2, 0, 8, 2, 9, 1, 1, 1, 0]$. As a consequence, neighborhood information can still be obtained in $O(1)$, even if information comes from other processors, and the parsing of local elements is cache-optimized. However, it is not possible with resulting arrays to determine communication scheme to proceed MPI exchanges. For this reason six additional tables are added in the parallel data structure to manage interprocess communications. These arrays rely on the cumulative degrees applied to processor ranks. Tables $cdeg^{tor}$ and $cdeg^{tos}$ are the cumulative degrees of nodes and edges to send to and to receive from other processors, where $|cdeg^{tor}| = |cdeg^{tos}| = p + 1$. And arrays N_E^{tor}, N_E^{tos}, N_V^{tor} and N_V^{tos} are the associated sets of nodes and edges indexes to send and receive.

The data structure presented in this section is independent from the graph partitioning method used to distribute the DAG. It is optimized to efficiently parse each sub-graphs and to allow communications/computations overlaps. However, the key point to obtain good performances of irregular structures lies in a good partition of the structure. This problem is known to be NP-complete, as a consequence, heuristics are used to approximate the solution. The network partitioning problem is not presented in this paper, a sibling-edges heuristic has been used for experiments and produces sensible results. Two other solutions, using the hypergraph partitioning model, with Mondriaan [13], are under study. Finally, ParMetis [12] and PTScotch [4] are known to obtain good partitioning for unstructured meshes, and could probably be used for a network partitioning.

4   SkelGIS Implementation for Network Simulations

SkelGIS is an implicit parallelism library for distributed memory architectures, which proposes a sequential programming view to the user while producing SPMD parallel programs. Figure 4 illustrates the user- and the real-view of a SkelGIS program. SkelGIS hides parallelization of codes through four concepts which are illustrated in Figure 4: *DDS* which represents a distributed data structure. The DDS is responsible for storing the domain and its connectivity and partitioning it automatically. In SkelGIS multiple DDSs are available to represent different kinds of domains and meshes. *DPMap* which maps data on the DDS. Each instantiation of such an object represents data used in the simulation and its mapping on the *DDS*. *AP* which is an applier. It is used to apply a sequential user code, called an *operation*, *OP*, to a set of DPMaps. An applier also transparently proceeds MPI communications between processors. I represents the programming interface of SkelGIS. I is used to navigate through DPMaps, read and update them. This interface is based on *iterators* and specific functions to access the *neighborhood* of elements (stencil). Applied to network simulations,

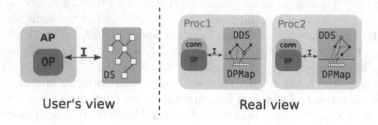

Fig. 4. SkelGIS user's view and its actual parallel execution

the DDS concept of SkelGIS is implemented using the distributed data structure presented in the previous section. Each of the three remaining concepts of SkelGIS, applied to networks, are implemented using this DDS, which makes possible and efficient the whole solution. Two DPMaps are needed for network simulations, one to map data on nodes and the other one to map data on edges. A DPMap can be compared to the array *values* of the CSR format. Using the DDS presented in the previous section, a DPMap is a light object which maps a distributed one-dimensional array to the local re-indexation of nodes and edges on each processor. This one dimensional array stores data associated to the DDS, and is able to store, for each edge or node, another one-dimensional array to implement complicated schemes. In this case, the order of the scheme gives information on needed communications. To be efficient with those different cases, partial template specializations [1] are used in SkelGIS. An applier is responsible for hiding communications from the user. As a result, *appliers* for networks use communication arrays $cdeg^{tor}$, $cdeg^{tos}$, N_E^{tor}, N_E^{tos}, N_V^{tor} and N_V^{tos} of the DDS. Three kinds of *iterators* are available to move through DPMaps applied to a network in SkelGIS. The first kind moves through all local nodes or edges of the *DDS*. The second kind moves through local nodes and edges which do not need communications to be computed, or on the contrary through local nodes and edges which need communications to be computed. This kind of iterators makes possible an overlap of computations with communications. Finally, the last kind of iterators moves through roots and leaves of the DAG, to manage the physical border of the domain. All moves of iterators are unordered as there are no dependencies in the numerical scheme (1), but all elements are guaranteed to be parsed by the iterator. All *iterators* use the re-indexation described in the previous section, to move contiguously in memory. Finally, functions to access neighborhood values directly use arrays $cdeg^+$, $cdeg^-$, N_E^+, N_E^-, N_V^+ and N_V^-. As a result, neighborhood values can be obtained in $O(1)$.

5   Experiments

SkelGIS performances have been evaluated using three different clusters to compute an arterial blood flow simulation [14]. This simulation is exclusively composed of double precision operations. Configurations of the three clusters are detailed in Table 1. The first one, at the university of Paris 6, is a well-equipped mid-size cluster. The second one, the TGCC-Curie in France, is the 20th cluster in the top500 list of November 2013. Finally, the third one, Juqueen in Germany, is the 8th cluster of the same list. Each experiment were evaluated four times, and the standard deviation of observed execution times is less than 1%. No specific optimization are proposed in SkelGIS for vectorization, however the simulation was compiled with the -O3 compilation flag.

Table 1. Hardware specifications of clusters

Cluster	System (clock)	Cores/n	Mem./n	Comp -O3	Net
Paris 6	2×Intel Xeon (3GHz)	12	24 GB	OpenMPI	InfiniBand
TGCC	2×SandyBridge (2.7GHz)	16	64 GB	Bullxmpi	InfiniBand
Juqueen	IBM PowerPC (1.6GHz)	16	16 GB	mpich2	5D Torus 40 GBps

On the Paris 6 cluster has been analyzed performances of the overlap of computations with communications. A DAG with 15k nodes and edges, with an average degree of nodes equal to 2, and with a unique root, has been used. Results are shown in Figure 5(a) and clearly state that this optimization is convincing, as expected. For all other experiments, the overlap optimization is used. On the TGCC, the same 15k nodes/edges DAG has been used (Figure 5(b)) and the speedup scale linearly until 256 cores, which is inferior than on the Paris 6 cluster. However, the use of these clusters is very different. Indeed, on the Paris 6 cluster we were the unique user and we were sure that no other processes were running on the attributed machines. On the TGCC, which is massively used, machines are attributed at their maximum and it is almost sure that other processes were running on some machines. On the Juqueen cluster, three different sizes of DAGs have been used to evaluate performances: 50k, 100k and 500k nodes/edges DAGs. The three of them were similarly shaped with an average degree of nodes equal to 2, and with a unique root. Results are shown on Figures 5(c) and 5(d). Those computations were very long (8 hours for the 500k with 1024 cores), and hours of use on clusters are limited. Then for 50k and 100k DAGs speedups are relative to 256 cores, and for the 500k DAG, the speedup is relative to 1024 cores. The speedups scale linearly to 4098 cores for 50k and 100k DAGs, and to 8192 cores for the 500k DAG. One can note a knee in the scaling for the 50k DAG at 2048 cores. This is probably due to a weakness in the graph partitioning solution.

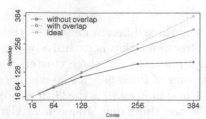

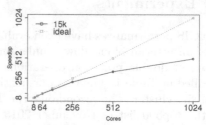

(a) Speedup obtained with comp/comm overlap on a 15k edges DAG on the LMM cluster.

(b) Speedup on a 15k edges DAG on the TGCC-Curie cluster.

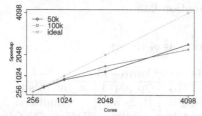

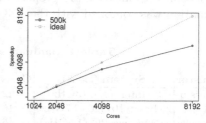

(c) Speedups on both 50k and 100k edges DAGs on the Juqueen cluster.

(d) Speedup on a 500k edges DAG on the Juqueen cluster.

Fig. 5. Results

6   Related Work

There are several well established implicit parallelism libraries to solve mesh-based PDEs. Some of them are more specific and some others are more generic, however, the purpose is always to find the good level of abstraction to obtain the easiest solution for the end-user. PETSc [2] proposes specific solutions for each kind of mesh possible (matrices, sparse matrices, unstructured meshes etc.). It is based on specific functions to solve PDEs such as, for example, functions to *interpolate* or execute a *jacobian*. PETSc is close to a standard function-based library but is specifically made to solve PDEs. The framework OP2 [11], to solve unstructured mesh-based PDEs, is closer to SkelGIS in the chosen abstraction level. It relies on four concepts, first to define unstructured meshes, then to apply data and make computations on it: *sets*, *data on sets*, *connectivity* between the sets and *operations* over sets. However, it differs from SkelGIS on several points. First, using OP2, the user can define the needed mesh and its connectivity, through the definition of different *sets*. This point offers a great flexibility, however it is adapted to unstructured meshes, and it is not possible to define a network with it. In addition to this, the OP2 *operation* concept is different from the SkelGIS one. Actually, with OP2, a higher level of abstraction is proposed to the user through *operations*, where loops do not have to be explicitly written. Thus, the programming style of OP2 is closer to an algorithmic skeleton library [10]. In a SkelGIS *operation*, the user is in charge of loops, as in a sequential program, through *Interfaces*. This last concept does not exist in the OP2 framework. Finally, SkelGIS is a library exclusively made of C++ header files (it is called a "h-only" library), while OP2 first generates code from code, before a final compilation. Liszt [7] is a *Domain Specific Language* (DSL) which stays close to a standard C programming style, where new language features and operators have to be used. Liszt, as OP2, is a solution to solve unstructured mesh-based PDEs, and the abstraction level is similar. The main difference is the way *sets* and their connectivity are defined. In OP2 the user is free to declare and connect as much sets as he wants. Using Liszt, on the other hand, *sets* are groups of mesh-elements pre-defined by the DSL: *vertices*, *edges*, *faces* and *cells*. Liszt is closer to SkelGIS than OP2 for its abstraction level. Actually, the Liszt code is close to a sequential program, as in SkelGIS. Loops are managed by the user through the concept of *for-comprehension*, which expresses computation on all mesh-elements in a set. Thus, *for-comprehension* could be compared to *iterators* of SkelGIS. However, it is not clear how the specific case of physical border elements can be parsed in Liszt, while using SkelGIS, specific *iterators* are available. Both OP2 and Liszt propose implicit parallelism solutions to solve unstructured mesh-based PDEs. The current version of SkelGIS can deal with two-dimensional regular meshes [5,6] but do not propose solution for unstructured meshes. This point is under study, and a specific new kind of *DDS* and its associated *DPMaps*, *appliers* and *interfaces* will be proposed. Note that SkelGIS, on the other hand, proposes a solution adapted to network simulations where nodes and edges do not form the cells of a mesh but a network. As far as we know, neither Liszt nor OP2 can manage such simulations. The same lack can be noticed for PETSc, however, using multiple sparse matrices, it seems possible but very complicated to work on networks.

7   Conclusion

SkelGIS is an implicit parallelism header-only library to solve mesh-based PDEs on distributed memory architectures. In this paper has been presented the implementation of SkelGIS for the specific case of networks which can be represented by DAGs. This implementation relies on an adaptation, a re-indexation and a parallelization of the CSR format for DAGs. The implementation of the associated *DPMaps*, *applier*, *iterators* and *neighborhood* is based on this new *DDS*, and its optimizations for cache lines and overlap of computations with communications. Experiments show that this solution scale on different architectures and different sizes of DAGs. Some improvement are under study to obtain a better graph partitioning algorithm and to use vectorization optimizations. Finally, SkelGIS is able to deal with two-dimensional meshes and network simulations, the next two steps are to propose implementations for unstructured meshes and for adaptive meshes. This last work will require mutable distributed data structures, not managed in the format presented in this paper.

References

1. Alexandrescu, A.: Modern C++ design: Generic programming and design patterns applied. Addison-Wesley Longman Publishing Co., Inc., Boston (2001)
2. Balay, S., Gropp, W.D., Curfman McInnes, L., Smith, B.F.: Efficient management of parallelism in object oriented numerical software libraries. In: Modern Software Tools in Scientific Computing, pp. 163–202. Birkhäuser Press (1997)
3. Barrett, R., Berry, M., Chan, T.F., Demmel, J., Donato, J., Dongarra, J., Eijkhout, V., Pozo, R., Romine, C., Van der Vorst, H.: Templates for the Solution of Linear Systems: Building Blocks for Iterative Methods, 2nd edn. SIAM (1994)
4. Chevalier, C., Pellegrini, F.: PT-Scotch: A tool for efficient parallel graph ordering. Parallel Computing 34(68), 318–331 (2008)
5. Coullon, H., Le, M.-H., Limet, S.: Parallelization of shallow-water equations with the algorithmic skeleton library SkelGIS. In: ICCS. Procedia Computer Science, vol. 18, pp. 591–600. Elsevier (2013)
6. Coullon, H., Limet, S.: Algorithmic skeleton library for scientific simulations: SkelGIS. In: HPCS, pp. 429–436. IEEE (2013)
7. DeVito, Z., Joubert, N., Palacios, F., Oakley, S., Medina, M., Barrientos, M., Elsen, E., Ham, F., Aiken, A., Duraisamy, K., Darve, E., Alonso, J., Hanrahan, P.: Liszt: A domain specific language for building portable mesh-based PDE solvers. In: Proc. of 2011 Intern. Conf. for High Performance Computing, Networking, Storage and Analysis, SC 2011, pp. 1–12. ACM (2011)
8. Nick Edmonds and Andrew Lumsdaine. Distributed compressed sparse row (2010)
9. Fishgold, L., Danalis, A., Pollock, L., Swany, M.: An automated approach to improve communication-computation overlap in clusters. In: Proceedings of the 20th International Conference on Parallel and Distributed Processing, IPDPS 2006, pp. 290–290. IEEE Computer Society, Washington, DC (2006)
10. Javed, N., Loulergue, F.: Parallel programming and performance predictability with Orléans Skeleton Library. In: HPCS, pp. 257–263. IEEE (2011)
11. Mudalige, G.R., Giles, M.B., Reguly, I., Bertolli, C., Kelly, P.H.J.: OP2: An active library framework for solving unstructured mesh-based applications on multi-core and many-core architectures. In: Innovative Parallel Computing (InPar), pp. 1–12. IEEE (2012)
12. Schloegel, K., Karypis, G., Kumar, V.: Parallel static and dynamic multi-constraint graph partitioning. Concurrency and Computation: Practice and Experience 14(3), 219–240 (2002)
13. Vastenhouw, B., Bisseling, R.H.: A two-dimensional data distribution method for parallel sparse matrix-vector multiplication. SIAM Rev. 47(1), 67–95 (2005)
14. Wang, X., Fullana, J.-M., Lagrée, P.-Y.: Verification and comparison of four numerical schemes for a 1D viscoelastic blood flow model. Technical report, Institut Jean Le Rond d'Alembert - IJLRA (2012)

GoFFish: A Sub-graph Centric Framework for Large-Scale Graph Analytics

Yogesh Simmhan[1], Alok Kumbhare[2], Charith Wickramaarachchi[2], Soonil Nagarkar[2],
Santosh Ravi[2], Cauligi Raghavendra[2], and Viktor Prasanna[2]

[1] Indian Institute of Science, Bangalore, India
[2] University of Southern California, Los Angeles, USA
simmhan@serc.iisc.in,
{kumbhare,cwickram,snagarka,sathyavi,raghu,prasanna}@usc.edu

Abstract. Vertex centric models for large scale graph processing are gaining
traction due to their simple distributed programming abstraction. However, pure
vertex centric algorithms under-perform due to large communication overheads
and slow iterative convergence. We introduce *GoFFish* a scalable sub-graph centric framework co-designed with a distributed persistent graph storage for large
scale graph analytics on commodity clusters, offering the added natural flexibility of shared memory sub-graph computation. We map Connected Components,
SSSP and PageRank algorithms to this model and empirically analyze them for
several real world graphs, demonstrating *orders of magnitude improvements*, in
some cases, compared to Apache Giraph's vertex centric framework.

1 Introduction

One defining characteristic of complexity in "Big Data" is the intrinsic interconnect-
edness, endemic to novel applications in both the Internet of Things and Social Networks. Such graph datasets offer unique challenges to scalable analysis, even as they are
becoming pervasive. There has been significant work on parallel algorithms and frameworks for large graph applications on HPC clusters [1][1], massively multi-threaded architectures [2], and GPUs [3]. Our focus here, however, is on leveraging *commodity
hardware* for scaling graph analytics. Such distributed infrastructure, including Clouds,
have democratized resource access, as evidenced by popular programming frameworks
like MapReduce. While MapReduce's tuple-based approach is ill-suited for many graph
applications [4], recent *vertex-centric programming abstractions* [5,6], like Google's
Pregel and its open-source version, Apache Giraph [7], marry the ease of specifying a
uniform logic for each vertex with a *Bulk Synchronous Parallel (BSP)* execution model
to scale[2]. Independent vertex executions in a distributed environment are interleaved
with synchronized message exchanges across them to form iterative *supersteps*.

However, there are short-comings to this approach. (1) Defining an individual vertex's logic forces costly messaging even within vertices in one partition. (2) Porting
shared memory graph algorithms to efficient vertex centric ones can be non-trivial. (3)

---

[1] The Graph 500 List, http://www.graph500.org
[2] Scaling Apache Giraph to a Trillion Edges, *Facebook Engineering*,
   http://on.fb.me/1czMarU

F. Silva et al. (Eds.): Euro-Par 2014, LNCS 8632, pp. 451–462, 2014.
© Springer International Publishing Switzerland 2014

The programming abstraction is decoupled from the data layout on disk, causing I/O penalties at initialization and runtime. A recent work [6] identified the opportunity of leveraging shared memory algorithms within a *partition*, but relaxed the programming model to operate on a whole partition, without guarantees of *sub-graph connectivity* within a partition or implicit use of *concurrency* across sub-graphs.

In this paper, (1) we propose a sub-graph centric programming abstraction, *Gopher*, for performing distributed graph analytics. This balances the flexibility of reusing shared-memory graph algorithms over *connected* sub-graphs while leveraging sub-graph concurrency within a machine, and distributed scaling using BSP. (2) We couple this abstraction with an efficient distributed storage, *GoFS*. GoFS stores partitioned graphs across distributed hosts while coalescing connected sub-graphs within partitions, to optimize sub-graph centric access patterns. Gopher and GoFS are co-designed as part of the *GoFFish* graph analytics framework, and are empirically shown here to scale for common graph algorithms on real world graphs, in comparison with Apache Giraph.

2   Background and Related Work

There is a large body of work on parallel graph processing [8] for HPC clusters [1], massively multi-threaded architectures [2], and GPGPUs [3], often tuned for specific algorithms and architectures [9]. For e.g., the STAPL Parallel Graph Library (SGL) [10] offers diverse graph data abstractions, and can express level-synchronous vertex-centric BSP and coarse-grained algorithms over sub-graphs, but not necessarily a sub-graph centric BSP pattern as we propose. SGL uses STAPL for parallel execution using OpenMP and MPI, which scales on HPC hardware but not on commodity clusters with punitive network latencies. Frameworks for commodity hardware trade performance in favor of scalability and accessibility – ease of use, resource access, and programming.

The popularity of MapReduce for large scale data analysis has extended to graph data as well, with research techniques to scale it to peta-byte graphs for some algorithms [11]. But the tuple-based approach of MapReduce makes it unnatural for graph algorithms, often requiring new programming constructs [12], platform tuning [4], and repeated reads/writes of the entire graph to disk. Google's recent Pregel [5] model uses iterative supersteps of vertex centric logic executed in a BSP model [13]. Here, users implement a `Compute` method for a single vertex, with access to its value(s) and outgoing edge list. `Compute` is executed concurrently for each vertex and can emit messages to neighboring (or discovered) vertices. Generated messages are delivered in bulk and available to the target vertices only after all `Compute`s complete, forming one barriered *superstep*. Iterative level-synchronized supersteps interleave computation with message passing. The vertices can `VoteToHalt` in their `Compute` method at any superstep; any vertex that has voted to halt is not invoked in the next superstep unless it has input messages. The application terminates when all vertices vote to halt and there are no new input messages available. Pseudocode to find the maximal vertex using this model is shown in Alg. 1.. Apache Giraph [7] is an open source implementation of Google's Pregel, and alternatives such as Hama [14], Pregel.NET [15] and GPS [16] also exist.

Despite the programming elegance, there are key scalability bottlenecks in Pregel: (1) the number of messages exchanged between vertices, and (2) the number of synchronized supersteps required for completion. Message passing is done either in-memory (for co-located vertices) or over the network, while barrier synchronization across distributed vertices is centrally coordinated. This often makes them communication bound on commodity hardware, despite use of `Combiners` [5] for message aggregation. Secondly, the default hashing of vertices to machines exacerbates this though better partitioning shows mixed results [16,6]. Even in-memory message passing causes memory pressure [15]. For e.g., GPS [16] performs dynamic partition balancing and replication on Pregel and our prior work [15] used a swathe-based scheduling to amortize messaging overhead. But these engineering solutions do not address key limitations of the abstraction, which also leads to large number of supersteps to converge for vertex centric algorithms (e.g.~30 for PageRank, or graph diameter for Max Vertex).

Recently, Tian, et al. [6] recognized these limitations and propose a *partition centric* variant, *Giraph++*. Here, users' `Compute` method has access to all vertices and edges in a partition on a machine, and can define algorithms that operate on a whole partition within a superstep before passing messages from *boundary vertices* of the partition to neighboring vertices. They also partition the graph to minimize average *ncuts*. Such local compute on the coarse partition can reduce the number of messages exchanged and supersteps taken, just as for us. But this approach falls short on several counts. (1) Though the partitions are called "sub-graphs" in Giraph++, these sub-graphs are not connected components. This limits the use of shared-memory graph algorithms that operate on connected graphs, and can lead to a suboptimal algorithm operating collectively on hundreds of sub-graphs in a partition. This also puts the onus on the user to leverage concurrency across sub-graphs in a partition. Our proposed abstraction and execution model *a priori* identifies *sub-graphs as locally connected components*; users define their `Compute` method on these. Our engine also automatically executes sub-graphs in parallel on the local machine. (2) Their `Compute` can send messages to only boundary vertices. We also allow messages to be sent to sub-graphs, fully exploiting the abstraction. (3) Our distributed graph storage is designed for sub-graph access patterns to offer data loading efficiencies, and extends beyond just prior graph partitioning.

Algorithm 1. Max Vertex Value using Vertex Centric Model

1: **procedure** COMPUTE(Vertex myVertex, Iterator⟨Message⟩ M)
2:     hasChanged = (superstep == 1) ? `true` : `false`
3:     **while** M.hasNext **do**   ▷ *Update to max message value*
4:         Message m ← M.next
5:         **if** m.value > myVertex.value **then**
6:             myVertex.value ← m.value
7:             hasChanged = `true`
8:     **if** hasChanged **then**   ▷ *Send message to neighbors*
9:         SENDTOALLNEIGHBORS(myVertex.value)
10:     **else**
11:         VOTETOHALT()

Distributed GraphLab [17] is another popular graph programming abstraction, optimized for local dependencies observed in data mining algorithms. GraphLab too uses an iterative computing model based on vertex-centric logic, but allows asynchronous execution with access to vertex neighbors. Unlike Pregel, it does not support graph mutations. There are other distributed graph processing systems such as Trinity [18] that offer a shared memory abstraction in a distributed memory infrastructure. Here, algorithms use both message passing and a distributed address space called *memory cloud*. However, this assumes large memory machines with high speed interconnects. We focus on commodity cluster and do not make such hardware assumptions.

3   Sub-graph Centric Programming Abstraction

We propose a sub-graph centric programming abstraction that targets the deficiencies of a vertex centric BSP model. We operate in a distributed environment where the graph is $k - way$ partitioned over its vertices across k machines. We define a **sub-graph** as a connected component within a partition of an undirected graph; they are weakly connected if the graph is directed. The Fig. 1(a) shows two partitions with three sub-graphs. Two sub-graphs do not share the same vertex but can have *remote edges* that connect their vertices (dotted edges in Fig. 1(a)), as long as the sub-graphs are on different partitions. If two sub-graphs on the same partition share a *local edge* (solid edges), by definition they are merged into a single sub-graph. A partition can have one or more sub-graphs and the set of all sub-graphs forms the complete graph. Specific partitioning approaches are discussed later, and each machine holds one partition. Sub-graphs behave like "meta vertices" with remote edges connecting them across partitions.

Formally, let $P_i = \{\mathbb{V}_i, \mathbb{E}_i\}$ be a graph partition i where V_i and E_i are the set of vertices and edges in the partition. We define a *sub-graph* S in P_i as $S = \{V, E, R | v \in V \Rightarrow v \in \mathbb{V}_i; e \in E \Rightarrow e \in \mathbb{E}_i; r \in R \Rightarrow r \notin \mathbb{V}_i; \forall u, v \in V \exists$ an undirected path between u, v; and $\forall r \in R \exists v \in V$ s.t. $e = \langle v, r \rangle \in E\}$ where V is a set of local vertices, E is a set of edges and R is a set of remote vertices.

Each sub-graph is treated as an independent unit of computation within a BSP superstep. Users implement the following method signature:

Compute(Subgraph, Iterator<Message>)

The Compute method can access the sub-graph topology and values of the vertices and edges. The values are mutable though the topology is constant. This allows us to fully traverse the sub-graph up to the boundary remote edges *in-memory, within a single*

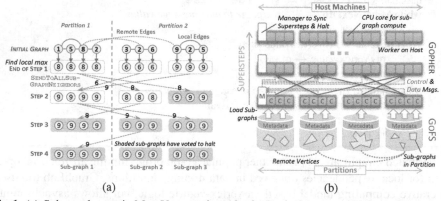

(a)   (b)

Fig. 1. (a) Sub-graph centric Max Vertex using Alg. 2.. Dashed arrows show messages passed. (b) Sub-graph centric data access from GoFS and BSP execution by Gopher.

superstep and accumulate values of the sub-graph or update values for the local vertices and edges. Different sub-graphs communicate by message passing, with messages exchanged at synchronized superstep boundaries in a BSP model. Several methods enable this messaging. Algorithms often start by sending messages to neighboring sub-graphs.

`SendToAllSubGraphNeighbors`(Message)

As other sub-graphs are discovered across supersteps, two other methods are useful:

`SendToSubGraph`(SubGraphID, Message)
`SendToSubGraphVertex`(SubGraphID, VertexID, Message)

We allow a (costly) broadcast to all sub-graphs, though it should be used sparingly.

`SendToAllSubGraphs`(Message)

As with Pregel, the `Compute` method can invoke `VoteToHalt`. The application terminates when all sub-graphs have halted and there are no new input messages.

Alg. 2. presents the sub-graph centric version for finding the maximum vertex value in a graph. Fig. 1(a) illustrates its execution. The `Compute` method operates on a sub-graph *mySG*. Lines 2–6 are executed only for the first superstep, where each sub-graph's value is initialized to largest of its vertices. Subsequently, the algorithm is similar to the vertex centric version: we send the sub-graph's value to its neighboring sub-graphs and update the sub-graph's value to the highest value received, halting when there is no further change. At the end, each sub-graph has the value of the largest vertex.

Algorithm 2. Max Vertex using Sub-Graph Centric Model

1: **procedure** COMPUTE(SubGraph mySG, Iterator⟨Message⟩ M)
2:     **if** superstep = 1 **then**   ▶ *Find local max in subgraph*
3:         mySG.value ← $-\infty$
4:         **for all** Vertex myVertex **in** mySG vertices **do**
5:             **if** mySG.value < myVertex.value **then**
6:                 mySG.value ← myVertex.value
7:     hasChanged = (superstep == 1) ? `true` : `false`
8:     **while** M.hasNext **do**
9:         Message m ← M.next
10:         **if** m.value > mySG.value **then**
11:             mySG.value ← m.value
12:             hasChanged = `true`
13:     **if** hasChanged **then**
14:         SENDTOALLSUBGRAPHNEIGHBORS(mySG.value)
15:     **else**
16:         VOTETOHALT()

Compared to the vertex centric algorithm, the sub-graph centric version reduces the number of supersteps taken since the largest value discovered at any superstep propagates through the entire sub-graph in the same superstep. For e.g., for the graph in Fig. 1(a), the vertex centric approach takes 7 supersteps while we use 4. Also, this reduces the cumulative number of messages exchanged on the network. In the worst case, when a sub-graph is trivial (has one vertex), we degenerate to a vertex centric model.
Benefits. Our elegant extension of the vertex centric model offers three key benefits.

1) Messages Exchanged. Access to the entire sub-graph enables the application to make a significant progress within each superstep while reducing costly message exchanges that cause network overhead, disk buffering or memory pressure, between supersteps. While Pregel allows `Combiners` per worker, they operate after messages are generated while we preclude message generation. Giraph++ has similar advantages, but no better; as sub-graphs in a partition are disconnected, they do not exchange messages.

2) Number of Supersteps. Depending on the algorithm, a sub-graph centric model can reduce the number of supersteps required compared to Pregel, thereby limiting synchronization overheads. Also, the time taken by a superstep is based on its slowest sub-graph, with a wide distribution seen across sub-graphs [15]. Reducing the supersteps mitigates this skew. For traversal algorithms, the number of supersteps is a function of the graph *diameter*. Using a sub-graph centric model, this reduces to the diameter of the meta-graph where the sub-graphs form meta-vertices. In the best case (a linear chain), the number of supersteps can reduce proportional to the number vertices in a sub-graph, while for a trivial sub-graph, it is no worse. These benefits translate to Giraph++ too.

3) Reuse of Single-machine Algorithms. Lastly, our approach allows direct reuse of efficient shared-memory graph algorithms on a sub-graph, while using a BSP model across supersteps. The change from a simple vertex-centric approach is incremental, but the performance improvement stark. e.g. In Alg. 2., but for the shaded lines 2–6 which operates on the whole sub-graph, other lines are similar to Alg. 1.. This has two benefits relative to Pregel and Giraph++: (1) We can leverage optimal single machines algorithms for sub-graphs, even leveraging GPGPU accelerators, with the added guarantee that the *sub-graphs are connected* (unlike Giraph++). This ensures traversals reach all sub-graph vertices and avoids testing every vertex in the partition independently. Second, when a partition has multiple sub-graphs, as is often, we can exploit concurrency across them automatically. While the degree of parallelism is not as high as vertex centric (Pregel), it is better than treating the partition as one computation unit (Giraph++).

4 Architecture

GoFFish is a scalable software framework for storing graphs, and composing and executing graph analytics[3]. A *Graph oriented File System (GoFS)* and *Gopher execution engine* are co-designed *ab initio* to ensure efficient distributed storage for sub-graph centric data access patterns. The design choices target commodity or virtualized hardware with Ethernet and spinning disks. GoFFish is implemented in Java.

GoFS Distributed Graph Store. GoFS is a distributed store for partitioning, storing and accessing graph datasets across hosts in a cluster. Graphs can have both a *topology* and *attributes* associated with each vertex and edge. The former is an adjacency list of uniquely labeled vertices and (directed or undirected) edges connecting them. Attributes are a list of name-value pairs with a schema provided for typing. Input graphs are partitioned across hosts, one partition per machine, using the METIS tool [19] to balance vertices per partition and minimize edge cuts (Fig. 1(b)).

GoFS uses a sub-graph oriented model for mapping the partition's content to *slice files*, which form units of storage on the local file system. We identify all sub-graphs

---

[3] https://github.com/usc-cloud/goffish

in the partition – components that are (weakly) connected through local edges, and a partition with n vertices can have between 1 to n sub-graphs. Each sub-graph maps to one *topology slice* that contains local vertices, local edges and remote edges, with references to partitions holding the destination remote vertex, and several *attribute slices* that hold their names and values. We use *Kryo*[4] for compact object storage on disk.

GoFS is a *write once-read many* scalable data store rather than a database with rich query support. The GoFS Java API allows clients to access a graph's metadata, attribute schema and sub-graphs present in the local partition. Specific sub-graphs and select attributes can be loaded into memory and traversed. Remote edges in a sub-graph resolve to a remote partition/sub-graph/vertex ID that can be used to send messages to.

Gopher Sub-graph Centric Framework. The Gopher programming framework implements our proposed sub-graph centric abstractions, and executes them using the *Floe* [20] dataflow engine on a Cloud or cluster in conjunction with GoFS. Users implement their algorithm in Java within a `Compute` method where they get access to a local sub-graph object and data messages from the previous superstep. They use `Send*` methods to send message to the remote sub-graphs in the next superstep and can `VoteToHalt()`. The same `Compute` logic is executed on every sub-graph in the graph, for each superstep.

The Gopher framework has a *compute worker* running on each machine and a *manager* on one machine. The workers initially load all local sub-graphs for that graph into memory from GoFS. For every superstep, the worker uses a multi-core-optimized task pool to invoke the `Compute` on each sub-graph, transparently leveraging concurrency within a partition. `Send*` messages are resolved by GoFS to a remote partition and host. The worker aggregates messages destined for the same host and sends them asynchronously to the remote worker while the compute progresses.

Once the `Compute` for all sub-graphs in a partition complete, the worker flushes pending messages to remote workers and signals the manager. Once the manager receives signals from all workers, it broadcasts a *resume* signal to the workers to start their next superstep and operate on input messages from the previous superstep. `Compute` is stateful for each sub-graph; so local variables are retained across supersteps. When a worker does not have to call `Compute` for any of its sub-graphs in a superstep, because all voted to halt *and* have no input messages, it sends a *ready to halt* signal to the manager. When all workers are ready to halt, the manager terminates the application.

Storage-Compute Co-design. Co-designing data layout and execution models is beneficial, as seen with Hadoop and HDFS. GoFFish uses sub-graphs as a logical unit of storage and computation; hence our data store first partitions the graph followed by sub-graph discovery. Partitioning minimizes network costs when loading sub-graphs into Gopher. We use existing partitioning tools (METIS) to balance vertices and minimize edge cuts. Ideally, we should also balance the number of sub-graphs per partition and ensure uniform size to reduce compute skew in a superstep. Further, having multiple sub-graphs in a partition can leverage the concurrency across sub-graphs. Such schemes are for future work. We also balance the disk latency against bytes read by slicing sub-graphs into topology and attributes files. For e.g. a graph with 10 edge attributes that uses only the *weight* attribute in an algorithm needs to load only one attribute slice.

---

[4] Kryo serialization framework, `https://github.com/EsotericSoftware/kryo`

5   Evaluation of Sub-graph Centric Algorithms on GoFFish

We present and evaluate several sub-graph centric versions of common graph algorithms, both to illustrate the utility of our abstraction and the performance of GoFFish. We comparatively evaluate against Apache Giraph, a popular implementation of Pregel's vertex centric model, that uses HDFS. We use the latest development version of Giraph, at the time of writing, which includes recent performance enhancements. Sub-graph centric Gopher and vertex centric Giraph algorithms are implemented for: *Connected Components*, *Single Source Shortest Path (SSSP)* and *PageRank*.

Experimental Setup and Datasets. We run these experiments on a modest cluster of 12 nodes, each with an 8-core Intel Xeon CPU, 16 GB RAM, 1 TB SATA HDD, and connected by Gigabit Ethernet. This is representative of commodity clusters or Cloud VMs accessible to the long tail of science rather than HPC users. Both Giraph and GoFFish are deployed on all nodes, and use Java 7 JRE for 64 bit Ubuntu Linux. The GoFFish manager runs on one node.

We choose diverse real world graphs (Table 1): California road network (**RN**), Internet topology from traceroute statistics (**TR**)), and LiveJournal social network (**LJ**). RN is a small, sparse network with a small and even edge degree distribution, and a large diameter. LJ is dense, with powerlaw edge degrees and a small diameter. TR has a powerlaw edge degree, with a few highly connected vertices. Unless otherwise stated, we report average values over three runs each for each experiment.

Table 1. Characteristics of graph datasets used in evaluation

Graph	Vertices	Edges	Diameter	WCC
RN	1,965,206	2,766,607	849	2,638
TR	19,442,778	22,782,842	25	1
LJ	4,847,571	68,475,391	10	1,877

Summary Results. We compare the end-to-end time (makespan) for executing an algorithm on GoFFish and on Giraph. This includes two key components: the time to load the data from storage, which shows the benefits of sub-graph oriented distributed storage, and the time to run the sub-graph/vertex centric computation. which shows relative benefits of the abstractions. Fig. 2(a) highlights the data loading time per graph on both platforms; this does not change across algorithms. Fig. 2(b) give the execution time as a *bar-plot* for various algorithms and datasets once data is loaded, as well as the makespan that includes the compute and load time, as a *dot-plot*. Also shown in Fig. 2(c) is the number of supersteps taken to complete the algorithm for each combination.

One key observation is that GoFFish's makespan is smaller than Giraph for all combinations but two, PageRank and SSSP on LJ. The performance advantage ranges from $81\times$ faster for Connected Components on RN to 11% faster for PageRank on TR. These result from abstraction, design and layout choices, as we discuss. In some, Giraph's data loading time from HDFS dominates (TR), in others, Gopher's algorithmic advantage significantly reduces the number of supersteps (RN for SSSP), while for a few, Gopher's compute time over sub-graphs dominates (PageRank on LJ).

Connected Components. Connected components identify maximally connected sub-graphs within an undirected graph such that there is path from every vertex to every

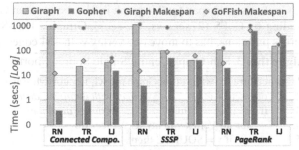

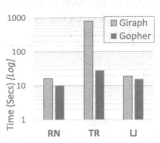

(a) Graph loading time (log scale) from disk to memory.

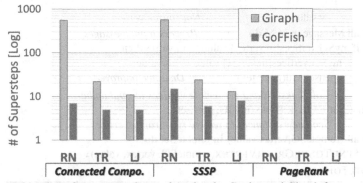

(b) Compute time and Makespan (incl. load) for GoFFish and Giraph for various graph algorithms and datasets (log scale)

(c) Number of supersteps (log scale) taken by Gopher and Giraph for various graph algorithms and datasets

Fig. 2. Comparison of GoFFish and Giraph for all Graph Algorithms and Datasets

other vertex in the sub-graph. The sub-graph and vertex centric algorithms are similar to the Maximum Vertex Value algorithm [21]. In effect, we perform a *breadth first traversal* rooted at the sub-graph with the largest vertex ID, with each superstep propagating the value one level deeper till the farthest connected sub-graph is reached. Finally, all vertices are labeled with the component ID (i.e. largest vertex ID) they belong to.

The computational complexity of this algorithm is $O((d+1) \times v/p)$, where d is the diameter of the graph (specifically, of the largest connected component) constructed by treating each sub-graph as a meta vertex, v is the number of vertices in the graph and p is the number of machines (partitions). The key algorithmic optimization here comes from reducing the number of supersteps $(d+1)$ relative to the vertex centric model.

As a result, Connected Components for GoFFish performs significantly better than Giraph for all three data sets – from $1.4\times$ to $81\times$. Fig. 2(c) shows the number of supersteps is much smaller for Gopher compared to Giraph, taking between 5 (TR, LJ) and 7 (RN) supersteps for Connected Components while Giraph takes between 11 (LJ) and 554 (RN). The superstep time in itself is dominated by the synchronization overhead. The ratio of compute times improvements between Giraph and Gopher is highly correlated ($R^2 = 0.9999$) with the vertex-based diameter of the graph (Table 1), *i.e., larger the vertex-based graph diameter, greater the opportunity to reduce sub-graph-based diameter, lesser the number of supersteps, and better that Gopher algorithm performs.*

Gopher's makespan for TR graph is $21\times$ better than Giraph due to much faster data loading by GoFS ($27secs$ vs. $798secs$). Giraph's HDFS, which balances the vertices across partitions, has to move one vertex with 1M edges that takes punitively long.

Algorithm 3. Sub-Graph Centric Single Source Shortest Path

1: **procedure** COMPUTE(SubGraph mySG, Iterator⟨Message⟩ M)
2:      openset ← ∅   ▸ *Vertices with improved distances*
3:      **if** superstep = 1 **then**   ▸ *Initialize distances*
4:          **for all** Vertex v **in** mySG.vertices **do**
5:              **if** v = SOURCE **then**
6:                  v.value ← 0   ▸ *Set distance to source as 0*
7:                  openset.add(v)   ▸ *Distance has improved*
8:              **else**
9:                  v.value ← −∞   ▸ *Not source vertex*
10:     **for all** Message m **in** M **do**   ▸ *Process input messages*
11:         **if** mySG.vertices[m.vertex].value > m.value **then**
12:             mySG.vertices[m.vertex].value ← m.value
13:             openset.add(m.vertex)   ▸ *Distance improved*
14:                 ▸ *Call Dijkstras and get remote vertices to send updates*
15:     remoteSet ← DIJKSTRAS(mySG, openset)
16:                 ▸ *Send new distances to remote sub-graphs/vertices*
17:     **for all** ⟨remoteSG,vertex,value⟩ **in** remoteSet **do**
18:         SENDTOSUBGRAPHVERTEX(remoteSG, vertex, value)
19:     VOTETOHALT( )

SSP. Intuitively, the sub-graph centric algorithm for Single Source Shortest Path (SSSP) finds the shortest distances from the source vertex to all internal vertices (i.e. not having a remote edge) in the sub-graph holding the source in one superstep using DIJKSTRAS (Alg. 3.). It then sends the updated distances from the vertices having a remote edge to their neighboring sub-graphs. These sub-graphs propagate the changes internally in one superstep, and to their neighbors across supersteps, till the distances quiesce.

DIJKSTRAS has a compute complexity of $O((e \cdot log(v)))$ per superstep, where e and v are typically dominated by the largest active sub-graph. The number of supersteps is a function of the graph diameter d measured through sub-graphs, and this takes $O(d)$ supersteps. For a partitions with large number of small sub-graphs, we can exploit concurrency across c cores on that machine. While the time complexity per superstep is relatively larger for DIJKSTRAS, we may significantly reduce the number of supersteps taken for the algorithm to converge.

SSSP's compute time for GoFFish out-performs Giraph by $300\times$ and $2\times$ for RN and TR, respectively, while it is the same for LJ. Gopher takes reduced supersteps on RN and TR for SSSP, that is able to offset its higher computational complexity per superstep. But this complexity impacts LJ which has high edge density, while its small world network diameter does not reduce the number of supersteps. Hence SSSP for Gopher only matches, rather than outperforms, Giraph's compute time for LJ.

PageRank. For each superstep in a vertex centric PageRank [5], a vertex adds all input message values into sum, computes $0.15/v + 0.85 \times sum$ as its new value, and sends $value/g$ to its g neighbors. The $value$ is $1/v$ initially, for v vertices in the graph. An equivalent sub-graph centric approach does not confer algorithmic benefits; it takes the same $\sim$30 supersteps to converge and each vertex operates independently in lock step, with an $O(30 \cdot \frac{v}{p \cdot c} \cdot g)$, for an average edge degree of g.

As shown in Fig. 2(b), Gopher under performs Giraph for PageRank for TR and LJ by $2.6\times$. It is $5.5\times$ faster for RN. TR's makespan offsets compute slowdown with data loading benefits. As observed, the fixed supersteps used for PageRank negates algorithmic benefits and the computation complexity per superstep for sub-graph centric is higher than for vertex centric. This also exacerbates the time skew across sub-graphs in a partition. For e.g., in LJ, many of the partitions complete their superstep within a range of $23 - 26secs$, but these are bound by single large sub-graphs in each partition which are stragglers, and cause 75% of the cores to be idle. Giraph, on the other hand, has uniform vertex distribution across machines and each worker takes almost the same time to complete a superstep while fully exploiting fine grained vertex level parallelism. This highlights the deficiencies of the default partitioning model used by GoFS that reduces edge cuts and balances the number of vertices per machine, *without considering the number of sub-graphs that are present per partition, and their sizes.*

6   Discussion and Conclusions

We introduce a sub-graph centric programming abstraction for large scale graph analytics on distributed systems. This model combines the scalability of vertex centric programming with the flexibility of using shared-memory algorithms at the sub-graph level. The connected nature of our sub-graphs provides stronger guarantees for such algorithms and allows us to exploit degrees of parallelism across sub-graphs in a partition. The GoFFish framework offers Gopher, a distributed execution runtime for this abstraction, co-designed with GoFS, a distributed sub-graph aware storage that pre-partitions and stores graphs for data-local execution.

The relative algorithmic benefits of using a sub-graph centric abstraction can be characterized based on the class of graph algorithm and graph. For algorithms that perform full graph traversals, like SSSP, BFS and Betweenness Centrality, we reduce the number of supersteps to a function of the diameter of the graph based on sub-graphs rather than vertices. This can offer significant reduction. However, for powerlaw graphs that start with a small vertex based diameter, these benefits are muted.

The time complexity per superstep can be larger since we often run the single-machine graph algorithm on each sub-graph. The number of vertices and edges in large sub-graph will impact this. If there are many small sub-graphs in a partition, the number of sub-graphs becomes the limiting factor as we approach a vertex centric behavior, but this also exploits multi-core parallelism. For graphs with high edge density, algorithms that are a linear (or worse) function of the number of edges can take longer supersteps.

We empirically showed that GoFFish performs significantly better than Apache Giraph. These performance gains are due to both the partitioned graph storage and sub-graph based retrieval from GoFS, and a significant reduction in the number of supersteps that helps us complete faster. This offers a high compute to communication ratio.

We do recognize some short comings, with further research opportunities. Sub-graph centric algorithms are vulnerable to imbalances in number of sub-graphs per partition and non-uniformity in their sizes. This causes stragglers. Better partitioning to balance the sub-graphs can help. The framework is also susceptible to small-world graphs with high edge degrees that have high sub-graph level computational complexity. Our software prototype offers opportunities for design and engineering optimizations.

References

1. Gregor, D., Lumsdaine, A.: The Parallel BGL: A Generic Library for Distributed Graph Computations. In: Parallel Object-Oriented Scientific Computing, POOSC (2005)
2. Ediger, D., Bader, D.: Investigating Graph Algorithms in the BSP Model on the Cray XMT. In: Workshop on Multithreaded Architectures and Applications, MTAAP (2013)
3. Harish, P., Narayanan, P.J.: Accelerating large graph algorithms on the gpu using cuda. In: IEEE High Performance Computing, HiPC (2007)
4. Lin, J., Schatz, M.: Design patterns for efficient graph algorithms in MapReduce. In: Workshop on Mining and Learning with Graphs, pp. 78–85. ACM (2010)
5. Malewicz, G., Austern, M.H., Bik, A.J., Dehnert, J.C., Horn, I., Leiser, N., Czajkowski, G.: Pregel: A system for large-scale graph processing. In: ACM International Conference on the Management of Data (SIGMOD), pp. 135–146. ACM (2010)
6. Tian, Y., Balmin, A., Corsten, S.A., Tatikonda, S., McPherson, J.: From "Think Like a Vertex" to "Think Like a Graph". Proc. of the VLDB (PVLDB) 7(3), 193–204 (2013)
7. Avery, C.: Giraph: Large-scale graph processing infrastructure on hadoop. In: Hadoop Summit (2011)
8. Lumsdaine, A., Gregor, D., Hendrickson, B., Berry, J.: Challenges in parallel graph processing. Parallel Processing Letters 17(01), 5–20 (2007)
9. Buluç, A., Madduri, K.: Parallel breadth-first search on distributed memory systems. In: IEEE/ACM International Conference for High Performance Computing, Networking, Storage and Analysis (SC). ACM (2011)
10. Harshvardhan, Fidel, A., Amato, N.M., Rauchwerger, L.: The STAPL Parallel Graph Library. In: Kasahara, H., Kimura, K. (eds.) LCPC 2012. LNCS, vol. 7760, pp. 46–60. Springer, Heidelberg (2013)
11. Papadimitriou, S., Sun, J.: DisCo: Distributed Co-clustering with Map-Reduce. In: IEEE International Conference on Data Mining, ICDM (2008)
12. Chen, R., Weng, X., He, B., Yang, M.: Large graph processing in the cloud. In: ACM International Conference on the Management of Data (SIGMOD), pp. 1123–1126. ACM (2010)
13. Gerbessiotis, A.V., Valiant, L.G.: Direct bulk-synchronous parallel algorithms. Journal of Parallel and Distributed Computing (JPDC) 22(2), 251–267 (1994)
14. Seo, S., Yoon, E.J., Kim, J., Jin, S., Kim, J.S., Maeng, S.: Hama: An efficient matrix computation with the mapreduce framework. In: IEEE International Conference on Cloud Computing Technology and Science (CloudCom). IEEE (2010)
15. Redekopp, M., Simmhan, Y., Prasanna, V.: Optimizations and analysis of bsp graph processing models on public clouds. In: IEEE Intl. Parallel & Distr. Proc. Symp., IPDPS (2013)
16. Salihoglu, S., Widom, J.: GPS: A Graph Processing System. In: International Conference on Scientific and Statistical Database Management, SSDBM (2013)
17. Low, Y., Bickson, D., Gonzalez, J., Guestrin, C., Kyrola, A., Hellerstein, J.M.: Distributed graphlab: A framework for machine learning and data mining in the cloud. VLDB 5(8), 716–727 (2012)
18. Shao, B., Wang, H., Li, Y.: Trinity: A distributed graph engine on a memory cloud. In: ACM International Conference on the Management of Data, SIGMOD (2013)
19. Karypis, G., Kumar, V.: Analysis of multilevel graph partitioning. In: IEEE/ACM Intl. Conf. for High Performance Computing, Networking, Storage and Analysis, SC (1995)
20. Simmhan, Y., Kumbhare, A., Wickramachari, C.: Floe: A dynamic, continusous dataflow framework for elastic clouds. Technical report, USC (2013)
21. Kang, U., Tsourakakis, C.E., Faloutsos, C.: Pegasus: A peta-scale graph mining system implementation and observations. In: IEEE Intl. Conf. on Data Mining, ICDM (2009)

Resolving Semantic Conflicts in Word Based Software Transactional Memory

Craig Sharp, William Blewitt, and Graham Morgan

Newcastle University, NE1 7RU, UK
{craig.sharp,william.blewitt,graham.morgan}@ncl.ac.uk

Abstract. In this paper we describe a technique for addressing semantic conflicts within word based Software Transactional Memory. A semantic conflict is considered to be some application condition which causes transactions to explicitly abort. Session locking and a companion Contention Management Policy are described which support the parallel exploration of multiple transaction schedules at run time, to resolve semantic conflicts. Performance figures are provided to demonstrate the effectiveness of our technique when semantic conflicts are introduced into established benchmarks.

Keywords: Transactional Memory, Contention Management, Shared Memory, Concurrency Control, STM.

1 Introduction

Software Transactional Memory (STM) has become a popular research area for concurrent programmers given that the STM abstraction offers ease of use in comparison to lock based approaches. More powerfully, composing sections of concurrent code can be achieved with ease using STM unlike a lock-based implementation [1]. At the time of writing, however, there exist a variety of STM implementations with two approaches gaining prominence: object based and word based. Object based STMs [2,3] are generally particular to object orientated languages and represent shared data in the form of *atomic objects*. Conversely, shared data in word based STMs [4,5] is represented at the level of *memory words*.

Felber et al observed in [4] that word based STMs allow transactional accesses to be mapped directly to the underlying memory system. As a result, word based STMs offer: (i) easier integration into existing programming languages and (ii) greater efficiency in the context of compiler support. *TinySTM* [4,6] has been provided as a lightweight and efficient word based STM. The (relatively) small code base makes *TinySTM* particularly attractive for STM development, allowing easy integration with the *STAMP* [7] benchmark suite. For these reasons, the developments in this paper have been integrated into *TinySTM*.

A significant feature of any STM system concerns the handling of aborted transactions under high contention for shared resources due to *concurrent* conflicts on shared data; a task typically delegated to the Contention Management

F. Silva et al. (Eds.): Euro-Par 2014, LNCS 8632, pp. 463–474, 2014.

Policy (CMP). Various CMPs exist to determine which transaction must abort upon a conflict (time-stamp CMP, for instance, gives priority to the transaction that began first). From the perspective of the application, however, there also exist *semantic* conflicts which can be conceived as conditions within the application which prevent a transaction from committing. Figure 1(A) provides an example of a semantic conflict with two threads executing a *withdrawal* and *deposit* transaction concurrently. Let us suppose that there is a concurrent conflict between the *withdrawer* and *depositor* transactions and that the CMP decides to abort the *depositor*. If the *withdrawer* requires that a deposit be made before it can perform the withdrawal, however, then it cannot continue and must (explicitly) abort. Both transactions re-execute until the *depositor* precedes the *withdrawer* (or the CMP aborts the *withdrawer*). If a CMP is employed which resolves conflicts based on transaction starting time or the amount of work completed, it is possible that the *withdrawer* may always succeed in aborting the *depositor* (if the *withdrawer* began before the *depositor* or has carried out more work, for instance).

Primitives exist to provide transaction coordination, which may in turn reduce the occurrence of semantic conflicts (e.g. Harris et al [1] provided primitives such as *retry* and *orElse*). Alternatively, a 'semantic transaction' can be avoided if simply allowed to commit rather than aborting explicitly (assuming no concurrent conflicts have occurred). The programmer may then specify that the transaction execute at some future time. Neither approach, however, alleviates the programmer from the burden of resolving the conflict. Conversely, [8] introduced a new CMP (*Hugh*) which resolves semantic conflicts without placing a burden on the programmer. *Hugh* was integrated with an object based STM and micro-benchmarks demonstrated some encouraging initial results. *Hugh2* has since been implemented with *TinySTM* (a word based STM). [9] describes the process of enabling transaction replication within *TinySTM* and severe implications for memory management are demonstrated (caused by the introduction of semantic conflicts). In this paper the following contributions are provided:

- The implementation of a novel *session* locking technique to resolve semantic conflicts in a manner both decoupled from the programmer and compatible with existing CMPs;
- Performance results showing the impact and resolution of semantic conflicts with several CMPs in large-scale benchmarks (e.g. *STAMP* benchmark suite [7]).

In Section 2 we describe the Implementation of our CMP and Section 3 summarises Related Work. Section 4 provides an Evaluation and, finally, Section 5 concludes the paper and summarises possible avenues for future work.

2   Implementation

2.1   Overview

Hugh2 CMP is activated once some $thread_x$ encounters a semantic conflict (causing $thread_x$ to explicitly abort its transaction). Before the aborted transaction

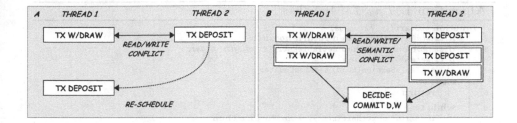

Fig. 1. Scenarios A and B contrast the approaches of a conventional CMP with the *Hugh2* CMP when a semantic conflict occurs

is restarted, *thread$_x$* enters a new *session* mode. During *session* mode, *thread$_x$* re-executes its own transaction in addition to the transactions of any other *session* mode threads. Each *session* mode thread executes a single permutation of transactions, to discover a schedule of transaction execution which resolves the semantic conflict(s). Figure 1(B) shows the re-execution of two transactions accessing a single account (specifically, a *depositor* and *withdrawer* transaction). Thread 2 executes a permutation which succeeds in resolving the semantic conflict (the deposit ensures that the withdrawal can occur).

When there are no further transactions to execute, each thread performs consensus to determine the permutation to be committed. Consensus is managed using a Universal Construction (hereafter UC). The UC is essentially a linked-list, which may be concurrently appended to by threads engaged in *session* mode. Each new entry of the UC identifies the transactions that have been committed during a particular *session*. Once a *session* has terminated each participating thread can determine whether its own transaction was committed or aborted by reading the log of the UC. Those threads whose transactions remain uncommitted perform a new *session*, while the threads of the committed transactions return to non-*session* mode.

2.2 Sessions

Hugh2 attempts to resolve semantic conflicts within the context of a *session*. A non-*session* mode thread will enter *session* mode if: (i) it encounters a semantic conflict while executing a transaction and (ii) it encounters data that is *session* locked while executing a transaction. In addition to the normal structures required by *TinySTM*, the following data structures are required to support *session* execution:

- A global *Transaction Table* is provided where the *n*-th entry into the table belongs to the *n*-th thread in the application. Threads in *session* mode retrieve and execute transactions stored in the table;
- A global UC is provided (a linked list) with a *session* counter (an integer). Each list entry corresponds to a *session* and the *session* counter identifies the

---

Algorithm 1. *TinySTM* Handlers

```
function onStart(tx, ftn, args)
1       if tx.state ≠ started then return nocalltx;
2       if tx.nbAborts = 0 then setTableEntry(tx.id, ftn, args);
3       if tx.sessionMode then
4           setTableSession(tx.id, sessionCounter );
        else
5           return calltx;
6       while true do
7           if (txcall ← getNextTx(tx)) = noMoreTx then
8               if onTimeout(tx) = 0 then break else continue;
9           if consensusReached(sessionNo(tx.id)) then break;
10          Invoke(txcall.ftn, txcall.arg);
11          if onTxSuccess(tx, txcall) = 0 then break;
12      return nocalltx;

function onPreCommit(tx)
13      if tx.state ≠ started then return;
14      logEntry ← UCLogEntry(sessionNo(tx.id));
15      if cas(&logEntry, logEntry, tx.txMask) = fail then
16          tx.state ← lostConsensus;
17          rollback();
        else
18          tx.state ← wonConsensus;

function onCommit(tx)
19      logEntry ← UCLogEntry(sessionNo(tx.id));
20      if tx.state = wonConsensus then
21          atomicIncrement(sessionCounter);
22      tx.state ← started;
23      if bitIsSet(logEntry, tx.id) then
24          tx.sessionMode ← false;
        else
25          rollback();
```

---

current *session*. Every entry contains a bit mask denoting which transactions were committed for that particular *session*;

– Each thread also uses several variables to manage *session* execution including: a flag indicating whether it is in *session* mode, a state variable to hold its progress (which may hold the value: *started*, *lostConsensus* or *wonConsensus*), and a bit mask to record the transactions executed during a *session* (The i-th bit of the mask corresponds to the i-th entry in the *Transaction Table*).

TinySTM allows custom handlers to be called upon the occurrence of several important events during the per-thread execution of a transaction. *Hugh2* is mostly implemented within these handlers, specifically: *onStart*, *onPreCommit*, *onCommit* and *onAbort*. Algorithms 1 and 2 provide the pseudo code:

OnStart performs the iterative execution of transactions when a thread enters *session* mode. When a thread first executes a transaction it inserts the transaction function and argument to the transaction table (line 2). Non *session* mode threads return from the *onStart* handler and executes their transactions normally (line 5). If the thread is in *session* mode, then the thread's table entry is updated to hold the current value of the *session* counter (line 4). Setting the *session* counter acts as a flag which other *session* mode threads can use to determine which transactions can be executed as part of their own *session*. Lines 6 to 11 perform the iterative execution of transactions. The thread first attempts to retrieve a new transaction to execute (line 7). If no more transactions are available, however, the thread calls an *onTimeout* handler (line 8). If the thread has not committed any transactions, it continues reading from the table. Otherwise, the thread breaks out of the loop and returns the *nocalltx* constant (line 12). If consensus has been reached (line 9) or the next transaction is successfully executed and no time remains (line 11), the thread breaks out of the loop and returns *nocalltx* (line 12).

OnPreCommit contains the code where *session* mode threads attempt to decide consensus. The *session*-mode thread invokes *compare-and-swap* (*CAS*) to set the status of the next entry in the UC (line 15). the thread updates its state, depending on the result of the *CAS* call (lines 16 and 18).

OnCommit is called after the *onPreCommit* handler has been invoked. If the calling thread is in *session* mode and it decided the consensus result, then it atomically increments the *session* counter (line 21) indicating to other threads that the *session* has terminated. In line 23, threads check the UC to determine whether their transaction was committed, and if so, the thread leaves *session* mode (line 24), otherwise the thread rolls-back execution and will attempt a new *session* (line 25).

OnAbort is invoked whenever any transaction aborts (see Algorithm 2, line 26). A flag is supplied to the abort handler to identify whether the abort was made implicitly (a concurrent conflict) or explicitly (a semantic conflict). In the case of explicit aborts, the aborting thread sets its *session* mode flag (effectively entering *session* mode).

OnTxSuccess is invoked when a transaction is successfully executed in *session* mode. The thread updates its bit mask (line 28), and decrements a private counter (line 29). If the counter has reached 0, the *onTimeout* handler is invoked (line 29). Threads invokes *onTimeout* (line 27) to determine whether they should continue executing transactions in the transaction table, or perform the *onPreCommit* handler (thus attempting consensus).

2.3   Session Locks

As with conventional *TinySTM*, locking is used to guarantee consistent reading and writing of shared data (*TinySTM* provides both read and write locks). To accommodate our CMP, however, we have added an extra type of lock, called a *session* lock, with the following properties:

- Once locked, a *session lock* grants access to a word of shared data for *any* thread operating in the same *session*, hence a *session lock* is locked only once per *session*;

– A *session lock* is never explicitly unlocked. A *session lock* has a viable lifetime for the duration of the *session* in which it was locked. Once the *session* has ended, the *session* lock is considered *stale* and may be removed at
the discretion of any encountering thread.

Algorithm 2. *TinySTM* and Session Lock Handlers

> **function** onAbort(*tx, explicit*)
> 26   if *explicit = true* **then** *tx.sessionMode ← true*;
>
> **function** onTimeout(*tx*)
> 27   **if** commitCount(*tx.txMask*) > 0 **then return** 0;
>   **else return** (*tx.counter ← newLimit*);
>
> **function** onTxSuccess(*tx, txcall*)
> 28   setBit(*tx.txMask, txcall.id*);
> 29   **if** decrement(*tx.counter*) = 0 **then return** onTimeout(*tx*);
> 30   **return** *tx.counter*;
>
> **function** onSharedAccess(*tx, lock*)
> 31   *ctr ←* sessionCounter;
> 32   **if** ¬*tx.sessionMode* **then**
> 33   **if** ¬sessionLocked(*lock*) **then return** *proceed*;
> 34   **if** *ctr ≠* sessionNo(*lock*) **then return** *stale*;
> 35   *tx.sessionMode ← true*;
> 36   **return** *killself*;
>
>   **if** consensusReached(sessionNo(*tx.id*)) **then return** *killself*;
>   **if** ¬sessionLocked(*lock*) **then return** *proceed*;
> 37   **if** *nextctr ≠* sessionNo(*lock*) **then return** *stale*;
> 38   **return** *sessionLocked*;
>
> **function** onLock(*tx, lock, accessResult, accessType*)
> 39   **if** ¬*tx.sessionMode* **then**
> 40   *lockval ←* createTinyStmLock(*lock, accessType*);
> 41   **return** (cas(*lock.addr, lock.val, lockval*) = success);
>
> 42   **if** *accessResult = sessionLocked* **then return** true;
> 43   *nextctr ←* sessionCounter;
> 44   *sLockValue ←* createSessionLock(*nextctr*);
> 45   **return** (cas(*lock.addr, lock.val, sLockVal*) = success);

In *TinySTM*, a lock is represented by a word-sized integer, with the value of
the last two bits denoting the type of lock (binary 0 is unlocked, 1 denotes *write*
locked and 2 denotes *read* locked). A *session* lock is represented by setting both
bits. The remaining bits of the word value hold the *session* number in which the
lock was set. Algorithm 2 (lines 31-45) shows two handlers which are invoked
when dealing with *session* locks:

OnSharedAccess is called before a shared word is locked for reading or writing.
Non *session* mode threads may attempt to lock shared data which is not *session* locked (line 33) or if the *session* lock is stale (line 34). Otherwise the thread
enters *session* mode (line 35) and aborts (line 36). Threads in *session* mode,
however, can attempt access of shared data as long as the *session* is still active.

OnLock is called whenever a thread attempts to lock shared data (lines 39-45).
Non *session* mode threads create a normal *TinySTM* type lock and attempt

to lock the data (line 41) while *session* mode threads can immediately access *session* locked data (line 42). If the shared word is not *session* locked, then a *session* mode thread must attempt to lock the data (line 45).

3   Related Work

A range of CMPs currently exist but which can be categorised as either wait based and schedule-based. Wait-based CMPs [10,11] (e.g. *Greedy*, *Karma*, *Polka* etc), are typically trivial to implement, versatile and offer good performance. Heber et al, however, noted in [12] an inefficiency with wait-based approaches due to the difficulty in finding an adequate back-off period, given the dynamic nature of execution in STMs. Conversely, schedule-based CMPs typically reschedule or serialise aborted transactions. [13] exemplifies one such approach. Bai et al produced several 'transaction executor' models with the aim of equitably distributing transactions as 'jobs' among the threads of an application. 'Keys' are also used to predict the likelihood that conflicts will arise between executing transactions. Transactions which are likely to conflict are scheduled to be executed by the same 'worker' thread (thus enforcing serialisation).

CAR-STM [14] and Steal on Abort [15] are also schedule-based CMPs where transactional jobs are assigned to per-thread work queues. Both CAR-STM and Steal on Abort move aborted transactions to the work queues of conflicting transactions upon the occurrence of a conflict, to serialise the conflicting transaction's execution. Steal on Abort experiments with various techniques when rescheduling transactions among work queues. Additional work queues can also be created when the number of transactional jobs is high. *Hugh2* differs from the cited approaches of both wait-based and schedule-based CMPs, insofar as *Hugh2* is the only approach which focuses on the resolution of semantic conflicts. In addition, *Hugh2* requires a single transaction table to hold transactional jobs, but does not require the overhead of a thread pool to administer such jobs. *Hugh2* also explores multiple schedules in parallel during the process of contention management.

Similarly with *Hugh2*, several approaches to STM have been developed which rely on a Universal Construction (UC). Herlihy [16] introduced the UC concept to enable multiple threads to access shared data structures via a wait-free algorithm. Wamhoff [17] and Chuong [18] combined the UC technique with transactions to handle certain failure conditions. Crain et al have shown that it is possible to remove the abort semantics of STM using a UC [19]. While the cited approaches apply the UC technique for a STM system, *Hugh2* uses the UC for contention management.

Finally, TL-STM [20] is an adaptation of *SwissTm* which incorporates Thread-Level-Speculation (TLS) into memory transactions. TL-STM bears similarity to *Hugh2* insofar that platform parallelism is exploited to explore different permutations of transactional elements. More specifically, TL-STM seeks to enhance transactional throughput by reordering the internal execution elements of a transaction to better reflect concurrent schedules of execution. Conversely,

Hugh2 seeks to reorder whole transactions to accommodate semantic schedules of execution. Whereas TL-STM applies *internal reordering* based on the semantics of a transaction, *Hugh2* applies *external reordering* based on the semantics of an application.

4   Evaluation

In this section we present results from a series of benchmarks to demonstrate the performance of our system. The tests were carried out on a desktop PC featuring 2 x dual-core 3.07GHz Intel(R) processors with 4GB of RAM. The Operating System used was Ubuntu (Linux) version 13.04 and the Transactional Memory software was *TinySTM* version 1.04 with the Write-Back, Eager Transactional Locking scheme using visible reads. Experiments were carried out with increasing numbers of threads (from 2 to 16) with each run executed 5 times with the average results provided. Two existing CMPs were used as a measure of comparison with *Hugh2*, specifically *Karma* and *Polka* [11].

Two benchmarks were used to test the performance of *Hugh2*. The first scenario (*bank*) is provided in the *TinySTM* software and allows the execution of a number of transaction types on a set of simulated bank accounts. The 'bank' in this case is an array of account data structures. The second scenario (*vacation*) is part of the *STAMP* benchmark suite [7] and provides transactional accesses over several red-black trees to represent a holiday booking database system. Both scenarios provide update, read-all and write-all transaction types which can be generated at varying intensities. Transactions from the *vacation* scenario differ from the *bank* simulation insofar as they tend to execute more statements of greater complexity.

Semantic transactions were introduced into *bank* and *vacation*. In the *bank* scenario, two extra transactions (called *service charge* and *pay interest*) were created which explicitly call abort based on the balance of certain bank accounts. In the *vacation* scenario an additional red-black tree was created and two transaction types (called *create customer* and *remove customer*) which add and remove nodes while explicitly aborting if the contents of the tree is deemed incorrect. The semantic transactions introduce a consumer-producer relationship where a producer transaction should precede a consumer to grant mutual success. The semantic transactions interact with numerous other shared data elements, so it is expected that if semantic transactions must abort frequently, this activity will also increase the frequency of concurrent conflicts. Increasing the number of semantic transactions in a scenario means we can measure the impact of semantic conflicts on the application (for example, we might set up a scenario with 16 threads and specify that 8 of the threads execute semantic transactions to observe the effects of 50% semantic conflicts on the throughput of the application).

4.1   Transaction Throughput

Figure 2 provides graphs showing results for transaction throughput. Y-axes shows the number of transactions committed per second and X-axes show the

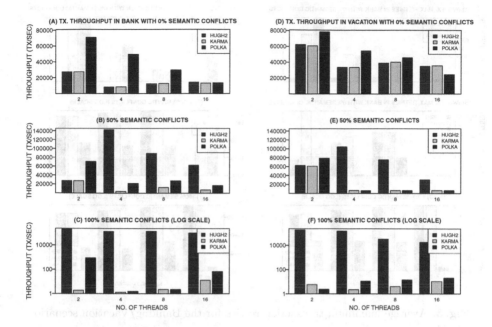

Fig. 2. Average transaction throughput for the Bank/Vacation scenario

number of threads used. Graphs 2(A) and 2(D) provide comparison between the *Karma*, *Polka* and *Hugh2* CMPs in the absence of semantic conflicts, for the *bank* and *vacation* scenarios respectively. The system which employs *Hugh2* for semantic conflicts, resorts to calling the *Karma* on occurrence of concurrent conflicts. As expected, with no semantic conflicts being generated in either graph, the performance of *Hugh2* and *Karma* are practically the same.

In Graphs 2(B) and 2(E) semantic conflicts have been introduced into both scenarios such that 50% of the threads generate semantic transactions in the case of thread numbers: 4, 8 and 16[1]. At this point the throughput for *Karma* and *Polka* have both fallen noticeably relative to the throughput for *Hugh2* which has increased substantially. In Graphs 2(C) and 2(F), semantic transactions are generated by 100% of the threads; once again the throughput for both *Karma* and *Polka* has reduced dramatically, whereas *Hugh2* outperforms both.

When comparing the *vacation* scenario to the *bank* scenario we can see that the *Polka* CMP mostly outperforms both the *Karma* and *Hugh2* CMPs when semantic conflicts are absent, and indeed, *Karma* CMP and has been cited as providing the best average performance of wait-based CMPs [15] (one notable exception, however, is in the *vacation* scenario when 16 threads are used). It is encouraging, however, to see that *Hugh2* can function in combination with an

---

[1] Two or more threads are required to resolve semantic conflicts (i.e. a producer and consumer). To show 50% semantic conflicts therefore requires at least four or more threads. The results for 2 threads show 0% semantic conflicts instead.

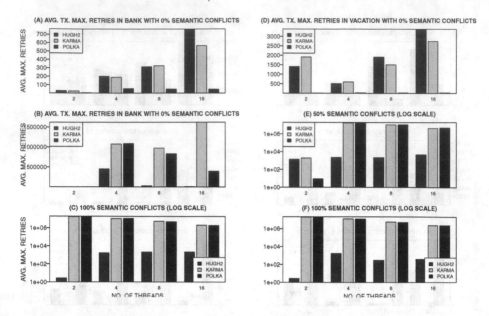

Fig. 3. Average maximum transaction retries for the Banking/Vacation scenario

existing CMP (in this case Karma), without degrading the performance with respect to resolving concurrent conflicts. Conversely, as semantic conflicts are introduced, neither *Karma* or *Polka* can approach the effectiveness of *Hugh2* in terms of transaction throughput. Although *Polka* almost always produces a higher throughput than *Karma*, neither approach maintains good performance when semantic conflicts are present (regardless of scenario). Throughput also diminishes for *Hugh2*, in the case of 50% semantic conflicts and to a lesser extent with 100% semantic conflicts. This suggests that the greater occurrence of threads producing concurrent conflicts has a negative impact on *Hugh2*.

4.2 Maximum Transaction Retries

Figure 3 presents results showing the average maximum retries for a transaction during the *bank* and *vacation* scenarios respectively. The format of the graphs in Figure 3 mirrors the previous results for transaction throughput with the exception that the Y-axis now shows average retries. A higher average number of retries is indicative of threads experiencing difficulty in resolving semantic conflicts. Hence, we expected that the average maximum retries should increase in tandem with an increase in semantic conflicts for the *Polka* and *Karma* managers, whereas this should not be the case for the *Hugh2* CMP.

Graphs 3(A) and 3(D) provide comparison between the *Karma*, *Polka* and *Hugh2* CMPs when no semantic conflicts are present. As expected, *Polka* CMP produces the smallest average maximum retries (graphs 2(A) and 2(D) have already shown that *Polka* produces the highest throughput in the absence of semantic conflicts). In Graphs 3(B) and 3(E), however, semantic conflicts have been introduced at a rate of 50% (half the threads in the scenario generate semantic transactions in the case of thread numbers: 4, 8 and 16). A substantial increase in average maximum transaction retries is now observable in all CMPs, although *Hugh2* produces the best performance.

In Graphs 3(C) and 3(F), semantic transactions are being created by 100% of threads. Once again the average maximum number of retries has increased for both *Karma* and *Polka* CMPs. In the case of *Hugh2*, the average maximum has fallen, with neither *Karma* or *Polka* tackling semantic conflicts more effectively than *Hugh2*. In addition, there is only a negligible difference in performance between *Polka* and *Karma* (suggesting that neither policy is more effective at resolving semantic conflicts).

5   Conclusion

This paper presents *Hugh2*, a CMP which deals with semantic conflicts via the speculative execution of aborted transactions. We have described how *Hugh2* can be integrated with a word based STM using a new *session* locking mechanism. Two substantial benchmarks demonstrated performance improvements once semantic conflicts are introduced. Given that *Hugh2* can be incorporated with any existing CMP, it would be interesting to test the performance of *Hugh2* against a wider range of CMPs. In addition, incorporating semantic conflicts into the remaining STAMP benchmarks may be useful in order to observe how semantic conflicts affect a diverse range of scenarios.

Going forward, we believe the *session* lock mechanism raises some exciting possibilities for exploring our work within a distributed STM application. In particular, *session* locks may provide a greater scalability in the context of DSTM, given *session* locks may be shared across threads and need not be explicitly unlocked.

References

1. Harris, T., Marlow, S., Peyton-Jones, S., Herlihy, M.: Composable memory transactions. In: Proceedings of the Tenth ACM SIGPLAN Symposium on Principles and Practice of Parallel Programming, pp. 48–60. ACM (2005)
2. Riegel, T., Felber, P., Fetzer, C.: A lazy snapshot algorithm with eager validation. In: Dolev, S. (ed.) DISC 2006. LNCS, vol. 4167, pp. 284–298. Springer, Heidelberg (2006)
3. Herlihy, M., Luchangco, V., Moir, M.: A flexible framework for implementing software transactional memory. In: ACM SIGPLAN Notices, vol. 41, pp. 253–262. ACM (2006)
4. Felber, P., Fetzer, C., Riegel, T.: Dynamic performance tuning of word-based software transactional memory. In: Proceedings of the 13th ACM SIGPLAN Symposium on Principles and Practice of Parallel Programming, pp. 237–246. ACM (2008)

5. Dragojević, A., Guerraoui, R., Kapalka, M.: Stretching transactional memory. In: ACM Sigplan Notices, vol. 44, pp. 155–165. ACM (2009)
6. Felber, P., Fetzer, C., Marlier, P., Riegel, T.: Time-based software transactional memory. IEEE Transactions on Parallel and Distributed Systems 21(12), 1793–1807 (2010)
7. Minh, C.C., Chung, J., Kozyrakis, C., Olukotun, K.: Stamp: Stanford transactional applications for multi-processing. In: IEEE International Symposium on Workload Characterization, IISWC 2008, pp. 35–46. IEEE (2008)
8. Sharp, C., Morgan, G.: Hugh: A semantically aware universal construction for transactional memory systems. In: Wolf, F., Mohr, B., an Mey, D. (eds.) Euro-Par 2013. LNCS, vol. 8097, pp. 470–481. Springer, Heidelberg (2013)
9. Sharp, C., Morgan, G.: Introducing semantic conflict resolution to word based software transactional memory. Technical report, 10 p. Newcastle University, UK (2014)
10. Guerraoui, R., Herlihy, M., Pochon, B.: Towards a theory of transactional contention managers. In: Annual ACM Symposium on Principles of Distributed Computing: Proceedings of the Twenty-fifth Annual ACM Symposium on Principles of Distributed Computing, vol. 23, pp. 316–317 (2006)
11. Scherer III, W.N., Scott, M.L.: Advanced contention management for dynamic software transactional memory. In: Proceedings of the Twenty-fourth Annual ACM Symposium on Principles of Distributed Computing, pp. 240–248. ACM (2005)
12. Heber, T., Hendler, D., Suissa, A.: On the impact of serializing contention management on stm performance. Journal of Parallel and Distributed Computing (2012)
13. Bai, T., Shen, X., Zhang, C., Scherer, W., Ding, C., Scott, M.: A key-based adaptive transactional memory executor. In: IEEE International Parallel and Distributed Processing Symposium, IPDPS 2007, pp. 1–8. IEEE (2007)
14. Dolev, S., Hendler, D., Suissa, A.: Car-stm: Scheduling-based collision avoidance and resolution for software transactional memory. In: Proceedings of the Twenty-seventh ACM Symposium on Principles of Distributed Computing, pp. 125–134. ACM (2008)
15. Ansari, M., Luján, M., Kotselidis, C., Jarvis, K., Kirkham, C., Watson, I.: Steal-on-abort: Improving transactional memory performance through dynamic transaction reordering. In: Seznec, A., Emer, J., O'Boyle, M., Martonosi, M., Ungerer, T. (eds.) HiPEAC 2009. LNCS, vol. 5409, pp. 4–18. Springer, Heidelberg (2009)
16. Herlihy, M.: Wait-free synchronization. ACM Transactions on Programming Languages and Systems (TOPLAS) 13(1), 124–149 (1991)
17. Wamhoff, J., Fetzer, C.: The universal transactional memory construction. Technical report, 12 p. University of Dresden, Germany (2010)
18. Chuong, P., Ellen, F., Ramachandran, V.: A universal construction for wait-free transaction friendly data structures. In: Proceedings of the 22nd ACM Symposium on Parallelism in Algorithms and Architectures, pp. 335–344. ACM (2010)
19. Crain, T., Imbs, D., Raynal, M.: Towards a universal construction for transaction-based multiprocess programs. In: Bononi, L., Datta, A.K., Devismes, S., Misra, A. (eds.) ICDCN 2012. LNCS, vol. 7129, pp. 61–75. Springer, Heidelberg (2012)
20. Barreto, J., Dragojevic, A., Ferreira, P., Filipe, R., Guerraoui, R.: Unifying thread-level speculation and transactional memory. In: Narasimhan, P., Triantafillou, P. (eds.) Middleware 2012. LNCS, vol. 7662, pp. 187–207. Springer, Heidelberg (2012)

Automatic Tuning of the Parallelism Degree in Hardware Transactional Memory*

Diego Rughetti[1], Paolo Romano[2], Francesco Quaglia[1], and Bruno Ciciani[1]

[1] Sapienza Universita' di Roma, Italy
[2] Instituto Superior Técnico, Universidade de Lisboa/INESC-ID, Portugal

Abstract. Transactional Memory (TM) is an emerging paradigm that promises to ease the development of parallel applications. Due to its inherently speculative nature, however, TM can suffer of performance degradations in presence of conflict intensive workloads.

A key technique to tackle this issue consists in dynamically regulating the number of concurrent threads, which allows for selecting the concurrency level that best fits the intrinsic parallelism of specific applications. In this area, several self-tuning approaches have been proposed for Software-based implementations of TM (STM). In this paper we investigate the effectiveness of these techniques when applied to Hardware TM (HTM), a theme that is particularly relevant and timely given the recent integration of hardware supports for TM in next generation of mainstream Intel processors. Our study, conducted on Intel's implementation of HTM, identifies several issues associated with the employment of techniques originally conceived for STM. Motivated by these findings, we propose an innovative machine learning based technique explicitly designed to take into account peculiarities of HTM systems, and demonstrate its advantages, in terms of higher accuracy and shorter learning times, using the STAMP benchmark suite.

1 Introduction

Transactional Memory (TM) [12,20] is an attractive programming paradigm for developing parallel/concurrent applications. By relying on the notion of atomic transaction, TM stands as a simper alternative to traditional lock-based synchronization. In more detail, with TM code blocks accessing shared-data can be marked as transactions. The complexity associated with enforcing coherency of concurrent data accesses is then delegated to the TM layer, rather than to any hand crafted synchronization scheme defined by the programmer. The maturing of the intense research that targeted TM over the last decade has recently led to the development of TM supports for the most popular open source compiler (GCC), and to the integration of hardware implementations of TM (HTM) in the last generations of processors produced by major vendors, such as Intel or IBM.

Even though TM shows a big potential for simplifying the software development process, another aspect that is central for the success of TM systems is the actual level

* This work was supported by national funds through FCT (Fundação para a Ciência e Tecnologia) under project PEst-OE/EEI/LA0021/2013, by the COST Action IC1001 Euro-TM and by project GreenTM EXPL/EEI-ESS/0361/2013.

F. Silva et al. (Eds.): Euro-Par 2014, LNCS 8632, pp. 475–486, 2014.

of performance they can deliver. In such a context, one core issue to cope with is related to maximize parallelism, while avoiding thrashing phenomena due to excessive data contention and high transaction abort rates.

For the case of Software-based implementations of TM (STM), several approaches have been proposed to cope with thrashing avoidance (see, e.g., [5,18,1,2,23]). One of the key techniques exploited in these approaches consists in (dynamically) regulating the actual level of concurrency, i.e. the number of concurrently active threads. All these approaches rely on performance models (either white-box, e.g. analytic [18,5], or black-box, e.g. machine-learning [1]), which are used to predict the expected performance, depending on the application's workload, while varying the number of threads.

On the other hand, we are not aware of any study in literature that investigates the issue of how to optimize the degree of parallelism in HTM systems. In this paper we aim to fill this gap, whose relevance is particularly strong given the recent integration of HTM in mainstream processors. We start by showing that the problem cannot be effectively addressed by reusing techniques originally conceived to operate in STM contexts, due to two key reasons:

1. Existing techniques targeting STM rely on models that do not consider transaction abort causes that are specific to HTM, and that are completely absent in STM systems. Particularly, in HTM a large number of transaction aborts is due to capacity constraints of processors' caches, as well as to a plethora of different microarchitectural reasons [13] (e.g. interrupts, faults or traps).
2. STM-oriented approaches are typically based on software instrumentation and runtime monitoring of specific parameters (whose values serve as input to instantiate performance models aimed to guide concurrency optimization). Monitoring these same parameters in the context of HTM is however unaffordable: existing HTM implementations do not externalize them, and monitoring them at the software level would induce overheads analogous to those of implementing an STM, defeating the whole purpose of HTM.

In the light of these considerations, this paper makes an additional contribution, by proposing a novel machine learning based technique to dynamically adapt the concurrency degree of HTM-based applications. The proposed self-tuning mechanism is explicitly designed to take into account the peculiarities of HTM systems, and avoids the issues that affect existing STM-oriented solutions. Via an extensive experimental evaluation based on the well known STAMP benchmark suite [14], and on a HTM-equipped Intel Haswell processor (8 virtual cores - 4 physical with hyper-threading), we show that the proposed approach achieves, on average, twice the accuracy of existing methods, while imposing negligible overheads and abating learning times dramatically.

The remainder of this paper is structured as follows. Section 2 discusses the state of the art on adaptive solutions for TM systems. In Section 3, we discuss issues associated with the employment, in the context of HTM, of solutions originally designed to self-tune the degree of parallelism in STM. Section 4 presents the proposed solution for optimizing the parallelism level in HTM applications. Section 5 presents the results of the experimental evaluation based on the STAMP benchmark. Finally, Section 6 concludes the paper.

2 Related Work

Several analytical models of STM [17,11] have been presented in literature. These models adopt a white-box approach to capture execution dynamics of STM and allow for predicting applications' performance in different configurations. Employing these techniques for the self-tuning of HTM systems is however infeasible for several of reasons. First, as they rely on white-box models tailored to STM, they fail to capture important peculiar aspects of HTM, in particular aborts induced by hardware-imposed restrictions. Further, these solutions typically require extensive instrumentation to gather a large set of parameters that serve as input for the white-box performance prediction model. Such instrumentation is not supported by existing HTM, and implementing it via software would induce unaffordable overheads, as we will also show in Section 3.

Other works have been based on black-box approaches, relying on various types of statistical/machine learning techniques to capture STM performance trends. These include techniques based on fitting to predetermined families of functions [8,16], or more generic regressors such as neural networks [15] and decision trees [5]. As we will discuss in more detail in the next section, employing these techniques in HTM systems would induce prohibitive instrumentation overheads. Also, being designed to operate in STM environments, the input parameters used by these models turn out to be inadequate to capture the proper dynamics of HTM.

Other black-box approaches adopt a model-free feedback-based method, implementing hill-climbing techniques that adapt the parallelism degree by reacting to variations of some key performance indicator, such as throughput [4] or abort rate [1]. Due to their model-free/exploratory nature, these approaches suffer of two main issues: slow convergence to the optimal solution [19], and risk of being trapped in local maxima.

Another related topic is transaction scheduling [23,9], in which the mapping of transactions to threads is dynamically adapted in order to minimize data contention. Such a technique has the effect of adapting the degree of parallelism, because rescheduled threads are removed from the execution for a while. Existing scheduling techniques employ different types of information, ranging from high level statistics on the abort ratio [23], to details on transaction's readset and writeset [9]. As already discussed, obtaining information on transactions' data access patterns is not feasible with existing HTM implementations.

Other related works, exploit machine learning to optimize orthogonal configuration parameters of STM, such as selecting the best performing conflict detection and management algorithm [22] or the most suitable mapping of threads to CPU-cores [3].

Our work is also related to recent research in the area of performance evaluation of HTM, both for Intel [7,10] and IBM implementations [21]. To the best of our knowledge, the only existing work in the area of self-tuning for HTM [6] copes with an issue orthogonal to the one tackled in this work, namely the tuning of the retry logic and fall-back path.

3 Concurrency Regulation Approaches: STM vs HTM

In this section we assess the effectiveness of existing approaches for self-tuning the degree of parallelism of STM, when employed in the context of HTM. We focus our study on model-based approaches that rely on machine learning [15,16]. This choice is motivated by the fact that, as discussed in Section 2, we are not aware of any analytical model capable of predicting the performance of HTM. Also, model-based approaches are known to achieve faster convergence than model-free ones [19], and avoid the issue of getting stuck in local maxima.

The performance models adopted in these approaches [15,16] aim at predicting the transaction wasted time (namely the CPU time spent in the execution of transaction instances that are eventually aborted) as a function of the number of concurrent threads. These models take as input a set of parameters, some of which are used to capture the data access pattern, and provide in output the expected wasted time. Specifically, these models can be seen as implementing the following function:

$$w_{time} = f(rs_{size}, ws_{size}, rw_{aff}, ww_{aff}, t_{time}, ntc_{time}, k) \qquad (1)$$

where k denotes the number of concurrent threads supposed to run the application, w_{time} is the average transaction wasted time, rs_{size} (resp. ws_{size}) is the average read-set (resp. write-set) size of transactions, rw_{aff} – read-write affinity (resp. ww_{aff} – write-write affinity) is an index providing an estimation of the likelihood that an object read (resp. written) by a transaction is also written by another transaction, t_{time} is the average execution time of the committed transaction runs, and ntc_{time} is the average execution time of non-transactional code blocks. As for the latter parameter, it is typical for TM applications interleave, in the same thread, the execution of transactional and non-transactional code blocks. The non-transactional blocks are typically used for tasks such as the interaction with an external user/application and/or the acquisition of input parameters for the transaction to be run.

In the solutions in [15,16] the shape of the function f is determined either by fitting data in the training set using generic neural networks, or by using a specialized family of analytical functions (which is used to build sub-functions whose composition determines the actual shape of f). In both cases, the predicted value of the transaction wasted time is used to compute the value of the expression $k/(w_{time}+t_{time}+ntc_{time})$, which represents the system throughput, and so to predict the value of k that is expected to maximize the throughput.

As pointed out before, both approaches rely on the run-time monitoring of the input parameters of function f. This is requested both for the initial model instantiation phase, as well as for performance prediction and concurrency regulation (once the application is already deployed). Particularly, the run-time monitoring of rs_{size}, ws_{size}, rw_{aff} and ww_{aff} allows for determining whether workload shifts occur, which may require a change of the parallelism degree k in order to ensure optimal performance.

These approaches adopt a further refinement of the performance model, which takes into account the fact that, besides w_{time}, also t_{time} and ntc_{time} can actually vary significantly with k. This phenomenon is imputable to hardware level contention, such as cross-core cache contention at lower cache-levels in the multi-core architecture. Hence, the observed values of t_{time} and ntc_{time} cannot be immediately used as input to the function f when carrying out predictions with values of k different from the ones used when those values were observed. Rather, *correction functions* are used to predict the values of t_{time} and ntc_{time} in the target configuration of the parallelism level for which

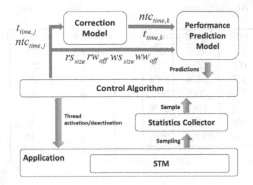

Fig. 1. STM-oriented concurrency regulation architecture

estimation is being carried out. These correction functions are typically much simpler than f (in fact, they are often linear), and have been shown to be identifiable in various ways, e.g., via a simple polynomial regression approach [16]. Overall, the final equation used for dynamically computing the best suited parallelism level, via maximization vs the value of k, is

$$\frac{k}{w_{time,k} + t_{time,k} + ntc_{time,k}} \qquad (2)$$

where the subscript 'k' exactly expresses the above depicted parameter dependency (also involving t_{time} and ntc_{time}). The architecture that has been proposed for exploiting the above model in order to dynamically regulate concurrency in STM systems is schematized in Figure 1.

When porting the above approaches (that are naturally conceived for STM) on top of HTM-based systems, the following two issues arise:

1. *Monitoring overhead* - tracing the features to be used as input to the performance model in Eq. 1 would be too costly in HTM. Specifically, obtaining information on readset/writeset size would require instrumenting every single transactional operation, paying a cost analogous to the one paid when handling transactional accesses via software techniques (just like in STM). Also, the relative cost for computing parameters like rw_{aff} and ww_{aff} (which are based on the scalar product of relative read/write access rates to individual transactional objects kept by the TM) would dominate, when compared to the actual transaction processing time in HTM based systems. These overheads would hinder performance severely, especially when considering that the key advantage of HTM systems is to avoid any cost related to additional software instrumentation.

2. *Inadequacy of the input features* - as already mentioned, a key difference between STM and HTM is that, in the former, data conflicts are the unique source of transaction aborts. In fact, the input parameters for Eq. 1, used as the base performance model by the works in [15,16], are targeted to characterise the data access profile as the unique cause for transaction aborts, and do not capture the dynamics of aborts due to architectural constraints. As shown in Table 1, this kind of aborts actually represents the dominant source of aborts for all the STAMP benchmark applications.

Table 1. Abort reasons

Benchmark	conflict	capacity	other
vacation	1%	41%	58%
kmeans	0%	2%	98%
genome	1%	35%	64%
intruder	1%	40%	59%
labyrinth	0%	79%	21%
ssca2	0%	2%	98%
yada	34%	37%	29%

Table 2. Sampling overhead

Conc. level	kmeans	intruder	genome
1	2%	3%	3%
2	2%	4%	3,5%
3	3%	1,3%	3,5%
4	2%	1,8%	1,3%
5	4%	0,1%	3,5%
6	3,5%	0,1%	3%
7	1,6%	0,1%	3,5%
8	4,5%	4,5%	1,7%

Hence, the need for devising models capable of explicitly capturing these phenomena, and to overcome the inadequacy of existing STM-oriented models.

These considerations led us to reconsider the set of input parameters to be used in the performance model, and to investigate on the ability of the following variant of the model to capture the dynamics proper of HTM:

$$w_{time} = f(t_{time}, ntc_{time}, abort_{conflict}, abort_{capacity}, abort_{other}, k) \qquad (3)$$

where t_{time} and ntc_{time} have the already explained meaning, whereas the explanation of the other parameters is the following: $abort_{conflict}$ is the abort rate due to data-conflict, $abort_{capacity}$ is the abort rate due to overflows of cache capacity, and $abort_{other}$ is the abort rate due to other architectural reasons.

We evaluated this approach considering an instantiation of Eq. 3 based on neural networks, and two alternative instantiations of the correction function for t_{time} and ntc_{time}, one using linear regression and the other using again neural networks (NN). We refer to the whole approach as 2-layered, due to the presence of the correction function. Table 3 shows the discrepancy in the throughput (compared to the optimal throughput, statically determined by exploring all the concurrency levels between 1 and 8 for all the different phases of each benchmark run) which is achieved by regulating concurrency via the reliance on the model in Eq. 3. Instead, in Table 2 we report the run-time monitoring overhead for sampling the input parameters of the performance model as the number of thread varies (again between 1 and 8). We can see that the sampling overhead is very limited, confirming the adequacy of our choice in relation to the input features for the performance model in Eq. 3, from the perspective of efficiency. Concerning effectiveness while regulating concurrency, which is a reflection of the performance model accuracy, the results are less exciting, with errors (expressed in terms of throughput penalty with respect to the optimal achievable throughput) of up to 18% for the approach using linear regression, and 15% for the one using neural networks.

The key reason for this is that, contrary to the base performance model developed for STM (expressed by Eq. 1), in the proposed model for HTM in Eq. 3, all the input parameters may exhibit a dependency on the level of parallelism. So specific correction functions should be used for each of them (which might exhibit non-linear shape), increasing significantly the complexity of the approach, and ultimately degrading its accuracy. In order to back this claim, in the third column of Table 3 we provide data related to the performance that could be reached by the 2-layered approach if a set of

Table 3. Throughput penalty with the 2-layered approach

Benchmark	2-layered-linear	2-layered-NN	2-layered-optimal
intruder	8%	$6,3\%$	$3,2\%$
genome	10%	$4,4\%$	$2,7\%$
kmeans	18%	15%	$5,6\%$
vacation	18%	14%	$3,4\%$
ssca2	$0,80\%$	$0,74\%$	$0,55\%$
yada	0%	0%	0%
labyrinth	10%	9%	$3,2\%$

optimal correction functions for input parameters were available. As we can see comparing the third column with the first two, the performance delivered by the 2-layered approach strictly depends on the accuracy of the correction functions.

4   A Classification Based Approach

In order to cope with the issues pointed out in the previous section, we worked on an alternative way of approaching the problem of instantiating the performance model used to guide the adaptation of the concurrency level. To this end, we cast the performance prediction problem as a classification, and not a regression, problem. Specifically, given a workload profile, instead of predicting the system performance for every possible concurrency level (and then picking the optimal one), we aim to determine directly the optimal parallelism level, among the (finite set of) possible ones.

In this way we operate according to a "1-step" approach that does not require the use of correction functions, which were shown to be the Achilles' heel of existing approaches in Section 3. We decided to use and compare two different machine learning approaches to cope with this classification problem: Decision Trees and Neural Networks. However, as we will see in Section 5, both the algorithms provide very similar accuracy levels.

The fulcrum of the new approach is the construction of the training set for the classification algorithms. Particularly, each sample we relied on is a couple $< \mathbf{i}, \mathbf{o} >$ where $\mathbf{i} = [t_{time}, ntc_{time}, abort_{conflict}, abort_{capacity}, abort_{other}]$ and $\mathbf{o} = [k_{opt}]$, with k_{opt} representing the optimal level of parallelism, namely the concurrency level that ensures the best throughput given the workload profile expressed by $\mathbf{i}$.

The training set can be populated by executing a few runs of the application with different inputs and configuration parameters. For each input, the application is executed for any level of parallelism, namely varying the number of threads from 1 to the maximum number of hardware-threads supported by the target system. This way, for each workload/configuration tested during the training phase, it is always possible to determine the best performing concurrency level.

As we will show in Section 5, the new approach achieves consistently better accuracy than the 2-layered approach based on the performance model expressed by Eq. 3, namely the variation of the STM performance model originally exploited in [15,16]. Further, a relevant advantage of the new approach, beyond its higher accuracy, consists of its simplicity. On the other hand, a drawback with respect to the 2-layered approach, is that it does not allow to estimate the absolute performance achievable when using a degree of parallelism not considered in the training phase, which could be instead useful, for instance, to support what-if analysis. This aspect is inter-twinned with, e.g., provisioning processes in the Cloud, since what-if analysis with non-observed parallelism levels may lead to planning for provisioning adequately powerful multi-core machines (or scaling up/down already in use resources) in order to meet specific performance levels (while optimizing the costs). On the other hand, the new 1-step approach based on classification is targeted at optimizing the application run-time in scenarios where the available resources (and hence the set of possible parallelism levels for the hosted application) are known and could be tested during the training phase used to instantiate the performance model. Note that this is a means for optimizing already done investments.

5   Experimental Results

In this section we report experimental data for a comparison between the 2-layered approach derived by adapting the proposals in [16], [15] and the new classification based approach. We executed our tests on top of system equipped with an Intel Haswell Xeon E3-1275 3,5 GHz processor (8 virtual cores: 4 physical with hyper-treading[1]) with 32 GB RAM. Intel TSX extension (i.e., Intel's implementation of HTM) requires that a software-based fall-back method is specified, in case a transaction cannot be executed in hardware. In the evaluation we consider a fall-back path based on a single global lock. We keep on relying on the STAMP benchmark suite [14] also in this comparative study.

Let us start by analyzing the results considering the usage of a global lock on the fall-back path. Table 4 shows the mean penalty, with respect to the optimal throughput, due to wrong concurrency level choices. The first and the second columns report results for the classification approach implemented resp. with decision trees and neural networks. The third and fourth columns show results for the 2-layered approach using neural networks for the performance prediction model, and linear regression (column 3) or neural networks (column 4) for the correction function. Note that for all the considered approaches we are here considering the set of features specified by Eq. 3.

As we can see by comparing the first two columns, excluding the row related to the Intruder benchmark, using neural network or decision tree to implement classification approaches yields approximately the same performance. Looking at the third and fourth column, it emerges clearly that the proposed classification approach can provide significant benefits in terms of accuracy: the average throughput penalty (across all benchmarks) is in fact equal to 3, 71% and 3, 39%, for the classification-based approach using, respectively, decision tree (DT) and neural network (NN), whereas the average throughput penalty for the 2-layered approach is of about 9, 33% when using a linear correction function and of approximately 7, 06% when using neural networks. This means, on average, a relative increase of accuracy by a factor 2.

---

[1] At the time of writing, this is the largest degree of parallelism achievable using HTM-equipped Intel processors.

Table 4. Throughput penalty comparison

Benchmark	classification-DT	classification-NN	2-layered-linear	2-layered-NN
intruder	7, 8%	2, 7%	8%	6, 3%
genome	5, 2%	7, 1%	10%	4, 4%
kmeans	5, 4%	5, 9%	18%	15%
vacation	3, 1%	3, 8%	18%	14%
ssca2	0, 70%	0, 72%	0, 80%	0, 74%
yada	0%	0%	0%	0%
labyrinth	3, 8%	3, 5%	10%	9%
average	3, 71%	3, 39%	9, 33%	7, 06%

The graphs in Figure 2 show how the performance penalty due to wrong prediction varies with respect to the number of samples used to train two different performance predictors, the one based on the proposed classification approach and the one based on the 2-layered approach. Each point is the mean value of the results of experiments executed with a fixed number of predictors that have been trained varying the composition of the training set and the configuration of the predictors (e.g. the number of hidden nodes in the neural networks). If we look at the left graph, which shows the results for the labyrinth, genome and kmeans benchmarks, we can see that the classification approach consistently outperforms the 2-layered one. Moreover the proposed approach requires less samples to ensure optimal performance and presents less variation in the results as shown by the bars on top of the histograms. These trends are confirmed by the right graph, which shows the performance penalty for other three benchmarks, namely intruder, vacation and ssca2. We avoid to present results related to the yada benchmark because, as shown in Table 4, for this benchmark all the approaches always ensure optimal performance (this is due to the fact that, at any point in time, the optimal configuration for yada never varies).

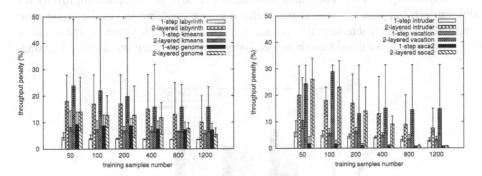

Fig. 2. Performance penalty varying predictor's training set size

The graphs in Figure 3 show the application speedup with respect to a non-instrumented sequential version, while varying the degree of parallelism, for two benchmarks of the STAMP suite, respectively Intruder and Genome. When running with no

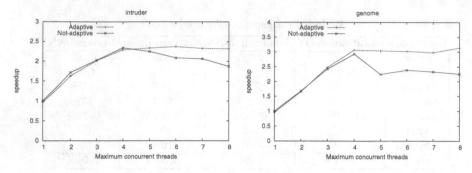

Fig. 3. Speedup

adaptive regulation of concurrency, we fix the degree of parallelism statically at start-up. On the other hand, when considering the adaptive version, we set the initial *and maximum* parallelism level according to the value reported on the x-axis of the figure, but then let the concurrency regulation mechanism adjust the parallelism level according to the indications of the performance model.

For the Intruder benchmark, when increasing the level of parallelism, the performance of the non-adaptive version of the application increases until it reaches a concurrency level equal to 4. Beyond this optimal level of parallelism, the performance decreases due to an excessive number of transaction aborts. The adaptive version of the application, instead, is able to determine at runtime which is the optimal concurrency level. As the dotted line in the graph shows, if we execute the application with a number of maximum available threads larger than 4, the adaptive version ensures the same speed-up that the application can reach when it is executed with the optimal concurrency level. Similar results can be obtained with the Genome benchmark as shown by the right plot.

Finally, in Figure 4 we report data showing the relative performance improvements achievable by approaches that dynamically regulate concurrency vs the static case where all the 8 available virtual cores are always employed for running the application. In this study we considered both our 1-step proposal, based on machine learning,

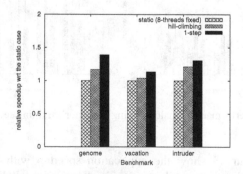

Fig. 4. Speedup (vs the static configuration employing 8 threads) of hill-climbing [4] and 1-step

and the hill climbing based technique investigated in [4]. The data refer to three different benchmark applications from STAMP, namely genome vacation and intruder. The
plots highlight that the 1-step approach constantly outperforms the hill-climbing technique. This is as a result of the ability of the proposed approach to avoid sub-optimal
exploration phases (unlike hill-climbing) and of identifying the optimal configuration
in a prompt and accurate way.

6 Conclusions

In this paper we presented the results of a study aimed at evaluating the feasibility of
re-using concurrency regulation techniques originally conceived for STM systems, or
adaptations of them, in the context of HTM systems.

We have shown, also via experimentation, that these techniques do not fully fit HTM
scenarios for two main reasons. On the one hand, the inadequacy of the parameters
selected as input to the performance models used to drive the concurrency regulation
process. On the other hand, the overhead for the monitoring of the model's input parameters, which becomes unaffordable in HTM.

We then devised and investigated a machine learning approach, based on classification and specifically tailored for HTM, which we have shown to yield higher accuracy,
reduced overhead and shorter learning time. The assessment of this approach has been
based on experimental results achieved by running the STAMP benchmark suite on
top of a machine equipped with and Intel 8 virtual cores CPU (4 physical plus hyper-
threading) with HTM support.

As future work along the concurrency regulation path we plan to investigate how to
combine performance prediction models, and how to devise innovative models, for contexts where STM and HTM co-exist as an hybrid support for shared-data management
in parallel/concurrent applications.

References

1. Ansari, M., Kotselidis, C., Jarvis, K., Luján, M., Kirkham, C., Watson, I.: Advanced concurrency control for transactional memory using transaction commit rate. In: Luque, E.,
   Margalef, T., Benítez, D. (eds.) Euro-Par 2008. LNCS, vol. 5168, pp. 719–728. Springer,
   Heidelberg (2008)
2. Blake, G., Dreslinski, R.G., Mudge, T.: Proactive transaction scheduling for contention management. In: Proc. of MICRO, pp. 156–167. ACM (2009)
3. Castro, M., Goes, L.F.W., Ribeiro, C.P., Cole, M., Cintra, M., Mehaut, J.F.: A machine
   learning-based approach for thread mapping on transactional memory applications. In: Proc.
   of HiPC, pp. 1–10. IEEE Computer Society (2011)
4. Didona, D., Felber, P., Harmanci, D., Romano, P., Schenker, J.: Identifying the optimal level
   of parallelism in transactional memory applications. In: Gramoli, V., Guerraoui, R. (eds.)
   NETYS 2013. LNCS, vol. 7853, pp. 233–247. Springer, Heidelberg (2013)
5. Didona, D., Romano, P., Peluso, S., Quaglia, F.: Transactional auto scaler: elastic scaling of
   in-memory transactional data grids. In: Proc. of ICAC, pp. 125–134. ACM (2012)
6. Diegues, N., Romano, P.: Self-tuning intel transactional synchronization extensions. In: Proc.
   of ICAC (2014)

7. Diegues, N., Romano, P., Rodrigues, L.: Virtues and limitations of commodity hardware transactional memory. In: Proc. of PACT (2014)
8. Dragojević, A., Guerraoui, R.: Predicting the scalability of an STM: A pragmatic approach. In: TRANSACT (2010)
9. Dragojević, A., Guerraoui, R., Singh, A.V., Singh, V.: Preventing versus curing: Avoiding conflicts in transactional memories. In: Proc. of PODC, pp. 7–16. ACM (2009)
10. Goel, B., Titos, R., Negi, A., McKee, S.A., Stenstrom, P.: Performance and energy analysis of the restricted transactional memory implementation on haswell. In: Proc. of IPDPS. IEEE Computer Society (2014)
11. He, Z., Hong, B.: Modeling the run-time behavior of transactional memory. In: Proc. of MASCOTS, pp. 307–315 (2010)
12. Herlihy, M., Moss, J.E.B.: Transactional memory: Architectural support for lock-free data structures. SIGARCH Comput. Archit. News 21(2), 289–300 (1993)
13. Intel Corporation: Intel Transactional Synchronization Extensions (Intel TSX) - Programming Considerations
14. Minh, C.C., Chung, J., Kozyrakis, C., Olukotun, K.: STAMP: Stanford Transactional Applications for Multi-Processing. In: Proc. of IISWC, Seattle, WA, USA, pp. 35–46 (2008)
15. Rughetti, D., Di Sanzo, P., Ciciani, B., Quaglia, F.: Machine learning-based self-adjusting concurrency in software transactional memory systems. In: Proc. of MASCOTS, pp. 278–285. IEEE Computer Society (2012)
16. Rughetti, D., Di Sanzo, P., Ciciani, B., Quaglia, F.: Regulating concurrency in software transactional memory: An effective model-based approach. In: Proc.of SASO. IEEE Computer Society (2013)
17. di Sanzo, P., Ciciani, B., Palmieri, R., Quaglia, F., Romano, P.: On the analytical modeling of concurrency control algorithms for software transactional memories: The case of commit-time-locking. Performance Evaluation 69(5), 187–205 (2012)
18. di Sanzo, P., Palmieri, R., Ciciani, B., Quaglia, F., Romano, P.: Analytical modeling of lock-based concurrency control with arbitrary transaction data access patterns. In: Proc. of WOSP/SIPEW (2010)
19. Schroeder, B., Harchol-Balter, M., Iyengar, A., Nahum, E., Wierman, A.: How to determine a good multi-programming level for external scheduling. In: Proc. of ICDE (2006)
20. Shavit, N., Touitou, D.: Software transactional memory. In: Proc. of PODC, pp. 204–213. ACM (1995)
21. Wang, A., Gaudet, M., Wu, P., Ohmacht, M., Amaral, J.N., Barton, C., Silvera, R., Michael, M.M.: Software support and evaluation of hardware transaction memory on blue gene/q. IEEE Transactions on Computers 99 (2013)
22. Wang, Q., Kulkarni, S., Cavazos, J.V., Spear, M.: Towards applying machine learning to adaptive transactional memory. In: Proc. of TRANSACT (2011)
23. Yoo, R.M., Lee, H.H.S.: Adaptive transaction scheduling for transactional memory systems. In: Proc. of SPAA, pp. 169–178. ACM (2008)

A Distributed CPU-GPU Sparse Direct Solver

Piyush Sao[1], Richard Vuduc[1], and Xiaoye Sherry Li[2]

[1] Georgia Institute of Technology
{piyush3,richie}@gatech.edu
[2] Lawrence Berkeley National Laboratory
xsli@lbl.gov

Abstract. This paper presents the first hybrid MPI+OpenMP+CUDA implementation of a distributed memory right-looking unsymmetric sparse direct solver (i.e., sparse LU factorization) that uses static pivoting. While BLAS calls can account for more than 40% of the overall factorization time, the difficulty is that small problem sizes dominate the workload, making efficient GPU utilization challenging. This fact motivates our approach, which is to find ways to aggregate collections of small BLAS operations into larger ones; to schedule operations to achieve load balance and hide long-latency operations, such as PCIe transfer; and to exploit simultaneously all of a node's available CPU cores and GPUs.

1 Introduction

Given a sparse matrix A, we consider the problem of factoring it into the product $A = L \cdot U$, where L is a unit lower triangular matrix and U is an upper triangular matrix. This problem ("sparse LU") is usually the most expensive step in a *sparse direct solver*, the use of which appears in a variety of computational science and engineering applications. It typically needs a lot of memory, thereby benefiting from the use of a distributed memory system. A natural question is, given the increased reliance on some form of GPU-like acceleration for such systems, how to exploit all forms of available parallelism, whether distributed memory, shared memory, or "accelerated."

The challenge is that sparse LU factorization is, computationally, neither strictly dominated by arithmetic, like high-performance LINPACK is when A is dense, nor is it strictly dominated by communication, as is often the case with iterative linear solvers. Thus, it is an open question whether or by how much we should expect to speed up sparse LU factorization using distributed CPU+GPU machines [9]. Additionally, the facts of indirect irregular memory access, irregular parallelism, and a strong dependence on the input matrix's structure—known only at runtime—further complicate its implementation. These complications require carefully designed data structures and dynamic approaches to scheduling and load balancing. Indeed, perhaps due to these myriad issues, there are many studies offering distributed algorithms and hybrid single-node CPU+GPU implementations but, to date, no fully distributed hybrid CPU+GPU sparse direct solver of which we are aware (§ 2).

F. Silva et al. (Eds.): Euro-Par 2014, LNCS 8632, pp. 487–498, 2014.
© Springer International Publishing Switzerland 2014

This paper presents the first such algorithm and implementation that can run scalably on a cluster comprising hybrid CPU+GPU nodes. We extend an existing distributed memory sparse direct solver, SUPERLU_DIST [5], by adding CPU multithreading and GPU acceleration during the LU factorization step. To effectively exploit intranode CPU and GPU parallelism, we use a variety of techniques (§ 4). These include aggregating small computations to increase the amount of compute-bound work; asynchronously assigning compute-bound work to the GPU and memory-bound work to the CPU, thereby minimizing CPU-GPU communication and improving system utilization; and careful scheduling to hide various long-latency operations. We evaluate this implementation on test problems derived from applications (§ 5). We show speedups of over 2× (§ 5) over a highly scalable MPI-only code; and, provide the required explanation when our approach does not yield speedups.

2   Related Work

The last five years have seen several research developments on accelerating sparse factorization algorithms using GPUs. Most of these efforts rely on the GPU for solving large dense matrix subproblems, performing any other processing on the host CPU with data transfer as needed. There exist methods for multi-frontal Cholesky [4,12,9,6]; and, in single-precision, left-looking sparse LU [8]. In essence, all of these methods use the GPU as a BLAS accelerator.

George et al. go beyond BLAS acceleration for their single-node multifrontal sparse Cholesky algorithm, implemented in WSMP [3]. They examine three compute-intensive kernels associated with each frontal matrix: factoring the diagonal block, triangular solution, and Schur complement update. These computations are selectively offloaded to the GPU depending on the workload distribution of the flops, which in turn depends on the input matrix. Their method achieves 10-25× speedups over a single-core.

Yeralan et al. developed a sparse multifrontal QR factorization algorithm using one CPU-GPU combination [11]. Since sparse QR has intrinsically higher arithmetic intensity than sparse LU, the pay-off of GPU acceleration should be higher.

Our approach also offloads the most arithmetic-intensive part of the workload to GPUs. However, one distinction of our work is that we aim to exploit the maximum available parallelism of a distributed memory system, namely, distributed memory parallelism via MPI combined with intranode parallelism through multithreading and GPU acceleration. While our implementation is specific to SUPERLU_DIST, we believe techniques discussed in this paper can be extended to other direct solvers.

3   Overview of SuperLU_DIST

Solving a linear system $Ax = b$ using SUPERLU_DIST involves a number of steps [10,7]. However, the most expensive step is numerical factorization, which is the focus of this paper. For test matrices in our study, numerical factorization

---

Algorithm 1. SUPERLU_DIST Numerical Factorization

1: **for** $k = 1, 2, 3 \ldots n_s$ **do**
    Panel Factorization
2:    Column computation of $L_{:,k}$.
3:    **if** $p_{id} \in P_c(k)$ **then**
4:       compute the block column $L_{k:n_s,k}$
5:       (communicate $U_{k,k}$ among $P_c(k)$)
6:       send $L_{k:n_s,k}$ to required processes in $P_r(:)$
7:    **else**
8:       receive $L_{k:n_s,k}$ if required
    Row computation of $U_{k,:}$.
9:    **if** $p_{id} \in P_r(k)$ **then**
10:      wait for $U_{k,k}$
11:      compute the block row $U_{k,k+1:n_s}$
12:      send $U_{k,k+1:n_s}$ to required processes in $P_c(:)$
13:    **else**
14:      receive $U_{k,k+1:n_s}$ if required
    Schur Complement Update
15:    **if** $L_{:,k}$ and $U_{k,:}$ are locally non-empty **then**
16:      **for** $j = k + 1, k + 2, k + 3 \ldots n_s$ **do**
17:        **for** $i = k + 1, k + 2, k + 3 \ldots n_s$ **do**
18:          **if** $p_{id} \in P_r(i) \cap P_c(j)$ **then**
19:            $A_{i,j} \leftarrow A_{i,j} - L_{i,k} U_{k,j}$

---

accounts for at least 75% of the total solve time, and in fact more often accounts for 90% or more. Therefore, we focus on just the numerical factorization phase. Accelerating the remaining steps is a good avenue for future research.

SUPERLU_DIST uses a fan-out (right-looking, outer-product) *supernodal* algorithm. A *supernode* is a set of consecutive columns of L with a dense triangular block just below the diagonal and with the same nonzero structure below the triangular block. To achieve good parallelism and load balance, the MPI processes are assigned to the supernodal blocks in a 2D cyclic layout.

Algorithm 1 shows the pseudocode of the factorization algorithm, where n_s is the number of supernodes, p_{id} is the ID of this process, and $P_c(k)$ and $P_r(k)$ are the groups of processes assigned to the k-th supernodal column and the k-th supernodal row, respectively. Step 1 is the k-th panel factorization, where the k-th supernodal column of L and the k-th supernodal row of U are computed. Subsequently, each process in $P_c(k)$ and $P_r(k)$ sends its local blocks of the factors to the processes assigned to the same row and column, respectively. Consequently, Step 2 updates the trailing submatrix using the k-th supernodal column and row of the LU factors. The block $A_{i,j}$ is updated only if both blocks $L_{i,k}$ and $U_{k,j}$ are not empty. A more detailed description appears elsewhere [10].

4   New Intranode Enhancements

Our work enhances the intranode performance and scaling of alg. 1. The panel factorization and row computation phases primarily are concerned with communication. By contrast, the Schur complement update phase (lines 15–19) is the local computation that dominates intranode performance. Thus, it is our main target for optimization.

Baseline Schur complement update. The Schur complement update step at iteration k of alg. 1 computes $A_{k+1,n_s:k+1,n_s}$ as

$$A_{k+1,n_s:k+1,n_s} = A_{k+1,n_s:k+1,n_s} - L_{k+1:n_s,k}U_{k,:k+1:n_s}. \tag{1}$$

SuperLU_DIST uses an owner-computes strategy, where each process updates the set of blocks, $\{A_{i,j}\}$, which it owns once it has received the required blocks $L_{:,k}$ and $U_{k,:}$.

Each GEMM subproblem computes one $A_{i,j}$, which is line 19 of alg. 1. In the baseline SuperLU_DIST implementation, a process updates each of its $A_{i,j}$ blocks in turn, traversing the matrix in a columnwise manner (outermost j-loop at line 18 of alg. 1). The update takes place in three steps: packing the U block, calling BLAS GEMM, and unpacking the result. We refer to the first two steps as the *GEMM* phase, and the last step as the *Scatter* phase.

Packing allows the computation to use a highly optimized BLAS implementation of GEMM. Packing converts the $U_{k,j}$, which is stored in a sparse format, into a dense BLAS-compliant column major format, $\tilde{U}_{k,j}$. This packing takes place once for each $U_{k,j}$. The $L_{i,k}$ operand need not be packed, as it is already stored in a column major form as part of a rectangular supernode.

The second step is the BLAS GEMM call, which computes $V \leftarrow L_{i,k}\tilde{U}_{k,j}$, where V is a temporary buffer.

The final *Scatter* step updates $A_{i,j}$ by subtracting V from it. Since only the nonzero rows of L and U are stored, the destination block $A_{i,j}$ usually has more nonzero rows and columns, than $L_{i,k}$ and $U_{k,j}$. Thus, this step must also map the rows and columns of V to the rows and columns of $A_{i,j}$ before the elements of $A_{i,j}$ can be updated, which involves indirect addressing. This final unpacking step is what we refer to as the *Scatter* phase.

Aggregating small GEMM subproblems. Relative to the baseline (above), we may increase the intensity of the GEMM phase by aggregating small GEMM subproblems into a single, larger GEMM. This aggregated computation then becomes a better target for GPU offload, though it also works well even in the multicore CPU-only case.

Our approach to aggregation, illustrated in fig. 1, has two aspects. First, we process an entire block column at once. That is, instead of calling GEMM for every block multiply $L_{i,k}\tilde{U}_{k,j}$, we aggregate the L-blocks in column k into a single GEMM call that effectively computes $V \leftarrow L_{k+1:n_s,k}\tilde{U}_{k,j}$, thereby reusing $\tilde{U}_{k,j}$. Secondly, the packed block $\tilde{U}_{k,j}$ may still have only a few nonzero columns. Thus, we group multiple consecutive U-blocks to form a larger $\tilde{U}_{k,j_{st}:j_{end}}$ block, where j_{st} and j_{end} are the starting and the ending block indices. This large block has some minimum number of columns N_b, a tuning parameter. We schedule the computation of $L_{k+1:n_s,k}\tilde{U}_{k,j_{st}:j_{end}}$ onto the GPU, using CUDA streams as explained below.

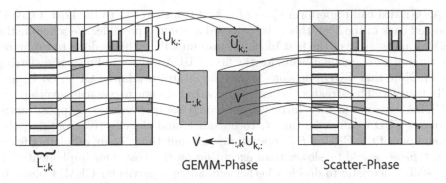

Fig. 1. Aggregating Small GEMM subproblems

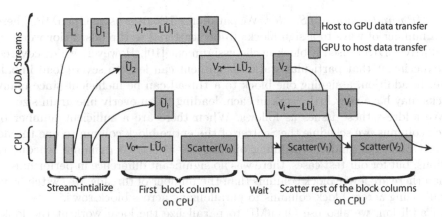

Fig. 2. Overlapping GEMM with Scatter

Aggregation may increase the memory footprint relative to the baseline. In particular, we may need to store a large U-block, U, and a large intermediate output, V. Our implementation preallocates these buffers, using N_b as a tunable parameter to constrain their sizes.

Pipelined execution. Given aggregated GEMMs, we use a software pipelining scheduling scheme to overlap copying the GEMM operands to the GPU with execution of both the GEMMs themselves as well as the CPU Scatter.

Our pipelining scheme, illustrated in fig. 2, uses CUDA's streams facility. Our scheme divides $\tilde{U}$ into n_s partitions, where n_s is the number of desired CUDA streams, a tuning parameter. To perform this division, our scheme first ensures that each partition has a minimum of N_b columns. It also ensures that the number of columns in each partition does not cross the boundary of the block columns. It then uses a greedy algorithm to ensure that each partition has a number of columns of at most the average number of columns, except for the last partition which has all the remaining columns.

The pipelining begins with the transfer of L to the GPU. Now each CUDA stream asynchronously initializes transfer of i-th partition, $\tilde{U}_i$, and a CUDA

BLAS GEMM call to perform $V_i \leftarrow L\tilde{U}_i$, and transfer of V_i to the host. Once V_i is copied back to the host, this V_i is scattered as soon as possible. We schedule the GEMM and scatter of the first block column on CPU. This is done to minimize idle time of CPU, while it waits for the first CUDA stream to finish transferring the V_1. Note that CUDA streams mainly facilitates overlap of CPU, GPU, and PCIe transfer. The streams themselves may, but do not necessarily, overlap

CUDA streams facility carries a nontrivial setup overhead. Suppose asynchronous CUDA calls take time t_s to initialize, and the effective floating-point throughput of the CPU is F_{cpu} operations per unit time. Then, offloading fewer than $t_s F_{CPU}$ would be slower than executing on the host. Our implementation uses such a heuristic to decide whether offloading a particular GEMM phase to the GPU will pay off, or otherwise executes on the CPU.

OpenMP parallelization of Scatter. We parallelized Scatter using OpenMP. There are a number of ways to assign blocks to be scattered to threads. Prior work on SUPERLU_DIST used a block cyclic assignment [10]. However, we discovered by experiment that particular static assignment can lead to severe load imbalance. In addition, assigning one block to a thread can be inefficient since many blocks may have very little work in each, leading to an overly fine grain size.

We address these issues as follows. When there are a sufficient number of block columns, we schedule the Scatter of the entire block column to one thread using OpenMP's guided scheduling option. We also tried dynamic scheduling options, but for our test cases, there was no significant difference in performance. When there are fewer block columns than the number of threads, we switch from parallelizing across block columns to parallelizing across block rows.

In addition, we also use OpenMP to parallelize the local work at the look-ahead phase and the panel factorization phase. However, doing so does not affect performance by much because these phases are dominated by MPI communication.

5 Experiments and Results

We used two GPU clusters in our evaluation (table 2). We tested our implementations on the input matrices in table 2, which derive from real applications [2].

We evaluated 6 implementation variants. (All variants use double-precision arithmetic, including on the GPU.) The baseline is SUPERLU_DIST. We *modified* this baseline to include the BLAS aggregation technique of § 4. Since all variants derive from SUPERLU_DIST, they all *include* distributed memory parallelism via MPI. Their mnemonic names describe what each variant adds to the MPI-enabled baseline.

- MKL₁ is the baseline, based on SUPERLU_DIST Version 3.3 "out-of-the-box." It uses MPI-only within a node and uses Intel's MKL, a vendor BLAS library, running in single-threaded mode. This implementation is what we hope to improve by exploiting intranode parallelism. Unless otherwise noted,

Table 1. Evaluation testbeds for our experiments

Parameter	Jinx-Cluster	Dirac-GPU test bed
# GPUs per node	2	1
Type of GPU	Tesla M2090 "Fermi"	Tesla C2050 "Fermi"
GPU double-precision peak	665 GF/sec	515 GF/sec
GPU DRAM / Bandwidth	6 GB / 177 GBytes/sec	3 GB / 144 GBytes/sec
Host	Intel Xeon X5650 @2.67 GHz	Intel Xeon X5530 @2.4 GHz
PCIe / Bandwidth	PCIe x16 /8GB/s	PCIe x16 /8GB/s
Sockets × Cores / socket	2 × 6	2 × 4
CPU double-precision peak	128 GF/sec	76.8 GF/sec
L3 Cache	2 × 12M	2× 8M
Memory	24GB	24GB
Network /Bandwidth	InfiniBand/ 40 Gbit/s	InfiniBand/ 32 Gbit/s

Table 2. Different test problems used for testing solvers. * See the University of Florida Sparse Matrix Collection [2]; † from NERSC users

Name	n	nnz	$\frac{nnz}{n}$	symm	Fill-in Ratio	Application
audikw_1*	943695	77651847	82.28	yes	31.43	structural
bone010*	986703	47851783	48.49	yes	43.52	model reduction
nd24k*	72000	28715634	398.82	yes	22.49	2D/3D
RM07R*	381689	37464962	98.15	no	78.00	fluid dynamics
dds.quad†	380698	15844364	41.61	no	20.18	cavity
matrix211†	801378	129413052	161.48	no	9.68	Nuclear Fusion
tdr190k†	1100242	43318292	39.37	no	20.43	Accelerator
Ga19As19H42*	133123	8884839	66.74	yes	182.16	quantum chemistry
TSOPF_RS_b2383_c1*	38120	16171169	424.21	no	3.44	power network
dielFilterV2real*	1157456	48538952	41.93	yes	22.39	electromagnetics

we try all numbers of MPI processes within a node up to 1 MPI process per physical core, and report the performance of the best configuration.

- MKL$_p$ is the same as MKL$_1$, but with multithreaded MKL instead. It uses 1 MPI process per socket; within each socket, it uses multithreaded MKL with the number of threads equal to the physical cores per socket.
- {cuBLAS,Scatter} is MKL$_p$ but with most GEMM calls replaced by their NVIDIA GPU counterpart, via the CUDA BLAS (or "cuBLAS") library. (Any other BLAS call uses MKL$_p$.) Additionally, cuBLAS may execute asynchronously; therefore, there may be an additional performance benefit from partial overlap between cuBLAS and Scatter, as the mnemonic name suggests. Like MKL$_1$, we try various numbers of MPI processes per node and report results for the best configuration. (When there are more MPI processes than physical GPUs, the cuBLAS calls are automatically multiplexed.)

- OpenMP+MKL$_1$ exploits intranode parallelism *explicitly* using OpenMP. It parallelizes all phases using OpenMP. For phases that use the BLAS, we use explicit OpenMP parallelization and with single-threaded MKL. Scatter and GEMM phases run in sequence, i.e., they do not overlap.
- OpenMP+{MKL$_p$,cuBLAS} shares the work of the GEMM phase between *both* the CPU and GPU, running them concurrently. This tends to reduce the time spent in GEMM compared to OpenMP+MKL$_1$ implementation, but may not hide the cost completely.
- OpenMP+{MKL$_p$,cuBLAS,Scatter}+pipeline adds pipelining to OpenMP+{MKL$_p$, cuBLAS}. We use $n_s = 16$ CUDA streams and $N_b = 128$.

The first three implementations use implicit parallelism via multithreaded or GPU-accelerated BLAS; the last three involve explicit parallelism. We used $X_s = 144$ as maximum supernode size. To profile the computation's execution time, we use TAU. When we evaluate memory usage, we use the IPM tool [1].

Overall impact of intranode optimization. Our first analysis answers the question, by how much can *explicit* intranode optimization techniques improve performance above and beyond having a highly tuned multicore and/or GPU-accelerated BLAS? These experiments use just two nodes of the cluster. The

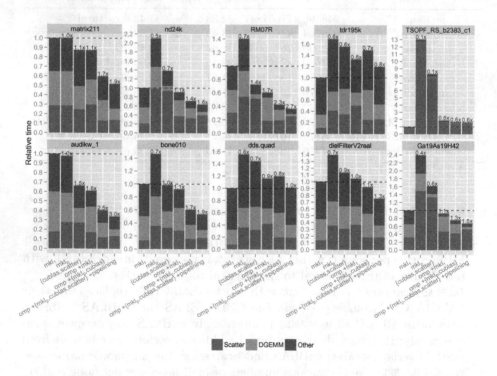

Fig. 3. Performance of different implementations for different test problems on Jinx cluster. Each bar is labeled by its speedup relative to the baseline (MKL$_1$).

results show best-case improvements of up to $3\times$ using our techniques, and high-light scenarios in which our methods may yield a slowdown.

We show results for the Jinx system in fig. 3. (Dirac results are similar [7], and so omitted for space.) It shows time (y-axis) versus implementation variant (x-axis) for a given matrix. The time is normalized to the baseline, with actual baseline execution times in the range of 10 to 1,000 seconds (not shown). Each bar breaks down the execution time into its components, which correspond to different phases of SuperLU. The **GEMM** phase and **Scatter** phase are as described in § 4. The **Scatter** phase includes any CUDA stream setup and wait time. The "**Other**" phase has three major components: MPI_Wait, MPI_Recv, and triangular solve. When phases may overlap, the bar shows only the *visible* execution time, i.e., the part of the execution time that does *not* overlap. Thus, the total height of the bar is the visible wall-clock time.

Both the MKL_p and {cuBLAS,Scatter} variants are slower or just comparable to MKL_1 in many cases. Though they may improve **GEMM**, **Scatter** and **Other** may slowdown since they tend to improve with more MPI processes. Thus, only relying on accelerating BLAS calls—whether by multithreading or offload—tends not to yield a significant overall speedup, and can in fact decrease performance.

The OpenMP+MKL_1 variant reduces the cost of **Scatter** and **Other** phases compared to MKL_p and {cuBLAS,Scatter}. While **Other** for OpenMP+MKL_1 is better than with MKL_1, **Scatter** is worse. OpenMP+MKL_1 often matches the baseline MKL_1. The OpenMP+{MKL_p,cuBLAS} variant reduces the time spent in **GEMM** compared to OpenMP+MKL_1 implementation, but cannot hide the cost of **GEMM** completely.

Our combined OpenMP+{MKL_p,cuBLAS,Scatter}+pipeline implementation outperforms MKL_1 on 7 of the 10 test matrices on either platform, yielding speedups of up to $3\times$ (fig. 3, audikw_1). Compared to MKL_1, this variant hides the cost of **GEMM** very well. However, **Scatter** still cannot achieve the same parallel efficiency as with MKL_1. The worst case occurs with TSOPF_RS_bs2383_c1, which derives from a power network analysis application. On Jinx, it is nearly $2\times$ slower than MKL_1 (fig. 3). However, even with a slowdown our implementation can reduce the memory requirement of this problem; see below.

Strong Scaling. Part of the benefit of intranode parallelism is to enhance strong scaling. We consider this scenario, for configurations of up to 8 nodes and 64 cores (Dirac) or 96 cores (Jinx), showing results for Jinx in fig. 4. (Dirac results are better than Jinx [7].) We present results for just two "extremes": Matrix nd24k, on which our implementation does well, and TSOPF_RS_b2383_c1, on which it fairs somewhat poorly.

We focus on three of our implementation variants: the baseline MKL_1, OpenMP+MKL_1, and OpenMP+{MKL_p,cuBLAS,Scatter}+pipeline. For the MKL_1 variant, we use 1 MPI process per core. For OpenMP+MKL_1 and OpenMP+{MKL_p,cuBLAS,Scatter}+pipeline cases, we use 1 MPI process per socket and one OpenMP thread per core.

Figure 4 shows scalability as a log-log plot of time (y-axis) versus configuration as measured by the total number of cores (x-axis). Each series shows one of the three implementation variants. Each column is a phase, with the leftmost column, **Total**, showing scalability of the overall computation, inclusive of all

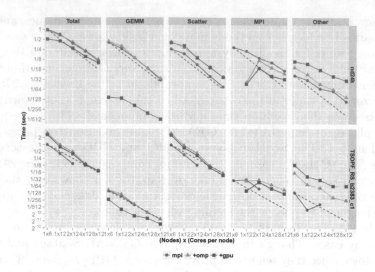

Fig. 4. Strong scaling on up to 8 nodes (96 cores and 16 GPUs) on Jinx

phases. Time is always normalized by the *total* MKL$_1$ time when running on the smallest configuration (1 node and 1 socket), to reveal the relative time spent in each phase. Dashed lines indicate ideal linear speedup for MKL$_1$; perfect scaling would be parallel to this line, while sublinear scaling would have a less steep slope and superlinear scaling would have a more steep slope.

On Dirac (not shown), both test matrices exhibit good scaling behavior for nearly all the phases; by contrast, Jinx scaling (fig. 4) exhibits sublinear behavior. At 96 cores and 16 GPUs (2 GPUs per node), all three implementations differ by only a little on nd24k. This is due largely to the relatively poor scaling of the **Other** phase, which eventually becomes the bottleneck for OpenMP+{MKL$_p$,cuBLAS,Scatter}+pipeline.

On TSOPF_RS_b2383_c1, the baseline MKL$_1$ is always fastest on both clusters, when it ran successfully. On Jinx, there was not enough memory per node to accommodate the 48 and 96 MPI processes cases, due to the fundamental memory scaling requirement of SUPERLU_DIST; for more analysis, see below.

Matrix TSOPF_RS_b2383_c1 case shows superlinear scaling. The **Scatter** phase is a major contributing factor in cost. As noted previously, the **Scatter** phase scales with increasing MPI processes, primarily due to better locality.

Overall, OpenMP+MKL$_1$ shows good strong scaling. By contrast, the scaling of OpenMP+{MKL$_p$,cuBLAS,Scatter}+pipeline can be worse, as observed on Jinx. However, this owes largely to Amdahl's Law effects due to **Other**. That component is primarily a triangular solve step, which our work has not yet addressed.

Time and memory requirements. Sparse direct solvers like SUPERLU_DIST may exhibit a *time-memory tradeoff*. We show an example on three representative problems in fig. 5. This example includes nd24k, which shows common-case

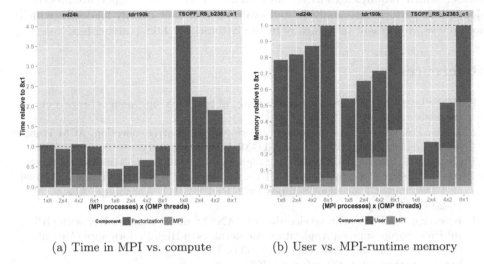

(a) Time in MPI vs. compute   (b) User vs. MPI-runtime memory

Fig. 5. Effect of intranode threading on memory and time

behavior; as well as TSOPF_RS_b2383_c1, which was a worst-case in execution time for our approach. The experiment tests the OpenMP+MKL$_1$ variant on one node of Dirac, which has 8 cores per node, under all configurations of (# of MPI processes) × (# of OpenMP threads) = 8.

Matrix TSOPF_RS_b2383_c1 exhibits the time-memory tradeoff. The **Scatter** phase dominates execution time, as observed above; since **Scatter** scales with MPI processes, the all-MPI configuration wins. However, memory usage actually *increases* with increasing numbers of MPI processes. Among user allocated memory, it turns out that the memory required by the L and U factors remains fairly constant, whereas the buffers used for MPI_Send and MPI_Recv increase. Memory allocated by MPI runtime also increases. Thus, even if our intranode threading approach is slower than the all-MPI case, there can be a large reduction in the memory requirement.

6   Conclusions and Future Work

The high-level question this paper considers is how to exploit intranode parallelism in emerging CPU+GPU systems for distributed memory sparse direct solvers. At the outset, one expects a highly tuned multicore and/or GPU BLAS will yield much of the potential performance benefits. The real question, then, is how much *additional* performance gain is possible from explicit parallelization. Our results for SUPERLU_DIST suggest that on today's systems, there may be up to a factor of 2× more to gain above and beyond BLAS-only parallelization.

Other avenues to pursue would include alternative accelerator platforms (e.g., Intel Xeon Phi, near-memory processing solutions); accelerating the Scatter phase, which requires extensive data structure changes; deeper architecture-dependent performance analysis; and evaluation of time-energy tradeoffs, which we believe are present intrinsically in the SUPERLU_DIST algorithm.

References

1. IPM : Integrated performance monitoring, http://ipm-hpc.sourceforge.net/ (accessed: January 26, 2014)
2. Davis, T.A., Hu, Y.: The university of florida sparse matrix collection. ACM Transactions on Mathematical Software (TOMS) 38(1), 1 (2011)
3. George, T., Saxena, V., Gupta, A., Singh, A., Choudjury, A.: Multifrontal factorization of sparse spd matrices on GPUs. In: Proc. of IEEE International Parallel and Distributed Processing Symposium (IPDPS 2011), Anchorage, Alaska, May 16-20 (2011)
4. Krawezik, G., Poole, G.: Accelerating the ANSYS direct sparse solver with GPUs. In: Proc. Symposium on Application Accelerators in High Performance Computing (SAAHPC). Urbana-Champaign, IL (2009), http://saahpc.ncsa.illinois.edu/09
5. Li, X.S., Demmel, J.W.: SuperLU_DIST: A scalable distributed-memory sparse direct solver for unsymmetric linear systems. ACM Trans. Mathematical Software 29(2), 110–140 (2003)
6. Lucas, R.F., Wagenbreth, G., Davis, D.M., Grimes, R.: Multifrontal computations on GPUs and their multi-core hosts. In: Palma, J.M.L.M., Daydé, M., Marques, O., Lopes, J.C. (eds.) VECPAR 2010. LNCS, vol. 6449, pp. 71–82. Springer, Heidelberg (2011), http://vecpar.fe.up.pt/2010/papers/5.php
7. Sao, P., Vuduc, R., Li, X.: A distributed CPU-GPU sparse direct solver. Technical report, Georgia Institute of technology (2014)
8. Schenk, O., Christen, M., Burkhart, H.: Algorithmic performance studies on graphics processing units. J. Parallel and Distributed Computing 68(10), 1360–1369 (2008)
9. Vuduc, R., Chandramowlishwaran, A., Choi, J., Guney, M., Shringarpure, A.: On the limits of GPU acceleration. In: Proc. of the 2nd USENIX Conference on Hot Topics in Parallelism, HotPar 2010, Berkeley, CA (2010)
10. Yamazaki, I., Li, X.S.: New scheduling strategies and hybrid programming for a parallel right-looking sparse LU factorization algorithm on multicore cluster systems. In: 2012 IEEE 26th International Parallel & Distributed Processing Symposium (IPDPS), pp. 619–630. IEEE (2012)
11. Yeralan, S.N., Davis, T., Ranka, S.: Sparse QR factorization on gpu architectures. Technical report, University of Florida (November 2013)
12. Yu, C.D., Wang, W., Pierce, D.: A CPU-GPU hybrid approach for the unsymmetric multifrontal method. Parallel Computing 37, 759–770 (2011)

Parallel Computation of Echelon Forms[*]

Jean-Guillaume Dumas[1], Thierry Gautier[2],
Clément Pernet[3], and Ziad Sultan[1,2]

[1] LJK-CASYS, UJF, CNRS, Inria, G'INP, UPMF, Grenoble, France
[2] LIG-MOAIS UJF, CNRS, Inria, G'INP, UPMF, Grenoble, France
[3] LIP-AriC UJF, CNRS, Inria, UCBL, ÉNS de Lyon, France

Abstract. We propose efficient parallel algorithms and implementations
on shared memory architectures of LU factorization over a finite field.
Compared to the corresponding numerical routines, we have identified
three main specifities of linear algebra over finite fields. First, the arithmetic complexity could be dominated by modular reductions. Therefore,
it is mandatory to delay as much as possible these reductions while mixing fine-grain parallelizations of tiled iterative and recursive algorithms.
Second, fast linear algebra variants, e.g., using Strassen-Winograd algorithm, never suffer from instability and can thus be widely used in
cascade with the classical algorithms. There, trade-offs are to be made
between size of blocks well suited to those fast variants or to load and
communication balancing. Third, many applications over finite fields require the rank profile of the matrix (quite often rank deficient) rather
than the solution to a linear system. It is thus important to design parallel algorithms that preserve and compute this rank profile. Moreover,
as the rank profile is only discovered during the algorithm, block size has
then to be dynamic. We propose and compare several block decompositions: tile iterative with left-looking, right-looking and Crout variants,
slab and tile recursive. Experiments demonstrate that the tile recursive
variant performs better and matches the performance of reference numerical software when no rank deficiency occurs. Furthermore, even in
the most heterogeneous case, namely when all pivot blocks are rank deficient, we show that it is possbile to maintain a high efficiency.

1 Introduction

Triangular matrix factorization is a main building block in computational linear
algebra. Driven by a large range of applications in computational sciences, parallel numerical dense LU factorization has been intensively studied since several
decades which results in software of great maturity (e.g., LINPACK is used for
benchmarking the efficiency of the top 500 supercomputers. More recently, efficient sequential exact linear algebra routines were developed [5]. They are used in
algebraic cryptanalysis, computational number theory, or integer linear programming and they benefit from the experience in numerical linear algebra. In particular, a key point there is to embed the finite field elements in integers stored as

---

[*] This work is partly funded by the HPAC project of the French Agence Nationale de
la Recherche (ANR 11 BS02 013).

F. Silva et al. (Eds.): Euro-Par 2014, LNCS 8632, pp. 499–510, 2014.

floating point numbers, and then rely on the efficiency of the floating point matrix multiplication dgemm of the BLAS. The conversion back to the finite field, done by costly modular reductions, is delayed as much as possible. Hence a natural ingredient in the design of efficient dense linear algebra routines is the use of block algorithms that result in gathering arithmetic operations in matrix-matrix multiplications. Those can take full advantage of vector instructions and have a high computation per memory access rate, allowing to fully overlap the data accesses by computations and hence deliver close to peak performance efficiency. In order to exploit the power of multi-core and many-core architectures, we now investigate the parallelization of the finite field linear algebra routines. We report in this paper the conclusions of our experience in parallelizing exact LU decomposition for shared memory parallel computers. We try to emphasize which specificities of exact computation domains led us to use different approaches than that of numerical linear algebra. In short, we will illustrate that numerical and exact LU factorization mainly differ in the following aspects:

- the pivoting strategies,
- the cost of the arithmetic (of scalars and matrices),
- the treatment of rank deficiencies.

Those have a direct impact on the shape and granularity of the block decomposition of the matrix used in the computation.

Types of block algorithms. Several schemes are used to design block linear algebra algorithms: the splitting can occur on one dimension only, producing row or column slabs [11], or both dimensions, producing tiles [2]. Note that, here, we denote by tiles a partition of the matrix into sub-matrices in the mathematical sense regardless what the underlying data storage is. Algorithms processing blocks can be either iterative or recursive. Figure 1 summarizes some of the various existing block splitting obtained by combining these two aspects. Most numerical dense Gaussian elimination algorithms, like in [2], use tiled iterative block algorithms. In [4] the classic tiled iterative algorithm is combined with a slab recursive one for the panel elimination. Over exact domains, recursive algorithms are preferred to benefit from fast matrix arithmetic (see below). Slab recursive exact algorithms can be found in [10] and references therein and [6] presents a tiled recursive algorithm.

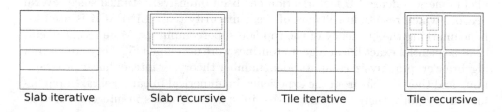

Slab iterative   Slab recursive   Tile iterative   Tile recursive

Fig. 1. Main types of block splitting

The granularity is the block dimension (or the dimension of the smallest blocks in recursive splittings). Matrices with dimensions below this threshold are treated by a base-case variant (often referred to as the panel factorization). It is an important parameter for optimizing efficiency: a finer grain allows more flexibility in the scheduling when running numerous cores, but it also challenges the efficiency of the scheduler and can increase the bus traffic.

The cost of the arithmetic. In numerical linear algebra, the cost of arithmetic operations is more or less associative: with dimensions above a rather low threshold (typically a few hundreds), the BLAS sequential matrix multiplication attains the peak efficiency of the processor. Hence the granularity has very little impact on the efficiency of a block algorithm run sequentially. On the contrary, over a finite field, a small granularity can imply a larger number of costly modular reductions, as we will show in Section 3.1. Moreover, numerical stability is not an issue over a finite field, and asymptotically fast matrix multiplication algorithms, like Winograd's variant of Strassen algorithm [8, §12] can be used on top of the BLAS. Their speed-up increases with matrix dimension. The cost of sequential matrix multiplication over finite field is therefore not associative: a larger granularity delivers better sequential efficiency.

Pivoting strategies and rank deficiencies. In dense numerical linear algebra, a pivoting strategy is a compromise between the two competing constraints: ensuring good numerical stability and avoiding data movement. In the context of dense *exact* linear algebra, stability is no longer an issue. Instead, only certain pivoting strategies will reveal the echelon form or, equivalently, the rank profile of the matrix [10,6]. This is a key invariant used in many applications using exact Gaussian elimination, such as Gröbner basis computations [7] and computational number theory [13].

In the case of numerical LU factorization, quite often all panel blocks have full rank. Therfore the splitting can be done statically according to a granularity parameter. Over exact domains, on the contrary, the large blocks are almost always rank deficient. Thus, the tiles or slabs have unpredictable dimensions and the block splitting necessarily dynamic, as will be illustrated in Section 4.

Consequently the design of a parallel exact matrix factorization necessarily differs from the numerical algorithms as follows:

- granularity should be as large as possible, to reduce modular reductions and benefit from fast matrix multiplication;
- exact algorithms should preferably be recursive, to group arithmetic operations in matrix products as large as possible;
- block splitting and pivoting strategies must preserve and reveal the rank profile of the matrix.

It also implies several requirements on the parallel run-time being used:

- the block splitting has to be dynamically computed;
- the computing load for each task is not known in advance (some panel blocks may have high rank deficiency), making the tasks very heterogeneous.

This motivated us to look into parallel execution runtimes using tasks with work-stealing based scheduling.

All experiments have been conducted on a 32 cores Intel Xeon E5-4620 2.2Ghz (Sandy Bridge) with L3 cache(16384 KB). The numerical BLAS is ATLAS v3.11.4, LAPACK v3.4.2 and PLASMA v2.5.0. We used X-KAAPI-2.1 version with last git commit: xkaapi_2.1-30-g263c19c638788249. The gcc compiler version used is gcc 4.8.2 that supports OpenMP 3.1.

We introduce in Section 2 the algorithmic building blocks on which our algorithms will rely and the parallel programming models and runtimes that we used in our experiments. In order to handle each problem separately, we focus in Section 3 on the simpler case where no rank deficiency occur. In particular Section 3.1 presents detailed analysis of the number of modular reductions required by various block algorithms including the tiled and slab recursive, the left-looking, right-looking and Crout variants of the tiled iterative algorithm. Lastly Section 4 deals with elimination with rank deficiencies. We there present and compare new slab iterative, tiled iterative and tiled recursive parallel algorithms that preserve rank profiles. We then show that the latter can match state of the art numerical routines, even when taking rank deficiencies into account.

2   Preliminaries

2.1   Auxiliary Sequential Routines

All block algorithms that we will describe rely on four types of operations that we denote using the BLAS/LAPACK naming convention:

gemm: general matrix multiplication, computing $C \leftarrow \alpha A \times B + \beta C$,
trsm: solving upper/lower triang. syst. with matrix right/left h.s $B \leftarrow BU^{-1}$.
laswp: permuting rows or columns by sequence of swaps.
getrf: computing (P, L, U, Q), L and U stored in place of A, s.t. $A = PLUQ$.

A first prefix letter d or f specifies if the routine works over double precision floating point numbers or finite field coefficients and an optional prefix p stands for parallel implementation. Our implementations use the sequential routines of the fflas-ffpack library[1] [5]. There, the elements of a finite $\mathbb{Z}/p\mathbb{Z}$ for a prime p of size about 20 bits are integers stored in a double precision floating point number. The sequential fgemm routine combines recursive steps of Winograd's algorithm calls to numerical BLAS dgemm and reductions modulo p when necessary. The ftrsm and fgetrf routines use block recursive algorithms to reduce most arithmetic operations to fgemm. More precisely fgetrf is either done by a slab recursive algorithm [5] or a tile recursive algorithm [6].

2.2   Parallel Programming Models

We base our implementation on the task based parallel features of the OpenMP standard. This is motivated by the use of recursive algorithms where tasks are

---

[1] http://linalg.org/projects/fflas-ffpack

mandatory. Now in tile iterative algorithms, loops with tasks happen to perform at least as well as parallel loops.

libgomp is the GNU implementation of the OpenMP API for multi-platform shared-memory parallel programming in C/C++ and Fortran. Alternatively, we also used libkomp [1], an optimized version of libgomp, based on the XKaapi runtime, that reduces the overhead of the OpenMP directives and handles more efficiently threads creation, synchronization and management. In the experiments of the next sections, we will compare efficiency of the same code linked against each of these two libraries.

2.3   Parallel Matrix Multiplication

In the iterative block algorithms, all matrix product tasks are sequential, whereas the recursive block algorithms must call parallel matrix products pfgemm, which we describe here. Operation pfgemm is of the form $C \leftarrow \alpha A \times B + \beta C$. In order to split the computation into independent tasks, only the row dimension of A and the column dimension of B only are split. The granularity of the split can be chosen in two different ways: either as a fixed value, or by a ratio of the input dimension (e.g. the total number of cores). We chose the second option that maximizes the size of the blocks while ensuring a large enough number of tasks for the computing resources. All our experiments showed that this option performs better than the first one. When used as a subroutine in a parallel factorization, it will create more tasks than the number of available cores, but this heuristic happens to be a good compromise in terms of efficiency.

Figure 2 shows the computation time on 32 cores of various matrix multiplications: the numerical dgemm implementation of Plasma-Quark, the implementation of pfgemm of fflas-ffpack using OpenMP tasks, linked against the libkomp library. This implementation is run over the finite field $\mathbb{Z}/131071\mathbb{Z}$ or over field of real double floating point numbers, with or without fast Strassen-Winograd's matrix product. One first notices that most routine perform very similarly. More precisely, Plasma-Quark dgemm is faster on small matrices but the effect of Strassen-Winograd's algorithm makes pfgemm faster on larger matrices, even on the finite field where additional modular reductions occur. In terms of speed-up, the pfgemm reaches a factor of approximately 27 (using 32 cores) whereas the numerical dgemm of Plasma-Quark reaches a factor of 29, but this mostly reflects the fact that dgemm has a less efficient sequential reference timing since it does not use Strassen-Winograd's algorithm.

Similarly, other basic routines used in the recursive block algorithms, such as ftrsm (solving matrix triangular systems) and flaswp (permuting rows or columns), have been parallelized by splitting a dimension into a constant number of blocks (typically the number of cores).

3   Eliminations with No Rank Deficiency

In this section, we make the assumption that no rank deficiency occurs during the elimination of any of the diagonal block. This hypothesis is satisfied by

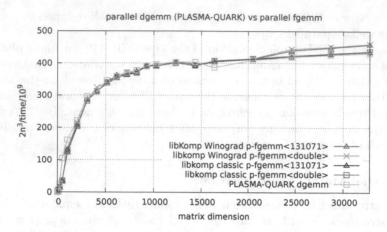

Fig. 2. Speed of exact and numerical matrix multiplication routines

matrices with generic rank profile (i.e. having all their leading principal minor non zero). This assumption allows us to focus on the problem of reducing the modular reduction count.

3.1 Modular Reductions

When computing over a finite field, it is of paramount importance to reduce the number of modular reductions in the course of linear algebra algorithms. The classical technique is to accumulate several multiplications before reducing, namely replacing $\sum_{i=1}^{n}(a_i b_i \mod p)$ with $(\sum_{i=1}^{n} a_i b_i)$ while keeping the result exact. If a_i and b_i are integers between 0 and $p-1$ this is possible with integer or floating point units if the result does not overflow, or in other words if $n(p-1)^2 < 2^{\text{mantissa}}$, see, e.g., [5] for more details.

This induces a splitting of matrices in blocks of size the largest n^* satisfying the latter condition. Now the use of block algorithms in parallel, introduces a second blocking parameter that interferes in the number of reductions. We will therefore compare the number of modular reductions of three variants of the tile iterative algorithm (left-looking, right-looking and Crout, see [3]), the slab recursive algorithm of [5], and the tile recursive algorithm of [6]. For the sake of simplicity, we will assume that the block dimensions in the parallel algorithms are always below n^*. In other words operations are done with full delayed reduction for a single multiplication and any number of additions: operations of the form $\sum a_i b_i$ are reduced modulo p only once at the end of the addition, but $a \cdot b \cdot c$ requires two reductions. For instance, with this model, the number of reductions required by a classic multiplication of matrices of size $m \times k$ by $k \times n$ is simply: $R_{\text{gemm}}(m, k, n) = mn$. From [6, Theorem 3], this extends also for triangular solving with an $m \times n$ unknown matrix: with unit diagonal, $R_{\text{utrsm}}(m, m, n) = mn$ (actually the computation of the last row of the solution requires no modulo reduction as it is just a division by 1, we will therefore rather use $R_{\texttt{utrsm}}(m,m,n) = (m-1)n$ and $R_{\texttt{trsm}}(m,m,n) = 2mn$ (with the previous refinement for $R_{\texttt{utrsm}}(m,m,n)$, this also reduces to $R_{\texttt{trsm}}(m,m,n) = (2m-1)n$. Table 1 sketches the different shapes of the associated routine calls in the main loop of each variant.

Then the number of modular reductions required for these different LU factorization strategies is given in Table 2. The last two rows of the table corresponds to [6, Theorem 4] where $R_{\texttt{utrsm}}$ has been refined to $(m-1)n$ as mentioned above. The first three rows are obtained by setting $k = 1$ in the following block versions. The next three rows are obtained via the following analysis where the base case (i.e. the $k \times k$ factorization) always uses the best unblocked version, that is the Left variant described above. Following Table 1, we thus have:

Table 1. Main loops of the Left looking, Crout and Right looking tile iterative block LU factorization, n and k are respectively matrix and block dimensions (see [3, Chapter 5])

Left looking	Crout	Right looking
for i=1 to n/k **do**	**for** i=1 to n/k **do**	**for** i=1 to n/k **do**
utrsm ((i-1)k,(i-1)k,k)	gemm (n-(i-1)k,(i-1)k,k)	pluq (k,k)
gemm (n-(i-1)k,(i-1)k,k)	gemm (k,(i-1)k,n-ik)	utrsm (k,k,n-ik)
pluq (k,k)	pluq (k,k)	trsm (k,k,n-ik)
trsm (k,k,n-ik)	utrsm (k,k,n-ik)	gemm (n-ik,k,n-ik)
	trsm (k,k,n-ik)	

The right looking variant performs $\frac{n}{k}$ such $k \times k$ base cases, pluq(k,k), then, at iteration i, $(\frac{n}{k} - i)(\texttt{utrsm}(k,k,k) + \texttt{trsm}(k,k,k))$, and $(\frac{n}{k} - i)^2$ gemm (k,k,k), for a total of $\frac{n}{k}(\frac{3}{2}n^2 - \frac{5}{2}n + 1) + \sum_{i=1}^{\frac{n}{k}}(n - ik)\left((3k-2) + (\frac{n}{k} - i)k\right) = \frac{1}{3k}n^3 + \left(1 - \frac{1}{k}\right)n^2 + \left(\frac{1}{6}k - \frac{3}{2} + \frac{1}{k}\right)n.$

The Crout variant requires, at each step, except the first one, to compute $R_{\texttt{gemm}}(n - ik, ik, k)$ reductions for the pivot and below and $R_{\texttt{gemm}}(k, ik, n - (i-1)k)$ for the other block; at each step, to perform one base case for the pivot block, to solve unitary triangular systems, to the left, below the pivot, using $(\frac{n}{k} - i)R_{\texttt{utrsm}}(k,k,k)$ reductions and to solve triangular systems to the right, using $(\frac{n}{k} - i)R_{\texttt{trsm}}(k,k,k)$ reductions.

Similarly, the Left looking variant requires $R_{\texttt{gemm}}(n - ik, ik, k) + R_{\texttt{pluq}}(k) + R_{\texttt{utrsm}}(ik, ik, k) + R_{\texttt{trsm}}(k, k, n - ik)$ reductions in the main loop.

In Table 2 we see that the left looking variant always performs less modular reductions. Then the tiled recursive performs less modular reductions than the Crout variant as soon as $2 \le k \le \frac{n}{2+\sqrt{2}}$. Finally the right looking variant clearly performs more modular reductions. This explains the respective performance of the algorithms shown on Table 3 (except for larger dimensions where fast matrix multiplication comes into play). Also, we see that even when the number of modular reductions is an order of magnitude lower than that of the integer operations the cost of the divisions is nonetheless not negligible. Moreover, the best algorithms here may not perform well in parallel, as will be shown next.

Table 2. Counting modular reductions in full rank block LU factorization of an $n \times n$ matrix modulo p when $np(p-1) < 2^{\text{mantissa}}$, for a block size of k dividing n

Iterative Right looking	$\frac{1}{3}n^3 - \frac{1}{3}n$
Iterative Left Looking	$\frac{3}{2}n^2 - \frac{5}{2}n + 1$
Iterative Crout	$\frac{3}{2}n^2 - \frac{5}{2}n + 1$
Tile Iterative Right looking	$\frac{1}{3k}n^3 + \left(1 - \frac{1}{k}\right)n^2 + \left(\frac{1}{6}k - \frac{3}{2} + \frac{1}{k}\right)n$
Tile Iterative Left looking	$\left(2 - \frac{1}{2k}\right)n^2 - \frac{5}{2}kn + 2k^2 - 2k + 1$
Tile Iterative Crout	$\left(\frac{5}{2} - \frac{1}{k}\right)n^2 + \left(-2k - \frac{3}{2} + \frac{1}{k}\right)n + k^2$
Tiled Recursive	$2n^2 - n\log_2 n - 2n$
Slab Recursive	$(1 + \frac{1}{4}\log_2 n)n^2 - \frac{1}{2}n\log_2 n - n$

Table 3. Timings (in seconds) of sequential LU factorization variants on one core

	$k = 212$			$k = \frac{n}{3}$			Recursive	
	Right	Crout	Left	Right	Crout	Left	Tile	Slab
n=3000	3.02	2.10	**2.05**	2.97	2.15	2.10	2.16	2.26
n=5000	11.37	8.55	8.43	9.24	8.35	8.21	**7.98**	8.36
n=7000	29.06	22.19	21.82	22.56	22.02	21.73	**20.81**	21.66

3.2   Parallel Experiments

In Figure 3 we compare the tiled iterative variants with the tiled recursive algorithm. The latter uses as a base case an iterative Crout algorithm too which performs fewer modular operations, The tiled recursive algorithm performs better than all other tiled iterative versions. This can be explained by a finer and more adaptive granularity and a better locality. The left looking variant performs poorly for it uses an expensive sequential trsm task. Although Crout and right-looking variant perform about the same number of matrix products, those of an iteration of the right-looking variant are independent, contrarily to those of the Crout variant, which explains a better performance despite a larger number of modular reductions.

Figure 4 shows the performance without modular reductions, of the tiled recursive parallel implementation on full rank matrices compared to Plasma-Quark. The best block size for the latter library was determined by hand for each matrix size. The two possible data-storage for Plasma-Quark are used: the collection of tiles or the row-major data-storage. Our tiled recursive parallel PLUQ implementation without modular reductions behaves better than the Plasma-Quark getrf_tile. This is mainly due to the bi-dimensional cutting which allows for a

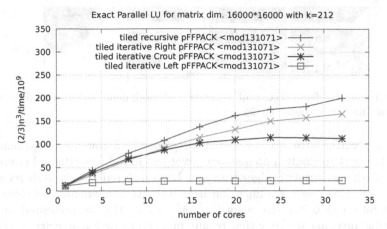

Fig. 3. Parallel LU factorization on full rank matrices with modular operations

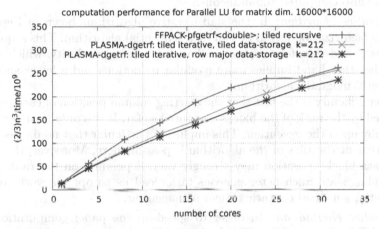

Fig. 4. Speed (normalized to $2/3n^3$ of parallel LU factorization on full rank matrices without modular operations

faster panel elimination, parallel `trsm` computations, more balanced `gemm` computations and some use of Strassen-Winograd's algorithm. This explains why performance become similar again on more than 24 cores: the size of the sequential blocks get below the threshold where this algorithm speeds up computations (typically 2400 on this machine).

4   Elimination with Rank Deficiencies

4.1   Pivoting Strategies

We now consider the general case of matrices with arbitrary rank profile, that can lead to rank deficiencies in the panel eliminations. Algorithms computing the row rank profile (or equivalently the column echelon form) used to share

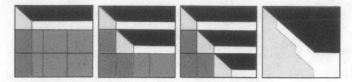

Fig. 5. Slab iterative factorization of a matrix with rank deficiencies, with final reconstruction of the upper triangular factor

a common pivoting strategy: to search for pivots in a row-major fashion and consider the next row only if no non-zero pivot was found (see [10] and references therein). Such an iterative algorithm can be translated into a slab recursive algorithm splitting the row dimension in halves (as implemented in sequential in [5]) or into a slab iterative algorithm. More recently, we presented in [6] a more flexible pivoting strategy that results in a tile recursive algorithm, cutting both dimensions simultaneously. As a by product, both row and column rank profiles are also computed simultaneously.

A slab iterative algorithm. In the slab iterative algorithm shown in Figure 5, each panel factorization has to be run by a sequential algorithm. This sequential task is costly and therefore imposes a choice of a fine granularity, which, as we saw, on the other hand implies more modular reductions and a lesser speed-up of Strassen-Winograd's algorithm.

Another difficulty is the fact that the starting column position of each panel is determined by the rank of the blocks computed so far. It can only be determined dynamically upon the execution. This implies in particular that no data-storage by tiles, that fit the tiles of the algorithm is possible here. Moreover, the workload of each block operation may strongly vary, depending on the rank of the corresponding slab. Such heterogeneous tasks lead us to opt for work-stealing based runtimes instead of static thread management.

Tiled iterative elimination. In order to speed-up the panel computation, we can split it into column tiles. Thanks to the pivoting strategy of [6], it is still possible to recover the rank profiles afterwards. Now with this splitting, the operations remain more local and updates can be parallelized. This approach shares similarities with the recursive computation of the panel described in [4]. Figure 6 illustrates this tile iterative factorization obtained by the combination of a row-slab iterative algorithm, and a column-slab iterative panel factorization.

This optimization used in the computation of the slab factorization improved the computation speed by a factor of 2, to achieve a speed-up of 6.5 on 32 cores with `libkomp`.

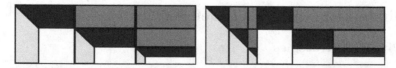

Fig. 6. Panel PLUQ factorization: tiled sub-calls inside a single slab and final reconstruction

Tiled recursive elimination. Recursive algorithms in dense linear algebra is a natural choice for hierarchical memory systems [14]. For large problems, the geometric nature of the recursion causes that the total area of operands for recursive algorithms is less compared to iterative algorithms [9]. We use the tile recursive algorithm described in [6]: the recursive splitting is done in four quadrants. Pivoting is done first recursively inside each quadrant and then between quadrants. It has the interesting feature that if the top-left tile is rank deficient, then the elimination of the bottom-left and top-right tiles can be parallelized. Thus it can be run in parallel using recursive tasks and the pfgemm, ftrsm and flaswp routines.

Figure 7 shows performance obtained for the tiled recursive and the tiled iterative factorization. Both versions are tested using libgomp and libkomp libraries. The input S16K is a 16000×16000 matrix with low rank deficiency (rank is 15500). Linearly independent rows and columns of the generated matrix are uniformly distributed on the dimension.

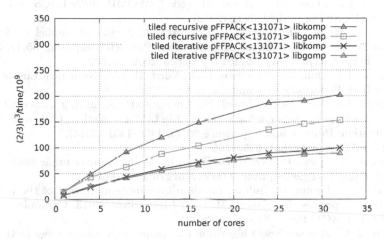

Fig. 7. Performance of tiled recursive and tiled iterative factorizations using libgomp and libkomp. Matrix dimension $n = 16000$ with rank 15500

The implementation with OpenMP of the tiled recursive LU maintained high efficiency in the case of rank deficient matrices. It attained a speed-up of 13.6 on 32 cores. Besides the fact that it benefits from Strassen-Winograd implementation, it is adapted to minimize memory accesses and optimize data placement. Using libkomp instead of libgomp library and numactl, for round and robin interleave memory placement, that helps reducing dependency on bus speed, we manage to obtain high performance for our tiled recursive LU factorization.

5 Conclusion

We analyzed five different algorithms for the computation of Gaussian elimination over a finite field. The granularity surely optimizes the parallelization of these algorithms but at the cost of more modular operations. Algorithms optimizing modular reductions are unfortunately not the most efficient in parallel. The best compromise is obtained with our recursive tiled algorithm that performs best in both aspects.

Perspective. Our future work focuses on two main issues. First, the use of specific allocators that can be used for a better mapping of data in memory and reduce distant accesses. Second, parallel programming frameworks for multicore processors [12] could be more effective than binding threads on each NUMA node. Dataflow based dependencies, like when using OpenMP 4.0 directives, can ensure more parallelism for recursive implementation using `libkomp` [1] library.

References

1. Broquedis, F., Gautier, T., Danjean, V.: libKOMP, an Efficient OpenMP Runtime System for Both Fork-Join and Data Flow Paradigms. In: Chapman, B.M., Massaioli, F., Müller, M.S., Rorro, M. (eds.) IWOMP 2012. LNCS, vol. 7312, pp. 102–115. Springer, Heidelberg (2012)
2. Buttari, A., Langou, J., Kurzak, J., Dongarra, J.: A class of parallel tiled linear algebra algorithms for multicore architectures. Parallel Computing 35(1), 38–53 (2009), http://dx.doi.org/10.1016/j.parco.2008.10.002
3. Dongarra, J.J., Duff, L.S., Sorensen, D.C., Vorst, H.A.V.: Numerical Linear Algebra for High Performance Computers. SIAM (1998)
4. Dongarra, J.J., Faverge, M., Ltaief, H., Luszczek, P.: Achieving numerical accuracy and high performance using recursive tile LU factorization. Concurrency and Computation: Practice and Experience 26(7), 1408–1431 (2014), http://hal.inria.fr/hal-00809765
5. Dumas, J.-G., Giorgi, P., Pernet, C.: Dense linear algebra over prime fields. ACM TOMS 35(3), 1–42 (2008), http://arxiv.org/abs/cs/0601133
6. Dumas, J.-G., Pernet, C., Sultan, Z.: Simultaneous computation of the row and column rank profiles. In: Kauers, M. (ed.) Proc. ISSAC 2013, Grenoble, France, pp. 181–188. ACM Press, New York (2013)
7. Faugère, J.-C.: A new efficient algorithm for computing Gröbner bases (F4). Journal of Pure and Applied Algebra 139(1–3), 61–88 (1999)
8. Gathen, J.V., Gerhard, J.: Modern Computer Algebra. Cambridge University Press, New York (1999)
9. Gustavson, F.G.: Recursion leads to automatic variable blocking for dense linear-algebra algorithms. IBM Journal of Research and Development 41(6), 737–756 (1997)
10. Jeannerod, C.-P., Pernet, C., Storjohann, A.: Rank-profile revealing Gaussian elimination and the CUP matrix decomposition. J. Symb. Comp. 56, 46–68 (2013)
11. Klimkowski, K., van de Geijn, R.A.: Anatomy of a parallel out-of-core dense linear solver. In: ICPP, vol. 3, pp. 29–33. CRC Press (August 1995)
12. Kurzak, J., Ltaief, H., Dongarra, J., Badia, R.M.: Scheduling dense linear algebra operations on multicore processors. Concurrency and Computation: Practice and Experience 22(1), 15–44 (2010)
13. Stein, W.: Modular forms, a computational approach. Graduate studies in mathematics. AMS (2007), http://wstein.org/books/modform/modform
14. Toledo, S.: Locality of reference in lu decomposition with partial pivoting. SIAM Journal on Matrix Analysis and Applications 18(4), 1065–1081 (1997)

Time-Domain BEM for the Wave Equation: Optimization and Hybrid Parallelization

Berenger Bramas[1], Olivier Coulaud[1], and Guillaume Sylvand[2]

[1] Inria Bordeaux, Sud-Ouest, 33405 Talence, France
[2] Airbus Group Innovations, Applied Mathematics and Simulation, Toulouse, France
{Berenger.Bramas,Olivier.Coulaud}@inria.fr, Guillaume.Sylvand@eads.net

Abstract. The problem of time-domain BEM for the wave equation in acoustics and electromagnetism can be expressed as a sparse linear system composed of multiple interaction/convolution matrices. It can be solved using sparse matrix-vector products which are inefficient to achieve high Flop-rate. In this paper we present a novel approach based on the re-ordering of the interaction matrices in slices. We end up with a custom multi-vectors/vector product operation and compute it using SIMD intrinsic functions. We take advantage of the new order of the computation to parallelize in shared and distributed memory. We demonstrate the performance of our system by studying the sequential Flop-rate and the parallel scalability, and provide results based on an industrial test-case with up to 32 nodes.

Keywords: Boundary element method (BEM), time domain, sparse matrix-vector product (SpMV), shared/distributed memory parallelization, SIMD.

1 Introduction

Airbus Group Innovations is an entity of Airbus Group devoted to research and development for the usage of Airbus Group divisions (Airbus Civil Aircraft, Airbus Defence & Space, Airbus Helicopters). The numerical analysis team has been working for more than 20 years on integral equations and boundary element methods for wave propagation simulations. The resulting software solutions are used on a daily basis in acoustics for installation effects computation, aeroacoustic simulations (in a coupled scheme with other tools), and in electromagnetism for antenna siting, electromagnetic compatibility or stealth. Since 2000, these frequency-domain Boundary Element Method (BEM) tools have been extended with a multipole algorithm (called Fast Multipole Method) that allows to solve very large problems, with tens of millions of unknowns, in reasonable time on parallel machines. More recently, H-matrix techniques have enabled the design of fast direct solvers, able to solve with a very high accuracy problems with millions of unknowns without the usual drawback associated with the iterative solvers (no control on the number of iterations, difficulty to find a good preconditioner, etc.). At the same time, we are working on the design and optimization of time

F. Silva et al. (Eds.): Euro-Par 2014, LNCS 8632, pp. 511–523, 2014.

domain BEM (TD-BEM) that allows to obtain with only one calculation the equivalent results of many frequency-domain computations. In this paper, we do not focus on the mathematical formulation of this TD-BEM (based on [2]), but rather on the parallel implementation of the algorithm.

In [3], the authors have implemented a TD-BEM application and their formulation is similar to the one we use. They show results up to 48 CPU and rely on sparse matrix-vector product without giving details on the performance. In [4], the author uses either multi-GPU or multi-CPU parallelization and accelerates the TD-BEM by splitting near field and far field. In [6], they give an overview of an accelerated TD-BEM using Fast Multipole Method. The paper does not contain any information on the sequential performance or even the parallelization which makes it difficult to compare to our work.

The optimization of the Sparse Matrix-Vector product (SpMV) operator has been widely studied because this is an essential operation in many scientific applications. Our work is not an optimization or an improvement for the general SpMV because we use a custom operator that matches our needs. Nevertheless, the optimizations of our implementation have been inspired by the historical work on SpMV which are the reordering of rows/columns, the management of the memory accesses, the blocking of the contiguous data or the data reuse, see [7],[8],[10],[9],[11],[12]. The performance is limited by the memory access pattern, the memory bandwidth and the instruction pipelining. It achieves 20% of the peak performance on common $X86$ architecture.

This paper addresses two major problems of the TD-BEM solver. First, we by-pass the low performance of SpMV by reordering the computation and by using a custom multi-vectors/vector product. Second, based on this new ordering we propose novel parallelization strategies for shared and distributed memory platforms.

The rest of the paper is organized as follows. Section 2 provides background and mathematical formulation of the problem. Section 3 describes the new organization of computations and the multi-vectors SIMD operator. Section 4 details the parallelization strategies inherited from the new computational order. Finally, in Section 5 we provide an experimental performance evaluation of our multi-vectors/vector operator and of the different parallelization strategies.

2   Formulation

Our formulation has been originally defined in [2] but in order to keep this paper self-explanatory, we introduce the relevant aspects of the TD-BEM. An incident wave w with a velocity c and a wavelength λ is emitted on a boundary Ω. This surface Ω is discretized by N unknowns. The problem is also discretized in time with a step Δt and a finite number of iterations driven by the frequency study. In fact, increasing the number of time steps improves the results towards the bottom of the frequency range considered. At iteration time $t_n = n\Delta t$, the vector l^n contains the illumination of w over the unknowns from one or several emitters. The wave illuminates the location where the unknowns are defined and is reflected by these ones over the mesh. It takes a certain amount of time for the waves from the emitter or an unknown to illuminate some others. This relation is characterized by the interaction/convolution matrices M^k. A matrix M^k contains the interactions between unknowns that are separated by a distance around $k.c.\Delta t$ and contains zero for unknowns that are closer or further than this. These $N \times N$ matrices, where N is the number of unknowns, are positive definite and sparse in realistic configuration. They have the following properties:

- The number of non-zero values for a given matrix M^k depends on the structure of the mesh (the distance between the unknowns) and the physical properties of the system c, λ and Δt.
- For $k > K_{max} = 2 + \ell_{max}/(c\Delta t)$, with $\ell_{max} = max_{(x,y)\in\Omega\times\Omega}(|x - y|)$ the maximum distance between two unknowns, the matrices M^k are null.

The construction of these matrices is illustrated in Figure 1. The matrices are filled with values depending on the delay taken by a wave emitted by an unknown to pass over another one.

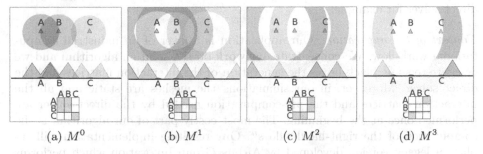

(a) M^0 (b) M^1 (c) M^2 (d) M^3

Fig. 1. Example of M^k matrices for three unknowns A, B, C in 1D. A wave emitted from each unknown is represented at each time step. When a wave is around an unknown, a value is added in the matrix which is symbolized by a gray square. All matrices M^k with $k > 3$ are zero since the longest distance between elements is lower than $3.c.\Delta t$.

Convolution system. Using the convolution matrices M^k, and the incident wave l^n emitted by a source on the mesh, the objective is to compute the state of the unknowns a^n at time n for a given number of time iterations. The problem to solve at time step n is defined in Equation (1)

$$\sum_{k\geq0}^{K_{max}} M^k \cdot a^{n-k} = l^n . \tag{1}$$

Equation (1) can be rewritten as in Equation (2) where the left hand side is the state to compute and the right-hand side is known from the previous time steps and the test case definition

$$a^n = (M^0)^{-1}\left(l^n - \sum_{k=1}^{K_{max}} M^k \cdot a^{n-k}\right). \tag{2}$$

Solution algorithm. The solution is computed in two steps. In the first step, the past is taken into account using the previous values of a^p with $p < n$ and the interaction matrices as shown in Equation (3). The result s^n is subtracted from the illumination vector, see Equation (4)

$$s^n = \sum_{k=1}^{K_{max}} M^k \cdot a^{n-k}, \tag{3}$$

$$\widehat{s}^n = l^n - s^n. \tag{4}$$

In the second step, the state of the system at time step n is obtained by solving the following linear system where $\widehat{s}^n$ is the right-hand side

$$M^0 a^n = \widehat{s}^n. \tag{5}$$

The first step is the most expensive part, from a computational standpoint. The solution of Equation (5) is extremely fast, since the matrix M^0 is symmetric, positive definite, sparse and almost diagonal. One can solve it using a sparse direct solver for example.

Context of the application. Our application is a layer of an industrial computational work-flow. We concentrate our work on the solution algorithm and we delegate to some black-boxes the generation of the interaction matrices and the direct solver. Moreover, in our simulations the meshes are static and all the interaction matrices and the pre-computation needed by the direct solver are performed once at the beginning. The most costly part of our algorithm is the computation of the right-hand side s^n. Our resulting implementation will replace a legacy version developed by Airbus Group Innovation which performs the solution algorithm using SpMV.

3   Summation Algorithm

3.1   Summation Ordering

We refer to the process of computing s^n as the summation stage. The summation uses the interaction matrices M^k and the past values of the unknowns a^{n-k}. A natural implementation of this computation is to perform K_{max} independent SpMV. That is implemented with four nested loops. The first loop is over the time step denoted by index n. The second loop is over the interaction matrices and is controlled by index k in our formulation and goes from 1 to K_{max}. Finally, the two remaining loops are over the rows and the columns of the matrices and are indexed by i and j respectively. The indices i and j cover the unknowns and go from 1 to N. The complete equation is written in Equation (6) where all indexes n, k, i and j are visible.

$$1 \le i \le N, s^n(i) = \sum_{k=1}^{k_{max}} \sum_{j=1}^{N} M^k(i,j) \times a^{n-k}(j) \tag{6}$$

In term of implementation, there is no need to keep the outer loop on index k and two other orders of summation are possible using i or j. The three possibilities are represented in Figure 2 where all interaction matrices M^k are shown one behind the other and represented as a $3D$ block. This figure illustrates the three different ways to access the interaction matrices according to the outer loop index. The natural approach using k is called by *front* and usually relies on SpMV. We propose to use a different approach called by *slice* using j as outer loop index. One can see the data access pattern of the interaction matrices in *slice* which is illustrated by Figure 2c.

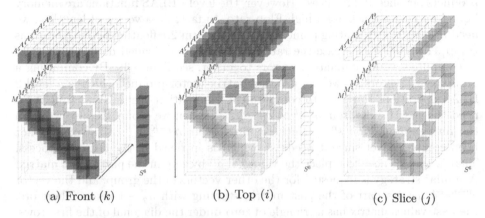

$\quad$ (a) Front (k) $\qquad\qquad$ (b) Top (i) $\qquad\qquad\qquad$ (c) Slice (j)

Fig. 2. Three ways to reorder the computation of s^n with current time step $n - 6$, number of unknowns $N = 8$ and $K_{max} = 6$. For *front* the outer loop is on the different M^k matrices. For *top* the outer loop is over the row index of M^k and s^k. For *slice* the outer loop is over the column index of M^k.

3.2 Slice Structure

We use the word *slice* to name the data that are used when the outer loop index of the summation is j. A $Slice^j$ is composed of the concatenation of each column j of the interaction matrices $[M^1(*, j)\, M^2(*, j) ... M^{K_{max}}(*, j)]$. Therefore, a slice is a sparse matrix of dimension $(N \times (K_{max} - 1))$. It has a non-zero value at line i and column k if $d(i, j) \approx k \cdot c \cdot \Delta t$, where $d(i, j)$ is the distance between the unknowns i and j. This definition is induced by the relation $M^k(i, j) = Slice^j(i, k)$. From the formulation, an interaction matrix represents the interaction between the unknowns for a given time/distance k. Whereas a $Slice^j$ represents the interaction that one unknown j has with others over the time. This provides an important property to the sparse structure of a slice: **the non-zero values are contiguous on each line**. In fact, it takes several iterations for a wave to cross over an unknown. In other words, for a given row i and column j all the interaction matrices M^k that have a non zero value at this position are consecutive in index k. In the slice format, it means that each slice has one vector per line but each of this vector may start at a different column k. If it takes p time steps for the wave from j to cross over i, then $Slice^j(i,k) = M^k(i,j) \neq 0$, $k_s \leq k \leq k_s+p$ where $k_s = d(i,j)/(c\Delta t)$.

3.3   Slice Computation

The Figure 3a shows a slice and how the values are contiguous on each line. It is natural to use level 1 BLAS dot-product instead of SpMV in order to take advantage of this particular structure. Therefore, for the entire summation defined in Equation (6), there are $N \times N$ dot-products to compute s^n (N dot-products per slice and N slices). However, the level 1 BLAS functions are memory bound and cannot achieve a high Flop-rate. In fact, for a vector of length v, we need to load $2.v+1$ floating point values to perform $2.v$ floating point operations (Flop). In order to increase the ratio of Flop against loaded data, we propose to compute several summation vectors together, see Figure 3b. By computing a group of n_g vectors s^*, we can use the matrix-vector product which is a level 2 BLAS operation. However, to compute the summation vector s^n at time n we need the past results from a^{n-1} to $a^{n-K^{max}}$. When we group, we also work on the future summation s^{n+1} which requires a^n to $a^{n-K^{max}+1}$. But a^n has not been computed yet since it needs s^n which is involved in the current process. That is why we need to replace the values of a^n by zero in the past values matrix. A similar strategy is requested for the other vectors of the group, and the vector s^{n+n_g-1} has its part of the past matrix starting with $n_g - 1$ zeros. Therefore, the past values matrix has a triangle of zero under the diagonal of the first rows. At time n, the algorithm computes $N \times N$ matrix-vector products and obtains n_g summation vectors where only the first one is complete. Like in the original algorithm, a direct solver gives a^n from $\widehat{s}^n$ (Equations (4) and (5)). Because the

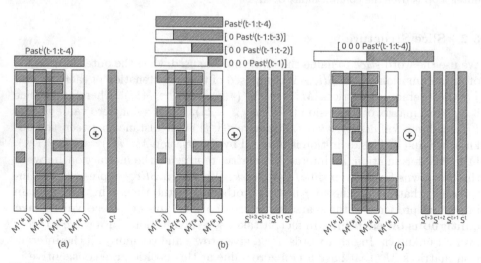

Fig. 3. Three ways of computing a slice product: (a) using dot-products, (b) by grouping with $n_g = 4$ and using matrix-vector product and (c) by grouping $n_g = 4$ and using custom multi-vectors/vector product

values of a^n were replaced by zeros in the summation the algorithm needs to update the incomplete summation vectors. The algorithm computes the action of the current values of a^n (at time step n) on the partial summation vectors from s^{n+1} to s^{n+n_g-1} (corresponding to future time steps $n+1$ to $n+n_g-1$) using SpMV and the n_g first interaction matrices. This operation is called radiation and it has to be repeated n_g times at each iteration.

The past matrix which is used in the slice computation using matrix-vector product has a particular structure. Each column is a copy of the previous column shifted by one and padded with zero (as illustrated on Figure 3b). Thus, instead of storing these data in a matrix of size $n_g \times K^{max}$, it is possible to use a special vector of size $n_g + K^{max} - 1$ with the values of a^{n-1} to $a^{n-K^{max}}$ at its end and with $n_g - 1$ zeros at its beginning as shown in Figure 3c. By grouping n_g vectors and using the special vector, we improve the ratio of Flop against loaded data: for a slice vector of length v, we need to load $2 \cdot v + 2 \cdot n_g - 1$ floating point values and we can perform $2 \cdot v \cdot n_g$ Flops. In such configuration we should be able to call an external matrix-vector product with a leading dimension of one for the past matrix. However, most of the BLAS libraries check the validity of the leading dimension and one is not a correct value. Moreover, a general matrix-vector product cannot take completely advantage of the pattern of the special past vector.

That is why we propose an implementation of an optimized operator to perform this operation and we refer to it as the multi-vectors/vector product. In our implementation, we reduce the memory access by re-using the past values, see Algorithm 1 that computes just one row in the set of output vectors s^n, s^{n+1}, ..., s^{n+n_g-1}.

Algorithm 1. Multi vectors/vector product

Data: n_g the number of result vectors to compute simultaneously (should be ≥ 2)
function MultiVectorsVector(vec[$SIZE\_VEC$], past[$SIZE\_VEC + n_g - 1$]) : res[n_g]

register res[n_g] = 0;
// We store the first past values (to load them once)
register buffer[n_g-1];
for idxBuffer = 0 → n_g-2 do
  | buffer[idxBuffer] = load(past[idxBuffer]);
end
// For all values in the vec
for idxVec = 0 → SIZE_VEC-1 do
  // Copy the current vec value
  register value = load(vec[idxVec]);
  for idxRes = 0 → n_g-3 do
    res[idxRes] += value * buffer[idxRes];
    // Shift the buffer value for the next idxVec loop
    buffer[idxRes] = buffer[idxRes+1];
  end
  res[n_g-2] += value * buffer[n_g-2];
  // Load a new value from the past vector
  buffer[n_g-2] = load(past[idxVec+n_g]);
  res[n_g-1] += value * buffer[n_g-2];
end
return res ;

---

4   Parallelization Strategies

4.1   Distributed Memory Parallelization

The parallelization over distributed memory is realized using Message Passing Interface (MPI) [16] and we name a MPI process a *process*. A slice interval is assigned to each process. This interval from j_{start} to j_{end} can be obtained in different ways: for example by dividing the number of N slices equally or by taking into account the amount of work in each slice. Each process needs to have the past values of the unknowns which match its slice interval. In a first stage, each process computes a part of the summation vectors without communicating with others. Then, all processes synchronize and call a sparse direct method to solve (5) and obtain the current solution a^n. With a number of threads per process equal to one, this algorithm is detailed in Algorithm 2.

At every iteration, the result is saved to disk for later work and it also has to be distributed to let each process have the current result for its interval j_{start} to j_{end}.

4.2   Shared Memory Parallelization

The straightforward parallelization in shared memory is implemented by splitting the slices computation and the radiation between threads. This is done using OpenMP $for pragma$ [17] and it is detailed in Algorithm 2. If the number of threads per process is 1 and the parallelism relies on MPI only, we refer to the algorithm 2 as the Full-MPI implementation. If the number of threads is larger than 1, we refer to it as the Hybrid-MPI/OpenMP implementation.

5   Numerical and Performance Studies

5.1   Experimental Setup

Hardware configuration. We use up to 32 nodes and each node has the following configuration: 2 Quad-core Nehalem Intel Xeon X5550 at $2.66GHz$ and $24GB$ (DDR3) of shared memory.

Compiler and libraries. We use the Gcc 4.7.2 compiler and Open-MPI 1.6.5. The compilation flags are -m64 -march=native -O3 -funroll-loops -freorder-blocks-and-partition -ftree-vectorize -msse -msse2 -msse3 -mfpmath=sse. The direct solver is a state of the art solver Mumps 4.10.0 [15] which relies on Parmetis 3.2.0 and Scotch 5.1:12b. The calculation is performed in 64 bit arithmetic.

Test case. The test case is an airplane composed of 23 962 unknowns shown in Figure 4. The simulation should perform 10 823 time iterations. There are 341 interaction matrices. The total number of non-zero values in the interaction matrices, except M^0, is 5.5×10^9. For one iteration the total amount of Flops to compute the summation s^n is around $11\,GFlops$. If we consider that the direct

Algorithm 2. Complete simulation with Hybrid-MPI/OpenMP parallelization

---

Data: *Slices*[N] the interaction matrices in slice/vectors shape. Each process is working on an interval [j_start; j_end] that cover the entire slices.
Result: $PastValues[j\_end - j\_start + 1][NB\_STEPS + n_g - 1]$ the state of the unknowns for all time step

```
begin
    // Direct Solver initialization (factorize/inverse M⁰)
    invM⁰_handle = direct_solver(M[0]);
    // For all time step with progression by n_g
    for n = 0 → NB_STEPS-1 by n_g do
        S[n_g][N] = 0;
        // Compute n_g vectors with each slices in my interval
        #pragma omp parallel reduce(+:S);
        for j = j_start → j_end do
            foreach Vec v in Slices[j].blocks do
                S[:][v.row] += MultiVectorsVector(v.values, PastValues[j][v.col - n_g + 1
                :v.col + v.length]) ;
            end
        end
        // Finalization
        for idx = 0 → n_g-1 do
            distributed_reduce(S[n_g - idx -1][:]);
            aⁿ = solve(invM⁰_handle, L[n+idx][:] - S[n_g - idx - 1][:]);
            master saves aⁿ to disk;
            // Copy result in Pastvalues format
            PastValues[j_start:j_end][NB_STEPS - n - 1] = aⁿ[j_start:j_end];
            // Radiation
            #pragma omp parallel;
            for past = idx + 1 → n_g-1 do
                S[n_g - past][:] += SpMV(M^{past-idx}[j_start:j_end],aⁿ[j_start:j_end]);
            end
        end
    end
end
```

---

solver has the cost of a matrix vector product, the total amount of Flop for the entire simulation is 130 651 *GFlop*. Storing all the data of the simulation takes more than 70 *GB*. Our application can execute out-of-core simulations, but we concentrate our study on in-core executions. We need at least 4 nodes to have the entire test case fitting in memory.

Fig. 4. Illustration of the Airplane test case

Parallel Efficiency. Usual parallel efficiency is defined by $e_n = T_1/(T_p * p)$ where T_1 is the sequential elpased time to execute the simulation and T_p the elapsed time using p cores. In our case, we use a modified version of the definition because we use at least 4 nodes (to remain in-core) and never execute the simulation sequentially. Using 1 core as a reference would artificially improve efficiency, since we would compare sequential out-of-core computations with parallel in-core computations. Hence, we replace the sequential time T_1 by T_r the time taken by the lowest number of cores which gives the new efficiency formula $\tilde{e}_n = (r * T_r)/(T_p * p)$ where r is the number of cores for the time reference.

5.2   Multi-vectors/Vector Product

We compare three implementations of the multi-vectors/vector product. We choose to have $n_g = 8$ as it is enough to by-pass the memory bandwidth limitation without paying too much extra cost in the radiation stage. The first implementation comes out of the Equation (6) and is implemented in C. Some important compilation flags are used in order to enable loop unrolling and the use of SSE instructions by the compiler. This is referred to as the Compiler Version implementation. The second version is written in C and comes out of the Algorithm 1. It is written with intrinsic SSE functions proposed by the compiler and SSE data types ($\_m128d$). We refer to it as the SSE-Intrinsic implementation. We have analyzed the assembly code the compiler has generated and we have considered that it is not optimal for both implementations. Thus, we have developed a third implementation in asm64 assembly to maximize the data re-use. With $n_g = 8$ it is possible to use all 16 SSE registers in order to read each value only once from the main memory. We refer to it as the SSE-Asm implementation. Figure 5 shows the Flop-rate for all three operators for different lengths of vector v. The two SSE based implementations are close but the SSE-Asm can achieve a slightly higher Flop-rate for large vectors. Both implementations suffer from small cache effects for $N_r = 1\,000$ and $v = 100$ (Figure 5a) and for $N_r = 20\,000$, $v = 25$ and $v = 80$ (Figure 5b). However, the length of the vectors of the slices in real test cases depends on Δt the time step, and the size of the elements on the mesh. In the airplane test case, each vector has a length between 1 and 15 and the average length is 9.5. In this configuration, the SSE-Asm implementation achieves $3.9\,GFlop/s$ per core (Compiler Version achieves $1.7\,GFlop/s$) for a peak performance of $10.64\,GFlop/s$.

5.3   Scalability

We compare the Full-MPI and the Hybrid-MPI/OpenMP implementations to compute the airplane test case. We use 4 to 32 nodes and 8 cores per node. In Figure 6 we give the total execution time and the parallel efficiency. The efficiency is worthy for both implementations but in terms of execution time, the Full-MPI is better. Even if the number of processes involved in the global communications becomes larger because there are 8 MPI processes on each node, there is no advantage to reduce this number by having one process per node

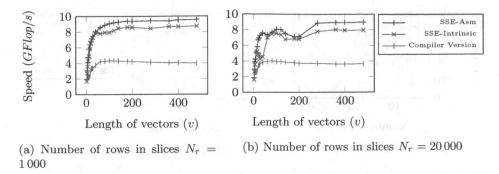

(a) Number of rows in slices $N_r = 1\,000$

(b) Number of rows in slices $N_r = 20\,000$

Fig. 5. Performance evaluation in *GFlop/s* for the multi-vectors/vector slice computation code for three implementation methods with $n_g = 8$. The test cases are slices of dimension $N_r \times v$.

and intra-node parallelism using threads. Figure 7 gives the percentages of time taken by the different operations. The time spent for the summation decreases as the number of nodes increases for both implementations. However, we can see that the Hybrid-MPI/OpenMP implementation exhibits more idle time than the Full-MPI when the number of nodes increases. In the Hybrid-MPI/OpenMP implementation some parts of the code are sequential, the threads share data, they parallelize small operations like the radiation for instance and the work is balanced statically between threads. In consequence, there are less MPI-processes in the Hybrid-MPI/OpenMP implementation but the threads are less balanced and they have to wait longer in the synchronization/reduction points.

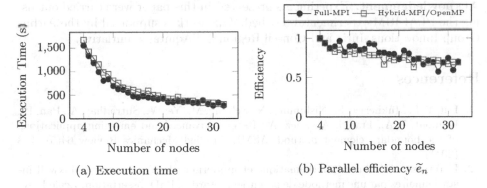

(a) Execution time

(b) Parallel efficiency $\widetilde{e}_n$

Fig. 6. Execution time and parallel efficiency of the airplane simulation for the Full-MPI and the Hybrid-MPI/OpenMP implementations using 4 to 32 nodes, 8 CPU per node and $n_g = 8$

The previous application used by Airbus Group takes $13\,500$ seconds to compute the airplane simulation on 6 nodes. The new version presented in this paper takes only $1\,200$ seconds, which is around 10 times faster.

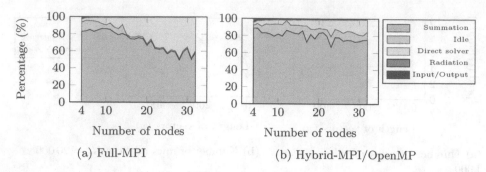

(a) Full-MPI   (b) Hybrid-MPI/OpenMP

Fig. 7. Percentage of the time taken for the different operations to compute the airplane simulation for the Full-MPI and the Hybrid-MPI/OpenMP implementations using 4 to 32 nodes, 8 CPU per node and $n_g = 8$

6 Conclusion

We have presented a new parallelization and efficient implementation of a TD-BEM solver. We showed that the method scales efficiently and how the reordering of the computation leads to a good Flop-rate despite the sparse structure of the data. Moreover, our current application has a speedup of 10 against the previous implementation. In future work, we intend to compute larger simulations and in the longer term to use accelerators. We intend to investigate how a *Slice* product can be performed efficiently on accelerators using the abundant research that has been developed for the SpMV.

Acknowledgement. Experiments presented in this paper were carried out using the PLAFRIM experimental test bed. This work is supported by the Airbus Group Innovations, Inria and Conseil Régional d'Aquitaine initiative.

References

1. Liu, Y.J., Mukherjee, S., Nishimura, N., Schanz, M., Ye, W., Sutradhar, A., Pan, E., Dumont, N.A., Frangi, A., Saez, A.: Recent advances and emerging applications of the boundary element method. ASME Applied Mechanics Review 64(5), 138 (2011)
2. I. Terrasse, Résolution mathématique et numérique des équations de Maxwell instationnaires par une méthode de potentiels retardés, PhD dissertation, Ecole Polytechnique Palaiseau France (1993)
3. Abboud, T., Pallud, M., Teissedre, C.: SONATE: A Parallel Code for Acoustics Nonlinear oscillations and boundary-value problems for Hamiltonian systems, Technical report (1982),
   http://imacs.xtec.polytechnique.fr/Reports/sonate-parallel.pdf
4. Hu, F.Q.: An efficient solution of time domain boundary integral equations for acoustic scattering and its acceleration by Graphics Processing Units. In: 19th AIAA/CEAS Aeroacoustics Conference, ch. (2013), doi:10.2514/6.2013-2018

5. Langer, S., Schanz, M.: Time Domain Boundary Element Method. In: Marburg, S., Nolte (eds.) Computational Acoustics of Noise Propagation in Fluids - Finite and Boundary Element Methods, pp. 495–516. Springer, Heidelberg (2008)
6. Takahashi, T.: A Time-domain BIEM for Wave Equation accelerated by Fast Multipole Method using Interpolation, pp. 191–192 (2013), doi:10.1115/1.400549
7. Karakasis, V., Goumas, G., Koziris, N.: Perfomance Models for Blocked Sparse Matrix-Vector Multiplication Kernels. In: International Conference on Parallel Processing 2009, pp. 356–364 (2009), doi:10.1109/ICPP.2009.21
8. Nishtala, R., Vuduc, R.W.: When Cache Blocking of Sparse Matrix Vector Multiply Works and Why. In: Proceedings of the PARA 2004 Workshop on the State-of-the-art in Scientific Computing (2004)
9. Toledo, S.: Improving the memory-system performance of sparse-matrix vector multiplication. IBM Journal of Research and Development 41(6), 711–725 (1997)
10. Pinar, A., Heath, M.T.: Improving performance of sparse matrix-vector multiplication. In: Proceedings of the 1999 ACM/IEEE Conference on Supercomputing. ACM (1999)
11. Yzelman, A.N., Bisseling, R.H.: Cache-Oblivious Sparse MatrixVector Multiplication by Using Sparse Matrix Partitioning Methods. SIAM Journal on Scientific Computing 31(4), 3128–3154 (2009), doi:10.1137/080733243
12. Vuduc, R.W., Moon, H.-J.: Fast sparse matrix-vector multiplication by exploiting variable block structure. In: Yang, L.T., Rana, O.F., Di Martino, B., Dongarra, J. (eds.) HPCC 2005. LNCS, vol. 3726, pp. 807–816. Springer, Heidelberg (2005)
13. Goto, K., Advanced, T.: High-Performance Implementation of the Level-3 BLAS, 117 (2006)
14. Morton, G.M.: A Computer Oriented Geodetic Data Base and a New Technique in File Sequencing. International Business Machines Company (1966)
15. Amestoy, P.R., Duff, I.S., L'Excellent, J.-Y.: MUMPS MUltifrontal Massively Parallel Solver Version 2.0 (1998)
16. Snir, M., Otto, S., et al.: The MPI core, 2nd edn (1998)
17. OpenMP specifications, Version 3.1 (2011), http://www.openmp.org

Structured Orthogonal Inversion
of Block p-Cyclic Matrices on Multicores
with GPU Accelerators*

Sergiy Gogolenko[1], Zhaojun Bai[2], and Richard Scalettar[2]

[1] Donetsk National Technical University, Donetsk, 83001, Ukraine
sergiy.gogolenko@gmail.com
[2] University of California, Davis, CA 95616, USA
{bai@cs,scalettar@physics}@ucdavis.edu

Abstract. We present a block structured orthogonal factorization (BSOF) algorithm and its parallelization for computing the inversion of block p-cyclic matrices. We aim at the high performance on multicores with GPU accelerators. We provide a quantitative performance model for optimal host-device load balance, and validate the model through numerical tests. Benchmarking results show that the parallel BSOF based inversion algorithm attains up to 90% of `DGEMM` performance on hybrid CPU+GPU systems.

Keywords: p-cyclic matrix, matrix inversion, structured orthogonal factorization, performance modelling, GPU acceleration.

1 Introduction

Since the pioneering works of Varga, Young, Romanovsky, and others in the 1950s, p-cyclic matrices have been found to be a very useful class of structured matrices with applications in numerical methods for differential equations, Markov chain modeling and quantum Monte Carlo simulations. The concept of block p-cyclic matrices in its modern term refers to matrices which can be transformed to the following *normalized block p-cyclic form* by row and/or column permutations:

$$
H = \begin{bmatrix}
A_1 & & & & B_p \\
B_1 & A_2 & & & \\
& B_2 & A_3 & & \\
& & \ddots & \ddots & \\
& & & B_{p-1} & A_p
\end{bmatrix},
\tag{1}
$$

* This work was supported by the National Science Foundation under grant NSF-PHY-1005503. SG would like to thank the Fulbright Program Office in Ukraine and the Institute of International Education for financial support during this study. This research used resources of the National Energy Research Scientific Computing Center, which is supported by the Office of Science of the U.S. Department of Energy under Contract No. DE-AC02-05CH11231.

F. Silva et al. (Eds.): Euro-Par 2014, LNCS 8632, pp. 524–535, 2014.
© Springer International Publishing Switzerland 2014

where A_i and B_i are non-zero blocks. For the sake of simplicity, in this paper, we are concerned entirely with the normalized block p-cyclic matrices, and furthermore, we assume that A_i and B_i are n-by-n square blocks, although in some applications A_i and B_i are rectangular. The fact that we discuss only matrices with the square blocks A_i and B_i does not limit the generality of approaches presented in this paper.

The early studies of p-cyclic matrices were closely related to numerical solution of differential equations [3,9,10]. In these applications, the p-cyclic matrices are also referred to as bordered almost block diagonal (BABD) matrices. An incomplete list of BABD-based numerical algorithms includes multiple shooting and finite difference schemes for two-point boundary value problems (BVPs), orthogonal spline collocation methods for separable elliptic BVPs, method of lines and Keller's box scheme for various initial BVPs [3,9]. The p-cyclic matrices also appear in Markov chain modeling, where the p-cyclic stochastic matrices represent infinitesimal generators of continuous-time Markov chains with periodic transition graphs for queuing networks and stochastic Petri nets [2]. In quantum Monte Carlo (QMC) simulations of Hubbard models for strongly correlated materials, the inverses of p-cyclic matrices, referred to as Green's functions, are required to be repeatedly computed *explicitly* for physical observables (see [1,6] and references therein). Other sources of applications of p-cyclic matrices include some linear least-square problems and parameter estimation with non-linear differential algebraic equations (DAE) models.

In contrast to the subject of solving block p-cyclic linear systems, where we observe tremendous progress over the last six decades, the problem of computing p-cyclic matrix inversion explicitly remains in a state of infancy. The recent advances are mainly related to computing some particular blocks in the inverse of a p-cyclic matrix using well-known explicit expressions [1]. For instance, the paper [6] addresses stabilized algorithms for calculation of diagonal blocks of the inverse of block p-cyclic matrices. To the best of our knowledge, there is no previous work focused on numerical algorithms for the entire inversion of block p-cyclic matrices, which is required for time-dependent physical measurements in the quantum Monte Carlo simulation [1]. Filling this gap is the main purpose of our paper.

In this paper, we pay particular attention to algorithmic solutions designed specifically for high performance computing on GPU accelerated multicore systems. We should point out that numerical libraries for GPGPU computing, including widely used CuSPARSE, CuLA, Paralution, and CUSP, do not support inversion of structured matrices. Furthermore, solvers in dense linear algebra libraries for GPUs such as CuBLAS, Magma [7], and CuLA, do not implement mechanisms for avoiding redundant computations with zero-blocks.

2 Previous Work

Historically, the studies of p-cyclic matrices were primarily focused on iterative and direct methods for p-cyclic linear systems. The vast literature on iterative

methods covers in detail successive overrelaxation, aggregation and disaggrega-
tion, Chebyshev semi-iterative, and Krylov subspace methods [2]. On the other
hand, the attention to the direct solvers is also remarkable. Researchers explored
numerous variations of Gaussian elimination and orthogonal factorization approaches for solving p-cyclic systems. There is a large volume of literature on
Gaussian elimination dealing with a special case of p-cyclic systems, called almost block diagonal (ABD) systems [9]. Nevertheless, while handling the ABD
systems successfully, Gaussian elimination processes could fail in more general
cases of p-cyclic systems. In fact, in [10], it is shown that the Gaussian elimination with row partial pivoting produces exponential error growth for p-cyclic
systems arising from multiple shooting for some linear BVPs with mixed two-
point boundary conditions. There is a number of approaches that enlarge the
class of linear systems for which numerical stability is ensured, such as certain
forms of pre-scaling and replacing row-by-row pivoting with more accurate panel
pivoting strategies. In the recent paper [5] Khabou et al. propose to use a panel
rank-revealing pivoting strategy based on strong rank revealing QR, which significantly reduces the growth factor, and thus results in practical stability of
Gaussian elimination in most cases.

Due to numerical stability issues of Gaussian elimination algorithms, Wright
proposed to use a structured orthogonal factorization (SOF) [9]. He described a
serial and two parallel block SOF algorithms. The first parallel algorithm uses
the recursive factorization process similar to cyclic reduction, whereas the second
one factorizes p-cyclic matrix in two steps, at first splitting the entire matrix in
parts and factorizing these parts concurrently, and then performing factorization
of the reduced p-cyclic matrix formed from border blocks of the parts factorized
in the previous step. A proof of the stability of SOF is presented in [9].

3   Basic Algorithms

This section gives a brief overview of an algorithm for structure-exploiting orthogonal inversion of block p-cyclic matrices. It is referred to as BSOFI. For
more details of the BSOFI and its modifications such as blocking and batching,
we refer readers to our technical report [4].

The algorithmic framework of BSOFI is composed of three phases. The first
one is the block SOF of H: $H = QR$. Once factors Q and R are computed,
the inverse is calculated by the identity $H^{-1} = R^{-1}Q^T$ in two phases, namely
inversion of the factor R and applying the transpose of the factor Q.

Block structured orthogonal factorization (BSOF) is a block structured QR
factorization algorithm introduced in [9], and has an identical complexity to the
best known block structured Gaussian elimination based algorithms. The essence
of this algorithm is in transformation of the matrix H through a sequence of $p-1$
block row updates (Fig. 1).

Data: H, n, p
Result: $R, \{Q^{(k)} | 1 \leq k < p-1\}$

1 $R \leftarrow O;\ \tilde{A}_1 \leftarrow A_1\ ;\ \tilde{B}_1 \leftarrow B_p;$
2 **for** $k \in \{1, 2, ..., p-2\}$ **do**

3 $\quad$ Compute regular QR: $Q^{(k)} \begin{bmatrix} R_{kk} \\ 0 \end{bmatrix} = \begin{bmatrix} \tilde{A}_k \\ B_k \end{bmatrix};$

4 $\quad \begin{bmatrix} R_{k,k+1} & R_{k,p} \\ \tilde{A}_{k+1} & \tilde{B}_{k+1} \end{bmatrix} \leftarrow \left(Q^{(k)} \right)^T \begin{bmatrix} 0 & \tilde{B}_k \\ A_{k+1} & 0 \end{bmatrix};$

5 Compute the QR: $Q^{(p-1)} \begin{bmatrix} R_{p-1,p-1} & R_{p-1,p} \\ 0 & R_{p,p} \end{bmatrix} = \begin{bmatrix} \tilde{A}_{p-1} & \tilde{B}_{p-1} \\ B_{p-1} & A_{p,p} \end{bmatrix};$

Fig. 1. BSOF – Wright's serial version of SOF algorithm

This reduction process results in the factorization $H = QR$, where Q is a product of the orthogonal $2n$-by-$2n$ matrices $Q^{(k)}$ extended by identity blocks:

$$Q = \prod_{k=1}^{p-1} Q_k = \prod_{k=1}^{p-1} I_{n(k-1)} \oplus Q^{(k)} \oplus I_{n(p-k-1)}, \quad Q^{(k)} = \begin{bmatrix} Q_{11}^{(k)} & Q_{12}^{(k)} \\ Q_{21}^{(k)} & Q_{22}^{(k)} \end{bmatrix},$$

and R has block upper bidiagonal form with full last block column:

$$R = \begin{bmatrix} R_{11} & R_{12} & & & R_{1,p} \\ & R_{22} & R_{23} & & R_{2,p} \\ & & \ddots & \ddots & \vdots \\ & & & R_{p-1,p-1} & R_{p-1,p} \\ & & & & R_{p,p} \end{bmatrix}. \tag{2}$$

Inversion of matrix R via block back substitution is the second phase. The inverse $X = R^{-1}$ is block upper triangular, and its non-zero blocks can be computed via block back substitution (BBS). We obtain a row version of the BBS Fig. 2a by taking into account the zero-blocks of R, while solving the matrix equation $RX = I$ for X. Likewise, the column version of the BBS algorithm is based on solving $XR = I$.

Both versions of the BBS have their virtues and flaws. The columnwise BBS requires two times more floating point operations (flops) compared to its row version. On the other hand, we are able to perform SOF and the column version in parallel, which overcomes lack of parallelism in the factorization phase (see Fig. 1). In contrast, the latter is impossible in the row version.

Applying the orthogonal factor Q^T to R^{-1} is the last phase. Due to the orthogonality of $Q^{(k)}$, the inverse of Q is equal to

$$Q^{-1} = Q^T = \prod_{k=1}^{p-1} Q_{p-k}^T = \prod_{k=1}^{p-1} I_{n(p-k-1)} \oplus \left(Q^{(p-k)} \right)^T \oplus I_{n(k-1)}. \tag{3}$$

---

[1] Batched denotes group of kernels that can be implemented in a single batched run.

<table>
<tr><td>

Data: R, n, p
Result: X

1 $X \leftarrow O$;
2 $X_{p-2:p,p-2:p} \leftarrow R_{p-2:p,p-2:p}^{-1}$;
3 Batched $_{i=1:p-3}$ $\{X_{ii} \leftarrow R_{ii}^{-1}\}$;
4 $X_{1:p-3,p} \leftarrow R_{1:p-3,p}X_{p,p}$;
5 Batched $_{i=1:p-3}$
   $\{X_{i,p} \leftarrow -X_{ii}R_{i,p},$
   $X_{i,i+1} \leftarrow -X_{ii}R_{i,i+1} \}$;
6 for $i \in \{p-3, p-4, ..., 1\}$ do
7   $\lfloor$ $X_{i,i+2:p} \leftarrow$
       $X_{i,i+2:p} + X_{i,i+1}X_{i+1,i+2:p}$;
8   $X_{i,i+1} \leftarrow X_{i,i+1}X_{i+1,i+1}$;

</td><td>

Data: R, n, p
Result: X

1 $X \leftarrow O$;
2 Batched $_{j=3:p}$ $\{X_{jj} \leftarrow R_{jj}^{-1}\}$;
3 Batched $_{j=3:p-1}$
   $\{X_{j-1,j} \leftarrow -R_{j-1,j}X_{jj}\}$;
4 $X_{1:2,1:2} \leftarrow R_{1:2,1:2}^{-1}$; $X_{1,p} \leftarrow X_{11}X_{1,p}$;
5 for $j \in \{3, ..., p-1\}$ do
6   $\lfloor$ Batched $\{X_{1:j-1,j} \leftarrow X_{1:j-1,j-1}X_{jj},$
       $X_{1:j-1,p} \leftarrow$
       $X_{1:j-1,p} + X_{1:j-1,j-1}R_{j-1,p}\}$
7 $X_{1:p-1,p} \leftarrow X_{1:p-1,p} + X_{1:p-1,p-1}X_{p-1,p}$;
8 $X_{1:p-1,p} \leftarrow -R_{1:p-1,p}X_{p,p}$;

</td></tr>
</table>

(a) BSTRI_RV – Row Version of the BBS   (b) BSTRI_CV – Column Version of the BBS

Fig. 2. Inversion of matrix R via block back substitution[1]

<table>
<tr><td>

Data: $X, \{Q^{(k)}|1 \le k < p-1\}, n, p$
Result: X

1 for $k \in \{p-1, p-2, ..., 1\}$ do
2   $\lfloor$ $X_{1:p,k:k+1} \leftarrow X_{1:p,k:k+1}Q^{(k)T}$

</td><td>

Data: $X_{1:p,k:k+1}, Q^{(k)}, n, p$
Result: $X_{1:p,k:k+1}$

1 $W_{1:k+1,k:k+1} \leftarrow X_{1:k+1,k:k+1}Q^{(k)T}$;
2 $W_{k+2:p,k:k+1} \leftarrow X_{k+2:p,k:k+1}Q_{1:2,2}^{(k)T}$;
3 $X_{1:p,k:k+1} \leftarrow W$;

</td></tr>
</table>

(a) BSOI – Update X via applying Q^T (b) BSOI_Qk – Applying Q_k^T

Fig. 3. Applying the orthogonal factors (Householder reflectors) to R^{-1}

Thus, computing product $R^{-1}Q^T$ is equivalent to applying Householder reflectors of $\left(Q^{(k)}\right)^T$ to the pairs of column panels of R^{-1} from right in a backward order, as shown in Fig. 3a. This is the gist of the last phase of BSOFI.

If matrices $Q^{(k)}$ are given in an explicit form, we benefit from the upper triangular structure of matrix R^{-1} by means of replacing line 2 in Fig. 3a by the algorithm BSOI_Qk from Fig. 3b. This simple modification reduces the number of flops in the algorithm shown in Fig. 3a from $8n^3p(p-1)$ to $2n^3(3p^2-p-4)$. Note that complete reconstruction of matrices $Q^{(k)}$ from Householder reflectors requires $O(n^3p)$ extra flops.

Computational complexity of the BSOFI algorithms is shown in Table 1. If BSTRI_RV is used, the total flops is $\Theta(7nN^2)$, where $N = n{\times}p$. This is roughly just two times more than the minimum flops count $\Theta(\frac{7}{2}nN^2)$ for the unstable Gaussian elimination based inversion without pivoting.

---

[2] The lower order terms are omitted for the sake of simplicity. More accurate formulae are presented in [4].

Table 1. Operation counts for the three phases of BSOFI algorithm[2]

Phase	Routine	Additions	Multiplications	Total Flops
I	BSOF	$\frac{1}{6}n^2(46np-60n+15p)$	$\frac{1}{6}n^2(46np-60n+39p)$	$\frac{1}{3}n^2(46np-60n+27p)$
II	BSTRI_RV	$\frac{1}{6}n^3\left(3p^2+7p-21\right)$	$\frac{1}{6}n^3\left(3p^2+7p-21\right)$	$\frac{1}{3}n^3\left(3p^2+7p-21\right)$
	BSTRI_CV	$\frac{1}{6}n^3\left(6p^2-11p+12\right)$	$\frac{1}{6}n^3\left(6p^2-11p+12\right)$	$\frac{1}{3}n^3\left(6p^2-11p+12\right)$
III	BSOI	$n^2p\left(3np-2n+p\right)$	$n^2p\left(3np-2n+p\right)$	$2n^2p\left(3np-2n+p\right)$

4 Parallel Implementation on Multicore with GPU Accelerators

Parallel "host-device" BSOFI algorithm. We design our parallel "host-device" algorithm in a way to maximally benefit through extensive use of well optimized vendor-specific linear algebra kernels. The latter implies paying attention to the limited choice of batched linear algebra kernels for GPUs and the diversity in the kernel's performance on throughput and latency oriented processors.

Specifically, our design is inspired by the following well-known observation. The performance efficiency highly varies for different numerical kernels, and the matrix-matrix multiplication routine DGEMM tends to be the most efficient among other BLAS/LAPACK kernels. Furthermore, performance gaps between DGEMM and other kernels are usually much lower for latency oriented processors compared to the throughput oriented ones. At the same time, in both cases, the gaps become smaller as the size of the problems grows. Hence, to attain better performance of hybrid CPU+GPU algorithm, it is preferable to exploit the throughput oriented GPU accelerators only for DGEMM and, conversely, to use the latency oriented CPUs for the whole variety of required kernels. In addition, such work distribution strategy avoids those LAPACK kernels for GPU platforms, which require CPU resources, and thus may interfere with pure CPU kernels executed in parallel. Specifically, following the recipes given in [8], QR factorization routines from the state-of-the-art LAPACK API implementations for GPUs, such as MAGMA [7] and CuLA, usually use an approach, where column panels are factorized on CPU and afterwards sent to GPU for trailing matrix update.

Since a vast part of computations in the BSOFI is spent on DGEMM, this algorithm has a great potential to be reorganized in accordance with the work distribution strategy discussed above. The necessary modifications are sketched in Fig. 4. To overcome the lack of parallelism and DGEMM operations in the factorization phase, we modify the basic BSOFI algorithm by merging the first two phases – factorization of H and inversion of factor R – in a single factorization/inversion algorithm BSOFTRI. Hence, in the BSOFTRI, factorization is a part of computation process which utilizes both host and devices in parallel.

The merged factorization/inversion phase consists of three steps. At the first step, we perform partial factorization of input p-cyclic matrix H on the host, where we run l_F loop iterations of BSOF algorithm (see Fig. 1). This step is

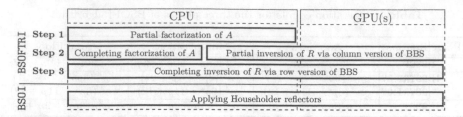

Fig. 4. Framework of the BSOFI adopted to execution on hybrid CPU+GPU platforms

aimed at preparing columns of R for further inversion and avoiding idles related to synchronizing concurrent threads in the next step. Since the optimal number of iterations l_F is usually relatively small, this step does not influence the overall performance of the algorithm much. At the second step, we fork the computational process on two asynchronous threads. The first thread completes factorization on CPU, whereas the second one computes upper left corner of matrix R^{-1} performing iterations of the column-wise inversion algorithm BSTRI_CV (see Fig. 2b). Once the SOF is completed, we join both threads and proceed to the third step, where we continue computing R^{-1} via row version of the BBS algorithm BSTRI_RV (see Fig. 2a) omitting treatment of the j_F already inverted blocks columns of R^{-1}. Switching from column-wise to row-wise inversion algorithm reduces computational complexity of BSOFTRI compared to the algorithm which uses only column version of BBS.

Depending on the ratio between multicores and device performance and the value of p, we make a decision on the need for processing the last column panel in BSOFTRI inversion thread. If device performance is insufficient to invert more than first $p - 2$ column panels of R while H is factorizing, we postpone processing the last column panel in order to avoid doubling of computational costs introduced by the original column version of BBS shown in Fig. 2b (see table 1).

In order to minimize data transfers from host to device in BSOFTRI algorithm, we employ devices in computing only those blocks of R^{-1}, which correspond to the zero blocks of R. The workload distribution between CPU and GPU(s) is controlled by parameters l_j and l_i respectively as illustrated in Fig. 5a and 5b.

In the phase of applying Householder reflectors to R^{-1}, we update block column pairs by means of explicit reconstruction of matrices $Q^{(k)}$ and the scheme similar to the algorithm shown in Fig. 3b. In this way, we replace DORMQR calls for applying reflectors to column panels in favor of more efficient DGEMM calls under the small computational overhead. The upper parts of block columns are updated on the host, whereas devices are used to update lower parts. Since the lower part of R^{-1} has more zero blocks, this approach requires less data transfers from CPU to GPUs. In order to avoid physical data transfers inside devices, we store block columns of the input matrix W in the reversed order with respect to the natural order of columns in matrix X. Namely, the $(k + 1)$th block column

---

[3] White – zero blocks, light gray – input non-zero blocks, dark gray – blocks processed (partially or fully) in the preceding iteration. Irrelevant zero blocks are omitted.

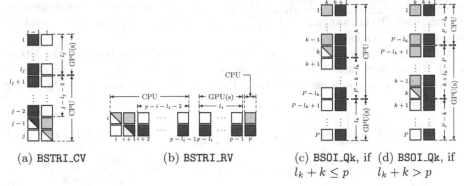

(a) BSTRI_CV   (b) BSTRI_RV   (c) BSOI_Qk, if   (d) BSOI_Qk, if
                                            $l_k + k \leq p$ $l_k + k > p$

Fig. 5. Workload distribution between host and device(s) while processing jth block column and ith block row of R^{-1} (a,b) and applying Q_k^T to R^{-1} (c,d)[3]

of X corresponds to $W_{:,1}$ and the kth block column of X corresponds to $W_{:,2}$. Herewith we use the following equality to update column pairs on device

$$X_{p-l_k:p,k:k+1}Q^{(k)T} = \begin{bmatrix} X_{p-l_k:p,k+1} & X_{p-l_k:p,k} \end{bmatrix} \begin{bmatrix} Q_{1:2,2}^{(k)} & Q_{1:2,1}^{(k)} \end{bmatrix}^T \qquad (4)$$

The workload distribution between host and device is controlled by l_k. If $l_k + k \leq p$ (Fig. 5c), then $X_{p-l_k:p,k} = 0$, and hence device does not require sub-matrix $Q_{1:2,1}^{(k)}$ to compute update according to (4). In contrast, if $l_k + k > p$ (Fig. 5c), whole matrix $Q^{(k)}$ and non-zero blocks of kth column panel of X should be sent from host to device for further processing. For more details on the algorithm presented in this paragraph, see [4].

Performance modelling and load balancing. The parameters l_i, l_j, l_k and l_F introduced in the previous paragraph, control workload distribution between host and devices, and play a crucial role in performance tuning. The following text is an excerpt of results related to choosing above-mentioned parameters and performance modelling. These results are based on the following assumptions: (i) the elapsed time for multiplying mn-by-n and kn-by-n matrices is nearly mk times more than the wall time for computing the product of two n-by-n matrices; (ii) the performance of numerical kernel is roughly proportional to the number of CPU cores utilized in its computing. These assumptions are consistent with benchmarking results for moderate and large values of n [4]. For more details and derivation of formulae, we refer to [4].

The formulae presented below use the following notation for time measures. $T_{R(P)}^{cr}$ denotes the wall time for BLAS and LAPACK routines R with a tuple of parameters P on the computational resource CPU or GPU, respectively. E.g., $T_{DGEMM(m,n,k)}^{cpu}$ is an elapsed time for computing a product of m-by-k and k-by-n matrices by means of the routine DGEMM on the CPU. We alias the routines for copying rectangular matrices to and from GPU with SET and GET respectively. We use braces if these data exchange operations can be executed algorithmi-cally in parallel with some numerical kernel(s). I.e., $\{T_{DGEMM(n,n,n)}^{gpu}, T_{GET(n,n)}^{gpu}\}$ is equal to $\max\{T^{\text{gpu}}_{\text{DGEMM(n,n,n)}}, T^{\text{gpu}}_{\text{GET(n,n)}}\}$ if copying is asynchronous and implemented via `cublasGetMatrixAsync`, and $T^{\text{gpu}}_{\text{DGEMM(n,n,n)}} + T^{\text{gpu}}_{\text{GET(n,n)}}$ if synchronous routine `cublasGetMatrix` is used.

The optimal values of the parameters l_j, l_i, and l_k correspond to the situation if the elapsed time of processing assigned kernels on both host and devices are roughly the same in each iteration. These conditions result in the following approximations

$$l_j \approx \frac{1}{1+\kappa_C}(j+c_j), \quad l_i \approx \frac{1}{1+\kappa_R}(p - \min\{i, j_F\} + 1 + c_i), \quad (5)$$

$$l_k \approx \begin{cases} \dfrac{1}{1+\kappa_Q}(p + k + 2 + c'_k - c''_k), & \text{if } k \leq \dfrac{\kappa_Q p - 2 - c'_k}{\kappa_Q + 2}, \\[3mm] \dfrac{1}{1+\kappa_Q}\left(p + \dfrac{\kappa_Q}{2}(p-k) + 1 + c'_k/2 - c''_k\right), & \text{if } k > \dfrac{\kappa_Q p - 2 - c'_k}{\kappa_Q + 2}, \end{cases} \quad (6)$$

where

$$\kappa_C = \frac{\{T^{\text{gpu}}_{\text{DGEMM(n,n,n)}}, T^{\text{gpu}}_{\text{GET(n,n)}}\}}{T^{\text{cpu}}_{\text{DGEMM(n,n,n)}}/(1+\eta)}, \quad c_j = 2\frac{T^{\text{cpu}}_{\text{DTRTRI(n)}} + 2T^{\text{cpu}}_{\text{DTRMM(n,n)}}}{2T^{\text{cpu}}_{\text{DGEMM(n,n,n)}}} - 1 > \frac{1}{6},$$

$$\kappa_R = \frac{\{T^{\text{gpu}}_{\text{DGEMM(n,n,n)}}, T^{\text{gpu}}_{\text{GET(n,n)}}\}}{T^{\text{cpu}}_{\text{DGEMM(n,n,n)}}}, \quad c_i = 2\frac{T^{\text{cpu}}_{\text{DTRTRI(n)}} + 3T^{\text{cpu}}_{\text{DTRMM(n,n)}}}{2T^{\text{cpu}}_{\text{DGEMM(n,n,n)}}} - 2 > -\frac{1}{3},$$

$$\kappa_Q = \frac{\{T^{\text{gpu}}_{\text{DGEMM(2*n,n,n)}}, T^{\text{gpu}}_{\text{GET(n,n)}}\}}{T^{\text{cpu}}_{\text{DGEMM(2*n,n,n)}}}, \quad c'_k = \frac{T^{\text{cpu}}_{\text{DORGQR(2*n,2*n)}}}{T^{\text{cpu}}_{\text{DGEMM(2*n,n,n)}}} - 2 > \frac{1}{3}, \quad c''_k = \frac{T^{\text{gpu}}_{\text{SET(n,n)}}}{T^{\text{cpu}}_{\text{DGEMM(2*n,n,n)}}},$$

η is a ratio between the number of cores involved in factorization of H and the number of cores involved in inversion of R in the second step of `BSOFTRI` (e.g., the typical values of η for single hexa-core are $3:3$, $4:2$, or $5:1$).

In order to reduce idle time related to the synchronization of parallel threads in the merged factorization/inversion phase, the total elapsed time for inversion of the first j_F columns should be less than the elapsed time for performing $j_F - l_F$ factorization steps. This condition leads to the following lower bound for l_F

$$l_F(\delta) \geq \frac{1}{2} - c_j + \frac{\delta\eta}{10\beta_F}\left(c_j^2 + c_j - \frac{1}{4}\right) + \frac{5\beta_F}{2\delta\eta}, \quad (7)$$

where

$$\beta_F = \frac{T^{\text{cpu}}_{\text{DGEQRF(2*n,n)}} + T^{\text{cpu}}_{\text{DORMQR('R','N',2*n,n,n)}}}{5T^{\text{cpu}}_{\text{DGEMM(n,n,n)}}},$$

$\delta = 1$ if the last column panel inversion is postponed in the second step of `BSOFTRI`, and $\delta = 2$ otherwise. The latter inequality usually holds true for some $2 \leq l_F \leq 6$. If $\delta = 1$, l_F and j_F are linked by expression

$$\hat{l}_F(j_F) = p - \frac{1}{5}\left(\frac{\eta}{\beta_F}\left(\frac{1}{2}\frac{\kappa_C}{1+\kappa_C}(j_F^2 + (1 + 2c_j)j_F - 4c_j - 6) + 1\right) - 3p + 10\right).$$

Hence, postponed processing of the last column panel in the second step of `BSOFTRI` makes sense only if $l_F(1) > \hat{l}_F(p-2)$ for minimal l_F which satisfies (7).

Table 2. Performance model of parallel "host-device" BSOFI, where Metric 1 is the number of flops on GPU, Metric 2 is the number of words CPU$\rightleftharpoons$GPU and Metric 3 is the number of messages CPU$\rightleftharpoons$GPU

Metric	BSOFTRI	BSOI
1	$\frac{n^3 p}{1+\kappa_R}\left(\theta^2\beta_F\left(1+\frac{\delta-1}{\delta\eta}\left(1+\frac{1}{\kappa_C}\right)\right)\right)+p+1+2c_i$	$\frac{2n^3 p}{1+\kappa_Q}\left(3p+1+2c_k'-4c_k''\right)$
2	$\frac{n^2 p}{1+\kappa_R}\frac{1}{2}\left(\frac{\theta^2\beta_F}{\delta}+p+5+2\kappa_R+2c_i\right)$	$\frac{n^2 p^2}{1+\kappa_Q}\frac{1}{2}\frac{3\kappa_Q+4}{\kappa_Q+2}$
3	$2p+2(2-\delta)\theta\sqrt{\frac{\beta_F}{\delta\eta}\left(1+\frac{1}{\kappa_C}\right)}(p-2)+2\delta-12$	$2p-2$

Results of the theoretical performance study are summarized in the table 2. For the sake of simplicity, the lower order terms are neglected. θ is a decreasing function of l_F. Its upper bound is $2\sqrt{2}$. The lower bound on θ is $\sqrt{3}$ if $\delta=1$.

5   Experimental Results and Analysis

Experimental setup. In order to examine our algorithmic solutions, we developed codes for stand-alone CPU and GPU processing, as well as hybrid CPU+GPU implementation. Our solvers receive p-cyclic matrix H in an unpacked form as input, and replace it with its inverse H^{-1} by performing in-place inversion. The POSIX threads are used for threading in the second step of BSOFTRI. For performance data presented below, the codes were compiled with ICC and linked against CuBLAS, Magma, and Intel's MKL library. Our codes are publicly available from https://github.com/SGo-Go/BSOFI. The performance data were collected on a 2-socket Intel Xeon X5070 coupled with NVIDIA GeForce GTX480 GPU. Intel Xeon X5670 is a 6-core processor with 2.9GHz clock rate. GTX480 is a CUDA-enabled NVIDIA GPU, which implements Fermi architecture, and has 15 streaming multiprocessors with 32 CUDA cores in each. For multi-GPU studies, we used a multi-GPU Fermi node on the Dirac cluster, housed at NERSC of Lawrence Berkeley National Laboratory. This node contains 2 Intel 5530 2.4GHz Quad core Nehalem processors, and 4 C1060 NVIDIA Tesla GPUs.

Performance tuning. In order to make our hybrid CPU+GPU codes architecture-aware, we perform benchmarking of basic kernels used in the modified BSOFI algorithm, evaluate parameters for (5)–(7), and embed their approximate models into the code. Our experiments have shown that parameters κ_R, κ_C, and κ_Q depend dramatically on the block size n if n is small, and this dependence can be sufficiently well approximated by the first order rational functions. We obtain parameters of these rational functions by Gauss-Markov estimator. The correction parameters c_i, c_j, c_k', and c_k'' are approximated by descending stepwise functions of n. At first, we filter curves for these parameters received after

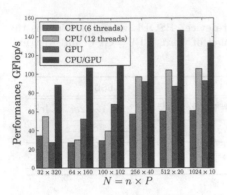
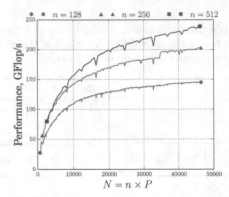

(a) Performance of the CPU, GPU and hybrid BSOFI codes

(b) Performance of the hybrid BSOFI codes

Fig. 6. Performance of BSOFI on a 2-socket Intel Xeon X5670 coupled with NVIDIA GeForce GTX480 GPU

benchmarking, and afterwards round the filtered curves to the closest integers. The same approach is used to build a step-wise approximation for parameter l_F.

Benchmarking results. To investigate the quality of exploiting structure by BSOFI algorithm, we compare performance of our CPU implementation with naïve BLAS3 LU inversion and inversion by multifrontal sparse LU solvers from UMFPACK. Benchmarking shows significant speed-up of BSOFI with respect to LU inversion. We observe up to 22× speed-up if $n \times p < 10^4$ and $n \geq 32$. The general tendency is an increase of speed-up with a decrease of n.

Fig. 6a shows the performance of BSOFI codes on different platforms for $N = 10240$. Hybrid implementation is up to 1.7× faster over the best of CPU and GPU codes. Its peak performance is higher than peak performance of DGEMM on CPU and is only 1.1× lower than the peak of DGEMM on GPU. Moreover, the difference in performance in the interval $32 \leq n \leq 1024$ does not exceed 1.5× for our hybrid CPU+GPU implementation. Fig. 6b compares the performance of CPU+GPU codes for different sizes of p-cyclic matrices if n is fixed. If n is large, performance of subroutine BSOI on the single GPU node is two times more in the case of CPU+GPU implementation than in the case of pure CPU implementation. At the same time, performance improvements for subroutine BSOFTRI are less significant than for BSOI. If $n \gtrsim 512$, performance curves are close to each other. This is a consequence of reaching maximum performance for DGEMM on both CPU and GPU.

More benchmarking results on both single and multi-GPU platforms can be found in [4].

6   Conclusions and Further Directions

We presented serial and parallel algorithms for structured orthogonal inversion of block p-cyclic matrices. We provided a performance model and discussed host-device load balance. Finally, we developed and explored CPU, GPU and hybrid CPU+GPU codes for in-place inversion of p-cyclic matrices. Benchmarking has shown that our codes for multicores with GPU accelerators maintain sustainable performance for different values of problem size n, and attain up to 90% of realistic peak performance in terms of the operation of the matrix-matrix multiplication.

There are numerous ways to extend the results presented in this paper. Since GPUs have a lot in common with Intel MIC architecture, it seems natural to verify the approaches on multicores with MIC accelerators. Another promising direction is in coupling of BSOFI with inversion based on explicit formulae. We conclude by mentioning that the solutions proposed here can be extended to the problems with other block structured matrices such as block upper Hessenberg matrices. This leads us to believe that the BSOFI could be a vital substitute to conventional Gaussian elimination based inversion for broader classes of block structured matrices.

References

1. Bai, Z., Chen, W., Scalettar, R., Yamazaki, I.: Numerical methods for Quantum Monte Carlo simulations of the Hubbard model. In: Hou, T.Y., Liu, C., Liu, J.G. (eds.) Multi-Scale Phenomena in Complex Fluids. Contemporary Applied Mathematics, ch. 1, vol. 12, pp. 1–100. World Scientific (2009)
2. Ernst, O.G.: Equivalent iterative methods for p-cyclic matrices. Numerical Algorithms 25(1-4), 161–180 (2000)
3. Fairweather, G., Gladwell, I.: Algorithms for almost block diagonal linear systems. SIAM Review 46(1), 49–58 (2004)
4. Gogolenko, S., Bai, Z.: A structured orthogonal inversion of block p-cyclic matrices on multicores with GPU accelerators. Tech. Rep. CSE-2013-78, CS Dept., UC Davis (2013),
   http://www.cs.ucdavis.edu/research/tech-reports/2012/CSE-2013-78.pdf
5. Khabou, A., Demmel, J., Grigori, L., Gu, M.: LU factorization with panel rank revealing pivoting and its communication avoiding version. SIAM J. Matrix Analysis Applications 34(3), 1401–1429 (2013)
6. Tomas, A., Chang, C.C., Scalettar, R., Bai, Z.: Advancing large scale many-body QMC simulations on GPU accelerated multicore systems. In: Proceedings of IPDPSW 2012, pp. 308–319. IEEE, Washington, DC (2012)
7. Tomov, S., Nath, R., Ltaief, H., Dongarra, J.: Dense linear algebra solvers for multicore with GPU accelerators. In: Proceedings of IPDPSW 2010, pp. 1–8. IEEE, Atlanta (2010)
8. Volkov, V., Demmel, J.: LU, QR and Cholesky factorizations using vector capabilities of GPUs. Tech. Rep. UCB/EECS-2008-49, EECS Dept., UC Berkeley (2008)
9. Wright, S.J.: Stable parallel algorithms for two-point boundary value problems. SIAM J. Sci. Stat. Comput. 13(3), 742–764 (1992)
10. Wright, S.J.: A collection of problems for which Gaussian elimination with partial pivoting is unstable. SIAM J. Sci. Comput. 14(1), 231–238 (1993)

High-Throughput Maps on Message-Passing Manycore Architectures: Partitioning versus Replication

Omid Shahmirzadi, Thomas Ropars, and André Schiper

Ecole Polytechnique Fédérale de Lausanne (EPFL),
Lausanne, Switzerland
firstname.lastname@epfl.ch

Abstract. The advent of manycore architectures raises new scalability challenges for concurrent applications. Implementing scalable data structures is one of them. Several manycore architectures provide hardware message passing as a means to efficiently exchange data between cores. In this paper, we study the implementation of high-throughput concurrent maps in message-passing manycores. Partitioning and replication are the two approaches to achieve high throughput in a message-passing system. Our paper presents and compares different strongly-consistent map algorithms based on partitioning and replication. To assess the performance of these algorithms independently of architecture-specific features, we propose a communication model of message-passing manycores to express the throughput of each algorithm. The model is validated through experiments on a 36-core TILE-Gx8036 processor. Evaluations show that replication outperforms partitioning only in a narrow domain.

1 Introduction

Manycore architectures, featuring tens if not hundreds of cores, are becoming available. Taking advantage of the high degree of parallelism provided by such architectures is challenging and raises questions about the programming model to be used [22, 13]. Most existing architectures are still based on cache-coherent shared memory but some provide message passing, through a highly efficient network-on-chip (NoC), as a basic means to communicate between cores [10, 21, 11]. Designing a scalable concurrent algorithm for cache-coherent architectures is a difficult task because it requires understanding the subtleties of the underlying cache coherence protocol [5]. On the other hand, message passing looks appealing because it provides the programmer with explicit control of the communication between cores. However, compared to the vast literature on concurrent programming in shared-memory systems [9], programming message-passing processors is not yet a mature research topic.

Implementing scalable data structures is one of the basic problems in concurrent programming. To increase the throughput of data structures in shared memory architectures, several well-known techniques can be used including fine-grained

F. Silva et al. (Eds.): Euro-Par 2014, LNCS 8632, pp. 536–547, 2014.

locking, optimistic synchronization and lazy synchronization [9]. In the case of message-passing systems, partitioning and replication are the two main approaches to improve the throughput of concurrent data structures [7]. Using partitioning, a data structure is partitioned among a set of servers that answer clients requests. Using replication, each client has a local copy of the data structure in its private memory. Both have been considered in recent work on message-passing manycores [2, 24, 4], but performance comparisons are lacking. In this paper we present a performance comparison of these two approaches for the implementation of high-throughput concurrent objects in message-passing manycores, considering the case of a linearizable map. Note that existing studies made in distributed message-passing systems are only of little help because the high performance of NoCs provides a completely different ratio between computation and communication costs compared to large scale distributed systems.

Maps are used in many systems ranging from operating systems [2, 24] to key-value stores [4]. Their performance is often crucial to the systems using them. A map is an interesting case study because it is a good candidate to apply both partitioning and replication techniques. Since operations on different keys are independent, maps are easily partitionable [4]. Because a large majority of operations are usually lookup operations [1], replication can help handling a large number of local lookup requests concurrently.

Since message-passing manycores are a new technology, only few algorithms targeting this kind of architectures are available. Thus, to compare partitioning and replication in this context, we devise simple map algorithms that have been chosen to be representative of the design space. To compare our algorithms, we present a model of the communication in message-passing manycores, and express the throughput of our algorithms in this model. Using a performance model allows us to compare the algorithms independently of platform-specific features and to cover a large scope of manycore architectures. We use a 36-core Tilera TILE-Gx8036 processor to validate our model. Evaluations on the TILE-Gx shows an extremely poor performance for replication compare to partitioning. However some limitations of this platform, *i.e.* costly interrupt handling and lack of broadcast service, can be blamed for the poor performance. Our model allows us to come up with a hypothetical platform based on the TILE-Gx, which does not suffer form its limitations. Our evaluations on this *ideal* platform show that even in the best setting in favor of replication, *i.e.* having highly efficient interrupt handling and a hardware-based broadcast service, replication can outperform partitioning only when update operations are rare and replicas are located in the cache system of the cores.

This paper is organized as follows. Section 2 specifies the underlying assumptions and goal of the study. Section 3 introduces the algorithms. Section 4 presents the modeling methodology and its validation on the TILE-Gx processor. Section 5 studies performance of the algorithms on different architectures. Related work and conclusion are presented in Sections 6 and 7.

2   Assumptions and Goal

The study assumes a fault-free manycore architecture where a large number of threads, each pinned to a single-threaded core during its lifetime, communicate through an on-chip network using the following operations: $send(m, i)$ sends message m to thread i; $bcast(m)$ sends m to all threads; $mcast(m, list)$ sends m to all threads in the $list$; $rcv(m)$ blocks until message m can be received. A thread can be interrupted to deliver a new message m upon its receipt, which is denoted as $arcv(m)$. Communication channels are asynchronous and FIFO.

The study considers the most general consistency criteria, linearizability, and compares the maximum achievable throughput of different linearizable map implementations. A map is a set of items indexed by unique keys that provides $lookup$ and $update$ operations: $lookup(key)$ returns the value indexed by key ($null$ if no value is associated with key); $update(key, val)$ updates the value indexed by key to val (deleting a key can be done using $update(key, null)$).

3   Algorithms

The two basic techniques to implement scalable concurrent maps on message-passing manycores are partitioning and replication. For each technique, we consider a few algorithms which are representative of the design space. Algorithmic details and correctness proofs can be found in our technical report [20].

3.1   Partitioning

Partitioning a map among a set of server threads can parallelize accesses to different map items. We study two algorithms based on partitioning. In the first algorithm, PART_SIMPLE, a map is partitioned among a set of s servers, $i.e.$ item $< key, val >$ is located on server $key \bmod s$. A client accesses the corresponding server upon executing a map operation on a key. In the second algorithm, PART_CACHING, recently accessed items are cached on client side. Cached values need to be invalidated if they are updated by other clients. To ensure linearizability, after multicasting an invalidation message, the server waits to receive the acknowledgement from all invalidated clients to finish the update.

3.2   Replication

Replicating a map on each client thread can localize accesses to map items during lookup operations. Unlike in large scale distributed systems, in message-passing manycores locating a replica close to a set of clients is not that beneficial. Even accessing a map replica located in a neighboring core is much more expensive than accessing it locally, since the main access cost is the network cycles used to pack and unpack the payload rather than traversing the hops. In this case replication and partitioning have similar lookup costs, while the former needs expensive updates to ensure consistency. Therefore we only consider the case where each client has its own local map replica.

In replication algorithms, clients deliver updates upon receiving inter-core interrupts. An alternative is to buffer updates and apply them before executing the next map operation. We eliminate this option due to the need for potentially large network buffers, which is not the case in current architectures [21]. To ensure linearizability the following conditions are necessary with respect to each key: (i) updates should be totally ordered; (ii) lookups should be synchronized with updates. We address each condition before describing the algorithms.

Atomic broadcast can be used for total ordering of updates. Among the five classes of atomic broadcast protocols mentioned in [6], we select the one based on a fixed sequencer. In a fixed sequencer algorithm, a sequencer server is in charge of assigning sequence numbers to updates. Three reasons motivate this choice: (a) it needs only one broadcast; (b) updates on different keys can propagate in parallel (by partitioning the sequencing service among multiple sequencer servers, if using a single sequencer can become the bottleneck); (c) replicas can issue requests independently of each other. Other classes lack some of these properties, and so, would provide much lower throughput. Alternatively atomic commitment, *e.g.* two-phase commit, can be used for total ordering of updates. Atomic commit ensures that only one update is applying in the system at a time. This can circumvent the need for dedicating sequencer threads. Therefore we also consider a variant of two-phase commit for total ordering of updates.

Executing lookups without synchronization can violate linearizability, as illustrated by Figure 1, and must be avoided. In this scenario, client c issues an operation *update(key,newval)*, which is applied on the map replicas on c' and c'' at time t_1 and t_2 respectively. If lookups can return immediately with no synchronizing, linearizability can be violated: *lookup(key)* on c_1 returns the new value while, at a later time, the same operation on c_2 returns the old value.

We describe three algorithms satisfying the two mentioned conditions: two based on atomic broadcast and one based on atomic commit. For simplicity we describe the algorithms from the perspective of only one key. We partition the sequencer service among s sequencer servers, each responsible for a subset of keys. In the first algorithm, REP_REMOTE, clients atomically broadcast their updates and return. Lookups need to contact the corresponding sequencer to know the sequence number sn of the last issued update. Lookups can return only when the update with sequence number sn has been delivered. In the second algorithm, REP_LOCAL, lookups do not need any remote communication to synchronize with updates. This makes updates more complex: After atomic broadcast of an update, the source waits until all other clients acknowledge delivery of this update before broadcasting a final acknowledgement and terminating the operation. Lookups issued after delivering an update should wait until the final acknowledgement is delivered in order to return. In the third algorithm, REP_2PC, a client, before issuing an update, requests from all other clients whether they are applying a conflicting update or not. If no client is applying a conflicting update, it broadcasts the new update and waits to receive an acknowledgement from all to terminate the operation. Otherwise it aborts its own update. Lookups apply a similar technique as in REP_LOCAL to synchronize with updates.

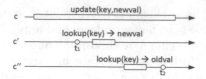

Fig. 1. Non-linearizable execution with a replicated map

4   Performance Modeling

We model the throughput of our map algorithms on message-passing manycores to be able to compare them independently of architecture-specific features and to help manycore programmers to decide about their implementation choice on different platforms. In this section we describe the modeling methodology and we validate it using an existing manycore architecture.

4.1   Methodology

To model the throughput of our algorithms, we assume threads are divided into c *clients*, which issue map operations, and s *servers*, which execute map related code[1]. Client and server threads are located in different cores. Keys are distributed evenly among the servers and are accessed uniformly by the clients.

In manycore architectures with highly efficient NoCs, cores are the main performance bottleneck. We define the following computation parameters to express throughput of our algorithms. We consider a generic map implementation defined by three parameters o_{pre}, o_{lup} and o_{upd}: o_{pre} is the computation time on the client before accessing the map, *e.g.* executing a hash function if the map is implemented using a hash table; o_{lup} and o_{upd} are the computation times corresponding to accessing the underlying data structure during a *lookup* and an *update* respectively. In a configuration with multiple servers, o_{sel} stands for the server selection overhead on the clients. We also associate an overhead with each of the communication primitives introduced in Section 2. Moreover, we introduce the parameter T_{rtt}, to represent round-trip times. More precisely, $T_{rtt}(send\_op, rcv\_op)$ is the round-trip time for the initial message sent with the $send\_op$ operation (*i.e.* send, bcast or mcast) and received with the rcv_op operation (*i.e.* rcv or arcv). The answer is always sent back using *send* and received using *rcv*. If the round trip is initiated with *bcast* or *mcast*, it finishes when the answers from all destinations have been received. We assume that all other computational costs related to the execution of the algorithms, *e.g.* L1 cache accesses, are negligible. Model parameters are summarized in Table 1.

We define T_{lup} and T_{upd}, the number of CPU cycles required to execute a *lookup* and an *update* respectively. For each operation op, T_{op} can be divided into the CPU cycles it takes on the client (T_{op}^c) and on the server (T_{op}^s). Considering

---

[1] REP_2PC includes no servers.

Table 1. Model parameters and their values ("-" : the same as on TILE-Gx)

parameter	description	TILE-Gx	int.	ideal
c	number of clients			
s	number of servers			
p	probability of a *lookup* operation			
o_{pre}	computation before a map access			
o_{lup}	access to the map for a *lookup*			
o_{upd}	access to the map for an *update*			
o_{sel}	server selection overhead	if $s = 2^x$ 17,else 90	-	-
o_{send}	overhead of *send(m)*	$8 + \lvert m \rvert$	-	-
o_{bcast}	overhead of *broadcast(m)*	$c \cdot o_{send}$	-	o_{send}
o_{mcast}	overhead of *multicast(m, list)*	$\lvert list \rvert \cdot o_{send}$	-	o_{send}
o_{rcv}	overhead of a *synchronous* receive	$2 \cdot \lvert m \rvert$	-	-
o_{arcv}	overhead of an *asynchronous* receive	$138 + o_{rcv}$	$4 + o_{rcv}$	$4 + o_{rcv}$
L	average communication latency	16	-	-
$T_{rtt}(send, rcv)$	round-trip time with *send* and *rcv*	$2 \cdot (o_{send} + o_{rcv} + L)$	-	-
$T_{rtt}(send, arcv)$	round-trip time with *send* and *arcv*	$2 \cdot (o_{send} + o_{arcv} + L)$	-	-
$T_{rtt}(bcast, arcv)$	round-trip time with *bcast* and *arcv*	$o_{bcast} + o_{arcv} +$ $o_{send} + o_{rcv} + 2 \cdot L$	-	-
$T_{rtt}(mcast, arcv)$	round-trip time with *mcast* and *arcv*	$o_{mcast} + o_{arcv} +$ $o_{send} + o_{rcv} + 2 \cdot L$	-	-

a load where the probability of having a *lookup* operation is p, the maximum throughput $\mathcal{T}^c$ achievable by clients (and equivalently by the servers) is:

$$\mathcal{T}^c = \frac{c}{p \cdot T^c_{lup} + (1 - p) \cdot T^c_{upd}} \tag{1}$$

Hence, the maximum throughput $\mathcal{T}$ of a map is:

$$\mathcal{T} = min(\mathcal{T}^c, \mathcal{T}^s) \tag{2}$$

As an example we model the throughput of the PART_SIMPLE algorithm. The communication pattern is described in Figure 2. It is similar for a *lookup* and an *update* operation. The only difference is that during an update operation, applying the update on the map can be removed from the critical path of the client. Computing T^s_{op} (where *op* is *upd* or *lup*), T^c_{lup} and T^c_{upd} is as follows:

$$T^s_{op} = o_{rcv} + o_{op} + o_{send} \tag{3}$$
$$T^c_{lup} = o_{pre} + o_{sel} + T_{rtt}(send, rcv) + o_{lup} \tag{4}$$
$$T^c_{upd} = o_{pre} + o_{sel} + T_{rtt}(send, rcv) \tag{5}$$

Unlike PART_SIMPLE, modeling the throughput of other algorithms involves some complexity. In replication algorithms, a client can deliver asynchronous messages *for free* during idle periods. This increases the throughput of the clients and alters the general Formula 1. Moreover in PART_CACHING, the probability of hitting the local cache as well as the number of clients which need to be invalidated should be computed. The detailed performance model of the other algorithms can be found in [20].

4.2 Validation

We use a Tilera TILE-Gx8036 processor [21] as a representative of current message-passing manycore architectures to validate our model. It consists of 36

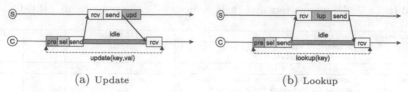

(a) Update   (b) Lookup

Fig. 2. PART_SIMPLE algorithm

cores communicating through a mesh interconnect. Cores and mesh operate at the same frequency, 1.2 Ghz. Each core is provided with a 32 KB L1 instruction cache, a 32 KB L1 data cache, a 256 KB L2 cache and four independent FIFO receive buffers where each can contain up to 118 64-bit words. Threads located on different cores can communicate using *send* and *rcv* primitives with no operating system intervention. A *send* puts the data in one of the four receive buffers of the destination and a *rcv* blocks until this data is available. Upon receipt of a message in any of the four buffers, an interrupt can be raised to perform an asynchronous receive. There is no hardware support for collective operations.

We obtain the model parameters for the TILE-Gx processor through microbenchmarks. Each *send* has a fixed overhead of 8 cycles plus 1 cycle per word. Due to the lack of collective operations, we implement *bcast* and *mcast* as a set of consecutive *send* operations, so their cost is a linear function of o_{send}[2]. Each *rcv* needs 2 cycles to deliver each word from the receive buffers. Each *arcv*, in addition to the cycles needed for receiving messages from the buffers, requires an overhead of 138 cycles to save and retrieve the execution context. We compute the round trip times, as the length of the critical path on the source thread from the first send operation to the last receive operation. Round-trip times take into account the average communication latency L, which involves a fixed packing and unpacking overhead of 10 network cycles plus an average traversal cost of 6 network cycles (1 cycle per hop). Finally o_{sel} is 17 cycles if the number of servers is a power of two, otherwise 90 cycles (*mod* function is implemented using bitwise operations). Table 1 summarizes the TILE-Gx parameters.

To validate our model, we pin each thread to a different core. Clients issue map operations with 90% probability a lookup ($p = 0.9$). Keys are evenly distributed among the servers and are accessed uniformly by the clients. We consider a map implemented using a hash table which fits into the L1 cache of the cores: $o_{lup} = o_{upd} = 0$ cycles[3]. We use the DJB hash function to generate 4 bytes long keys from 36 bytes long strings: $o_{pre} = 156$ cycles. We consider a collision-free scenario. Experiments are run with version 2.6.40.38-MDE-4.1.0.148119 of Tilera's custom Linux kernel, compiled using GCC 4.4.6 with O3 flag.

Figure 3(b) presents the maximum throughput of the five algorithms, obtained through experiments and model, for different total number of threads. Each point in the experimental results is the average throughput of 6 runs, where in each

---

[2] Effects of such an implementation will be later removed by considering a platform with a hardware-based broadcast service.

[3] We consider L1 to better evaluate the accuracy of our communication model.

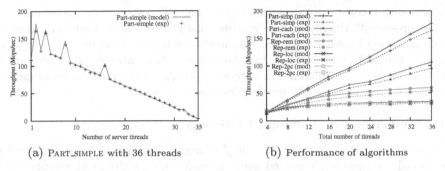

(a) PART_SIMPLE with 36 threads   (b) Performance of algorithms

Fig. 3. Model validation on TILE-Gx processor (p=0.90)

run every client issues 10000 operations on the map. Keys are distributed among the servers uniformly and clients randomly select the key for the next operation with a uniform distribution. For a given number of threads, the corresponding throughput for each algorithm represents the throughput obtainable from the best possible configuration of clients and servers. For example, the throughput of the simple partitioning algorithm with 36 threads in Figure 3(b) is obtained through the graph shown in Figure 3(a), where the configuration with 2 servers and 34 clients leads to the best throughput (hiccups are due to o_{sel}). These figures show that we manage to model the throughput of the algorithms with good approximation (a maximum of 12% deviation in the case of PART_CACHING). However the throughput obtained through the model is slightly higher than through experiments. This is mainly because in practice other computational costs are involved (*e.g.* operations on the cached variables).

5   Evaluation

Studying algorithms only on the TILE-Gx leads to architecture-specific results. Two limitations of this processor can decrease the performance: (i) asynchronous receives, although relatively efficient compared to existing architectures, are still much more costly than synchronous ones; (ii) there is no efficient broadcast service[4]. These limitation could impair the performance of all replication algorithms and of PART_CACHING and so, could be the reason for the higher throughput of PART_SIMPLE observed in Figure 3(b). Using our model, we define two platforms based on TILE-Gx to avoid the harmful effects of the mentioned limitations. We define an *intermediate* platform where synchronous and asynchronous receives have similar costs. We also define an *ideal* platform, which enhances the *intermediate* platform with broadcast operation in hardware. In this case the cost of *bcast* is equal to the cost of a single *send*. The *ideal* platform provides the best setting for the replication algorithms. These assumptions are realistic. In [18], a

---

[4] When broadcast is implemented using asynchronous communication, the throughput of the system is independent from the broadcast algorithm [16].

solution with a constant 4 cycles cost of saving and restoring an execution context is presented. Moreover some existing manycores, *e.g.* Kalray [11], provide hardware-based broadcast. Table 1 summarizes parameter values for these platforms. In this section we compare the algorithms performance on these platforms. We also discuss how different consistency, configuration and load assumptions can alter the results (see [20] for detailed discussions).

5.1   Comparison on Different Platforms

To compare the algorithms on different platforms, we apply our analytical model. We consider a map implemented using a hash table as the most popular map implementation. To avoid orthogonal issues, we consider a collision free scenario where the keys are evenly distributed among servers and are accessed uniformly by the clients. To assess different computational costs, we identify three use cases with different hash function costs (depending on its input type) and hash table sizes (small enough to fit in the L2 cache or otherwise in memory). Namely we consider (i) a small hash table with an integer hash function ($o_{pre} = 12$, $o_{op} = 11$); (ii) a small hash table with a string hash function ($o_{pre} = 156$, $o_{op} = 11$); (iii) a big hash table with a string hash function ($o_{pre} = 156$, $o_{op} = 88$). The first two are representative use cases in operating systems [12] while the latter is a representative use case in key-value stores [14][5].

Considering the first use case, we compare the performance of the algorithms on different platforms with 90% and 99% of lookups (see Figure 4). We apply the same methodology as in model validation to obtain throughput graphs. Three main conclusions can be taken from the results. First, with 90% of lookups PART_SIMPLE outperforms other algorithms on all platforms at almost all scales. Second, with 99% of lookups REP_LOCAL outperforms the partitioning algorithms only if asynchronous receives are handled efficiently. Actually on the *ideal* platform the minimum ratio of lookups for replication to outperform partitioning is 98%. Third, having broadcast in hardware does not change the relative performance of the algorithms dramatically (compare Figures 4(e) and 4(f)).

Considering other use cases, the mentioned conclusions remain valid. The only exception is the scenario where the hash table is located in the main memory. In this case even with 99% of lookups, PART_CACHING shows best performance on all platforms. This is due to the fact that replicated maps are not able to leverage the locality if map replicas are not cached.

5.2   Discussion

To assess the effects of weakening the consistency criteria, we also study the case of sequential consistency. Replicated maps are able to exploit sequential consistency by removing the synchronization between lookups and updates. On the contrary partitioned maps are not able to exploit sequential consistency, mainly because sequential consistency is not compositional. Evaluations show that replication still needs the same conditions as with the case of linearizability

---

[5] We did not find any use cases for a big hash table applying a cheap hash function.

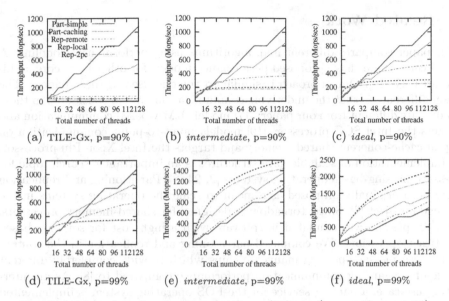

Fig. 4. Analytical performance on the three platforms ($o_{pre} = 12$, $o_{op} = 11$)

to outperform partitioning. Study of even weaker consistency criteria [23], using a similar methodology, can complement this study.

Clients and servers can be collocated on the same core. This configuration avoids dedicating resources to play the server role. On the TILE-Gx, this is not a desirable choice since a costly asynchronous receive will be involved in every request sent to the servers. Evaluations on the *ideal* platform show that, despite efficient asynchronous receives, this collocation only leads to a negligible performance gain. The main reason is that in the best configurations, the number of servers which can be collocated with the clients is small.

Client can access the servers non-uniformly, *e.g.* when the map is implemented using a hash table with a non-uniform hash function. This phenomenon decreases the throughput of the servers, and consequently of the overall map (except for REP_2PC). Moreover a non-uniform access of the clients to different keys increases the throughput of the PART_CACHING algorithm, by increasing the probability of local lookups and decreasing the number of invalidations. For a given distribution of the client accesses among servers and the key accesses among clients, throughput of the maps can be quantified using our model.

We considered the TILE-Gx, a general purpose message-passing manycore, as the baseline for our evaluations. We believe that our conclusions remain valid on similar architectures since: (i) TILE-Gx provides efficient inter-core communication; (ii) using our model we could consider cases where broadcast operations and asynchronous receives are very efficient. Still, using our model, one can directly do a comparison on other architectures. One exception is the architectures with one-sided communication primitives, *e.g.* Intel SCC [10]. The main reason is that inter-core communication in these architectures involves some synchronization costs [17] which are not included in our model.

6   Related Work

This paper compares different map algorithms using performance modeling. A few recent studies have proposed performance models for other manycore architectures [17, 19]. Our approach is similar to the one used in these papers. The main difference is that the underlying communication system considered in these studies are different from our paper: [17] models RMA-based communication and targets the Intel SCC processor; [19] models point-to-point communication on top of cache-coherent shared memory and targets the Intel Xeon Phi processor.

Implementation of scalable data structures is an important research topic for message-passing-based operating systems [2, 24, 8]. Partitioning and replication were both originally proposed as a mean to scale the operating systems in the Tornado project [8]. Since Tornado was designed for shared-memory processors, message-passing was emulated in software with a high cost for software-based multicast operations. We compared partitioning and replication in the context of modern message-passing manycore chips which provide completely different trade-offs regarding communication performance compared to [8]. As an interesting use-case, a naming service for the FOS operating system is implemented using a weakly-consistent replicated hash map [3]. The replication algorithm used in this study is a variant of REP_2PC, but is not compared to other alternatives.

Optimization of in-memory key-value stores for manycores is another area where our results could be used [4, 15]. The authors of [4] and [15] both propose a partitioning approach similar to the PART_SIMPLE algorithm. The solution proposed in [15] is based on message-passing emulated on top of shared memory whereas [4] takes advantage of hardware message-passing provided by Tilera. Our paper complements these studies by comparing replication and partitioning.

7   Conclusion

The paper studies the implementation of strongly-consistent maps in message-passing manycores. Using a communication model it compares the performance of partitioned and replicated maps under different settings. A Tilera TILE-Gx8036 processor is used to validate the model and serves as a baseline for the evaluations. The results show that replication can outperform partitioning only if handling interrupts is highly efficient, update operations are rare and map replicas are located in the cache system of the cores.

References

[1] Atikoglu, B., Xu, Y., Frachtenberg, E., Jiang, S., Paleczny, M.: Workload analysis of a large-scale key-value store. In: Proceedings of the 12th ACM SIGMETRICS/PERFORMANCE, pp. 53–64 (2012)

[2] Baumann, A., Barham, P., Dagand, P., et al.: The multikernel: a new OS architecture for scalable multicore systems. In: Proceedings of the ACM SIGOPS 22nd Symposium on Operating Systems Principles, pp. 29–44 (2009)

[3] Beckmann, N.: Distributed naming in a factored operating system. Master's thesis, Massachusetts Institute of Technology (2010)

[4] Berezecki, M., Frachtenberg, E., Paleczny, M., Steele, K.: Many-core key-value store. In: Proceedings of the 2011 International Green Computing Conference and Workshops, pp. 1–8 (2011)
[5] Calciu, I., Dice, D., Lev, Y., Luchangco, V., Marathe, V.J., Shavit, N.: NUMA-aware reader-writer locks. In: Proceedings of the 18th ACM SIGPLAN Symposium on Principles and Practice of Parallel Programming (2013)
[6] Défago, X., Schiper, A., Urbán, P.: Total order broadcast and multicast algorithms: Taxonomy and survey. ACM Computing Surveys 36(4), 372–421 (2004)
[7] Devlin, B., Gray, J., Laing, B., Spix, G.: Scalability terminology: Farms, clones, partitions, and packs: Racs and raps. Technical Report MS-TR-99-85, Microsoft Research (1999)
[8] Gamsa, B., Krieger, O., Appavoo, J., Stumm, M.: Tornado: Maximizing locality and concurrency in a shared memory multiprocessor operating system. In: The Third Symposium on Operating Systems Design and Implementation, pp. 87–100 (1999)
[9] Herlihy, M., Shavit, N.: The Art of Multiprocessor Programming. Morgan Kaufmann (2012)
[10] Howard, J., Dighe, S., Hoskote, Y., et al.: A 48-core IA-32 message-passing processor with DVFS in 45nm CMOS. In: International IEEE Solid-State Circuits Conference Digest of Technical Papers (ISSCC), pp. 108–109 (2010)
[11] Kalray, http://www.kalray.eu
[12] Lever, C.: Linux kernel hash table behavior: analysis and improvements. Technical Report TR 00-1, University of Michigan (2000)
[13] Martin, M.M.K., Hill, M.D., Sorin, D.J.: Why on-chip cache coherence is here to stay. Communications of the ACM 55(7), 78–89 (2012)
[14] Memcached, http://www.memcached.org
[15] Metreveli, Z., Zeldovich, N., Kaashoek, M.F.: Cphash: A cache-partitioned hash table. In: Proceedings of the 17th ACM SIGPLAN Symposium on Principles and Practice of Parallel Programming, pp. 319–320 (2012)
[16] Petrović, D., Shahmirzadi, O., Ropars, T., Schiper, A.: Asynchronous broadcast on the Intel SCC using interrupts. In: Proceedings of the 6th Many-core Applications Research Community Symposium, pp. 24–29 (2012)
[17] Petrović, D., Shahmirzadi, O., Ropars, T., Schiper, A.: High performance RMA based broadcast on the Intel SCC. In: Proceedinbgs of the 24th ACM Symposium on Parallelism in Algorithms and Architectures, pp. 121–130 (2012)
[18] Rafla, N., Gauba, D.: Hardware implementation of context switching for hard real-time operating systems. In: 54th IEEE International Midwest Symposium on Circuits and Systems (2011)
[19] Ramos, S., Hoefler, T.: Modeling communication in cache-coherent SMP systems: A case-study with Xeon Phi. In: Proceedings of the 22nd International Symposium on High-Performance Parallel and Distributed Computing, pp. 97–108 (2013)
[20] Shahmirzadi, O., Ropars, T., Schiper, A.: High-throughput maps for message-passing manycore architectures: partitioning versus replication. Technical Report 196582, EPFL (2014)
[21] Tilera, http://www.tilera.com
[22] Torrellas, J.: Architectures for Extreme-Scale Computing. IEEE Computer 42(11), 28–35 (2009)
[23] Vogels, W.: Eventually consistent. Communications of the ACM 52(1), 40–44 (2009)
[24] Wentzlaff, D., Agarwal, A.: Factored operating systems (FOS): the case for a scalable operating system for multicores. ACM SIGOPS Operating Systems Review 43(2), 76–85 (2009)

A Fast Sparse Block Circulant Matrix
Vector Product

Eloy Romero, Andrés Tomás, Antonio Soriano, and Ignacio Blanquer

Instituto de Instrumentación para Imagen Molecular (I3M),
Centro Mixto CSIC – Universitat Politècnica de València – CIEMAT,
Camino de Vera s/n, 46022 Valencia, Spain
{elroal,antodo,asoriano}@i3m.upv.es, iblanque@dsic.upv.es

Abstract. In the context of computed tomography (CT), iterative image reconstruction techniques are gaining attention because high-quality images are becoming computationally feasible. They involve the solution of large systems of equations, whose cost is dominated by the sparse matrix vector product (SpMV). Our work considers the case of the sparse matrices being block circulant, which arises when taking advantage of the rotational symmetry in the tomographic system. Besides the straightforward storage saving, we exploit the circulant structure to rewrite the poor-performance SpMVs into a high-performance product between sparse and dense matrices. This paper describes the implementations developed for multi-core CPUs and GPUs, and presents experimental results with typical CT matrices. The presented approach is up to ten times faster than without exploiting the circulant structure.

Keywords: Circulant matrix, sparse matrix, matrix vector product, GPU, multi-core, computed tomography.

1 Introduction

Iterative approaches to image reconstruction have cut down the radiation dose delivered to the patient in computed tomography (CT) explorations [5], because they are less sensitive to noisy acquisitions than filtered backprojection (FBP). Iterative methods consider the reconstruction problem as a system of linear equations $y = Ax$. The probability matrix A constitutes a mathematical model of the tomographic system that links the reconstructed attenuation map x with the estimation of the measurement y. The large number of projections and the high spatial resolution (≈ 0.1 mm) in CT require the solution of huge systems. This is the reason why CT image reconstruction has been dominated by analytic methods like FBP [3]. However the availability of cheaper and more powerful hardware has favoured a novel interest in the use of iterative methods in CT image reconstruction [1,18,15].

Like in many other engineering and scientific applications, A is usually a large, sparse matrix, *i.e.*, with relatively few non-zeros. Operating with sparse matrices is computationally efficient: the storage requirements and the time of a product

F. Silva et al. (Eds.): Euro-Par 2014, LNCS 8632, pp. 548–559, 2014.

by a vector are almost linear to the number of non-zeros, instead of quadratic to the matrix dimension for dense matrices. In spite of this good asymptotic behavior, the performance shown by sparse matrices is far from exhausting the computing throughput of modern processors, mainly because of low count of operations per memory transaction. As an example, results testing the matrix-vector (SpMV) product on several multi-core processors in [23] show disparate peak performance between 3% and 40%. This has aimed the development of optimizations techniques and enhanced formats specialized for matrices with dense blocks [7,22], dense triangles, diagonals, symmetry [12,11] and general patterns [10].

In the same way, this work addresses block circulant matrices, block matrices where each row of blocks is rotated one element to the right relative to the previous row. Examples of these matrices can be found in applications involving discretization aware of cylindrical or cyclical symmetries in the domain [4,9,13,20]. Particularly in the context of CT scanners, mathematical descriptions based on polar coordinates take advantage of the rotational symmetries in the tomographic system, because it is easy to find an ordering of the unknowns so that projections share the same pattern of weights in the probability matrix, although shifted by a fixed number of columns [19,16]. The probability matrix A constructed like this corresponds to a block circulant matrix, in which the rows associated to a projection form a row of blocks with the displacement being the number of columns in every block. Implicit representations of A can save storage and speed up its construction by a factor of the number of projections, which is around 100 in practice. Nevertheless, the cost of the associated SpMV product remains the same, in terms of the number of floating-point operations.

In general the SpMV products dominate the time spent on the solution of the system of linear equations by iterative methods such as the maximum likelihood expectation maximization (MLEM) algorithm [17], one of the most used in CT. In this paper, we propose to accelerate these products by rewriting them as sparse matrix-dense matrix (SpMM) products. The results we obtained show a reduction of time by a factor up to ten.

The remainder of this paper is organized as follows. In section 2 it is explained the approach based on the SpMM product and possible implementations. Sections 3 and 4 detail several implementations for multi-core CPUs and GPUs, respectively, and show performance results. And finally section 5 concludes.

Notation. We denote matrices with uppercase letters (A, B...) and vectors with bold lowercase letters ($\boldsymbol{x}$, $\boldsymbol{y}$...). Indices in vectors and matrices start by zero. $X_{i,j}$ or $\mathsf{X}[i,j]$ refer to the element on row i and column j of the matrix X. We refer to the BLAS-1 functions, AXPY as $\boldsymbol{y} \leftarrow \boldsymbol{y} + \alpha \cdot \boldsymbol{x}$, and MAXPY with cardinality k as $\boldsymbol{y} \leftarrow \boldsymbol{y} + \alpha_0 \cdot \boldsymbol{x}_0 + \alpha_1 \cdot \boldsymbol{x}_1 + \cdots + \alpha_{k-1} \cdot \boldsymbol{x}_{k-1}$.

2   Circulant Matrix Product Approach

Let C being a block circulant matrix of size $m_C \times n_C$, made by $k \times k$ matrix blocks A_i of size $m_B \times n_B$. Then $m_C = k \cdot m_B$ and $n_C = k \cdot n_B$. The matrix-vector product $\boldsymbol{y} \leftarrow C\boldsymbol{x}$ takes the form

$$
\begin{pmatrix} \boldsymbol{y}_0 \\ \boldsymbol{y}_1 \\ \vdots \\ \boldsymbol{y}_{k-2} \\ \boldsymbol{y}_{k-1} \end{pmatrix} \leftarrow \begin{pmatrix} A_0 & A_1 & \cdots & A_{k-2} & A_{k-1} \\ A_{k-1} & A_0 & \cdots & A_{k-3} & A_{k-2} \\ \vdots & \vdots & & \vdots & \vdots \\ A_2 & A_3 & \cdots & A_0 & A_1 \\ A_1 & A_2 & \cdots & A_{k-1} & A_0 \end{pmatrix} \begin{pmatrix} \boldsymbol{x}_0 \\ \boldsymbol{x}_1 \\ \vdots \\ \boldsymbol{x}_{k-2} \\ \boldsymbol{x}_{k-1} \end{pmatrix}, \tag{1}
$$

where $\boldsymbol{x}_i$ are subvectors of length n_B and $\boldsymbol{y}_i$ are of length m_B. The block circulant matrix C is fully specified by the first block of rows, which we named $A = (A_0 \ A_1 \ \dots \ A_{k-1})$. Basic implementations avoid storing explicitly the matrix C, for instance by rewriting the whole product as products by the blocks A_i,

$$
\boldsymbol{y}_i \leftarrow \sum_{j=0}^{k-1} A_{(j-i) \bmod k} \, \boldsymbol{x}_j, \qquad \text{for } i \text{ from } 0 \text{ to } k-1. \tag{2}
$$

This approach employs the SpMV product, which in practice has a performance mostly limited by the memory bandwidth. Instead, we propose to rewrite the block circulant matrix-vector product into a matrix-matrix product, which offers better performance even in simple implementations, as we show further. Then the product in (1) can be reformulated as $Y \leftarrow A\mathring{X}$, which is in detail

$$
\begin{pmatrix} \boldsymbol{y}_0 \ \boldsymbol{y}_1 \cdots \ \boldsymbol{y}_{k-1} \end{pmatrix} \leftarrow \begin{pmatrix} A_0 \ A_1 \ \dots \ A_{k-1} \end{pmatrix} \begin{pmatrix} \boldsymbol{x}_0 & \boldsymbol{x}_1 & \cdots & \boldsymbol{x}_{k-2} & \boldsymbol{x}_{k-1} \\ \boldsymbol{x}_1 & \boldsymbol{x}_2 & \cdots & \boldsymbol{x}_{k-1} & \boldsymbol{x}_0 \\ \vdots & \vdots & & \vdots & \vdots \\ \boldsymbol{x}_{k-2} & \boldsymbol{x}_{k-1} & \cdots & \boldsymbol{x}_{k-4} & \boldsymbol{x}_{k-3} \\ \boldsymbol{x}_{k-1} & \boldsymbol{x}_0 & \cdots & \boldsymbol{x}_{k-3} & \boldsymbol{x}_{k-2} \end{pmatrix}. \tag{3}
$$

Therefore, the circulant property has transfered from C to the vector $\boldsymbol{x}$, converting the latter in a kind of *anti-circulant* block matrix $\mathring{X}$, where the rows of blocks rotate to the left instead. The matrix $\mathring{X}$ is of size $n_C \times k$ and, as earlier, it is fully specified by the first row of blocks, which we named $X = (\boldsymbol{x}_0 \ \boldsymbol{x}_1 \ \dots \ \boldsymbol{x}_{k-1})$. In the process, also the output vector $\boldsymbol{y}$ is transformed into the matrix form $Y = (\boldsymbol{y}_0 \ \boldsymbol{y}_1 \ \dots \ \boldsymbol{y}_{k-1})$.

An efficient (at least, in memory) implementation of the product needs to maintain $\mathring{X}$ implicit. In a SpMM product code, a way to do so is by replacing the $\mathring{X}$ accesses by accesses to X like this,

$$
\mathring{X}_{i,j} = X_{i',j'}, \quad \text{where} \quad i' = i \bmod n_B \quad \text{and} \quad j' = (\lfloor i/n_B \rfloor + j) \bmod k. \tag{4}
$$

This solution can be useful if either the SpMM product routine allows to reimplement the behaviour of the operators (for instance, because matrices are implemented as classes in an object oriented language like C++), or the source code is available.

Nevertheless, we propose an alternative when it is not possible, for instance in the case of using a commercial numerical library. If the routine requires the dense matrix to be stored in column-major (*i.e.*, elements in consecutive rows and in

Data: $A : \mathbb{R}^{m \times n}$ sparse matrix; $\mathsf{X} : \mathbb{R}^{n \times k}$, dense matrix
Result: $\mathsf{Y} : \mathbb{R}^{m \times k}$, dense matrix with the product $A\mathsf{X}$
1 $\mathsf{Y} \leftarrow 0$
2 **for** $i \leftarrow 0$ **to** $m - 1$ **do (in parallel)**
3 | **foreach** *nonzero with column index* j *and value* v *in row* i *of* A **do**
4 | | **for** $p \leftarrow 0$ **to** $k - 1$ **do** // Done as an AXPY
5 | | | $\mathsf{Y}[i, p] \leftarrow \mathsf{Y}[i, p] + v \cdot \mathsf{X}[j, p]$

Fig. 1. Generic sparse-dense matrix product, $Y \leftarrow AX$

the same column are contiguous in memory), then the next relation between $\overset{\circ}{X}$ and a vector $\hat{x}$ that contains two contiguous copies of x can be useful,

$$\overset{\circ}{X}_{i,j} = j'\text{-th element in } \hat{x}, \qquad \text{where} \quad j' = i + j \cdot n_B \quad \text{and} \quad \hat{x} = \begin{pmatrix} x \\ x \end{pmatrix}. \quad (5)$$

Then the routine is passed the sparse matrix A, and $\hat{x}$ as the dense matrix, indicating the leading dimension n_B (the number of elements in between two elements with consecutive indices in the dimension that is not contiguous in memory).

Otherwise, if the dense matrix has to be stored in row-major (*i.e.*, elements in the same row are contiguous in memory) instead, column indices of the non-zeros in the sparse matrix has to be updated in the next way,

$$A_{i,j} = \hat{A}_{i,j'}, \text{ where } j' = 2 \cdot k \cdot (j \bmod n_B) + (\lfloor j/n_B \rfloor) \bmod k. \quad (6)$$

Then the routine is passed the modified sparse matrix $\hat{A}$ (with size $m_B \times 2 \cdot n_C$) and the dense matrix $\overset{\circ}{X} = (X \ X)$ in row-major, indicating the leading dimension 1.

3   Multi-Core CPU Implementation

Earlier we discussed how to perform the block circulant SpMV product by using a SpMM product. Although the SpMM product is algorithmically simple, it admits several implementations. One of them consists on multiple calls to the SpMV product kernel, but in the case of implementing (3) it is equivalent to do the product in the original way of (1).

From the rest of implementations, we conveniently choose the one that for every nonzero value in a sparse matrix A with row i and column j, an AXPY operation is done involving the j-th row of the input matrix X and the i-th row of the output matrix Y. The algorithm is illustrated in Fig. 1.

The product is not computationally heavy, then the performance is conditioned to the capability of the machine's cache system to take advantage of the reference locality of the implementation. Considering the spatial locality (*i.e.*, the use of data elements within relatively close address locations), the memory access pattern is efficient if the vectors involved in the AXPYs are contiguous.

Table 1. Description of tested matrices

Matrix	Rows	Columns	Blocks	Nnz A	Nnz/row	A^t Nnz/row
CT small	19,600	1,284,000	150	7,029,618	358.7	821.2
CT medium	19,600	5,583,600	150	18,845,735	961.5	506.3
CT big	19,600	15,767,700	150	40,601,519	2,071.5	386.2
CT large	78,400	29,764,800	150	120,506,745	1,537.1	607.3
CT huge	78,400	116,660,700	150	304,228,353	3,880.5	391.2

Table 2. Description of the test machines

CPU Name	Freq.	PUs	Cores	L1	L2	L3	Mem.	Bandwidth
Intel Xeon X3450	2.7 GHz	8	4	32 KiB	256 KiB	8 MiB	4 GiB	21 GB/s
Intel i7 3930K	3.2 GHz	12	6	32 KiB	256 KiB	12 MiB	32 GiB	51 GB/s
NVIDIA GTX680	1.1 GHz	8	192	48 KiB	512 KiB	–	4 GiB	192 GB/s

This is the case of the input X and output Y dense matrices stored in row-major. Considering the temporal locality (*i.e.*, the use of the same data elements within a relatively small time duration), per nonzero value in A read it is done k read accesses of X, and k read and write accesses of Y. Along a row in the sparse matrix A, all the accesses go to the same row of Y. Then it seems an optimal strategy to visit the non-zeros on the sparse matrix by rows. A similar conclusion is found on [7].

In addition, the straightforward parallelization is that every task carries on the AXPYs of several rows of the sparse matrix A, which corresponds to distribute the iterations of the loop at line 2 in Fig. 1. This strategy prevents two tasks accessing the same row of Y. The distribution of work will be balanced if every task performs almost the same number of AXPYs, *i.e.*, every task processes almost the same number of non-zeros from A.

3.1   Custom Product for Circulant Block Sparse Matrices

We developed several kernels that implement the product for sparse circulant matrices in CSR format. They are written in C++ and parallelized using threads by means of OpenMP directives. We present performance results of the kernels compiled with GNU GCC 4.8 and the options `-Ofast -march=native -mtune=native`, running on two Intel multi-core processors detailed on Table 2. The test set comprises five matrices from a CT scanner, whose characteristics are detailed on Table 1. They come from reconstructions with different spatial resolutions. Their patterns are quite similar and, as an example, Fig. 2.a shows the pattern of the first rows for some blocks of the smaller matrix on the set.

Figure 3 summarizes the performance of the kernels grouped by processor and matrix. In order to emulate the behavior of an iterative solver (like MLEM), it

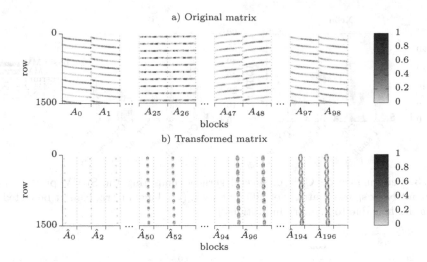

Fig. 2. Fragments of nonzero pattern in a) the matrix CT small and b) after applying the transformation of (6)

is performed 20 products alternating the direct and the transposed matrix. The results correspond to the shorter time of three attempts.

The first kernel, tagged *basic MV*, uses the matrix-vector product approach and it is parallelized by every thread computing a y_i as (2) indicates.

The second kernel, tagged *MM*, uses the matrix-matrix product approach (indicated in (3)) and the implicit circulant matrix formulas for $\mathring{X}$ (indicated in (4)) over the input vector, stored as a row-major matrix. It corresponds to the algorithm in Fig. 5 without the code under the *while* loop at line 4. The *for* loop at line 9 is implemented as two calls to an AXPY kernel, one from $p \leftarrow 0$ to $p_0 - 1$ and other from $p \leftarrow p_0$ to $k - 1$, where p_0 is $k - \lfloor \text{Aj}[j]/n_B \rfloor \bmod k$. Otherwise GNU GCC fails to vectorize the loop. The results suggest a gain of this kernel up to four times with respect to *basic MV*.

If the kernel is passed the matrix $\hat{X} = (X\ X)$ instead of X, then the *for* loop at line 9 can be implemented as a single call to an AXPY kernel with k-length vectors. This variant, tagged *MM-2*, obtains an extra performance of up to 70% respect to *MM*.

Finally, some memory transactions from the output matrix Y can be saved by merging s AXPYs originated from the same row, in a single MAXPY operation, as shown on Fig. 5. Although it can make worse the temporal locality of X (because s different parts of X are being visited at a time), simple tests shown in Fig. 4 suggest that in general the performance is improved with larger s, while the compiler is able to vectorize the innermost loop of MAXPY, which corresponds to *for* at line 5 in Fig. 5. Codes using MAXPYs with $s > 8$ vectors fail to be vectorized by the tested compiler. The performance of this optimization for $s = 8$, tagged as *MM-2-8*, is about 25% better than *MM-2*, and about 10 times better than the *basic MV* kernel.

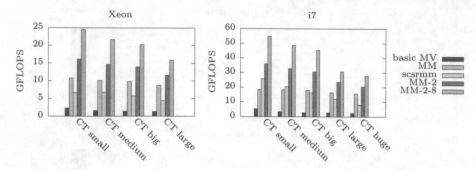

Fig. 3. Performance on CPU of several kernels computing the SpMV product with circulant block sparse matrices of different sizes. (CT huge matrix cannot be tested on Xeon machine due to memory limitations.)

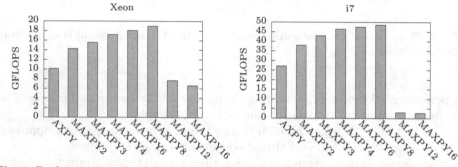

Fig. 4. Performance on both processors of AXPY and MAXPY (with different cardinalities) adding 50 vectors with 100 elements. GCC reports that it failed to vectorize the loops in the routines MAXPY12 and MAXPY16.

3.2   Using a SpMM Kernel in a Numerical Library Software

We found two open source implementations of the SpMM product. One is in the Scipy library (the core library of SciPy [8]), in which the input and output matrices are stored in row-major. And other is in Epetra (a core linear algebra package in Trilinos [6]), which merges multiple AXPYs in MAXPYs, but the dense matrices are stored in column-major. We do not show results with any of these libraries because none of them include both optimizations at the same time. Other popular libraries, like OSKI [21] or CUSP [2], offer an interface to perform the SpMM product but the implementation relies on multiple calls to the SpMV product kernel.

Regarding commercial high-performance numerical libraries, only Intel® Math Kernel Library (Intel® MKL) offers several routines for SpMM product. Concretely we tested the function *csrmm, in which the sparse matrix is introduced in CSR format and the input and the output dense matrices are stored in row-major. For that, the original sparse matrix A has to be modified as indicated in (6) (the new nonzero pattern is shown in Fig. 2.b), and the input dense matrix introduced is the replicated $\hat{X}$ in row-major. As Fig. 3 shows, its performance is superior to the *basic MV* and *MM* kernels in few cases, and *MM-2-8* can double the performance of the MKL kernel.

Data: Ai : $\mathbb{N}^{m_B+1}$, Aj : $\mathbb{N}^{nnz}$, Av : $\mathbb{R}^{nnz}$, CSR vectors of a $m_B \times (n_B \cdot k)$, nnz non-zeros sparse matrix representing the first block row of a $k \times k$ block circulant matrix; X : $\mathbb{R}^{n_B \times k}$, dense matrix.

Result: Y : $\mathbb{R}^{m_B \times k}$ dense matrix with the product of the sparse matrix by X.

1 Y $\leftarrow 0$
2 **for** $i \leftarrow 0$ **to** $m_B - 1$ **do (in parallel)**
3     $j \leftarrow$ Ai$[i]$
4   **while** $j + s \leq$ Ai$[i+1]$ **do** // Optional: take s vector at a time
5   **for** $p \leftarrow 0$ **to** $k - 1$ **do** // MAXPY
6           $Y[i,p] \leftarrow Y[i,p] + \sum_{l=j}^{j+s-1}$ Av$[l] \cdot$ X$[$Aj$[l]$ mod $n_B, (\lfloor$Aj$[l]/n_B\rfloor + p)$ mod $k]$
7        $j \leftarrow j + s$
8   **while** $j \leq$ Ai$[i+1]$ **do** // Take the last vectors
9   **for** $p \leftarrow 0$ **to** $k - 1$ **do**
10         $Y[i,p] \leftarrow Y[i,p] +$ Av$[j] \cdot$ X$[$Aj$[j]$ mod $n_B, (\lfloor$Aj$[j]/n_B\rfloor + p)$ mod $k]$

Fig. 5. Product of block circulant sparse matrix by dense matrix, taking s by s vectors at a time (CPU)

4 Circulant Sparse Product Implementation on GPU

Current GPU accelerators provide a cost-effective platform for CT applications. These applications require single precision arithmetic only, allowing to use low cost graphics hardware. Furthermore, the sparse matrix vector product performance is limited by memory bandwidth and GPU accelerators provide much higher bandwidth than CPU main memory.

In this paper a NVIDIA Geforce GTX 680 is selected as the hardware platform and CUDA as the software counterpart. The CUDA software package includes an implementation of the SpMM product in the CUSPARSE library [14]. However, this routine checks the input parameters and, unlike the MKL library, forbids to set the leading dimension of the dense matrix to a value smaller than its number of rows. Therefore, an implementation based on the CUSPARSE SpMM routine cannot be tested, and we present only results performing several calls to the SpMV routine from the same library.

We developed a custom CUDA kernel based on the SpMM approach from (3), following many of the considerations detailed earlier on the CPU. In particular, the data layout of the dense matrices X and Y is also row-major. However, these matrices are stored without any redundancy, this is important as GPU memory is not as large as CPU memory.

The work distribution among GPU processors is completely different from the CPU implementation. The key to obtain high performance in a GPU is to keep

Data: Ai : $\mathbb{N}^{m+1}$, Aj : $\mathbb{N}^{nnz}$, Av : $\mathbb{R}^{nnz}$, CSR vectors of a $m \times n$, nnz nonzeros
  sparse matrix representing the first block row of a $k \times k$ block circulant
  matrix; X : $\mathbb{R}^{n_B \times k}$, dense matrix.
Result: Y : $\mathbb{R}^{m \times k}$ dense matrix with the product of the sparse matrix by X.

```
1  for i ← 0 to m − 1 do (in parallel) // block parallelism
2      for p ← 0 to k − 1 do (in parallel) // thread parallelism
3          w ← 0
4          for j ← Ai[i] to Ai[i + 1] do
5              c ← Aj[j]/n_B + p
6              if c > n_B then
7                  c = c − n_B
8              l ← Aj[j] mod n_B
9              w ← w + Av[j] · X[l, c];
10         Y[i, p] ← w;
```

Fig. 6. Product of block circulant sparse matrix by dense matrix (GPU)

all of the computing elements busy with a minimum of communications among
them. Therefore, a straightforward work distribution is to assign to each thread
the computation of just one element from the product result vector Y.

Figure 6 contains the GPU implementation pseudocode for the circulant
sparse matrix product. The CUDA runtime environment provides blocks of
threads, that is, two levels of parallelism. The first level (blocks) is presented
in Fig. 6 as the first loop, while the second level (threads) corresponds to the
second loop. The actual implementation does not contain these two loops, they
are implicitly created by the kernel invocation parameters.

First, to obtain good performance in the GPU a large number of thread blocks
must be created, in this case one block per matrix row. The actual amount of
work per block is determined by the matrix pattern and could be quite different
from row to row. However, this is not an issue because there are enough blocks to
keep busy all GPU processors. If the execution time of a block is too short, the
hardware scheduler could easily select another block from the execution queue.

Second, the number of threads inside a block should be a small multiple of
32 (warp size) to obtain good performance on the GPU. In this implementation
there are as many threads as blocks has the circulant matrix. Although this
number might not be a multiple of 32 (150 in our tests), it is sufficiently large
to occupy several warps.

Last but not least, GPU performance is very dependent on memory access
patterns. In this case, all data is stored in device memory with a similar distribution as presented before for the CPU implementation. The vector X is read in
coalesced form via a texture cache to further increase the effective bandwidth.
Each element of vectors Ai, Aj and Av is read simultaneously by all threads in
a block. This memory access is quite efficient and saturate most of the device

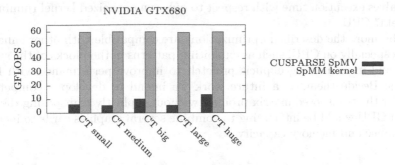

Fig. 7. Performance on GPU of kernels based on the SpMV and SpMM approaches with different matrix sizes

memory bandwidth. Our tests show no tangible benefits in using shared or constant memory for this access pattern.

One small optimization different to the CPU implementation is that Aj (column index) is stored in two separate vectors, one with values $\lfloor Aj[j]/n_B \rfloor$ and another with $Aj[j] \bmod n_B$. Both operations have a low throughput on the GPU, and precomputing them on the CPU improves performance of the whole circulant sparse product.

Figure 7 compares the performance of two circulant sparse matrix product implementations on the GTX680 GPU. The first is based on CUSPARSE SpMV routines while the second is our custom SpMM kernel implementation, which is several times faster than the SpMV implementation. The performance of SpMM is almost constant (about 60 GFLOPS) for all matrix sizes, and up to two times faster than our optimized SpMM on the CPU. The main advantage of the GPU over the CPU is that performance does not decrease with large matrices.

5   Conclusions and Future Work

In this paper, we have described optimization techniques to improve the performance of the sparse matrix vector product (SpMV) for block circulant matrices. This matrix structure allows to rewrite the SpMV into a product of two matrices, one sparse and other dense (SpMM). Moreover, we propose to replicate vector data and to join several AXPY products into a MAXPY. Both optimizations simplify data access and improve cache locality.

Our optimized SpMM kernel reduces execution time by 10 times on an Intel i7 CPU compared to a trivial SpMV implementation. We also tested alternative implementations using the SpMV and SpMM products from high-performance libraries (Intel MKL), but all of them obtain worse performance than our kernels.

On GPU, we propose a similar distribution of data which allows to fully exploit the device raw bandwidth via coalesced and textured memory accesses. This SpMM implementation is about 6 times faster than the SpMV from the CUSPARSE library on a NVIDIA GTX680 graphics card. For very large matrices, this

GPU halves execution time with respect to our own optimized kernel running on the Intel i7 CPU.

Furthermore the described optimizations are compatible with other enhancements, especially on CPU, such as exploiting patterns in the blocks of the sparse matrix and implementing explicit prefetch to improve performance with large matrices. Beside them, as a future work we intend to develop a competitive kernel for the transposed matrix product without explicitly transposing the matrix. On GPU would be interesting to combine several graphics cards to increase performance and memory capacity.

References

1. Bian, J., Siewerdsen, J.H., Han, X., Sidky, E.Y., Prince, J.L., Pelizzari, C.A., Pal, X.: Evaluation of sparse-view reconstruction from flat-panel-detector cone-beam ct. Physics in Medicine and Biology 55, 6575–6599 (2010)
2. Dalton, S., Bell, N.: CUSP: A C++ templated sparse matrix library version 0.4.0 (2014), http://cusplibrary.github.com/
3. Feldkamp, L., Davis, L., Kress, J.: Practical cone-beam algorithm. Journal of the Optical Society of America 1, 612–619 (1984)
4. Ganine, V., Legrand, M., Michalska, H., Pierre, C.: A sparse preconditioned iterative method for vibration analysis of geometrically mistuned bladed disks. Computers & Structures 87(5-6), 342–354 (2009)
5. Hara, A.K., Paden, R.G., Silva, A.C., Kujak, J.L., Lawder, H.J., Pavlicek, W.: Iterative reconstruction technique for reducing body radiation dose at CT: Feasibility study. American Journal of Roentgenology 193, 764–771 (2009)
6. Heroux, M.A., Bartlett, R.A., Howle, V.E., Hoekstra, R.J., Hu, J.J., Kolda, T.G., Lehoucq, R.B., Long, K.R., Pawlowski, R.P., Phipps, E.T., Salinger, A.G., Thornquist, H.K., Tuminaro, R.S., Willenbring, J.M., Williams, A., Stanley, K.S.: An overview of the Trilinos project. ACM Trans. Math. Softw. 31(3), 397–423 (2005)
7. Im, E.J., Yelick, K., Vuduc, R.: Sparsity: Optimization framework for sparse matrix kernels. International Journal of High Performance Computing Applications 18(1), 135–158 (2004)
8. Jones, E., Oliphant, T., Peterson, P., et al.: SciPy: Open source scientific tools for Python (2001), http://www.scipy.org/
9. Kaveh, A., Rahami, H.: Block circulant matrices and applications in free vibration analysis of cyclically repetitive structures. Acta Mechanica 217(1-2), 51–62 (2011)
10. Kourtis, K., Goumas, G., Koziris, N.: Optimizing sparse matrix-vector multiplication using index and value compression. In: Proceedings of the 5th Conference on Computing Frontiers, CF 2008, pp. 87–96. ACM, New York (2008)
11. Krotkiewski, M., Dabrowski, M.: Parallel symmetric sparse matrix–vector product on scalar multi-core CPUs. Parallel Computing 36(4), 181–198 (2010)
12. Lee, B., Vuduc, R., Demmel, J., Yelick, K.: Performance models for evaluation and automatic tuning of symmetric sparse matrix-vector multiply. In: International Conference on Parallel Processing, ICPP 2004, vol. 1, pp. 169–176 (2004)
13. Leroux, J.D., Selivanov, V., Fontaine, R., Lecomte, R.: Accelerated iterative image reconstruction methods based on block-circulant system matrix derived from a cylindrical image representation. In: Nuclear Science Symposium Conference Record, NSS 2007, vol. 4, pp. 2764–2771. IEEE (2007)

14. NVIDIA: CUSPARSE library (2014), https://developer.nvidia.com/cusparse

15. Pan, X., Sidky, E.Y., Vannier, M.: Why do commercial CT scanners still employ traditional, filtered back-projection for image reconstruction? Inverse Problems 25, 123009 (2008)

16. Rodríguez-Alvarez, M.J., Soriano, A., Iborra, A., Sánchez, F., González, A.J., Conde, P., Hernández, L., Moliner, L., Orero, A., Vidal, L.F., Benlloch, J.M.: Expectation maximization (EM) algorithms using polar symmetries for computed tomography CT image reconstruction. Computers in Biology and Medicine 43(8), 1053–1061 (2013)

17. Sheep, L., Vardi, Y.: Maximum likelihood reconstruction for emmision tomography. IEEE Transactions on Medical Imaging 1, 113–122 (1982)

18. Sidky, E.Y., Pan, X.: Image reconstruction in circular cone-beam computed tomography by constrained, total-variation minimization. Physics in Medicine and Biology 53, 4777–4807 (2008)

19. Soriano, A., Rodríguez-Alvarez, M.J., Iborra, A., Sánchez, F., Carles, M., Conde, P., González, A.J., Hernández, L., Moliner, L., Orero, A., Vidal, L.F., Benlloch, J.M.: EM tomographic image reconstruction using polar voxels. Journal of Instrumentation 8, C01004 (2013)

20. Thibaudeau, C., Leroux, J.D., Pratte, J.F., Fontaine, R., Lecomte, R.: Cylindrical and spherical ray-tracing for ct iterative reconstruction. In: 2011 IEEE Nuclear Science Symposium and Medical Imaging Conference (NSS/MIC), pp. 4378–4381 (2011)

21. Vuduc, R., Demmel, J.W., Yelick, K.A.: OSKI: A library of automatically tuned sparse matrix kernels. Journal of Physics: Conference Series 16(1), 521 (2005)

22. Vuduc, R.W., Moon, H.-J.: Fast sparse matrix-vector multiplication by exploiting variable block structure. In: Yang, L.T., Rana, O.F., Di Martino, B., Dongarra, J. (eds.) HPCC 2005. LNCS, vol. 3726, pp. 807–816. Springer, Heidelberg (2005)

23. Williams, S., Oliker, L., Vuduc, R., Shalf, J., Yelick, K., Demmel, J.: Optimization of sparse matrix-vector multiplication on emerging multicore platforms. Parallel Computing 35(3), 178–194 (2009)

Scheduling Data Flow Program in XKaapi: A New Affinity Based Algorithm for Heterogeneous Architectures

Raphaël Bleuse[1], Thierry Gautier[2], João V.F. Lima[4],
Grégory Mounié[1], and Denis Trystram[1,3]

[1] Univ. Grenoble Alpes, France
{raphael.bleuse,gregory.mounie,denis.trystram}@imag.fr
[2] Inria Rhône-Alpes, France
thierry.gautier@inrialpes.fr
[3] Institut universitaire de France
[4] Universidade Federal de Santa Maria (UFSM), Brazil
jvlima@inf.ufsm.br

Abstract. Efficient implementations of parallel applications on heterogeneous hybrid architectures require a careful balance between computations and communications with accelerator devices. Even if most of the communication time can be overlapped by computations, it is essential to reduce the total volume of communicated data. The literature therefore abounds with *ad hoc* methods to reach that balance, but these are architecture and application dependent. We propose here a generic mechanism to automatically optimize the scheduling between CPUs and GPUs, and compare two strategies within this mechanism: the classical Heterogeneous Earliest Finish Time (HEFT) algorithm and our new, parametrized, Distributed Affinity Dual Approximation algorithm (DADA), which consists in grouping the tasks by affinity before running a fast dual approximation. We ran experiments on a heterogeneous parallel machine with twelve CPU cores and eight NVIDIA Fermi GPUs. Three standard dense linear algebra kernels from the PLASMA library have been ported on top of the XKaapi runtime system. We report their performances. It results that HEFT and DADA perform well for various experimental conditions, but that DADA performs better for larger systems and number of GPUs, and, in most cases, generates much lower data transfers than HEFT to achieve the same performance.

Keywords: Heterogeneous architectures, scheduling, cost models, dual approximation scheme, programming tools, affinity.

1 Introduction

With the recent evolution of processor design, the future generations of processors will contain hundreds of cores. To increase the performance per watt ratio, the cores will be non-symmetric with few highly powerful cores (CPU) and numerous, but simpler, cores (GPU). The success of such machines will rely on the ability to schedule the workload at runtime, even for small problem instances.

F. Silva et al. (Eds.): Euro-Par 2014, LNCS 8632, pp. 560–571, 2014.

One of the main challenges is to define a scheduling strategy that may be able to exploit all potential parallelisms on a heterogeneous architecture composed of multiple CPUs and multiple GPUs. Previous works demonstrate the efficiency of strategies such as static distribution [14,15], centralized list scheduling with data locality [6], cost models [1–4] based on Heterogeneous-Earliest-Finish-Time scheduling (HEFT) [16], and dynamic for some specific application domains [5,10]. Locality-aware work stealing [9], with a careful implementation to overlap communication by computation [13], improves significantly the performance of compute-bound linear algebra problems such as matrix product and Cholesky factorization.

Nevertheless, none of the above cited works considers scheduling strategies from the viewpoint of a compromise between performance and locality. In this paper, we propose a scheduling algorithm based on dual approximation [12] that uses a performance model to predict the execution time of tasks during scheduling decision. This algorithm, called Distributed Affinity Dual Approximation (DADA), is able to find a compromise between transfers and performance. This trade-off is tuned thanks to a parameter α. The main advantage of dual approximation algorithms is their theoretical performance guarantee as they have a constant approximation ratio. On the contrary, the worst case of HEFT can be arbitrarily bad [12].

We compare these two different scheduling strategies for data-flow task programming. These strategies are implemented on top of the XKaapi scheduling framework with performance models for task execution time and transfer prediction. The contributions of this paper are first the design and implementation of dual approximation scheduling algorithms (with and without affinity) and second their evaluation in comparison to the well-known HEFT algorithm on three dense linear algebra algorithms in double precision floating-point operations from PLASMA [7]: namely Cholesky, LU, and QR. To our knowledge, this paper is the first report of experimental evaluations studying the impact of data transfer model and contention on a machine with up to 8 GPUs.

The main lesson of this work is that scheduling algorithms need extra information in order to take the right decisions. Such extra information could be obtained in a precise communication model to predict processing time of each task or in a more flexible information such as the affinity in DADA. Even if HEFT remains a good candidate for scheduling such linear algebra kernels, DADA is highly competitive against it for multi-GPU systems: the experimental results demonstrate that it achieves the same range of performances while reducing significantly the communication volume.

The remainder of this paper is organized as follows. Section 2 provides an overview of XKaapi runtime system, describes the XKaapi scheduling framework and the cost model applied for performance prediction. Section 3 details the two studied scheduling strategies. Section 4 presents our experimental results on a heterogeneous architecture composed of 12 CPUs and 8 GPUs. In Section 5 we briefly survey related works on runtime systems, scheduling strategies and performance prediction. Finally, Section 6 concludes the paper and suggests future directions.

2   Scheduling Framework in XKaapi

The XKaapi[1] data-flow model [8] – as in Cilk, Intel TBB, OpenMP-3.0, or OmpSs [6] – enables non-blocking task creation: the caller creates the task and proceeds with the program execution. Parallelism is explicit while the detection of synchronizations is implicit [8]: dependencies between tasks and memory transfers are automatically managed by the runtime system.

XKaapi runtime system is structured around the notion of *worker*: it is the internal representation of kernel threads. It executes the code of the tasks and takes local scheduling decisions. Each worker owns a local queue of ready tasks. Our interface is mainly inspired by work stealing scheduler and is composed of three operations that act on workers' queues of tasks: *pop*, *push* and *steal*. In our previous work, we demonstrated the efficiency of XKaapi locality-aware work stealing as well as the corresponding multi-GPU runtime support [9] using specialized implementation of these operations. A new operation, called *activate*, has been defined to push ready tasks to a worker's queue.

2.1   Execution Flow

The sketch of the execution mechanism is the following: at each step, either the own queue of worker is not empty and the worker uses it; or the worker emits a steal request to a randomly selected worker in order to get a task to execute. According to the dependencies between tasks, once a worker finishes a task, it calls the *activate* operations in order to activate the successors of the task which become ready for execution.

The XKaapi runtime system gets information from each internal events (such as start-end of task execution, or start-end of communication toward GPU) to calibrate the performance model and corrects erroneous predictions due to unpredictable or unknown behavior (*e.g.* operating system state or I/O disturbance). StarPU [4] uses similar runtime measurements in order to correct the performance predictions in its HEFT implementation.

All of our scheduling strategies follow this sketch. Every worker terminates its execution when all the tasks of the application have been executed.

2.2   Pop, Push, Steal and Activate Operations

A framework interface for scheduling strategies is not a new concept in heterogeneous systems. Bueno *et al.* [6] and Augonnet *et al.* [4] described a minimal interface to design scheduling strategies with selection at runtime. However, there is little information available on the comparison of different strategies. Most of

---

[1] http://kaapi.gforge.inria.fr

them reported performance on centralized list scheduling and performance models. Our framework is composed of three classical operations in the work stealing context, plus an action to activate tasks when their predecessors have completed.

- The *push* operation inserts a task into a queue. A worker can push a task into any other workers' queue.
- A *pop* removes a task from the local queue owned by the caller worker.
- A *steal* removes a task from the queue of a remote worker. It is called by an idle thread – the *thief* – in order to pick tasks from a randomly selected worker – the *victim*.
- The *activate* operation is called after the completion of a task. The role of this operation is to allocate the tasks that are ready to be executed. Hence, most of the scheduling decision are done during this operation.

2.3 Performance Model

Cost models depend on a certain knowledge of both application algorithm and the underlying architecture to predict performance at runtime. In order to predict performance, we designed a StarPU [3] like performance model for task execution time and communication. Our task prediction relies on an history-based model, and transfer time estimation is based on asymptotic bandwidth. They are associated with scheduling strategies that are based on task completion time such as HEFT and DADA with and without affinity.

In order to balance efficiently the load, for each processor XKaapi maintains a shared time-stamp of the predicted time when it has completed its tasks. The completion date of the last executed task is also kept. The update and incrementation of the time-stamps are efficiently implemented with atomic operators.

3 Scheduling Strategies

This section introduces the scheduling strategies designed on top of the XKaapi scheduling framework. We consider a multi-core parallel architecture with m homogeneous CPUs and k homogeneous GPUs. First, we describe our implementation of HEFT [16]. Then, we recall the principle of the dual approximation scheme [11]. We propose a new algorithm – Distributed Affinity Dual Approximation (DADA) – based on this paradigm which takes into account the affinity between tasks.

In the following, the number of tasks is denoted by n. We denote by p_i^{CPU} the processing time of task T_i on a CPU and p_i^{GPU} on a GPU. We define the speedup S_i of task T_i as the ratio $S_i = p_i^{CPU}/p_i^{GPU}$.

3.1 HEFT within XKaapi

The Heterogeneous Earliest-Finish-Time algorithm (HEFT), proposed by [16], is a scheduling algorithm for a bounded number of heterogeneous processors. Its

---

Algorithm 1. HEFT – *activate* operation

Input   : A list of ready tasks T_i LR
Output: Tasks T_i pushed to the worker's queues

1 **foreach** $T_i \in$ LR **do**
2 | $S_i \leftarrow p_i^{CPU} / p_i^{GPU}$
3 **end**
4 Sort all ready tasks T_i by decreasing speedup S_i
5 **foreach** $T_i \in$ LR **do**
6 | Schedule T_i on the worker w_j achieving the earliest finish time
7 | push T_i into queue of worker w_j
8 | Update processor load time-stamps on worker w_j
9 **end**

---

time complexity is in $O(n^2 \cdot (m+k))$. It has two major phases: *task prioritizing* and *worker selection*. Our XKaapi version of HEFT implements both phases during the *activate* operation. The *task prioritizing* phase computes for all ready tasks T_i its speedup S_i relative to an execution on GPU. Next, it sorts the list of ready tasks by decreasing speedups. Whereas the original HEFT rule sorts the tasks by decreasing upward rank (average path length to the end), our rule gives priority on minimizing the sum of the execution times. In the *worker selection* phase, the algorithm selects tasks in the order of their speedup S_i and schedules each task on the worker which minimizes the completion time. Algorithm 1 describes the basic steps of HEFT over XKaapi.

3.2   Dual Approximation and Affinity

Dual Approximation. Let us first recall that a ρ-dual approximation scheduling algorithm considers a *guess* λ (which is an estimation of the optimal makespan) and either delivers a schedule of makespan at most $\rho\lambda$ or answers correctly that there exists no schedule of length at most λ [11]. The process is repeated by a classical binary search on λ up to a precision of ϵ. We target $\rho = 2$. The dual approximation part of Algorithm 2 consists in the following steps:

- Choice of the initial guess λ (lines 2 and 4);
- Extract the tasks which fit only into GPUs ($p_i^{CPU} > \lambda$), and symmetrically those which are dedicated to CPUs (line 9);
- Keep this schedule if the tasks fit into λ (line 12). Otherwise, reject it if there is a task larger than λ on both CPUs and GPUs (line 15);
- Add to the tasks allocated to the GPU those which have the largest speedup S_i up to overreaching the threshold λ (line 19) which guarantees the ratio $\rho = 2$;
- Put all the remaining tasks in the m CPUs and execute them using an earliest-finish-time scheduling policy (line 19).

Algorithm 2. DADA – *activate* operation

Input : A list of ready tasks T_i LR
Output: Tasks T_i pushed to the worker's queues

1 $lower \leftarrow 0$
2 $upper \leftarrow \sum_i max(p_i^{CPU}, p_i^{GPU})$
3 **while** $(upper - lower) > \epsilon$ **do**
4      $\lambda \leftarrow (upper + lower)/2$
5   **begin** *local affinity phase*
6   Schedule tasks of LR per affinity score on its affinity processor, loading each processor up to overreaching $\alpha\lambda$
7   **end**
8   **begin** *global balance phase*
9   Schedule LR to minimize finish time using λ as hint
10   **if** *tasks do fit into* $(\rho + \alpha)\lambda$ **then**
11             $upper \leftarrow \lambda$
12   Keep current schedule
13   **else**
14             $lower \leftarrow \lambda$
15   Reject current schedule
16   **end**
17   **end**
18 **end**
19 Push each task T_i of LR on queue of worker w_j based on the last fitting schedule and update processor load time-stamps

---

Affinity. DADA builds a compromise taking into account both raw performance and transfers. The principle consists in two successive phases: a first local phase targeting the reduction of the communications through the abstraction described below and a second phase which counter-balances the induced serialization aiming at a global balance. Any algorithm optimizing the makespan could be used for the second phase. We use a basic dual-approximation. In order to gain a finer control, the length of the first phase is controlled by a parameter (denoted by α, $0 \leq \alpha \leq 1$). A value of 0 for α means that the affinity is not taken into account: DADA is then a basic dual-approximation. While at the opposite a value close to 1 allows a length up to λ for the first phase, thus giving a greater weight to affinity.

Each pair (task, computation resource) is given an affinity score. Maximizing the score over the whole schedule enables to consider local impacts. The affinity scores are computed using extra information automatically gathered by the runtime system. In our implementation, they were computed using the amount of data updated by each task. For instance, a task that *writes* or *modifies* a data stored on a resource R has a high score and is prone to be scheduled on R.

4   Experiments

4.1   Experimental Setup: Platform and Benchmarks

Platform. All experiments have been conducted on a heterogeneous, multi-GPU system. It is composed of two hexa-core Intel Xeon X5650 CPUs running at 2.66 GHz with 72 GB of memory. It is enhanced with eight NVIDIA Tesla C2050 GPUs (Fermi architecture) of 448 GPU cores (scalar processors) running at 1.15 GHz each (2688 GPU cores total) with 3 GB GDDR5 per GPU (18 GB total). The machine has 4 PCIe switches to support up to 8 GPUs. When 2 GPUs share a switch, their aggregated PCIe bandwidth is bounded by the one of a single PCIe 16x. Experiments using up to 4 GPUs avoid this bandwidth constraint by using at most 1 GPU per PCIe switch.

Benchmarks. All benchmarks ran on top of a GNU/Linux Debian 6.0.2 *squeeze* with kernel 2.6.32-5-amd64. We compiled with GCC 4.4 and linked against CUDA 5.0 and the library ATLAS 3.9.39 (BLAS and LAPACK). All experiments use the tile algorithms of PLASMA [7] for Cholesky (`DPOTRF`), LU (`DGETRF`), and QR (`DGEQRF`). The QUARK API [17] has been implemented and extended in XKaapi to support task multi-specialization: the XKaapi runtime system maintains the CPU and GPU versions for each PLASMA task. At the task execution, our QUARK version runs the appropriate task implementation in accordance with the worker architecture. The GPU kernels of QR and LU are based on previous works from [1,2] and adapted from PLASMA CPU algorithm and MAGMA from [15]. Each running GPU monopolizes a CPU core to manage its worker. The remaining CPU cores are involved in the application computations.

Methodology. Each experiment has been executed at least 30 times for each set of parameters and we report on all the figures (Fig. 1, 2, 3 and 4) the mean and the 95% confidence interval. The factorizations have been done in double precision floating-point operations with a PLASMA internal block (*IB*) of size 128 and tiles of size 512. For each of them, we plot the highest performance obtained on various matrix sizes with the discussed scheduling strategies.

In the following, DADA(α) represents DADA parametrized by α. We denote by DADA(α)+CP the algorithm using Communication Prediction as supplementary information. HEFT strategy always computes the earliest finish time of a task taking into account the time to transfer data before executing the task.

4.2   Impact of the Affinity Control Parameter α

This section highlights the impact of the affinity control parameter α on the compromise between performance and data transfers. The measures have been done with the Cholesky decomposition on matrices of size 8192×8192 and 16384×16384. However, we present only results for the smallest size as we observe similar behaviors for both matrix sizes.

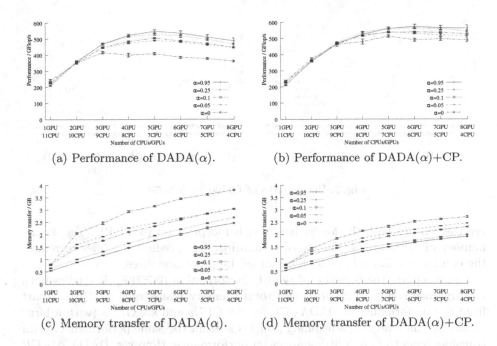

(a) Performance of DADA(α).   (b) Performance of DADA(α)+CP.

(c) Memory transfer of DADA(α).   (d) Memory transfer of DADA(α)+CP.

Fig. 1. Impact of parameter α on Cholesky (`DPOTRF`) with matrix of size 8192×8192

Fig. 1 shows both performance (Fig. 1(a) and 1(b)) and total memory transfers (Fig. 1(c) and 1(d)) for several values of α with respect to the number of GPUs. Both metrics are shown without (Fig. 1(a) and 1(c)) and with (Fig. 1(b) and 1(d)) communication prediction taken into account. Once affinity is considered (*i.e.* $\alpha \neq 0$), the higher the value of α, the better the policy scales. Using as little information as possible (*i.e.* DADA(0) and no communication prediction), the policy performance does not scale with more than two GPUs due to a too huge amount of transfers.

4.3 Comparison of Scheduling Strategies

We present in this section the results for the three kernels with matrix size 8192×8192. Other tested sizes have the same behavior. The idea is to evaluate the behavior of each strategy with different work loads. Both performance and data transfers of the policies introduced above: HEFT, DADA(0), DADA(α) and DADA(α)+CP are studied.

Experimental Evaluation. Fig. 2 reports the behavior of the Cholesky decomposition (`DPOTRF`) with respect to the number of GPUs used. It studies both performance results (Fig. 2(a)) and total memory transfers (Fig. 2(b)). All scheduling algorithms have similar performances. DADA(α)+CP scales slightly better with the number of GPU. As expected DADA(α)+CP and DADA(α)

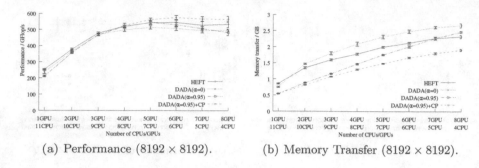

(a) Performance (8192 × 8192).   (b) Memory Transfer (8192 × 8192).

Fig. 2. Benchmarks of Cholesky (`DPOTRF`)

are the policies with the lowest bandwidth footprint up to 6 GPU. Yet, as the number of GPU grows, the use of communication prediction allows to reduce the communication volume with sustained high performances.

Fig. 3 reports the behavior of the LU factorization (`DGETRF`). It studies both performance results (Fig. 3(a)) and total memory transfers (Fig. 3(b)). Apart from the performance of DADA+CP for six CPUs and six GPUs (with a large confidence interval), all scheduling policies sustain the same performance. Data transfers seem to have a little impact on performance. However, DADA(α)+CP generates less memory movements than other strategies. DADA(0) is the most costly policy while DADA(α) and HEFT have similar impacts. The total memory transfers of the LU and the Cholesky factorizations behave in a similar way. Still, the gap between the curves is widening: DADA(α)+CP is 3.5 less demanding in bandwidth than HEFT for only a slowdown of about 1.13 in performance for 8 GPU.

Finally, Fig. 4 reports the behavior of the QR factorization (`DGEQRF`) with respect to the number of GPUs used. Both performance results (Fig. 4(a)) and total memory transfers (Fig. 4(b)) are studied. All dual approximations (DADA(0), DADA(α), DADA(α)+CP) behave the same and are outperformed by HEFT. Even the low transfer footprint of both DADA(α) is not able to sustain performance. It seems that the dependencies between tasks for QR factorization have a strong impact on the schedule computed by all dual approximation algorithms. We are still investigating this particular point.

Discussion

Communication Prediction Affinity is a viable alternative to communication modeling. Indeed, DADA without communication prediction is comparable to HEFT in terms of performance. Moreover, affinity based policy combined with communication prediction allows to reduce further more memory transfers (up to a factor 3.5 when compared to HEFT).

Comparison with Work Stealing Scheduling Algorithm For the sake of completeness, we also tested the work stealing algorithm. However we did not plot the

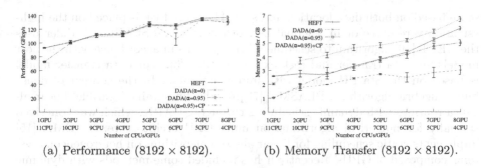

(a) Performance (8192 × 8192).   (b) Memory Transfer (8192 × 8192).

Fig. 3. Benchmarks of LU (`DGETRF`)

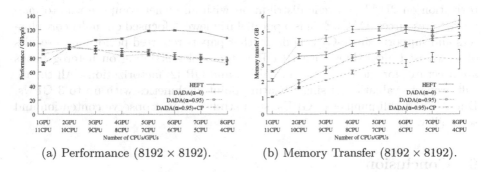

(a) Performance (8192 × 8192).   (b) Memory Transfer (8192 × 8192).

Fig. 4. Benchmarks of QR (`DGEQRF`)

results in previous figures for the sake of readability. We briefly discuss them now. The naïve work stealing algorithm is cache unfriendly, especially with small matrices as its random choices are heavily penalizing [9]. On the contrary, the affinity policies proposed here are suitable for this case. When scheduling for medium and large matrix sizes, the impact of modeling inaccuracies grows. Model oblivious algorithms such as work-stealing behave well by efficiently overlapping communications and computations while HEFT is induced in error by the imprecise communication prediction. Hence, our approach is much more robust than work stealing and HEFT since it does not need a too precise communication model and adapts well to various matrix sizes.

5 Related Works

StarPU [4], OmpSs [6] and QUARK [17] are programming environments or libraries that enables to automatically schedule tasks with data flow dependencies. OmpSs is based on OpenMP-like pragmas while StarPU and QUARK are C libraries. QUARK does not schedule tasks on multi-GPU architecture and implements a centralized greedy list scheduling algorithm. OmpSs locality-aware scheduling, similar to our data-aware heuristic from [9], computes an affinity score based on both data location and size. Then, the task is placed on the highest affinity resource or in a global list, otherwise. The StarPU scheduler uses the HEFT [16] algorithm to schedule all ready tasks in accordance with the cost models for data transfer and task execution time [3]. Our data transfer model is based on the StarPU model with minor extension. In the context of dense linear algebra algorithms, PLASMA [7] provides fine-grained parallel linear algebra routines with dynamic scheduling through QUARK, which was conceived specially for numerical algorithms on multi-CPU architecture. MAGMA [15] implements static scheduling for linear algebra algorithms on heterogeneous systems composed of GPUs. Recently it has included some methods with dynamic scheduling in multi-CPU and multi-GPU sytems on top of StarPU, in addition to the static multi-GPU version. In [14] the authors based their Cholesky factorization on 2D block cyclic distribution with an owner compute rule to map tasks to resources. DAGuE [5] is a parallel framework focused on multi-core clusters and supports single-GPU nodes. Other papers reported performance results of task-based algorithms with HEFT cost model scheduling on heterogeneous architectures for the Cholesky [4], LU [1], and QR [2] factorizations. All the results report evaluation of single floating point arithmetics with up to 3 GPUs. Due to the small number of GPUs, such studies cannot observe contention and scalability.

6   Conclusion

We presented in this paper a new scheduling algorithm on top of the XKaapi runtime system. It is based on a dual approximation scheme with affinity and has been compared to the classical HEFT algorithm for three tile algorithms from PLASMA on an heterogeneous architecture composed of 8 GPUs and 12 CPUs. Both algorithms attained significant speed up on the three dense linear algebra kernel. Moreover, if HEFT achieves the best absolute performance with respect to DADA on QR, while DADA has similar or better performances than HEFT on Cholesky and LU for large numbers of GPU. Nevertheless, DADA allows to significantly reduce the data transfers with respect to HEFT. More interesting, thanks to its affinity criteria DADA can introduce communication in the scheduling without too precise communication cost model which are required in HEFT to predict the completion time of tasks.

We would like to extend the experimental evaluations on robustness of scheduling with respect to uncertainties in cost models, especially on the communication cost which is very sensitive to contentions that may appear at runtime. Another interesting issue would be to study other affinity functions.

Acknowledgments. This work has been partially supported by the French Ministry of Defense – DGA, the ANR 09-COSI-011-05 Project Repdyn and CAPES/Brazil.

References

1. Agullo, E., Augonnet, C., Dongarra, J., Faverge, M., Langou, J., Ltaief, H., Tomov, S.: Lu factorization for accelerator-based systems. In: IEEE/ACS, AICCSA 2011, pp. 217–224. IEEE Computer Society, Washington, DC (2011)
2. Agullo, E., Augonnet, C., Dongarra, J., Faverge, M., Ltaief, H., Thibault, S., Tomov, S.: QR Factorization on a Multicore Node Enhanced with Multiple GPU Accelerators. In: IEEE IPDPS. EUA (2011)
3. Augonnet, C., Thibault, S., Namyst, R.: Automatic calibration of performance models on heterogeneous multicore architectures. In: Lin, H.-X., Alexander, M., Forsell, M., Knüpfer, A., Prodan, R., Sousa, L., Streit, A. (eds.) Euro-Par 2009 Workshops. LNCS, vol. 6043, pp. 56–65. Springer, Heidelberg (2010)
4. Augonnet, C., Thibault, S., Namyst, R., Wacrenier, P.A.: StarPU: A unified platform for task scheduling on heterogeneous multicore architectures. Concurrency and Computation: Practice and Experience 23(2), 187–198 (2011)
5. Bosilca, G., Bouteiller, A., Danalis, A., Herault, T., Lemarinier, P., Dongarra, J.: DAGuE: A generic distributed DAG engine for High Performance Computing. Parallel Computing 38(1–2), 37–51 (2012)
6. Bueno, J., Planas, J., Duran, A., Badia, R.M., Martorell, X., Ayguadé, E., Labarta, J.: Productive Programming of GPU Clusters with OmpSs. In: IEEE IPDPS (2012)
7. Buttari, A., Langou, J., Kurzak, J., Dongarra, J.: A class of parallel tiled linear algebra algorithms for multicore architectures. Parallel Computing 35(1), 38–53 (2009)
8. Gautier, T., Besseron, X., Pigeon, L.: KAAPI: A thread scheduling runtime system for data flow computations on cluster of multi-processors. In: PASCO 2007. ACM, London (2007)
9. Gautier, T., Lima, J.V., Maillard, N., Raffin, B.: XKaapi: A Runtime System for Data-Flow Task Programming on Heterogeneous Architectures. In: IEEE IPDPS, pp. 1299–1308 (2013)
10. Hermann, E., Raffin, B., Faure, F., Gautier, T., Allard, J.: Multi-GPU and Multi-CPU Parallelization for Interactive Physics Simulations. In: D'Ambra, P., Guarracino, M., Talia, D. (eds.) Euro-Par 2010, Part II. LNCS, vol. 6272, pp. 235–246. Springer, Heidelberg (2010)
11. Hochbaum, D.S., Shmoys, D.B.: Using dual approximation algorithms for scheduling problems theoretical and practical results. J. ACM 34(1), 144–162 (1987)
12. Kedad-Sidhoum, S., Monna, F., Mounié, G., Trystram, D.: Scheduling independent tasks on multi-cores with GPU accelerators. In: an Mey, D., et al. (eds.) Euro-Par 2013. LNCS, vol. 8374, pp. 228–237. Springer, Heidelberg (2014)
13. Lima, J.V.F., Gautier, T., Maillard, N., Danjean, V.: Exploiting Concurrent GPU Operations for Efficient Work Stealing on Multi-GPUs. In: 24th SBAC-PAD, pp. 75–82. IEEE, New York (2012)
14. Song, F., Dongarra, J.: A scalable framework for heterogeneous GPU-based clusters. In: ACM SPAA, pp. 91–100. ACM, New York (2012)
15. Tomov, S., Dongarra, J., Baboulin, M.: Towards dense linear algebra for hybrid GPU accelerated manycore systems. Parallel Computing 36(5-6), 232–240 (2010)
16. Topcuoglu, H., Hariri, S., Wu, M.Y.: Performance-effective and low-complexity task scheduling for heterogeneous computing. IEEE TPDC 13(3), 260–274 (2002)
17. YarKhan, A., Kurzak, J., Dongarra, J.: Quark users' guide: Queueing and runtime for kernels. Tech. Rep. ICL-UT-11-02, University of Tennessee (2011)

Delegation Locking Libraries for Improved Performance of Multithreaded Programs*

David Klaftenegger, Konstantinos Sagonas, and Kjell Winblad

Department of Information Technology, Uppsala University, Sweden

Abstract. While standard locking libraries are common and easy to use, delegation algorithms that offload work to a single thread can achieve better performance in multithreaded applications, but are hard to use without adequate library support. This paper presents an interface for delegation locks together with libraries for C and C++ that make it easy to use *queue delegation locking*, a versatile high-performance delegation algorithm. We show examples of using these libraries, discuss the porting effort needed to take full advantage of delegation locking in applications designed with standard locking in mind, and the improved performance that this achieves.

1 Introduction

In many programming languages, locking is still the dominant synchronization mechanism that multithreaded programs use to protect their critical sections. Especially in systems programming languages, lock-based multicore programming is supported by libraries which are readily available and easy to use. Recently, particularly in programs manipulating shared data structures protected by a single lock, researchers have investigated ways of offloading critical sections to a single processor core and letting them be executed by the same thread [3, 4, 7, 9–11]. Such *delegation algorithms*, which effectively bring the operations of critical sections to the data instead of bringing data to where the operations execute, have significant performance advantages on modern multicores and are often superior to implementing concurrent data structures either by fine-grained locking or in lock-free ways [3, 4]. Alas, this style of multicore programming is very hard to employ without adequate library support.

This paper presents an interface for delegation locks and two libraries for C and C++ that make a versatile high-performance delegation algorithm, called *queue delegation locking* (Sect. 2), easy to use. More specifically, we describe the most important aspects of the programming interfaces of our libraries (Sect. 3 and 4), and our experiences in porting code of significant size ($\approx 16\,300$ LOC) to using this library both in effort required as well as in performance improvements that this brought (Sect. 5). To the best of our knowledge, our libraries[1] are the first to provide portable support for delegation. By portable we mean that they only require the presence of a compiler that adheres to the C11/C++11 standards. In addition, we discuss issues that are involved when one wants to modify existing multithreaded programs that have been written with standard locking in mind to take full advantage of delegation locking (Sect. 7).

---

* Research supported in part by EU project RELEASE (IST-2011-287510) and by UPMARC.
[1] http://www.it.uu.se/research/group/languages/software/qd_lock_lib
(Publicly available)

F. Silva et al. (Eds.): Euro-Par 2014, LNCS 8632, pp. 572–583, 2014.

2 Queue Delegation Locking

The delegation algorithm we use, called *Queue Delegation (QD) locking* [6], is a new efficient delegation algorithm whose idea is simple. When, e.g., a shared data structure protected by a single lock is contended, the threads do not wait for the lock to be released. Instead, they try to delegate their operation to the thread currently holding the lock (called the *helper*). If the operation does not read from the shared structure, successful delegation allows a thread to immediately continue execution, possibly delegating more operations or doing other work. The helper thread is responsible for eventually executing delegated operations in the order they arrived to ensure linearizability. This implies that reading from the shared data structure needs to wait for all prior operations so that no outdated data is ever read. Most kinds of critical sections can be delegated with this scheme, and waiting is only needed when effects of a critical section need to be visible.

QD locking is realized by placing delegated operations in a *delegation queue*. The operations are stored in order of their arrival, and thus their linearization point is the successful enqueueing into the delegation queue. However, the enqueueing can fail when the lock holder is not accepting any more operations. This happens when the queue is already full or when the helper already executed all operations it found and is about to release the lock. If delegation fails, the thread has to retry until it succeeds to either take the lock itself or delegate its operation to a new lock holder.

The delegation queue is implemented as a fixed size buffer which stores operations together with arbitrarily sized parameters, e.g. some data to insert. This avoids the allocation of additional memory to pass data for each operation. An atomically incremented offset is used to access the buffer and automatically close the queue when it is full. If the required data exceeds the remaining space in the queue, the queue still closes, but the delegation has to be retried. A standard mutual exclusion (mutex) lock is used only to determine the helper thread to which operations are delegated.[2] Our libraries also come with a lock which allows multiple readers in parallel. We base our multiple readers QD (MRQD) lock on the mutex lock agnostic write-preference readers-writer lock algorithm of Calciu et al. [2]. As a *reader indicator* we use reader groups [5], which essentially is a counter that is distributed over many cache lines to avoid false cache invalidations.

The QD lock is accessed using a `delegate` function. When needed, e.g. for reading data, *futures* can be used to wait until the data is available. Futures can be as simple as having the delegated operation setting a flag upon completion or writing data to a predetermined location. MRQD locks come with an additional trade-off: For consistency, readers have to wait immediately for previously delegated operations before they can all access in parallel. By the time the read operation is performed it is guaranteed that any previously delegated operation on the same QD lock has finished. Read-only critical sections using the `rlock` and `runlock` functions work exactly as in traditional readers-writer locks. To ease porting of existing code we also provide `lock` and `unlock` on QD and MRQD locks, which are simply forwarded to the underlying mutex lock. For more information on the queue delegation algorithm, e.g. hierarchical NUMA variants or susceptibility to starvation, see a companion paper [6] describing QD locking in detail.

---

[2] Our libraries use a test-and-test-and-set lock for this; for the reasoning of this choice refer to [6].

3   C Library

We will present the C API of our QD locking library through examples. Let us first consider the implementation of a shared integer (ShInt) that can be accessed concurrently by several threads. All operations on ShInts are supposed to be atomic. A ShInt can be represented with the following C structure which employs an MRQD lock to coordinate concurrent accesses to it.

```
1 typedef struct { MRQDLock lock; int value; } ShInt;
```

Now consider a `mult` operation that multiplies a ShInt with an integer value and stores the result back on the ShInt. Since MRQD locks support the traditional locking operations `lock` and `unlock`, the `mult` function could be implemented like this:

```
1 void mult1(ShInt* v1, int v2) {
2   LL_lock(&v1->lock); v1->value = v1->value * v2; LL_unlock(&v1->lock);
3 }
```

This implementation is easy to understand, but it may not be very efficient when a ShInt is contented on a multicore machine. One reason is that every thread has to wait for the thread currently holding the lock to release it before its execution can proceed. With thread preemption, the OS can force the lock holding thread to be suspended for an arbitrary amount of time. Since `mult` does not return any value, we could instead delegate the responsibility of executing the critical section to another thread that has already acquired the lock. This is easy to do using the `LL_delegate` function from the QD locking library:

```
1 typedef struct { ShInt* v1; int v2; } MultMsg;
2 void mult_cs(unsigned int sz, void* msgP) {
3   MultMsg* msg = (MultMsg*)msgP;
4   msg->v1->value = msg->v1->value * msg->v2;
5 }
6 void mult2(ShInt* v1, int v2) {
7   MultMsg msg = {.v1 = v1, .v2 = v2};
8   LL_delegate(&v1->lock, mult_cs, sizeof(msg), &msg);
9 }
```

The `LL_delegate` call (line 8) either executes the `mult_cs` function in the current thread while holding the lock or delegates the responsibility to execute it to the current lock holder. As long as all accesses to the ShInt are done by threads that have acquired the lock, `mult1` and `mult2` are equivalent in the sense that it is impossible to detect which one is used. The parameters to `LL_delegate` are the lock, the function with the code of the critical section, the message size and a pointer to the message data. The message data and the message size will be passed to the delegated function when it is executed. The programmer cannot rely on that the `mult_cs` function is executed by the current thread or that the message data is not copied to another location. Many threads can delegate critical sections to the same helper, which has the performance advantage that the manipulated data can stay in the same private cache while it is being manipulated.

Extending the example, suppose we now also want the result of the multiplication as a return value. We can create the function `mult_res` for that purpose:

```
1  typedef struct { ShInt* v1; int v2; int* retval; } MultResMsg;
2  void mult_res_cs(unsigned int sz, void* msgP) {
3    MultResMsg* msg = (MultResMsg*)msgP;
4    msg->v1->value = msg->v1->value * msg->v2;
5    *msg->retval = msg->v1->value;
6  }
7  int mult_res(ShInt* v1, int v2) {
8    int res;
9    MultResMsg msg = {.v1 = v1, .v2 = v2, .retval = &res};
10   LL_delegate_wait(&v1->lock, mult_res_cs, sizeof(msg), &msg);
11   return res;
12 }
```

The delegated function writes back the result to the location pointed to by `retval` in `MultResMsg` (line 5). Here we are using a variant of `delegate` called `LL_delegate_wait` (line 10), which waits for the delegated function's execution before it returns. Unsurprisingly, `LL_delegate_wait` also guarantees that the lock is held by the thread that executes the delegated function. Instead of returning the actual value from `mult_res` one could return at this point a future that will contain the result when it is ready. However, in a low-level language such as C, constructing this future is something that needs to be done by the program itself. In the next section we will see how the situation changes in C++.

The QD locking library also supports read-only critical sections:

```
1  int read(ShInt* v) {
2    int res;
3    LL_rlock(&v->lock);    res = v->value;    LL_runlock(&v->lock);
4    return res;
5  }
```

Using read-only critical sections is a powerful way to support multiple parallel read operations. Mixing read-only critical sections with delegated critical sections can give excellent performance. Since threads can delegate critical sections without waiting for the actual execution they can continue and issue a read-only critical section. Read-critical sections are thus more likely to bulk up so that more can execute in parallel than if a readers-writer lock without delegation was used.

We have almost gone through all functions in the locking library for C. The only ones left are the `LL_delegate_or_lock` family of functions. These provide the same functionality as `LL_delegate` but avoid the overhead that `LL_delegate` has in creating a separate buffer for copying the message for the delegated critical section to the current lock holder. Creating this buffer can be particularly expensive when the size of the buffer is not known at compile time and needs to be allocated dynamically. Dynamic memory allocation is expensive and can be a scalability problem on multicores. The code at the top of the next page shows how this family of functions is used. The `enqueue` function is for a concurrent queue. The function `enq` is not shown for lack of space but we can assume that it is a non-thread-safe enqueue function which copies the data into the queue data structure. The `LL_delegate_or_lock` function (line 5) attempts to get a message buffer of the specified size for a critical section. If `LL_delegate_or_lock` succeeds a buffer address will be returned, otherwise NULL is returned and the lock is acquired.

```
1 void enqueue_cs(unsigned int sz, void* m) {
2   enq(*((Queue**)m), sz - sizeof(Queue*), &((char*)m)[sizeof(Queue*)]);
3 }
4 void enqueue(Queue* q, int dSize, void* d) {
5   void* buff = LL_delegate_or_lock(q->lock, dSize + sizeof(Queue*));
6   if (buff == NULL) {
7     enq(q, dSize, d);
8     LL_delegate_unlock(lock);
9   } else {
10    memcpy(buff, &q, sizeof(Queue*));
11    memcpy(&((char*)buff)[sizeof(Queue*)], d, dSize);
12    LL_close_delegate_buffer(q->lock, buff, enqueue_cs);
13  }
14 }
```

The function `LL_delegate_unlock` (line 8) is used to unlock the lock when no message buffer was acquired. `LL_close_delegate_buffer` (line 12) will indicate to the lock holder that the message buffer is fully written. After the `LL_close_delegate_buffer` call, the delegated function (provided as parameter) can be executed with the message buffer given as parameter.

4   C++ Library

While the C library performs very well, its interface restrictions mean that a C++ programmer has to write many function wrappers so that operations could be delegated. For this reason, we also developed a C++11 implementation of QD locking, which makes delegation in C++ code easier. It provides the same variants of QD locks as the C library, namely `qdlock` and `mrqdlock`. For the user, it provides two delegation interfaces: `delegate_n`, which detaches the execution entirely, and `delegate_f`, which returns a future that is bound to the critical section. The initial example in C could look similar to this in C++:

```
1 mrqdlock lock;
2 void mult_cs(int* a, int b) { *a = *a * b; }
3 void mult(int* v1, int v2) {
4     lock.lock(); mult_cs(v1, v2); lock.unlock();
5 }
```

From the parameters to the critical section, it is clear what data needs to be transferred. As the type of each object is known at compile time, the compiler can produce code to forward the data to the critical section.

```
3 void mult(int* v1, int v2) {
4     lock.delegate_n(&mult_cs, v1, v2);
5 }
```

Furthermore, with C++11 lambda functions it is not even necessary to have a separate named function, like `mult_cs` above, for the critical section.

```
3   void mult(int* v1, int v2) {
4       lock.delegate_n([](int* a, int b) { *a = *a * b; }, v1, v2);
5   }
```

Even with these simple examples one can see the flexibility of the library. Using functors – which lambda functions are – or normal function pointers, the library takes them together with their parameters and passes them to the QD lock, serializing each element as needed. However, this flexibility comes at a price. To determine the types of the parameters, a function is constructed by the compiler, which can deserialize the parameters and passes them to the function or functor specified by the user. This additional function pointer needs to be passed to the lock together with the parameters, resulting in a one word overhead when compared to the C version of the library. This can be avoided only for non-overloaded functions by passing the function address as a template parameter to the library code.

```
4       lock.delegate_n<void (*)(int*, int), &mult_cs>(v1, v2);
```

Due to language restrictions, we need to specify the function signature as well, so that the compiler can type-check it later. For convenience, we provide a macro which inserts the function signature automatically.

```
4       lock.DELEGATE_N(&mult_cs, v1, v2);
```

To return values from critical sections or wait for their actual execution, we use futures. This allows the programmer to execute an arbitrary amount of code between issuing a critical section and the point where the return value or side effect of it needs to be visible to the system.

```
1    int read(int* shared) {
2        auto future = lock.delegate_f([=shared]() -> int { return *shared; });
3        return future.get();
4    }
5    void add_two_and_wait_for_first(int* shared) {
6        auto future = lock.delegate_f([=shared]() -> void { *shared += 1; });
7        lock.delegate_n([=shared]() -> void { *shared += 1; });
8        future.wait();
9    }
10   void add_two_and_block_both(int* shared) {
11       auto future1 = lock.delegate_f([=shared]() -> void { *shared += 1; });
12       auto future2 = lock.delegate_f([=shared]() -> void { *shared += 1; });
13       future2.wait();
14   }
```

In the last example the waiting for the second future is sufficient, as the order of delegations is preserved. If a future is destructed, the behaviour depends on the implementation used, which is currently std::future. To avoid ambiguity it is best to always store the return value of delegate_f and explicitly decide when the future needs to be invoked.

For a more complicated example, we will use std::map in a thread-safe way. While the example does not actually use concurrency, the code could be plugged into a concurrent program. It first inserts two values, then reads one back using a delegation, and finally reads the other value back using rlock. Remember that rlock has to wait for the completion of prior delegated sections, which means the future.get() call at the end will always immediately return the value.

```
1  #include<map>
2  #include "qd.hpp"
3  int main() {
4    std::map<int, double> map;
5    mrqdlock lock;
6    lock.delegate_n([&map]() { map.insert(std::make_pair(21, 2.56)); });
7    lock.delegate_n([&map]() { map.insert(std::make_pair(42, 3.14)); });
8    auto future = lock.delegate_f([&map](int key) {return map[key];}, 42);
9    lock.rlock(); double r2 = map[21]; lock.runlock();
10   double r1 = future.get();
11 }
```

5   Queue Delegation Locking for the Erlang Term Storage

In this section we will discuss the applicability of delegation locking to protect a shared key-value store, namely the Erlang Term Storage (ETS). ETS is a heavily used part of the Erlang programming language and is implemented in C for efficiency reasons. Erlang programs can use ETS as shared memory between threads (Erlang processes). Being shared memory, ETS has become a scalability concern on multicore machines [5]. Because of the complexity of ETS, it is difficult to apply efficient fine grained locking or lock-free techniques. This is especially true for the ordered_set ETS table type that is implemented as an AVL tree. Such ETS tables are currently protected by a single readers-writer lock. We will describe the steps we went through when porting the ETS code to use an MRQD lock instead of a readers-writer lock and the performance we got.

5.1   Porting

We have chosen to focus on the ETS operations insert, delete and lookup when porting. The first two operations are interesting since they do not have any return value and can thus be delegated to the current lock holder without any need to wait for their execution. The lookup operation is interesting because it can help us show how well QD locking works together with the multiple-readers extension. We divided the porting work into three steps of increasing difficulty, where each step produced working code that we could benchmark to measure the resulting performance. We started from an ETS code base of eight files with a total of 16 277 lines of code.

Step 1, delegate and wait: In this step we just delegate the original critical section and wait for its actual execution with the LL_delegate_wait function from the C library. In most situations this works without any semantic change of the original code. However, if thread-local variables are accessed inside the critical section, as was the case in ETS, care must be taken so the right thread-local variable is accessed. In ETS, the thread-local variable access was subtle since it was done in the read-unlock call of a readers-writer lock. To fix this issue we simply moved the read-unlock call to after the issuing of the critical section. Another way to deal with this problem would have been to pass a reference to the thread-local variable to the delegated function. In total this step required changing about 400 lines of code (60 of which were changes and 340 were additions, many to integrate with the existing locking structure).

Step 2, delegate without wait: To delegate without waiting for the actual execution of the critical section required more changes. The original code did some checking of parameters inside the critical section that could result in a return value indicating an error. These checks did not need to be done inside the critical section and could simply be lifted out. The parameters to the `insert` and `delete` functions are allocated on the heap of the issuing thread (process in Erlang terminology) and can be deallocated as soon as the functions have returned. Therefore it is not safe to send references to these values to delegated critical sections. Instead, we changed the original code to allocate a clone of the value and send a reference to the clone. For the `insert` case, the clone is in a form that can be inserted directly into the table data structure. The effort of allocating a clone is therefore not wasted since a clone would need to be created anyway to store the object. Furthermore, since the cloning is done outside the critical section, this modification can also decrease the length of the critical section. However, if the object being inserted is replacing an existing larger object, the original code had less memory management cost because it would just overwrite the existing object. For the `delete` operation, both the allocation of the cloned key and its subsequent freeing incurs an overhead compared to the original code. This step required changes in about 400 more lines of code (760 if one starts counting the differences from the original code).

Step 3, delegate and copy directly into the QD queue: In this step we got rid of the need to do more memory management than the original code by copying all parameters needed in the critical section directly into the queue buffer of the QD lock. This also had the benefit of improving the cache locality for the helper thread that is executing the critical sections. Because all needed data for the critical sections is stored in a continuous array, data for several operations can potentially be read with a single cache miss. The only additional porting effort required in this step was the serialization of the key and the object to a form that can be stored directly into the QD queue. This step required changing only about 100 more lines of code.

5.2 Performance Evaluation

We used ets_bench, a benchmark from BenchErl [1] to evaluate the performance and scalability of ETS tables of type ordered_set after applying each porting step described in the previous section. A detailed description of ets_bench can be found in a paper about the scalability of ETS [5], but basically it measures the performance of ETS under variable contention levels and distributions of operations. We ran the benchmark on an Intel(R) Xeon(R) E5-4650 (2.70GHz) chip with eight cores and two hardware threads per core (i.e., a total of 16 hardware threads running on eight cores). The machine ran Debian Linux 3.10-0.bpo.2-amd64 and had 128GB of RAM. All code was compiled using GCC version 4.7.2 with -O3. We pinned the software threads to logical processors so that the first eight software threads in the graphs were pinned to separate cores. Each configuration was run three times and we report the average run time. The minimum and maximum are shown as bars when varying enough to be visible.

The update only scenario presented in Fig. 1(a) shows the run time of N threads (Erlang processes) performing $2^{22}/N$ operations each. The inserted objects are Erlang tuples with an integer key randomly selected from the range $[0, 2^{16}]$. The operations are

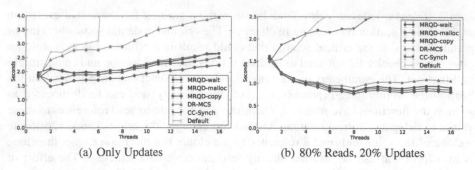

(a) Only Updates   (b) 80% Reads, 20% Updates

Fig. 1. Scalability Benchmarks for ETS. Dataset size is 2^{16}.

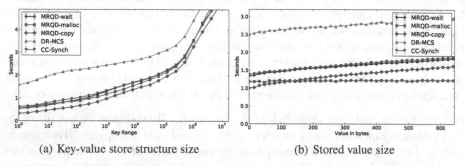

(a) Key-value store structure size   (b) Stored value size

Fig. 2. Benchmarks varying the size of data. Using eight threads for all measurements.

`insert` or `delete` with equal probability. The line labeled Default represents the default readers-writer lock used by ETS. It is optimized for frequent reads and the uncontended case. Therefore, it does not scale well with parallel writers. We also include the state-of-the-art readers-writer lock DR-MCS presented by Calciu *et al.* [2]. The MCS lock [8] that DR-MCS uses to synchronize writers is good at minimizing cache coherence traffic in the lock hand over. However since MCS is a queue based lock, the thread that executes critical sections is likely to alternate between the cores. This is causing a lot of expensive cache coherence traffic inside the critical section which is one reason why its performance is worse than all delegation based locks. CC-Synch [3] is included in our comparison to show an alternative delegation locking mechanism that can be used with the same interface as QD locking. MRQD-copy, which is corresponding to porting step 3 in the previous section, performs best in all contended cases. MRQD-copy is closely followed by MRQD-wait, CC-Synch (both step 1) and MRQD-malloc (step 2). MRQD-wait, CC-Synch and MRQD-malloc are almost indistinguishable except for the case with two threads. MRQD-malloc performs better in this case because of its ability to continue directly after delegating work.

Figure 2(a) shows how the performance varies with the set size (key range) while the thread count is fixed to eight. The figure shows that the performance advantage of delegation based locks compared to DR-MCS is larger with smaller set sizes. This is expected since with smaller set sizes, the length of the critical sections is smaller and the helper thread can keep most data in the private cache while executing operations. The larger slowdown is caused by running out of shared cache and hitting memory.

Figure 2(b) shows performance with varied value size and thread count fixed to eight. MRQD-malloc is least affected by the size of the value passed together with the key to the insert operation. The reason is that MRQD-malloc clones the key and the value before the critical section so that the size of the critical section stays largely unaffected by the value size. MRQD-copy, which is the best performing variant for value sizes up to a few cache lines, has to read the whole value from the queue inside the critical section. In Fig. 2(b) we use the key range $[0, 2^{10}]$ to make the effect of the value size more visible.

In Fig. 1(b) we show the performance when 80% of the operations are lookups and the rest are inserts and deletes with equal probability. Unsurprisingly, since they use the same read synchronization algorithm, the order between MRQD-copy, MRQD-malloc, MRQD-wait and DR-MCS is the same as in the update only scenario. With 99% lookup operations the difference between MRQD-copy, MRQD-malloc, MRQD-wait and DR-MCS is very small, but the performance advantage of the four delegation based algorithms gets larger and larger with more updates. Due to space limitations we only show measurements for 80% lookups in this paper.

6   Related Synchronization Algorithms

QD locking comes from the same line as other delegation locking techniques such as the detached contexts algorithm by Oyama *et al.* [9], the flat combining algorithm by Hendler *et al.* [4], and the Synch algorithms by Fatourou and Kallimanis [3]. The common property of all these techniques is that a helper thread can execute critical sections for other threads. Under contention this means that the same processor core can execute many critical sections, one after the other, and thereby keep the protected data in the same fast private cache. In the uncontended case the delegation locking algorithms behave like traditional locking algorithms, although most of them have a small overhead for opening the delegation data structure.

The algorithm of Oyama *et al.* shares with QD locking the ability to continue a thread's execution immediately after delegation. However, unlike QD locking, under high contention it will starve the helper thread. Furthermore, its need to allocate contexts for critical sections can easily become another bottleneck. While flat combining has a very efficient handover of critical sections to the helper thread, it does not execute critical sections in arrival order, which means that threads have to block until their delegated section is executed in order to maintain linearizability. The Synch algorithms execute the critical sections in arrival order and have efficient handover of critical sections. To avoid the problem of starving helper threads, they allow the helper to stop helping. In this case the thread owning the next delegated section becomes the new helper, which means that all threads must wait until their section is executed as well.

In short, QD locking offers delegation without waiting, and does not starve helper threads, which we have not found possible in other algorithms. This is achieved through a preallocated queue buffer which enables both a fast handover and limiting the amount of work a helper thread has to do. Experiments reported elsewhere [6] show that QD locking performs better than other delegation algorithms at various contention levels.

7   Discussion

Many delegation algorithms have been shown to outperform non-delegating locking approaches, but compared to traditional locks the support for programming with delegation has been somewhat limited so far. Code for using flat combining[3] and the Synch algorithms[4] is available online, but significant work is required to use them in programs other than the benchmarks these implementations were written for. Making use of delegation based locking thus requires a substantial investment from programmers. The libraries presented in this paper aim to make it easier to use delegation locking, lowering the entrance barrier and enabling more programs to take advantage of them. In fact the APIs of our libraries can be used for other delegation locking schemes as well.

As has been illustrated in this paper, many types of critical sections can be ported straightforwardly. However, some other types of critical sections cannot use delegation algorithms. As an example, hand-over-hand locking interleaves lock and unlock calls, resulting in partially overlapping critical sections, which cannot be delegated. This is not a problem for many applications, as the most common use of locks allows critical sections to be tranformed into subroutines.

For latency critical programs a complaint could be that the helper can get stuck executing critical sections for other threads. This is actually not a big problem as the maximum amount of help that a thread does can be limited using a parameter to the lock. Furthermore, if the critical section allows for delegating without waiting for the actual execution, threads can continue where they would have needed to wait with traditional locking. The ability to continue without waiting for the actual execution of a critical section could even make QD locking an attractive alternative if otherwise only non-blocking algorithms would be considered.

8   Future Work and Concluding Remarks

To ease the porting of large programs with many locks and critical sections, it would be useful to have a tool that detects critical sections that can be used with delegation locking. Such a tool would need to detect if the critical section can be factored into a function or if it uses thread local variables. Additionally, the tool could detect implicit return values from the critical sections and decide whether delegation without waiting for the actual execution can be used or not.

More options for performance tuning in the libraries will be added in the future. For example, a companion paper presents a hierarchical QD (HQD) lock variant for NUMA systems [6]. On such systems, it has faster delegation and execution at the cost of more often having to wait for delegate calls to succeed. This means that it is not always better to use this variant on NUMA systems, but rather depends on the workload. Another extension would be to make delegate wait passively instead of spinning. The libraries also could incorporate other locking and delegation algorithms to facilitate comparisons. For the C library it is already possible to use it to compare against a few other locking algorithms, including DR-MCS and CC-Synch as used in this paper.

---

[3] http://github.com/mit-carbon/Flat-Combining
[4] https://code.google.com/p/sim-universal-construction/

All in all, there is room to improve the libraries, but also potential to apply them. For writing new code, the idea to `delegate` operations is fairly intuitive, but when porting from `lock` and `unlock` some effort is required to achieve optimal performance. Even then, experiments in this and other papers show that delegation can improve performance twofold and sometimes more. For many applications this may be enough incentive to give QD locking a try, and the libraries presented here make it a lot easier to get started.

References

1. Aronis, S., Papaspyrou, N., Roukounaki, K., Sagonas, K., Tsiouris, Y., Venetis, I.E.: A scalability benchmark suite for Erlang/OTP. In: Proceedings of the Eleventh ACM SIGPLAN Workshop on Erlang Workshop, pp. 33–42. ACM, New York (2012)
2. Calciu, I., Dice, D., Lev, Y., Luchangco, V., Marathe, V.J., Shavit, N.: NUMA-aware reader-writer locks. In: Proceedings of the 18th ACM SIGPLAN Symposium on Principles and Practice of Parallel Programming, pp. 157–166. ACM, New York (2013)
3. Fatourou, P., Kallimanis, N.D.: Revisiting the combining synchronization technique. In: Proceedings of the 17th ACM SIGPLAN Symposium on Principles and Practice of Parallel Programming, pp. 257–266. ACM, New York (2012)
4. Hendler, D., Incze, I., Shavit, N., Tzafrir, M.: Flat combining and the synchronization-parallelism tradeoff. In: Proceedings of the 22nd ACM Symposium on Parallelism in Algorithms and Architectures, pp. 355–364. ACM, New York (2010)
5. Klaftenegger, D., Sagonas, K., Winblad, K.: On the scalability of the Erlang term storage. In: Proceedings of the Twelfth ACM SIGPLAN Workshop on Erlang, pp. 15–26. ACM, New York (2013)
6. Klaftenegger, D., Sagonas, K., Winblad, K.: Queue delegation locking (2014), http://www.it.uu.se/research/group/languages/software/qd_lock_lib
7. Lozi, J.-P., David, F., Thomas, G., Lawall, J., Muller, G.: Remote core locking: Migrating critical-section execution to improve the performance of multithreaded applications. In: Proceedings of the 2012 USENIX Annual Technical Conference, Berkeley, CA, USA, pp. 65–76. USENIX Association (2012)
8. Mellor-Crummey, J.M., Scott, M.L.: Algorithms for scalable synchronization on shared-memory multiprocessors. ACM Trans. Comput. Syst. 9(1), 21–65 (1991)
9. Oyama, Y., Taura, K., Yonezawa, A.: Executing parallel programs with synchronization bottlenecks efficiently. In: Proceedings of the International Workshop on Parallel and Distributed Computing for Symbolic and Irregular Applications, pp. 182–204. World Scientific (1999)
10. Sridharan, S., Keck, B., Murphy, R., Chandra, S., Kogge, P.: Thread migration to improve synchronization performance. In: Workshop on Operating System Interference in High Performance Applications (2006)
11. Suleman, M.A., Mutlu, O., Qureshi, M.K., Patt, Y.N.: Accelerating critical section execution with asymmetric multi-core architectures. In: Proceedings of the 14th International Conference on Architectural Support for Programming Languages and Operating Systems, pp. 253–264. ACM, New York (2009)

A Generic Strategy for Multi-stage Stencils

Mauro Bianco and Benjamin Cumming

Swiss National Supercomputing Centre (CSCS)

Abstract. Stencil computations on regular grids are widely used in scientific simulations. Optimization techniques for such stencil computations typically exploit temporal locality across time steps. More complex stencil applications, like those in meteorology and seismic simulations, cannot easily take advantage of these techniques, since the number of physical fields and computation stages to consider at each time step flush all data present in the cache at the beginning of the next time step. In this paper we present a technique for improving performance of such computations, based only on spatial tiling, which is implemented as a generic algorithm.

More specifically, we investigate how to take advantage of producer-consumer relations of stencil loops, in a single time step, to improve memory hierarchy utilization. This approach makes it possible to balance computation and communication to improve resource usage. We implement our methods using generic programming constructs of C++, which we compare with hand-tuned implementations of the stencils. The results show that this technique can improve both single-threaded and multi-threaded performance to closely match that of hand-tuned implementations, with the convenience of a high-level specification.

1 Introduction

Stencil computations are an important algorithmic motif in scientific computing. When applied on regular grids, stencil computation is essentially a set of nested for loops in which the body of the innermost loop computes a function using grid values at fixed offsets from the coordinates specified by the loop variables. Stencil computations are often used in the solution of (partial) differential equations with explicit temporal integration. Such applications use a time loop which applies the same stencils on each iteration. Scientific simulations often employ 3D stencils because they map better to real world cases. From an algorithmic point of view, the 3D stencil computations typically used in scientific computing pose specific challenges when optimizing the use of memory hierarchy [10]. The literature focusing on this kind of algorithms is abundant, and very clever techniques have been developed to improve their performance.

Many of these optimization strategies take advantage of the fact that, for simple differential equations at least, temporal locality may be exploited across time steps (among others, [4,9,12,6,13]). However, for more complicated applications, such as meteorological simulations, the number of stencil functions applied in each time step is very high. In such applications, it is not possible, or very hard,

F. Silva et al. (Eds.): Euro-Par 2014, LNCS 8632, pp. 584–595, 2014.

```
for(i=bi−b10; i<ei+e10; ++i)
  for(j=bj−b12; j<ej+e11; ++j)
    for(k=bk−b12; k<ek+e12; ++k)
      t[i][j][k] = in[i+2][j][k]...

for(i=bi; i<ei; ++i)
  for(j=bj; j<ej; ++j)
    for(k=bk; k<ek; ++k)
      out[i][j][k] = t[i−1][j][k−1]...
```

(a)

```
struct  stencil_operator  {
  template <class S1, class S2>
  void
  operator()(S1 &v, S2 const& u) const
  {
    v() = 1.0/36.0 *(6*u()
      − u(1,0,0) − u(−1,0,0)
      − u(0,1,0) − u(0,−1,0)
      − u(0,0,1) − u(0,0,−1));
  } };
```

(b)

Fig. 1. (a) Example of a typical structure of a stencil application. (b) Example of a GSCL stencil operator implementation for a 7-point Laplacian.

to retain data in cache between time steps, due to the complicated dependencies between the different stencil stages in each time step.

However, it is possible to exploit temporal locality in such applications. Here we investigate temporal locality in the producer-consumer relations between consecutive stencil loops. A trivial example of this is illustrated in Figure 1.a, where the output of the first stencil loops, stored in t is used in the second loop.

In this paper, we refer to a nested loop as a *stencil stage*, and a sequence of such stages as a *multi-stage stencil computation*. An example stencil from the numerical weather forecasting code COSMO (Consortium for Small-scale Modeling) [5] is the horizontal diffusion (HD) stencil, which applies a fourth-order dispersion operator to an input field, and writes the result to an output field. The horizontal diffusion stencil can be expressed using four stages: the first computes the Laplacian of the input field, then two independent stages that use the Laplacian values to compute orthogonal fluxes in the horizontal plane, and a final stage that combines the fluxes to compute the output.

In our work we distinguish between data that is the output of a multi-stage stencil, and temporary data that is produced and consumed in intermediate stages of a multi-stage stencil. For instance, the Laplacian and fluxes in the horizontal diffusion stencil are only consumed by the stages inside the stencil, so they can be discarded after the output has be computed. For such data fields that are only consumed in the stencil where they are computed, we take advantage of blocking techniques that allow us to balance computation intensity and memory bandwidth. We call the stencil stages that produce intermediate output *intermediate stages*, and in this paper we focus on multi-stage stencil computations with at least one intermediate stage.

We will describe an algorithm that each thread in a shared memory parallel program, uses to trade computation intensity and communication bandwidth of multi-stage stencils, and show how this improves both the performance and scalability of the multi-stage stencil computation. We present our solution implemented in context of the Generic Stencil Computing Library (GSCL) [2], which is a generic C++ library for specifying stencil computations on different architectures, including multicore processors, graphic accelerators, up to large parallel machines. The library expresses computations as *stencil operators* applied to some data fields according to *iteration spaces*, which specify data dependencies. An example of a stencil operator can be found in Figure 1.b. We show that our technique is capable of matching the performance of hand-tuned versions, while retaining ease of use through the generic interface of GSCL. Being generic, our solution also is suitable for being implemented in other contexts, such as a DSL.

2   Related Work

Stencil computations are typically bandwidth limited. As such, much of the research in this field has focused on optimizations that reduce global memory bandwidth by taking advantage of cache hierarchies. In [4,9,12] the optimization of simple stencil computations inside time loops was investigated. Similar stencils were studied in [6,13] in the context of cache obliviousness. The most complicated stencil computation investigated in the aforementioned papers is Jacobi iteration with two grids, while real applications like climate modeling or earthquake simulations [11,5] have between 5 to 15 grids. It is not clear to what extent the reasoning behind many optimizations for simpler stencils might be directly ported to real-world use cases. A similar problem is addressed in [10], in which, however, the Authors discuss solutions for other cases.

In this paper we use GSCL which is a C++ template library, as opposed to [3], which employs a DSL, and [8] which heavily uses macros. This gives us the ability to reach good expressivity in design and a robust implementation. In [7,3] Authors use auto-tuning techniques, which we are planning to investigate in future papers, but are not the aim of current work. More specific compiler approaches, such as [1], are also out of our scope, but try to solve similar problems.

3   Tiling and Buffering

In this section we describe how each thread in a multithread stencil execution can optimize the trade-off between computation intensity and memory bandwidth in order to improve execution time.

These computations are specified in GSCL by using *functional stencils*, or **f_stencils**. Functional stencils specify that the value needed at the point of evaluation depends on a stencil operator computed at a given offset, specified through relative coordinates. The syntax is as follows: **f_stencil <F, i,j,k>(a,b ,...)** where **i**, **j** and **k** are coordinates relative to the current point of evaluation where **F** is to be computed, and **(a,b ,...)** is the list of arguments to be passed to **F**.

Figure 2 shows an implementation of the stencil operator **simpleHD** that computes a simplified version of the Horizontal Diffusion (HD) stencil from the COSMO weather forecasting code. Computing HD first requires the computation of a Laplacian (**lap**), then two fluxes (**fluxx** and **fluxy**). Finally, the **simpleHD** computes the output values. The figure also illustrates the call graph.

Functional stencils employ a functional specification of the stencil operation instead of the imperative approach illustrated in Figure 1.a. Loop bounds are

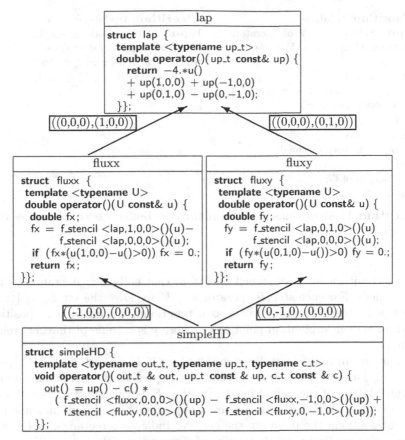

Fig. 2. The illustration of the GSCL implementation of the HD multi-stage stencil

determined automatically from the output dimensions, removing the burden of manually adjusting the loop limits **b10**, **b11**, **e10**, etc.. When executed as functions, functional stencils reduce memory transactions in memory-bound stencil computations by computing intermediate fields on the fly, at the expense of increasing the number of arithmetic operations. Hence, as the depth and arity of the call tree increases, the use of functional stencils can make the computation compute-bound with possible poor performance. However, the functional flavor of the algorithm specification allows the implementation to choose to buffer intermediate results in order to trade memory pressure with computation redundancy, thus transforming calls to functional stencils into *reads* from pre-computed buffers.

3.1 The Algorithm

The algorithm for executing a multi-stage stencil has two phases. The first is an analysis phase that computes the sizes of the intermediate buffers, the second is the computation of the stencil itself.

```
Algorithm: Analysis                    Algorithm: Update_Φ
Input: Sets E_u, set V of operators    Input: Current node u, graph G
Output: Graph G = (V, E, φ)            Output: Updated Φ_v values
E ← ∅;                                 for v such that (u, v) ∈ E do
for u, v ∈ V do                            Φ_v ← MBR(Φ_v, Φ_u ⊕ φ_uv);
    φ_uv ← MBR{p : (u, v, p) ∈ E_u};       Update_Φ(v, G);
    Insert (u, v) in E;                end
end
for v ∈ V do
    Φ_v ← Empty rectangle;
end
s ← Source of G;
Update_Φ(s, G);
```

Algorithm 1. Algorithms for determining the buffer sizes of the nodes of the call graph

We start with a set V of stencil operators that call other operators as functional stencils. For each stencil operator $u \in V$ we have the set $E_u = \{(v, p)\}$, where v is a stencil operator called as a functional stencil by u at position p relative to current evaluation point of u, where p is a tuple of (integer) relative coordinates.

We can obtain a weighted direct graph $G = (V, E, \phi)$ such that $E = \{(u, v) : (v, p) \in E_u$ for some $p\}$, and the weight ϕ_{uv} represent the minimum bounding rectangle (MBR) of the points in $\{p : (v, p) \in E_u\}$, the set of all the offsets at which u calls v. A rectangle is a pair of tuples with minimum and maximum coordinates among the points in the set. We indicate a rectangle as (p^b, p^t) to indicate the coordinates of the "bottom" (typically with non positive coordinates) and the "top" corners (typically with non negative coordinates) of the rectangle. The structure of the graph G for the HD stencil is shown in Figure 2 along with the weights. We are interested in computations where graph G is acyclic (a DAG) (an operator cannot call a predecessor in the graph) and with a single source node that we indicate as s.

After having obtained the DAG G, we need to compute the extent (a rectangle) at which each of the nodes $v \in V$ is needed during the computation and we call it Φ_v. To do this, we first set $\Phi_s = (\mathbf{0}, \mathbf{0})$ as an empty rectangle, centered at the origin, representing the point of evaluation. Next we traverse the graph in pre-order. When node u is visited we update the values Φ_v, of nodes v adjacent to u, to the MBR including the rectangles Φ_v and $\Phi_u \oplus \phi_{uv}$, where the sum for two rectangles (p^b, p^t) and (q^b, q^t) is defined as $(p^b, p^t) \oplus (q^b, q^t) = (p^b + q^b, p^t + q^t)$. When Φ_v is updated for the first time, it is set to $\Phi_u \oplus \phi_{uv}$, which are defined since G is traversed in pre-order. Algorithm 1 shows the pseudo-code for this procedure.

Proof: We now offer an informal proof that the node v is never invoked outside of the bounding box Φ_v computed using Algorithm 1. If we assume that all the ϕ_{uv} are correct, then if v was needed at a coordinate outside Φ_v, a predecessor u

of v would have to be accessed outside of Φ_u. Likewise, if u is not the source we can apply the same reasoning backward. When we reach the source it means that it is accessed outside the point of evaluation, which is against the hypotheses. We can also see that if there are no conditional branches that can falsify this statement in particular cases, the *edges* of the rectangles are always accessed, so the bounding is tight.

There may be values in the rectangles that are not needed. However, if the call tree is wide enough, the additional storage overheads are compensated for by the use of simple affine expressions to access data. The final objective is to tile the computation with blocks of size $B_I \times B_J \times B_K$. Before doing so, given $\Phi_v = (p^b, p^t)$, we associate a buffer with each stencil operator in G, where the buffer b_u has dimension $(B_I - p_i^b + p_i^t) \times (B_J - p_j^b + p_j^t) \times (B_K - p_k^b + p_k^t)$ with origin set to $-p_b$ so that accesses that touch the halo region are valid.

To balance the computation/communication ratio, nodes in the DAG can be marked be either buffered or to computed on the fly. Execution of the stencil then proceeds as a post order visit on the DAG G, so first the adjacency list of a node is evaluated and then the node itself. If a node is marked to compute values in a buffer, it is executed, otherwise nothing is done, and the node will be invoked as a functional stencil in subsequent stages.

3.2 Implementation

The algorithm described in the previous subsection is modified for implementation in GSCL because some of the required information is computed during compilation. Since C++ does not allow introspection, the structure of the unweighted version of the DAG G has to be provided to GSCL in the form of a *call graph* object. The object type encodes the topology of the graph as a list of levels corresponding to the topological sort of the DAG to guarantee the producer consumer relations of the computation. The interface requires the first level to be a **procedure**, i.e. it behaves as a regular GSCL stencil operator that writes the results into some of the output arguments. The other levels can either be **function**s, or a list of functions that are **independent**, all of which will be called as functional stencils. Additionally, since GSCL cannot know which arguments will be passed to the functional stencils, an argument mapping is also needed. For the simple HD stencil in Figure 2, the call-graph type is

```
typedef call_graph_type <procedure<simpleHD>,
              independent<function<fluxx,arg_map<1> >,
                          function <fluxy,arg_map<1> > >,
              function <lap,arg_map<1> > > cg_type;
```

We would like to emphasize that, although our implementation uses C++, the technique is more general. For instance a specialized compiler could collect the information about the call graph from the code without user intervention.

To execute the multi-stage stencil, an object of type **call_graph_type**, which is the implementation of call graph object mentioned before, can then be passed to a **do_all_ms**, i.e., a special iteration space that process call graph types, where the suffix **ms** stands for multi-stage. After some transformations to adapt

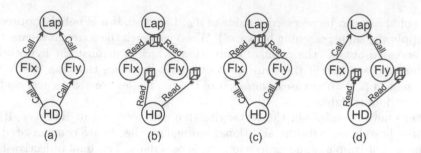

Fig. 3. Graphical representation of the different implementations that GSCL provides for the HD stencil. Circles are procedure/function nodes, while rectangles are node buffers.

the call graph, **do_all_ms** computes the rectangles ϕ and Φ for determining the sizes of the blocks by simulating the computation passing to the operators **test_stencils** to collect the proper information.

To mark nodes to compute on the fly and other to buffer, two compile time constant parameters are given as **do_all_ms<low, high>(...)**, where **low** and **high** indicates where to turn buffering on and off, respectively. This mechanism allows the programmer to specify *different thresholds for different computations in the same program*, and incurs no runtime overhead by virtue of being performed at compile time. Figure 3 shows different implementations for the horizontal diffusion (HD) stencil. If the thresholds for turning on and off the buffering define an empty interval, the implementation turns all of the functional stencils into function calls to compute values on the fly (Figure 3.a). If the thresholds include all levels then all functional stencil calls read results from previously computed blocks (Figure 3.b). We can specify that levels 1 and 2 are to be buffered, and have the fluxes computed on the fly as in Figure 3.c, or that levels 0 and 1 are to be buffered, and get the behavior shown in Figure 3.d.

At this point the execution of the multi-stage by stencil computation is performed through a post-order visit of the call-graph, which is inlined and has virtually no runtime overhead. The OpenMP implementation of GSCL, first partitions the global iteration space, then each thread applies the multi-stage stencil on its partition.

3.3 Analysis

The versions of **simpleHD** obtainable by GSCL, and depicted in Figure 3, plus the base version that does not use loop tiling, have different computation to main memory access ratios. By analyzing the code in Figure 2, it is not difficult to see that the a base version, that does not use **f_stencils**, perform 18 operations per output value. For the tiling, in this example the operation count does not depend on B_k (no *halo* in the third dimension). By picking $B_i = B_j = 8$, we obtain block sizes that provide good cache usage. In this case the version that computes everything on the fly, corresponding to Figure 3.a, needs 61 operations

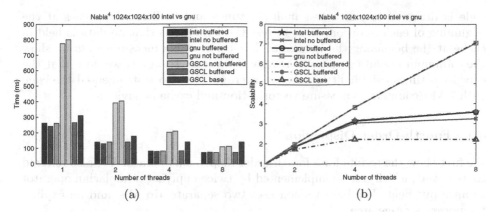

Fig. 4. Comparison of execution times and scalability of hand-coded implementations of ∇^4 (Intel C++ and GNU C++ compilers) and GSCL (only GNU)

per output value. When we buffer all the intermediate results, Figure 3.b, we obtain 21.8 operations per output value, which is higher that the base version since the computation on the tiles is redundant. The cases of Figure 3.c and Figure 3.d have respectively 28.8 and 36.5 operations per output value.

Assuming that the block sizes are small enough to keep all the intermediate storage in cache, the characteristics of memory accesses of the GSCL implementations, other than the base, are similar thanks to the loop tiling. Counting the number of operations is then enough to give an indication of the ratio between computation and main memory requests, whose rate is limited by the physical bandwidth. We would expect the versions that buffer only the Laplacian to perform better than the version the buffer the fluxes, since the computation intensity is quite high for the latter version and because two buffers have to be kept in cache instead of one, thus increasing the cache pressure. In general the performance of the actual computation depends on the *arity* and depth of the call three and it not easy to predict a priori which implementation is the best.

For the base version we draw a somewhat different conclusion. As the problem size increases we should see a gap between this and the tiled versions as the intermediate fields for the base version become to large to reside in cache.

4   Results

In this Section we show and discuss some performance results obtained with our algorithm. We test on the cores of a single socket in this paper to avoid NUMA effects, and with the understanding that GSCL typically has one MPI process per NUMA domain. Testing was performed on an eight-core Intel Sandybridge processor (Xeon E5-2670) running at 2.60GHz, without hyper-threading. Each core of the chip has 32KB of L1 cache, with all 8 cores sharing 256KB of L2 on-chip cache and 20MB of L3 off-chip cache. Version 4.7.1 of the GNU C++ compiler and version 13.0.1 of the Intel C++ compiler were used. The benchmark code is designed to run a test multiple times and to flush the caches at the beginning of each iteration, so as to test the hypothesis that no data is held in cache at the beginning the iterations. To obtain stable measurements we show the minimum execution times of several iterations. However, we note that the execution times exhibit little noise on average. We also instrumented the code with PAPI counters to measure vectorization and cache behaviors.

4.1   Fourth-Order Dispersion

We first show the results for a fourth-order dispersion operator ∇^4, also referred to as $nabla^4$, which can be implemented by twice applying a Laplacian operator to an input field. The base version uses two separate **do_alls** and an explicit temporary storage area.

To validate performance, we implemented hand-tuned versions of compute-on-the-fly and buffered implementations. They were developed in a distinct source files, since the modularity is reduced in these versions. It should be noted that the hand-tuned versions are not generic at all and their code is much longer than GSCL code. It is made of several loop nests (for tiling and iterating within blocks), plus pointer arithmetic, and specific **#pragmas** for the compiler[1].

In Figure 4.a we show the execution times of ∇^4 for different number of threads (one per core on the chip) and a fairly large input size (in the context of COSMO). The versions not labelled with "GSCL" are hand-tuned versions. The GNU compiler did not perform well when no buffering is employed in GSCL, that is, when we compute all values needed by ∇^4 on the fly. In this case the GNU compiler is unable to exploit vectorization, and because this version is the most computationally intense, the penalty for not using vector instruction is the highest. On the other hand this results in almost ideal scalability. As we can see, the base implementation scales poorly due to bandwidth memory limitations do to lack of loop-tiling (Figure 4.b).

For this input size, GSCL performs comparably to hand tuned versions. On smaller inputs GSCL is slightly slower but still competitive (results not showed for space constraints). The compute-on-the-fly hand-tuned version is quite fast compared to the corresponding GNU compiled version. This is because unlike the GNU compiler, the Intel compiler can vectorize this computation very well, which is important for this computationally intensive case.

4.2   SimpleHD

In this section we discuss the performance of the **simpleHD** example we analyzed throughout the paper. **simpleHD** implementation corresponds to Figure 2 which allows us to test with turning on and off buffering. First, we show how performance varies as we tune the levels for turning buffering on and off. Figure 5 shows a comparison of the base GSCL version against the four different

---

[1] For a fair comparison of compiler generated code, explicit prefetching and intrinsics were not used in the hand-tuned codes.

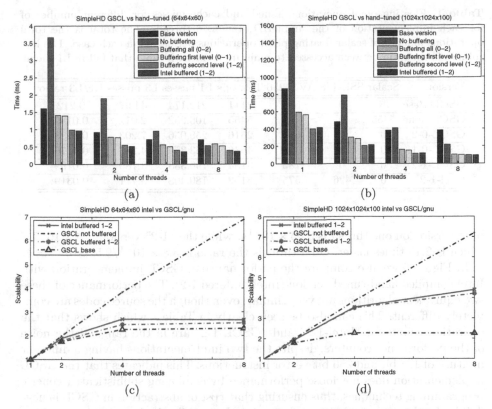

Fig. 5. Comparison of hand-tuned implementation and different thresholds to trigger buffering on and off in the simpleHD example. The versions are indicated by the thresholds used to turn on buffering. (a) and (b) shows times, (c) and (d) scaling.

combinations shown in Figure 3. When we turned off buffering at all levels the performance was low on a single thread. This is mostly due to the inability of the GNU compiler to employ vectorization in this compute bound case, as can be seem in Table 1 entry for "GSCL-none", which is the version that does not employ buffering. As the number of threads and problem size increases (Figure 5.a and .b) the performance increases, getting better than the base version, due to better memory use. This observation is also evident in Figure 5.c and .d, which shows scaling with thread count for the implementations.

As expected from the analysis in Section 3.3, the performance of buffering all the nodes (threshold from 0 to 2, dubbed 0-2) was similar to buffering the computation of the fluxes while computing the Laplacian on the fly (threshold from 0 to 1, so dubbed 0-1). Buffering the Laplacian and computing the fluxes on the fly (dubbed 1-2) gave the best performance for both the small and large meshes. As the number of threads increased, the advantage of on the fly computation increased since it is less bandwidth-eager. The execution time for the

Table 1. Floating point operations issued and cache misses for different number of for each implementation of the simpleHD stencil, 8 threads. The total is the total operations amount of scalar floating point operations performed in each case. The last column is the ratio between accessed to main memory with those that fail in L1 cache.

Version	Scalar	SSE-128	AVX-256	Tot. ops	L1 misses	L3 misses	L1/L3 ratio
GSCL-Base	91	0	505	2111	212.174	44.97	0.212
GSCL-none	5455	0	0	5455	106.252	2.012	0.0189
GSCL-0-2	0	0	654	2616	250.056	7.203	0.0288
GSCL-0-1	0	0	1134	4536	153.379	4.235	0.0276
GSCL-1-2	0	0	785	3154	190.338	3.789	0.0199
Intel-1-2	0	426	575	3152	180.408	5.771	0.0319

base version on one thread is $8.63 \times 10^{-1}s$, while the "1-2" version is $4 \times 10^{-1}s$, which is 2.15 times faster. On 8 threads the ratio is $3.8 \times 10^{-1}/9.5 \times 10^{-2} \simeq 4$.

In Figure 5 we also compare the performance of GSCL implementation with Intel compiled hand-tuned version (Intel buffered 1-2). The performance of these two equivalent algorithms are very similar, even though the source codes are completely different. This can also be seen clearly in Table 1 which shows that the operation counts for "Intel-1-2" and "GSCL-1-2" are in the range of the noise of the performance counters, despite the two implementations having a different mixture of 128 bit and 256 bit vector instructions. This indicates that the GSCL implementation does not loose performance by employing sophisticated generic programming techniques, thus ensuring that cost of abstraction in GSCL is negligible. In the same table it can be noted that, while the base implementation has very poor cache performance, since 21% of the accesses that fails to L1 reach main memory. The other implementations shows ratios of 2-3%. It is interesting to note that GSCL-none has the best ratio, since there the computation does not use buffers at all, while GSCL-1-2 exhibits the best ration between cache accesses and operation counts, which explains why Intel-1-2, even though with a similar operation count, is slower than the GSCL one.

5   Conclusions

We presented a generic method to optimize complex stencil applications by expressing the computation using a functional approach to fuse otherwise distinct loops, and buffer intermediate results for best memory hierarchy exploitation. The implementation can be tuned by selecting for which levels to use buffering and for which to compute on the fly, thus trading computation for memory bandwidth. We shown that we can achieve the performance of hand tuned implementations of the same computations.

In future we also plan to employ auto-tuning techniques to select tile sizes and to select which nodes to buffer. For the latter case it is possible to work at the finer granularity of single nodes instead of levels.

References

1. Bandishti, V., Pananilath, I., Bondhugula, U.: Tiling stencil computations to maximize parallelism. In: Proc. of the 2012 ACM/IEEE Conference on Supercomputing, SC 2012, pp. 40:1–40:11. IEEE Computer Society Press, Los Alamitos (2012)
2. Bianco, M., Varetto, U.: A generic library for stencil computations. CoRR, abs/1207.1746 (2012)
3. Christen, M., Schenk, O., Cui, Y.: Patus for convenient high-performance stencils: Evaluation in earthquake simulations. In: SC, p. 11 (2012)
4. Datta, K., Kamil, S., Williams, S., Oliker, L., Shalf, J., Yelick, K.: Optimization and performance modeling of stencil computations on modern microprocessors. SIAM Rev. 51, 129–159 (2009)
5. Doms, G., Schätter, U.: A description of the nonhydrostatic regional model lm, part i, dynamics and numerics (2002)
6. Frigo, M., Strumpen, V.: Cache oblivious stencil computations. In: Proc. of the 19th Annual International Conference on Supercomputing, ICS 2005, pp. 361–366. ACM, New York (2005)
7. Kamil, S., Chan, C., Oliker, L., Shalf, J., Williams, S.: An auto-tuning framework for parallel multicore stencil computations. In: IPDPS, IPPS 2010, pp. 1–12 (2010)
8. Maruyama, N., Nomura, T., Sato, K., Matsuoka, S.: Physis: An implicitly parallel programming model for stencil computations on large-scale gpu-accelerated supercomputers. In: Proc. of 2011 ACM/IEEE Conference on Supercomputing, SC 2011, pp. 11:1–11:12. ACM, New York (2011)
9. Nguyen, A., Satish, N., Chhugani, J., Kim, C., Dubey, P.: 3.5-d blocking optimization for stencil computations on modern cpus and gpus. In: Proc. of the 2010 ACM/IEEE Conference on Supercomputing, SC 2010, pp. 1–13. IEEE Computer Society, Washington, DC (2010)
10. Rivera, G., Tseng, C.-W.: Tiling optimizations for 3D scientific computations. In: Proc. of the 2000 ACM/IEEE Conference on Supercomputing, SC 2000. IEEE Computer Society, Washington, DC (2000)
11. Rojas, O., Dunham, E.M., Day, S.M., Dalguer, L.A., Castillo, J.E.: Finite difference modelling of rupture propagation with strong velocity-weakening friction. Geophysical Journal International 179(3), 1831–1858 (2009)
12. Shimokawabe, T., Aoki, T., Takaki, T., Endo, T., Yamanaka, A., Maruyama, N., Nukada, A., Matsuoka, S.: Peta-scale phase-field simulation for dendritic solidification on the tsubame 2.0 supercomputer. In: Proc. of 2011 ACM/IEEE Conference on Supercomputing, SC 2011, pp. 3:1–3:11. ACM, New York (2011)
13. Strzodka, R., Shaheen, M., Pajak, D., Seidel, H.-P.: Cache oblivious parallelograms in iterative stencil computations. In: Proc. of the 24th ACM International Conference on Supercomputing, ICS 2010, pp. 49–59. ACM, New York (2010)

Evaluation of OpenMP Task Scheduling
Algorithms for Large NUMA Architectures

Jérôme Clet-Ortega, Patrick Carribault, and Marc Pérache

CEA, DAM, DIF F-91297, Arpajon, France
{jerome.clet-ortega,patrick.carribault,marc.perache}@cea.fr

Abstract. Current generation of high performance computing platforms tends to hold a large number of cores. Therefore applications have to expose a fine-grain parallelism to be more efficient. Since version 3.0, the OPENMP standard proposes a way to express such parallelism through tasks. Because the task scheduling strategy is implementation defined, each runtime can have a different behavior and efficiency. Notwithstanding, the hierarchical characteristic of current parallel computing systems is rarely considered. This might come down to a loss of performance on large multicore NUMA systems. This paper studies multiple task scheduling algorithms with a configurable scheduler. It relies on a topology-aware tree-based representation of the computing platform to orchestrate the execution and the load-balacing of OPENMP tasks. High-end users can select the task-list granularity according to the tree structure and choose the most convenient work-stealing strategy. One of these strategies takes into account data locality with the help of the hierarchical view. It performs well with unbalanced codes, from BOTS benchmarks, in comparison to INTEL and GNU OPENMP runtimes on 16-core and 128-core systems.

1 Introduction

Conceiving parallel algorithms is getting more and more intricate in accordance with the evolution of computer architectures. Multi-core and many-core systems are widespread in the high performance computing landscape. The number of computing units per node massively increase and the future processor design announced by constructors, for example INTEL *Xeon Phi* [6], continues this upward trend. In order to help the parallel application programmer in getting the best performance from the hardware, work has been conducted to integrate inside programming model implementations several mechanisms [1,2,3] that take into account the memory hierarchy of the underlying node. The programming models themselves evolve to offer features fitted with current processors structure. One could cite the adjonction of task parallelism to the OPENMP *de facto* standard [4] (in the 3.0 version) that allow the programmer to express a fine-grained parallelism. Currently, most of the OPENMP implementations support task programming, like in GNU OPENMP [5] or INTEL OPENMP [7]. Thus, each of them relies on a particular task management system which directly affects the application performance, according to the system architecture. Indeed,

F. Silva et al. (Eds.): Euro-Par 2014, LNCS 8632, pp. 596–607, 2014.

C. Terboven and al. [8] point out that the topology needs to be taken into account, especially on NUMA architectures. In this article, we propose to draw a list of parameters that control task scheduling and evaluate the different configurations with representative applications over a highly hierarchical system. In this way, we characterize the models of task-based applications and we map each category to the right OPENMP task scheduling configuration. We implemented our work inside the MPC framework [9,21], which now includes an OPENMP 3.0 implementation.

This paper is structured as follows. The next section presents some related work on task scheduling. Section 3 introduces the task scheduling parameters (topology-driven task-list granularity and work-stealing policy) and the design of our customizable OPENMP task runtime. Evaluation results of the different combinations provided by our proposal are presented in section 4. The last section sums up these results and deals with future work.

2 Related Work

To extract the most relevant runtime parameters shaping the performance of task scheduling, we first focus on several up-to-date task implementations. One of the most common impementation is the GNU OPENMP runtime (LIBGOMP) embedded within the GNU compiler collection. For the task scheduling, it allocates a single list per OPENMP team. Each access to this global list (creation of a deferred task or regular task scheduling) is synchronized with a mutex. Therefore, when a large amount of threads execute tasks, it quickly becomes a memory bottleneck.

The other major implementation, INTEL OPENMP *Runtime Library*, attaches a task list to each OPENMP thread of every team. Each time a thread creates a task that will not be executed immediatly, that task is placed inside the thread's deque (double ended queue). A random stealing strategy between deques is set up for load balancing purpose. This implementation design is used by several other approaches: OPENUH, X-KAAPI and OMPI. The first one, OPENUH, is a branch of the OPEN64 compiler suite providing OPENMP tasking feature [10]. Inspired by the CILK scheduler [11], the tasks are created in a breadth-first way and executed in depth-first manner. It also uses a cut-off (on the number of total tasks created and the depth in the task graph) to avoid task overload which could happen with recursive algorithm like Fibonacci sequence computing. Based on the runtime system for data-flow parallel applications X-KAAPI [15], LIBKOMP [16] implements the OPENMP task model. Load balancing is realized with a work-stealing technic, inspired by CILK. They also propose several extensions to the standard to deal with task data dependencies now present in OPENMP 4.0. Nevertheless, in this article we do not deal with this part of the standard which add some interesting constraints to task scheduling. Finally, OMPI [17] is an OPENMP 3.0 infrastructure for C language, including a source-to-source compiler and a runtime library. In order to implement a breadth-first algorithm, it uses a circular deque per thread to manage deferred tasks. Load balancing is managed with a lock-free work-stealing algorithm where each thread thief traverses other thread queues.

The ROSE compiler infrastructure [12] exposes an approach beyond per-thread list and random stealing. Its OPENMP task scheduling implementation [13] relies on *Qthreads* user-level thread runtime library [14]. It targets multi-core systems through a hierachical scheduling strategy. They point out a strategy which regroups threads in *shepherds* using one LIFO task queue per *shepherd*. A work-stealing mechanism between *shepherds* maintains the load balancing.

Finally, other approaches deal with task list placement and topology-driven work-stealing. Thus, the FORESTGOMP software [2] proposes work-stealing technics according to the memory hierarchy. However this takes place when dealing with nested parallelism and the stealing objects are threads and their data. Beside OPENMP runtimes, STARPU [18] is well-known in HPC domain and is based on data-flow dependencies to schedule tasks. A set of parameters is available to define the kind of task list (FIFO, LIFO, deque) and its granularity (one per thread or a single global one).

From this overview of task schedulers and their internal mechanisms, we decide to build an environment in which we could play with different parameters like the granularity of task lists and the work stealing policy.

3 Task Scheduling Control

OPENMP tasking support implies for a runtime developer to take some significant decisions concerning the implementation, especially the type of datastructure for task management (list, stack, deque, ...) which bears directly on application performance. Indeed, the task paradigm often leads OPENMP applications to generate a large amount of tasks. That means the runtime has to minimize the overhead of the numerous operations linked to task managing: creation, browsing, sharing and/or stealing, ... Additionally, the runtime has to control the load balancing, through a work stealing mechanism in most cases.

This section details some relevant runtime parameters shaping the performance of task scheduling and the design of our customizable OPENMP task scheduling engine. It gives us the possibility to evaluate multiple configurations inspired from the existing runtimes described in the previous section. The next section will illustrate such configurations with experimental results.

3.1 Task List Granularity

The omnipresence of multicore architectures in the High Performance Computing landscape constrains the application and runtime developers to take care of the underlying hardware topology. Some work on OPENMP task scheduling [2,13,8] has shown that the difficulty comes from mapping of task execution scheme with the memory hierarchy of the system. The first relevant parameter is therefore the placement of task lists according to the hardware topology.

We rely on the HWLOC software package [19], used in several parallel runtimes and MPI implementations, to discover the entire topological structure of the system. It allows us to build a topology tree for OpenMP teams based on a restricted view of the original one: it ignores the levels that do not bring any structure information (one-to-one links). Thus this tree holds all the groups of threads defined according to the memory hierarchy, as in the ForestGOMP runtime system with its hierarchical scheduler. For example, on a dual-socket eight-core Intel *Sandy Bridge EP*, each core owns a L1 and a L2 cache memory and the L3 cache is shared between the eight cores of a socket. Each socket is linked with a memory bank, constituting a NUMA node. Thus, there are eight levels but only three are relevant in the hierarchy structure. The first one concerns the processing units, the cores, the L1 and L2 cache memories. The second one regroups the L3 cache and the NUMA node levels. The last one is the whole machine.

With this representation, the user can decide at which level the task lists are allocated and accessed by the OpenMP threads. This parameter allows to check the impact of access contention to the list(s) and data locality, noticed as a main challenge [8]. Thus we extend the *shepherds* concept of S.L. Olivier and al. [13] to the whole hierarchical levels of a computing node.

3.2   Stealing Strategies

The second parameter identified in Section 2 is the stealing strategy. Indeed, since the development of *Cilk* [11], the work-stealing algorithm is the most studied one for dynamic load balancing purpose. It provides pretty good performance on average and is implemented inside a large majority of task schedulers. When it comes to starvation for a thread, it becomes a thief looking for work inside other task pools. Most of the time the victim is randomly chosen: it often avoids contention for multiple thieves at the same time and is a quick decision algorithm which matters at such critical point. However, this strategy does not take into account the memory position of the stolen data according to the binding of the thief thread. On a SMT system or a small scale system, that does not really matter. When executing this algorithm on a large multiprocessor and multicore machine, the impact over the performance may not be negligible anymore. So, for this second parameter, we designed several policies for the selection of the victim. This can be divided into three categories.

The first category of stealing strategy is based on random-victim choice. We can extract two approaches: *Random* and *Random Order*. The first one looks for a randomly-chosen victim and the second one generates a random-ordered sequence of all task lists to look for. The second category exploits the hierarchical aspect of the underlying topology. The *Hierarchical* strategy starts from the closest list in the hierarchical order determined with the physical architecture structure to choose a list to steal. For example, in case of one task list per thread, a thread whose list is empty will start to steal a task from the lists of threads running on the cores of the same processor, before looking further. Another hierarchical approach is called *Round Robin*: it browses the lists for a task to steal according to a static global topology ordering. A starving thread would look inside the first neighbor of its own list, then the second, and so on. The first neighbor is likely to be close according to the hardware topology but may not be the closest one. The advantage of this approach is the low overhead to choose the victim. The final category is based on a per-list statistic: the *Producer* algorithm selects the list which contains the largest number of tasks enqueued and the *Producer Order* strategy builds a sequence of task lists according to this indicator.

3.3 Implementation

To evaluate the impact of the 2 parameters (task-list granularity and stealing strategy), we implemented a customizable OPENMP task scheduling engine. This work has been realized inside the unified parallel-runtime framework called MPC [9], by extending the current OPENMP library to conform to the OPENMP 3.0 standard. The MPCOMP library uses a tree-based representation of the computing platform to schedule OPENMP threads. We relied on this tree to develop our task scheduling engine. Task lists are allocated on the appropriate NUMA node thanks to this structure and stealing strategies functions use it to retrieve tasks to execute. The compilation step, which turns OPENMP directives into runtime calls, is performed by a patched version of the GNU C compiler. Finally, we could control at user level the behavior of the scheduler by specifying the number of task lists and choosing the work stealing policy.

4 Evaluation

This section reports the results of our experiments on the BOTS benchmarks suite to evaluate our different strategies in comparison to two other OPENMP implementations: the INTEL OPENMP *Runtime Library* coming with version 13.1.3 of the INTEL C compiler and the GNU OPENMP library with the version 4.7 of the GNU C compiler.

4.1 Experiments Platforms

Our experiments were conducted on a 128-core node of the *Curie* supercomputer (GENCI) and composed of 16 eight-core INTEL *Nehalem-EX* processors at 2.27 GHz and associated to 512 GB of memory (32 GB per NUMA node). This structure comes from the association of 4 motherboards inter-connected through a Bull network. Each processor exposes three levels of cache memory: 32 KB of L1 and 256 KB of L2 cache owned by each core and 24 MB of L3 shared by eight cores.

In our implementation in MPC, the hierarchical representation of the system, used for OPENMP thread scheduling, is a four-level tree. The root (level 0) corresponds to the whole computational node, the next level (1) to the motherboard, the next one (level 2) to the socket and L3 cache memory and the leaves (level 3) represent the cores with their L1 and L2 cache memories. That means the task-list granularity (first parameter) could be defined among four values: a single one for whole system (1 list), one list per motherboard (4 lists), one list per socket (16 lists) and one list per core (128 lists).

4.2 Results

The results come from the execution of the *Barcelona OpenMP Tasks Suite* (BOTS). These benchmarks, inspired from real-life applications, evaluate the performance of OPENMP tasks runtimes. Several versions of each benchmark are available and described in [20]. The next array presents the main characteristics of those benchmarks we took interested in. Thus, some kernels use a single thread to produce all the tasks (with a *single* construct) whereas for others, all threads generate a certain amount of tasks. Three of them use tasks that may generate tasks (nesting). Finally, only the SPARSELU benchmark exhibits an irregular parallelism.

Application	Creation pattern	Task type	Load-balancing	#Tasks
Alignment	Single & Multiple	Final	Regular	$\approx 50K$
FFT	Multiple	Nested	Regular	$\approx 10M$
Fibonacci	Multiple	Nested	Regular	$\approx 860M$
Sort	Single	Nested	Regular	$\approx 2M$
Sparse LU	Single & Multiple	Final	Irregular	$\approx 40K$

One has to specify that each compiler provides different sequential performance. For example, the modified version of LIBGOMP used for MPCOMP is 4.4 and the version used for comparisons is 4.7. Because of this difference, the MPCOMP version is on average 30-35 % less effective than LIBGOMP on serial execution of these benchmarks. There is a similar impact with the INTEL compiler which generates most of the time a faster serial code on the target INTEL-based architecture.

4.3 Alignment

Alignment is an application where the data locality really matters. Indeed, the quantity of write operations to non-private memory is very low as presented in [20]. The great majority of stores are to the private memory of the task.

Figures 1 and 2 present the speed-up obtained on 128 cores with 128 OPENMP threads for two versions: multiple producers and single producer. Regarding the first parameter, the task scheduling with a single global list, as for LIBGOMP, is the worst solution whereas giving one list per thread, like INTEL OPENMP, seems to be more efficient. For the second parameter (work-stealing approaches), all strategies deliver more or less the same performance. Gaps between strategies execution time are just a bit less perceptible with the *single* construct version.

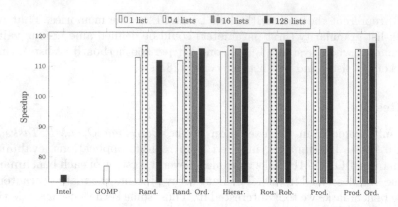

Fig. 1. Speedup for *Alignment* multiple producer benchmark with 128 threads

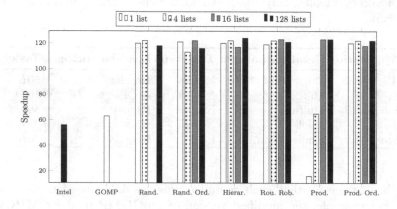

Fig. 2. Speedup for *Alignment* single producer benchmark with 128 threads

Overall, a hierarchical strategy seem to give the best performance (either hierarchical or round robin).

Of interest, for both single and multiple producers versions, MPCOMP performs worse than INTEL OPENMP and even than LIBGOMP in serial: the run takes 2,791 seconds for MPCOMP whereas INTEL OPENMP performs it in 1,312 seconds and LIBGOMP in 2,105 seconds. The performance follow the same trend with 8, 16, 32, 64 threads. When it reaches the number of 128 threads, MPCOMP distinguishes itself and outperforms LIBGOMP. For a well balanced code, like the multiple producer version, INTEL OPENMP still reaches better performance. However with the *single* construct, the benchmark is unbalanced and MPCOMP outperforms INTEL OPENMP. The best results comes from the *Hierarchical* stealing policy, always with one task list per thread. This is consistent with the fact that hierarchical strategy favors local data accesses for the benefit of this benchmark.

4.4   FFT

The *FFT* benchmark computes the *Fast Fourier Transform* of a vector of n complex values. INTEL OPENMP gave the best results in this benchmark even if the speedup is not really significant (10 on a 128 cores). For its own part, LIBGOMP does not scale and performs really worse than INTEL OPENMP (approximately 50 times longer). Among several policies given by MPCOMP, the ones using a single list per core show the best performance, leading to an execution time 10 times faster but still 5 times longer than INTEL OPENMP. Moreover all other policies deliver a consequent deterioration of the execution time. One may notice that, with 32 threads, the best approach uses one list per socket and the producer strategy for work-stealing.

There are a really large number of tasks to manage for the runtime. In order to limit the impact of the overhead for managing so many elements, GCC use a static threshold on the number of tasks generated at one time.[1] We also choose this solution. However the parallelism of the application is limited by this threshold. This may explain the performance difference between the INTEL runtime and the LIBGOMP and MPCOMP implementations.

4.5   Fibonacci

This application benchmark generates a large number of fine grained OPENMP task to compute the nth Fibonacci number thanks to a recursive algorithm. For our run we use the parameter $n = 42$.

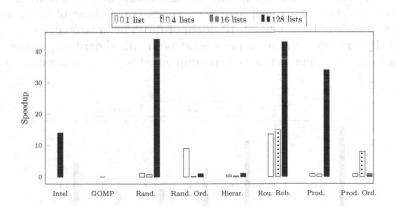

Fig. 3. Speedup for *Fibonacci* benchmark with 128 threads

Figure 3 shows the results for this benchmark. Among all strategies, only the ones with a low overhead like *Random*, *Round Robin* and *Producer*, deliver a good speedup, even better than INTEL OPENMP. Indeed, in this *Fibonacci*

---

[1] Actually, the threshold is defined to 64 times the number of threads.

algorithm, the duration of executing a task code is so tiny that the steal decision step becomes more critical. A way to reduce the overhead might be to steal more than one task. It would nevertheless require a study to determine the amount of tasks to steal, like in LIBKOMP or in the OPENMP runtime developed over the ROSE compiler. As for LIBGOMP, there are so many accesses to the global list during the whole run that it didn't finished in a reasonnable duration.

4.6 Sort

The *Sort* benchmark sorts a random permutation of n numbers with a fast parallel sorting variation of the classical mergesort. As seen in Figure 4, the best speed-up for MPCOMP corresponds to the *one list per thread* granularity (first parameter). Regarding the second parameter (stealing strategy), the *Random* policy is the most performant. This can be explained by the fact that this application is well balanced with nested tasks. Therefore, the strategy with the lowest overhead performs better. This is confirmed by the INTEL OPENMP performance which goes a little further probably because of some additional runtime optimizations.

4.7 SparseLU

The SPARSE LU application computes a LU matrix factorization over sparse matrices. We focus on the multiple producer version. A group of submatrices is assigned to each thread and, due to the sparseness of the matrix, some of them may not be allocated which explains the unbalance of the algorithm. INTEL OPENMP performs really well here with an execution time of 25.52 seconds with 128 threads whereas LIBGOMP does not finish in a reasonable time. As for MPCOMP strategies, the one using one list per motherboard and a hierarchical stealing is the best approach with a speedup equal to 27 corresponding to a run

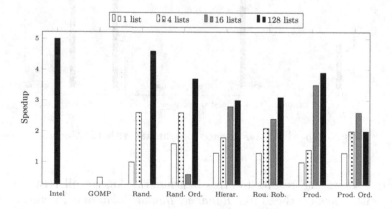

Fig. 4. Speedup for *Sort* benchmark with 128 threads

of 32.78 seconds. Even though the speedup of INTEL OPENMP is far better (near 110), one has to notice that it comes from a long serial execution time for INTEL OPENMP, equal to 2 993 seconds, in comparison to LIBGOMP with 1 005 seconds or to MPCOMP with 985 seconds.

Thus, a work-stealing strategy that takes care of data locality is the recommended one. Indeed, this benchmark presents a large percentage of accesses to shared data. Moreover, unlike the previous algorithms which employ nesting task creation, those sharings do not happen between tasks and their children. So there is less likely for an OPENMP thread to get tasks that will work on the same data.

4.8 Analysis

This experimental section shows that the two parameters highlighted in this paper for task scheduling are relevant. For the first parameter (task-list granularity), one list per core seems to be the best suitable configuration in most cases. Even if this result might be surprising on such manycore architecture (2 NUMA levels and 16 sockets), allocating one specific list per OPENMP thread in the team allows to reach decent performance. However, this study does not focus on memory consumption, but this aspect might become important on future generations of manycore architectures. In such situation, the solution of one list per thread may not be possible anymore depending on the amount of memory used by the application data.

Regarding the second parameter (work-stealing strategy), the performance really depends on the characteristics of the benchmark. Even if our implementation of each strategy can be optimized, the overhead to decide the target list to steal is crucial. For example, in the Fibonacci benchmark, each task is tiny. It explains why a low-overhead strategy, like random, performs well. Nevertheless, the round robin approach is able to reach high performance in such cases because it allows an approximate hierarchical traversal with a lower overhead. For benchmarks with tasks containing a larger amount of work, strategies with a higher overhead (hierarchical and producer) can be considered. The hierarchical approach allows to select the target list with respect to the data locality: this is an important parameters on such manycore architectures.

5   Conclusion and Future Work

High-Performance Computing platforms are getting embarassingly parallel for application developers. They need to split up their algorithm structure to offer enough parallel work to the massive number of cores forming the current and future architectures. The evolution of the parallel programming models, like OPENMP with the task support, allows them to express their problem in a finer-grained parallelism. Nevertheless, the hierarchical structure of the underlying system is barely considered in most of the OPENMP task schedulers. On large NUMA nodes it can be really penalizing due to the overhead of distant memory accesses over local ones. We proposed in this paper an evaluation of two key parameters for task scheduling. We designed a configurable task scheduler which allows us to control: (i) the granularity of task list, according to the hardware topology, and (ii) the work-stealing strategy. Thus, we compared those technic combinations through the execution of *Barcelona OpenMP Task Suite*. We noticed that the approach chosen by the INTEL OPENMP RUNTIME LIBRARY is suitable for the first parameter (list granularity) and sometimes for the second too. However the design adopted by LIBGOMP cannot scale on a large NUMA node for several applications. Finally, we show that hierarchical work-stealing strategies can lead to better performance in specific cases.

For future work, this study would benefit from using the same compiler to avoid performance difference for the computational part of the applications. Thus, we are actually working on the support of both INTEL C compiler and recent GCC compiler in the MPC framework for further fair comparisons. Regarding the current key parameters, our approaches may be optimized and tested on more applications to derive a static/dynamic cost model to choose the right strategy. Finally, some new parameters could be taken into account to refine this study. For example, the cut-off value can be used to artificially stop the parallelism extraction and reduce the runtime overhead. The memory consumption is another aspect that could be of interest for a task runtime. Indeed, this metric may become more important on next-generation of manycore processors (e.g., INTEL *Xeon Phi*) with an hybrid programming model like MPI+OPENMP.

References

1. Ma, T., Bosilca, G., Bouteiller, A., Goglin, B., Squyres, J.M., Dongarra, J.J.: Kernel Assisted Collective Intra-node MPI Communication among Multi-Core and Many-Core CPUs. In: International Conference on Parallel Processing (ICPP), pp. 532–541 (2011)
2. Broquedis, F., Furmento, N., Goglin, B., Wacrenier, P.-A., Namyst, R.: ForestGOMP: An efficient OpenMP environment for NUMA architectures. International Journal on Parallel Programming, 418–439 (2010)
3. Jin, H., Jespersen, D., Mehrotra, P., Biswas, R., Huang, L., Chapman, B.: High performance computing using MPI and OpenMP on multi-core parallel systems. Parallel Computing, 562–575 (2011)
4. The OpenMP API specification for parallel programming, http://www.openmp.org
5. An OpenMP implementation for GCC, http://gcc.gnu.org/projects/gomp
6. Intel Xeon Phi Coprocessor - The Architecture. http://software.intel.com/en-us/articles/intel-xeon-phi-coprocessor-codename-knights-corner
7. Intel OpenMP Runtime Library, https://www.openmprtl.org
8. Terboven, C., Schmidl, D., Cramer, T., an Mey, D.: Assessing OpenMP Tasking Implementations on NUMA Architectures. In: Chapman, B.M., Massaioli, F., Müller, M.S., Rorro, M. (eds.) IWOMP 2012. LNCS, vol. 7312, pp. 182–195. Springer, Heidelberg (2012)
9. Pérache, M., Jourdren, H., Namyst, R.: MPC: A unified parallel runtime for clusters of NUMA machines. In: Luque, E., Margalef, T., Benítez, D. (eds.) Euro-Par 2008. LNCS, vol. 5168, pp. 78–88. Springer, Heidelberg (2008)

10. Addison, C., LaGrone, J., Huang, L., Chapman, B.: OpenMP 3.0 tasking implementation in OpenUH. Open64 Workshop at CGO (2009)
11. Blumofe, R.D., Joerg, C.F., Kuszmaul, B.C., Leiserson, C.E., Randall, K.H., Zhou, Y.: Cilk: An Efficient Multithreaded Runtime System. Journal of Parallel and Distributed Computing, 207–216 (1995)
12. Liao, C., Quinlan, D.J., Panas, T., de Supinski, B.R.: A ROSE-Based OpenMP 3.0 research compiler supporting multiple runtime libraries. In: Sato, M., Hanawa, T., Müller, M.S., Chapman, B.M., de Supinski, B.R. (eds.) IWOMP 2010. LNCS, vol. 6132, pp. 15–28. Springer, Heidelberg (2010)
13. Olivier, S., Porterfield, A., Wheeler, K.B., Spiegel, M., Prins, J.F.: OpenMP task scheduling strategies for multicore NUMA systems. International Journal of High Performance Computing Applications, 110–124 (2012)
14. Wheeler, K.B., Murphy, R.C., Thain, D.: Qthreads: An API for programming with millions of lightweight threads. In: IEEE International Symposium on Parallel and Distributed Processing, IPDPS 2008, pp. 1–8 (2008)
15. Gautier, T., Ferreira Lima, J.V., Maillard, N., Raffin, B.: XKaapi: A Runtime System for Data-Flow Task Programming on Heterogeneous Architectures. In: IEEE International Parallel and Distributed Processing Symposium (IPDPS), pp. 1299–1308 (2013)
16. Broquedis, F., Gautier, T., Danjean, V.: LIBKOMP, an Efficient OpenMP Runtime System for Both Fork-Join and Data Flow Paradigms. In: Chapman, B.M., Massaioli, F., Müller, M.S., Rorro, M. (eds.) IWOMP 2012. LNCS, vol. 7312, pp. 102–115. Springer, Heidelberg (2012)
17. Agathos, S.N., Kallimanis, N.D., Dimakopoulos, V.V.: Speeding up OpenMP tasking. In: Kaklamanis, C., Papatheodorou, T., Spirakis, P.G. (eds.) Euro-Par 2012. LNCS, vol. 7484, pp. 650–661. Springer, Heidelberg (2012)
18. Augonnet, C., Thibault, S., Namyst, R., Wacrenier, P.-A.: StarPU: A unified platform for task scheduling on heterogeneous multicore architectures. In: Sips, H., Epema, D., Lin, H.-X. (eds.) Euro-Par 2009. LNCS, vol. 5704, pp. 863–874. Springer, Heidelberg (2009)
19. Broquedis, F., Clet-Ortega, J., Moreaud, S., Furmento, N., Goglin, B., Mercier, G., Thibault, S., Namyst, R.: Hwloc: a Generic Framework for Managing Hardware Affinities in HPC Applications. In: The 18th Euromicro International Conference on Parallel, Distributed and Network-Based Computing, PDP, pp. 180–186 (2010)
20. Duran, A., Teruel, X., Ferrer, R., Martorell, X., Ayguade, E.: Barcelona OpenMP Tasks Suite: A Set of Benchmarks Targeting the Exploitation of Task Parallelism in OpenMP. In: Proceedings of the 2009 International Conference on Parallel Processing, pp. 124–131 (2009)
21. Mahéo, A., Koliaï, S., Carribault, P., Pérache, M., Jalby, W.: Adaptive OpenMP for Large NUMA Nodes. In: Chapman, B.M., Massaioli, F., Müller, M.S., Rorro, M. (eds.) IWOMP 2012. LNCS, vol. 7312, pp. 254–257. Springer, Heidelberg (2012)

Power-Aware Replica Placement in Tree Networks with Multiple Servers per Client

Guillaume Aupy[1], Anne Benoit[1], Matthieu Journault[1], and Yves Robert[1,2]

[1] École Normale Supérieure de Lyon, CNRS & INRIA, France
{guillaume.aupy,anne.benoit,yves.robert}@ens-lyon.fr
[2] University of Tennessee Knoxville, USA

Abstract. In this paper, we revisit the well-studied problem of replica placement in tree networks. Rather than minimizing the number of servers needed to serve all client requests, we aim at minimizing the total power consumed by these servers. In addition, we use the most general (and powerful) server assignment policy, where the requests of a client can be served by multiple servers located in the (unique) path from this client to the root of the tree. We consider multi-modal servers that can operate at a set of discrete speeds, using the dynamic voltage and frequency scaling (DVFS) technique. The optimization problem is to determine an optimal location of the servers in the tree, as well as the speed at which each server is operated. A major result is the NP-completeness of this problem, to be contrasted with the minimization of the number of servers, which has polynomial complexity. Another important contribution is the formulation of a Mixed Integer Linear Program (MILP) for the problem, together with the design of several polynomial-time heuristics. We assess the efficiency of these heuristics by simulation. For mid-size instances (up to 30 nodes in the tree), we evaluate their absolute performance by comparison with the optimal solution (obtained via the MILP). The most efficient heuristics provide satisfactory results, within 20% of the optimal solution.

1 Introduction

In this paper, we revisit the well-studied problem of replica placement in tree networks. Replica placement in tree networks is an important problem [8,20,3], with a broad spectrum of applications, such as electronic, ISP, or VOD service delivery (see [12,8,14] and additional references in [20]). The problem is the following: one is given a tree-shaped network where clients are periodically issuing requests to be satisfied by servers. The clients are known (both their position in the tree and their number of requests per time unit), while the number and location of the replicas (also called servers) are to be determined. Clients are leaves of the tree, and requests can be served by one or several internal nodes. Note that the distribution tree (clients and nodes) is fixed in the approach.

Initially, there is no replica; when a node is equipped with a replica, it can process a number of requests, up to its capacity limit. Nodes equipped with a

F. Silva et al. (Eds.): Euro-Par 2014, LNCS 8632, pp. 608–619, 2014.

replica, also called servers, can only serve clients located in their subtree (so that the root, if equipped with a replica, can serve any client); this restriction is usually adopted to enforce the hierarchical nature of the target application platforms, where a node has knowledge only of its parent and children in the tree. More precisely, there are three classical policies to serve the requests of a client [3]: (i) *Closest*: All requests of a client must be served by the first server located in the path from this client to the root; (ii) *Single*: All requests of a client must be served by a single server, located anywhere in the path from this client to the root; and (iii) *Multiple*: The requests of a client can be served by several servers, all located in the path from this client to the root. For instance in the *Multiple* policy, half the requests of a client can be served by one server, and the other half by another server located higher in this path. In this paper, we study the *Multiple* policy, because it is the most flexible, hence it will lead to the most efficient solution in terms of both the number of servers and total consumed power.

The classical optimization objective in the literature is the number of servers needed to serve all requests. However, minimizing the total power consumed by the servers has recently become a very important objective, both for economic and environmental reasons [16]. To help reduce power dissipation, multi-modal servers are used: each server has a *discrete* number of predefined speeds, which correspond to different voltages that the server can be subjected to. State-of-the-art processors can only be operated with a restricted number of voltage levels, hence with a few speeds [13,11]. The power consumption is the sum of a static part (the cost for a server to be on and operated) and a dynamic part. This dynamic part is a strictly convex function of the server speed, so that the execution of a given amount of work costs more power if a server runs at a higher speed [11]. More precisely, a server operated at speed s dissipates s^3 watts [6,5,18]. Faster speeds allow servers to handle more requests per time unit, but at the price of a much higher (supra-linear) power consumption.

A major contribution of this paper is to show that minimizing power consumption is an NP-complete problem, even if the servers are already placed in the network (and without static power). This is to be contrasted with the polynomial complexity of minimizing the number or servers [3]. Another major contribution is the design of a set of heuristics to minimize power consumption. These heuristics work in two steps: (i) server placement and (ii) request assignment. The placement step relies on an interesting theoretical result: given a fixed set of servers that should all be used, and assuming continuous speeds, it is possible to optimally assign the requests to these servers in polynomial time. We can therefore easily derive a greedy algorithm to place the servers in the continuous case, because for a given placement, we can directly compute the corresponding optimal power consumption. Of course, assuming continuous speeds is not realistic, but it is a handy simplification of the problem: with continuous speeds, once requests are assigned to servers, each server can operate just at the right speed, namely the sum of its requests, so that selecting the server speeds is immediate. With discrete speeds, the problem is more challenging and may well lead to re-assign the requests, for a given placement of servers. To see this, start from the solution with continuous speeds (including the greedy placement and optimal request assignment). Let r be the number of requests processed by a given server N in the solution with continuous speeds. With discrete speeds, we have to use the smallest speed s that is larger than r, thereby losing a lot of power if the difference $s - r$ is large. If it is the case, we can try and re-assign some requests to another server N' located upper in the path from N to the tree root. There would then remain only s' requests to be served by N, where s' is the largest speed that is smaller than r: this saves power locally by avoiding the large $s - r$ gap, but we have to re-assign $r - s'$ requests to another server, and this has a cost that should be balanced with the local gain. Such trade-off decisions are exactly those taken in the request assignment step of the heuristics.

To the best of our knowledge, this paper is the first to propose heuristics for power minimization with multiple servers, hence we cannot use any heuristic from the literature as reference. However, we have derived a Mixed Integer Linear Program (MILP) to compute the optimal solution to the power minimization problem. Using this linear program has (potentially) exponential cost, but it enables us to assess the absolute performance of the heuristics, at least for small-size problems.

Related Work. Many papers considering the replica placement problem deal with general graphs, while we focus in this work on tree networks. In the problem with a general graph network, it is already difficult to decide which spanning tree to use, in order to optimize some global objective function. A survey of work targeting performance issues can be found in [15]. Recently, some work start to tackle energy-related problems. For instance, in [19], the authors discuss thermal and power-aware task scheduling and data placement heuristics, in the context of a Hadoop system. All problems are NP-hard, and there is no tree structure but rather a set of racks, and a set of data nodes per rack.

For tree networks, a large effort has been spent to optimize the performance of replica placements, assuming that the spanning tree was given, or that the network had a tree structure initially. Most work has focused on the *Closest* policy, where a client has to be served by the closest server on the path towards the root of the tree, see for instance [8,14]. Kalpakis et al. [12] studied a variant with bi-directional links, and therefore the tree structure may not be respected anymore, and a client may be served by a node that is not its ancestor in the tree. While the problem with a tree structure has polynomial complexity, the bi-directional problem becomes NP-complete.

Following this line of work, we had investigated in our previous work [4] the complexity of the power-aware replica placement problem with the *Closest* policy, and proved that the problem becomes NP-complete when the objective is to minimize the total power consumption. We considered servers with several distinct possible speeds, and a server operating at a given speed consumes a power composed of a static part and a dynamic part proportional to the cube of the speed. We keep the same model in this paper, because it is a classical model extensively used when considering dynamic voltage and frequency scaling (DVFS) technique [6,5,18].

The *Multiple* policy is more flexible than *Closest* because it loosens placement rules: the requests of a client can be processed by several servers located anywhere in the path from the client to the root. As for the *Closest* policy, the problem of minimizing the cost of the replica placement can be solved in polynomial time [3]. However, we are not aware of any other work aiming at optimizing the power consumption on tree networks for this *Multiple* policy.

Paper Organization. The rest of the paper is organized as follows. Section 2 is devoted to a precise statement of the framework. Section 3 assesses the complexity of the power minimization problem, through an intricate NP-completeness proof. This section also provides the MILP to compute the optimal solution. Section 4 introduces several heuristics to solve the problem. The placement step is an incremental greedy procedure, whose evaluation is based on the optimal solution for request assignment with fixed servers, when assuming continuous speeds. Section 5 reports experimental results and comparisons of the heuristics, together with their absolute performance evaluation: the distance to the optimal solution is computed through the linear program for instances with up to 30 servers.

2 Framework

Replica Placement Problem. We consider a distribution tree whose nodes are partitioned into a set of clients $\mathcal{C}$, and a set of N nodes, $\mathcal{N}$. The clients are leaf nodes of the tree, while $\mathcal{N}$ is the set of internal nodes. Each client $i \in \mathcal{C}$ (leaf of the tree) is sending r_i requests per time unit to a database object. Internal nodes equipped with a replica (also called *servers*) can process requests from clients in their subtree. If a server $j \in \mathcal{N}$ is operated at speed s_j, then it can process up to s_j requests per time unit. Both the r_i's and the s_j's are assumed to take rational values. Note that it would be easy to allow *client-nodes* that play both the rule of a client and of a node (possibly a server), by dividing such a node into an internal node and a leaf in the tree.

For each client $i \in \mathcal{C}$ and each node $j \in \mathcal{N}$, $r_{i,j}$ is the number of requests from client i processed by server j. We must have $\sum_{j \in \mathcal{N}} r_{i,j} = r_i$ for all $i \in \mathcal{C}$, i.e., all requests are processed. Furthermore, a server cannot process more requests than its assigned speed, i.e., $w_j = \sum_{i \in \mathcal{C}} r_{i,j} \leq s_j$ for all $j \in \mathcal{N}$, where w_j is the load of server j. The set of replicas is defined as $\mathcal{R} = \{j \in \mathcal{N} | \exists i \in \mathcal{C}, r_{i,j} > 0\}$.

Power Consumption Model. We (realistically) consider discrete speeds. Servers may operate only at a set $\{s_1, \ldots, s_K\}$ of different (rational) speeds, depending upon the number of requests that they have to process per time unit. We assume that $0 \leq s_1 \leq \cdots \leq s_K$, and therefore no server can handle more than s_K requests. A server with a load w will therefore operate at speed s_k, where $s_{k-1} < w \leq s_k$ (letting $s_0 = -1$ for the limit case). The power consumption of a server $j \in \mathcal{R}$ operated at speed $s(j)$ obeys the classical model,

$$\mathcal{P}(j) = \mathcal{P}_{\text{static}} + s(j)^3,$$

and the total power consumption $\mathcal{P}(\mathcal{R})$ of the solution is the sum of the power consumption of all server nodes:

$$\mathcal{P}(\mathcal{R}) = \sum_{j \in \mathcal{R}} \mathcal{P}(j) = \sum_{j \in \mathcal{R}} (\mathcal{P}_{\text{static}} + s(j)^3) = |\mathcal{R}| \times \mathcal{P}_{\text{static}} + \sum_{j \in \mathcal{R}} s(j)^3, \quad (1)$$

where $|\mathcal{R}|$ is the total number of servers in the solution.

Optimization Problems. The main optimization problem is the DISCRETE problem: given a distribution tree (with a number of requests per client), decide where to place the servers, and how to distribute client requests among them (which can also be seen as assigning the speed of each server), in order to minimize the total power consumption.

We also consider the sub-problem where the servers are already placed in the tree, DISCRETE-PLACED. The goal is then only to decide how to distribute requests among servers, hence at which speed to operate each server, in order to minimize total power consumption.

3 Complexity Results

Theorem 1. *The* DISCRETE *and* DISCRETE-PLACED *problems are NP-complete, even with* $\mathcal{P}_{static} = 0$.

We provide a sketch of the proof here; the detailed proof is very long and technical and can be found in the companion research report [1]. The reduction comes from 2-Partition [10], and the tree consists of a root with n children. There is a server on each node, hence the proof works for both problems. Each child node has a number of requests that is very different from the other children, but depends on the a_i from 2-Partition. The server has therefore the choice between only two speeds among those belonging to the set of possible speeds: either it takes the lower speed and let a_i requests go up in the tree (but the root node can only accommodate $\sum a_i/2$ requests), or it takes the upper speed but the loss in power also is linear in terms of the a_i. The problem then amounts to select which servers run at their lower speed, and it is equivalent to 2-Partition.

Theorem 2. *The following Mixed Integer Linear Program (MILP) characterizes the* DISCRETE *problem, where the unknown variables are the* $x_{j,k}$'s *(Boolean variables) and the* $y_{i,j}$'s *(rational variables), for* $j \in \mathcal{N}$, $1 \le k \le K$ *and* $i \in \mathcal{C}$:

$$\begin{aligned}
&Minimize \sum_{j \in \mathcal{N}} \sum_{1 \le k \le K} x_{j,k}(\mathcal{P}_{static} + s_k^3) \text{ subject to} \\
&(i) \ \sum_{j \in \mathcal{N}} y_{i,j} = r_i, && i \in \mathcal{C} \\
&(ii) \ \sum_{1 \le k \le K} x_{j,k} \le 1, && j \in \mathcal{N} \qquad (2) \\
&(iii) \ \sum_{i \in \mathcal{C}} y_{i,j} \le \sum_{1 \le k \le K} x_{j,k} s_k, && j \in \mathcal{N}
\end{aligned}$$

Proof. The constants are the r_i's for $i \in \mathcal{C}$, and the s_k's for $1 \le k \le K$, and we consider the following variables:

- $x_{j,k}$ is a boolean variable equal to 1 if j is a server operated at speed s_k, for $j \in \mathcal{N}$ and $1 \leq k \leq K$; $x_{j,k} = 0$ otherwise.
- $y_{i,j}$ is a rational variable equal to $r_{i,j}$, the number of requests of client $i \in \mathcal{C}$ processed by server $j \in \mathcal{N}$; if j is not an ancestor of i in the tree, we directly set $y_{i,j} = 0$.

Then the constraints are:

- For all $i \in \mathcal{C}$, all requests of client i are processed: $\forall i \in \mathcal{C}, \sum_{j \in \mathcal{N}} y_{i,j} = r_i$;
- Each server is assigned at most one speed: $\forall j \in \mathcal{N}, \sum_{1 \leq k \leq K} x_{j,k} \leq 1$; note that a node j is equipped with a server if and only if $\sum_{1 \leq k \leq K} x_{j,k} = 1$;
- The processing capacity of any server cannot be exceeded: $\forall j \in \mathcal{N}, \sum_{i \in \mathcal{C}} y_{i,j} \leq \sum_{1 \leq k \leq K} x_{j,k} s_k$.

Finally, we minimize the total power consumption. Overall, there are $|\mathcal{C}| + 2|\mathcal{N}|$ constraints and $|\mathcal{N}| \times (|K| + |\mathcal{C}|)$ variables in this MILP.

4 Heuristics

In this section, we propose some polynomial-time heuristics for the DISCRETE problem. We start by outlining the general principles that have guided their design before exposing the details for each heuristic.

As already mentioned in Section 1, the heuristics work in two steps: (i) server placement and (ii) request assignment. The placement step of the heuristics relies on the following result, whose proof is long and technical (see the companion research report [1] for full details):

Proposition 1. *Given a fixed set of servers deployed on a tree of size $t = |\mathcal{C}| + |\mathcal{N}|$ and assuming continuous speeds, the optimal assignment* ALG-CONT-PLACED *of requests to servers that uses all these servers and minimizes power consumption can be determined in time $O(t^2)$.*

The placement step works incrementally: to compute a solution with k servers, the heuristic starts from a solution with $k-1$ servers, and then greedily tests the addition of one additional server. It uses Proposition 1 to compute the optimal assignment of requests with this additional server, computes the corresponding power, and returns the best solution over all possible choices for the additional server. This placement step assumes continuous speeds, hence the loads assigned by ALG-CONT-PLACED to each server do not take the set of actual speeds into account. The second step of the heuristics involves determining a discrete speed for each server, which usually leads to re-assigning some requests, as explained in Section 1. While the first step of the heuristics is common to all heuristics, we outline below three different methods to perform this request assignment step.

We provide three different heuristics to determine the actual speed of each server. In the first heuristic, GREEDY, we assign the smallest speed equal to or greater than the load given by ALG-CONT-PLACED to each server. While simple, GREEDY provides a $\left(1 + \frac{\max_i (s_{i+1} - s_i)}{s_{\min}}\right)^3$-approximation for the problem with the placement given by ALG-CONT-PLACED, where s_{min} is the smallest speed available ($s_{min} = s_1$). Finally, we point out that if there is no speed greater than the value determined by ALG-CONT-PLACED for some server, then there does not exist a solution for this (given) placement (see [1] for further details).

The next two heuristics, SPEED and EXCESS, improve the GREEDY heuristic by trying to modify the load of each server, via request re-assignment. The goal is to decrease the speed of some servers. More precisely, in the procedure, which is called EQUILIBRATE and detailed in [1], if a server is not loaded up to its full capacity (meaning its load is equal to its capacity), then the heuristics take some load out of its children until this server reaches its capacity. The capacity of a server is defined as the maximum between its actual speed and the maximum speed of its children, hence we transfer even more load to this server if one of its children has a higher speed (and thus we should be able to reduce the speed of at least one child). This may happen if we have decreased the speed of the current node in a previous step of the algorithm, but not the speed of its children.

The main difference between the two heuristics SPEED and EXCESS lies in the selection of the children whose load is taken out:

- In the SPEED heuristic, we favor the children whose servers have the largest speeds. To break ties if two children of a given server have the same speed, we favor the one with the smallest load. The idea is that the gain in power will be more important if we can decrease the execution speed of a server with a large speed (favor large speeds); and if there is a tie, there is more chance to decrease the speed of a server if its load is small.
- On the contrary, in the EXCESS heuristic, we favor children with small *excess*. The excess of a server is defined as the difference between its load and the largest speed below it. The idea is that we will be able to decrease the speed of more servers if we favor small excess. Finally, when two children have the same excess, we favor the one with the largest load.

Recall that K is the number of speeds and $t = |\mathcal{C}| + |\mathcal{N}|$. The complexity of the GREEDY heuristic is $O(t^2)$, the most costly part being the call to ALG-CONT-PLACED. For the EQUILIBRATE procedure, and hence for the SPEED and EXCESS heuristics, the complexity becomes $O(Kt^2 \log t)$ [1].

5   Simulations

In this section, we report extensive simulations to assess the performance of the heuristics presented in Section 4. All the source code, together with scripts to obtain additional results that were omitted due to lack of space, are publicly available [2]. The heuristics have been coded using the programming language OCaml, while the MILP computing the optimal solution is generated using the C language and solved using IBM Cplex [9].

In order to evaluate the heuristics, we have generated more than 100 random trees for each simulation. To simplify the generation, each internal node in the tree has a unique client leaf, which is assigned a random rational number of requests between 0 and 100. For processor speeds, unless stated otherwise, we use five speeds spaced as those of the Intel Xscale, following [7,17]: we suppose that the largest speed can process 150 requests, and the ratio of the different speeds to the largest speed is then: $(0.15, 0.4, 0.6, 0.8, 1)$. In [7,17], the static power is equal to the power consumed in the lowest speed, which here corresponds to $(0.15 * 150)^3 \approx 11,000$.

We have conducted four different sets of simulations to assess the impact of the number of nodes, of static power, of the number of available speeds and of the total load of requests. Note that for the first and the last sets of simulations, additional plots with more values of static power can be found in the companion research report [1].

Impact of the Number of Nodes. In the first set of simulations, we study the impact of the number of nodes on power consumption: in Figure 1, we plot the ratio of the power returned by the heuristics over the power of the optimal solution, with a static power of 5,000, 20,000, and 100,000 respectively. Note that Figure 1d is different from the others and provides results at larger scale: there we plot the ratio of the power returned by SPEED and EXCESS over the power consumption of GREEDY, with a static power of 50,000, but for a larger number

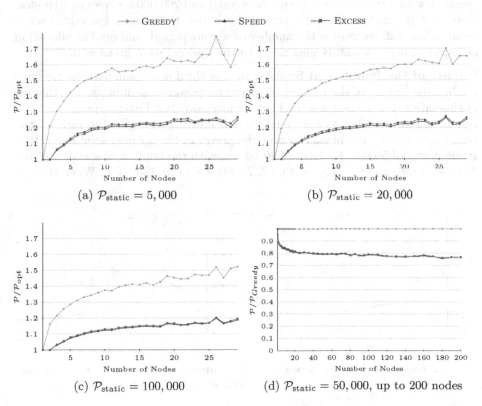

Fig. 1. Study of the impact of the number of nodes, for random requests between 0 and 100, average on 100 tests

of nodes (up to 200 nodes). While one could expect that the performance of the heuristics would decrease for larger trees, it seems that SPEED and EXCESS reach a plateau after $\approx$ 15 nodes, and that on average the maximum waste is between 20 and 25%. Furthermore, when the static power is higher (100,000), this maximum waste is even below 20%. This observed plateau is very likely correlated to the set of speeds and to the static power. This plateau makes sense in practice if we assume that the first step (the placement step) of the heuristics is not too far from the optimal solution because the GREEDY heuristic is an approximation algorithm. SPEED and EXCESS are just improvements of the GREEDY heuristic. It would be interesting to see how much they improve the approximation factor, though probably complicated. Note that in Figure 1d, we see that SPEED and EXCESS are still consistently better than GREEDY even with a larger number of nodes, with a power consumption of around 80% of the power consumption for GREEDY.

Impact of the Static Power. In the second set of simulations, we have studied the impact of the static power on total power consumption. In Figure 2a, we plot the ratio of the power returned by the heuristics over the power of the optimal solution, with a static power varying between 0 and 200,000 for trees of 20 nodes. Note that the higher the static power, the better the results. Indeed, at some point, what matters most is the number of servers placed, and not the allocation of requests, hence GREEDY gets closer to the optimal solution as well.

Impact of the Number of Speeds. In this third set of simulations, we have studied the impact of the number of speeds on power consumption. For this set of simulations, we do not use Intel speeds anymore, but instead speeds that are equally distributed between 0 and 150. In Figure 2b, we plot the ratio of the power returned by the heuristics over the power of the optimal solution, with a static power of 50,000, for trees of 20 nodes, with the number of speeds varying from one (150) and ten (15, 30, 45, 60, 75, 90, 105, 120, 135, 150). When there is

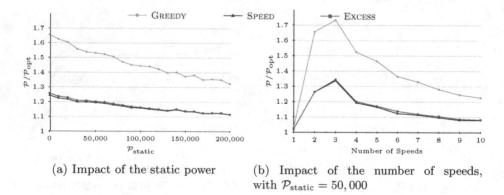

(a) Impact of the static power

(b) Impact of the number of speeds, with $\mathcal{P}_{\text{static}} = 50,000$

Fig. 2. Study of the impact of the static power and of the number of speeds, for trees of 20 nodes, for random requests between 0 and 100, average on 100 tests

only one speed, obviously the results are as good as they can be and only depend on the allocation heuristic. Then starting from three speeds, we observe that the more speeds, the better the results. This was expected since the more speeds we have, the closer we can get to the optimal solution computed by ALG-CONT-PLACED, and the better the results. The fact that the results are better with two speeds than three can be explained by the fact that with only two speeds, it is still easier to find the optimal speed (hence a lower ratio than with three speeds), but a mistake is very expensive, hence a result that is not as good as with four speeds. A final remark: when speeds are equally distributed, the (proven) approximation ratio of the GREEDY heuristic is 8. However in Figure 2b, we see that the ratio never goes above 1.8.

Impact of the Total Load of the Tree. Finally, in the last set of simulations, we have studied the impact of the total load of the tree on the power consumption. In Figure 3, we plot the ratio of the power returned by the heuristics over the power of the optimal solution, for trees of 20 nodes, and for a static power of 5,000 and 100,000 respectively. Overall, the total number of requests does not impact the performance of the heuristics: the average ratio stays constant with the total load of the tree, for all values of static power (see additional plots in [1]).

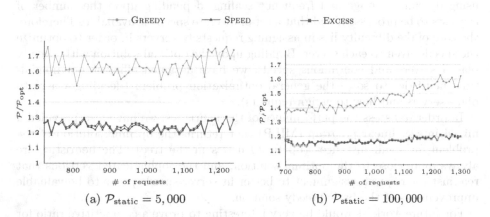

(a) $\mathcal{P}_{\text{static}} = 5,000$ (b) $\mathcal{P}_{\text{static}} = 100,000$

Fig. 3. Study of the impact of the total load, for trees of 20 nodes, for random requests between 0 and 100, average on 100 tests

Summary of Simulation Results. To conclude on the different studies, the first observation is somewhat expected: there is a huge gap between the GREEDY heuristic, and the SPEED and EXCESS heuristics: there is a degradation w.r.t. the optimal of 50 to 70% when using the GREEDY heuristic with 10 to 30 nodes, while it is only approximately 20% (or less with larger static power) when using the SPEED or EXCESS heuristic. The difference between the SPEED and EXCESS heuristics is negligible, although it should be noted that on average, the SPEED heuristic performs slightly ($\approx$ 1%) better than the EXCESS heuristic. Furthermore, it seems that what matters most for the competitiveness of the heuristics is the set of speeds and the static power $\mathcal{P}_{static}$. In particular, the number of speeds is very important: the closer the speeds are to each other, the better the results. Above a certain number of nodes (≈ 15), the ratio of the results of the heuristics over the optimal solution seems to reach a threshold (independently of the load and the static power), but the value of this threshold depends on the set of speeds and on the static power. Higher static power lowers the value of the threshold: at some point, what matters most is the number of servers, even if they are all at maximum speed. Similarly, the smaller the gap between two consecutive speeds, then the closer we can get to the optimal solution computed by ALG-CONT-PLACED, and the better the results.

6   Conclusion

In this paper, we have revisited the well-known replica problem in tree networks under power constraints, in the most flexible scenario where requests of a client can be split between multiple servers. While the problem of minimizing the number of servers has polynomial complexity, we have proved that the problem of minimizing the power consumption is NP-complete, even if the servers are already placed in the tree. We assume that the server speeds can be modified using dynamic voltage and frequency scaling, depending upon the number of requests to be processed, and that a set of discrete speeds is available. Therefore, the core of the difficulty lies in assigning requests to servers in order to optimize the speeds given to each server. Building upon the optimal solution with already placed servers and continuous speeds, we have designed efficient polynomial-time heuristics to solve the general optimization problem (deciding where to place servers and how to assign requests).

In order to assess the performance of the heuristics, we have also provided a mixed integer linear program (MILP) that returns the optimal solution of the problem for small instances (up to 30 nodes in the tree). The heuristics are always quite close to the optimal solution, and the sophisticated versions that readjust the request assignment to better fit server speeds prove to be valuable improvements of the basic greedy solution.

For future work, it would be very interesting to prove a competitive ratio for the heuristics that we have designed. However, this is quite a challenging work for arbitrary trees, and one may try to design approximation algorithms only for special tree structures, e.g. binary trees.

Acknowledgements. This work was supported in part by the French Research Agency (ANR) through the *Rescue* project. Anne Benoit and Yves Robert are with Institut Universitaire de France.

References

1. Aupy, G., Benoit, A., Journault, M., Robert, Y.: Power-aware replica placement in tree networks with multiple servers per client. Research Report 8474, INRIA (February 2014), http://graal.ens-lyon.fr/~abenoit/

2. Aupy, G., Journault, M.: Source code for the simulations,
   https://github.com/Gaupy/replica
3. Benoit, A., Rehn-Sonigo, V., Robert, Y.: Replica placement and access policies in tree networks. IEEE Trans. Parallel and Distributed Systems 19(12), 1614–1627 (2008)
4. Benoit, A., Renaud-Goud, P., Robert, Y.: Power-aware replica placement and update strategies in tree networks. In: Proceedings of the 25th IEEE Int. Parallel and Distributed Processing Symposium, IPDPS 2011 (May 2011)
5. Chandrakasan, A.P., Sinha, A.: Jouletrack: A web based tool for software energy profiling. In: Design Automation Conference. IEEE, pp. 220–225 (2001)
6. Chen, J.J., Kuo, T.W.: Multiprocessor energy-efficient scheduling for real-time tasks. In: Proceedings of Int. Conf. on Parallel Proc (ICPP), pp. 13–20. IEEE (2005)
7. Chen, J.J.: Expected energy consumption minimization in DVS systems with discrete frequencies. In: Proc. of SAC 2008, Symp. on Applied Computing, pp. 1720–1725 (2008)
8. Cidon, I., Kutten, S., Soffer, R.: Optimal allocation of electronic content. Computer Networks 40, 205–218 (2002)
9. Cplex: ILOG CPLEX: High-performance software for mathematical programming and optimization, http://www.ilog.com/products/cplex/
10. Garey, M.R., Johnson, D.S.: Computers and Intractability, a Guide to the Theory of NP-Completeness. W.H. Freeman and Company (1979)
11. Hotta, Y., Sato, M., Kimura, H., Matsuoka, S., Boku, T., Takahashi, D.: Profile-based optimization of power performance by using dynamic voltage scaling on a PC cluster. In: The IEEE Int. Parallel and Distributed Processing Symposium Proceedings of IPDPS (2006)
12. Kalpakis, K., Dasgupta, K., Wolfson, O.: Optimal placement of replicas in trees with read, write, and storage costs. IEEE Trans. Parallel and Distributed Systems 12(6), 628–637 (2001)
13. Larabel, M.: Intel EIST SpeedStep
14. Liu, P., Lin, Y.F., Wu, J.J.: Optimal placement of replicas in data grid environments with locality assurance. In: Int. Conf. on Parallel and Distr. Syst. (2006)
15. Loukopoulos, T., Ahmad, I., Papadias, D.: An overview of data replication on the Internet. In: Proc. Int. Symp. on Parallel Architectures, Algorithms and Networks ISPAN 2002. IEEE Computer Society Press (2002)
16. Mills, M.P.: The internet begins with coal. Environment and Climate News (1999)
17. Niu, L.: Energy Efficient Scheduling for Real-Time Embedded Systems with QoS Guarantee. In: Proc. of RTCSA, the 16th Int. Conf. on Embedded and Real-Time Computing Systems and App., 163 –172 (August 2010)
18. Pruhs, K., van Stee, R., Uthaisombut, P.: Speed scaling of tasks with precedence constraints. Theory of Computing Systems 43, 67–80 (2008)
19. Shi, B., Srivastava, A.: Thermal and Power-Aware Task Scheduling and Data Placement for Storage Centric Datacenters. In: Ranka, S., Ahmad, I. (eds.) Handbook of Energy-Aware and Green Computing, vol. 1, CRC Press (2012)
20. Wu, J.J., Lin, Y.F., Liu, P.: Optimal replica placement in hierarchical Data Grids with locality assurance. J. Parallel and Distributed Computing 68(12), 1517–1538 (2008)

On Constructing DAG-Schedules with Large AREAs

Scott T. Roche, Arnold L. Rosenberg, and Rajmohan Rajaraman

Northeastern University,
College of Computer and Information Science,
Boston, MA 02115, USA
{rraj,str,rsnbrg}@ccs.neu.edu

Abstract. The Area of a schedule Σ for a DAG $\mathcal{G}$ measures the rate at which Σ renders $\mathcal{G}$'s nodes eligible for execution. Specifically, $AREA(\Sigma)$ is the average number of nodes that are eligible for execution as Σ executes $\mathcal{G}$ node by node. Extensive simulations suggest that, for many distributions of processor availability and power, schedules having larger Areas execute DAGs faster on platforms that are *dynamically* heterogeneous: their processors change power and availability status in unpredictable ways and at unpredictable times. While Area-maximal schedules exist for every DAG, efficient generators of such schedules are known only for well-structured DAGs. We prove that the general problem of crafting Area-maximal schedules is NP-complete, hence likely computationally intractable. This situation motivates the development of heuristics for producing DAG-schedules that have large Areas. We build on the *Sidney decomposition* of a DAG to develop a *polynomial-time* heuristic, SIDNEY, whose schedules have quite large Areas. (1) Simulations on DAGs having *random structure* indicate that SIDNEY's schedules have Areas: (a) at least 85% of maximal; (b) at least 1.25 times larger than those produced by previous heuristics. (2) Simulations on DAGs having the structure of *random "LEGO®"* DAGs indicate that SIDNEY's schedules have Areas that are at least 1.5 times larger than those produced by previous heuristics. The "85%" result emerges from an LP-based formulation of the Area-maximization problem. (3) Our results on random DAGs are roughly matched by a second heuristic that emerges directly from the LP formulation.

1 Introduction

The problem. Many modern computing platforms—notably clouds [31,32], desktop grids [3], and volunteer-computing projects [9,16]—exhibit extreme levels of *dynamic* heterogeneity. The availability and relative powers of the platforms' computing resources can change at unexpected times and in unexpected ways. Scheduling a computation for efficient execution on such a platform can be quite challenging, particularly when there are dependencies among the computation's constituent *chores*[1] (jobs, tasks, etc.); as is traditional, we model such computations as DAGs (*directed acyclic graphs*). The *Area* of a schedule Σ for a DAG $\mathcal{G}$ measures the rate at which schedule Σ renders nodes eligible for execution: the larger the better. Specifically, $AREA(\Sigma)$ is the average number of nodes of $\mathcal{G}$ that are eligible as Σ executes $\mathcal{G}$ node by node.

---

[1] We use the granularity-neutral term "chore" to avoid nuances of coarseness.

F. Silva et al. (Eds.): Euro-Par 2014, LNCS 8632, pp. 620–631, 2014.

The motivating intuition is that increasing the likelihood of having nodes eligible for execution increases the opportunities for concurrency and decreases the likelihood of a computation's stalling for lack of eligible work. Although this is just intuition—the definition of Area does not mention any properties of the computing platform—extensive simulations ([5,6,13,20]) suggest that, for many distributions of processor availability and power, schedules having larger Areas execute DAGs faster on dynamically heterogeneous platforms. The current paper is motivated by the fact that, while all DAGs admit Area-maximizing schedules, we know how to derive such schedules *efficiently* only for a variety of specific families of DAGs [5,8].

Our Contributions. Our first main result establishes the NP-completeness (hence, likely computational intractability) of the AREA-MAX *problem*: the problem of generating Area-maximizing schedules for general DAGs (Sect. 3). While our search for *approximation schemes* for AREA-MAX, i.e., algorithms whose DAG-schedules have Areas within a fixed bound of maximal, has thus far been unsuccessful, it has not been fruitless. Our second main result is a *polynomial-time* heuristic, SIDNEY, for producing DAG-schedules, which is based on the *Sidney decomposition* of a DAG [27]. Simulation experiments suggest that SIDNEY's schedules have quite large Areas (Sect. 4.1). Simulations on DAGs having:

1. *random structure* suggest that SIDNEY's schedules have Areas: (a) at least 85% of maximal; (b) at least 1.25 times larger than those of previous heuristics' schedules.
2. the structure of *random* LEGO®-DAGs [6] suggest that SIDNEY's schedules have Areas at least 1.5 times larger than those of previous heuristics' schedules.

Our third main result is a new formulation of AREA-MAX as a Linear Program (LP) (Sect. 4.2). (i) The Area-value produced by the (unrounded) LP for a DAG $\mathcal{G}$ provides an upper bound on the maximum Area achievable by any schedule for $\mathcal{G}$. We thereby observe the "85%" result just mentioned for SIDNEY. (ii) The LP formulation yields a second new polynomial-time heuristic, LP for AREA-MAX. While LP's schedules essentially match SIDNEY's schedules' random-DAG Areas, the heuristic promises to yield valuable information about the structure of Area-maximizing schedules; see Sect. 4.2.

Related Work. How to minimize the completion times of computations on parallel computing platforms has been studied since such platforms emerged [26]. Most variants of this problem provide nontrivial computational challenges, especially in the presence of interchore dependencies that constrain execution order, as when computations are modeled as DAGs. Despite differences in detail, virtually all strategies for scheduling DAGs rely on knowing, possibly in a stochastic sense ([33]), (almost) exact chore execution-times; therefore, *dynamically heterogeneous* platforms resist standard scheduling strategies. Many attempts have been made to adapt earlier DAG-scheduling heuristics, such as HEFT [29] and FCP [24], to the new platforms, but none adequately addresses the range of challenges posed by dynamic heterogeneity. Among the bold approaches to scheduling for dynamic heterogeneity are the partial-order schedules of [23], which strive for temporal flexibility that is fixed only at run time. A similar delay-of-commitment approach is advocated in [2,14]. Yet other sources propose strategies wherein a precomputed schedule is reorganized at run time in response to changes in processors' powers [19,33]; in [22], e.g., planned checkpoints allow dynamic response to unexpected volatility. The scheduling strategy underlying our study was the *IC-scheduling* paradigm of

[25,21]. This strategy advocates ignoring the (unknowable) characteristics of the host platform and, instead, deploying a DAG's chores in an order that maximizes the rate of producing more chores that are eligible for deployment—to increase the likelihood of having work to allocate to available processors; simulation experiments in [13,20] validate this intuition. But an unrecoverable flaw in IC-scheduling is that many DAGs do not admit optimal schedules under the paradigm [21] (although many computationally significant DAGs do [7]). This flaw led to the development of *Area-maximizing* DAG-scheduling [5], whose study we continue here. One sees in [5] that (*a*) every DAG admits an Area-maximizing schedule and (*b*) Area-maximizing schedules and optimal IC-schedules coincide for any DAG that admits both. Since *efficient* generators of Area-maximizing schedules are not known for general DAGs, a heuristic was developed in [6] that converts a DAG $\mathcal{G}$ to a *series-parallel* version $\sigma(\mathcal{G})$ and then obtains a schedule for $\mathcal{G}$ by "filtering" an Area-maximizing schedule for $\sigma(\mathcal{G})$ (using an algorithm in [8]). Simulation experiments suggest that Area-maximizing DAG-scheduling has computational benefits similar to those of IC-scheduling, although to a moderated degree [6]. An interesting comparison of two dynamic approaches to DAG-scheduling appears in [15]: replicated allocation of chores vs. deadline-triggered reallocation. Other sources have analyzed the reliability of scheduling DAGs under execution-time uncertainty [11,18]. Finally, one finds in [1] a framework for minimizing makespan when processors asynchronously execute DAGs having unit-time chores.

2   Computation-DAGs and Their Schedules

A. Basics. A *(computation-)*DAG $\mathcal{G}$ has a set $\mathcal{N}_\mathcal{G}$ of $N_\mathcal{G}$ nodes, each representing a chore in a computation, and a set $\mathcal{A}_\mathcal{G}$ of $A_\mathcal{G}$ arcs, each representing an interchore dependency. For $(u \to v) \in \mathcal{A}_\mathcal{G}$: • chore v cannot be executed until chore u is; • u is a *parent* of v; v is a *child* of u in $\mathcal{G}$; • *ancestorhood* is inherited from parenthood; • a parentless node is a *source*; a childless node is a *sink*; • $\mathcal{G}$ is *bipartite of type* $(X \to Y)$ if $\mathcal{N}_\mathcal{G}$ can be partitioned into X and Y, and each arc $(u \to v)$ has $u \in X$ and $v \in Y$.

DAG-schedules and quality. When one executes a DAG $\mathcal{G}$, a node v becomes eligible (for execution) after all of its parents have been executed. We do not allow recomputation of nodes, so a node loses eligible status once it is executed. In compensation, executing node v may render new nodes eligible—when v is their last-executed parent. A *schedule* Σ for $\mathcal{G}$ is a rule for selecting which eligible node to execute at each step of an execution of $\mathcal{G}$; Σ is, thus, a *topological sort* of $\mathcal{G}$, i.e., a linear ordering of $\mathcal{N}_\mathcal{G}$ in which all of each node v's children appear after v. We measure the quality of schedule Σ via the rate at which its successive node-executions produce new eligible nodes—the more, the better. One cannot always execute nodes so that the number of eligible nodes on $\mathcal{G}$ is maximized *at every step of a computation* [21], so we seek schedules that maximize the *average* number of eligible nodes on $\mathcal{G}$ (over all steps of the computation). A schedule that achieves this goal is said to be *AREA-maximizing*, in the following sense.

B. AREA-maximizing schedules. The AREA metric. For any schedule Σ for a DAG $\mathcal{G}$ and any integer $T \in [0..N_\mathcal{G}]$, we denote by $E_\Sigma(T)$ the number of nodes that are eligible at step T when Σ executes $\mathcal{G}$.[2] Σ's *eligibility profile* is the $(N_\mathcal{G} + 1)$-tuple

---

[2] We measure time in an event-driven manner, as the number of nodes executed to that point.

$\Pi(\Sigma) = \langle E_\Sigma(0), \ldots, E_\Sigma(N_\mathcal{G}) \rangle$. Σ's *Area* is the sum[3]

$$AREA(\Sigma) = E_\Sigma(0) + E_\Sigma(1) + \cdots + E_\Sigma(N_\mathcal{G}). \tag{1}$$

We seek an *AREA-maximizing schedule (A-M schedule)* for $\mathcal{G}$: a schedule Σ^* such that

$$AREA(\Sigma^*) = \max_{\Sigma \text{ a schedule for } \mathcal{G}} AREA(\Sigma) \stackrel{\text{def}}{=} AREA(\mathcal{G}).$$

We refer to the quest for A-M schedules as the **AREA-MAX** problem.

C. Two simplifications of the problem. We cite from [5].
1. *Every DAG admits an A-M schedule that executes all sinks only after all nonsinks.*
2. Say that $\mathcal{G}$ has n nonsinks, N nonsources, s sources, and S sinks. If schedule Σ executes all nonsinks before any sinks, then we can maximize $AREA(\Sigma)$ by maximizing

$$Area(\Sigma) \stackrel{\text{def}}{=} \sum_{i=0}^{n} E_\Sigma(i) = AREA(\Sigma) - \binom{S}{2}. \tag{2}$$

Letting $e_\Sigma(t)$ be the number of nodes that are rendered eligible by Σ's tth node-execution, we note that

$$area(\Sigma) \stackrel{\text{def}}{=} \sum_{t=0}^{n} \sum_{j=1}^{t} e_\Sigma(j) = n \cdot e_\Sigma(1) + (n-1) \cdot e_\Sigma(2) + \cdots + 1 \cdot e_\Sigma(n) \tag{3}$$

is the only portion of $Area(\Sigma)$ that actually depends on choices made by Σ.

We henceforth study a connection between **AREA-MAX** and the *Minimum Weighted-Completion-Time* problem for DAGs, MWCT. Building on [30], we prove that AREA-MAX is NP-Complete (Sect. 3); inspired by [17], we develop new heuristics that produce schedules with large-Areas (Sect. 4.1); we test the heuristics' schedules in Sect. 5.

3 The NP-Completeness of AREA Maximization

Clearly, the (decision version of the) **AREA-MAX** problem lies within the class NP. One just "guesses" a topological sort for a DAG and calculates the Area of the resulting schedule. We show now that **AREA-MAX** is also NP-hard, via reduction from the 0-1 *Minimum Weighted-Completion-Time* problem for a class of bipartite DAGs. This problem, which we refer to as $(0, 1)$-MWCT, is defined as follows. One is given a bipartite DAG $\mathcal{G}$ with source-set S and sink-set T. Every source $u \in S$ has computation time $C_u = 1$ and weight $w_u = 0$; every sink $v \in T$ has computation time $C_v = 0$ and weight $w_v = 1$. Under this model, the makespan of $\mathcal{G}$ is not changed when we execute any (eligible) sink; so, for definiteness, we execute a sink "greedily," as soon as it becomes eligible. We can, therefore, view a schedule as an ordering of $\mathcal{G}$'s s sources. The *weighted completion time* for $\mathcal{G}$ associated with schedule Σ is

$$W_\Sigma \stackrel{\text{def}}{=} \sum_{j=1}^{s} w_j C_j = 1 \cdot e_\Sigma(1) + 2 \cdot e_\Sigma(2) + \cdots + s \cdot e_\Sigma(s). \tag{4}$$

---

[3] The term *Area* arises by analogy with the approximation of integrals by Riemann sums.

$(0, 1)$-MWCT is the NP-Complete problem [30]: find a schedule Σ with minimal W_Σ. This is a $1|prec|\sum w_j C_j$ problem: there is a single processor (1) with interjob precedences $(prec)$ that strives to minimize $\sum w_j C_j$. We reduce $(0, 1)$-MWCT to AREA-MAX.

Lemma 1. *Any AREA-maximizing schedule Σ for the 0-1 bipartite DAG $\mathcal{G}$ minimizes $\mathcal{G}$'s weighted completion time; hence, it solves the $1|prec|\sum w_j C_j$ problem for $\mathcal{G}$.*

Proof. Say that $\mathcal{G}$ has s sources and S sinks. Adding Eqs. (3) and (4), we find that

$$Area(\Sigma)+W_\Sigma = (S+1)s-\binom{s+1}{2}+(s+1)\sum_{k=1}^{s}e_\Sigma(k) = (S+1)s-\binom{s+1}{2}+(s+1)S,$$

since each of $\mathcal{G}$'s S sinks becomes eligible exactly once. It follows that any AREA-maximizing schedule minimizes weighted completion time.

4   Two New DAG-Scheduling Heuristics

4.1   A DAG-Scheduling Heuristic Based on the Sidney Decomposition

We now develop the SIDNEY DAG-scheduling heuristic, which transforms a DAG $\mathcal{G}$ into a DAG $\mathcal{G}'$ such that: finding an A-M schedule for $\mathcal{G}$ is *equivalent* to finding a schedule for $\mathcal{G}'$ that minimizes the MWCT, $\sum_{v\in\mathcal{N}_{\mathcal{G}'}} w_v C_v$. We reduce AREA-MAX to MWCT and invoke a known approximation algorithm for MWCT to derive the SIDNEY scheduler. (This complements Sect. 3's reduction of an NP-hard case of MWCT to AREA-MAX.)

We construct the 0-1 *version* $\mathcal{G}_{0,1}$ of a DAG $\mathcal{G}$ as follows. The nodes of $\mathcal{G}_{0,1}$ are obtained by splitting each node $v \in \mathcal{N}_\mathcal{G}$ into two nodes, v_0 and v_1. We give each node of $\mathcal{G}_{0,1}$ that has a 0 subscript (the *zero-nodes*) a processing time of 0 and a weight of 1: symbolically, $p_{v_0} = 0$ and $w_{v_0} = 1$; we give each node of $\mathcal{G}_{0,1}$ that has a 1 subscript (the *one-nodes*) a processing time of 1 and a weight of 0: $w_{v_1} = 0$ and $p_{v_1} = 1$. Finally, we give $\mathcal{G}_{0,1}$ an arc $(u_1 \to v_0)$ for each $(u \to v) \in \mathcal{A}_\mathcal{G}$ and an arc $(u_0 \to u_1)$ for each $u \in \mathcal{N}_\mathcal{G}$ (i.e., for each pair $u_0, u_1 \in \mathcal{N}_{\mathcal{G}_{0,1}}$). Schedule Σ' for $\mathcal{G}_{0,1}$ is a 0-1 *version* of schedule Σ for $\mathcal{G}$ if Σ' executes $\mathcal{G}_{0,1}$'s one-nodes in an order consistent with Σ's order of executing $\mathcal{G}$'s nodes; i.e., if Σ executes $\mathcal{G}$'s nodes in the order $v_1, \ldots, v_N$, then Σ' executes $\mathcal{G}_{0,1}$'s nodes in the order $v_{1,1}, \ldots, v_{N,1}$.

Lemma 2. *Let $\mathcal{G}$ be any DAG and $\mathcal{G}_{0,1}$ its 0-1 version. If Σ is an A-M schedule for $\mathcal{G}$, then any 0-1 version of Σ minimizes WCT for $\mathcal{G}_{0,1}$.*

Proof. Every zero-node v_0 has $p_{v_0} = 0$, so any MWCT schedule for $\mathcal{G}_{0,1}$ will execute v_0 as soon as it is eligible. Hence, the WCT for a 0-1 version of a schedule Σ for $\mathcal{G}$ is:

$$W_{\Sigma'} = \sum_{i\in\mathcal{N}_\mathcal{G}} w_i \cdot \max_{j \text{ a parent of } i} C(j) = \sum_{i\in\mathcal{N}_\mathcal{G}} w_i \cdot E(i), \tag{5}$$

where $C(k)$ (resp., $E(k)$) denotes the step when node k completes execution (resp., becomes eligible). By similar reasoning:

$$AREA(\Sigma) = \sum_{i\in\mathcal{N}_\mathcal{G}} ((C(i) - 1) - E(i)) = \binom{n+1}{2} - \sum_{i\in\mathcal{N}_\mathcal{G}} E(i). \tag{6}$$

It follows from eqs. (5, 6) that if one could replace Σ' by a schedule Σ'' for $\mathcal{G}_{0,1}$ that has $W_{\Sigma''} < W_{\Sigma'}$, then there would be a schedule $\widehat{\Sigma}$ for $\mathcal{G}$ such that $AREA(\widehat{\Sigma}) > AREA(\Sigma)$. But the existence of $\widehat{\Sigma}$ would contradict Σ's assumed AREA-maximality.

The duality between $AREA(\mathcal{G})$ and $WCT(\mathcal{G}_{0,1})$ gives us access to an approximation algorithm for MWCT that we sketch here; details appear in [4,27]. The algorithm decomposes a DAG $\mathcal{G}$ whose nodes v each has a *processing time* p_v and a *weight* w_v. The *rank* of $v \in \mathcal{N}_{\mathcal{G}}$ is $r_v = p_v/w_v$; by extension, the rank of $S \subseteq \mathcal{N}_{\mathcal{G}}$ is $r(S) = \sum_{v \in S} p_v/w_v$. Following [4], a sub-DAG $\mathcal{G}'$ of $\mathcal{G}$ is *precedence-closed* if every ancestor of each $v \in \mathcal{N}_{\mathcal{G}'}$ is also in $\mathcal{N}_{\mathcal{G}'}$. $\mathcal{G}^*$ denotes precedence-closed subgraph of $\mathcal{G}$ of minimum rank. Finally, a *segment* in a schedule Σ is a consecutively-scheduled set of nodes. One can generalize Smith's rule for DAGs [28] as follows.

Lemma 3 ([4,27]). *There exists an* WCT-*minimizing schedule Σ for any DAG $\mathcal{G}$ in which an optimal schedule for $\mathcal{G}^*$ occurs as an initial segment of Σ.*

Thus, in an optimal schedule Σ for $\mathcal{G}$, an optimal ordering of the nodes of the minimum-rank precedence-closed subgraph $\mathcal{G}^*$ appears as the first segment of Σ. A polynomial-time algorithm **A** is developed in [4], which recursively finds $\mathcal{N}_{\mathcal{G}^*}$ (plus the residual graph $\mathcal{G} \setminus \mathcal{G}^*$); then schedules the nodes within each set in a feasible schedule. Building on the Sidney decomposition of $\mathcal{G}$, **A** produces a schedule for $\mathcal{G}$ whose WCT is no greater than double the optimal WCT for $\mathcal{G}$. In detail: Rather than specifically looking for the minimum-rank precedence-closed sub-DAG $\mathcal{G}^*$, algorithm **A** finds a sub-DAG whose rank is $\leq$ a given positive constant λ (specified as an input). It accomplishes this by constructing an associated *capacitated* graph $\mathcal{G}_\lambda$, with the following properties:

- The nodes of $\mathcal{G}_\lambda$ consist of the nodes of $\mathcal{G}$ along with a source s and a sink t.
- The arcs of $\mathcal{G}_\lambda$ are: $\{(s \to t), (i \to t) | i \in \mathcal{N}(\mathcal{G})\} \bigcup \{(i \dashrightarrow j) | j$ is an ancestor of $i\}$.

We associate a capacity $c(e)$ with every arc e, as follows:

$$c(e) = \begin{cases} p_i, & \text{if } e = e(i, t) \\ \lambda w_i, & \text{if } e = (s, i) \\ \infty, & \text{otherwise} \end{cases}$$

Finding subgraph $\mathcal{G}^*$ is thus reduced to finding a (s, t)-minimum cut for $\mathcal{G}_\lambda$ with cut value $\leq \lambda w(\mathcal{G})$. Lemma 3 in [4] guarantees that if (A, B) is such a cut, then the rank of $A \setminus \{s\}$ is $\leq \lambda$, and $A \setminus \{s\}$ is precedence-closed in $\mathcal{G}$. Hence, one can find $\mathcal{G}^*$ by performing a binary search on λ, and then recurse on the residual DAG $\mathcal{G} \setminus \mathcal{G}^*$ until all of $\mathcal{G}$ has been decomposed. Alternatively, one can use an algorithm such as that in [10] to find all points λ in a single max-flow computation (making use of a variable of the push-relabel algorithm), thereby decomposing $\mathcal{G}$ in a single pass. This alternative provides an efficient running time of $O(\min(n^{2/3}, m^{1/2})m \log(n^2/m) \log U)$, where $n = N_{\mathcal{G}}$, $m = A_{\mathcal{G}}$, and U is the maximum (finite) capacity, which is $\leq n$ in our case. Thus, for sparse DAGs ($m = O(n)$), the running time is $O(n^{5/3} \log^2 n)$, while for dense DAGs ($m = \Theta(n^2)$), the running time is $O(n^{5/2} \log^2 n)$.

Our final ingredient in devising SIDNEY is the DYNAMIC-GREEDY heuristic, which maintains a MAX-priority queue of the eligible nodes, (partially) ordered by *yield*.

The *yield* of an eligible node $v \in \mathcal{N}_{\mathcal{G}}$ at step t of Σ's execution of $\mathcal{G}$ is the number of nodes that would be rendered eligible if Σ were to execute v at that step.

At each step, DYNAMIC-GREEDY selects a maximal-yield node for execution. When a node completes executing, all newly eligible nodes are inserted into the priority queue, in random order. (The heuristic thus makes an optimal choice for this step—but ignores future ramifications of this choice.)

We can now specify the SIDNEY heuristic for computing large-AREA DAG-schedules.

The SIDNEY heuristic

Given a DAG $\mathcal{G}$:

1. Construct the associated 0-1 DAG $\mathcal{G}_{0,1}$.
2. Use a max-flow computation to perform a Sidney decomposition of $\mathcal{G}_{0,1}$.
3. Let $S_1, \ldots, S_k$ be the node-sets computed in the Sidney decomposition:
   (a) Remove all 0-nodes from each task-set S_i.
   (b) For each task-set S_i, use the DYNAMIC-GREEDY heuristic to produce a schedule Σ_i for the nodes in S_i.
4. Output schedule $\Sigma = \Sigma_1 \Sigma_2 \ldots \Sigma_k$, the concatenation of the k subschedules.

4.2   A DAG-Scheduling Heuristic Based on Linear Programming

We exploit the structure of AREA-MAX to formulate the problem as a Linear Program (LP). Our formulation serves two purposes: (1) the (unrounded) solution to the LP for a DAG $\mathcal{G}$ bounds $Area(\mathcal{G})$ from above; (2) rounding the solution to yield *integer* values, provides a valid schedule for $\mathcal{G}$. This (solve LP)-(then round) procedure comprises the *LP heuristic* LP for scheduling DAGs. Of course, obtaining *optimal* integer solutions to an LP is the NP-hard *ILP problem*, but the ILPs that arise in AREA-maximization may be computationally simpler; at least, they give us access to approximate solutions via the unrestricted (non-integer) form of the LP. Our LP-formulation of AREA-MAX for an n-node DAG employs three classes of indicator (i.e., 0-1 valued) variables, each of size roughly n^2. For $i \in [1..n]$ and $t \in [0..n]$:

Variable	Interpretation
$x_{i,t}$	*Task/node i is executed at step t of schedule Σ.*
$y_{i,t}$	*Task/node i is eligible at step t of schedule Σ.*
$z_{i,t}$	*Task/node i has been executed prior to step t of schedule Σ.*

The AREA-MAX problem can be formulated as follows.

$$\textbf{Maximize} \sum_{t=0}^{n} \sum_{i=0}^{n} y_{i,t} \textbf{ subject to:}$$

$$
\begin{array}{lll}
\text{C1} & \sum_{t=0}^{n} x_{i,t} = 1 & \forall\, i \in \mathcal{N}_{\mathcal{G}} \\
\text{C2} & \sum_{i=0}^{n} x_{i,t} = 1 & \forall\, t \in [0..n] \\
\text{C3} & z_{i,T} = \sum_{t<T} x_{i,t} & \forall\, i \in \mathcal{N}_{\mathcal{G}},\, T \in [1..n] \\
\text{C4} & y_{i,T} = 1 - z_{i,T} & \forall\, i \in (\text{Sources of } \mathcal{G}),\, T \in [1..n] \\
\text{C5} & y_{i,T} \leq z_{j,T} - z_{i,T} & \forall\, T \in [0..n],\, j \in (\text{ancestors of } i) \\
\text{C6} & z_{i,T+1} \leq z_{j,T} & \forall\, T \in [0..n],\, j \in (\text{ancestors of } i) \\
\text{C7} & x_{i,t}, y_{i,t}, z_{i,t} \in \{0,1\} & \forall\, i \in \mathcal{N}_{\mathcal{G}},\, t \in [0..n]
\end{array}
$$

The various constraints play the following roles: C1 and C2 ensure, resp., that each node/task is completed and that no processor is ever idle; C3 ensures that the cumulative-execution variable z tallies all work done on each node prior to time T; C4 ensures that the eligibility of a source node is 1 minus (the work completed in prior time steps); C5 ensures that for each precedence constraint (j must be executed before i), the eligibility of a node is bounded by (the work already done on it) minus (the work already done on its ancestors); C6 ensures that for each constraint (j must be executed before i), the work done on node i is no greater than the work done on all of its ancestors.

We create an LP from this ILP by replacing the integrality constraints C7 by:

$$[0 \le y_{i,t} \le 1 \text{ for all } i, t] \quad \text{and} \quad [0 \le x_{i,t} \le 1 \text{ for all } i, t]$$

The major difference between the ILP and LP formularion of **AREA-MAX** is that the latter allows fractional execution (and eligibility) of tasks—which is equivalent to allowing preemption in schedules. The LP thus provides an upper bound for the optimal value of $AREA(\mathcal{G})$. It also naturally yields the following DAG-scheduling heuristic.

The LP heuristic LP on a DAG $\mathcal{G}$:

1. Construct the LP from $\mathcal{G}$; solve it.
2. For each $i \in \mathcal{N}_\mathcal{G}$, calculate a completion time C_i as the first time step T such that $\sum_{t=0}^{T} x_{i,t} = 1$
3. Sort the set of completion times $\{C_i\}_{i=0}^n$, breaking ties arbitrarily.
4. The resulting ordering of $\mathcal{N}_\mathcal{G}$ is schedule Σ for $\mathcal{G}$.

5 Simulation Experiments

5.1 Experimental Procedure

Overview. To test the Area-quality of heuristics SIDNEY and LP, we generated synthetic DAGs that share structural characteristics with a variety of "real" computation-DAGs, especially those encountered in scientific computing. We constructed schedules for each DAG using three heuristics: SIDNEY (Sect. 4.1) and the two "best" known heuristics (described below) as determined by experiments in [6]. We compared the Areas of the three schedules for each DAG. For some small DAGs (having ≤ 100 nodes), we also considered the Areas of the schedules produced by LP (Sect.4.2). Although LP is polynomial-time, its current implementation is prohibitively computationally intense on even moderate-size DAGs. We continue to seek better implementations of the LP computation since its specification for a DAG $\mathcal{G}$ exactly reflects $AREA(\mathcal{G})$.

The tested DAGs. We generated random DAGs from the following families.

1. *Random n-node DAGs.* We randomly ordered n nodes into a sequence $1, 2, \ldots, n$, designating the last five nodes as sinks. Then, for each node $i \in [1..n-5]$, we randomly selected five children, $j_1 > i, \ldots, j_5 > i$ and generated arcs $(i \to j_k)$.
2. *Random n-node* LEGO®-DAGs. We tested LEGO®-DAGs as defined in [21]. These are built from a repertoire of *Bipartite Building Block* DAGs *(BBBs)*, that represent (parallel) steps in a computation. As in [21] (q.v.), we employed BBBs that reflect a single: *expansive step* (as in an out-tree), *reductive step* (as in an in-tree), *group*

step (as in computations exemplified by convolutions or parallel-prefix operations). We selected BBBs, randomized according to both size and structure, and composed them to create multi-step, multi-level computations; we continued this process until a DAG reached the desired size range. We created two classes of LEGO®-DAGs: one used BBBs with sizes drawn from a uniform distribution in the range [2..20]; the other used BBBs with sizes drawn from a harmonic distribution that produced BBBs of expected size 10.

The tested heuristics. We used three schedulers to generate schedules:

1. The SIDNEY scheduler of Sect. 4.1.
2. The AOSPD scheduler [8]. This heuristic takes a DAG $\mathcal{G}$ and invokes an algorithm from [12] to convert $\mathcal{G}$ to a *series-parallel* DAG $\sigma(\mathcal{G})$ (while retaining much of $\mathcal{G}$'s parallel structure); if $\mathcal{G}$ is already a series-parallel DAG, then $\sigma(\mathcal{G}) = \mathcal{G}$. AOSPD then generates an Area-maximizing schedule for $\sigma(\mathcal{G})$, using an algorithm from [8]. Experiments in [6] show that AOSPD produces schedules with quite large Areas.
3. The DYNAMIC GREEDY scheduler (Sect. 4.1). This heuristic achieves the second-best Area performance, after AOSPD, in the experiments in [6,8].

Methodology. For each $n \in \{100, 200, 300, 500\}$, we generated 100 n-node DAGs of random structure. We also generated 100 random LEGO®-DAGs of each approximate size $n = 200k$ where $k \in [1..20]$, using both the uniform and harmonic distributions. For each generated DAG, we had each of our three heuristics generate a schedule, and we computed the Areas of the resulting schedules.

5.2 Experimental Results

The SIDNEY heuristic. The plots in Fig. 1(a) illustrate that, for the DAG-classes and -sizes tested, the Areas of the schedules generated by SIDNEY far exceed those of the schedules generated by both AOSPD and DYNAMIC GREEDY.

1. The advantage of SIDNEY is particularly remarkable with both classes of LEGO®-DAGs. For these DAGs, SIDNEY's schedules have Areas 2.3 times greater than DYNAMIC-GREEDY's and nearly 1.5 times greater than AOSPD's. These factors are heartening because of LEGO®-DAGs' structural similarity with "real" DAGs.
2. SIDNEY exhibited a notable Area-advantage over the other heuristics when executing random DAGs, albeit by a smaller factor, 1.3. We can not yet interpret this decreased advantage, but it may relate to random DAGs' often-pathological structure (e.g., their often high expansion). We note that AOSPD also displays negligible Area-advantage over DYNAMIC-GREEDY for random DAGs.

The preceding suggests that SIDNEY finds large-Area schedules for a broader class of DAGs than do the regimens studied in [8,6].

The LP heuristic. The results with LP lead us to classify it as an "auxiliary" scheduler:

The cons. We know of no LP solvers that can efficiently handle even moderate size DAGs—and our LPs are enormous. For example, 400-node DAGs yield LPs with $\approx 5 \times 10^5$ variables and $\approx 10^6$ (mostly non-sparse) constraints. We therefore were able to generate LP schedules for only small random DAGs (≤ 100 nodes).

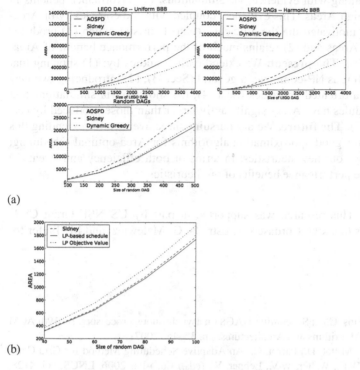

(a)

(b)

Fig. 1. (a) Area-qualities of our schedulers on tested DAGs. (b) LP vs. SIDNEY on random DAGs.

The pros. LP's schedules compete well experimentally with SIDNEY's in terms of Area. Both produced roughly the same mean Areas for the same DAGs (Fig. 1(a)).

Using LP as an "auxiliary" scheduler for small DAGs could be beneficial:

> *We conjecture that* SIDNEY *would produce higher-Area schedules if sub-*DAGs *were scheduled via* LP *rather than* DYNAMIC-GREEDY.

Testing this conjecture is high on our to-do list. At least as important is the direct application of the LP formulation of AREA-MAX:

> *The objective value of an LP for a* DAG $\mathcal{G}$ *provides a (possibly unachievable) upper bound on* $Area(\mathcal{G})$, *the maximum possible Area of any schedule for* $\mathcal{G}$.

Perspective. Fig. 1(b) indicates that on the tested DAGs: (a) SIDNEY ony slightly outperforms LP; (b) both heuristics produce schedules whose Areas achieve an average of 85% of the true value of $Area(\mathcal{G})$.

6 Conclusion

The past. The Area metric for DAG-schedules is a step toward achieving high performance on dynamically heterogeneous platforms. The basic properties of the metric were derived in [5], along with evidence, via simulations, of performance benefits in schedules that have high Areas. This evidence, coupled with the complexity of Area-maximal scheduling, motivated the the efficient AOSPD heuristic which (1) produces schedules with large Areas and (2) retains much of the performance benefit of Area-optimal schedules [8,6]. **The present.** We extend earlier studies by: (1) showing that Area-optimal scheduling is NP-complete in general (Sect. 3); (2) introducing two new polynomial-time Area-oriented heuristics (Sect. 4); (3) showing via simulations that both heuristics' schedules have Areas significantly larger than those produced by earlier heuristics (Sect. 5). **The future.** We are pursuing three avenues for extending this work: (1) searching for good approximation algorithms for Area-optimal scheduling; (2) seeking to improve our new heuristics, in terms of both efficiency and Area; (3) beginning to study the performance benefits of our heuristics.

Acknowledgments. This research was supported in part by US NSF Grant CSR-1217981. The authors thank G. Cordasco, T. Estrada, G. Malewicz, and M. Taufer for helpful conversations.

References

1. Bender, M.A., Phillips, C.A.: Scheduling DAGs on asynchronous processors. In: 19th ACM Symp. on Parallel Algorithms and Architectures, pp. 35–45 (2007)
2. Boutammine, S.-S., Millot, D., Parrot, C.: An Adaptive Scheduling Method for Grid Computing. In: Nagel, W.E., Walter, W.V., Lehner, W. (eds.) Euro-Par 2006. LNCS, vol. 4128, pp. 188–197. Springer, Heidelberg (2006)
3. Casanova, H., Dufossé, F., Robert, Y., Vivien, F.: Scheduling parallel iterative applications on volatile resources. In: 25th IEEE Int'l Parallel and Distributed Processing Symp. (2011)
4. Chekuri, C., Motwani, R.: Precedence constrained scheduling to minimize sum of weighted completion times on a single machine. Discrete Applied Math. 98, 29–38 (1999)
5. Cordasco, G., De Chiara, R., Rosenberg, A.L.: On scheduling DAGs for volatile computing platforms: Area-maximizing schedules. J. Parallel and Distr. Computing 72, 1347–1360 (2012)
6. Cordasco, G., De Chiara, R., Rosenberg, A.L.: An AREA-oriented heuristic for scheduling DAGs on volatile computing platforms (2013) (submitted for publication), See also Assessing the Computational Benefits of AREA-Oriented DAG-Scheduling. In: Jeannot, E., Namyst, R., Roman, J. (eds.) Euro-Par 2011, Part I. LNCS, vol. 6852, pp. 180–192. Springer, Heidelberg (2011)
7. Cordasco, G., Malewicz, G., Rosenberg, A.L.: Applying IC-scheduling theory to some familiar computations. In: Wkshp. on Large-Scale, Volatile Desktop Grids (2007)
8. Cordasco, G., Rosenberg, A.L.: On scheduling series-parallel DAGs to maximize AREA. In: Int'l J. Foundations of Computer Science (to appear, 2014)
9. Estrada, T., Taufer, M., Reed, K.: Modeling job lifespan delays in volunteer computing projects. In: 9th IEEE Int'l Symp. on Cluster, Cloud, and Grid Computing (2009)
10. Gallo, G., Grigoriadis, M.D., Tarjan, R.E.: A fast parametric maximum flow algorithm and applications. SIAM J. Comput. 18, 30–55
11. Georgiou, C., Kowalski, D.R.: Performing dynamically injected tasks on processes prone to crashes and restarts. In: Peleg, D. (ed.) DISC 2011. LNCS, vol. 6950, pp. 165–180. Springer, Heidelberg (2011)

12. González-Escribano, A., van Gemund, A., Cardeñoso-Payo, V.: Mapping unstructured applications into nested parallelism. In: High Performance Computing for Computational Sci. (2002)
13. Hall, R., Rosenberg, A.L., Venkataramani, A.: A comparison of DAG -scheduling strategies for Internet-based computing. In: 21st IEEE Int'l Parallel and Distr. Processing Symp. (2007)
14. Isard, M., Prabhakaran, V., Currey, J., Wieder, U., Talwar, K., Goldberg, A.: Quincy: Fair scheduling for distributed computing clusters. In: ACM Symp. on Operating Systs. Principles (2009)
15. Kondo, D., Casanova, H., Wing, E., Berman, F.: Models and scheduling mechanisms for global computing applications. In: 16th Int'l Parallel and Distr. Processing Symp. (2002)
16. Korpela, E., Werthimer, D., Anderson, D., Cobb, J., Lebofsky, M.: SETI@home: massively distributed computing for SETI. In: Dubois, P.F. (ed.) Computing in Science and Engineering. IEEE Computer Soc. Press (2000)
17. Lawler, E.L.: Sequencing jobs to minimize total weighted completion time subject to precedence constraints. Annals of Discrete Math. 2, 75–90 (1978)
18. Lombardi, M.: Robust scheduling of task graphs under execution time uncertainty. IEEE Trans. Computers 62, 98–111 (2013)
19. Millot, D.: Scheduling on unspecified heterogeneous distributed resources. In: IEEE Int'l Symp. on Parallel and Distributed Processing: Wkshps. and PhD Forum, pp.45–56 (2011)
20. Malewicz, G., Foster, I., Rosenberg, A.L., Wilde, M.: A tool for prioritizing DAGMan jobs and its evaluation. J. Grid Computing 5, 197–212 (2007)
21. Malewicz, G., Rosenberg, A.L., Yurkewych, M.: Toward a theory for scheduling sc DAGs in Internet-based computing. IEEE Trans. Comput. 55, 757–768 (2006)
22. Nurmi, D., Wolski, R., Brevik, J.: Model-based checkpoint scheduling for volatile resource environments. In: Cluster 2005 (2005)
23. Policella, N.: Scheduling with uncertainty: A proactive approach using partial order schedules. AI Communications 18, 165–167 (2005)
24. Radulescu, A., van Gemund, A.J.C.: On the complexity of list scheduling algorithms for distributed memory systems. In: 13th Int'l Conf. on Supercomputing, pp.68–75 (1999)
25. Rosenberg, A.L.: On scheduling mesh-structured computations for Internet-based computing. IEEE Trans. Comput. 53, 1176–1186 (2004)
26. Sarkar, V.: Partitioning and Scheduling Parallel Programs for Multiprocessors. MIT Press, Cambridge (1989)
27. Sidney, J.B.: Decomposition algorithms for single-machine sequencing with precedence relations and deferral costs. Operations Res. 23(2), 283–298 (1975)
28. Smith, W.: Various optimizers for single-stage production. Naval Res. Logistics Quart. 3, 59–66 (1956)
29. Topcuoglu, H., Hariri, S., Wu, M.Y.: Performance-effective and low-complexity task scheduling for heterogeneous computing. IEEE Trans. Parallel and Distr. Systs. 13, 260–274 (2002)
30. Woeginger, G.J.: On the approximability of average completion time scheduling under precedence constraints. Discr. Appl. Math. 131, 237–252 (2003)
31. Yao, S., Lee, H.-H.S.: Using mathematical modeling in provisioning a heterogeneous cloud computing environment., pp. 55–62. IEEE Computer (August 2011)
32. Zaharia, M., Konwinski, A., Joseph, A.D., Katz, R., Stoica, I.: Improving MapReduce performance in heterogeneous environments. In: 7th USENIX Symp. on Operating System Design and Implementation (2008)
33. Zheng, W.: A monte-carlo approach for full-ahead stochastic DAG-scheduling. In: 26th IEEE Int'l Parallel and Distributed Processing Symp.: Wkshps. and PhD Forum, pp. 99–112 (2012)

Software Defined Multicasting for MPI Collective Operation Offloading with the NetFPGA

Omer Arap[1], Geoffrey Brown[2], Bryce Himebaugh[2], and Martin Swany[1]

[1] Center for Research in Extreme Scale Technologies,
Indiana University, Bloomington, IN 47405, USA
{omerarap,swany}@crest.iu.edu
[2] School of Informatics and Computing,
Indiana University, Bloomington, IN 47405, USA
{geobrown,bhimebau}@cs.indiana.edu

Abstract. Collective operations play a key role in the performance of many high performance computing applications and are central to the widely used Message Passing Interface (MPI) programming model. In this paper we explore the use of programmable networking devices to accelerate the implementation of collective operations by offloading functionality to the underlying network. In our work we utilize a networked FPGA in conjunction with commercial OpenFlow switches supporting multicast. The union of hardware configurable network interfaces with Software Defined Networking (SDN) provides a significant opportunity to improve the performance of MPI applications that rely heavily on collective operations. The programmable interfaces implement collective operations in hardware using OpenFlow supported multicast. In our 8-node cluster, we observed up to 12% reduction in MPI_Allreduce latency in dynamic schemes employing SDN; and up to 22% reduction in static topologies. The results suggest more benefits if our approach is deployed in larger settings with low latency switches.

Keywords: SDN, OpenFlow, MPI, NetFPGA, MPI_Allreduce, MPI_Barrier.

1 Introduction

This work introduces a powerful new capability in high performance computing (HPC) environments based on the widely-used Message Passing Interface (MPI) [4]. Many MPI-based applications depend heavily on collective operations, which encapsulate multi-process communication and operation patterns in ways that are amenable to optimization. By enabling reconfiguration of the network based on the selected collective algorithm utilizing Software Defined Networking (SDN) capabilities, and incorporating MPI functionality in programmable network elements based on Field Programmable Gate Arrays (FPGA), we can improve performance and reduce overhead for this important class of parallel program functionality.

The MPI collectives can be implemented in various ways and major MPI suites [6] [5] [3], select the specific collective algorithm based upon runtime parameters such as message size, number of processes, underlying topology etc. Each algorithm constructs a virtual topology between the processes. If the underlying physical topology does not

F. Silva et al. (Eds.): Euro-Par 2014, LNCS 8632, pp. 632–643, 2014.

overlap with the selected algorithm's virtual topology, the performance of the collective operation may suffer. Determining the underlying topology in advance and choosing the best fitting collective algorithm has been studied in the past [13]. In addition, for the specific topologies more efficient algorithms have been proposed [21]. In contrast, in this work we configure the network according to the chosen algorithm in the runtime benefiting SDN capabilities. We benefit from software defined multicast rules rather than specific protocol's static multicasting capabilities to enhance the performance of collective operations.

Collective operations involving implicit synchronization mostly benefit from our multicasting architecture when the release phase of the algorithm is executed. In tree based algorithms, the root process receives the data from its children and it produces the final outcome along with generating release message. Multicasting reduces extra copies of the same data packets for different recipients after the release is issued by the root. We also have a modified version of the recursive doubling algorithm [10] which significantly benefits from the underlying network's multicasting capabilities.

Specialized interconnects have been extensively considered in HPC environments and indeed HPC has driven interconnect technology at times. The NetFPGA platform [17] has a significant code-base and provides the fine-grained programmability with hardware logic performance compared to the non-FPGA interconnects. We study collective operation offloading utilizing the NetFPGA platform. The NetFPGA platform is mainly used for prototyping networking devices such as switches and routers that are are broadly deployed in the core of the network. Therefore, the platform builders did not focus on optimizing the communication between the host and the NetFPGA; and it does not have features such as zero-copy, early memory registration, interrupt coalescing that are commonly provided in modern HPC interconnects. Therefore, our goal in this work is enhancing the collective operation after it is offloaded to the network.

The remainder of this paper is organized as follows: Section 2 presents background information and related work. Section 3 outlines the implementation details and architectural design. Section 4 presents the method of evaluation and performance results. Section 5 provides discussion about future work and concludes the paper.

2   Background and Related Work

The NetFPGA is an open-source network interface device and software ecosystem developed at Stanford University. Field-Programmable Gate Arrays (FPGA) are hardware devices that implement programmable logic. An FPGA consists of reconfigurable logic blocks that are programmed with a high-level description language (HDL) such as Verilog and VHDL. The NetFPGA platform has been used extensively for network experimentation [12, 18, 19, 22]. The hardware design and supporting software are open source. The NetFPGA project provides a framework consisting of an OS driver, reusable hardware modules, and designs for reference projects.

The first generation of the NetFPGA has four 1Gb/second Ethernet ports. Recently, a new version of the NetFPGA, the NetFPGA 10G [9], was released with four 10Gb/second Ethernet ports and a more capable FPGA component. Due to the increased performance requirements for operating four 10G ports at line rate, much of the infrastructure for the 1G platform must be substantially reworked. Those efforts are ongoing and making rapid progress toward providing the same functionality and stability as the previous iteration.

SDN is emerging as a powerful new paradigm in network architecture that enables fine-grained programming of the network's "forwarding plane". SDN is implemented by the burgeoning OpenFlow protocol, and indeed the development and adaption of OpenFlow drove the shift toward thinking of network hardware behavior being defined by software rather than protocols. OpenFlow enables software definition of switching hardware forwarding decisions, which can operate at the speed of the hardware. Researchers are interested in OpenFlow as it is possible to implement new approaches to networking on real hardware without suffering the overheads of software routers.

There is not much published work related to HPC employing SDN. However, it is becoming very popular in the HPC community and there are efforts incorporating SDN into the HPC. Kawai [15] provides brief discussion about HPC and SDN and claims that there is a high potential in SDN to support HPC community. [16] presents MPI_Bcast implementation using an SDN framework. Our work is distinct from this work in several respects. We provide a generic environment to implement any MPI collective operations with flexibility of reconfiguration of network in the runtime based on the selected algorithms. In contrast, they study MPI_Bcast using a single multicast scheme which does not even require SDN. While this work only focuses on software level optimizations on MPI_Bcast, we provide collective operation offload, which significantly increases the performance of any collective operation.

Collective operation offload has been studied in the past on various platforms. Out of many, CORE-Direct [1] technology by Mellanox is very popular nowadays among its industry competitors. The CORE-Direct feature was first presented by Graham et al. [11] demonstrating how task lists could be generated to implement offloaded versions of collective operations. Moreover, Kandalla et al. [14] studied non-blocking MPI_Allreduce on an InfiniBand cluster employing this collective offload mechanism. They created a task list for the non-blocking MPI_Allreduce operation by performing an offloaded version of the recursive doubling algorithm. This function employs explicit wait tasks between stages. Our work provides a modified version of recursive doubling algorithm which removes the wait operation between stages to utilize multicasting feature of underlying network [10]. One disadvantage of the CORE-Direct is that it can only support binary operations of scalar values. Offloaded reductions on vector data requires more advanced hardware support which we provide in our NetFPGA implementation.

Mamidala et al. [20] studied MPI_Barrier and MPI_Allreduce on InfiniBand cluster utilizing hardware level multicast. They also focus on the cases where there are processes reaching the collective point later than other processes on tree based schemes. Their adaptive algorithm does not have static root, and when there is a late process the preassigned root passes the token to the skew process and it becomes the new root and finally generates the release message. Our work shares similar motivation but differs from this work in various aspects. We utilize multicasting in tree-based schemes but also for recursive doubling. Further, our approach has the potential to be extended to other algorithms. Our multicasting scheme also is not static and with the help of SDN we create multicasting rules and addresses based on the collective algorithm. In addition, we do not rely on single multicast address. We generate forwarding rules and multicast addresses for each single rank that may have different roles in the overall algorithm.

3 Architecture and Implementation Details

In this section we present our experimental architecture and provide more information about supported collective operations and associated algorithms. We conclude with a detailed micro-architecture discussion about each component.

3.1 Overall Architecture

Our experimental architecture consists of the following major components: MPI processes on the host(s) communicating through NetFPGA based network interfaces, connected by an OpenFlow switch, which is controlled by an OpenFlow controller. MPI Communicators define the subset of the processes in an MPI job that participate in the collective operation. MPI_COMM_WORLD is the communicator that includes all the ranks in the MPI job.

When a new communicator is created, initialization code is also executed. The initialization code sets up the environment in the network for the offloading of collective operations associated with that communicator. When a collective operation is run on that specific communicator, the NetFPGAs, in conjunction with the OpenFlow switches, identify which algorithm will be used to perform the specific collective.

The OpenFlow controller installs a rule in the switch in order to recognize initialization requests. These requests get forwarded to the controller. An MPI process generates an initialization UDP packet and sends it to the NetFPGA. The NetFPGA updates some packet fields so that the OpenFlow switch distinguishes this packet from regular Ethernet traffic and forwards it to the controller. The controller creates custom multicasting rules and addresses after it receives the initialization request from all ranks in the communicator. The generated multicast addresses are sent to the NetFPGAs and stored for further processing of the collective algorithm. The controller installs the forwarding rules whose actions are based on the multicast address and incoming port. We call this *software defined multicasting* which is different than the static multicasting defined by a specific networking protocol.

3.2 Solution Space

Currently, our implementation supports MPI_Barrier and MPI_Allreduce operations. MPI_Barrier is a synchronization mechanism for participating processes to ensure that all processes have reached the barrier point in their execution. MPI_Allreduce combines the values of all processes by applying the reduction operation, and finally all processes receive the same result. While MPI supports many reduction operations on diverse data types, our current NetFPGA implementation is restricted to MPI_SUM, MPI_MIN and MPI_MAX over MPI_INT and MPI_DOUBLE data. The remaining discussion is limited to MPI_Allreduce of which MPI_Barrier can be considered a special case.

3.3 Micro-architecture

In this section, we provide details of the major components of our design.

3.3.1 NetFPGA Processing

The NetFPGA is the major component of our architecture. Our NetFPGA configuration for MPI leverages the existing NetFPGA code base; our MPI module resides in the *user data path* defined by the NetFPGA architecture. Figure 1 shows the block diagram of the *MPI module* in the *user data path*. The *MPI Preprocessor* submodule detects if the received packet is an MPI packet and retrieves necessary information from the MPI header. Parsed MPI header fields are *latched* in the *MPI Info Fifo* and based on these MPI header fields, the module uses the appropriate network-level state machine. Not all the components of the module are utilized for every collective operation. We integrated a pipelined version of the double precision floating point unit (FPU) [2]. We only utilize this core when the data type is MPI_DOUBLE and the operation is MPI_SUM and the collective operation is MPI_Allreduce. The MPI module itself employs two state machines: a word-level state machine and a packet-level state machine. The word-level state machine is to make changes in the packet fields or data being streamed through the NetFPGA. The packet-level state machine employs the logic of the collective algorithm and state transitions are based on the packet types it receives. For reduction based collectives such as MPI_Allreduce, we need packet buffers to store the result of the reduction operation of the previous state. When new data arrives and the state of the collective operation is in a state that requires reduction, the state machine applies the reduction operation on received data and previously stored data in the packet buffers.

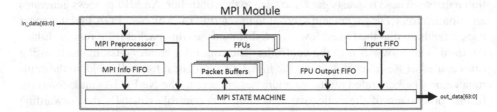

Fig. 1. Block diagram of MPI Verilog module embedded in *user data path*

3.3.2 Controller

We selected OpenDaylight [7] as our controller implementation platform. Our implementation is built on top of a learning switch module that is available with the distribution. At boot time, the controller inserts a specific rule for communicator initialization. When each rank calls MPI_Init or a new communicator is created, the communicator initialization routine generates a UDP packet with the specific port number so that the NetFPGA can distinguish it from regular Ethernet traffic. When the NetFPGA recognizes that packet type, it updates the MAC header's source field with the UDP port number and forwards it to the switch. Because of the rule installed in the boot time, the switch is configured for that address and forwards the received packet to the controller.

The controller parses the packet and extracts the information about the communicator. If it is the first packet for that communicator it creates a dictionary entry to store the information about this communicator. The controller also maps the ranks to the incoming ports. When each rank in that communicator makes the call, the controller generates the multicast addresses and forwarding rules according to the algorithm associated with this communicator.

3.3.3 Multicast Addresses

Each algorithm implicitly defines a collection of ranks, and how a specific rank communicates. For example, for the ring algorithm, rank i only sends a packet to rank $i+1$. In the case of binary tree scheme, the root rank sends packets to its children, while an internal rank sends packets to both its children and parent. A leaf rank only sends packets to its parents. For the recursive doubling pattern, a rank communicates with $\log_2 P$ number of other ranks. Therefore, based on the algorithm and rank's role, each NetFPGA needs different set of multicast addresses according to the state it is in. The controller generates those addresses for each ranks NetFPGA and installs the forwarding rules on the OpenFlow switch.

When a collective operation is offloaded to the network, the host is not involved until the final outcome is generated. Because OpenFlow switches forward based upon L2/L3 headers and all communication occurs between programmed NICs, we have the freedom to generate our own L2/L3 multicast protocol. To support multicast, we generate multicast addresses as MAC addresses.

The 48-bit MAC address is divided into two parts. The first part is the base address which is the *Comm_ID*, specific identifier of the communicator. The second part provides an encoding of neighbor ranks of a specific rank for a specific stage of an algorithm. For the ring algorithm, it is trivial since each rank only sends packet to the next rank. So, the multicasts address would be {*Comm_ID:00:00:00:01*} for each NetFPGA. For the binary tree, it is also deterministic. Only the last three bits are used and the first bit is for sending a packet to the left child, the second bit is for sending a packet to right child and the third bit is for sending a packet to the parent rank. Because there is no state in the scheme where a rank sends packets to both its children and its parent, there is no need to generate an address and rule for that behavior. Therefore, the controller generates {*Comm_ID:00:00:00:03*} address for sending packets to the children and {*Comm_ID:00:00:00:04*} for sending packets to its parent.

Unlike tree based patterns, the traditional recursive doubling algorithm does not utilize multicasting; ranks exchange messages with a single other rank during each step. However, the algorithm assumes every rank arrives at the collective point in their execution at essentially the same time. This is almost impossible as we showed in [10]. Therefore, ranks need to deal with unexpected messages if they arrive at the collective operation point later than other ranks in the communicator. To recover from that kind of situation we could apply multicasting to the recursive doubling algorithm with the support of message tagging. Indeed, message tagging is not even necessary for the collectives that do not involve any reduction operation on the data such as MPI_Allgather and MPI_Barrier. The communication pattern is equivalent to that of the release state of a binomial tree if there is a single late rank. Figure 2.a depicts the schedule of the message when each rank reaches collective point at the same time and runs a perfect

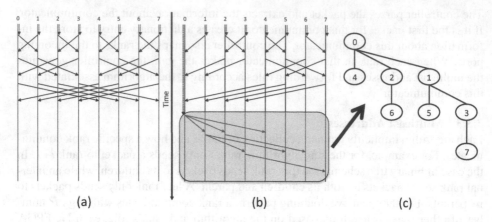

Fig. 2. Recursive doubling pattern: a. Perfect recursive doubling b. One late rank c. Corresponding binomial tree

recursive doubling. On the other hand, in Figure 2.b, rank 0 is the late process arriving at the collective after all the other ranks are finished exchanging messages between each other and Figure 2.c presents how the ranks would be dynamically organized as a binomial tree if that scenario occurs. The multicast addresses generated for this scheme requires deeper analysis, which we provide in the next section.

3.3.4   Multicast Rule Space

The number of forwarding rules installed is important because of the limited rule capacity of the OpenFlow switch. We need to determine how many forwarding rules a scheme requires. The analysis is trivial for ring algorithm where there is no actual multicasting but simple forwarding between the ranks. Each rank is connected to the next rank, so if the number of processes is P we need to install P of rules.

In the case of a *full complete* binary tree, if the depth of the tree is d, there are at most 2^d leaf ranks that need only one rule to send messages to their parents. There are at most $2^d - 2$ internal ranks which need 2 separate rules for sending message to their parents and children. The root rank only needs a rule to send a message to its children. So, the total number of rules for the *full complete* binary tree would be at most $2^d + 2 * (2^d - 2) + 1$ which is $3 * 2^d - 3$. The maximum number of nodes in a *full complete* binary tree, P, can be at most $2^{d+1} - 1$. So the total rules need to be installed on the switch would be at most $3 * \frac{P+1}{2} - 2$.

For the recursive doubling, in the traditional algorithm each rank communicates with a single rank in each stage and the total number of ranks it communicates is $\log_2 P$. Since there are P processes the total number of rules would be $P * \log_2 P$. However, with our modified algorithm each rank has the ability to send multicast messages to ranks. There are $\log_2 P$ ranks a rank can send messages to. Therefore, there are $2^{\log_2 P} - 1$ possible multicast addresses. Indeed, we do not need to create all those addresses since a rank can only send multicast message to the ranks that are consecutive in the stages of the recursive doubling algorithm. For example, if the communicator size is 8, rank 0 communicates with rank 1,2 and 4. According to our modified algorithm, a rank can only send messages to consecutive ranks. So, there is no need to have a multicast address to send multicast message to rank 1 and 4 at the same time. As explained in the previous section, the ranks that a given rank sends messages to are encoded. A bit position represents the stage and the rank to be communicated in that stage. Thus, for rank 0, bit position 0 indicates if it is sending a packet to rank 1, bit position 1 indicates if it is sending a packet to rank 2 and the bit position 2 indicates if it is sending a packet to rank 4. Since there are $log_2 P$ bit slots for an address, there are $log_2 P$ possible address if the consecutive rank size is 1, $log_2 P - 1$ if the consecutive rank size is 2, $log_2 P - 2$ if the consecutive rank size is 3 and so on. So, the total would be $\frac{log_2 P*(log_2 P+1)}{2}$. Since this is the number of addresses generated for each process, the total number of rules to be installed in the OpenFlow switch would be $P * \frac{log_2 P*(log_2 P+1)}{2}$. For an 8-process setting, these are going to be the multicast addresses for the recursive doubling algorithm: $\{Comm\_ID:00:00:00:01\}$, $\{Comm\_ID:00:00:00:02\}$, $\{Comm\_ID:00:00:00:04\}$, $\{Comm\_ID:00:00:00:03\}$, $\{Comm\_ID:00:00:00:06\}$, $\{Comm\_ID:00:00:00:07\}$.

4 Evaluation

In this section, we present performance improvements of multicasting with SDN on the recursive doubling algorithm and provide the details of the methodology of our empirical study. Then, we present latency measurements of MPI_Allreduce employing the recursive doubling algorithm focusing on various aspects of offloaded operation. We did not provide separate results for MPI_Barrier since it can be considered a special case of MPI_Allreduce with data size 0. We also do not present results for the ring and binary tree implementations since there is no multicasting benefit provided by the ring topology and static multicasting would also achieve the same benefit for the binary tree scheme. Finally, we provide estimated results for the newest generation NetFPGA-10G.

Our experimental setup consists of a Pronto-3290 OpenFlow enabled switch, 8 NetF PGAs in hosts with Intel(R) Core i5-2400 at 3.10GHz CPUs, 4GB RAM, and dual Gigabit Ethernet NICs. We also present performance results for static network topologies where the NetFPGAs were directly connected to the each other. In this paper, we present micro-benchmark results obtained running a modified version of the OSU Micro-Benchmark Suite [8] for MPI_Allreduce.

Even though we could estimate the time spent after the collective operation is offloaded to the network, in our design the NetFPGA has a feature to measure the time for the collective operation after it is offloaded. It records the time when it receives the offload request from the host. When it reaches a release state, it attaches the elapsed time to the overall collective result for that specific host. Our modification to the benchmark utilizes this feature and isolates the host's operating system overhead and the network's processing time. In addition, based on the use of generated multicast addresses, the NetFPGA keeps track of the message transfers saved for each collective operation and notifies the host process along with the collective result.

Figure 3 shows the percentage savings for number of messages generated by the ranks running the recursive doubling algorithm. When a rank sends a message with

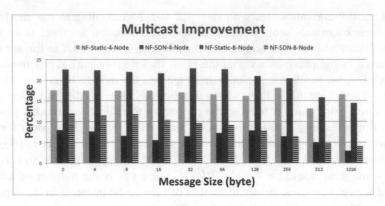

Fig. 3. Percentage savings of generated messages by all ranks compared to the traditional recursive doubling algorithm

multicast address that sends a message to 2 different ranks, we record that as a benefit of 1 message. The NetFPGA accumulates those savings and reports it to the host process. Our modified benchmark sums up all the savings of each rank and calculate final percentage saving. For the recursive doubling scheme there are $nlog_2n$ messages being exchanged between ranks if there were no multicasting. For an 8-node setting if there is a single late rank, instead of 24 messages, there are 20 messages generated and it results in 16.67% savings. There are various scenarios where the saving is even more. Increase in the communicator size would also increase the probability of multicasting. The recursive doubling scheme does not benefit from multicasting when each rank reaches the collective point at the same time and messages are received in each stage at the same epoch. In our previous work [10], we demonstrated that it is very unlikely to occur in larger settings.

The static network configuration in which the NetFPGAs connect directly to the each other provides more benefit. The point-to-point latency is less because of the absence of the OpenFlow switch processing overhead. An increase in the point-to-point latency reduces the probability of unexpected messages, which would increase the chance of

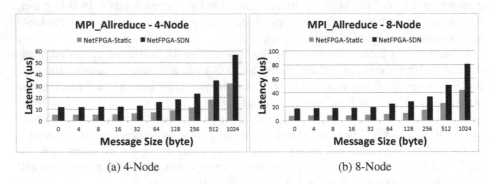

(a) 4-Node

(b) 8-Node

Fig. 4. Average MPI_Allreduce latency introduced by the NetFPGA network for recursive doubling algorithm on MPI_DOUBLE applying MPI_MIN operation

perfect recursive doubling. Because the packet processing time is a portion of the point-to-point latency, it is evident that an increase in the message size results in an increase of the probability to observe perfect recursive doubling behavior.

As we state in previous sections, we did not focus on optimizing the NIC's host interface. Therefore, the latency results presented are significantly higher than modern interconnects. Figure 4 presents results after the collective operation is offloaded to the network and Figure 5 provides results for overall latency including the host overhead for offloading the collective to the NIC. When the NetFPGAs are directly connected, it provides promising results. The newest generation NetFPGA has great potential to improve those results. When we utilize the OpenFlow switch to make our design dynamic, we pay the price of switching cost. The OpenFlow switch in our scheme seems to be the bottleneck and is not a low latency switch. The latency is more than double for short messages. When the message size increases for MPI_Allreduce the difference is reduced but is still significant.

We provide estimated results for the new generation NetFPGA-10G in Figure 6b based on the single packet processing times. Figure 6a also presents single packet processing times for various message sizes. When the size of the message increases, the

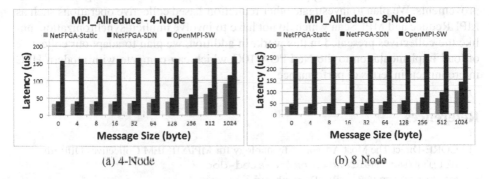

(a) 4-Node

(b) 8 Node

Fig. 5. Average MPI_Allreduce latency on host processes for recursive doubling algorithm on on MPI_DOUBLE applying MPI_MIN operation

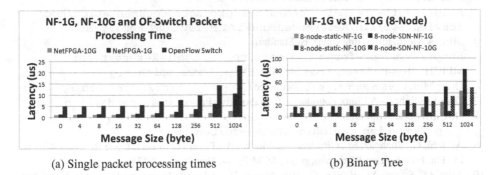

(a) Single packet processing times

(b) Binary Tree

Fig. 6. Single packet processing times for various message sizes and estimated results for NetFPGA-10G based on single packet processing times

NetFPGA-10G network provides significant performance benefits. In addition, when the message size increases, the OpenFlow switch's overhead ratio against the NetF-PGA's processing time also decreases.

5   Conclusion and Future Work

In this paper, we presented an experimental study showing how MPI collective operations can benefit from SDN using software defined multicasting in conjunction with a highly programmable NIC, the NetFPGA. When the collective operations are offloaded to the underlying network, the network has an opportunity to utilize multicasting scheme independent of the host's L2/L3 protocols. We also designed our multicasting scheme based on the collective operation algorithm. The SDN controller configures the network and creates custom forwarding rules for the offloaded collective operation in the runtime.

SDN is a new paradigm that is not widely utilized in HPC community. This is our first attempt to utilize OpenFlow switches in an HPC cluster. We believe there is great potential for further research in this area. This approach provides not only performance benefits for various parallel applications but also supports potential algorithmic improvements. We plan to investigate other reduction-based collective operations such as MPI_Reduce and MPI_Scan which do not have to involve implicit synchronization, unlike the collectives presented in this work. In addition, we plan to adapt our collective offload implementation to the NetFPGA-10G which can compete with modern HPC interconnects in terms of performance.

References

1. CORE-Direct The Most Advanced Technology for MPI/SHMEM Collectives Offloads, http://www.mellanox.com/related-docs/whitepapers/TB_CORE-Direct.pdf
2. double_fpu_verilog: Overview: OpenCores, http://opencores.org/project,double_fpu
3. Intel MPI Library Reference Manual for Linux OS, http://software.intel.com/sites/products/documentation/hpc/ics/impi/41/lin/Reference_Manual/I_MPI_ADJUST_Family.htm
4. MPI: A Message-Passing Interface Standard, http://www.mpi-forum.org/docs/mpi-2.2/mpi22-report.pdf
5. MPICH : High-Performance Portable MPI, http://www.mpich.org
6. Open MPI: Open Source High Performance Computing, http://www.open-mpi.org
7. OpenDaylight — A Linux Foundation Collaborative Project, www.opendaylight.org/
8. OSU Micro-Benchmarks 4.0, http://mvapich.cse.ohio-state.edu/benchmarks/
9. Antichi, G., Shahbaz, M., Giordano, S., Moore, A.: From 1G to 10G: Code Reuse in Action. In: The First Edition Workshop, p. 31. ACM Press, New York (2013)
10. Arap, O., Swany, M., Brown, G., Himebaugh, B.: Adaptive Recursive Doubling Algorithm for Collective Communication Operations. In: Submitted to 2014 IEEE International Conference on Cluster Computing, CLUSTER (2014)

11. Graham, R., Poole, S., Shamis, P., Bloch, G., Bloch, G., Chapman, H., Kagan, M., Shahar, A., Rabinovitz, I., Shainer, G.: ConnectX-2 InfiniBand Management Queues: First Investigation of the New Support for Network Offloaded Collective Operations. In: 2010 10th IEEE/ACM International Conference on Cluster, Cloud and Grid Computing (CCGrid), vol. 2, pp. 53–62 (2010)

12. Hanay, Y., Dwaraki, A., Wolf, T.: High-Performance Implementation of in-Network Traffic Pacing. In: 2011 IEEE 12th International Conference on High Performance Switching and Routing (HPSR), pp. 9–15 (2011)

13. Kandalla, K., Subramoni, H., Vishnu, A., Panda, D.K.: Designing Topology-aware Collective Communication Algorithms for Large Scale Infiniband Clusters: Case Studies with Scatter and Gather. In: 2010 IEEE International Symposium on Parallel & Distributed Processing, Workshops and Phd Forum (IPDPSW), pp. 1–8. IEEE (2010)

14. Kandalla, K., Yang, U., Keasler, J., Kolev, T., Moody, A., Subramoni, H., Tomko, K., Vienne, J., De Supinski, B., Panda, D.: Designing Non-blocking Allreduce with Collective Offload on InfiniBand Clusters: A Case Study with Conjugate Gradient Solvers. In: 2012 IEEE 26th International on Parallel Distributed Processing Symposium (IPDPS), pp. 1156–1167 (2012)

15. Kawai, E.: Can SDN Help HPC? In: 2012 IEEE/IPSJ 12th International Symposium on Applications and the Internet (SAINT), pp. 210–210 (July 2012)

16. Dashdavaa, K., Date, S., Yamanaka, H., Kawai, E., Watashiba, Y., Ichikawa, K., Abe, H., Shimojo, S.: Architecture of a high-speed mpi_bcast leveraging software-defined network. In: an Mey, D., et al (eds.) Euro-Par 2013 Workshops. LNCS, vol. 8374, pp. 885–894. Springer, Heidelberg (2014)

17. Lockwood, J., McKeown, N., Watson, G., Gibb, G., Hartke, P., Naous, J., Raghuraman, R., Luo, J.: NetFPGA - An Open Platform for Gigabit-rate Network Switching and Routing. In: IEEE International Conference on Microelectronic Systems Education, MSE 2007, pp. 160–161. IEEE (2007)

18. Lombardo, A., Panarello, C., Reforgiato, D., Santagati, E., Schembra, G.: A Module for Packet Hijacking in NetFPGA Platform. In: 2011 14th Euromicro Conference on Digital System Design (DSD), pp. 283–286 (2011)

19. Lombardo, A., Reforgiato, D., Schembra, G.: An Accelerated and Energy-Efficient Traffic Monitor Using the NetFPGA. In: Proceedings of the 19th ACM/SIGDA International Symposium on Field Programmable Gate Arrays, pp. 277–277. ACM (2011)

20. Mamidala, A., Liu, J., Panda, D.: Efficient Barrier and Allreduce on Infiniband Clusters Using Multicast and Adaptive Algorithms. In: 2004 IEEE International Conference on Cluster Computing, pp. 135–144 (September 2004)

21. Sack, P., Gropp, W.: Faster Topology-aware Collective Algorithms Through Non-minimal Communication. In: ACM SIGPLAN Notices, vol. 47, pp. 45–54. ACM (2012)

22. Salmon, G., Ghobadi, M., Ganjali, Y., Labrecque, M., Steffan, J.G.: NetFPGA-based Precise Traffic Generation. In: Proc. of NetFPGA Developers Workshop 2009 (2009)

MapReduce over Lustre:
Can RDMA-Based Approach Benefit? *

Md. Wasi-ur-Rahman, Xiaoyi Lu, Nusrat Sharmin Islam,
Raghunath Rajachandrasekar, and Dhabaleswar K. (DK) Panda

Department of Computer Science and Engineering,
The Ohio State University
{rahmanmd,luxi,islamn,rajachan,panda}@cse.ohio-state.edu

Abstract. Recently, MapReduce is getting deployed over many High Performance Computing (HPC) clusters. Different studies reveal that by leveraging the benefits of high-performance interconnects like InfiniBand in these clusters, faster MapReduce job execution can be obtained by using additional performance enhancing features. Although RDMA-enhanced MapReduce has been proven to provide faster solutions over Hadoop distributed file system, efficiencies over parallel file systems used in HPC clusters are yet to be discovered. In this paper, we present a complete methodology for evaluating MapReduce over Lustre file system to provide insights about the interactions of different system components in HPC clusters. Our performance evaluation shows that RDMA-enhanced MapReduce can achieve significant benefits in terms of execution time (49% in a 128-node HPC cluster) and resource utilization, compared to the default architecture. To the best of our knowledge, this is the first attempt to evaluate RDMA-enhanced MapReduce over Lustre file system on HPC clusters.

Keywords: MapReduce, RDMA, Lustre, HPC Clusters.

1   Introduction

The explosive growth of 'Big Data' has caused many industrial firms to adopt HPC technologies to meet the requirements of huge amount of data to be processed and stored. According to the IDC study [6] in 2013, 67% of HPC sites were running High-Performance Data Analysis (HPDA) workloads. Hadoop MapReduce [21] and Hadoop Distributed File System (HDFS) [16] are increasingly being used on modern HPC clusters [17,4] to process HPDA workloads.

The default Hadoop design mainly focuses on the commodity servers which are typically equipped with low-bandwidth interconnects. These clusters often have multiple large-capacity local HDDs to achieve better data-locality for MapReduce jobs. In contrast, modern HPC clusters [17,4] have quite different execution environments, where

---

* This research is supported in part by National Science Foundation grants #OCI-1148371, #CCF-1213084 and #CNS-1347189. It used the Extreme Science and Engineering Discovery Environment (XSEDE), which is supported by National Science Foundation grant number OCI-1053575.

F. Silva et al. (Eds.): Euro-Par 2014, LNCS 8632, pp. 644–655, 2014.

high-speed interconnects, like InfiniBand, 10 Gigabit Ethernet (10 GigE), and high performance but smaller capacity local disks are commonly used. In addition, a global file system, like Lustre [24], is often shared by all the compute nodes to meet the storage requirements of HPC applications. If we directly run default Hadoop on HPC clusters, it is hard to achieve optimal performance; because, recent studies [14,23,8,13,10,2,5] have shown that default Hadoop components can not leverage HPC cluster features, like Remote Direct Memory Access (RDMA) enabled high performance interconnects, high-throughput and large capacity parallel file systems, etc. efficiently. InfiniBand is the most popular RDMA-enabled high-performance interconnect in TOP500 [22], while Lustre [24] is widely deployed on modern HPC clusters.

1.1 Motivation and Related Studies

The use of Lustre, in particular, with the MapReduce architecture has attracted significant attention within the Big Data community. The evaluations in [9,2,15] argue for the use of Lustre as the back-end file system for Apache Hadoop MapReduce in HPC clusters. On the other hand, recent studies [14,13] show that by leveraging the benefits of RDMA, the overall performance of Hadoop MapReduce can be significantly improved with many additional design features. Both default and RDMA-enhanced designs of MapReduce have been well studied and evaluated with default and RDMA-enhanced HDFS designs.

Table 1. Existing Performance Studies on MapReduce Designs

	Apache HDFS	RDMA HDFS	Lustre
Apache MapReduce	[21,16]	[8]	[2,15,9]
RDMA MapReduce	[14,23,13]	[11]	N/A (this paper)

Table 1 summarizes the existing studies on different combinations of MapReduce designs with different file systems. As shown here, the benefits of RDMA-enhanced MapReduce over Lustre are not yet discovered. In this regard, an obvious question arises: *Can RDMA-based Approaches Benefit MapReduce over Lustre?*

1.2 Contributions

This paper addresses this issue by comparing our RDMA-enhanced MapReduce [14] solution with default MapReduce over Lustre. The primary contributions of this paper are as follows:

1. A demonstration of the potential of RDMA-enhanced MapReduce over Lustre deployments on leadership-class HPC systems,
2. A comprehensive methodology, to evaluate MapReduce solutions over parallel file systems provisioned on such HPC systems, and to understand the behavior of Hadoop on HPC resources, and
3. A thorough evaluation of both default and RDMA-enhanced designs of MapReduce, to give insights into the benefits of RDMA in terms of scalability, performance, and resource utilization efficiency.

In our performance evaluations, we observe 49% benefit in job execution time for the Sort benchmark with an increasing cluster size of up to 128 nodes in Cluster TACC-Stampede. On SDSC-Gordon, a 43% benefit in job execution time is observed in comparison to the default architecture, on evaluations up to 64 nodes. To the best of our knowledge, this is the first paper to show the benefits of RDMA-enhanced MapReduce over Lustre in production HPC clusters.

2   Evaluation Methodology

In this section, we discuss our evaluation methodology in detail.

2.1   Evaluation Platforms

Most of the modern HPC clusters follow a hybrid topological solution of traditional Beowulf architecture [19,20] with separate I/O service nodes. The architecture of these clusters opens the possibility of keeping lean compute nodes with lightweight operating system and limited storage capacity [3], connected to a sub-cluster of dedicated I/O nodes with enhanced parallel file systems, such as Lustre, to provide fast and scalable solutions. Figure 1(a) shows such a deployment where dedicated I/O nodes are reserved as Metadata Servers (MDS) and Object Storage Targets (OST) for Lustre, that are connected to the client compute nodes through high performance interconnects, typically InfiniBand or 10 GigE. Each of the compute nodes has small local storage as well as Lustre client to read/write data to Lustre. When a MapReduce framework is configured to run in such a cluster, TaskTrackers and Map/Reduce Tasks are launched in compute nodes. These processes use the local storage for temporary data and Lustre for persistent storage. Typically, a MapReduce application can be CPU-, I/O-, and/or network-bound as it goes through different stages involving any or a combination of these operations. Thus, we propose an evaluation methodology that considers application behavior for all system and configuration settings.

2.2   Dimensions in Methodology

To propose an evaluation methodology for such deployment, we emphasize three broad dimensions, shown in Figure 1(b).

Different HPC Clusters: Popular clusters used in the HPC community vary based on the number of system, network, and I/O resources available which brings variations in application performance behavior. Also, difference in configuration and problem size add further variability on performance for MapReduce jobs over any file system. In this paper, we choose three clusters with MapReduce over Lustre deployment. Among these, TACC-Stampede [17] is one of the largest supercomputing system based on 6,400+ Dell PowerEdge server nodes. According to TOP500 [22] list in November 2013, this cluster is listed as the 7th fastest supercomputer worldwide with a delivered performance of 5,168.1 TFlops. SDSC-Gordon [4], ranked 129th in the same list, is another large HPC cluster that we use for our evaluation. We choose these clusters to bring enough variations in our experimental setup. For example, these two clusters differ in Lustre

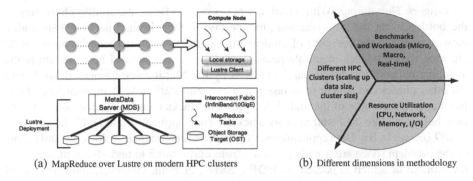

(a) MapReduce over Lustre on modern HPC clusters   (b) Different dimensions in methodology

Fig. 1. Evaluation basis and dimensions

interconnect (10 GigE in SDSC-Gordon and InfiniBand FDR in TACC-Stampede) as well as interconnect for compute nodes (InfiniBand QDR vs FDR). The third cluster we choose has InfiniBand QDR as the interconnect for both Lustre and compute nodes.

Benchmarks and Workloads: We select a set of benchmarks and workloads to facilitate variations in workload characteristics. We categorize the benchmarks into three different types: micro-benchmarks, macro-benchmarks, and real-world workloads. For micro-benchmark, we select the Sort, as this is one of the simplest and most popular MapReduce benchmarks with minimal user-defined map() and reduce() functionality. For macro-benchmarks, we select five different benchmarks from Purdue MapReduce Benchmark Suite (PUMA) [12,1] based on the benchmark characteristics. In particular, we consider the ratio of the data volume that gets shuffled to the data volume in computation and choose two shuffle-intensive (Adjacency List and Self Join) and two compute-intensive (Word Count and Inverted Index) benchmarks to introduce enough variation in our evaluation. However, we also pick Sequence Count benchmark that qualifies for both as it has both computation and shuffle over large volume of data. We also choose the Statistical Workload Injector for MapReduce (SWIM) [18] that provides real-world workload from production clusters in Facebook. This workload consists of many short-duration MapReduce jobs that run one after another in an overlapped manner to mimic the workload characteristics in the data center environment.

Resource Utilization: Resource utilization determines the ability of a framework to provide fast and scalable solutions. In this purpose, we select the following parameters.

CPU Usage: For most MapReduce applications, map() and reduce() phases consume most of the CPU cycles, as these are user-defined functions that directly operate on the data. To provide more CPU cycles to these functions, the underlying framework must keep the CPU free most of the time during its execution. Hence, it is critical to understand CPU utilization patterns for any MapReduce framework.

Memory Usage: Most of the modern HPC clusters provide large amount of memory on each machine that can be utilized during execution of MapReduce or any Big Data applications to achieve faster job execution throughput. Although default MapReduce relies heavily on both disk and memory usage, faster solutions are possible by utilizing memory space more than disk. In this perspective, this parameter is crucial.

Network Throughput: With traditional network interfaces, the shuffle phase acts as the bottleneck in the job execution pipeline due to their limited network bandwidth. However, due to the presence of modern high performance interconnects in the HPC clusters, the bottleneck in shuffle phase turns into the question of how efficiently the available network bandwidth can be utilized by the MapReduce framework so that all the other phases can benefit from faster data communication. With the profiling of this parameter, differences of the underlying protocol stacks can also be discovered which may help to realize the better network stack for such applications in HPC clusters.

I/O Usage: In Big Data applications, I/O usage is fundamental as the input and output of the problem space are usually provided from and written to underlying file systems, the storage of which is backed by HDDs, SSDs, or both. However, abundant use of disks may cause slowness in the pipeline which reduces the performance of MapReduce applications. In this perspective, I/O usage parameter is useful to visualize whether a particular MapReduce framework can observe benefits by reducing significant number of I/O operations. For any MapReduce framework, the initial read and final write phases are obligatory. Thus, only the local I/O operations during shuffle phase are those that can be reduced to have an impact in the overall job execution. In our evaluation, we measure the IOPS (I/O per second) for the local disk.

2.3   Evaluation Methods

To measure different parameters mentioned in Section 2.2, we use Linux performance monitoring tool, `sar`, provided as a part of the `sysstat` package. `sar` can be used to measure real-time data for CPU, memory, and I/O usage. We measure all of the metrics on the entire cluster to monitor all the concurrent tasks for overall performance. The sampling rate we use is two seconds. For reporting CPU usage, we use an arithmetic average over all CPUs' usage obtained from different machines in the cluster. For memory and I/O usage, similar methods are followed by measuring the parameters, free memory (kbmemfree) and transaction per second (tps), respectively. For network throughput measurement, we profile the shuffle stage to report the amount of data transfer at each point of time. We sum the total data transfer at the second granularity and average over all data transfers in the cluster. This resembles the overall data transfer capability in the shuffle phase of the corresponding framework.

3   Performance Evaluation

In this section, we discuss experimental setups and detailed performance evaluations.

Table 2 summarizes our three clusters' configurations. The Lustre deployments at OSU and TACC-Stampede are accessible through the InfiniBand interconnect, while that at SDSC-Gordon uses a 10 GigE transport. We used hadoop-0.20.2 and Java 1.7 for our experiments. As InfiniBand software stacks provide a driver for implementing the IP layer, we evaluate the default MapReduce over this layer. This is indicated as "IPoIB" (IP-over-InfiniBand) in the subsequent graphs. The "RDMA" legends in the graphs represent RDMA-enhanced MapReduce architecture [14] which uses native IB for communication. QDR and FDR are mentioned as 32Gbps and 56Gbps, respectively.

Table 2. Experimental setups used in this paper

Cluster	OSU	SDSC-Gordon	TACC-Stampede
Nodes (cores)	25 (200)	65 (1040)	129 (2064)
Processor	Intel Xeon E5640 dual quad-core (2.67 GHz)	Intel EM64T Xeon E5 dual octa-core (2.7 GHz)	Intel Sandy Bridge E5-2680 dual octa-core (2.6 GHz)
Memory	12/24 GB per node	64 GB per node	32 GB per node
Local disk	single 160 GB HDD per node	single 80 GB HDD per node	single 80 GB HDD per node
Lustre	12 TB	4 PB	14 PB
OS	Red Hat Enterprise Linux Server 6.4	CentOS 6.4 (Final)	CentOS 6.3 (Final)
Interconnect (compute nodes)	InfiniBand QDR (32Gbps)	InfiniBand QDR (32Gbps)	InfiniBand FDR (56Gbps)
Interconnect (Lustre)	InfiniBand QDR (32Gbps)	10GigE	InfiniBand FDR (56Gbps)

3.1 Tuning of Lustre Stripe Size

The total number of launched map tasks in a MapReduce job execution depends on the file system block size as each map reads one block of data. Tuning the block size can get a good trade-off point between I/O and parallel task execution. For MapReduce over Lustre, the Lustre stripe size is set to the block size to ensure that each block resides in single OST, rather than a multiple number of OSTs. We use the Sort micro-benchmark with different stripe sizes for both default architecture and RDMA-enhanced design. For these experiments, we have used a cluster size of four with a data size of 20 GB. A stripe size of 64 MB is proved to be optimum for IPoIB in Cluster OSU. However, for RDMA-enhanced design, 256 MB stripe size obtains the best performance in terms of job completion. For SDSC-Gordon, both IPoIB and RDMA have an optimum stripe size of 256 MB. In Cluster TACC-Stampede, stripe size is tuned to a value of 128 MB for IPoIB. For RDMA, performance is mostly similar across different stripe sizes starting from 64 MB to 512 MB. We pick 256 MB as the optimum stripe size for RDMA-enhanced design in TACC-Stampede. For the remaining experiments, we have used the optimum Lustre stripe size obtained from these tunings.

3.2 Comparison of Progress in Different Phases

We measure the execution progress with respect to time for map and reduce phases and compare the results in Figure 2. We show these results for Cluster TACC-Stampede and SDSC-Gordon.

Figure 2(a) shows the map execution progress for 20 GB Sort in a cluster size of four. Here, we can see that, map phase in RDMA-enhanced design finishes a little early compared to that of default architecture. This is because RDMA-based shuffle allows more CPU cycles to be available for map() execution. Also, the difference of map progress between Cluster TACC-Stampede and SDSC-Gordon occurs because of the difference in local disk write throughput between these two clusters (shown later in Figure 8(c) and Figure 8(b)). For the reduce progress shown in Figure 2(b), we see that the RDMA-enhanced approach is much faster in progress in both the clusters compared to the default architecture because of its design features. However, the difference in progress between the two clusters, TACC-Stampede and SDSC-Gordon, is primarily due to the difference in the underlying Lustre write throughput. We perform write experiments with IOzone [7] benchmark to measure throughput of Lustre file system in

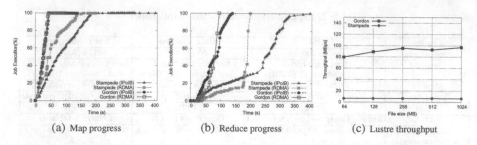

(a) Map progress   (b) Reduce progress   (c) Lustre throughput

Fig. 2. Map and reduce phase progress comparison in different clusters

both clusters. As shown in Figure 2(c), SDSC-Gordon Lustre deployment has much improved throughput (90 MBps average) compared to that (6.5 MBps average) of TACC-Stampede.

3.3   Evaluation of Micro-benchmark

In these experiments, we measure the job execution time for both architectures and compare them with varying cluster and data sizes.

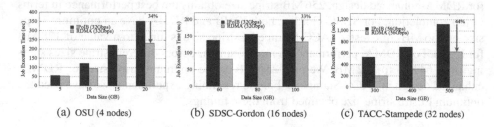

(a) OSU (4 nodes)   (b) SDSC-Gordon (16 nodes)   (c) TACC-Stampede (32 nodes)

Fig. 3. Sort benchmark evaluation with variation in data size

Figure 3 presents the Sort benchmark evaluation on different clusters based on data size variation. In Figure 3(a), we present the job execution times in Cluster OSU varying the data size from 5 GB to 20 GB. For increased data size, we observe a trend of increase in improvement for RDMA-enhanced design. For 20 GB data size, it has a performance benefit of 34% compared to IPoIB. For similar experiments in SDSC-Gordon (Figure 3(b)), we vary data size from 60 GB to 100 GB. For this experiment, the performance benefit of RDMA-enhanced approach is 33% for 100 GB Sort. In TACC-Stampede (Figure 3(c)), we vary the data size from 300 GB to 500 GB. Here, we observe a benefit of 44% for 500 GB Sort.

We also conduct experiments with simultaneous variations in both cluster and data sizes. We present these results in Figure 4. Here, in Figure 4(a), we increase cluster size from 4 to 16 with a data size increase of 20 to 80 GB for Cluster OSU. RDMA-enhanced approach observes a benefit of 49% here for cluster size 16. For similar experiments in SDSC-Gordon, we vary cluster size from 4 to 64 with data size increase of

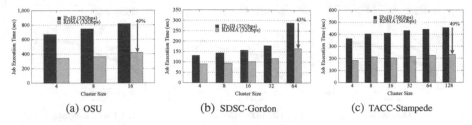

(a) OSU   (b) SDSC-Gordon   (c) TACC-Stampede

Fig. 4. Sort benchmark evaluation with variation in cluster and data size

up to 320 GB and observe a performance benefit of 43% for the largest cluster and data size. For TACC-Stampede (Figure 4(c)), we vary the cluster size up to 128 nodes with 640 GB data size and achieve a performance benefit of 49%. In all these experiments, we observe a trend of increase in performance benefit for RDMA-enhanced design as we scale up both the cluster size and the data size. For TACC-Stampede, the benefit is more compared to SDSC-Gordon because of the InfiniBand FDR interconnect.

3.4 Evaluation of Resource Utilization

In this section, we use profiling analysis to find out different system resource utilization. We use Sort benchmark to evaluate all the metrics in a cluster size of four.

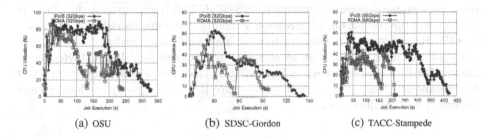

(a) OSU   (b) SDSC-Gordon   (c) TACC-Stampede

Fig. 5. Profiling CPU usage

CPU: We present the CPU usage for different clusters in Figure 5. Here, X-axis represents the job execution in seconds and Y-axis represents the average CPU usage at each point of time during job execution. We profile CPU idle% on each machine in the cluster and average across all the CPUs. As shown in Figure 5, in all the clusters, default architecture is more CPU hungry compared to RDMA-enhanced approach. The major reason behind this observation is that, RDMA-enhanced communication does not require remote end's CPU to perform data transmission. Besides, during the early stage when all maps are running, the default architecture tries to shuffle the map output data as much as possible, keeping the ReduceTasks busy and taking longer CPU cycles. However, in RDMA-enhanced design, during this phase, the ReduceTasks are shuffling only a small portion of map output data to build up the Priority Queue and thus takes

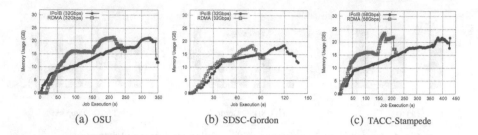

(a) OSU   (b) SDSC-Gordon   (c) TACC-Stampede

Fig. 6. Profiling memory usage

less CPU cycle. The average reductions in CPU usage for the three clusters in the order of Figure 5 are 14%, 13%, and 28%, respectively.

Memory: We observe memory usage for both the architectures and present the comparisons in Figure 6. The memory requirements during the entire job execution are similar for both architectures. However, RDMA-enhanced design utilizes free memory better compared to the default architecture. From the time of initialization, the RDMA-enhanced design capitalizes on using the available free memory space to achieve faster job completion and thus reduces the duration of memory consumption for Cluster OSU, SDSC-Gordon, and TACC-Stampede by 27%, 35%, and 57% respectively.

Network: In Figure 7, we present the comparison of shuffled data transfer during the job execution. The X-axis represents the job execution progress in seconds and the Y-axis represents the average data transfer from a single TaskTracker to all ReduceTasks at each point of time during the job execution. It clearly shows that the default architecture over IPoIB can not take advantage of network bandwidth as it transfers data during the entire job execution process with an average throughput of only 24.75 Mbytes/sec in Cluster TACC-Stampede (shown in Figure 7(c)). This also demonstrates the fact that the pipeline efficiency in the default architecture is not good enough to handle large amount of data shuffle at once.

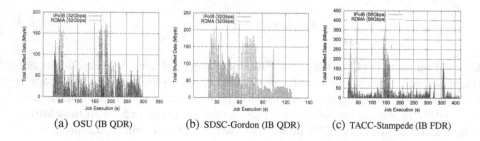

(a) OSU (IB QDR) (b) SDSC-Gordon (IB QDR) (c) TACC-Stampede (IB FDR)

Fig. 7. Profiling network throughput

However, at the early stage of the job execution, ReduceTasks in RDMA-enhanced design build the Priority Queue with the least amount of data transferred from each map location. As soon as the map phase completes, it utilizes the network more and achieves an average throughput of 77 Mbytes/sec, thus observing 211% improvement over default architecture. However, the average throughput after the map phase is as high as 197 Mbytes/sec that clearly reflects how efficiently this architecture utilizes network bandwidth as soon as it gets the opportunity. This also states the fact that, in the RDMA-enhanced design, the pipeline efficiency after the map phase is good enough to consider a high network throughput. For Cluster OSU (Figure 7(a)) and SDSC-Gordon (Figure 7(b)), the absolute values of achievable network bandwidth for both the architectures are less due to the data rate of the network cards (QDR). However, RDMA-enhanced design still observes an improvement in average network throughput of 29% in both of these clusters.

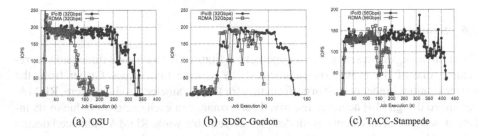

(a) OSU   (b) SDSC-Gordon   (c) TACC-Stampede

Fig. 8. Profiling I/O operations in local disk

Disk I/O: Figure 8 presents the profiling of local I/O operations. We present the I/O operations per second (IOPS) against job execution time for both the architectures. Here, we can see that, because of the in-memory merge operations, RDMA-enhanced design reduces IOPS to almost zero as soon as map phase completes. The reductions in IOPS for Clusters OSU, SDSC-Gordon, and TACC-Stampede are 59%, 43%, and 58%, respectively. The reason for difference in these values is due to the fact that the default architecture uses local file system for merge operation if the available memory space is not enough. So, depending on the local memory space and disk throughput, the IOPS value can vary in different clusters.

3.5 Evaluation of Macro-Benchmarks

For space limitation, we present macro-benchmarks performance comparisons in Cluster TACC-Stampede only. We use a cluster size of 32 for PUMA [12] benchmarks. As shown in Figure 9(a), we observe 35% improvement for Adjacency List with a data size of 30 GB. For Sequence Count, the benefit is 36% for 80 GB data size. With compute-intensive workloads, such as Word Count and Inverted Index, the total shuffled data volume is not significant [1]. Thus, we observe less benefits in job execution time. For SWIM [18], shown in Figure 9(b), we evaluate 50 short-duration jobs for which the data is generated from real-time workloads. We observe an average benefit of 16% in terms of job execution time with a cluster size of four.

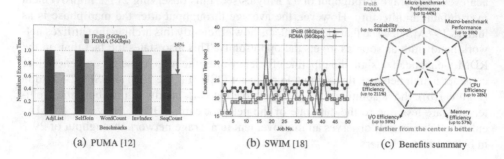

Fig. 9. Macro benchmark evaluation and summary

3.6 Summary

To summarize, we present a 7-axis hypothetical Figure 9(c) with each dimension representing one of the evaluation parameters. We assume that values farther from the center signifies higher benefit in performance for that parameter. As shown here, RDMA-enhanced design [14] achieves improved performance in each dimension due to its inherent design enhancements. Both designs are scalable while RDMA-enhanced design achieves better performance with scaling up in both cluster and data size.

4   Conclusion and Future Work

In this paper, we propose a methodology to evaluate MapReduce over Lustre file system in modern HPC clusters. Our performance evaluations based on this methodology show that RDMA-enhanced MapReduce can achieve significant performance benefits compared to the default architecture in every aspect of system and resource utilization. The centerpiece of our evaluation demonstrates that RDMA techniques help reduce the job execution time by 49% on 128 node cluster, in comparison to the default architecture. As part of the future work, we would like to explore more involved techniques that help improve the performance of MapReduce over HPC file systems such as Lustre.

References

1. Ahmad, F., Chakradhar, S.T., Raghunathan, A., Vijaykumar, T.N.: Tarazu: Optimizing MapReduce on Heterogeneous Clusters. In: ASPLOS (2012)
2. Castain, R.H., Kulkarni, O.: MapReduce and Lustre: Running Hadoop in a High Performance Computing Environment, https://intel.activeevents.com/sf13/connect/sessionDetail.ww?SESSION_ID=1141
3. Engelmann, C., Ong, H., Scott, S.L.: Middleware in modern high performance computing system architectures. In: Shi, Y., van Albada, G.D., Dongarra, J., Sloot, P.M.A. (eds.) ICCS 2007, Part II. LNCS, vol. 4488, pp. 784–791. Springer, Heidelberg (2007)
4. Gordon at San Diego Supercomputer Center, http://www.sdsc.edu/us/resources/gordon/

5. Huang, J., Ouyang, X., Jose, J., Rahman, M.W., Wang, H., Luo, M., Subramoni, H., Murthy, C., Panda, D.K.: High-Performance Design of HBase with RDMA over InfiniBand. In: IPDPS, Shanghai, China (2012)
6. International Data Corporation (IDC): New IDC Worldwide HPC End-User Study Identifies Latest Trends in High Performance Computing Usage and Spending, http://www.idc.com/getdoc.jsp?containerId=prUS24409313
7. IOzone: IOzone Filesystem Benchmark, http://www.iozone.org/
8. Islam, N.S., Rahman, M.W., Jose, J., Rajachandrasekar, R., Wang, H., Subramoni, H., Murthy, C., Panda, D.K.: High Performance RDMA-based Design of HDFS over InfiniBand. In: SC (2012)
9. Kulkarni, O.: Hadoop MapReduce over Lustre, http://www.opensfs.org/wp-content/uploads/2013/04/LUG2013_Hadoop-Lustre_OmkarKulkarni.pdf
10. Lu, X., Islam, N.S., Rahman, M.W., Jose, J., Subramoni, H., Wang, H., Panda, D.K.: High-Performance Design of Hadoop RPC with RDMA over InfiniBand. In: ICPP, France (2013)
11. OSU NBC Lab: RDMA for Apache Hadoop: High-Performance Design of Apache Hadoop over RDMA-enabled Interconnects, http://hadoop-rdma.cse.ohio-state.edu
12. Purdue MapReduce Benchmarks Suite (PUMA), http://web.ics.purdue.edu/
13. Rahman, M.W., Islam, N.S., Lu, X., Jose, J., Subramoni, H., Wang, H., Panda, D.K.: High-Performance RDMA-based Design of Hadoop MapReduce over InfiniBand. In: HPDIC, in Conjunction with IPDPS, Boston, MA (2013)
14. Rahman, M.W., Lu, X., Islam, N.S., Panda, D.K.: HOMR: A Hybrid Approach to Exploit Maximum Overlapping in MapReduce over High Performance Interconnects. In: ICS, Munich, Germany (2014)
15. Rutman, N.: Map/Reduce on Lustre, http://www.xyratex.com/sites/default/files/Xyratex_white_paper_MapReduce_1-4.pdf
16. Shvachko, K., Kuang, H., Radia, S., Chansler, R.: The Hadoop Distributed File System. In: MSST, Incline Village, Nevada (2010)
17. Stampede at TACC, http://www.tacc.utexas.edu/resources/hpc/stampede
18. Statistical Workload Injector for MapReduce, https://github.com/SWIMProjectUCB
19. Sterling, T., Lusk, E., Gropp, W.: Beowulf Cluster Computing with Linux. MIT Press, Cambridge (2003)
20. Sterling, T.L., Salmon, J., Becker, D.J., Savarese, D.F.: How to Build a Beowulf: A Guide to the Implementation and Application of PC Clusters. MIT Press, MA (1999)
21. The Apache Software Foundation: The Apache Hadoop Project, http://hadoop.apache.org/
22. Top500 Supercomputing System, http://www.top500.org
23. Wang, Y., Que, X., Yu, W., Goldenberg, D., Sehgal, D.: Hadoop Acceleration through Network Levitated Merge. In: SC, Seattle, WA (2011)
24. Xyratex: Lustre, http://wiki.lustre.org/index.php/Main_Page

Random Fields Generation on the GPU with the Spectral Turning Bands Method

Lars Hunger[1,4], Biagio Cosenza[2], Stefan Kimeswenger[1,3], and Thomas Fahringer[2]

[1] Institute for Astro- and Particle Physics, University of Innsbruck, Austria
[2] Institute of Computer Science, University of Innsbruck, Austria
[3] Instituto de Astronomía, Universidad Católica del Norte Antofagasta, Chile
[4] BrainLinks-BrainTools, University of Freiburg, Germany

Abstract. Random field (RF) generation algorithms are of paramount importance for many scientific domains, such as astrophysics, geostatistics, computer graphics and many others. Some examples are the generation of initial conditions for cosmological simulations or hydrodynamical turbulence driving. In the latter a new random field is needed every time-step. Current approaches commonly make use of 3D FFT (Fast Fourier Transform) and require the whole generated field to be stored in memory. Moreover, they are limited to regular rectilinear meshes and need an extra processing step to support non-regular meshes.

In this paper, we introduce TBARF (Turning BAnd Random Fields), a RF generation algorithm based on the turning band method that is optimized for massively parallel hardware such as GPUs. Our algorithm replaces the 3D FFT with a lower order, one-dimensional FFT followed by a projection step, and is further optimized with loop unrolling and blocking. We show that TBARF can easily generate RF on non-regular (non uniform) meshes and can afford mesh sizes bigger than the available GPU memory by using a streaming, out-of-core approach. TBARF is 2 to 5 times faster than the traditional methods when generating RFs with more than 16M cells. It can also generate RF on non-regular meshes, and has been successfully applied to two real case scenarios: planetary nebulae and cosmological simulations.

Keywords: gpu, random field, turning band, fft, astrophysics, non uniform mesh, non-regular mesh, gpgpu, spectral methods.

1 Introduction

A Random Field (RF) is a spatial distribution of correlated random values. One RF point consists of a random value, and its corresponding spatial coordinates. The correlation function describes how the values of RF points behave depending on their relative position to each other. For instance, for a correlation function with high correlation on short ranges, closeby points have very similar values. This leads to the formation of clusters of points with similar values. The size distribution of these clusters is described by the power spectrum. The correlation function and the power spectrum are two different ways to describe a RF. The power spectrum can be transformed into a corresponding correlation function and vice versa, according to requirement of the Wiener-Khinchin theorem [27].

F. Silva et al. (Eds.): Euro-Par 2014, LNCS 8632, pp. 656–667, 2014.

RF generation algorithms are of crucial importance for many scientific areas. They are used to generate initial conditions for cosmological structure formation simulations like the Millenium simulation [5], to create winds in planetary nebulae simulations (see Sec.6) and for the initialization of N-body simulations [19]. In simulations that use a turbulence driving technique like the one proposed in [8], a RF has to be generated in each time-step of the Magneto-hydrodynamical simulation. RFs are also often used in geostatistical research [24] together with a technique called Kriging for creating topological maps. In other words, RFs are used when the statistical properties of a scalar field are known and distinct realizations are to be generated.

We focus on three-dimensional (3D) RF. Traditional approaches to compute 3D RFs make extensive use of 3D Fast Fourier transforms (3D FFT). These 3D FFT-based methods are limited to regular meshes for generating random fields.

In this paper we introduce TBARF (Turning BAnd Random Fields), a new random field generation implementation based on the Turning band (TB) method that has been highly optimized to run on GPUs. The proposed algorithm replaces the 3D FFT used in a traditional approaches with a two step approach: a faster, lower dimensional FFT to generate lines (which uses a smaller set of points with respect to the traditional approach); and a multi-dimensional projection step, where all of the lines affect each mesh point of the random field. TB RF generators are not commonly used for generating large RFs since, on the CPU, they are much slower than a traditional 3D FFT approach. TB methods are slower, on the CPU, since each grid point is affected by all off the lines, while in the 3DFFT approach the field is generated in one pass. In this work we demonstrate that TB methods can be highly optimized for GPUs and allow the out-of-core generation of RF on regular and non-regular meshes.

The contribution of this paper are as follows:

- TBARF, a TB-based RF generation algorithm optimized for GPUs exploiting loop blocking and unrolling;
- Support for the fast generation of RF on irregular meshes;
- Out-of-core streaming computation of a RF which allows the generation of a very large RF, not possible with the traditional approach on the GPU;
- Practical application of TBARF to two real test cases: planetary nebulae and cosmological simulations.

2   Related Work

Random field generation. The TB method itself was first proposed in [23]. The spectral TB method was then first proposed in Mantoglou [3] where a TB method like TBARF is first described in combination with a spectral line generation algorithm. A Matlab version of the TB method can be found in Xavier et al. [4].

GPU. Graphics Processing Units (GPUs) are used not only for 3D graphics rendering but also in general-purpose computing because of their huge computational power. GPUs' programmability has significantly improved thanks to high-level parallel programming languages such as the CUDA [1] and OpenCL [2]. The

GPUs' huge potential computational power comes with some drawbacks: The available device memory is limited to few GBs (e.g. 6GB on NVIDIA Tesla K20); it requires slow host-device communications for big datasets. Moreover, optimizing code for GPUs means writing algorithms which are better suited for the hardware, but also exploring low level optimizations. Traditional compiler optimizations such as loop tiling (blocking) [16] and loop unrolling [14] have been successfully tested on GPUs [17,15]. However, the search space is quite big [21,18] and highly optimized codes still requires manual, problem-specific exploitation of the optimization space.

FFT. Our work also focuses on one- and multi-dimensional FFT methods. For small-scale FFTs, if the data can be held entirely on a GPU, the computation can benefit from the high device memory bandwidth [12,13,10,11]. However, if the data does not fit the available device memory, the overhead to transfer data between host memory (i.e. the CPU main memory) and device memory is a bottleneck [22]. This problem applies whenever the dataset is bigger than the available device memory, e.g. out-of-core computation or cluster computing [22].

3   The Turning Band Method

Correlation function and power spectrum. The (auto-)correlation function describes the correlation of two values of a RF depending on their spatial positions. The power spectrum describes the size distribution of clusters in the RF. For well behaved correlation functions these two ways of describing a RF are interchangeable. This transformation is not always possible, but TBARF is able to create a RF from both a spectral density or a correlation function. The TB method is an asymptotically correct approach of generating multidimensional RFs which we use for generating 3D RFs. The TBARF algorithm has multiple steps. First, discrete 1D RFs, i.e. lines, have to be generated. The correlation function or the power spectrum that the 1D lines have to follow is calculated by

$$C_{1D}(r) = \frac{d}{dr}[r \cdot C_{3D}(r)]$$

$$S_{1D}(\omega) = \frac{4\pi \left|\omega^2\right|}{6} \cdot S_{3D}(\omega)$$

where C_{3D} is the correlation function, S_{3D} the power spectrum of the 3D field to be generated, r the distance between points and ω the angular frequency corresponding to a structure of a certain size. To generate these lines according to a power law power spectrum, we use a simple 1D Fourier transform approach [25]. For lines with an arbitrary power spectrum we use a pulse train method [26]. Lines according to a correlation function are generated using a circulant embedding approach [6].

Number of lines and line directions. The TB method is an approximate method. The statistical quality depends on the number of lines used to create the multidimensional field. Empirical studies have shown that for a 3D field of any size 1000 lines are sufficient to avert banding artifacts [3,4]. A schematic picture of the TB method is shown in Fig. 1(right). The lines are laid out along unit vectors (u_i), starting at the origin, so that the surface of the unit sphere is covered

Algorithm 1. Turning bands method.

```
1:  S ← computeHaltonSequence()
2:  Dir ← computeLineDirection(S)
3:  L ← computeLines(Y) // requires 1D FFT
4:  for all line ∈ L do
5:      for all cell(x, y, z) ∈ domain do
6:          lineCoord ← −(x, y, z) · Dir[line]
7:          linePoint ← round(lineCoord × resolutionFactor) + lineLength × 0.5 + 1
8:          index = line.index * linelength + linepoint
9:          value = L[index]
10:         field[index] = field[index] + value
11:     end for
12: end for
```

as uniformly as possible. We create the unit vectors with the help of a pseudo-random Halton sequence, which leads to a closer to optimal coverage of the unit sphere than random vectors. After the direction vectors have been created, we rotate all vectors together by a random angle around the three major Cartesian axes. This assures that we do not produce statistical artifacts if we generate a large number of fields.

Projection step. The last step is the projection in which the 3D RF is generated (Fig. 1(right)). A point P of the 3D RF is generated by projecting its location vector X_P onto the line i and adding the corresponding value of this line $L_i(P)$ to the value of the point P. For P, this projection is then repeated for each line. After doing the projection step for each point, we have generated the full 3D RF.

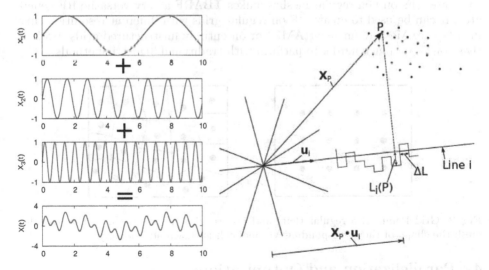

Fig. 1. In the FFT method (left), components with different frequencies (or wavevectors) are summed up according to their amplitude. This summing is done by performing the inverse FT. In The TB algorithm (right) the point positions P are projected onto the lines $X_p \cdot u_i$, and the corresponding values $L_i(P)$ are then summed over all lines.

Traditional 3D FFT method. As a comparison, we also show a traditional 3D Fourier Transform algorithm for creating a RF with a power law power spectrum and a power law index between -3 and -5. This algorithm is much less versatile than our TB algorithm. For the input data we choose the amplitude A for each 3D wavevector $\mathbf{k}$ according to the desired power spectrum. For each wavevector we also choose a random phase Φ to be able to generate different realizations of the RF. We choose the random phases of our input data so that $\Phi(\mathbf{k}) = -\Phi(\mathbf{-k})$, making sure that the result of the following inverse Fourier transformation is real. After filling the 3D array with the input data $(A \cdot \Phi)$ we only have to perform a 3D inverse Fourier transformation on the array to get our final field with the correct power spectrum. With the inverse Fourier transform, contributions with different wavevectors are summed up according to their amplitude to generate a real valued field (see Fig. 1(left)). For the power law indexes outside the range -3 to -5, this method does not work because the resulting field will show very strong generation artifacts. There are more complex 3D FFT methods that can generate RF according to arbitrary power spectra but that is beyond the scope of this paper. To compare the results of both methods, we calculate the power spectrum of the resulting field and compare it with the theoretical power spectrum we aimed to generate. Both methods generate RFs with the correct power spectrum.

Non-regular (Non-uniform) Fields. One advantage of the TB method is its ability to generate RF on non-regular meshes. The difference between regular and non-regular meshes is shown in Fig. 2. The 3D FFT methods can only generate RF on regular rectangular meshes since FFT works only on equally spaced points. In the projection step, the TB method can generate RF with arbitrary point positions. The resolution of the 1D lines has to be chosen high enough so that the smallest distance between two grid points can be sufficiently resolved. The ability to create RFs on non-regular meshes makes TBARF a very versatile RF generator. It can be used to create RF on regular grids with different resolutions like in Adaptive Mesh Refinement(AMR) or on entirely unstructured grids. Both of these tasks are much harder to perform with traditional 3D FFT methods.

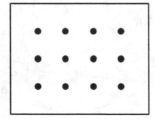 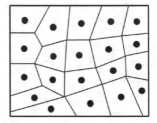

Fig. 2. Grid Points of a regular (left) and non-regular (right) mesh. In the irregular mesh the shape of the corresponding Voronoi cell is shown additionally.

4   Parallelization and Optimizations

The TB method, as described by Algorithm 1, comprises four main steps: the Halton sequence (line 1) and line direction generation (line 2), the one-dimensional field generation (line 3) , and the final projection step (lines 4-11). Step 1 and 2 are fast. Step 3 includes multiple 1D FFT calls with very small sizes, which are quite fast (cuFFT has an optimized *cufftPlanMany* function for this). Therefore, the *projection code* is the main bottleneck and is where we focus our optimization efforts. In the following section we describe how we map that algorithm, and in particular the projection phase, onto the GPU hardware.

OpenCL. We use the OpenCL [2] model and terminology: the platform model comprises of a *host* connected to one or more *devices* (e.g. a GPU). Each device consists of one or more compute units (CUs) which are further divided into processing elements (PEs). A program running on a device is called *kernel*, and represents the parallel part of an OpenCL application. A single OpenCL thread is called *work-item*. Several work-items form a *work-group*. OpenCL provides a fast *local memory* which is shared between work-items belonging to the same work-group. Similarly, OpenCL offers fast local synchronization between work-items inside the same group. Host and device exchange data through memory buffers, which are passed as arguments to the kernel before its execution.

Parallelization strategy. Algorithm 1 can be parallelized in two different ways. Following the original sequential formulation, it is possible to run a different OpenCL work-item for each line (*line parallelization*). Alternatively, it is possible to apply a loop interchange between the two for loops, therefore mapping a different OpenCL work-item to each cell, i.e. *cell parallelization*. The *line parallelization* approach has two drawbacks. First, writing cell values happens concurrently from different threads, therefore requiring an atomic addition. Unfortunately, atomic addition for double floating point precision is not included in OpenCL 1.1, but can be implemented by exploiting a 64-bit compare and exchange operation (*atom_cmpxchg*). However, atomic operations are extremely expensive on GPUs. The second drawback is the lower parallelism: while applying our approach to a real dataset, the number of lines is too low (ranging from 1024 up to 8192) to exploit GPUs' massively parallel architecture. On the other hand, cell parallelization exposes a high level of parallelism and does not require the use atomic operations. We tested the two parallelizations on a 128^3 mesh with 1024 lines of length 2600, where the cell parallelization was 50 times faster than the line parallelization.

```
1  __kernel void make_reg_field(int nr_lines,
2      int dim_x, int dim_y, int dim_z, int linelength,
3      __global double4* dir, __global double* L,
4      __global double* RF, double resfactor) {
5      const size_t dim_yz  = dim_y*dim_z;
6      int gid = get_global_id(0);
7      int k = gid / dim_yz;
8      int j = (gid % (fielddim_yz  )) / fielddim_y;
9      int i = gid - j * dim_y - k * dim_yz;
10     double4 id4 = {k, j, i, 0};
11     double rf_value = 0;
12     for(int l=0; l<nr_lines; l++) {
13         double linecoord = - dot(id4, dir[l]);
14         size_t linepoint = round(linecoord*resfactor)+linelength*0.5+1;
15         rf_value += L[l*linelength+linepoint];
16     }
17     RF[gid] = rf_value;
18 }
```

Listing 1.1. Non optimized OpenCL kernel for the cell parallelization projection kernel.

Loop blocking and unrolling. Starting from the cell parallelization, we applied two loop optimizations to the for loop in line 12 (Listing 1.1). First, we tried to apply *loop blocking* (i.e. tiling) by partitioning the loop iteration space into smaller blocks (matching the work-group size), to ensure data used in a loop stays in the fast local memory available on the GPU. This technique can be applied to the line *dir* vector (line 13) which has coalesced memory accesses. However, the *L* array (line 15) is accessed randomly and cannot be prefetched.

We also applied *loop unrolling* (i.e. unwinding) to the same loop. The goal of loop unrolling is to reduce the number of iterations and branch penalties, as well as hiding memory access latencies while reading data from the memory [14]. The latter is particularly important in our case, as the inner loop performs many random accesses to the (slower) global memory. We applied to the projection code all the combinations of loop blocking and unrolling, with group size of 64, 128, 256 and 512, and unroll factors of 1, 2, 4 and 8.

Streaming out-of-core field generation. GPU architecture has a limited amount of memory with respect to the RF size needed in some applications (already 30 GB for an 1024^3 grid). Especially while working with astrophysical datasets, RFs commonly exceed the memory available on a single GPU. This is a limitation for the standard approach based on 3D FFT [22]. Our approach only requires the lines to be stored on the GPU, and can be further distributed to work over multiple devices (e.g. on a multi-GPU or cluster of GPUs) or to perform an out-of-core streaming computation of the field in a single machine. TBARF splits the field in fragments of 128^3 cells to allow out-of-core RF generation.

Non-regular fields The TB method can also be used to generate a non-regular RF. We applied the same optimizations to a non-regular version of the projection kernel (note that other parts of the algorithm do not change), and tested different point distributions.

5   Results

Test settings We ran different versions of the TBARF code on a Intel Core i7 CPU 960 (3.20GHz 4 cores, 8 logical procs) and an NVIDIA GeForce GTX 550 (with 1280MB of OpenCL global memory). All tests were performed with double precision. OpenCL drivers were Intel OpenCL 1.2 SDK, OpenCL 1.1. CUDA and CUDA Driver API 5.5 (CC 2.0). We used the libWater CUDA extension [20] to support both CUDA and OpenCL kernels. For the FFT implementations, we used FFTW [9] on the CPU and CUFFT [11] for the CUDA version.

TBARF vs traditional approach. We compared the traditional approach based on 3D FFT with our approach running on the GPU and CPU. Figure 3 shows the performance for different grid sizes and line lengths. For all the tests, we used 1024 lines and line length scaling according to the the grid size (e.g. 512^3 cells line length is 1064). The standard approach on the CPU uses 3D FFTW and supports very big grid sizes. The erratic behavior of the FFTW approach can be explained by the different algorithms employed by the FFTW library when the number of points is not equal to a power of two. The GPU version of the same approach based on cuFFT

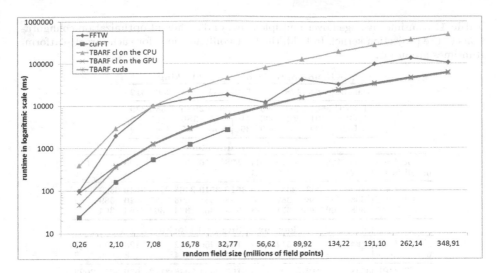

Fig. 3. Performance behavior of our out-of-core RF generation on different target architectures with varying problem sizes (i.e. the number of cells)

is faster, but it is limited by the amount of memory available on the GPU (up to 32.77 million cells for our test cases). 3D FFT methods require an extra cell per dimension (i.e. to generate a field of 256^3 elements we need a 257^3 3D FFT). We tested TBARF OpenCL on both CPU and GPU, and a CUDA version on the latter. Each TBARF code was running on its optimized configuration (see next paragraph). Despite being slower than the 3D cuFFT for small datasets, the TBARF CUDA version can quickly generate RFs bigger than the available device memory; on such datasets, it is always faster than the 3D FFTW approach. TBARF CUDA is about 4 to 6% faster than TBARF OpenCL on the NVIDIA GPU.

Projection kernel optimizations. Table 1 shows the runtimes for the projection kernel on a uniform mesh generation with 128^3 cells. The use of local memory highly improves performance of GPU kernels, in the projection kernel this optimization can only be applied to the relatively small line buffer. Unfortunately there is no simple way to apply the same optimization to the line array. Applying both loop unrolling and blocking is not always beneficial for the CPU. On the GPU, the fastest CUDA configuration uses loop unrolling (factor 4) while the fastest OpenCL configurations utilize both loop unrolling and blocking.

Non-regular fields. Finally, we tested the non-regular version of the RF generation algorithm against different mesh structures in order to understand how the point distribution affects the locality of the memory accesses. The first, named *regular*, has exactly the same distribution of the regular, uniform grid used before. The second uses a *jitter* sampling approach where each point has a regular position plus a random offset. The third is a completely *random* point distribution, where two close points in the input array may be very distant in space. Figure 4 shows that regular and jitter distribution are very similar in performance. However, the random distribution is noticeably slower than a regular one (10 to 25% slower) as it exposes poor memory accesses locality.

Table 1. Runtime, averaged over multiple runs, of 32 different optimization configurations of the projection kernel. In bold, the best configurations for each target platform. Runtimes are in ms.

	non optimized				blocking			
local size	64	128	256	512	64	128	256	512
CL CPU	3600	3594	3590	3603	2966	**2945**	3038	3329
CL GPU	391	391	396	416	387	**386**	388	392
CUDA	369	368	369	368	**363**	365	366	369

	loop unrolling											
local size	64	128	256	512	64	128	256	512	64	128	256	512
unroll factor	2	2	2	2	4	4	4	4	8	8	8	8
CL CPU	3702	3628	3634	3632	3510	3516	3510	3468	3556	3510	3523	3515
CL GPU	388	387	389	387	**386**	388	388	393	387	**386**	389	394
CUDA	368	369	369	371	**363**	364	366	364	364	364	364	364

	loop unrolling and blocking											
local size	64	128	256	512	64	128	256	512	64	128	256	512
unroll factor	2	2	2	2	4	4	4	4	8	8	8	8
CL CPU	3248	3130	3121	3121	3098	3105	3064	3048	3113	3079	3051	3023
CL GPU	388	390	400	417	**386**	388	390	403	**386**	**386**	**386**	391
CUDA	369	372	385	412	367	369	372	381	364	367	366	370

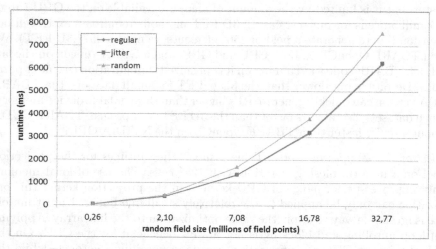

Fig. 4. Non-regular field with three different point distributions

6   Applications

Astrophysics: Planetary Nebulae. The code presented here has already been implemented to create a wind with density fluctuations in a Planetary Nebulae clump simulation. To have an inflowing wind entering on one side of the computation domain we create a RF tube of size 256 x 256 x 5000 with a power law power spectrum. The size of the tube will be larger for higher resolutions. For this problem we already use the out-of-core version of TBARF since the whole field is too large to fit into the main memory. Examples of the fields used can be found in Fig.5, for these simulations the power law index of the power spectrum is a free

Fig. 5. 2D plane slices through 3D RF used in the Planetary Nebulae simulations. Red values are positive while blue values are negative. (left) shows a field with a power spectrum $P(k) \propto k^{-3.9}$ that emphasizes larger structures while (right) shows a field with a power spectrum of $P(k) \propto k^{-2.0}$ where larger structures are less prominent.

parameter, so we show RFs for different power law indices. With the optimized out-of-core CUDA kernel it takes 28241 ms to generate a RF with 256 x 256 x 5000 points using 1024 lines with a linelength of 4350.

Astrophysics: Cosmology Simulations. In the astrophysical community moving mesh techniques for calculating hydrodynamical simulations have become more popular. The most prominent example is AREPO, the new moving mesh n-body code by Volker Springel [7]. In these codes hydrodynamic simulations are performed on a non-regular mesh.TBARFs ability to create RFs on a non-regular mesh is a clear advantage over the traditional 3D FFT methods for all simulations performed with these moving mesh codes.

TBARF is able to generate RFs that can be used as initial conditions for cosmological structure formation simulations with AREPO. A realization of such a RF following a Harrison Zeldovich spectrum is shown in Fig. 6 (left). These new moving mesh codes can also be used to perform turbulence driven simulations.

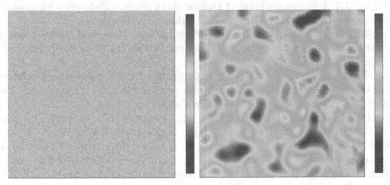

Fig. 6. Red values are positive while blue values are negative. (left) shows a 2D slice through a 3D RF with a power spectrum of $P(k) \propto k^{1.0}$ sometimes proposed as the initial fluctuations (Harrison Zeldovich Spectrum) of cosmological structure formations. (right) shows a slice through a 3D RF with a power spectrum of $P(k) \propto k^6 \cdot e^{(-k)}$ that is used for turbulence driving simulations.

These simulations are typically quite large so the ability of TBARF to create the fields out-of-core is another advantage. A RF is needed in every time-step, making the RF generation a major contributor to the computational cost of the whole simulation. Until now the runtime of TB methods prohibited them from being used in this manner. With the increased performance on the GPU, TB methods, like TBARF, are now a viable option for turbulence driven simulations on non-regular meshes. In Fig. 6 (right) we show a slice of a RF that can be used for this kind of turbulence driven simulations. With the optimized out-of-core CUDA kernel it takes 22803 ms to generate a RF with 512^3 points using 1024 lines with a linelength of 1065.

7   Conclusions

In this paper we demonstrated that TB methods can be significantly sped up by porting them onto the GPU. We present TBARF, our implementation of the turning band method. TBARF efficiently generates random fields on both regular and non-regular meshes on the GPU. We showed that TBARF is able to create random fields which are bigger than the available device GPU memory quickly, thanks to its ability to do out-of-core streaming computation. Traditional methods based on 3D FFT are limited to the available device memory and can not generate random fields on non-regular meshes. These advantages make TBARF much better suited to be used in combination with, for example, moving mesh hydrodynamic codes than traditional 3D FFT RF generators. The project source is available at https://github.com/LarsHunger/TBARF under the LGPL License.

Acknowledgment. This project was funded by the FWF Doctoral School CIM Computational Modelling under contract W 1227-N16 (DK-plus CIM) and by the Austrian Research Promotion Agency under contract 834307 (AutoCore).

References

1. NVIDIA: CUDA Compute Unified Device Architecture Reference Manual
2. Khronos OpenCL Working Group: The OpenCL Specification 1.1
3. Mantoglou, A.: Digital Simulation of Multivariate Two- and Three-Dimensional Stochastic Processes with a Spectral Turning Bands Method. Mathematical Geology 19(2), 129–149 (1987)
4. Emery, X., Lantuéjoul, C.: TBSIM: A computer program for conditional simulation of three-dimensional Gaussian random fields via the turning bands method. Computers & Geosciences 32, 1615–1628 (2006)
5. Springel, V., White, S.D.M., Jenkins, A., Frenk, C.S., Yoshida, N., Gao, L., Navarro, J., Thacker, R., Croton, D., Helly, J., Peacock, J.A., Cole, S., Thomas, P., Couchman, H., Evrard, A., Colberg, J., Pearce, F.: Simulations of the formation, evolution and clustering of galaxies and quasars. Nature 435, 629–636 (2005)
6. Dietrich, C.R., Newsam, G.N.: Fast and Exact Simulation of Stationary Gaussian Processes through Circulant Embedding of the Covariance Matrix. SIAM Journal on Scientific Computing 18(4), 1088–1107 (1997)
7. Springel, V.: E pur si muove: Galilean-invariant cosmological hydrodynamical simulations on a moving mesh. Monthly Notices of the Royal Astronomical Society 401(2), 791–851 (2010)

8. Stone, J.: Direct Numerical Simulations of Compressible Magnetohydrodynamical Turbulence Interstellar Turbulence. In: Proceedings of the 2nd Guillermo Haro Conference, p. 267. Cambridge University Press (1999)
9. Frigo, M., Johnson, S.G.: The Design and Implementation of FFTW3. Proceedings of the IEEE 93(2), 216–231 (2005)
10. Volkov, V., Kazian, B.: Fitting FFT onto G80 Architecture Report. University of California, Berkeley (2008)
11. NVIDIA: CUDA CUFFT Library, Version 2.3 (2009)
12. Govindaraju, N., Lloyd, B., Dotsenko, Y., Smith, B., Manferdelli, J.: High performance discrete fourier transforms on graphics processors. In: Proceedings of the Conference on High Performance Computing Networking, Storage and Analysis (SC), pp. 2:1–2:12 (2008)
13. Nukada, A., Matsuoka, S.: Auto-tuning 3-D FFT Library for Cuda GPUs. In: Proceedings of the Conference on High Performance Computing Networking, Storage and Analysis (SC), pp. 30:1–30:10 (2009)
14. Sarkar, V.: Optimized Unrolling of Nested Loops. International Journal of Parallel Programming 2(5), 545–581 (2001)
15. Yang, Y., Xiang, P., Kong, J., Zhou, H.: A GPGPU compiler for memory optimization and parallelism management In: Proceedings of the 2010 ACM SIGPLAN PLDI, pp. 86–97 (2010)
16. Wolfe, M.: More Iteration Space Tiling. In: Proceedings of the ACMIEEE Conference on Supercomputing, pp. 655–664 (1989)
17. Murthy, G.S., Ravishankar, M., Baskaran, M.M., Sadayappan, P.: Optimal Loop Unrolling For GPGPU Programs. In: IEEE International Symposium on Parallel & Distributed Processing (IPDPS), pp. 1–11 (2010)
18. Kofler, K., Grasso, I., Cosenza, B., Fahringer, T.: An Automatic Input-Sensitive Approach for Heterogeneous Task Partitioning. In: Proceedings of the 27th International ACM Conference on International Conference on Supercomputing, pp. 149–160 (2013)
19. Kofler, K., Steinhauser, D., Cosenza, B., Grasso, I., Schindler, S., Fahringer, T.: Kd-tree Based N-Body Simulations with Volume-Mass Heuristic on the GPU. In: Workshop on Parallel and Distributed Scientific and Engineering Computing (PDSEC)
20. Grasso, I., Pellegrini, S., Cosenza, B., Fahringer, T.: LibWater: Heterogeneous Distributed Computing Made Easy. In: Proceedings of the 27th International ACM Conference on International Conference on Supercomputing, pp. 161–172 (2013)
21. Jordan, H., Thoman, P., Durillo, J.J., Pellegrini, S., Gschwandtner, P., Fahringer, T., Moritsch, H.: A Multi-Objective Auto-Tuning Framework for Parallel Codes. In: Proceedings of the International Conference on High Performance Computing, Networking, Storage and Analysis (SC), pp. 10:1–10:12 (2012)
22. Chen, Y., Cui, X., Mei, H.: Large-scale FFT on GPU Clusters. In: Proceedings of the 24th ACM International Conference on Supercomputing (ICS), pp. 315–324 (2010)
23. Matheron, G.: The intrinsic random functions and their application. Adv. Appl. Prob. 5, 439–468 (1973)
24. Chiles, J.P., Delfiner, P.: Geostatistics: Modeling Spatial Uncertainty. John Wiley & Sons, New York (1999)
25. Kasdin, N.J., Walter, T.: Discrete Simulation of Power Law noise. In: 46th Proceedings of the 1992 IEEE Frequency Control Symposium, pp. 274–283 (1992)
26. Carrettoni, M., Cremonesi, O.: Generation of noise time series with arbitrary power spectrum. Computer Physics Communications 181(12), 1982–1985 (2010)
27. Engelberg, S.: Random signals and noise: A mathematical introduction, p. 130. CRC Press (2007)

Fast Set Intersection through Run-Time Bitmap Construction over PForDelta-Compressed Indexes

Xiaocheng Zou[1,2], Sriram Lakshminarasimhan[3], David A. Boyuka II[1,2],
Stephen Ranshous[1,2], Houjun Tang[1,2], Scott Klasky[2], and Nagiza F. Samatova[1,2,*]

[1] North Carolina State University, Raleigh, NC 27695, USA
[2] Oak Ridge National Laboratory, Oak Ridge, TN 37830, USA
[3] IBM India Research Lab, Bangalore - 560045, India
samatova@csc.ncsu.edu

Abstract. Set intersection is a fundamental operation for evaluating conjunctive queries in the context of scientific data analysis. The state-of-the-art approach in performing set intersection, compressed bitmap indexing, achieves high computational efficiency because of cheap bitwise operations; however, overall efficiency is often nullified by the HPC I/O bottleneck, because compressed bitmap indexes typically exhibit a heavy storage footprint. Conversely, the recently-presented PForDelta-compressed index has been demonstrated to be storage-lightweight, but has limited performance for set intersection. Thus, a more effective set intersection approach should be efficient in both computation and I/O.

Therefore, we propose a fast set intersection approach that couples the storage light-weight PForDelta indexing format with computationally-efficient bitmaps through a specialized on-the-fly conversion. The resultant challenge is to ensure this conversion process is fast enough to maintain the performance gains from both PForDelta and the bitmaps. To this end, we contribute two key enhancements to PForDelta, *BitRun* and *BitExp*, which improve bitmap conversion through bulk bit-setting and a more streamlined PForDelta decoding process, respectively. Our experimental results show that our integrated PForDelta-bitmap method speeds up conjunctive queries by up to 7.7x versus the state-of-the-art approach, while using indexes that require 15%-60% less storage in most cases.

1 Introduction

Set intersection is a fundamental operation for evaluating conjunctive queries in the context of scientific data analysis, as well as in other fields [1,2]. For example, consider the following conjunctive query used in detecting atmospheric rivers [3]: "water vapor > 20mm, length > 2000km and width <1000km, and spatial constraints". In order to answer this query (i.e., retrieve the common records satisfying all constraints), it is necessary to intersect multiple record sets, each of which satisfies an individual query constraint. Indexes are often used in support of such intersection operations, as they accelerate the evaluation of the individual constraints.

Compressed bitmap indexing methods are commonly used in scientific data analysis to support set intersections [4–6]. These methods successfully provide computationally-efficient set intersections by means of cheap bitwise operations. However, this efficiency

---

* Corresponding author.

F. Silva et al. (Eds.): Euro-Par 2014, LNCS 8632, pp. 668–679, 2014.

may be nullified by the I/O bottleneck common in High-Performance Computing (HPC) environments, as compressed bitmap indexes often have large storage footprints [7]. Thus, effective set intersections in an HPC context require not only efficient computation, but also low I/O overhead.

Recently, PForDelta-compressed indexes have been demonstrated as a promising alternative to compressed bitmap indexes [8, 9]. By using PForDelta compression [10–12], a dynamic data-locality-based encoding, these indexes are often able to achieve multi-fold storage reduction relative to compressed bitmap indexes. However, existing algorithms for set intersections on PForDelta-compressed indexes are not able to deliver good compute performance in the context of HPC. For example,"comparison-based" set intersection methods [13–15] usually require sorted set operands, whereas a PForDelta-compressed index over scientific data is typically value-partitioned (see Section 2.2), resulting in a partially-sorted data structure that is expensive to sort on-the-fly. Likewise, the "skipping" method [2, 16] shares this sorting requirement, and further assumes that at least one individual constraint is highly selective, a condition not always met in scientific analysis. Thus, while PForDelta indexes surmount the I/O bottleneck challenge, existing PForDelta set intersection methods conversely fall short in computational efficiency.

Therefore, we propose a new set intersection approach based on coupling the PForDelta indexing format and bitmaps through a specialized on-the-fly conversion. Our key insight is that PForDelta indexing and bitmap intersection can bring lightweight I/O and computational-efficiency benefits to the set intersection operation, respectively.

The challenge is to ensure this conversion process is fast enough to avoid diminishing the performance gains from this integrated approach. To this end, we contribute two key enhancements to PForDelta, *BitRun* and *BitExp*, that greatly improve bitmap conversion through bulk bit-setting and a more streamlined PForDelta decoding process, respectively. Our experimental results show that our integrated PForDelta-bitmap approach speeds up conjunctive queries by up to 7.7x versus the state-of-the-art pure bitmap-based method, while using 15–60% less index storage space in most cases.

2   Related Work and Background

2.1   Set Intersection

Methods for achieving efficient set intersection are a focus in several fields of research. For scientific data analysis, compressed bitmaps are the state-of-the-art approach for set intersections. Word-aligned Hybrid (WAH) [4–6], a prominent compressed-bitmap approach, achieves compression by capturing long runs of 0-bits and 1-bits with *fill words*. Each fill word begins with a "fill flag bit," followed by the fill type (0 or 1) and count. Bits not part of a run are encoded using *literal words*, denoted by a "literal flag bit," which simply contain the exact bits to encode. During set intersection, words from multiple bitmaps are "matched up" in a bitwise AND operation. Fill words enable large segments of bitmap to be processed in bulk, saving a substantial compute time. However, compressed bitmaps often exhibit heavy storage footprints [7], which is an impediment in an HPC context due to the ubiquitous I/O bottleneck.

In fields such as information retrieval and web search, "comparison-based" set intersection methods are more common [13–15]. Most research on such methods aims to reduce the asymptotic complexity and/or practical run time of set intersections over uncompressed, sorted integer lists. Another, similar technique is the "skipping" method [2, 16], which performs set intersection over PForDelta-compressed sets. By leveraging min/max element metadata in each chunk, this method is able to entirely skip some compressed chunks, reducing overall decompression cost.

While well-suited for their designed purposes, these set intersection methods do not translate well to scientific data indexing and querying. First, most are not designed to operate on compressed indexes (unlike our approach); second, they assume sorted operand sets, which is not the case for finely-partitioned value-binning indexes (explained next); third, some additional, method-specific limitations may apply (e.g., the skipping method depends on high skewness in query constraint selectivities, which does not hold for many scientific queries). Our methodology aims to overcome these barriers.

2.2   PForDelta-Compressed Indexes

PForDelta-compressed indexing is a recent approach to scientific data indexing. It is built on *value binning*, an indexing approach which groups data that have similar values into histogram bins to produce broader bin values. "Similar" may be defined several ways, such as bit-level binning [7], interval binning [6], and equality binning [6]. In this work, we elect to use bit-level binning, which partitions data according to the 16 most significant bits of their floating-point representation (equivalent to roughly 1 to 2 base-10 significant digits in scientific notation). The binning process collects the *record IDs* (or *RIDs*, integer IDs specifying datapoint locations via some linearization) of all values contained in each bin. These bins of RIDs are then compressed using PForDelta.

PForDelta compression operates on a list of integers (record IDs, in this case) in a chunk-wise manner. Within each fixed-size chunk, PForDelta computes the deltas between consecutive integers, then selects a reduced bit-width b (bits-per-element) that can encode the majority of these deltas. The remaining deltas that can not be encoded with b bits are termed *exceptions*, and are stored uncompressed alongside the bit-packed deltas. Since most delta values may typically be encoded using far fewer bits than the standard word size, a high compression ratio can be achieved, especially when some data locality is present in the original RIDs, which translates to many small deltas.

Some refinements to the base PForDelta encoding have been proposed. For example, Zhang et al. [11] use a flexible number of bits to encode exceptions, and Yan et al. [12] use the vacant b-bit-wide slots at the exception positions in the delta list to store the low bits of exception values. In this work, we leverage the version of PForDelta used in our previous work [9], as its design is targeted to achieve good compression on scientific data indexes. Specifically, we use 0 delta values to identify exception positions, instead of the explicit offset list used in other works. We also incorporate Zhang et al. [11]'s variable exception bit-width approach. These modifications form a baseline for our work; we present additional, new PForDelta enhancements in Section 3.

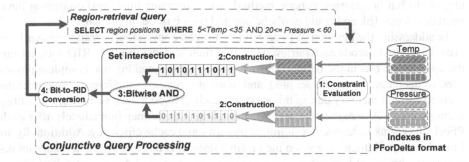

Fig. 1. Overview of our set intersection approach using PForDelta-compressed indexes fits into conjunctive query processing

3   Method

To recap, both I/O and computational efficiency barriers must be overcome to achieve fast set intersection in an HPC context. Our approach is to couple the storage-lightweight PForDelta indexing format with computationally-efficient bitmaps for set intersections via on-the-fly PForDelta-to-bitmap conversion. However, to retain the benefits of PForDelta and bitmaps, it is critical to ensure the efficiency of the conversion process.

To this end, after reviewing the flow of conjunctive query processing in Section 3.1, we present two techniques, *BitRun* (Section 3.2) and *BitExp* (Section 3.3), that enhance PForDelta to increase bitmap conversion throughput. *BitRun* uses a run-length encoding approach to speed up bitmap construction for high-data-locality scientific datasets, whereas *BitExp* tunes PForDelta to increase decoding throughput on data that show moderate locality. Additionally, in Section 3.4, we explain how to apply *BitRun* and *BitExp* simultaneously in a flexible, combined approach.

3.1   The Role of Set Intersection in Conjunctive Query Processing

Figure 1 illustrates an overall flow of conjunctive query processing, which is the context of our methods. Initially, each scientific dataset is indexed by *value binning*, which partitions the record IDs (RIDs) of data elements into a series of bins, each of which has associated value interval. Each index bins is then compressed using PForDelta, which compresses the list of RIDs in a chunk-wise manner.

When a conjunctive query arrives, each individual constraint in the conjunction is evaluated using its respective index, causing a subset of bins to be retrieved. These retrieved bins serve as the inputs to the set intersection operation, which proceeds in three steps. First, these retrieved bins for each query constraint are converted to a single bitmap (which is also an implicit union operation). Second, the bitmaps built from these constraints are then intersected via bitwise AND operations, which yield a single, final bitmap. Last, the final bitmap is transformed to a list of RIDs (using a lookup table for speed), which serves as the region result for the original query. Note that, in this work, we limit our consideration to region-retrieval queries with value constraints aligned to bin boundaries; generic methods for supporting unaligned constraint have been developed [6], and could easily be applied on top of our approach.

In addressing the key step of PForDelta-to-bitmap conversion, a straightforward approach is to first decode each retrieved bin, and then scan the resulting RID lists, setting the appropriate bits in the bitmap. However, this requires making two complete passes (first to decompress, then to set bits), and mandates retaining the intermediate uncompressed form in memory during this process, leading to poor cache efficiency and high memory usage. As a refinement, we instead set bits in the bitmap immediately after each PForDelta chunk is decoded, resulting in memory and cache efficiency. Additionally, to limit the output bitmap size when the original dataset is large (since each datapoint requires one bit in the bitmap), we perform "data partitioning" during index building to split the dataset into manageable blocks, preventing bitmaps from becoming unwieldy during query processing.

However, there is still substantial room for improvement, and thus, we devote our effort to improving the efficiency of bitmap conversion in the following subsections.

3.2   *BitRun*: Incorporating Run-length Encoding into PForDelta

A frequently observed phenomenon in scientific simulations is the data locality, in which data from contiguous time-steps or spatial regions exhibits very close value. Consequently, when the value binning is applied on the datasets, many RIDs in the indexes show a high degree of consecutiveness.

However, PForDelta is not efficient for building a bitmap from consecutive RIDs, and so a more specialized encoding within PForDelta is needed to optimize for this case. To see this, consider the example illustrated in Figure 2, which shows how PForDelta encodes a chunk of mostly-sequential RIDs. The first step of PForDelta encoding calculates the deltas between consecutive RIDs, producing a list of deltas, most of which are equal to 1. In the second step, the encoding bit-width is determined to be 1, since most deltas can be encoded in a single bit. Lastly, the deltas are bit-packed, producing the packed delta array B and the exception array E.

In the above example, suppose this encoded chunk were converted to a bitmap. This bitmap would then exhibit a few long sequences of 1-bits and 0-bits. Unfortunately, during this conversion, each 1-bit in the bitmap is set individually, because each corresponding RID is decoded separately in PForDelta. If we had a more concise encoding for long sequences of consecutive 1-bits, then these bits could be set in bulk, which is potentially more efficient.

In response to this, we develop *BitRun*, a method inspired by run-length encoding, to speed up bitmap construction by capturing the bit consecutiveness of high-locality chunks. Within such a chunk, instead of encoding the deltas as before, we encode the lengths of alternating runs of 1-bits and 0-bits in the expected bitmap. These lengths are stored in a bit-setting (S) and a bit-clearing (C) array, respectively.

To compute S and C, we could directly scan through the original chunk data, counting the number of consecutive RIDs and measuring gaps between them. However, since

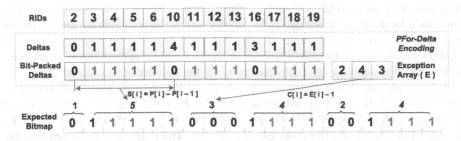

Fig. 2. An example of how PForDelta encodes a chunk of mostly-sequential RIDs, and the bitmap resulting from decoding this chunk. Note how each 1-bit in the expected output bitmap (except the first in each consecutive run) is encoded with a separate delta value. Also shown is the calculation of the S and C arrays used in our more-concise *BitRun* encoding.

PForDelta has already computed the exception (E) and exception position (P) arrays for the chunk (with length denoted by n), we can instead compute S and C as follows:

$$\text{for } i = 1, \ldots, |E|: \quad C_i = E_i - 1, \; S_i = \begin{cases} P_{i+1} - P_i & \text{if } i < |E| \\ n - P_i & \text{otherwise} \end{cases}$$

This computation only requires $|E|$ iterations, rather than n. After this, S and C serve as the encoding output for the chunk (instead of the normal PForDelta chunk output). Since this S and C computation relies on the intermediate state of PForDelta *BitRun* only replaces the last step of PForDelta (delta bit-packing), leaving the other steps identical.

The corresponding decoding algorithm for *BitRun* recovers the bitmap encoded by the S and C arrays. It works by starting at the beginning of the bitmap, then alternately skipping $C[i]$ bits followed by setting the next $S[i]$ bits to 1 for $1 \leq i \leq |E|$. The bit-setting step is accomplished using highly-efficient bitmask OR operations. Additionally, the contiguous 0-bits described by C can merely be skipped, not cleared, because the bitmap is zero-initialized at the start. Since both 0-bit and 1-bit runs are handled in bulk, this decoding process is a substantially faster alternative to standard PForDelta for chunks with $b = 1$.

3.3 *BitExp*: Expanding the PForDelta Encoding Bit-Width

In addition to *BitRun*, which is designed for high chunk data locality, we also develop *BitExp*, a complementary approach for the case when chunk data displays less locality. The key insight of *BitExp* comes from profiling each PForDelta decoding step. By doing so, we are able to improve PForDelta decoding throughput, and thus, to improve the efficiency of the bitmap construction .

We start by looking at the performance of each of the three main steps in PForDelta decoding: 1) *unpack deltas*, which expands the packed deltas to a delta array; 2) *exception patch*, which patches exceptions back to the delta array; and 3) *cumulative sum*, which recovers the original values by summing the deltas. The performance of the *cumulative sum* step is relatively stable, as the execution time of sum operation is determined only by the fixed chunk size D. In contrast, the performance of the *unpack deltas* and *exception patch* steps fluctuate. The former depends on the bit-width b, which determines the number of bitwise operations in the step, whereas the latter is affected by the number of exceptions ($|E|$), which determines the number of patch operations.

We next measure the performance sensitivity of the *unpack deltas* and *exception patch* steps as b and $|E|$ vary. We accomplish this by collecting PForDelta decoding performance on compression chunks generated with every combination of b and $|E|$ varying from 2 to 31 and from 0 to 64, respectively. The range of b is chosen because $b = 1$ is already covered by *BitRun* and PForDelta mandates $b < 32$, and the range of $|E|$ covers most realistic encoding cases. We uniformly distribute exceptions in our compression chunks.

The results are shown in Figure 3. We see that the decompression time is almost linear with $|E|$ when b is fixed, whereas the decompression time is quite stable regardless of b while fixing $|E|$. Thus, the number of exceptions plays a dominant role in determining the decoding throughput.

Given this trend, one could maximize decoding throughput by expanding b in every chunk to eliminate all exceptions; however, this would lead to a large storage increase, increasing I/O time and potentially countering any improved decoding throughput. Therefore, *BitExp* opts for another approach: rather than choosing every chunk for b-expansion, *BitExp* selects only those chunks where all exceptions can be eliminated via a small increase in b, leaving other, "harder" chunks untouched. This way, only some chunks use a larger b, balancing decreased compression ratio and increased decoding throughput. Specifically, when encoding each chunk, *BitExp* considers two options: 1) using a larger b to produce an "exceptionless chunk" (which has a larger compressed size, but is faster to decode), or 2) retaining the original b and chunk encoding. The decision is made using a threshold ratio: if the increase in compressed size by using an exceptionless chunk is below this threshold, b is expanded; otherwise, the original b is retained. This b-expansion only affects the encoding process, and does not change the PForDelta format; thus, the usual decoding process is still used, though it now benefits from improved decoding throughput.

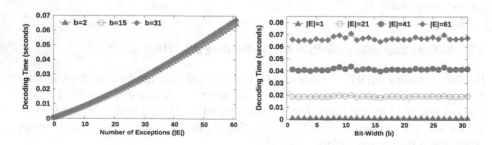

Fig. 3. PForDelta decoding time when varying $|E|$ while keeping b fixed (left), and when varying b while keeping $|E|$ fixed (right). Reported timings are for decoding 1000 PForDelta chunks. Trends seen are representative of experiments with other b and $|E|$ parameters.

3.4   BitRun-BitExp: Handling Set Intersections across Heterogeneous Datasets

Often, queries over scientific data induce set intersections across datasets with differing levels of locality. However, neither *BitRun* nor *BitExp* can effectively tackle this scenario, as they each target a specify level of data locality. Fortunately, these methods are both complementary and have compatible output forms (bitmaps). Therefore, by using *BitRun* for high-locality datasets and *BitExp* for low-locality datasets simultaneously, or even by interleaving *BitRun* and *BitExp* in a single dataset on a PForDelta-chunk basis, we can attain performance beyond what either method can provide alone. We term this approach "BitRun-BitExp (*BRBE*)."

4   Results

4.1   Experimental Setup

Computing Environment: All experiments are executed on the "Sith" cluster at Oak Ridge National Lab. Sith consists of 40 compute nodes, each equipped with four 2.3 GHz 8-core AMD Opteron processors and 64 GB of memory. All data are stored on the Lustre parallel file system using the default striping parameters.

Index Preparation: We use double-precision floating-point datasets from the S3D combustion [17] and FLASH astrophysics [18] simulations. Selected datasets have three locality categories: low, medium, and high. The category indicates the compressibility of dataset. "High" means the dataset is easy to be compressed, whereas, "low" means the dataset is hard to be compressed. All selected datasets have 2GB data size. We construct 5 indexes on each variable: our three index types (*BitRun, BitExp, BRBE*), PForDelta index, and FastBit's *WAH* compressed bitmap index. The index sizes of these datasets obtained from these 5 indexes methods are shown in Table 1. Additionally, these indexes are all binned using ALACRITY-style [8] significant-bit-based method, which roughly corresponds to binning with between 1 and 2 significant digits in base-10 scientific notation. Since FastBit does not normally support ALACRITY-style binning, in order to ensure a fair comparison, we emulate this binning strategy using a mapping technique to produce an equivalent set of bins in FastBit to match those in our methods. For *BitExp* and *BRBE*, we use an expansion threshold ratio of 1.6, as this value gives reasonable performance based on preliminary experimentation. Finally, *BRBE* is configured to use *BitRun* indexes on S3D datasets marked "medium locality" in Table 1, and *BitExp* indexes for those marked "low locality."

Conjunctive Query Processing and Queries: Our conjunctive query processing (shown in Section 3.1) is built as an extension of the ALACRITY univariate query processing engine. To clearly evaluate our method, all queries used for evaluation are region-retrieval queries, and use constraints that are aligned to index bin boundaries as value-retrieval so that candidate checks are not needed. We use a set of queries in our experiments: 5 overall selectivities ranging from 0.001% to 10% in powers of 10, using 3 or 4 query constraints. We choose these queries as the scientific queries typically have multi-variate constraints and relatively low selectivities [19].

4.2   Comparison with WAH Bitmap Indexes

We compare our PForDelta-based indexing against *WAH*-based indexing, in two respects: storage size, and query performance as both of these are important aspects of set intersection performance.

The index storage footprints shown in Table 1 demonstrate that the storage requirement for our main method. The index size of *BRBE* is substantially lower, ranging from 15% to 60%, than that of *WAH* for most datasets, except the high locality one. We believe several factors are at play here. First, fewer consecutive runs of bits occur in a *WAH* index for low locality datasets, leading to significant drops in compression due to loss of fill word encoding. In contrast, PForDelta is delta-oriented, and thus its compression degrades more gracefully in the face of slight losses in consecutiveness of RIDs. Furthermore, *BitRun* does not exhibit the same penalty as *WAH* because its run-length encoding mode is only rarely triggered in low locality datasets, minimizing any increase in index size.

Complementarily, Figure 4(a) and 4(b) show the comparison of end-to-end query processing times between a FastBit's *WAH* bitmap index and a PForDelta-compressed index using our method. As FastBit currently does not support performance breakdown, we show this by comparing the total response time, which includes CPU and I/O time.

We see that *BRBE* yields query response times that are 2.1x to 7.7x faster than *WAH* on this range of queries. We attribute this trend to *BRBE*'s relatively higher index compression ratio, which leads to less I/O than that induced by *WAH*. A "flattening-off" effect is also apparent in *WAH*'s times for lower selectivities. One possible explanation is the query optimization in *WAH* (which is also common in database management systems): when selectivity on some query constraint is very low, a sequential scan is used instead of the index (for that constraint only), thus avoiding the cost of processing a large portion of index. With *BRBE*'s smaller index, however, this strategy does not appear to be necessary.

4.3   Performance Breakdown of PForDelta-Compressed Index Approaches

We breakdown the end-to-end query processing time to gain further insight of our methods. In addition to evaluating our three methods (*BitRun*, *BitExp*, and *BRBE*), we also include methods "*RawIndex*" and "*Simple*" as comparison baselines to demonstrate the benefit of our refinements. The *RawIndex* method uses a simple, uncompressed

Table 1. Storage footprints of different indexing methods on several scientific datasets

Dataset	Data Locality	Index Size (as % of Original Data Size)				
		PForDelta	*BitRun*	*BitExp*	*BRBE*	*WAH*
FLASH_gamc	High	2.5%	2.0%	2.5%	2.0%	0.3%
FLASH_vely	Medium	4.4%	5.4%	4.4%	5.7%	6.8%
S3D_temp	Medium	5.3%	6.7%	5.9%	7.0%	8.8%
S3D_uvel	Medium	6.6%	10.6%	7.4%	11.0%	15.1%
S3D_vvel	Low	15.1%	19.2%	17.7%	21.1%	55.0%
S3D_wvel	Low	15.1%	18.9%	17.6%	20.8%	55.0%

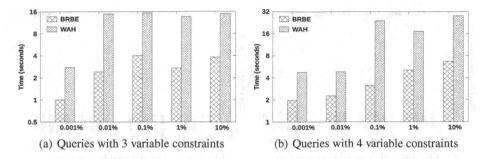

(a) Queries with 3 variable constraints   (b) Queries with 4 variable constraints

Fig. 4. Comparison of query response times between *BRBE* and *WAH*. Results for two-constraint queries are similar, but are omitted for space considerations.

inverted index, and build an uncompressed bitmap directly from this representation before performing set intersection. The *Simple* method instead stores its inverted indexes in standard PForDelta-compressed form, and fully decompresses retrieved bins before building the uncompressed bitmap in the same manner as *RawIndex*. We show results for *RawIndex* to illustrate the need for a storage-lightweight approach, and *Simple* to demonstrate the need for an efficient PForDeltato-bitmap conversion process.

The performance breakdown includes each component in the query evaluation process: "I/O," "Decode," "Bitmap Build," "Bitwise AND," and "RID Recovery." "I/O" measures the time to read the compressed or uncompressed index bins from storage. We would like to point out there is a relatively stable "I/O" performance throughout our experiments as we observe the average standard deviation and variance of "I/O" are 0.1024 and 0.0133, respectively. "Decode" indicates the time to decompress the compressed index bins (this phase is not present for *RawIndex*). "Bitmap Build" shows the time to build the uncompressed bitmap from these bins (this phase is not present for *BitRun, BitExp* or *BRBE*, as they do this in situ during the "Decode" step). Finally, "Bitwise AND" is the time to intersect the bitmaps from each constraint into the final output bitmap, and "RID Recovery" measures the last step of extracting RIDs from this result bitmap (both of these steps are shared by all five methods).

Figures 5(a) and 5(b) show the performance breakdown of each component in the query evaluation. Performance of the *RawIndex* and *Simple* approaches are predictable: *RawIndex*'s performance is dominated by long I/O times due to its lack of compression, whereas *Simple* suffers from having separate decompression and bitmap construction steps, demonstrating the need for a more efficient bitmap conversion process.

We see that *BitRun, BitExp*, and *BRBE* are consistently faster than *RawIndex* and *Simple* in almost all cases. This is because decoding time is greatly reduced for our methods, more than offsetting their slightly higher I/O cost. This decoding speedup is partly because all three of our methods employ a cache-efficient, in-place bitmap construction technique. Additionally, both *BitRun* and *BitExp* add their own optimizations to the decoding process (as described in Sections 3.3 and 3.2).

Between *BitRun* and *BitExp*, we see *BitRun* demonstrates the larger performance gain, presumably because it exploits the more "lucrative" possibility of setting runs of bits in bulk. However, *BRBE* generally performs better than when either *BitRun* or

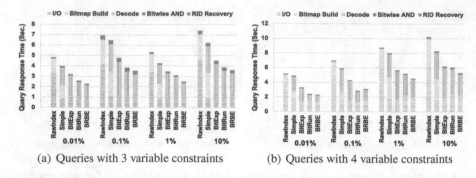

(a) Queries with 3 variable constraints   (b) Queries with 4 variable constraints

Fig. 5. Comparison of query response times among *BitRun*, *BitExp*, and *BRBE*, as well as two baseline index methods

BitExp is applied alone. This is because *BRBE* combines the benefits of both its component methods, and thus can handle a mix of higher-locality and lower-locality dataset variables, whereas *BitRun* or *BitExp* alone can only effectively handle one of these cases.

5   Conclusion and Future Work

Set intersection is a critical operation for conjunctive query processing in scientific data analysis. In this work, we present a fast set intersection approach based on coupling the storage-lightweight PForDelta indexing format with computationally-efficient bitmaps via an on-the-fly conversion process. We address the key challenge of minimizing the bitmap conversion cost through enhancements to PForDelta, which drastically improve bitmap construction time. Results indicate our method achieve speedups of between 2.1x and 7.7x versus state-of-the-art method while only requiring 15-60% less storage space.

In the future, we plan to extend this work in two directions: 1) we will evaluate the end-to-end impact of our method in real scientific applications by integrating our work in two widely used I/O middlewares: HDF5 and ADIOS; 2) we will consider parallelizing our method in the GPU environment, in which the massive number of parallel threads helps to decompress tremendous PForDelta chunks simultaneously.

Acknowledgment. We would like to thank the Leadership Computing Facilities at Argonne National Laboratory and Oak Ridge National Laboratory for the use of resources. Oak Ridge National Laboratory is managed by UT-Battelle for the LLC U.S. D.O.E. under Contract DE-AC05-00OR22725. This work was supported in part by the U.S. Department of Energy, Office of Science, Advanced Scientific Computing Research and the U.S. National Science Foundation (Expeditions in Computing and EAGER programs).

References

1. Demaine, E., López-Ortiz, A., Munro, J.: Adaptive set intersections, unions, and differences. In: Proc. Symposium on Discrete Algorithms, SODA (2000)
2. Moffat, A., Zobel, J.: Self-indexing inverted files for fast text retrieval. ACM Transactions on Information Systems (1996)
3. Byna, S., Wehner, M., Wu, K., et al.: Detecting atmospheric rivers in large climate datasets. In: Proc. Workshop on Petascal Data Analytics: Challenges and Opportunities (2011)
4. Wu, K., Otoo, E., Shoshani, A.: Compressing bitmap indexes for faster search operations. In: Proc. Scientific and Statistical Database Management, SSDM (2002)
5. Wu, K., Otoo, E., Shoshani, A.: On the performance of bitmap indices for high cardinality attributes. In: Proc. Very Large Data Bases (VLDB), vol. 30 (2004)
6. Wu, K.: FastBit: An efficient indexing technology for accelerating data-intensive science. Journal of Physics: Conference Series (2005)
7. Jenkins, J., et al.: Analytics-driven lossless data compression for rapid in-situ indexing, storing, and querying. In: Liddle, S.W., Schewe, K.-D., Tjoa, A.M., Zhou, X. (eds.) DEXA 2012, Part II. LNCS, vol. 7447, pp. 16–30. Springer, Heidelberg (2012)
8. Jenkins, J., et al.: Alacrity: Analytics-driven lossless data compression for rapid in-situ indexing, storing, and querying. In: Hameurlain, A., Küng, J., Wagner, R., Liddle, S.W., Schewe, K.-D., Zhou, X. (eds.) TLDKS X. LNCS, vol. 8220, pp. 95–114. Springer, Heidelberg (2013)
9. Lakshminarasimhan, S., Boyuka II, D., et al.: Scalable in situ scientific data encoding for analytical query processing. In: Proc. High-performance Parallel and Distributed Computing HPDC 2013 (2013)
10. Zukowski, M., Heman, S., Nes, N., Boncz, P.: Super-scalar RAM-CPU cache compression. In: Proc. International Conference on Data Engineering, ICDE (2006)
11. Zhang, J., Long, X., Suel, T.: Performance of compressed inverted list caching in search engines. In: Proc. World Wide Web, WWW (2008)
12. Yan, H., Ding, S., Suel, T.: Inverted index compression and query processing with optimized document ordering. In: Proc. World Wide Web, WWW (2009)
13. Barbay, J., López-Ortiz, A., Lu, T.: Faster adaptive set intersections for text searching. In: Álvarez, C., Serna, M. (eds.) WEA 2006. LNCS, vol. 4007, pp. 146–157. Springer, Heidelberg (2006)
14. Baeza-Yates, R.: A fast set intersection algorithm for sorted sequences. In: Sahinalp, S.C., Muthukrishnan, S.M., Dogrusoz, U. (eds.) CPM 2004. LNCS, vol. 3109, pp. 400–408. Springer, Heidelberg (2004)
15. Chatchaval, J., Boonjing, V., Chanvarasuth, P.: A skipping SvS intersection algorithm. In: Proc. International Conference on Computing, Engineering and Information, ICC (2009)
16. Jonassen, S., Bratsberg, S.E.: Efficient compressed inverted index skipping for disjunctive text-queries. In: Clough, P., Foley, C., Gurrin, C., Jones, G.J.F., Kraaij, W., Lee, H., Mudoch, V. (eds.) ECIR 2011. LNCS, vol. 6611, pp. 530–542. Springer, Heidelberg (2011)
17. Chen, J., Choudhary, A., Supinski, B., et al.: Terascale direct numerical simulations of turbulent combustion using S3D. Computational Science & Discovery (2009)
18. Fryxell, B., Olson, K., Ricker, P., et al.: FLASH: An adaptive mesh hydrodynamics code for modeling astrophysical thermonuclear flashes. The Astrophysical Journal Supplement Series (2000)
19. Sinha, R.R., Winslett, M.: Multi-resolution bitmap indexes for scientific data. ACM Transactions on Database Systems, TODS (2007)

Hybrid CPU/GPU Acceleration of Detection of 2-SNP Epistatic Interactions in GWAS

Jorge González-Domínguez[1], Bertil Schmidt[1],
Jan Christian Kässens[2], and Lars Wienbrandt[2]

[1] Parallel and Distributed Architectures Group,
Johannes Gutenberg University - Mainz, Germany
{j.gonzalez,bertil.schmidt}@uni-mainz.de
[2] Department of Computer Science,
Christian-Albrechts-University of Kiel, Kiel, Germany
{jka,lwi}@informatik.uni-kiel.de

Abstract. High-throughput genotyping technologies allow the collection of up to a few million genetic markers (such as SNPs) of an individual within a few minutes of time. Detecting epistasis, such as 2-SNP interactions, in Genome-Wide Association Studies is an important but time consuming operation since statistical computations have to be performed for each pair of measured markers. In this work we present EpistSearch, a parallelized tool that, following the log-linear model approach, uses a novel filter to determine the interactions between all SNP-pairs. Our tool is parallelized using a hybrid combination of Pthreads and CUDA in order to take advantage of CPU/GPU architectures. Experimental results with simulated and real datasets show that EpistSearch outperforms previous approaches, either using GPUs or only CPU cores. For instance, an exhaustive analysis of a real-world dataset with 500,000 SNPs and 5,000 individuals requires less than 42 minutes on a machine with 6 CPU cores and a GTX Titan GPU.

Keywords: Bioinformatics, GWAS, Epistasis, Pthreads, CUDA.

1 Introduction

High-throughput genotyping technologies allow the collection of hundreds of thousands to a few million genetic markers, such as Single Nucleotide Polymorphisms (SNPs) of an individual within a few minutes of time. In Genome-Wide Association Studies (GWAS) these genotypes are typically measured for several thousand individuals and then linked to a given phenotype of each individual, such as the presence (case) or absence (control) of an associated disease. In classical single-locus GWAS each genetic marker is then analyzed individually in order to identify markers that are significantly different for cases and controls. Unfortunately, this approach is generally not powerful enough to model complex traits for which the detection of joint genetic effects (epistasis) needs to be considered [1,2]. In 2-way statistical epistasis each pair of measured markers is therefore tested in order to discover interactions between SNP-pairs that explain the given phenotype.

F. Silva et al. (Eds.): Euro-Par 2014, LNCS 8632, pp. 680–691, 2014.

Consequently, a number of algorithms and tools have been developed to address the problem of detecting epistasis in recent years using one or several statistical tests over all SNP-pairs [3]. The main goal of these approaches is to find SNP-pairs whose joint values show a statistically significant difference compared to the individual SNP values. One of the most popular approaches uses statistical regression methods [4,5]. These tests are very precise but the pair-wise analyses are very computationally-expensive. As an example, it is necessary to apply the statistical tests to 125 billion pairs when analyzing a moderately-sized dataset consisting of half million SNPs [6,7].

Many recent approaches are filtration-based; i.e. they firstly apply a computationally faster filter and subsequently perform the full statistical analysis only to the SNP-pairs not discarded by the preliminary filter. SNPHarvester [8] uses path algorithms to identify several groups of SNPs associated to the same disease. Then, it applies the statistical method only to the pairs generated within each group. SNPRuler [9] narrows the search space through a learning approach based on predictive rule learning. BOOST [10] introduces the Kirkwood Superposition Approximation (KSA) as preliminary filter. This last tool was taken as basis for our work because it is currently widely used by biologists (see e.g. [11,12,13]). Furthermore, it is faster than previous approaches not only for CPU but also for GPU computation (GBOOST [14]).

As the development of epistasis tools has attracted extensive research interests, even more recent work that try to improve precision using different statistical methods has arisen. iLOCi [15] uses a statistical method based on the difference of the dependency of controls and cases, but our preliminary benchmarking demonstrated that it is much slower than BOOST. GWIS [16], which presents a GPU implementation of a method based on ROC-curves, could not be tested since merely a web interface is publicly available. Thus, these tools and their statistical methods are not as commonly used by biologists as BOOST and GBOOST. In this paper we present EpistSearch. In order to further improve the speed of this approach our tool introduces a novel preliminary filter and takes advantage of heterogeneous CPU/GPU architectures through inter-task hybrid parallelism to perform fast epistasis search in GWAS datasets.

The rest of the paper is organized as follows. Section 2 describes the BOOST method that is adapted by our tool. Our novel preliminary KSASA filter is presented in Section 3. Section 4 describes our hybrid parallelization approach. Runtime performance is evaluated and compared in Section 5 using both simulated and real-world datasets. Section 6 concludes the paper.

2   Background

2.1   Contingency Tables

We work with datasets of biallelic genetic markers where major alleles are denoted with capital letters and minor alleles with lowercase letters. Therefore, for each SNP there are three genotypes $\{AA,Aa,aa\}$, which are numerically represented as $\{0,1,2\}$. The number of SNPs and individuals are denoted as M

Table 1. Example of contingency table

Cases	SNP2=0	SNP2=1	SNP2=2	Controls	SNP2=0	SNP2=1	SNP2=2
SNP1=0	n_{000}	n_{010}	n_{020}	SNP1=0	n_{001}	n_{011}	n_{021}
SNP1=1	n_{100}	n_{110}	n_{120}	SNP1=1	n_{101}	n_{111}	n_{121}
SNP1=2	n_{200}	n_{210}	n_{220}	SNP1=2	n_{201}	n_{211}	n_{221}

and N, respectively. The individuals are categorized as cases (value 0) and controls (value 1). The filters that select the SNP-pairs that present interaction use a 3x3x2 contingency table per pair. As seen in the example of Table 1, each cell ijk stores the count of individuals categorized as k (case or control) with the value of the first SNP as i, and the second SNP as j. We can also fill the contingency table with probabilities: $\pi_{ijk} = n_{ijk}/N$.

2.2 Log-Linear Models and the KSA Filter

The purpose of a 2-SNP statistical epistasis tool is to identify SNP-pairs whose joint values are significantly different from the joint values expected from the individual SNP values. In [10] Wan et al. prove that the search for interaction with regression models can be simplified using log-linear models. They define interaction from the perspective of the log-linear models as the information contained in the joint distribution but not in its lower-order factorization. This definition led to measure interaction as $\hat{L}_S - \hat{L}_H$, where $\hat{L}_S$ and $\hat{L}_H$ represent the maximum log-likelihood of the saturated and the homogeneous association models, respectively. It can be calculated from the values of the contingency table as:

$$N \sum_{ijk} \left[\hat{\pi}_{ijk} \log \left(\frac{\hat{\pi}_{ijk}}{\hat{p}_{ijk}} \right) \right]$$

where $\hat{\pi}_{ijk}$ is the joint distribution obtained under the saturated model and $\hat{p}_{ijk}$ the distribution obtained under the homogeneous association model. They establish that all pairs with log-linear measure higher than certain threshold T present epistasis. Although this log-linear model is affordable, it still requires a lot of computation as $\hat{p}_{ijk}$ has to be computed through iterative methods. This is the reason why BOOST applies a simpler filter based on the Kirkwood Superposition Approximation (KSA). The authors proved the following upper bound:

$$\hat{L}_S - \hat{L}_H \leq \hat{L}_S - \hat{L}_{KSA}$$

$$\hat{L}_S - \hat{L}_{KSA} = N \sum_{ijk} \left[\hat{\pi}_{ijk} \log \left(\frac{\hat{\pi}_{ijk}}{\hat{p}_{ijk}^k} \right) \right]$$

$$\hat{p}_{ijk}^k = \frac{1}{\eta} \frac{\pi_{ij.}\pi_{i.k}\pi_{.jk}}{\pi_{i..}\pi_{.j.}\pi_{..k}}$$

$$\eta = \sum_{ijk} \frac{\pi_{ij.}\pi_{i.k}\pi_{.jk}}{\pi_{i..}\pi_{.j.}\pi_{..k}}$$

The equations above show that the KSA value can be directly calculated from the cells of the contingency table without iterative methods. Therefore, BOOST and GBOOST accelerate their analyses using the KSA filter ($\hat{L}_S - \hat{L}_{KSA}$). From now, we call the value of $\hat{L}_S - \hat{L}_{KSA}$ for a specific SNP-pair its "KSA value". As the KSA value is an upper bound of the log-linear measure, these tools calculate it for all SNP-pairs and discard those with a KSA value lower than T. Finally, they only apply the log-linear filter to the remaining pairs. For simplicity, we refer to [10] to find the proofs and further explanation of the KSA and log-linear filters.

3   KSA's Superposition Approximation (KSASA)

Although the KSA filter does not need iterative methods, a relatively large amount of numerical computations still have to be performed on each pair. Thus, we have designed a novel simpler filter called KSA Superposition Approximation (KSASA). EpistSearch applies the KSASA filter (upper bound for KSA) to all SNP-pairs, discarding all that have a value below the threshold, and only calculating the KSA and log-linear values for the other. The pseudo-code of EpistSearch is summarized in Algorithm 1.

```
foreach SNP-pair P do
    v = KSASA_Value(P)
    if v > T then
        v = KSA_Value(P)
        if v > T then
            v = LogLinear_Value(P)
            if v > T then
                | Print P in the output file as pair with epistasis
            end
        end
    end
end
```

Algorithm 1. Pseudo-code of EpistSearch

In order to prove that KSASA is an upper bound for KSA, let E and O denote the counts of expected (control) and observed (case) studies, then the total variation distance and the total spread are:

$$\delta(E, O) = \frac{1}{2} \sum_x |E_x - O_x| = \frac{1}{2} \sum_{ij} |\pi_{ij1} - \pi_{ij0}|$$

$$D_{\text{spread}}(E, O) = \sum_x (E_x - O_x)^2 = \sum_{ij} (\pi_{ij1} - \pi_{ij0})^2$$

Following a similar approach as for the design of the log-linear and KSA filters, we use the discrete Kullback-Leibler divergence as measure:

$$D_{\text{KL}}(E, O) = \sum_x E_x \log\left(\frac{E_x}{O_x}\right) = \sum_{ij} \pi_{ij1} \log\left(\frac{\pi_{ij1}}{\pi_{ij0}}\right)$$

This Kullback-Leibler divergence between the empirical distributions of the input classes is much faster to calculate than the KSA value. However, we need to prove that it is an upper bound of the KSA value in order to be used as prefilter:

$$\hat{L}_S - \hat{L}_H \leq \hat{L}_S - \hat{L}_{KSA} \leq N * D_{KL}(E, O)$$

This inequality reduces to prove that the Kullback-Leibler divergence between the maximum likelihood estimate of the joint distribution obtained from a homogeneous association model and the maximum likelihood estimate of the joint distribution obtained from the Kirkwood superposition approximation is bounded by the Kullback-Leibler divergence of the empirical distributions of the input classes:

$$\sum_{ijk} \left[\hat{\pi}_{ijk} \log \left(\frac{\hat{\pi}_{ijk}}{\hat{p}_{ijk}^k} \right) \right] \leq c \sum_{ij} \pi_{ij1} \log \left(\frac{\pi_{ij1}}{\pi_{ij0}} \right)$$

Reducing the inequality further we obtain:

$$\sum_{ijk} \frac{n_i jk}{N} \left[\log \left(\frac{n_i jk}{N} \right) + \log (\eta) - \log \left(\frac{n_{ij.} n_{i.k} n_{.jk}}{n_{i..} n_{.j.} n_{..k}} \right) \right] \leq$$
$$c \sum_{ij} \left[\frac{n_{ij1}}{n_{..1}} \log \left(\frac{n_{ij1}}{n_{..1}} \right) - \frac{n_{ij0}}{n_{..0}} \log \left(\frac{n_{ij0}}{n_{..0}} \right) \right]$$

Since it can be shown that the last inequality holds[1], $N \cdot D_{KL}(E, O)$ is a valid upper bound that can be used as our KSASA prefilter.

4   Parallelization Approach

4.1   Optimization of the Calculation of Contingency Tables

A boolean representation of genotype data is employed in BOOST in order to calculate the values of the 18 cells of the contingency tables in a fast manner. EpistSearch optimizes this approach further by reducing the number of explicitly calculated cells to only 8 (shown without "-" in the Table 2). When loading the datasets, the sums of the AA and aa biallelic values are calculated per SNP. This information is also provided to the filters and can then be used to calculate the remaining cells of the table if necessary. As the sums are only calculated once per SNP, this approach is faster than calculating the values of 10 additional cells per SNP-pair.

4.2   Inter-Task Hybrid CPU-GPU Parallelism

Although a heterogeneous CPU-GPU architecture is the common platform for GPU-based applications, the CPU usually performs tasks that are inherently sequential or have a low computational intensity. Therefore, GPU applications

---

[1] Because of the page limitation the detailed proof is omitted in this paper.

Table 2. Values of the contingency table explicitly calculated by EpistSearch

Cases	SNP2=0	SNP2=1	SNP2=2	Controls	SNP2=0	SNP2=1	SNP2=2
SNP1=0	n_{000}	-	n_{020}	SNP1=0	n_{001}	-	n_{021}
SNP1=1	-	-	-	SNP1=1	-	-	-
SNP1=2	n_{200}	-	n_{220}	SNP1=2	n_{201}	-	n_{221}

usually waste most of the computational power of CPU multicores. For instance, GBOOST [14] applies intra-task parallelism where the GPU computes the KSA filter for all pairs and the CPU computes only the log-linear filter of the pairs that were not discarded. As the percentage of pairs that pass the KSA filter is usually very low, the CPU is often idle. On the contrary, EpistSearch applies inter-task parallelism so that the CPU and GPU threads perform the whole computation but for different SNP-pairs. This hybrid parallelism has already been shown to be effective in biological sequence database search [17] and next generation sequencing read alignment [18]. Furthermore, the CPU computation is also parallelized with the POSIX Threads Programming technology (Pthreads) [19] to take advantage of CPU multicore platforms.

4.3   CUDA Implementation

We use the CUDA programming model [20] for the GPU implementation of EpistSearch. A single kernel that performs the whole analysis of a set of SNP-pairs is developed. The overall approach works as follows:

1. The whole information of the SNPs is transferred to the device memory through pinned copies at the beginning of the execution.
2. The CUDA kernel that analyzes the interaction of a subset of pairs is launched several times. In the kernel each thread creates the contingency table of a number of SNP-pairs independently and performs the necessary filters.

The execution finishes when all pairs have been processed. When assigning the GPU resources to the different parts of the code, we gave the highest priority to the KSASA filter, as it is executed for all SNP-pairs. Therefore, this filter is implemented using registers and it does not directly accesses the device memory.

The current implementation of EpistSearch can only work with datasets that fit into the device memory. The largest currently available WTCCC dataset contains about 500,000 SNPs from 5,000 individuals. This can be stored in around 600MB of memory, which is available in almost any modern GPU. For example, a Tesla K40 GPU, with 12GB of memory, would be able to analyze datasets with more than 5 million SNPs from 25,000 individuals. This should be sufficient to analyze most large-scale datasets in the near future.

Depending on the results of the KSASA filter, GPU threads that test pairs discarded by this preliminary filter would be idle while other threads are performing the KSA and Log-Linear filters. For instance, in a scenario where the probability of a SNP-pair passing the KSASA filter is 0.01, 99% of threads would finish their computation in the kernel after the KSASA filter, but they would have to wait for the remaining 1%. As mentioned in Section 4.2, GBOOST addresses this thread divergence problem by performing the calculation of the KSA and log-linear values on the CPU. Although this approach eliminates CUDA thread divergence, it significantly decreases performance if many SNP-pairs pass the first filter. An alternative solution would be the division of the computation in two different kernels: the first one for the generation of the contingency tables and the KSASA filter (performed for all SNP-pairs), and the second kernel for the KSA and log-linear filters. However, the overhead of copying the contingency tables of pairs that pass the KSASA filter between kernels would cause a significant performance overhead. Therefore, EpistSearch maintains only one kernel with all the computation but, in order to reduce thread divergence, each thread evaluates 64 SNP-pairs every time the kernel is launched.

5   Performance Evaluation

The performance of EpistSearch has been evaluated by looking for interactions between SNP-pairs in several simulated datasets and one real dataset. All the experiments have been conducted on a system with a hex-core Intel Core i7 Sandy Bridge 3.20GHz CPU with 12MB cache, and two different NVIDIA Kepler GPUs, whose specifications are shown in Table 3. The runtime of EpistSearch is compared to BOOST and GBOOST using the same dataset and threshold. Note that EpistSearch and (G)BOOST produce the same output for all the experiments. Thus, the accuracy of EpistSearch and (G)BOOST is identical, and therefore we just compare the runtime performance.

Table 3. Specifications of the two GPUs used for the experimental evaluation

Name	Number of SMs	Number of cores	Core frequency	Memory size
GTX 650Ti	4	768	980MHz	2GB
GTX Titan	14	2688	875.5MHz	6GB

Our first evaluation uses only CPU cores and 6 different simulated datasets generated with the genomeSIMLA tool [21]. All the datasets are based on the same penetrance table (epi1 model in the supplementary material of [10]), but vary in terms of the number of SNPs and individuals.

Table 4 shows the percentage of pairs that pass the KSASA and log-linear filters for each dataset explored on the CPU. The percentage for the KSA filter is not included because it is always very similar to the reported log-linear percentage. It can be seen that the KSASA filter discards much less SNP-pairs than the KSA and log-linear filters. The percentages vary from 8.88% to 25.46% (almost 3x) and from 0.0006% to 0.017% (more than 28x) in the KSASA and log-linear filters, respectively. Thus, we can assert that the evaluation is performed in very different scenarios. Figure 1 shows the execution times of BOOST and

Table 4. Percentage of pairs that pass the KSASA and log-linear filters in the CPU experiments

Num. Inds. →	800		1600		3200	
Num. SNPs →	10K	40K	10K	40K	10K	40K
KSASA	18.84	15.95	12.17	8.88	25.46	14.27
log-linear	11×10^{-4}	6×10^{-4}	27×10^{-4}	8×10^{-4}	170×10^{-4}	19×10^{-4}

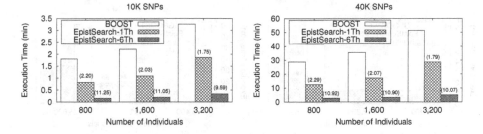

Fig. 1. Execution times of BOOST and EpistSearch (with 1 and 6 threads) in the CPU. Speedups compared to BOOST are shown in brackets.

EpistSearch when running only on the multicore CPU part of the test platform. Additionally, it shows the speedups for each EpistSearch execution (in parenthesis) compared to BOOST. As BOOST does not have support for parallelism it can only exploit one of the cores. For EpistSearch we present results using only one core and the whole hex-core processor. EpistSearch significantly outperforms BOOST even when using only one core: it is more than 2x faster for all experiments with 800 and 1600 individuals and more than 1.7x faster in any case. Moreover, the Pthreads implementation achieves a speedup of around 5x for all experiments when using the 6 cores ($\simeq 85\%$ of parallel efficiency). Therefore, EpistSearch finishes the analyses of the datasets between 9.5x and 11.3x faster than BOOST on the studied hex-core machine.

The characteristics of the datasets used for the evaluation of the GPU-based code are shown in Table 5. Due to the power of the GPUs, we use larger datasets. Furthermore, the variability of the percentage of SNP-pairs that pass each filter is even higher than in the CPU experiments: from 6.13% to 52.02% (8.5x) for the KSASA filter and from 0.0006% to 0.4% (667x) for the log-linear filter. Figures 2 and 3 compare the performance of GBOOST and EpistSearch working with the GTX 650Ti and GTX Titan GPU, respectively. Regarding EpistSearch, we provide the runtimes for GPU-only as well as for hybrid CPU/GPU execution. The results indicate the following trends:

- EpistSearch is always faster than GBOOST, either using the 6 CPU cores or not, and independently of the characteristics of the dataset and the GPU.
- In cases where a high percentage of pairs present interaction the improvement of performance achieved by EpistSearch is the most significant. For instance, in the experiment with 40K SNPs and 25,600 individuals EpistSearch is more

Table 5. Percentage of pairs that pass the KSASA and log-linear filters in the GPU experiments

Num. Inds. →	6400		12800		25600	
Num. SNPs →	40K	160K	40K	160K	40K	160K
KSASA	20.27	6.13	35.49	7.03	52.02	9.35
log-linear	110×10^{-4}	6×10^{-4}	800×10^{-4}	7×10^{-4}	4000×10^{-4}	12×10^{-4}

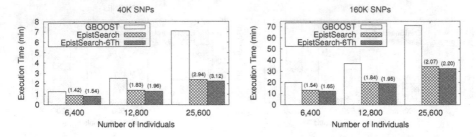

Fig. 2. Execution times of GBOOST and EpistSearch (with and without 6 additional CPU threads) on the GTX 650 Ti GPU. Speedups compared to GBOOST are shown in brackets.

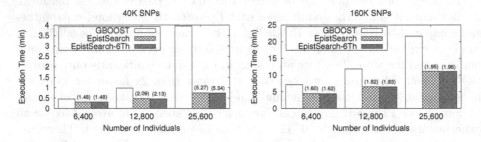

Fig. 3. Execution times of GBOOST and EpistSearch (with and without 6 additional CPU threads) on the GTX Titan GPU. Speedups compared to GBOOST are shown in brackets.

than 3x and 5x faster than GBOOST on the GTX 650 Ti and the GTX Titan GPUs, respectively.

- The speedup obtained by our tool compared to GBOOST in the other cases is always between 1.4x and 2.2x on both GPUs.
- EpistSearch runs between 2.8x and 3.2x faster on the GTX Titan than on the GTX 650 Ti GPU, while the improvement of GBOOST is only between 1.7x and 3.0x. It means that EpistSearch shows better scalability on larger number of SMs.
- The hybrid GPU/CPU combination consistently improves performance compared to the GPU-only execution. However, the improvement is relatively small (around 1.1x faster for the GTX 650 Ti GPU and 1.03x faster for the

GTX Titan GPUs) since the speedups of the GPU compared to the CPU are relatively high (40x for GTX 650 Ti and 122x for GTX Titan).

Finally, we have also applied EpistSearch and GBOOST to analyze a real-world dataset obtained from the WTCCC project. This datasets contains valuable information with cases of seven common human diseases: bipolar disorder, coronary artery disease, "Crohn disease", hypertension, rheumatoid arthritis, type 1 diabetes and type 2 diabetes. The project provides information about 3,000 shared controls and 2,000 cases per disease. Table 6 compares the runtime of EpistSearch, GBOOST and other two GPU-based tools (EpiGPU [22] and SHEsisEPI [23]) when analyzing the bipolar disorder disease (500,000 SNPs and 5,000 individuals) on different GPUs. Some results are obtained from the publications of the corresponding authors. Besides the execution time, we also show performance in terms of millions of evaluated SNP-pairs per second. Again, EpistSearch is faster than GBOOST on all GPUs. Although results for EpiGPU and SHEsisEPI must be treated carefully since the comparison is done over different architectures, we can infer that they are significantly slower than EpistSearch (as mentioned in Section 1, even slower than GBOOST).

Table 6. Performance comparison of different tools when looking for epistasis in a dataset with 500,000 SNPs and 5,000 samples. Results obtained from the publications of the corresponding authors are marked with (*).

Tool	Architecture	Time	Speed (10^6 tests per second)
EpistSearch	GTX Titan + 6 Intel Core i7	42 m	49.81
EpistSearch	GTX Titan	43 m	49.04
GBOOST	GTX Titan	1 h 01 m	34.23
EpistSearch	GTX 650Ti + 6 Intel Core i7	1 h 48 m	19.29
EpistSearch	GTX 650Ti	1 h 57 m	17.81
GBOOST	GTX 650Ti	2 h 41 m	12.97
GBOOST*	GTX 285	2 h 43 m	12.81
EpiGPU*	GTX 580	2 h 55 m	11.90
SHEsisEPI*	GTX 285	27 h	1.29

6   Conclusions

We have presented EpistSearch, a tool to search for epistasis between SNP-pairs in a fast manner taking advantage of CPU and GPU parallelism. The results produced by this tool can help to find genetic expressions for multiple common human diseases. Similar to BOOST and its GPU variant (GBOOST), which are currently two of the fastest and most popular available tools, EpistSearch is based on a definition of interaction via logistic regression models. Although our tool outputs the same list of pairs with epistasis than BOOST for all the experiments included in this paper (thus, providing the same accuracy), EpistSearch has been optimized by calculating less elements of the contingency tables and by applying a novel preliminary filter. Therefore, EpistSearch uses a three-stage approach where only the simplest (but less precise) filter is applied to all the SNP-pairs.

The most precise and most computationally expensive filters are only applied to the pairs that were not discarded by the preliminary test. In addition, an inter-task hybrid CPU-GPU parallelism has been implemented using Pthreads and CUDA in order to concurrently work on both multicore CPUs and GPUs.

We have also compared the performance of EpistSearch to BOOST and GBOOST on a hex-core modern machine with two available GPUs using simulated and real datasets. This experimental evaluation shows that EpistSearch is consistently faster in all the experiments, even though the characteristics of the input datasets are very different. For CPU computation, our tool obtains a speedup higher than 2x compared to BOOST using the same resources (only one CPU core) and it is able to accelerate the computation up to 11.3x by exploiting the 6 cores of the machine. Moreover, depending on the characteristics of the dataset of SNPs, EpistSearch obtains a speedup of more than 3x and 5x on a GTX 650 Ti and a GTX Titan GPU, respectively.

As future work, we will extend EpistSearch so it can work with a larger number of SNPs, even if they do not fit in the GPU memory. Furthermore, we will develop a multiGPU version.

References

1. Maher, B.: Personal Genomes: the Case of the Missing Heritability. Nature 456(7218), 18–21 (2008)
2. Moore, J.H., Asselbergs, F.W., Williams, S.M.: Bioinformatics Challenges for Genome-Wide Association Studies. Bioinformatics 26(4), 445–455 (2010)
3. Cordell, H.J.: Detecting Gene-Gene Interactions that Underlie Human Diseases. Nature Reviews Genetics 10(6), 392–404 (2009)
4. Zhao, J., Jin, L.: Test for Interaction Between Two Unlinked Loci. The American Journal of Human Genetics 78(1), 15–27 (2006)
5. Purcell, S., et al.: PLINK: a Tool Set for Whole-Genome Association and Population-Based Linkage Anlyses. The American Journal of Human Genetics 81(3), 559–575 (2007)
6. Wellcome Trust Case Control Consortium, http://www.wtccc.org.uk/ (last visit: January 2014)
7. Wellcome Trust Case Control Consortium: Genome-Wide Association Study of 14,000 Cases of Seven Common Diseases and 3,000 Shared Controls. Nature 447(7145), 661–678 (2007)
8. Yang, C., He, Z., Wan, X., Yang, Q., Xue, H., Yu, W.: SNPHarvester: a Filtering-Based Approach for Detecting Epistatic Interaction in Genome-Wide Association Studies. Bioinformatics 25(4), 504–511 (2009)
9. Wan, X., Yang, C., Yang, Q., Xue, H., Tang, N.L., Yu, W.: Predictive Rule Inference for epistatic Interaction Detection in Genome-Wide Association Studies. Bioinformatics 26(1), 30–37 (2010)
10. Wan, X., Yang, C., Yang, Q., Xue, H., Tang, N.L., Yu, W.: BOOST: A Fast Approach to Detecting Gene-Gene Interactions in Genome-Wide Case-Control Studies. The American Journal of Human Genetics 87(3), 325–340 (2010)
11. Bi, J., Gelernter, J., Sun, J., Kranzler, H.R.: Comparing the Utility of Homogeneous Subtypes of Cocaine Use and Related Behaviors with DSM-IV Cocaine Dependence as Traits for Genetic Association Analysis. American Journal of Medical Genetics 165(2), 148–156 (2014)

12. Chu, M., et al.: A Genome-Wide Gene-Gene Interaction Analysis Identifies an Epistatic Gene Pair for Lung Cancer Susceptibility in Han Chinese. Cancinogenesis 32(3), 572–577 (2014)
13. Milne, R.L., et al.: A Large-Scale Assessment of Two-Way SNP Interactions in Breast Cancer Susceptibility Using 46,450 Cases and 42,461 Controls from the Breast Cancer Association Consortium. Human Molecular Genetics 23(7), 1934–1946 (2014)
14. Yung, L.S., Yang, C., Wan, X., Yu, W.: GBOOST: A GPU-Based Tool for Detecting Gene-Gene Interactions in Genome-Wide Case Control Studies. Bioinformatics 27(9), 1309–1310 (2011)
15. Piriyapongsa, J., Ngamphiw, C., Intarapanich, A., Kulawonganunchai, S., Assawamakin, A., Bootchai, C., Shaw, P.J., Tongsima, S.: iLOCi: a SNP Interaction Priorization Technique for Detecting Epistasis in Genome-Wide Association Studies. BMC Genomics 13(suppl. 7) (2012)
16. Goudey, B., Rawlinson, D., Wang, Q., Shi, F., Ferra, H., Campbell, R.M., Stern, L., Inouye, M.T., Ong, C.S., Kowalczyk, A.: GWIS - Model-Free, Fast and Exhaustive Search for Epistatic Interactions in Case-Control GWAS. BMC Genomics 14(suppl. 3) (2012)
17. Liu, Y., Wirawan, A., Schmidt, B.: CUDASW++ 3.0: Accelerating Smith-Waterman Protein Database Search by Coupling CPU and GPU SIMD Instructions. BMC Bioinformatics 14(177) (2013)
18. Liu, Y., Schmidt, B.: CUSHAW2-GPU: Empowering Faster Gapped Short-Read Alignment Using GPU Computing. IEEE Design & Test of Computers (in press)
19. POSIX Threads Programming, https://computing.llnl.gov/tutorials/pthreads/ (last visit: January 2014)
20. NVIDIA Developer CUDA Zone, https://developer.nvidia.com/category/zone/cuda-zone (last visit: January 2014)
21. genomeSIMLA Webpage, http://chgr.mc.vanderbilt.edu/genomeSIMLA/genomeSIMLA/Introduction.html (last visit: January 2014)
22. Hemani, G., Theocharidis, A., Wei, W., Haley, C.: EpiGPU: Exhaustive Pairwise Epistasis Scans Parallelized on Customer Level Graphic Cards. Bioinformatics 27(11), 1462–1465 (2011)
23. Hu, X., Liu, Q., Zhang, Z., Li, Z., Wang, S., He, L., Shi, Y.: SHEsisEpi, a GPU-Enhanced Genome-Wide SNP-SNP Interaction Scanning Algorithm, Efficiently Reveals the Risk Genetic Epistasis in Bipolar Disorder. Cell Research 20(7), 854–857 (2010)

IFM: A Scalable High Resolution Flood Modeling Framework

Swati Singhal[1], Sandhya Aneja[2], Frank Liu[1], Lucas Villa Real[1],
and Thomas George[1]

[1] IBM Research
[2] Universiti Brunei Darussalam, Brunei Darussalam

Abstract. Accurate and timely flood forecasts are essential for effective management of flood disasters, which has become increasingly frequent over the last decade. Obtaining such forecasts requires high resolution integrated weather and flood models with computational costs optimized to provide sufficient lead time. Existing overland flood modeling software packages do not readily scale to topography grids of large size and only permit coarse resolution modeling of large regions. In this paper, we present a highly scalable, integrated flood forecasting system called IFM that runs on both shared and distributed memory architectures, effectively allowing the computation of domains with billions of cells. In order to optimize IFM for large areas, we focus on the computationally expensive overland routing engine. We describe a parallelization scheme and novel strategies to partition irregular domains to minimize load imbalance in the presence of memory constraints that results in 40% reduction in time compared to best uniform partitioning. We demonstrate the scalability of the proposed approach for up to 8192 processors on large scale real-world domains. Our model can provide a 48-hour flood forecast on a watershed of 656 million cells in under 5 minutes.

1 Introduction

Operational flood forecasting is becoming increasingly important due to the changing global climate and frequent incidence of flood disasters [1]. The most common causes for flooding are sudden precipitation in urban areas with poor drainage or seasonal storms resulting in persistent rainfall, which results in overflowing water bodies. Hence, in recent years there has been a strong focus on two stage mechanisms to predict flooding events. The first stage employs a weather model to predict precipitation. The second stage uses these predictions as input to an overland flood model, which computes surface runoff and routes the flow taking into account surface characteristics such as variation in land use type and topography. In such a system, the weather forecasting is performed using fine resolution atmospheric models that discretize the partial differential equations representing evolution of atmospheric flows in time [12], while the overland flows are simulated via equations based on conservation of mass and momentum with the vertical effects simplified to yield the 2-D shallow water equation [14].

F. Silva et al. (Eds.): Euro-Par 2014, LNCS 8632, pp. 692–703, 2014.

Advances in scaling high resolution weather models using contemporary HPC systems have made it feasible to obtain highly accurate fine-grained forecasts for large geographical regions [4, 5]. Unfortunately, most of the existing flood modeling packages [13], [2] primarily focus on usability and are designed for hydrologists to work on medium size desktop machines, which does not permit scaling to large size fine resolution domains for which weather forecasts are available. The domains considered in this paper for operational flood forecasting include a grid with 1 km horizontal resolution for the precipitation estimates and 1m LiDAR [9] topography data from the city of Rio de Janeiro – the latter consisting of 2.4 billion cells. With existing flood modeling software it is not feasible to perform modeling on such a large grid due to the large memory requirements and running times. On the other hand, efficient parallelization of the modeling requires a load-balanced partitioning of the domain, which is non-trivial due to domain irregularity and processor memory constraints.

Contributions:

– We describe an integrated flood forecasting system that readily handles grid sizes up to a billion cells and also incorporates high resolution meso-scale weather forecasts and other fine resolution topographical information for a target region with minimal human effort. To the best of our knowledge, this is the first high resolution operational flood forecasting with such capabilities.
– We propose and implement a distributed memory (MPI) parallelization strategy for diffusive water routing algorithms. Our approach is based on statistical modeling of the true workload using observed computational times and a novel iterative partitioning scheme, which improves load balance while taking into account memory constraints on individual processors.
– We evaluate the serial version and the various parallelization strategies on HPC systems for up to 8192 processors on real world domains and demonstrate that a large domain of 656 million cells can be solved under 5 minutes.

The rest of the paper is organized as follows: Section 2 discusses related work on parallelization of flood routing engines. Section 3 provides an overview of our integrated flood modeling framework. Section 4 discusses our distributed memory parallelization strategy whereas Section 5 introduces the various approaches to domain partitioning. Section 6 describes empirical evaluation of our approach on real world domains. Concluding remarks are presented in Section 7.

2   Related Work

Prior approaches on scaling water routing in flood modeling employ multiprocessor distributed architecture and divide the computation either via functional or domain decomposition.

Methods based on functional decomposition involve parallelization of nested loops to process the grid cells more efficiently. Neal et al. [7] explored the intrinsic parallelism in the functions that looped around the floodplain cells of a domain via OpenMP and demonstrated a speedup up to 5.8× relative to the serial algorithm for 8 cores with domain sizes varying from 3,000 to 3 million cells. The key limiting factors for the parallel speedup were the serial time and processor load imbalances. For the scale of problems we are interested in, such a simple shared memory implementation would not suffice due to scalability limits.

The second class of methods employ domain decomposition, where the grid to be simulated is split into smaller domains that are processed in parallel. The main challenge here is to is figure out a partitioning that achieves load balance. This task is particularly difficult due to three main reasons: (a) irregularity of domain, (b) dependence of computation costs on not only static properties of the domain, but also on dynamic attributes (e.g., wet cells in the neighborhood make the routing computation much more expensive than that of dry neighborhoods), and (c) memory constraints of individual processors. For our work, we adopt the domain decomposition approach due to its better scalability.

There is a large body of literature [8,10,16] on using domain decomposition to improve scalability of hydrological models via message-passing interfaces. These modeling approaches involve partitioning into regular rectangular shaped sub-domains primarily due to the huge software changes required to handle irregular shaped sub-domains. In particular, Yu [16] presents an approach to parallelize a two-dimensional model by spatially dividing the target region into sub-regions of equal size and dimension according to the number of available processors. Empirical performance evaluation of that approach on a large domain (232,000 cells) indicates a maximum speedup of $1.75\times$, $1.98\times$ and $2.71\times$ for MPI simulations using 2, 4, and 8 nodes, respectively, with associated efficiencies of 0.87, 0.50 and 0.33. A recent work [11] presents a hybrid MPI-OpenMP version that incorporates a master-slave model of MPI workload balancing for independent watersheds and OpenMP based shared memory parallelization within each basin. With this hybrid approach, the speedup was reported to be $13\times$ on a 16 core machine. While this approach works on moderate sized systems with large shared memory, it does not scale to large watersheds due to memory limitations at a single processor and load imbalance due to a wide range of basin sizes.

3   Integrated Flood Modeling System

The Integrated Flood Model (IFM) is a hydrological model developed at IBM Research aimed at providing high resolution flood forecasts. IFM consists of two main components, a soil and an overland routing model, shown in Figure 1. Precipitation forecasts are provided by a state of the art weather model. The soil model estimates the *surface-runoff* based on the incoming precipitation, soil, and land use properties. These runoff estimates are input to the overland flood routing engine, which calculates the water in-flows and out-flows on a two-dimensional grid based on topological characteristics. The remnant water-flow from a simulation step is then fed back to the soil model to more accurately determine the water height in the next simulation step. In the serialized implementation of IFM, the overland routing dominates the execution time. Hence, we mainly focus on parallelizing the overland routing component described next.

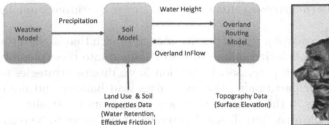

Fig. 1. IBM Integrated Flood & Weather Modeling System

Fig. 2. Rio domain delimited by a bounding box

Overland Flood Routing. Overland water movement in IFM is implemented as diffusive routing, which allows the distribution of lateral inflow in both space and time [6] with significant reduction in computation cost. To be specific, the inflow in the X direction for the ith cell denoted by $OLR_X[i]$ is given by the Manning formula [15] as $OLR_X[i] = \frac{1}{N[j]}\sqrt{|S[i,j]|} * \Delta d * H[j]^{\eta}$, where the jth cell adjoins the ith cell along the X-direction, $H[j]$ denotes the water height or surface-runoff of the jth cell estimated by the soil model, $N[j]$ is the Manning's friction coefficient determined by land use data, $\eta = 5/3$ is based on the laminar and mixed laminar-turbulent conditions of the flow, Δd is the distance between the two cells and the terrain slope $S[i,j]$ indicates a net dip towards the jth cell (i.e., $S[i,j] > 0$). This slope itself is calculated as $S[i,j] = \frac{1}{\Delta d}(H[i] + h[i] - H[j] - h[j])$, where $h[i]$ denotes the natural elevation of the ith cell. The above routing is implemented on a 2D grid along both X and Y directions. First, the flow rate is calculated in the X direction (row-wise), letting the fluid flow from cell i to its neighbors or the other way round. Then, the flow rate is calculated in the Y direction (column-wise) to determine the in-flow in Y direction $OLR_Y[i]$ and the resulting in-flows are used to re-estimate the water height $H[i]$.

4   Distributed Memory Parallelization

In this section, we describe a distributed memory MPI implementation that partitions the domain into disjoint sub areas to be assigned to individual processors. To achieve effective parallelization, we need to address two main challenges:

Partitioning Irregular Shaped Domains. Watersheds tend to be highly irregular in shape as shown in Figure 2. Direct domain decomposition of such grids into possibly irregular sub-regions is non-trivial and the software changes required to support it are enormous. On the other hand, mapping to a regular grid results in grid cells that are not required for simulation and leads to wasted computation and extra book-keeping. Further, balancing the grid point count alone might result in heavy load imbalance among the processors. The processor memory limits also narrow the space of feasible partitionings.

Handling Common Boundaries. Even though the disjoint areas are processed independently, the parallel processing of the domains requires communication of the shared boundary cells (*halo region*) after every time step to synchronize among the different processors.

In our current work, we adopt a simple partitioning approach that divides the bounding rectangular grid of the irregular real world domain into tiles (possibly of different sizes), one for each processor. In Section 5, we discuss strategies to identify such a rectangular partitioning that optimizes load balance and minimizes communication costs in the presence of processor memory constraints.

The regularity of the tile structure allows the common boundaries to be readily handled. To avoid loading the entire dataset on a single processor, processor 0 streams each row of the mask file to identify the valid cells. Once the partitions are decided, processor 0 sends their coordinates and the neighbors at each boundary with their respective extent of overlap. The rest of the processes wait to receive their partition information. Afterwards, each process loads the subdomain based on the received data using a collective parallel I/O operation [3].

To process the partitions in parallel, we define a halo region of fixed width around each partition to store all the required information from neighbors during a simulation. Since the water flow in the domain is simulated from bottom to top and left to right, the top and right halo regions are used for runoff computations while left and bottom halo regions are simply used to pass information. The simulation starts by exchanging static information, e.g., the elevation and Manning's coefficients. In every iteration, the water heights are first updated based on the amount of runoff received from the left and bottom neighbors. After this step, computation is performed using the updated height values. However, processing of top and right boundaries is deferred and performed only after receiving the updated height values from the top and right neighbors. Note that since the tiles are not all of the same size, there can be multiple neighbors in each direction.

5   Domain Partitioning Approaches

Desiderata. Our primary objective is to identify a partitioning of the bounding grid of an irregular region into rectangular tiles that minimizes the net simulation time. This requires balancing workload across nodes while keeping communication costs low. Due to the nature of the computations in overland routing, the workload assigned to a node largely depends on the number of *valid grid points* assigned to it, i.e., all the points in the original irregular domain. Hence, it is highly likely that achieving load balance will require non-uniform tile sizes. Communication costs borne by a node, on the other hand, depend on the number of tiles adjoining the assigned tile and are minimized when the tile boundaries are aligned as in the case of a uniform partitioning. In addition to the load balance and communication reduction, it is also critical that the rectangular tile assigned to each node does not exceed its memory limit.

Partition Representation. Let $m_x \times m_y$ be the size of the bounding rectangular grid and N the number of processor nodes. Common partitioning strategies include: (a) 1-D decomposition where the N processors are arranged in a chain and the resulting tiles are row or column-wise slices of the original domain, (b)

2-D decomposition where the processors themselves are arranged in a $N_x \times N_y$ grid and the original domain is divided into $N_x \times N_y$ tiles slicing along one dimension and then another for better alignment of tiles. In non-uniform slicing, it is preferable to divide along the longer dimension of the domain grid. Without loss of generality, we assume that the tile construction involves a vertical slicing followed by a horizontal slicing of each of the vertical slices. Given a processor grid $N_x \times N_y$ (1-D case corresponds to $N_x = N$ and $N_y = 1$), the partitioning can then be represented in terms of the vertical boundaries $\{x(i), [i]_1^{N_x}\}$ and horizontal boundaries $\{y(i,j) \, [j]_1^{N_y}, \, [i]_1^{N_x}\}$. In the 2-D decomposition case, it is preferable to choose the processor grid dimensions N_x and N_y to the closest two factors of N, i.e., nearly equal to each other, for better distribution of communication costs. To ensure a balanced aspect ratio for each individual tile, the factors N_x and N_y can be assigned to the X-Y dimensions so that the larger domain dimension corresponds to the larger of N_x and N_y. In each of the above cases, the decomposition could be based either on ensuring that the tiles are nearly equal in size (i.e., number of total grid points) which reduces communication costs or nearly equal in workload (i.e., roughly proportional to the number of valid grid points). These correspond to different variants: (a) 1D-uniform, (b) 1D-nonuniform, (c) 2D-uniform, and (d) 2D-nonuniform. The first three variants are relatively simple, but less likely to achieve load balance and more prone to violate processor memory constraints. For the flood modeling, since computation tends to cost more than communication, the last variant is likely to perform better in terms of net simulation time on large grids. Determining its optimal partition, however, especially in the face of memory constraints, is non-trivial.

5.1 Two Dimensional Non-uniform Partitioning

We now focus on 2-D partitioning where the workload needs to be balanced while satisfying memory constraints. Although it is natural to assume that the workload depends only on valid cells, empirical observations point to a significant variation in computation time among tiles with nearly identical valid cells, as shown in Table 1. Hence, we assume the workload to be a linear function of the number of valid and invalid cells. Let $C^v(x,y)$, $C^a(x,y)$ and $C^w(x,y)$ denote the number of valid grid points, the total number of cells, and the workload in the sub-grid with corners $[(0,0), (x,0), (0,y), (x,y)]$ inclusive of the boundaries. Then, the assumption on the workload translates to $C^w(x,y) = C^v(x,y) + \alpha(C^a(x,y) - C^v(x,y))$, where $0 \le \alpha < 1$ is the weighting factor for invalid cells. The optimal value for α can be chosen based on empirically observed computation times ($\alpha = 0$ equals to focusing on valid cells alone). Experiments in Section 6 are based on choosing $\alpha = 1/73$, which was computed from empirical data.

The total workload of the grid is given by $C^w_{tot} = C^w(m_x, m_y)$ and the workload up to and including the xth column is $C^w(x, m_y)$. Let $W(i,j)$ denote the workload in the jth horizontal tile of ith vertical slice. Using the notation for tile boundaries, this can be computed as $W(i,j) = C^w(x(i), y(i,j)) - C^w(x(i), y(i,j-1)) - C^w(x(i-1), y(i,j)) + C^w(x(i-1), y(i,j-1))$. The number of

Table 1. Computation times of partitions with comparable number of valid cells

	Invalid cells	Valid cells	Time (sec.)
Partition 1	2,457,186	79,998	622.92
Partition 2	840,252	80,708	566.58
Partition 3	418,072	80,808	541.46

valid cells $V(i,j)$ can be similarly obtained while the total number of cells $T(i,j)$ can be computed more efficiently as $T(i,j) = (x(i)-x(i-1))*(y(i,j)-y(i,j-1))$.

In the absence of memory constraints, the ideal 2D partitioning corresponds to the case where $W(i,j) = C_{tot}^w/(N_x \times N_y), \forall i,j$. Such a perfect partitioning is, often, not feasible since the tiles need to be rectangular. However, one can obtain a nearly equal distribution via a two step approach, where in the first step, the vertical slices are each chosen to approximately contain workload equal to C_{tot}^w/N_x and each of these slices is further horizontally partitioned into tiles that roughly contain $1/N_y$ of the workload in entire slice. The ith vertical boundary $x(i)$ is picked so that it is the smallest column index such that the workload over all rows and up to the $x(i)^{th}$ column exceeds $\frac{iC_{tot}^w}{N_x}$, i.e.,

$$C^w(x(i) - 1, m_y) < \frac{iC_{tot}^w}{N_x} \leq C^w(x(i), m_y), \ [i]_1^{N_x}. \tag{1}$$

Similarly, for each vertical slice i, we pick the jth horizontal boundary $y(i,j)$ with the smallest row index such that the workload on all the slice columns and up to the $y(i,j)^{th}$ row exceeds $\frac{j}{N_y}$ fraction of the total workload in that slice.

The above two-step slicing approach results in a fairly equitable partitioning of workload, but the resulting tiles might not fit into the memory available at a single node of a distributed memory cluster, in which case the partitioning cannot be used for simulation. When there are memory constraints that place an upper bound T_{max} on the tile size (i.e., total number of cells, not just valid ones) that can be accommodated at each node, some of the processors will need to be assigned tiles with total size close to T_{max}, but much smaller number of valid cells. Typically, these would correspond to ocean and land portions outside of the targeted watersheds. To make up for the lighter workload of the maximal tile nodes, it is necessary to increase the workload for all the other nodes in a balanced fashion. Figuring out the optimal partitioning for this scenario is hard since the tiles need to be contiguous and one cannot estimate the number of maximal size tiles and the desired workload distribution in a single step.

Typically, the first stage of vertical slicing results in vertical slices with width much smaller than T_{max}. Hence, for ease of presentation, we consider partitioning taking into account the tile size limit T_{max} only in the second stage of horizontal slicing.[1] To eliminate inefficiencies, we only consider the grid allocation and workload contributions from the set of rows $R(i)$ that have at least one valid cell in the chosen vertical slice. Algorithm 1 provides details of the horizontal

---

[1] When T_{max} is small, the first stage of horizontal slicing can also be adapted in a similar fashion as in Algorithm 1 to account for memory constraints.

partitioning developed for the ith vertical slice. The key idea in this approach is to perform multiple iterations scanning the vertical slice and in each iteration, construct tiles from one end to another while dynamically re-estimating an equitable distribution of remaining workload among the remaining processors. In the very first iteration, the dynamic estimation of workload share depends only on allocations till that point, whereas in the later iterations, we also incorporate information from the previous iteration on the number of maximal size tiles and the workload covered in those tiles.

Let $W(i) = W$ denote the total workload of the ith vertical slice (based on the rows in $R(i)$) and L_{max} the maximum allowed tile length based on T_{max} and the width of the ith slice. At any stage in the kth scan, let $N_A^{(k)}$ denote the number of nodes that have been assigned tiles and $W_A^{(k)}$ denote the already allocated workload. In the first iteration, the best one can do is to assume that the rest of the workload is going to equally shared among yet to be allocated nodes and the desired workload for the next tile is given by

$$W_{eq}^A = \frac{W - W_A^{(k)}}{N_y - N_A^{(k)}}.$$

If the next tile length required to cover workload of W_{eq} is greater than L_{max}, then the tile length is chosen to be exactly L_{max}. In such a case, the workload to be shouldered by the remaining processors goes up even further resulting in a high load imbalance. Further, the last tile itself may reach the maximal size with additional unassigned workload due to an early under allocation.

To address this issue, we perform additional rounds of assignment where a more balanced workload share is computed incorporating information from the previous iteration. Let $N_M^{(k)}$ and $W_M^{(k)}$ denote the number of nodes that attain maximum tile size and the net workload assigned to them in the kth iteration (or up to that point in case of current iteration). Let $N_E^{(k)}$ and $W_E^{(k)}$ denote the minimum number of tiles required to cover the unassigned region at the end and the associated workload for the kth iteration. In the earlier stages in the $(k+1)^{th}$ iteration, it would be reasonable to assume that among the remaining $(N_y - N_A^{(k)})$ nodes, approximately $(N_M^{(k)} - N_M^{(k+1)} + N_E^{(k)})$ would have to be assigned maximal size tiles roughly accounting for $W_M^{(k)} - W_M^{(k+1)} + W_E^{(k)}$ of the workload. Keeping this in view, a better estimate of the workload to be shared is given by

$$W_{eq}^B = \frac{W - W_A^{(k+1)} - W_M^{(k)} + W_M^{(k+1)} - W_E^{(k)}}{N_y - N_A^{(k+1)} - N_M^{(k)} + N_M^{(k+1)} - N_E^{(k)}}.$$

This estimate tends to overload the processors aggressively from the very beginning and might result in relatively no less or no work for the last few processors. Often, W_{eq}^B is higher than W_{eq}^A, but to address scenarios with complicated arrangement of sparse workload regions, we consider the maximum of the two choices. When T_{max} is large enough to allow a feasible partitioning, it can be shown that the above algorithm converges to a solution (not necessarily optimal) in a finite number of rounds since $W_E^{(k)}$ decreases after each iteration.

Algorithm 1. Two-dimensional partitioning with memory constraints

---

Input: Vertical slice with column indices $x(i)$ and $x(i-1)$, Workload matrix C^w computed over rows in $R(i)$ with at least one valid cell, Max. tile size T_{max}, Processors along Y dimension N_y, Max. iterations $Kmax$

Output: Partitioning of the slice into horizontal tiles $y(i,j)$, $[j]_1^{N_y}$

Method: $k \leftarrow 1$;

Max. tile length $L_{max} \leftarrow ceil(\frac{T_{max}}{x(i)-x(i-1)})$

Last valid row $y_{max} \leftarrow \max(R(i))$

Total workload of ith slice, $W \leftarrow C^w(x(i), m_y) - C^w(x(i-1), m_y)$;

while $(k \leq 2)$ or $((k <= Kmax)$ and $(W_E^{(k-1)} > 0))$ **do**

$\quad (N_A^{(k)}, W_A^{(k)}, N_M^{(k)}, W_M^{((k)}, y[i,0]) \leftarrow (0,0,0,0,0)$

$\quad$ **for** $j = 1$ to N_y **do**

$\qquad W_{eq}^A \leftarrow \dfrac{W - W_A^{(1)}}{N_y - N_A^{(1)}}$

$\qquad$ **if** $(k > 1)$ **then**

$\qquad\qquad W_{eq}^B = \dfrac{W - W_A^{(k)} - W_M^{(k-1)} + W_M^{(k)} - W_E^{(k-1)}}{N_y - N_A^{(k)} - N_M^{(k-1)} + N_M^{(k)} - N_E^{(k-1)}}$

$\qquad\qquad W_{eq}^A = \max(0, W_{eq}^A, W_{eq}^B)$

$\qquad y_{tmp} \leftarrow \arg\min_y = \{y | C^w(x(i), y) - C^w(x(i-1), y) > W_A^{(k)} + W_{eq}^A\}$

$\qquad$ **if** $(y_{tmp} - 1 < \min(y(i, j-1) + Lmax, y_{max}))$ **then**

$\qquad\qquad y(i,j) \leftarrow y_{tmp} - 1$

$\qquad$ **else**

$\qquad\qquad y(i,j) \leftarrow \min(y(i, j-1) + Lmax, y_{max})$

$\qquad\qquad N_M^{(k)} \leftarrow N_M^{(k)} + 1$

$\qquad\qquad W_M^{(k)} \leftarrow W_M^{(k)} + W(i,j)$

$\qquad N_A^{(k)} \leftarrow N_A^{(k)} + 1$

$\qquad W_A^{(k)} \leftarrow W_A^{(k)} + W(i,j)$

$\quad N_E^{(k)} \leftarrow ceil(\frac{|R(i) \cap \{y(i,N_y), \cdots, m_y\}|}{Lmax})$

$\quad W_E^{(k)} \leftarrow W - W_A^{(k)}$

---

6 Empirical Evaluation

6.1 Experimental Setup

Hardware & Software Configurations. For our experiments, we used an IBM Blue Gene BG/P computer that has four 850 MHz embedded PowerPC 450 cores with a peak floating point throughput of 13.6 GF/node. For compiling the software, we used IBM XLC compilers on BG/P with -O3 optimization. In order to handle various platform independent binary files as input and output, we incorporated Network Common Data Format (NetCDF) support for I/O. A version of NetCDF dubbed PnetCDF [3] that is built on top of MPI-IO provides an easy to use interface to perform parallel I/O on large scale supercomputers and was, therefore, integrated into IFM for all I/O.

Experiments were performed on two real world domains (Brunei and Rio) using multiple partitioning schemes, with details given in Table 2. For the Brunei domain, a topography grid with spatial resolution of 90m and 1688×1318 cells (of which 72% are valid) was used. The Rio domain was processed with a grid of 1-meter resolution derived from LiDAR, with 46% of its 18369×35726 cells being valid.

Table 2. Details of the partitioning schemes

Partitioning Scheme	Description
1D-N	Uniform 1D split along longer dimension
1D-VM	1D split that balances #valid cells under memory constraints
2D-N	Uniform 2D split that balances #total cells
2D-VM	2D split that balances #valid cells under memory constraints
2D-WVM	2D split that balances workload assumed to be linear function of #valid and #invalid cells with $\alpha = 1/73$ (see Section 5.1)

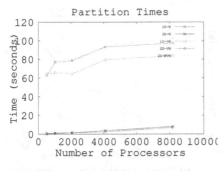

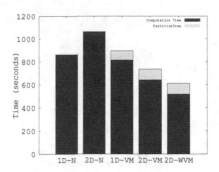

Fig. 3. Partitioning times for varying number of processors

Fig. 4. Partition vs total times on 4096 processors (Rio domain)

6.2 Results

We now present results of empirical evaluation of our partitioning strategies.

Partitioning Costs. Figure 3 shows the partitioning costs for the various schemes with increasing number of processors. As the number of processors grow, a modest increment in partitioning costs is seen. Figure 4 shows the split up of partitioning and total computation times for a 48 hour forecast for the Rio domain based on 1440 simulation steps. The naïve partitioning schemes take negligible time. However, the computation times for 2D-N partitioning scheme is almost double that of the best case (2D-WVM). These figures indicate that it is worthwhile to spend the extra partitioning time since it is a one time cost that can be amortized while simulating larger number of timesteps. (and which can be cached to save computation time in future runs)

Effect on Load Balancing. Table 3 shows the load balance achieved by the various partitioning schemes. 2D-N has the highest load imbalance (116.34%) and our weighted 2D-WVM partitioning scheme has the lowest load imbalance (6.36%), which is also significantly superior to the unweighted version 2D-VM(32%). Improving the load balance results in a 40% reduction in total time over the best naïve partitioning scheme, which is 1D-N for the Rio domain.

Scaling of MPI Implementation. We now present the results of experimentation with the various partitioning schemes for varying number of processors. Figure 5a shows the scaling behavior for Brunei domain for 8 – 512 processors. The 1D-N scheme outperforms the 2D-N scheme for almost all the processor

Table 3. Cell distribution for partitions with maximum times and the percentage imbalance with respect to average time across all processors (Rio domain)

Scheme	Invalid Cells	Valid Cells	Max Time(s)	Avg. Time (s)	%Imbalance
1D-N	35357	129964	860.20	495.77	73.51
2D-N	0	160433	1061.27	490.57	116.34
1D-V	39937	125384	815.50	486.44	67.65
2D-VM	2440289	81151	642.28	486.43	32
2D-WVM	0	75775	520.86	489.72	6.36

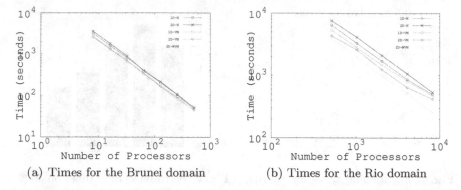

(a) Times for the Brunei domain   (b) Times for the Rio domain

Fig. 5. Log-log plot of scaling behavior with increasing number of processors

configurations. Since this domain has a high number of valid cells in comparison to the total number (72%), 2D-N partitioning does almost as well as 2D-VM and 2D-WVM schemes for 512 processors. This is because only a small fraction of processors are not completely explored and there is only a slight load imbalance even for the 2D-N scheme. Overall we observe a 15–27% improvement in performance for the 2D-WVM scheme in comparison to a naïve 2D decomposition for this range of processors. Figure 5b shows the scaling behavior for all the partitioning schemes for the Rio domain. Here, the 1D-N naïve partitioning scheme consistently outperforms the 2D-N scheme for up to 8192 processors. This can be due to the fact that very few processors are kept idle at times due to the distribution of valid and invalid cells in the Rio domain. However, we do see signs of flattening of the curves beyond 4096 for all the schemes except 2D-WVM.

7   Conclusion

Operational flood forecasting is an important problem requiring a scalable high resolution integrated modeling solution. Our current work presents such an integrated modeling system IFM comprising soil model, and a water routing engine. In particular, we focus on the routing process, which is the most compute intensive and propose a distributed memory parallelization scheme to scale it up to large grid sizes. We also present novel partitioning techniques to minimize load imbalance subject to memory constraints. Empirical evaluation of our proposed approach on large scale real-world domains demonstrates that it scales well up to 8192 processors, and can enable a number of applications and services to be built around flood forecasts that are delivered in a timely fashion. Though inspired by the constraints of the flood-modeling problem, the proposed 2D-WVM partitioning scheme presents two key ideas that are likely to have broad applicability in other areas (e.g., computational seismology) that involve irregular and/or heterogeneous domains and resources constraints: (a) iterative refinement of partitioning by using information from previous iteration(s) on partitions that achieve the constraints (b) statistical modeling of the true workload of a partition in terms of the constituent grid cell properties.

References

1. 10 costliest floods worldwide ordered by overall losses, http://www.munichre.com/app_pages/www/res/pdf/NatCatService/significant_natural_catastrophes/2012/NatCatSERVICE_significant_floods_eco_en.pdf
2. Gill, M.A.: Flood routing by the Muskingum method. Journal of Hydrology 36(34), 353–363 (1978)
3. Li, J., Liao, W.K., Choudhary, A., Ross, R., Thakur, R., Gropp, W., Latham, R., Siegel, A., Gallagher, B., Zingale, M.: Parallel netCDF: A High-Performance Scientific I/O Interface. In: SC (2003)
4. Malakar, P., et al.: A divide and conquer strategy for scaling weather simulations with multiple regions of interest. In: SC 2012, pp. 37:1–37:11 (2012)
5. Michalakes, J., et al.: WRF Nature Run. In: SC (2007)
6. Moussa, R., Bocquillon, C.: Algorithms for solving the diffusive wave flood routing equation. Hydrological Processes 10(1), 105–123 (1996)
7. Neal, J., Fewtrell, T., Trigg, M.: Parallelisation of storage cell flood models using OpenMP. Environmental Modelling & Software 24(7), 872–877 (2009)
8. Neal, J.C., Fewtrell, T.J., Bates, P.D., Wright, N.G.: A comparison of three parallelisation methods for 2D flood inundation models. Environ. Model. Softw. 25(4), 398–411 (2010)
9. Priestnall, G., Jaafar, J., Duncan, A.: Extracting urban features from LiDAR digital surface models. Computers, Environment and Urban Systems 24(2) (2000)
10. Sanders, B.F., Schubert, J.E., Detwiler, R.L.: ParBreZo: A parallel, unstructured grid, Godunov-type, shallow-water code for high-resolution flood inundation modeling at the regional scale. Advances in Water Resources 33(12), 1456–1467 (2010)
11. Singhal, S., Villa Real, L., George, T., Aneja, S., Sabharwal, Y.: A hybrid parallelization approach for high resolution operational flood forecasting. In: HiPC 2013 (2013)
12. Skamarock, W.C., et al.: A description of the Advanced Research WRF version 3. Tech. Rep. TN-475, NCAR (2008)
13. Todini, E.: The ARNO rainfall runoff model. J. Hydrology 175(14), 339–382 (1996)
14. Vreugdenhil, C.: Numerical Methods for Shallow-Water Flow. NATO Asi Series. Series C, Mathematical and Physical Science. Springer (1994)
15. Yen, B.: Channel Flow Resistance: Centennial of Manning's Formula. Water Resources Pub. (1992)
16. Yu, D.: Parallelization of a two-dimensional flood inundation model based on domain decomposition. Environmental Modelling & Software 25(8), 935–945 (2010)

High Performance Pseudo-analytical Simulation of Multi-Object Adaptive Optics over Multi-GPU Systems

Ahmad Abdelfattah[1], Eric Gendron[2], Damien Gratadour[2], David Keyes[1],
Hatem Ltaief[1], Arnaud Sevin[2], and Fabrice Vidal[2]

[1] Extreme Computing Research Center, Division of Computer, Electrical, and
Mathematical Sciences and Engineering, KAUST, Thuwal, KSA
{Ahmad.Ahmad,David.Keyes,Hatem.Ltaief}@kaust.edu.sa
[2] LESIA, Observatoire de Paris, CNRS, UPMC, Universite Paris Diderot
{Eric.Gendron,Damien.Gratadour,Arnaud.Sevin,Fabrice.Vidal}@obspm.fr

Abstract. Multi-object adaptive optics (MOAO) is a novel adaptive optics (AO) technique dedicated to the special case of wide-field multi-object spectrographs (MOS). It applies dedicated wavefront corrections to numerous independent tiny patches spread over a large field of view (FOV). The control of each deformable mirror (DM) is done individually using a tomographic reconstruction of the phase based on measurements from a number of wavefront sensors (WFS) pointing at natural and artificial guide stars in the field. The output of this study helps the design of a new instrument called MOSAIC, a multi-object spectrograph proposed for the European Extremely Large Telescope (E-ELT)[1]. We have developed a novel hybrid pseudo-analytical simulation scheme that allows us to accurately simulate in detail the tomographic problem. The main challenge resides in the computation of the tomographic reconstructor, which involves pseudo-inversion of a large dense symmetric matrix. The pseudo-inverse is computed using an eigenvalue decomposition, based on the divide and conquer algorithm, on multicore systems with multi-GPUs. Thanks to a new symmetric matrix-vector product (SYMV) multi-GPU kernel, our overall implementation scores significant speedups over standard numerical libraries on multicore, like Intel MKL, and up to 60% speedups over the standard MAGMA implementation on 8 Kepler K20c GPUs. At 40,000 unknowns, this appears to be the largest-scale tomographic AO matrix solver submitted to computation, to date, to our knowledge and opens new research directions for extreme scale AO simulations.

1 Introduction

Astronomical programs characterizing high redshift galaxies to study their formation and evolution, require to observe a large number of objects in parallel in

---

[1] http://www.eso.org/public/teles-instr/e-elt

F. Silva et al. (Eds.): Euro-Par 2014, LNCS 8632, pp. 704–715, 2014.

the largest field possible to achieve a sufficient statistic for a reasonable observing time. This is the principle of multi-object spectroscopy. Moreover, it is also necessary to resolve these galaxies so as to perform integral field spectroscopy on their structures. The required resolution should be much better than atmospherical seeing, typically 50 to 100 milli-arcseconds, and therefore requires the implementation of adaptive optics (AO), an instrumental technique for the compensation of dynamically evolving aberrations in an optical system (i.e., due to atmospheric turbulence in the case of a ground based telescope). One of the instruments proposed for the future European Extremely Large Telescope (E-ELT) is MOSAIC [8], a multi-object integral field (multi-IFU) spectrograph for the analysis of distant galaxies, a merger of the EAGLE and OPTIMOS-EVE phase A projects [5,15]. It must be equipped with a specific AO concept, called multi-object AO (MOAO).

In this paper, we present an efficient approach for simulating the behavior of a MOAO system on extremely large telescopes, based on a novel hybrid, pseudo-analytical simulation scheme, somewhere in between the end-to-end and purely analytical approaches, that allows us to simulate in detail the tomographic problem as well as noise and aliasing with a high fidelity. The advantage of this pseudo-analytical approach is its accuracy, as compared to a pure Fourier approach (as developed for instance in [16]), since it is using the same reconstructor as the one that would be used on sky, while being extremely fast as compared to a standard end-to-end approach. The main challenge resides in the computation of the tomographic reconstructor which is split in three phases: 1) the eigen decomposition of a large dense symmetric matrix (typically 40 000 × 40 000 elements, or greater) corresponding to the covariance matrix of the turbulence using a divide-and-conquer algorithm, 2) the explicit pseudo-inversion computation of the covariance matrix and 3) the computation of the tomographic reconstructor using matrix-matrix multiplication kernel. Thanks to their high memory bandwidth and their compute-intensive capabilities (high ratio floating point operations per memory byte loaded i.e., the so-called *surface to volume* effect), hardware accelerators, such as GPUs, are natural candidates for such workloads. Our contributions are twofold. We have further optimized the existing multi-GPU symmetric eigensolver [21] from the Matrix Algebra on GPU and Multicore Architectures library [2] (MAGMA) by integrating a new symmetric matrix-vector product (SYMV), which represents one of the main performance bottlenecks for symmetric eigensolvers due to its memory-bound nature (phase 1). We have also developed a linearly scaling matrix-matrix multiplication kernel on multi-GPUs (phases 2 and 3).

The remainder of the paper is organized as follows. Section 2 introduces the novel MOAO approach. Section 3 presents the mathematical model for simulating the MOAO technique. Section 4 recalls the major computational steps of the dense symmetric eigensolver. Section 5 describes the parallel implementation of the overall tomographic reconstructor which includes an efficient matrix-matrix multiplication kernel on multi-GPUs. Section 6 highlights the performance results on multi-GPUs. Also, performance comparisons against the state of the art, high performance dense linear algebra software libraries are shown on x86 as well as GPUs i.e., Intel MKL [13], CULA [1] and the standard MAGMA implementation. Finally, Section 8 summarizes the results of this paper and presents the ongoing work.

2   The Multi-Object Adaptive Optics Technique

Measuring the wavefront disturbances is achieved, by conventional AO systems, using a wavefront sensor (WFS), which is of a Shack-Hartmann type for most of systems currently in operations [6]. The WFS splits optically the telescope pupil into a number of sub-apertures and makes as many images of a sufficiently bright stellar guide source in each sub-apertures. The exact position of each image, influenced by the turbulence, allows to determine the local slope (i.e., derivative) of the wavefront in front of each sub-aperture. The WFS measurement ends up with a vector field, sampled as the sub-aperture pattern, and describing the wavefront gradient over the pupil area.

The high redshift galaxies are much too faint to provide guide sources for the wavefront measurement for AO and one should find field stars bright enough to ensure this measurement. To obtain 100% sky coverage, a critical aspect for cosmological programs, it is necessary to create artificial guide stars by the backscattering of a laser beam on the Sodium layer of the atmosphere [10] so as to deal with the low stars density found in cosmological fields. These artificial stars are called Laser Guide Stars (LGS) as opposed to Natural GS (NGS). Whatever type of GS, natural or laser, they can be used to measure the atmospheric turbulence in directions that are not those directions of interest (those galaxies to be observed). Tomography algorithms must thus be developed to allow optimal reconstruction of the turbulent volume and the calculation, by projection on the different directions of interest, of the correction to be applied.

Moreover, the fields of interest are very large (5 to 10 arc minutes) compared to the capabilities of conventional AO and a deformable mirror (DM), or even several, compensating the whole field of view is not an adequate solution. Additionally, serious problems arise when trying to implement such optical designs. In fact, only the galaxies must be corrected in this large field, i.e., small patches of few arcseconds, but not the entire field. In the MOAO concept, a specific optical train is placed in the direction of each object of interest including a dedicated DM to ensure correction. Aligned with the linear approach of wavefront reconstruction used in classical AO systems, the tomographic reconstructors proposed up to now in the literature are linear operators [7]. The input data is a vector that concatenates all the measurements taken at a given moment of all the WFSs staring at NGS and LGS. On output, the multiplication by the tomographic matrix will produce a vector that will represent either the phase in the volume (expressed in a suitable basis), or the voltages of a DM.

We have chosen to follow an approach that we have used on the CANARY experiment [9]: the "Learn & Apply". The tomographic reconstructor is aimed at retrieving the wavefront measurements that a virtual sensor would see when looking at a source located on the scientific target and called *truth* sensor (TS). As finding this reconstructor is an inverse problem, it is searched using a minimal mean square error (MMSE) approach, relying on priors on turbulence parameters (Kolmogorov assumption, global Fried parameter, $C_n^2(h)$ profile, wind speed profile, etc.) in order to constraint it and provide regularization. This reconstructor can then be used either to control a real system, or in our case to compute the reconstruction error using an analytical model for the various terms of the system error budget. From this reconstructor, we derive numerically the covariance matrix of the tomographic error, including aliasing and propagated noise. We are then able to simulate the point-spread function (PSF) associated to this covariance matrix of the residuals. The obtained long exposure PSF is then multiplied, in the Fourier space, by the product of the optical transfer functions (OTF) corresponding to bandwidth and fitting errors.

3   Mathematical Model

Because we aim to simulate the image quality attained on the E-ELT using MOAO, the end product we are looking for is the long-exposure point spread function (PSF). The latter is the Fourier transform of the optical transfer function (OTF). Under the hypothesis of stationarity of the phase, it has been shown, for instance in [19] that the OTF can be written as $OTF(\rho/\lambda) = OTF_{\text{tel}}(\rho/\lambda)$ $\exp(-\frac{1}{2}D_\phi(\rho))$, with OTF_{tel} the optical transfer function of the telescope, and $D_\phi(\rho)$ the structure function of the residual phase.

We will assume that the residual errors induced by the AO correction will be made of three independent terms: 1) a term due to the DM fitting error induced by the limited number of actuators on the DM, 2) a term due to temporal error, induced by the finite system bandwidth and 3) a term made of the tomographic error, the associated aliasing, and the noise propagated from the measurements through the tomographic reconstructor. A structure function will be associated to each of these terms, that will be computed from the power spectral density of the residual phase for the first two items, exactly as proposed in [17,14]. The computation of the third term is explained below. We will assume that these 3 terms behave as independent processes. Thus, the structure function of the residual phase can be written as the following sum: $D_\phi(\rho) = D_{\text{fit}}(\rho) + D_{\text{bw}}(\rho) + D_{\text{tomo}}(\rho)$.

While the computation of the first two structure functions: $D_{\text{fit}}(\rho)$ and $D_{\text{bw}}(\rho)$ is not compute intensive, the computation of the last term: $D_{\text{tomo}}(\rho)$ requires a lot of computing power, especially in the case of the E-ELT, as explained below. As mentioned in the previous section, in our current design for MOAO, an on-axis "truth sensor" is used to calibrate the interaction matrix of the system, that will allow us to control the DM from this virtual WFS measurements minimizing the calibration errors. If we call t the measurements of the truth sensor and v the voltages applied on the DM, we can calibrate the interaction matrix D by soliciting each actuator of the DM one by one : $t = Dv$ and we can control the DM from the TS measurements using $v = D^\dagger t$, where $D^\dagger$ is the generalized inverse of D, possibly with some filtered modes. $D^\dagger$ is usually computed by doing a singular value decomposition (SVD) of $D = U \cdot [\mathrm{diag}(\lambda_i)] \cdot V^t$. The negligible singular values are then filtered out and $D^\dagger$ can then be calculated as follows:

$$D^\dagger = V \cdot [\mathrm{diag}(1/\lambda_1, 1/\lambda_2, \cdots, 1/\lambda_k)] \cdot U^t, \tag{1}$$

where k is the numerical rank of D. The tomographic error vector e, as it would be measured by a noiseless truth sensor, would be $e = t - Rm$, where R is the tomographic reconstructor used on the system to drive the DM. Given a particular reconstructor, we can thus compute the covariance matrix C_{ee} of e as follows:

$$C_{ee} = C_{tt} - C_{tm}R^t - RC_{tm}^t + RC_{mm}R^t. \tag{2}$$

The structure function of the phase tomographic error $D_{\mathrm{tomo}}(\rho)$ can then be deduced from the statistical covariance matrix of the DM actuators, C_{vv} (the subscript v stands for *volts*). The matrix C_{vv} is computed using $C_{vv} = D^\dagger C_{ee} D^{\dagger t}$, with C_{ee} given in Eq. 2 and $D^\dagger$ explained in Eq. 1. To compute C_{ee} it is thus necessary to introduce a given tomographic reconstructor. It has been shown, for instance in [20], that the Minimum Mean Square Error (MMSE) tomographic reconstructor can be written as:

$$R = C_{tm} \cdot C_{mm}^{-1}, \tag{3}$$

where C_{mm} stands for the covariance matrix between all the measurements of all the WFS of the instrument, and C_{tm} is the covariance matrix between the measurements of the factious truth sensor, and all the other system measurements. In the case of the E-ELT, C_{mm} is an extremely large matrix (40k x 40k or greater) and its inversion is thus the most compute intensive part of our pseudo-analytical model. It must be noted that the inversion of matrix C_{mm} in the previous equation is not a strict inversion, as the null space of C_{mm} may not be empty. Inverting C_{mm} may be done using eigen decomposition, and filtering out the negligible eigenvalues.

4   Dense Symmetric Eigensolver Algorithm

The LAPACK dense symmetric eigensolver (DSYEVD) is composed of three computational stages. The matrix is first reduced to tridiagonal (DSYTRD) form using orthogonal transformations based on Householder reflectors, which guarantees numerical stability. The reflectors are saved in the reduced lower or upper part of the matrix, depending on which part is considered, since they will be required at the last stage. The second stage extracts all eigenvalues from the tridiagonal matrix and optionally computes all eigenvectors using a divide-and-conquer algorithm (DSTEDC). The third stage corresponds to the back transformation where all orthogonal transformations from the first stage are applied by block to the eigenvector matrix (DORMTR). If only eigenvalues are needed, the routine DYSTRD is called followed by DSTERF, which calculates only the eigenvalues out of the tridiagonal matrix and has an algorithmic complexity of $O(n^2)$

compared to $O(n^3)$ for DSYTRD. One of the main performance bottlenecks of DSYEVD is DSYTRD due to its expensive panel factorization, which requires loading into memory the whole unreduced part of the matrix (i.e., the trailing submatrix) at each single reduction step to perform Level 2 BLAS operations (memory-bound) i.e., the symmetric matrix-vector product (DSYMV). The update of the trailing submatrix is however compute-intensive and relies on high performance Level 3 BLAS operations (compute-bound). When all eigenvectors are additionally needed, DSTEDC and DORMTR are also based on successive calls to Level 3 BLAS kernels and easily achieve high performance close to the matrix-matrix multiplication kernel performance (DGEMM) on modern parallel architectures.

5   Implementation Details

The DSYMV is a memory-bound kernel that represents the main bottleneck in the DSYEVD algorithm. We present an optimized DSYMV kernel, which is a variant of a previously version proposed by some of the authors [3]. The new version has some improvements, such as the elimination of the need to a workspace for global reduction, and the use of atomic operations to allow multiple threads working on the same output location. These new optimizations are suitable for the Kepler architecture[2]. In contrast with the old design [3], the DSYMV is BLAS compliant and achieves higher occupancy on the GPU for relatively small matrices. For the multi-GPU DSYMV, the matrix layout over the GPUs is decided by the upper level algorithm (DSYTRD). A multi-GPU version of this algorithm is proposed by MAGMA [21]. The matrix layout is block-column 1D cyclic distribution. Since we intend to integrate our DSYMV into MAGMA, we use the same layout.

Once the eigenvalue decomposition is complete, the pseudo inverse of the covariance matrix can be computed, $C_{mm}^{-1} = U \cdot E^{-1} \cdot U^t$, where U is the matrix of eigenvectors and E is a diagonal matrix containing the eigenvalues. Afterwards, the tomographic reconstructor can be computed as in Equation 3, where C_{tm} is a rectangular matrix of a typical size 3.5k × 40k. It is not trivial, though, to perform such operations on huge matrices. One optimization for the pseudo inverse is to compute the square root of E^{-1} and multiply it by U. This multiplication is simplified to scaling the columns of U by the square roots of E^{-1}. The resulting matrix (say $\bar{U}$) can then be used to compute C_{mm}^{-1}, since $C_{mm}^{-1} = \bar{U} \cdot \bar{U}^T$. We propose a statically scheduled DGEMM on multi-GPU systems. The proposed kernel performs the standard BLAS operation, $C = \alpha A \cdot B + \beta C$, where A, B, and C have the dimensions $m \times k$, $k \times n$, and $m \times n$, respectively[3]. The design is based on processing matrices with tiles. cuBLAS DGEMM [18] is used to perform the

---

[2] http://www.nvidia.com/content/PDF/kepler/
NVIDIA-Kepler-GK110-Architecture-Whitepaper.pdf

[3] NVIDIA's cuBLAS-XT library provides a similar kernel, but it is not freely available on multi-GPUs.

product at the tile level. It is a highly optimized kernel that achieves approximately 1.1 Tflop/s in double precision on a Kepler GPU. Since the matrices might not fit into GPUs' main memory, our implementation is an out-of-core DGEMM. The tiles are exchanged between CPU and GPU(s) as needed during computation. The communication overhead should be hidden by useful computation. Figure 1 shows how the work is assigned among four GPUs, where A and B are both processed in the non-transposed mode. For simplicity, assume that m, n, and k can be fully divided into a given tile size. The block rows of A are assigned to GPUs in a 1D cyclic manner. Each GPU reads a block row of A, tile by tile, and does all the computation associated with it. A GPU reads B in block columns, tile by tile, and writes the corresponding result in C (1D cyclic block row, tile by tile). An important point is the memory consumption per GPU.

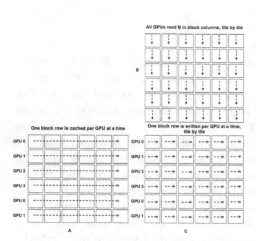

Fig. 1. Strategy and memory requirement for the proposed DGEMM-MGPU

From Figure 1, we can determine the device memory requirement for the proposed DGEMM-MGPU, for a sample matrix whose dimension k fits into six tiles. Each GPU requires as many tiles as necessary to store a block row of A. The implementation uses double buffers for B and C tiles in order to overlap communication with computation. The total memory requirement (M), in bytes, per GPU is given by, $M = (kT + 4T^2)P$, where P is the precision, expressed in bytes, and T is the tile size. Only tile sizes higher than 1000 are considered, to ensure approximately 1.1 Tflop/s performance per tile. Even with a large tile size of 5k, the kernel can process square matrices beyond 100k in double precision (on a K20c GPU), which is beyond the targeted size here.

6   Experimental Results

The experiments have been conducted on a system equipped with Intel Sandy Bridge CPU (2 sockets × 8 cores per socket), and accelerated with eight Kepler K20c GPUs (ECC off), each with 5 GB of memory. We use CUDA Toolkit 5.5 and Intel MKL (Intel Composer XE 2013) to build MAGMA-1.4.0. CULA R17 does not distribute DSYEVD and provides only the DSYEV algorithm (symmetric eigensolver using the QR iteration) on single GPU. All computations are done in double precision. Results are properly averaged across multiple runs.

Starting with the DSYMV, The proposed kernel outperforms the state-of-the-art implementations, including MAGMABLAS-1.4.0, cuBLAS-5.5, and CULA-R17. Figure 2(a) shows the performance of the proposed kernel against the

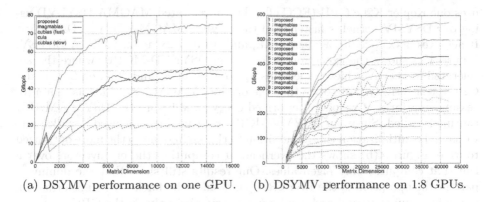

(a) DSYMV performance on one GPU. (b) DSYMV performance on 1:8 GPUs.

Fig. 2. DSYMV performance on single and multi-GPUs (Kepler K20c - ECC off)

aforementioned high performance libraries, on a single Kepler K20c GPU. The Figure shows an asymptotic improvement of 97% against CULA-R17, 56% against cuBLAS-5.5, and 44% against MAGMABLAS-1.4.0. For small matrix dimensions (less than 2000), the improvement is up to 2x against the best implementation, which is a crucial result for the DSYTRD algorithm. The performance is about 88% of the sustained peak bandwidth performance. cuBLAS appears twice in the Figure, since it provides two implementations. In addition to our multi-GPU implementation, only MAGMABLAS provides the DSYMV kernel on multi-GPUs. Figure 2(b) shows the performance of both implementations, on a single node with 8 GPUs. The asymptotic performance speedup over 8 GPUs is up to 40%.

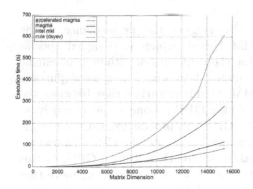

Fig. 3. DSYEVD Execution time using one GPU against multi-core system.

The dominant part of DSYEVD is the DSYTRD stage, which is, in turn, dominated by symmetric matrix-vector product. Thanks to MAGMA being open source, we were able to replace MAGMABLAS DSYMV kernel with the one we propose. For the single GPU case, we compare the three libraries offering symmetric eigenvalue decomposition, Intel MKL, MAGMA-1.4.0, and CULA-R17. For MAGMA, we run an additional accelerated version (from now on referred to as accelerated MAGMA) where our proposed DSYMV is used. All eigenvalues and eigenvectors are computed here, although our application, in principle, will filter out up to 20% of the eigenpairs with very low magnitude. Figure 3 shows the execution time of the DSYEVD algorithm for the aforementioned libraries. GPU accelerated libraries uses one Kepler K20c GPU (ECC off). The accelerated MAGMA DSYEVD using our DSYMV kernel is faster than the original MAGMA DSYEVD by 35%. It achieves 3.4x speedup against MKL, and up to 7.2x against CULA DSYEV. Figure 4(a) shows the execution time for the DSYEVD-MGPU, where the accelerated MAGMA achieves speedups up to 45%, 60%, and 70%, on 2, 4, and 8 GPUs, respectively. We notice that the original MAGMA routine has a preprocessing step for a workspace, performed every time before the DSYMV-MGPU routine is called. Since our DSYMV-MGPU routine does not need a workspace, we save the initialization time in addition to the saving due to the more optimized routine. Figure 4(b) shows the overhead of computing the eigenvectors over a run that computes only eigenvalues. Our results still show that the dominant part in the operation is the DSYTRD part, since the backward transformation phase is compute-bound and can be done very efficiently on the GPU.

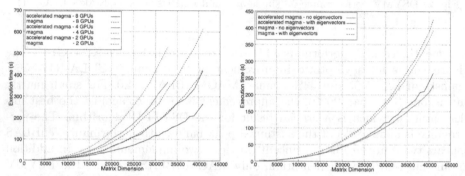

(a) DSYEVD scalability against the num- (b) Overhead of eigenvector computations
ber of GPUs.   on 8 GPUs.

Fig. 4. DSYEVD execution time analysis

Table 1. Performance (Tflop/s) of the pseudo inversion

Tile size	4 GPUs	8 GPUs
1000	3.50	5.39
1600	3.60	6.04
2000	3.99	6.36
2500	4.03	7.74
4000	3.52	5.23
5000	4.16	8.05

We also present the performance of the DGEMM kernel, which is designed specifically for the application, although it can be easily modified to serve as general purpose DGEMM. Communicating tiles between the CPU and the GPU is done asynchronously, so that the GPU can process existing tiles while receiving new ones, and the CPU can do useful work concurrently with the GPU. In this case, the useful work is scheduling more tiles to be processed. Figure 1 shows that our static scheduling strategy may suffer from load imbalance, which will result in a performance drop. However, for the matrix sizes of the application, we can achieve performance that is very close to the peak, if we choose the right tile size. The computation of the pseudo inverse involves multiplication of two 40k×40k matrices. Using different tile sizes, the performance is summarized in Table 1, for 4 and 8 GPUs. It is clear that the larger the tile, the better the performance. Tile size 5000 achieves performance that is very close to the sustained peak.

Finally, we present the overall simulation performance. Thanks to the proposed DSYMV and DGEMM kernels, the accelerated MAGMA finishes the simulation in 263.49s. This is 60% better than an original MAGMA implementation (421.10s). It is also 17.5x faster than Intel MKL on 16 core Intel Sandy Bridge processor (4656.25s). To prove how dominant the DSYEVD is, our results show that it takes 241.07s on accelerated MAGAM, 399.15s with an original MAGMA, and 4370.50s using Intel MKL. The other phases are less than 10% of the total run time, for the accelerated MAGMA case.

7 Related Work

It is noteworthy to mention that there exist other numerical algorithms for dense symmetric eigensolver, which tries to workaround DSYTRD's bottlenecks by introducing a two-stage tridiagonal reduction. The original dense matrix is first reduced to band form using efficient compute-intensive kernels from which a bulge chasing algorithm is applied to chase down the off-diagonal elements until the final tridiagonal matrix is formed. This allows to cast most of Level 2 BLAS operations into Level 3 BLAS operations and increases significantly the overall symmetric eigensolver. This two-stage approach has been first introduced by Bischof et. al [4]. Haidar et. al [11,12] have further improved it on shared-memory multicore architecture. All aforementioned implementations run only on multicore and are very challenging to port on GPUs due to the non-conventional kernels involved in the bulge chasing procedure. The authors presented only performance results based on a MATLAB implementation.

8 Conclusion and Future Work

This paper has presented 1) an efficient implementation of the DSYMV kernel on multi-GPUs, which is a critical Level 2 BLAS operation for the dense symmetric eigensolver DSYEVD and 2) an optimized asynchronous DGEMM kernel on multi-GPUs. Thanks to both implementations and the multi-object adaptive optics approach, the overall application accurately solves unprecedented problem scale in the adaptive optics field (up to our knowledge) and reaches high performance on multi-GPUs compared to the standard MAGMA implementation on 8 Kepler K20c GPUs (up to 60% speedup). New research directions for extreme scale AO simulations can be envisaged by replacing the actual dense symmetric eigensolver to compute the tomographic reconstructor with the Cholesky-based symmetric matrix inversion. This would permit to calculate the explicit inverse directly without intermediary computational steps as well as to port this overall application to distributed-memory systems with GPUs more easily. This method would also allow to capture and to better handle the noise propagated from the measurements through the tomographic reconstructor. In addition, the covariance matrix generation has not been investigated here since the time taken to compute it is not dominant for the problem sizes studied in the paper. However, it would have to be considered for large problem sizes, especially when targeting distributed-memory environment. Future possibilities also include exploitation of the low rank character of the co-variance matrix and reuse of information between instances that are currently treated as independent.

Acknowledgment. This work is supported by the ANR grant ANR-12-MONU-0022 of the French Ministry of Research. We thank NVIDIA for their continuous support and hardware donations. We also thank the CSCS Swiss National Supercomputing Centre for granting us access on their GPU computing platforms.

References

1. CULA Dense Free Edition, http://www.culatools.com/
2. Matrix Algebra on GPU and Multicore Architectures. Innovative Computing Laboratory, University of Tennessee, http://icl.cs.utk.edu/magma/
3. Abdelfattah, A., Dongarra, J., Keyes, D., Ltaief, H.: Optimizing Memory-Bound SYMV Kernel on GPU Hardware Accelerators. In: Daydé, M., Marques, O., Nakajima, K. (eds.) VECPAR. LNCS, vol. 7851, pp. 72–79. Springer, Heidelberg (2013)
4. Bischof, C.H., Lang, B., Sun, X.: Algorithm 807: The SBR Toolbox—software for successive band reduction. ACM Transactions on Mathematical Software 26(4), 602–616 (2000)
5. Cuby, J.-G., Morris, S., Fusco, T., Lehnert, M., Parr-Burman, P., Rousset, G., Amans, J.-P., Beard, S., Bryson, I., Cohen, M., Dipper, N., Evans, C., Ferrari, M., Gendron, E., Gimenez, J.-L., Gratadour, D., Hastings, P., Hubert, Z., Hugot, E., Jagourel, P., Laporte, P., Lebrun, V., Le Mignant, D., Madec, F., Myers, R., Neichel, B., Morris, T., Robert, C., Schnetler, H., Swinbank, M., Talbot, G., Taylor, W., Vidal, F., Vivès, S., Vola, P., Welikala, N., Wells, M.: EAGLE: a MOAO fed multi-IFU NIR workhorse for E-ELT. In: Society of Photo-Optical Instrumentation Engineers (SPIE) Conference Series. Society of Photo-Optical Instrumentation Engineers (SPIE) Conference Series, vol. 7735 (July 2010)
6. Davies, R., Kasper, M.: Adaptive Optics for Astronomy. Annual Review of Astronomy and Astrophysics 50, 305–351 (2012)
7. Ellerbroek, B.L., Vogel, C.R.: TOPICAL REVIEW: Inverse problems in astronomical adaptive optics. Inverse Problems 25(6), 063001 (2009)
8. Evans, C., Puech, M., Barbuy, B., Bastian, N., Bonifacio, P., Caffau, E., Cuby, J.-G., Dalton, G., Davies, B., Dunlop, J., Flores, H., Hammer, F., Kaper, L., Lemasle, B., Morris, S., Pentericci, L., Petitjean, P., Schaerer, D., Telles, E., Welikala, N., Ziegler, B.: ELT-MOS White Paper: Science Overview and Requirements. ArXiv e-prints (February 2013)
9. Gendron, E., Vidal, F., Brangier, M., Morris, T., Hubert, Z., Basden, A., Rousset, G., Myers, R., Chemla, F., Longmore, A., Butterley, T., Dipper, N., Dunlop, C., Geng, D., Gratadour, D., Henry, D., Laporte, P., Looker, N., Perret, D., Sevin, A., Talbot, G., Younger, E.: MOAO first on-sky demonstration with CANARY. Astronomy and Astrophysics 529, L2 (2011)
10. Gratadour, D., Gendron, E., Rousset, G.: Intrinsic limitations of Shack-Hartmann wavefront sensing on an extended laser guide source. Journal of the Optical Society of America A 27(26), A260000 (2010)

11. Haidar, A., Ltaief, H., Dongarra, J.: Parallel Reduction to Condensed Forms for Symmetric Eigenvalue Problems using Aggregated Fine-Grained and Memory-Aware Kernels. In: Proceedings of 2011 International Conference for High Performance Computing, Networking, Storage and Analysis, SC 2011, pp. 8:1–8:11. ACM, New York (2011)
12. Haidar, A., Ltaief, H., Dongarra, J.: Toward a High Performance Tile Divide and Conquer Algorithm for the Dense Symmetric Eigenvalue Problem. SIAM J. Scientific Computing 34(6) (2012)
13. Intel. Math Kernel Library,
    http://software.intel.com/en-us/articles/intel-mkl/
14. Jolissaint, L., Christou, J., Wizinowich, P., Tolstoy, E.: Adaptive optics point spread function reconstruction: lessons learned from on-sky experiment on Altair/Gemini and pathway for future systems. In: Society of Photo-Optical Instrumentation Engineers (SPIE) Conference Series. Society of Photo-Optical Instrumentation Engineers (SPIE) Conference Series, vol. 7736 (July 2010)
15. Navarro, R., Chemla, F., Bonifacio, P., Flores, H., Guinouard, I., Huet, J.-M., Puech, M., Royer, F., Pragt, J.H., Wulterkens, G., Sawyer, E.C., Caldwell, M.E., Tosh, I.A.J., Whalley, M.S., Woodhouse, G.F.W., Spanò, P., di Marcantonio, P., Andersen, M.I., Dalton, G.B., Kaper, L., Hammer, F.: Project overview of OPTIMOS-EVE: the fibre-fed multi-object spectrograph for the E-ELT. In: Society of Photo-Optical Instrumentation Engineers (SPIE) Conference Series. Society of Photo-Optical Instrumentation Engineers (SPIE) Conference Series, vol. 7735 (July 2010)
16. Neichel, B., Fusco, T., Conan, J.-M., Petit, C., Rousset, G.: PSD-based simulation algorithm for Wide FoV AO design: application to ELT studies. In: Society of Photo-Optical Instrumentation Engineers (SPIE) Conference Series. Society of Photo-Optical Instrumentation Engineers (SPIE) Conference Series, vol. 7015 (July 2008)
17. Rigaut, F.J., Veran, J.-P., Lai, O.: Analytical model for Shack-Hartmann-based adaptive optics systems. In: Bonaccini, D., Tyson, R.K. (eds.) Adaptive Optical System Technologies. Society of Photo-Optical Instrumentation Engineers (SPIE) Conference Series, vol. 3353, pp. 1038–1048 (September 1998)
18. Tan, G., Li, L., Triechle, S., Phillips, E., Bao, Y., Sun, N.: Fast Implementation of DGEMM on Fermi GPU. In: Proceedings of 2011 International Conference for High Performance Computing, Networking, Storage and Analysis, SC 2011, pp. 35:1–35:11. ACM, New York (2011)
19. Veran, J.-P., Rigaut, F., Maitre, H., Rouan, D.: Estimation of the adaptive optics long-exposure point-spread function using control loop data. Journal of the Optical Society of America A 14, 3057–3069 (1997)
20. Vidal, F., Gendron, E., Rousset, G.: Tomography approach for multi-object adaptive optics. Journal of the Optical Society of America A 27(26), A260000 (2010)
21. Yamazaki, I., Dong, T., Solc, R., Tomov, S., Dongarra, J., Schulthess, T.: Tridiagonalization of a dense symmetric matrix on multiple GPUs and its application to symmetric eigenvalue problems. In: Concurrency and Computation: Practice and Experience (2013)

Parallel Dual Tree Traversal on Multi-core and Many-core Architectures for Astrophysical N-body Simulations

Benoit Lange[1,2,*] and Pierre Fortin[2]

[1] Sorbonne Universités, UPMC Univ Paris 06, ICS, F-75005, Paris, France
[2] Sorbonne Universités, UPMC Univ Paris 06, UMR 7606,
LIP6, F-75005, Paris, France;
CNRS, UMR 7606, LIP6, F-75005, Paris, France
{benoit.lange,pierre.fortin}@lip6.fr

Abstract. In astrophysical N-body simulations, Dehnen's algorithm, implemented in the serial *falcON* code and based on a dual tree traversal, is faster than serial Barnes-Hut tree-codes, but outperformed by parallel CPU and GPU tree-codes. In this paper, we present a parallel dual tree traversal, implemented in the *pfalcON* code, targeting multi-core CPUs and many-core architectures (Xeon Phi). We focus here on both performance and portability, while preserving Dehnen's original algorithm. We first use task parallelism, with either OpenMP or Intel TBB, for the dual tree traversal. We then rely on the SPMD (single-program, multiple-data) model for the SIMD vectorization of the near field part thanks to the Intel SPMD Program Compiler. We compare the *pfalcON* performance to related work, and finally obtain performance results that match one of the best current tree-code implementations on GPU.

Keywords: dual tree traversal, task parallelism, SIMD, SPMD model, N-body problem.

1 Introduction

The N-body problem describes the computation of all pairwise interactions among N bodies (or particles). In astrophysics, such N-body simulations are essential and widely used for galactic dynamics studies. The direct computation of all pairwise interactions among N bodies leads to a prohibitive $\mathcal{O}(N^2)$ runtime complexity. Hierarchical methods [2,5] have therefore been introduced to reduce this runtime complexity: thanks to an octree data structure, the force field is decomposed in a near field part, directly computed, and a far field part approximated with various expansions. In astrophysics, the Barnes-Hut tree-code is one of the most used algorithms for serial and parallel CPU executions (see for example *treecode1* in NEMO[1] and GADGET-2 [12]). Recently, parallel implementations

---

[*] This work undertaken (partially) in the CALSIMLAB framework is supported by the public grant ANR-11-LABX-0037-01 of the French National Research Agency (ANR) as part of the "Investissements dAvenir" program (ANR-11-IDEX-0004-02).
[1] A Stellar Dynamics Toolbox: http://bima.astro.umd.edu/nemo

F. Silva et al. (Eds.): Euro-Par 2014, LNCS 8632, pp. 716–727, 2014.
© Springer International Publishing Switzerland 2014

on GPUs (Graphics Processing Units) [3, 4] have also been developed which outperform multi-core CPUs. Dehnen's algorithm [6], implemented in the serial *falcON* code (Force ALgorithm with Complexity $\mathcal{O}(N)$), is one order of magnitude faster than serial executions of Barnes-Hut tree-codes [6, 8], mainly thanks to its dual tree traversal (DTT). But parallel tree-codes implementations, on one or two multi-core CPUs or on one GPU, then manage to outperform *falcON* [8]. The parallelization of *falcON* is therefore crucial to exploit its algorithmic asset on current parallel architectures. But contrary to tree-codes algorithms, this DTT does not exhibit natural parallelism.

In this paper, we present a parallel dual tree traversal, implemented in the *pfalcON (parallel falcON)* code, that efficiently exploits two levels of parallelism on one single shared-memory node (we do not consider distributed-memory parallelism here). We first target multi-core parallelism on CPUs whose number of cores is constantly increasing, as well as on new many-core architectures like the Intel Xeon Phi whose compute power is similar to high end GPUs. We also target SIMD parallelism because of its increasing importance in the overall CPU performance: 128-bit SSE, 256-bit AVX, and 512-bit Xeon Phi vector units.

Contributions. Our contributions are thus two-fold. Firstly, we use task parallelism for the DTT on both multi-core CPUs and on the Xeon Phi. This requires a recursive formulation of the *falcON* code, as well as adequate atomic operations and memory barriers in order to obtain an efficient implementation. We detail how this can be achieved for both OpenMP tasks and Intel TBB (Threading Building Blocks) tasks, and how we manage to preserve Dehnen's original algorithm in the parallel tree traversal. Secondly, we use Intel SPMD Program Compiler (`ispc`) and its SPMD (single-program, multiple-data) model for the SIMD vectorization of the direct computation required for the near field part. We show that such approach enables us to have one single portable source code for this direct computation which is very efficient on both SSE and AVX, as well as on Xeon Phi vector instructions. Best performance is here obtained via a hybrid strategy that efficiently combines scalar and vector code. In the end, we show performance results that match the GPU `Bonsai` code which is currently one of the fastest GPU tree-codes [3].

Related work. An MPI parallelization of Dehnen's algorithm has been briefly presented in [10], but is based on a complete rewriting of the algorithm in Fortran 90, not on the highly optimized C++ *falcON* code. Recently, the `exaFMM-dev` software has included an implementation of Dehnen's algorithm that also uses task parallelism for the dual tree traversal [13, 14], but in a different way that requires the rewriting of this traversal. As for SIMD programming, `exaFMM-dev` uses C++ template metaprogramming for the hand-tuned kernel of the direct computation part. In the following, we will thus highlight the differences between *pfalcON* and `exaFMM-dev` and compare their performance.

In the rest of this paper, Sect. 2 describes N-body algorithms, especially Dehnen's algorithm. In Sect. 3, we detail how we have used task parallelism and SPMD programming in the *pfalcON* code. Section 4 presents performance results

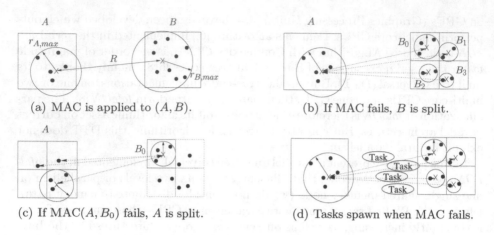

(a) MAC is applied to (A, B).

(b) If MAC fails, B is split.

(c) If MAC(A, B_0) fails, A is split.

(d) Tasks spawn when MAC fails.

Fig. 1. Dual tree traversal in Dehnen's algorithm

and comparisons with other codes. Finally, concluding remarks will be presented in Sect. 5. More technical details are available in the research report [9].

2 N-body Algorithms

We focus here on galactic simulations and on hierarchical N-body algorithms, where the 3D particle space is hierarchically decomposed thanks to an octree whose leafs contain at most $Ncrit$ particles.

The Barnes-Hut tree-code algorithm [2] computes the gravitational forces among N particles with a $\mathcal{O}(N \ln N)$ runtime complexity thanks to monopole (and possibly quadrupole) moments. For each target body, the octree is here recursively traversed and "body-cell" or "body-body" interactions are evaluated depending on a multipole acceptance criterion (MAC). The loop on the target bodies is parallel which enables CPU parallel implementations with multi-threading and/or with MPI [12]. Recently, this inherent parallelism has been efficiently exploited to develop GPU implementations that run entirely on the GPU [3, 4]. For example, the Bonsai code, which relies on monopole and quadrupole moments and on a specific MAC, enables speedups around 20 on GPU compared to a multi-core CPU implementation [3].

Dehnen's algorithm [6] can be considered as a nontraditional fast multipole method [5], specific to the relatively low precisions required in astrophysics. This $\mathcal{O}(N)$ algorithm indeed relies on "cell-cell" interactions. This requires specific, low precision local expansions based on cartesian Taylor expansions, and a specific MAC that can balance (along with the expansion order, which is fixed to 3) the accuracy and the computation cost. This MAC is defined for two cells (A, B) (see Fig. 1(a)) as: $\frac{r_{A,max} + r_{B,max}}{R} < \theta$, where θ is an input parameter ($\theta = 0.6$ by default) that balances accuracy and computation cost, and $r_{C,max}$ denotes an upper limit for the distance of any body within the node C from its center of mass [6].

Once the octree has been built and the multipole moments have been calculated, the interactions are computed in two steps.

The first step (*interaction phase*) relies on the dual tree traversal (DTT) presented in Figs. 1(a),1(b),1(c). If the MAC succeeds between two cells (A, B), their interactions can be approximated: both local expansions of A and B are updated thanks to the mutuality of gravity (see Fig. 1(a)). If the MAC fails, the larger cell (B here) is split and the MAC is applied between A and all the children of B (see Fig. 1(b), with 8 children in 3D). This is applied recursively, and A can then be split when the MAC fails with A as the larger cell (see Fig. 1(c)). This thus leads to a dual recursive traversal of the octree. When the MAC fails for two octree leafs, or when the number of particles is too low (depending on empirical thresholds [6]), the direct computation is used instead of the expansions. Thanks to this DTT, Dehnen's algorithm consistently uses the mutuality of gravity to halve the computation cost in the near field part as well as in the far field part. After the interaction phase, the *evaluation phase* is recursively used to evaluate the local expansion of each cell for each body within this cell.

All these features have been implemented in the *falcON*[2] code (Force ALgorithm with Complexity $\mathcal{O}(N)$) which offers $\mathcal{O}(N)$ computation times one order of magnitude smaller than serial executions of Barnes-Hut tree-codes [6, 8]. Moreover, these computation times are much less sensitive to the distribution of particles: this is very important for astrophysical simulations where the particle distributions representing galaxies or groups of galaxies are highly non-uniform.

The interaction and evaluation steps correspond together to the most time consuming part. The octree construction has a non-negligible computation time, but it does not have to be performed at every time-step. Moreover, the interaction step represents around 95% of the total time for both the interaction and evaluation steps, which makes it crucial for the overall performance of *falcON*. In the following, we will thus see how the interaction and evaluation steps of Dehnen's algorithm can be efficiently parallelized in a new *pfalcON* code.

3   *pfalcON*: A Parallel *falcON*

The dual tree traversal of the interaction step was described as a recursive algorithm in [6], but was implemented using a stack-based approach in the *falcON* code. In practice when an interaction fails the MAC, it is pushed in one of the available stacks according to its type ("cell-cell", "body-cell"...). The stacks are then regularly popped in a specific order. When using tasks to process interactions, the task runtime will have to store the tasks (i.e. the interactions) in memory. The original stacks in *falcON* then become redundant. We have thus removed these stacks and rewritten *falcON* as a recursive code (more convenient for task parallelism), where recursive calls process interactions in the same order as in *falcON*. This new code will be hereafter referred to as *rfalcON*.

---

[2] Available in http://carma.astro.umd.edu/nemo/, version 3.6. We use here the *gyrfalcON* full-fledged N-body code (GalaxY simulatoR using falcON).

Besides, local Taylor expansions are allocated on the fly during the dual tree traversal in the original *falcON* code. This enables to save memory by allocating these expansions only when they are effectively required for each cell. In parallel executions, concurrent memory allocations have to be serialized at the system level, which can become a performance bottleneck. In *rfalcON* we thus allocate these expansions for each non-empty cell during the step which computes multipole moments. This implies some memory overhead, which is not problematic since current N-body simulations on one single node are more limited by the compute power than by the available memory. With such features, *rfalcON* is slightly faster than *falcON* (around 8%) for the interaction step.

3.1   Task Parallelism for the Dual Tree Traversal

On multi-core CPUs, loop-based parallelism (like in OpenMP) is suitable for treecodes, but clearly not here for the DTT of the *rfalcON* interaction phase since there is no explicit parallel loop. Task parallelism, firstly introduced in Cilk and now available in OpenMP (since version 3.0) and in Intel TBB, is here much more suitable for such recursive algorithm. Tasks are specified in the source code by the programmer, and then managed during the execution by a runtime which dynamically schedules these tasks on the available threads. Such dynamic load balancing is especially useful in astrophysical N-body simulations where the particle distributions, hence the computation loads, are highly non-uniform.

In *pfalcON*, each time an interaction fails the MAC, we thus simply create one task for each of the (up to) eight interactions involving the children of the larger cell: see Fig. 1(d). However, due to the consistent use of the mutuality of gravity in Dehnen's algorithm, a task updates both cells A and B (either local expansions or particles) when the interaction is effectively computed. Hence different tasks can update the same cells concurrently which requires synchronization among the tasks to avoid conflicts. We need here the lightest synchronization mechanism to have the smallest overhead on the parallel execution. That is why we use here atomic operations and memory barriers on one specific flag per cell to indicate if the cell is already being updated or not.

More precisely, we use here one bit (the Most Significant Bit - MSB) in one 32-bit integer variable (named `val` in the *falcON* code). Such variable is stored in each octree cell to describe various features of this cell, and only 25 bits are currently used. When a task needs to update a given cell, it first has to set this bit to 1 while checking that the bit was not already set to 1 (by another task): the two operations must be performed atomically. In case the bit was already set to 1, we use busy waiting since the cell update is a very fast operation. Another possibility is to suspend the current task and make the underlying thread treat another task: no performance gain was obtained in our tests in doing so. When the update is over, the bit is reset to 0: such write must include a memory barrier to ensure that (i) the write is performed after the computation and that (ii) subsequent reads are performed after this write. With OpenMP, we use `atomic capture` and `atomic update` operations. With TBB, the whole field `val` is declared as an atomic integer and we use a `compare_and_swap` operation to check the bit value and set it to 1.

In practice, we expect very few concurrent accesses to the same cells (which may increase the overhead of using atomics operations) since the number of cells in the octree is many orders of magnitude higher than the number of threads used.

In the exaFMM-dev software [13,14], task parallelism is applied to the DTT differently. In order to avoid conflicts, the traversal is strongly rewritten using one list of children cells for cell A and one list for cell B [13]. These two lists are halved which results in up to four tasks that must be computed among the four half-lists. Task barriers are then used to isolate tasks that can be performed in parallel without conflicts. As mentioned in [13], this implies some extra computations since cells A and B can be opened at the same time, whereas only one cell would have been opened in the original Dehnen's algorithm. On the contrary, in *pfalcON* we do not require a rewriting of the DTT and we do not introduce extra computations.

Besides, we also have to control the task computation grain for efficient parallel executions. Spawning too small tasks may not enable to offset the task creation overhead, whereas spawning only large tasks may result in an overall load imbalance among threads. We thus introduce a threshold (*TCT*, *Task Creation Threshold*) to stop task creation: when there are less than *TCT* particles in the two cells A and B (or in the cell A if $A = B$) no task is created for the remainder of this traversal (but atomic operations are still required). According to the $\mathcal{O}(N)$ runtime complexity, such linear threshold is indeed well-suited to control the computation grain size. Appropriate *TCT* values for OpenMP and TBB are around 1000 or 10000. It can be noticed that a similar threshold is used in exaFMM-dev in order to reduce the number of extra computations introduced by the exaFMM-dev task parallelism.

As far as the evaluation step is concerned, the task parallelism is straightforward to implement since there is no conflict among the tasks. We also use a threshold like *TCT* in order to control the task computation grain.

3.2 Portable and Efficient SIMD Direct Computation

SPMD model. Many works have already been published on the efficient vectorization of the direct computation for the near field part (see for example [1,7,14]). We target here both efficiency and portability on various vector instruction sets (SSE, AVX, Xeon Phi). We thus focus on the SPMD (single-program, multiple-data) model, where all computations are written as scalar ones and it is up to the compiler to merge such scalar computations in SIMD instructions. The main advantages are the ease of programming and the portability: the programmer needs neither to write the specific SIMD intrinsics for each architecture, nor to know the vector width, nor to implement data padding with zeroes according to this vector width. On CPU, such programming model is available in OpenCL (OpenCL implicit vectorization), as well as in the Intel SPMD Program Compiler (ispc) [11]. Compared to OpenCL, ispc has especially the following advantages [11]: (i) ispc kernel launches are faster and (ii) the same memory space and data structures can be shared between the C/C++ code and the ispc code. These are very important for *pfalcON* since SIMD computations are performed with small computation grains (usually a few tens of particles per leaf) and require a tight integration in the dual tree traversal and in the octree data structure. We will therefore rely here on the SPMD-on-SIMD model of `ispc`.

ispc technical features. In `ispc`, each scalar control flow corresponds to a *program instance* (similar to an OpenCL work-item). The group of program instances will be merged in one *gang* (similar to a CUDA warp or to an AMD OpenCL wave-front) to be processed concurrently with SIMD instructions. The gang size (denoted *gs*) of the gang is usually set to one or two time(s) the width of the underlying SIMD vector. Depending on the available instruction level parallelism and on the register pressure, it can be indeed more efficient (or not) to use twice the vector width. When the number of items to process is greater than the gang size, the programmer implements the mapping via an explicit loop over all items (contrary to CUDA and OpenCL, where warps/wave-fronts are scheduled by the runtime) [11]. This gives us more control to efficiently and safely implement the direct computation with the mutuality of gravity.

Direct computation kernels. We first focus on the direct computations between two different leafs A and B (*pair* computations). We first determine the leaf with the greatest number of particles (say A here). Each program instance is then in charge of one of the first *gs* particles in A, which leads to a SIMD processing of these *gs* particles. Interactions between these *gs* particles and the first particle of B are then processed concurrently: the first particle in B is therefore replicated in the underlying SIMD vector. Force and potential are then updated in A (no conflict among the program instances), as well as in the first particle of B (with `ispc` reductions among the program instances in the gang). This is iterated over all particles in B. Once all particles in B have been treated, the whole process is restarted for the next *gs* particles in A.

We now focus on the direct computations among all particles within one given leaf (*own* computations). In this case, we proceed as in [7] by using as much as possible the (efficient) pair computation along with the mutuality of gravity, and we start by isolating the first *gs* particles. Interactions between these first *gs* particles and the remaining particles are then computed by the pair computation kernel (with the mutuality of gravity). After this, the interactions among the first *gs* particles are then computed (similarly to the pair computation, but without the mutuality of gravity here). The whole process is restarted with the remaining particles, whose first *gs* particles are isolated.

Besides, moving from arrays of structures (AoS - as in the scalar *falcON*) to structures of arrays (SoA - more efficient for vector loads and stores) in *falcON* would have required very important programming efforts: we therefore keep the AoS data layout (like in `exaFMM-dev` for example) and rely on the fact that for direct computations the $\mathcal{O}(N)$ memory access times can be rapidly overlapped with the $\mathcal{O}(N^2)$ computation times. Moreover, we also use software pipelining in *pfalcON* with double buffering: we process two interactions at the same time, the first one being computed while data for the next one are being loaded in registers. This has been implemented in both the scalar *pfalcON* (referred to as *pfalcON-scalar*) and the SIMD code. Finally, we rely on the rsqrt_ps intrinsic SIMD function as a

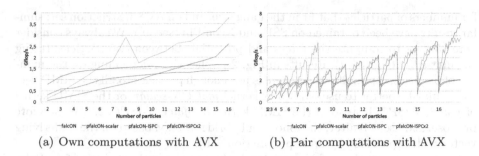

(a) Own computations with AVX   (b) Pair computations with AVX

Fig. 2. Performance of the different kernels for direct computations on AVX instruction set. For pair computations between cells A and B, only the number of particles N_A in cell A is indicated: for each value of N_A, N_B ranges from 1 to N_A.

floating-point reciprocal square root estimate, followed by one Newton-Raphson iteration to match floating point single precision.

4 Performance Results

For performance tests, we use three compute servers: *SSE-server* with two Intel X5650 CPUs (each having 6 SSE cores with 2-way SMT at 2.67 GHz) and 48 GB of memory, *AVX-server* with two Intel E5-2660 CPUs (each having 8 AVX cores with 2-way SMT at 2.20 GHz) and 32 GB of memory, and *Xeon-Phi* which is a 5110P Xeon Phi (60 cores with 4-way SMT at 1.053 GHz) used in native mode as a distant server. For *pfalcON*, we use OpenMP (3.1) and TBB (4.1) with GCC (4.7.3), since GCC specific optimizations are used in *falcON*, and with ICC (14.0.0) on *Xeon-Phi* for the SIMD intrinsics. exaFMM-dev[3] is used with ICC and TBB, and Bonsai[4] is run on NVIDIA GPUs (C2070 or K20c, both in *SSE-server*) with CUDA 5.0.

We will use two distributions of 10M particles: an artificial uniform distribution inside a 3D cube, and a Plummer distribution as a classical (non-uniform) astrophysical model [8]. All codes compute both forces and potentials, for all particles, with single precision floating point arithmetic. We also use in each code appropriate softenings for the near field part of the gravity [8].

4.1 SIMD Direct Computation

Figure 2 presents the performance of different direct computation kernels presented in Sect. 3.2; namely the original scalar implementation in *falcON*, *pfalcON-scalar* and two SIMD versions in *pfalcON*: with the gang size set to the underlying vector width (*pfalcON-ISPC*) or to twice this vector width (*pfalcON-ISPCx2*). This last ispc feature is however not yet available on the Xeon Phi, where we will therefore only use *pfalcON-ISPC*. The comparison is here performed

---

[3] https://bitbucket.org/rioyokota/exafmm-dev, commit 4bd77a5, 2013-09-12.
[4] https://github.com/treecode/Bonsai, version 8d8e4c0d19, 2013-04-21.

for numbers of particles that fit in the gang size, and on AVX instruction set: similar results have been obtained on SSE and Xeon Phi (see [9]). We always consider here 25 flops to compute the forces and potentials between two particles (using the mutuality of gravity). Results in Fig. 2 implies that, depending on the number of particles, especially when there is not enough particles to fill the SIMD vector, it may be better to use our scalar kernel *pfalcON-scalar*, or the SIMD kernel of *pfalcON-ISPC*, instead of the SIMD kernel of *pfalcON-ISPCx2*. We therefore propose, and use hereafter, the following hybrid strategy, based on the underlying vector width (provided by an `ispc` function call).

For own computations of N particles, we first compute the number of particles $N_m = \lfloor N/w \rfloor \times w$ that correspond to multiples of the vector width w, and the remainder $N_r = N - N_m$. Then we apply specific thresholds for each SIMD architecture to process N_m and N_r (with AVX: $T_1 = 6$, $T_2 = 72$; see [9] for SSE and Phi). For example for N_m, we use: *pfalcON-ISPCx2* if $T_2 \leq N_m$; *pfalcON-ISPC* if $T_1 \leq N_m < T_2$; *pfalcON-scalar* if $N_m < T_1$.

For pair computations of cells A and B with N_A and N_B particles ($N_A \geq N_B$), we first compute $N_{m,A}$ and $N_{r,A}$. We then apply specific thresholds (with AVX: $T_{S,1} = 8$, $T_{B,1} = 2$, $T_{S,2} = 32$, $T_{B,2} = 13$) following this strategy (firstly for $N_{m,A}$ and secondly for $N_{r,A}$): we use *pfalcON-ISPCx2* if $N_{m,A} \geq 2 \times VectorWidth$ and $N_{m,A} + N_B \geq T_{S,2}$ and $N_B \geq T_{B,2}$; otherwise, we use *pfalcON-ISPC* if $N_{m,A} + N_B \geq T_{S,1}$ and $N_B \geq T_{B,1}$; otherwise we use *pfalcON-scalar*.

Figures 3(a),3(b),3(c) show that our `ispc` hybrid strategy leads on SSE and AVX to performance that is mainly similar or better than the hand-tuned kernels of `exaFMM-dev` [14] for low numbers of particles. For higher numbers of particles, `ispc` clearly outperforms `exaFMM-dev` thanks to a gang size set to twice the vector width. On the Xeon Phi, we also obtain similar or better performance than `exaFMM-dev`, except for the high values of N with own computations: this is mainly due to the current lack of *pfalcON-ISPCx2* on the Xeon Phi.

Finally, we evaluate in Fig. 3(d) the SIMD performance gain on the overall interaction step: values on top of each bar correspond to the speedups of *pfalcON* with `ispc` over the scalar *rfalcON*. We optimally choose here the *Ncrit* value for each code on each architecture: for *rfalcON* the optimal *Ncrit* value is 8, whereas for the SIMD *pfalcON* code this is 32 for AVX and Xeon Phi, and 8 for SSE. The SIMD *pfalcON* code offers thus performance gains over *rfalcON* of 5% on one SSE core, but of up to 24% (resp. 92%) on one AVX (resp. Xeon Phi) core.

4.2   Task Parallelism

Figure 4 presents speedups of *pfalcON* over the serial *rfalcON* code. With both OpenMP and TBB, and for both uniform and non-uniform distributions of particles, we obtain very good speedups up to 15.8 on *AVX-server* and up to 60 on *Xeon-Phi*. Similar or better parallel efficiencies have been obtained on *SSE-server* (speedups up to 13.8, not shown here). Once the overhead of using task and atomic operations is taken into account (for 1 thread), we indeed obtain linear speedups on up to 32 physical CPU cores. On the Xeon Phi, using two hardware threads per core (denoted as 2-way SMT) enables us to improve the speedup from 50 (with 60

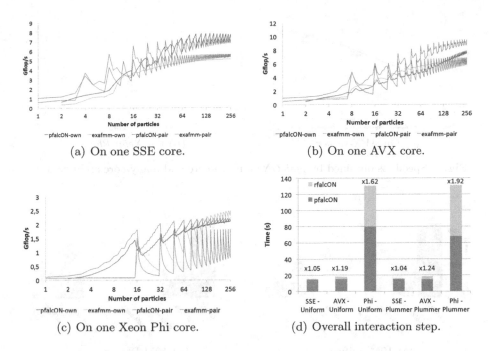

(a) On one SSE core.

(b) On one AVX core.

(c) On one Xeon Phi core.

(d) Overall interaction step.

Fig. 3. Figs. 3(a),3(b),3(c): performance comparison for direct computations (only up to 256 particles because of the *Ncrit* limit within each leaf). For pair computations, we use the same number of particles in both cells. Fig. 3(d): computation times on one CPU core for the overall interaction step on the two 10M distributions.

threads) to 60 (with 120 threads on 60 cores). Using two hardware threads is indeed required to reach best performance on this architecture, but performance drops for too many threads (with 4 hardware threads per core - 4-way SMT). These results show that our task parallelism with atomic operations is very well suited for multi-core CPUs, and scales well on the Xeon Phi. For the evaluation step, good speedups (around 12 on *AVX-server*, and around 32 on *Xeon-Phi*, not shown here) are obtained, these speedups being mainly limited by the very small computation times of this step in our tests.

4.3   Comparison with exaFMM-dev and Bonsai

Finally, we now compare in Fig. 5 the following codes: (i) the original *falcON*, (ii) the SIMD *pfalcON* on *AVX-server* (GCC+OpenMP with 32 hardware threads) and on *Xeon-Phi* (ICC+TBB with 120 hardware threads), (iii) the SIMD exaFMM-dev code with 1 or 32 threads on *AVX-server* (ICC+TBB), (iv) and finally Bonsai on one C2070 GPU and on one K20c GPU. We compare here two multi-core CPUs (*AVX-server* TDP: $2 \times 95W$) with one GPU (maximum power consumption: 238W for C2070 and 225W for K20c) and with one Xeon Phi (TDP: $225W$), since this corresponds to the same power consumption. Optimal *Ncrit*

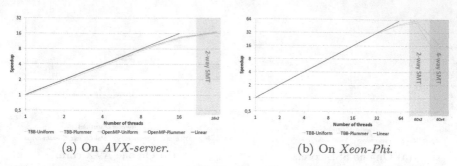

(a) On *AVX-server*.   (b) On *Xeon-Phi*.

Fig. 4. Speedups obtained by *pfalcON* on multi-core and many-core architectures

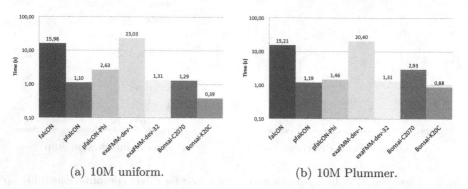

(a) 10M uniform.   (b) 10M Plummer.

Fig. 5. Computation times (interaction and evaluation steps) for various *N*-body codes

values are used for *falcON*, *pfalcON* and `exaFMM-dev`, whereas `Bonsai` uses its own specific thresholds ($N_{leaf} = 16$ and $N_{crit} = 64$, see [3]). As recommended for astrophysical *N*-body simulations [8], we use $\theta = 0.6$ for *falcON*, *pfalcON* and `exaFMM-dev`, and $\theta = 0.75$ for `Bonsai` (default value) whose expansions and MAC are different [3]. For *falcON*, *pfalcON* and `exaFMM-dev`, we consider here only the interaction and evaluation steps, and for `Bonsai` we consider the corresponding "tree-traverse" step.

Speedups between *pfalcON* and `exaFMM-dev` are similar. Since *falcON* is somewhat faster for serial executions, *pfalcON* is then also somewhat faster than `exaFMM-dev` for parallel executions. As far as the Xeon Phi is concerned, there is no performance gain compared to the two multi-core CPUs, mainly because astrophysical *N*-body simulations offer small computation grains for the direct computations: there is usually too few particles per leaf to fill at best the vector units of the Xeon Phi. The Xeon Phi however outperforms the C2070 for the non-uniform Plummer distribution. Finally, *pfalcON* on *AVX-server* outperforms `Bonsai` on the C2070 GPU. Using the newer K20c GPU, `Bonsai` outperforms *pfalcON* on *AVX-server* for the uniform distribution, but the performance results are much more closer for the more realistic Plummer distribution. Non-uniform distributions are indeed more challenging for GPU codes, whereas *pfalcON* on *AVX-server* is few sensitive to the particle distribution. Lastly, we emphasize that 50M distributions can be run on *SSE-server* and *AVX-server*, but not on any GPU.

5   Conclusion and Future Work

We have presented a parallel version of the dual tree traversal which is the most challenging and time consuming part in Dehnen's algorithm. Very good speedups are obtained, Dehnen's original algorithm is preserved, no extra computations are introduced, and the SPMD model is shown to be suitable for efficient and portable SIMD vectorization. Since *falcON* is faster than serial Barnes-Hut tree-codes, *pfalcON* with such parallel speedups should outperform any parallel tree-code on one single node with multi-core CPUs. Besides, *pfalcON* is faster than or almost as fast as GPU tree-codes like `Bonsai` for astrophysical distributions, but we emphasize that GPU tree-codes are limited by the GPU memory, and MPI communications on multiple nodes with GPU are usually penalized by the PCI bus. The *pfalcON* code is available at `https://pfalcon.lip6.fr`.

Future work will be focused on the other parts of *falcON* (mainly the octree construction [13]), on distributed-memory parallelism, and on applying such parallel algorithm to other applications than astrophysics. Another (challenging) task would be to efficiently combine the best algorithm, namely the dual tree traversal, with the most powerful hardware currently available, namely GPUs.

References

1. Arora, N., Shringarpure, A., Vuduc, R.: Direct n-body kernels for multicore platforms. In: Proc. of the Int. Conf. on Parallel Processing (ICPP), pp. 379–387 (2009)
2. Barnes, J.E., Hut, P.: A hierarchical O(N log N) force-calculation algorithm. Nature 324(4), 446–449 (1986)
3. Bédorf, J., Gaburov, E., Zwart, S.P.: A sparse octree gravitational N-body code that runs entirely on the GPU processor. J. Comp. Phys. 231(7), 2825–2839 (2012)
4. Burtscher, M., Pingali, K.: An Efficient CUDA Implementation of the Tree-Based Barnes Hut n-Body Algorithm. GPU computing Gems Emerald edition, p. 75 (2011)
5. Cheng, H., Greengard, L., Rokhlin, V.: A Fast Adaptive Multipole Algorithm in Three Dimensions. Journal of Computational Physics 155, 468–498 (1999)
6. Dehnen, W.: A Hierarchical O(N) Force Calculation Algorithm. J. Comp. Phys. 179, 27–42 (2002)
7. Fortin, P., Lamotte, J.L.: Fast Multipole Method on the Cell B.E.: the Near Field Part. In: Int. Parallel Computing Conf. (ParCo), vol. 19, pp. 323–330 (2009)
8. Fortin, P., Athanassoula, E., Lambert, J.-C.: Comparisons of different codes for galactic N-body simulations. Astronomy & Astrophysics 531, A120 (2011)
9. Lange, B., Fortin, P.: Parallel dual tree traversal on multi-core and many-core architectures for astrophysical N-body simulations, `http://hal.upmc.fr/hal-00947130`
10. Londrillo, P., Nipoti, C., Ciotti, L.: A parallel implementation of a new fast algorithm for N-body simulations. In: Comp. Astro. in Italy: Methods and Tools (2002)
11. Pharr, M., Mark, W.R.: ispc: A SPMD compiler for high-performance CPU programming. In: Innovative Parallel Computing (InPar 2012), pp. 1–13. IEEE (2012)
12. Springel, V.: The cosmological simulation code GADGET-2. Monthly Notices of the Royal Astronomical Society 364(4), 1105–1134 (2005)
13. Taura, K., Nakashima, J., Yokota, R., Maruyama, N.: A Task Parallel Implementation of Fast Multipole Methods. In: SC Companion, pp. 617–625 (2012)
14. Yokota, R.: An FMM Based on Dual Tree Traversal for Many-core Architectures. Journal of Algorithms and Computational Technology 7(3), 301–324 (2013)

Customizing Driving Directions with GPUs*

Daniel Delling[1], Moritz Kobitzsch[2], and Renato F. Werneck[1]

[1] Microsoft Research
{dadellin,renatow}@microsoft.com
[2] Karlsruhe Institute of Technology
kobitzsch@kit.edu

Abstract. Computing driving directions interactively on continental road networks requires preprocessing. This step can be costly, limiting our ability to incorporate new optimization functions, including traffic information or personal preferences. We show how the performance of the state-of-the-art customizable route planning (CRP) framework is boosted by GPUs, even though it has highly irregular structure. Our experimental study reveals that our method is an order of magnitude faster than a highly-optimized parallel CPU implementation, enabling interactive personalized driving directions on continental scale.

1   Introduction

The past decade has seen intense research on the computation of driving directions in road networks [2, 20]. This problem can be modeled as computing shortest paths on a weighted graph and solved by classical algorithms such as Dijkstra's [4]. For continental road networks (with tens of millions of arcs), however, queries can take seconds, which is too slow for interactive applications. To overcome this, modern specialized algorithms [1, 3, 12, 14] generally work in two phases: a *preprocessing stage* precomputes some auxiliary data, which is then used to answer on-line *queries*. The fastest algorithms [1, 3] answer queries in microseconds or less after a few minutes of preprocessing on a standard server.

Such queries are certainly fast enough, but since preprocessing must be rerun whenever arc weights change, these methods do not support dynamic scenarios such as real-time traffic. The recent *customizable route planning* (CRP) algorithm [7, 10] (see also [8]) offers a different trade-off by working in *three* phases. The initial *preprocessing* phase is *metric-independent*: it takes as input only the graph topology. The *customization* phase takes as input the cost function (metric) and the output of the previous phase. Finally, *queries* use the outputs of both phases to compute point-to-point shortest paths. Queries are just fast enough (milliseconds rather than microseconds) for interactive applications, but a new cost function can be incorporated in mere seconds (by running only the customization phase), enabling CRP to handle frequent traffic updates. The algorithm is currently used by Bing Maps to compute driving directions.

We investigate how we can use GPUs to accelerate customization even further. Our approach is to set up all necessary data structures on the GPU during the metric-independent preprocessing, such that we only need to invoke a few GPU kernels when

---

* The second author worked on this project while at Microsoft Research.

F. Silva et al. (Eds.): Euro-Par 2014, LNCS 8632, pp. 728–739, 2014.
© Springer International Publishing Switzerland 2014

a metric change occurs. This enables a degree of personalization well beyond what is available in current systems. Most notably, one could define a cost function at query time and still obtain driving directions in a fraction of a second. At first sight, computing driving directions is not a natural application for GPUs. Through careful engineering, however, we can harness the power of GPUs to make customization not only faster, but also more energy-efficient than CPU-based (even multicore) implementations.

We are not aware of previous work that uses GPUs to process dynamic continental road networks effectively. PHAST [6] can efficiently answer one-to-all (rather than point-to-point) queries on a GPU, but only after heavy CPU-based *metric-dependent* preprocessing, and is thus not dynamic. Parallelizing a single shortest-path computation on sparse and high-diameter graphs (such as road networks) is generally hard [16, 18] even on multicore CPUs. It is even harder on GPUs [5, 17, 19], since access patterns and operations are far from regular. We get around this issue by parallelizing more than a single shortest-path computation.

2   Preliminaries

The standard representation [2] of a road network is as a directed graph $G = (V, A)$, where each vertex $v \in V$ represents an intersection (junction) and each arc $a \in A$ represents a (directed) road segment. A *cost function* (or *metric*) $\ell : A \to \mathcal{N}$ maps each arc $a \in A$ to a positive *cost* (or *length*) reflecting the effort to traverse it. We use a more realistic model that incorporates turn costs and restrictions. The customization phase takes as input an *expanded graph* where vertices correspond to the heads of original arcs, and arcs are the concatenation of an original turn and an original arc. For queries and to store the graph in main memory, we use a more compact representation [7, 13].

Each original arc in our application is modeled as a collection of *static properties*, such as physical length (in meters), road category (freeway, local road, or ferry, for example), number of lanes, and speed limit. Similarly, each turn has a *type* (left turn, right turn, and so on). A *metric decoder* is a function that maps these properties to the cost of traversing the arc or making the turn. We could model special cases (such as traffic) by storing costs explicitly for some exceptional arcs. We assume all costs are integral and that the length of any shortest path fits in 32 bits.

A *path* in the graph is a sequence of arcs of the form (v_0, v_1), (v_1, v_2), (v_2, v_3), ..., (v_{k-1}, v_k). The *cost* (or *length*) of a path is the sum of the costs of its arcs and the turns between them. The *point-to-point shortest path* problem takes as input the graph $G = (V, A)$ and two arcs a_s and a_t, and returns the shortest (minimum-length) path that starts at a_s and ends at a_t in G.

Customizable Route Planning. The *preprocessing phase* of CRP starts by computing a nested L-level partition. A partition of V is a collection of *cells* such that each vertex $v \in V$ belongs to exactly one cell. A nested L-level partition of V is a family of partitions such that, for any level $i < L$ and each cell C, there exists a cell C' on level $i + 1$ that contains C; we say that C is a subcell of C'. (For simplicity, define a level-0 partition consisting of singletons.) CRP uses the PUNCH [9] graph-partitioning algorithm to generate an L-level partition top-down, partitioning level L first, then (recursively) each

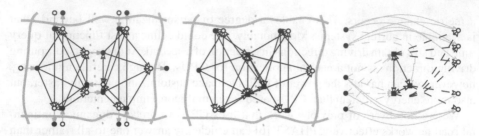

Fig. 1. A cell C with the overlays of its two subcells (left), its compact graph (center), and the abstracted subgraph with entry (filled circles), inner (squares), and exit (hollow circles) vertices

cell thus created. For each level l, PUNCH finds cells with no more than U_l (an input parameter) vertices and minimizes the number of boundary arcs between cells.

The CRP preprocessing phase also sets up the topology of a multilevel overlay graph [15]. Figure 1 (left) shows a cell C on some level. Every incoming boundary arc (u, v) (with $u \notin C$ and $v \in C$) corresponds to an *entry vertex* for C, and every outgoing boundary arc (v, w) (with $v \in C$ and $w \notin C$) defines an *exit vertex* for C. The overlay of a cell is the complete bipartite graph with directed *shortcuts* (black arrows in the figure) between its entry (filled circles) and exit (hollow circles) vertices. The overlay of level l is the union of all cell overlays and boundary arcs (gray arrows) on this level.

The CRP *customization phase* computes the costs of all shortcut arcs on the overlay. It computes, for each cell C, the distances between each entry vertex and each exit vertex: a shortcut (p, q) in C represents the shortest p–q path restricted to C. The algorithm processes cells bottom-up, starting at level one; when processing a level-l cell C, it works on the (small) overlay graph for level $l - 1$. One could simply run Dijkstra's algorithm from each entry vertex until all exit vertices are scanned [7], but one can do better (even on CPUs [10]) using Bellman-Ford [4] or contraction [12]. Sections 3 and 4 detail these approaches and show how they can be effectively realized on the GPU.

A point-to-point CRP *query* runs bidirectional Dijkstra on the overlay graph, but only entering cells that contain either the source s or the target t.

3   Search-Based Customization

The main subroutine of the CRP customization phase computes arc lengths of bipartite graphs. The fastest [10] approach based on graph traversal is based on the classical Bellman-Ford algorithm. To process a cell C at level i, it first builds a compact graph $G_C = (V_C, A_C)$ consisting of the shortcuts and boundary arcs on level $i - 1$ that are in C, but with the head vertices of the internal boundary arcs (i.e., those not on level i) removed and their incident arcs concatenated. See Figure 1 (center). Let N_C and X_C be the sets of entry and exit vertices of C, respectively. The algorithm maintains, for each vertex in V_C, a *distance array* with $|N_C|$ values; the k-th position for the k-th entry vertex is initialized with zero, and all others with infinity. Then it runs Bellman-Ford as long as there is an improvement on any of the distance labels. Eventually, the distance labels of the exit vertices will reflect their distances from each of the entry vertices.

Basic Algorithm. On small diameter graphs, Bellman-Ford works well on GPUs [5], but we can make it even more efficient for our purposes. We can classify the vertices in V_C into three categories: entry (N_C), exit (X_C), and inner (I_C). Figure 1 (center) shows that entry vertices have only outgoing arcs, and exit vertices only incoming arcs. Moreover, there are four types of arcs in A_C (illustrated in Figure 1 (right), obtained by rearranging Figure 1 (center)). The *init* arcs A_C^j (dashed gray) link entry to inner vertices, the *inner* arcs A_C^i (solid black) connect inner vertices to one another, the *collection* arcs A_C^c (dashed black) link inner to exit vertices, and the *mapping* arcs A_C^m (solid gray) link entry to exit vertices. Note that init and mapping arcs are shortcuts, while each inner or collection arc is the concatenation of a shortcut and a cut arc (all from level $i - 1$). When running on G_C, Bellman-Ford touches each mapping and init arc only once, at which point it sets exactly one distance value at its head vertex. We can exploit this.

For a cell C, let $G_C^i = (I_C, A_C^i)$ be its *inner graph* and $V_C^c = (X_C, A_C^c)$ be its *collection graph*. In general, on level i, we compute the costs of shortcuts on level i (to be stored in a *shortcut array S_i*) from costs of level-$i - 1$ shortcuts and boundary arcs (stored in a *boundary array B*). Our algorithm processes a cell in five phases. The *mapping phase* copies the costs of the mapping arcs from S_{i-1} to S_i. The subsequent *aggregation* phase computes the costs of the inner arcs from S_{i-1} and B. The third phase (*injection*) copies the init arc costs from S_{i-1} into the distance array (which now has size $|N_C| \cdot |I_C|$). The fourth phase, *search*, runs Bellman-Ford on the inner graph, stopping when there is no improvement. The final *collection* phase first aggregates the costs of the collection arcs (as in the aggregation phase); then, for each exit vertex v, it iterates over its incoming collection arcs to compute the costs of the level-i shortcuts ending at v, updating S_i. We propose two GPU implementations of this approach: global and local.

Global Implementation. The global implementation is orchestrated by the CPU and invokes multiple kernels per level i. We maintain one global distance array representing the distance values of all inner vertices of all cells on level i.

For each of the first three phases of customization (mapping, aggregation, and injection), we create a single kernel with one thread for each relevant arc. We support these threads by maintaining *auxiliary arrays* with the relevant information in global memory; thread t reads position t from this array. For aggregation, we arrange the data in global memory such that threads also write their output to consecutive positions.

More precisely, the *mapping* phase has one thread per mapping arc: it uses the auxiliary array to learn the position it must read from (in S_{i-1}) and write to (in S_i). During the *aggregation* phase, thread t computes the length of inner arc t; the corresponding auxiliary array contains the positions in B_{i-1} and S_{i-1} the thread must read from. Similarly, *injection* has one thread per init arc, and its auxiliary array stores a position in S_{i-1} (for reading) and another in the distance array (for writing).

The *search* phase uses one thread per distance value. Recall that we have one distance per pair (inner vertex, entry vertex). A thread processes all incoming arcs for a fixed inner vertex v and updates a single distance value (for one entry vertex). The corresponding index array contains the vertex ID it has to process, as well as an index (a number from 0 to $|N_C| - 1$) indicating which of its distances to update. This information can be packed into 32 bits. Also, rather than storing the tail ID, an arc stores the position of the first distance of its tail; the thread then uses the index as an offset. Since global synchronization is required, each Bellman-Ford iteration runs as a single kernel. Each thread writes to a timestamp array (indexed by cell number) whenever it updates some value; Bellman-Ford stops after an iteration in which this array does not change.

The *collection phase* is similar to the search phase, but operates on the exit vertices and is limited to one round. Moreover, it stores its information directly to S_i. To make these accesses more efficient, shortcuts are ordered by tail in global memory.

Note that our implementation has no write-write conflict. During Bellman-Ford, a thread may read a position that is being updated by another. Since integers are atomic and values only improve from one round to the next, this does not affect correctness.

Local Implementation. The local implementation invokes one kernel per level and operates block-wise. For simplicity, we first describe our algorithm assuming it processes one cell per thread block, then generalize it. Since we no longer have one thread for each value we deal with, we use a small *block header* to store relevant information the threads require. It includes the numbers of all types of arcs (mapping, injection, inner, and collection) and vertices (inner, entry, and exit). It also has pointers to the positions in global memory where we store the topology of the inner and collection graphs.

The algorithm starts by reserving space in shared memory for the distance values it will compute (initialized with ∞). The mapping phase is exactly as before. The *aggregation phase* is also similar, but stores the values in shared memory; it also copies the inner graph topology to shared memory. Similarly, *injection* works as before, but writing into the distance array in shared memory. The *search phase* now operates entirely in shared memory and uses the GPU block-based synchronization between Bellman-Ford rounds. Note that thread t (within the block) can deduct from the block header both the vertex it has to work on ($\lfloor t/|I_C| \rfloor$) and the entry vertex number ($t \bmod |I_C|$). The *collection phase* first copies the collection graph to shared memory (overwriting the inner graph, which is no longer needed), aggregating the costs of the collection arcs. It then performs a single Bellman-Ford round and stores the final distances to global memory. We use global memory as fallback if any of these phases does not fit in shared memory.

We use 16 bits for indexing; if that is not enough for a given cell, we process the entire level using the global implementation instead. This happens only very rarely, and can usually be avoided by optimizations we introduce later.

Since we know in advance how much shared memory each cell occupies, we can often group multiple cells into the same block. We reorder the cells in GPU memory to ensure their shortcuts appear consecutively. For regularity, we only group cells that have the same number of entry vertices. The algorithm works exactly as before: it just sees the input as a bigger, disconnected graph.

Comparing the local and global approaches, the latter is more space-consuming, since it needs to store additional data for each distance value in global memory. It is still a good option when there are few cells or when graphs are too large to fit in shared memory. We thus use the global implementation on levels with fewer than 100 cells (about 6 times the typical number of multi-processors of current GPUs), or when the number of collection or inner arcs exceeds 65 536, the maximum number the local approach can index with 16 bits.

We have been assuming that we can use a level-$i - 1$ overlay to compute the overlay of level i, but this is not true for the first level, when we must operate on the underlying original graph. We can handle this by adapting the routine that aggregates arc costs. Mapping and init arcs represent an original graph arc, and all other arcs are a concatenation of a turn and an original arc. Therefore, for a mapping or init arc, we store its physical properties (rather than a position in S_{i-1}); for other arcs, we store the turn type as well. In all cases, we apply the current metric decoder during aggregation.

An important optimization is to use *mezzanine levels* [10], partition levels that are used to accelerate customization, but discarded for queries (to save space). Mezzanine levels help reduce the size of inner graphs (which are expensive to deal with) by turning more arcs into init, mapping, or collection arcs (which are accessed a constant number of times). This reduces the number of Bellman-Ford iterations, our main bottleneck. Mezzanine levels are not free, though: there is some overhead for mapping the extra levels, but this is very cheap on the GPU (not so on CPUs [10]). Moreover, they increase both the number of cells and the space consumption on the GPU. Note, however, that we can overwrite shortcut weights for mezzanine level i as soon as level $i + 1$ is processed.

4 Contraction-Based Customization

For lower levels of the hierarchy, customization is faster [10] if one uses *graph contraction* instead of graph searches (Dijkstra or Bellman-Ford). We first recap how the CPU-based approach works on the CPU, then explain how it can be adapted to the GPU.

When processing a cell C on the CPU, we can compute the lengths of the shortest paths (in G_C) from its entry vertices to its exit vertices using the *shortcut* operation [12]. Shortcutting an inner vertex v means removing it from the graph and, for each incoming arc (u,v) and outgoing arc (v,w), creating a *shortcut arc* (u,w) with length $\ell(u,w) = \ell(u,v) + \ell(v,w)$. If (u,w) does not yet exist, we insert it; if it does, we update its length if the new arc is shorter. By repeatedly applying this operation to all inner vertices in G_C, one ends up with a bipartite graph with arcs between entry and exit vertices of C, where arc lengths represent the corresponding distances (missing arcs represent infinite distances). Any contraction order leads to the same final topology, but a carefully chosen (during preprocessing) order based on nested dissections leads to fewer operations overall and a faster algorithm [10].

The fundamental operation of contraction is to read the costs of two arcs, add them up, compare the result with the cost of a third arc, and update its cost if needed. Instead of using a graph during customization, Delling and Werneck [10] propose simulating the contraction process during preprocessing to create an *instruction array* representing these fundamental operations (*microinstructions*) compactly as triples (a,b,c), where a and b are the positions to be read and c the position to write to. These positions refer to a *memory array* M and correspond to arc costs. Each cell C has its own instruction and memory arrays. Moreover, they use an *arc instruction* array to initialize M.

Building the GPU Microinstructions. Microinstructions provide a natural starting point for implementing contraction-based customization on the GPU. Although the microinstruction array can be fairly large, it is only read once (and sequentially), so we keep it in global memory. Since M is much smaller and has a less rigid access pattern (each position can be accessed multiple times), we keep it in shared memory. For optimal performance, however, we must address several issues: decreasing the space used by microinstructions (for fewer accesses to slower memory), reducing the memory array (to keep multiple cells in shared memory at once), and parallelization within a cell (for efficiency on GPU). We do so by preprocessing and enriching the microinstructions before copying them to the GPU (the arc instructions can be copied essentially as is).

First, we make the microinstructions more compact. Since each entry in the memory array M takes 32 bits of shared memory, it can have at most 12 288 positions in the GPUs we test. These can be addressed with 14 bits, or 42 bits per triple in the instruction array. For most cells, however, 32 bits are enough. To achieve this, we first ensure that $a < b$ in each instruction triple (a,b,c) (we swap a and b otherwise), then store the triple $(a, b-a, c-b)$ using 14, 8, and 9 bits, respectively (we reserve the 32nd bit for later). This means a can be any position in shared memory, b can refer to positions $a+1$ to $a+256$, and c can refer to $b-256$ to $b+255$. If a cell has at least one instruction that cannot use this compact representation (with b too far from a or c too far from b), we use a full 48-bit representation for all of its microinstructions.

To parallelize within a cell, we group independent instructions by layers. Note that two instructions in a cell are independent if they do not write to the same memory position. We create these layers by working in rounds, from latest to earliest, greedily assigning instructions to the latest possible layer (after accounting for the dependencies between them); we then apply a postprocessing step to make the layers more balanced.

Next, we reduce the memory array. Once a shortcut is eliminated by the contraction routine, the memory position that stores its cost could be reused for another shortcut, thus saving on shared memory. We identify such reusage opportunities during preprocessing as follows. We process the layered microinstructions from earliest to latest. We interpret each entry in a triple (a,b,c) as a *shortcut* (rather than positions in M, which is what we are trying to determine). We keep counters of pending reads and writes for each shortcut and a candidate pool of free memory positions (initially, all but those used by the arc instructions); when a read counter becomes zero for some shortcut, we add its position to the pool for potential reuse in future layers. When processing an instruction (a,b,c) that writes to shortcut c for the first time, we assign c to the free position that is closest to b; in addition, we use the 32nd bit (mentioned above) to *mark* this instruction, indicating that the GPU must simply write to the target position (ignoring the value already there) when executing this instruction. As an optimization, if an instruction (a,b,c) performs the last read from a (or b) and the first to c, we can immediately assign c to a's (or b's) position. If after running this basic algorithm the new instructions still cannot be represented in compact form (32 bits), we perturb the positions of the original arcs and retry; this is cheap and helps in some cases. Since the final shortcuts do not necessarily have consecutive positions in M, we use a map to translate them to the corresponding (consecutive) positions in S_1, the shortcut array on level 1. Note that we use microinstructions only to compute the shortcuts on the lowest level.

Finally, for better block utilization, we greedily pack cells as long as their combined memory arrays fit in shared memory. For better memory access patterns, we do not mix compact and full cells. We prefer to group cells with the same number of layers within a block, but we may combine blocks with different depth if needed. When we finally store the instruction array on the GPU, we reorder it to reflect the block assignments:

instructions within the same block are sorted by layer (across cells). Since the GPU must synchronize between layers, we store layer sizes in the block header.

GPU Execution. With the data structures set up, we compute S_1 on the GPU as follows. We invoke one kernel for the full computation, since synchronization is only needed within a block. On each block, we first run the arc instructions. The block header stores the number of arc instructions in each of its cells; each thread can use this information (and its own ID) to determine where in shared memory to store the result of the arc instruction it is responsible for. We then execute the microinstructions, layer by layer, also with one thread per instruction. Finally, we map the costs of the output shortcuts to S_1, using one thread per value. For each block, we store its first position in S_1, allowing each thread to determine (using its own ID) where to write to.

5   Putting Everything Together

During the metric-independent phase of CRP, we set up all necessary data structures on the GPU, including arc instructions to aggregate the costs of the boundary arcs.

The work flow of the customization phase is as follows. We start by transferring the current metric decoder (less than a kilobyte) from main to GPU memory. Then we invoke two streams on the GPU, one computing the lowest level (using either Bellman-Ford or microinstrutions), and one setting the costs of the boundary arcs of the overlay graph. When both are done, one stream processes all remaining levels, while another asynchronously copies shortcut levels to main memory as soon as they are ready. This hides the time needed for the GPU-CPU data transfer almost completely.

Our implementation can use multiple GPUs in a single machine simply by allocating all top-level cells (and their subcells) among them so as to balance the (estimated) work. This approach requires no GPU to GPU communication during customization.

6   Experiments

We implemented all algorithms in C++ and CUDA, and compiled them with Visual C++ 2012 and CUDA 5.5. We ran most tests on a desktop computer running Windows 8.1. It has an Intel Core-i7 4770 (4 cores, 8 threads, 3.4 GHz, 4x64 KB L1, 4x256 KB L2, and 8 MB L3 cache) and 32 GiB of 1600-DDR3 RAM. Moreover, it has an ASUS NVIDIA GTX Titan with 6144 MiB of DDR5 RAM (6 GHz) and 14 multiprocessing units, each with 192 cores (2688 cores in total). The GPU has a normal clock rate of 837 MHz, but operates at 1 GHz as long as it stays cool enough (which was the case for all of our experiments).

Our focus is on the overall *customization time*, the total time from a metric change to the point we can compute driving directions (on the CPU). Thus, in our GPU setting, we include the time needed for data transfer (copying the metric decoder to the GPU and the shortcut costs back). All GPU times are averages over 1000 executions.

Our default input represents the road network of (Western) Europe and was made available by PTV AG for the 9th DIMACS Implementation Challenge [11]. This graph

Table 1. Impact of mezzanine levels on customization done by local and global Bellman-Ford

	LOCAL BELLMAN-FORD								GLOBAL BELLMAN-FORD							
	TIME ON LEVEL [MS]						TOTAL		TIME ON LEVEL [MS]						TOTAL	
Z	0	1	2	3	4	5	[ms]	[MiB]	0	1	2	3	4	5	[ms]	[MiB]
0	73.8	37.9	23.0	25.5	40.7	—	—	2212	157.6	82.1	56.9	45.8	43.7	40.4	477	3679
1	52.2	26.5	14.4	12.6	16.7	65.8	244	2816	94.9	48.9	28.6	25.9	25.6	22.8	295	4363
2	51.9	26.8	14.6	11.3	16.5	50.7	228	3412	99.3	47.9	26.1	23.0	23.7	21.3	289	5559
3	56.0	27.2	14.0	10.6	12.4	38.5	212	3911	114.9	47.7	25.5	20.4	20.0	18.8	297	5913
4	61.7	28.7	15.3	10.6	13.9	42.3	224	4342	133.1	52.0	44.7	21.3	21.2	19.7	344	7318

has $|V| = 18 \cdot 10^6$ vertices, $|A| = 42 \cdot 10^6$ arcs, and travel times as the cost function. As in previous work [7], we augment it by U-turn costs of 100 s (other turns are free). Our default CRP setup has 5 levels, with maximum cell sizes of $U_1 = 2^8$, $U_2 = 2^{11}$, $U_3 = 2^{14}$, $U_4 = 2^{17}$, and $U_5 = 2^{20}$; it requires about 72 MiB to store all shortcut costs.

Table 1 evaluates the global (GBF) and local (LBF) Bellman-Ford implementations, as well as how mezzanine levels affect them. As in previous work [7], we always keep two *phantom* levels (these are fixed mezzanine levels) of size $U_{-1} = 4$ and $U_0 = 32$. We always use LBF to compute the lowest level (cell size 4); this takes about 50 ms. We then vary the number of mezzanine levels (Z) between two consecutive levels; maximum mezzanine cell sizes are set so that their ratios across levels remain roughly constant. The table reports the times spent on each level (starting from the level below) for $0 \leq Z \leq 4$. A "—" entry means that LBF could not be executed because at least one cell has more than 65 535 inner arcs (see Section 3). We also report the total customization time (including all mezzanine levels) and the space consumption on the GPU.

We observe that mezzanine levels reduce customization times in general. One mezzanine level is enough on lower levels, but we can use up to three on higher levels, since more mezzanine levels can make more inner graphs fit into shared memory. Moreover, LBF is faster than GBF for all levels but the highest one, on which the number of cells is small and LBF is unbalanced. GBF consumes more space, mostly due to the distance array and thread data we need to store in global memory. For the rest of the paper, our default setting is to use $Z = 1$ up to level 1 and $Z = 3$ for higher levels; moreover, we use GBF for levels with fewer than 100 cells, and LBF otherwise. With this combination, customization takes 182.0 ms and uses 3034 MiB of GPU memory.

With this default setup, we now evaluate the effect of microinstructions. Figure 2 (left) reports the (relative) increase in customization time and GPU space when we use microinstructions up to a certain (possibly mezzanine) level, and Bellman-Ford afterwards. Using microinstructions up to cell size 32 reduces customization times by up to 20% (to 150.4 ms), but increases the overall space consumption by 25% (to 3792 MiB). Interestingly, using microinstructions for bigger or smaller cells does not help: many bigger cells cannot use instructions packed into 32 bits, and for smaller cells the overhead for initializing the memory array by arc instructions is too high. For the remaining experiments, we use microinstructions to process cells of size up to 32.

Figure 2 (right) reports the speedup when we vary the core clock rate of the GTX Titan between 900 and 1200 MHz (recall that 1000 is the default) and the memory clock rate between 5400 and 7200 MHz (the default is 6000). We observed no data errors

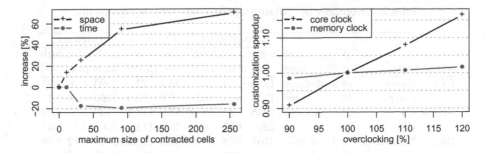

Fig. 2. Left: Impact of microinstructions on GPU space consumption and customization times for varying cell sizes. Right: Impact of clock rates on customization times.

when overclocking in these ranges. The results indicate we are computation bound: increasing the core clock by 20% accelerates customization by almost 17%, whereas the memory clock rate has very little impact on the overall performance.

Table 2 compares our novel GPU implementation of CRP with the previous (highly tuned) CPU implementation [10], which uses microinstructions up to cell sizes of 256. We test various machines and GPU setups: M1-4 is our default machine (Core i7 4770), M2-12 has two 6-core Intel Xeon X5680 (3.33 GHz, 6x64 KB L1, 6x256 KB L2, and 12 MB shared L3 cache) with 96 GiB of DDR3-1333 RAM, and M2-16 has two 8-core Intel Xeon E5-2690 (2.9 GHz, 8x64 KB L1, 8x256 KB L2, and 20 MB shared L3 cache) with 384 GiB of DDR-1066 RAM. (We turn hyperthreading off for M2-12 and M2-16 because it does not help performance in our setting.) Finally, we test different GPU setups in M1-4: our default Titan, the Titan with core clock rate overclocked by 20%, two EVGA GTX 780 Ti OC (15 multiprocessors, 2880 CUDA cores, 1.2 GHz core, and 3 GiB of 7 GHz memory), as well as four GTX 780 Ti. (Note that a single GTX 780 Ti does not have enough memory for our default setup.) Besides customization times, we report the number of CPU threads used (t), the space occupied by all data structures in main and GPU memory, the (system-wide) power usage during customization, and the resulting average energy consumption for a single customization.

The GPU implementation always outperforms the CPU implementation. Using a single GPU, our algorithm is about 20 times faster than a sequential CPU execution.

Table 2. Key figures for various hardware setups

machine	t	GPU	RATE [GHz] core	mem	MEM [MiB] main	GPU	TIME [ms]	POW [W]	ENER. [J]
M1-4	1	Titan	1.0	6.0	484	3791	150.4	248	37.3
M1-4	1	Titan	1.2	6.0	484	3791	129.3	280	36.2
M1-4	2	2x780 Ti	1.2	7.0	484	3800	67.3	574	38.6
M1-4	4	4x780 Ti	1.2	7.0	484	3821	35.8	1045	37.4
M1-4	1	–	–	–	3119	–	2654	54	143.3
M1-4	8	–	–	–	3119	–	645	94	60.6
M2-12	12	–	–	–	3119	–	371	332	123.2
M2-16	16	–	–	–	3119	–	346	401	141.5

Table 3. Performance of CRP with GPU customization on other inputs

source	input	$\|V\|$ [$\times 10^6$]	cost func	setup [s]	space[MiB] main	GPU	time [ms]	space [MiB]	nmb. scans	dist [ms]	path [ms]
					DATA STRUCT.		CUSTOM		QUERIES		
PTV	Europe	18.0	distance	1736	484	3821	36.3	72.3	2993	1.30	5.95
	Europe	18.0	time	1736	484	3821	35.8	72.3	3050	1.17	3.17
TIGER	US	23.9	distance	2005	682	6939	57.9	113.1	3149	1.30	8.05
	US	23.9	time	2005	682	6939	56.6	113.1	3006	1.14	5.47
Bing	N. America	30.3	default	2767	908	8590	68.4	139.1	3387	1.12	3.98
	Europe	47.9	default	3618	1128	6707	62.8	124.1	3661	1.35	4.03

Increasing the number of GPUs linearly decreases customization times; with 4 GPUs, we are still 10 times faster than the best CPU setup (on 16 cores). Moreover, GPU customization is 2 to 3 times more energy-efficient, which is consistent with previous observations on related problems [6]. We also note that, since we store microinstructions on the GPU, the memory footprint on the CPU is reduced significantly.

Finally, we test more benchmark instances. Besides PTV Europe, we use TIGER USA from the 9th DIMACS Implementation Challenge, both with two cost functions: driving times (enriched by 100s U-turns) and distances. We also evaluate instances from Bing Maps, which build on Navteq data and include actual turn costs and restrictions; the proprietary "default" metric correlates well with driving times. We use the 4xGTX 780 Ti setup. Table 3 reports, besides customization times and CPU/GPU space consumption, the overall time spent (using all CPU cores) in the metric-independent phase (partitioning, microinstruction generation, and setting up the GPU data structures). For reference, it also reports the average performance for 10 000 random queries, given by the number of vertices scanned and the times to find the distance and a full description of the path (including the distance). Note that we do not cache path unpacking [10], thus capturing the average time to execute the *first* query after a metric change.

We can apply a metric change on every input in less than 70 ms, which is 10–12 times faster than on all 12 cores of M2-12 [10]. Preprocessing takes an hour or less, which is fast enough to incorporate topology changes in a timely manner. About 90% of that time is spent partitioning the graph; setting up our GPU data structures only takes a few minutes. On our Bing instances, computing (on the CPU) the first path after a metric changes takes about 4 ms, still considerably less time than customization.

7   Final Remarks

We have shown how to use GPUs to quickly incorporate a new cost function when computing shortest path on road networks. Although computing shortest paths on arbitrary graphs is not a natural fit for GPUs (given its irregular nature), we can still take advantage of their architecture by carefully exploiting various features of our application. Since we work on a graph with fixed topology, we use preprocessing to carefully plan the computation and prepare GPU-friendly data structures. Instead of operating on the entire graph at once, we decompose it into small graphs (cells) with low diameter, which usually fit in shared memory and can be processed in parallel. Finally, cost functions are described compactly, saving on communication overhead.

References

1. Abraham, I., Delling, D., Goldberg, A.V., Werneck, R.F.: Hierarchical hub labelings for shortest paths. In: Epstein, L., Ferragina, P. (eds.) ESA 2012. LNCS, vol. 7501, pp. 24–35. Springer, Heidelberg (2012)
2. Bast, H., Delling, D., Goldberg, A.V., Müller–Hannemann, M., Pajor, T., Sanders, P., Wagner, D., Werneck, R.F.: Route planning in transportation networks. MSR-TR-2014-4 (2014)
3. Bast, H., Funke, S., Sanders, P., Schultes, D.: Fast routing in road networks with transit nodes. Science 316(5824), 566 (2007)
4. Cormen, T.H., Leiserson, C.E., Rivest, R.L., Stein, C.: Introduction to Algorithms. MIT Press (2009)
5. Davidson, A.A., Baxter, S., Garland, M., Owens, J.D.: Work-efficient parallel GPU methods for single-source shortest paths. In: IPDPS. IEEE (2014)
6. Delling, D., Goldberg, A.V., Nowatzyk, A., Werneck, R.F.: PHAST: Hardware-accelerated shortest path trees. Journal of Parallel and Distributed Computing 73(7), 940–952 (2013)
7. Delling, D., Goldberg, A.V., Pajor, T., Werneck, R.F.: Customizable route planning. In: Pardalos, P.M., Rebennack, S. (eds.) SEA 2011. LNCS, vol. 6630, pp. 376–387. Springer, Heidelberg (2011)
8. Delling, D., Goldberg, A.V., Pajor, T., Werneck, R.F.: Customizable route planning in road networks (2013) (submitted for publication)
9. Delling, D., Goldberg, A.V., Razenshteyn, I., Werneck, R.F.: Graph partitioning with natural cuts. In: IPDPS, pp. 1135–1146. IEEE (2011)
10. Delling, D., Werneck, R.F.: Faster customization of road networks. In: Bonifaci, V., Demetrescu, C., Marchetti-Spaccamela, A. (eds.) SEA 2013. LNCS, vol. 7933, pp. 30–42. Springer, Heidelberg (2013)
11. Demetrescu, C., Goldberg, A.V., Johnson, D.S. (eds.): The Shortest Path Problem: Ninth DIMACS Implementation Challenge, DIMACS Book 74. AMS (2009)
12. Geisberger, R., Sanders, P., Schultes, D., Vetter, C.: Exact routing in large road networks using contraction hierarchies. Transportation Science 46(3), 388–404 (2012)
13. Geisberger, R., Vetter, C.: Efficient routing in road networks with turn costs. In: Pardalos, P.M., Rebennack, S. (eds.) SEA 2011. LNCS, vol. 6630, pp. 100–111. Springer, Heidelberg (2011)
14. Hilger, M., Köhler, E., Möhring, R.H., Schilling, H.: Fast point-to-point shortest path computations with arc-flags. In: Demetrescu, et al. (eds.) [11], pp. 41–72
15. Holzer, M., Schulz, F., Wagner, D.: Engineering multilevel overlay graphs for shortest-path queries. ACM Journal of Experimental Algorithmics 13(2.5), 1–26 (2008)
16. Madduri, K., Bader, D.A., Berry, J.W., Crobak, J.R.: Parallel shortest path algorithms for solving large-scale instances. In: Demetrescu, et al. (eds.) [11], pp. 249–290
17. Martín, P.J., Torres, R., Gavilanes, A.: CUDA solutions for the SSSP problem. In: Allen, G., Nabrzyski, J., Seidel, E., van Albada, G.D., Dongarra, J., Sloot, P.M.A. (eds.) ICCS 2009, Part I. LNCS, vol. 5544, pp. 904–913. Springer, Heidelberg (2009)
18. Meyer, U., Sanders, P.: Δ-stepping: A parallelizable shortest path algorithm. Journal of Algorithms 49(1), 114–152 (2003)
19. Ortega-Arranz, H., Torres, Y., Llanos, D., Gonzalez-Escribano, A.: A new GPU-based approach to the shortest path problem. In: HPCS, pp. 505–511 (2013)
20. Sommer, C.: Shortest-path queries in static networks. ACM Comp. Surveys 46(4) (2014)

GPU Accelerated Range Trees with Applications

Manoj Kumar Maramreddy and Kishore Kothapalli

International Institute of Information Technology, Hyderabad,
Gachibowli, Hyderabad, India, 500 032

Abstract. Range searching is a primal problem in computational geometry with applications to database systems, mobile computing, geographical information systems, and the like. Defined simply, the problem is to preprocess a given a set of points in a d-dimensional space so that the points that lie inside an orthogonal query rectangle can be efficiently reported.

Many practical applications of range trees require one to process a massive amount of points and a massive number of queries. In this context, we propose an efficient parallel implementation of range trees on manycore architectures such as GPUs. We extend our implementation to query processing. While queries can be batched together to exploit inter-query parallelism, we also utilize intra-query parallelism. This inter- and intra-query parallelism greatly reduces the per query latency thereby increasing the throughput. On an input of 1 M points in a 2-dimensional space, our implementation on a single Nvidia GTX 580 GPU for constructing a range tree shows an improvement of 12X over a 12-threaded CPU implementation. We also achieve an average throughput of 10 M queries per second for answering 4 M queries on a range tree containing 1 M points on a Nvidia GTX 580 GPU. We extend our implementation to an application where we seek to report the set of maximal points in a given orthogonal query rectangle.

1 Introduction

Manycore accelerators such as GPUs have occupied a prominent place in the theory and practice of parallel computing. This is aided in part by their ubiquitous nature, low cost, and importantly compute power. Several programming models and utility libraries such as CUDA [12], Thrust (See http://thrust.github.io/), and OpenAcc (See http://www.openacc-standard.org/) are being currently supported for writing general purpose programs on GPUs. It is possible to arrive at very efficient implementations of general purpose computations using such programming support [11,2].

On the other hand, there is very little work on how to efficiently build and operate on data structures on architectures such as GPUs. Hierarchical data structures such as trees and multi-dimensional data structures render the nature of the problem more difficult. In fact, there are very few such reported instances in the literature. Some early work in this direction by Lefohn et al. [10] proposes

F. Silva et al. (Eds.): Euro-Par 2014, LNCS 8632, pp. 740–751, 2014.

a template library that can be used to build data structures and also identify common themes across existing GPU based data structures. It is to be noted that very few of the existing data structures deal with hierarchical ones [3,6].

We posit that it is possible to build hierarchical data structures on GPUs by introducing novel techniques that improve the way the data structures are built and accessed. Given the plethora of programming support available for programming GPUs, we show that it is also possible to build such data structures with a minimal programming effort. Our work indicates that one should make use of available primitives such as sort, merge, and scan.

As a case-study, we consider data structures for multi-dimensional datasets such as the range tree. A d-dimensional range tree is a data structure that can store a set of points in a d-dimensional space so that operations such as searching on d-dimensional datasets is efficiently supported. A d-dimensional range tree for storing n points requires a space of $O(n \log^{d-1} n)$ and involves creating a nested set of d trees. In a sequential setting, this construction can be done efficiently in time $O(n \log^{d-1} n)$, and the data structure can be stored using pointers. However, creating and accessing pointer based data structures is difficult in many-threaded settings. Hence, one has to identify alternate ways to represent the data structure while keeping access to the data structure as efficient as possible. Fortunately, the nested trees that arise in the range tree are all full binary trees, i.e., for n nodes where n is a power of 2, these trees have exactly $\log n$ levels. We use this fact, along with additional novel considerations to represent a d-dimensional range tree. For building a 2-dimensional range tree on an input dataset of 2^{20} points we achieve a speed up of 12X compared to the 12-threaded CPU implementation.

We also show that accessing the range tree in our representation is also efficient by considering two canonical applications. One of the prominent applications of range trees is range searching. In range searching, one is interested in reporting the points that lie in a given orthogonal query rectangle. An orthogonal query rectangle is a rectangle whose sides are parallel to the axes of the d-dimensional space. Such a query finds applications in several areas such as database systems, geographical information systems, mobile computing, CAD tools and the like [1]. In this case, it is easy to notice that there is natural inter-query parallelism. However, we also modify the querying algorithm to exploit also intra-query parallelism. The combination of the two help us in increasing the query throughput.

The second application we consider is that of reporting the set of maximal points that lie in a given orthogonal query rectangle. A point $P = (x_1, x_2, \cdots, x_d)$ is said to be *maximal* if no point $P' = (x'_1, x'_2, \cdots x'_d)$ exists with $x_i < x'_i$ for $1 \leq i \leq d$. The set of maximal points, also called as *skyline points* offer a good summarization of the points. For this problem also, we exploit intra-query parallelism and by introducing a standard primitive called the All-Nearest-Larger-Values (ANLV) [7]. This primitive that we develop as part of this work can be of independent interest to the parallel computing community.

For both of our applications, on trees with 2^{10} points and 1 M queries, our implementation on an NVidia GTX 580 GPU achieves around 7x more throughput compared to a 12-threaded implementation on an Intel i7 X980 CPU.

1.1 Related Work

Efficient constructions of hierarchical data structures on modern architectures is an emerging research theme. Construction of B+ trees is studied in [5], and of KD-trees in [6]. Kim et al [9] had proposed solutions for implementing R-trees on GPUs. They propose solutions to avoid irregular memory access and improved efficiency. A Massively Parallel Three-phase Scanning (MPTS) algorithm for R-tree traversal for processing multi-dimensional range queries is proposed in [9]. Both of the works focuses on R-tree search algorithms, but not on constructing the trees in parallel. To the best of our knowledge this is the first attempt to implement range trees on GPUs. We provide solutions for both efficient construction and accessing of range trees on GPUs.

2   Preliminaries

For ease of exposition, we describe the 2-dimensional range tree in the following. In this case, we assume that each point has a x-coordinate and a y-coordinate. In a 2-dimensional range tree, we start with a *primary tree* that is a balanced binary search tree T built on x-coordinate of points in P. Each internal node in the primary tree can be the median of the canonical subset of v. Further, every node v in T contains a pointer to a *secondary tree* that is a binary search tree on y-coordinate of the canonical subset of v. The space required for a 2-dimensional range tree is $O(n \log n)$. An example is shown in Figure 1. The time required for constructing a 2-dimensional range tree is $O(n \log n)$. Points stored in the leaves of a subtree rooted at an internal node v are called the *canonical subset* of v and v is called the canonical node of the subset.

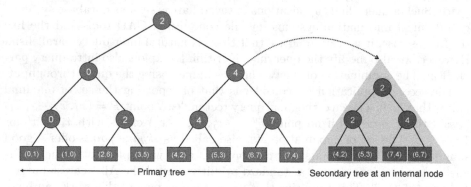

Fig. 1. A 2-dimensional range tree. Each node in the primary tree has a corresponding secondary tree.

2.1   Range Querying

We first describe a 1-dimensional range query. To report the points in a 1-dimensional query $[a, b]$ we proceed as follows. We first search for a and b in the 1-dimensional range tree. Let u and v be the leaves where this search ends. The points in the interval $[a, b]$ are the points stored in the leaves in between u and v and possibly the points stored at u and v. Let r_{split} be the node where the search paths to u and v separate. Starting from r_{split} we then follow the search path to u. At each node where the path goes left we report all the leaves in the right subtree. Similarly, we follow the path to v and report all the points in the left subtree when the path goes right.

For a 2-dimensional query $[a, b] \times [c, d]$, we first perform a 1-dimensional query $[a, b]$ on primary tree. At each node where the search path to u goes left we do a 1-dimensional range query on y-coordinate in the secondary tree associated at the right child of the node. Similarly, at each node where the search path to v goes right we do a 1-dimensional range query on y-coordinate in the secondary tree associated at the left child of the node.

3   A Parallel Range Tree

In this section we describe our new implementation of a multi-dimensional range tree. We argue that our new representation is efficient on GPU architectures in the way that it is represented and accessed in parallel. In a standard two-dimensional range tree (cf. Section 2), every node in the primary and secondary tree contains left and right child pointers. Porting this representation of range tree directly on to the GPU platform is not efficient due to the below mentioned reasons.

- Accessing multiple levels of pointer indirection will lead to massively increased memory access latency and will break the little cache coherency available on the GPU.
- The irregular tree traversals cause thread divergence when implemented on GPUs. Also, one needs to regularize the work done by each thread in order to achieve maximum efficiency.
- Copying a complex structure such as range trees, consisting of nested pointers, on to GPU requires a *deep copy* functionality for which there is no available API. Copying back the same structure poses the same problem in reverse.

For addressing the above mentioned challenges, we use an array based representation of complete range tree. We flatten-out the hierarchical structure of the range tree into a structure containing two 1-dimensional arrays, one storing x-coordinates and other storing y-coordinates. We first store the primary tree in an array, followed by the secondary trees from bottom up approach. We label the nodes in the tree in inorder starting from '0'. Rather than storing inorder traversal of the complete tree, we only store the leaves of primary and secondary trees. By using bitwise representation of the nodes it is possible to dynamically

Table 1. Conversion formulas between array representation and standard range tree

converting array index i to corresponding index j of the leaf in primary tree	$j = 2 \times i + 1$
converting internal node(range tree) index i to array index j	$j = i/2 - 1$
computing offset of secondary tree at node i of primary tree	$h = \log_2(i \& - i)$ offset $= h \times n + i \times 2^{(h+1)} \times (i \& - i)$

compute the offset of secondary trees and corresponding internal nodes of the trees. Formula for converting indices from array representation to virtual range tree is given in table 1. An example of this representation is given in Figure 2. The point set used is same as in Figure 1.

This simple structure also helps in building the range tree using existing primitives such as sorting and merging. The representation not only helps us in regularizing the work done by threads while processing the queries but also avoids the increased memory access latency that might arise due to multiple levels of pointer indirection. We use the bit representation to exploit intra-query parallelism as explained in Section 4. Further, our representation requires the same space asymptotically as the standard representation. Finally, though we perform our experiments in a two dimensional space, the same representation can be extended to higher dimensions.

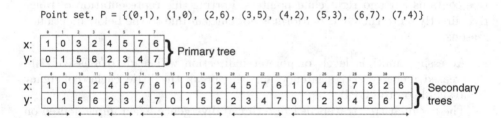

Point set, P = {(0,1), (1,0), (2,6), (3,5), (4,2), (5,3), (6,7), (7,4)}

Fig. 2. In the new representation only leaves of each tree (primary & secondary) are stored in an array. The trees are stored contiguously. The offset of secondary trees and the corresponding internal nodes can be dynamically computed.

3.1 Implementation Details

Our array based representation of range trees helps us in using existing primitives for construction. In the following, we show the steps for constructing a 2-dimensional range tree.

1. Sort the points on their x-coordinates. Sorting is a well studied problem on GPUs. For this purpose, we use sort_by_key implementation provided by Thrust library.

2. Merge the points recursively on their y-coordinates and store the merged result in each iteration. The merged result at each iteration in fact represents secondary trees from bottom to top. Though **thrust** provides a merge implementation, we use a more recent merge sort implementation (**kernelMerge**) provided by Baxter (See http://nvlabs.github.io/moderngpu/).

Algorithm 1. BUILDRANGETREE(P)

1: *Input.* Set of points in a two dimensional plane $P := \{p_1, p_2, ..., p_n\}$.
2: *Output.* A 2d Range tree T.
3: $T[1...n] \leftarrow$ **sort_by_key**(P)
4: $numPasses \leftarrow log(n)$
5: **for** $pass = 0, numPasses$ **do**
6:    $coop = 2^{(pass+1)}$
7:    $source = T[n \times pass...n \times (pass + 1)]$
8:    $dest = T[n \times (pass + 1) + 1...n \times (pass + 1) + n]$
9:    **kernelMerge**(source, dest, coop)

3.2   Results and Performance Analysis

Platform: All our experiments are performed on a machine with Intel core i7 X980 CPU and Nvidia Geforce GTX 580 GPU. The Intel core i7 X980 is a 3.33-GHz six-core CPU with Intel's hyper-threading technology. It can work on 12 streams at once. It has a 12MB L3 cache. GTX 580 has 512 CUDA cores. For all our experiments we used OpenMP specification 3.0 and the CUDA 5.0 programming model for programming multi-core CPUs and Nvidia many-core GPUs respectively.

Dataset: For input data we have randomly generated points from a uniform distribution. We perform our experiments on data sets with small trees containing few thousand points to large trees with over 1 M points.

Our simplified structure of range tree enables us to achieve faster construction times using existing primitives such as sorting and merging. With minimal programing effort we are able to achieve faster construction times. Figure 3 shows the speed up of constructing a range tree on GPU over a multi-core CPU implementation. It is evident from the graph that our implementation can easily scale to huge datasets. For constructing a range tree on a dataset with 1 M points, we achieve a speed up of 12X on GPU over 12-threaded CPU implementation.

4   Application I: Range Searching

The problem of range searching is to report the set of points that lie in a given orthogonal query rectangle. An orthogonal query rectangle has its sides parallel to the axes of the underlying space. An orthogonal rectangle can then be

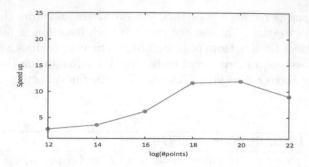

Fig. 3. Speedup of building range tree on GPU vs 12-threaded CPU implementation

represented by considering the cross product of ranges in each dimension. In particular, in a 2-dimensional setting, the rectangle $[a, b] \times [c, d]$ refers to the rectangle consisting of points whose x-coordinates are in $[a, b]$ and y-coordinates are in $[c, d]$. Given a range tree for n points in a 2-dimensional space and a range query q of the form $[a, b] \times [c, d]$, the algorithm to process the query has the following three main steps (cf. Section 2).

1. Finds the nodes that are closest to a and b in the primary tree
2. Find the canonical nodes in the primary tree, and
3. Find the result by repeating the above steps in the secondary tree for each canonical node of the primary tree
4. Transfer results to host CPU

In the following, we show how each of the above steps can be also performed in parallel for a given query. This helps us extract intra-query parallelism apart from the standard inter-query parallelism[1].

1. **Binary Search on Primary tree:** In the first phase, we binary search for a and b in the primary tree. We assign a search key per thread. In order to avoid conditional branching of threads we store our sorted array in level-order rather than in-order. This technique was used in [11] to avoid conditional branching of threads.

    Let u and v are the indices of the nodes where the binary search for a and b in the primary tree ends. The split node r_{split} is computed by taking xor of u and v. The number of canonical nodes can be obtained by counting the number of set bits. The result of the binary search and the split nodes are saved and passed as input to Phase-2.

2. **Find canonical nodes:** In the second phase, we compute the indices of the canonical nodes in parallel. While the standard range search implementation is bounded by sequential search for canonical nodes, we present a method to find all the canonical nodes in parallel. In order to get the total number of

---

[1] Detailed pseudocode is available at
http://cstar.iiit.ac.in/~kkishore/rangetree.pdf

canonical nodes for the batch of queries we perform a parallel reduce on the number of canonical nodes for each query obtained from Phase-I.

The inorder labeling of the nodes in the tree provides information about the path traced from root to that node. A $'0'$ bit at i^{th} position from right indicates the path has traversed left and a $'1'$ bit indicates the path has traversed right. Using this path information and the corresponding split node obtained in Phase-I, we give a technique to compute the canonical nodes in parallel.

In the path from split node to u, a $'0'$ bit indicates the presence of a canonical node. Similarly, for the right path to v a $'1'$ bit indicates the presence of a canonical node.

3. **Binary Search on Secondary tree:** For every canonical node found in Phase-2, we perform binary search for c and d in the corresponding secondary tree. The output of the binary search for each canonical node is stored.

4. **Reporting results:** The number of output points generated per query can be of the order of $O(n)$. Copying back such huge data to the host CPU consumes a significant amount of time. We alleviate this problem substantially by reporting only the left and right indices of our search in secondary trees. A sequential scan of these ranges on the host would output the points on the host side. This greatly reduces the amount of data to be transfered to $O(\log n)$ per query. In order to further hide the copy time we process our queries in batches so that the copy time of output of the ith batch can be completely hidden by computation of the $(i-1)^{th}$ batch.

4.1 Performance Analysis

Dataset: To generate the queries, we study three different datasets. These datasets are dictated by the number of canonical nodes that each query results in. Since the number of canonical nodes in each query directly impacts the work done in Phase II and III of our querying algorithm, this study helps us understand the efficacy of our implementation. It is easy to note that in a range tree containing n points, the average number of canonical nodes in a query whose range is generated uniformly at random is $O(\log n/2)$. Based on this average, we study the following query datasets.

1. **Short-range Queries:** We define a query as a short-range query if the number of canonical nodes for the query is between zero and $\log n/2$.
2. **Medium-range Queries:** A medium-ranged query has canonical nodes between $\log n/2$ and $3\log n/4$.
3. **Long-range Queries:** Any query with canonical nodes greater than $3\log(n)/4$ is defined as a long-range query.

Throughput: In our experiments, we consider trees with 2^{10} points as small trees and trees with 2^{20} points as large trees. The throughput graph for the three datasets is show in Figure 4. We see from Figure 4 that our algorithm scales

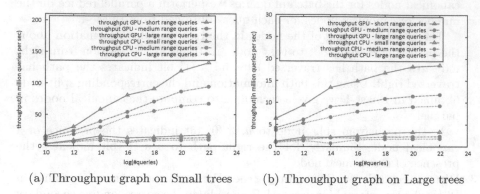

(a) Throughput graph on Small trees   (b) Throughput graph on Large trees

Fig. 4. Throughput of GPU range searching vs. a 6-core CPU

for both small trees and large trees and also over the three query datasets. This suggests that a batch of queries that come with a mix of short-range to long range queries can also be processed without any further rearrangement of the queries. We do notice a higher throughput for the Short-range Query dataset compared to other datasets. This is due to the fact that as the number of canonical nodes is small in that dataset, the amount of computation spent in phase 2 and 3 is minimal.

Batch Size: We finally study the impact of batch size on our implementation. Recall from Section 4, Phase IV of our querying algorithm can be made to overlap with Phases I-III of the querying algorithm a scenario, finding the right value for the batch size is crucial. In Figure 5 we show the throughput achieved by our algorithm as a function of the batch size. As can be intuitively observed, the throughput increases with increasing batch size up to a certain point. This is due to the fact that the time spent in Phase IV can be completely hidden by the time spent in Phase I-III, except for the time spent in Phase IV for the last batch. However, as we increase the batch size further, the increase in time spent in Phase IV will decrease the throughput achieved. From Figure 5, we notice that for a dataset of 2^{16} points and 2^{16} queries, a batch size of 2^{13} is ideal.

5   Application II: Reporting Maximal Points in an Orthogonal Query

A traditional range search query focuses on returning all the points inside a given range. But when dealing with large datasets, the resulting number of points may be huge and hence it is impractical to return the entire result. One such scenario may be server returning results to mobile devices where bandwidth and screen resolution are constrained. In such scenarios, it is beneficial to return a summary of the result. Maximal points offer a good summary of the results [1]. Using range trees, a sequential algorithm to report the set of maximal points in

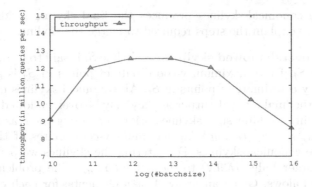

Fig. 5. Variation of query throughput with batch size for a dataset of 2^{16} points and 2^{16} queries

a given orthogonal query region is proposed in [4]. In this section, we use our GPU-based construction of a range tree to provide a parallel solution to problem of reporting the maximal points in a given orthogonal query region.

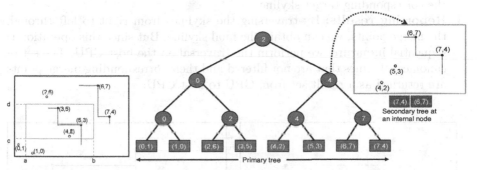

(a) Skyline points in-(b) In the associated structure we only store the skyline of the side a rectangle points rooted at that internal node

Fig. 6. An application of range trees to find maximal points inside a query rectangle

In order to efficiently report the maximal points, also called as the *skyline points*, or simply the *skyline*, inside a given range, we preprocess the input point set into a data structure. This data structure is similar to range tree we described in Section 3 with a difference that we store the maximal points of the canonical subset of points at each internal node of the secondary tree. This solution is described in detail in [8].

The algorithm for reporting skyline points inside an orthogonal range query is similar to that of range searching described in Section 4. At the end of Phase-3, we get a skyline corresponding to each canonical node in the primary tree.

Merging these canonical-skylines produces the final skyline inside the query range. Below we explain the steps required to merge the skylines.

1. **Filtering overshadowed skylines:** A skyline S_i is said to be overshadowed by skyline S_j if the maximum y-coordinate of points in S_j is greater than maximum y-coordinate of points in S_i. All canonical-skylines may not contribute to the final merged output as they may be overshadowed by a skyline to their right. We filter such skylines prior to merging them as follows.

   Let $Y_{max} = \{y_1, y_2, ... y_k\}$ be maximum y-coordinates of the points in each of the canonical-skylines. For filtering the skylines we perform an All Nearest Larger Value (ANLV) to the left on Y_{max}. The problem of ANLV is defined as follows. Given an array A of n elements, for each element $A[i]$, find the element closest to the left of i that is greater than $A[i]$. ANLV is a well studied problem in parallel algorithms [7]. For solving this problem, we use the algorithm from [7]. For every canonical-skyline we find a target skyline to be merged with. An example of the problem is illustrated in Figure 7.

2. **Merging skylines:** Assuming S_i and S_j are the two skylines to be merged where S_i lies left of S_j. Let y_i be the maximum y-coordinates of the points in S_j. In order to merge S_i and S_j we find the merge point by searching for y_i in S_i. For all the canonical-skylines that are not filtered in the above step we find the merge point by searching their maximum y-coordinate in the corresponding target skyline.

3. **Reporting results:** By traversing the skylines from right to left through the merge points, we can obtain the final skyline. But since this operation is sequential in nature, we perform the traversal on the host CPU. The set of canonical-skylines that are not filtered and their corresponding merge points are returned as a result set from GPU to host CPU.

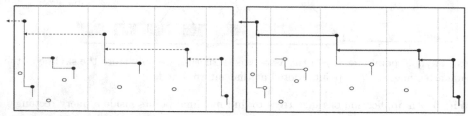

(a) We compute ANLV on the maximum y-coordinates of points in skylines

(b) Final skyline is obtained by merging individual skylines

Fig. 7. Finding skyline inside an orthogonal range query

5.1   Performance Results

For the experiments, we generate random queries from a uniform distribution. The throughput graph is show in Figure 8. As can be seen, our implementation offers a good speed-up over a corresponding multi-core CPU.

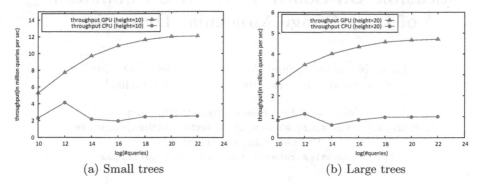

(a) Small trees (b) Large trees

Fig. 8. Throughput graph of GPU vs 6-core CPU

6 Conclusions

In this paper, we show that hierarchical data structures can be efficiently constructed on modern parallel architectures. Our method involves identifying efficient ways to store and represent the data structure without compromising on the access efficiency of the representation. As a case-study, we considered the range tree along with two applications of the same.

References

1. Agarwal, P.K., Erickson, J.: Geometric range searching and its relatives. In: Advances in Discrete and Computational Geometry, vol. 223, pp. 1–56
2. Bell, N., Garland, M.: Efficient sparse matrix-vector multiplication on cuda. Technical report, NVIDIA Technical Report NVR-2008-004 (2008)
3. Coombe, G., Harris, M.J., Lastra, A.: Radiosity on graphics hardware. In: Proceedings of the 2004 Conference on Graphics Interface, pp. 161–168 (2004)
4. Das, A.S., Gupta, P., Srinathan, K.: On Finding Skyline Points for Range Queries in Plane. In: CCCG (2011)
5. Fix, J., Wilkes, A., Skadron, K.: Accelerating Braided B+ Tree Searches on a GPU with CUD. In: Proc. ISCA Workshops (2011)
6. Foley, T., Sugerman, J.: Kd-tree acceleration structures for a gpu raytracer. In: Proc. Graphics Hardware, pp. 15–22 (2005)
7. Jaja, J.: An Introduction To Parallel Algorithms. Addison-Wesley (2004)
8. Kalavagattu, A.K., Agarwal, J., Das, A.S., Kothapalli, K.: Counting Range Maxima Points in Plane. In: Smyth, B. (ed.) IWOCA 2012. LNCS, vol. 7643, pp. 263–273. Springer, Heidelberg (2012)
9. Kim, J., Kim, S.-G., Nam, B.: Parallel multi-dimensional range query processing with R-trees on GPU. J. Par. Dist. Comp. 73(8), 1195–1207 (2013)
10. Lefohn, A.E., Sengupta, S., Kniss, J., Strzodka, R., Owens, J.D.: Glift: Generic, Efficient, Random-access GPU Data Structures. ACM Trans. Graph. 25(1), 60–99 (2006)
11. Leischner, N., Osipov, V., Sanders, P.: GPU sample sort. In: IEEE International Parallel and Distributed Processing Symposium, IPDPS (2010)
12. NVidia Corporation, Cuda: Compute Unified Device Architecture programming guide. Technical report, Nvidia. Tech. Rep. (2007)

Scalable On-Board Multi-GPU Simulation of Long-Range Molecular Dynamics

Marcos Novalbos[1], Jaime González[2], Miguel A. Otaduy[1],
Roberto Martinez-Benito[2], and Alberto Sanchez[1]

[1] Universidad Rey Juan Carlos, Madrid, Spain
{marcos.novalbos,miguel.otaduy,alberto.sanchez}@urjc.es
[2] Plebiotic S.L., Madrid, Spain
{jaime.gonzalez,roberto.martinez}@plebiotic.com

Abstract. Molecular dynamics simulations allow us to study the behavior of complex biomolecular systems by modeling the pairwise interaction forces between all atoms. Molecular systems are subject to slowly decaying electrostatic potentials, which turn molecular dynamics into an n-body problem. In this paper, we present a parallel and scalable solution to compute long-range molecular forces, based on the multilevel summation method (MSM). We first demonstrate an optimization of MSM that replaces 3D convolutions with FFTs, and we achieve a single-GPU performance comparable to the particle mesh Ewald (PME) method, the de facto standard for long-range molecular force computation. But most importantly, we propose a distributed MSM that avoids the scalability difficulties of PME. Our distributed solution is based on a spatial partitioning of the MSM multilevel grid, together with massively parallel algorithms for interface update and synchronization. We demonstrate the scalability of our approach on an on-board multi-GPU platform.

1 Introduction

Molecular dynamics consists of studying the behavior of molecular systems by modeling the motion of individual atoms due to inter-atom forces. Molecular dynamics simulations enable the prediction of the shape and arrangement of molecular systems that cannot be directly observed or measured, and it has demonstrated its impact on applications of drug and nanodevice design [16].

However, molecular dynamics is a computationally expensive problem, due to both high temporal and high spatial resolution. The trajectories and arrangements of molecules over temporal scales in the order of $1\mu s$ are dictated by vibrations taking place at scales as fine as $1fs = 10^{-15}s$; therefore, effective analysis requires the computation of many simulation steps. At the same time, meaningful molecular systems are often composed of even millions of atoms. Most importantly, the motion of atoms is affected by distant electrostatic potentials, which makes molecular dynamics an n-body problem with quadratic cost.

Typical solutions to molecular dynamics separate short-range forces, which are computed exactly, from long-range ones, and approximate such long-range

F. Silva et al. (Eds.): Euro-Par 2014, LNCS 8632, pp. 752–763, 2014.

forces. The Particle Mesh Ewald (PME) method [3] is probably the most popular approximation to long-range molecular forces, and it discretizes atom charges on a grid, computes a grid-based potential using a FFT, and finally interpolates the potential back to the atoms. Its cost is dominated by the FFT, which yields an asymptotic complexity $O(N \log N)$.

Molecular dynamics computations can be further accelerated through parallel algorithms, including massive parallelization on GPUs [8,15], or even multi-GPU parallelization [11]. The PME method is suited for single GPU parallelization, but not for distributed computation, thus limiting the scalability of long-range molecular dynamics.

In this paper, we propose a scalable solution to long-range forces in molecular dynamics using on-board multi-GPU architectures. Our solution to long-range molecular dynamics is based on the Multilevel Summation Method (MSM), proposed by Izaguirre et al. [10] for the solution to general n-body problems, and parallelized on a single GPU by Hardy et al. [5] for molecular dynamics.

In section 3 we outline the overall molecular dynamics simulation algorithm and we overview MSM. We also propose an optimization of the original MSM, based on the summations of potentials on each level using an FFT. As a result of this optimization, the performance of MSM on a single GPU turns out to be comparable to that of PME.

But most importantly, MSM is better suited for a distributed implementation. In section 4, we present a distributed multi-GPU on-board version of MSM, and we discuss its implementation. Our distributed MSM deals efficiently with periodic boundary conditions and with the synchronization of interfaces between computing nodes. All interface-related computations are designed as massively parallel algorithms running on each GPU independently, and data is transferred between pairs of GPUs directly. With our solution, it is possible to execute molecular dynamics analysis on large molecular systems (with over one million atoms in our examples), and the performance of molecular dynamics is not limited by the compute bounds of a single GPU.

2   Related Work

There are many approaches to improve the quadratic cost of long-range molecular dynamics, either using approximate solutions or parallel implementations (See [14] for a survey). Massively parallel solutions on GPUs have also been proposed, although GPUs are mostly used as co-processors [15].

As mentioned in the introduction, PME [3] is the most popular method to compute long-range molecular forces. Lattice Ewald methods solve the long-range potential on a grid using an FFT. Regular PME uses spectral differentiation and a total of four FFTs per time step, while Smooth PME (SPME) [4] uses B-spline interpolation reducing the number of FFTs to two. PME is widely used in parallel molecular dynamics frameworks such as NAMD [15], GROMACS [9] or ACEMD [8]. PME can be massively parallelized on a single GPU, but it is difficult to distribute over multiple GPUs due to the all-to-all communication needed by the FFT. However Nukada et al. [12] propose a scalable multi-GPU 3DFFT to minimize all-to-all comunications. Cerutti et al. [2] proposed Multi-Level Ewald (MLE) as an approximation to SPME by decomposing the global FFT into a series of independent FFTs over separate regions of a molecular system, but they did not conduct scalability analysis.

Other long-range force approximation are based on multigrid algorithms. Multigrid approaches utilize multiple grid levels with different spatial resolutions to compute long-range potentials with $O(N)$ cost. In molecular dynamics, multigrid methods have been demonstrated to be superior to other methods [17], such as the Fast Multipole Method (FMM) [19], because they achieve better scalability while keeping acceptable error levels. The Meshed Continuum Method (MCM) [1] and MSM [6] are the two most relevant multigrid methods for long-range force computation. MCM uses density functions to sample the particles onto a grid and calculates the potential by solving a Poisson equation in a multigrid fashion. On the other hand, MSM calculates the potential directly on a grid by using several length scales. The scales are spread over a hierarchy of grids, and the potential of coarse levels is successively corrected by contributions from finer levels up to the finest grid, which yields the final potential. This approach exhibits higher options for scalability than PME or other multigrid algorithms. MSM has been massively parallelized on a single GPU [5], although its performance is notably worse than PME. With our optimized MSM, even its single-GPU performance is comparable to PME.

Multigrid methods have been used extensively in a variety of scientific fields, but molecular dynamics suffers the added difficulty of dealing with periodic boundary conditions. Izaguirre and Matthey [10] developed an MPI-based parallel multigrid summation on clusters and shared-memory computers for n-body problems. Our approach presents a solution for long-range molecular dynamics on board multi-GPU platforms, and our improvements could be extended to other types of n-body problems.

3   Optimized MSM

3.1   Overview of Molecular Dynamics

In computer simulations of molecular dynamics, atoms are modeled as particles in a virtual 3D spatial coordinate system. Their motion is computed by solving Newtonian mechanics under the action of three types of forces: bonded forces, non-bonded short-range forces (composed of Van der Waals forces and electrostatic interactions between atoms closer than a cutoff radius R_c), and non-bonded long-range forces (consisting of electrostatic interactions between atoms separated by a distance greater than R_c). The simulation time is divided into steps of very small size, in the order of $1\text{fs} = 10^{-15}\text{s}$. Given atom positions X_i and velocities V_i at time T_i, the simulation algorithm evaluates the interaction forces and integrates them to obtain positions X_{i+1} and velocities V_{i+1} at time T_{i+1}. In biological systems, the molecules of interest are surrounded by water molecules, and *periodic boundary conditions* are imposed on the simulation volume, i.e., the simulation volume is implicitly replicated infinite times. A more comprehensive description of the basics of molecular dynamics can be found in [16].

Most of the time in a molecular dynamics simulation is spent calculating non-bonded forces. In the remaining of this paper, we address only non-bonded long-range forces, and we rely on an existing on-board multi-GPU algorithm for bonded and non-bonded short-range forces [11].

3.2 The Multilevel Summation Method

For a particle system with charges $\{q_1, \ldots q_N\}$ at positions $\{\mathbf{r}_1, \ldots \mathbf{r}_N\}$, the electrostatic potential energy is

$$U(\mathbf{r}_1, ...\mathbf{r}_N) = \frac{1}{2} \sum_{i=1}^{N} \sum_{j=1, j \neq i}^{N} \frac{q_i\, q_j}{||\mathbf{r}_i - \mathbf{r}_j||}. \tag{1}$$

Its exact computation has $O(N^2)$ complexity.

MSM is a fast algorithm for computing an approximation to the electrostatic interactions with just $O(N)$ computational work. MSM splits the potential into short-range and long-range components. The short-range component is computed as a direct particle-particle interaction while the long-range one is approximated through a hierarchy of grids.

For the long-range component, the method first distributes atom charges onto the finest grid. This process is called *anterpolation*. A nodal basis function $\phi(\mathbf{r})$ with local support about each grid point is used to distribute charges. Once all atom charges are distributed onto the finest grid, charges are distributed onto the next coarser grid, using the same basis functions. This process is called *restriction*, and it is repeated until the coarsest grid is reached.

On each level, the method computes direct sums of nearby grid charges up to a radius of $\lfloor 2\,R_c/h_0 \rfloor$ grid points, where h_0 is the resolution of the finest grid. Hardy and Skeel [6] indicate that a resolution h_0 between 1Å and 3Å is sufficient for molecular dynamics simulations. Note that the resolution is halved on each coarser grid, hence direct sums cover twice the distance with the same number of points. The direct sum of pairwise charge potentials is analogous to the one for short-range non-bonded forces, with the exception that grid distances are fixed and can be computed as preprocessing, hence the computation is simply an accumulation of weighted grid charges.

A GPU optimized version of the direct sum was developed by Hardy et al [5]. The weighted grid is stored in constant memory and charges in shared memory. A sliding window technique is used to achieve an efficient reading. Hardy's algorithm computes the finest levels on GPU, while the coarsest levels are computed on CPU. Our method runs the whole simulation on an on-board multi-GPU architecture by allocating a portion of the system to each GPU and using a boundary interface to communicate updates directly between portions.

Once direct sums are computed on each level, potentials are interpolated from coarse to finer levels, and contributions from all levels are accumulated. This process is called *prolongation*. Finally, potentials from the finest grid are interpolated on the atoms.

Algorithm 1 highlights the differences between our distributed MSM and the original algorithm. See also [6] for a thorough description of the method. Note that the direct sums are independent of each other, and the direct sum on a certain level and the restriction to the coarser level can be executed asynchronously.

3.3   FFT-Based Sums

To perform the direct sum part on each level, the original MSM applies a 3D convolution over all grid points using a kernel with $2 \lfloor 2\,R_c/h \rfloor + 1$ points in each dimension [6]. However, Hardy shows that the direct sum part is the most computationally expensive part. We substitute this convolution with a product in frequency domain. Specifically, we compute grid potentials in three steps:

1. Forward FFT of the grids of charges and kernel weights.
2. Complex point-wise product of the two resulting vectors
3. Inverse FFT to obtain the potentials.

The grids of charges and kernel weights should have identical dimensions; therefore, we extend the kernel. Note that the kernel is constant, hence we only compute its FFT once per level as a preprocess.

Even though the FFT has $O(N \log N)$ complexity as opposed to $O(N)$ complexity of the convolution, in practice large kernels yield a steep linear complexity for the convolution approach. For very large molecules, the $\log N$ factor of the FFT would dominate, but with our distributed MSM presented next in Section 4, FFTs are computed on each partition separately, hence N is bounded. We have compared the performance of efficient GPU implementations of massively parallel MSM using the convolution and FFT approaches, and the FFT approach enjoys a speed-up of almost $10\times$. Table 1 shows timing comparisons for two molecular systems. The examples were executed on an Intel Core i7 CPU 860 at 2.80GHz with a NVIDIA GTX Titan GPU and CUDA Toolkit 5.5. FFTs were computed using NVIDIA's highly efficient cuFFT library [13].

The cutoff distance R_c has a great impact on both error and performance. Error is lower for higher cutoffs, and this can be observed from the fact that a larger cutoff distance increases the kernel size as well. For our performance analysis, we used a cutoff radius of 9.0 Å, which is a standard value for molecular dynamics simulations. Assuming a fixed grid size, the resolution of the grid h, which is automatically set for each level and each axis, determines the overall performance and accuracy. Smaller values of h for the same number of levels implies higher accuracy, but this also translates into a larger kernel size $2 \lfloor 2\,R_c/h_0 \rfloor + 1$, hence adding to the computational cost. The table shows the grid resolution on each axis (in Å), as well as the kernel size.

Table 1 also compares the performance of MSM and PME under the same grid resolutions. We implemented an efficient GPU version of the Smooth PME

Table 1. Performance comparison for long-range force computation on two molecular systems, using regular MSM with 3D convolution, our optimized MSM based on FFTs, and PME. Timings correspond to one simulation step and are given in ms. All cases were executed using a $64 \times 64 \times 64$ grid.

#Atoms	$h_{x,y,z}$	Kernel size	t_{MSM}	$t_{MSM_{FFT}}$	t_{PME}
256,436	{1.88,1.87,2.65}	9x9x6	31.901	4.79	5.095
90,849	{1.56,1.56,1.56}	11x11x11	43.694	5.09	2.22

(SPME) algorithm [4], following the optimizations described by Harvey and De Fabritiis [7]. We also implemented the previously mentioned GPU version of the MSM algorithm proposed by Hardy. With our FFT-based optimization, the performance of MSM becomes comparable to that of PME.

4   Distributed MSM

We propose a distributed MSM (DMSM) that partitions a molecular system and the multilevel grid of MSM among multiple GPUs. As a computing element, each GPU handles in a parallel manner the computation and update of its corresponding portion of the molecular system, as well as the communications with other GPUs. In this section, we first describe the partition of the molecular system, then the handling of periodic boundary conditions across all MSM levels, and finally our parallel algorithms for interface update and synchronization.

4.1   Multigrid Partitions

Following the observations drawn in [11] for short-range molecular forces, we partition a molecular system linearly along its longest axis, as this approach reduces the cost to communicate data between partitions. Then, for DMSM, we partition each level of the MSM grid into regular portions using planes orthogonal to the longest axis. Each GPU device stores a portion of the grid at each level, including two types of grid points: i) interior grid points owned by the GPU itself. ii) interface grid points owned by neighboring GPUs.

The size of the interface corresponds to the half-width of the convolution kernel, i.e., $\lfloor 2\,R_c/h \rfloor$ points to the left and right of the interior ones, as shown in Figure 1. The interface stores replicas of the grid points of neighboring partitions, which are arranged in device memory just like interior points, to allow seamless data access. The interface is used both to provide access to charges of neighboring partitions and to store partial potentials corresponding to those same partitions. Note that, due to the use of a linear partitioning strategy, the neighboring nodes along the shorter directions are the result of periodic boundary conditions, and they do not need to be stored as interface points as they are readily available as interior points.

The partitions are made only once at the beginning of the simulation. At runtime, interface values need to be communicated when needed as part of restriction, direct sum of potentials, and prolongation.

4.2   Periodic Boundary Conditions on Multiple GPUs

As outlined in Section 3.1, molecular dynamics are performed on infinite systems formed by replicating periodically images of the molecular system under study along all three spatial directions [18]. Periodic replication is also applied to the MSM grid; therefore, on the boundary of the molecular system interfaces represent images of grid points on the opposite sides, as shown in Figure 1.

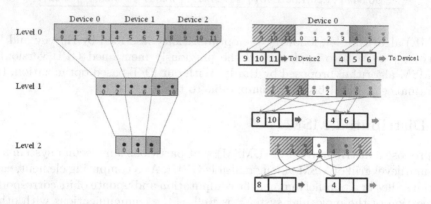

Fig. 1. Partition of the multilevel grid under periodic boundaries. Left: All grid points on each level, distributed into 3 GPU devices. Right: Data structure of GPU device 0 (blue) on all levels, showing: its interior grid points, interface points for an interface of size 3, and buffers to communicate partial sums to other devices. Interface points due to periodic boundary conditions are shown striped. Arrows indicate sums of interface values to the output buffers. With interfaces of size 3, in levels 1 and 2 several interface points contribute to the same buffer location, and in level 2 there are even interior points that map to interface points.

In higher levels of the multilevel grid, where the total number of grid points along the longest axis is similar to the convolution kernel size, periodic boundaries complicate the management of interface points. Two main complications may occur, shown in Figure 1: the same point may map to two or more interface points, and even interior points may map to interface points. To deal with interface handling, each GPU device stores the following data on each level:

- Begin and end indices of neighbor partitions, to know what part of the interface belongs to each GPU device.
- Periodic begin and end indices of the interfaces of neighbor partitions, to know what interior points constitute interfaces for other GPU devices.

Since the multilevel grid is static during the simulation, the auxiliary indices of neighbor partitions are created and shared between GPUs once as a preprocessing step. Once each GPU knows the indices of its neighbors, it creates the incoming and outgoing data buffers to share interface data, and sets static mappings that allow efficient read/write operations with these buffers as shown in Figure 1.

4.3   Parallel Update and Synchronization of Interfaces

Algorithm 1 DMSM method main loop.

1: **procedure** COMPUTEDMSM
2:     $n = nlevels$
3:     $q^0 \leftarrow Anterpolation()$
4:     $* \; accumulateInteriorCopies(q^0)$
5:     $* \; updateInterfaces(q^0)$
6:     **for** $i = 0 \ldots n - 2$ **do**
7:         $V^i \leftarrow DirectSum(q^i)$
8:         $q^{i+1} \leftarrow Restriction(q^i)$
9:         $* \; updateInterfaces(q^{i+1})$
10:     **end for**
11:     $V^{n-1} \leftarrow DirectSum(q^{n-1})$
12:     $* \; accumulateInteriorCopies(V^{n-1})$
13:     $* \; updateInterfaces(V^{n-1})$
14:     **for** $i = n - 2 \ldots 0$ **do**
15:         $V^i \leftarrow Prolongation(V^{i+1})$
16:         $* \; accumulateInteriorCopies(V^i)$
17:         $* \; updateInterfaces(V^i)$
18:     **end for**
19:     $Interpolation(V^0)$
20: **end procedure**

Our DMSM algorithm needs to update and synchronize interfaces at multiple stages of the original MSM algorithm. There are two synchronization operations:

1. *accumulateInteriorCopies*: In the charge anterpolation, the coarsest direct sum and prolongation steps, values are accumulated onto the interface grid points in each GPU device. These interface points are local copies of interior points of other GPUs, hence the values stored on interface points need to be accumulated onto their true owners. This operation is executed in 3 steps. First, the values from the interface points are accumulated into the output buffers. Second, the buffers are transferred to their destination GPUs. And third, the receiver GPUs accumulate the incoming values into their interior grid points. Thanks to the preprocessing of mappings described previously, the accumulation to the output buffers is executed efficiently in a massively parallel manner on each GPU. Periodic boundary conditions are also handled efficiently, and the accumulation of multiple copies of the same point is dealt with during the accumulation to output buffers, prior to data transfer.

2. *updateInterfaces*: Once interior grid values are set, it may be necessary to update their copies in other GPUs, i.e., the interface grid points of other GPUs. Data is transferred between pairs of GPUs directly. This step is necessary after charge anterpolation, after restriction, after the direct sum of potentials, and after prolongation.

Algorithm 1 shows our DMSM algorithm, highlighting in blue and with a star the steps that augment the original MSM algorithm. We distinguish charge values q from potential values V, which are used as arguments of the *accumulate InteriorCopies* and *updateInterfaces* procedures when appropriate. Superscripts indicate grid levels. With our DMSM algorithm, all operations to set up, transfer, and collect data packages are highly parallelized, thus minimizing the cost of communications and maximizing scalability.

5   Evaluation

This section analyzes the scalability of our proposal. We carried out our experiments on a machine outfitted with Ubuntu GNU/Linux Precise Pangolin 12.04, two Intel Xeon Quad Core 2.40GHz CPUs with hyperthreading, 32 GB of RAM and four NVidia GTX580 GPUs connected to PCIe 2.0 slots in an Intel 5520 IOH Chipset of a Tyan S7025 motherboard.

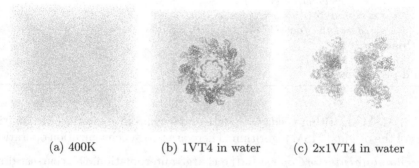

(a) 400K   (b) 1VT4 in water   (c) 2x1VT4 in water

Fig. 2. Benchmark molecules

Given our testbed architecture, we have tested the scalability of our proposal by measuring computation and transmission times for 1, 2, and 4 partitions running on different GPUs. We have used three molecular systems as benchmarks (see Figure 2), all three with a large number of atoms:

- 400K (399,150 atoms) is a well-balanced system of 133,050 molecules of water designed synthetically.
- 1VT4 (645,933, atoms) is a multi-molecular holoenzyme complex assembled around the adaptor protein dApaf-1/DARK/HAC-1.
- 2x1VT4 (1,256,718 atoms) is a complex system formed by two 1VT4 molecules.

5.1   Scalability Analysis

Figure 3a shows the speedup and running times for the three molecules using our proposal with the settings shown in Table 3b. Note that running times have been measured using a GTX580 GPU, being affected by NVidia's CUDA AtomicAdd() operation, whose implementation depends on the hardware architecture. We also show the results obtained with the CPU implementation of PME in NAMD, one of the most used tools for molecular dynamics, as a baseline for comparison. The results show that our method benefits from larger molecules. The reason is that anterpolation, whose workload is easier to share among GPUs, dominates the cost of updates in this case.

The scalability of the system is limited because of interface updates between GPUs. Figure 3c shows the data transfers between GPUs to update their interfaces for the 2x1VT4 molecule for a single step of DMSM. We have selected 2x1VT4 due to its higher complexity and data size, with more than 1.2 Million atoms. The figure indicates that, as expected, the data size of interface cells grows linearly, since each new partition adds a constant data transfer that depends on the grid resolution h and its corresponding interface size. Furthermore, the average data size transfered per GPU is similar to the data needed in a single-GPU implementation in order to account for periodic boundary conditions, as shown in Figure 3c.

Finally, Figure 3d shows how the total simulation time split between computation and interface updates for the 2x1VT4 molecule, to analyze the importance of the transferred data size. With up to 4 partitions, the cost is dominated by

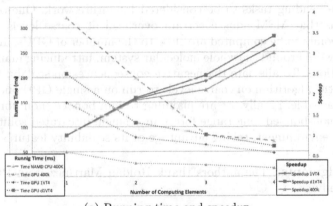

(a) Running time and speedup

Molecule	$h_{x,y,z}$
400K	{2.57,2.57,2.57}
1VT4	{1.86,1.86,0.93}
2x1VT4	{1.89,1.87,1.78}

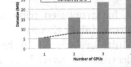 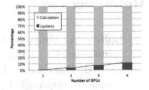

(b) Evaluation Settings   (c) Interface size (2x1VT4)   (d) Simulation cost (2x1VT4)

Fig. 3. Scalability Analysis

computations, with interface transfers adding up to only a low percentage. In this way, the speedup grows almost linearly with each additional GPU. All in all, the results show that our proposal presents very good scalability in on-board multi-GPU platforms.

6   Conclusions and Future Work

This article presents a scalable parallel algorithm to execute long-range molecular dynamics using on-board multi-GPU architectures. The approach extends and optimizes the Multilevel Summation Method, takes advantage of direct GPU-GPU communications, and introduces massively parallel algorithms to update and synchronize the interfaces of spatial partitions on GPUs.

We first improve the performance of MSM by using an FFT instead of 3D convolution in the computation of direct sums on individual GPUs. The paper demonstrates the benefits of our approach in contrast to the original MSM and the well known long-range molecular dynamics algorithm PME. We then show how to perform a spatial partitioning of the multilevel grid, dividing atom data between GPUs, and designing massively parallel algorithms to minimize communications and efficiently update and synchronize interfaces. Our experiments allow us to conclude that our on-board multi-GPU molecular dynamics approach presents very good behavior in terms of performance and scalability.

There are pending tasks to be considered for future work. One of the main drawbacks is that MSM adds a certain overhead at coarse levels, where the number of points to be computed are close to the number of GPUs, and periodic boundaries wrap around the whole molecular system, introducing many-to-many communications. To alleviate the negative consequences on scalability, we plan to redesign the algorithm on coarse levels to run on a single GPU once the work load is manageable. Finally, we are planning to join bonded, non-bonded short-range, and non-bonded long-range forces in a single integrated solution to run on a cluster environment, taking advantage of its scalability features.

Acknowledgments. The authors thank Roldán Martínez from Plebiotic for his helpful advice.

References

1. Bolten, M.: Multigrid methods for structured grids and their application in particle simulation. Dr., Univ. Wuppertal, Jülich (2008)
2. Cerutti, D.S., Case, D.A.: Multi-level ewald: A hybrid multigrid / fast fourier transform approach to the electrostatic particle-mesh problem. J. Chem. Theory Comput. 6(2), 443–458 (2010)
3. Darden, T., York, D., Pedersen, L.: Particle mesh ewald: An nlog(n) method for ewald sums in large systems. The Journal of Chemical Physics 98(12), 10089–10092 (1993)

4. Essmann, U., Perera, L., Berkowitz, M.L., Darden, T., Lee, H., Pedersen, L.G.: A smooth particle mesh ewald method. The Journal of Chemical Physics 103(19), 8577–8593 (1995)
5. Hardy, D.J., Stone, J.E., Schulten, K.: Multilevel summation of electrostatic potentials using graphics processing units. Parallel Computing 35(3), 164–177 (2009); revolutionary Technologies for Acceleration of Emerging Petascale Applications
6. Hardy, D.J., Skeel, R.D.: Multilevel summation for the fast evaluation of forces for the simulation of biomolecules. University of Illinois at Urbana-Champaign, Champaign (2006)
7. Harvey, M.J., De Fabritiis, G.: An implementation of the smooth particle mesh ewald method on gpu hardware. Journal of Chemical Theory and Computation 5(9), 2371–2377 (2009), http://pubs.acs.org/doi/abs/10.1021/ct900275y
8. Harvey, M.J., Giupponi, G., Fabritiis, G.D.: ACEMD: Accelerating Biomolecular Dynamics in the Microsecond Time Scale. Journal of Chemical Theory and Computation 5(6), 1632–1639 (2009)
9. Hess, B., Kutzner, C., van der Spoel, D., Lindahl, E.: GROMACS 4: Algorithms for Highly Efficient, Load-Balanced, and Scalable Molecular Simulation. Journal of Chemical Theory and Computation 4(3), 435–447 (2008)
10. Izaguirre, J.A., Hampton, S.S., Matthey, T.: Parallel multigrid summation for the n-body problem. J. Parallel Distrib. Comput. 65(8), 949–962 (2005)
11. Novalbos, M., Gonzalez, J., Otaduy, M.A., Lopez-Medrano, A., Sanchez, A.: On-board multi-gpu molecular dynamics. In: Wolf, F., Mohr, B., an Mey, D. (eds.) Euro-Par 2013. LNCS, vol. 8097, pp. 862–873. Springer, Heidelberg (2013)
12. Nukada, A., Sato, K., Matsuoka, S.: Scalable multi-GPU 3-D FFT for TSUBAME 2.0 Supercomputer. In: Proceedings of the International Conf. on High Performance Computing, Networking, Storage and Analysis (SC 2012), pp. 44:1–44:10 (2012)
13. NVidia: CUFFT:: CUDA Toolkit Documentation, http://docs.nvidia.com/cuda/cufft/ (accessed January 2014)
14. Rachinger, C.: Scalable Computation of Long-Range Potentials for Molecular Dynamics. Master's thesis, KTH, Numerical Analysis, NA (2013)
15. Rodrigues, C.I., Hardy, D.J., Stone, J.E., Schulten, K., Hwu, W.M.W.: Gpu acceleration of cutoff pair potentials for molecular modeling applications. In: Proceedings of the 5th Conference on Computing Frontiers, CF 2008, pp. 273–282 (2008)
16. Schlick, T.: Molecular Modeling and Simulation: An Interdisciplinary Guide. Springer-Verlag New York, Inc., Secaucus (2002)
17. Skeel, R.D., Tezcan, I., Hardy, D.J.: Multiple grid methods for classical molecular dynamics. Journal of Computational Chemistry 23(6), 673–684 (2002)
18. de Souza, O.N., Ornstein, R.L.: Effect of periodic box size on aqueous molecular dynamics simulation of a dna dodecamer with particle-mesh ewald method. Biophys. J. 72(6), 2395–2397 (1997)
19. Yokota, R., Bardhan, J.P., Knepley, M.G., Barba, L., Hamada, T.: Biomolecular electrostatics using a fast multipole BEM on up to 512 GPUs and a billion unknowns. Computer Physics Communications 182(6), 1272–1283 (2011)

Resolution of Linear Algebra for the Discrete Logarithm Problem Using GPU and Multi-core Architectures

Hamza Jeljeli

CARAMEL project-team, LORIA, INRIA / CNRS / Université de Lorraine,
Campus Scientifique, BP 239, 54506 Vandœuvre-lès-Nancy Cedex, France
Hamza.Jeljeli@loria.fr

Abstract. In cryptanalysis, solving the discrete logarithm problem (DLP) is key to assessing the security of many public-key cryptosystems. The index-calculus methods, that attack the DLP in multiplicative subgroups of finite fields, require solving large sparse systems of linear equations modulo large primes. This article deals with how we can run this computation on GPU- and multi-core-based clusters, featuring InfiniBand networking. More specifically, we present the sparse linear algebra algorithms that are proposed in the literature, in particular the block Wiedemann algorithm. We discuss the parallelization of the central matrix–vector product operation from both algorithmic and practical points of view, and illustrate how our approach has contributed to the recent record-sized DLP computation in $GF(2^{809})$.

Keywords: Discrete logarithm problem, sparse linear algebra, parallel computing, GPU acceleration, multi-core processors, InfiniBand.

1   Introduction

The security of several public-key cryptosystems and protocols relies on the hardness of the computation of the discrete logarithm problem (DLP) in a given cyclic group [20]. To name but a few, we can mention the Diffie–Hellman key exchange protocol [11], the ElGamal encryption system [13] or the pairing-based cryptography [12].

In this context, a family of algorithms, known as *index-calculus* methods, is used to attack the DLP on finite fields. The majority of these algorithms propose to solve it in time sub-exponential in the size of the finite field. While a stream of recent algorithmic improvements for fields of small characteristic, including a quasi-polynomial algorithm [7], have produced several record-sized computations [23], the sub-exponential methods appear to be most competitive for fields of prime extension degree, at least so far.

Index calculus algorithms require solving large sparse systems of linear equations over finite fields. It is important to mention that, most considerations and methods in the case of numerical computations do not apply here. Several papers have focused on efficient implementations of sparse linear algebra over finite fields. For instance, Schmidt et al. [24] treated linear algebra over GF(2) for integer factorization; Boyer et al. [9] worked on the case of small finite rings and fields.

F. Silva et al. (Eds.): Euro-Par 2014, LNCS 8632, pp. 764–775, 2014.

Problem Statement. Let $GF(q)$ be the field in which the DLP is to be solved. The linear algebra is performed modulo a large prime ℓ that divides $q - 1$. We consider ℓ between 160 and 650 bits, along with an N-by-N sparse matrix A defined over $\mathbb{Z}/\ell\mathbb{Z}$. The size N ranges from hundreds of thousands to millions. Each row of A contains $O\left((\log N)^2\right)$ non-zero coefficients. The very first columns of A are relatively dense, then the column density decreases gradually. The row density does not change significantly (cf. Figure 2). The so-called linear algebra step in the DLP computation consists in finding a non-trivial vector $w \in (\mathbb{Z}/\ell\mathbb{Z})^N$ such that $Aw = 0$.

We assume that we have access to one or several high-performance computing clusters, containing multi-core CPUs and/or GPUs, interconnected by fast communication links (typically InfiniBand). We want to optimize the use of these resources in order to solve the linear algebra problem efficiently. In particular, we aim to minimize the overall wall-clock time for solving the problem. First, at an algorithmic level, we study how these heavy computations can be distributed into smaller parallel subtasks. Then, we focus on more practical concerns, for instance the communication within these different subtasks.

Organization. This article is organized as follows: Section 2 gives an overview of the relevant algorithms for sparse linear algebra, while we discuss the parallelization of the matrix–vector product operation and focus on the communication concerns in Section 3. Finally, Section 4 details how our implementation has been used in concrete DLP computations with different hardware setups.

2   Algorithms for Sparse Linear Algebra

To solve systems of linear equations, two families of algorithms are available: *direct methods*, such as Gaussian elimination or LU/QR decompositions, and *iterative methods*, such as the conjugate gradient method and, in the context of linear algebra over finite fields, the Lanczos [19] and Wiedemann [27] algorithms.

The first set of algorithms requires $O(N^\omega)$ field operations, where ω is, for implementation concerns, 2.81 at best using the Strassen algorithm for matrix multiplication [25]. However, these methods tend to densify the matrix, which quickly raises storage issues. The second set of algorithms does not modify the matrix and requires $O(N)$ sparse-matrix–vector products (SpMVs). As long as an SpMV can be performed faster than $O\left(N^{\omega-1}\right)$ field operations, the iterative methods are asymptotically faster. This condition is reasonable, since the complexity of an SpMV is $O(N\gamma)$, where γ is the average number of non-zero coefficients per row. From both storage and complexity points of view, the iterative methods appear to be more suited to sparse linear algebra.

Still, in our case, despite the fact that the matrix is extremely sparse, the cost of an iterative solver remains high because the matrix is very large. The exact nature of the computation calls for no less than N iterations, or a number proportional to N depending on some fine points. The approach following is applied to tackle that problem. First, a structured Gaussian elimination (SGE) is run as a preprocessing step so as to reduce the size of the matrix [21]; then an iterative solver is used. Although the Gaussian elimination increases the average

row weight, it nevertheless allows us to decrease the cost of the iterative solver
and to reduce the amount of required memory, which is a major implementation
concern as will be seen in the following. It is important that we stop the SGE
when the projected cost of the iterative solver starts to increase again or when
memory requirements are small enough so as to fit on the hardware at hand [8].

The Lanczos and Wiedemann algorithms are the most commonly used iterative algorithms in the context of finite fields linear algebra. The Lanczos
algorithm is known to have a better complexity than the Wiedemann algorithm.
However, the block extension of Wiedemann algorithm (*a.k.a* block Wiedemann)
offers the opportunity to split the computation into several independent subtasks, which is an important practical advantage [18,3].

The Wiedemann algorithm and block Wiedemann algorithms return both a
vector w of the kernel of A. This vector is non-trivial with high probability. In
practice, a single run of the solver is sufficient to find an appropriate solution.

Wiedemann Algorithm. The starting point of the Wiedemann algorithm is to
choose two random vectors $x, y \in (\mathbb{Z}/\ell\mathbb{Z})^N$. The algorithm is organized in three
steps [27], for which we use monikers borrowed from the CADO-NFS software
implementation [5].

- The first step computes the first $2N$ terms of the linearly recurrent sequence
  $(a_i)_{i\in\mathbb{N}} \in (\mathbb{Z}/\ell\mathbb{Z})^N$, where $a_i = {}^t x A^i y$. This step is usually called *Krylov* .
- Then, thanks to the Berlekamp–Massey algorithm, we compute the minimal
  polynomial of the sequence, which is the polynomial $F(X) = \sum_{i=0}^d f_i X^i$ of
  lowest degree d such that $\sum_{i=0}^d f_i a_{k+i} = 0$ for all $k \geq 0$. The degree d is
  close to N. We commonly call this step *Lingen* .
- The last step, called *Mksol* , finally computes $w = F(A)y$.

The Wiedemann algorithm requires $3N$ SpMVs for the *Krylov* and *Mksol*
steps and $O(N \log N)$ field operations for the *Lingen* step.

Block Wiedemann Algorithm. Wiedemann algorithm is fully sequential. In
[17,10], Coppersmith et al. presented a block variant that provides parallelism.
The block Wiedemann algorithm replaces the vector $y \in (\mathbb{Z}/\ell\mathbb{Z})^N$ by a block
of n vectors $y^{(0)}, \ldots, y^{(n-1)}$, each in $(\mathbb{Z}/\ell\mathbb{Z})^N$, and similarly uses a block of m
vectors for x. The sequence of scalars a_i is thus replaced by a sequence of m-by-n
matrices. There is a complete freedom in the choice of the blocking parameters
(m, n). For the efficiency of the *Lingen* run, m is chosen to be equal to $2n$ [5].

- The *Krylov* step now computes the first $\lceil \frac{N}{n} \rceil + \lceil \frac{N}{m} \rceil$ terms of the sequence
  $(a_i)_{i\in\mathbb{N}}$. Notice that the j-th column of the m-by-n matrix ${}^t x A^i y$ depends
  only on the j-th column of the block vector y. Thus, the computation of
  $\left({}^t x A^i y\right)_{i\in\mathbb{N}}$ can be distributed into n parallel tasks, each computing
  $\left({}^t x A^i y^{(j)}\right)_{i\in\mathbb{N}}$. These tasks need no synchronization nor communication, except at the end when all their results are combined.
- The *Lingen* step seeks a linear generator for the previous sequence. The complexity of this step becomes $O\left(n^{\omega-1} N \log N\right)$ with $m = 2n = o(\log N)$ [26].
  The output of *Lingen* is composed of n generators $F^{(0)}, \ldots, F^{(n-1)}$, each of
  them a polynomial over $\mathbb{Z}/\ell\mathbb{Z}$ of degree less than $\lceil \frac{N}{n} \rceil$.

– The *Mksol* step computes the following element of the null-space of A: $w = \sum_{j=1}^{n} F^{(j)}(A)y^{(j)}$. Similarly to the *Krylov* phase, the computation can be distributed into n independent computations.

In the rest of the paper, we focus on the *Krylov* and *Mksol* steps, as they dominate the overall cost and can benefit from parallel hardware. For the *Lingen* computation, we use the CADO-NFS software [5].

3   The Matrix–Vector Product

The *Lingen* step complexity depends roughly quadratically on the blocking parameter n. Therefore, we can not increase too much the blocking parameters (n, m). We observe also that the block Wiedemann algorithm does not distribute the matrix–vector product, so it does not reduce the amount of required memory per node. Thus, the parallelism provided by the block Wiedemann algorithm is soon limited. We need to explore how to carry out a *Krylov*/*Mksol* task on more than one computation node. Typically, this is related to performing each matrix–vector product in parallel on many computation nodes. In this section, we study how to accelerate this major operation on parallel hardware.

We assume that we have a set of identical *computing nodes* organized according to a 2D rectangular grid and interconnected by a network. Each node is identified by its coordinates (i, j) in the grid. At this level, we ignore the nature of the nodes. The nodes could be cores within a machine, independent machines or GPUs. The matrix A is split into square parts of equal size, such that each node (i, j) gets the part $A_{i,j}$.

3.1   Communication/Computation Scheme

An SpMV iteration takes an input vector u and computes $v = Au$. At the beginning of an iteration, a node (i, j) holds the sub-matrix A_{ij} and the j-th fragment u_j of the input vector u. The nodes collaborate together to compute the output vector, which will be the input vector to the next iteration. To be able to run the next iteration, the node A_{ij} only needs to know the j-th fragment v_j of the output vector v. More specifically, the parallel SpMV product is performed as follows.

1. Each node (i, j) computes the partial SpMV $A_{ij}u_j$.
2. Each diagonal node (i, i) collects and sums the partial results from the nodes of the row i. The sum corresponds to the i-th fragment of v.
3. Each diagonal node (i, i) broadcasts its fragment v_j to the nodes of the column i.

In Figure 1, we give an example of a run for 4 parallel nodes with a 2×2 split of the matrix. In this figure, the 4 nodes are, represented in gray, numbered from 0 to 3. On the left-hand side, we indicate how the matrix A and the input vector u are distributed among the nodes. We detail on the right-hand side the intermediate data present on each node after each step.

The communication scheme suffers from the fact that only one node per row collects the partial products. A parallelization of the Reduction/Broadcast operations is possible, typically using the ReduceScatter/AllGather operations. This

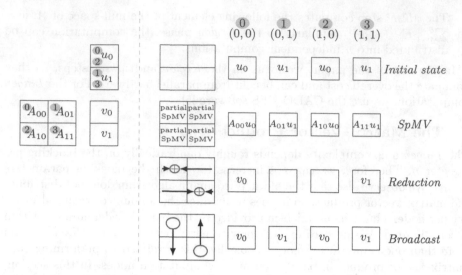

Fig. 1. Computation/Communication scheme for a 2×2 split of A

should yield to a significant speedup of the communication delay. However, the output of the iteration will be permuted, *i.e.*, the fragments of v will not be distributed as were those of u in the beginning of the iteration. In summary, it remains an improvement that can be explored.

3.2 Balancing the Workload

The particular distribution of the non-zero coefficients is such that the nodes will get unbalanced workloads, and the nodes working on the denser parts will take more time than those working on the sparser ones. For the particular kind of input, this unbalance problem can fortunately be solved efficiently. To fix this problem, we apply permutations of the rows and columns, so that the distribution of non-zero coefficients for each sub-matrix is close to that of the matrix A, as shown in Figure 2. One possibility to obtain this permutation is to sort the columns by their weight and distribute them evenly among the nodes, then proceed likewise with the rows. This is made possible by the fact that the standard deviation of the row weight is much smaller than that of the column weight.

3.3 The Partial SpMV

The matrix is stored in a sparse format, adapted from the *Compressed Sparse Row* (CSR) format for the particular distribution of the non-zero coefficients.

We chose to implement the arithmetic operations in $\mathbb{Z}/\ell\mathbb{Z}$ using the *Residue Number System* (RNS). The use of this representation for finite field arithmetic provides a fine grained parallelism, which can be exploited by Single Instruction, Multiple Data (SIMD) architectures.

In the remainder of the article, we consider the partial matrix–vector product as a *black box*, that is, a subroutine which, on inputs A and u returns the product Au. We give more details about how this subroutine is implemented in [14].

Initial   **Balanced**

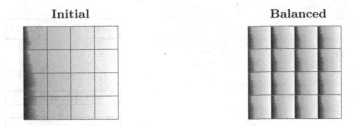

Fig. 2. Distribution of non-zero coefficients for initial and balanced matrices

3.4   Communication Concerns

We now focus on how to share data between the computing nodes, in the cases of CPU nodes and GPU nodes.

CPU Communications. The case of CPU-only setups is quite straightforward, as we use the MPI operation `MPI_Reduce` to collect and combine on a diagonal node the results of nodes belonging to the same row, and `MPI_Bcast` to broadcast the combined results to the nodes of each column. In the following subsections, we assume that we execute the application over a cluster of GPUs and we discuss the data movement. We restrict to NVIDIA graphics hardware. Distributing an SpMV on several GPUs requires considering two possible (and not mutually exclusive) cases: the first one where a single CPU node harbors two or more GPUs, and the second one where the GPUs are in different CPU nodes.

Intra-node GPU Communications. We are in the case of sharing data between two GPUs within the same CPU node. In order to do so, *CUDA*, the parallel programming model for NVIDIA GPUs [1] offers three possibilities:
- Staging through CPU: the communication has to involve the host CPU. Thus, it is composed of two transfers, a device to-host copy (D2H) then a host-to-device copy (H2D).
- Device-to-device copy (D2D): from the programmer's perspective, it is a direct copy of the GPU buffers. Although the transfer still passes through the host memory, the copy is fully pipelined.
- Peer-to-Peer Direct Access (P2P DMA): using this feature, the devices can share data independently of the CPU. P2P DMA requires to enable peer access for each GPU, which is supported by recent hardware.

The P2P DMA feature should decrease the host overhead and thus accelerate the memory copies. To verify it, we ran benchmarks to compare the bandwidth and latency of each approach (cf. Figure 3). The experiment is performed using two NVIDIA GeForce GTX 680 cards. The benchmarks measure the run time for sending messages of increasing size from one GPU to the other. The latencies for the first two options are 19.7 µs and 19.4 µs, respectively, and only 14 µs when the P2P DMA is enabled. The peak bandwidths are 6.1 GB/s for the explicit host staging transfer, 7.3 GB/s for the device to device transfer, and 10.4 GB/s for the P2P DMA transfer.

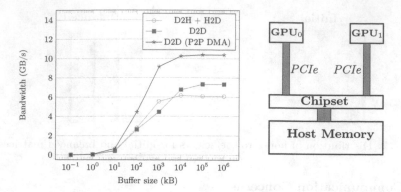

Fig. 3. Benchmarking Intra-node GPU communications

Inter-node GPU Communications. Now, we are interested in the case of sharing data between GPUs installed in different CPU nodes. The trivial option in this case is to perform the transfer in three steps: a data copy from device to host using CUDA routines, then use MPI to copy data between hosts, and finally a CUDA copy from host to device on the destination node (cf. Figure 4).

It is however possible to overcome the host staging using the *Cuda-aware MPI* feature which combines MPI and CUDA. It allows one to address GPU buffers directly in the MPI routines (cf. Figure 5). From the programmer's point of view, a data transfer boils down to one call to an MPI routine. With *Cuda-aware MPI*, the data transfers are fully pipelined, while without the feature, the transfers between hosts and those between the device and the host are pipelined separately. The *Cuda-aware MPI* feature is incorporated in several widely used MPI libraries and considerably improves the data movement latencies.

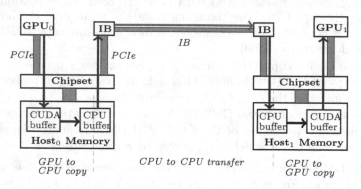

Fig. 4. Data copy from GPU$_0$ to GPU$_1$ without *Cuda-aware MPI*

In Figure 6, we report the results of bandwidth benchmarks for inter-node GPU-to-GPU communications. We ran the experiment using two NVIDIA GTX 680 installed in two nodes connected with QDR InfiniBand. We use CUDA 5.0 and Open MPI 1.7.3. In addition to benchmarks for the two ways of communication, we added the Host-to-Host (H2H) communication results as a reference, for

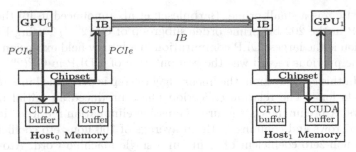

Fig. 5. Data copy from GPU_0 to GPU_1 with *Cuda-aware MPI*

which we measured the data movement from one CPU buffer to another CPU buffer using the regular MPI routines.

The latency of a plain Device-to-Device transfer is 11 µs. It becomes 9 µs if the feature *Cuda-aware MPI* is used. The latency of the Host-to-Host transfer is 1 µs. Without *Cuda-aware MPI*, the bandwidth is bounded by 2.3 GB/s. The *Cuda-aware MPI* feature allows to reach the Host-to-Host peak bandwidth, which is 3.7 GB/s.

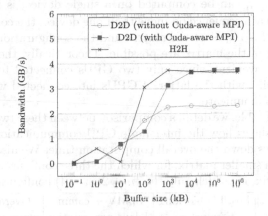

Fig. 6. Benchmarking Inter-node GPU communications

Another feature that further optimizes data transfers is *GPU Direct*. The *GPU Direct* offers lower latency for moving data compared to transfers staged through the host. However, its bandwidth is significantly limited. We could not deploy this feature in our application, as it is supported only by the recent Tesla and Quadro cards. A comparison of the performance of this feature with the transfers staged through host can be found in [22].

4 Examples of Computations

4.1 DLP in GF(2^{809})$^\times$ Using FFS

The function field sieve (FFS) [2] is an *index-calculus* algorithm designed to attack the DLP in the multiplicative subgroup of a finite field GF(p^n), where the characteristic p is a small prime. Barbulescu et al. announced in [6] the solving of the DLP in the 202-bit prime order subgroup of $GF(2^{809})^{\times}$ using FFS. This computation is the largest DLP computation in a binary field extension of prime degree. The previous record was the computation of a DLP in $GF(2^{613})^{\times}$ [16].

Matrix. In this computation, the linear algebra step is performed in $\mathbb{Z}/\ell\mathbb{Z}$ where ℓ is 202 bits long. The relation collection phase produced an initial matrix of 78.8M rows. A preliminary structured Gaussian elimination reduced the matrix to 3,602,667 rows and columns, with an average of 100 non-zero coefficients per row. Each non-zero coefficient of A fits in a single machine word. Around 90% of them are ± 1 [8], [6].

Linear Algebra Setup. At the time of the computation, we had access to a 4-node cluster, with 2.4 GHz Intel Xeon E5620 Westmere processors connected with InfiniBand network at 40 Gb/s. Each node is equipped with 2 NVIDIA Tesla M2050 graphics processors.

The total memory required to handle the matrix along with the input and output vectors is 3.16 GB. Since the available memory on one card is only 3 GB, the block Widemann configuration ($n = 8, m = 16$), for which a sequence $\left({}^{t}xA^{i}y^{(j)}\right)_{i\in\mathbb{N}}$ can be computed on a single device, is not feasible. We have to compute each sequence on more than one device; the configuration ($n = 4, m = 8$) with a 2×1 split of the matrix and the configuration ($n = 2, m = 4$) with a 2×2 split of the matrix are possible. Theoretically, the former appears to be the most convenient, since only two GPUs connected to the same node communicate, while, with the latter, 4 GPUs interconnected with the network are required to communicate.

In the following table, we detail a comparison between these two configurations. The comparison shows how the inter-node GPU communication for the second configuration slows down the overall computation time. We also present benchmarks related to a smaller matrix, for which the three configurations are possible and a bigger matrix, for which only the ($n = 2, m = 4$) configuration is feasible.

Matrix size (required memory)	Possible blocking parameters	SpMV + comm. delays per iteration	Overall comp. time	Ratio com. /iteration
3.6M × 3.6M (3.2 GB)	($n = 4, m = 8$)	142 + 27 ms	**4.5 days**	**16%**
	($n = 2, m = 4$)	72 + 41 ms	6 days	37%
3M × 3M (2.7 GB)	($n = 8, m = 16$)	**228 + 0 ms**	**2.5 days**	**0%**
	($n = 4, m = 8$)	115 + 23 ms	3 days	17%
	($n = 2, m = 4$)	58 + 35 ms	4.1 days	38%
6M × 6M (5.4 GB)	($n = 2, m = 4$)	**123 + 69 ms**	**16.7 days**	**36%**

With the ($n = 4, m = 8$) blocking parameters, an iteration takes 169 ms on each node, including 27 ms for the GPU communications. The initial sequence computation required 2.6 days in parallel on the 4 nodes. The linear generator computation was carried out in parallel using 16 threads running on 16 CPU cores. It required 2 hours. Finally, computing the kernel vector required 1.8 days in parallel on the 4 GPU nodes. The overall computation took a total wall-clock time of about 4.5 days.

4.2 DLP in a 596-bit Prime Field Using NFS

To compute discrete logarithms in a prime field $GF(p)$, the Number Field Sieve (NFS) algorithm is used [15]. The last NFS record was accomplished by T. Kleinjung et al. [4] for a 530-bit (160-decimal-digit) prime p using NFS. We are currently running an NFS-based computation to attack the DLP in a 596-bit (180-decimal-digit) prime field. The linear algebra step is defined over a 595-bit prime ℓ.

Matrix. The matrix contains 179M rows at the end of the relation collection. The preliminary structured Gaussian elimination reduced the number of rows to 7,287,476, with an average weight of 150 non-zero coefficients per row. The matrices issued from NFS computations contain a small number (5, here) of dense columns, whose elements live in $\mathbb{Z}/\ell\mathbb{Z}$. The rest of the matrix is similar to an FFS matrix in terms of distribution and coefficient size. Taking this dense part into account adds a non-negligible cost when compared to FFS matrices.

GPU Setup. For this computation, we have access to 8 NVIDIA GeForce GTX 680 graphics processors, plugged into a 4-node cluster of Intel Xeon E5-2609 processors running at 2.4 GHz, and connected with QDR Infiniband network. Each graphics card has 4 GB of memory. The total memory required to carry out the SpMV on one GPU is 9.8 GB. Thus, 4 GPUs should work on a single sequence, *i.e.*, at most two sequences can be computed in parallel, and the blocking parameters are ($n = 2, m = 4$). An iteration takes 615 ms on each group of 4 GPUs, with 195 ms for the GPU-to-GPU communications. The overall computation should take a total wall-clock time of about 65 days.

CPU Setup. Another option was tried, using our CPU implementation on a 768-core cluster. The cluster contains 48 nodes connected with FDR Infiniband. Each node hosts two 2-GHZ 8-core Intel Xeon E5-2650 processors. With this setup, we propose an 8×8 split of the matrix, so that 64 MPI processes running on 4 nodes work together to carry out a matrix–vector product, each process running on one core. This yields to a ($n = 12, m = 24$) block Wiedemann configuration. The processes are distributed so that the processes running on the same node are contiguous. This allows to accelerate the reduction/broadcast operations, since data sharing between threads belonging to the same node is performed on shared memory, not across the network. A speedup of 2.4 on the communication delay is observed when comparing with the default MPI processes mapping.

In the following table, we compare the GPU and CPU setups. We observe that starting from a certain matrix size and with these setups, the multi-core acceleration prevails over the GPU one. For comparison, we add a setup, where we have a cluster similar to the 48-node multi-core cluster, but containing two NVIDIA GeForce GTX 680 on each node. This setup is not speculative, the GPU setup obtained with 8 GPUs scales perfectly to 96 GPUs, thanks to the cost-free distribution of block Wiedemann algorithm.

With the CPU setup, an iteration is performed in 2.1 s by the 64 parallel threads, including 0.4 ms for communications. The *Krylov* phase required 22 in the 768-core cluster, which is equivalent to 46-core years. The *Lingen* phase required 15 hours running on 144 cores. The *Mksol* phase took 16 days in the 768-core cluster (i.e. 34-core years). The overall computation required around 80-core years.

Matrix size (Memory)	Setup	Blocking parameters	SpMV+com. delays [ms]	Overall comp. time	Ratio com.
7.3M × 7.3M (9.8 GB)	8 GPUs on 4 nodes	($n = 2, m = 4$) 4 GPUs ↔ 1 subtask	420 + 195	65 days	32%
	768 cores on 48 nodes	**($n = 12, m = 24$) 64 cores ↔ 1 subtask**	**1700 + 400**	**39 days**	**19%**
	96 GPUs on 48 nodes	($n = 24, m = 48$) 4 GPUs ↔ 1 subtask	420 + 195	5.5 days	32%

5   Conclusion

In this article, we presented how the block solvers, in our case block Wiedemann algorithm, distribute heavy computations without an additional overhead. We discussed a further parallelization of the matrix-vector product and detailed how we can efficiently run this computation in a cluster of GPUs or CPUs. In the examples that we ran, we did not combine the two architectures on the same computation. However, our final implementation can be run on a hybrid GPU/Multi-core architecture.

Acknowledgments. The author is grateful to Jérémie Detrey and Emmanuel Thomé. This work would not be possible without their support. We also thank the reviewers for their valuable comments.

References

1. CUDA Programming Guide Version 5.5 (2013), http://docs.nvidia.com/cuda/cuda-c-programming-guide/
2. Adleman, L.M.: The function field sieve. In: Huang, M.-D.A., Adleman, L.M. (eds.) ANTS 1994. LNCS, vol. 877, pp. 108–121. Springer, Heidelberg (1994)
3. Aoki, K., Franke, J., Kleinjung, T., Lenstra, A.K., Osvik, D.A.: A kilobit special number field sieve factorization. In: Kurosawa, K. (ed.) ASIACRYPT 2007. LNCS, vol. 4833, pp. 1–12. Springer, Heidelberg (2007), http://eprint.iacr.org/
4. Bahr, F., Franke, J., Kleinjung, T.: Discrete logarithms in GF(p) - 160 digits, Email to the NMBRTHRY mailing list (February 2007), http://perso.univ-rennes1.fr/reynald.lercier/file/BFK07.txt
5. Bai, S., Filbois, A., Gaudry, P., Kruppa, A., Morain, F., Thomé, E., Zimmermann, P.: CADO-NFS, Crible Algébrique: Distribution, Optimisation - Number Field Sieve, http://cado-nfs.gforge.inria.fr/
6. Barbulescu, R., Bouvier, C., Detrey, J., Gaudry, P., Jeljeli, H., Thomé, E., Videau, M., Zimmermann, P.: Discrete logarithm in GF(2^{809}) with FFS. In: Krawczyk, H. (ed.) PKC 2014. LNCS, vol. 8383, pp. 221–238. Springer, Heidelberg (2014)
7. Barbulescu, R., Gaudry, P., Joux, A., Thomé, E.: A quasi-polynomial algorithm for discrete logarithm in finite fields of small characteristic. In: Nguyen, P.Q., Oswald, E. (eds.) EUROCRYPT 2014. LNCS, vol. 8441, pp. 1–16. Springer, Heidelberg (2014)

8. Bouvier, C.: The filtering step of discrete logarithm and integer factorization algorithms, p. 22 (2013) (Preprint)
9. Boyer, B., Dumas, J.G., Giorgi, P.: Exact sparse matrix-vector multiplication on GPU's and multicore architectures. CoRR, abs/1004.3719 (2010)
10. Coppersmith, D.: Solving homogeneous linear equations over GF(2) via block Wiedemann algorithm. Math. Comput. 62(205), 333–350 (1994)
11. Diffie, W., Hellman, M.E.: New directions in cryptography. IEEE Transactions on Information Theory 22(6), 644–654 (1976)
12. Dutta, R., Barua, R., Sarkar, P.: Pairing-based cryptographic protocols: a survey. Cryptology ePrint Archive, Report 2004/064 (2004)
13. ElGamal, T.: A public key cryptosystem and a signature scheme based on discrete logarithms. IEEE Transactions on Information Theory 31(4), 469–472 (1985)
14. Jeljeli, H.: Accelerating iterative SpMV for Discrete Logarithm Problem using GPUs, p. 11 (2013) (Preprint), http://hal.inria.fr/hal-00734975
15. Joux, A., Lercier, R.: Improvements to the general number field sieve for discrete logarithms in prime fields. a comparison with the Gaussian integer method. Mathematics of Computation 72(242), 953–967 (2003)
16. Joux, A., Lercier, R.: Discrete logarithms in $GF(2^{607})$ and $GF(2^{613})$. E-mail to the NMBRTHRY mailing list (September 2005), http://listserv.nodak.edu/archives/nmbrthry.html
17. Kaltofen, E.: Analysis of Coppersmith's block Wiedemann algorithm for the parallel solution of sparse linear systems. Mathematics of Computation (1995)
18. Kleinjung, T., et al.: Factorization of a 768-bit rsa modulus. In: Rabin, T. (ed.) CRYPTO 2010. LNCS, vol. 6223, pp. 333–350. Springer, Heidelberg (2010), http://eprint.iacr.org/
19. C. Lanczos. Solution of systems of linear equations by minimized iterations. J. Res. Natl. Bur. Stand, 49:33–53, 1952.
20. Odlyzko, A.M.: Discrete logarithms in finite fields and their cryptographic significance. In: Beth, T., Cot, N., Ingemarsson, I. (eds.) Advances in Cryptology - EUROCRYPT 1984. LNCS, vol. 209, pp. 224–314. Springer, Heidelberg (1985)
21. Pomerance, C., Smith, J.W.: Reduction of huge, sparse matrices over finite fields via created catastrophes. Experiment. Math. 1, 89–94 (1992)
22. Potluri, S., Hamidouche, K., Venkatesh, A., Bureddy, D., Panda, D.K.: Efficient inter-node mpi communication using gpudirect rdma for infiniband clusters with nvidia gpus. In: ICPP, pp. 80–89. IEEE (2013)
23. Zumbragel, J., Granger, R., Kleinjung, T.: Discrete logarithms in $GF(2^{9234})$. E-mail to the NMBRTHRY mailing list (January 2014), http://listserv.nodak.edu/archives/nmbrthry.html
24. Schmidt, B., Aribowo, H., Dang, H.-V.: Iterative sparse matrix-vector multiplication for integer factorization on GPUs. In: Jeannot, E., Namyst, R., Roman, J. (eds.) Euro-Par 2011, Part II. LNCS, vol. 6853, pp. 413–424. Springer, Heidelberg (2011)
25. Strassen, V.: Gaussian elimination is not optimal. Numerische Mathematik 13(4), 354–356 (1969)
26. Thomé, E.: Subquadratic computation of vector generating polynomials and improvement of the block Wiedemann algorithm. Journal of Symbolic Computation 33(5), 757–775 (2002)
27. Wiedemann, D.H.: Solving sparse linear equations over finite fields. IEEE Trans. Inf. Theor. 32(1), 54–62 (1986)

Toward OpenCL Automatic Multi-Device Support

Sylvain Henry[1], Alexandre Denis[2], Denis Barthou[3], Marie-Christine Counilh[3], and Raymond Namyst[3]

[1] Exascale Computing Research Laboratory, France
sylvain.henry@exascale-computing.eu
[2] Inria Bordeaux – Sud-Ouest, France
alexandre.denis@inria.fr
[3] Univ. of Bordeaux, France
denis.barthou@inria.fr, {counilh,raymond.namyst}@labri.fr

Abstract. To fully tap into the potential of today heterogeneous machines, offloading parts of an application on accelerators is no longer sufficient. The real challenge is to build systems where the application would permanently spread across the entire machine, that is, where parallel tasks would be dynamically scheduled over the full set of available processing units. In this paper we present SOCL, an OpenCL implementation that improves and simplifies the programming experience on heterogeneous architectures. SOCL enables applications to dynamically dispatch computation kernels over processing devices so as to maximize their utilization. OpenCL applications can incrementally make use of light extensions to automatically schedule kernels in a controlled manner on multi-device architectures. We demonstrate the relevance of our approach by experimenting with several OpenCL applications on a range of heterogeneous architectures. We show that performance portability is enhanced by using SOCL extensions.

1 Introduction

Heterogeneous architectures are becoming ubiquitous in high-performance computing centers as well as in embedded systems [1]. The number of top supercomputers using accelerators such as GPU or Xeon Phi keeps growing. As a result, for an increasing part of the HPC community, the challenge has shifted from exploiting hierarchical multicore machines to exploiting heterogeneous multicore architectures. The Open Computing Language (OpenCL) [2] is part of this effort. It is a specification for heterogeneous parallel programming, providing a portable programming language together with a unified interface to interact with the different processing devices. In OpenCL, programmers explicitly define code fragments (*kernels*) to be executed on particular devices. Kernel executions, synchronizations, and data transfers are then explicitly triggered by the host and dependencies are enforced by user-defined events. OpenCL applications are portable over a wide range of supported platforms. However, performance

F. Silva et al. (Eds.): Euro-Par 2014, LNCS 8632, pp. 776–787, 2014.

portability is still difficult to achieve because high performance kernels have to be adapted in term of (i) parallelism, (ii) granularity and (iii) memory working set to the target device architecture. Adapting parallelism requires that the implicit kernel dependence graph built by the programmer exposes enough parallelism to feed all computing devices. This effort has to be achieved by the user. As each task has to be mapped to a particular device in OpenCL, load-balancing strategies for heterogeneous architectures have also to be hand-tuned. Load-balancing issues for heterogeneous platforms are clearly a limiting performance factor for OpenCL codes. Likewise, adapting granularity is a strong scalability requirement, and since different devices may have very different memory hierarchies, granularity and working sets have also a high impact on performance. While OpenCL kernels are compiled at load-time, their granularity are determined by the user. Adapting granularity thus results in writing as many kernels as there are different devices. Performance comes therefore at the expense of portability, reducing the competitive edge of OpenCL compared to other parallel languages.

Our contribution lies in the design, implementation and validation of new OpenCL mechanisms that tackle load-balancing issues on heterogeneous devices. Kernels submitted by users are automatically scheduled on devices by our OpenCL runtime system. It handles load-balancing issues and maintains the coherency of data across all devices by performing appropriate data transfers between them. These mechanisms have been implemented in our unified OpenCL platform, named SOCL. We show that existing OpenCL codes, where devices and memory transfers are managed manually can be migrated incrementally to automatic scheduling and memory management with SOCL. With little impact on the code, making OpenCL codes use SOCL implementation is a way to adapt transparently to multi-device architectures.

The remainder of this paper is organized as follows: we present SOCL, our unified OpenCL platform in Sect. 2, and its implementation in Sect. 3; in Sect. 4, we evaluate the performance of SOCL; in Sect. 5, we compare our work with existing related works; finally we draw conclusions in the last section.

2 Dynamic Adaptation of Parallelism to Heterogeneous Architectures

We aim at bringing dynamic architecture adaptation features into an OpenCL framework called SOCL. In this section we show how OpenCL applications can benefit from the following advantages: (1) a unified OpenCL platform, (2) an automatic memory management over all devices, and (3) an automatic command scheduler.

2.1 SOCL: A Unified OpenCL Platform

The OpenCL specification defines a programming interface (API) for the *host* to submit commands to *computing devices*, and a programming language called OpenCL C language for writing the *kernels* — the tasks to execute on the

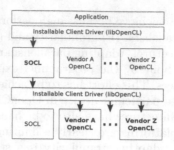

Fig. 1. SOCL unified platform uses OpenCL implementations from other vendors and can be used as any other implementation using the ICD. Thus, SOCL is both an OpenCL implementation and an OpenCL (client) application.

devices. Kernels can be dynamically compiled during the execution of the application for any available accelerator device that supports OpenCL.

To handle the case where multiple OpenCL devices from different vendors are available on a given machine, each vendor provides an implementation of the OpenCL specification, called a *platform*. The Installable Client Driver (ICD) exposes all platforms available for an application. Devices that need to be synchronized, to share or exchange data can be grouped into *context* entities. However OpenCL is restrictive about interaction between devices: devices in a context must all belong to the same platform. Thus it prevents synchronization commands between devices from different vendors — as is often found on heterogeneous architectures.

As an answer to this issue we propose a *unified platform* provided by SOCL. It can be used like any other OpenCL implementation with the OpenCL host API. As the ICD extension is supported, it can be installed side-by-side with other OpenCL implementations and applications can dynamically choose to use it or not among available OpenCL platforms, as depicted in Fig. 1.

A distinctive feature of SOCL is that it wraps all entities of the other platforms into entities of its own unified platform. SOCL implements everything needed to make this unified platform support every OpenCL mechanism defined in the specification. Hence, applications using SOCL unified platform can create contexts mixing devices that were initially in different platforms. In particular, it is possible to use command queues, context and events for tasks to schedule on different devices.

2.2   Automatic Memory Management

SOCL provides a global virtual memory encompassing every device memory and part of the host memory with a relaxed consistency model. Every buffer can be accessed by any command (kernel execution, transfer, etc.) on any device because the runtime system ensures that a valid copy of the buffer is present in the device memory before executing the command, performing appropriate data transfers beforehand if required. Moreover it ensures that two commands accessing the

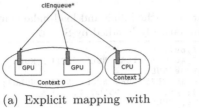

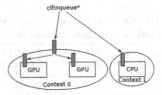

(a) Explicit mapping with OpenCL contexts

(b) Explicit or automatic mapping with SOCL scheduling contexts

Fig. 2. (a) Command queues are attached to single devices (b) Context queues are attached to contexts and SOCL automatically schedules commands on devices in the context

same buffer are not executed simultaneously if one of them is writing, while a buffer can be concurrently accessed for reading. Finally, as commands can be enqueued in advance (into command queues), SOCL can anticipate some data transfers for commands whose dependencies have not yet completed.

In addition to device memories, SOCL uses host memory space to store buffers that have to be evicted from a device memory to make some room for other buffers as well as to perform indirect data transfers between device memories. When buffers are created using host memory mapping (CL_MEM_USE_HOST_PTR flag), the host memory space is aggregated to the SOCL managed host memory and must not be used directly anymore (i.e., without using OpenCL API) by the application. Temporarily direct access to a buffer in the managed host memory can be obtained using OpenCL buffer mapping in host address space facilities (clEnqueueMapBuffer).

Using the CL_MEM_USE_HOST_PTR flag is the preferred way to create initialized buffers with SOCL as it avoids any superfluous data transfer. Nevertheless other mechanisms such as explicitly writing into a buffer (i.e., WriteBuffer command) or writing into a buffer mapped in host address space are fully supported.

2.3 Automatic Command Scheduler

In OpenCL applications, commands such as kernel executions, memory transfers or synchronizations are submitted to a command queue attached to a single device. Synchronization between commands from different queues is possible using *event* entities. Events give a fine control of the dependencies between commands. As such they subsume command queue ordering and barriers. Each command can trigger an event when the command completes, and depends on a list of events triggered by other commands. Events can only be defined and used *within the same context*.

We propose to attach command queues to contexts, independently of any particular device, as illustrated on Fig. 2. It enables the runtime system to schedule commands submitted to these queues onto any device of the context. This extends the notion of context to what we call *scheduling contexts*, and these

Listing 1.1. Context queue creation example. Scheduling and load-balancing of commands submitted in these queues are automatically handled by SOCL.

```
cl_context ctx1 = clCreateContextFromType(NULL,
    CL_DEVICE_TYPE_GPU | CL_DEVICE_TYPE_ACCELERATOR, NULL, NULL, NULL);
cl_context ctx2 = clCreateContextFromType(NULL,
    CL_DEVICE_TYPE_CPU | CL_DEVICE_TYPE_ACCELERATOR, NULL, NULL, NULL);
cl_command_queue cq1 = clCreateCommandQueue(ctx1, NULL, 0,
 CL_QUEUE_OUT_OF_ORDER_EXEC_MODE_ENABLE, NULL);
cl_command_queue cq2 = clCreateCommandQueue(ctx2, NULL, 0,
 CL_QUEUE_OUT_OF_ORDER_EXEC_MODE_ENABLE, NULL);
```

Listing 1.2. Context properties are used to select the scheduling policy.

```
cl_context_properties properties[] = { CL_CONTEXT_SCHEDULER_SOCL, "heft", 0 };
cl_context ctx =
 clCreateContextFromType(properties, CL_DEVICE_TYPE_CPU, NULL, NULL, NULL);
```

command queues are named *context queues*. Thanks to context queues, programmer may rely on automatic task placement by the runtime system, rather than to decide placement manually. On another hand, it does not forbid manual placement if programmer wants so for optimization purposes. Several contexts may be created to ease application development, e.g., programmer may create a context queue with all accelerators for data parallel tasks (GPU, Xeon Phi) and another context queue for code with more control (CPU, Xeon Phi). Listing 1.1 shows an example of code with two scheduling contexts and two context queues. Note that command queues are created with a NULL device since they are *context queues*.

The runtime scheduling strategy has to take into account various device properties such as: *memory capacity*, so as not to saturate a device memory; *affinity between tasks*, i.e., schedule tasks on the same device as their input buffer already is; *performance* of devices, i.e., schedule tasks on the most efficient device for the task. A predefined set of scheduling strategies assigning commands to devices is available for SOCL, brought by StarPU. They can be selected through context properties. For instance, the code in Listing 1.2 selects the *heft* scheduling policy, implementing the Heterogeneous Earliest Finish Time heuristic [3], based on estimated tasks and transfers durations. Other heuristics are available, such as *eager* where every device picks a task in a shared queue when it becomes idle, and additional strategies can be user-defined if need be.

3   SOCL Implementation

SOCL currently implements the whole OpenCL 1.0 specification (except imaging), and parts of newer specifications. SOCL relies on StarPU [4] runtime system. Namely, SOCL is an OpenCL frontend for StarPU with unified platform, and is distributed as open-source software together with StarPU. StarPU uses a task-based programming model with explicit dependencies; SOCL extends StarPU memory management and event mechanism in order to handle all OpenCL specification.

When a kernel is created using OpenCL, the SOCL implementation automatically handles the allocation and configuration of a StarPU kernel. When an OpenCL kernel is enqueued for execution, a StarPU task is created and configured to be executed on appropriate devices (all the devices of the target context or a selected device). OpenCL provides two mechanisms to order task executions: events, i.e., explicit dependencies, and synchronization on command queues. Implicit dependencies between kernels placed in an in-order command queue are converted by SOCL into explicit dependencies for StarPU. Similarly, barriers are also translated into explicit dependencies between tasks separated by these synchronizations.

To implement OpenCL buffer allocation, SOCL triggers the allocation of StarPU data, of the "variable" flavor, following StarPU terminology. To implement OpenCL buffer initialization mechanisms, SOCL circumvents StarPU limitations. Indeed, StarPU only provides a registering mechanism similar to OpenCL buffer allocation when the CL_USE_HOST_PTR is set. All the other allocation modes in OpenCL have been implemented within SOCL. Moreover, data transfers between host memory and buffers are not supported directly by StarPU, where transfers are the consequence of data dependence between tasks. In SOCL, the implementation of ReadBuffer and WriteBuffer commands for instance resorts to StarPU tasks with no computational part but dependent on the data to transfer.

4   Performance Evaluation

In this section, we present performance figures to show the benefits of our approach. Three OpenCL benchmarks are considered: Black-Scholes, LuxRender and HDR Tone Mapping. Experiments are conducted on the following hardware platforms: hannibal — Intel Xeon X5550 2.67GHz with 24GB, 3 Nvidia Quadro FX 5800; alaric — Intel Xeon E5-2650 2.00GHz with 32GB, 2 AMD Radeon HD 7900; averell — Intel Xeon E5-2650 2.00GHz with 64GB, 2 Nvidia Tesla M2075. The software comprises Linux 3.2, AMD APP 2.7, Intel OpenCL SDK 1.5 and Nvidia CUDA 4.0.1.

4.1   Black-Scholes

The Black-Scholes model is used by some option market participants to estimate option prices. Given three arrays of n values, it computes two new arrays of n values. The code is easily parallelized in any number of blocks of any size. We use the kernel provided by Nvidia OpenCL SDK, using float values for each array.

Figures 3a, 3b and 3c present performance obtained on hannibal with blocks of fixed size of 1 million, 5 millions and 25 millions options, comparing Intel OpenCL, Nvidia OpenCL, and SOCL. Intel and Nvidia OpenCL tests have been performed using a static round-robin distribution of the blocks on devices. Since

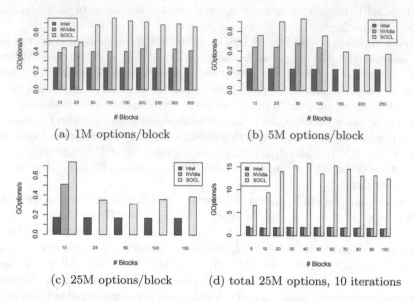

(a) 1M options/block   (b) 5M options/block

(c) 25M options/block   (d) total 25M options, 10 iterations

Fig. 3. Performance of Black-Scholes algorithm with blocks containing 1M (a), 5M (b) and 25M options (c). Performance of 10 iterations with a total of 25M options (d).

Nvidia OpenCL implementation is restricted to GPU memory, it fails in case the problem does not fit graphic card memory, which explains why some results are missing for Nvidia. SOCL tests were obtained with automatic scheduling mode, able to schedule tasks on any device (GPU or CPU). On this example, SOCL automatic scheduling always reaches better performance than round-robin approach, nearly doubling performance in the case of 1M options (for 100 blocks). This is due to the fact that both computing devices (CPU and GPU) are used, while Nvidia and Intel OpenCL implementations use only one type of device.

Figure 3d shows results obtained on 10 iterations on the same data set using the same kernel, with a total option count of 25 millions. It illustrates the benefits of automatic memory management associated with scheduling, when there is some temporal locality. The test was conducted on `averell`. The *heft* algorithm clearly outperforms the other approaches in this case, and avoids unnecessary memory transfers. Indeed, this algorithm takes into account memories into which data are stored to schedule tasks. This advantage comes with very little impact on the original OpenCL code, since it only requires to define a scheduling strategy for the context, and to remove device information in the definition of command queues.

Overall, this example shows the benefits of a unifying platform, able to use both CPU and GPUs with an efficient dynamic memory management allowing large computations to be performed on GPUs, contrary to Nvidia OpenCL implementation. It exhibits a performance gain up to 85% without data reuse and way higher in case of data reuse.

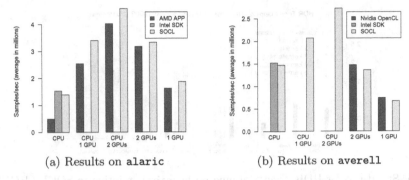

(a) Results on `alaric`   (b) Results on `averell`

Fig. 4. LuxRender benchmark results (average number of samples rendered per second)

4.2 LuxRender

LuxRender [5] is a rendering engine that simulates the flow of light using physical equations and produces realistic images. LuxRays is a part of LuxRender that deals with ray intersection using OpenCL to benefit from accelerator devices. SLG2 (SmallLuxGPU2) is an application that performs rendering using LuxRays and returns some performance metrics. SLG2 can only use a single OpenCL platform at a time. As such, it is a good example of an application that could benefit from SOCL property of grouping every available device in a single OpenCL platform.

For this experiment, we use the existing SLG2 OpenCL code unmodified, and run on Nvidia, AMD, Intel OpenCL and SOCL with the example "luxball" scene with default parameters. We use batch mode and run rendering for 120 seconds. We disable CPU compute threads to avoid conflicts with OpenCL CPU devices.

The average amount of samples computed per second for each OpenCL platform is shown in Fig. 4. When a single device is used (CPU or GPU), SOCL introduces only a small overhead compared to the direct use of the vendor OpenCL. However in the case of a single AMD GPU, SOCL outperforms the vendor implementation, presumably thanks to a better data pre-fetching strategy.

On `alaric`, CPU is better handled with the Intel OpenCL implementation than with AMD OpenCL. The best performance is obtained with the SOCL platform using 2 GPUs and the CPU, combining the use of the AMD implementation for the GPUs and the Intel for the CPU. On `averell`, the best performance is also obtained with SOCL when it uses both Nvidia and Intel implementations.

This test shows that an OpenCL application designed for using a single OpenCL platform can directly benefit from using the SOCL unified platform without any change in its code.

4.3 HDR Tone Mapping

HDR Tone Mapping is an image processing technique to render a high dynamic range image on a device with a limited dynamic range. Intel has implemented [6]

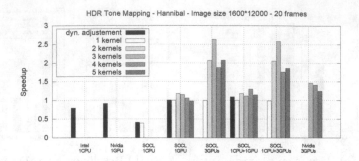

Fig. 5. Speed-ups for HDR Tone Mapping on `hannibal`, relative to SOCL / 1 GPU.

this technique in OpenCL. Their code features multi-device support, both CPU and GPU, given that both devices are in the same platform (Intel GPU and CPU). Each frame is split to balance load between CPU and GPU, the splitting ratio being dynamically computed based on processing times measured for previous frames.

We have modified the code to run more than two kernels, with an equal amount of data between kernels, in order to let SOCL perform kernel scheduling using the *heft* scheduler. Kernels are submitted to SOCL command queue attached to context with out-of-order execution. The number of kernels can be greater than the number of devices.

Our benchmark consists in rendering 20 frames for an image of size 1600 × 12000. The results are shown in Fig. 5. Original code with dynamic load balancing is referred to as "dynamic adjustment". Since our test machine has an Nvidia GPU, not Intel, the original dynamic adjustment code runs on CPU (Intel platform) or GPU only (Nvidia platform). It can use CPU+GPU through our SOCL platform which unifies both devices on a single virtual platform, and gives only a small performance boost compared to CPU or GPU only. The modified code running on SOCL gets similar performance to the original code on GPU and CPU+GPU. It is slower on CPU alone, which is explained by the fact that SOCL considers CPU as a regular OpenCL device and performs memory transfers that could be optimized out in a future version. When all 3 GPUs are used by SOCL, we get a speed-up of 2.6 with the modified code, and Nvidia OpenCL gets a speed-up of 1.5; the difference may be explained by StarPU managing data transfers better than the application code. For CPU+3 GPUs, SOCL performance is roughly the same since CPU is slow on this example; thanks to SOCL scheduler, adding a slow CPU to device set does not degrade performance.

This benchmark demonstrates that SOCL is able to efficiently aggregate performance of multiple OpenCL devices. Contrary to original Intel code, it is able to aggregate performance of devices from multiple platforms, and more than two devices. Moreover, it handles kernel scheduling and load balancing in a generic fashion in the runtime system, rather than hard-coded in the application. The speed-ups we obtain are convincing.

5   Related Works

About unifying OpenCL devices. IBM OpenCL Common Runtime [7] provides a unified OpenCL platform consisting of all devices provided by other available implementations, like SOCL does. However OpenCL Common Runtime does not provide automatic scheduling. Multicoreware GMAC (Global Memory for Accelerator) [8] allows OpenCL applications to use a single address space for both GPU and CPU kernels. However, it defines its own API on contrary to SOCL. Kim *et al.* [9] propose an OpenCL framework that considers all available GPUs as a single GPU. It partitions the work-groups among the different devices, so that all devices have the same amount of work. Their approach does not handle heterogeneity among GPUs, nor a hybrid architecture with CPUs and GPUs, and the workload distribution is static. Besides, data dependences between tasks are not considered since work-groups are all independent. De La Lama *et al.*[10] propose a compound OpenCL device in order to statically divide the work of one kernel among the different devices. Maestro[11] is a unifying framework for OpenCL, providing scheduling strategies to hide communication latencies with computation. Maestro proposes one unifying device for heterogeneous hardware. Automatic load balance is achieved thanks to an autotuned performance model, obtained through benchmarking at install-time. This mechanism also help to adapt the size of the data chunks given as parameters to kernels. On contrary to SOCL, Maestro assumes the kernels can be tuned at compile-time, while SOCL applies dynamic scheduling strategy at runtime which is more flexible. SnuCL [12] is an OpenCL framework for clusters of CPUs and GPUs. The SnuCL runtime does not offer automatic scheduling between CPUs and GPUs, on contrary to SOCL and the scheduling is performed by the programmer. Moreover, SnuCL does not handle multi-device on the same node. The approach of SnuCL (multiple nodes, one device per node) is complementary to SOCL (single node, mutliple devices).

About automatic scheduling on heterogeneous architectures. Grewe and O'Boyle [13] propose a static approach to load partitioning and scheduling. At runtime, the decision to schedule code uses a predictive model based on decision trees built at compile time from microbenchmarks. However, the case of multiple GPU is not directly handled, and the decision to schedule a code to a device does not take into account memory affinity considerations. Besides, some recent works use OpenCL as the target language for other high-level languages (for instance, CAPS HMPP [14] and PGI [15]). Grewe *et al.* [16] propose to use OpenMP parallel programs to program heterogeneous CPU/GPU architectures, based on their previous work on static predictive model. The work proposed here for SOCL could be used in these contexts. Finally, several previous works have proposed dedicated API and runtimes for the automatic scheduling on heterogeneous architectures. StarPU [4] is a runtime system that provides both a global virtual memory and automatic kernel scheduling on heterogeneous architectures. SOCL currently relies on it internally and provides the additional OpenCL implementation layer that was not available initially in StarPU which only supports its own programming interface. Qilin, StarSS and Kaapi [17,18,19] are other examples of runtimes for heterogeneous architectures, that do not rely on the standard OpenCL programming interface but on special APIs or code annotations. Boyer *et al.*[20] propose a dynamic load balancing approach, based on an adaptive chunking of data over the heterogeneous devices and the scheduling of the kernels. The technique proposed focuses on how to adapt the execution of one kernel on multiple devices. SOCL offers a wider range of applications made of multiple kernels, scheduled using dependencies.

6   Conclusion and Future Work

The OpenCL language is a *rosetta stone* to program heterogeneous parallel computing platforms. It is portable across a range of different devices and make them usable through a unified interface. However it lacks mechanisms to make multiple devices usable seamlessly.

In this paper we have presented several extensions to OpenCL to simplify programming of applications on heterogeneous architectures. We have proposed the SOCL platform, able to make OpenCL mechanisms usable equally with all devices regardless of their initial platform. In addition, SOCL offers a mechanism to automatically schedule commands on devices belonging to a context.

The unified platform proposed in SOCL means that OpenCL applications do not have to worry about data transfers and kernel scheduling. These operations are automatically performed. It requires only minor changes to existing OpenCL code to use context queues rather than explicit device queues. This brings significant performance gain on multi-GPU, multi-core machines, compared to solutions using only the GPUs. Moreover, we have shown that automatic memory management in SOCL enabled large computations to be performed on GPUs, on contrary to other OpenCL implementations.

As future work, we currently study a preliminary strategy to adapt dynamically the granularity of kernels, in order to adapt to the heterogeneity. The user explicitly gives a function to divide work; the runtime calls it whenever it needs more parallelism to feed devices. Preliminary results are promising but need further exploration about strategies to choose the best suited granularity for given devices.

References

1. HSA Foundation: Heterogeneous System Architecture (2012),
   http://hsafoundation.com
2. Khronos OpenCL Working Group: The OpenCL Specification, Version 1.2 (2011)
3. Topcuoglu, H., Hariri, S., Wu, M.Y.: Performance-effective and low-complexity task scheduling for heterogeneous computing. IEEE Transactions on Parallel and Distributed Systems 13(3), 260–274 (2002)
4. Augonnet, C., Thibault, S., Namyst, R., Wacrenier, P.-A.: StarPU: a unified platform for task scheduling on heterogeneous multicore architectures. In: Sips, H., Epema, D., Lin, H.-X. (eds.) Euro-Par 2009. LNCS, vol. 5704, pp. 863–874. Springer, Heidelberg (2009)

5. LuxRender: GPL physically based renderer (2013), http://www.luxrender.net
6. Intel: Hybrid HDR tone mapping for post processing multi-device version (2013), http://software.intel.com/en-us/vcsource/samples/hdr-tone-mapping-multi-device
7. IBM: OpenCL Common Runtime for Linux on x86 Architecture (version 0.1) (2011)
8. Multicoreware, Inc.: GMAC: Global Memory for Accelerator, TM: Task Manager (2011), http://www.multicorewareinc.com
9. Kim, J., Kim, H., Lee, J.H., Lee, J.: Achieving a single compute device image in opencl for multiple gpus. In: Proceedings of the 16th ACM Symposium on Principles and Practice of Parallel Programming, PPoPP 2011, pp. 277–288. ACM, New York (2011)
10. de La Lama, C., Toharia, P., Bosque, J., Robles, O.: Static multi-device load balancing for opencl. In: 2012 IEEE 10th International Symposium on Parallel and Distributed Processing with Applications (ISPA), pp. 675–682 (2012)
11. Spafford, K., Meredith, J., Vetter, J.: Maestro: data orchestration and tuning for OpenCL devices. In: D'Ambra, P., Guarracino, M., Talia, D. (eds.) Euro-Par 2010, Part II. LNCS, vol. 6272, pp. 275–286. Springer, Heidelberg (2010)
12. Kim, J., Seo, S., Lee, J., Nah, J., Jo, G., Lee, J.: SnuCL: an OpenCL framework for heterogeneous CPU/GPU clusters. In: Proceedings of the 26th ACM International Conference on Supercomputing, ICS 2012, pp. 341–352. ACM, New York (2012)
13. Grewe, D., O'Boyle, M.F.P.: A Static Task Partitioning Approach for Heterogeneous Systems Using OpenCL. In: Knoop, J. (ed.) CC 2011. LNCS, vol. 6601, pp. 286–305. Springer, Heidelberg (2011)
14. Dolbeau, R., Bihan, S., Bodin, F.: HMPP: A hybrid Multi-core Parallel Programming Environment (2007)
15. Wolfe, M.: Implementing the PGI accelerator model. In: GPGPU (2010)
16. Grewe, D., Wang, Z., O'Boyle, M.F.: Portable mapping of data parallel programs to opencl for heterogeneous systems. In: ACM/IEEE International Symposium on Code Generation and Optimization, Shenzen, China (February 2013)
17. Luk, C.K., Hong, S., Kim, H.: Qilin: exploiting parallelism on heterogeneous multiprocessors with adaptive mapping. In: Proceedings of the 42nd Annual IEEE/ACM International Symposium on Microarchitecture, MICRO 42, pp. 45–55. ACM, New York (2009)
18. Ayguadé, E., Badia, R.M., Igual, F.D., Labarta, J., Mayo, R., Quintana-Ortí, E.S.: An Extension of the StarSs Programming Model for Platforms with Multiple GPUs. In: Sips, H., Epema, D., Lin, H.-X. (eds.) Euro-Par 2009. LNCS, vol. 5704, pp. 851–862. Springer, Heidelberg (2009)
19. Gautier, T., Besseron, X., Pigeon, L.: KAAPI: A thread scheduling runtime system for data flow computations on cluster of multi-processors. In: Proceedings of the 2007 International Workshop on Parallel Symbolic Computation, PASCO 2007, pp. 15–23. ACM, New York (2007)
20. Boyer, M., Skadron, K., Che, S., Jayasena, N.: Load balancing in a changing world: Dealing with heterogeneity and performance variability. In: IEEE Computing Frontiers Conference (2013)

Concurrent Kernel Execution on Xeon Phi within Parallel Heterogeneous Workloads

Florian Wende[1], Thomas Steinke[1], and Frank Cordes[2]

[1] Zuse Institute Berlin, Takustraße 7, D-14195 Berlin, Germany
{wende,steinke}@zib.de
[2] GETLIG&TAR GbR, Bachstelzenstraße 33A, D-14612 Falkensee, Germany
cordes@getlig.com

Abstract. Computations with a sufficient amount of parallelism and workload size may take advantage of many-core coprocessors. In contrast, small-scale workloads usually suffer from a poor utilization of the coprocessor resources. For parallel applications with small but many computational kernels a concurrent processing on a shared coprocessor may be a viable solution. We evaluate the Xeon Phi offload models Intel LEO and OpenMP4 within multi-threaded and multi-process host applications with concurrent coprocessor offloading. Limitations of OpenMP4 regarding data persistence across function calls, e.g. when used within libraries, can slow down the application. We propose an offload-proxy approach for OpenMP4 to recover the performance in these cases. For concurrent kernel execution, we demonstrate the performance of the different offload models and our offload-proxy by using synthetic kernels and a parallel hybrid CPU/Xeon Phi molecular simulation application.

1 Introduction

Throughout the different kinds of applications from science and economy performance gains by up to one order of magnitude are demonstrated by using coprocessors like GPGPUs (General Purpose Graphics Processing Units) or Intel's Xeon Phi instead of traditional multi-core CPUs when the problem is large-scale and highly regular [1,2]. In contrast, small-scale computations usually suffer from a poor utilization of the coprocessor device as a whole. A usual means to achieve acceptable utilization in these cases is executing many such computations in a concurrent manner. This can be done either by merging multiple small compute kernels into a larger "super kernel," or by offloading multiple small kernels for a "concurrent kernel execution" on the coprocessor.

Our work addresses application scenarios of the said type with offloads to the Xeon Phi ("Phi" for short hereafter) from within multi-threaded and multi-process workloads. Our contributions are:

1. A performance evaluation of concurrent offloading to Xeon Phi using Intel's Language Extension for Offload (LEO) and OpenMP4.
2. We study the impact of thread placements on Xeon Phi: Multiple concurrent offloads should not perturb each other.

F. Silva et al. (Eds.): Euro-Par 2014, LNCS 8632, pp. 788–799, 2014.
© Springer International Publishing Switzerland 2014

3. We demonstrate how multiple simultaneous offload data transfers between host and Xeon Phi can affect the overall program performance.
4. For OpenMP4, we propose an offload-proxy pattern to enable data persistence across different function scopes.

In Section 2 we discuss related work. Section 3 is on the Xeon Phi coprocessor and it briefly introduces the Intel LEO and OpenMP4 offload programming model. In Section 4 we use synthetic kernels to get information about the achievable performance in the case of compute and memory bound computations. Section 5 focuses on a real-world application implementing a simulation of a small molecule solvated within a nanodroplet. The application serves as a representative of a parallel heterogeneous workload. Section 6 concludes.

2   Related Work

The offload model and runtime system for the Intel Xeon Phi coprocessor is detailed by Newburn et al. [3].

Johnson et al. [4] explore the support for, what the authors call, Many-Task Computing (MTC) on the Xeon Phi platform. The authors' framework GeMTC is interfaced to Intel's SCIF communication API. It is based on a client server architecture with persistent threads or processes on the Phi. The authors investigate the overhead associated with the task offload itself. With 90% efficiency their approach outperforms OpenMP's offload mechanism.

Somehow related to our real-world application, Pennycook et al. [5] analyze the miniMD benchmark (Sandia) on Xeon Phi. The authors present a variety of optimizations, e.g. taking advantage of the Phi's SIMD units. They achieve performance improvements of about a factor $4 - 5$ depending on the problem size and the cut-off value. With their minimal size of 32,000 atoms, the authors consider problem sizes that are more than one order of magnitude above what is addressed by our real world application.

Prior to Xeon Phi, concurrent kernel execution [6] has been known from Nvidia GPGPUs of the Fermi architecture and later. A major drawback of Fermi is false-serialization of concurrent kernels as a result of the GPU is fed by just one task queue [7]. Current Nvidia GPGPUs provide 32 hardware queues (Hyper-Q) to improve concurrent kernel execution. Investigations on using Hyper-Q from within parallel workloads on the host can be found in [8]. However, a comparison of Xeon Phi offloading with its GPGPU counterpart is not part of this work.

3   Intel Xeon Phi Offload Programming

The Xeon Phi coprocessor is based on Intel's Many Integrated Core (MIC) architecture. It presently holds up to 61 64-bit compute cores [9], each of which with fully-coherent L1 and L2 cache, a 512-bit SIMD vector unit, and 4-way hardware multi-threading. Current Xeon Phis are used as coprocessors to a distinguished host system, where communication with the host is over PCIexpress

(PCIe). The Phi runs its own Linux OS, enabling for a flexible integration into cluster- and supercomputer setups.

From the programmers point of view there are two approaches to involve the Phi into computations: (i) native program execution with support for message passing, e.g. via MPI, and (ii) offload execution with the Phi as a coprocessor to the CPU. While native execution on Xeon Phi requires the entire application be parallelizable, the offload model is the common means to involve the Phi into codes with both serial and parallel sections. In this work, we therefore focus on the offload model and compare against native executions only where meaningful.

Intel LEO and OpenMP4. The Intel Language Extension for Offload (LEO) is a non-shared memory offload model for the Intel Xeon Phi coprocessor [9]. It provides a set of directives to the programmer that allow to mark code regions within a host program to be executed on the coprocessor if present. Since host and coprocessor are physically separate compute devices, memory transfers between the two are necessary in order to provide data for and get results of the computation(s). The models are appropriate for dealing with flat data structures that can be moved bitwise between host and coprocessor. For array-based data structures the copy direction, and the amount of elements to be moved need to be specified in the offload clauses – the actual copy process is implicit.

Figure 1 gives a code snippet that adds two vectors a and b into c using LEO and OpenMP4 – Xeon Phi device 0 is used. a and b are moved from the host to the coprocessor, and c is copied back after the computation. Except for different directives and clauses OpenMP4 is compatible with LEO.

Persistent Data on the Coprocessor. The execution of the offload regions in Fig. 1 go along with the (de)allocation of memory buffers on the coprocessor and the actual data transfers into/from these buffers before and after the offload computation. Repeated offloading with intensive data transfers thus can result in non-negligible overhead and hence reduced overall performance.

Both LEO and OpenMP4 allow for the allocation of memory on the coprocessor, retaining and reusing it across multiple offload regions within the same thread (process) context, and releasing it after the computation [9,10]. Enabling data persistence in LEO is done via the `alloc_if(cond)` and the `free_if(cond)` clause – memory is allocated or freed only if `cond` is `true` respectively 1. In the OpenMP4 model, keeping data on the coprocessor across multiple offloads is possible within `omp target data` regions only. Offload regions that are enclosed by

```
float a[size],b[size],c[size];
// Offload using Intel LEO:              // Offload using OpenMP4:
#pragma offload target(mic:0)\           #pragma omp target device(0)\
   in(a[0:size]) in(b[0:size])\             map(to:a[0:size]) map(to:b[0:size])\
   out(c[0:size])                           map(from:c[0:size])
   { c[0:size]=a[0:size]+b[0:size]; }       { c[0:size]=a[0:size]+b[0:size]; }
```

Fig. 1. Vector addition using the LEO and the OpenMP4 offload model, respectively

a `target data` region inherit memory allocations associated with variables listed in the surrounding `target data` directive clauses.

Figure 2 illustrates the use of persistent memory on the coprocessor: Ⓐ Allocate memory and transfer data from host to coprocessor without freeing it. Ⓑ Reuse data for computation and copy content of b to the host. Ⓒ same as Ⓑ, but memory is freed eventually. For OpenMP4 the regions marked Ⓧ, Ⓨ, Ⓩ correspond to Ⓐ, Ⓑ, Ⓒ. Note the `target update` construct in Ⓨ, where data is moved from the coprocessor to the host within the `target data` region.

Although both models allow for persistent data on the coprocessor, LEO is more flexible since memory allocated via `alloc_if(1)` can be used anywhere in the same thread (process) context. As OpenMP4's `target data` region cannot extend across different function scopes, function calls need to be enclosed by it and variables representing persistent data have to be explicitly passed through. Using OpenMP4 offload e.g. within libraries thus requires the user of the library to create the `target data` region within its code. Contrary to design principles, the user gets involved into the library's memory management on the coprocessor.

OpenMP4 Offload within Libraries Using an Offload-Proxy. One solution to the `target data` problem when using OpenMP4 offload within libraries is using an offload-proxy that is instantiated by the library itself. The proxy creates a `target data` region, enters it, and remains within that region. Library calls create tasks and use a signaling mechanism to wake up the proxy and make it execute the tasks. When finished a task the proxy signals back to the caller.

A similar offload-proxy approach has been already evaluated by the authors in the context of concurrent kernel execution on Nvidia Fermi GPGPUs [7]. Although using the proxy pattern requires code modifications – when not included into the library design from the first – the following benefits can be noted: (i) it implements asynchronicity regarding coprocessor offloads, and (ii) for OpenMP4 it enables data persistence across different function scopes. The latter is also relevant for the integration of OpenMP4 offloading into C++ class designs.

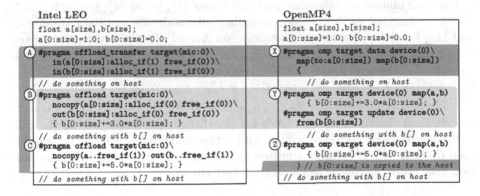

Fig. 2. Persistent data on the coprocessor using LEO and OpenMP4. White, gray- and light-gray-shaded regions have the same meaning in the two models.

4   Synthetic Benchmarks

In this section we assess the performance that can be achieved with LEO and OpenMP4 (+proxy), where multiple concurrent host threads (processes) offload (i) a compute bound, and (ii) a memory bound kernel to the coprocessor each. On the coprocessor itself OpenMP is used within the kernels. As representatives for (i) and (ii) we decided for the Intel MKL SGEMM and the STREAM Copy and Triad benchmark. Our intention is for multiple concurrent "small-scale" setups to determine the fraction of the performance achievable compared to "large-scale" setups, and to find out meaningful thread placements on the coprocessor.

Hardware and Software Setup. We use a compute node hosting two Xeon E5-2670 octa-core CPUs (Hyper-Threading enabled), 64 GB RAM, and two Intel Xeon Phi 7120P connected to the host via PCIe x16. Each Phi has 61 physical (244 logical) cores, and 16 GB ECC RAM – for benchmarking we use 60 physical cores (one core is reserved for the Phi's OS) and have ECC enabled. The host runs a CentOS 6.3 Linux with kernel 2.6.32-279. We use the Intel MPSS 2.1.6720-19, Intel compilers 14.0.3 (C++) and 14.0.1 (Fortran), and Intel MPI 4.1.1.036.

Benchmarking Setup and Methodology. For both SGEMM and STREAM we vary the number of OpenMP threads and MPI processes on the host between $p = 1, \ldots, 60$. Each host thread (process) offloads a set of SGEMM kernels – we call SGEMM directly on the Phi – or a STREAM kernels to the coprocessor by means of LEO respectively OpenMP4. Each offload uses $x = 1, \ldots, 4$ OpenMP threads on the Phi for computation. The benchmarks are written as libraries to allow for portability and ease of integration.

A single benchmark run consists of $N = 50$ successive offloads per thread (process) using respective library calls. To determine the performance of a single benchmark run, we measure the execution time of all offloads and use this value to estimate the compute performance in case (i), and the bandwidth in case (ii). The benchmark runs are repeated 10 times for each setup.

For each offload we take start and end times $\{t_{i,k}^{s}\}$ and $\{t_{i,k}^{e}\}$ ($i = 1, \ldots, N$ and $k = 1, \ldots, p$) of the offload (including all overheads and data transfers), and $\{\tau_{i,k}^{s}\}$ and $\{\tau_{i,k}^{e}\}$ for kernel execution on Xeon Phi – time stamps are taken with `clock_gettime(CLOCK_REALTIME,..)`. We approximate the degree of concurrency $\mathcal{C}_t$ across all p host threads (processes) as follows: Let $t^s = \max\{t_{1,k}^s\}$, $t^e = \min\{t_{N,k}^e\}$, $\Delta t = t^e - t^s$, and $\Delta t_{i,k} = t_{i,k}^e - t_{i,k}^s$. With $W_t = \{\Delta t_{i,k} : t_{i,k}^s \geq t^s \wedge t_{i,k}^e \leq t^e\}$, we have $1 \leq \frac{1}{\Delta t} \sum_{\omega \in W_t} \omega \leq p$. Hence, $\mathcal{C}_t \approx \frac{1}{p-1}\left(\frac{1}{\Delta t} \sum_{\omega \in W_t} \omega - 1\right) \in [0,1]$. A similar expression holds for the thread concurrency $\mathcal{C}_\tau$ on the Phi.

If computations perfectly overlap, and if the offloading overhead is negligible then $\mathcal{C}_\tau \leq \mathcal{C}_t \approx 1$. If memory transfers before and/or after the actual computation take place, $\mathcal{C}_t$ can be significantly larger than $\mathcal{C}_\tau$.

Thread Affinity on the Coprocessor. Since the Xeon Phi runs a Linux operating system, assigning threads to specific compute cores can be done by means of cpu-set masks directly within the offload kernel using the Linux scheduler interface. For our setups we use up to 60 threads (processes) on the host, each with a thread group of size up to 4 on Xeon Phi. We establish a "scatter-compact" thread pinning with "scatter" on the level of the groups and "compact" within the groups. The creation of the per-thread cpu-set mask is illustrated in Fig. 3 – on Xeon Phi the 0th and the last 3 logical cores are reserved for the Phi's OS.

```
#pragma omp parallel num_threads(4) // groupId=0..59
{
    cpu_set_t cpuMask; CPU_ZERO(&cpuMask);
    CPU_SET(1+(4*groupId+omp_get_thread_num())%(4*60),&cpuMask);
    sched_setaffinity(0,sizeof(cpu_set_t),&cpuMask);
}
```

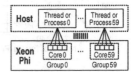

Fig. 3. Setting the thread affinity via `sched_setaffinity()` on Xeon Phi 7-series devices. The pinning model considered is "scatter-compact" (see text).

In many cases this low-level approach can be replaced by setting specific environment variables: e.g. `OMP_PLACES=threads|cores` results in successive logical respectively entire physical cores are assigned to OpenMP threads within multi-threaded offload kernels in the order the threads are created. We found using `KMP_AFFINITY` in multi-offload setups places OpenMP threads within different offload kernels on the same cores, resulting in oversubscription, potentially causing performance degradation.

Intel MKL SGEMM Benchmark. We consider two different benchmarking modes: all data is copied to Xeon Phi at the beginning, and is reused throughout all computations (M1) without any additional data transfers between host and Phi, and (M2) with data transfers containing 25%, 50%, and 100% of the problem size – 100% means two matrices are copied to the Phi, and one is copied back to the host. Benchmark results using matrices of size 1024^2 are illustrated in Fig. 4. Selected results for matrices of size 256^2, 512^2, and 2048^2 are given in Tab. 1.

With `OMP_PLACES=threads` and 1 thread per offload only 15 cores of the Phi are used if $p = 60$, whereas with `OMP_PLACES=cores` one thread resides on every physical core. The difference in the performance can be seen in sub-plots a) and

Table 1. Selected SGEMM performance results for runs using 60 host threads (processes) with 4 threads on the Xeon Phi each. Matrices have size 256^2, 512^2, 2048^2.

Intel MKL SGEMM	OpenMP on Host			MPI on Host		
	256^2	512^2	2048^2	256^2	512^2	2048^2
(M1) Performance [GFlops/s]	396±2	1226±4	1577±2	328±5	1157±5	1564±2
Concurrency $\mathcal{C}_t|\mathcal{C}_\tau$	0.92|0.92	0.93|0.93	0.93|0.93	0.90|0.88	0.91|0.90	0.95|0.94
(M2) Performance [GFlops/s]	94±2	440±3	798±7	234±1	677±2	1452±10
Concurrency $\mathcal{C}_t|\mathcal{C}_\tau$	0.94|0.10	0.93|0.29	0.94|0.48	0.85|0.34	0.89|0.46	0.92|0.88

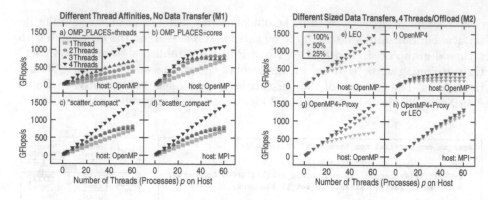

Fig. 4. Performance for p concurrent SGEMM offload computations on Xeon Phi. Left-hand side: Different thread affinities and numbers of threads used per offload. Right-hand side: Impact of data transfers between host and coprocessor. Threads (processes) are created either by means of OpenMP or MPI (right bottom corner of the sub-plots).

b). Increasing the number of threads per offload from 1 to 2, 3, and 4 results in significant performance gains, supporting the point that at least 2 threads per physical Xeon Phi core should be used [9]. However, in b) the 4-thread performance is behind that in a). We found using OMP_PLACES=threads|cores for concurrent offloads does not guarantee for a particular host thread (process) that its OpenMP threads on Xeon Phi are assigned cores with contiguous logical core IDs. We observed that it is more likely for b) to have all threads of the same group on different cores than it is for a). We assume the performance discrepancy between a) and b) in Fig. 4 is caused by unfortunate thread placements.

Sub-plots c) and d) show the performance obtained with by-hand thread pinning using the "scatter-compact" scheme. The 1-thread performance is identical to b). In the 4-thread case, the performance is measurably larger than in a), since all 4 threads within the same group execute on the same physical core. Cache-optimized kernels can benefit from sharing the L1-cache in this case. A comparison of c) and d) shows that MPI- and OpenMP-based executions perform almost equivalent for large matrices. We achieve $\approx 65\%$ efficiency in these cases – the Xeon Phi 7120P provides about 2.4 TFlops/s single precision peak performance. Native Xeon Phi executions of SGEMM with larger matrices achieve about 86% efficiency [2]. The performance shown in sub-plots a) – d) is independent of whether LEO or OpenMP4 is used for the offload.

The right-hand side sub-plots display the performance impact of data transfers between successive offload computations. If the entire problem size is transferred, for all executions with multi-threading on the host the performance breaks down significantly. Although each host thread has a corresponding Xeon Phi thread linked by a COIPipeline (Coprocessor Offload Infrastructure) for kernel invocations and data transfers [3], concurrency across multiple pipelines suffers from the current COI implementation uses just one DMA channel. As a consequence, data transfers are serialized, possibly causing kernel executions be serialized too

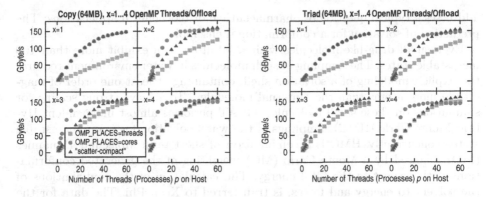

Fig. 5. STREAM copy and triad benchmark for different numbers p of concurrent host threads (processes) and $x = 1, \ldots, 4$ OpenMP threads on the Xeon Phi

(see the decrease of the in-kernel concurrency $\mathcal{C}_\tau$ for (M2) in Tab. 1). When using MPI the number of DMA channels equals the number of MPI ranks. The performance compared to no data transfers thus decreases only a little.

Sub-plot f) shows reduced performance when using OpenMP4 within libraries with frequent data transfers between host and Phi. Our offload-proxy approach recovers the performance achievable with LEO to almost 100% (Fig. 4, g).

STREAM Benchmark. The STREAM copy benchmark refers to `b[0:size]=a[0:size]`, while the STREAM triad is `c[0:size]=a[0:size]+q*b[0:size]`. We aim to measure the streaming performance that can be achieved when accessing main memory from within concurrent memory bound kernels. The streaming performance for different thread affinities and different numbers of OpenMP threads is shown in Fig. 5 – array size: 64 MB. Host threads were created using OpenMP. For kernel offloading Intel LEO was used. Performance results for OpenMP4 and MPI are almost identical as the host just initiates the offloads.

Using `OMP_PLACES=cores` the Phi's physical cores are populated faster than with `OMP_PLACES=threads`. Hence, the streaming performance is higher for both copy and triad. The "scatter-compact" thread pinning scheme gives the same performance as `OMP_PLACES=cores` if a single thread is used per offload. With 60 host threads (processes) and two OpenMP threads per offload, the streaming performance starts to saturate at about 162 GB/s, which is close to the value of 174 GB/s (ECC enabled) for native Phi execution of STREAM triad by 93% [2].

5 Strong Scaling for Simulations of Small Molecules

The program package GLAT (Global Local Adaptive Thermodynamics) overcomes the problem of critical slowing down of conventional thermodynamical simulations by decomposing the conformational space into metastable subregions, which can be investigated almost independently. The current paper addresses a typical question of pharmaceutical or biochemical applications: The prediction of solvation for a conformational ensemble.

Even small drug-like molecules with < 50 atoms can exhibit more than 100 metastable states. The sampling of such molecules in water environment requires the explicit modeling of a solvation shell, containing at least one order of magnitude more atoms than the "internal molecule." To achieve strong scaling for simulations on these small molecules, GLAT performs almost independent Hybrid Monte Carlo (HMC) samplings of the water solvation for many metastable states concurrently. HMC is a combination of short term Molecular Dynamics (MD) followed by a Monte Carlo (MC) weighting of the generated conformations with respect to the total energy. The calculation of the contributions of the solvent to energy and forces, is transferred to Xeon Phi. The data for the water environment remains on the Phi, whereas the forces of the water on the internal molecule, as well as the potential/kinetic energy of the water are sent back to the host for the HMC step.

Figure 6 illustrates the workflow of a simulation within one metastable state: First the simulation is initialized with coordinates, velocities, and force-field parameters of the internal molecule in a given metastable conformation. Followed by an automatic modeling and minimization of the water environment, the result is a water droplet containing the molecule of interest. Then the water data as well as the positions of the internal molecule are transferred to the Phi where the calculation of the covalent contributions and the forces of the water on the internal molecule is started. Meanwhile the host carries out the force calculation of the internal molecule with itself. At the following barrier the host receives the forces on the internal molecule, completes the MD step, and copies the updated coordinates of the internal molecule to the Phi, whereas the coprocessor calculates the water-water interactions and performs the MD step for the water. Since the whole simulation is embedded into an HMC scheme, the host performs some statistical weightings after a sequence of ≈ 10 MD steps. The HMC sampling is repeated for a given water environment several times until about 10^3 MD steps are reached. The final convergence check will either finish the simulation or restart it with another randomly created water environment.

- The GLAT core is written in Fortran, whereas the coprocessor portion of the code is encapsulated into a C++ library. We introduced the possibility to fall back to the CPU when calling the library. For both Xeon Phi and CPU, kernels have been optimized using SIMD intrinsics.

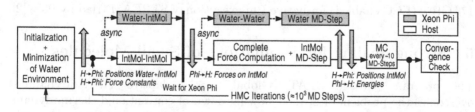

Fig. 6. Workflow of GLAT. The schematic displays an entire simulation cycle.

Benchmarking Setup and Methodology. We consider three different sized problems: An internal molecule consisting of 27 atoms embedded into a water droplet containing 101 (P1), 302 (P2), and 505 (P3) molecules. As a performance measure we determine the number of particle-particle interactions per second for (A) the MD loop only, and (B) an entire simulation cycle including the water minimization, the HMC step, and the final convergence check. Runtimes for 2000 iteration steps are measured using `clock_gettime(CLOCK_REALTIME,..)`.

For each setup we use OpenMP4, with and without our offload-proxy approach (Sec. 3), and Intel LEO for coprocessor offloading. Concurrency on the host is achieved by means of multiple OpenMP threads and/or MPI processes, each of which creating a Markov chain throughout the HMC sampling, and offloading kernels to the Phi to speed up force computations.

The system used for benchmarking is described in Sec. 4. It provides 16 physical respectively 32 logical CPU cores. When using a single Xeon Phi, we create 1...16 concurrent host threads (processes). On Xeon Phi we use 15 OpenMP threads per offload computation for a total of up to 240 threads – we use 60 out of 61 physical cores (see Sec. 4). Computations with two Xeon Phis use either 2...32 MPI ranks on the host, or two multi-threaded MPI ranks with up to 16 OpenMP threads per rank. When redirecting the offload to the host – CPU-only computation –, two OpenMP threads are used for kernel execution.

Benchmarking Results. The benchmarking results are displayed in Fig. 7. For each sub-plot the left hand side graphics are for the MD loop only, whereas the right hand side ones are for an entire simulation cycle – the performance on the right thus is lower. In all cases larger values are better.

Throughout all sub-plots the OpenMP4 performance, when not using our offload-proxy approach, is significantly behind the others due to data transfers (Sec. 3). The performance loss can be compensated to a certain extent with our proxy approach. However, it is below the one obtained with LEO as our offload-proxy performs busy-waiting during the OpenMP4 offloads, and hence consumes CPU resources on the host. Since best performance values can be achieved with LEO, the implementation of the entire simulation uses LEO. The right hand side sub-plots in Fig. 7 thus do not contain data for OpenMP4.

Using MPI on the host can result in measurable performance gains over using OpenMP if problems are small, e.g. (P1) and (P2). With OpenMP concurrent data transfers suffer from just one DMA channel is used by the current COI implementation, causing serialization of data movements between Xeon Phi and host. In case of small problem sizes, where kernel execution times are of the same order as the associated data transfer times and the offload overhead, serialization of data transfers implicitly serializes kernel executions (Tab. 1).

Executions using two Xeon Phis achieve almost twice the overall performance compared to single-Phi executions if the setup becomes large – e.g. (P3). Best performance in these cases can be obtained with a hybrid MPI/OpenMP approach on the host. However, with significantly more than 16 host threads (processes) concurrency on the host, and hence on the Phi, suffers from contention due to oversubscription of CPU resources. It thus would be meaningful to extend

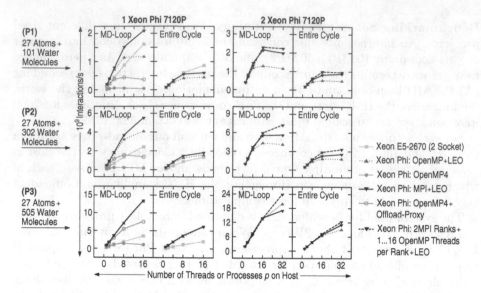

Fig. 7. Particle-particle interaction rates obtained with GLAT for three different sized problems (P1) – (P3) (see the text). Each host thread (process) offloads computations to Xeon Phi via OpenMP4 or LEO. Note the different scales. Larger values are better.

the computation across more than one compute node. Since the current offload models can use coprocessors within the same node only, hybrid approaches like MPI+X are necessary in this case. For GLAT the offloads to Xeon Phi are independent of each other and thus not affected by MPI traffic.

Since GLAT draws on a legacy Fortran code base containing a non-negligible amount of sections that are not highly parallel, comparing our results against native Xeon Phi execution of GLAT (as a whole) would suffer from insufficient performance of its serial parts and the low performance of the internal-molecule kernels.

6   Summary and Conclusion

In this work we investigated the performance of multi-threaded/-process applications with concurrent offloading of many small-scale computational kernels to Xeon Phi. We evaluated the two offload models Intel LEO and OpenMP4 including our offload-proxy approach. For a small synthetic compute bound kernel performing an SGEMM computation, we achieved a high degree of concurrency with up to 60 host threads (processes) offloading to the Phi. For scenarios without data transfers LEO and OpenMP4 perform equally. We observed deficiencies in the OpenMP4 offload model regarding data persistence across different function scopes, limiting its usability within libraries offloading computations to a coprocessor. To partly compensate for this issue, we proposed and evaluated an offload-proxy approach. For a real-world application implementing a simulation of drug-like molecules solvated within a nanodroplet, we demonstrated its viability. By using OpenMP4 respectively LEO offloading to Xeon Phi speedups of about a factor 2 – 3 over an optimized and parallelized CPU implementation could be achieved.

Acknowledgments. The Intel Xeon Phi nodes are kindly donated by Intel. The authors would like to thank Michael Klemm and Chris J. Newburn (both Intel Corp.) for in-depth discussions of Xeon Phi specifics. This work was partly supported by the Deutsche Forschungsgemeinschaft (DFG), Priority Program "Software for Exascale Computing" (SPP-EXA), DFG-SPP 1648, project FFMK (Fast Fault-tolerant Microkernel), and by Intel Corp. within the "Intel Parallel Computing Centers" initiative.

References

1. Hwu, W.M.W.: GPU Computing Gems Jade Edition, 1st edn. Morgan Kaufmann Publishers Inc., San Francisco (2011)
2. Intel Corporation: Intel Xeon Phi Product Family Performance, rev. 1.0. (December 2012), http://www.intel.com/performance
3. Newburn, C.J., Dmitriev, S., Narayanaswamy, R., Wiegert, J., Murty, R., Chinchilla, F., Deodhar, R., McGuire, R.: Offload Compiler Runtime for the Intel Xeon Phi Coprocessor. In: IPDPS Workshops, pp. 1213–1225. IEEE Computer Society (2013)
4. Johnson, J., Krieder, S.J., Grimmer, B., Wozniak, J.M., Wilde, M., Raicu, I.: Understanding the Costs of Many-Task Computing Workloads on Intel Xeon Phi Coprocessors. In: 2nd Greater Chicago Area System Research Workshop (GCASR). Northwestern University, Evanston (2013)
5. Pennycook, S.J., Hughes, C.J., Smelyanskiy, M., Jarvis, S.A.: Exploring SIMD for Molecular Dynamics Using Intel Xeon Processors and Intel Xeon Phi Coprocessors. In: IEEE International Parallel & Distributed Processing Symposium, pp. 1085–1097. IEEE Computer Society, Los Alamitos (2013)
6. Wang, L., Huang, M., El-Ghazawi, T.: Towards Efficient GPU Sharing on Multicore Processors. In: Proceedings of the 2nd International Workshop on Performance Modeling, Benchmarking and Simulation of HPC Systems, PMBS 2011, pp. 23–24. ACM, New York (2011)
7. Wende, F., Cordes, F., Steinke, T.: On Improving the Performance of Multithreaded CUDA Applications with Concurrent Kernel Execution by Kernel Reordering. In: Proceedings of the 2012 Symposium on Application Accelerators in High Performance Computing, SAAHPC 2012, pp. 74–83. IEEE Computer Society, Washington, DC (2012)
8. Wende, F., Cordes, F., Steinke, T.: Multi-threaded Kernel Offloading to GPGPU using Hyper-Q on Kepler Architecture. Technical Report 14-19, ZIB, Takustr. 7, 14195 Berlin (June 2014)
9. Jeffers, J., Reinders, J.: Intel Xeon Phi Coprocessor High Performance Programming, 1st edn. Morgan Kaufmann Publishers Inc., San Francisco (2013)
10. OpenMP Architecture Review Board: OpenMP Application Program Interface, Version 4.0. 4.0 edn. (July 2013), http://www.openmp.org

Writing Self-adaptive Codes
for Heterogeneous Systems

Jorge F. Fabeiro, Diego Andrade, Basilio B. Fraguela, and Ramón Doallo

Depto. de Electrónica e Sistemas, Universidade da Coruña, Spain
{jorge.fernandez.fabeiro,diego.andrade,basilio.fraguela,doallo}@udc.es

Abstract. Heterogeneous systems are becoming increasingly common. Relatedly, the popularity of OpenCL is growing, as it provides a unified mean to program a wide variety of devices including GPUs or multicore CPUs. More recently, the Heterogeneous Programming Library (HPL) targets the same variety of systems as OpenCL, intending to improve their programmability. The main drawback of such unified approaches is the lack of performance portability, as codes written using OpenCL or HPL may obtain a good performance in a given device but a poor performance in a different one. HPL allows to generate different versions of kernels at run-time by combining C++ and the HPL embedded language. This paper explores the development of self-adaptive kernels that exploit this characteristic so that their code depends on configuration parameters that are tuned using a genetic algorithm through an iterative optimization process. The results show that these self-adaptive kernels are faster than those generated by hand following heuristics.

1 Introduction

One of the most important problems that hamper the wider use of heterogeneous systems is the current poor portability of the codes for these devices. The truly portable programming of heterogeneous system needs: (1) a unified programming language for any kind of device and, (2) a method to achieve performance portability. OpenCL [1] solves the first challenge as it enables the programming of a wide variety of devices. The second requirement, performance portability, has been widely addressed in the bibliography. For example, the framework [2] separates functionality from implementation details using specialized functions that allow to explore a great variety of implementations and to select the optimal one for a certain platform. VForce [3] provides performance portability in a transparent way across different kinds of accelerators to programs written in a domain-specific language focused on image and signal processing.

Performance portability can also be achieved through iterative processes. For example, [4] uses iterative compilation to select the optimal parameters for GPU codes according to a set of pre-defined, parametrized templates for linear algebra problems. An auto-tuning approach that selects the best execution plan for the SkePU skeleton programming framework in multi-GPU systems based on

F. Silva et al. (Eds.): Euro-Par 2014, LNCS 8632, pp. 800–811, 2014.
© Springer International Publishing Switzerland 2014

predictions is presented in [5]. The PARTANS framework [6], which is specifically designed to express stencil computations in multi-GPU systems, includes auto-tuning mechanisms to optimize this kind of computations.

Focusing on OpenCL, uCLbench [7] characterizes the properties of the device and the OpenCL implementation where the code is intended to run, seeking to guide programmers in the hand-tuning of their codes. The main changes required to port the performance of OpenCL codes that have been tuned for GPUs to CPUs are discussed in [8][9]. GLOpenCL [10] is a development framework consisting of a compiler and a runtime library that supports OpenCL on different types of multicores. OCLoptimizer [11] searches optimal unroll factors for OpenCL kernels based on compiler directives and a configuration file. Finally, Dolbeau et al [12] discuss the performance that the same OpenCL code achieves on different platforms. They use the CAPS compiler to generate auto-tuned OpenCL code.

The Heterogeneous Programming Library (HPL) [13] is a C++ framework that improves the programmability of heterogeneous systems by combining special data types and an embedded language to write kernels, which express the parallelized computations to run in the devices. HPL is a unified approach for programming heterogeneous systems as it uses as backend OpenCL, so that its kernels can run on any device. It also provides appropriate tools to provide performance portability, as the combination of its embedded language and C++ to write the kernels enables run-time code generation (RTCG), which can be used to write self-adaptive generic kernels. While other tools enable RTCG using similar mechanisms [14][15], they only target regular CPUs, and therefore they have sought other purposes. This way, this paper explores the development of kernels with portable performance by combining C++ and the HPL embedded language to generate parametrized generic kernels. The configuration parameters of each kernel change certain aspects of how its code is optimized, and they are adjusted using a genetic algorithm through an iterative process. The performance of the kernel generated using each combination of values of its parameters is evaluated by executing the code. The configuration parameters select the optimal unroll factors for some loops, the optimal granularity for the work performed by each instance of the kernel, the base version of the algorithm used, and which data structures are stored in local memory. The performance results, focused on a matrix product code, show that our approach generates kernels that can be up to 4.67 times faster than kernels generated following heuristics.

The rest of the paper is organized as follows. Section 2 briefly introduces the HPL library. Section 3 explains how RTCG can be used in HPL to write parametrized generic kernels. Section 4 explains the method derived to select the optimal values for the configuration parameters of the kernel using iterative optimization. Section 5 shows the experimental results and Section 6 concludes.

2 The Heterogeneous Programming Library

The Heterogeneous Programming Library (HPL), which is publicly available at http://hpl.des.udc.es, intends to improve the programmability of heterogeneous systems while providing portability through an approach where the computational kernels that exploit heterogeneous parallelism are written in a language embedded in C++. This characteristic enables run-time code generation (RTCG), which is a powerful tool to provide performance portability, as we will see through this paper. HPL provides portability because OpenCL is the intermediate representation (IR) it currently generates, thus this library targets the same range of devices supported by OpenCL.

The HPL library supports the same programming model as CUDA and OpenCL. Its hardware model is composed by a host equipped with a standard CPU and memory, with a number of computing devices attached. The host runs the sequential parts of the code, while the devices run the parallel parts. Each device has processors that execute SPMD parallel code on data present in the memory of their device. As in OpenCL or CUDA, we can create groups of threads that can be synchronized through barriers and share a small scratchpad memory.

The memory model distinguishes the same kinds memory as OpenCL (global, local, constant and private) and with the same properties. As kernels can only work with data available in the devices, data must be transferred between host and devices, but this process is totally automated by the library.

Several instances of each kernel, or work-items using OpenCL terminology, can be executed in parallel, each instance being univocally identified. The number of instances of the kernels and their identifiers are defined by a global domain of non-negative integers with up to 3 dimensions. This way, instances are identified inside this domain with tuples of global ids. In turn, these instances can be associated in groups. With this purpose, we can define local domains as equal portions of the global domain. Instances are identified inside its group using tuples of local ids. Now, Section 2.1 explains how to program using HPL.

2.1 Programming Using HPL

The library provides three main components to the programmers:

- A template class `Array` to define both the variables to be transferred between the host and the devices, and the variables that are local to the kernels.
- The kernels, which are functions written in a language embedded in C++. This embedded language is an API in C++ consisting of data types, functions, macros and predefined variables.
- An API that will be used by the code to inspect the devices available in a given platform and to order the execution of the kernels.

All the kernel variables must have type `Array<type, n [, memFlag]>`, which represents an n-dimensional array of elements of a C++ `type`, or a scalar for n=0. Scalars and vectors can also be defined with special data types like `Int`, `Float`, `Int4`, `Float8`, etc. The optional `memFlag` can specify one of the kinds of memory supported (`Global`, `Local`, `Constant` or `Private`). The arrays passed as parameters to the kernels must be declared in the host using the same type. These variables are initially stored in the host memory, but when they are used as

Listing 1.1. SAXPY HPL code

```
void saxpy(Array<float,1> y, Array<float,1> x, Float a) {
    y[idx] = a * x[idx] + y[idx];
}

int main(int argc, char *argv) {
    Float a;
    Array<float, 1> x(1000), y(1000);
    //x, y and a are filled in with data (not shown)
    eval(saxpy).global(1000).local(10)(y, x, a);
}
```

kernel parameters they are automatically transferred to the device. The outputs are also automatically transferred to the host when needed.

HPL kernels also require that their control flow structures are written using special keywords. The embedded language uses the same constructs as C++ but their name finishes with an underscore (if_, for_, ...). Also, the arguments to for loops are separated by commas instead of semicolons. The library provides an API based on predefined variables to obtain the global, local and group identifiers as well as the sizes of the domains and numbers of groups. For example, idx provides the global id of the first dimension, while szx provides the globalsize of that dimension. If we add the l prefix to these keywords we obtain their local counterparts and if we replace the letter x with y or z, we obtain the same values for the second and the third dimensions respectively.

Kernels are written as regular functions or functors that use these elements and whose parameters are passed by value if they are scalars, and by reference otherwise. The saxpy routine in Listing 1.1 implements using this language the SAXPY (Single-precision real Alpha X Plus Y) vector BLAS routine, which computes $Y = a \times X + Y$. In this kernel, each instance idx computes a different position of the result y[idx].

Regarding the host interface, its most important component is the function eval, which requests the execution of the kernel f with the syntax eval(f)(arg1, arg2, ...). The execution of the kernel can be parametrized by inserting specifications, in the form of methods, between eval and the argument list. For example, the global and the local sizes can be specified using methods called global and local respectively. This way, the saxpy routine is invoked in Listing 1.1 with a global domain of 1000 elements and a local domain of 10 elements.

3 Performance Portability in HPL

HPL generates the internal representation (IR) of its kernels by running them as regular code in the host when an eval requests their execution for the first time. Subsequent requests just reuse the IR generated the first time, which is stored in an internal cache, unless this cache is erased in order to force the regeneration of the IR. The HPL macros and data types capture all the expressions in which they are involved during the execution of the kernel in the host, allowing the runtime to generate the associated IR. However, regular C++ sentences found within the kernel are simply executed and they do not appear in the resulting IR. This characteristic enables RTCG, which can be used, for example, to choose between different versions of the same code, or to parametrize the generation of code. The method proposed in this paper combines RTCG and generic kernels to generate different versions of the same kernel based on different input parameters. In this context, generic kernels are those written for generic values of some parameter, such as the granularity, which can be adjusted at run-time.

First, we describe the strategy we have followed to parameterize the kernels. We have defined the HPL kernels using functors, so that for each kernel we define a class with the name of the kernel that defines the `operator()`. The arguments and the body of this method are the arguments and the body of the kernel, respectively. The parameters that will be used to parametrize the kernel at runtime, are defined as properties of this class, thus, they can be accessed from the `operator()` method. Besides, they can be set from the host before the generation of the kernel code is initiated by an `eval` invocation.

Based on a set of parameters, we have used RTCG and generic kernels to generate codes that at the same time: (1) apply the unrolling technique to one or several loops using a given unroll factor, (2) select the best granularity of the computation performed by each instance of the kernel, (3) select the most suitable variant of an algorithm depending on the device that will be used and (4) decide which data structures are stored in local memory. The methods used to introduce these features in the kernels are now explained in turn.

Unrolling: Loop unrolling is a popular optimization technique whose main benefits are that it unveils instruction level parallelism, minimizes branch penalty and reduces the number of control instructions executed. Loop unrolling using arbitrary unroll factors can be introduced in HPL kernels using RTCG. The C++ code will be used in conjunction with the embedded language to generate the unrolled loops. Let us see an example starting from the matrix-vector product (MxV) code shown in Listing 1.2. This code defines the HPL kernel in lines 2-6. Each instance of the kernel processes one row from the input matrix, thus a single loop is required to multiply each element of the row by the corresponding element of the input vector.

Listing 1.3 shows an unrolled version of the kernel. The loop between lines 4-7 is an unrolled version of the original loop, thus, its stride is now the unroll factor (`uf`). The body of the loop is replicated `uf` times by a native C++ loop (lines 5-6). As the number of iterations of the loop N may not be a multiple of `uf`, to prevent out of range array accesses, the loop limit is `N-uf`. If there are some iterations left after that loop, they are processed without unrolling by the code in lines 8-9. The value for the unroll factor is passed to the kernel from the main procedure by setting the appropriate attribute of the class that defines the kernel (line 15).

Granurality: HPL creates one instance (or thread in HPL terminology) of the kernel for each point of the global domain. The optimal amount of work performed by each thread must be tuned for each platform in order to maximize

Listing 1.2. MxV code: original version

```
1   class MxV {
2     void operator()(Array<float,2> a, Array<float,1> x, Array<float,1> y) {
3       Int k;
4       for_(k=0, k<N, k++)
5         y[idx] += (a[idx][k] * x[k]);
6     }
7   };
8   int main(...) {
9     //Declare and initialize ax,xv and yv Arrays
10    MxV matvec
11    eval(matvec).global(M)(av, xv, yv);
12  }
```

Listing 1.3. MxV code: unrolled version

```
1   class MxV { //Other portions of the class have been elided
2     void operator()(Array<float,2> a, Array<float,1> x, Array<float,1> y) {
3       Int k;
4       for_(k=0, k <= (N - uf), k += uf) {
5         for(aux=0; aux<uf; aux++)
6         y[idx] += (a[idx][k+aux] * x[k+aux]);
7       }
8       for_(k,k<N,k++)
9         y[idx] += (a[idx][k] * x[k]);
10    }
11  }
12  int main(...) {
13    ...
14    MxV matvec
15    matvec.set_uf(unrolling_factor);
16    eval(matvec).global(M)(av, xv, yv);
17  }
```

the performance. For example, CPUs tend to be more effective using threads with larger workloads than GPUs. It is interesting to be able to tune that granularity at run-time depending on the type of device we are using. We can do that in HPL by changing the number of points in the global domain. For example, in our MxV code, the number of threads created is equal to the number of rows of the input matrix, thus, each thread processes one row of this matrix. If we reduce the number of threads, each thread should process several rows from the input matrix. This modification requires that the code is rewritten for a generic grain size, the grain size being in this case the number of rows of the input matrix processed by each thread. In our proposal, the rows are distributed using a block-cyclic policy, thus, grains of bszx rows are assigned cyclically to the threads available. The optimal value of bszx is found for each device. In the MxV code, this block size will not have a big influence in the performance, but in other problems some values of bszs may benefit locality or coalescing, so, they will have a big impact in the performance.

In order to implement this distribution of the rows, the MxV kernel code must be changed to add two outer loops that process the blocks of bszx rows assigned

```
     Listing 1.4. MxV code: auto-adjustable granularity version
1    class MxV { //Other portions of the class have been elided
2      void operator()(Array<float,2> a, Array<float,1> x, Array<float,1> y) {
3        Int ii, i, ilim, k;
4        for_(ii = idx*bszx, ii < M, ii += szx*bszx)
5          for_(i = ii,i < min(xx+bszx, M), i++)
6            for_(k = 0, k < N, k++)
7              y[i] += a[i][k] * x[k];
8      }
9    }
10   int main(...) {
11     ...
12     int szx = <# threads of the global domain>;
13     int bszx = <block size>;
14     ...
15     eval(matvec).device(dev).global(szx)(av, xv, yv);
16   }
```

```
     Listing 1.5. MxV code: algorithm version selection
1    class MxV { //Other portions of the class have been elided
2      void operator()(Array<float,2> a, Array<float,1> x, Array<float,1> y) {
3        if (device==CPU) {
4        //Version better suited to CPUs
5        } else {
6        //Version better suited to other devices
7        }
8      }
9    }
```

to each thread. Loop headers in lines 4-5 of Code 1.4 select the appropriate set of rows to be processed by each thread following the block-cyclic policy. The resulting kernel does not use RTCG but it is written in a generic way, so that if different values are provided for the size of the global domain and the block size, the granularity of the work performed by each thread is automatically adjusted at run-time.

Algorithm selection: The type of device used for a kernel execution is known at run-time. HPL can use this information to choose between different versions of the same algorithm, or portions of the algorithm, using RTCG. For example, a version that exploits local memory is good for GPUs but it may introduce unnecessary synchronization points in CPUs. The best strategy to divide the work among the threads varies depending on the type of device. RTCG can be used to select the appropriate base version or implementations of portions of the algorithm at run-time. Figure 1.5 shows the skeleton of a MxV vector kernel where a different variant of the algorithm is selected depending on the type of device. In the same vein, the size of the problem can advise the usage of different base versions of the algorithm.

Local memory: The usage of local memory is crucial for some devices like GPUs. We propose a technique to dynamically adjust the usage of local memory in HPL kernels. The idea is to write kernels where one or several data structures

```
     Listing 1.6. MxV code: local memory usage
1    class MxV { //Other portions of the class have been elided
2      void operator()(Array<float,2> a, Array<float,1> x, Array<float,1> y,
3              Array<float,1,Local> lx) {
4        Int k;
5        if(copyX) {
6          for_(k=lidx, k<N, k+=lszx)
7            lx[k] = x[k];
8          barrier(LOCAL);
9        }
10       for_(k=0, k<N, k++)
11         y[idx] += a[idx][k] * (copyX ? (Float)lx[k] : (Float)x[k]);
12     }
13   }
14   int main(...) {
15     ...
16     eval(matvec).device(dev).global(M).local(localsize_x)(av, xv, yv, lxv);
17   }
```

may optionally be stored in local memory or not. For example, in the MxV code, we can choose vector x for this purpose. A boolean parameter copyX will be set in the host to indicate whether we want to place that array in local memory. Listing 1.6 contains the MxV kernel modified to implement this behavior. The kernel uses RTCG to make the copy of x to local memory if copyX is activated, see lines 5-9. When the computation is done, the global array x or its local copy will be used depending on the value of the copyX parameter in line 11.

4   HPL Portable Kernels through Iterative Optimization

The search of the optimal parameters for the kernel is performed using an iterative optimization process guided by a Genetic Algorithm (GA). Concretely, we have built the iterative search on top of the sequential version of the GAlib genetic algorithm package [16]. The chromosomes of our GA, which are potential solutions to our problem, have one gene per configuration parameter of the kernel. The initial population of the algorithm is composed of a configurable number of individuals that have been fixed by experimentation. The individuals and chromosomes of the initial population are randomly generated. Each individual generates a different version of the kernel using the values selected for each configuration parameter. These versions are evaluated using their fitness function, which is its execution time.

The minimum execution time obtained by a member of the population is used to decide whether the search must finish. The condition for this is that the fitness function (the execution time) has not improved for five generations. When this happens, the chromosomes that provided the best solution are used to generate the optimal kernel. If the condition has not been reached, a new generation of individuals is generated. This generation is created starting from the best individuals of the previous generation, and using mechanisms such as crossover and mutations. The process is repeated until the fitness function has not improved for five generations.

5   Experimental Results

The techniques just described have been applied to implement a self-adaptive version of a matrix multiplication ($C = A \times B$) that has been tested on a **CPU** socket of two Intel Xeon E5-2660 Sandy Bridge with eight 2.2Ghz cores and hyper-threading (8×2 threads per processor, for a total of 32) and 64 GB of RAM, an Intel Xeon Phi 5110P **Accelerator** with sixty 1.053GHz cores with 8 GB of RAM, and an NVIDIA Tesla Kepler K20m **GPU** with 5 GB GDDR5. The Intel OpenCL 2013 R3 was used for the CPU and the accelerator, and the NVIDIA CUDA 5.0.35 toolkit for the GPU.

At the top level, our kernel chooses between two base versions of the algorithm in which matrices are processed following a block-cyclic approach. One version is more suitable for CPUs and the Xeon Phi, as it uses neither local memory nor cooperation among threads and each thread works on blocks of sizes specified by the user at runtime. The other version, where the work is distributed among the threads in tiles of a given size, and the data of each one of the input matrices used by each thread group can be copied or not to local memory, so that local domain sizes play an important role, better fits GPUs for this algorithm. Both versions also allow to adjust the size of the global domain of the execution as well as the degree of unroll of the innermost loop at runtime. Table 1 lists the configuration parameters of the kernel that are adjusted by the GA through the iterative process, and their baseline values. The N/A labels indicate the combinations in which the parameter is not applicable to the device, whose type is obtained at run-time. The baseline of the experiments is the parametrized HPL code. In this baseline, the global domain has been chosen following policies adequate to each platform and the usage of local memory is disabled. This way, the CPU baseline uses a global domain of (8,4) threads, as there are 32 threads available in the socket, and a consecutive block distribution. The baseline of the Xeon Phi and the GPU version has a global workspace with the shape of the destination matrix (so each kernel instance computes a single item) and it directly reads the input matrices from global memory. Furthermore, in all the baselines the size of the local workspace was automatically selected by the OpenCL driver, and no innermost loop unrolling was applied. The usage of an HPL baseline over an OpenCL implementation allow us to measure the impact of the tuning of the parameters.

Table 2 shows for each one of the platforms and for three matrix sizes the execution time of the baseline HPL version of the kernel, the execution time of the version tuned using our tool, the speedup of this version with respect to the baseline, and the execution time of the tool itself. Although HPL has very small overheads with respect to native OpenCL [13], we have exclusively measured the runtime of the underlying OpenCL kernel generated to provide maximum accuracy. We can see that speedups of between 1.01 and 4.67 were achieved in all the platforms over hand-tuned baselines, justifying the interest of this approach. The high execution time of the tools is due to the fact that the search process is guided by the execution time. This time could be reduced if the search is guided, or at least pruned, using analytical models [17,18].

Table 1. Parameters adjusted by the genetic algorithm and their baseline values, where c and r are the number of columns and rows of the destination matrix C, respectively. N/A=not applicable.

Name(s)	Description	Baseline		
		CPU	ACC	GPU
uf	Unroll factor	1		
szx, szy	Global size of both dimensions	(8,4)	(c,r)	(c,r)
lszx, lszy	Local size of both dimensions	Auto		
bszx, bszy	Block size of the block-cyclic distribution	(c/szx,r/szy)		N/A
T	Tile size for the copies of A and/or B	N/A		-
CopyA, CopyB	Copy or not arrays A and B respectively	N/A		false

Table 2. Execution times and speedups achieved by generated kernels

Device	Size	Baseline time (s)	Kernel time (s)	Speedup	Tool time (s)
CPU	1024	0.176	0.092	1.91	207
	2048	1.252	0.706	1.77	627
	4096	114.369	24.478	4.67	20651
ACC	1024	0.034	0.031	1.09	1534
	2048	0.246	0.243	1.01	2598
	4096	2.207	2.129	1.03	4479
GPU	1024	0.016	0.013	1.24	198
	2048	0.167	0.108	1.54	490
	4096	1.509	0.996	1.52	2241

Table 3 shows the optimal values found for each test case. The wide variety of solutions indicates the difficulty of finding a priori heuristics to choose the best parameters, making search necessary. In fact, some results are counterintuitive. For example, large numbers of workitems, much larger than the number of cores available, yielded always the best performance in the CPU and the Xeon Phi. The reasons are probably that in these devices the OpenCL framework coarsens multiple kernel instances into a single task ([19] indicates a work group is the smallest task scheduled on a software thread in the Xeon Phi), and that it may use several software threads per hardware thread in order to achieve the best performance. In fact this selection matches for example the manufacturer recommendation for the Xeon Phi [19], which was also followed to choose its baseline parameters. Still, the tool is able to further tune the parameters to increase the performance of the code in this platform. Similarly, copying the input matrices to the local memory not always achieved the best performance in the GPU, as we can see in the experiment with the 2048×2048 matrix. It is also interesting that adjusting isolatedly some of the parameters to their optimum value in the original kernels can actually generate slowdowns, which justifies the need to take into account all the parameters simultaneously in the search process.

Table 3. Optimal values selected for each generated kernel

Device	Size	Optimal values					
		szx, szy	lszx, lszy	bszx, bszy	T	CopyA, CopyB	uf
CPU	1024	(1024,8)	(8,4)	(1,256)	-	-	2
	2048	(1024,8)	(8,8)	(1,1024)	-	-	8
	4096	(1024,256)	(1024,1)	(1,4)	-	-	4
ACC	1024	(1024,1024)	(64,1)	(1,1)	-	-	2
	2048	(2048,2048)	(64,1)	(1,1)	-	-	1
	4096	(4096,4096)	(32,1)	(1,1)	-	-	1
GPU	1024	(128,1024)	(16,16)	-	16	true, true	4
	2048	(2048,256)	(32,16)	-	4	false, true	4
	4096	(2048,1024)	(16,32)	-	4	true, true	1

6 Conclusions

Performance portability is an open problem in heterogeneous systems. This work proposes a set of techniques to generate codes that self-adapt to different devices at run-time. Our approach generates HPL kernels that can be tuned through a set of parameters whose optimal values are searched following an iterative process based on a genetic algorithm. The results show that our strategy generates versions of the kernels up to 4.67 faster than baselines based on heuristics. Such improvement is observed in a CPU, whereas the improvements achieved in a Xeon Phi and a GPU reach 9% and 54%, respectively. We plan to explore the application of more optimization techniques using our approach and to enhance the search process with effective heuristics or analytical models.

Acknowledgements. This work was supported by the Xunta de Galicia under the Consolidation Program of Competitive Reference Groups (Ref. GRC2013/055) and by the Spanish Ministry of Science and Innovation (Ref. TIN2010-16735), both of them cofunded by FEDER funds of the European Union.

References

1. Munshi, A., Gaster, B., Mattson, T.G., Fung, J.: OpenCL Programming Guide. Addison-Wesley Professional (2011)
2. Wernsing, J.R., Stitt, G.: Elastic computing: a framework for transparent, portable, and adaptive multi-core heterogeneous computing. SIGPLAN Not. 45(4), 115–124 (2010)
3. Moore, N., Leeser, M., Smith King, L.: VForce: An environment for portable applications on high performance systems with accelerators. J. Parallel Distrib. Comput. 72(9), 1144–1156 (2012)
4. Du, P., Weber, R., Luszczek, P., Tomov, S., Peterson, G., Dongarra, J.: From CUDA to OpenCL: Towards a performance-portable solution for multi-platform GPU programming. Parallel Comput. 38(8), 391–407 (2012)

5. Dastgeer, U., Enmyren, J., Kessler, C.W.: Auto-tuning SkePU: a multi-backend skeleton programming framework for multi-GPU systems. In: Proc. 4th Intl. Workshop on Multicore Software Engineering, IWMSE 2011, pp. 25–32 (2011)
6. Lutz, T., Fensch, C., Cole, M.: PARTANS: An autotuning framework for stencil computation on multi-GPU systems. ACM Trans. Archit. Code Optim. 9(4), 59:1–59:24 (2013)
7. Thoman, P., Kofler, K., Studt, H., Thomson, J., Fahringer, T.: Automatic OpenCL device characterization: Guiding optimized kernel design. In: Jeannot, E., Namyst, R., Roman, J. (eds.) Euro-Par 2011, Part II. LNCS, vol. 6853, pp. 438–452. Springer, Heidelberg (2011)
8. Lan, Q., Xun, C., Wen, M., Su, H., Liu, L., Zhang, C.: Improving performance of GPU specific OpenCL program on CPUs. In: Proc. 13th Intl. Conf. on Paral. and Distrib. Computing, Applications and Technologies (PDCAT 2012), pp. 356–360 (2012)
9. Shen, J., Fang, J., Sips, H., Varbanescu, A.: Performance traps in OpenCL for CPUs. In: Proc. 21st Euromicro Intl. Conf. on Parallel, Distributed and Network-Based Processing (PDP 2013), pp. 38–45 (2013)
10. Daloukas, K., Antonopoulos, C.D., Bellas, N.: GLOpenCL: OpenCL support on hardware- and software-managed cache multicores. In: Proc. 6th Intl. Conf. on High Performance and Embedded Architectures and Compilers, pp. 15–24 (2011)
11. Fabeiro, J.F., Andrade, D., Fraguela, B.B.: OCLoptimizer: An iterative optimization tool for OpenCL. In: Proc. Intl. Conf. on Computational Science, ICCS 2013, pp. 1322–1331 (2013)
12. Dolbeau, R., Bodin, F., de Verdiere, C.: One OpenCL to rule them all? (2013)
13. Viñas, M., Bozkus, Z., Fraguela, B.B.: Exploiting heterogeneous parallelism with the Heterogeneous Programming Library. J. Parallel Distrib. Comput. 73(12), 1627–1638 (2013)
14. Beckmann, O., Houghton, A., Mellor, M.R., Kelly, P.H.J.: Runtime code generation in C++ as a foundation for domain-specific optimisation. In: Lengauer, C., Batory, D., Blum, A., Odersky, M. (eds.) Domain-Specific Program Generation. LNCS, vol. 3016, pp. 291–306. Springer, Heidelberg (2004)
15. Newburn, C., So, B., Liu, Z., McCool, M., Ghuloum, A., Toit, S.D., Wang, Z.G., Du, Z., Chen, Y., Wu, G., Guo, P., Liu, Z., Zhang, D.: Intel's array building blocks. A retargetable, dynamic compiler and embedded language. In: 9th IEEE/ACM Intl. Symp. on Code Generation and Optimization (CGO 2011), pp. 224–235 (2011)
16. Wall, M.: GAlib: A C++ Library of Genetic Algorithm Components (1996)
17. Fraguela, B.B., Carmueja, M.G., Andrade, D.: Optimal tile size selection guided by analytical models. In: Procs. of Parallel Computing (ParCo), pp. 565–572 (2005)
18. Fraguela, B.B., Voronenko, Y., Püschel, M.: Automatic tuning of discrete fourier transforms driven by analytical modeling. In: Proc. of Intl. Conf. on Parallel Architectures and Compilation Techniques, pp. 271–280 (2009)
19. Intel Corp.: OpenCL design and programming guide for the Intel Xeon Phi coprocessor (2014), http://software.intel.com/en-us/articles/opencl-design-and-programming-guide-for-the-intel-xeon-phi-coprocessor (accessed May 29, 2014)

A Pattern-Based Comparison of OpenACC and OpenMP for Accelerator Computing

Sandra Wienke[1,2], Christian Terboven[1,2], James C. Beyer[3], and Matthias S. Müller[1,2]

[1] IT Center, RWTH Aachen University, 52074 Aachen, Germany
[2] JARA – High-Performance Computing, Schinkelstr. 2, 52062 Aachen, Germany
{wienke,terboven,mueller}@itc.rwth-aachen.de
[3] Cray Inc., 380 Jackson Street, Suite 210 St. Paul, MN, USA
beyerj@cray.com

Abstract. Nowadays, HPC systems frequently emerge as clusters of commodity processors with attached accelerators. Moving from tedious low-level accelerator programming to increased development productivity, the directive-based programming models OpenACC and OpenMP are promising candidates. While OpenACC was completed about two years ago, OpenMP just recently added support for accelerator programming. To assist developers in their decision-making which approach to take, we compare both models with respect to their programmability. Besides investigating their expressiveness by putting their constructs side by side, we focus on the evaluation of their power based on structured parallel programming patterns (aka algorithmic skeletons). These patterns describe the basic entities of parallel algorithms of which we cover the patterns *map, stencil, reduction, fork-join, superscalar sequence, nesting* and *geometric decomposition*. Architectural targets of this work are NVIDIA-type accelerators (GPUs) and specialties of Intel-type accelerators (Xeon Phis). Additionally, we assess the prospects of OpenACC and OpenMP concerning future development in soft- and hardware design.

Keywords: OpenACC, OpenMP 4, GPU, Xeon Phi, programmability, parallel patterns.

1 Introduction

Heterogeneity and specialized accelerating hardware add a further level of complexity to parallel programming. Although, accelerator programming with low-level APIs like CUDA or OpenCL opens up opportunities for performance tuning, it also challenges the software design or may lead to error-prone tasks or even hardware-specific implementations. By attempting to overcome these difficulties, directive-based models for accelerator programming gained more interest, lately. Up to now, the most prominent one is OpenACC [13] that was released as industry standard in November 2011 and incorporates two years of maturity now. While OpenMP [14] has been the de-facto standard for programming multi-core CPUs for over ten years, it also covers high-level accelerator programming since version 4.0 (July 2013). Having two well-promoted directive-based models for accelerators around, developers are currently wondering which programming model to chose. Emerging questions relate to the power of the programming paradigm, opportunities for performance and the long-term perspective of the usage of the programming model and its mapping to future hardware architectures.

F. Silva et al. (Eds.): Euro-Par 2014, LNCS 8632, pp. 812–823, 2014.

In this paper, we discuss answers to most of these questions to assist developers in their decision-making process between OpenACC and OpenMP. We examine the programmability and potency of the two models by comparing both the available constructs side by side and the expressiveness taking a pattern-based approach, following the classification by McCool et al [12]. Covered patterns are *map, stencil, reduction, fork-join, superscalar sequence, nesting* and *geometric decomposition*. Implementations are illustrated for NVIDIA-type accelerators (GPGPUs) and occasionally for Intel-type accelerators (Intel Xeon Phis). From these, we derive similarities and differences in programmability. A comparison of performance measurements is currently not possible since OpenACC/ OpenMP implementations for the same device hardware do not exist.

The paper is structured as follows: Section 2 covers related work. In Section 3, we give an overview on available accelerator directives in OpenACC and OpenMP and show fundamental differences in their expressiveness. The pattern-based comparison is carried out in Section 4 and examines the fit for certain algorithmic tasks. Finally, we conclude our findings in Section 5 and discuss future perspectives of both models.

2 Related Work

Over the years, numerous approaches to characterize parallel algorithms have been undertaken. An early work [5] classifies algorithms into *skeletons*. A pattern language for parallel programming that uses *design patterns* and makes up four design spaces is defined by Mattson et al [11]. A famous categorization is given by Berkley's dwarfs (or motifs) [1] that characterize workloads for the evaluations of parallel architectures, for instance, dense/ sparse linear algebra, (un-)structured grids or n-body applications. We chose a lower level of abstraction by applying parallel patterns for structured programming defined by McCool et al [12]. While few works applied different categorizations of parallel algorithms to accelerator paradigms (e.g. [4]), we are the first to our knowledge that use the novel characterization by McCool et al. The relative low abstraction level and the applicability to scientific programming makes this characterization specifically suitable to compare parallel programming paradigms.

Various directive-based paradigms fed into the current OpenACC and OpenMP standards. Some of these approaches (PGI Accelerator, hiCUDA, HMPP, OpenMPC, R-Stream) have been compared to OpenACC (CAPS, PGI, accULL) in [6,15,9]. Groundwork for OpenMP for accelerators [3] was done by our author Beyer (et al).

While few works deal with OpenMP for accelerators so far, much research has been carried out on OpenACC in the last years. However, most of it focuses on performance evaluations rather than on programmability—as we do. In [7], the authors compare the performance of Cray's, PGI's and HMPP's OpenACC implementation to a low-level CUDA version using two micro-benchmarks and one real-world code. Our previous work [17] covers performance results on two real-world applications comparing OpenCL with Cray's OpenACC and the PGI Accelerator Model. Performance investigations also cover different architectures such as Intel Xeon Phi and NVIDIA GPUs [16]. Some of these works [17,9,6] also include programmability aspects with respect to learning curve, code size, development effort or adaptability. For evaluating expressiveness, we follow a more general approach and exhibit a structured comparison by well-defined parallel patterns. With respect to the OpenMP accelerator model, only few investigations have been published yet at all. The research implementation *HOMP* is introduced in [10] for NVIDIA GPUs. The authors compare performance of HOMP to PGI's and HMPP's OpenACC versions. To the best of our knowledge, we provide the first comparison of programmability between OpenACC and OpenMP for accelerator programming (basing on Beyer's webinar [2]). Wolfe [19] makes rather skeptical comments on the extension of accelerator offload regions to OpenMP. We contribute our own view that bases on experiences in academia, industry and our work in the OpenMP/OpenACC committees on the prospects of both standards in Section 5.

3   Overview on OpenACC and OpenMP for Accelerators

OpenMP has been the de-facto standard for shared-memory multi-core programming since about ten years. Additionally, the OpenMP language committee has been working on the integration of accelerator support since 2009, which resulted in the `target` construct as part of OpenMP 4.0. In between, the independent sub group of Cray, CAPS, PGI, and NVIDIA released their own industry standard as OpenACC in 2011. OpenMP aims to extend known concepts from multi-core programming to accelerators and allows heterogeneous programming with just one paradigm, while OpenACC was motivated by GPGPU users being tired of low-level APIs. OpenACC's specification 2.0 from June 2013 contains advances and feedback gathered from the last two years. Similarly, the OpenMP language committee is already working on improving the accelerator support for the next (minor) standard update.

Both models build on a host-directed execution model in which the host offloads data and compute-intensive loops to an accelerator (or as fallback to the host itself). An abstract machine model is presented in [20, p. 5]. Both models also exhibit a weak device memory model so that memory coherence between operations executed by different threads is not assured. The memory entities between host and device are presumed to be separate. However, the devices may share memory with the host [13, p. 9f.] [14, p. 17ff.]. OpenACC and OpeMP both contain constructs, clauses, runtime library routines and environment variables to control the workflow and express parallelism. A direct comparison of important features is given in Table 1.

4   Pattern-Based Comparison

Patterns are the basic structural entities of algorithms and represent common control flows and data organizations in applications. We apply these parallel patterns as defined by McCool et al to accelerator programming models and focus on these special accelerator features rather than on the base language characteristics of C/C++ or Fortran. By parallel patterns, we show concepts and differences of the programmability and potency of OpenACC and OpenMP.

4.1   Map

The elementary map pattern is the foundation of numerous algorithms (e.g. Monte Carlo sampling) and other patterns. It represents a parallel version of a serial iterating loop of

Table 1. Comparison of constructs and clauses of OpenACC and OpenMP

OpenACC	OpenMP	Remark
parallel	target	offload of computational work to the device (synchronously)
parallel	teams, parallel	creation of in parallel running threads
kernels		compiler may find parallelism in associated block automatically
data	target data	structured data management between host & device
loop	distribute, do, for, simd	worksharing across the parallel units
host data		interoperability with low-level languages like CUDA
cache		move object closer to the execution units in the memory hierarchy
update	target update	data movement between host & device within data environment
declare	declare target	declaration of global, file static or extern objects used inside a parallel region
routine	declare target	declaration of functions called inside a parallel region
enter data		unstructured data management to the device
exit data		unstructured data management from the device
	tasks	creation of explicit tasks for task parallelism
async(*int*)	task depend	asynchronous execution with dependencies
wait		synchronization of streams
async wait		asynchronous waiting on a specific stream
parallel in parallel	parallel in parallel or team	nested parallelism on the device
tile		strip-mining of data collections
device_type		device-specific tuning of clauses
atomic	atomic	atomic operations
	sections, critical, barrier, master, single	non-iterative workshare, critical sections, synchronization, control flow for single thread

which all iterations of the body are independent and the number of iterations is known in advance. This pattern *maps* in parallel the different elements of the input data within the index space to an output collection using a so-called elemental function.

The elemental function f of the map example in Listings 1.1–1.4 describes a naive scaled matrix transpose: $B = p \cdot A^T$ with $p \in \mathbb{R}$, $A \in \mathbb{R}^{n \times m}$, $B \in \mathbb{R}^{m \times n}$. OpenACC and OpenMP both support the map pattern. Listings 1.1 and 1.2 show implementations for NVIDIA-type accelerators that leverage the GPU's two levels of parallelism. While the parallel construct in OpenACC directly starts the parallel execution on the device, an additional target construct must be specified in OpenMP to differentiate between host and device execution. OpenMP is also verbose on the different hierarchies of parallelism: on a GPU, the teams distribute spreads the work of the outer loop in independent chunks onto the compute units (as defined in [8, p. 23f.]). Here, teams creates a parallel teams region; distribute indicates the workshare. It does not contain an implicit barrier at its end and must be closely nested in or combined with teams. Then, the parallel for distributes the work of the inner loop across the processing elements [8, p. 23f.] within a compute unit. With OpenACC, the loop directive is sufficient for worksharing, but should be extended by an efficient loop

Listing 1.1. Map with two levels of parallelism in OpenACC (GPU)

```
1  #pragma acc routine seq
2  double f(double p, double aij) {
3    return (p * aij);
4  }
5
6  // [..]
7  #pragma acc parallel
8  #pragma acc loop gang
9  for(i=0; i<n; i++) {
10 #pragma acc loop vector
11   for(j=0; j<m; j++) {
12     b[j][i] = f(5.0,a[i][j]);
13 } }
```

Listing 1.2. Map with two levels of parallelism in OpenMP (GPU)

```
1  #pragma omp declare target
2  double f(double p, double aij) {
3    return (p * aij);
4  }
5  #pragma omp end declare target
6  // [..]
7  #pragma omp target
8  #pragma omp teams distribute
9  for(i=0; i<n; i++) {
10 #pragma omp parallel for
11   for(j=0; j<m; j++) {
12     b[j][i] = f(5.0,a[i][j]);
13 } }
```

Listing 1.3. Map in OpenACC (Phi)

```
1
2  #pragma acc routine seq
3  double f(double, double);
4
5  // [..]
6  #pragma acc parallel
7  #pragma acc loop gang vector
8  for(i=0; i<n; i++) {
9    for(j=0; j<m; j++) {
10     b[j][i] = f(5.0,a[i][j]);
11 } }
```

Listing 1.4. Map in OpenMP (Phi)

```
1  #pragma omp declare target
2  #pragma omp declare simd
3    double f(double, double);
4  #pragma omp end declare
5  // [..]
6  #pragma omp target
7  #pragma omp parallel for simd
8  for(i=0; i<n; i++) {
9    for(j=0; j<m; j++) {
10     b[j][i] = f(5.0,a[i][j]);
11 } }
```

scheduling clause. Here, `loop gang` and `loop vector` equal the work distribution of the OpenMP example. Additionally, OpenACC provides the "magical" `kernels` directive that delegates the responsibility of finding parallelism to the compiler.

Closely related to the map pattern is the elemental function that is implemented as function call. OpenACC (2.0) supports function calls by the `routine` construct which needs the declaration of a parallelism level (gang, worker, vector, seq). A seq clause is used in the example to denote that the function does not express any parallelism itself, as it is already sufficiently exploited at the loop level. In turn, OpenMP has a more flexible way by denoting the `declare target` directive without specifying the parallelism. Thus, the function can be called from different contexts. Contrary, the absence of this hint might prevent some optimizations. In the following, we express the elemental function of the fundamental map pattern in formulas for better reading.

The same implementations will also work on an Intel Xeon Phi as OpenACC and OpenMP guarantee portability. However, performance portability may be implementation dependent. A more appropriate approach applies another level of parallelism (no hierarchy) and emphasizes vectorization (compare Listings 1.3 and 1.4). The mapping of work onto the threads on the Phi is employed by `loop gang` and `parallel for`. Vectorization is requested by `vector` and `simd` clauses, respectively.

Listing 1.5. Stencil in OpenACC (GPU)

```
1  #pragma acc parallel
2  #pragma acc loop tile(64,4) gang vector
3    for(i=1; i<n-1; i++) {
4      for(j=1; j<m-1; j++) {
5
6  #pragma acc cache(a[i-1:3][j-1:3])
7
8      anew[i][j] = (a[i-1][j] + a[i+1][j] +\
                     a[i][j-1]+ a[i][j+1]) * 0.25;
9    }
10 }
```

Listing 1.6. Stencil in OpenMP (GPU)

```
1  #pragma omp target
2  #pragma omp teams distribute collapse(2)
3    for(i=1; i<n-1; i+=64) {
4      for(j=1; j<m-1; j+=4) {
5  #pragma omp parallel for collapse(2)
6        for(k=i; k<min(n-1,i+64); k++){
7          for(l=j; l<min(m-1,j+4); l++){
8            anew[k][l] = (a[k-1][l] +          \
                          a[k+1][l] + a[k][l-1] + \
                          a[k][l+1]) * 0.25;
9  } } } }
```

4.2 Stencil

The elemental function of the stencil pattern allows several input elements that can be accessed in a regular way, i.e. with fixed offsets. This structure of neighboring input elements enables data reuse and cache optimizations. To fit data into the software- or hardware-managed cache (especially) for multi-dimensional stencils, the 'layer condition' must be fulfilled. A common solution is the spatial blocking of data that is also known as strip-mining.

In Listings 1.5 and 1.6, a small part of a Jacobi solver for the Laplace equation is presented, omitting the matrix swap and the convergence iteration. The presented two-dimensional stencil can be tiled into blocks using OpenACC. The tile clause hides loop splitting and collapsing. This is illustrated in the OpenMP example since tiling must be explicitly expressed in OpenMP. Here, distribute teams collapse(2) combines the index space of the outer two loops for distribution to the compute units of a GPU and parallel for collapse(2) for distribution across the processing elements within the compute units. In addition to blocking, OpenACC provides the cache-ing capability (line 6) to let the developer specify that sub arrays should be fetched into the highest-level memory for data reuse. OpenMP does not yet support leveraging the on-chip caches explicitly. Summarizing, both models do not have built-in functions for stencils, but OpenACC provides some features for optimization.

4.3 Reduction

Another pattern that is often required in linear algebra is the reduction pattern. It combines every element of an input data set into a single element using a certain reduction operation (combiner function). For parallelization, the combiner function must be associative to support reordering of operations.

OpenACC and OpenMP allow directly to compute reductions with a clause. Reductions are supported at worksharing levels and parallel regions (parallel, teams). Listings 1.7 and 1.8 present an example for reductions on different levels of parallelism, i.e. a matrix vector multiply extended with a checksum computation: $b = A \cdot x$, checksum $= \sum_{i=1}^{n} b_i$ with $b \in \mathbb{R}^n$, $x \in \mathbb{R}^m$, $A \in \mathbb{R}^{n \times m}$ and $b_i \in \mathbb{R}$. The reduction value of the scalar tmp is already needed right after the inner loop to compute the checksum. For vector parallelism in OpenACC (line 5), it is necessary that the variable also appears in a private clause to get it updated right at the exit of the loop and

Listing 1.7. Reduction in OpenACC (GPU)

```
1  #pragma acc parallel private(tmp)
2  #pragma acc loop gang                    \
       reduction(+:checksum)
3  for(i=0; i<n; i++) {
4    tmp = 0;
5  #pragma acc loop vector reduction(+:tmp)
6    for(j=0; j<m; j++) {
7      tmp += A[i][j] * x[j];
8    }
9    b[i] = tmp;
10   checksum += tmp;
11 }
```

Listing 1.8. Reduction in OpenMP (GPU)

```
1  #pragma omp target
2  #pragma omp teams distribute private(tmp)\
       reduction(+:checksum)
3  for(i=0; i<n; i++) {
4    tmp = 0;
5  #pragma omp parallel for reduction(+:tmp)
6    for(j=0; j<m; j++) {
7      tmp += A[i][j] * x[j];
8    }
9    b[i] = tmp;
10   checksum += tmp;
11 }
```

Listing 1.9. Fork-join in OpenMP (Phi)

```
1  #pragma omp declare target
2  int fib(int n) {
3    int x, y;
4    if (n < 2) {return n;}
5  #pragma omp task shared(x)
6    x = fib(n - 1);
7  #pragma omp task shared(y)
8    y = fib(n - 2);
9  #pragma omp taskwait
10   return (x+y);
11 }
12 #pragma omp end declare target
13 // [..]
14 #pragma omp target
15 #pragma omp parallel
16 #pragma omp single
17 result=fib(n);
```

Listing 1.10. Unstructured data lifetime in OpenACC (GPU)

```
1  class CArray {
2  public:
3    CArray(int n) {
4      a = new double[n];
5  #pragma acc enter data create(a[0:n])
6    }
7    ~CArray() {
8  #pragma acc exit data delete(a[0:n])
9      delete(a);
10   }
11   void fillArray(int n) {
12 #pragma acc parallel loop
13     for(int i=0; i<n; i++) { a[i]=i; }
14   }
15 private:
16   double *a;
17 };
```

not only at the end of the parallel region. Correspondingly, the checksum variable is put properly in the reduction at the gang parallelism (line 2). For OpenMP, there are corresponding rules.

As an advantage, OpenMP supports user-defined reductions, especially useful on structured data types, which is currently not possible with OpenACC. Furthermore, the OpenMP simd construct also supports reduction operations.

4.4   Fork-Join

The fork-join pattern directs the workflow to be split (forked) into multiple parallel and independent flows and get merged (joined) later again. OpenACC and OpenMP both support parallel regions on the device that actually fork control into multiple threads and later return to a single master thread (compare Section 4.1). However, worksharing constructs in parallel regions only support data parallel execution across threads. OpenMP additionally provides task parallel execution on the device via sections or tasks. It enables parallel execution of instances with different computational work and efficient load balance. The fork-join pattern can also be applied for recursive algorithms such as divide-and-conquer. A simple recursive application is the

Listing 1.11. Superscalar sequence in OpenACC (GPU)

```
1
2
3
4
5   #pragma acc parallel loop async(1)
6
7   // F = f(A)
8
9
10  #pragma acc parallel loop async(2)
11  // G = g(B)
12  #pragma acc wait(1,2) async(3)
13
14
15  #pragma acc parallel loop async(3)
16  // H = h(F,G)
17  #pragma acc wait(1)
18  // S = s(F)
19  #pragma acc wait
20
```

Listing 1.12. Superscalar sequence in OpenMP (GPU)

```
1   #pragma omp parallel
2   #pragma omp single
3   {
4   #pragma omp task depend(inout:F)
5   #pragma omp target teams distribute \
            parallel for
6   // F = f(A)
7   #pragma omp task depend(inout:G)
8   #pragma omp target teams distribute \
            parallel for
9   // G = g(B)
10  #pragma omp task depend(in:F,G)     \
            depend(inout:H)
11  #pragma omp target teams distribute \
            parallel for
12  // H = h(F,G)
13  #pragma omp task depend(in:F)
14  // S = s(F)
15  #pragma omp taskwait
16  }
```

computation of Fibonacci numbers in Listing 1.9. This algorithm forks for each recursive call a new `task` and joins them by using the `taskwait` directive. This conceptual behavior can be approximated by host-directed nested parallel constructs in OpenACC.

4.5   Superscalar Sequence

The superscalar sequence pattern describes the parallelization of the serial sequence which executes an ordered list of tasks. In a superscalar sequence, the specific order can be lifted by parallel execution as long as all data dependencies are satisfied. On multi-core processors with attached accelerators, the superscalar sequence can also be interpreted as heterogeneous or hybrid parallelization for the combination of host and device using asynchronous execution.

To denote data dependencies, OpenACC follows a streaming concept that is known from CUDA programming. As seen in Listing 1.11, the streams are expressed by `async` clauses that take a positive integer as stream label. Data that contains dependencies must be put into the same stream (same integer) for sequential ordering. Tasks that can be executed in parallel should be in different streams. The `wait` construct and clause help with the synchronization across different streams. For OpenMP, the tasking model can be applied with the extension of data dependency capabilities. Tasks that do not depend on each other can be employed in parallel. In Listing 1.12, all tasks (except the last one listed) start a target region for execution on the device. Other than in OpenACC, the OpenMP host thread that picks up the scheduled task has to wait until the task has been completed to return to the thread pool to execute further tasks.

4.6   Nesting

The nesting pattern is a compositional pattern for creating hierarchies. They are needed for a modular code structure and the incorporation of libraries. Here, we look

Listing 1.13. Update in OpenACC (GPU)

```
1  void stencilOnAcc(double **a, double **\
       anew, int n, int m) {
2  #pragma acc parallel present              \
       (a[1:n-2][0:m], anew[1:n-2][0:m])
3  #pragma acc loop
4      // stencil computation
5  }
6  // [..]
7  #pragma acc data create(Anew[0:n][0:m]) \
       copyin(A[0:n][0:m]) if(test)
8  {
9
10   while (iter < iter_max) {
11     stencilOnAcc(A,Anew,n,m);
12  #pragma acc update host(Anew[1:n-2][0:m])
13
14     swapOnHost(A,Anew,n,m);
15  #pragma acc update device(A[1:n-2][0:m])
16
17     iter++;
18  } }
```

Listing 1.14. Update in OpenMP (GPU)

```
1  void stencilOnAcc(double **a, double **  \
       anew, int n, int m) {
2  #pragma omp target map(tofrom:            \
       a[1:n-2][0:m], anew[1:n-2][0:m])
3  #pragma omp teams distribute parallel for
4      // stencil computation
5  }
6  // [..]
7  #pragma omp target data                   \
       map(alloc:Anew[0:n][0:m])             \
       map(to:A[0:n][0:m]) if(test)
8  {
9    while (iter < iter_max) {
10     stencilOnAcc(A,Anew,n,m);
11  #pragma omp target update                 \
       from(Anew[1:n-2][0:m])
12     swapOnHost(A,Anew,n,m);
13  #pragma omp target update                 \
       to(A[1:n-2][0:m])
14     iter++;
15  } }
```

especially at nested parallelism. In OpenACC, a modular composition can be explored by the ability of nesting `parallel` regions or `kernels` into each other. For OpenMP, some restrictions are imposed to with `target` and `teams` constructs: both are not allowed to be nested in themselves. Only `parallel` directives can be applied inside of `target/teams/parallel` directives.

4.7 Parallel Update

While various parallel data management patterns are defined by McCool et al, no specific pattern displays the data relationship between a host and an accelerator. Therefore, we extend the parallel patterns by defining a *parallel update* pattern. The parallel update pattern does not have a pendant in serial execution, as it exposes capabilities to synchronize data between host and device.

Both programming models support basic parallel update methods like data clauses, data regions and update constructs. The usage of these patterns is illustrated in Listings 1.13 and 1.14 that show a simplified iterative Jacobi solver with stencil computations. Data movement is controlled by data clauses next to the `parallel`, `kernels` or `target` construct, which take a variable list and a map type determining the data transfer direction or creation/deletion. Basic OpenACC map types are `create`, `copy`, `copyin` and `copyout`. OpenMP provides `alloc`, `tofrom`, `to` and `from`, respectively, in combination with the `map` clause. The variable list must only denote arrays or pointers, as scalar variables are transfered automatically. Statically-allocated arrays can be automatically recognized and moved by the compiler. Thus, we did not have to specify them in previous examples. In contrast, the size of dynamically-allocated memory must be manually denoted in the form of array sections or sub arrays (e.g. line 12) representing rectangular or contiguous memory (depending on the construct, base programming language and vendor implementation). Besides data clauses, OpenACC and OpenMP also support data regions (`data`, `target data`) which decouple the data movement from computational regions. The same data map types apply. Hitherto un-

Listing 1.15. Partition in OpenACC (GPU)

```
1  // determine idDev, stIdx & #rows per dev
2  acc_set_device_num(idDev, \
       acc_device_nvidia);
3  #pragma acc parallel loop copy(x[stIdx:\
       rows][0:n],y[stIdx:rows][0:n])
4     // y = a * x (on distributed rows)
```

Listing 1.16. Partition in OpenMP (GPU)

```
1  // determine idDev, stIdx & #rows per dev
2
3  #pragma omp target device(idDev) map(x[\
       stIdx:rows][0:n],y[stIdx:rows][0:n])
4  #pragma omp teams distribute parallel for
5     // y = a * x (on distributed rows)
```

mentioned are the present checks employed for data on the device. OpenACC provides `present_or_copy` (and similar) clauses that test the existence of data on the device and moves the data if necessary. The OpenMP runtime implies this check for all data transfers. OpenACC also allows to explicitly express that a variable is and must be already `present` in a given data context (see line 2). If the variable is not accessible on the device (`if(test)` evaluates to false), the runtime will throw an error. OpenMP applications must specify the `map` clause with inclusive present check. Thus, the program continues executing. The `update` directive allows solely data movement between host and device and can be used flexibly within the corresponding data environment.

Additionally, both models enable an automatic deep copy of flat objects to the device, i.e. structs and classes with static member types. With OpenACC's data API, a manual deep copy of pointer structures is further possible, but tedious. The concept is called unstructured data lifetime and can also be expressed by directives. In Listing 1.10, `enter data create` allocates memory on the device as soon as the constructor of class `CArray` is called. Respectively, `enter data delete` in the destructor destroys the data on the device. Copy clauses are also possible. An OpenMP counterpart does not exist, momentarily.

4.8 Geometric Decomposition

Data reorganization is a necessary pattern for many algorithms. The geometric decomposition pattern divides the data collections into sub domains. For parallel execution on independent data sections, the sub domains should be non-overlapping at best. If this is the case and the sub domains are uniform in size, we call this the partition pattern.

The partition pattern is illustrated by a vector scaling in Listings 1.15 and 1.16: $y = \alpha \cdot x$ with $x, y \in \mathbb{R}^n, \alpha \in \mathbb{R}$. Using OpenACC or OpenMP, data subdivision can take place between host and accelerator or between multiple accelerators. The decomposition between host and device can be employed using asynchronous call capabilities covered in Section 4.5. The distribution across multiple accelerators of the same type can be applied by API calls (OpenACC: line 2) or clauses (OpenMP: line 3), respectively, specifying a certain device ID.

The distribution across multiple accelerators of different types (e.g. GPU, Xeon Phi) is only supported by OpenACC. OpenACC provides API calls for setting the current device type (`acc_set_device_type(type)`) and additionally `device_type` clauses that enable device-specific clause tuning for computational work.

5 Conclusion

In the context of structured parallel patterns, we compared the power of OpenACC and OpenMP for accelerators. A summary table is provided in [18]. We conclude that

OpenACC is one step ahead of OpenMP, momentarily. Although OpenACC does not directly support the fork-join pattern, it provides more features concerning the remaining patterns. Contrary, the OpenMP model provides more general concepts such as sections and task parallelism today. Thus, if developers want to start directive-based programming on GPGPUs now, we recommend to use OpenACC. A port to OpenMP 4.0 can be easily carried out, any time, if only features from OpenACC 1.0 were used. Similarly to OpenACC, OpenMP aims to quickly add missing functionality.

Assessing the long-term perspective of both models, the question is whether they will co-exist, converge or diverge. Based on our work in the OpenACC and OpenMP accelerator committees, we assume that they will continue to live independently because of business interests. However, if users advocate for a certain model, vendors cannot neglect their need. While accelerator capabilities of OpenMP, that target a broad user base, might always lag behind OpenACC's, OpenMP might have the advantage in the long term: It is widely excepted in the user community and supported by numerous vendors for broad portability. Additionally, it provides a unified model for programming accelerators and CPUs. On the other hand, the effort for a complete OpenMP 4.0 implementation is significant, possibly preventing full support of all OpenMP concepts in offload regions.

A further uncertainty is the development of future architectures. It is likely that accelerators will get closer to the host processor and/ or might share the same memory. Not forgetting, Amdahl's law still holds. Then, the offload model of OpenACC and OpenMP might lose importance and hosts with large-scaling capabilities might be superior. While in principle OpenACC can also be compiled for the host, OpenMP is already well-known for a productive usage on CPUs. Thus, OpenMP might take the lead with its non-offload parallel features then.

At the end, developers look out for one productive parallel programming model that also delivers performance. While directive-based models might deliver lower performance than low-level approaches, performance differences between equivalent approaches in OpenACC and OpenMP are not expected, if compared on the same target architecture. The only dissimilarity might occur if the general concept differs, for instance, as with asynchronous streams and asynchronous tasks. Unfortunately, we could not investigate performance measurements so far since current OpenACC implementations only exist for GPUs and an OpenMP 4.0 implementation with device offloading capabilities is only existent for Intel's Xeon Phi. These performance examinations are left for future work. Further investigations will also cover a pattern-based comparison between low-level and directive-based accelerator models.

References

1. Asanovic, K., Bodik, R., Catanzaro, B.C., Gebis, J.J., Husbands, P., Keutzer, K., Patterson, D.A., Plishker, W.L., Shalf, J., Williams, S.W., Yelick, K.A.: The Landscape of Parallel Computing Research: A View from Berkeley. Tech. Rep. UCB/EECS-2006-183 (2006)
2. Beyer, J.C.: OpenACC 2.0 vs OpenMP 4.0 Programming Comparison. GTC Express Webinars, ID GTCE058 (2013)
3. Beyer, J.C., Stotzer, E.J., Hart, A., de Supinski, B.R.: OpenMP for Accelerators. In: Chapman, B.M., Gropp, W.D., Kumaran, K., Müller, M.S. (eds.) IWOMP 2011. LNCS, vol. 6665, pp. 108–121. Springer, Heidelberg (2011)

4. Che, S., Boyer, M., Meng, J., Tarjan, D., Sheaffer, J., Lee, S.H., Skadron, K.: Rodinia: A benchmark suite for heterogeneous computing. In: IEEE International Symposium on Workload Characterization, IISWC 2009, pp. 44–54 (2009)
5. Cole, M.: Algorithmic Skeletons: Structured Management of Parallel Computation. MIT Press, Cambridge (1991)
6. Ghosh, S., Liao, T., Calandra, H., Chapman, B.: Experiences with OpenMP, PGI, HMPP and OpenACC Directives on ISO/TTI Kernels. In: High Performance Computing, Networking, Storage and Analysis (SCC), 2012 SC Companion, pp. 691–700 (2012)
7. Hoshino, T., Maruyama, N., Matsuoka, S., Takaki, R.: CUDA vs OpenACC: Performance Case Studies with Kernel Benchmarks and a Memory-Bound CFD Application. In: 13th IEEE/ACM International Symposium on Cluster, Cloud and Grid Computing (CCGrid), pp. 136–143 (2013)
8. Khronos OpenCL Working Group: The OpenCL Specification, v2.0 (2014)
9. Lee, S., Vetter, J.S.: Early Evaluation of Directive-based GPU Programming Models for Productive Exascale Computing. In: Proceedings of the International Conference on High Performance Computing, Networking, Storage and Analysis, pp. 23:1–23:11. IEEE Computer Society Press, Los Alamitos (2012)
10. Liao, C., Yan, Y., de Supinski, B.R., Quinlan, D.J., Chapman, B.: Early Experiences with the OpenMP Accelerator Model. In: Rendell, A.P., Chapman, B.M., Müller, M.S. (eds.) IWOMP 2013. LNCS, vol. 8122, pp. 84–98. Springer, Heidelberg (2013)
11. Mattson, T., Sanders, B., Massingill, B.: Patterns for Parallel Programming, 1st edn. Addison-Wesley Professional (2004)
12. McCool, M., Reinders, J., Robison, A.: Structured Parallel Programming: Patterns for Efficient Computation, 1st edn. Morgan Kaufmann (2012)
13. OpenACC-Standard.org: The OpenACC Application Programming Interface, v2.0 (2013)
14. OpenMP ARB: OpenMP Application Program Interface, v. 4.0 (2013)
15. Reyes, R., Lopez, I., Fumero, J., De Sande, F.: Directive-based Programming for GPUs: A Comparative Study. In: 2012 IEEE 14th International Conference on High Performance Computing and Communication 2012 IEEE 9th International Conference on Embedded Software and Systems (HPCC-ICESS), pp. 410–417 (2012)
16. Wang, Y., Qin, Q., See, S.C.W., Lin, J.: Performance Portability Evaluation for OpenACC on Intel Knights Corner and Nvidia Kepler. HPC China (2013)
17. Wienke, S., Springer, P., Terboven, C., an Mey, D.: OpenACC – First Experiences with Real-World Applications. In: Kaklamanis, C., Papatheodorou, T., Spirakis, P.G. (eds.) Euro-Par 2012. LNCS, vol. 7484, pp. 859–870. Springer, Heidelberg (2012)
18. Wienke, S., Terboven, C., Beyer, J.C., Müller, M.S.: A Pattern-Based Comparison of OpenACC and OpenMP for Accelerator Computing, slides (2014),
https://sharepoint.campus.rwth-aachen.de/units/rz/HPC/
public/Shared%20Documents/WienkeEtAl_OpenACC-OpenMP-
PatternComparison.pdf
19. Wolfe, M.: Compilers and More: Accelerated Programming. HPC Wire (2013)
20. Wolfe, M.: Programming Heterogeneous X64+GPU Systems Using OpenACC. IEEE Comupter Society Webinar (2013)

Author Index

Printed in the United States
By Bookmasters